P9-BZC-596

Multistate Testing Practice Questions

Volume 1

Multistate Advantage™

To be used in conjunction with the Summer 2009 and Winter 2010 BAR/BRI Bar Review Courses

MPQ1

Copyright © 2009 by BAR/BRI, a Thomson Reuters business. All rights reserved. No part of this publication may be reproduced or transmitted in any form or by any means, electronic or mechanical, including photocopy, recording, or any information storage and retrieval system, without permission in writing from the publisher. Printed in the United States of America.

TABLE OF CONTENTS

STUDY SMARTER
with
StudySmart® Bar Review Software.

Get StudySmart® from the BAR/BRI website and do the question sets in this book assigned in your Paced Program™

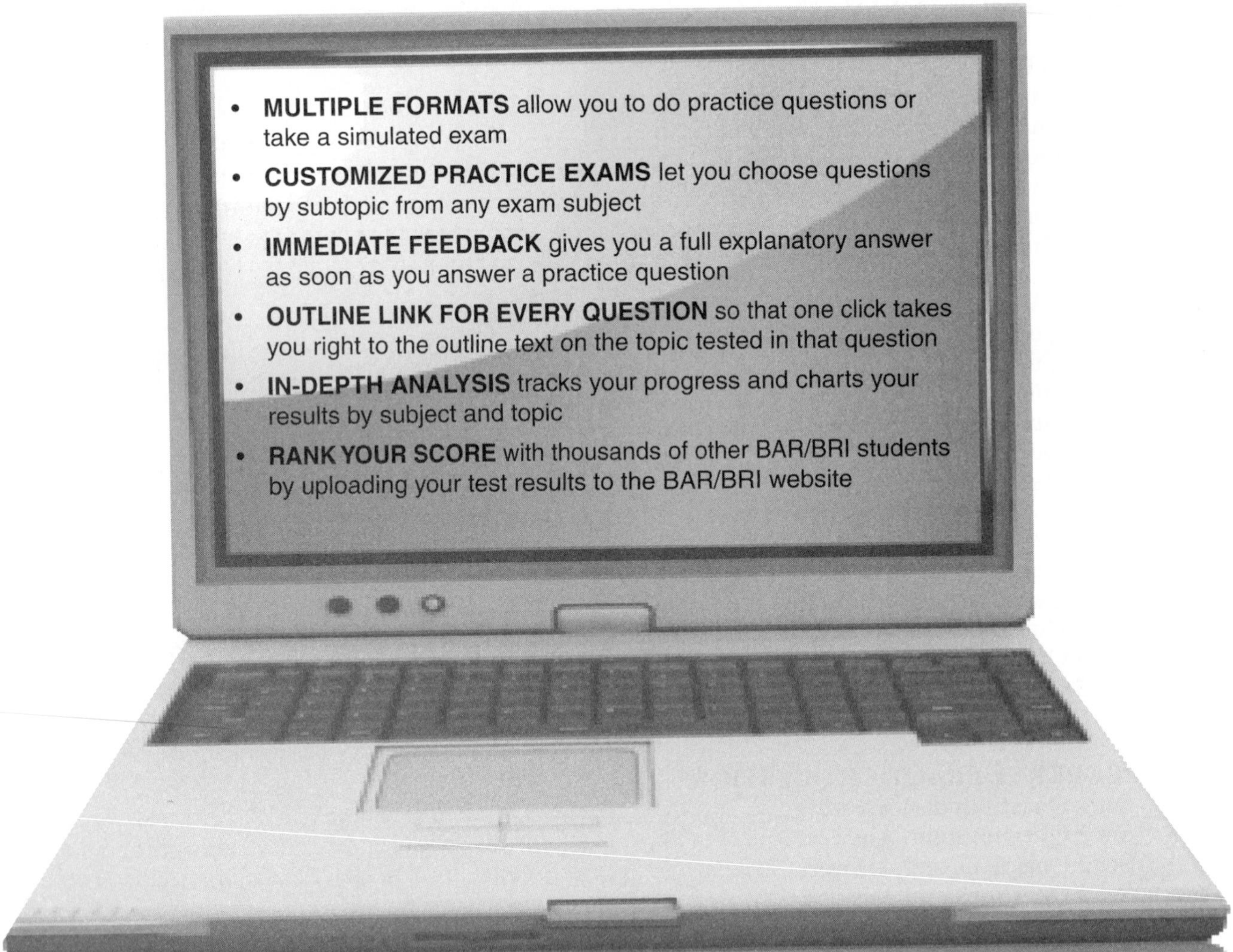

- **MULTIPLE FORMATS** allow you to do practice questions or take a simulated exam
- **CUSTOMIZED PRACTICE EXAMS** let you choose questions by subtopic from any exam subject
- **IMMEDIATE FEEDBACK** gives you a full explanatory answer as soon as you answer a practice question
- **OUTLINE LINK FOR EVERY QUESTION** so that one click takes you right to the outline text on the topic tested in that question
- **IN-DEPTH ANALYSIS** tracks your progress and charts your results by subject and topic
- **RANK YOUR SCORE** with thousands of other BAR/BRI students by uploading your test results to the BAR/BRI website

With StudySmart®, you'll know where you stand before you sit for the exam

HOW TO USE THE MULTISTATE PRACTICE QUESTIONS BOOKS

The Multistate Testing Practice Questions books are the backbone of BAR/BRI's ***Multistate Advantage***™ program—an unparalleled collection of workshops and workbooks that give you ***everything you need*** to succeed on the Multistate Bar Exam.

There are two Practice Questions books—Volume 1 and Volume 2. Together they contain over 1,700 MBE-type multiple choice questions. Additional questions will be offered online through the BAR/BRI website during the course. However, we do ***NOT*** recommend that you do all of the questions offered, ***especially at the expense of reading through the outlines and working on essay questions.*** Your course will probably provide a Paced Program™ with specific assignments from these books, or you can follow the suggested approach below to focus your MBE preparation.

Step 1: After you've had the substantive lecture on an MBE subject, go to www.barbri.com to do the ***Multistate Enhancer*** online workshops. If you haven't already done so, start with the Introductory Workshop, which contains the National Conference of Bar Examiners subject matter outlines showing topics tested on the MBE. Then do the question set for the subject that you have just studied. Finally, access the corresponding lecture in the online workshop to review the questions and learn test-taking techniques for that subject.

Step 2: Do the ***Question Sets*** arranged by subject in this book. There are six question sets for each subject. The question sets are of ***gradually increasing difficulty*** so that you will continue to be challenged as you master the techniques for answering MBE questions. Goals for each question set are provided in the front of this book so that you can gauge how you are doing. If you want to obtain a more detailed diagnostic analysis of your performance, ***including a ranking of your performance against that of other students taking the course at this time,*** do these questions using the BAR/BRI StudySmart® software (choose the Paced Program mode from the Take a Test screen to do the questions arranged by question set).

Step 3: Once you have had the substantive lectures on all six MBE subjects, you will participate in the ***Multistate Maximizer*** 3-day workshop, in which you will take a ***Simulated MBE*** under timed conditions and have it computer graded. We strongly recommend that you take this exam when it is scheduled by your course. There is no substitute for experiencing the time pressures imposed by a pace of 1.8 minutes per question.

Step 4: If assigned by your Paced Program™, or if you want additional exposure to questions in a mixed subject format, you can do the two ***Mixed Question Sets*** in this book. You can also do the Half Day Practice Exam or the Full Day Practice Exam in ***Volume 2.*** If you can, do these questions under timed conditions; *i.e.*, set aside a block of time (*e.g.*, one hour per 33 questions) and try to answer that set of questions within that time period.

Step 5: ***Don't panic.*** The MBE is not an easy exam, but you can miss a lot of questions and still get a passing score. As long as you keep on a reasonable schedule and use BAR/BRI's suggested approach for working through the questions, you will be prepared for the MBE.

QUESTION SET GOALS

Introduction

The goals listed below for each question set are based on the performance of previous BAR/BRI students on these questions.

Use these goals to track your progress as you work through the questions. If your scores in one or two subjects are lower than the average, spend more time reviewing the blackletter law for that subject or subjects. If your scores in all of the subjects are lower than average, consider doing the 100-question Half Day Practice Exam and/or the 200-question Full Day Practice Exam in Volume 2.

Remember that your scores on these question sets are raw scores; on the actual MBE, the bar examiners will add points to your raw score to obtain a scaled score, which is what states use to compute overall passing grades. The bottom line is that you can miss a lot of questions and still pass the exam.

Constitutional Law Goals
Sets 1 and 2 (18 questions each) – 12 correct per set (66%)
Sets 3 and 4 (18 questions each) – 10 correct per set (55%)
Sets 5 and 6 (36 questions each) – 18 correct per set (51%)

Contracts Goals
Sets 1 and 2 (18 questions each) – 11 correct per set (61%)
Sets 3 and 4 (18 questions each) – 9 correct per set (50%)
Sets 5 and 6 (36 questions each) – 17 correct per set (48%)

Criminal Law Goals
Sets 1 and 2 (18 questions each) – 11 correct per set (61%)
Sets 3 and 4 (18 questions each) – 10 correct per set (55%)
Sets 5 and 6 (36 questions each) – 17 correct per set (48%)

Evidence Goals
Sets 1 and 2 (18 questions each) – 12 correct per set (66%)
Sets 3 and 4 (18 questions each) – 10 correct per set (55%)
Sets 5 and 6 (36 questions each) – 18 correct per set (51%)

Real Property Goals
Sets 1 and 2 (18 questions each) – 10 correct per set (55%)
Sets 3 and 4 (18 questions each) – 9 correct per set (50%)
Sets 5 and 6 (36 questions each) – 16 correct per set (46%)

Torts Goals
Sets 1 and 2 (18 questions each) – 11 correct per set (61%)
Sets 3 and 4 (18 questions each) – 10 correct per set (55%)
Sets 5 and 6 (36 questions each) – 17 correct per set (48%)

Mixed Subject Goals
Set 1 (36 questions) – 20 correct per set (55%)
Set 2 (36 questions) – 19 correct per set (53%)

Constitutional Law

Question Sets and Analytical Answers

Set 1 Answer Sheet

1. Ⓐ Ⓑ Ⓒ Ⓓ
2. Ⓐ Ⓑ Ⓒ Ⓓ
3. Ⓐ Ⓑ Ⓒ Ⓓ
4. Ⓐ Ⓑ Ⓒ Ⓓ
5. Ⓐ Ⓑ Ⓒ Ⓓ
6. Ⓐ Ⓑ Ⓒ Ⓓ
7. Ⓐ Ⓑ Ⓒ Ⓓ
8. Ⓐ Ⓑ Ⓒ Ⓓ
9. Ⓐ Ⓑ Ⓒ Ⓓ
10. Ⓐ Ⓑ Ⓒ Ⓓ
11. Ⓐ Ⓑ Ⓒ Ⓓ
12. Ⓐ Ⓑ Ⓒ Ⓓ
13. Ⓐ Ⓑ Ⓒ Ⓓ
14. Ⓐ Ⓑ Ⓒ Ⓓ
15. Ⓐ Ⓑ Ⓒ Ⓓ
16. Ⓐ Ⓑ Ⓒ Ⓓ
17. Ⓐ Ⓑ Ⓒ Ⓓ
18. Ⓐ Ⓑ Ⓒ Ⓓ

CONSTITUTIONAL LAW QUESTIONS - SET 1

Question 1

A state Occupational Health and Safety Board recently issued regulations valid under its statutory mandate requiring that all employers in the state provide ionizing air purification systems for all employee work areas. These regulations replaced previous guidelines for employee air quality that were generally not mandatory and did not specify the method of air purification used.

The requirements regarding air purification systems are likely to be unconstitutional as applied to which of the following employers?

(A) A wholly owned subsidiary of a Japanese corporation with seven retail outlets within the state.

(B) The state supreme court, which recently completed construction of its new courthouse with a non-ionizing air purification system which the builder is contractually bound to maintain for the next three years.

(C) A United States Armed Forces Recruiting Center located adjacent to the state capitol building.

(D) A privately operated community service center funded by donations and constructed through use of a loan provided by the United States Veterans Administration and repayable to that agency.

Question 2

A man committed a particularly brutal series of crimes that, because of their interstate character, were violations of a federal criminal statute. The man was convicted in federal court and sentenced to life imprisonment. Six months after the man was incarcerated, the President pardoned him. There was a great public outcry, amid charges that the President issued the pardon because the man's uncle had made a large contribution to the President's reelection campaign fund. Responding to public opinion, Congress passed a bill limiting the President's power to pardon persons convicted under the specific statute that the man had violated. The President vetoed the bill, but three-quarters of the members of each house voted to override the veto.

The legislation is:

(A) Unconstitutional, because the power to pardon is expressly granted to the President in the Constitution and is an unqualified power (except as to impeachment).

(B) Unconstitutional, because the President has the duty to enforce the laws, and therefore has plenary powers.

(C) Constitutional, under Article I, Section 1.

(D) Constitutional, because Congress wrote the federal criminal statutes and has the right to determine who should be convicted under such statutes.

Question 3

A state with a number of automobile manufacturing facilities within its borders and a high unemployment rate because of declining sales of automobiles, especially ones built domestically, enacted a statute calling for a $100-per-car tax on all foreign-built automobiles sold within the state. The tax revenues were to be placed into a state fund to be used to retrain the state's unemployed automobile workers.

A major automobile importer and dealership owner brings suit in federal district court seeking to halt the enforcement of the statute on constitutional grounds.

The court should find the statute:

(A) Constitutional, because it is a proper exercise of a state's rights under the Import-Export Clause.

(B) Constitutional, if consented to by Congress.

(C) Unconstitutional, because the statute violates the Privileges and Immunities Clause of Article IV.

(D) Unconstitutional, unless the state can show that the statute is necessary to promote a compelling state interest.

Question 4

The federal government recently constructed a radio telescope in Puerto Rico. In addition to receiving radio signals, the telescope was set up to beam radio waves far out into space. As part of the bill providing for operational funding for the facility, Congress provided for a program to "inform any aliens who might be listening in outer space of the 'American Way of Religion.'" A $10 million appropriation was provided; any religious group whose membership exceeded 500 members in the United States was permitted to prepare a five-minute presentation, and the federal government would pay for the recording of the presentations and broadcast them into space using the transmitter in Puerto Rico. The President signed the bill and it became law. A religious group with a large following in Europe, but only 100 members in the United States, protested and filed suit.

Will the court find the religious broadcasts to be constitutional?

(A) Yes, because the power to regulate commerce with foreign nations and among the several states implies that commerce with outer space is included as well.

(B) Yes, because the commerce power is not limited by First Amendment prohibitions.

(C) No, because the First Amendment prohibits state involvement with religion without a compelling state interest.

(D) No, because the broadcasts are a waste of money and exceed the spending powers of Congress.

Question 5

The director of a one-person field station of the United States Department of Agriculture ("USDA") in a small town was instructed by his superiors to sell surplus government cheese and butter to local low income residents at 10% of market value. All sales were conducted at the USDA warehouse next to the field station.

Pursuant to state statutes allowing municipal governments to establish reasonable regulations governing the retail sale of foodstuffs, the town in which the field office is located requires any establishment for the retail sale of food to pass a health and sanitation inspection and meet other specified criteria for obtaining a city license. The director of the field office failed to obtain a license from the town and was prosecuted for the failure.

Which of the following will provide the best defense for the director in this prosecution?

(A) The ordinance under which the director is being prosecuted is invalid as an undue burden upon interstate commerce.

(B) The ordinance under which the director is being prosecuted violates the Equal Protection Clause of the Fourteenth Amendment.

(C) The ordinance under which the director is being prosecuted deprives him of property without due process of law.

(D) The ordinance under which the director is being prosecuted violates the principles of intergovernmental immunity as applied to him.

Question 6

Congress has enacted a law providing that all disagreements between the United States and a state over federal grant-in-aid funds shall be settled by the filing of a suit in the federal district court in the affected state. The law further provides: "The judgment of the federal court shall be transmitted to the head of the federal agency dispensing such funds, who, if satisfied that the judgment is fair and lawful, shall execute the judgment according to its terms."

This law is:

(A) Constitutional, because disagreements over federal grant-in-aid funds necessarily involve federal questions within the judicial power of the United States.

(B) Constitutional, because the spending of federal monies necessarily includes the authority to provide for the effective settlement of disputes involving them.

(C) Unconstitutional, because it vests authority in the federal court to determine a matter prohibited to it by the Eleventh Amendment.

(D) Unconstitutional, because it vests authority in a federal court to render an advisory opinion.

Question 7

A city council passed an ordinance providing: "No person may contribute more than $100 annually to any group organized for the specific purpose of supporting or opposing referenda to be voted on by the city electorate or regularly engaging in such activities."

If the ordinance is challenged in federal court, how should the court rule on the constitutionality of this ordinance?

(A) Strike it down, because it violates First Amendment rights of free speech and freedom of association.

(B) Strike it down as a violation of due process, because no hearing mechanism has been provided for.

(C) Uphold it, because the city council has a legitimate interest in controlling such contributions.

(D) Dismiss the case, because it involves a political question and is thus a nonjusticiable matter.

Question 8

The President of the United States accepted an invitation to give a commencement address at a small, Midwestern university in its auditorium. Pursuant to school rules, no one is permitted to bring posters, banners, or signs of any kind larger than the size of a piece of notebook paper into any event at the auditorium. The main purpose of the rule is to prevent obstruction of the view within the auditorium. Nevertheless, at the commencement ceremony, a student in a front row balcony seat unfurled a banner that he had hidden in his coat with a message supporting the President. The student was promptly arrested and charged in municipal court with trespassing. The student filed suit in federal court to enjoin the municipal prosecution and to have the trespass ordinance declared unconstitutional as applied to him.

Will the federal court likely hear the student's case?

(A) Yes, if he argues that the trespass ordinance is invalid on its face.

(B) Yes, if he argues that the prosecutor had no hope of conviction and was proceeding to harass him.

(C) No, if the prosecution argues that the student lacks standing.

(D) No, if the prosecution argues that the case involves a political question.

Question 9

A state that is subject to severe winters generally allows the use of studded tires between October 1 and March 31. However, the legislation allows counties to opt out and prohibit the use of studded tires year round, because studded tires tend to tear up pavement more than nonstudded tires, thus necessitating more frequent road repairs. No other state in the region allows use of studded snow tires at all. The state law contains one exception: it excludes "doctors" from any county ban on the use of snow tires because they might have to cross county lines in emergencies. After the passage of the legislation, only one county in the state invoked its right to ban the use of studded snow tires.

A lawyer who lives in the state was angered that the legislature had given special privileges to doctors but not to lawyers. One January day, with studded tires on his car, he drove from his home county, which allowed use of studded tires, into the county that banned them. A sheriff's officer noticed the lawyer's studded tires and cited him. After being convicted and fined, the lawyer appealed.

The lawyer's best argument for getting the ban invalidated is:

(A) The statute interferes with his fundamental right to practice his profession in violation of the Privileges and Immunities Clause of Article IV.

(B) The statute violates his right to travel.

(C) The statute violates the Commerce Clause by placing an unreasonable restraint on interstate commerce.

(D) The ban on studded snow tires is not rationally related to a legitimate state interest because it will likely result in an increased loss of life.

Question 10

An ordinance of a city prohibits leafleting on the grounds of any hospital or on the sidewalks within five feet of the hospital entrances during visiting hours. A member of a religious group advocating prayer to restore the sick to good health is arrested for violating the ordinance, is fined $100, and is convicted. She appeals her conviction, claiming that her constitutional rights were violated.

The case was heard by the state supreme court, which ruled that while the ordinance was permissible under the United States Constitution, it was unconstitutional under the state constitution because the fine money was designated to go to the city's only hospital, which was privately owned, rather than to the city. The city seeks to bring the case before the United States Supreme Court.

Should the United States Supreme Court grant certiorari?

(A) No, because the case was decided on independent state grounds.

(B) No, because the case is moot.

(C) No, because this is a political question.

(D) Yes, the Supreme Court should hear the case on its merits, because it involves an important federal question.

Question 11

A state bans the use of disposable diapers to reduce the volume of nonbiodegradable material in its landfills. The ban was a boon for diaper services within the state, but many parents of young children were displeased with the use of conventional diapers. With support from retail establishments that lost business from the disposable diaper ban, a grass roots coalition formed to fight the ban funded a study showing that the trucks and cleaning supplies used by diaper services within the state harmed the environment more than disposable diapers. The coalition and retailers then filed suit seeking to have the ban on disposable diapers declared unconstitutional.

If the court strikes down the statute, on which of the following constitutional provisions would its decision most likely be based?

(A) The Equal Protection Clause of the Fourteenth Amendment.

(B) The Due Process Clause.

(C) The Impairment of Contracts Clause.

(D) The Privileges and Immunities Clause of the Fourteenth Amendment.

Question 12

A town in a rural state facing financial difficulties passed a variety of "sin taxes," including one aimed at electronic game arcades frequented by local juveniles. The tax is a one-cent per game tax imposed on the manufacturers of the games based on the estimated number of plays over a machine's lifetime. There are no electronic game manufacturers in the state.

Which of the following constitutional provisions would support the best argument ***against*** enforcement of the tax?

(A) The Equal Protection Clause.

(B) Substantive due process.

(C) The Privileges and Immunities Clause of Article IV.

(D) The Commerce Clause.

Question 13

A state's highway speed limits were 65 miles per hour in its flat land regions and 55 miles per hour its mountainous regions. To reduce traffic fatalities and combat the fact that most of the vehicles on state highways were exceeding posted speed limits, the state legislature proposed banning the use of radar detectors. Citizens in the mountainous regions of the state, where most of the state's highway fatalities occurred, generally supported the ban, but citizens in the flat regions of the state opposed the ban, so the legislature adopted a law banning use of radar detectors on any road with a speed limit below 60 miles per hour.

A driver whose car was equipped with a radar detector lived in the mountainous region of the state but frequently drove to the state's flat region. While on a mountain highway with a posted speed limit of 55 miles per hour, the driver was pulled over by a state trooper for speeding. While approaching the driver's car, the state trooper noticed that the driver's radar detector was turned on. The trooper ticketed the driver for both speeding and illegal use of a radar detector. The driver challenges his ticket for use of the radar detector, arguing that it is unfair to allow people in the flat lands to use radar detectors while prohibiting residents of the mountainous region from using them.

Which of the following statements is correct regarding the burden of proof in such a case?

(A) The state will have to prove that the ban serves a compelling state interest.

(B) The state will have to prove that the ban is rationally related to a legitimate state interest.

(C) The driver will have to prove that the ban does not serve a compelling interest.

(D) The driver will have to prove that the ban is not rationally related to a legitimate state interest.

Question 14

A town's public high school lost its French teacher shortly before the school year began and the board of education was unable to find a replacement. Faced with the prospect of canceling all French classes, the board agreed to a proposal offered by the principal of the parochial high school, whereby the parochial school's state-qualified French teacher would teach at the parochial school in the mornings and at the public school in the afternoons, and the board would reimburse the parochial school for half of the teacher's salary and benefits package costs. The board began forwarding monthly checks to the parochial school to cover 50% of teacher's salary and benefits once the school year began. A local group favoring complete separation of church and state learned of the arrangement and filed suit in federal court to block the payments.

Assuming that there are no problems with jurisdiction or standing, the group will most likely:

(A) Lose, because the arrangement is for a secular purpose, has a primary effect of neither advancing nor inhibiting religion, and does not unduly entangle a governmental body with religion.

(B) Lose, because the school board had a compelling need for the French teacher's services.

(C) Prevail, because by paying half of the parochial school's teacher's salary, the town is favoring the parochial school's religious sect over others.

(D) Prevail, because it is unconstitutional to transfer public funds to a parochial school.

Question 15

Which of the following acts would be improper for the United States Senate to perform?

(A) Adjudicating a border dispute between states.

(B) Defining certain qualifications for being a member in good standing of the United States Senate.

(C) Sitting in joint session with the House of Representatives.

(D) Passing a resolution directing the President to pursue a particular course of foreign policy.

Question 16

Congress passed legislation banning the hunting of snipe birds within the United States. The range of the snipe is quite limited; they are found primarily in only one state, although they migrate annually to several nearby states. Hunters from throughout the United States have traditionally traveled to the snipe's home state during snipe hunting season, bringing considerable revenue into the state. A state statute allows hunting of snipe during a two-week period in November and charges a $50 license fee for state residents and a $250 fee for hunters from other states. The bag limit is one snipe bird per licensed hunter.

The state statute allowing snipe hunting is:

(A) Valid, because states have the right to control their own natural resources and wildlife.

(B) Valid, because the power exercised is reserved to the states by the Tenth Amendment.

(C) Invalid, because of the Supremacy Clause.

(D) Invalid, because of the Commerce Clause.

Question 17

A state adopted legislation making it a crime to be the biological parent of more than two children. The stated purpose of the statute is to preserve the state's natural resources and improve the quality of life for the state's residents. A married couple has just had their third child. They have been arrested and convicted under the statute.

Which of the following is the strongest argument for voiding the convictions of the couple?

(A) The statute is an invalid exercise of the state's police power because there is no rational basis for concluding that the challenged statute would further the government's stated interests.

(B) The statute places an unconstitutional burden on the fundamental privacy interests of married persons.

(C) The statute places too much discretion in state officials to determine who will be permitted to bear children.

(D) The statute denies married persons equal protection of law.

Question 18

To reduce air pollution, a town adopted an antipollution ordinance prohibiting the burning of trash, garbage, leaves, or similar matter, with an exception for materials used in outdoor barbecue grills. On the night of October 31, a town resident raked a large quantity of leaves into a pile in her back yard and set them on fire as part of a nontraditional religious ritual. Although she was careful in building the fire so that there was no danger that it could spread to any structure, her neighbor reported the fire to the police and fire departments. Firefighters doused the fire and the resident was charged under the antipollution ordinance. At trial, the resident truthfully told the court she was merely observing one of the important tenets of her faith. The trial judge summarily fined the resident $250, and she appealed the conviction in federal court, asserting that her freedom of religion has been infringed.

Will the fine likely be upheld?

(A) Yes, because the resident does not belong to a traditional established religion.

(B) Yes, because the ordinance was adopted to reduce air pollution and not to prohibit religious practices.

(C) No, because the town could accomplish its goal through less restrictive means.

(D) No, because the ordinance is not necessary to promote a compelling interest.

CONSTITUTIONAL LAW ANSWERS - SET 1

Answer to Question 1

(C) The armed forces recruiting center is least likely to be required to comply with the new state law. A state has no power to regulate activities of the federal government unless Congress consents to the regulation. Accordingly, agents and instrumentalities of the federal government, such as the armed forces recruiting center, are immune from state regulations relating to performance of their federal functions. (D) is incorrect because, although the recreation center's construction was funded by a loan from the Veterans Administration, the center itself is privately operated and funded by donations. As a result, the center has only a tenuous connection with the federal government, so that it cannot claim the immunity afforded to a federal agency or instrumentality. Accordingly, in the same sense as is employed in the federal tax immunity cases, the agency does not "stand in the shoes" of the federal government. Thus, the application of the state regulations to the recreation center would not present constitutional problems. (A) apparently refers to the principle that the power to regulate foreign commerce lies exclusively with Congress. However, the mere fact that the regulated outlets are part of a wholly owned subsidiary of a Japanese corporation does not mean that the state regulations affect foreign commerce. The subsidiary's activities are conducted entirely within the state, and do not touch upon foreign commerce in any way. Therefore, application of the regulations so as to require the subsidiary to provide an ionizing air purification system for its employee work areas will not constitute a proscribed state regulation of foreign commerce. Thus, (A) is incorrect. (B) is more troubling, but does not offer as compelling an argument as (C). The Contract Clause prohibits states from acting to ***substantially*** impair contract rights (*i.e.,* destroy most or all of a party's rights under an existing contract). Under the Clause, the Supreme Court will subject state actions that impair their own contracts to strict scrutiny. In any case, even if state action substantially impairs rights under an existing contract, the action still may be upheld if it: (i) serves an important and legitimate public interest; and (ii) is a reasonable and narrowly tailored means of promoting that interest. Here, the state supreme court, as an instrumentality of the state, would probably not have grounds for complaining that its rights under the contract have been impaired, but the builder might have grounds (*e.g.,* the builder might have future economic interests during the three-year service period that will be substantially impaired if the court is required to install an ionizing system). Nevertheless, the regulation still may be valid if the state can prove that it truly serves the important public interest of protecting the health and safety of workers in the state and is narrowly tailored to promoting that interest. In any case, because it is uncertain whether the vendor's rights have been substantially impaired and, if so, whether the state can prove the worth of the regulation, (C) is a better choice.

Answer to Question 2

(A) The legislation is unconstitutional because the President has exclusive power to pardon. Article II, Section 2 of the United States Constitution grants the President the power to grant reprieves and pardons for offenses against the United States, except in cases of impeachment. This pardon power is not subject to control by Congress and it includes the power to commute a sentence on any conditions the President chooses (as long as the conditions do not offend some other constitutional provision). As applied to the facts here, Congress quite simply lacks the authority to circumscribe the President's power to pardon persons convicted under the statute at issue. (B) is incorrect because it is too broad. It is true that the President has the duty to enforce the laws, and that certain powers are part of and emanate from this duty. However, the call of this question clearly points toward the need to address the pardon power specifically, as well as any possible

congressional limitations on that power. (C) is incorrect because Article I, Section 1 of the Constitution simply vests all legislative powers in the Congress. As explained above, this legislative power does not include the authority to set limitations on the President's pardon power. Consequently, the congressional action undertaken here is unconstitutional. (D) is incorrect because it also concludes that Congress is empowered to limit the pardon power. In addition, the language of (D) amounts to a bill of attainder if applied to the man pardoned. A bill of attainder is a legislative act that inflicts punishment without a judicial trial upon individuals who are designated either by name or in terms of past conduct. Both the federal and state governments are prohibited from passing bills of attainder. The assertion by Congress of the right to determine who should be convicted under a statute would amount to an attempt to pass a bill of attainder, because conviction would be imposed without a judicial trial.

Answer to Question 3

(B) The court should find the statute constitutional as long as Congress has consented to the tax. Article I, Section 10, Clause 2 provides: "No state shall, without the Consent of the Congress, lay any Imposts or Duties on Imports or Exports, except what may be absolutely necessary for executing its inspection Laws." Hence, the Import-Export Clause prohibits the states from imposing any tax on imported goods as such or on commercial activity connected with imported goods as such (*i.e.*, taxes discriminating against imports), except with congressional consent. Thus, (B) is correct and (A) is incorrect. (C) is wrong because the Privileges and Immunities Clause does not apply to corporations or aliens. (D) is wrong because without congressional consent, the statute is unconstitutional despite the compelling nature of the state's interest.

Answer to Question 4

(C) The legislation, which is not narrowly tailored to promote a compelling state interest, violates the Establishment Clause. The Establishment Clause of the First Amendment prohibits any law "respecting an establishment of religion." While usually a three-part test based on *Lemon v. Kurtzman* is used to determine whether legislation creates improper government involvement with religion, the "compelling state interest" test is used if a law or government program discriminates among religions. Here, the law differentiates among different religious groups, allowing only those with larger memberships to record presentations. There is no compelling state interest for discriminating among the religious groups in this way; thus the legislation is unconstitutional. (A) is incorrect despite the fact that the federal commerce power could be interpreted as extending to commerce with outer space should the occasion arise. Nevertheless, the commerce power does not override independent constitutional restrictions (*e.g.*, the Establishment Clause) on the conduct in question here. (B) is an incorrect statement of law. The federal commerce power cannot be used to abrogate freedom of speech or to discriminate in favor of religious groups. (D) is incorrect. Regardless of merit, almost all expenditures made by Congress are permissible under its spending power. [U.S. Const. art. I, §8] Rather than limit the power only to spending for accomplishment of other enumerated powers, this provision grants Congress broad power to spend for the "general welfare" (*i.e.*, any public purpose). As long as the expenditure is not conditioned on requiring a recipient to forgo an individual constitutional right, it is within the spending power of Congress.

Answer to Question 5

(D) The town licensing requirement unconstitutionally impinges upon a duly authorized federal program. The United States Government, as well as its agencies and instrumentalities, is immune from state regulation that interferes with federal activities, functions, and programs. To the extent that state regulations substantially interfere with an authorized federal program, the state laws must yield. Here, the director, as an agent of the federal government, was carrying out a duly authorized program of the Department of Agriculture by conducting sales of surplus government food at a federally owned warehouse. To sustain the power of the town to prosecute the director for not having a retail food sale license would give the town overriding authority over the selection of personnel to administer a federal program, as well as over the means by which this program is to be implemented. Thus, the licensing requirement would substantially interfere with the proper functioning of this federal program by directly interfering with a federal employee in the carrying out of his orders. (A) is incorrect because the facts do not indicate that the licensing requirement is in any way a measurable burden upon interstate commerce, much less an ***undue*** burden. The licensing regulation appears to affect, almost exclusively, the peculiarly local concerns of health and sanitation. (B) is incorrect because an equal protection violation exists where a law limits the liberty of some persons but not others, *i.e.,* where a law treats similar persons in a dissimilar manner. The licensing regulation at issue here is apparently being applied in an even-handed fashion, and the director is not being treated differently from anyone else who does not have the required license. Thus, there is no equal protection problem. (C) is incorrect because the director is not being deprived of any property or interest to which he has a legitimate claim; *e.g.,* he is not being deprived of employment to which he is entitled. Because there is no deprivation of property, there is no due process issue.

Answer to Question 6

(D) The law is unconstitutional because it gives the federal district courts authority to render advisory opinions. The Supreme Court has interpreted the constitutional power of the federal courts to hear "cases and controversies" to mean that federal courts may not render advisory opinions. Under the law here, the district court's decision is not binding on an agency dispensing funds, because the agency head is given discretion to decide whether the court's judgment is fair. Therefore, the judgment is merely advisory and so is not within the jurisdiction of the federal courts. (A) is incorrect because while it is true that the cases would present a federal question, it is not enough merely that a federal question exists; there must be a case or controversy. (B) is incorrect for the same reason. Congress certainly has authority to provide for the settlement of disputes under federal grant programs, but that authority does not permit Congress to violate the case or controversy requirement. (C) is incorrect because the Eleventh Amendment only prohibits the federal courts from hearing an action by a citizen of a state against his state; actions between the federal government and a state are not barred.

Answer to Question 7

(A) The federal court should strike the ordinance for violating the First Amendment. While the government may limit the amount of contributions that an individual can contribute to a candidate's campaign (to avoid corruption or the appearance of corruption), the government may not limit the contributions to a political committee that supports or opposes a ballot referendum, because such a law does not serve a sufficiently important interest to outweigh the restraints that it puts on the First Amendment freedoms of speech and association. (B) is incorrect because the Due Process Clause does not require that every law provide for a hearing, but only those laws involving the deprivation of life, liberty, or property of an ***individual***. The law here does not involve a deprivation of life or property, and liberty is not being denied to individuals on a judicial basis (*i.e.,* according to the facts of each case), but rather is being denied to all persons on a legislative basis. In such a case, individual hearings are not required to satisfy due process;

as long as the law was lawfully adopted (*e.g.,* with notice to all interested parties), the Due Process Clause has been satisfied. (C) is incorrect because a legitimate interest in controlling contributions to a political committee for ballot referendum is not enough. The statute must be "closely drawn" to match a "sufficiently important interest," which is an intermediate scrutiny standard, and the Supreme Court has invalidated limitations on contributions to influence referendum elections. (D) is incorrect because political questions, which are nonjusticiable, arise when the issue is committed to another branch of the government by the Constitution or is incapable of resolution and enforcement by the judiciary. Determining whether a law is valid is within the realm of the judiciary and certainly is capable of resolution (*i.e.,* the law could be invalidated). Thus, there is no political question here.

Answer to Question 8

(B) The federal court will hear the student's case if the student argues that the prosecutor was merely trying to harass him. The federal courts generally will abstain from enjoining pending state criminal proceedings, such as the one here, even if they have jurisdiction over the case. For purposes of this rule, a case is deemed to be pending as soon as it is filed. Thus, the federal court would ordinarily not hear the student's claim here until after the state prosecution has ended. However, there is an exception to the general rule—a federal court will hear an action to enjoin a pending state court prosecution if it is being conducted in bad faith; *e.g.,* merely to harass the defendant. Thus, (B) is correct. (A) is incorrect because the abstention rule does not distinguish between claims that ordinances are invalid on their face and claims that they are invalid as applied. (C) is incorrect because the student clearly has standing. A person has standing to challenge a governmental action if he can show an injury in fact from the action that is greater than the injury everyone suffers when the government acts unlawfully, and that a decision in his favor will remedy the injury. If the ordinance here is being applied unconstitutionally, the student has suffered a sufficient injury, and a decision in his favor will remedy his injury. (D) is incorrect because whether an ordinance is being applied in an unconstitutional manner is not a political question. Political questions are those committed by the Constitution to another branch of the government or that are inherently incapable of resolution and enforcement by the judicial process. This case is properly within the judiciary branch and the courts can resolve it.

Answer to Question 9

(D) The best argument for getting the law invalidated is that it is not rationally related to a legitimate state interest. The lawyer would argue that the statute violates equal protection because it singles out one class of citizens for special treatment. Because neither a fundamental right nor a suspect nor quasi-suspect class is involved here, the case would be decided under the rational basis standard. For a law to be held invalid under the rational basis standard, the plaintiff must show that the law is not rationally related to a legitimate state interest. Toward this end, the lawyer might argue that the law will really cost more money than it will save, perhaps because the resulting number of injuries due to the absence of studded tires will more than offset the money saved in road repair. (This argument will likely fail, however, because courts give legislatures broad discretion in making such determinations, and the statute does appear to be rational. Nevertheless, this is the lawyer's best argument.) (A) is incorrect because the Privileges and Immunities Clause of Article IV applies only to discrimination by a state against nonresidents, and here the lawyer is a resident of the state that enacted the legislation. (B) is incorrect because nothing in the facts indicates that the right to travel is involved. The right to travel involves ***interstate*** travel, and here, all travel concerns are wholly intrastate. (C) is incorrect because there is no unreasonable restraint on interstate commerce. If Congress has not allowed or prohibited state regulation in the area, a nondiscriminatory state regulation will be upheld only if its burden on commerce does not outweigh a legitimate local interest. Here, because no other state allows studded snow tires, the ban does not discriminate against out-of-state vehicles and does not burden commerce. (If other states allowed these snow tires, there might be a viable Commerce Clause issue.)

Answer to Question 10

(A) The Court should refuse to grant certiorari because the case was decided on independent state grounds. The Supreme Court will not hear a case from a state court, even though it has jurisdiction over the parties and the subject matter, if there are adequate and independent state grounds to support the decision. Here, the state court held the law invalid on state, rather than federal, constitutional grounds. Therefore, the Supreme Court should refuse to grant certiorari. (B) is incorrect because mootness goes to whether there is a real, live controversy at this stage of the proceeding. The case here is not moot because the city wants to challenge the ruling that the law was unconstitutional under the state constitution. If the city wins, it may enforce the ordinance. (C) is incorrect because no political question is involved here. A political question, which is nonjusticiable, is one involving an issue that the Constitution has committed to another branch of the government or that is inherently incapable of judicial resolution and enforcement. Whether a law is constitutional—a determination of law—is certainly capable of judicial resolution and is properly within the judiciary branch's powers. Thus, a political question is not involved. (D) is incorrect because, as explained above, the basis for the decision was a state, not federal, violation. Therefore, there is no federal question.

Answer to Question 11

(B) Of the choices presented, the only likely basis to strike down the statute is that it would violate substantive due process. Substantive due process tests the reasonableness of a statute; it prohibits arbitrary governmental action. Under substantive due process, when government action limits a fundamental right, the government must prove that the action is necessary to promote a compelling interest. If a fundamental right is not involved, the challenging party must prove that the act is not rationally related to any legitimate government interest. The retail sale of diapers is not a fundamental right, and so a challenger must prove that there is no rational basis for the statute. Almost any law can be justified under the rational basis standard. The law need not be the best law for accomplishing the government's goal. Thus, even if it is true that the disposable diaper ban causes more pollution than it prevents, because the ban is rationally related to reducing the volume of trash in landfills, the challenge is unlikely to succeed. Nevertheless, none of the other choices states a viable ground for invalidating the statute, and so (B) is the best choice. (A) is wrong because equal protection applies where a statute or governmental action treats similar people in a dissimilar manner (*i.e.,* classifies people), and here there is no classification—under the statute ***no one*** can sell disposable diapers for use within the state. Thus, an equal protection argument is not applicable. (C) is wrong because the Impairment of Contracts Clause prohibits only the ***substantial*** impairment of existing contracts (and there are exceptions even where there is substantial impairment), and nothing in the facts indicates that forbidding the retail sale of disposable diapers would substantially impair any existing contract. (D) is wrong because the privileges and immunities covered by the Fourteenth Amendment are those attributes peculiar to United States citizenship (*e.g.,* the right to petition Congress for redress or the right to vote for federal officers). The statute here does not affect such rights.

Answer to Question 12

(D) The best argument against enforcement of the tax is that it violates the Commerce Clause. If Congress has not adopted laws regarding a subject, local governments are free to tax or regulate

local aspects of the subject area as long as the tax or regulation does not discriminate against interstate commerce or unduly burden it. Here, the tax does not discriminate against interstate commerce, since it does not single out interstate commerce for taxation in order to benefit the local economy. However, it could be argued that the tax unduly burdens interstate commerce. A local tax will be held to unduly burden interstate commerce if the locality's need for the revenue does not outweigh the burden on interstate commerce. The Supreme Court will consider whether there is a substantial nexus between the activity or property taxed and the taxing state, whether the tax is fairly apportioned, and whether there is a fair relationship between the tax and the benefit the taxed party receives from the state. Here, there is little nexus between the manufacturer and the town. The facts indicate that out-of-state manufacturers' machines are used in the town, but do not indicate whether the manufacturers conduct any selling activity in the town. Similarly, nothing indicates that there is a relationship between the tax and any benefit that the manufacturers derive from the town. Thus, the tax would probably be unconstitutional under the Commerce Clause. (A) is not as good an argument as (D) because the Equal Protection Clause prohibits the states from treating similarly situated persons differently without sufficient justification. Where a classification does not involve a suspect or quasi-suspect class or a fundamental right, the classification will be upheld as long as it is rationally related to a legitimate government interest. While the tax here singles out arcade game manufacturers for special tax treatment, no suspect or quasi-suspect class is involved, nor is a fundamental right affected. Thus, the tax will be valid under the Equal Protection Clause because it is rationally related to the legitimate government interest of raising revenue. (B) is not a good argument because substantive due process requires that laws not be arbitrary. When laws do not involve a fundamental right, they will be held valid under the Due Process Clause as long as they are rationally related to a legitimate government interest. As established above, no fundamental right is involved and the tax is rationally related to a legitimate government interest. Thus, under the Due Process Clause the tax may be enforced. (C) is not a good argument because the Privileges and Immunities Clause of Article IV prohibits states from discriminating against out-of-state residents when a fundamental right is involved, and the tax here does not differentiate between residents and nonresidents.

Answer to Question 13

(D) The driver will have to prove that the ban is not rationally related to a legitimate state interest. Whether the law here is examined under the substantive provisions of the Due Process Clause or the Equal Protection Clause, the analysis is the same: If no fundamental right or suspect or quasi-suspect class is involved, the law will be assessed under the rational basis standard. Under that standard, government action will be upheld unless a challenger can prove that it is not rationally related to a legitimate government interest. Here, the right involved (using a radar detector) is not fundamental, and no suspect or quasi-suspect class is involved. Thus, the regulation will be assessed under the rational basis standard. (A) is incorrect because, as explained above, the compelling interest standard does not apply when neither a fundamental right nor a suspect classification is involved. (B) is incorrect because, although it states the correct standard, it placed the burden of proof on the wrong party. The challenger must prove that the law is irrational; the government need not prove that it is rational. (C) is incorrect because it states the wrong standard (compelling interest). Moreover, if the compelling interest test were applicable, the government would have to prove that the standard was met; the burden would not be on the driver.

Answer to Question 14

(A) The group will lose because the action does not violate the Establishment Clause. Where government aid is given to a religious body and no sect preference is involved (the case here, because the school board did not require that the teacher be from a particular religious sect), the aid will be upheld if: (i) it has a secular purpose; (ii) its primary effect neither advances nor inhibits religion; and (iii) it does not produce excessive government entanglement with religion. Here, the payments made to the parochial school constitute government aid, because the government is sending money to the school. However, all three requisites to constitutional validity are met: the program serves the secular purpose of providing the public school with a French teacher; the primary effect of the program does not promote religion, rather it promotes the learning of French; and no excessive government entanglement is involved because all the school board is required to do is to send the parochial school a check for half of the teacher's compensation. Thus, the program is valid. (B) is incorrect because it refers to the wrong standard. As explained above, there is no sect preference here. Therefore, a compelling interest need not be shown. Moreover, it is uncertain whether offering French classes is a compelling government interest. (C) is incorrect because, as explained above, the Establishment Clause is not violated. (D) is incorrect because it is too broad; while usually a transfer of public funds to a parochial school would violate the Establishment Clause, such transfers are permissible where the three-part test (above) is satisfied.

Answer to Question 15

(A) It would be improper for the Senate to adjudicate a border dispute between states. The Constitution divides the power of the federal government among the three branches. The power to adjudicate actions where two or more states are involved, which would include actions to adjudicate border disputes, is vested in the judicial branch by Article III of the Constitution. Thus, it would be improper for the Senate to adjudicate such a border dispute. (B) is incorrect because it would be proper for the Senate to define certain qualifications for being a member in good standing of the Senate. The Constitution lists certain minimal requirements for Senators, but grants each House of Congress the power to be the judge of member qualifications and allows each to determine rules for proceedings. [U.S. Const. art. I, §5] (C) is incorrect because the Constitution contains no prohibition against joint sessions of Congress and, as mentioned above, it grants both Houses the power to regulate their proceedings, which would include the manner of their meetings. (D) is incorrect because Congress has some power over foreign affairs—through its war power, its treaty power, and its power to regulate foreign commerce—and a resolution would probably be proper pursuant to such power. Moreover, while the President's power over foreign affairs is paramount, a resolution such as the one here amounts to nothing more than a suggestion to the President, and so would not be a usurpation of the executive.

Answer to Question 16

(C) The state statute is invalid because of the Supremacy Clause. Under the Clause, if the federal government adopts legislation that it has the power to adopt, the federal legislation is supreme, and a conflicting state law is rendered invalid. The federal law here, banning the hunting of snipe, is within the federal government's power under the Commerce Clause, which gives the government power to regulate anything that might affect interstate commerce. Because the birds themselves are found in a few states, they probably cross state lines. Also, hunters come from out of state and generate revenue in the state, so interstate commerce is involved. The state law directly conflicts with the federal law because it allows hunting of snipe. Therefore, the state law will be held invalid under the Supremacy Clause. (A) is incorrect because, while states do have a limited right to control their natural resources, the right is concurrent with the federal government's power, and cannot be exercised to conflict with federal regulation in the area. Note further that a state's power to control its natural resources is also limited even if Congress does not act: A state

may not adopt a law discriminating against interstate commerce or excessively burdening interstate commerce, even absent federal legislation. Regarding (B), the Tenth Amendment reserves all powers not granted to the federal government to the states. (B) is incorrect because the Court will not likely strike down on Tenth Amendment grounds a federal regulation that subjects state governments to the same regulations as apply to the private sector. In such cases, the states' interests are best protected by the states' representation in Congress. (D) is incorrect because the Commerce Clause does not render the state's action invalid; it merely gives Congress the power to act. It is the Clause that makes the interfering state law invalid.

Answer to Question 17

(B) The couple's strongest argument is that the law burdens their fundamental right of privacy. The right of privacy is not specifically mentioned in the Constitution, but the Supreme Court has recognized the right on a number of occasions. The right is strong when it involves acts of procreation by married couples. When the government restricts a fundamental right, such as the right here, the government must show a ***compelling interest*** in the regulation and that the regulation is ***necessary*** to achieve that purpose. This is a difficult standard to meet, and thus the statute will probably be struck down. Here, the stated purposes for the law (improving the quality of life and preserving natural resources) may be found by the Court to be compelling, but the limitation on the number of children that couples may have certainly is not ***necessary*** for these purposes. Thus, this is the couple's best argument. (A) is not a good argument for two reasons: (i) because a fundamental right is involved, the rational basis standard (suggested by this choice) is improper, as strict scrutiny is the appropriate standard; and (ii) the statute here in fact is ***rationally*** related to its stated purpose because this standard is a very easy one to meet. (C) is not as good an argument as (B) because the facts do not indicate that any official discretion is involved. The statute is violated when anyone is the biological parent of more than two children. (D) is incorrect because the Equal Protection Clause merely prohibits treating classes of persons differently without adequate justification, and here, the statute applies equally to all persons; it does not classify.

Answer to Question 18

(B) The fine will be upheld because the ordinance was enacted to reduce air pollution. The First Amendment provides that government may not make a law prohibiting the free exercise of religion. This prohibition, however, is not absolute, and the Supreme Court has held that a law of general applicability will not be struck down on free exercise grounds unless it was enacted for the purpose of burdening religion. [Employment Division v. Smith (1990)] The ordinance here was clearly enacted to reduce air pollution, and thus is valid as applied to the resident. The court will not force the town to carve out an exception to this prohibition on religious grounds. (A) is incorrect because it is irrelevant what religious group the resident belongs to; the result would be the same even if she belonged to a traditional religion. Moreover, the fact that the resident's religion is not traditional cannot even be considered by the court, because a court is not allowed to assess the validity of religious belief; it may only assess whether a person sincerely holds the religious belief that she claims. (C) is incorrect because it goes to the balancing test formerly used by the Supreme Court to assess whether a law was valid under the Free Exercise Clause. Since *Employment Division v. Smith,* factors such as less restrictive means are irrelevant. (D) is incorrect because the compelling interest test is no longer important in judging laws affecting religious ***conduct***. (This was also a factor under the old balancing test.) As stated above, a law of general application not enacted to burden religion is valid, and the Court does not consider whether the state's interest is compelling.

Set 2 Answer Sheet

1. Ⓐ Ⓑ Ⓒ Ⓓ
2. Ⓐ Ⓑ Ⓒ Ⓓ
3. Ⓐ Ⓑ Ⓒ Ⓓ
4. Ⓐ Ⓑ Ⓒ Ⓓ
5. Ⓐ Ⓑ Ⓒ Ⓓ
6. Ⓐ Ⓑ Ⓒ Ⓓ
7. Ⓐ Ⓑ Ⓒ Ⓓ
8. Ⓐ Ⓑ Ⓒ Ⓓ
9. Ⓐ Ⓑ Ⓒ Ⓓ
10. Ⓐ Ⓑ Ⓒ Ⓓ
11. Ⓐ Ⓑ Ⓒ Ⓓ
12. Ⓐ Ⓑ Ⓒ Ⓓ
13. Ⓐ Ⓑ Ⓒ Ⓓ
14. Ⓐ Ⓑ Ⓒ Ⓓ
15. Ⓐ Ⓑ Ⓒ Ⓓ
16. Ⓐ Ⓑ Ⓒ Ⓓ
17. Ⓐ Ⓑ Ⓒ Ⓓ
18. Ⓐ Ⓑ Ⓒ Ⓓ

CONSTITUTIONAL LAW QUESTIONS—SET 2

Question 1

A housing development contained one-, two-, and three-bedroom units. All units were suitable for occupancy, and the developers of the project filed the appropriate documents, including a Declaration of Restrictions that limited ownership and occupancy of the units to families or to groups of unrelated adults of not more than three in number. Each deed to the individual units also contained the restriction.

One of the two-bedroom units was purchased by a woman and her boyfriend. They immediately moved into the unit with another unmarried couple who were friends of theirs. Other unit owners brought suit against the woman and her boyfriend to enjoin the occupancy by the other couple.

If the other unit owners prevail, it will be because:

(A) The litigants are private parties and the restriction was not enacted by the government.

(B) Enforcement of the restriction is rationally related to a legitimate government interest.

(C) Notice was not given by the woman and her boyfriend to the sellers of the unit that they intended to occupy the residence with another couple.

(D) The restriction constitutes a lawful restraint on alienation.

Question 2

A city ordinance provided that anyone who wanted to speak in a public park must have a permit to do so issued by the city. The ordinance granted the mayor discretion to issue or deny such permits based on the mayor's judgment of whether the speech would be "in the public interest." The mayor has never denied a permit to anybody desiring to speak on a political topic.

A city resident who was unhappy with the city government went to a public park in the city square. There, he made a 10-minute speech accusing the mayor and the city council of gross incompetence and urging voters to "throw the rascals out" at the next election. The city resident had not applied for a permit. After the resident completed his oration, the police arrested him and charged him with violating the permit ordinance.

Would a conviction of the resident be constitutional?

(A) Yes, because the resident did not have a permit to speak, and a municipality has the right to regulate the time, place, and manner of speech.

(B) Yes, because the mayor would have issued the permit, because the resident's speech was on a political topic.

(C) No, because the ordinance is void on its face.

(D) No, but only if the resident could prove that the mayor would not have issued him a permit to speak.

Question 3

The federal government owned an old but functional building in a warm southern state. Its furnace was quite outmoded, but because of the building's location, the furnace was used only a few days a year. However, on the days it was used, it emitted a noticeable quantity of smoke and particulate matter. The amount of pollutants exuded into air on those days exceeded the state's stringent environmental regulations.

If the state attempts to enforce its environmental standards and compel compliance by the federal building, who will likely prevail?

(A) The state, because a state may regulate the quality of its own air under its police power.

(B) The state, because the states and the federal government have joint responsibility for clean air, and the federal government should give full faith and credit to the state's laws and regulations in the area.

(C) The federal government, because the Supremacy Clause of Article VI prevents the state from imposing its regulations on the federal government.

(D) The federal government, because the emissions from the building occur so seldom as to be minimal, and the state cannot assert sufficient harm to the health of its citizens to constitute a compelling interest.

Question 4

A pool hall seeking to attract more afternoon business advertised a $2 per hour table rental discount between the hours of 2 and 6 p.m. The ad caught the attention of students who attended a high school in the city where the pool hall was located, and soon the hall was bristling with students in the afternoon. To discourage city youth from frittering away their afternoons, the city council passed an ordinance imposing a $2 per hour rental tax on pool tables rented before 6 p.m. on weekdays.

A lawsuit to challenge the tax could be brought by any of the following ***except***:

(A) A civic watchdog and good government group.

(B) The owner of the pool hall.

(C) A citizen of the city who opposes every new tax and who has taken advantage of the discount on several occasions.

(D) A 16-year-old boy who regularly plays pool at the hall after school.

Question 5

A state statute made it unlawful to sell milk for home consumption in containers less than one quart in size. Violation of the statute was a misdemeanor, punishable by a $500 fine and loss of the retail business license. The owner of a convenience store within the state who specialized in sales of pints of milk to walk-in lunchtime buyers had her retail license immediately revoked when a state inspector discovered that the owner was selling milk in pints.

The owner's best argument in a suit to defeat the revocation is that the action of the state agency:

(A) Impaired her contract with wholesale distributors of pint cartons of milk.

(B) Was a denial of equal protection.

(C) Was a denial of procedural due process.

(D) Was a denial of substantive due process.

Question 6

A student activist at a state-supported university filed a defamation suit in federal court against the school, seeking a cease and desist order. The suit alleged that several university officials had been making statements to the local press about the student, falsely accusing her of both bizarre sexual activities and former felonious crimes. In addition, the student alleged that she had found herself generally harassed on campus by university personnel and that the university's actions against the student were intended to silence her criticisms. Within a week after the suit was filed, the defamations and harassments ceased. When the case came before the federal court four months later, both sides stipulated that the defamations and harassments had ceased.

What action should the district court take?

(A) Dismiss the suit for lack of standing.

(B) Dismiss the suit for mootness.

(C) Dismiss the suit, because the case is not ripe.

(D) Hear the case on the merits.

Question 7

A music show promoter was handing out leaflets at a county fair, advertising a commercial country and western music concert scheduled at the fairgrounds two weeks after the county fair was due to end. The fair manager approached the promoter and politely asked him to stop distributing leaflets because it was in contravention of the fair's rules. The promoter refused to stop, and the manager summoned a county police officer. In the officer's presence, the manager again told the promoter to stop handing out the leaflets. The promoter ignored the manager again and continued to hand out leaflets, at which point he was arrested for criminal trespass and charged in municipal court. At trial, the promoter defended against the charges by claiming a violation of his First Amendment rights.

Which of the following, if true, is most damaging to the promoter's First Amendment claims?

(A) The place where the promoter distributed leaflets was private property leased to the county for holding the fair.

(B) The rules of the county fair clearly prohibit all leafleting or other solicitations on fair property, except at designated hours other than the time the promoter was engaged in distributing leaflets.

(C) The means of communication was printed leaflets rather than oral speech.

(D) The message on the leaflets promoted a commercial event.

Question 8

A city zoning board recently denied a request from the local library for a variance needed to expand the library building. In order to put pressure on the board to change their vote, a library patron went to the library, stood next to the front door, and handed each person entering the library a leaflet asking the person to contact each city zoning board member named in the leaflet and threaten to vote each member out of office unless the member changed his or her vote regarding the library's request for a zoning variance. The head librarian noticed the patron handing out the leaflets and asked her to stop, correctly explaining that the distribution was in violation of a city ordinance. The patron refused to comply, and the head librarian summoned the police. When an officer arrived, the librarian again asked the patron to stop distributing leaflets, but the patron again refused. The officer then arrested patron for violating a city ordinance. At trial, the patron defended against the charges by claiming a violation of her First Amendment rights.

Which of the following variations of fact would be most helpful to the patron's First Amendment claim?

(A) The librarian did not repeat the "cease and desist" request in the police officer's presence.

(B) The library is completely surrounded by public sidewalks.

(C) The librarian has permitted some people to distribute leaflets at the front door of the library at all hours.

(D) The leaflets also requested campaign contributions to be used to oppose board members who failed to change their vote.

Question 9

A city passed an ordinance prohibiting persons on a public sidewalk within 100 feet of a health care facility from approaching within eight feet of those seeking access to the facility for purposes of protest, education, or counseling. The day after the city's new ordinance became effective, a person advocating against abortion went to an abortion clinic within the city, stood 25 feet from its entrance, stopped the first woman whom she saw about to enter the clinic, and gave her a leaflet espousing the leafletter's religious views and discouraging abortion. The leafletter was promptly arrested for violating the city's ordinance. At trial, the leafletter challenges the ordinance on First Amendment grounds.

How should the court rule on the leafletter's First Amendment defense?

(A) In favor of the leafletter, because the ordinance violates the Free Exercise Clause.

(B) In favor of the leafletter, because the ordinance infringes on the freedom of speech.

(C) In favor of the city, because the ordinance is reasonable as to time, place, and manner.

(D) In favor of the city, because patients' and visitors' freedom of association right to be let alone is being infringed by the leafletter.

Question 10

A state passed a statute requiring all employers in the state to provide a medical insurance plan for full-time employees. A state trade association to which many state employers belong brought suit in federal court, asking the court to strike down the statute as unconstitutional.

Which of the following best reflects the burden of persuasion in this case?

(A) The burden is on the trade association to prove that the statute is not rationally related to a legitimate state interest.

(B) The burden is on the trade association to prove that the statute is not necessary to achieve a compelling state interest.

(C) The burden is on the state to prove that the statute is rationally related to a legitimate state in interest.

(D) The burden is on the state to prove that the statute is necessary to achieve a compelling state interest.

Question 11

To boost the slumping cruise ship trade, Congress passed a bill providing that six outmoded United States Navy vessels would be sold to a private cruise company for $1 each, on condition that the company refurbish the ships at its own expense and operate the ships as cruise ships for at least four years. The conditions for the refurbishing were highly specific, and it would cost the company at least $3 million to refit each ship as a modern cruise liner. The company agreed to the conditions, but a competitor cruise company filed suit in federal court to block the sale.

Which of the following statements is most correct concerning disposition of the case?

(A) The federal court should treat the sale as presumptively valid, because the Constitution expressly gives Congress the power to dispose of property of the United States.

(B) The federal court should treat the sale as presumptively invalid, because the Constitution expressly denies Congress the right to deprive persons of property without due process of law.

(C) The federal court should rule the statute constitutional only if the President or the Secretary of Defense has certified that the Navy ships are obsolete for defense purposes.

(D) The federal court should rule the statute unconstitutional, because it denies other cruise ship operators the equal protection of the laws.

Question 12

Congress passed a law forbidding the United States mails to be used for the distribution of unsolicited advertising for contraceptives.

Although the legislation was cheered by some religious groups and organizations fearful of a "birth dearth" among the American middle class, the legislation was strongly opposed by a number of family planning and civil liberties groups. This eventually led to litigation in the federal courts regarding the constitutionality of the statute.

The best argument against the constitutionality of the statute is that:

(A) The statute offends certain rights that give rise to a constitutional right of privacy.

(B) The statute constitutes a taking without due process of law.

(C) The statute improperly infringes on the commercial speech protection of the First Amendment.

(D) The statute unduly burdens interstate commerce.

Question 13

A city passed an ordinance prohibiting door-to-door solicitation of contributions by charitable organizations that did not use at least 75% of their receipts for "charitable purposes." The ordinance further provided that anyone wishing to solicit for purposes of charity must obtain a permit and present satisfactory proof that at least 75% of the proceeds of such solicitation will be used directly for the charitable purposes of the organization. An organization seeking to solicit support within the city applied for and was denied a permit because it did not meet the 75% requirement.

As applied to the organization, is the ordinance constitutional?

(A) Yes, because the 75% rule serves a legitimate state interest in preserving the integrity of charities.

(B) Yes, because the right to solicit for a charity is balanced against the interest of the state in preventing fraud and crime.

(C) No, because the ordinance violates the protections afforded by the First Amendment.

(D) No, because the ordinance has as a purpose the protection from undue annoyance and the preservation of residential privacy.

Question 14

Concerned about the number of households headed by single teenage mothers, and the deleterious effects of overpopulation, a state enacted legislation requiring any person under the age of 25 to obtain a certificate of responsibility before having children. Any child born whose parents do not have a certificate of responsibility will be placed for adoption. A pregnant 21-year-old resident of the state challenges the legislation.

If the woman's action proceeds to substantive determination, which of the following statements regarding the parties' burden of proof is most accurate?

(A) The state bears the burden of proving that its law is necessary to achieve a compelling government purpose, because it has a substantial impact on a fundamental right.

(B) The state bears the burden of proving that its law is necessary to achieve a compelling government purpose, because it creates a suspect classification.

(C) The woman bears the burden of proving that the law is not necessary to achieve a compelling government purpose, because it is presumed valid.

(D) The woman bears the burden of proving that the law is not necessary to achieve a compelling government purpose, because it is an exercise of the state's police power.

Question 15

To ease the desperate plight of the thousands of auto workers suffering layoffs, plant closures, and pay cuts from lost sales to foreign competitors, a state legislature enacted an excise tax on any automobile sold in the state that had not been manufactured within the state. The tax was graduated from 5% of the sales price of inexpensive automobiles down to 1% for automobiles selling for more than $100,000. A corporation that manufactures automobiles in a neighboring state brought an appropriate action in federal court to enjoin enforcement of the automobile tax statute as to its products.

Which of the following is the strongest constitutional argument supporting the invalidity of the special tax?

(A) It is an undue burden on interstate commerce.

(B) It violates the Equal Protection Clause of the Fourteenth Amendment.

(C) It violates the Fourteenth Amendment's protection of the privileges and immunities of national citizenship.

(D) It violates the Due Process Clause of the Fourteenth Amendment.

Question 16

After the dictator of a Caribbean island country was deposed, the President of the United States extended official recognition to the country's new government. As ambassador to the newly recognized government, the President nominated an aging industrialist who was a close personal friend of the deposed dictator. Unable to muster enough votes to block approval of the new ambassador, the President's political opponents in the Senate caused a resolution to be passed requiring that all consular staff below the rank of ambassador be selected from a list of "approved" candidates who have been certified as acceptable by the new country's government. The President refused to consider any of the Senate's list of approved candidates.

Which of the following is the President's strongest constitutional basis for refusing to obey the Senate resolution?

(A) The Senate could have effectuated its policies by a less intrusive method, such as refusing to appropriate funds to staff the new embassy if the President's selections were inappropriate.

(B) The President has the authority to nominate and appoint the diplomatic representatives of the United States.

(C) The President has exclusive authority, as commander-in-chief, to protect American interests abroad.

(D) The President's control over the foreign policy of the United States may not be limited by other branches of government.

Question 17

A state statute prohibited individuals from donating more than $1,000 per year to any group that lobbies for or against any matter up for consideration before the state legislature. A voter who wanted to donate $5,000 to a lobbying group challenged the statute on constitutional grounds in federal court.

Is the court likely to uphold the statute?

(A) Yes, because the statute is reasonably related to the state's legitimate interest in controlling such contributions.

(B) Yes, because the statute does not restrict the core political speech right to donate directly to legislative candidates.

(C) No, because the statute places a restraint on core political speech and association rights without sufficient justification.

(D) No, because a state may not place any limits on the amount of money that may be spent to support political campaigns.

Question 18

A candidate for a state legislature brought an action under the Fourteenth Amendment against a privately owned cab company to compel the company to accept his political advertisements on its vehicles. The cab company is licensed by a rural county within the state in which the candidate is running. As part of its taxi business, the cab company uses pickup trucks to ferry its largely rural-based customers and the agriculturally related items they often carry around. The company sells space on the wooden slats surrounding the bed of each pickup truck to commercial advertisers, but it refuses to carry any political advertising.

Which of the following is the strongest justification for the trial court's denying the candidate any relief?

(A) The sides of the cab company's pickup trucks are not public forums.

(B) The candidate has reasonable alternative methods of getting his message to the public.

(C) The Fourteenth Amendment provides no basis on which to compel the cab company to accept the candidate's ads.

(D) The right of the cab company to choose what messages to display outweighs the candidate's right to insist that the cab company accept his advertising.

CONSTITUTIONAL LAW ANSWERS - SET 2

Answer to Question 1

(B) If the other owners prevail, it will be because the court's enforcement of the regulation is rationally related to a legitimate government interest. The Supreme Court has held that court enforcement of restrictive covenants in deeds constitutes state action, and thus a court may enforce a restrictive covenant only if it is constitutional. Under the Due Process Clause, unless fundamental rights are involved, government action is constitutional as long as it is rationally related to any conceivable legitimate end of government. Zoning regulations prohibiting three or more unrelated persons from living together have been held not to infringe on any fundamental rights in *Village of Belle Terre v. Boraas* (1974); hence, judicial enforcement of a private covenant with that prohibition likely would also be valid for that reason. (A) is wrong because, as discussed above, government action includes court enforcement of restrictive covenants between private parties, and deed restrictions based on race have been held unenforceable in *Shelley v. Kraemer* (1948), because enforcement would constitute government action supporting discrimination against a suspect class. Here, however, no suspect class or fundamental right is involved. (C) is wrong because it is not relevant to a determination of whether the restriction can be properly enforced by the court. (D) is wrong because the issue here involves occupancy of the unit rather than transfer or sale.

Answer to Question 2

(C) A conviction of the resident would not be constitutional because the ordinance is void on its face. Although a municipality can place reasonable time, place, and manner restrictions on certain aspects of speech, it may not adopt a regulation that gives officials broad discretion over speech issues. If a statute gives licensing officials unbridled discretion, it is void on its face, and speakers need not even apply for a permit. They may exercise their First Amendment rights even if they could have been denied a permit under a valid law, and they may not be punished for violating the licensing statute. Here, the law allows the mayor to grant or deny permits based on his assessment of public interest. This is too much discretion to be valid. Therefore, the ordinance is void. (A) is wrong because, as explained above, the ordinance was void on its face and thus need not be obeyed. Therefore, the resident did not need to apply for the permit. Also, although it is true that the municipality has a right to reasonable restrictions, this ordinance is not reasonable because it gives too much discretion to the mayor. (B) is wrong because even if the mayor has not abused his discretion, the ordinance is void on its face and thus need not be obeyed. (D) is wrong because, as stated above, the resident's case does not depend on whether the mayor would grant or deny the permit.

Answer to Question 3

(C) The United States will win because of the Supremacy Clause. Where the federal government and the state government share power to regulate a particular subject matter, the Supremacy Clause provides that federal law is the supreme law of the land, and consequently a conflicting state law will be superseded by a federal law. A corollary of this rule is that the states have no power to regulate the legitimate activities of the federal government unless Congress consents. Running a government building is a legitimate governmental activity, and so the Supremacy Clause prevents the state regulation here. (A) is incorrect because although regulation of air quality is certainly within the scope of a state's police power (the power to legislate for the health, safety, and morals of the community), it does not allow the state to regulate the legitimate activities of the federal government. An immunity is afforded the federal government by the Supremacy Clause, and the state's police power cannot overcome that immunity. (B) is incorrect because while it is true that the power to regulate air quality is shared, this means that when the federal government acts, conflicting state law will be superseded by virtue of the Supremacy Clause. The federal government does not have to defer to the state. (D) is incorrect because it is based on an inappropriate premise—that the state's interference would be justified if it was related to a compelling interest. The strength of the state's interest is irrelevant under the Supremacy Clause.

Answer to Question 4

(A) The civic watchdog group is not likely to have standing to challenge the tax. To have standing, a plaintiff must show that it has a concrete stake in the outcome of the litigation sufficient to ensure its zealous participation. On a constitutional issue, the plaintiff must be able to show that it is or will be injured by the government action involved and that its injury can be remedied by a decision in its favor. The civic watchdog group is not likely to have standing because it has no concrete stake in the outcome. It has not shown that it will be injured by the tax in any manner other than the way in which everyone is injured by unlawful governmental conduct, and that is not a sufficient injury to sustain standing. (Note that an organization may have standing to represent its members if there is a sufficient injury to the members that is related to the organization's purpose, and the nature of the claim and the relief sought does not require participation of the members; but since this organization is not limited to pool hall owners or customers, its injury is not sufficient to allow standing.) (B) is incorrect. The tax could have its intended consequence of discouraging high school students from shooting pool in the afternoon. If that happens, the owner's revenues would decrease. Thus, he has a concrete stake in the outcome and his injury could be prevented by removing the tax. Therefore, the owner has standing. (C) is incorrect. Anyone who plays pool regularly in the afternoon would be injured by the tax even though its purpose is to keep high school students from shooting pool. Note that the rule that there is no "citizen standing" is not applicable here—while the citizen generally opposes new taxes, this is not a case where he is attempting to challenge the tax as a mere citizen—he has patronized the pool hall in the afternoon and would be directly impacted by the tax. (D) is incorrect for much of the same reason that (C) is incorrect. As a regular patron of the hall, the student would be directly impacted by the tax and eliminating the tax would eliminate any harm caused by the tax. Therefore, the student has standing.

Answer to Question 5

(C) The lack of notice and hearing prior to termination of the owner's license points to procedural due process as being the strongest argument. Procedural due process requires that fair procedure be used before a government agency takes away a person's life, liberty, or property. At the very least, this requires notice of the government's proposed action and an opportunity to present objections to an unbiased decisionmaker. A person has a protectable property interest whenever she has a legitimate claim to a benefit under state law. The owner has a protectable property interest in her business license because presumably the license cannot be terminated without cause. Thus, revocation of the owner's license violates procedural due process since she was not given notice or an opportunity to respond. (A) is incorrect because it is not the strongest argument; it is not clear that there is any substantial impairment of any contract between the owner and her wholesale distributors. The Impairment of Contracts Clause prohibits only ***some*** government action substantially impairing existing contracts. Nothing here indicates that a contract with wholesalers will be substantially impaired by the owner's no longer ordering pints. Even if there would be substantial impairment, the law may be valid if it serves an important state interest and is a narrowly tailored means of promoting that interest. Here, an important state interest will likely be found (*e.g.*, reduction of litter on the streets and highways or reduction of trash in state landfills), and this law could be seen as narrowly tailored to that interest. Thus, the law would probably be valid despite its impairment of the contract. Therefore, this is not the owner's best argument. (B) is incorrect because the state agency's action does not indicate that the owner has been subjected to a governmental classification in which similar people are treated in a dissimilar manner. The owner was apparently not singled out for a license revocation while certain other retailers were not obliged to comply with the statute. As far as can be known, all sellers of milk for home consumption are required to comply with the statute. (D) is incorrect because violation of substantive due process is not a very strong argument in this case. Because no fundamental right was involved, the rational basis standard would be applied. Most statutes tested under this standard are upheld because the statute need be rational in light of ***any*** legitimate government interest. The law here, for example, could be said to reduce litter or trash and this is a legitimate government interest, and so the government would probably win on this basis. Therefore, this is not the owner's best argument.

Answer to Question 6

(D) The court should hear the case on the merits. This question is best answered by eliminating the incorrect choices. (A) is incorrect because the student has standing. To have standing, one must have a concrete stake in the outcome of the controversy. To have such a stake, the person must be suffering an injury in fact caused by governmental action that is greater than the injury that all persons suffer when the government acts improperly, and her injury must be able to be remedied by a decision in her favor. The student here is suffering an injury to her reputation, and more importantly from a constitutional law point of view, a governmental body (the university officials) is attempting to suppress her First Amendment speech and assembly rights. A cease and desist order will remedy her harm. Thus, she has standing. (B) is incorrect because the case is not moot, even though the officials are currently not harassing the student. Under the mootness doctrine, a federal court will not hear a case unless there is a real, live controversy at all stages of the proceedings. However, there is an exception to this rule: Controversies capable of repetition but evading review will be heard even though the controversy might not continue for the entire case. The exception applies where the controversy involves issues of short duration (*e.g.*, pregnancy) or where, as here, the defendant voluntarily stops the offending practice (because the defendant could resume the offending practice as soon as the case is dismissed). (C) is incorrect because the case here is ripe. Ripeness is a bar to hearing actions ***before*** a controversy arises, and here the controversy has already arisen, as the officials have already harassed the student. Therefore, the case is ripe. Thus, because there are no grounds presented on which to refuse jurisdiction, the court should hear the case on the merits.

Answer to Question 7

(B) The most damaging fact to the promoter's First Amendment claims is that the fair's rules clearly prohibit leafleting except at designated hours other than the time the promoter was distributing leaflets. The First Amendment freedom of speech is not absolute. To avoid chaos and to protect other governmental interests, government is allowed to adopt reasonable time, place, and manner regulations on speech in public forums and designated public forums. To be valid, such regulations must be content neutral, narrowly tailored to serve a significant government interest, and leave open alternative channels of communication. The fact that the rule here allows solicitation at specified times indicates that it is narrowly tailored and leaves open alternative channels of communication. The rule also seems to be content neutral and it serves the government's significant

interest of keeping the fair orderly. Therefore, the rule would probably be valid if (B) is true. (A) would not be damaging to the promoter because the First Amendment protects against government infringement on speech by the government, regardless of whether the speech is on private or public property; the fact that the fairgrounds are private property does not preclude the property from being a public forum during the time that the county was leasing it and conducting a fair on it. Hence, the fairgrounds would be considered to be government property for purposes of application of the public forum rule. (C) is not damaging because the First Amendment protections extend to most forms of speech, including certain symbolic acts and the right not to speak. It certainly also extends to leafleting. (D) is not very damaging because the First Amendment protects commercial speech, although the standard for regulation differs from other speech—the government may ban false or misleading commercial speech and may regulate (including content regulation) other commercial speech with narrowly tailored regulations that directly advance a substantial government interest. The regulation here appears to meet this standard.

Answer to Question 8

(C) The most helpful additional fact for the patron is that the head librarian allowed other people to distribute leaflets at all hours. Although the government may adopt reasonable time, place, and manner restrictions in public forums and designated public forums, such restrictions must be content neutral. The head librarian's allowing some people to distribute leaflets at all hours shows that the restriction here is probably being used as a content regulation, which would be prohibited under these facts. Additionally, if the head librarian is allowing others to distribute leaflets at all hours, the discriminatory application of the ordinance might also violate the Equal Protection Clause. (A) is not very helpful because the fact that the patron was informed once of the rule would be sufficient to give her notice that she was violating the law. There is no requirement that persons be warned twice that they are violating speech regulations. (B) might help the patron because she could claim that because the library is surrounded by a public forum (sidewalks), the front door step also is a public forum. This argument will probably not prevail, however, because the Supreme Court has never made such a holding (and indeed has held that although the sidewalks around the Supreme Court building are public forums, the Supreme Court building itself is not a public forum). This fact might even hurt the patron, because it indicates that alternative public forums were readily available. (D) is not very helpful because political fundraising receives no more First Amendment protection than pure political speech; indeed, more regulation is allowed in the fundraising arena.

Answer to Question 9

(C) The Court should rule in favor of the city, upholding the ordinance as a valid time, place, and manner restriction on the exercise of First Amendment rights. The First Amendment protects the freedoms of speech and assembly; however, the protection is not absolute. The government is allowed to adopt regulations concerning the time, place, and manner of the exercise of speech and assembly in public forums and designated public forums to facilitate order and to protect other important government interests. To be valid, such a law must: (i) be content neutral; (ii) be narrowly tailored to serve a significant government interest; and (iii) leave open alternative channels of communication. The ordinance here, although it restricts speech on public sidewalks, serves a significant government interest—the health and welfare of health care facility patients. It is content neutral because it prohibits all protesting, educating, and counseling around health care facilities and not just such conduct concerning a particular message. It is narrowly tailored because it applies only to activities within 100 feet of a health care facility and within eight feet of another person. Finally, the law leaves open alternative channels of communication, because people are allowed to engage in such activities outside the limited range. Thus, the ordinance is valid. (A) is incorrect because the Free Exercise Clause does not protect the leafletter's conduct here. The Free Exercise Clause provides that the government may not prohibit the free exercise of religion. However, the Clause does not provide an absolute right, and the Supreme Court has held that the government may regulate general conduct without violating the Constitution, even if the regulation happens to interfere with a person's or group's religious practices. The Clause merely prohibits the regulation of conduct because it is religious. Because the statute here is a broad regulation and is not specifically aimed at religious conduct, it does not violate the Constitution. (B) is incorrect because it is too broad. As explained above, some infringement of speech is constitutionally allowed (*i.e.,* reasonable time, place, and manner restrictions on speech in public forums are allowed). (D) is incorrect because, as a general rule, the Constitution does not protect people from the acts of other people, but rather from the acts of the government. Thus, the rationale of (D) does not make sense—a law will not be held "constitutional" because it prevents persons from violating others' constitutional rights.

Answer to Question 10

(A) The trade association will have to prove that the statute is not rationally related to a legitimate state interest. Whether the statute is treated as a due process challenge (because it affects all employees), or as an equal protection problem (because employers are singled out for special treatment), the same standard will apply. Because there is no fundamental right involved and employers are neither a suspect nor quasi-suspect class, the rational basis standard will apply. Under the rational basis standard, the party challenging the government action has the burden of proving that the action is not rationally related to any legitimate state interest—a very difficult burden to meet. Thus, the burden will be on the trade association and (A) is correct. (B) is incorrect because it states the wrong standard. (C) and (D) are incorrect because they place the burden on the wrong party.

Answer to Question 11

(A) The court should hold the sale presumptively valid pursuant to Congress's property power. Article IV, Section 3 of the Constitution gives Congress the power to dispose of all property belonging to the federal government. There are no express limits placed on this power, and a disposal has never been invalidated on the ground that it places a competitor of the purchaser at a disadvantage. (B) is incorrect because the Due Process Clause would not prevent the sale here. The Due Process Clause prohibits the government from denying persons life, liberty, or property without due process of law. For the restrictions of the Clause to apply, a person must have a legitimate property interest in the property taken. "Property" includes more than personal belongings, but a mere expectation or desire for the benefit is not enough. One must have a legitimate claim or entitlement to the benefit before one may make a procedural due process challenge, and here the competitor has no claim to a right to be offered the ships that were sold to the first cruise company. (C) is incorrect because, as indicated above, there is no express limit on Congress's power to dispose of government property; nothing in the Constitution requires Congress to get the President's (or any other executive officer's) permission to exercise the power. (D) is incorrect because there is no denial of equal protection here. While the Equal Protection Clause is not applicable to the federal government, equal protection guarantees are applicable through the Fifth Amendment Due Process Clause. Nevertheless, there is no equal protection violation here: Because no suspect class or fundamental right is involved, the action would be tested under the rational basis standard (discriminatory government action is valid as long as it is rationally related to any legitimate government interest) and would be upheld since the sale is rationally

related to the government's interest in reviving the cruise ship industry. It does not matter that the government is not doing all that it can; a first step is permissible.

Answer to Question 12

(C) The statute here unconstitutionally infringes on the commercial speech protections of the First Amendment because it forbids truthful advertisement of a lawful product. Commercial speech is protected by the First Amendment, but it can be subject to significantly more regulation than noncommercial speech. In determining whether a restriction on commercial speech is valid, a court first asks whether the speech concerns lawful activity and is not misleading or fraudulent. The activity here is lawful, and nothing indicates fraud or falsity. Next, the court will determine whether: (i) the government interest in the regulation is substantial; (ii) the regulation directly advances that interest; and (iii) the regulation is narrowly tailored to the substantial interest. The facts do not indicate what interest the government seeks to promote with this regulation. Prevention of the "birth dearth" might be one purpose; however, even assuming that prevention of the "birth dearth" is a significant government interest, the regulation still will not stand because it does not directly advance that interest; *i.e.,* it does not directly encourage having babies, but rather only limits one method of advertisement of contraceptives. Thus, the restriction on commercial speech is invalid. (A) is not the best argument against the statute because it is not as direct as (C). It is true that the right to privacy is protected by the Constitution and the right to contraceptives is probably included within that right, but the regulation here does not make contraceptives illegal (it merely bans one form of advertisement) and limits can be placed on advertisements. Because advertisement is commercial speech, the appropriate place to look for constitutional protection is the First Amendment. (B) is incorrect because regulation will amount to a taking only when it unjustly reduces the economic value of property, so that there cannot be a fair return on investment. Nothing here indicates that the ban is unjust, but more importantly nothing indicates that makers of contraceptives will not be able to obtain a fair return if they are prohibited from soliciting through the mail. (D) is incorrect because while the statute indeed burdens interstate commerce, Congress has the power to control interstate commerce in nearly any manner it desires (as long as it does not violate some other constitutional provision). Only the states are prohibited from unduly burdening interstate commerce.

Answer to Question 13

(C) The Court should declare the ordinance unconstitutional, because charitable solicitations for funds in residential areas are within the protection of the First Amendment. In *Village of Schaumburg v. Citizens for a Better Environment* (1980), the Supreme Court held unconstitutional a municipal ordinance that prohibited the door-to-door solicitation of contributions by charitable organizations that did not use at least 75% of their receipts for charitable purposes. After review, the Court stated that the precedent of earlier decisions established clearly that the charitable appeal for funds involves a variety of speech interests that are within the protection of the First Amendment. The Court concluded that the ordinance unduly intruded on the rights to free speech because the justifications for the restriction were not sufficiently compelling. (A) is wrong because the state's "legitimate interest" is not enough to justify violation of First Amendment rights. Similarly, (B) and (D) are wrong because the First Amendment rights outweigh the state's purposes and there are less intrusive ways of accomplishing the state's goals.

Answer to Question 14

(A) If the case goes to trial, the state will have the burden of proving that the statute is necessary to achieve a compelling government purpose because it has a substantial impact on a fundamental right. The right to have children involves the fundamental right of privacy, and when a statute imposes on a fundamental right, it will violate due process unless the state can show that it is necessary to promote a compelling interest. (B) is incorrect because no suspect class is involved here. It is true that if a law impacts a suspect class, it is unconstitutional unless the state can prove that the law is necessary to achieve a compelling interest, but age—the only classification involved in the question—is not a suspect class. (C) is incorrect because statutes are presumed to have a sufficient relationship to a government interest only if they are tested under the rational basis test (*i.e.,* where neither a suspect class nor a fundamental right is involved), and the statute here will be tested under strict scrutiny because a fundamental right is involved. (D) is incorrect because it is an incorrect statement of law—the burden of persuasion is not placed on the challenger merely because the law is within the state's police power.

Answer to Question 15

(A) The strongest argument against the tax is that it burdens interstate commerce. The Commerce Clause of the Constitution gives Congress plenary power to authorize or forbid state taxation that affects interstate commerce. Unless approved by Congress, state taxes that discriminate against interstate commerce are invalid. The special tax here does not pass muster because it directly discriminates against out-of-state competition. Thus, the tax violates the Commerce Clause and (A) is correct. (B) is not a good argument because the Equal Protection Clause is not violated here. The Equal Protection Clause prohibits government from treating similarly situated people differently without good reason. What constitutes a good reason depends on the classification and the right involved. If the class is suspect or the right is fundamental, a compelling reason is required. Otherwise, the reason need only be rational. For most state or local government taxes, equal protection requires only that the tax classifications have a rational relationship to a legitimate government interest. Here, there is a rational reason for the regulation—protection of local jobs. Thus, the tax does not violate the Equal Protection Clause. (C) is incorrect because the Fourteenth Amendment clause protecting the privileges and immunities of national citizenship does not apply here. The clause protects only those rights attributable to being a United States citizen, *e.g.,* the right to petition Congress. The clause is inapplicable here. (D) is incorrect because the Due Process Clause is not violated here. For state taxation of interstate commerce to be valid under the Due Process Clause, the benefits and protection afforded by the taxing state must have a sufficient relationship to the subject matter taxed such that it is reasonable for the taxed party to expect to be subject to the taxing state's jurisdiction. Here, the tax is imposed on autos sold in the taxing state; this is a sufficient relationship to satisfy the Due Process Clause.

Answer to Question 16

(B) Article II, Section 2 provides that the President shall nominate, and with the advice and consent of the Senate shall appoint, ambassadors and other officers of the United States. The section also provides that Congress may vest the appointment of inferior officers in the President alone, in the courts of law, or in the heads of departments. Under separation of powers principles, however, Congress may not vest in itself any broader appointment powers than what is provided for by the Constitution. Where Congress has not vested the appointment power in courts of law or the heads of departments, it is not permitted to restrict the candidates that the President may nominate for appointment. Thus, the Senate's attempt here to exert some control over the President's choice of lower-level diplomatic representatives is an unconstitutional violation of the separation of powers. (A) is incorrect for two reasons: First, if the Senate's action had been constitutionally permissible, there would be no requirement of using a "less intrusive method" to effectuate such action. The President would simply be required to seek the approval of the Senate. Second, if the

Senate refused to appropriate funds to staff the embassy because it deemed the President's selections inappropriate, this would simply be another way of exerting control over the President's selection of lower-level diplomatic personnel, and would be as unconstitutional as the resolution passed by the Senate. (C) is incorrect because the President's status as commander in chief is not at issue here. The President does have rather extensive military powers as commander in chief of the armed forces. However, the appointment of a consular staff involves the President's power in foreign relations, not his power as commander in chief. In addition, (C) incorrectly states that the President has ***exclusive*** authority to protect American interests abroad. Although the President has broad authority to protect American interests abroad, Congress also has some authority in this field. For example, Congress has the power to declare war, to raise and support armies, and to give its advice and consent in the making of treaties. Similarly, (D) incorrectly asserts a limitless presidential control over foreign policy. While the President's authority in foreign policy is quite broad, it has some limits; *e.g.,* the requirement of senatorial advice and consent in the making of treaties.

Answer to Question 17

(C) The federal court would likely find that the statute violates the First Amendment. While the government may limit the amount of contributions that an individual may contribute to a candidate's campaign, it may not limit contributions to groups that lobby for or against matters before the legislature, because the Supreme Court has found that such a law does not serve a sufficiently important interest to outweigh the restraints that it puts on the First Amendment freedoms of speech and association. (A) is incorrect because it states an incorrect result (the statute likely will be found invalid for the reason stated above) and because it states an improper standard (a statute limiting campaign contributions is tested under intermediate scrutiny—it must be closely drawn to achieve a sufficiently important interest). (B) is incorrect. As mentioned above, the government ***may*** limit the amount of contributions that an individual may contribute to a candidate's campaign, because the government has a sufficiently important interest in preventing the corruption or the appearance of corruption from large contributions that outweighs First Amendment issues. (D) is incorrect because it is too broad. While states may not limit the amount that an individual may spend on a political campaign, there is an exception for amounts that a nonideological corporation may spend.

Answer to Question 18

(C) The strongest basis for denying the candidate relief is that there is no state action on which the Fourteenth Amendment can operate. The cab company is privately owned and operated. For state action to be present, the government must be significantly involved in the private entity; mere county licensing does not convert the private company's operations into state action. (A), (B), and (D) are incorrect because they ignore this critical factor. If state action were involved, these justifications—based on the First Amendment prohibitions against government infringement of speech—would tend to support the cab company's position, but there is no need to apply First Amendment doctrines because the government is not involved.

Set 3 Answer Sheet

1. Ⓐ Ⓑ Ⓒ Ⓓ
2. Ⓐ Ⓑ Ⓒ Ⓓ
3. Ⓐ Ⓑ Ⓒ Ⓓ
4. Ⓐ Ⓑ Ⓒ Ⓓ
5. Ⓐ Ⓑ Ⓒ Ⓓ
6. Ⓐ Ⓑ Ⓒ Ⓓ
7. Ⓐ Ⓑ Ⓒ Ⓓ
8. Ⓐ Ⓑ Ⓒ Ⓓ
9. Ⓐ Ⓑ Ⓒ Ⓓ
10. Ⓐ Ⓑ Ⓒ Ⓓ
11. Ⓐ Ⓑ Ⓒ Ⓓ
12. Ⓐ Ⓑ Ⓒ Ⓓ
13. Ⓐ Ⓑ Ⓒ Ⓓ
14. Ⓐ Ⓑ Ⓒ Ⓓ
15. Ⓐ Ⓑ Ⓒ Ⓓ
16. Ⓐ Ⓑ Ⓒ Ⓓ
17. Ⓐ Ⓑ Ⓒ Ⓓ
18. Ⓐ Ⓑ Ⓒ Ⓓ

CONSTITUTIONAL LAW QUESTIONS - SET 3

Question 1

A state law provides that all persons who have been residents of the state for more than three years shall be entitled to free tuition at the state's main university. It further provides that persons who have resided in the state for three years or less shall pay the nonresident tuition rate, which is significantly higher. A student at the state's university who had been a state resident for less than three years filed a class action in federal court on behalf of himself and other similarly situated university students, seeking a declaration that the state statute is unconstitutional. When the case came to trial, the student had been a resident of the state for more than three years and was no longer required to pay tuition. By that time, a number of amicus curiae briefs had been filed in the case, some supporting and some opposing the student's position. Nevertheless, the state moved to dismiss the case as moot.

Should the state's motion to dismiss be granted?

(A) Yes, because the student is now a three-year resident.

(B) Yes, because the student lacks standing.

(C) No, because amicus curiae briefs have been filed.

(D) No, because there is a live controversy.

Question 2

Congress passed a law imposing a 50% excise tax on each pack of cigarettes manufactured for sale in the United States. An amendment was successfully added to the original bill requiring that all proceeds from the tax be used for antismoking educational programs in the audio, video, and print media and elsewhere. The amendment also provided for the establishment of federal stop-smoking clinics funded through the excise tax. The various tobacco companies were required to pay the tax directly to the federal government. A tobacco company filed suit in the appropriate federal court, contending that the tax should be struck down as unconstitutional.

Is the court likely to find the tax constitutional?

(A) Yes, because the tax is severable from its purpose.

(B) Yes, because the broad provisions of the General Welfare Clause would condone it.

(C) No, because it does not provide equal time for the tobacco companies to present their side of the smoking controversy.

(D) No, because it abridges the First Amendment rights of tobacco manufacturers by forcing them to pay for messages with which they may not agree.

Question 3

To reduce deer overpopulation in state forests, state Blue adopted a statute allowing anyone with a valid deer hunting license from any state to hunt deer within state Blue. The act also imposed a $0.25 per pound tax on each deer killed within the state. Funds from the tax were earmarked to support state forest land. State Red is adjacent to state Blue and also has an overabundance of deer. To encourage hunting, state Red does not impose a tax on deer taken from its forests.

A hunter who is a resident of state Red and who is licensed to hunt there earns his living by supplying wild game to several high-end restaurants in state Red. While legally hunting deer within state Red, the hunter inadvertently crossed the state line and killed a deer in state Blue. Upon hearing the hunter's shot, a state Blue game warden arrived at the scene, approximated the weight of the kill, and handed the hunter a tax bill based on the approximation. The bill provided a method for challenging the approximated weight of the deer, but the hunter

refused to pay any tax on his kill. He instead filed suit in federal court to enjoin collection of the state Blue tax on constitutional grounds.

Which of the following results is most likely?

(A) The hunter will prevail because the tax is invalid under the Commerce Clause.

(B) The hunter will prevail because the tax is invalid under the Interstate Privileges and Immunities Clause of Article IV, Section 2.

(C) State Blue will prevail because the tax is valid under the Commerce Clause.

(D) State Blue will prevail because the tax is valid under the Import-Export Clause.

Question 4

Pursuant to an edict recently issued by the elders of their religion, a mother and father instructed their son who just turned age 14 to report to a community woodworking shop instead of school. A state law requires all children to attend school until the age of 16, and the woodshop does not qualify as a school under state law. Because the parents did not report their son's absence, a truant officer visited the family and warned them that parents who willfully refuse to comply with the mandatory attendance law are subject to a $500 fine and up to 30 days in jail for each day of noncompliance. The parents listened, but informed the officer that they could not comply with the state law because of their religious views. The following day, the 14-year-old again went to work in the community woodshop instead of to school. His parents were then arrested and charged with violating the state mandatory school attendance law.

At the parents' criminal trial, which of the following may the court constitutionally consider in determining guilt or innocence?

(A) Whether the tenets of the parents' religion are true.

(B) Whether the parents' religion is a traditional, established one.

(C) Whether the parents believe that the tenets of their religion are derived from a supreme being.

(D) Whether the parents sincerely believe the tenets of their religion.

Question 5

A man who belonged to an ancient religion whose rituals require the use of bald eagle feathers traveled to an area where bald eagles were known to roost. After searching the area, he found a fallen eagle feather and returned home. A few weeks later, the man showed the feather to an acquaintance, who happened to be a national park ranger, and explained how the feather was obtained. The ranger informed the man that a federal anti-poaching law makes any possession of a bald eagle feather without a special permit a crime. The ranger then cited the man for possession of the feather and confiscated it.

At the man's trial for violating the federal bald eagle feather possession statute, which of the following constitutional arguments is most appropriate for the prosecution to make?

(A) The statute is a neutral law that only incidentally burdens the man's rights under the First Amendment.

(B) The Free Exercise Clause applies only to belief and not to conduct.

(C) The government has a substantial and important interest in protecting bald eagles and there is no other feasible way to achieve the legislative purpose.

(D) Making an exception for the man on religious grounds would violate the Establishment Clause of the First Amendment.

Question 6

To stabilize state corn prices, a state purchased large quantities of corn from resident farmers and converted the corn into biodegradable plastics. The state then sold the plastics to

state residents at cost and to out-of-state residents at cost plus 25%. An out-of-state corporation purchased biodegradable plastics from the state at a cost substantially below the price other companies charge. Nevertheless, the corporation believes that it is unconstitutional for the state to charge out-of-state purchasers more than resident purchasers. The out-of-state corporation, therefore, brings suit in federal court challenging the state pricing scheme.

Assuming that the court has jurisdiction, should it uphold the constitutionality of the pricing scheme?

(A) Yes, because as a market participant the state is free to charge nonresidents more than residents.

(B) Yes, because the state is selling plastics to nonresidents at prices substantially below that of other companies.

(C) No, because the scheme discriminates against nonresidents in violation of the Commerce Clause.

(D) No, because charging nonresidents more for plastics than residents pay violates the Privileges and Immunities Clause guaranteeing benefits of state citizenship.

Question 7

A town with a population of 30,000 merged with a city of 60,000. To protect voting rights of the citizens of the former town, a proposal was made that for a period of 20 years, beginning at the date of the merger, the city council of the merged city would consist of six persons. Each formerly separate municipality would be divided into three council districts. Each district from the former town would have approximately 10,000 residents, and each district from the former city would have 20,000 residents. A mayor would be elected at large. Before this proposal was placed on the ballot, the state attorney general issued an advisory opinion stating that the proposal was not in violation of any state statutory or constitutional provision. The proposal was placed on the ballot and was carried by large majorities in both the town and the city, and the districts were carved out.

Three taxpayers filed suit to enjoin the holding of an election with council districts of such disparate proportions. The suit reached the state supreme court, which ruled that the governmental formula was constitutional under both the state and United States Constitutions. The plaintiffs wish to take the case to the United States Supreme Court.

The Supreme Court should:

(A) Rely on the attorney general's opinion and not hear the case on its merits.

(B) Not hear the case, because it was decided below on an independent state ground.

(C) Not hear the case, but remand it to federal district court.

(D) Hear the federal issues involved, but decline to rule on state issues.

Question 8

A state set up an intrastate message routing system to carry messages to and from the various state agency offices located throughout the state. This proved to be cheaper and more efficient than the United States Postal Service. The message service worked so well that the state offered the messenger service to its employees as a fringe benefit. Moreover, it expanded delivery options beyond state offices to any address in the state and permitted the employees to use the service for personal correspondence as well as for official business.

Are the state's actions constitutional?

(A) Yes, because the messenger service operates entirely within the state borders.

(B) Yes, because the Commerce Clause does not prohibit states from acting as a market participant.

(C) No, because the Equal Protection Clause prohibits this singling out of state employees for special benefits.

(D) No, because it violates the federal postal monopoly.

Question 9

Congress enacted a statute appropriating money to the states on condition that the states use the money to support "public performances of classical ballet open to the public." The statute provided that the money was not to be used to support any other type of dance, and that tickets to any performance paid for with these funds were to be distributed to the public on a first come, first served basis.

A state that accepted a grant of $500,000 under the federal statute gave half of the grant to a state-sponsored ballet company. The company had been started 20 years earlier as part of a state effort to bring culture to poor, inner city areas. By state law enacted when the company was formed, no less than 35% of the tickets to each performance of the ballet company must be distributed to the inner-city school systems to be given to minority school children.

Is the state's method of distributing tickets to the state ballet company's performances constitutional?

(A) Yes, because the state ballet company is state-operated and the doctrine of federalism prohibits the federal government from directly interfering with state operations.

(B) Yes, because the state ballet ticket distribution system substantially conforms with the underlying purpose of the federal ticket distribution scheme.

(C) No, because the state distribution system violates the Supremacy Clause.

(D) No, because the state distribution system violates equal protection.

Question 10

The President of the United States and the king of a foreign nation entered into a treaty agreeing that citizens of the foreign nation who reside in the United States would not be taxed by the United States and that United States citizens who reside in the foreign nation would not be taxed by it. The treaty was ratified by the United States Senate and the royal council of the foreign nation. One year after the treaty became effective, the foreign nation began to tax United States citizens within its borders. The President immediately declared the tax treaty to be void and ordered the Internal Revenue Service to tax citizens of the foreign nation living in the United States.

Is the President's action constitutional?

(A) Yes, because the President has emergency powers to protect United States citizens.

(B) Yes, under the foreign policy powers of the President.

(C) No, because the treaty is the supreme law of the land, on par with federal legislation, and the President is not free to ignore it.

(D) No, unless the President receives the advice and consent of the United States Senate.

Question 11

Congress enacted a statute that purported to ban all discrimination against African-Americans in any commercial transaction taking place within the United States.

The statute would most likely be held:

(A) Constitutional, under Thirteenth Amendment provisions barring badges or incidents of slavery.

(B) Constitutional, because the federal government has an important interest in furthering the equal protection provisions of the Fourteenth Amendment.

(C) Unconstitutional, because Congress's powers under the Commerce Clause do not extend so far as the statute would require.

(D) Unconstitutional, because commercial transactions are not among the privileges and immunities of national citizenship.

Question 12

A pregnant woman wished to obtain an abortion but she was poor and could not afford one. Her home state did not provide financial assistance for abortions, but a neighboring state did for women who had been living within the state for at least three months prior to the procedure. The woman went to see a doctor in the neighboring state. He told her of the residency requirement. He also told the woman that he thought the residency requirement was unconstitutional and suggested that the woman bring an action in federal court challenging the residency requirement. She complied, bringing an action in forma pauperis, naming the doctor as the only defendant. The doctor responded that he believed that the requirement was unconstitutional and would like to be able to perform the abortion for the woman.

The court should:

(A) Dismiss the action because the woman lacks standing.

(B) Dismiss the action because there is no case or controversy.

(C) Abstain from hearing the action because deciding whether to fund abortions is a highly political issue.

(D) Issue a declaratory injunction upholding the residency requirement because the state has a compelling interest in preventing nonresidents from draining local welfare funds.

Question 13

State Green passed a statute requiring all commercial trucks passing through the state to use Type A tires, even though all other states permit the use of either Type A or Type B tires on commercial vehicles. The United States Supreme Court struck down the state Green statute and stated in its opinion that Type A and Type B tires are equally safe. Subsequent to the Supreme Court decision, the legislature of state Yellow enacted a statute requiring the use of Type B tires by commercial vehicles and banning the use of Type A tires by commercial vehicles. The statute states that the reason for the prohibition is that Type A tires are dangerous.

The best argument for striking down the state Yellow statute as unconstitutional would be based on:

(A) The fact that Type A and Type B tires are equally safe.

(B) The Supremacy Clause.

(C) The Commerce Clause.

(D) Res judicata.

Question 14

The United States was involved in a dispute with a small island nation over the ownership of an archipelago. On discovering that the archipelago was rich in oil, the President announced that he would appoint an ambassador to negotiate a treaty with the island nation to jointly exploit the oil reserve. A majority of Senators believed that the island clearly belonged to the United States and did not want to negotiate with the island nation. They passed a resolution requiring the President to include a Senator in his diplomatic mission to ensure that the Senate's view was presented in any negotiation with the island nation.

What is the strongest constitutional ground for the President's refusal to do so?

(A) As commander-in-chief, the President has the exclusive power to determine how to protect our national interest abroad.

(B) The resolution is unreasonable because it includes a Senator and not any Representatives.

(C) The President has the exclusive power to select diplomatic representatives of the United States.

(D) The Senate, if it does not like the President's actions, can refuse to appropriate the necessary monies for the President to implement his policies.

Question 15

A man from a foreign country obtained a doctorate in political science from a state university and applied to teach there. The man was denied employment at the university under a state law requiring all teachers within the state to be United States citizens.

Is the state's citizenship requirement constitutional as it applies to the man?

(A) Yes, because states have the right to set minimal standards for state employees under the Tenth Amendment.

(B) Yes, because a university political science teacher would exert a great deal of influence over the attitudes of students toward government, the political process, and citizenship.

(C) No, because the citizenship requirement is not rationally related to a legitimate state interest.

(D) No, because the citizenship requirement is not necessary to achieve a compelling state interest.

Question 16

A state statute makes it a felony for anyone in the corridors or on the grounds of any building in which a court may be in session to make a speech or carry a sign intended to improperly influence judicial proceedings. During a murder trial, a friend of the defendant was arrested under the statute for carrying a sign on the steps of the courthouse bearing the message: "Free the defendant or the judge will die."

Can the friend constitutionally be convicted under the statute?

(A) No, because the statute could apply to others whose speech is constitutionally protected.

(B) No, unless she personally intended to harm the judge.

(C) Yes, if there was a clear and present danger that the judge would be influenced by the sign.

(D) Yes, because the statute does not violate the freedom of expression guaranteed by the First Amendment.

Question 17

A state statute provides: "Any merchant desiring to sell within this state any product or goods manufactured outside of the United States must (i) obtain a special license from the state for $50 and (ii) clearly mark the goods as to specify their country of origin." The statute makes it a misdemeanor for any merchant to willfully sell goods without complying with these statutory requirements.

Which of the following statements is correct regarding the constitutionality of the statute?

(A) The portion of the statute requiring the license fee can be sustained on the ground that reasonable inspection fees are proper; but the balance of the statute is invalid.

(B) The portion of the statute requiring that the goods be labeled as to country of origin can be sustained because it only requires disclosure; but the balance of the statute is invalid.

(C) The statute is constitutionally valid as long as the burden on foreign commerce is minimal and is justified by legitimate state interests.

(D) The statute is unconstitutional in its entirety.

Question 18

A state enacted a law banning the use within the state of computerized telephone solicitation devices, and requiring that all telephone solicitation calls to numbers within the state be dialed by human beings. Federal legislation and administrative regulations control only the rates to be charged for telephone calls.

The legislation is:

(A) Valid, because it involves wholly intrastate commerce that is not subject to federal regulation.

(B) Valid, because the statute does not conflict with federal legislation or the negative implications of the Commerce Clause.

(C) Invalid, because the statute is preempted by federal legislation under the Supremacy Clause.

(D) Invalid, because the statute is an unconstitutional attempt by a state to regulate interstate commerce.

CONSTITUTIONAL LAW ANSWERS - SET 3

Answer to Question 1

(D) There is a live controversy and the case is not moot. A federal court will not hear a case unless there is a real, live controversy at all stages of the proceeding, not merely when the case is filed. Because the student is no longer required to pay nonresident tuition, there is arguably no controversy and the case may seem moot. However, a class action is not moot, and the class representative may continue to pursue it—even if the representative's own controversy has become moot—because the claims of others in the class are still viable. Here, the student filed his suit as a class action for university students with less than three years' residency; undoubtedly some of those students will still have a real controversy at this time. Thus, the case is not moot. (A) is wrong although it states a true fact. (A) implies that the case should be dismissed because the student's claim is moot. As explained above, this is a class action and other members of the class have a viable case. Thus, even though the named student's case by itself would be moot, he may continue the case as a representative of the class action. (B) is wrong because standing (the requirement that a plaintiff have a concrete stake in the outcome of the case) is determined at the beginning of a lawsuit. At the beginning of this case, the student had standing because he had suffered an injury (*i.e.*, had to pay nonresident tuition), caused by the government, that was remediable by the court. Thus, he had a concrete stake in the outcome of the case and had standing. (C) is wrong because it is irrelevant; the fact that amicus curiae briefs have been filed has no effect on mootness. A moot case will not be heard simply because amicus briefs have been filed.

Answer to Question 2

(B) The tax is constitutional because it represents a proper exercise of the power of Congress to tax and spend for the general welfare. Pursuant to the Constitution, Congress may tax and spend to provide for the general welfare. A congressional tax measure will be upheld if it bears some reasonable relationship to revenue production or if Congress has the power to regulate the taxed activity. Congress may spend for any public purpose, not merely the accomplishment of other enumerated powers. The tax at issue here bears a reasonable relationship to revenue production. Also, the purchase and sale of cigarettes in the United States is subject to congressional regulation, as an activity having a substantial economic effect on interstate commerce. Thus, the tax itself is valid. The amendment to the original tax bill is also valid, as a reflection of a congressional determination to use the proceeds of the tax for the promotion and implementation of an antismoking program, presumably in furtherance of public health. This is a public purpose for which Congress can spend pursuant to the General Welfare Clause. (A) is incorrect because it implies that the purpose of the tax is not constitutional. The purpose of the tax is to raise revenue to fund a federal antismoking program. As explained above, this is a proper exercise of the congressional taxing and spending power. Therefore, the constitutionality of the tax does not hinge on the severability of its purpose. (C) is incorrect because there is no "fairness doctrine" under the Constitution; *i.e.*, when Congress determines a course of action pursuant to its power to tax and spend for the general welfare, it need not provide equal time for opponents of the action to express their views. (D) is incorrect because the tax in no way abridges the First Amendment rights of the manufacturers. While the freedom of speech is very broad and includes the freedom to not speak and to refrain from endorsing views with which one does not agree, it does not invalidate the tax here because the tax does not force the tobacco companies to endorse the stop-smoking clinics or the government's antismoking stance. Neither does the tax forbid or control the tobacco manufacturers from endorsing a pro-smoking message. The manufacturers' First Amendment rights are simply not burdened here.

Answer to Question 3

(C) State Blue will prevail because the tax is valid under the Commerce Clause. A tax is valid under the Commerce Clause if: (i) the tax does not discriminate against interstate commerce; (ii) there is a substantial nexus between the activity taxed and the taxing state; (iii) the tax is fairly apportioned; and (iv) the tax fairly relates to services or benefits provided by the state. The state of Blue tax is applicable equally to residents of Blue and nonresidents. Thus, there is no discrimination against interstate commerce. Because the taxed deer are taken from within the state, there is a substantial nexus between the activity taxed and the taxing state. There is fair apportionment if a tax is based on the extent of the taxable activity or property in the state. Here, the killing of a deer within state Blue obviously occurs entirely within the state. Thus, the state tax is fairly apportioned. Also, there is a fair relationship between the tax and any benefits provided by the taxing state, because the state is permitting those engaged in hunting to take deer from its forest lands, in return for a rather modest amount of $0.25 per pound. That revenue, in turn, is used to support state Blue forest land, which provides hunters with a place to hunt. Thus, the state tax meets all of the requirements for validity under the Commerce Clause. (A) incorrectly states that the tax is invalid under the Commerce Clause. (B) is incorrect because the Interstate Privileges and Immunities Clause prohibits discrimination by a state against nonresidents when such discrimination involves fundamental rights, such as those involving important commercial activities. Here, while the tax may affect the hunter's commercial activity (because he earns a living from hunting and selling meat), the tax treats residents and nonresidents equally. Thus, there is no constitutional violation under the Privileges and Immunities Clause. (D) is incorrect because the Import-Export Clause applies to the authority of a state to tax foreign commerce. This question here does not deal with imported or exported goods. Thus, the Import-Export Clause is inapplicable to these facts.

Answer to Question 4

(D) The sincerity of the parents' religious beliefs is a factor that can be inquired into as a way of determining whether they can avail themselves of the protection of the Free Exercise Clause. The Free Exercise Clause of the First Amendment, applicable to the states through the Fourteenth Amendment, prohibits punishing people for their religious beliefs. When a person claims that he is being punished for his religious beliefs, the court may consider whether the person challenging the law sincerely holds those beliefs. Thus, the court may consider whether the parents' beliefs are sincerely held. (A) is incorrect because the First Amendment forbids a court from determining whether a person's religious beliefs are true. A court must respect a sincerely held religious belief, even if it appears to be illogical or incapable of proof. (B) is incorrect because the Free Exercise Clause protects all sincerely held religious beliefs, regardless of whether a specific religion is deemed to be "established" or "traditional." (C) is incorrect because religious beliefs need not be theistic to qualify for constitutional protection. An asserted religious belief must occupy a place in the believer's life parallel to that occupied by orthodox religious beliefs. Even an internally derived belief is entitled to protection.

Answer to Question 5

(A) The best argument for the prosecution is that the Free Exercise Clause does not afford a right to a religious exemption from a neutral law that happens to impose a substantial burden on a religious practice, if the law is otherwise constitutionally applied to persons who engage (or fail to engage) in the particular conduct for nonreligious reasons. Here, the federal law interferes with the man's religious beliefs. However, the statute prohibits ***any possession*** of a bald eagle feather without a

permit. Thus, the state should argue that the law was enacted to protect eagles and not merely to interfere with the religious beliefs of people such as the man here. (B) is incorrect because it is too broad. Conduct is protected (although the protection is limited). For example, the government cannot punish conduct merely because it is religious (although if the law affects both religious and nonreligious conduct, it is generally valid). [*See, e.g.,* Employment Division v. Smith (1990)] (C) is incorrect because it states the former rule in these cases. In the past, the Court used a balancing test to determine whether a religious exemption had to be granted from a law with a secular purpose that happened to burden religious practices or beliefs. The Court would consider the severity of the burden, the strength of the state's interest, and the existence of alternative means. Now, however, the Court no longer uses a balancing test; the state need not establish a strong interest or a lack of alternative means if the challenged statute is neutral. (D) could be successfully argued, but its chances for success are not as certain as for the argument in (A). The Establishment Clause prohibits laws respecting the establishment of religion. If a law includes a preference for one religious sect over another, the law will be held invalid unless it is narrowly tailored to promote a compelling interest. If there is no sect preference, the law is valid if: (i) it has a secular purpose; (ii) its primary effect neither advances nor inhibits religion; and (iii) it does not produce excessive government entanglement. Here, no sect preference appears, because nothing indicates that an exception would apply only to members of the man's religion. It could be argued, however, that the only purpose for an exemption here is to favor religious believers over nonbelievers. If that is the purpose, the exemption would not have a secular purpose and would fail the secular purpose test above. On the other hand, the state could argue that free exercise of religion is also protected, and an exemption protects sincerely held religious beliefs. [*See, e.g.,* Wisconsin v. Yoder (1979)] Thus, the outcome of the argument in (D) is uncertain, and (A) is the state's most appropriate argument.

Answer to Question 6

(A) The court will likely reject the company's challenge to the state pricing scheme. Although the Commerce Clause generally prohibits states from discriminating against out-of-state businesses to benefit local economic interests, the market participant exception applies here. The Commerce Clause does not prevent a state from preferring its own citizens when the state is acting as a market participant (*e.g.,* buying or selling products, hiring labor, giving subsidies, etc.). Because the pricing scheme here involves the sale of goods, the state can constitutionally charge whatever prices it desires to whomever it desires. Therefore, (A) is correct and (C) is incorrect. (B) reaches the right result but for the wrong reason. But for the market participant exception, the state pricing scheme would violate the Commerce Clause for discriminating against nonresidents. It would not matter that the state's prices to nonresidents are lower than anyone else's price, because the state is charging its own residents an even lower price. (D) is incorrect. Although the Privileges and Immunities Clause of Article IV entitles citizens of each state to the privileges and immunities of citizens of the several states, and thus prohibits discrimination by a state against nonresidents, the Clause does not apply to corporations, such as the purchaser here. Therefore, the Clause cannot be the basis for the court's ruling.

Answer to Question 7

(D) The Supreme Court may grant certiorari to review a case from the highest court in a state that can render an opinion on the matter if a state statute's validity is called into question under the federal Constitution. [28 U.S.C. §1257] The Court may decide the federal issues, but cannot rule on the state law issues. (A) is incorrect for several reasons: (i) the attorney general evaluated only the proposal's validity under the state constitution; and (ii) even if her opinion had addressed the

proposal's federal constitutional validity, the Supreme Court is not bound by advisory opinions of state attorneys general. (B) is incorrect even though the state supreme court may have had an independent state ground for finding the law constitutional under its state constitution. The Supreme Court will refuse to hear the case only if the state ground is ***adequate*** by itself to support the decision as well as independent, so that the Court's review of the federal ground for the decision would have no effect on the outcome of the case (such as if the state court had found the law invalid under both the state and federal Constitutions). Here, the Supreme Court's review of the state court opinion on the law's federal constitutional status may have an outcome on the case regardless of the state court's decision on the state constitutional issue; the Court therefore will hear the federal issues involved. (C) is incorrect because 28 U.S.C. section 1257 provides that appellate review of a matter from a state's highest court is to the Supreme Court by petition for a writ of certiorari, rather than to a federal district court.

Answer to Question 8

(D) The legislation is unconstitutional because it violates the federal postal monopoly. Article I, Section 8, Clause 7 of the Constitution grants Congress the power to establish post offices and post roads. This power grants Congress a monopoly over the delivery of mail. No other system for delivering mail—public or private—can be established absent Congress's consent. Congress has delegated to the Postal Service the power to decide whether others may compete with it, and the Postal Service has carved out an exception to its monopoly for extremely urgent letters. However, this exception would not apply to the state messenger service here since the state service extends to every letter or package of an employee deliverable within the state. (A) is irrelevant because the postal monopoly applies even to wholly intrastate competing systems. The rationale is that the Postal Service must be protected from companies that would deliver only on profitable routes at a low cost, leaving the Postal Service only expensive, money-losing routes. (B) also is irrelevant. While it is true that there is a market participant exception to the Commerce Clause, the Commerce Clause is not the controlling law here; the controlling law is the federal postal power. (C) is incorrect because the Equal Protection Clause would not prohibit the special treatment here. Because no suspect class or fundamental right is involved, the program would be judged under the rational basis standard. Under this standard, a law is upheld if it is rationally related to ***any*** legitimate government interest. Here, the law would be upheld because there is a conceivable rational basis for the program (*e.g.*, to make government employment more attractive), and the law is rationally related to that interest.

Answer to Question 9

(C) The state ticket distribution system is unconstitutional because of the Supremacy Clause. A valid act of Congress supersedes any state or local action that conflicts with it. The act here is valid because Congress has the power to spend for the general welfare, and in so doing may place conditions on grants as it sees fit. The state law directly conflicts with the federal law because the federal law requires that tickets be distributed on a first come, first served basis, and the state law requires that 35% of the tickets be given to minority school children. Because the state law conflicts with the federal law, it is invalid. (A), based on the Tenth Amendment, is incorrect because, even if Congress lacks the power to directly regulate the distribution of the tickets in question, the regulation here would still be valid as a spending power condition. The Supreme Court has held that Congress may condition grants under the spending power even where it cannot directly regulate. [*See* South Dakota v. Dole (1987)—conditioning federal highway grants on prohibiting minors from drinking] (B) is incorrect because the Supremacy Clause invalidates ***all*** conflicting state laws where there is a clash, no matter how complementary the state law may

be viewed. (D) is incorrect because the state program probably is valid under the Equal Protection Clause. State programs that ***favor*** racial and ethnic minorities are subject to the same strict scrutiny standards as programs that discriminate against minorities: They must be narrowly tailored to promote a compelling government interest. There is a compelling government interest in remedying past discrimination, and the facts indicate that the ballet company was established to remedy the prior lack of cultural opportunities that existed in the inner city. The program also appears to be narrowly tailored, and so would likely survive an equal protection challenge.

Answer to Question 10

(B) The President's action is constitutional pursuant to his power over treaties and foreign relations. The power to enter into treaties is vested in the President, and his power to act for the United States in day-to-day foreign affairs is paramount. Even as to foreign relations that require congressional consent, the President's powers are much broader than in the realm of internal affairs. No significant judicial control has been exercised over such declarations. Thus, this action is allowable under these broad powers. (A) is incorrect because the President's emergency power to protect United States citizens is unclear. While he has power to act concerning foreign nations, it is unclear whether he could "legislate" concerning the internal affairs involved here (*e.g.,* tax collection) merely because he thought that United States citizens needed protection. In any case, the power to act here more properly arises from the President's power over foreign affairs and not from a power to protect United States citizens. (C) is incorrect because while it is true that properly ratified treaties are the supreme law of the land, that only means that conflicting state or local laws must yield. If the President has power to override the treaty (which he does have, as explained above), the Supremacy Clause is not controlling. (D) is incorrect because the Constitution only requires the President to obtain the advice and consent of the Senate to enter into treaties; it does not require him to obtain Senate consent to void a treaty.

Answer to Question 11

(A) The statute is constitutional as a legitimate exercise of congressional enforcement powers under the Enabling Clause of the Thirteenth Amendment. The Thirteenth Amendment prohibits slavery. The Enabling Clause of the amendment has been held to confer on Congress the authority to proscribe almost any private racially discriminatory action that can be characterized as a badge or incident of slavery. Because the statute at issue bans ***all*** discrimination against African-Americans in commercial transactions, it necessarily reaches private conduct. Such congressional action is constitutionally permissible pursuant to the Thirteenth Amendment. (B) is incorrect. Application of the Fourteenth Amendment has been limited to cases involving state action. [*See* United States v. Morrison (2000)] The statute here reaches private action, and so the Thirteenth Amendment is the correct source for the law, since that amendment addresses private action. (C) is incorrect because, even if Congress's power over interstate commerce would not reach every commercial transaction, the statute would be enforceable under the Thirteenth Amendment, as discussed above. (D) is incorrect because it is irrelevant. While it is true that the commercial transactions here are not among the privileges and immunities of citizenship (which include rights such as the right to petition Congress for redress and the right to interstate travel), the law can be based on the Commerce Clause or the Thirteenth Amendment, and thus is constitutional.

Answer to Question 12

(B) The federal court should dismiss the action because there is no case or controversy. The federal courts will not issue advisory opinions and so will not hear collusive actions. The fear is that if

interested parties are not on both sides of an issue, the court will not have an opportunity to fairly address all of the sides to each issue. Here, there is no interested party opposing the pregnant woman, and so the federal court should dismiss. (A) is incorrect because the woman has standing. To have standing, a person must have a concrete stake in the outcome of the controversy. A plaintiff will have to show an injury in fact caused by the government that can be remedied by a decision in her favor. The woman here would be able to get an abortion if the statute is stricken, and so she has standing. (C) is incorrect because a political question is not involved. A political question is an issue committed by the Constitution to another branch of the government or an issue inherently incapable of resolution and enforcement by the political process. Whether a residency requirement is constitutional is not a political question. (D) is incorrect. When a state uses a durational residency requirement (a waiting period) for dispensing benefits, the government usually must show that the requirement is tailored to promote a compelling interest because it interferes with an individual's fundamental right to migrate from state to state. However, even assuming that the community interest in preventing nonresidents from draining local welfare funds is compelling, the court should decline jurisdiction because there is no case or controversy here.

Answer to Question 13

(C) The best argument for striking down the statute as unconstitutional is the Commerce Clause. Under the Commerce Clause, states may regulate local aspects of interstate commerce as long as the regulation does not discriminate against interstate commerce or unduly burden interstate commerce. The statute here does not discriminate against interstate commerce because it treats all trucks alike. To determine whether the statute unduly burdens interstate commerce, the court will balance the incidental burden on interstate commerce from the statute against the benefits produced by the legislation. Here, the burden on commerce is great, because the statute will force everyone who wants to travel through state Yellow to have Type B tires. The Supreme Court, in its opinion on the benefit produced by the statute from the previous case, found Type A tires and Type B tires equally safe. Thus, the statute provides little, if any, benefit. Because the burden on interstate commerce outweighs the benefits of the statute, the statute will be struck down. (A) is incorrect because the fact that the tires are equally safe does not itself render a ban against one type of tire unconstitutional. Such an argument might arise under the Due Process Clause (*i.e.*, the law is arbitrary), but the issue is not fully discussed in choice (A). In any case, the mere fact that the tires are equally safe is not itself a constitutional rationale for striking down a law. (B) is incorrect because the Supremacy Clause is used to strike down state laws that conflict with federal laws or regulations or that involve a field that Congress has preempted. Under the facts here, there is no conflicting federal law and nothing indicates that Congress has preempted the field. Rather, the actual basis for invalidating this law is the "dormant" or "negative" Commerce Clause. (D) is incorrect because res judicata (the fact that the issue has been litigated before) is not a constitutional doctrine, and the Court need not follow its previous decision.

Answer to Question 14

(C) The President's strongest argument is that the power to select ambassadors is vested by the Constitution in the President, and the Senate's only power in this respect is to advise and give (or withhold) its consent. The Senate is not given the power to force ambassadors on the President. (A) is not a strong argument because the President's power as commander-in-chief is not involved here. That power involves the President's role as the supreme military leader, and military issues are not involved under the facts. (B) is not a strong argument because as far as foreign relations are concerned, the Senate does have more powers than the House. As stated above,

ambassadors may be selected only with the advice and consent of the Senate, and the President's treaty power is also similarly limited. Thus, but for the fact that the resolution is not within the Senate's power to enforce, it would be appropriate to exclude the House from participating, because foreign affairs are involved. (D) may be a true statement, because Congress controls appropriations, but it is not a strong argument because it merely states that the Senate has another remedy (*i.e.,* besides forcing an ambassador on the President), and the fact that the Senate has another method for achieving its goals has no bearing on whether its action here is permissible.

Answer to Question 15

(D) A state generally may not discriminate against aliens absent a compelling state interest, and no compelling interest is served by prohibiting aliens from teaching at a state university. (A) is incorrect. The Tenth Amendment reserves to the states power not granted to the federal government. The Constitution vests the power to regulate aliens in Congress, and thus the states do not have power to control aliens under the Tenth Amendment. (B) is incorrect because it states the standard that the Supreme Court has applied to primary and secondary school teachers. The Supreme Court has upheld state statutes prohibiting aliens from teaching primary or secondary school on the rationale that teachers at the elementary and high school level have a great deal of influence over the attitudes of students toward government, the political process, and citizenship. It is doubtful that the Court would extend this rationale to university teachers. (C) is incorrect because it states the wrong standard. If state discrimination against aliens relates to participation of aliens in the functioning of state government, the rational basis test applies. Merely teaching political science at a state university is not equivalent to participating in the political process.

Answer to Question 16

(D) The friend can constitutionally be convicted because the statute does not violate the First Amendment. Certain public property (*e.g.,* public streets or parks) is so historically associated with the exercise of First Amendment rights that speech thereon can be regulated only by content neutral proscriptions. Other places controlled by the government, however, are not so historically linked to speech activities, and in such locations free speech might interfere with the intended use of such locations. Thus, the government can regulate access to these nonpublic forums based on the subject matter of the speech, as long as the regulation is reasonably related to the purpose served by the property and is not designed merely to suppress a particular point of view. A courthouse and its grounds is not a public forum. (The surrounding sidewalks are, but that is not in issue here.) The statute, although based on the subject matter of speech, is viewpoint neutral and reasonably related to the courthouse purpose of promoting a stable, orderly atmosphere in which judicial proceedings can take place free of improper outside influence or coercion. Thus, the statute is valid and the friend can be convicted for her actions. (A) is wrong because it is based on an overbreadth argument and the statute here is not overbroad. A regulation of speech that restricts substantially more speech than necessary is unenforceable, even if the speech in question could have been properly restricted by a narrower statute. This doctrine is inapplicable here because the statute is not overbroad: it reaches only speech ***in the courthouse or on its grounds*** and only that speech ***that might improperly influence the judicial proceedings***; it does not limit all speech at that location. (B) is wrong because the friend's intent to harm the judge is irrelevant. The statute makes it a crime to make a speech or carry a sign intended to influence the judicial proceeding. The statute does not require that the violator intend to harm anyone. Because the state is entitled to regulate speech or conduct in the courthouse or on its grounds that might interfere with the judicial proceedings, it is entitled to convict the friend for her actions here regardless of her intent to harm the judge. (C) is wrong because it improperly applies the "clear

and present danger" test to these facts. Under the current version of the "clear and present danger" test, a state cannot forbid advocating the ***use of force or violation of law*** unless such advocacy is (i) directed to producing or inciting imminent lawless action, and (ii) likely to produce such action. The state statute here does not purport to punish advocacy of force or lawlessness, but rather seeks to further the purpose of maintaining the stability and integrity of the judicial proceedings by regulating access to certain nonpublic areas. Therefore, the restrictions are constitutionally valid and the "clear and present danger" test is inapplicable.

Answer to Question 17

(D) The statute is an unconstitutional violation of the Commerce Clause. Regulation of foreign commerce is exclusively a federal power because of the need for the federal government to speak with one voice when regulating commercial relations with foreign governments. The existence of legitimate state interests underlying state legislation will not justify state regulation of foreign commerce. The state statute, in imposing requirements for a license costing $50 and for a clear marking of goods as being from a foreign country, clearly is an attempt by the state to restrict or even eliminate the flow of such goods in foreign commerce. Thus, the statute is unconstitutional. (A) is incorrect because even if the $50 fee represents a reasonable inspection fee, the fee would still constitute an interference with foreign commerce. In addition, the facts do not indicate that the license fee has anything to do with inspection, or that the amount of the fee bears any relation to legitimate inspection purposes. (B) is incorrect because the labeling requirement imposes a burden on goods that flow in the stream of foreign commerce. Although this burden may be relatively small, it is still impermissible in light of the exclusive power held in this area by the federal government. (C) is incorrect because it states factors that would be relevant in a matter involving regulation of interstate commerce, rather than foreign commerce. Congress's power over interstate commerce is shared with the states, so that a state law may regulate local aspects of interstate commerce if it does not discriminate against out-of-state competition to benefit local economic interests and its incidental burden on interstate commerce does not outweigh the legitimate local benefits arising therefrom. However, Congress's power over foreign commerce is exclusive, so that factors such as a minimal burden on foreign commerce and the presence of legitimate state interests will not save a state law from a challenge based on the power to regulate foreign commerce.

Answer to Question 18

(B) The legislation is valid because the statute does not conflict with federal legislation or violate the Commerce Clause. The states may regulate local aspects of interstate commerce as long as Congress has not adopted regulations concerning the subject matter or preempting the entire area of regulation. Even absent federal legislation, under the negative implications of the Commerce Clause the state regulation must not discriminate against interstate commerce or unduly burden it. Here, there is no federal legislation directly conflicting with the state law, as the facts state that the federal government only regulates the rates that may be charged by phone companies. Neither has Congress preempted the field. Preemption occurs when Congress shows an intent to occupy an entire field, thus precluding any state regulation. If the law does not state whether state law is to be preempted, the Court will look to the comprehensiveness of the scheme and whether Congress has created an agency to administer over the area. Here, the legislative scheme does not seem comprehensive, and although the facts indirectly mention the existence of an agency (since there are relevant administrative rules), it may be presumed that Congress did not intend to preempt the field here (the agency's only power presumably is over rate regulation). Finally, nothing in the facts indicates that the state law discriminates against out-of-state competition, and the

law does not unduly burden interstate commerce, because the incidental burden on interstate commerce does not appear to outweigh the legitimate local benefits produced by the regulation. Thus, (B) is correct. (A) is incorrect because the federal commerce power allows Congress to regulate the channels of intestate commerce, and telephone and similar communications devices would be considered to be channels of interstate commerce. Thus, Congress could regulate the dialing devices even if they are used wholly within one state. (C) is incorrect for the reasons stated above regarding preemption. (D) is incorrect because, as indicated above, states may regulate local aspects of interstate commerce under certain circumstances.

Set 4 Answer Sheet

1. Ⓐ Ⓑ Ⓒ Ⓓ
2. Ⓐ Ⓑ Ⓒ Ⓓ
3. Ⓐ Ⓑ Ⓒ Ⓓ
4. Ⓐ Ⓑ Ⓒ Ⓓ
5. Ⓐ Ⓑ Ⓒ Ⓓ
6. Ⓐ Ⓑ Ⓒ Ⓓ
7. Ⓐ Ⓑ Ⓒ Ⓓ
8. Ⓐ Ⓑ Ⓒ Ⓓ
9. Ⓐ Ⓑ Ⓒ Ⓓ
10. Ⓐ Ⓑ Ⓒ Ⓓ
11. Ⓐ Ⓑ Ⓒ Ⓓ
12. Ⓐ Ⓑ Ⓒ Ⓓ
13. Ⓐ Ⓑ Ⓒ Ⓓ
14. Ⓐ Ⓑ Ⓒ Ⓓ
15. Ⓐ Ⓑ Ⓒ Ⓓ
16. Ⓐ Ⓑ Ⓒ Ⓓ
17. Ⓐ Ⓑ Ⓒ Ⓓ
18. Ⓐ Ⓑ Ⓒ Ⓓ

CONSTITUTIONAL LAW QUESTIONS - SET 4

Question 1

A city condemned all of the buildings in a decaying warehouse district and offered them to developers at no cost, provided the developer submits a building revitalization plan to the city's planning commission, the commission approves the plan, and the developer pays the city's redevelopment authority to perform the work needed to revitalize the building. An experienced developer submitted a plan to revitalize a block-long building, and his plan was approved by the planning commission. However, the developer wanted to perform the revitalization work himself, both to ensure that the job was done correctly and to save a substantial amount of money. Although he offered to post a surety bond to insure his performance, the city refused his offer.

As applied to the contractor, is the city's requirement that the developer use the city's redevelopment authority constitutional?

(A) No, because it violates the privileges and immunities protected by Article IV.

(B) No, because it constitutes an improper exaction under the Fifth Amendment.

(C) Yes, because the city is seeking just compensation for the building that it would provide to the developer.

(D) Yes, because the requirement is rationally related to a legitimate government interest.

Question 2

Congress passed a bill to relocate a special forces training center. The bill included funds to facilitate the move and mandated that the funds be so spent. The bill was signed into law by the President. Thereafter, the senators from the state in which the training center is currently located informed the President that they would withdraw their support for an important bill he favored if the move takes place.

Which of the following statements is most accurate regarding the power of the President on this issue?

(A) The President has no power to decline to spend the funds appropriated for the move because he is doing so for political reasons.

(B) The President has no power to decline to spend the funds appropriated for the move because they were specifically appropriated for the relocation of the training center.

(C) The President, as part of his authority as commander in chief of the armed forces, has the power to leave the special forces training center where it is.

(D) The President, as part of his authority to balance the budget, has the power to decline to spend appropriated funds.

Question 3

Which of the following clauses of the Constitution would most likely permit Congress to impose on the states a uniform child custody law?

(A) The Commerce Clause.

(B) The Police Power Clause.

(C) The Privileges and Immunities Clause.

(D) The Taxing and Spending Power Clause.

Question 4

Shortly after a professor at a state university completed her second year of teaching, she was informed that her contract was not being renewed for the following year. By state law, a professor does not acquire tenure until after she has completed three consecutive years of teaching. Before acquiring tenure, state law does not require either a statement of reasons or a hearing when a professor's contract is not renewed, and the university administration refused to give either to the professor.

Which of the following, if established, sets forth the strongest constitutional argument that the professor could make to compel the university to furnish her a statement of reasons for the failure to rehire her and an opportunity for the hearing?

(A) She purchased a home in anticipation of renewal of her contract, because most professors who had taught two years were rehired.

(B) She had been voted the most popular professor on campus in each of her first two years of teaching.

(C) She was the only teacher at the university whose contract was not renewed that year.

(D) There is evidence to indicate that the decision not to rehire the professor was not based on her ability to teach.

Question 5

Due to complaints about the "secondary effects" of adult book stores, such as increases in petty crimes, a city council passed an ordinance banning the operation of adult-oriented businesses in any "residential" or "commercial" zone of the city. Such businesses were allowed to operate only in areas zoned "industrial." The owner of a profitable adult bookstore and video-rental operation located in a commercially zoned area of the city filed suit in federal court to prevent enforcement of the statute against him and others in adult-oriented businesses, claiming violation of his free speech rights.

The court's ruling is likely to favor:

(A) The city, because speech-related activities may be regulated to prevent effects that are offensive to neighboring businesses and residents.

(B) The city, because the ordinance is designed to serve a substantial governmental interest and does not unreasonably limit alternative avenues of communication.

(C) The business owner, because the city is improperly regulating speech based on its content.

(D) The business owner, because the city has not established that he is selling obscene materials.

Question 6

A city passed an ordinance prohibiting all of its police officers and firefighters from "moonlighting" (working a second job). The ordinance was passed to ensure that all police officers and firefighters were readily available in case an emergency should arise and for overtime work when the situation warranted it. Other city employees, including members of the city council and the city manager, had no such restrictions placed on secondary employment. A police officer who wanted to moonlight as a dancer at a nightclub within city limits brought suit in federal court, alleging that the ordinance violated her constitutional rights.

How should the court rule on the constitutionality of the ordinance?

(A) The ordinance is unconstitutional, because it restricts the officer's First Amendment rights to freedom of expression.

(B) The ordinance is unconstitutional, because the singling out of police officers and firefighters violates equal protection.

(C) The ordinance is constitutional, because the city has a significant interest that it seeks to regulate.

(D) The ordinance is constitutional, because there is a rational basis for the ordinance.

Question 7

An author who was about to release a book on military censorship in war zones was interviewed by a newspaper reporter. During the interview, the author spoke generally of military censorship in war zones, but would not give the reporter any specific instances of censorship that he intended to include in his book. During the interview, the author received a phone call and excused himself. While the author was out of the room, the reporter found a pre-publication copy of the author's book and quickly took photographs of several pages. The reporter later printed the pictures and published an article that included the photographed sections of the book verbatim. The author brought an appropriate action against the reporter for copyright infringement.

Assuming that the court properly concludes that any fair use exception in the copyright laws is not applicable, it should:

(A) Not award the author damages because his book included matters of public concern, and so the reporter had a right under the First Amendment to publish it.

(B) Not award the author damages because newspapers have an absolute right under the First Amendment to print whatever information they receive.

(C) Award the author damages because he has a Fifth Amendment property right in his book.

(D) Award the author damages because the newspaper did not get his permission to print the pages from his book.

Question 8

Congress enacted a statute requiring state-supported institutions of higher education that provide federal student loan funds to their students to fund women's sports according to a complex formula intended to fairly support woman's athletics and remedy past funding discrimination. Under the formula, a particular state military school will be required to allocate 25% of its athletic budget to its female athletics programs even though only 10% of the school population is female. A male student whose athletic program will be discontinued because of the budget allocation filed suit in federal court challenging the federal statute on various constitutional grounds.

Is the court likely to find that the statute is constitutional?

(A) No, because the government will be unable to prove that the discriminatory funding requirements required by the statute are necessary to achieve a compelling government interest.

(B) No, because the federal government does not have the power to dictate the budget allocations of state-supported educational institutions.

(C) Yes, because remedying past discrimination is a legitimate government interest, and the student will be unable to prove that the statute's funding requirements are not rationally related to that interest.

(D) Yes, because the government will be able to prove that the statute's funding requirements are substantially related to an important government interest.

Question 9

A man who lived in the state of Green was injured when the automobile that he was driving crossed over the yellow line and crashed into an automobile being driven by a woman in the state of Green. The woman was a domiciliary of the state of Orange. The man suffered severe injuries in the crash and his automobile was totally destroyed. The woman's automobile was severely damaged, but she received only minor cuts and bruises as a result of the crash. At the time of the crash, the man was legally intoxicated.

The woman brought suit against the man in a proper Green state court to recover $20,000 for the damages to her car. The man filed a counterclaim against the woman for $400,000 for his personal injuries and damages to his automobile. The state of Green has adopted a pure comparative negligence rule. The court found that the man was 90% at fault and the woman was 10% at fault and entered a final judgment against the woman for $22,000 after offsetting her damages against the man's damages.

The man then filed suit in the state of Orange to enforce his judgment against the woman. The state of Orange has adopted partial comparative negligence by statute. The woman appeared at the state of Orange proceeding and argued that the Green judgment should not be enforced because the state of Orange has a strong public policy against both drunk driving and allowing a tortfeasor who was more than 50% at fault from recovering from someone who was less than 50% at fault.

How should the Orange state court rule?

(A) In favor of the man because the Green state court had adequate and independent grounds on which to base its judgment.

(B) In favor of the man because the Green judgment is entitled to full faith and credit.

(C) In favor of the woman because, under recent Supreme Court precedent, allowing a person who is 90% at fault to recover from a person who is 10% at fault violates due process.

(D) In favor of the woman because the Tenth Amendment reserves to the states the right to enforce their strong public policies regarding torts and drunk driving.

Question 10

A duly enacted federal statute sets aside a $5 million grant to study whether after-school dance classes could help prevent teenagers from joining gangs. A nonpartisan taxpayer's group, dedicated to restoring fiscal integrity in the federal government, has filed suit in federal court against appropriate federal officials to enjoin their expenditure of the $5 million provided by the statute. The suit challenges the statute as an improper exercise of congressional power.

Which of the following best reflects the likely result of the case on a proper challenge?

(A) The court will dismiss the case because a federal court lacks jurisdiction to enjoin expenditure of funds voted by Congress, under the doctrine of separation of powers.

(B) The court will dismiss the case because the nonpartisan group lacks standing to maintain the action.

(C) The court will hear the case on its merits and will find that the grant is a valid exercise of the federal taxing and spending powers.

(D) The court will hear the case on its merits and will find that the grant is an invalid exercise of the federal taxing and spending powers.

Question 11

To protect its faltering lobster industry, the state of Blue enacted a statute providing that no lobster shall be taken from lobster beds lying within three miles of the state shoreline unless it is at least one pound in weight (the purpose of which is to enable young lobsters to reproduce before being caught). At the same time, Congress enacted a lobster conservation act that provides $5 million for research funds to develop and improve breeding grounds for lobsters and imposes a special excise tax of $1,000 on each lobster caught in violation of state law if later shipped in interstate commerce. A lobsterman who lives in the state of Green, which is just south of the state of Blue, crossed over into waters lying within three miles of the Blue coastline. He was arrested by state Blue law enforcement officers for taking lobsters that weighed less than one pound. The man defended the charge by challenging the constitutionality of the state Blue statute.

Which of the following results is most likely?

(A) The statute will be upheld because it does not violate the Constitution in any way.

(B) The statute will be upheld because the Commerce Clause does not apply when a state is seeking to protect natural resources.

(C) The statute will be held invalid because it violates the Interstate Privileges and Immunities Clause of Article IV, Section 2.

(D) The statute will be held invalid because it is preempted by the federal lobster conservation act.

Question 12

A state enacted a statute requiring the parents of every child to have the child vaccinated for smallpox before the child's third birthday. Failure to comply was a misdemeanor punishable by a fine of $500 or six months in the county jail. The parents of an infant living within the state objected to application of the statute to their child on the ground that any injections or vaccinations violated the tenets and beliefs of their religion. The parents have commenced an action in federal court to declare the statute unconstitutional on the ground that it violates their right to the free exercise of their religion under the First Amendment to the United States Constitution.

The best argument to defeat their action is that:

(A) A proceeding for declaratory judgment is not the proper vehicle for asserting this claim.

(B) The state legislature has repeatedly defeated bills to repeal the statute.

(C) There is no substantial threat that the statute will be enforced.

(D) The federal courts should abstain until the state courts have had an opportunity to construe the statute.

Question 13

A woman decided to run for office as a park district trustee in the next general election. A city ordinance provided that all candidates running for the office of park district trustee must present to the city clerk within 90 days of the election petitions signed by at least 500 qualified voters, a $500 filing fee, and a personal financial statement that will be open to the public for inspection. The woman timely filed the petitions with sufficient signatures, but refused to file the financial statement or pay the filing fee. When the clerk refused to put her name on the ballot, she filed suit, claiming that the filing fee and personal financial statement requirements are unconstitutional.

Which of the following statements best describes the likely outcome of the woman's suit?

(A) The filing fee requirement will be held invalid if the woman is indigent, but the financial statement requirement will be upheld.

(B) The filing fee requirement will be upheld, but the financial statement requirement will be held invalid because it impairs the woman's right of personal privacy.

(C) Both requirements will be held invalid and the woman will be entitled to have her name placed on the election ballot.

(D) Both requirements will be held invalid unless the requirements are shown to serve some legitimate state purpose.

Question 14

The United States entered into a treaty with a foreign nation in which the foreign nation agreed to give up its quest for a nuclear arsenal and the United States agreed to allow the foreign nation to export automobiles to the United States. After the treaty was signed, evidence was discovered indicating that the foreign nation might not be living up to its end of the treaty. Before an investigation could be completed, an enraged Congress enacted a statute that specifically terminated permission for the foreign nation to export automobiles to the United States.

Which of the following statements is most correct?

(A) The federal legislation is invalid because the agreement with the foreign nation was a treaty rather than an executive agreement.

(B) The federal legislation is invalid as interfering with the executive power over foreign affairs.

(C) The federal legislation works to repeal the substance of the treaty.

(D) The federal legislation works to repeal the treaty only if signed by the President (rather than being passed over his veto) and ratified by two-thirds of the Senate.

Question 15

A state adopted a statute making the ritual slaughter of chickens illegal. The legislative debates made clear that the purpose of the statute was to prevent unnecessary cruelty to animals. The religious leader of a church located within the state, whose core religious beliefs require ritual slaughter of chickens during worship services, brought suit to have the statute declared unconstitutional for violating her right to practice her religion.

The court will most likely:

(A) Uphold the statute, because of the compelling state interest involved.

(B) Uphold the statute, because it is a neutral law of general application.

(C) Invalidate the statute, because ritual slaughter is a core tenet of the plaintiff's religious beliefs.

(D) Invalidate the statute, because it targets only ritual slaughter.

Question 16

A group of parents advocating abstinence among teenagers developed a seminar that it presents to middle school students throughout the country. The seminar includes lectures by trained professionals accompanied by slides, some of which depict explicit sexual activity between nude males and females. Parents are required to give their consent before any child may participate. A school administrator invited the group to present its program. However, a law in the state in which the school is located provides in its entirety, "It is unlawful to sell, give, or display to any person under the age of 17 any lewd or obscene article, picture, or depiction." The district attorney for the district in which the school is located learned of the planned presentation and threatened to prosecute the school's administrative board and program's presenter under the state statute if they carried out the planned program.

If the school's administrators seek relief in federal court, which of the following statements regarding the likely result of the case is correct?

(A) The federal court has power to grant a declaratory judgment that the statute is unconstitutional, either on its face or as applied to the program.

(B) The federal court has power to enjoin the district attorney from prosecuting the administrators and presenter only if there is diversity of citizenship between them and the district attorney.

(C) The federal court is more likely to grant an injunction or declaratory relief after the state criminal prosecution has commenced than beforehand.

(D) Under no circumstances will the federal court enjoin a state criminal prosecution.

Question 17

A state statute makes it unlawful to willfully cause or permit the life or health of a child under the age of 18 to be endangered or to willfully cause or permit a child to be placed in circumstances that endanger the child's life or health. A local prosecutor brought charges against parents who brought their child to their church's religious service in which venomous snakes were passed around, and the parents were convicted.

Which of the following best describes the likely result if the parents appeal their convictions on constitutional grounds?

(A) Their convictions will be upheld because the parents lack standing to challenge the statute on "free exercise of religion" grounds.

(B) Their convictions will be upheld because the state's interest in regulating activities involving children necessarily outweighs any rights of members of a church under the Free Exercise Clause of the First Amendment.

(C) Their convictions will be reversed if it can be shown that the statute is being applied only to interfere with religion.

(D) Their convictions will be reversed because the freedom to engage in conduct connected with one's religion is absolutely protected under the First and Fourteenth Amendments.

Question 18

A state passed a statute containing numerous provisions regulating abortion. The statute was challenged by appropriate parties in federal court.

The court is likely to find which of the following statutory provisions unconstitutional?

(A) The person seeking the abortion must have resided within the state for at least 30 consecutive days.

(B) If it is a nontherapeutic abortion and is to be performed at a public hospital, it must be performed by a qualified physician.

(C) The person seeking the abortion must notify her parents or a court of the planned abortion if she is a minor.

(D) The person seeking the abortion must reimburse the state for the costs of a nontherapeutic abortion performed at a public hospital.

CONSTITUTIONAL LAW ANSWERS - SET 4

Answer to Question 1

(D) The city's requirement that the developer use the city's redevelopment authority is constitutional. When a city acts and the actions do not affect a fundamental right or involve a suspect or quasi-suspect classification, the action will be upheld unless the challenging party can prove that the action is not rationally related to a legitimate government interest. The city's desire to use its own work crews to do all redevelopment work in the warehouse district is rationally related to many possible legitimate government interests; *e.g.,* ensuring consistency and quality, providing work for government employees, and even making a profit or recouping some of the funds that the city expended to condemn the buildings. Moreover, the city does not classify developers, treating some differently from others, so no suspect or quasi-suspect class is involved, and as will be explained below, no fundamental right is involved either. (A) is incorrect because the Privileges and Immunities Clause is not applicable here. The Article IV Privileges and Immunities Clause prohibits states from discriminating against nonresidents regarding "fundamental" rights, and the right to remodel a particular building using the labor force of one's choice simply is not a fundamental right. (B) is incorrect. It is based on the Taking Clause of the Fifth Amendment. That clause prohibits government from taking private property without just compensation. It has been held that under the clause, government may not condition a building permit on a landowner's conveying title to part of his land to the government or granting the public access to the property unless the government can show that the condition relates to a legitimate government interest and the adverse impact of the proposed development is roughly proportional to the loss caused to the owner by the forced transfer. Here, the contractor does not own the building—the city is willing to give it to the builder only if certain conditions are met. Thus, the conditions do not amount to an exaction. (C) is incorrect. It also is based on the Taking Clause. That clause is not a source of power. Thus, it cannot be a constitutional basis for upholding the city's requirement.

Answer to Question 2

(B) The President has no power to decline to spend funds specifically appropriated by Congress when Congress has expressly mandated that they be spent, regardless of Congress's reason for making the appropriation. The President has no "legislative" power in internal affairs, and has a duty under Article II to "see that the laws are faithfully executed." In contrast, Congress clearly has the power to spend to "provide for the common defense and general welfare." [U.S. Const. art. I, §8] Hence, the Supreme Court has ruled that there is no constitutional basis for the President to "impound" (*i.e.,* refuse to spend) funds whose expenditure Congress has expressly mandated. [Kendall v. United States (1838)] Here, since the bill included an appropriations provision mandating that funds be spent on the relocation of the training center, the President must carry out the congressional directive. (A) is wrong because there is no requirement that the President exercise in a nonpolitical manner any power that he has over expenditures; the fact that he may have refused to authorize expenditures to obtain votes on an unrelated matter would not by itself invalidate his action. (C) is wrong because the President's authority is very limited when he is taking action in the domestic arena against the express will of Congress. [*See* Youngstown Sheet & Tube v. Sawyer (1952)] Here, Congress has specifically directed that the training center be relocated, and there is no indication in the facts that there is a military necessity in keeping the center at that location. (D) is wrong because the scope of the President's authority on budget matters does not extend to refusing to spend funds specifically appropriated by Congress.

Answer to Question 3

(D) The most likely method the United States could use to impose a uniform child custody law on all the states is through the taxing and spending power, making an allocation of funds available to each state that adopts the uniform law. No other selection would pass constitutional muster. The Commerce Clause has not been applied to child custody matters, and it is unlikely that Congress would use its commerce powers to regulate in this area. Indeed, were it to do so, such a measure might well lead the Supreme Court to find a violation of this power. Thus, (A) is not the most likely basis for such a statute. (B) is wrong; there is no general federal police power. (C) is wrong because neither of the Privileges and Immunities Clauses would apply to this matter: Article IV does not apply, since this is an action of the federal government, and the Fourteenth Amendment does not apply since child custody matters are not among the list of privileges or immunities the Court has recognized under that provision.

Answer to Question 4

(D) The professor is an at-will employee, and under most circumstances may be discharged "for any reason or no reason at all." Thus, normally, evidence regarding the motives for dismissal is irrelevant. The question here, however, is what is the ***strongest*** argument that the professor could make, and (D) creates at least an inference that an impermissible motive might be present (gender, free speech, etc.). (A) is a weaker answer because the professor has no property interest in continued employment; a mere expectation in continued employment is not enough, even when coupled with reliance (her buying a house). There must be a legitimate claim or entitlement—created by a contract or clear policy—that employment can be terminated only for cause. The bases alleged in (B) are arguably irrelevant; the professor's popularity may or may not have anything to do with her ability, and even if it does, she remains an at-will employee. (C) might under some circumstances offer an argument, but there could be any number of valid explanations for keeping others and letting a particular professor go, including budget constraints, subject needs, etc. (D) is, accordingly, the strongest of the possibilities.

Answer to Question 5

(B) The city is likely to prevail because the zoning ordinance is a constitutional restriction on the operation of adult-oriented businesses. The Supreme Court has held that businesses selling material that is sexually explicit, although not necessarily obscene, may be regulated through land use ordinances designed to reduce the secondary effects of such businesses. Thus, a zoning ordinance prohibiting the location of adult bookstores and theaters in areas close to residential zones and restricting such theaters to a limited area of the city is permissible if it is designed to promote substantial government interests (*e.g.*, property interests) and does not prohibit all such entertainment in the community. [City of Renton v. Playtime Theaters, Inc. (1986)] Because the city's ordinance is a legitimate part of its zoning scheme and does not prevent the businesses from operating in other areas of the town, it will probably be upheld. (A) is incorrect because it is too broad. The type of regulation in this question cannot be based simply on what residents find "offensive"; only regulations that are based on substantial government interests and do not entirely prohibit the activity have been permitted by the Supreme Court. (C) is incorrect because the regulation here, even if it is arguably content-based, is permissible because it is based on the legitimate local interest of preserving property values from the secondary effects of such businesses. (D) is incorrect because a city may restrict the location of speech-related businesses under the circumstances here without having to establish that the content of the speech is obscene.

Answer to Question 6

(D) The ordinance is constitutional. Because the ordinance is not related to the exercise of a fundamental right or based on a suspect trait, it need only rationally relate to some legitimate governmental interest. Under the Equal Protection Clause, which is implicated because the ordinance treats some city employees differently from others, a governmental classification must be necessary to promote a compelling state interest when it relates to who may exercise a fundamental right or when it is based on a suspect trait (*e.g.*, race or national origin). If a quasi-suspect classification (*e.g.*, gender or legitimacy) is involved, the classification will be upheld if it is substantially related to an important government interest. In all other cases, the classification is valid if there is any conceivable basis on which it might relate to any legitimate governmental interest. This "rational basis" test is used for all classifications that relate only to matters of economics or social welfare. The right of police officers and firefighters to hold second jobs is not a fundamental right that will trigger strict scrutiny. In addition, the ordinance is not based on a suspect or quasi-suspect classification. Therefore, the validity of the ordinance is judged according to the "rational basis" test. A party attacking a classification under this test bears the difficult burden of demonstrating to the court that the classification does not have a rational relationship to a legitimate interest of government. The ordinance is intended to and does in fact promote the legitimate governmental interests of public safety and social welfare—it increases the likelihood that there will be sufficient numbers of police and firefighters to deal with emergencies. Thus, the ordinance is valid. (C) is incorrect because, as detailed above, the test applicable here is the "rational basis" test, which requires only that the city have a "legitimate" interest rather than a "significant" interest. (B) is incorrect. Although the ordinance treats police officers and firefighters differently from other city employees, this treatment, as discussed above, is rationally related to legitimate governmental interests. Regarding (A), it is doubtful from the facts that the police officer's job as a dancer was a means of exercising the freedom of expression. However, even if the officer were "expressing" herself by means of this job, the ordinance's content-neutral restriction on this freedom is only incidental, is in furtherance of the governmental interests of public safety and social welfare, and is narrowly tailored to the furtherance of those interests. Note also that the city is not prohibiting the officer from expressing herself by means of the dance art form as such, but is only prohibiting her from holding a job in addition to that of police officer. Presumably, the officer is free to join a dance troupe or otherwise engage in dance, as long as such activities do not involve her being employed outside the police force. For these reasons, (A) is incorrect.

Answer to Question 7

(D) The author can obtain damages from the reporter because he had a property right in his manuscript that can be protected by the copyright laws regardless of the public importance of the content. The best way to answer this question is to eliminate the wrong choices. (A) is wrong because there is no First Amendment exception to copyright laws. It does not matter that the author may have been a public figure or that his book discussed a matter of public concern; magazines have no right to publish copyrighted material without permission beyond the statutory fair use exception, not the case here. [Harper & Row Publishers v. Nation Enterprises (1985)] (B) is wrong because it is too broad; the press generally has no greater freedom to speak than does the public. (C) is wrong because the Fifth Amendment is not applicable here. The Fifth Amendment prohibits ***government*** from taking private property without due process or just compensation, and here a private party has acted. Therefore, (D) is correct; the author will prevail in an appropriate action for copyright infringement against the reporter because the reporter published portions of the author's work without permission.

Answer to Question 8

(D) The statute will likely be held constitutional because the attempt to compensate for past discrimination against women is substantially related to an important government objective. When examining federal government action involving classifications of persons, the Supreme Court, using the Due Process Clause of the Fifth Amendment, applies the same standards that it applies to state actions under the Fourteenth Amendment Equal Protection Clause. When analyzing government action based on gender classifications, the Court will apply an intermediate standard and strike the action unless the government proves, by an exceedingly persuasive justification, that the action is substantially related to an important government interest. Applying this standard, the Court has generally upheld classifications benefiting women that are designed to remedy past discrimination against women, because remedying past gender discrimination is an important government interest. Here, the federal statute establishes a formula designed not only to ensure current "gender equity" in funding of intercollegiate athletic programs but also to correct specific past inequities, and the school's required funding allocation in favor of women is designed to correct inequitable allocations by the school in prior years. Hence, even though the statute's allocation requirement may discriminate against the student and other males at the school, the government can satisfy its burden of showing a substantial relationship to an important government interest. (A) is incorrect because classifications based on gender are subject to an intermediate standard rather than a strict scrutiny standard; in other words, the government need not show that the classification is necessary to achieve a compelling interest, only that it is substantially related to an important interest. Furthermore, if the classification were one subject to strict scrutiny, remedying past discrimination based on the classification would probably be considered a compelling government interest. (B) is incorrect because Congress may "regulate" states through the spending power by imposing conditions on the grant of money to state governments. Even if Congress lacked the power to directly regulate the activity that is the subject of the spending program, attaching conditions on the spending does not violate the states' Tenth Amendment rights. (C) is incorrect because it imposes the burden of proof on the wrong party and relies on the wrong standard. Because the statute results in gender discrimination, the government has the burden of proof, and that burden is to prove that the statute is substantially related to an important government interest.

Answer to Question 9

(B) The court should rule in favor of the man on full faith and credit grounds. Under the Full Faith and Credit Clause of the United States Constitution, states must give full faith and credit to the judgment of another state if the judgment is final, on the merits, and rendered by a court with jurisdiction. These requirements appear to have been satisfied here. (A) is incorrect because it is irrelevant. The doctrine of adequate and independent grounds comes into play when the United States Supreme Court is asked to review a state court ruling in a case that might have constitutional dimensions, but has been disposed of on state law grounds that are adequate to support the judgment and independent of any federal law. (C) is incorrect because no such precedent exists. (D) is incorrect because the Tenth Amendment provides that powers not delegated to the United States Government nor prohibited to the states are reserved to the states. Here, operation of the Full Faith and Credit Clause effectively prohibits the state of Orange from enforcing its public policy because the man obtained a final judgment on the merits of his counterclaim against the woman in a Green state court with jurisdiction. There is no public policy defense to the Full Faith and Credit Clause.

Answer to Question 10

(B) The court will likely hold that the nonpartisan taxpayer's group lacks standing to maintain the action because its interest is too remote. As an organization representing the interests of its members, the nonpartisan group would have standing to challenge government actions that injure the organization or its members. A party must have standing to mount a constitutional challenge; *i.e.,* the party must demonstrate a concrete stake in the outcome of a controversy. To show the existence of such a stake, the plaintiff must be able to assert that it is injured by a government action or that the government has made a clear threat to cause injury to it if it fails to comply with a law, regulation, or order. Also, the plaintiff must show that the injury in fact will be remedied by a decision in its favor. As a general rule, people do not have standing as taxpayers to challenge the manner in which the federal government spends tax dollars, because their interest is too remote. Under an exception to this general rule, federal taxpayers have standing to challenge federal appropriation and spending measures if they can establish that the challenged measure: (i) was enacted under the taxing and spending power of Congress; and (ii) exceeds some specific limitation on the power. The only such limit found by the Court to date on the taxing power is the Establishment Clause. Here, the nonpartisan group of taxpayers is trying to challenge the way in which the federal government is spending tax money, which falls within the general rule that such people cannot demonstrate a sufficient stake in the outcome of the controversy as to confer on them standing. In addition, the group cannot claim standing under the exception to this rule, because the challenge raised by the group does not allege that the Establishment Clause, or any other specific limitation on the taxing and spending power, has been exceeded. (A) is incorrect because, although there is no explicit constitutional statement of the power of federal courts to determine the constitutionality of acts of other branches of government, such judicial review of other branches of the federal government was established in *Marbury v. Madison.* The Constitution is law, and the judiciary has the authority and duty to declare what the law is. For instance, if a plaintiff can show that a particular spending measure exceeds the limitations of the Establishment Clause, a federal court has the power to prevent such an unconstitutional expenditure of funds. (C) is not as good an answer as (B) even though, if the court were to reach the merits of the case, it would likely uphold the spending measure. Pursuant to the taxing and spending powers, Congress may lay and collect taxes, as well as spend to provide for the common defense and general welfare. Such spending may be for any public purpose, not merely for the accomplishment of other enumerated powers. The statute here was enacted for the public purpose of deterring gang membership. Consequently, the statute is a valid exercise of the federal taxing and spending powers. Nevertheless, the court will never reach the merits on a proper jurisdictional challenge, as discussed above. (D) is incorrect both because the court will never reach the merits and because the statute would be upheld if the court did reach the merits.

Answer to Question 11

(A) The statute will be upheld because it does not discriminate against out-of-state economic interests and it is not unduly burdensome. A state or local government may regulate local aspects of interstate commerce if such regulation: (i) does not discriminate against out-of-state competition to benefit local economic interests; and (ii) is not unduly burdensome (*i.e.,* the incidental burden on interstate commerce does not outweigh the legitimate local benefits produced by the regulation). The state of Blue statute does not discriminate against out-of-state elements of the lobster fishing industry. The statute is designed to maintain the lobster population by allowing lobsters to reproduce. By maintaining the lobster population, the state is attempting to further the legitimate interest of reviving its faltering lobster fishing industry, rather than trying to protect a local business against interstate competition. In addition, the statute is applied evenhandedly (*i.e.,* it does not merely regulate the activities of out-of-state lobster fishers while exempting in-state fishers from those same regulations). Therefore, the statute does not discriminate against interstate commerce. The statute may impose some incidental burden on interstate commerce by

requiring out-of-state lobster fishers to refrain from taking lobsters weighing less than one pound from lobster beds within three miles of the state shoreline. However, this burden should not result in any great difficulty for out-of-state lobster fishers who wish to catch lobsters in state Blue waters. There is nothing especially burdensome or restrictive about the statute's provisions, and certainly the incidental burden that does exist does not outweigh the state's legitimate interest in maintaining its lobster population and the vitality of its lobster fishing industry. Consequently, the statute is not unduly burdensome. Because the statute is not unduly burdensome and is nondiscriminatory against out-of-state competition, it does not violate the Commerce Clause. (B) is incorrect because it is overbroad. The Commerce Clause does apply even when a state seeks to protect natural resources. (C) is incorrect because the Interstate Privileges and Immunities Clause prohibits discrimination by a state against nonresidents when such discrimination concerns fundamental rights, such as those involving important commercial activities or civil liberties. The Blue statute does not discriminate in favor of its own citizens, because ***no one*** is permitted to take a lobster from a lobster bed lying within three miles of the state shoreline unless the lobster weighs at least one pound, regardless of whether that person is a resident of the state of Blue. Therefore, the statute confers no advantage on state residents and there is no violation of the Privileges and Immunities Clause of Article IV, Section 2. (D) is incorrect because the statute is not preempted by the federal act. Under the Supremacy Clause, a state law that directly conflicts with a federal law will be held invalid. Even if a state law does not directly conflict with a federal law, it may still be held invalid if it appears that Congress intended to preempt the entire field of regulation. Preemption may be explicit in the federal law or the Court might find preemption from a pervasive federal scheme. In any case, the state statute here seems to be in harmony with the federal act, since both seek to preserve lobster fishing. Moreover, no preemption will be found since the act recognizes and reinforces state laws on the subject by providing a penalty for shipping lobsters taken in violation of state law. Thus, (D) is incorrect.

Answer to Question 12

(C) If there is no substantial threat that the statute will be enforced, then there are no constitutional issues ripe for review. A federal court will resolve only constitutional issues that are necessarily presented, ripe for review, and unavoidable for decision of the case. Someone seeking a declaration that a statute is unconstitutional must demonstrate that she has engaged (or will engage) in specific conduct, and that the challenged statute poses a real and immediate danger to her interests. The court will not determine the constitutionality of a statute when the statute has not been enforced and there is no immediate threat that it will be enforced. Thus, if the state statute is not likely to be enforced, it is not a substantial threat to the parents and so they will be unable to demonstrate any real and immediate harm (or threat thereof) to their interest. Therefore, this case is not ripe, and this choice gives the state a chance to defeat the parents' argument. The other choices do not present the state with viable arguments. (A) is incorrect because, if ripeness were present, an action for declaratory judgment ***would*** be proper. A federal court may not issue advisory opinions, but where there is a real controversy, it may issue a final judgment declaring the rights and liabilities of the parties even though no affirmative relief is sought. Maintenance of such an action requires an actual dispute between parties with adverse legal interests. If the parents were being prosecuted for violating the statute (or threatened with prosecution), the requisites for a declaratory judgment would be met and it would be an appropriate means of determining the constitutionality of the state statute. (B) is incorrect because the refusal of the state legislature to repeal the statute indicates a legislative intent that the statute remain in effect, thus implying a greater likelihood that the statute ***would be enforced***. This would make the parents' case ripe and so would help them rather than defeat their action. (D) is incorrect because the grounds for abstention are absent. When a federal constitutional claim is premised on an unsettled question of state law, the federal court should abstain, to give the state courts a chance to settle the underlying state law question. Here, there is no unsettled question of state law. Therefore, abstention by the federal court would be inappropriate.

Answer to Question 13

(A) The filing fee is invalid if the woman is indigent, but the financial statement requirement is valid. A state may not impose on candidates a fee that renders it impossible for indigents to run for office. Even as applied to nonindigent candidates, an unreasonably high filing fee that is not tailored to promote a substantial or overriding state interest might be held invalid. However, even a reasonable and otherwise valid fee would have to be waived for an indigent candidate unable to pay the fee. If the woman is indigent, then a $500 filing fee would certainly preclude her running for office. Other types of restrictions on the ability of persons to be candidates must be examined to see if the restrictions violate either the First Amendment right of political association or the Fourteenth Amendment Equal Protection Clause. A ballot access regulation must be a reasonable, nondiscriminatory means of promoting important state interests (such as running an honest, efficient election system). The financial statement requirement here is a reasonable means of promoting the important state interest of disclosing possible conflicts of interest that might compromise the integrity of elected officials. (It also might be a legitimate method for determining whether a candidate is truly indigent, thus justifying waiver of the filing fee.) This requirement is nondiscriminatory because it is applied to all candidates, rather than only some candidates. Any impairment of a candidate's right of privacy resulting from this requirement is slight in comparison to the important governmental interest served thereby. Thus, the financial statement requirement is valid. (B) is incorrect in stating the invalidity of the financial statement requirement. Also, (B) is incorrect because it cannot be said with any certainty that the filing fee requirement is valid. The fee requirement will certainly be invalid as applied to indigent candidates, and it might be so high and lacking in promotion of a substantial state interest that it will be invalid as applied to all candidates. (C) is incorrect because it states that the financial statement requirement is unconstitutional in addition to the filing fee requirement. As noted above, the requirement of a financial statement is valid. (D) is incorrect because the validity of restrictions on the ability of persons to be candidates is determined by a balancing test: A severe restriction such as a filing fee making it impossible for indigents to run for office would require a ***compelling*** state purpose to be valid.

Answer to Question 14

(C) The federal statute would work to repeal the treaty. Although a treaty has supremacy over conflicting state law, a treaty is only on a supremacy parity with an act of Congress. Any conflict between an act of Congress and a treaty is resolved by order of adoption; *i.e.,* the last in time prevails. Here, the congressional legislation conflicts with the treaty by specifically terminating the permission to freely export automobiles from the foreign nation that was conferred by the treaty. Because this statute was enacted after the treaty, the terms of the statute prevail, thus repealing the substance of the treaty. (A) is incorrect because the legislation has the same effect in this case regardless of whether the agreement was a treaty or an executive agreement; as discussed above, the legislation will prevail over the treaty. (B) is incorrect because there is no unconstitutional interference with the executive's powers here. Both the President and Congress have some authority over foreign relations (*e.g.,* the Commerce Clause allows Congress to regulate foreign commerce), and Congress has a right to exercise its power here. As stated above, the last expression of the sovereign (here, the statute) controls. (D) states the requirements for adoption of a treaty (*i.e.,* the treaty power is granted to the President by and with the advice and

consent of the Senate, providing two-thirds of the Senators present concur). Legislation that has the effect of repealing a treaty need not be signed by the President (*i.e.,* it may be passed over the President's veto), nor must such legislation be ratified by two-thirds of the Senate (unless an attempt is being made to override a presidential veto, in which case a two-thirds vote of each house is required). Therefore, (D) is incorrect.

Answer to Question 15

(D) The court will most likely strike the statute because it targets ritual slaughter. The First Amendment provides that the free exercise of religion shall not be abridged; however, the prohibition is far from absolute. The Supreme Court has stated that the amendment prohibits the government from outlawing religious beliefs and it has struck down a statute similar to the one here that outlaws conduct merely because it is religious (*i.e.,* ritual slaughter of chickens is prohibited but not other instances of chicken slaughter), at least when the law is not necessary to achieve a compelling interest. (A) is incorrect because even if prevention of cruelty to animals is a compelling interest, a statute prohibiting all ritual slaughter of chickens probably is not necessary to achieving the goal of preventing unnecessary cruelty to animals; a statute prohibiting cruel methods of slaughter would serve such a purpose. (B) is incorrect because it states the rule that the Court would use for government action that does not target religious practice. A religiously neutral law of general application may validly proscribe general conduct; *i.e.,* a law of general application will not be held invalid under the First Amendment merely because it happens to proscribe conduct that is required by one's religious beliefs. Neither will the state be required to provide religious exemptions from the statute. [Employment Division v. Smith (1990)] However, the statute here is clearly aimed at religious practices only, as it prohibits only ritual slaughter. Thus, (B) reflects the wrong standard to be applied. (C) is incorrect because it is irrelevant whether the religious practice interfered with is a core religious belief or merely a minor belief—the Court will not assess the centrality of religious belief, but will only inquire into whether a person's belief is sincere and the government action targets that belief.

Answer to Question 16

(A) The federal court may grant a declaratory judgment that the statute is unconstitutional. A federal court has the authority to issue a final judgment declaring the rights and liabilities of parties (*i.e.,* a declaratory judgment) only if there is an actual controversy. A complainant must show that he has engaged (or wishes to engage) in specific conduct and that the challenged governmental action poses a real and immediate danger to his interests. Here, the school administrators are planning to present a program of sex education and they are presented with an immediate danger of criminal prosecution from the district attorney. This threat of prosecution presents an immediate threat of interference with the administrators' First Amendment rights; *i.e.,* as is commonly stated in the First Amendment context, their rights have been "chilled." Thus, there is an actual dispute such as would authorize a court to issue a declaratory judgment that the state criminal statute (under which a prosecution is genuinely threatened) is unconstitutional, either on its face or as applied. (C) is incorrect because the commencement of a state criminal prosecution actually makes it less likely that a court will grant an injunction or declaratory relief. Generally, a federal court will not enjoin ***pending*** state criminal proceedings because of principles of equity, comity, and federalism. Thus, commencement of a state criminal prosecution would have the opposite effect of that described in (C). (D) is incorrect because it is too broad. Although a federal court will generally refrain from enjoining a ***pending*** state criminal prosecution, it could enjoin a prosecution before it is brought. Moreover, even if a prosecution is pending, a federal court could enjoin the proceeding in cases of proven harassment or prosecutions undertaken in bad faith (*i.e.,* without hope of a valid conviction). (B) is incorrect because a federal court has jurisdiction over a civil action arising under the Constitution or laws of the United States (federal question jurisdiction). Here, if the administrators are alleging a right that is founded on federal constitutional law, the court will have jurisdiction over the matter regardless of the existence of diversity of citizenship.

Answer to Question 17

(C) The convictions will be reversed if it can be shown that the statute is being applied only to interfere with religion. The Free Exercise Clause prohibits government from punishing religious belief. The Clause prevents government from punishing conduct merely because it is religious and from regulating conduct for the purpose of interfering with religion. However, the Clause does not prohibit government from regulating general conduct, even if the regulation happens to interfere with a person's ability to conform conduct to sincerely held religious beliefs. Thus, if it can be shown here that the statute is not really a regulation of general conduct but rather is being applied only to interfere with religion, the convictions will be reversed. (A) is incorrect because the parents would have standing. All that is required is a concrete stake in the outcome of the litigation; having been prosecuted for violating the statute, the parents' stake is about as concrete as it can get. (B) is incorrect because it implies that the court will balance the interests involved in determining the validity of the application of the statute here. Under the former constitutional test, the Court would make such a determination, but since *Employment Division v. Smith* (1990), the Court has abandoned the balancing approach in favor of the approach discussed above. (D) is incorrect because, as stated above, a person's conduct can be regulated by a generally applicable conduct regulation; religiously motivated conduct has very narrow protection.

Answer to Question 18

(A) The 30-day residence requirement to obtain an abortion is least likely to be constitutional because it violates the rights to privacy and to travel. Certain constitutional rights are deemed to be fundamental and can be interfered with only to promote compelling government interests. Among these are the right to privacy and the right to travel interstate. The right to privacy, among other things, protects a woman's constitutional right to have an abortion. Thus, a government cannot restrict a woman's decision to have an abortion except to promote a compelling interest (*e.g.,* protecting the life and health of the pregnant woman or protecting a viable fetus). Where, as here, the fetus is not yet viable, the state may not adopt regulations that impose an "undue burden" on the woman's right to have an abortion. The duration requirement here does not appear to serve any purpose other than to deter obtaining an abortion, and so it violates the right of privacy. The requirement also appears to violate the right to travel as well. The right to travel interstate protects a person's right to migrate from state to state. Generally, government action interfering with the right to migrate from state to state (*e.g.,* durational residency requirements) must be narrowly tailored to a compelling interest. A short durational requirement (*e.g.,* 24 hours) to obtain an abortion might be justified, but the 30-day waiting period here burdens a woman's ability to migrate for no apparent legitimate reason; rather, as stated above, the purpose appears to be to deter abortions. Thus, the right to travel is violated. (B) is constitutional because, as explained above, the government has a compelling interest in protecting a pregnant woman's health, and a requirement of obtaining a qualified physician seems to be narrowly tailored to promote that interest. (C) has been held to be constitutional as long as the court bypass procedure is available. (D) is constitutional because while government is restricted in its ability to interfere with a woman's right to have an abortion, it is not required to fund abortions. Thus, a state may require reimbursement for nontherapeutic abortions performed in public hospitals.

Set 5 Answer Sheet

1. Ⓐ Ⓑ Ⓒ Ⓓ
2. Ⓐ Ⓑ Ⓒ Ⓓ
3. Ⓐ Ⓑ Ⓒ Ⓓ
4. Ⓐ Ⓑ Ⓒ Ⓓ
5. Ⓐ Ⓑ Ⓒ Ⓓ
6. Ⓐ Ⓑ Ⓒ Ⓓ
7. Ⓐ Ⓑ Ⓒ Ⓓ
8. Ⓐ Ⓑ Ⓒ Ⓓ
9. Ⓐ Ⓑ Ⓒ Ⓓ
10. Ⓐ Ⓑ Ⓒ Ⓓ
11. Ⓐ Ⓑ Ⓒ Ⓓ
12. Ⓐ Ⓑ Ⓒ Ⓓ
13. Ⓐ Ⓑ Ⓒ Ⓓ
14. Ⓐ Ⓑ Ⓒ Ⓓ
15. Ⓐ Ⓑ Ⓒ Ⓓ
16. Ⓐ Ⓑ Ⓒ Ⓓ
17. Ⓐ Ⓑ Ⓒ Ⓓ
18. Ⓐ Ⓑ Ⓒ Ⓓ
19. Ⓐ Ⓑ Ⓒ Ⓓ
20. Ⓐ Ⓑ Ⓒ Ⓓ
21. Ⓐ Ⓑ Ⓒ Ⓓ
22. Ⓐ Ⓑ Ⓒ Ⓓ
23. Ⓐ Ⓑ Ⓒ Ⓓ
24. Ⓐ Ⓑ Ⓒ Ⓓ
25. Ⓐ Ⓑ Ⓒ Ⓓ
26. Ⓐ Ⓑ Ⓒ Ⓓ
27. Ⓐ Ⓑ Ⓒ Ⓓ
28. Ⓐ Ⓑ Ⓒ Ⓓ
29. Ⓐ Ⓑ Ⓒ Ⓓ
30. Ⓐ Ⓑ Ⓒ Ⓓ
31. Ⓐ Ⓑ Ⓒ Ⓓ
32. Ⓐ Ⓑ Ⓒ Ⓓ
33. Ⓐ Ⓑ Ⓒ Ⓓ
34. Ⓐ Ⓑ Ⓒ Ⓓ
35. Ⓐ Ⓑ Ⓒ Ⓓ
36. Ⓐ Ⓑ Ⓒ Ⓓ

CONSTITUTIONAL LAW QUESTIONS - SET 5

Question 1

In compliance with a federal statute that permits government agencies to sell or give away surplus government property, the Secretary of State directed that one of the State Department's surplus airplanes be given to a church. The Secretary knew that the church planned to use the plane to fly medical supplies to its missions in Third World countries. These missions provide medical assistance, but they also attempt to evangelize residents of the countries in question, and the Secretary was aware that, in addition to medical supplies, the plane might transport Bibles and religious tracts translated into local languages. Had the Secretary not ordered the plane to be given to the church, it would have been sold at a very reasonable cost to a nonprofit organization that helps teach young people the fundamentals of piloting and maintaining aircraft.

Which of the following parties would be most likely to have standing to sue to prevent the Secretary of State from making the gift to the church?

(A) A taxpayer.

(B) A citizen of the United States.

(C) A member of the nonprofit flying organization.

(D) The attorney general of the state in which the airplane is located.

Question 2

A state statute prohibits merchants from selling goods manufactured in a foreign country unless the merchant clearly marks the goods with their country of origin. The United States has a treaty with a foreign country that allows each country to import and sell goods and products from the other country. If a person is prosecuted under the state law for refusing to mark goods as being of that foreign country's origin, which of the following statements reflects the most likely outcome of the case?

(A) The person should be acquitted because the state statute is unconstitutional.

(B) The person will be acquitted, but only if the treaty with the foreign country preceded the state statute in point of time.

(C) The person will be found guilty because the treaty with the foreign country is no defense to a criminal prosecution in state courts for violating state laws.

(D) The person will be found guilty because the treaty is no defense to the criminal prosecution in the absence of effectuating legislation by Congress.

Question 3

A town adopted an ordinance providing that a person must have been a resident of the town for at least one year to be eligible to vote in school board elections. A resident who moved to the town seven months ago attempted to register to vote in the school board elections scheduled for the next month. However, the town clerk refused to register the resident because he will not have resided in the town for a full year prior to the election. The resident filed a class action suit on behalf of all of the new residents of the town, challenging the validity of the one-year residency requirement.

Which of the following statements is correct?

(A) If the resident's suit is not heard before the election, it will be dismissed as moot, because the resident will have met the residency requirement by the time of the next annual election.

(B) The resident will prevail even if the matter is not decided until after next month's election.

(C) As long as there is some legitimate purpose for the one-year residency requirement, such as the need to prepare voting lists, the residency requirement will be upheld.

(D) The resident will lose because one-year residency requirements have been held permissible restrictions on the right to vote in local elections.

Question 4

A city's water board election laws provide that, although members of the board are elected at large, one member of the board is required to live within each of the five designated water districts within the city. The city's population was more or less evenly distributed among the districts when this election law was enacted. A resident and registered voter of the city investigated the district residency requirement and discovered that most of the city's newer residents had moved into the same two water districts, so that the city's population was no longer evenly distributed among the five water districts. Instead, 80% of the city's residents lived within its central and eastern water districts, while the other 20% of the city's residents were scattered among its three other, more rural, districts.

If the resident files suit in federal court challenging the constitutionality of the residency requirement, the court will most likely rule that:

(A) The residency requirement is unconstitutional because it impairs the voters' equal protection rights, in that it gives the voters in the less populous districts more effective representation on the water board.

(B) The residency requirement is unconstitutional because it violates the candidates' equal protection rights.

(C) The residency requirement is constitutionally permissible because the water board members do not exercise legislative power.

(D) The residency requirement is constitutionally permissible because the water board members are elected at large.

Question 5

Which of the following suits would not fall within the United States Supreme Court's original jurisdiction under Article III, Section 2?

(A) A suit seeking to assert the interest of state citizens in retaining diplomatic relations with a foreign nation.

(B) A suit seeking to protect a state's timber from allegedly illegal cutting by residents of another state.

(C) A suit seeking to enjoin enforcement of an allegedly unconstitutional executive order that will greatly limit the state's authority to make policy decisions regarding admission to state universities.

(D) A suit by the United States government seeking to enjoin state construction of a bridge over a navigable waterway.

Question 6

The state passed a law stating that "only persons living with their parents or guardians who are bona fide residents of the state shall be entitled to free public education; all others who wish to attend public schools within the state may do so, but they must pay tuition of $3,000 per semester." A 15-year-old girl moved in with her friend so that she could attend the public schools in the state, and the state legislature passed the tuition statute just as she completed her junior year. The girl wants to complete her senior year in the state high school, but cannot afford to pay tuition.

If the girl sues in federal court to strike down the tuition statute, the court is likely to rule that the statute is:

(A) Constitutional, provided that the state can show that the statute is necessary to promote a compelling state interest.

(B) Constitutional, unless the girl can show that the statute is not rationally related to a proper state interest.

(C) Unconstitutional, because it infringes on the girl's fundamental right to an education.

(D) Unconstitutional, because it interferes with the girl's fundamental right to interstate travel.

Question 7

An employee of the United States Department of Labor was instructed by his superior to solicit subscriptions to the Department's bulletin on a door-to-door basis in the city in which he worked. While doing so, the employee was arrested for violation of a city ordinance that prohibited commercial solicitation of private residences.

The employee's best defense is:

(A) Intergovernmental immunity.

(B) The First Amendment freedom of expression as it applies to the states through the Fourteenth Amendment.

(C) The Equal Protection Clause as it applies to the states through the Fourteenth Amendment.

(D) The city ordinance effectively restricts interstate commerce.

Question 8

A federal statute taxing residential real property will most likely be upheld if it:

(A) Is applied to residences located in the various Indian lands in the United States.

(B) Is enacted under the Commerce Clause.

(C) Applies to residences located in the District of Columbia.

(D) Is applied uniformly throughout the United States.

Question 9

Intending to encourage long-time resident aliens to become American citizens, a state passed a law denying numerous state and municipal jobs to persons who had been resident aliens for longer than 10 years. Those already in the state had to apply for American citizenship within a year after the law took effect. Persons who had acquired resident alien status prior to achieving the age of majority had until age 30 to acquire such status or be automatically disqualified from obtaining such a job. A 40-year-old man who has been a resident alien in the state for 15 years applied for a job as a police emergency response telecommunications expert. He had not filed for citizenship within the one-year grace period.

May the state constitutionally rely on the statute to refuse to hire the man?

(A) Yes, because a police department performs an integral governmental function and the state law does not discriminatorily classify resident aliens by race or ethnicity.

(B) Yes, because aliens are not entitled to the privileges and immunities of state citizenship.

(C) No, because the law does not apply equally to all aliens.

(D) No, because the reasons for application of the law to the man do not appear compelling.

Question 10

A federal statute just signed into law by the President provided that school districts no longer needed to recognize the tenure of elementary school teachers—all tenured teachers would lose their status and would be treated the same as nontenured teachers. The effect of the law would be to allow all tenured teachers to be fired more easily if their performance was not adequate. The law also allowed the salaries of tenured teachers to be lowered, at least until a new contract with the teachers could be negotiated. The law had a two-year grace period before it was to take effect, to give schools and teachers time to adjust to the law; however, it specifically provided that once it is in effect, school board actions under the law supersede any existing contract terms.

A public elementary school district is in the first year of a three-year union contract with its teachers. The school board has stated that it plans to abolish tenured positions as soon as the law takes effect. The union, believing that numerous terms of the contract will be invalidated when the law takes effect, filed an action in federal court on behalf of the teachers, asking for an injunction to prevent the school board from abolishing tenured positions and for a declaratory judgment stating that the law is invalid.

Should the federal court hear the case?

(A) No, because a ruling on the law at this point is premature.

(B) No, because the union does not have standing to sue on behalf of the teachers.

(C) Yes, because the federal law encourages improper interference with a contract in violation of the Contract Clause of the Constitution.

(D) Yes, because the teachers' rights and benefits are threatened by the law and the school board's stated plans.

Question 11

A new federal law prohibited the use of various pesticides in areas with a certain population density near navigable waters. A city located in the southeastern United States was plagued by a sharp increase in disease-carrying mosquitoes. The city's board of health recommended that all residential areas be sprayed with a pesticide proven to be highly effective against mosquitoes. Despite the fact that the federal law would prohibit use of that pesticide in these areas, the city council passed an ordinance adopting the board of health plan, relying on the opinions of several independent experts that the health benefits of reducing the mosquito population outweighed the risks of spraying. An environmentally minded citizen of the city brought an action in federal court challenging the ordinance.

Assuming that the citizen has standing, the court will most likely find the ordinance:

(A) Valid, because pursuant to the police power, cities have a compelling interest in laws designed to protect the health, safety, and welfare of their citizens.

(B) Valid, because controlling health hazards is an integral governmental function.

(C) Invalid, because it is superseded by the power of Congress to adopt laws to protect the health, safety, and welfare of citizens.

(D) Invalid, because it conflicts with a federal law that Congress had the power to make under the Commerce Clause.

Question 12

In order to raise revenue, a city erected billboards on the sides of all government buildings and planned to sell the space for commercial advertising. A city ordinance provided that any advertiser could rent the space, provided that the activity or product advertised was legal and had "nothing to do with religion or politics" because the city sought to "avoid controversy."

The owner of a bookstore that specialized in books on all religions and "spiritual" subjects sought to lease a billboard on a city building to place an ad. In addition to selling books, the owner conducted daily reading and study groups in the store on all of the major religions. The proposed ad implored onlookers to come to the bookstore in order to find their own path to God and to attend study groups at the store held at 6 p.m. nightly. The ad was rejected by city officials.

If the owner files an appropriate suit against the city in federal district court asserting violation of her First Amendment rights, she is likely to:

(A) Win, because the city has made the sides of civic buildings public forums.

(B) Win, because restrictions on commercial speech must be narrowly tailored to serve a substantial government interest directly advanced by the restriction.

(C) Lose, because the restriction is viewpoint neutral and reasonably related to a legitimate government purpose.

(D) Lose, because the city must avoid excessive entanglement with religion.

Question 13

A state law required all automobile drivers to carry liability insurance; however, because of the high number of auto accidents in the state, the cost of insurance became prohibitive. A study sponsored by the state legislature showed that males under the age of 21 were four times more likely to get into automobile accidents than any other group, including females in the same age group. The study predicted that prohibiting males under the age of 21 from driving would result in a 15% reduction in all other persons' automobile insurance rates. Ultimately, the legislature raised the minimum age for obtaining a driver's license to age 21 for males. Females were still allowed to obtain licenses at age 16. An 18-year-old male living in the state when the limit was raised, and who worked as a pizza delivery driver, was fired from his job and replaced by a 17-year-old female.

If the young man sues to have the law set aside and prevails, it will most likely be because the state could not prove that the law was:

(A) The least restrictive means of achieving a compelling government purpose.

(B) Rationally related to a legitimate government purpose.

(C) Substantially related to an important government interest.

(D) Necessary to achieve a compelling government purpose.

Question 14

A state engaged a private company to run its lottery, but the state maintained close regulation of the manufacture and distribution of lottery equipment by the private company in order to prevent frauds. One lottery regulation required the company to submit to the state all applications of persons being considered for employment. The state ran background checks on the prospective employees to ensure that they did not have a criminal record. A prospective employee that did not pass the state background check could not be hired by the company.

An employee of the company who had a poor work record and called in sick often was spotted by her supervisor dancing at a bar one evening after she had called in sick during the day. The supervisor immediately told the employee that she should consider herself terminated, although the employee tried to explain that she in fact had been sick that morning but began feeling well by mid-afternoon.

A state law provided that employees of the state could not be fired from their positions except for cause. The woman sued in federal court, claiming that she was constitutionally entitled to a hearing to determine whether her supervisor had cause to fire her.

If the court rules correctly, it will probably find the employee's termination:

(A) Constitutional, because no hearing was required since the supervisor witnessed the employee's misconduct.

(B) Constitutional, because the employer is free to fire employees at will.

(C) Unconstitutional, because it violates the employee's right to procedural due process.

(D) Unconstitutional, because of the state's regulation of the hiring process.

Question 15

A critically acclaimed movie that had received a number of awards opened in a small town. The film had portrayals of nudity and scenes involving sexuality, but its advertising was very tasteful and concentrated on its critical acclaim and its receipt of seven Academy Award nominations. Nevertheless, when the movie opened in the small town, there was a public outcry against it, including picketing. The town, which had been founded in the late nineteenth century by a fundamentalist religious group, remained very conservative and highly religious, and was the only community in the state where a consensus of the community would find the movie to be obscene. The town prosecutor went to the local court seeking an injunction to halt the showing of the movie. The theater owner refused to voluntarily stop showing the film and appeared in court to defend against the proposed injunction.

What is the owner's best defense?

(A) The proper "community standards" should be those of the entire state rather than of the town.

(B) The film has some redeeming social value.

(C) The Establishment Clause of the First Amendment prevents the state from enforcing a particular set of religious beliefs.

(D) The film has proven artistic merit.

Question 16

A township located in a farming community was composed mostly of persons belonging to a specific religious sect. To help instill proper respect for authority in children, which was a central tenet of the sect, and to maintain order in the classroom, the local school board allowed teachers to inflict corporal punishment. Such punishment was inflicted on a fourth grader in a township school immediately after his teacher saw him pulling a girl's hair. Neither he nor his parents belonged to the religious sect. When the boy's parents learned of the incident, they hired an attorney. Rather than suing the teacher for battery as permitted under state law, the attorney brought an action against the teacher under a federal statute providing a cause of action for damages against any government employee who deprives a person of his constitutional rights.

Should the court find the policy allowing corporal punishment to be constitutional?

(A) No, because the punishment policy violates the First Amendment Establishment Clause.

(B) No, because the boy was denied any kind of hearing, in violation of his right to procedural due process under the Fourteenth Amendment.

(C) Yes, because under the doctrine of parens patriae states may impose any punishment they see fit.

(D) Yes, because the punishment was not grossly disproportionate under the Eighth and Fourteenth Amendments.

Question 17

A cattle-producing state adopted a statute requiring any food service business operating in the state to serve beef raised in the United States. A licensed hot dog vendor who worked at a football field within the state and who had been buying hot dogs made with foreign beef for the past several years estimated that switching to an all-beef hot dog made from United States beef would reduce his profits by 10%. An attorney hired by the vendor to challenge the statute discovered during research into the case that most of the footballs used at the football field at which the vendor worked were made of foreign leather.

Which of the following grounds is the vendor's best argument against the constitutionality of the state statute?

(A) The statute burdens foreign commerce.

(B) The statute violates equal protection guarantees because it is not rational to prohibit the sale of foreign beef but not foreign leather.

(C) The statute substantially interferes with the vendor's right to earn a living under the Privileges and Immunities Clause of the Fourteenth Amendment.

(D) The statute constitutes a taking without due process of law.

Question 18

A man was arrested in a state for armed robbery. A combined preliminary hearing to determine probable cause and initial appearance was held within 20 hours of his arrest. Probable cause was found, and bail was properly denied under the state's Bail Reform Act. A state statute provided that when a defendant is in custody, his trial must begin within 50 days of his arrest. After 50 days had passed since the man's arrest and no trial had been held, he filed a motion for dismissal for violation of his right to a speedy trial under the state constitution, which tracked verbatim the speedy trial provision of the United States Constitution. The trial judge held that he was bound to follow federal interpretations of the speedy trial provision and granted the man's motion on that basis. On appeal, the state supreme court agreed with the trial judge. The state prosecutor seeks to challenge the ruling in the United States Supreme Court.

If the Supreme Court thinks that the state court wrongly decided that the man was denied his right to a speedy trial under federal standards, it should:

(A) Reverse the decision because the state speedy trial provision cannot be interpreted in a manner different from federal interpretations.

(B) Reverse the decision and remand it to state court because the state speedy trial issue was so intertwined with the federal question that it would be difficult to determine on which ground the state court relied.

(C) Decline jurisdiction because the Eleventh Amendment prohibits a state from challenging a decision of its supreme court in federal court.

(D) Reverse the decision and remand the case to be decided on the independent state grounds only.

Question 19

To combat rising unemployment, a state offered a $25,000 prize to anyone who could devise a scheme to create at least 200 jobs within the state and demonstrate its viability. While hiking through a national park within the state, a geologist noticed rock containing titanium. Knowing that titanium was commonly used in military aircraft built within the state and that mining and refining titanium could provide the state with thousands of jobs, the geologist chipped out a sample of the ore and took it back to the state employment division. After reviewing the geologist's ideas, the state announced in a press release that he was the first recipient of the $25,000 prize. Within a few days, the federal ranger in charge of the valley from which the sample was taken had the geologist arrested for violating a federal law making it illegal to remove any "plants, animals, or minerals from federal lands." The geologist was convicted and fined $5,000. He appeals the conviction to the federal court of appeals, claiming that the fine is unconstitutional.

How should the court rule?

(A) For the geologist, because the state has a compelling interest in reducing unemployment and the federal statute unreasonably interferes with the state interest.

(B) For the geologist, because removing the ore was a purely intrastate act and had no effect on interstate commerce.

(C) For the government, because the federal statute providing for the fine is constitutional under the Property Clause of Article IV, Section 3 of the federal Constitution.

(D) For the government, because the federal statute providing for the fine is constitutional under the Commerce Clause.

Question 20

Congress passed a law allowing widespread oil exploration on federal lands in the western United States. A large deposit of oil sand was discovered in one western state and Congress authorized an oil sand refining plant to be built on federal park land within the state. The refinery was built in compliance with federal pollution regulations. Pursuant to state law, the plant manager allowed the state to inspect the plant before putting it into operation. Because state refinery standards were more strict than the federal standards (in order to better protect state citizens from pollution associated with refineries), the refinery did not pass the inspection, and the state inspector refused to give the manager a permit to run the refinery. The refinery manager nevertheless began to run the refinery and was fined by the state.

Which of the following is the manager's best defense against imposition of the fine?

(A) The state does not have a compelling interest in regulating the refinery, because it is within a federal park.

(B) The state regulation is invalid because Congress has preempted the field of pollution control.

(C) The state pollution regulation is invalid because it is inconsistent with the state's compelling interest in providing jobs.

(D) The state law violates the principles of intergovernmental immunity as applied to the manager.

Question 21

Adherents of a particular religion whose tenets focused mostly on business practices forbade women from studying their sacred texts. A group of college students who were adherents of that religion applied to use an empty room at their state college to study sacred texts. The school permitted numerous student groups to use its facilities for extracurricular activities during times when classes were not in session. However, the school administration denied the requests from the group in question, claiming that it would be in violation of a state statute forbidding any group using public facilities to discriminate on the basis of race or gender. The students brought an action in federal court challenging application of the statute to them by the school administration.

If the court finds the actions of the school valid, it would most likely be because:

(A) Permitting the religious group to hold the meeting in a public school facility would violate the Establishment Clause, applicable to the state under the Fourteenth Amendment.

(B) The statute is the least restrictive means of advancing the state's compelling interest in ending discrimination by groups using public facilities.

(C) Allowing student groups to use classroom facilities when classes are not in session does not constitute state action for purposes of the Fourteenth Amendment.

(D) The right of freedom of association does not apply to groups involved in business and commercial activities.

Question 22

A counselor was provisionally employed at a public high school in the state of Green. Pursuant to state law, provisional employees could be terminated with or without cause at any time. Among her job duties, the counselor was required

to counsel students who became pregnant. A school policy required counselors to present students with materials from all public and private agencies that provided aid to pregnant teens, including brochures from the county, several religious organizations, and the local family planning agency.

Within two months after the counselor began working, school administrators were informed that she was not distributing brochures from the local family planning agency to pregnant students. The superintendent of the school district met with the counselor and asked her if the information was true, and if so the reasons for the failure. The counselor acknowledged that it was true, and that she did not distribute the family planning agency's brochures because that agency counseled students regarding abortion, which was against the counselor's religious views. The superintendent fired the counselor.

If the counselor brings a suit in federal court claiming that her firing was unconstitutional, is she likely to prevail?

(A) Yes, because she has a liberty interest in freedom of speech that gives rise to the right to a post-deprivation hearing.

(B) Yes, because the firing violates her freedom of speech rights regarding a matter of public concern.

(C) No, because the firing did not violate her First Amendment rights.

(D) No, unless she can prove that she sincerely held the religious belief that abortion is immoral.

Question 23

Congress created the National Agency for Burglar Alarms ("NABA"), giving it the power to regulate both burglar alarm hardware and installation personnel. NABA adopted a regulation requiring that all burglar alarm installation companies be licensed, and providing that anyone installing an alarm without a license could be fined. The regulation also provided that any company in the installation business on the day the regulation was adopted automatically would receive a license, but to obtain a license thereafter, an applicant would have to show that he has worked as an installer at a licensed company for at least three years.

A man who has been installing alarm systems for eight years sold his installation business a few months before the NABA regulation was adopted and went to work for the purchaser servicing his old accounts. A few months after the NABA regulation was adopted, a representative from a national department store chain approached the man with an offer to hire him as an independent contractor to revamp the chain's alarm systems. The man quit his job and applied for an NABA installer's license. His application was denied because he was not in business on the day the NABA regulation was adopted and had worked for a licensed installer for only a few months. The man decided to install the alarm systems anyway.

Can the man properly be fined for installing alarms?

(A) Yes, because the NABA was established under Congress's power to legislate for the general welfare, and Congress may take whatever steps are necessary and proper to enforce its laws.

(B) Yes, because the regulation falls within the scope of Congress's commerce power, and Congress may delegate its authority to regulate as it has done here.

(C) No, because the regulation interferes with the man's fundamental right to earn a living without a substantial justification and so violates the Privileges and Immunities Clause of Article IV, Section 2.

(D) No, because a government agency cannot itself levy fines for a violation of its regulations.

Question 24

An attorney was employed by the United States Department of Health and Human Services in a regional office located in a tobacco-growing state. A labor contract between the agency and the clerical workers union contained a policy providing for termination of union employees only for certain specified grounds. The attorney, however, was not a member of the union and not covered by such a policy. The attorney was angered by the regional director's refusal to adopt a no-smoking policy for employees and visitors in the office. She posted a notice in the employee cafeteria ridiculing what she called the hypocrisy of an agency promoting health issues and nonsmoking programs while refusing to provide its employees with those same opportunities. The notice prompted a great deal of debate among the employees and was brought to the attention of the regional director, who was very displeased.

Which of the following statements is most accurate regarding the director's right to dismiss the attorney?

(A) The attorney has a liberty interest in the exercise of her First Amendment rights that entitles her to a hearing to contest the grounds of her dismissal.

(B) The attorney has a property interest as a public employee that precludes her from being fired without notice and an opportunity to respond.

(C) The attorney has no right to a hearing because her statements were not an expression of views on public issues.

(D) The attorney has both a liberty interest and a property interest that entitles her to a pre-termination evidentiary hearing.

Question 25

A state provided for a public school system based primarily on property tax revenues from the various districts. School districts that had a property tax base below a certain threshold received supplemental funds from the state that were derived from state lottery revenues. The school districts receiving the supplemental funds served a predominately Hispanic population as compared to the school districts funded only from property tax revenues.

To help balance its budget this year, the state legislature passed a statute terminating the supplemental funds program and earmarking the lottery revenues for deficit reduction. A group of parents of Hispanic schoolchildren in one of the school districts formerly receiving supplemental funds filed suit in federal court, alleging that the state's action in terminating the funding violates the Equal Protection Clause of the Fourteenth Amendment.

Which of the following best describes the appropriate standard by which the court should review the constitutionality of the state action?

(A) Because the state statute results in discrimination against a suspect class, the state will have to demonstrate that the statute is necessary to vindicate a compelling state interest.

(B) Because the right to education burdened by the statute is not a fundamental right, the parents will have to demonstrate that the statute is not substantially related to an important state interest.

(C) Because no suspect class or fundamental right is improperly burdened in this case, the parents will have to demonstrate that the statute is not rationally related to any legitimate state interest.

(D) Because the state statute is not discriminatory in intent, the state will have to demonstrate only that the statute is rationally related to a legitimate state interest.

Question 26

An automotive engineer announced that he had developed a carburetor that will enable cars to achieve 100 miles per gallon of fuel, and that he will allow the carburetor to be inspected next month. Soon after, a former employer of the engineer brought an action to prohibit the engineer from displaying the carburetor, claiming that the engineer probably had stolen the carburetor's design from the employer. The court granted the employer a temporary restraining order prohibiting the engineer from disclosing any mechanical details of his carburetor, and ordered a hearing to be held in one week to determine whether a preliminary injunction should be issued. Because each party would have to reveal the mechanical details of his designs at the hearing, the employer requested that the hearing be closed to the public and that the record be sealed to avoid revelation of his designs. The court granted the request. A reporter for a monthly automobile magazine heard about the case and wanted to attend the hearing. When he was told that the hearing would be closed, he filed an action to have it opened.

What is the reporter's best argument for opening the hearing?

(A) Closure is not necessary to preserve an overriding interest here.

(B) The right of freedom of the press is extensive and allows the press to attend all hearings of interest to the public.

(C) Closure here amounts to a prior restraint.

(D) Under the fairness doctrine, the magazine will be required to give each litigant an opportunity to present his side of the case.

Question 27

Small, prolific mussels called zebra mussels were first introduced into the Great Lakes by a foreign cargo ship. They became a serious problem because they attached themselves to smooth, hard surfaces, and often clogged water intake pipes. Congress determined that zebra mussels posed a great threat to the economic welfare of the Great Lakes region and passed a statute requiring all Great Lakes water intakes to be coated with a special chemical compound that repels zebra mussels. Studies by biologists at a major state university showed that while the special chemical compound that the federal government has required was effective, it also was toxic to other aquatic life. The biologists recommended that Great Lakes intake pipes be coated with a less toxic and less expensive copper-based paint. On the basis of those studies and the recommendation, three Great Lakes states adopted laws permitting municipal water districts to coat their intake pipes with copper paint.

Can municipalities using copper-based paint on their intake pipes successfully be prosecuted for violating the federal law?

(A) No, because the Tenth Amendment prevents Congress from interfering with integral government functions.

(B) No, because the municipalities are taking effective steps to combat zebra mussels in compliance with the spirit and purpose of the federal law.

(C) Yes, because Congress is in a better position to regulate the entire Great Lakes region than the individual states.

(D) Yes, because Congress may adopt laws regulating navigable waters.

Question 28

To increase tourism, a city began sponsoring laser light shows, which proved to be very popular. Several charitable organizations received permission from the council to sponsor a show and charge admission to raise money to help support their causes. One of them hired a famous laser light artist to give their show. When the artist arrived, he began setting up his lasers for the show. A city official soon stopped him, informing him that he could use only the city's lasers because the city feared that outsiders might use powerful lasers that could cause eye damage to viewers. The artist told the charitable organization that had hired him that the success of his art depends on the power of his lasers and that he could not produce desirable effects using the city's lasers. The charitable organization appealed to the city, but the city held fast to its rule requiring all laser light artists to use the city's lasers.

If the charitable organization files an action against the city, the court will most likely:

(A) Find for the charitable organization, because art is protected by the First Amendment and the city rule interferes with the artist's freedom of expression.

(B) Find for the charitable organization, because the city rule is not the least restrictive method for achieving the city's goals.

(C) Find for the city, because the laser light show is not speech and therefore is not protected by the First Amendment.

(D) Find for the city, because the rule is a reasonable time, place, and manner restriction.

Question 29

Due to budget shortages and a critical need of funding to fight a war, Congress enacted a $25 tax on each person flying into an airport in the five most popular vacation destinations in the country, as determined by Congress. The tax was implemented, and officials in the five destinations were outraged, fearing that the number of vacationers to the taxed destinations would decrease due to the tax.

If the tax is challenged in federal court by an official with standing, the most likely result is that the tax will be held:

(A) Unconstitutional, because it makes it significantly more difficult for persons to travel between the states.

(B) Unconstitutional, because the tax unfairly discriminates against certain vacation destinations by taxing them and not taxing other, similar vacation destinations.

(C) Constitutional, because the tax is necessary to achieve a compelling government interest.

(D) Constitutional, because Congress has plenary power to impose taxes to raise revenue.

Question 30

To prevent the Supreme Court from whittling away the protections that previous Supreme Court decisions had created for individuals accused of crimes, Congress passed a law eliminating from Supreme Court jurisdiction all cases in which a state supreme court has decided that a defendant's federal constitutional rights have been violated.

If the statute is held unconstitutional, it will most likely be because:

(A) The determination of the extent of constitutional rights is precisely the domain of the Supreme Court.

(B) Congress's power to limit jurisdiction applies only to cases originating in the federal courts.

(C) To be effective, the action taken by Congress here would require a constitutional amendment.

(D) Congress may not eliminate all avenues for Supreme Court review of issues vested within the judicial power of the federal courts.

Question 31

The mayor of a town received several complaints from residents regarding the growing number of adult theaters and nude dancing establishments in a nearby town. To allay fears, the mayor asked the town's attorney what could be done to prevent or at least limit such establishments from setting up business in their town, which currently follows a zoning plan that provides for residential, commercial, and light industrial uses.

Which of the following most correctly describes the town's constitutional options?

(A) The town may revise its zoning ordinance to prohibit adult theaters and nude dancing establishments because erotica is unprotected speech.

(B) The town may revise its zoning ordinance to limit the location of adult theaters and nude dancing establishments only if this serves a compelling interest.

(C) The town may revise its zoning ordinance to limit the location of adult theaters and nude dancing establishments to control the secondary effects of such businesses.

(D) The town may not limit the location of either adult theaters or nude dancing establishments in any manner different from limitations on other commercial establishments.

Question 32

Residents of a village in a desert state that allows gambling and has several military bases within the state's borders adopted an ordinance prohibiting "any gambling, mining, or military activities within village limits" and also prohibiting any devices related to such activities from entering the village. The only road into the village was the one that served as the most convenient exit from a nearby military base. In the past, the military would drive tanks and trucks with armed troops through the village to go to training exercises in the desert.

Can the military continue to drive through the village?

(A) Yes, because the village ordinance interferes with the federal right to bear arms.

(B) Yes, because states and municipalities may not interfere with legitimate federal operations.

(C) No, if other routes are only slightly less convenient.

(D) No, because the village ordinance is a legitimate exercise of the municipality's police power to protect the health, morals and safety of its citizens.

Question 33

A wife married to her husband for five years filed for divorce because her husband had become extremely abusive. She was told that the state required a $150 court fee to grant her divorce. The wife challenges the required fee.

Which of the following statements is most correct concerning the wife's challenge?

(A) Because the wife is poor, the state will have to show that its divorce fee is necessary to achieve a compelling interest.

(B) Because the wife is poor, she will have to show that requiring her to pay the divorce fee is irrational.

(C) Because the wife has a compelling interest in obtaining a divorce, the state will have to show that its divorce fee is narrowly tailored to serve an important state interest.

(D) Because the wife has a fundamental right to a divorce, the state will have to prove that requiring her to pay the fee is necessary to achieve a compelling state interest.

Question 34

A state statute has detailed classifications of civil servants for both state and city positions. It provides that all civil servants who have been employed for over 18 months may be dismissed only for "misconduct" and also requires that state and city agencies comply with all procedures set forth in any personnel handbook issued by that agency. The personnel handbook of the state tollway authority sets forth detailed procedures for dismissal of civil servant employees. The handbook provides that written notice of the grounds for dismissal must be given to the employee prior to dismissal, and that the employee must, on request, be granted a post-dismissal hearing within three months after the dismissal takes effect. An employee is entitled to present witnesses and evidence at the post-dismissal hearing, and is entitled to reinstatement and back pay if the hearing board decides that the employer has not shown by a preponderance of the evidence that the dismissal was justified.

A state tollway employee who had been employed for three years recently was fired. After an investigation by state auditors, the employee was notified by registered letter that he was being dismissed because of evidence that he took bribes from construction firms in exchange for steering contracts to them. He was informed of his right to a hearing and requested one as soon as possible. Three weeks after his dismissal, the state personnel board conducted a hearing at which the employee denied the charges and presented witnesses to attest to his honesty. At the conclusion of the hearing, the board upheld his dismissal, finding that it was supported by a preponderance of the evidence.

If the employee files suit in federal court challenging his dismissal on constitutional grounds, will he be likely to prevail?

(A) Yes, because the employee had a right to a pre-termination hearing at which he could present witnesses to support his side of the story.

(B) Yes, because the employee had a right to have an opportunity to respond to the charges prior to his dismissal.

(C) No, because the state may establish the required procedures for terminating an interest that it created by statute.

(D) No, because the procedures taken for termination of the employee's job satisfied due process requirements.

Question 35

A state study indicated that an inordinately high percentage of homeless in the state were afflicted by alcoholism or addiction to illegal drugs. The legislature therefore decided to levy a special tax, with all proceeds marked for rehabilitative services for the homeless. However, the legislators determined that direct taxes on alcoholic beverages would be resented by the citizenry. Lobbyists from the state's growing wine industry also objected to anything that would retard the industry's development. There were no breweries or distilleries within the state. Thus, a tax was eventually passed requiring newspapers and magazines of general circulation published in the state to be taxed at a rate of 20% on all advertising space sold for beer or distilled spirits promotions.

For certain historical reasons, a high proportion of the advertising revenue of a particular small newspaper within the state came from beer and wine ads. The publisher of the small paper filed suit to have the tax declared unconstitutional. A major wholesale beer and liquor distributor located within the state and several out-of-state brewers and distillers who sold and advertised their products in the state also joined in the suit as plaintiffs.

If the tax is declared unconstitutional, it will most likely be because:

(A) The tax burdens interstate commerce by exempting advertisements for the local wine industry from the tax, while the ads of out-of-state brewers and distillers are subject to the tax.

(B) The tax infringes on freedom of the press, which is guaranteed by the First and Fourteenth Amendments.

(C) The tax is unconstitutional because it is not properly apportioned.

(D) The tax violates the Equal Protection Clause of the Fourteenth Amendment, because it does not treat all alcoholic products equally.

Question 36

A city entered into a contract with a cable and Internet provider allowing the provider to be the exclusive cable and Internet provider in the city in exchange for certain rights. To facilitate installation of the provider's fiber optic cables for all of the city's residents, the city passed an ordinance requiring all apartment owners to allow the provider to install cables in their buildings. Installation of the cables involved drilling a hole in one exterior wall of the building and running the cables between the interior walls of the buildings.

The owner of an apartment building within the city did not want to allow new cables to be installed in his building, as he had gone through a similar process with another company three years earlier and he believed that the other company had damaged his property. To deter the installation, the owner filed suit against the city, claiming that the ordinance amounts to a taking under federal law.

How should the court rule?

(A) For the owner, because the ordinance amounts to a taking without just compensation.

(B) For the owner, because the government does not have a right to require owners of private property to allow private installation of cable lines.

(C) For the city, because the ordinance is a regulation and not a taking.

(D) For the city, because any taking here is de minimis.

CONSTITUTIONAL LAW ANSWERS - SET 5

Answer to Question 1

(C) A member of the nonprofit flying association is most likely to have standing to challenge the gift. To have standing to challenge government action on constitutional grounds, a person must show that he has a concrete stake in the outcome of the litigation. This is to ensure adequate presentation of the issues. To have such a stake, the potential litigant must show that he has an injury in fact caused by the government that is more than the theoretical injury that all persons suffer when the government engages in unconstitutional acts, and that a decision in his favor will eliminate his harm. A member of the flying association can show both components here: If the gift is unconstitutional, the association has suffered more than a theoretical injury—it has lost the opportunity to purchase the airplane from the federal government at a good price, and a decision in the club's favor will eliminate the injury because it will then be able to purchase the plane. Thus, the member of the nonprofit flying organization has standing. (B) is incorrect because the only injury that a citizen would suffer here is the theoretical injury that we all suffer from the government's unconstitutional acts. People have no standing merely as "citizens" to claim that government action violates federal law or the Constitution. (A) is incorrect because a person's injury as a taxpayer is generally held to be insufficient to establish standing. There is an exception where the federal government acts under the taxing and spending power and that action allegedly violates the Establishment Clause, but the government action here falls under the Property Clause and not the Spending Clause; thus, the exception does not apply. (D) is incorrect because the state attorney general has no stake in the outcome of the litigation, and it is not sufficient even if he is deemed to represent the interests of all the citizens in the state.

Answer to Question 2

(A) The person should be acquitted because the statute is unconstitutional. Like other federal law, a treaty is the supreme law of the land. Consequently, any state action or law that conflicts with a United States treaty is invalid. Some treaties are expressly or impliedly self-executing (*i.e.*, they are effective without any implementation by Congress). Others are not effective unless and until Congress passes legislation to effectuate their ends. The federal treaty with the foreign country, pursuant to which the United States and that country agree to permit the importation and sale of goods and products from each other, does not appear to be in need of congressional action to implement its terms. The treaty on its face allows goods from the foreign country to be imported and sold in this country. With the permission for such importation and sale having thus been granted, there should be no need for any further action to bring about the terms of the treaty. Thus, the treaty is impliedly self-executing, and it has supremacy status over any conflicting state law. Because the state statute places obstacles in the way of the sale of products from foreign countries, the statute is in conflict with the treaty, and is therefore invalid. (D) is incorrect because, as explained above, there is no indication that effectuating legislation is necessary with relation to this treaty. (C) is incorrect because, if the statute under which the person is prosecuted is invalid by reason of a conflict with the federal treaty, then obviously the prosecution can proceed no further. Thus, the treaty does provide a defense to the state criminal prosecution. (B) is incorrect because a federal treaty has supremacy over conflicting state law regardless of the time sequence in which the treaty and the state statute came into being. Consequently, the person will be acquitted even if the treaty was made after the enactment of the state statute.

Answer to Question 3

(B) The resident will prevail even if the matter is not decided until after the election, because the suit is not moot and the residency requirement is unconstitutional. The resident's suit is not moot even if the matter will not be decided until after the election because other members of the class might have a live controversy. Under the case and controversy requirement of the Constitution, there must be a real, live controversy at all stages of the suit. If through the passage of time, the controversy between the parties is resolved, the case is said to be moot. However, there are exceptions to the mootness doctrine. In a class action, it is not necessary that the suit by the named plaintiff be viable at all stages, as long as the claim is viable by some member of the class. Thus, the suit here would not be moot. Moreover, the residency requirement here violates the resident's fundamental rights to vote and to interstate travel. A restriction on the right to vote is subject to strict scrutiny and is valid only if it is necessary to achieve a compelling state interest (otherwise the restriction violates the Equal Protection Clause by treating new residents differently from old residents). Relatively short residency requirements (*e.g.,* 30 days) have been upheld as being necessary to promote the compelling interest of assuring that only bona fide residents vote. However, the Supreme Court has struck down longer durational requirements for lack of a compelling justification. Thus, the one-year requirement here probably unconstitutionally impinges on the right to vote. The residency requirement also impinges on the fundamental right to travel in the same manner (*i.e.,* it discourages people from migrating by denying them the right to vote without a compelling reason). Thus, the requirement is invalid. (A) is incorrect because, as indicated above, the case will not be moot since other members of the class might have a live controversy. (C) is incorrect because it applies the wrong standard. Because fundamental rights are affected by the residency requirement here, the government must show a ***compelling*** justification; a mere rational or legitimate basis is not enough. (D) is incorrect because, as stated above, the Supreme Court has found that there was no compelling interest for a one-year residency requirement in order to vote.

Answer to Question 4

(D) The residency requirement is permissible because the water board is elected at large. The Equal Protection Clause prohibits state dilution of the right to vote, so that when a governmental body establishes voting districts for the election of representatives, the number of persons in each district may not vary significantly. This is known as the principle of "one person, one vote." This principle applies to almost every election where a person is being elected to perform normal governmental functions (*e.g.,* an election for trustees for a junior college district). However, the principle of one person, one vote generally is inapplicable where there is an at-large system of election (except where the system is adopted for discriminatory purposes). Here, the water board members are elected by all of the qualified voters in the city in an at-large system (rather than having the voters of each individual district select one board member apiece), and no discriminatory intent is evident. Thus, the statutory provision requiring board members to reside in each of the five districts does not result in an imbalance or a dilution of the voting rights of the citizens of the city. Consequently, (A) is incorrect, and (D) presents an accurate statement of the constitutionality of the residency requirement. (Note that the answer might be different under federal ***statute*** because the city would have to prove a valid, nondiscriminatory purpose.) (C) is incorrect even though it reaches the correct result. While the Supreme Court has exempted special purpose water storage districts from the one person, one vote requirement, the basis of the decision was the specialized nature of the entity. The constitutional requirements apply not only to legislators, but also to elected administrative and executive officials. (B) is incorrect because, even assuming that the residency requirement violates the candidates' equal protection rights, the resident would not have standing to raise the issue. Generally, a claimant must assert his own constitutional rights and cannot assert the rights of third parties.

Answer to Question 5

(A) The suit to assert state citizens' rights is not within the Supreme Court's original jurisdiction. Under Article III, Section 2, the United States Supreme Court has original jurisdiction in all cases affecting ambassadors, other public ministers, and consuls, and in which a state is a party. In (A), the state is not really seeking to advance or protect any interest of its own. Rather, the state is attempting to act in parens patriae (*i.e.,* to act as a representative of its citizens, thereby asserting their interests). Thus, the state is not an actual party in this case in the sense that the Supreme Court has traditionally required to justify exercise of original jurisdiction. (B) would be a proper case for institution under the Supreme Court's original jurisdiction because it involves an attempt by a state to protect its own economic interest rather than to assert the interests of its citizens in a representative capacity. Similarly, (C) sets forth a situation in which a state is attempting to defend its asserted right to render decisions affecting admissions policies relative to its own state universities. Thus, in (C) the state is an actual party to the case. Finally, (D) describes an attempt by the federal government to prevent state construction of a bridge (presumably pursuant to the admiralty power). Clearly, this case involves an alleged grievance that will be directly committed by a state. Therefore, the state is an actual party.

Answer to Question 6

(B) The court is likely to rule that the statute is constitutional. A bona fide residence requirement, such as this statute, that is not based on a suspect classification and does not limit the exercise of a fundamental right, is judged by the rational basis test. Thus, (A) is incorrect. The statute provides free education for all children who are bona fide residents of the state. Thus, it uniformly furthers the state interest in assuring that services provided for its residents are enjoyed only by residents. (C) is incorrect because education is not a fundamental right. (D) is incorrect because this statute does not impair the right of interstate travel. Any person is free to move to the state and establish residence there. This statute does not deter people from moving into the state.

Answer to Question 7

(A) The employee's best defense is intergovernmental immunity. State and local governments cannot tax or regulate the activities of the federal government. This principle is often termed "intergovernmental immunity." The arrest and prosecution of a federal employee who was on the job violates this principle, which is based on the supremacy of the federal government and federal law. (B) is not a bad answer because door-to-door solicitation is protected by the First Amendment. However, at best, (B) would subject the city's actions to strict scrutiny and allow the city to prevail if it could prove that its action was necessary to achieve a compelling government purpose. In contrast, (A) would automatically invalidate the city's enforcement of the law against the employee, and so (A) is a better answer. (C) is irrelevant because the Fourteenth Amendment's restriction on the states has to do with persons, not the federal government, and here there is no claim that the city was discriminating against the employee. The city's ordinance, as briefly described, does not seem to provide the basis for an equal protection claim. (D) is wrong because nothing in the facts shows any burden on interstate commerce. Moreover, at most such a claim would trigger heightened scrutiny; it would not automatically invalidate the enforcement of the law as would (A).

Answer to Question 8

(C) The statute will most likely be upheld applied to the District of Columbia. Under Article I, the right of Congress to legislate over the District of Columbia is the same as the state legislatures'

right to regulate their internal matters. This has been held to include the right to tax real property. (A) is incorrect since the Indian lands are considered independent sovereignties and as such could not be taxed by a "foreign" government. (B) could conceivably be correct given Congress's plenary powers over interstate commerce. (D) is also arguably correct for the same reason; *i.e.*, assuming Congress acted pursuant to its plenary power, a "uniform" tax would be valid. But the question asks for the "most likely" result, and (C) is the best answer because of federal power over the District of Columbia.

Answer to Question 9

(D) The law probably is unconstitutional as applied to the man in question. An equal protection issue is involved. Under the Equal Protection Clause, state classifications based on alienage are subject to strict scrutiny and so must serve a compelling interest to be constitutional. No compelling purpose seems to be present here. Thus, (D) is correct. (A) is incorrect because, although there is an exception from the strict scrutiny standard where a state or local government discriminates against aliens when hiring persons for jobs involving "self-government" process, the job here (emergency communications for a police department) is a technical position and probably would not be found to be related to the self-government process; in any event, the statute applies to all positions and not just to jobs involving only the self-government process. (B) is incorrect because, although it is true that aliens are not entitled to the privileges and immunities of state citizenship, the law here is still unconstitutional under the Equal Protection Clause, as discussed above, which applies to aliens. (C) is incorrect because the discrimination would be unconstitutional even if it did apply to all aliens equally, as discussed above.

Answer to Question 10

(A) The federal court should not hear the case because it is not yet ripe for review. A federal court will not hear a case unless there exists a "case and controversy." This has been interpreted to mean, among other things, that a plaintiff generally is not entitled to review of his claim unless he has been harmed or there is an immediate threat of harm. This is to prevent the federal courts from hearing unnecessary actions. There is no immediate threat of harm to the union here because the law does not take effect for another two years. Before that happens, Congress might change the law or repeal it altogether, or the school board may decide to keep the old contract system after all. Thus, (A) is correct and (D) is incorrect. (B) is incorrect because the union would have standing. An association has standing if (i) there is an injury in fact to its members that would give them standing, (ii) the injury is related to the organization's purpose, and (iii) neither the nature of the claim nor the relief requested requires participation of the individual members in the lawsuit. All three of the conditions are met here; thus, the union would have standing. (C) is incorrect because the Contract Clause does not limit federal power, only state power, and because the state would be acting pursuant to a federal law here, there would be no Contract Clause violation. Moreover, even if the Contract Clause limited the state's actions here, it still is not clear that there would be a constitutional violation. The Clause bans only substantial interference with existing contracts (*i.e.,* destruction of almost all of a party's rights under a contract), and it is not clear here that the impairments would be sufficiently substantial.

Answer to Question 11

(D) Congress's power to regulate commerce has been construed broadly, so that it may regulate any activity, local or interstate, that either in itself or in combination with other activities has a substantial economic effect on interstate commerce. If Congress has determined that the use of chemical pesticides and their runoff into waterways (which are channels of interstate commerce) will have an overall detrimental impact on the environment, this determination will be sufficient in this case to satisfy the standards established by the Supreme Court. Therefore, the law probably is a valid exercise of the commerce power. Any state or local action that conflicts with a valid act of Congress is invalid under the Supremacy Clause. (A) is incorrect because while the police power (the power to adopt regulations for the health, safety, and welfare of citizens) belongs to the states, a police power regulation that conflicts with a federal law is invalid under the Supremacy Clause. (B) is incorrect because state and local government activities may be regulated by a general law that applies to both the public and private sectors, even if the regulation affects integral governmental functions, as long as there is a constitutional basis for the law. (C) is incorrect because Congress does not have a general "police power" to adopt laws on health and safety. The laws that Congress has passed banning activities that it has deemed harmful to public health have been based on its power to regulate interstate commerce.

Answer to Question 12

(C) The restriction will probably be upheld because it is viewpoint neutral and reasonably related to a legitimate government purpose. The billboards are not traditional public forums; rather, they will be found to be "commercial ventures" by the city. In a similar setting, the Supreme Court held that cities could differentiate between broad categories of speech in accepting advertising on city-owned buses (*i.e.,* the Court allowed a city to refuse political advertising and accept only commercial advertising) [*see* Lehman v. Shaker Heights (1974)], as long as the restriction was viewpoint neutral and reasonably related to a legitimate government interest. The city rule here is constitutional because it is viewpoint neutral (it distinguishes between broad categories of speech but does not distinguish based on content within a category) and it is reasonably related to the legitimate government interest of avoiding controversy. (A) is incorrect because the Supreme Court has held that allowing advertising on government-owned property does not make that property a public forum; rather, the property is a commercial forum. [*See* Lehman v. Shaker Heights, *supra*] (B) is incorrect because, although it states the general rule for regulation of commercial speech, the more specific Supreme Court precedents regarding advertising on ***city-owned*** property used for a proprietary venture (discussed above) would apply here. (D) is incorrect because nothing in the city policy would cause an excessive entanglement with religion; rather, the policy seeks to avoid excessive entanglement by prohibiting religious ads on government property.

Answer to Question 13

(C) The young man will prevail if the state cannot establish that the restriction is substantially related to an important government interest. Classifications based on gender usually are tested against an intermediate standard of review; *i.e.,* the Supreme Court will strike down the classification unless the government offers an exceedingly persuasive justification that the classification is substantially related to an important government interest. Classifications intentionally discriminating against men generally are invalid, and (C) states the proper standard for review. (A) and (D) are substantially the same and incorrect because they state the standard to be applied to classifications involving a suspect class or fundamental right. However, a gender-based distinction is characterized as a ***quasi-suspect*** classification. (B) is incorrect because it states the standard to be applied when no fundamental right or suspect or quasi-suspect class is involved.

Answer to Question 14

(B) The employer was free under the Constitution to fire the employee without a hearing because she was an employee at will. Unless prohibited by a state statute, a private employer usually can fire

an employee for any reason or no reason at all, absent a contract providing otherwise. (C) and (D) are related to each other and are both incorrect. Most constitutional guarantees prohibit state action and do not impose duties on private parties. That is not to say that state action can never be found in the acts of a private party—it will be found if the private party performs exclusive public functions or has significant state involvement in its activities. However, there is no state action here. Running a lottery is not an exclusive public function, and merely being the exclusive lottery supplier for a state does not constitute significant state involvement, even where the state controls who may be hired. State action will not be found merely because the state has granted a monopoly to a business or heavily regulates it. (A) is incorrect because whether a hearing is required does not turn on whether the supervisor witnessed the misconduct—if state action were involved, a hearing would have been required because a public employee who is subject to removal only for "cause" has a property interest in her job that cannot be taken without fair process. Since there was no state action, no hearing was necessary.

Answer to Question 15

(D) The theater owner's best defense is that the film has proven artistic merit. The First Amendment generally protects the right of freedom of speech, and this freedom includes the right to show movies. Thus, to enjoin the showing of the movie here, the city will have to prove that the speech involved is unprotected speech. Obscenity is the category of unprotected speech most relevant here. The Court has defined obscenity as a depiction of sexual conduct that, taken as a whole, by the average person, using contemporary community standards: (i) appeals to the prurient interest in sex; (ii) portrays sex in a patently offensive way; and (iii) using a rational, reasonable person standard, does not have serious literary, artistic, political, or scientific value. If the theater owner shows that the film has proven artistic merit, it cannot be held to be obscene because the third element of the above definition will have failed. Thus, (D) is his best argument. (A) is not as good an argument as (D) because the Supreme Court has held that while a statewide community standard ***may*** be used, it is not mandatory—a local community standard is sufficient to evaluate whether the film is "patently offensive." Thus, the town's community standards would be sufficient. (B) is not as good an argument as (D) because it is not sufficient that there is ***some*** redeeming social value; it must have ***serious*** redeeming value, as indicated above. For example, it would not be sufficient that an otherwise obscene movie included short tips on the importance of brushing teeth. (C) is not a good argument. The Establishment Clause forbids the government from adopting a law or program that establishes religion. It is inapplicable here because the town is not trying to enforce a particular set of religious views; rather, it is trying to prohibit obscenity. The Supreme Court has held that the government has a legitimate interest in prohibiting obscenity, and the fact that this happens to coincide with the beliefs of a particular religious group does not render such bans void.

Answer to Question 16

(D) The punishment here is constitutional because it does not violate any constitutional provision. The best answer reflecting this reasoning is (D)—there was no Eighth Amendment violation here—because paddling students as a disciplinary measure has not been found to be cruel and unusual punishment. (A) is incorrect because there is no Establishment Clause violation here. Under the Establishment Clause, if there is no sect preference, government action generally will be upheld if the action serves a secular purpose, its primary effect neither advances nor inhibits religion, and it does not excessively entangle government with religion. There is no sect preference under the school board's corporal punishment rule here, the rule has the secular purpose of maintaining order in the classroom (the fact that this coincides with the tenets of a local religion does not change that conclusion), its main purpose neither advances nor inhibits religion, and there is no excessive entanglement. (B) is incorrect because there has been no deprivation of procedural due process. The Supreme Court has held that although corporal punishment may involve a liberty interest, no hearing is required prior to inflicting such punishment; the possibility of a common law action in tort is sufficient procedural protection. [Ingraham v. Wright (1977)] (C) is incorrect because it is too broad. The doctrine of parens patriae allows the state to stand in the shoes of a parent, but even a parent may not impose ***any*** punishment he sees fit (*e.g.,* a parent may not break a child's arm as punishment for stealing).

Answer to Question 17

(A) The best argument against the constitutionality of the state statute is that it burdens foreign commerce. For all practical purposes, the power to regulate foreign commerce lies exclusively with Congress. Therefore, a state that adopts legislation requiring private vendors to favor United States products over foreign products, as the state did here, may be acting outside the scope of its powers. (B) is incorrect because the statute is a rational method of protecting local beef interests. The rational basis standard applies when an economic law, such as the one here, is challenged on equal protection grounds. Under the standard, the Supreme Court will usually defer to a legislature's decision that the law is rational notwithstanding the fact that the statute is underinclusive. In other words, the law need not address all of the problems that prompted its passage; it will be upheld even if it is only a "first step" toward a legitimate goal. Here, prohibiting the use of foreign beef appears to be a rational method of protecting state beef raisers. Thus, it is irrelevant that the statute is underinclusive in that it allows the use of both United States beef and foreign leather. (C) is incorrect because the right to earn a living is not a privilege under the Fourteenth Amendment, which protects against infringement of rights of national citizenship, such as the right to petition Congress for redress. (Neither would the statute violate the Privileges and Immunities Clause of Article IV, because that clause only prohibits discrimination against citizens of other states and the statute here treats citizens of all states the same.) (D) is incorrect because the vendor had all of the process that was due him. Because the government action here was a general act and not an individualized adjudication, the vendor had no right to an individual hearing; the normal procedure for adopting a statute is all the process that is due.

Answer to Question 18

(D) The best way to approach this question is to eliminate the wrong answers first. (A) is incorrect because state constitutional provisions do not have to be interpreted exactly the same as federal provisions; the federal Constitution provides the minimum rights that states must provide, but states are free to grant broader rights. Thus, even though a 50-day delay may be constitutional under the federal Constitution, it can still be held unconstitutional under a state constitution. (B) is incorrect because the facts make it clear that the state court was relying on federal case interpretations. Moreover, if the Supreme Court could not decide whether the case was based on federal or state grounds, it would not reverse the case, because a federal court will not hear a case that can be based on adequate and independent state grounds; rather, it would dismiss the case or remand it to the state for clarification. (C) is incorrect because the Eleventh Amendment generally prohibits federal courts from hearing actions by a private party or foreign government against the state government; it does not bar a state from appealing a ruling from its own court system. Thus, (D) is correct. The Supreme Court had jurisdiction to hear the case, because it has jurisdiction to hear appeals from a state's highest court concerning the constitutionality of a state statute, and as indicated above, the state court's decision was not based on independent state grounds; the decision was based on federal case law interpreting an identical federal provision.

Thus, jurisdiction was proper and the Court could reverse the state court decision and hold that a 50-day delay does not violate the federal Constitution. However, the case should be remanded so that the state may decide whether the delay was too long under state law, since a state is free to provide its citizens with more civil protection than is required by the federal Constitution.

Answer to Question 19

(C) The court should affirm the geologist's conviction. The fine is constitutional under the Property Clause, which gives Congress the power to "make all needful rules and regulations respecting the territory or other property belonging to the United States." This power permits Congress to acquire and dispose of all kinds of property, and to protect its property with a law such as the one here. (D) is not as good an answer as (C) because the Commerce Clause is not as directly applicable to regulation of acts on federal lands as is the Property Clause. Nevertheless, (B) is incorrect because the fine could probably be upheld under the Commerce Clause. Under the Clause, Congress may regulate any act that may itself or in combination with other activities have a substantial effect on interstate commerce, even intrastate activities. If everyone removed minerals from federal lands, the necessary substantial effect on interstate commerce would be present. (A) is incorrect because, notwithstanding the state's compelling interest, by virtue of the Supremacy Clause a valid act of Congress supersedes any state or local action that actually conflicts with the federal rule.

Answer to Question 20

(D) The state law violates intergovernmental immunities principals. The states have no power to regulate the activities of the federal government unless Congress consents to the regulation. Thus, instrumentalities and agents of the federal government are immune from state regulations that interfere with their federal functions. Here, the regulation clearly interferes with the manager's duties to run the refinery. While it might be argued that the manger agreed to comply with the state regulations, because he allowed the state inspection, nothing indicates that Congress consented, and so the state regulation cannot be applied to the manager. (A) is factually incorrect; a state may still have a compelling interest in activities on federal lands, and the interest here of preventing pollution that may spread beyond federal lands probably is compelling. Nevertheless, the argument is without merit because it is irrelevant whether the state has a compelling interest in regulating federal activities; a state simply is not allowed to interfere with federal activities. (B) is incorrect because not enough facts are given to make this determination. The Supremacy Clause prohibits states from adopting laws that interfere with federal laws, and this prohibition extends to any law—even one that seeks to support the federal scheme—when Congress has preempted the field. In determining whether a field has been preempted, courts will consider the comprehensiveness of the federal scheme. The question does not give enough facts to make the determination here. (C) is incorrect because it is irrelevant. The Constitution does not require the state to favor one compelling interest over another, and so states are free to adopt laws that interfere or are inconsistent with other state goals, unless the laws are arbitrary, in which case they would violate substantive due process. The laws here do not appear to be arbitrary, and so (C) does not offer a viable defense.

Answer to Question 21

(B) If the school's action is valid, it will be because the state statute is the least restrictive means of advancing the state's compelling interest in ending discrimination by groups using public facilities. While schools are generally not public forums, they may become a designated public forum

by being held open to student groups for meetings. In that case, the First Amendment may be violated if a college restricts use of its classrooms based on the content of a student group's speech. To justify content-based regulation of otherwise protected speech, the government must show that the regulation is necessary to achieve a compelling state interest that cannot be satisfied by less restrictive means. Similarly, the right to associate for expressive purposes is not absolute. Infringements on the right may be justified by compelling state interests, unrelated to the suppression of ideas, that cannot be achieved through means significantly less restrictive of associational freedoms. Here, the state's interest in not allowing its facilities to be used by groups practicing discrimination of various types is compelling. [*See* Roberts v. United States Jaycees (1984)] The denial of access to the student group based on the students' religious principles, while it may be viewed as content-based discrimination, is the most narrowly drawn means of advancing the state's interest. [*See* Bob Jones University v. United States (1983)] (A) is incorrect because a school does not violate the Establishment Clause by permitting a religious student group the same after-class access to its facilities that other student groups have. [Good News Club v. Milford Central School (2001)] (C) is incorrect because the actions of administrators of a state college in allowing or denying access to its facilities is clearly state action that brings the Fourteenth Amendment into play. (D) is incorrect. While the right to join together for expressive or political activity, which is protected by the First Amendment, may be less strong for large organizations that engage in both commercial and expressive activity than for smaller and more selective groups, it is still a recognized right. [*See* Roberts v. United States Jaycees, *supra*] Furthermore, the student group's discussion of business activity in this case is tied to its religion. Hence, the association rights of the student group are based on freedom of religion as well as freedom of expression. The state would probably have to show a compelling interest to support a restriction on the group's association rights.

Answer to Question 22

(C) The counselor will fail in her lawsuit because the firing did not violate her free speech rights. The United States Supreme Court has held that a government employer may punish a government employee's speech whenever the speech is made pursuant to the employee's official duties, and this is true even if the speech touches on a matter of public concern. The counselor's official duties required her to disseminate information from the family planning agency. Thus, her refusal to speak (*i.e.* her refusal to disseminate the information) was not entitled to First Amendment protection. (B) is incorrect for this reason. (A) also is incorrect. A person has a liberty interest and is entitled to a hearing when government action deprives the person of a fundamental constitutional right. As indicated above, the Supreme Court has found that a person does not have a constitutional free speech right regarding speech that is made pursuant to government employment. Because the counselor's speech (or refusal to speak) here was pursuant to her government employment, it was not protected by the First Amendment and so no liberty interest arose. (D) is incorrect. Under the Free Exercise Clause the government may not punish religious beliefs, but it may punish violations of rules of general applicability that incidentally impinge on a person's religious beliefs. Here, nothing indicates that the school rule requiring the counselor to distribute materials from all agencies offering help to pregnant teens was targeted at undermining any specific religious belief. Therefore, it does not matter whether the counselor can prove that she sincerely held a religious belief that abortion is immoral.

Answer to Question 23

(B) The man can be fined. Congress has the power to regulate alarm installation companies under the Commerce Clause because the clause permits Congress to regulate any local or interstate activity

that, either in itself or in combination with other activities, has an effect on interstate commerce. Burglar alarm companies use instrumentalities of interstate commerce such as phone lines and have a cumulative effect on interstate commerce even though some may only do business locally. Hence, their activities can be regulated by Congress. The delegation to the NABA is valid because Congress has broad discretion to delegate its legislative power; the Supreme Court will uphold almost any delegation of congressional power. Therefore, the man can be fined. (A) is incorrect because it improperly mixes two concepts. Congress does not have the power to ***legislate*** for the general welfare—there is no federal police power— but rather Congress has the power to ***spend*** for the general welfare. (C) is incorrect because, even assuming that the regulation here interferes with the man's right to make a living, it would not violate the interstate Privileges and Immunities Clause of Article IV because the clause restricts states, not the federal government. (D) is incorrect. Congress can provide that violation of an agency's regulations is a criminal offense that can be enforced through the imposition of fines. Furthermore, an agency has the power to impose civil fines and penalties for a violation of its regulations.

Answer to Question 24

(A) If the attorney is fired, she has a right to a hearing to determine whether her First Amendment rights were violated by her dismissal. Under the Due Process Clause of the Fifth Amendment, a person has a liberty interest in the exercise of specific rights provided by the Constitution, including freedom of speech. If a government employer seeks to fire an employee for speech-related conduct when the speech involved a matter of public concern, the courts must carefully balance the employee's rights as a citizen to comment on a matter of public concern against the government's interest as an employer in the efficient performance of public service. Under the Court's expansive interpretation of what is a public issue in this context [*see* Rankin v. McPherson (1987)], the attorney's statement would probably qualify. At the very least, she can make a sufficient showing that her termination violates her free speech rights to be entitled to a hearing on the issue under procedural due process principles. [*See* Givhan v. Western Line Consolidated School District (1979)] (B) is wrong because the attorney does not appear to have a property interest in her job. A public employee who is subject to removal only for "cause" has a property interest in her job and generally must be given notice of the charges against her that are to be the basis for her job termination, and a pre-termination opportunity to respond to those charges. Here, however, the attorney did not have a property interest in her job; she could have been dismissed for no reason at all. She was not covered by the labor contract between the agency and its clerical workers, and there appears to be no other basis for her to claim an entitlement to continued employment. (C) is wrong because the attorney is entitled to a hearing as long as she can raise a prima facie claim that her speech, which was regarding an important health issue and the perception of her agency, was on a public issue and therefore protected by the First Amendment. (D) is wrong for two reasons. As discussed above, the attorney does not have a property interest in her job. Also, due process does not necessarily entitle her to a pre-termination evidentiary hearing; a post-termination evidentiary hearing is probably sufficient. [*See* Cleveland Board of Education v. Loudermill (1985)]

Answer to Question 25

(C) To prevail, the parents will have to show that the statute does not meet the rational basis test. Under that test, a law is presumed to be valid and will be upheld unless the challenger can make the difficult showing that it is not rationally related to a legitimate state interest. Here, the statute terminating the funds did not target a suspect class and did not burden a fundamental right, so the rational basis test applies. (A) is incorrect because it is not enough to show that legislation has a discriminatory effect on a suspect class; there must be an intent to discriminate. To establish a racial, national origin, or ethnicity classification, the party challenging the law must show that (i) the racial classification appears in the law itself (facial discrimination), (ii) the law was applied in a purposefully discriminatory manner, or (iii) the law was enacted or maintained for a discriminatory purpose. None of these situations appears to be indicated under these facts. (B) is incorrect because it states the wrong standard. As that choice indicates, the Supreme Court has not held education to be a fundamental right under the Due Process Clause, nor has it found classifications based on wealth to require strict scrutiny. Hence, the test that is applied is the rational basis standard; the standard in (B) is an intermediate scrutiny test applied to gender and legitimacy classifications. (D) is incorrect because it imposes the burden of proof on the wrong party. For a statute that does not discriminate against a suspect class, the plaintiff bears the burden of proving that the statute is not rationally related to a legitimate state interest.

Answer to Question 26

(A) The reporter's best argument is that the closure here is not necessary to preserve an overriding interest because trials and pretrial hearings generally must be open to the public. The Supreme Court has held, at least in the context of criminal cases, that trials and pretrial proceedings can be closed only if closure is necessary to preserve an overriding interest and the closure order is narrowly tailored to serve the overriding interest. While the Court has not yet established the standard for civil matters such as the case here, several Justices and commentators have suggested that the same standard will be applied in civil cases since they too have historically been open to the public. (B) is a false statement of the law—freedom of the press is not absolute and does not allow the press unlimited access to any hearing of interest to the public; the hearing may be closed where an overriding interest in protecting the privacy of the parties is established. (C) is not as good an argument as (A) because, while closure here would amount to a prior restraint (any government action that prevents a communication from reaching the public), the prior restraint would be justified if the government proves that it was narrowly tailored to achieve a compelling interest. The argument in (A) negates this possibility and so is a better argument. (D) is incorrect because the fairness doctrine is irrelevant to the issue of whether a hearing should be open to the public. It was a rule of the Federal Communications Commission that required, among other things, that the media give political candidates an opportunity to oppose candidates or views endorsed by the media.

Answer to Question 27

(D) The cities can be prosecuted because state or local government action that conflicts with valid federal laws is invalid under the Supremacy Clause. The federal law here could be found valid as an exercise of the commerce power (Congress can regulate any activity that either in itself or in combination with other activities has a substantial economic effect on interstate commerce) or under the admiralty power (Congress can regulate all navigable waterways). The action of the municipalities directly conflicts with the directives of the federal law and can therefore be stopped. (B) is incorrect because the fact that the copper paint may be as effective as the special compound does not change the result. The action by the municipalities can be prohibited under the Supremacy Clause. (A) is incorrect because for regulations that apply to both the public sector and the private sector, the Supreme Court has held that states' Tenth Amendment rights are best protected by the states' representation in Congress; hence, the Tenth Amendment is not a likely ground for striking this federal legislation because it is not directed only at state or local governments. (C) is incorrect because it is irrelevant; the federal law is superior to the states' laws because it is within Congress's power, not because Congress is in a better position than the states to adopt the legislation involved.

Answer to Question 28

(D) The city will prevail because its rule is a reasonable time, place, and manner restriction. Speech protected by the First Amendment includes not only verbal communication, but also conduct that is undertaken to communicate an idea. The laser light show, like other art, probably is protected speech. While the content of speech generally cannot be limited, the conduct associated with speech in public forums can be regulated by reasonable time, place, and manner restrictions. To be valid, the regulation must be content neutral, narrowly tailored, and leave open alternative channels of communication. The city's rule meets these requirements: the types of images displayed are not controlled, just the means of showing them; the rule is narrowly tailored because it does not regulate substantially more speech than is necessary to further a significant government interest (here, preventing eye damage and disturbing boaters); and alternative channels of communication are available because the artist can use the city's equipment, albeit with less spectacular results. (A) is incorrect because while the artist's art is protected by the First Amendment, it may still be regulated by reasonable time, place, and manner regulations, as indicated above. (B) is incorrect because it states the wrong standard. To be valid, a time, place, and manner regulation need not be the least restrictive means for achieving the desired result, but rather only narrowly tailored to the result. [*See* Ward v. Rock Against Racism (1989)] (C) is incorrect because art, including performance art such as the laser light show, is protected by the First Amendment. As discussed above, the First Amendment guarantee of freedom of speech protects more than merely spoken or written words; it includes conduct and other forms of expression undertaken to communicate an idea.

Answer to Question 29

(D) The destination tax will likely be held constitutional under Congress's taxing power. Congress has the power to lay taxes under Article II, Section 2, and a tax measure will usually be upheld if it bears some reasonable relationship to revenue production or if Congress has the power to regulate the taxed activity. Despite the protest from the officials of the affected locations, the tax here does appear to be related to revenue production and so will be upheld. (C) is incorrect because it is based on the wrong standard—the compelling interest test does not apply here. (A) is incorrect because the extent of the right to travel is not clearly defined. The Supreme Court has established that the right to travel from state to state is a fundamental right that may be violated by ***state*** laws designed to deter persons from moving into a state; however, the Court has not specifically applied this rule to the federal government or to the type of tax legislation present here. (B) also is incorrect. While the federal government is not subject to the Equal Protection Clause of the Fourteenth Amendment, it is prohibited from unfair discrimination by the Due Process Clause of the Fifth Amendment. Nevertheless, the discrimination here is not unfair. If a governmental act, such as the tax here, does not involve a fundamental right or a suspect or quasi-suspect class, it will be upheld as long as it is rationally related to a legitimate governmental interest. The government has a legitimate interest in taxing, and so the tax will be upheld.

Answer to Question 30

(D) The most likely ground for holding the statute unconstitutional is that Congress may not limit all avenues for Supreme Court review of federal constitutional issues. Article III, Section 2 provides that the Supreme Court shall have appellate jurisdiction under such regulations as the Congress shall make. Although *Ex parte McCardle* (1868) gives Congress broad power to regulate the Supreme Court's appellate jurisdiction, it has been suggested that Congress may not eliminate all avenues for Supreme Court review of issues vested within the federal judicial power. This argument is the most likely basis for finding the law here unconstitutional because none of the other choices is viable. (A) is not the best argument. As indicated above, Congress has the power to regulate the appellate jurisdiction of the Supreme Court, and since the Supreme Court's primary role as an appellate court is to determine constitutional issues, it follows that Congress can eliminate from the Supreme Court's review the determination of certain cases involving constitutional issues, as long as jurisdiction remains in some lower federal courts. (B) is incorrect because Congress's power is limited to regulating the Supreme Court's appellate jurisdiction; it has no power to restrict or enlarge the Court's original jurisdiction. (C) is incorrect because Congress has the authority to adopt laws modifying appellate jurisdiction; modification of the Court's original jurisdiction would require a constitutional amendment.

Answer to Question 31

(C) The town may constitutionally limit the location of these establishments to control the secondary effects of these businesses. A municipality may use zoning to limit the location of adult theaters and nude dancing establishments as long as the ordinance (i) is designed to promote important government interests (*e.g.,* eliminate the secondary effects of such businesses—lowering of property values, increased traffic, etc.) and (ii) does not prohibit all such entertainment in the community. [*See* City of Renton v. Playtime Theatres, Inc. (1986)] (A) is incorrect because nude dancing (and by implication other erotica) is marginally protected speech. The Supreme Court has held erotica to be symbolic conduct (*i.e.,* conduct undertaken to convey a message), and like other symbolic conduct, it can be regulated to serve important government interests unrelated to the suppression of speech. [*See* Barnes v. Glen Theatre, Inc. (1991)—allowing state to prohibit public nudity, including nude dancing] (B) reaches a correct result—municipalities can limit the location of such establishments—but uses the wrong standard. As discussed above, erotica is only marginally protected speech and can be regulated to serve important, rather than compelling, interests. Protecting community morals and property values are important enough to justify regulation. (D) is incorrect because the Supreme Court has allowed municipalities to treat adult theaters differently from other theaters, despite the fact that this appears to be regulation based on the content of speech. For example, in *City of Renton* the Court allowed the municipality to prohibit adult theaters from being located within 1,000 feet of residential zones, schools, and parks.

Answer to Question 32

(B) The village ordinance is invalid to the extent that it restricts the passage of troops through the town. The states have no power to regulate the activities of the government unless Congress consents. Thus, instrumentalities of the federal government are immune from state regulations relating to performance of their federal functions. A state or local law that attempts to restrict United States military traffic in this manner is not enforceable. (A) is incorrect. The precise meaning of the Second Amendment right to bear arms has not been established, but in any case the rights it protects are those of citizens, not the United States military. (C) is incorrect because it is irrelevant whether there are equally convenient alternative means of performing the military activities; as long as the activities are within the legitimate scope of federal activities (and military exercises certainly fall within the scope of federal power), they cannot be regulated by the states. (D) is incorrect because even assuming that the ordinance is a police power regulation, it cannot interfere with the legitimate functions of the federal government.

Answer to Question 33

(D) Because marriage and divorce are within the fundamental right of privacy, the state will have to show that requiring the wife to pay the fee is necessary to achieve a compelling state interest.

The Supreme Court applies one of three standards to determine whether state action that classifies people is valid. A classification based on suspect criteria (*e.g.,* race, religion, or nationality) or affecting a fundamental right will be strictly scrutinized—the state must prove that it is necessary to achieve a compelling state interest. A classification based on quasi-suspect criteria (*e.g.,* gender and legitimacy) will be given intermediate scrutiny—it must be established that the action is substantially related to an important state interest. All other classifications will be upheld unless the complainant shows that the classification is not rational. The law here has the effect of classifying people into those who can obtain a divorce and those who cannot. While the classification is based on wealth (those who can afford to pay the fee and those who cannot), which is neither a suspect nor quasi-suspect class, it also affects a fundamental right; the right to marry and be divorced, which is controlled by the state through access to its courts, is part of the fundamental right of privacy. [Boddie v. Connecticut (1971)] Therefore, the classification will be subjected to strict scrutiny and the state will be required to waive its divorce fee here, since the wife cannot afford to pay, unless the state can show that the fee is necessary to serve a compelling state interest. (A) is incorrect because while it states the proper strict scrutiny standard, it gives the wrong reason for applying the standard. Strict scrutiny will be applied here not because the wife is poor, but because the right to divorce is fundamental. (B) is incorrect because it states the wrong standard—while a classification based solely on wealth would be tested under the rational basis standard, the standard to be applied here is based on the wife's fundamental right to a divorce. (C) is incorrect because it states both the wrong standard to be applied (the intermediate standard) and an improper rationale for applying the standard—it is irrelevant that the wife has a compelling interest in obtaining a divorce; what is relevant is that the right to obtain a divorce is encompassed within the fundamental right of privacy.

Answer to Question 34

(B) The employee will likely prevail because the procedures taken to terminate his employment did not satisfy due process. Under the Due Process Clause of the Fourteenth Amendment, a public employee who is subject to removal only for "cause" under a statute, ordinance, or personnel document has a property interest in continued employment that cannot be taken away without due process of law. The Court has held that such an employee generally must be given notice of the charges and ***a pre-termination opportunity to respond to those charges***. The employee must also be given a subsequent evidentiary hearing regarding the termination (with reinstatement if the employee prevails). [Cleveland Board of Education v. Loudermill (1985)] Here, the employee was notified of the charges but was not given any opportunity to respond to the charges until after his termination. Hence, his termination did not satisfy due process requirements. (A) is incorrect because the employee does not have to be given a full, formal hearing before his termination, as long as he is given oral or written notice of the charges, an explanation of the employer's evidence, and an opportunity to tell his side of the story. (C) is incorrect because the fact that the state created the employee's property interest in his job does not permit the state to define what procedures may be used to terminate the interest. The procedures to which the employee was entitled are determined by independent constitutional standards. (D) is incorrect because, as discussed above, the procedures followed here did not satisfy due process standards. The Supreme Court has held that an employee can be suspended from his job without a prior hearing if the government has a significant reason for removing the employee from the job and providing him with only a post-termination hearing. [Gilbert v. Homar (1997)—campus police officer suspended after being arrested and charged with felony drug offense] Here, however, there is no substantial reason why the employee could not have been given the opportunity to respond to the charges prior to dismissal.

Answer to Question 35

(B) The tax unconstitutionally burdens the freedom of the press. Press and broadcasting companies can be subject to general business taxes, but a tax applicable only to the press or based on the content of a publication will not be upheld absent a compelling justification. Mere need for revenue probably is not a sufficiently compelling interest. (A) is incorrect because there is no unconstitutional burden on interstate commerce here. The law treats all businesses subject to the tax (namely breweries and distilleries) equally, and so is not protecting local business against out-of-state competition. The fact that the law treats breweries and distilleries differently from wineries and that the state has no breweries or distilleries but does have wineries probably does not change this, because a court will probably find these to be distinct businesses for purposes of advertising. (C) is incorrect. When a sales tax is imposed on a sale taking place entirely within one state, there is no apportionment problem because the sale cannot be taxed by any other state (because no other state has a sufficient nexus). (D) is incorrect because there is no equal protection violation here even though brewers and distillers are being treated differently from wine makers. Because no suspect class or fundamental right is involved, nor is a quasi-suspect class involved, the tax will pass constitutional muster as long as it is rationally related to a legitimate government purpose, and the tax here certainly seems to be related to revenue production.

Answer to Question 36

(A) The court should rule for the owner. The Fifth Amendment to the United States Constitution, which is applicable to the states through the Due Process Clause of the Fourteenth Amendment, provides that private property shall not be taken for public use without just compensation. Where there is a physical appropriation of property, there is a per se taking. Here, the ordinance requires apartment owners to relinquish their right to exclude the cable company from their property. Moreover, the ordinance requires the owners to cede space between the walls of their buildings to the cable company. Although the amount of property taken is small and might not have much value, the physical appropriation here still amounts to a taking. The de minimis doctrine does not apply. Thus, (D) is incorrect. (B) is incorrect because it is untrue. A city can require a property owner to turn over property to another private party as long as the it is for a public purpose. The Supreme Court has defined the term "public purpose" very broadly, and cable access for all residents of a city surely would fall within the Court's definition of a public purpose. (C) is incorrect because, as discussed above, at least to the extent that the city has denied apartment owners the right to exclude the cable company and has required the owners to cede space in their buildings to the cable company, there is a physical appropriation for which just compensation is due.

Set 6 Answer Sheet

1.	Ⓐ Ⓑ Ⓒ Ⓓ	19.	Ⓐ Ⓑ Ⓒ Ⓓ
2.	Ⓐ Ⓑ Ⓒ Ⓓ	20.	Ⓐ Ⓑ Ⓒ Ⓓ
3.	Ⓐ Ⓑ Ⓒ Ⓓ	21.	Ⓐ Ⓑ Ⓒ Ⓓ
4.	Ⓐ Ⓑ Ⓒ Ⓓ	22.	Ⓐ Ⓑ Ⓒ Ⓓ
5.	Ⓐ Ⓑ Ⓒ Ⓓ	23.	Ⓐ Ⓑ Ⓒ Ⓓ
6.	Ⓐ Ⓑ Ⓒ Ⓓ	24.	Ⓐ Ⓑ Ⓒ Ⓓ
7.	Ⓐ Ⓑ Ⓒ Ⓓ	25.	Ⓐ Ⓑ Ⓒ Ⓓ
8.	Ⓐ Ⓑ Ⓒ Ⓓ	26.	Ⓐ Ⓑ Ⓒ Ⓓ
9.	Ⓐ Ⓑ Ⓒ Ⓓ	27.	Ⓐ Ⓑ Ⓒ Ⓓ
10.	Ⓐ Ⓑ Ⓒ Ⓓ	28.	Ⓐ Ⓑ Ⓒ Ⓓ
11.	Ⓐ Ⓑ Ⓒ Ⓓ	29.	Ⓐ Ⓑ Ⓒ Ⓓ
12.	Ⓐ Ⓑ Ⓒ Ⓓ	30.	Ⓐ Ⓑ Ⓒ Ⓓ
13.	Ⓐ Ⓑ Ⓒ Ⓓ	31.	Ⓐ Ⓑ Ⓒ Ⓓ
14.	Ⓐ Ⓑ Ⓒ Ⓓ	32.	Ⓐ Ⓑ Ⓒ Ⓓ
15.	Ⓐ Ⓑ Ⓒ Ⓓ	33.	Ⓐ Ⓑ Ⓒ Ⓓ
16.	Ⓐ Ⓑ Ⓒ Ⓓ	34.	Ⓐ Ⓑ Ⓒ Ⓓ
17.	Ⓐ Ⓑ Ⓒ Ⓓ	35.	Ⓐ Ⓑ Ⓒ Ⓓ
18.	Ⓐ Ⓑ Ⓒ Ⓓ	36.	Ⓐ Ⓑ Ⓒ Ⓓ

CONSTITUTIONAL LAW QUESTIONS - SET 6

Question 1

A man is subpoenaed to appear before the House of Representatives Armed Services Committee and answer certain questions. When he appears, he refuses to answer and is cited for contempt of Congress.

Which of the following is the man's best defense to the charge of contempt of Congress?

(A) He demonstrates that the questions asked him did not relate to any matter on which Congress could legislate.

(B) He establishes that he is an employee of the Department of Defense and may not be questioned relating to his duties as an officer of the executive branch of the federal government.

(C) He establishes that he holds an office by appointment of the President and may not be questioned as to his duties except by the Senate.

(D) He demonstrates that the questions asked him did not relate to any matter as to which funds appropriated by the House were expended.

Question 2

In which of the following cases does Congress have the power to restrict the jurisdiction of the United States Supreme Court?

(A) A case involving an ambassador.

(B) A case involving a dispute between two states.

(C) A case involving maritime jurisdiction.

(D) A case involving a state and the federal government.

Question 3

In an effort to protect the dwindling California condor population, Congress enacted the Condor Preservation Act, which made it illegal to take, possess, or sell any part of a California condor. The constitutionality of the Act is challenged by a seller of gifts and artifacts, including artifacts made out of California condor feathers.

Is the statute valid?

(A) No, the statute violates due process because the absolute prohibition on sale is an effective taking under the Fifth Amendment Due Process Clause without just compensation.

(B) No, because the statute is discriminatory as applied.

(C) Yes, because the statute is rationally related to interstate commerce.

(D) Yes, because the statute is designed to protect a dwindling national resource.

Question 4

A state was suffering from a near-depression caused by layoffs in the tourist service industry. In an attempt to alleviate the problem, the state enacted a statute providing for the immediate hiring of 100,000 employees to repair, maintain, and otherwise work at the discretion of the state director of highways. The statute further stated that preference would be given to persons who had worked in the tourist service industry for five years and had been laid off.

Which of the following constitutional provisions would be most relevant in determining the constitutionality of the preference for tourist service industry workers?

(A) The Privileges and Immunities Clause of Article IV.

(B) The Equal Protection Clause of the Fourteenth Amendment.

(C) The reserved powers of the state under the Tenth Amendment.

(D) The Privileges and Immunities Clause of the Fourteenth Amendment.

Question 5

To provide jobs for its citizens, stimulate future tourism, and help the environment, a state legislature enacted a statute authorizing the state's department of parks and recreation to hire up to 5,000 persons to plant trees on land in the state that has been denuded of trees by overlogging. Among other things, the statute provides that resident aliens may be employed only if no United States citizens are available to fill the necessary positions.

In a challenge to the constitutionality of that provision by a plaintiff with standing to raise the claim, which of the following constitutional provisions would be most helpful to the plaintiff?

(A) The Privileges and Immunities Clause of the Fourteenth Amendment.

(B) The reserved powers of the state under the Tenth Amendment.

(C) The Equal Protection Clause of the Fourteenth Amendment.

(D) The Fourteenth Amendment Due Process Clause.

Question 6

A state statute was struck down by the supreme court of the state on the grounds that it was in conflict with the Supremacy Clause of the United States Constitution as well as the Equal Protection Clause of the state constitution.

Does the United States Supreme Court have jurisdiction to hear an appeal of the state supreme court's decision?

(A) Yes, because the Supreme Court has original jurisdiction of all cases in which a state is a party.

(B) Yes, because the requirements for an appeal to the United States Supreme Court are met under the facts.

(C) No, because the requirements of certiorari are not met under the facts.

(D) No, because of the "adequate and independent state ground" theory.

Question 7

A state enacted a statute to provide financial aid for residents of the state who attend public or private colleges and universities in the state. Under this statute, eligible students receive varying amounts of money, depending on need. A student living in the state who has never paid taxes applied for a grant of funds under this statute to attend a private college in a different state. His application was denied because the college was outside of his home state. The student filed suit in federal court against the appropriate state official, challenging the constitutionality of the denial on equal protection grounds and to compel the granting of his application.

Which of the following statements is most correct?

(A) The suit is barred by the Eleventh Amendment.

(B) The student has standing to maintain the action despite the fact that he has never paid taxes in the state.

(C) The federal court will not grant the injunctive relief sought by the student in the absence of "extraordinary circumstances."

(D) The doctrine of sovereign immunity bars the student's action.

Question 8

A Delaware corporation with its business headquarters in Illinois conducts bar preparation courses for law school graduates. In addition to its national headquarters, the corporation rents local administrative headquarters in at least one city in each state.

Its instructors are law school professors and other lawyers who are paid an hourly, or occasionally bi-annual, fee, but each instructor is considered an independent contractor and prepares his or her own lecture outlines and respective study outlines that are provided to students. Some instructors lecture only in one or more cities in the same state, while other instructors lecture in cities throughout the United States. A professor who is a resident of the state of Virginia gives lectures on Constitutional Law in more than 20 states, including California.

The printer that publishes all of the bar preparation company's instructional materials is located in New York and ships the materials by commercial carriers to the respective state offices of the bar preparation company. The printer does not solicit business and does not have officers or agents outside of New York.

Which of the following taxes is most likely valid?

(A) A Virginia income tax on all of the Virginia professor's income.

(B) An Illinois income tax on all of the Virginia professor's income.

(C) A New York use tax on instructional materials shipped to and sold in California.

(D) A California ad valorem property tax on each item of instructional material received in that state.

Question 9

As part of a program to meet the needs of a growing homeless population, a city council appropriated funds to construct a shelter and community center in the downtown area and sought bids from organizations interested in operating the center. The group submitting the lowest bid was a religious organization, which ran a number of shelters and food kitchens in adherence to the religion's central tenet of aiding the needy. While church members never actively preached to people using the shelters, it did make available reading materials about its religion. The only other bidder was a local nonprofit foundation not affiliated with any church. The nonprofit foundation concluded that it was underbid because it was subject to a state tax imposed on all facilities offering overnight lodging, whether run for profit or not for profit; the only exemption was for facilities run by an organized religion.

If the nonprofit foundation seeks to challenge the application of the state tax to its operation of the homeless shelter, which of the following statements is most correct?

(A) Imposing the tax on the church's operation of homeless shelters, which is mandated by the religious beliefs of its members, would improperly inhibit their free exercise of religion.

(B) Maintaining the tax exemption for the church's operation of homeless shelters is a proper means of avoiding excessive government entanglement with religion.

(C) Permitting a tax exemption for the church-run shelter and not for a shelter run by other not-for-profit institutions has the unconstitutional effect of advancing religion.

(D) The tax exemption only for church-run shelters violates the Equal Protection Clause of the Fourteenth Amendment because the state does not have a compelling interest justifying application of the tax to some organizations that operate shelters and not others.

Question 10

A comprehensive federal health-care reform statute created a Federal Health Policy Board,

which was directed to monitor the fees charged for various medical procedures covered by insurance. The board also had the power to subpoena records to determine whether fee increases were a true reflection of cost increases. Nothing in the statute provided for caps on fee increases.

Because of the continuing escalation of health-care costs while the statute was being debated, several states had passed health-care legislation on their own. One state passed legislation that prohibited most fee increases of 10% or more per year for specified health-care services covered by insurance, and created a health-care review board to regulate these costs and impose monetary penalties on health-care providers or insurers that tried to circumvent the cap.

Which of the following would be the best basis for finding the state provision unconstitutional?

(A) The federal legislation was passed after the state legislation and therefore supersedes it.

(B) The Federal Health Policy Board was constituted with many of the same powers as the state board but was not given the power to impose sanctions.

(C) The state provision impairs existing contracts between health-care providers and insurers in violation of the Contract Clause.

(D) Health-care fee caps create an undue burden on interstate commerce even in the absence of federal regulation.

Question 11

A city council and park board announced joint plans to tear down some old buildings and erect a park. Before the contracts were made, in order to garner the greatest political benefit from such projects, the city council adopted an ordinance requiring that 35% of the work force of contractors working on city-funded projects be residents of the city.

One of the contractors working on the park project employed several people from the city, but most of his employees came from a town in a neighboring state that was a few miles west of the city. When the city projects inspector discovered that the contractor did not employ the required 35%, he told the contractor that if he did not hire a sufficient number of city workers within 20 days the contractor would forfeit the opportunity to work on the project. The contractor immediately filed an action in federal court seeking to have the employment requirement declared unconstitutional.

The court should rule in favor of:

(A) The city, because it is acting as a "market participant" here.

(B) The city, because there is a rational basis for favoring city residents here.

(C) The contractor, because the requirement interferes with his rights under the Privileges and Immunities Clause of Article IV.

(D) The contractor, because the requirement interferes with his Contract Clause rights.

Question 12

A federal law requiring that all automobiles driven on United States military bases be equipped with air bags would most probably be justified by:

(A) The Property Clause of Article IV, Section 3.

(B) The General Welfare Clause of Article I, Section 8.

(C) The Supremacy Clause of Article VI, Section 2.

(D) The Commerce Clause of Article I, Section 8.

Question 13

Congress has recently enacted legislation that makes it a federal crime for any person to interfere with any right conferred by the Equal Protection Clause of the Fourteenth Amendment.

The statute may be applied constitutionally in which of the following situations?

(A) A person who hates Asians bribes a federal official so that he fails to distribute free dairy products to otherwise eligible Asians.

(B) A person who believes women are inferior to men persuades the dean of a private school licensed by the state to deny admission to otherwise qualified women because of their sex.

(C) By threats of violence, a person coerces the coach of a public high school's basketball team to exclude white athletes from the team solely because of their race.

(D) A person persuades the members of his church council to deny shelter and food to homosexual men who seek aid at the church-run downtown relief center.

Question 14

As an aide to a member of the Congress of the United States, you are expected to provide an analysis of the constitutionality of proposed legislation that your employer is called to vote on. A bill has been proposed that would create a mandatory price schedule for every motor vehicle sold in the United States.

Which of the following should you tell your employer is the strongest constitutional basis for the proposed legislation?

(A) All motor vehicle transactions in the United States, taken as a whole, have a significant impact upon interstate commerce.

(B) Because the purchase or sale of a motor vehicle, by definition, involves commerce, the federal government may regulate such transactions under the commerce power.

(C) Congress has the power to regulate transportation in the United States.

(D) Congress has the power to legislate for the general welfare of the people of the United States.

Question 15

A package delivery service that operates throughout the United States is based in a southwestern state. The company specializes in transporting packages to airports, where air freight companies or commercial airlines transport the packages to their cities of destination. However, the company's entire fleet of trucks operate only in the state in which it is based. The company purchased the trucks from dealers within the state. The company's drivers pick up packages from shippers within the state and the packages are then delivered to an airport located in the state, where employees of the airlines load the packages onto their planes. Each shipper is charged a service fee by the company. The state wishes to impose a 5% transaction tax on each of the fees collected by the company for the services that the company renders in the state.

The federal courts would probably rule that such a tax is:

(A) Constitutional, because the tax is imposed before the packages enter the stream of commerce.

(B) Constitutional, because the tax is severable from any effect it might have on interstate commerce.

(C) Unconstitutional, because the packages are already in the stream of commerce.

(D) Unconstitutional, because the tax exposes the company to the possibility of multiple taxation.

Question 16

It was common practice in a particular state for a security interest in land to be structured as a deed absolute, which gave a lender absolute title to the borrower's property as security for the loan. The lender would reconvey only on complete payment of the loan by the debtor party, and could dispose of the land immediately without a foreclosure sale on default. A new governor of the state whose campaign platform was built around abolishing the deed absolute mortgage encouraged the legislature to enact a bill that immediately outlawed use of the deed absolute, declaring that all such deeds would be considered mere liens against the secured property. The law applied not only to loans made in the future, but also to the thousands of such loans in existence at the time the legislation was passed. As soon as the governor signed the legislation, lending institutions and individuals who had loaned money secured through deeds absolute challenged the constitutionality of the new law.

The strongest argument that the challengers can make is:

(A) As applied to loans outstanding at the time the bill was enacted, the law is an ex post facto law, and such laws are banned by the federal Constitution.

(B) Lenders using the deed absolute have been singled out by the governor and his followers in the legislature as political scapegoats, and such discrimination against the lenders violates the Equal Protection Clause.

(C) Lenders had property rights in the secured property and such rights were summarily abrogated by the new law, constituting an unconstitutional taking of property without due process of law.

(D) As applied to loans outstanding at the time the bill was enacted, the law impairs the contract rights of the lenders and such rights are guaranteed by the Contracts Clause of the federal Constitution.

Question 17

After the release of various news stories about the President's possible violation of political campaign funding laws, a federal grand jury investigation and an investigation by a special Senate subcommittee were initiated. The Senate subcommittee subpoenaed documents and records from several top officers of the executive branch. Learning of the subpoenas, the President ordered all executive officials to refuse to turn over materials, claiming "executive privilege."

Which of the following statements is most accurate?

(A) The subpoena violates the constitutional principle of separation of powers.

(B) The President's executive privilege is absolute, except in cases of impeachment.

(C) The presidential papers are presumptively privileged, but the privilege must yield to a demonstrated specific need for evidence in a pending legislative proceeding.

(D) The President's executive privilege applies to proceedings by Congress, but not to proceedings by the courts.

Question 18

A state passed a law requiring that anyone holding himself out to be a private investigator in the state must be licensed by the state. Licensure requirements included a thorough background check into the person's criminal record and mental health. It also required passing a test on ethical obligations of a private investigator. Finally, the investigator was required to sign a two-part oath. Part one was a loyalty oath, which stated: "I solemnly swear (or affirm) that I will be loyal to the United States and to the state and will uphold their Constitutions." Part two stated: "I solemnly swear (or affirm) that I am not now a member of any organization that advocates illegal acts, nor will I become a member of any such organization while I am a licensed private investigator in this state."

An experienced investigator with a master's degree in criminal justice administration applied for a private investigator's license. He easily passed both background checks, but he refused to take the oaths, claiming that they inhibited his freedoms of speech and association as guaranteed by the federal Constitution. The state professional licensure board denied him a private investigator's license solely on the basis of his refusal to take the oaths. The investigator sued in federal court to require the state to grant him a license and to strike down the oath requirements in the licensure statute.

The court is likely to find that:

(A) Both the loyalty oath and the membership oath are constitutional.

(B) The loyalty oath is constitutional, but the membership oath is unconstitutional.

(C) The membership oath is constitutional, but the loyalty oath is unconstitutional.

(D) Neither the loyalty oath nor the membership oath is constitutional.

Question 19

A state legislature adopted a statute requiring that state school districts be funded equally on a per capita basis, because the previous method of funding school districts based on the amount of taxes paid by residents of the district resulted in schools in the state's wealthiest district receiving twice as much funding per pupil as did schools located in poorer districts. A resident of the wealthy district whose children attend public schools brought an action in state court to have the new statute declared invalid. He established at trial that the disparities in the previous funding system were not based in any way on racial or ethnic discrimination. Nevertheless, when the case reached the state supreme court, it ruled that, based on a provision in the state constitution similar to the Fourteenth Amendment Equal Protection Clause of the United States Constitution, all school districts in the state must be funded equally on a per capita basis.

Subsequent to this decision, a taxpayer in a neighboring state sued in federal court, demanding equal per capita funding in his state's school districts. The taxpayer's case eventually reached the United States Supreme Court, which ruled that the Fourteenth Amendment does not compel equal funding, provided there is no probable racial discrimination in the funding. After that decision, the resident of the wealthy district who had lost his state court case filed a petition for a writ of certiorari to have the decision by his state supreme court overturned.

The resident is most likely to:

(A) Prevail, because the Supremacy Clause renders the state decision invalid.

(B) Prevail, because the issue is res judicata.

(C) Not prevail, because the state decision turned on state law grounds.

(D) Not prevail, because the resident lacks standing.

Question 20

A state statute provides that no alien may own a restaurant within the state and that it is unlawful for anyone to give, sell, or otherwise convey a restaurant to an alien. A citizen of Canada who legally resides in the state has entered into a contract to buy a restaurant located within the state from a restaurant owner.

If the buyer and the seller join in a declaratory judgment action to test the state statute in a federal court:

(A) The case may not be heard because the buyer does not have standing.

(B) The burden of proof is on the buyer and seller to show that the statute is rationally related to a legitimate state interest.

(C) The burden of proof is on the state to show that the statute is necessary to achieve a compelling state interest.

(D) The burden of proof is on the state to show that the statute is substantially related to an important state purpose.

Question 21

A state statute prohibits aliens from owning land and makes it illegal to sell land to aliens, even if they are legally residing in the state. A legal resident alien who entered into a contract to buy land within the state brought suit challenging the constitutionality of the statute.

The alien will most likely:

(A) Win, because the statute impinges on Congress's power to legislate with respect to aliens and foreign affairs.

(B) Win, because the statute denies the privileges and immunities guaranteed by Article IV of the Constitution even though the alien is not a citizen.

(C) Win, because the statute denies the alien equal protection of the laws even though the alien is not a citizen.

(D) Lose, because of the alien's noncitizen status.

Question 22

A state statute prohibits aliens from owning land and makes it illegal to sell land to aliens. A landowner who entered into a contract to sell property to an alien brought an action to challenge the statute. The alien, however, did not participate in the action.

The landowner's strongest constitutional argument against the validity of the statute is that:

(A) The statute denies the equal protection of the laws to aliens.

(B) The statute unconstitutionally impairs the landowner's contract for the sale of land to a buyer.

(C) The statute is a direct restraint on the alienation of the landowner's real property.

(D) The statute denies the landowner of a property right without due process of law.

Question 23

During extensive hearings, a state legislature determined that double tractor-trailer rigs—trucks consisting of a tractor (the motorized portion) towing two large, connected trailers—caused the roadway to deteriorate faster than other freight vehicles and autos because of their weight. Traffic safety experts also produced evidence showing that double tractor-trailer vehicles were involved in more accidents than other freight vehicles, primarily due to "jack-knifing," where the rear trailer loses traction and swerves violently, causing the entire vehicle to be upended. Consequently, the legislature passed a statute requiring the owners and users of double tractor-trailer vehicles to pay a user's fee, in addition to normal vehicle licenses, of 10 cents per mile traveled over state highways and an annual registration fee of $5,000.

The owner of 30 tractors in a neighboring state that almost exclusively pull double trailer rigs through the state imposing the fees determined that about 30% of the total mileage of all of the owner's vehicles is accumulated in that state, and that there is no easy way to avoid traveling through that state to get to the delivery destinations in other states. The mileage fees and registration fees for 30 trucks in a year would be about 60% of the owner's gross annual income. The owner brought suit in federal district court seeking a judicial declaration that the fees imposed by the state statute are unconstitutional. At trial, attorneys for the state produced evidence of highway destruction and safety hazards from the double tractor-trailer rigs as found by legislative committee hearings. The owner proved the relevant facts about his operations and the cost the statute would impose.

If the court finds the tax unconstitutional, it will most likely be because:

(A) It seeks to regulate by taxation what it could not do directly, *i.e.,* regulate interstate commerce.

(B) The state's interests in preserving its highways and in promoting traffic safety are outweighed by the interference with interstate transportation of goods.

(C) It violates the owner's right to the equal protection of the laws.

(D) A use tax on companies engaged in interstate commerce violates the Commerce Clause.

Question 24

A state legislature recently enacted a statute imposing a "land utilization tax" on those operating businesses within the state who pay no property taxes. The state seeks to apply the tax to the owner of a small restaurant and store that is located in a national park within the state. The owner operates the restaurant and store pursuant to a contract with the United States government and pays no property taxes.

Which of the following is the owner's best constitutional argument against application of the tax to her?

(A) The owner has been denied the privileges and immunities of national citizenship, protected by the Fourteenth Amendment, because the state tax impairs her fundamental right to conduct business on federal lands.

(B) The tax is unconstitutional as applied to the owner, because it interferes with interstate tourism in violation of the federal commerce power.

(C) The owner is being denied equal protection of law, because those operating businesses on federal lands in other states are not subject to the tax.

(D) The tax is unconstitutional as applied to the owner, because under the property power the federal government has plenary power to regulate federal lands.

Question 25

The Federal Communications Commission ("FCC") issued a lengthy set of regulations regarding personal radar detectors. The regulations deal with the safety of such detectors and the frequencies on which they may operate, so as not to interfere with FCC-licensed radio and television stations or with radar used by commercial airliners and private aircraft.

May a state constitutionally ban the use of radar detectors given their regulation by the FCC?

(A) No, because the regulation of radio transmissions is within the purview of the FCC rather than the states, and state laws that attempt to regulate devices such as radar detectors are preempted.

(B) No, because such a ban would burden interstate commerce.

(C) Yes, because such a ban would not conflict with the FCC regulations.

(D) Yes, because the state has a legitimate interest in regulating the use of radar detectors in order to promote safe driving.

Question 26

A state's constitution authorizes a state reapportionment board to redraw state legislative districts every 12 years. During the most recent reapportionment process, consultants had provided the board with two alternative plans for reapportionment. One plan provided for districts with less than a 3% difference in proportional representation between districts. The other plan was drawn up to conform state legislative districts as nearly as possible to county borders, resulting in differences in proportional representation between districts of up to 12%. The current apportionment of legislative districts results in differences of up to 15% between districts. The board ultimately selected the reapportionment plan based on county borders, and this plan was approved by the state legislature.

A Caucasian resident and registered voter of the state brought a constitutional challenge to the reapportionment in federal court. His claim is based on the fact that, as a result of the plan that the board selected, the percentage of the African-American voting population in the district in which he lives increased from 45% to 55%. Had the other plan been selected, the percentage would have been unchanged in his district.

In the absence of a federal statute applicable to the state, is the resident likely to prevail?

(A) Yes, because an alternative plan with more equal apportionment is available.

(B) Yes, because any legislative apportionment discriminating in favor of or against racial minority groups is subject to strict scrutiny, and there is no evidence of past discrimination or any other compelling state interest to justify adopting the plan.

(C) No, because preserving political subdivisions is a legitimate state interest that justifies the plan's variance in representation.

(D) No, because the reapportionment plan results in less of an overall variance between districts than the current legislative apportionment.

Question 27

A city's airport board that oversees a large international airport in the United States has adopted a policy of reviewing current vendor licensees every three years. During the process, the board reviews customer comments, assesses the utility of the vendor's services, and reviews the profitability of the vendor (licensees pay rent based on a percentage of their gross profit). The licensee is entitled to present evidence on all of the issues reviewed.

The owner of a franchised currency exchange on wheels had a license to operate the cart within the airport until last week, when his license came up for review. After an appropriate hearing, the board refused to renew the owner's license mainly because of an excessive number of customer complaints. Nevertheless, the owner continued operating his cart pursuant to a license granted to him under the Federal Borders Act that allowed him to operate his cart at all borders or their functional equivalent. A city police officer patrolling the airport asked to see the owner's license. The owner showed his federal license, but the officer issued the owner a citation because he did not have a city license.

Which of the following is the owner's best constitutional defense?

(A) The city deprived the owner of his license without due process of law.

(B) The licensing scheme was arbitrary and capricious.

(C) The licensing scheme substantially interferes with interstate and foreign commerce.

(D) The license requirement here was superseded by the owner's federal license.

Question 28

To protect its citizens from the fluctuating price of energy, a state formed a state-owned electric company that operated exclusively within the state. The company provided electricity to residents of the various cities within the state on the basis of a rate schedule that reflected the historic costs associated with servicing each city. Under the schedule, electricity rates for citizens of a particular city were 15% higher than the premiums for any other city in the state. A group of residents from that city brings suit in state court to require the state electric company to make the premiums equal for everyone.

The most likely result is:

(A) The residents will prevail, unless the state electric company shows a compelling reason for the discrimination.

(B) The state electric company will prevail, unless the residents show that there is no rational basis for higher rates.

(C) The suit will be dismissed, because the state electric company is organized as a private business and thus is acting as a market participant.

(D) The suit will be dismissed, because it is an instrument of the state, and thus immune under the Eleventh Amendment from suits by citizens of the state.

Question 29

To combat rising insurance rates, a state formed a state-owned insurance company that operated exclusively within the state. The company provided insurance on the basis of premiums calculated according to a schedule of fees. Under the schedule, premiums for residents of a particular city were 25% higher than the premiums for any other municipality in the state. Forty percent of that city's residents were of Mexican descent compared with a state-wide Mexican-American population of approximately 15%. A Mexican-American citizen living in the city brings suit, alleging that the state insurance company's rate structure violates the Equal Protection Clause.

The most likely result is:

(A) The citizen will prevail, because the higher rates have the effect of discriminating against the Mexican-American population.

(B) The citizen will prevail, unless the state insurance company shows a compelling reason for the discrimination.

(C) The state insurance company will prevail, unless the citizen shows that Mexican-American citizens pay higher rates than similarly situated non-Mexican-American citizens of that city.

(D) The state insurance company will prevail, because discriminatory economic regulations are not a suspect classification.

Question 30

In an effort to standardize laws pertaining to the solicitation of business by mail, Congress adopted a statute establishing certain requirements that must be met before an organization can solicit business through the mails. A national religious organization that solicited charitable contributions by mail determined that the federal statute would substantially interfere with the successful accomplishment of the organization's religious objectives. The organization files suit seeking a declaratory judgment that the federal law may not be applied to its solicitation activities.

Which of the following, as a matter of constitutional law, best describes the burden that must be sustained?

(A) The federal government must demonstrate that a rational legislature could believe that this law helps to achieve a legitimate national interest when applied to both religious and secular solicitation activities.

(B) The federal government must demonstrate that the application of this statute to the solicitation activities of this organization is necessary to vindicate a compelling governmental interest.

(C) The organization must demonstrate a specific congressional purpose to inhibit the accomplishment of the organization's religious objectives.

(D) The organization must demonstrate that no reasonable legislator could think that the application of the statute to this organization would be helpful in accomplishing a legitimate governmental objective.

Question 31

A citizen who is unhappy about a recent decision of his city council stood in front of city hall and gave an extemporaneous speech belittling each member of the city council. During the diatribe, the citizen made the following

statement: "If there is a God, the city council members will surely burn in hell forever." A state statute, enacted in 1898, prohibited "the public utterance of any blasphemy or sacrilege," and provided criminal penalties for its violation. On hearing the citizen's utterances, a police officer arrested him for violating the 1898 statute. The local district attorney decided to proceed with prosecution of the case, only the third recorded such prosecution in the state's history.

Which of the following arguments would not be helpful for the citizen's defense?

(A) Application of the statute to the citizen infringes his freedom of speech in violation of the Fourteenth Amendment.

(B) Application of the statute to the citizen denies him equal protection of the law in violation of the Fourteenth Amendment.

(C) The statute violates the Fourteenth Amendment because it is an establishment of religion.

(D) The statute violates the Fourteenth Amendment because it is vague.

Question 32

After a state supreme court overturned the conviction of a murder for failure to give proper *Miranda* warnings, a reporter asked the murder victim's father to comment on the case as he exited the supreme court building. The father made the following statement: "Each one of the so-called supreme court justices is worse than a murderer, because they make it possible for more sons and daughters to be murdered. I'd like to see every one of them strung up, like they should have done to the creep who was set free, and if someone will give me a rope I'll go in there and do it myself."

A state statute proscribes, with criminal penalties, "the making of any threat to the life or safety of a public official for any act the official performed as part of the official's duties in office."

Which of the following is correct regarding the statute?

(A) The victim's father could constitutionally be punished under the statute, but only if the state supreme court justices heard the threats he made.

(B) The victim's father could constitutionally be punished under the statute.

(C) The victim's father could not be constitutionally punished under these circumstances, but the statute is constitutional on its face.

(D) The statute is unconstitutional on its face.

Question 33

A state statute makes criminal "all speech-making, picketing, or public gathering of any sort on the steps of the supreme courthouse Monday through Friday, between the hours of 8:30 a.m. and 4:30 p.m., when court is in session." A citizen is upset about a supreme court decision that was just released and stands on the steps of the courthouse at noon, while court is in session, handing out leaflets and exhorting passersby to vote the state supreme court justices out of office.

If the citizen is prosecuted for violation of the statute, which of the following best describes the applicable burden of proof?

(A) The state will have to show that there was a compelling need for the statute and that no less restrictive alternatives existed to meet that need.

(B) The state will have to show that the statute was narrowly tailored to serve a significant government interest and leaves open alternative channels of communication.

(C) The citizen will have to show that there was no compelling need for the statute and that less restrictive alternatives were available to accomplish the same goals.

(D) The citizen will have to show that there was no reasonable basis for enacting the statute.

Question 34

A federal district court judge was accused of misconduct in office and was impeached by the House of Representatives. At trial in the United States Senate, the judge was convicted and removed from office. Nevertheless, the President directed the Attorney General to institute criminal proceedings against the judge. After presentation to a federal grand jury, an indictment was issued against the judge and signed by the Attorney General. At the opening of his trial, the judge moved to have the indictment dismissed.

Most likely the trial judge would:

(A) Dismiss, because the President had told the Attorney General to prosecute.

(B) Dismiss, because the criminal proceeding violates the Fifth Amendment's proscription against double jeopardy.

(C) Deny the dismissal, because the federal grand jury issued the indictment.

(D) Deny the dismissal, because the judge has not been previously tried in a criminal proceeding.

Question 35

A foreign student who had entered the United States on a student visa four years ago was notified by the Immigration and Naturalization Service that he was subject to being deported because his visa had expired. Federal law provided that an alien who is subject to being deported has the right to appear before an administrative officer appointed by the Attorney General's office for a hearing on whether he should be deported. This officer, appointed by the executive branch of the government, has the right under law to make a final order concerning whether the alien should be deported. After a hearing, the administrative officer entered an order allowing the student to remain in the United States as a permanent resident.

However, a congressional rule permitted the House of Representatives, by resolution, to deport "undesirable aliens." After the administrative judge entered his order, the House passed a resolution that the student should be deported. The student petitioned the federal court to declare the legislative resolution invalid.

The court should find the resolution:

(A) Valid, because Congress has plenary powers with regard to aliens and naturalization.

(B) Valid, because aliens are not "citizens" within the meaning of the Fourteenth Amendment.

(C) Invalid, because the federal law removed congressional power with regard to aliens in this circumstance, and the resolution of the House violates the separation of powers doctrine.

(D) Invalid, because the student was denied due process when he was not given a hearing before the House of Representatives.

Question 36

A civilian contract employee working for the United States Army was suspected of copying classified army documents onto a flash drive and selling the files to foreign governments. After a short investigation, the employee was arrested by military police. The employee was brought before a court martial, convicted of espionage, and sentenced by the court to 20 years' hard labor. The employee appeals his conviction and sentence on constitutional grounds.

How should the court rule?

(A) The sentence is unconstitutional because 20 years' hard labor is cruel and unusual punishment.

(B) The conviction is unconstitutional because the court martial did not have jurisdiction to try the employee.

(C) The sentence will be upheld because 20 years' hard labor is neither cruel nor unusual given the charges here.

(D) The conviction will be upheld because the court had jurisdiction over the employee.

CONSTITUTIONAL LAW ANSWERS - SET 6

Answer to Question 1

(A) The man's best defense is to show that the questions did not relate to a matter on which Congress could legislate. The power to investigate to secure information as a basis for potential legislation is very broad, but the investigation must be for purposes within the scope of Congress's power. Hence, (A) is the best choice. (D) is incorrect because, while Congress may investigate only matters on which it can legislate or otherwise act, it is not limited to matters as to which it has made appropriations of money. (B) is incorrect because executive privilege is not absolute. (C) is incorrect because both branches of Congress have investigatory powers.

Answer to Question 2

(C) Congress has the power to limit the Supreme Court's jurisdiction in maritime cases. The Supreme Court has original jurisdiction in all cases affecting ambassadors, other public ministers and consuls, and those in which a state shall be a party. Congress may neither restrict nor enlarge the Supreme Court's original jurisdiction. Thus, (A), (B), and (D) are incorrect. In all other cases, such as maritime disputes, the Supreme Court has only appellate jurisdiction, which Congress has extensive power to regulate and limit. Hence, (C) is correct.

Answer to Question 3

(C) The statute is valid because it is rationally related to interstate commerce. Regulating the possession or sale of an item made from a California condor clearly affects commerce. Thus, Congress can act under its broad commerce power. Because the regulations do not compel surrender of the artifacts, and there is no physical invasion or restraint on them, there is no taking of a property right without just compensation. Therefore, Congress's power to regulate is proper, even though it diminishes the opportunity to make a profit. Thus, (A) is incorrect. (B) is not supported by the facts—there does not appear to be a discriminatory application of the statute. (D) states the right conclusion, but for the wrong reason. The statutory authority here lies in Congress's broad power to regulate interstate commerce.

Answer to Question 4

(B) The Equal Protection Clause of the Fourteenth Amendment is the most relevant. The Equal Protection Clause is at issue when a law treats a person or class of persons differently from others. Here, the classification scheme makes a distinction between individuals who worked in tourism and those who did not, and those who worked for five years versus those with a lesser period of employment. (A) is wrong, because the Privileges and Immunities Clause of Article IV has no bearing: That clause prohibits discrimination by states against nonresidents, and here the state is not treating residents of other states differently. (C) is not the best answer, because the reserved powers doctrine helps, rather than hinders, the state by providing that all powers not delegated to the federal government by the Constitution are reserved to the states. (D) is wrong because employment is not within the narrow category of privileges protected by the Fourteenth Amendment Privileges and Immunities Clause.

Answer to Question 5

(C) The Equal Protection Clause of the Fourteenth Amendment is the most helpful provision. State classifications based on alienage that do not involve alien participation in the self-government

process are suspect under the Equal Protection Clause and are subject to strict judicial scrutiny. They will be upheld only if the government can show that the classification is necessary to achieve a compelling state interest. While the state's interests here in providing jobs, stimulating future tourism, and helping the environment may be compelling, it cannot be said that these goals can be achieved only by discriminating against resident aliens. Thus, the legislation would be found unconstitutional under the Equal Protection Clause. (A) is wrong because the Privileges and Immunities Clause of the Fourteenth Amendment protects the privileges and immunities of United States citizens, not aliens. (B) is wrong because, even if applicable, the Tenth Amendment could only help the state (by reserving to the state powers that are not delegated to the federal government); it does not carry any prohibitions. (D) might provide a viable argument, as a statute that affects a fundamental right can be struck down under the Due Process Clause under the same strict scrutiny test as set out above under the Equal Protection Clause. However, it is a less direct argument than (C) because strict scrutiny applies under the Due Process Clause only if the challenger can show that a fundamental right is involved.

Answer to Question 6

(D) The Supreme Court probably would not review the state decision because of the "adequate and independent state ground" theory. The Supreme Court will hear a case from a state court only if the state court judgment turned on federal grounds. Here, the judgment is, in part, based on a violation of the Equal Protection Clause of the state constitution, which is an adequate and independent state ground on which the decision would rest even if the federal issue were resolved (assuming that the state court's disposition of the state constitutional issue did not depend on federal doctrines). (A) is wrong because this is a question of appellate jurisdiction, not original jurisdiction. (B) is wrong because this type of case would not meet the very narrow requirements of appeal. (C) is wrong because if it were not for the adequate and independent state ground, this type of challenge could be heard by the Court in its discretion.

Answer to Question 7

(B) The student has standing. A person challenging the constitutionality of a government action must have standing to raise the issue. To have standing, a person must show that he is injured by a government action (injury in fact) and that a favorable decision will eliminate the harm. Generally, a taxpayer does not have standing to challenge the way tax money is spent because any alleged injury is too remote. However, here the student is not bringing suit as a taxpayer; rather he is alleging that the state policy of providing financial aid only for residents who attend schools in the state injures him by depriving him of such aid solely on the basis of attending a college outside the state, thus violating his right to equal protection. A ruling in the student's favor will eliminate the harm to him. Therefore, the student has a concrete stake in the outcome of this controversy, entirely independent of whether he has ever paid taxes in the state. Regarding (A), the Eleventh Amendment prohibits a federal court suit against a state by a citizen of that state or by a citizen of another state. However, the Eleventh Amendment does not bar a suit against a state official acting pursuant to state law but allegedly in violation of the plaintiff's constitutional rights. Here, the student is seeking an order that a particular state official be compelled to act in conformity with the student's right to equal protection. The lawsuit is not brought against the state, nor does it seek a retroactive recovery from state funds. The prospective payment of state funds that the student seeks through the compelled granting of his application for aid is not prohibited by the Eleventh Amendment. Thus, (A) is incorrect. Regarding (D), the doctrine of sovereign immunity refers to the rule that a governmental entity may not be sued unless it consents to be sued (which consent is generally afforded by statute). Here, the facts do not state

whether the state has consented to be sued. However, as detailed above, the student is not actually suing the state. He is suing a state official who is allegedly enforcing an unconstitutional enactment, and is seeking to compel the official to grant his application. Because the suit is not against the state, the doctrine of sovereign immunity is not applicable. (C) is incorrect because it is only with regard to state criminal statutes or prosecutions that a party seeking to enjoin such statutes or prosecutions must show irreparable injury or exceptional circumstances (*i.e.,* a showing of significant harm that could not be avoided by state adjudication and appellate review of the proceedings). Here, there is no criminal statute or prosecution at issue. Thus, there is no need to show "extraordinary circumstances."

Answer to Question 8

(D) An ad valorem tax on each item received in California is most likely to be held valid. An ad valorem property tax is a tax based on a percentage of the assessed value of the property in question. Although such a tax is generally valid, potential Commerce Clause problems arise when the property taxed moves in interstate commerce. Goods in transit are totally exempt from taxation. Interstate shipment usually ends when the goods reach their destination; thereafter, the goods are subject to local tax. Here, once each item of instructional material is received in California, it has clearly reached its destination, and the interstate shipment has come to an end. At this point, the materials become subject to the local ad valorem property tax. Thus, (D) sets forth a tax that is valid. (C) is incorrect because it misstates the concept of the use tax. A use tax is a tax imposed on the users of goods purchased out of state. Use taxes are imposed by the state in which the buyer resides. Here, New York is the state of the publisher and seller of the instructional materials. New York has no basis for imposing a use tax on materials that are being used in California. The income taxes described in (A) and (B) are invalid because they fail to satisfy the three-part test for determining the validity of a nondiscriminatory state tax affecting interstate commerce. The factors required to be satisfied are: (i) substantial nexus between the activity or property taxed and the taxing state; (ii) fair apportionment based on the extent of the taxable property or activity in the state; and (iii) a fair relationship between the tax and the services or benefits provided by the state. In (A), the professor is a resident of Virginia, and he also lectures in that state. Thus, there is a substantial nexus between his income-producing activity and the taxing state. However, the professor's income-producing activity is carried on in more than 20 states. Therefore, a Virginia income tax on ***all*** of the professor's income would not be fairly apportioned according to the extent of the taxable activity carried on in Virginia, and would potentially subject the professor to cumulative tax burdens. Consequently, the tax is invalid. The Illinois income tax in (B) also fails to fairly apportion the tax, because it taxes ***all*** of the professor's income. In addition, the Illinois tax is invalid because there is no indication of a substantial nexus between Illinois and the professor's income-producing activity. We are not told that the professor lectures in Illinois; indeed, the only mention of Illinois is a reference to its being the national headquarters of the bar prep company, which in no way establishes any nexus between Illinois and the professor's activity.

Answer to Question 9

(C) The tax exemption in this case probably violates the Establishment Clause. To be valid under this clause, a law favoring religion or authorizing governmental benefits to a religiously affiliated institution must (i) have a secular purpose, (ii) have a primary effect that neither advances nor inhibits religion, and (iii) not produce excessive government entanglement with religion. Although religious associations may be included in tax exemptions available to a variety of secular and religious organizations, a tax exemption that is available only for religious organizations or

religious activities and not for other organizations engaged in the same activity violates the Establishment Clause. [Texas Monthly, Inc. v. Bullock (1989)] Here, providing the tax exemption only to shelters run by religious groups and not to those run by other not-for-profit groups would seem to have a primary effect of advancing religion, because it provides religious groups with an advantage over nonreligious groups in providing services to the homeless. (A) is incorrect. While a broad exemption from property taxation for property used exclusively for religious, educational, or charitable purposes has been held not to violate the Establishment Clause [Walz v. Tax Commission (1970)], a narrower exemption applying only to religious groups is invalid, as discussed above. If the exemption here had applied to any not-for-profit group that operates a homeless shelter, it probably would have been valid. (B) is incorrect. While an exemption may involve less government entanglement than imposing the tax on church-run shelters, the other elements of the Establishment Clause test are not satisfied when shelters run by other groups are excluded from the exemption. (D) is incorrect because the state does not need to show a compelling interest to validate a tax classification that does not discriminate against a suspect class or burden a fundamental right. The tax exemption here need only have a rational relationship to a legitimate government interest.

Answer to Question 10

(B) The fact that the federal board was similar to the state board but was not given the power to restrict fee increases and impose sanctions in an otherwise comprehensive bill suggests that such provisions in the state law violate the Supremacy Clause. A state law may fail under the Supremacy Clause even if it does not directly conflict with a federal statute or regulation if it interferes with the achievement of a federal objective or the federal regulations occupy the entire field. The more comprehensive a federal scheme is, the more likely a finding of implied preemption. The fact that the health-care legislation was comprehensive but the federal board was not given regulatory or enforcement power suggests that Congress did not want specific restrictions in these areas and may have wanted free-market principles to determine fee increases at the outset. The state board's power to impose these restrictions may violate the Supremacy Clause under these circumstances. (A) is incorrect because the fact that the federal legislation was passed later does not automatically mean that the state legislation has been superseded. In areas of concurrent legislative power, a state regulation will be upheld if it does not conflict with and is not preempted by federal legislation. (C) is incorrect because the Contract Clause prevents only ***substantial*** impairments of existing contracts by state legislation, and only if the legislation does not serve an important and legitimate public interest or is not a reasonable and narrowly tailored means of promoting that interest. Here, the law has a prospective effect only, and even if existing contracts between health-care providers and insurers are affected by the legislation, the other requirements for the Contract Clause to apply are not likely to be satisfied. (D) is incorrect because states may regulate local aspects of interstate commerce in the absence of federal regulation as long as the regulation is nondiscriminatory and does not unduly burden interstate commerce, which is a case-by-case balancing test. Here, the legislation appears to be nondiscriminatory and there are insufficient facts to establish that it would constitute an undue burden; hence, (B) presents a stronger argument than (D).

Answer to Question 11

(C) The court should rule in favor of the contractor because the pursuit of a livelihood is a right protected by the Privileges and Immunities Clause, and the requirement here substantially interferes with that right. The Privileges and Immunities Clause of Article IV prohibits states and municipalities from discriminating against residents of other states. Not all discrimination is prohibited—only that which substantially interferes with important commercial activities or civil liberties. The Supreme Court has held that the right to pursue a livelihood is a right protected by the Privileges and Immunities Clause, and also has held that a requirement that private contractors on city projects employ a certain percentage of city residents substantially interferes with the right. [*See* United Building & Construction Trades Council v. Mayor of Camden (1984)] (A) is incorrect because there is no market participant exception under the Privileges and Immunities Clause. The market participant exception arises from the Commerce Clause and is not appropriate in privileges and immunities analysis. [*See* United Building & Construction Trades Council v. Mayor of Camden, *supra*] (B) is incorrect because the fact that a rational basis exists for the requirement does not justify it. The Supreme Court has stated that the Privileges and Immunities Clause prohibition on discriminating against nonresidents may be overcome if there is substantial justification for the discrimination. The exception will apply if nonresidents are causing a problem (*e.g.*, unemployment) and the discrimination is the least restrictive means of combating the problem. It is not apparent from the facts here that the city has an unemployment problem or that nonresidents are causing the problem. In any case, the choice states the wrong standard. Therefore, (B) is incorrect. (D) is incorrect because the Contract Clause is a limitation on states' rights to modify existing contracts retroactively; it is unrelated to a state's power to regulate contracts prospectively, which is the case here since the resident employee restriction predated Wright's contract.

Answer to Question 12

(A) Under Article IV, Section 3, Congress has the power "to make all needful rules and regulations respecting the territory or other property belonging to the United States." This power would encompass a regulation such as the air bag statute. Therefore, (A) is correct. (B) is incorrect because the General Welfare Clause is part of Congress's taxing and spending power; it does not authorize nonspending provisions that directly regulate an activity, such as the air bag provision. (C) is incorrect because the Supremacy Clause merely makes federal laws supreme over conflicting state laws. Here, there is no indication of any conflicting state law. (D) could be correct, but it is not the best answer. Congress does have plenary power over interstate commerce, and it could be argued that the regulation here affects interstate commerce, especially because transportation is involved. Nevertheless, (A) presents a more direct justification for the law because of its focus on federal property.

Answer to Question 13

(C) The facts of (C) are the only ones in which the person has compelled a state official to deny equal protection of the law to some person. The Fourteenth Amendment prevents states from depriving any person of life, liberty, or property without due process of law and equal protection of the law. Because the Equal Protection Clause protects against state action only, the federal statute at issue prohibits only behavior that causes or induces a state official, agency, or instrumentality to deny the equal protection of the law to some person. In (C), the person coerced a state agent (the coach of a public high school basketball team) to exclude people from participation in an activity at a state institution solely on the basis of race. Because this is a state governmental act that classifies people based on a suspect trait (race) in the absence of a compelling state interest, it violates equal protection. For bringing about this violation, the person is guilty of violating the federal statute. (A) is incorrect because the person there is inducing a ***federal*** official to discriminate in the distribution of free dairy products. The Fourteenth Amendment, unlike the Fifteenth Amendment, does not curtail the actions of the federal government. Therefore, the person acting has not interfered with any right conferred by the Fourteenth Amendment

Equal Protection Clause. (B) is incorrect because the person there has induced discriminatory action against women by the dean of a private school. The Fourteenth Amendment does not protect against the actions of private persons or institutions. The actions of a private entity may constitute state action if the state is significantly involved in the private entity. However, the mere granting of a license is not sufficient state involvement with a private entity so as to convert its action into state action. Thus, the fact that the private school in (B) is licensed by the state does not make the school's discriminatory treatment of women state action. (D) is incorrect because the person there has induced discriminatory action by his church, which is a private entity with no apparent significant state involvement. As explained above, the Fourteenth Amendment Equal Protection Clause does not protect against the actions of such an entity. Thus, the person has not interfered with a right conferred by the Equal Protection Clause.

Answer to Question 14

(A) As part of its power to regulate interstate commerce, Congress may regulate any activity, local or interstate, which either in itself or in combination with other activities has a substantial economic effect upon, or effect on movement in, interstate commerce. Because all motor vehicle transactions in the United States, in the aggregate, have a significant impact upon interstate commerce (as (A) states), Congress is constitutionally empowered to regulate such transactions by, *e.g.*, enacting a mandatory price schedule. (B) is incorrect because the price of a vehicle manufactured and sold in one state may have no effect upon ***interstate*** commerce; *i.e.*, it may not affect or involve more than one state. While Congress does have the power to determine that these individual transactions do in fact have an impact on interstate commerce, they do not come within the federal government's Commerce Clause power merely because they involve "commerce." (C) is incorrect because it is too broad. Congress is empowered to regulate transportation that constitutes interstate commerce. However, there is no congressional power to regulate transportation as such. (D) is incorrect because Congress may ***tax and spend*** to provide for the general welfare. The General Welfare Clause does not, however, authorize Congress to enact nonspending legislation or regulations for the general welfare.

Answer to Question 15

(B) The transaction tax in this case, which is being applied to the local activities of an interstate company, is valid because it is not discriminatory and does not unduly burden interstate commerce. A "transaction tax" is essentially a privilege or occupation tax—*i.e.*, a tax on the privilege of doing business in the state. This type of tax is constitutional if: (i) it does not discriminate against interstate commerce; (ii) the activity taxed has a substantial nexus to the taxing state; (iii) the tax is fairly apportioned; and (iv) the tax fairly relates to services provided by the taxing state. Here, there is nothing in the facts to indicate that the tax is being imposed only on shipments being made in interstate commerce or only on interstate shippers; thus, no discrimination against interstate commerce exists. The transaction tax is on fees paid by shippers in the state to the company for transport of the packages within the state using its state-registered trucks; hence, a substantial nexus exists between the taxed activity and the state. The tax is fairly apportioned because it is a percentage of the service fee that the company sets for its purely local activity (in other words, it is severable from any effect it might have on interstate commerce). Finally, the company's use of the state's transportation network (*e.g.*, roads and airport) in operating its business indicates that the transaction tax fairly relates to the services provided by the state. Therefore, this tax is valid. (A) is wrong because whether the packages have entered the stream of commerce is relevant only to an ad valorem property tax on the packages themselves. A tax on the packages, if they were already in the stream of commerce, would be invalid. Here the tax is on the service of transporting the packages,

and so a different test (*see* above) applies. (C) is wrong for a similar reason. The status of the packages in interstate commerce is not the critical factor for evaluating a tax on the shipping transaction; rather, the factors above are important. (D) is wrong because the tax on the company is being imposed only on its local activity in that state. A similar tax imposed on the company by other states would apply only to the company's local activity in those states; hence, this type of tax does not expose the company to the possibility of multiple taxation.

Answer to Question 16

(D) The best argument against the statute is that it violates the Contracts Clause. The Contracts Clause prohibits states from retroactively and substantially impairing contract rights unless the governmental act serves an important and legitimate government interest and is a reasonable and narrowly tailored means of promoting that interest. Here, the legislation by its terms affects existing contracts. It is arguable that the effect is a substantial impairment, because deeds absolute have been turned into mortgages by the statute. While protecting debtors may be a legitimate government interest, it could be argued that the statute is not narrowly tailored to that interest. It is doubtful that the plaintiffs' attorneys would win on this argument, but it is their best approach. (A) is not a good argument because ex post facto laws are laws that retroactively alter criminal law, and here the law is not criminal, but rather civil. (B) is not a good argument because the law does not violate the Equal Protection Clause. The law does not involve a suspect or quasi-suspect class or a fundamental right, and so its validity would be tested under the rational basis standard. A law that has any legitimate rational basis will be upheld under this standard, and as established above, the law here serves the legitimate government purpose of protecting debtors. Thus, equal protection is not violated. (C) is not a good argument because the Due Process Clause does not prohibit laws that "summarily take" property from a class in general; no individual hearing or other process is required for laws of general applicability. Substantive due process is not violated either; since no fundamental right is involved, the law will be judged under the rational basis standard, and as stated above, will be upheld.

Answer to Question 17

(C) Executive privilege is an inherent privilege necessary to protect the confidentiality of presidential communications. Under this privilege, presidential documents and conversations are presumptively privileged, but this privilege must yield to a demonstrated need for such materials as evidence in a criminal case in which they are relevant and otherwise admissible. [United States v. Nixon (1974)] Although the Supreme Court has not expressly decided that the privilege must also yield to a demonstrated need for evidence in a pending legislative proceeding, such an extension of *Nixon* is likely, and none of the other alternatives is at all accurate. (A) is incorrect because it is too broad. In *Nixon, supra,* the Court decided that an evidentiary subpoena to the President in a criminal case does not violate the separation of powers principle. By extension, a subpoena issued by a Senate subcommittee, pursuant to the well-established implied power of Congress to investigate, would not be deemed to violate separation of powers. (B) is also incorrect because it is too broad. As stated above, although a presumptive privilege applies to presidential documents and conversations, that privilege must yield to a demonstrated need in criminal cases. Thus, executive privilege is not absolute. (D) is incorrect because executive privilege does apply to proceedings by the courts; in fact, the privilege is overridden only on a specific showing of need for specific information.

Answer to Question 18

(B) The loyalty oath is constitutional, but the membership oath is unconstitutional. The First Amendment protects the rights of association and speech. State infringements on these rights must be

justified by a compelling state interest, unrelated to the suppression of ideas. In the area of public employment, neither standards of conduct nor loyalty oaths may be vague or overbroad. Precision is required because of the potential chilling effect on First Amendment rights. Here, the investigator is not applying for public employment, but the state is requiring him to take the oaths to obtain a state license, which involves the same First Amendment issues. The loyalty oath is virtually identical to oaths that have been held to be constitutional. The state has a compelling interest in seeing that both constitutions are upheld and there is nothing vague about the oath. Oaths similar to the membership oath, however, have been struck down as overbroad. The state has a compelling interest only in preventing ***knowing membership*** with the specific intent to ***further unlawful aims***. Persons cannot be denied a license because of mere membership in a particular group, and the state statute here addresses mere membership. Thus, (B) is correct and (A), (C), and (D) are incorrect.

Answer to Question 19

(C) The resident will not prevail because the state decision was based on state law grounds. The Supreme Court will hear a case from a state court only if it turned on federal grounds. If it finds adequate and independent state grounds for the decision, it will refuse jurisdiction. Here, the facts state that the state decision was based on a provision of the state constitution. The fact that the state provision is similar to the federal Equal Protection Clause is irrelevant to determining whether the decision here was based on state law, since the state court did not base its decision on interpretation of the federal provision, but rather interpreted the state provision. Therefore, the Supreme Court will refuse jurisdiction, and the resident will not prevail. (A) is incorrect because the Supremacy Clause renders state laws invalid only if they conflict with federal law or if Congress has preempted the field. Nothing in the facts indicates that Congress has preempted the issue of school funding, and the state decision is not in conflict with the Supreme Court decision here; the Supreme Court held that the federal Equal Protection Clause does not ***require*** equal funding, not that equal funding violates equal protection. Thus, the state court was free to grant its citizens more protection under the state equal protection provision than is granted under the federal provision. (B) is incorrect because res judicata is not a constitutional issue. Moreover, the Supreme Court did not decide whether equal funding was invalid, only that it was not required. (D) is incorrect because the resident has standing. To have standing, a party must have a concrete stake in the outcome of a controversy. This requires an injury in fact caused by the government action that can be remedied by a decision in the litigant's favor. The resident has an injury in fact since his children are being deprived of educational money under the new state statute. This injury could be remedied by a decision in his favor, because if the statute is held invalid, the state would go back to the unequal funding system.

Answer to Question 20

(C) Because the state statute is based on alienage, it is subject to strict scrutiny and, thus, the state has the burden of proof. State laws based on alienage are subject to the strict scrutiny test, except when the law concerns alien participation in the functioning of the state government (and possibly "illegal" alien adults), in which case the rational basis test is applied. Under the strict scrutiny test, the government bears the burden of showing that the law is necessary to a compelling state interest. The state law here does not concern alien participation in the functioning of state government (or illegal aliens), and thus the strict scrutiny test will be used. The state thus has the burden of proof. (A) is wrong because the buyer has standing. A person has standing if he can demonstrate a concrete stake in the outcome of the controversy; *i.e.,* he has been or will be injured by the governmental action and a decision in his favor will remedy the situation. The buyer has standing because he has been injured (the statute directly impairs his right to own a restaurant and thus violates his right to equal protection). A declaratory judgment in his favor will remedy this situation; the buyer will be able to buy a restaurant if the law is declared unconstitutional. Thus, he has standing. (B) is wrong because, as explained above, the burden of proof is on the government and not on the buyer and seller. (B) is also wrong because it implies that the validity of the statute would be determined by the rational basis test. Because the statute here is based on alienage and does not pertain to participation in the functioning of state government, the strict scrutiny standard, rather than the rational basis test, will be applied. (D) is wrong because, as discussed, the strict scrutiny standard applies.

Answer to Question 21

(C) The alien will win because legal aliens fall within the protection of the Equal Protection Clause. The Fourteenth Amendment prevents the states from denying any person within their jurisdiction equal protection of the laws. Legal aliens are "persons" within the meaning of this clause. The state statute subjects the resident alien here to disparate treatment solely on the basis of alien status. Thus, the state has denied the alien equal protection of the laws. (A) is incorrect because the statute does not intrude on any congressional power respecting aliens or foreign affairs. Although Congress has exclusive power over naturalization and denaturalization, as well as plenary power over admission, exclusion, and deportation of aliens, the state statute does not impinge on any of these areas. Neither does the statute concern the conduct of foreign affairs. Thus, the statute does not conflict with or otherwise intrude on any power belonging to Congress. (B) is incorrect because the Article IV Privileges and Immunities Clause does not protect the rights of aliens. This Privileges and Immunities Clause protects "citizens" of states from discrimination by other states. Aliens and corporations are not "citizens" for purposes of this clause. (D) incorrectly implies that the challenger's status as an alien excludes him from any protection under the Constitution. As noted above, legal aliens are protected by the Equal Protection Clause.

Answer to Question 22

(A) The landowner's strongest argument is based on the alien's equal protection rights. Although the state statute directly impairs the equal protection rights of the buyer rather than the seller, here the seller can assert the buyer's rights. A person who challenges the constitutionality of a governmental action must have standing; *i.e.*, she must demonstrate a concrete stake in the outcome of the controversy and that the governmental action at issue impairs her rights. Generally, a claimant must have suffered (or may presently suffer) a direct impairment of her own constitutional rights. However, a plaintiff may assert a third party's rights where the plaintiff has suffered injury and the injury adversely affects her relationship with third parties, resulting in an indirect violation of their rights. Here, the state statute causes injury to the seller by prohibiting her from contracting to sell land to an alien buyer. Such an injury would adversely affect the seller's relationship with aliens by prohibiting her from selling land to them, and would thus indirectly violate their right to equal protection. Consequently, the seller may assert the equal protection rights of aliens. (B) is incorrect because under the Contract Clause, which prohibits states from passing any law impairing the obligation of contracts, there is no impairment unless the law is retroactive. Here, it appears that the statute was in existence when the buyer and seller entered into their contract. Thus, the statute did not unconstitutionally impair that contract. (C) is incorrect because, even if the statute does constitute a direct restraint on the alienation of the seller's property, such a restraint does not rise to the level of a constitutional violation. Thus, an argument based on (C) would not be as strong as the assertion of aliens' equal protection rights, as

found in (A). (D) is incorrect because nothing here indicates that the seller's due process rights have been violated. The procedural due process proscription against the governmental taking of property without due process of law applies to individualized takings—*i.e.,* when the government takes property to which the individual has a legitimate claim. Here, the seller is not complaining about an action against her individually, but rather is complaining about a law of general application. Thus, a procedural due process argument is inapplicable. Substantive due process will not be helpful to the seller either. If a law limits a fundamental right (*i.e.,* voting, privacy, right to travel, or a First Amendment right), the strict scrutiny test is used. However, if a fundamental right is not involved, as here, the rational basis test is used. Under the rational basis test, it is unlikely that the seller can succeed with her claim because she will have the burden of proving that the government has no rational basis for its law. Because under this test almost any basis will support governmental action, this statute is likely to be upheld, and so this is not the seller's best argument.

Answer to Question 23

(B) If the court should find the statute unconstitutional, it will be because the state's safety concerns are outweighed by the burden on interstate commerce. Where a state enacts a law that does not discriminate against interstate commerce, it may still be invalid if the benefits from the law are outweighed by the burdens the law places on interstate commerce. The determination is made on a case-by-case basis, depending on the facts. Here, there is no discrimination against interstate commerce, and the state has shown that tandem trailer trucks are more dangerous than other vehicles and they cause more road damage. However, the owner has shown that the state law makes it expensive to operate his interstate trucks in that state. The court could easily find that the added expense on interstate carriers is not outweighed by the benefits to the state. (Note that the Supreme Court has twice addressed this issue in similar cases [Raymond Motor Transportation, Inc. v. Rice (1978); Kassel v. Consolidated Freightways Corp. (1981)] with a similar result.) (A) is incorrect because it assumes that the states cannot regulate interstate commerce in general or trucks in particular. As indicated above, safety aspects of interstate commerce can be regulated by the states as long as the regulation does not discriminate against or unduly burden interstate commerce. If a state has the power to regulate an aspect of interstate commerce, it has the power to tax it as well, and a tax such as the one here could be valid (*see* (D), below). (C) is incorrect because the Equal Protection Clause is not violated here. Under the Clause, a law that regulates economic interests where no suspect class or fundamental right is involved will be upheld as long as the classification is rationally related to any legitimate governmental interest. Preventing accidents and saving money on road repair are legitimate government interests; so the law here is valid. (D) is incorrect because states can impose use taxes on interstate businesses as long as the activity taxed has a substantial nexus to the taxing state; the tax is fairly apportioned; the tax does not discriminate against interstate commerce; and the tax is fairly related to the services provided by the state. The tax here appears to meet these conditions.

Answer to Question 24

(D) The best argument is that the tax interferes with the plenary power of Congress to regulate federal lands. Article IV, Section 3 of the Constitution gives Congress the power to make all necessary rules and regulations concerning property belonging to the federal government. The owner would argue that this power, when combined with the Supremacy Clause (which makes federal law the supreme law of the land, superseding conflicting state law) would prevent any attempt by a state to tax persons on federal land, absent congressional consent to the tax. In fact, this argument will probably fail because the Court has indicated that while the states may not

directly tax or regulate the federal government, they may indirectly do so by adopting taxes or regulations on persons dealing with the federal government, as long as the tax or regulation does not unduly burden the federal government. The tax here seems to fall into the permissible category; nevertheless, this is the owner's best argument. (A) is not a good argument because the Privileges and Immunities Clause of the Fourteenth Amendment does not protect the right to conduct business on federal lands. The Clause protects a narrow range of privileges of United States citizenship, such as the right to ***enter onto*** federal lands, the right to petition Congress for redress, and the right to vote for federal officers. The Clause does not protect the entire Bill of Rights against infringement, and the owner's right here falls outside the scope of the Clause. (B) is incorrect because the commerce power would not preempt the tax here. Generally, a state may adopt taxes that will affect interstate commerce as long as the tax does not discriminate against interstate commerce (the tax here does not), and (i) there is a substantial nexus between the state and the taxpayer (here, the owner does business on land within the state); (ii) the tax is fairly apportioned (the tax here is fair since it merely equalizes the tax burden on users of land within the state); and (iii) there is a fair relationship between the tax and the benefits provided by the state (this requisite is met because the owner gets the protection of doing business in the state in exchange for the tax). (C) is incorrect because there is no equal protection violation here. The Equal Protection Clause merely prohibits the states from treating similar people in a dissimilar manner without a valid reason. When, as in this case, the law does not involve a suspect or quasi-suspect class or a fundamental right, the law will be upheld as long as there is a rational basis for the discrimination. Here, it is questionable whether the law discriminates, since it is applicable to ***all*** persons using land in the state. Assuming that the law does discriminate on the basis of the location of land, the discrimination is permissible because it is rationally related to a legitimate state purpose (a state may impose taxes to raise revenues but may not impose a tax on land or activities outside of the state).

Answer to Question 25

(D) The state may ban the radar detectors. States may regulate local aspects of interstate commerce as long as the local regulation does not conflict with, or is not preempted by, federal regulation and the regulation meets the following tests: (i) the regulation does not discriminate against out-of-state competition in order to benefit local economic interests, and (ii) the incidental burden on interstate commerce does not outweigh the local benefits of the regulation. In this case, the federal regulations do not conflict with the state ban and are not so comprehensive as to preempt nonconflicting state regulation. With regard to the two-part test, the first standard is met because the regulation is not discriminatory against out-of-state products (because it bans ***all*** radar detectors regardless of origin). The second part is a balancing test, in which the court will consider whether the regulation promotes legitimate state interests and whether less restrictive alternatives are available. Here, the ban clearly promotes the state's legitimate interest in highway safety by making it harder for speeding motorists to evade detection. Anything less than a ban would not be effective in preventing the use of the detectors, and their use makes radar, the state's best means of preventing speeding, much less effective. On balance, the ban's local safety benefits outweigh its burden on interstate commerce and transportation. (A) is incorrect because a field will be held to be preempted only where the federal statute is so comprehensive that Congress impliedly occupied the whole field, and here the federal regulations concern only safety of the devices and use of frequencies. (B) is incorrect because it is too broad—not every law that burdens interstate commerce is unconstitutional. Rather, a balancing test will be applied. (C) is incorrect because it addresses only the preliminary issue. It is not enough that a statute regulating local aspects of interstate commerce does not conflict with federal regulations; even in the absence of any conflicting federal regulations, the statute must meet the tests described above.

Answer to Question 26

(C) The resident will not prevail because the reapportionment plan does not violate the Equal Protection Clause of the Fourteenth Amendment. That provision has been interpreted to prohibit state dilution of the right to vote, so that whenever a governmental body establishes voting districts for the election of representatives, the number of persons in each district may not vary significantly. However, for the purpose of electing representatives to a state or local governmental body, the variance in the number of persons included in each district can be greater than that permitted for congressional districts. If the deviation from mathematical equality between districts is reasonable and tailored to promote a legitimate state interest, the law establishing the districts will likely be upheld. The Court has held that maintaining the integrity of local political subdivision lines when establishing legislative districts is a legitimate state interest, as long as the final apportionment is substantially based on population. [*See* Mahan v. Howell (1973)—16% variance upheld] Here, the reapportionment attempted to conform legislative districts as nearly as possible to county borders and had a maximum variance of 12%. Thus, it will probably withstand the resident's challenge. (A) is incorrect because the fact that an alternative plan has a lesser variance between the districts does not make the selected plan invalid. Because it satisfies the less stringent requirements for state and local governmental bodies discussed above, the plan does not violate the Equal Protection Clause. (B) is incorrect because race can be considered in drawing up new voting districts, even though it cannot be the predominant factor. If a plaintiff can show that a redistricting plan was drawn up predominantly on the basis of racial considerations (as opposed to the more traditional factors, such as compactness, contiguity, and community interest), the plan will violate the Equal Protection Clause unless the government can show that the plan is narrowly tailored to serve a compelling government interest (such as eliminating past discrimination). However, if a legislative redistricting map can be explained in terms other than race, the Court will not find that the law constitutes racial discrimination on its face. In such a case, the person attacking legislative districts as being based on racial classifications would have to show that district lines were drawn predominantly for a racially discriminatory purpose. Here, as discussed above, the state's interest in preserving political subdivisions (counties) is a legitimate government interest, and the resident will be unable to prove that this was not the predominant factor in the reapportionment. (D) is incorrect because the fact that the reapportionment plan reduces the existing population variance among districts does not make it constitutionally valid. The plan must satisfy the equal protection requirements established by the Court in apportionment cases.

Answer to Question 27

(D) The owner's best defense is that the license requirement was superseded by the owner's federal license. The Supremacy Clause makes federal law the supreme law of the land. This means that whenever a valid federal law conflicts with a state law, the state law is inapplicable and the federal law controls. The federal law granting the owner a license here would be valid pursuant to Congress's power to regulate interstate and foreign commerce. In addition to actually regulating such commerce, Congress can adopt any law necessary or proper to implement its power, and providing licenses to vendors to ensure that people can exchange money at the border and its functional equivalents would certainly be within the scope of the broad federal power. Because the city license requirement interferes with the federal licensing scheme, it cannot be enforced against the owner. (A) is incorrect because the owner appears to have had all the process that was due. It may be that the owner had a property interest in his license under the Fourteenth Amendment Due Process Clause in that he could expect to keep the license as long as he performed well. He could not be deprived of his property interest in his license without due process of law, including a hearing. Here, he was given a hearing prior to revocation of his license at which he was allowed to present relevant evidence, and nothing in the facts indicates that the board was biased against the owner. Thus, due process was satisfied. (B) is incorrect because nothing in the facts indicates that the licensing scheme was arbitrary. An arbitrary licensing scheme would violate substantive due process, which requires at a minimum that laws be rational. Note also that this choice is something of a red herring—the "arbitrary and capricious" standard is the standard that courts use in reviewing determinations of fact by administrative agencies that are not "on the record." (C) is incorrect because nothing in the facts indicates that the city's licensing scheme interferes with foreign or interstate commerce—nothing in the scheme favors local economic interests over out-of-state or foreign interests, so there is no unlawful discrimination, and the scheme appears to place little if any burden on interstate or foreign commerce.

Answer to Question 28

(B) The legislation here is merely economic in nature and economic legislation will be upheld as long as there is a rational basis for the legislation. The residents would have the burden of proving that there is not a rational basis for the higher premiums here. (A) is incorrect because the compelling interest standard is not used to judge economic legislation, such as that involved here. (C) is incorrect because the market participant rule is an exception to the Commerce Clause ban on state action burdening interstate commerce. Here, the issue is not interstate commerce. Because this is a state-created and -operated company, it will be held to the same equal protection standards as any other arm of the state. The Eleventh Amendment refers to suits in federal court. Thus, (D) is not applicable because the facts indicate that the citizens sued in state court. This does not mean that the state is necessarily subject to the suit, because it might have its own sovereign immunity doctrines. However, even if that were an answer choice, the facts do not indicate to what extent the state has waived its sovereign immunity doctrines.

Answer to Question 29

(C) The state insurance company will prevail unless the citizen can show that the company charges Mexican-American citizens higher rates than other citizens of that city who are similarly situated. The mere fact that legislation or governmental action has a discriminatory effect is not sufficient to trigger strict scrutiny. There must be intent to discriminate on the part of the government, which can be shown by the discriminatory application of a law or regulation that appears neutral on its face. If the state insurance company is charging the city's Mexican-American citizens higher rates than citizens who are otherwise situated the same, the court will find that there is an intent to discriminate in the rate-setting process, triggering strict scrutiny because a suspect class is involved. (A) is incorrect because, as stated above, the citizens must show more than a discriminatory effect to prevail. The classification will be subject to strict scrutiny only if an intent to discriminate is established, which can be shown by (i) facial discrimination, (ii) discriminatory application, or (iii) discriminatory motive. (B) is incorrect. If the strict scrutiny standard applied, proof of a compelling interest would be required to uphold the discriminatory classification. However, as discussed, strict scrutiny will be triggered only if an intent to discriminate is shown; a discriminatory effect is not sufficient. (D) is incorrect because government actions or regulations that improperly discriminate against a suspect class may violate equal protection even if they are "economic" in nature.

Answer to Question 30

(C) The organization must prove that the legislation was motivated by a desire to inhibit the accomplishment of the organization's religious objectives. The Free Exercise Clause cannot be used to

challenge a law of general applicability unless it can be shown that the law was motivated by a desire to interfere with religion. [Employment Division v. Smith (1990)] Thus, states may regulate conduct even if the regulation happens to interfere with a person's religious practices, as long as that was not the purpose of the legislation. (A) is incorrect because the burden of proof is on the organization, as the party challenging the law, to show that it was motivated by improper considerations. Even if the rational basis test were applied, the burden of proof would be on the organization rather than the government. (B) is incorrect because it states the test for upholding a law that was designed to suppress conduct solely because it was religiously motivated. Such a law would be justified only if the government could show that it was necessary to further a compelling interest. (D) is incorrect because the rational basis test is not applied to a Free Exercise Clause challenge to a law regulating general conduct. As discussed above, the challenger must show that the legislation was motivated by a desire to interfere with religion.

Answer to Question 31

(B) A Fourteenth Amendment equal protection defense would be least helpful to the citizen. If a law treats a person or class of persons differently than others, it is an equal protection question. Here, the statute on its face does not treat different classes of persons differently, and there is nothing in the facts to suggest that the law, although infrequently enforced, has been applied to the citizen in a discriminatory manner. Hence, an equal protection argument would be weak. (A) is incorrect because it is presumptively unconstitutional for the government to place burdens on speech because of its content. To prevail, the government would have to show that the statute was necessary to serve a compelling state interest and narrowly drawn to achieve that end. Thus, free speech rights would provide an effective challenge to the statute. (C) is incorrect because the citizen could argue that the statute violates the Establishment Clause. A statute will be valid under that provision only if it (i) has a secular purpose, (ii) has a primary effect that neither advances nor inhibits religion, and (iii) does not produce excessive government entanglement with religion. The citizen can argue that a statute prohibiting the utterance of "blasphemy" and "sacrilege" violates that rule. (D) is incorrect because the citizen has a strong argument that the statute violates the Due Process Clause. If a criminal law or regulation fails to give reasonable notice as to what is prohibited, it violates the Due Process Clause. This principle is applied strictly when First Amendment activity is involved to avoid the chilling effect that a vague law might have on freedom of speech. Here, the citizen can defend by asserting that the statute does not define the prohibited speech except in the most general terms, and therefore the statute is unconstitutionally vague.

Answer to Question 32

(C) The statute is not unconstitutional. True threats are not protected by the First Amendment. Moreover, content-based restrictions on speech are permitted in cases where the speech creates a clear and present danger of imminent lawless action. A state can forbid advocating the use of force or of law violation if such advocacy (i) is directed to producing or inciting imminent lawless action, and (ii) is likely to produce or incite such action. Thus, a statute proscribing threats to the life or safety of a public official, such as the statute here, is valid. However, it cannot constitutionally be applied to the victim's father. It is doubtful that the father's words will be interpreted as a true threat of immediate harm. In context, the speech seems to be more a political commentary, which would be protected by the First Amendment. The father appeared to be merely venting his outrage. There was no indication that the father's words were inciting imminent lawless action or were likely to produce such action. It does not appear that the father was actually threatening the justices with harm or inciting anyone to storm into the court building.

Thus, his speech was protected and (B) is incorrect. (A) is incorrect because the father cannot constitutionally be punished for the reasons stated above. Moreover, whether the justices actually heard the threats would be irrelevant if the threats were otherwise punishable. (D) is incorrect because the statute is valid on its face, as discussed above.

Answer to Question 33

(D) The citizen will have to show that the statute was not reasonably related to a legitimate government purpose. Other than streets, sidewalks, parks, and designated public forums, most public property (including a court building and its grounds) is considered to be a nonpublic forum. The government can regulate speech in such a forum to reserve the forum for its intended use. Regulations will be upheld as long as they are (i) viewpoint neutral, and (ii) reasonably related to a legitimate government purpose. Here, the statute prohibited public gatherings on the steps of the courthouse at specified times while the court was in session, which appears to be a reasonable, viewpoint neutral effort to preserve government property for its intended use. The citizen would have the burden of proving that there was no reasonable basis for the statute. (A) and (C) are incorrect because the strict scrutiny standard enunciated in those choices applies only to content-based restrictions, and here the statute was not content-based. (B) is incorrect because it states the test for restrictions on speech in public forums. Unlike sidewalks and parks, a courthouse building and grounds are not a public forum even if they are open to the public during specified times.

Answer to Question 34

(D) The trial judge will most likely deny the motion to dismiss the indictment. The Fifth Amendment right to be free of double jeopardy for the same offense applies to subsequent criminal actions, but not to civil actions or impeachment proceedings, which are distinct from criminal proceedings. Article I, Section 3 of the Constitution specifically states that a conviction by impeachment does not prevent the party convicted from being subject to indictment, trial, judgment, and punishment according to the law. Hence, (B) is incorrect. (A) is incorrect because there is nothing in the facts to show that the Attorney General was not acting within his prosecutorial discretion even if he was complying with the wishes of the President. (C) is incorrect because the fact that the grand jury issued the indictment is irrelevant. If double jeopardy did apply or if the Attorney General had abandoned his prosecutorial discretion in instituting criminal proceedings, the fact that the grand jury issued an indictment would not prevent the indictment from being dismissed.

Answer to Question 35

(C) The court should find the resolution invalid. While Congress has broad power to delegate, the separation of powers doctrine forbids Congress from trying to control the exercise of the power delegated in various ways, such as by overturning an executive agency action without bicameralism (*i.e.*, passage by both houses of Congress). By enacting the federal law allowing the administrative law judge to enter a final order with regard to aliens, Congress has given up any control it may have had previously in these situations. The resolution by the House here is an unconstitutional legislative veto that violates the separation of powers doctrine. (A) is incorrect because, while Congress does have plenary power over aliens with regard to immigration and naturalization, here it has given up control over this area by enacting a law allowing an administrative officer appointed by the executive branch to make a final order concerning whether an alien should be deported. (B) is incorrect because the fact that aliens are not citizens has no bearing on

whether the House resolution violated the Constitution. (D) is incorrect because, while resident aliens are entitled to notice and hearing before they can be deported, the student did receive a hearing before the administrative officer. There is no requirement that persons affected by legislative action have the right to be heard by the legislative body taking the action. Thus, the better argument as to why the resolution was invalid is based on separation of powers.

Answer to Question 36

(B) The conviction is unconstitutional because of lack of jurisdiction. Court martial of a civilian generally is prohibited as long as actual warfare has not shut down the civilian courts. The employee is a civilian and nothing in the facts indicates that warfare has shut down the civilian courts. (A) is incorrect. Under the Eighth Amendment, a sentence cannot be grossly disproportionate to the crime committed. Twenty years' hard labor probably would not be considered grossly disproportionate to the crime of espionage, as the death penalty has commonly been used to punish espionage, and hard labor is a less drastic measure than that. (C) and (D) are incorrect because, as discussed above, the court lacked jurisdiction to impose any sentence.

Contracts

Question Sets and Analytical Answers

Set 1 Answer Sheet

1. Ⓐ Ⓑ Ⓒ Ⓓ
2. Ⓐ Ⓑ Ⓒ Ⓓ
3. Ⓐ Ⓑ Ⓒ Ⓓ
4. Ⓐ Ⓑ Ⓒ Ⓓ
5. Ⓐ Ⓑ Ⓒ Ⓓ
6. Ⓐ Ⓑ Ⓒ Ⓓ
7. Ⓐ Ⓑ Ⓒ Ⓓ
8. Ⓐ Ⓑ Ⓒ Ⓓ
9. Ⓐ Ⓑ Ⓒ Ⓓ
10. Ⓐ Ⓑ Ⓒ Ⓓ
11. Ⓐ Ⓑ Ⓒ Ⓓ
12. Ⓐ Ⓑ Ⓒ Ⓓ
13. Ⓐ Ⓑ Ⓒ Ⓓ
14. Ⓐ Ⓑ Ⓒ Ⓓ
15. Ⓐ Ⓑ Ⓒ Ⓓ
16. Ⓐ Ⓑ Ⓒ Ⓓ
17. Ⓐ Ⓑ Ⓒ Ⓓ
18. Ⓐ Ⓑ Ⓒ Ⓓ

CONTRACTS QUESTIONS - SET 1

Question 1

On December 6, the owner of an electronics store sent a written request to a computer manufacturer asking for the price of a certain laptop computer. The manufacturer sent a written reply with a catalog listing the prices and descriptions of all of his available computers. The letter stated that the terms of sale were cash within 30 days of delivery. On December 14, by return letter, the store owner ordered the computer, enclosing a check for $4,000, the listed price. Immediately on receipt of the order and check, the manufacturer informed the store owner that there had been a pricing mistake in the catalog, which should have quoted the price as $4,300 for that computer.

The store owner refuses to pay the additional $300, arguing that his order of December 14 in which the $4,000 check was enclosed was a proper acceptance to the manufacturer's offer. In a suit for damages, will the manufacturer prevail?

(A) Yes, because his first communication stated terms calling for cash within 30 days of delivery.

(B) Yes, because of the mistake as to price.

(C) Yes, because his first communication did not constitute an offer.

(D) No, because the store owner's December 14 letter was a proper acceptance to the manufacturer's offer.

Question 2

A wholesale seller of turquoise received a fax from a retail seller of Indian jewelry, a long-time customer, which read: "Send 200 16-inch strands of Kingman turquoise beads at your usual price of $45 per strand." The wholesaler faxed the customer back a confirmation, promising to ship the strands within 10 days. However, the wholesaler currently had no strands in stock and so began making phone calls to locate them in sufficient quantity. Ultimately, he secured the strands of beads. However, before he could ship the beads to the retailer, he received another fax from the retailer canceling the order without explanation. The wholesaler immediately set out to find another buyer for the beads, but found that Kingman turquoise had fallen out of favor. Consequently, the wholesaler was forced to sell the strands of beads at a "salvage" price of $4,000.

If the wholesaler sues the retailer for damages, how much should he receive?

(A) Nothing, because this was a contract between merchants and the retailer canceled within a reasonable time.

(B) The full contract price of $9,000 (because the retailer breached the contract and the price was fair), plus the wholesaler's incidental expenses.

(C) The full contract price plus incidentals, less the $4,000 salvage price.

(D) The full contract price, less the $4,000 salvage price.

Question 3

In March, a homeowner contracts with a buyer to sell his house for $280,000, with the purchase price to be paid and the deed to be delivered on July 1. On May 1, the buyer writes the homeowner a letter, stating that she has had second thoughts about buying the house, and she "won't pay that amount of money unless you repaint the house and fix up the yard."

If the homeowner wishes to treat the contract as breached:

(A) He may sue the buyer upon receipt of the letter.

(B) He must wait until July 1 to sue the buyer, the date on which the purchase price is to be paid.

(C) He must make a written demand to the buyer seeking adequate assurance of performance and wait a reasonable time for a response prior to filing suit.

(D) He cannot sue the buyer because the parties' promises are executory at this stage.

Question 4

In answer to a radio advertisement, a teenager two months shy of his 18th birthday contracted to buy a late model car from a car dealership. The agreement required a $1,500 down payment with the remainder of the $7,200 price to be paid in monthly installments to a local finance company. The teenager's first eight payments were made regularly until his driver's license was suspended. He then informed the company that no further payments would be forthcoming.

The finance company sues for the remaining payments. The age of majority in the teenager's state is 18 years. Would the teenager be liable for the balance of the payments?

(A) Yes, because the car dealership was liable on the contract from the outset, notwithstanding his minority.

(B) Yes, because he kept the car for six months after reaching the age of majority.

(C) No, because he was a minor at the time of contracting, and the contract was voidable by him.

(D) No, because he informed the finance company in a timely manner after his driver's license was suspended.

Question 5

On April 10, the owner of a small farm mailed a letter to a newcomer to the area who had expressed an interest in buying the farm. In this letter, the farm owner offered to sell the farm to the newcomer for $100,000. The offer expressly stated that the offer expires on June 1, "if acceptance by the offeree has not been received by the offeror on or before that date."

On the morning of June 1, the newcomer sent a written acceptance to the farm owner by messenger. However, through negligence of the messenger company, the acceptance was not delivered to the farm owner until June 2. On June 4, the farm owner entered into a contract to sell the farm to another buyer for more money but did not inform the newcomer of the transaction. When the newcomer followed up by phone on June 10, the farm owner told him that he had sold the farm to another buyer.

Which of the following is the most correct statement?

(A) No contract between the farm owner and the newcomer arose on June 2.

(B) An enforceable contract arose on June 1.

(C) The farm owner's silence constituted an acceptance of the newcomer's message on June 2.

(D) A voidable contract arose on June 1.

Question 6

A builder contracted to build a house for a newly married couple. Terms of the contract provided that the builder would receive the contract price when the building was fully completed. Just when the builder had completed one-half of the structure, a tornado struck the area and demolished the building.

What is the builder entitled to recover from the couple under the contract?

(A) Nothing.

(B) One-half of the contract price.

(C) One-half of the fair market value of what remains of the house.

(D) Cost of materials and reasonable labor costs.

Question 7

A wholesale seller sent a fax to a manufacturer with whom he had done business before: "Send 500 'Madewell' chairs at your usual price." The manufacturer responded, also by fax, that the line was being discontinued, but he would ship his last 500 chairs at $75 per chair, his usual price. The manufacturer immediately began the paperwork for processing the order and started preparing and packing the chairs for shipment. Before the chairs could be delivered, the wholesaler canceled his order, noting that the price was too high. The day after receiving the wholesaler's cancellation, the manufacturer sold the chairs to another buyer for $75 each.

If the manufacturer sues the wholesaler for damages, how much should he recover?

(A) Nothing, because this was a contract between merchants and the wholesaler canceled within a reasonable time.

(B) Nothing, because the manufacturer was able to cover by selling the chairs at the same price he would have received from the wholesaler.

(C) $37,500, the full contract price, because the wholesaler breached the contract and $75 per chair was a fair price.

(D) The incidental costs of preparing the paperwork and other office costs connected with preparing and packing the chairs for shipment to the wholesaler.

Question 8

A park board in a large suburb announced that it was accepting bids for renovation work on its recreation center. A builder advertised for sub-bids for the electrical work, and a local electrician submitted to the builder by electronic bidding service a sub-bid of $130,000. However, due to the bidding service's negligence, the sub-bid that the builder received from the electrician read $30,000 instead of $130,000. Because this was the lowest sub-bid that the builder received for the electrical work, and $60,000 less than the next lowest sub-bid, the builder awarded the subcontract to the electrician. Based in part on the electrician's sub-bid, the builder came up with a bid for the job that beat out all of the competition and won the job.

The electrician's best argument to successfully refuse to perform the resulting contract is:

(A) The contract would be unconscionable.

(B) The great difference between the $30,000 figure and the next lowest bid should have alerted the builder to the existence of a mistake in the sub-bid.

(C) The electrician was not responsible for the negligence of the bidding service.

(D) The builder's own negligence in not checking out all sub-bids precludes enforcement of the contract.

Question 9

A corporation whose subsidiaries include a major hotel chain planned to build a new hotel and advertised for bids to build the hotel within the next six months. Four bids were received, for $17 million, $17.2 million, $17.4 million, and $15 million. The corporation's chief financial officer reviewed the bids, then emphatically told the corporation's chief executive officer ("CEO") that there was "no way" the low bidder could make a profit on the $15 million bid. The CEO made no response.

In fact, the builder had stayed up for 72 hours without sleep preparing the bid for the hotel project and had neglected to include the plumbing expenses in the bid. Typically, the cost of plumbing, including the shop's profit, would have been about $2 million.

Shortly after the $15 million contract was signed by the CEO and the builder, the builder discovered his mistake and telephoned the CEO to tell her that he had forgotten to include the cost of plumbing, adding that he would normally charge $2 million for plumbing. The CEO agreed to pay the additional $2 million, but this arrangement was never reduced to writing.

After the builder completes the project on time, the CEO sends him a check for only $15 million. Can the builder compel the CEO to tender the additional $2 million?

(A) Yes, because the CEO was on notice of the builder's mistake.

(B) Yes, but only if there was additional consideration for the agreement to pay the additional $2 million.

(C) No, because the builder had a preexisting legal duty to complete the project for $15 million.

(D) No, because evidence of the agreement to pay the additional $2 million is barred by the parol evidence rule.

Question 10

A music promoter planned to open a discotheque and bar on the outskirts of town. He hired a builder to build it, with a completion date of September 15. Although the promoter was very optimistic that the disco would be a big success, its profitability could not be determined with certainty. First year profits were estimated to be about $1,000 per day. To encourage the builder to work in a timely manner, the contract included a liquidated damages clause, providing that the builder would pay the promoter $10,000 per day for each day the contract ran over its completion date. The builder's work progressed smoothly and would have been finished on time, except that the builder failed to place in a timely manner his order for the disco's specially manufactured dance floor lighting. Consequently, the work was not completed until October 15.

The promoter sues the builder for breach of contract. The builder calls a witness who testifies that the disco would have received $30,000 in income during that 30-day period and would have expended $20,000, leaving a profit of $10,000. How much should the builder be required to pay to the promoter in damages?

(A) $10,000, representing the disco's lost profits.

(B) $30,000, representing the disco's lost income.

(C) $300,000, representing damages provided in the contract.

(D) $310,000, representing damages provided in the contract, plus lost profits.

Question 11

The owner of an apartment building contracted with a painter to paint the porches of the apartments for $5,000. The contract was specifically made subject to the owner's good faith approval of the work. The painter finished painting the porches. The owner inspected the porches and believed in good faith that the painter had done a bad job. The painter demanded payment, but the owner told him that the paint job was poor and refused to pay. The painter pleaded that he was desperately in need of money. The owner told the painter that she would pay him $4,500, provided he repainted the porches. The painter reluctantly agreed, and the owner gave the painter a check in the amount of $4,500. The painter went to his bank, indorsed the check "under protest" and signed his name, then deposited the check in his account. He never returned to repaint the porches.

The painter sues the owner for $500, which he believes is still owed to him on his contract to paint the porches. Will he prevail?

(A) Yes, because he indorsed the check "under protest."

(B) Yes, but only if he repaints the porches.

(C) Yes, because he performed the contract by painting the porches the first time.

(D) No, even if he repaints the porches.

Question 12

A homeowner contracted with a local builder to build a wooden deck onto the back of her house. The contract called for half of the contract price of $20,000 to be paid to the contractor before he began work and the other half to be paid to him when the job was completed. The contractor began the work, and partway through the job, he got an offer for a rush job that paid better and abruptly quit.

The homeowner sues the contractor for specific performance. Will she prevail?

(A) Yes, because there has been a novation.

(B) Yes, because the contract between the parties was valid and the contractor had no legal justification for abruptly quitting.

(C) No, because by not paying the contractor for the second half of the job, the homeowner has not satisfied all of her conditions under the contract.

(D) No, because the contract is for personal services.

Question 13

On February 4, a newspaper printed an advertisement from an auto repair shop, which stated that, on September 5 only, anyone ordering a complete four-cylinder engine tune-up at the regular price of $249.95 (plus parts and lubricants) would receive, without charge, his or her choice of either a commemorative gold coin containing the likeness of the U.S. President or a set of baking pans. Because the coins were in short supply generally, and the President was immensely popular, the repair shop was inundated with tune-up customers on February 5, and they all wanted the coin. By 3:15 p.m. the shop had exhausted its entire supply of coins. At 3:17 p.m., a customer pulled her car into the shop's service bays, jumped out, and told the mechanic on duty that she wanted a complete four-cylinder engine tune-up plus the presidential gold coin. The mechanic, knowing that no more coins were available, briefly tried to talk the customer into taking the baking pans, which proved unavailing. He then looked quickly under her hood, pronounced her engine "in tip-top condition," and told her that her car did not need a tune-up. Finally, when she insisted that her car had been burning a quart of oil a week and frequently lost power going downhill, the mechanic stated that there was not enough time left before closing to complete the tune-up, and that she should try a car dealership shop down the street. In fact, it would have taken about four hours to complete a tune-up on the customer's car, and the shop closed at 5 p.m. that day, its regular closing time. The customer drove home without a tune-up and without the presidential coin.

The coin increased greatly in value, and the customer brought a breach of contract action against the shop. What is the shop's strongest defense?

(A) A tune-up of the customer's car could not have been completed in the time available before the shop closed.

(B) The advertisement in the newspaper was merely an invitation to offer, and the shop had the right to refuse to accept any offer made.

(C) Because the customer never expressly tendered payment of the $249.95, there was no acceptance of the shop's offer.

(D) The customer's unwillingness to accept the baking pans indicated lack of good faith on her part.

Question 14

A general contractor who wished to bid on a construction project solicited bids from a variety of subcontractors. Four electrical subcontractors submitted bids to the contractor in the amounts of $75,000, $85,000, $90,000, and $95,000, respectively.

As he was making out his company's bid, which was higher than he wanted it to be, the contractor called the low bidder on the electrical work and told him, "We won't be able to do it with your present bid, but if you can shave off $5,000, I'm sure that the numbers will be there for us to get that project." The low bidder told the contractor that he could not lower his bid, adding that the bid he submitted was based on a $15,000 error, and he could not do the job for less than $90,000. The contractor lost the construction job and subsequently sued the low bidder.

The low bidder is liable for:

(A) Breach of contract, because the mistake was not so unreasonably obvious as to make acceptance of his bid unconscionable.

(B) Breach of contract, because the mistake was unilateral.

(C) Nothing, because the low bidder rejected the contractor's counteroffer.

(D) Nothing, because even though the low bidder lacked authority to renege on its bid, the contractor suffered no damages because no bidder was willing to do the work for $70,000.

Question 15

A business owner hired a private detective to find an employee who had disappeared without a trace after leaving the workplace one afternoon with $40,000 in cash that the business owner had asked her to deposit at a local bank. The detective presented the business owner with a standard contract providing that the business owner pay him $10,000 upfront and another $10,000 when he found the employee, or in three months from the date the contract was signed, whichever came first. The business owner agreed in writing to those terms and paid the detective the first $10,000, and the detective began his search for the employee. Shortly thereafter, the detective told the business owner that when the balance of payment came due to give the money to his son. The son was not aware of the business dealings between the detective and the business owner, or that the detective made this statement to the business owner. Right before the three months were up, the detective changed his mind and told the business owner to pay him (the detective) directly.

If the son subsequently discovers the above facts, against whom, if anyone, may he enforce the agreement to pay him $10,000?

(A) The business owner.

(B) The detective.

(C) Either the business owner or the detective.

(D) Neither the business owner nor the detective.

Question 16

A homeowner hired a contractor to make some improvements on his house. They entered into a written contract providing that the contractor would do the improvements for $5,000. Shortly after the contract was signed, the contractor told the homeowner to give the money to his (the contractor's) daughter when the job was finished, adding, "She is getting married soon and I want her to have a nice wedding present from me." The daughter was aware that her father made this statement to the homeowner. She married, but soon thereafter the contractor told the homeowner to pay him the $5,000, and not the daughter, because his son-in-law had a gambling problem and would probably use the money to bet at the racetrack.

What is the best argument in favor of the daughter's being able to enforce a contract for $5,000 in her favor?

(A) Statute of Frauds.

(B) Parol evidence rule.

(C) The daughter was an intended third-party beneficiary.

(D) The daughter married in reliance on a promise.

Question 17

A college student was interested in renting a particular apartment because of its very distinctive features, but she was also considering a number of other options. Because she wanted some time to make up her mind, she contacted the building's rental agent and asked him to reserve her right to rent the particular apartment. They made the following written agreement:

> Upon payment of $200, the student shall have the right to inform the agent that she wishes to rent the apartment any time on or before July 1. If she fails to notify the agent that she wants the apartment on or before July 1, the agent shall keep the $200. However, if she does notify the agent on or before July 1 that she desires the apartment, the agent will apply the $200 to her first month's rent.

The student paid the agent $200.

On June 9, the agent rented the apartment to a third party who was unaware of the agent's agreement with the student. On July 1, the student told the agent that she wanted the apartment. He refused to rent it to her and returned her $200.

The student wants the court to compel the agent to rent her the apartment. The court determines that the agent has breached his agreement with the student. Would it be appropriate for the court to order the agent to rent the apartment to the student?

(A) Yes, because the agent should not have rented the apartment to the third party before July 2.

(B) Yes, because the student's harm cannot be remedied with money damages.

(C) No, because the contract was unconscionable.

(D) No, because the student's right to specific performance was cut off by the lease to the third party.

Question 18

The proprietor of a food brokerage entered into oral negotiations with a manufacturer of gourmet food products for restaurants and select retail outlets. The proprietor wished to secure an exclusive distributorship for the manufacturer's products in the six New England states. At the end of the first stage of oral negotiations, the parties had come to an agreement on the major points, and only a few minor points of disagreement remained. Both, however, were anxious to begin distribution of the food products in New England, and the manufacturer assured the proprietor, "Don't worry about it; we'll work these things out." Assuming from this that he would be the New England distributor for the food products, the proprietor leased larger facilities, bought a number of trucks, and hired new workers. Shortly thereafter, the manufacturer informed the proprietor that another distributor, and not the proprietor, would receive the New England distributorship.

If the proprietor prevails in a suit against the manufacturer, it will most likely be because the court applies which of the following theories?

(A) Implied-in-fact contract.

(B) Promissory estoppel.

(C) Unjust enrichment.

(D) Quasi-contract.

CONTRACTS ANSWERS - SET 1

Answer to Question 1

(D) The store owner's December 14 letter was an acceptance. Whether the letter was an acceptance depends on whether the manufacturer's letter was an offer, because an acceptance is a manifestation of assent to an offer. For a communication to be an offer, it must create a reasonable expectation in the offeree that the offeror is willing to enter into a contract on the basis of the offered terms. There must be a promise, undertaking, or commitment to enter into a contract with certain and definite terms. Courts usually hold that if a statement is made broadly, such as in an advertisement or catalog, it will not constitute an offer because it is not reasonable to expect that the sender intended to make offers to all who received the advertisement; rather, the courts usually find such advertisements to be invitations seeking offers. However, the courts will look to the surrounding circumstances, and here a court would probably determine that the catalog that the manufacturer sent ***was*** an offer because it was sent in response to the store owner's specific inquiries about prices on a specific computer and it included delivery terms and conditions of sale. (A) is incorrect because although the letter called for payment in cash, tender by check is sufficient unless the seller demands legal tender and gives the buyer time to obtain cash. Moreover, because the contract called for payment within 30 days of delivery, even if the check was not sufficient, the store owner still had time under the contract to obtain cash. (B) is incorrect because the mistake was unilateral. Generally, a unilateral mistake will not be grounds to rescind a contract unless the nonmistaken party knew or should have known of the mistake. Here, nothing in the facts indicates that the store owner knew of the mistake, and the mistake was not so large that it could be said that he should have known of it. (C) is incorrect because, as explained above, the manufacturer's catalog was sent in response to the store owner's request for information and his terms for sale constituted an offer.

Answer to Question 2

(C) The wholesaler is entitled to recover the incidental damages plus the difference between the contract price and the salvage price. When a buyer breaches a contract to purchase by repudiating his offer, the seller is entitled to recover incidental damages plus either the difference between the contract price and the market price or the difference between the contract price and the resale price, less expenses saved as a result of the breach. Because the wholesaler chose to resell the strands of beads, his damages would be the difference between the resale (salvage) price and the contract price, plus incidental damages. Thus, the wholesaler can recover $9,000 less $4,000, plus incidental damages. (A) is incorrect because there is nothing in the U.C.C., which governs this contract, that makes contracts between merchants cancelable within a reasonable time. (B) is incorrect because the U.C.C. remedy gives the seller the ***difference*** between the contract price and the resale price, not just the contract price. (D) is incorrect because it fails to account for the wholesaler's incidental damages.

Answer to Question 3

(A) The homeowner may sue the buyer when he receives the letter because an anticipatory breach situation exists. Anticipatory repudiation occurs where a promisor, prior to the time set for performance of her promise, indicates that she will not perform when the time comes. Anticipatory repudiation serves to excuse conditions if: (i) there is an executory bilateral contract with ***executory duties on both sides***; and (ii) the words or conduct of the promisor ***unequivocally*** indicates that she cannot or will not perform when the time comes. The requirements for anticipatory

repudiation are met here because the homeowner's duty to deliver the deed and the buyer's duty to pay have yet to be performed, and the buyer's writing unequivocally states that she will not pay unless the homeowner performs extra tasks. In the case of anticipatory repudiation, the nonrepudiating party has the option to treat the contract as being breached and sue immediately. Therefore, the homeowner may sue the buyer upon receipt of the letter. (B) is incorrect because, as stated above, the homeowner may sue upon receipt of the letter because of the buyer's anticipatory repudiation. The doctrine of anticipatory repudiation would not apply if both sides did not have executory duties to perform. In such a case, the nonrepudiator must wait to sue until the time originally set for performance by the repudiating party. However, as discussed above, the homeowner's duty was still executory at the moment of the buyer's repudiation. Therefore, the homeowner does not have to wait until July 1 to sue the buyer for breach. (C) is incorrect because seeking adequate assurances of the buyer's intent to perform is not necessary when the repudiating party has stated unequivocally that she will not perform. A party may in writing demand adequate assurance of due performance if "reasonable grounds for insecurity arise with respect to the performance of" the other party, after which the nonrepudiating party can treat the contract as repudiated if those assurances are not given within a reasonable time. However, here, it is clear from the buyer's writing that she is unwilling to perform and, therefore, the homeowner need not seek assurances of an intent to perform. (D) is incorrect because the homeowner can sue the buyer immediately ***because*** their promises are still executory. As discussed above, the doctrine of anticipatory repudiation is applicable only if there are executory duties on both sides. Here, the homeowner's duty to deliver a deed and the buyer's duty to pay are both executory, so the doctrine applies and the homeowner can sue the buyer now.

Answer to Question 4

(B) The court should rule that the teenager affirmed the contract and, thus, should be liable for the balance of the payments. Although infants generally lack capacity to enter into a contract that is binding on themselves, an infant may affirm, *i.e.*, choose to be bound by his contract, upon reaching majority. Affirmance may be either express or by conduct, *e.g.*, failing to disaffirm the contract within a ***reasonable time*** after reaching majority. Disaffirmance discharges all liability. Here, the teenager continued making payments on the car six months after reaching his 18th birthday, and did not disaffirm the contract. Thus, the court should hold that he affirmed the contract and was liable for the unpaid balance. (A) is incorrect because, although it is true that the car dealership was liable on the contract from the outset, that liability did not extend to the infant. A contract entered into between an infant and an adult is voidable by the infant but binding on the adult. (C) is incorrect because, although the teenager could have voided the contract while still a minor, he did not do so and, once he reached the age of 18, was left only with the option of disaffirming the contract within a reasonable time after reaching majority, which he also failed to do. Thus, his minor status at the time of contracting, without more, would not allow him to escape liability for the payments. (D) is incorrect because timely notice of a breach of contract does not mitigate the effects of his liability for the breach, and the teenager's affirmance of the contract, as discussed above, renders him liable for the unpaid balance.

Answer to Question 5

(A) No contract arose on June 2 because the farm owner's offer expired on June 1, when the farm owner did not receive the newcomer's acceptance. If a period of acceptance is stated in an offer, the offeree must accept within that period to create a contract. Failure to timely accept terminates the power of acceptance in the offeree (*i.e.*, a late acceptance will not be effective and will not create a contract). Under the mailbox rule, an acceptance generally is effective upon dispatch (*i.e.*, the acceptance creates a contract at the moment it is mailed or given to the delivery company). However, the mailbox rule does not apply where the offer states that acceptance will not be effective until received. In the latter case, acceptance is effective only upon receipt. Here, the farm owner's offer specifically stated that the acceptance must be received by June 1 to be effective. Thus, the farm owner opted out of the mailbox rule and no contract was created by delivery of the acceptance on June 2. Note that the newcomer will not be able to successfully argue that the acceptance was valid because the late delivery was the messenger company's fault. This would be a valid argument if the mailbox rule applied here, because the acceptance would have been effective on June 1, when the message was given to the messenger company. However, by opting out of the mailbox rule, the farm owner put the burden of any negligence in delivery on the newcomer. Thus, there was no valid acceptance. (B) is incorrect because of the requirement that acceptance be ***received*** by June 1. This requirement obviates the mailbox rule, so that the mere mailing of a letter (or sending of a message) does not operate as an effective acceptance. (C) is incorrect because the farm owner was not obligated to respond in any way to the message received on June 2. Once the specified time passed without receipt of acceptance, the offer (as well as the newcomer's power of acceptance) was terminated. Thus, receipt of the message on June 2 created neither a contract nor an obligation on the part of the agent to respond to the message. (D) is incorrect because no contract, voidable or otherwise, arose on June 1. As explained above, there could be no contract because acceptance of the offer was not received as specified by the offer. Also, the facts do not indicate circumstances under which a contract is usually held to be voidable. A voidable contract is a contract that one or both parties may elect to avoid or to ratify (*e.g.*, contracts of infants). The facts of this question provide no basis for concluding that any contract that might have arisen between these parties would be voidable.

Answer to Question 6

(A) The builder will not be able to recover anything from the couple under the contract because he has not performed his duty. Under the parties' contract, the builder's completion of the house was a condition precedent to the couple's duty to pay. The condition precedent was not discharged by the destruction of the work in progress because construction has not been made impossible, but rather merely more costly—the builder can rebuild. Thus, he is not entitled to any recovery. Note, however, that a number of courts will excuse ***timely*** performance because the destruction was not the builder's fault. (B) is incorrect because the contract is not divisible (*i.e.*, it is not divided into an equal number of parts for each side, each part being the quid pro quo of the other); thus, completion of one-half of the house did not entitle the builder to one-half of the price. (C) is incorrect because it is not a correct measure of recovery. As stated above, the builder cannot recover under the contract. However, he could recover under a quasi-contract theory if he determined that he could not perform under the contract by rebuilding. Quasi-contract is a remedy that prevents unjust enrichment by imposing on a recipient of requested goods or services a duty to pay for the benefit received when there is a failed contract or no contractual relationship between the parties. The measure of recovery here would be the fair market value of what remains of the house because that is the benefit conferred—it would not be cut in half merely because the house was only half completed. (D) is an incorrect contract recovery because the builder has not fulfilled the condition precedent to the couple's duty to pay. It is also an incorrect quasi-contract recovery where the claimant has breached his duty to perform, because such recovery is measured by the benefit conferred and not by the costs of conferring the benefit.

Answer to Question 7

(D) The manufacturer will recover only its incidental damages, *i.e.,* the costs of preparing to ship the chairs. An offer calling for shipment of goods, such as the offer here, may be accepted by prompt

shipment with notice or by a promise to ship. Acceptance forms a contract. Here, the manufacturer accepted the wholesaler's offer by promising to ship, and a contract was formed. The wholesaler breached the contract by canceling his order. When a buyer breaches by repudiating his offer, as the wholesaler did here, the seller has a right to recover his incidental damages plus either the difference between the contract price and the market price or the difference between the contract price and the resale price of the goods, reduced in either case by any expenses saved as a result of the breach. Here, the manufacturer made what he would have if the sale with the wholesaler had gone through—there was no difference between the contract price and the resale price. Thus, the manufacturer would be limited to his incidental damages. Lost profits would not be available because the chairs were the last ones that the manufacturer had and would have because the line was being discontinued. Therefore, the manufacturer would not have been able to sell them to another potential buyer. (A) is incorrect because there is no rule under the U.C.C., which governs the contract here, that makes contracts between merchants cancelable within a reasonable time. (B) is incorrect because, as indicated above, the U.C.C. allows the seller to recover incidental damages. (C) is incorrect because the U.C.C. seeks only to put the nonbreaching party in as good a position as it would have been had the other party performed, and here, awarding the manufacturer the full contract price would put him in a better position than performance would have, because it would give him a double recovery for selling the same goods. (The result would be different, however, if the manufacturer had had more chairs to sell, because in that case, the breach would have cost the manufacturer additional sales—*i.e.,* he could have sold to the wholesale seller ***and*** to the second buyer.)

Answer to Question 8

(B) The builder will not be permitted to snap up the electrician's offer because the great difference between the electrician's sub-bid, as transmitted, and the next lowest sub-bid should have alerted the builder to the obvious mistake in the electrician's sub-bid. Where only one of the parties entering into a contract is mistaken about facts relating to the agreement, the unilateral mistake will not prevent formation of a contract unless the nonmistaken party is or had reason to be aware of the mistake made by the other party, in which case the contract is voidable. Here, the difference between the $30,000 figure and the next lowest bid should have alerted the builder to the existence of a mistake, so the electrician should be able to refuse to perform the contract. (A) is incorrect because the concept of unconscionability concerns clauses in a contract that are so one-sided as to be unconscionable under the circumstances existing at the time the contract was formed. The concept is typically applied to one-sided bargains where one of the parties has substantially superior bargaining power and can dictate the terms of the contract to the other party. That is not what happened under the facts here. Rather, there was a unilateral mistake and, as discussed above, the builder should have known of the mistake. (C) is incorrect because, under the prevailing view, where there is a mistake in the transmission of an offer by an intermediary, the offer as transmitted is operative unless the other party knew or should have known of the mistake. Thus, the electrician would not be excused from performance based on the faulty transmission alone. (D) is incorrect because a builder has no duty to check out all bids and, thus, the builder's failure to check out the bids would not, by itself, be grounds for rescission.

Answer to Question 9

(A) The builder will be able to compel the CEO to pay the additional $2 million because the CEO was on notice of the mistake. The builder has the defense of unilateral mistake. Although the general rule is that a contract will not be avoided by a unilateral mistake, there is an exception

where the nonmistaken party either knew or should have known of the mistake. Here the facts clearly indicate that the CEO knew that the builder's bid could not be correct, yet relied on it anyway. Thus, the builder had grounds to avoid the contract. Rather than completely avoid the contract here, the parties agreed to reform it, but they failed to record the reformation in writing. Nevertheless, the court will allow the parties to show the reformed terms because of the mistake. (B) is incorrect because although consideration is usually required to modify a contract, it is not required where the parties are modifying ***merely to correct an error*** in the original contract. Also, it is not even clear that the parties here are modifying their contract; because the mistake would have served to discharge the builder from the contract completely, the reformed contract can be viewed as a new contract, which is enforceable even though it is not in writing because it is not within the Statute of Frauds (a contract to build a building is not within the Statute unless, by its terms, it cannot be performed within a year). (C) is incorrect because the unilateral mistake here was sufficient to discharge the builder from his duties under the contract, so there was no preexisting duty. (If the mistake had not been sufficient to discharge the shop, (C) would be correct because where one is under a preexisting legal duty to perform, performance of that same duty will not be sufficient consideration to support a promise to pay additional sums for the performance.) (D) is incorrect because the parol evidence rule only prevents introduction of oral statements made prior to or contemporaneously with a written contract. Here, the $2 million term, although oral, was agreed upon after the original contract was made; thus, the parol evidence rule would not be a bar.

Answer to Question 10

(A) The promoter will be able to recover $10,000, the disco's lost profits for the 30-day period. The purpose of contract damages is to put the nonbreaching party into as good a position as he would have been had the breaching party fully performed. This would be represented here by the disco's lost profits, which is income ($30,000) minus expenses ($20,000), or $10,000. (B) is incorrect because giving the promoter the $30,000 income would put him in a better position than he would have been in if the builder had performed, because such an award does not take into account the expenses that were saved by the disco not being in operation. (C) is incorrect because a court would not uphold the liquidated damages clause here. A liquidated damages clause is enforceable only if damages were difficult to estimate at the time the contract was formed, and the amount agreed upon is a reasonable forecast of the damages that would result from a breach. Here, the damages may have been difficult to predict when the contract was formed because it was not known just how well a new discotheque would do; however, the amount agreed upon seems to be too high. The facts indicate that a reasonable estimate at the time of the contract was about $1,000 per day, but because the liquidated damages amount ($10,000 per day) is 10 times that amount, it seems that this amount was unreasonable. (D) is incorrect because it seeks to combine the actual damages with the liquidated damages. Even if the liquidated damages clause were enforceable, this answer would still be incorrect because a party may recover either liquidated damages, or if not available, the actual damages, but not both.

Answer to Question 11

(D) The painter will be unable to recover the $500 because he did not satisfy the condition precedent to payment under the contract. A party does not have a duty to perform if a condition precedent to that performance has not been met. Here, the parties made the owner's satisfaction with the painter's paint job a condition precedent to the owner's duty to pay the $5,000. Because the owner was not satisfied with the paint job, her duty to pay the painter never arose. The fact that the owner offered to give the painter $4,500 if he repainted the porches has no effect on this analysis, because the offer constituted a ***new contract***, the owner having been excused from the old one. (A) is wrong because it does not matter whether the painter indorsed under protest. The indorsement will not change the result here because the new contract did not seek to ***discharge*** any contractual duty—the owner was already excused from her duties because the condition precedent was never met. (B) is wrong because the old contract is considered to be at an end due to the painter's breach (a material breach discharges the other party's duty to perform), and under the terms of the new contract, the painter is entitled only to $4,500. The terms of the old contract would have allowed payment of the $500, but the new contract was for $4,500 for repainting. Thus, if the painter repainted, all he would be entitled to is $4,500. (C) is wrong because the painter did not perform his contractual duties. It was his duty to paint to the owner's satisfaction, and the owner was under a duty of good faith. The courts have held such conditions to be valid—not illusory promises—because of the promisor's duty to exercise good faith in assessing satisfaction. Here, the facts state that the owner believed in good faith that the painter had done a bad job; thus, the painter did not perform his contractual duties. For that reason, he is not entitled to the $500.

Answer to Question 12

(D) The homeowner will not prevail in her suit for specific performance because the contract is for personal services. Specific performance is available only where the legal remedy (*i.e.*, money damages) is inadequate. Money damages can be inadequate for a number of reasons, such as where the goods or services sought are unique. Nevertheless, specific performance is not available as a remedy regarding a contract for services. If the services contracted for are not unique, then money damages would be adequate because the nonbreaching party could use the damages to hire someone else to perform. However, even if the services are unique, courts generally will not grant a decree of specific performance to force someone to work because of problems in overseeing performance and because it would be tantamount to involuntary servitude. (A) is wrong because a novation is a substitution of a third party for one of the parties to a contract by agreement of all the parties involved, and nothing in the facts indicates that such a substitution was involved here. Moreover, if a novation were involved, the homeowner would not be able to force the contractor to work because the contractor would have been the party released. (B) is wrong because a valid contract and no legal justification for breaching it do not, by themselves, mean that specific performance is available, as discussed above. (C) is wrong because, under the contract, the homeowner was not required to make the second half of the payment to the contractor until the contractor's work was completed. One of the prerequisites for specific performance is that all of the plaintiff's contractual conditions have been fulfilled. This includes the fulfillment of all conditions precedent and a readiness to perform any conditions concurrent. Here, the homeowner stood ready and able to perform under the contract when the contractor performs, so the homeowner's failure to pay the contractor for the second half of the job would not be a bar to specific performance.

Answer to Question 13

(B) The repair shop's strongest defense is that the advertisement was not an offer, but merely an invitation for offers. Statements of promise, undertaking, or commitment (*i.e.*, offers) must be distinguished from statements of future intent or preliminary negotiations. Advertisements are generally construed to be mere invitations to make offers, although some advertisements may be construed as offers, especially if they are very definite as to terms. Here, the advertisement is fairly specific in its terms and thus it is not easy to tell whether it is an offer or mere invitation for offers. Following the general rule that advertisements are mere invitations, and because none of the other choices provide the shop with a defense, this is the best answer. (A) is wrong because the advertisement, if it is construed as an offer, did not say anything about when the tune-up had to be performed or completed; it merely stated that the tune-up had to be ordered on that day. (C) is wrong because the "offer" called for acceptance by "ordering" the tune-up, not by actual payment or any other performance. (D) is wrong because the customer's refusal to take the baking pans is irrelevant. The "offer" gave her a choice of the baking pans or the presidential coin; she did not have to take the pans.

Answer to Question 14

(C) The low bidder is liable for nothing because no contract was formed between the contractor and the low bidder. Formation of a contract requires mutual agreement between the parties (offer and acceptance) and consideration. There was no contract here because there was no acceptance. The low bidder's bid constituted an offer—a certain and definite promise, undertaking, or commitment to enter into a contract communicated to the offeree. An offer gives the offeree the power to accept and create a contract until the offer is terminated. An offer can be terminated in a number of ways, including through a counteroffer from the offeree. A counteroffer serves as both a rejection terminating the original offer and a new offer from the original offeree, thus reversing the former roles of the parties and giving the original offeror the right to accept or reject the new offer. Here, the contractor's call constituted a rejection and a counteroffer that the low bidder rejected, and so no contract was formed. Therefore, the low bidder cannot be held liable. (A) and (B) are incorrect because, as stated above, a contract was never formed between the contractor and the low bidder. Thus, it is irrelevant whether the mistake was unilateral or obvious. (Note that the general rule is that a contract will not be set aside for a unilateral mistake unless the nonmistaken party either knew or should have known of the mistake. Thus if the contractor had not called the low bidder but had instead accepted his bid, the low bidder would be liable on the contract despite his mistake because (B) the mistake was unilateral and (A) it was not obvious.) (D) is incorrect for several reasons: First, it relies on the existence of a contract, and as stated above, there is no contract here. Second, the premise that the low bidder could not renege on its offer is untrue. The general rule is that offers are revocable until accepted. In a subcontractor bid situation, a bid is treated as irrevocable for a reasonable amount of time because of detrimental reliance (*i.e.,* the general contractor will rely on the mistaken bid in preparing his bid). However, here the contractor learned of the low bidder's mistake before any reliance on the bid. Moreover, it is unclear whether the contractor is complaining about the low bidder's reneging on his bid; the contractor appears to be complaining that the low bidder refused to lower the mistaken bid. The low bidder would have no duty to lower its bid in any case. The final premise in (D) is irrelevant. If the low bidder lacked the power to renege, the lack of power goes to the $75,000 bid; the fact that no one would do the job for $70,000 has no bearing on the issue.

Answer to Question 15

(D) The son cannot enforce the contract because the assignment of rights to him was properly revoked. He gave no consideration for the right to receive the $10,000 that was assigned to him. A gratuitous assignment generally is revocable unless the obligor has already performed or the assignee has relied on the promise to his detriment. Revocation of the assignment can be accomplished in a number of ways, including by giving notice to the obligor or assignee. Here, the obligor (the business owner) had not yet performed (paid the money), and the son did not rely on the promise because he did not even know about it. The detective revoked the assignment by giving notice to the business owner. Thus, the revocation was proper, and the son cannot enforce the assignment against either party. Therefore, (D) is correct and (A), (B), and (C) are incorrect.

Answer to Question 16

(D) The daughter's best argument to enforce the contract in her favor is that she married in reliance on the contract (detrimental reliance), although she will probably be unsuccessful. Here, the daughter was a gratuitous assignee (because she gave no consideration) and her rights under the contract were revoked. Thus, her strongest argument will be one that nullifies the revocation. The only possible choice here is (D), because under the doctrine of detrimental reliance, a promise will be enforced to the extent necessary to prevent injustice if it was made with a reasonable expectation that it would induce reliance, and such reliance was in fact induced. The problem with this argument here is that it is not clear that the daughter relied on the promise to give her $5,000, because she already had planned to get married. However, none of the other choices is a possible argument, so (D) is her best choice. (A) would not help her because the Statute of Frauds is a defense to enforcement of certain contracts when there is no writing, including contracts where the consideration is marriage, but here the daughter is seeking to ***enforce the contract***, not prevent its enforcement. (B) is incorrect because the parol evidence rule only prevents the introduction of prior or contemporaneous oral statements to contradict the terms of an integrated written contract, and here, the statement that gave the daughter her rights and the one that took them away were both ***subsequent*** oral statements. (C) does not help her because she was not an intended third-party beneficiary. If a contract between two parties contemplates performance to a third party, that third party may have rights to enforce the contract. To do so, the third party must be an intended beneficiary (*e.g.*, designated in the contract). An assignment, on the other hand, is a contract that does ***not*** contemplate performance to a third party when the contract is made. Rather, later one of the parties transfers his rights to another. Here, the contractor and the homeowner signed their contract and ***later***, the contractor assigned his rights to his daughter. Thus, the daughter was not an intended third-party beneficiary who could enforce the agreement, but merely an assignee who gave no consideration for the assignment. As such, she cannot recover the $5,000.

Answer to Question 17

(D) The court should not order the rental agent to rent the apartment to the student because her right to specific performance was cut off by the lease to the third party. A court will grant specific performance of a contract in certain circumstances (*e.g.*, if money damages would be inadequate). While money damages generally are considered inadequate when a transfer of an interest in land is involved (including a transfer of a leasehold estate), a court will not grant specific performance if the subject matter of the contract has been transferred to a bona fide purchaser for value. A third party lessee who was unaware of the agreement between the agent and the student would be considered a bona fide purchaser for value. Thus, even assuming that all of the elements for specific performance are present, the court still would not order the rental agent to lease the apartment to the student here. (A) would be correct if a bona fide purchaser were not involved. The student and the agent created an option contract, the terms of which required the agent to rent the apartment to the student if she notified the agent on or before July 1. The agent breached the contract by renting the apartment to a third party on June 9, because renting the apartment before July 2 prevented the agent from renting the apartment to the student. All land is considered unique (and the apartment here had some very distinctive features to make this point even clearer), so specific performance would generally be an appropriate remedy for breach but for the lease to the third party. (B) would also be a good choice but for the lease to the third party. The student's harm cannot be remedied with money damages (because the apartment is unique) and that generally is a ground for granting specific performance. However, as explained above, any right to specific performance will be cut off by the lease. (C) is wrong because nothing in the facts shows the contract to be unconscionable. Unconscionability prevents oppression and unfair surprise. The basic test is whether at the time the contract was formed the clauses involved were extremely one-sided. That was not the case here.

Answer to Question 18

(B) The doctrine of promissory estoppel under section 90 of the Restatement (Second) of Contracts provides that a promise that the promisor should reasonably expect to induce action or forbearance on the part of the promisee, and which does induce such action or forbearance, is binding if injustice can be avoided only by enforcement of the promise. When the manufacturer promised the proprietor that "we'll work these things out," he should have reasonably expected the proprietor to take exactly the sort of action he did to prepare for the distributorship, because the parties had already agreed on the major points of their arrangement. The manufacturer will therefore be liable for the proprietor's detrimental reliance on a theory of promissory estoppel. (A) is incorrect because an implied-in-fact contract arises when assent is manifested by conduct, as opposed to assent by oral or written language, which gives rise to an express contract. A typical example of an implied-in-fact contract is where a customer enters a barbershop, sits in the barber's chair, and receives a haircut from the barber without speaking a word. The circumstances imply that the customer has agreed to pay for the haircut, even though this was not discussed beforehand. There was no conduct under the facts from which assent to anything can be implied. (C) is incorrect because unjust enrichment arises in situations where there is no enforceable contract, yet one person has for some reason conferred a benefit on another with the expectation of being compensated. If the second person retains the benefit without paying for it, he will be unjustly enriched. The proprietor's expenditures did not serve to enrich the manufacturer, so the concept of unjust enrichment does not apply. (D) is incorrect because a quasi-contract action is used to provide restitution in situations of unjust enrichment. In some cases, courts will allow a plaintiff in a quasi-contract action to recover restitution for the market value of his services even if they do not directly benefit the defendant, provided they were given with the expectation of being compensated or they benefit a third party at the request of defendant. The costs incurred by the proprietor, on the other hand, were expenditures to enable him to perform the contract that he had been promised; hence, promissory estoppel is the appropriate theory for the proprietor to use.

Set 2 Answer Sheet

1. Ⓐ Ⓑ Ⓒ Ⓓ
2. Ⓐ Ⓑ Ⓒ Ⓓ
3. Ⓐ Ⓑ Ⓒ Ⓓ
4. Ⓐ Ⓑ Ⓒ Ⓓ
5. Ⓐ Ⓑ Ⓒ Ⓓ
6. Ⓐ Ⓑ Ⓒ Ⓓ
7. Ⓐ Ⓑ Ⓒ Ⓓ
8. Ⓐ Ⓑ Ⓒ Ⓓ
9. Ⓐ Ⓑ Ⓒ Ⓓ
10. Ⓐ Ⓑ Ⓒ Ⓓ
11. Ⓐ Ⓑ Ⓒ Ⓓ
12. Ⓐ Ⓑ Ⓒ Ⓓ
13. Ⓐ Ⓑ Ⓒ Ⓓ
14. Ⓐ Ⓑ Ⓒ Ⓓ
15. Ⓐ Ⓑ Ⓒ Ⓓ
16. Ⓐ Ⓑ Ⓒ Ⓓ
17. Ⓐ Ⓑ Ⓒ Ⓓ
18. Ⓐ Ⓑ Ⓒ Ⓓ

CONTRACTS QUESTIONS - SET 2

Question 1

A builder learned of a bid being let by the local school board for a new high school. Anxious to get the job, the builder immediately advertised for sub-bids. The lowest sub-bid came from a local contractor. It was for $160,000, which was $40,000 less than the next lowest sub-bid.

The builder submitted its general bid to the school board after computing it based, in part, on the lowest sub-bid. The builder's general bid was $30,000 lower than the school board had originally anticipated.

Pleasantly surprised by the low bid, the school board accepted. After the acceptance, the contractor who had submitted the lowest sub-bid informed the builder that there had been a mistake in computing the sub-bid. The correct sub-bid was $210,000. The builder had been unaware of this mistake.

In a suit for rescission of its contract with the builder, the contractor should:

(A) Not prevail, because the mistake in the figures was made before the bid was accepted.

(B) Not prevail, because nothing indicates that the builder actually knew or should have known of the mistake involved.

(C) Prevail, because the mistake was part of the basis of the bargain.

(D) Prevail, because this was a unilateral, not a bilateral, mistake.

Question 2

The owner of a pet shop received a flyer from a professional bird breeder that included the following: "Lovebirds! $119.95 a pair! Delivery in 4-6 weeks. Terms of sale, cash within 30 days of delivery." The shop owner wrote to the bird breeder on April 26, ordering one pair of lovebirds, and enclosing a check for $119.95. Immediately on receipt of the order and check, the bird breeder sent a letter to the shop owner indicating that there was a mistake in the advertisement; it should have read "$119.95 per bird." The bird breeder went on to state that she would ship a pair of the birds to the shop owner if she would pay the additional $119.95 upon receipt of the birds. By return mail, the shop owner authorized the breeder to ship the pair of lovebirds and agreed to pay the additional $119.95, but she noted that they must be delivered on or before May 21, because they are going to a customer for his sister's birthday gift and needed to be personally delivered. The bird breeder immediately sent a fax to the shop owner agreeing to deliver the birds to her by May 21. However, the birds did not arrive at her shop until June 1.

Is the shop owner's promise to pay $119.95 more than the price listed in the flyer enforceable?

(A) No, because the bird breeder did not ship the birds so that they would arrive at the shop owner's store by May 21.

(B) No, because it was only a counteroffer, which the bird breeder did not accept.

(C) No, because the bird breeder had a preexisting legal obligation to ship the birds to the shop owner.

(D) Yes, it is enforceable.

Question 3

The owner of a neighborhood tavern ordered 20 kegs of domestic beer from a brewery. The written contract between the parties provided that the brewery would deliver the beer by January 31, and the tavern owner would pay the brewery $1,400 upon delivery. The tavern owner was expecting a big crowd for Super Bowl Sunday, four days after the scheduled delivery date. The brewery did not deliver the beer to the tavern owner until February 16, but the tavern owner still accepted it.

Did a duty to pay the $1,400 arise upon the tavern owner's acceptance of the beer on February 16?

(A) No, but the tavern owner retained the right to sue for any damages incurred because of the delay in delivery.

(B) No, and the tavern owner lost the right to sue for any damages incurred because of the delay in delivery.

(C) Yes, but the tavern owner retained the right to sue for any damages incurred because of the delay in delivery.

(D) Yes, and the tavern owner lost the right to sue for any damages incurred because of the delay in delivery.

Question 4

A wholesale seller of widgets telephoned a retail seller of widgets and told him that he had 5,000 pounds of widgets ready for delivery at $5,000. The retailer agreed to purchase the widgets, but stated that he would appreciate it if the wholesaler would deliver 2,000 pounds now and 3,000 pounds next month. There were no further communications between the parties.

The most likely result of the conversation between the wholesaler and the retailer is:

(A) A contract was formed to deliver 2,000 pounds now and 3,000 pounds next month.

(B) A contract was formed to deliver 5,000 pounds now.

(C) No contract was formed, because the retailer's response was merely a counteroffer and a rejection.

(D) No contract was formed, unless the wholesaler notified the retailer within a reasonable time of his assent to the proposed schedule of delivery.

Question 5

A wholesale seller of DVD players e-mailed a message to the owner of a retail electronics store, stating that he had recently received a new shipment of 200 X-Brand DVD players that were available for sale to the store owner. In a return e-mail, the store owner agreed to purchase the DVD players, but added that it would be easier, given his limited space, if the wholesaler delivered 50 of the DVD players each month for the next four months. The wholesaler e-mailed back to the store owner, saying that he would only ship the entire order of 200 DVD players now.

If the wholesaler then tenders the 200 DVD players, the store owner:

(A) May reject the entire delivery.

(B) Must accept the entire delivery.

(C) May demand that the wholesaler deliver 50 DVD players a month for the next four months.

(D) Must accept or reject the entire delivery.

Question 6

On February 3, a property owner mailed an offer to a married couple who had expressed an interest in buying his property at 337 Green Street, consisting of a house and lot. The offer asked for $200,000, "terms $60,000 cash, with the balance secured by a first mortgage." The offer reached the couple on February 5. On February 8, the couple replied by fax that the offer had been received and was being considered, and added, "We would much prefer a straight cash deal. Would you consider an immediate purchase for $180,000 cash?" On February 10, this reply was received by the property owner, who responded with a one-word fax: "No." Receiving this fax on February 11, the couple faxed: "Fax received. We accept your

offer of February 3. Tender the deed c/o our agent, The First National Bank and Trust."

If the property owner now refuses to sell and the couple sues, the court would probably hold:

(A) A valid contract exists.

(B) No contract exists because the couple's response of February 8 operated to terminate the property owner's offer.

(C) No contract exists because the couple's communications to the property owner both contained alterations of the terms of the offer.

(D) No contract exists because the offer relates to real property, and the communications fail to establish the terms of the proposed agreement with sufficient definiteness.

Question 7

A doll collector knew that an acquaintance from her doll collectors' club coveted one particular doll that she owned. The doll collector mailed a letter to an acquaintance on May 3 offering to sell the doll to her for $750. Her letter arrived on May 4. On May 5, the doll collector changed her mind and immediately mailed a revocation to the acquaintance. This revocation arrived on May 7. As the mail carrier handed it to her, the acquaintance simultaneously handed to the mail carrier her own letter to the doll collector, unequivocally accepting her offer.

What is the result of the actions here?

(A) The revocation was effective upon mailing, and the acceptance would be treated as a counteroffer.

(B) The acceptance was effective, as long as the acquaintance had no knowledge of the contents of the doll collector's letter when she handed her letter to the mail carrier.

(C) The outcome would turn on the court's determination as to whether the doll collector's letter had been received by the acquaintance before she had entrusted the letter of acceptance to the mail carrier.

(D) Handing a letter to a mail carrier is not a proper posting of the acceptance, and hence the acquaintance's purported acceptance is not timely.

Question 8

An advertising agency specializing in aerial banners and skywriting signed a contract with a film production company that was premiering a new blockbuster film. The contract provided that the agency would advertise the film by flying over the city towing a giant streamer belonging to the film company heralding the film's catch phrase and title in large letters. This contract specified that the flight was to be conducted on the first Saturday in June at noon (when the film was showing locally) and the film company was to pay the advertising agency $500 for the flight.

On the designated Saturday, the advertising agency was unable to fly because of a defective fuel pump. The defective condition was entirely unforeseeable and did not occur through any negligence or fault of the agency. The film company did not pay the agency, and each of the parties has sued the other for damages.

Which of the following best states the rights and liabilities of the parties?

(A) The film company is entitled to recover damages from the advertising agency on account of the agency's failure to fly.

(B) The advertising agency is entitled to recover from the film company the $500 contract price, as the incapacity of the airplane was not the agency's fault.

(C) Neither party is entitled to recover against the other, because the advertising agency's duty to fly was discharged by impossibility, and the film company's duty to pay was contingent on the agency's flight.

(D) Neither party is entitled to recover against the other, because the film company's offer to pay $500 for the flight was in effect an offer for an act, and because the act was not performed, there was no valid acceptance.

Question 9

The owner of a high-style ladies' fashion store often did business with the designer of a world-famous line of original gowns. On April 1, the store owner and the designer signed a written agreement wherein the store owner was appointed the "sole and exclusive" retail distributor for the designer's clothes in the town in which her store is located. On May 1, the store owner handed the designer a written order for $50,000 worth of his original gowns, to be delivered to her store on September 1. The designer did not sign an acknowledgment of her order, but in her presence he set aside the originals designated in her order by putting her name on them.

To publicize her new line of merchandise, the store owner conducted a large advertising campaign announcing to the townspeople that she would have a wide selection of the designer's originals on display on September 1. She also made substantial improvements to the store to display these clothes in lush and expensive settings. On August 15, the designer canceled his order by fax. He explained to the store owner that a store in a neighboring town made an offer for the clothes "that I simply couldn't pass up." Upon receipt of the message, the store owner filed suit against the designer.

Assuming that an enforceable contract existed between the store owner and the designer, what legal effect would the designer's fax of August 15 have?

(A) It is a breach of contract by anticipatory repudiation, entitling the store owner to bring an immediate action to enforce the contract without waiting until September 1.

(B) It is a breach of contract by anticipatory repudiation allowing the store owner to sue, but only if she first demands adequate assurances of performance from the designer, and he fails to provide these within a reasonable time.

(C) It is an anticipatory breach, requiring the store owner to tender the purchase price on September 1, and sue after that date.

(D) Its legal effect depends on whether the designer was acting in good faith in refusing to perform, and because he was not, the store owner may bring an immediate action.

Question 10

On December 10, a housepainter entered into a contract with a homeowner to paint her house for $8,000, to be paid on completion of the work. On December 20, before the work was completed, the painter sent a letter to the homeowner telling her to pay the $8,000 to one of his creditors, whom he identified by name. The painter sent a copy of the letter to the creditor, then completed the work.

The homeowner refuses to pay the creditor, and the creditor sues the homeowner for the $8,000. Which of the following, if true, will act as her best defense?

(A) The creditor was not the intended beneficiary of the painter-homeowner contract.

(B) The creditor was incapable of performing the painter's work.

(C) The painter had not performed his work in a workmanlike manner.

(D) The assignment was not valid because it was made without consideration.

Question 11

A store selling secondhand office equipment advertised used Regal Typewriters for sale at its store, for $100 each. The resident adviser of a

college dormitory whose residents included a number of computer-phobic students mailed the store a check for $500 with a note ordering five used Regal Typewriters, as advertised.

Upon checking his stock, the store owner found that he had only two Regals left, but he had plenty of Overwoods, and therefore he sent the resident adviser two Regals and three Overwoods by common carrier.

The legal effect of the store owner's shipment of the two Regals and three Overwoods in response to the resident adviser's order for five Regals was:

(A) An acceptance of the resident adviser's offer with respect to the two Regals, and a counteroffer as to the three Over-woods.

(B) An acceptance of the resident adviser's offer to purchase five Regals, and a breach of the contract formed thereby.

(C) Neither an acceptance nor a counteroffer, because a mere shipment of goods is not a manifestation of assent to any particular terms.

(D) A mere offer to furnish substituted goods as an accommodation.

Question 12

An amateur sculptor ordered from an art museum's gift shop a miniature reproduction of a favorite statue, which the museum's flyer indicated was for sale only at the gift shop. He sent the museum an order form printed from its website and a check to cover the cost of the statue. The museum received and processed his order, but by mistake sent, by common carrier, a reproduction of a different statue. The statue was stolen from the carrier en route to the sculptor's home.

Between the buyer and the museum, who bears the loss?

(A) The loss falls on the museum because it was the museum that selected the carrier and made the arrangements for shipment.

(B) The loss falls on the museum because under the facts here, the seller bears the risk of loss.

(C) The loss falls on the buyer because the statue was advertised as being available for sale only at the museum's gift store, and therefore the risk of loss shifted to the buyer.

(D) The loss falls on the buyer because title to the statue passed to him upon shipment, and he therefore bears the risk of loss.

Question 13

A small-town actor offered to pay $500 to a publicity firm to put up a billboard advertisement (complete with a huge, close-up color photo of the actor's face) by the side of the highway leading into town, announcing his debut in a starring role in a community theater production. The publicity firm accepted. The actor wanted the billboard in place in two weeks' time, right before the opening of the play, because he had heard that an important talent scout would be in town that night. On the morning that the billboard advertisement was to go up (the day of the play's opening), the billboard was destroyed by fire, through the fault of neither party, and could not be replaced in time.

Which of the following best states the rights and liabilities of the parties?

(A) The publicity firm is entitled to recover from the actor the costs and expenses it would have incurred in performing the contract.

(B) The actor is entitled to at least nominal damages against the publicity firm, because destruction of the billboard was not the actor's fault, and therefore the publicity firm was in technical breach of contract in failing to perform under the contract.

(C) Neither party is entitled to recover against the other because destruction of the contemplated subject matter of the contract (the billboard) terminated the actor's offer by operation of law.

(D) Neither party is entitled to recover against the other because destruction of the billboard excused the publicity firm's duty to perform under the contract, the performance being a condition precedent to the actor's duty to pay.

Question 14

On May 1, a promoter for local fairs and festivals, in a series of phone calls with the owner of a champion pig, struck an agreement with the owner for the pig to perform entertaining tricks in three shows a day for 10 days beginning July 25, for a fee of $500. Shortly before the fair was scheduled to open, the pig contracted swine flu and was too sick to appear at the fair. The promoter demanded that the pig's owner either bring the pig to the fair to perform as scheduled or pay damages.

The pig's owner's best argument for not performing the contract would be based upon which of the following?

(A) Statute of Frauds.

(B) Parol evidence rule.

(C) Impossibility of performance.

(D) Failure of consideration.

Question 15

The owner of a mint-condition classic automobile wrote a letter to his trusted car mechanic offering to sell him the auto for $45,000, if he bought it before April 15.

The mechanic researched the current market value of the car online and discovered that comparable vehicles were being sold for $48,000. On April 1, he was just leaving his home to drive to the car owner's house to give him a check for $45,000 when he received a fax from the owner stating that he had changed his mind and the auto was no longer for sale. The mechanic drove to the auto owner's house anyway, where the auto was parked out front with a "for sale" sign in its window. The mechanic knocked on the owner's door and, when he answered, tendered the $45,000 certified check and demanded the auto. The car owner refused.

The mechanic brings an action for damages for breach of contract against the car owner. He will recover:

(A) Nothing, because the offer to sell the auto was withdrawn before he accepted.

(B) $45,000, because the auto owner has failed to perform under the contract of sale.

(C) $3,000, because his tender of the purchase price was an acceptance of the auto owner's offer.

(D) $3,000, because the auto owner's letter created an enforceable option.

Question 16

A large bookstore entered into a written agreement with the manager of a shopping center to rent space that the manager agreed to fix up to suit the bookstore's purpose. The contract between the parties provided that the store premises would be ready by June 1, or July 1 at the latest. The manager immediately contracted with a builder to do the construction work in accordance with the bookstore's requirements. When the premises were not ready by July 1, the bookstore notified the manager that it would rent store space elsewhere. Four days later, on July 5, the manager sent the bookstore a letter by certified mail stating that the construction had been delayed because the builder he had hired had breached his contract, and he had to employ another builder. However, the manager promised that the premises would be completed no later than July 15, and said that under the circumstances, he believed he was entitled to this short period of time to complete the agreement because the renovations, done especially for the bookstore, had already cost him $15,000. On July 15, the manager tendered performance to the bookstore, but it refused to accept the lease. The manager sought another tenant for the space, without success.

The manager brought suit against the bookstore for breach of contract. The most likely fact that will decide who prevails in this suit is:

(A) A substitute who was willing to rent the premises with the renovations done especially for the bookstore could not be found.

(B) The manager could not have foreseen that the builder would not complete the construction.

(C) The bookstore did not show that it would have suffered "undue hardship" if it waited until July 15 to see if the construction would be completed.

(D) The contract provision that the store premises will be ready by July 1 "at the latest" was a time of the essence provision.

Question 17

A manufacturer of heavy oak furniture entered into an agreement with a seller of industrial tools to purchase 50 of the seller's Series B saw blades. The agreement required the manufacturer to pay for the blades when he placed the order. The manufacturer gave the seller $5,000 in full payment at the time he placed his order. When the blades arrived the following week, the manufacturer inspected them and found that they were Series A saw blades. He immediately contacted the seller and demanded the return of his payment. The seller refused to accept the return of the blades or to return the manufacturer's payment, claiming that there was no significant difference between the Series B and Series A blades.

Which of the following statements is most accurate with regard to the consequences of the manufacturer's paying for the saw blades in advance of inspecting them?

(A) The payment in advance was an acceptance, and therefore the manufacturer waived his rights to reject the goods.

(B) The payment in advance did not act to waive the manufacturer's right to object to a total breach of contract, but it did act as an acceptance if the goods shipped substantially conformed to the manufacturer's requirements.

(C) The payment in advance impaired neither the manufacturer's right to inspect nor his right to assert his remedies for any breach of contract.

(D) The payment in advance had no effect, because goods are never deemed accepted until the buyer notifies the seller in writing that the goods are acceptable.

Question 18

A wholesaler who sold hair-care products to beauty salons and spas contracted to purchase 20 hand-held ionic hair dryers to be delivered no later than May 1. She paid for the hair dryers at the time she placed her order. When the hair dryers were delivered on May 1, the wholesaler noticed that they were hot air, and not ionic, hair dryers. She immediately contacted the manufacturer, which refused to grant the wholesaler any remedy.

The wholesaler brings a claim for breach of contract against the manufacturer, and the court determines that the hot-air hair dryers are nonconforming. What are the wholesaler's remedies?

(A) None, because the salon owner waived her rights when she paid for the hair dryers in advance.

(B) None, because the manufacturer has the right to cure by notice and a new tender of conforming goods.

(C) Damages based on the difference between the contract price and the price to buy conforming goods.

(D) Damages based on the difference between the contract price and the value of the hair dryers she received.

CONTRACTS ANSWERS - SET 2

Answer to Question 1

(B) The contractor should not prevail because its computation error was a unilateral mistake. Where only one of the parties entering into a contract is mistaken about facts relating to the agreement, this unilateral mistake will not prevent formation of a contract unless the nonmistaken party is or had reason to be aware of the mistake made by the other party. Here, the computation error was the contractor's mistake alone, and the contract may not be rescinded unless the builder actually knew or should have known of the mistake. While such errors may be canceled in equity if the nonmistaken party has not relied on the contract, the builder clearly relied upon the sub-bid provided by the contractor when it submitted its bid to the school board. (A) is incorrect because the fact that the mistake was made before the bid was accepted by the school board is irrelevant by itself. What ***is*** crucial to the contractor's suit is whether the builder knew or should have known of the mistake before submitting the bid to the school board. If so, as discussed above, grounds for rescission exist. (C) is incorrect because the contractor's error was not a mutual mistake that was part of the basis of the bargain. When both parties entering into a contract are mistaken about facts relating to the agreement, the contract may be voidable by the adversely affected party if, among other things, the mutual mistake concerns a basic assumption on which the contract is made. Here, the computation error was a unilateral, not a mutual mistake, and did not concern an assumption on which the agreement of both parties is based. While there is modern authority indicating that a unilateral mistake that is so extreme that it outweighs the other party's expectations under the agreement will be a ground for cancellation of the contract in equity, the error here probably is not sufficiently extreme to justify cancellation. (D) is incorrect because a unilateral mistake is generally ***not*** a defense to the formation of a contract. As discussed above, where only one of the parties is mistaken about facts relating to the agreement, the mistake will not prevent formation or enforcement of the contract unless the other party knew or had reason to know of the mistake. Therefore, the contractor will not prevail simply because the error was a unilateral mistake.

Answer to Question 2

(D) The shop owner's promise to pay $119.95 more than the price listed on the flyer is enforceable under the U.C.C., which governs because the contract is for the sale of goods. Under the U.C.C., a promise to modify an existing contract is enforceable even without consideration. The only requirement is that the proposal to modify be made in good faith. Here, the proposal was made in good faith, because it was to correct an error in the flyer. Thus, the shop owner's promise to pay the additional $119.95 is enforceable. (Note that this modification would be enforceable even in a non-U.C.C. case because the new shipping date would be consideration for the additional $119.95.) (A) is incorrect because even if shipping late was a breach of contract (and it probably was, because the shipment date was part of the modification sought in good faith), it would not give the shop owner the right to unilaterally decide not to pay a portion of the price. The breach would only give her the right to reject the birds and cancel or "cover," or accept them and sue for damages. (B) is incorrect because even if the shop owner's promise is a counteroffer, it was also an acceptance of the bird breeder's offer to modify. Under the U.C.C., unlike under common law, if a merchant accepts another merchant's offer and proposes additional or different terms, there is an effective acceptance and a contract is formed. Therefore, the shop owner's promise is enforceable. (C) is incorrect because the common law preexisting legal duty rule does not apply to modifications under the U.C.C. The common law enforces promises only if they are supported by consideration, and a promise to perform a preexisting duty is not valid consideration. But, as stated above, the U.C.C. allows good faith modifications even without consideration.

Answer to Question 3

(C) When the tavern owner accepted the beer on February 16, his duty to pay the $1,400 arose, but he retained the right to sue for damages because of the late delivery. When nonconforming goods are delivered, the buyer may: (i) reject them and cancel the contract or sue for damages; or (ii) accept any commercial units, reject the rest, and sue for damages. Once the goods are accepted, the buyer generally is bound on the contract and it is too late to cancel; however, the buyer retains the right to sue for damages for any nonconformity. Acceptance occurs when the buyer: (i) indicates that he will accept the goods after a reasonable opportunity to inspect them; (ii) fails to reject within a proper time; or (iii) does any act inconsistent with the seller's ownership. Here, the tavern owner accepted the beer even though he knew that it did not conform to the contract (because of the late delivery); thus, the time for rejection had passed. When the tavern owner accepted the beer, he became bound under the contract to pay for the beer. Nevertheless, he can sue for damages that arose from the late delivery. Therefore, (C) is correct, and (A), (B), and (D) are incorrect.

Answer to Question 4

(A) The conversation created a contract for 2,000 pounds of widgets now and 3,000 pounds next month. Because the contract is for the sale of goods, the U.C.C. governs. Under the U.C.C., a contract is formed whenever it appears from the parties' communications that they intended to enter into a contract. Here, it is clear that the parties intended to enter into a contract, but the acceptance contained terms additional to the offer terms. When this occurs, the U.C.C. provides for which terms govern: If the contract is between merchants, the additional terms in the acceptance are included in the contract, unless (i) the additional terms materially alter the contract, (ii) the offer expressly limits acceptance to the terms of the offer, or (iii) the offeror objects within a reasonable time. Here, both parties are merchants, and it does not appear that the delivery terms materially alter the contract. There is no indication that the offer limited acceptance to the terms of the offer or that the wholesaler objected to the terms; thus, there is a contract containing the additional terms. (B) would be correct if one of the parties were not a merchant, because under the U.C.C., when an acceptance proposes additional terms, a contract would be formed under the terms of the offer unless both parties are merchants. (C) would be correct if the U.C.C. did not apply, because under the common law, an acceptance must mirror the offer (the "mirror image" rule); if new terms are added in the acceptance, it is treated as a counteroffer. (D) is incorrect because under the U.C.C., no notice was necessary to form the contract. Notice would be required, however, if the wholesaler did not want to be bound by the additional terms.

Answer to Question 5

(B) Because the wholesaler objected to the store owner's new delivery term, the store owner must accept the entire delivery of 200 DVD players, because the new delivery term did not become part of the contract. Under the U.C.C., which applies here because the contract is for the sale of goods, additional terms in a contract between merchants usually become part of the contract when the acceptance does not mirror the offer; however, there are several exceptions to this general rule, and one applies here: If the offeror notifies the offeree within a reasonable time after receiving the acceptance that he objects to the offeree's new terms, the contract is formed according to the terms of the original offer. Thus, the contract was formed under the wholesaler's terms and a single delivery of 200 DVD players is a proper delivery; so the store owner must accept all

200 DVD players. (A), (C), and (D) might be correct if the store owner's additional terms were part of the contract, but because the contract was formed under the terms of the offer, these three choices constitute breach.

Answer to Question 6

(A) A contract was formed here because there was mutual assent and valid consideration. For there to be mutual assent, there must be a valid offer and an unequivocal acceptance before the offer is either rejected by the offeree or revoked by the offeror. Here, the property owner offered to sell his house and lot for $200,000. This was clearly an offer to the couple. The issue here is whether either of the couple's replies constitutes an unequivocal acceptance of this offer. A counteroffer serves as a rejection of the original offer as well as a new offer. However, a mere inquiry about additional terms or matters is not a counteroffer. The test of whether the reply is a counteroffer or inquiry is whether a reasonable person would believe that the offer was being rejected. Here, the couple's February 8 communication was a mere inquiry, rather than a counteroffer. The couple's statements do not show an outright rejection unless their terms are agreed to; they merely state what they would prefer and then ask the property owner to consider their proposal. Most likely this would be considered to be an inquiry. The February 11 communication is an acceptance. The couple clearly state that they accept the "offer of February 3" (showing that they are agreeing to the property owner's original terms). The additional language in their fax (about the deed and their agent) is not an alteration of the original terms because implicit in a sale of land contract is that a deed will be conveyed, and the use of an agent is immaterial. Statements by the couple that make implicit terms explicit do not prevent acceptance of the offer. Thus, their second communication unequivocally accepts the property owner's offer. Because promises were exchanged (a promise to sell the property for a promise to pay $200,000), valid consideration existed, and a contract was formed. (B) is wrong because, as explained above, the couple's February 8 communication did not constitute a counteroffer, which would act as a rejection of the offer. Because the communication was a mere inquiry, the offer was still viable and the couple could accept it. (C) is wrong because the first communication only inquired about altering the deal and the second merely expressed terms already implicit to the offer. Neither contained alterations of the offer's terms. (D) is wrong because a contract for the sale of land need only identify the land and contain a price term. Here, the offer adequately described the property and stated the price. It was a sufficiently definite offer.

Answer to Question 7

(C) At common law, an acceptance is effective upon dispatch (*e.g.*, upon mailing a properly addressed and stamped letter) under the mailbox rule. The mailbox rule does not apply to revocations, however—revocations are effective only upon receipt. Receipt does not require knowledge of the revocation, but merely possession of it. [*See* Restatement (Second) of Contracts §68] The facts here present a close question as to whether there has been a dispatch of the acceptance before the receipt of the revocation. The outcome of this question will depend on the court's determination as to what came first (the posting of the acceptance or receipt of the revocation). This will decide the existence or nonexistence of the contract. (A) is incorrect because, as indicated above, revocation is effective only upon receipt, not mailing. (B) is incorrect because whether the acceptance is effective depends on whether the revocation was received before the acceptance was dispatched, and whether the revocation was received first is not dependent on whether the acquaintance had knowledge of its contents, but rather it depends on whether she had possession of it. (D) is incorrect because the mailbox rule makes an acceptance effective upon

posting, and there is no reason to hold that handing a properly addressed, stamped letter to a mail carrier is not a valid posting.

Answer to Question 8

(A) The film company will be able to recover damages from the advertising agency because the agency's failure to fly constituted a breach of contract. The parties entered into a bilateral contract—the agency promised to fly with the streamer and the film company promised to pay for the flight. The agency breached the contract by failing to fly on the designated Saturday. Its duty to fly was not discharged by impossibility. A contractual duty to perform may be discharged by objective impossibility (*i.e.*, ***no one*** could have performed), but subjective impossibility (***defendant*** could not perform) is insufficient. Here, the defect in the plane constituted only subjective impossibility (if it amounted to impossibility at all) because the agency could have obtained another plane to pull the streamer. If the agency had been unable to fly the plane because of weather (*e.g.*, a severe ice storm), it would have been objective impossibility and the agency would be discharged. However, under the facts, the film company is entitled to damages for the agency's breach. (B) is incorrect because the film company's duty to perform (pay $500) was subject to the condition precedent of the agency's performance (flying), and, as discussed above, the agency breached the contract by failing to fly. Therefore, the film company's duty to pay never arose. The fact that the engine problem was not the agency's fault does not change things. The agency's inability to perform, even if it could be considered impossibility, would merely discharge the contract, and each party would be excused from performance. Thus, the film company would not have to pay the $500. (C) is incorrect because, as determined above, the agency's duty was not discharged because performance was only subjectively impossible. (If there had been objective impossibility, (C) would have been the correct choice.) (D) is incorrect because it suggests that the contract was a unilateral one (the offer to pay could be accepted only by completion of performance). This interpretation is clearly contrary to the facts. Although the film company offered to pay $500 for the flight, the agency accepted that offer by signing the contract. A promise to pay was given in exchange for a promise to fly. Thus, there was a contract to which both parties were bound.

Answer to Question 9

(A) The designer's fax constitutes anticipatory repudiation, which entitles the store owner to sue immediately. Anticipatory repudiation occurs where a promisor, prior to the time set for performance of his promise, indicates that he will not perform when the time comes. The contract must be executory on both sides and the repudiation must be unequivocal. Upon anticipatory repudiation, the nonrepudiating party has several options, including suing immediately for breach. Here, the designer unequivocally indicated that he would breach before the agreed-upon delivery date, and the contract was executory on both sides because the store owner had not paid for the gowns and the designer had not delivered them. Thus, the store owner could sue for damages immediately. (B) is incorrect because the store owner need not demand assurances before suing on the contract. As explained above, if there has been a repudiation of the contract, the other party may sue immediately. [U.C.C. §2-610] This choice would be correct if the designer's actions had not been so clearly a repudiation. U.C.C. section 2-609 provides that when actions or circumstances increase the risk of nonperformance, but do not clearly indicate that performance will not be forthcoming, there is no breach. Rather, the party has a right to demand assurances. If proper assurances are not given within a reasonable time, then the contract may be seen as having been breached. Here, the designer's statements were clear indications that he would not perform, and so section 2-609 does not apply. (C) is incorrect because anticipatory breach is the same as

anticipatory repudiation. Although the nonbreaching party has a number of options—including waiting for the performance date—she is not obliged to choose any particular option and, as indicated above, she may sue immediately. (D) is incorrect because whether a breach was made in good faith or bad faith is irrelevant. When there is a breach, the nonbreaching party is entitled to her U.C.C. remedies, and as stated above, the store owner may sue before September 1 without proving motive. The motive for the designer's breach has no bearing on her right to sue.

Answer to Question 10

(C) The homeowner's best defense is that the painter had not performed his work in a workmanlike manner. The painter apparently has assigned his claim against the homeowner to the creditor. In the absence of an enforceable agreement to the contrary, an assignee would take subject to defenses good against his assignor. Therefore, if the painter has not properly performed the work, the homeowner could use this as a defense in a suit brought by the creditor. (A) is wrong because the creditor is not claiming he is a third-party beneficiary, but rather is an assignee of the rights of the painter. (B) is wrong because the fact that the creditor is incapable of performing the painter's work is immaterial. (D) is wrong because consideration is not required for an assignment to be valid.

Answer to Question 11

(B) The store owner's shipment constituted both an acceptance of the resident adviser's offer and a breach of the resulting contract. The U.C.C. applies here because goods are involved. Under the U.C.C., an offer to buy goods can be accepted by the seller by either a promise to ship or by prompt shipment of conforming ***or*** nonconforming goods. Shipment of nonconforming goods will constitute an acceptance ***and a breach*** unless the seller notifies the buyer that the goods are offered only as an accommodation. Here, the store owner shipped nonconforming goods without a notice of accommodation; thus, the shipment was both an acceptance and a breach. (A) is incorrect because the shipment was not an acceptance of the conforming goods and a counteroffer as to the nonconforming goods. The resident adviser ordered five Regal typewriters. He did not receive what he ordered. Instead, he received three Overwoods. Because he did not receive what he ordered, the whole shipment is nonconforming. As mentioned above, under the U.C.C., shipment of nonconforming goods is an acceptance (and breach), not a counteroffer, unless notice of accommodation is given. Because the store owner gave no notice of accommodation, the shipment of the Regals and Overwoods is an acceptance. (C) is incorrect because under the U.C.C. shipment of requested goods, even nonconforming goods, is an acceptance [U.C.C. §2-206], and it could be a counteroffer if notice of accommodation is given. (D) is incorrect because under the U.C.C. the result of the shipment is more than a mere offer to furnish substituted goods. (*See* above.) For the shipment to function as an offer to furnish substituted goods, notice must be given that the goods are intended as an accommodation. Here, no such notice was given, so the shipment was an acceptance.

Answer to Question 12

(B) The museum suffers the loss because the risk of loss was still with it when the statue was stolen. Under the U.C.C., when the contract authorizes or requires the seller to ship the goods by carrier but does not explicitly require the seller to deliver them at a particular location, risk of loss passes to the buyer when the goods are duly delivered to the carrier. [U.C.C. §2-509] However, if the goods are so defective that the buyer has a right to reject them, the risk of loss does not pass until the defects are cured or the buyer accepts the goods. [U.C.C. §2-510(1)] Here, the shipment

of a nonconforming good constituted a breach, and the buyer had a right to reject it. Thus, the loss falls on the museum with respect to the theft. (A) is incorrect because risk of loss here is determined by the fact that the shipment was a breach of contract; it is not determined by who selected the carrier and made the arrangements. (C) is incorrect because it is irrelevant what the museum's advertisements say, since they are not part of the contract but rather are solicitations for offers. (D) is incorrect because, as stated above, risk of loss does not pass to the buyer if the good is so defective that the buyer has a right to reject it. (D) would be correct if not for the breach, because this is probably a shipment contract (requiring the museum to put the goods in the hands of a carrier, but not requiring delivery at a particular destination).

Answer to Question 13

(D) Neither party is entitled to recover from the other because destruction of the billboard without the fault of either party discharged the publicity firm's obligation under the contract, because it made performance impossible. Contractual duties will be discharged if it has become impossible to perform them. To result in discharge of the contract, the impossibility must be objective; *i.e., **no one*** would be able to perform. Here, performance was objectively impossible because the subject matter of the contract (the billboard) was destroyed without the fault of either party and could not be replaced in time. Thus, the publicity firm's duty to put up the billboard advertisement was discharged because of destruction of the thing necessary to fulfill the contract. Under the terms of the contract, the publicity firm's putting up of the billboard was a condition precedent to the actor's duty to pay. Therefore, the actor's duty to pay never arose. In this case, then, neither party may recover. (A) is incorrect because when a party is excused from performing by impossibility, the excuse is not a substitute for performance. Rather, the contract is discharged and each party is excused from contractual duties yet to be fulfilled. Therefore, the actor does not have to pay the publicity firm on the contract. (B) is incorrect because when the destruction of the subject matter of the contract is not the fault of either party, the parties are discharged from their duties to perform. It is not a breach of the contract—technical or otherwise. (C) is incorrect because it incorrectly states the effect of the destruction of the billboard. It is true that neither party may recover (*see* above), but the reason is that the ***contract*** between the parties was discharged by impossibility. The offer was not terminated by the impossibility; it had already been accepted when the parties signed the contract.

Answer to Question 14

(C) The pig's owner's best defense is impossibility. Contractual duties will be discharged where it has become impossible to perform them. For impossibility to operate, the duty must be objectively impossible (*i.e., **no one*** would be able to perform). One common situation where impossibility is applied is where either the means for carrying out the contract or the subject matter of the contract is destroyed or damaged. Here, the pig's illness can be seen as damaging the means of performing under the contract. Note that impossibility is also often applied where the person to perform is sick or injured, and the pig's illness here is analogous. In any case, the pig cannot perform, and apparently no other pig could take its place, so performance is impossible and its owner can avoid the contract. (A) is not a good defense because the Statute of Frauds is not applicable to the contract here because it is a contract to perform, which will by its terms be completed within a year. Such a contract is not covered by the Statute and may be enforced without a writing. (B) is not a good defense because the parol evidence rule merely prohibits introduction of prior or contemporaneous oral statements to contradict a written contract, and here there was no written contract, and even if there was, the pig's owner is not trying to contradict it. (D) is incorrect because failure of consideration does not apply to the pig's owner. Failure of consideration is not a claim that the contract lacked consideration when made, but rather that some element of the promised consideration cannot now be given. Failure of consideration is a ground for breach. Here, the promoter is apparently able to pay (perform under the contract), so failure of consideration does not excuse the pig's owner. (The promoter, on the other hand, could use this as a claim for not paying the pig's owner.)

Answer to Question 15

(A) The mechanic will recover nothing because no contract was formed. To create a contract, there must be an effective offer and acceptance. To be effective, an acceptance must be made before the offer is terminated. An offer may be terminated in a number of ways, including directly informing the offeree that the offer is being revoked. Here, the mechanic received a revocation of the offer from the auto owner before he accepted the offer. Thus, his acceptance was not effective if the auto owner's revocation was effective. An offeror has the power to revoke an offer any time before an acceptance has occurred, even if the offeror has promised to keep the offer open, unless (i) consideration has been paid to keep the offer open (thus forming an option contract), (ii) the offeree reasonably relies on the offer to his detriment, or (iii) the offer is a merchant's firm offer. Here, the mechanic did not pay the car owner to keep the offer open, there was no reasonable detrimental reliance on the offer before the revocation (the mechanic did not drive to the car owner's house until after receiving the revocation), and the auto owner could not make a merchant's firm offer with respect to the car because he is not an auto merchant. Thus, the auto owner had the power to revoke, his revocation was effective, and the mechanic's acceptance was therefore ineffective. (B) is incorrect for two reasons: (i) there was no contract between the parties (*see* above), and (ii) even if there were a contract, the mechanic would not recover $45,000. In a contract for the sale of goods, the basic remedy for nondelivery is the difference between the contract price and either the market price or the cost of cover, plus consequential and incidental damages. Here, there is a $3,000 difference between the contract price and the market price (and cover price), and so $3,000 would be the appropriate amount had there been a contract. (C) is incorrect because, as indicated above, the mechanic's power of acceptance was terminated by the auto owner's prior revocation of the offer. (D) is incorrect because, as indicated above, no option contract was created, because the mechanic did not pay to keep the offer open.

Answer to Question 16

(D) The factor most likely to have an impact on the resolution of this case is that the provision requiring the premises to be ready on July 1 "at the latest" was a time of the essence provision. The manager's failure to perform within the time specified was a material breach that gave the bookstore the absolute right to cancel the contract when the premises were not ready by that date. (A), (B), and (C) are incorrect because none of them bears on whether the manager's failure to perform on time is a material breach.

Answer to Question 17

(C) The manufacturer's payment in advance for the saw blades did not affect his rights with regard to them. Under U.C.C. section 2-512(2), paying for goods in advance impairs neither the buyer's right to inspect nor his right to assert his remedies. (A) and (B) are incorrect, because paying for goods in advance does not constitute an acceptance, and that fact does not change when the breach is minor. (D) is incorrect, because there is no requirement that goods be accepted by a written notice.

Answer to Question 18

(C) The wholesaler is entitled to damages based on the difference between the contract price and the price to buy conforming goods, plus any incidental and consequential damages. (This is the rule of U.C.C. section 2-712(A).) (A) is incorrect because paying for goods in advance does not constitute an acceptance. (B) is incorrect because a seller ordinarily has no right to cure beyond the original contract time, and the manufacturer here delivered the goods on the last day performance could be made. There is an exception under which a seller may cure within a reasonable time beyond the original contract time, if the seller reasonably believed that the tender would be acceptable. To fall within the exception, the seller must show that trade practices or prior dealings with the buyer led him to believe that the goods would be acceptable, or the seller could not have known of the defect despite proper business conduct. Here, the facts do not indicate that either criterion was met. (D) is an incorrect measure of damages.

Set 3 Answer Sheet

1. Ⓐ Ⓑ Ⓒ Ⓓ
2. Ⓐ Ⓑ Ⓒ Ⓓ
3. Ⓐ Ⓑ Ⓒ Ⓓ
4. Ⓐ Ⓑ Ⓒ Ⓓ
5. Ⓐ Ⓑ Ⓒ Ⓓ
6. Ⓐ Ⓑ Ⓒ Ⓓ
7. Ⓐ Ⓑ Ⓒ Ⓓ
8. Ⓐ Ⓑ Ⓒ Ⓓ
9. Ⓐ Ⓑ Ⓒ Ⓓ
10. Ⓐ Ⓑ Ⓒ Ⓓ
11. Ⓐ Ⓑ Ⓒ Ⓓ
12. Ⓐ Ⓑ Ⓒ Ⓓ
13. Ⓐ Ⓑ Ⓒ Ⓓ
14. Ⓐ Ⓑ Ⓒ Ⓓ
15. Ⓐ Ⓑ Ⓒ Ⓓ
16. Ⓐ Ⓑ Ⓒ Ⓓ
17. Ⓐ Ⓑ Ⓒ Ⓓ
18. Ⓐ Ⓑ Ⓒ Ⓓ

CONTRACTS QUESTIONS - SET 3

Question 1

A builder and a landowner enter into a valid written contract under which the builder agrees to erect a house on the landowner's land according to certain plans and specifications and the landowner agrees to pay the sum of $200,000 upon completion. During the course of construction, building costs increase significantly. The builder informs the landowner of the increased costs, and the parties agree in writing that the builder could omit installing the air conditioning unit called for by the specifications (thus saving the builder approximately $10,000) and nevertheless receive the full construction contract price.

Under the general rule, this subsequent written agreement is:

(A) Unenforceable for lack of consideration, even though in writing.

(B) Enforceable as a novation, which superseded the original construction contract.

(C) Enforceable, because an agreement modifying a contract for the sale of goods (the air conditioning unit) needs no consideration to be binding.

(D) Enforceable, on the theory that the builder gave up his right to breach the contract (walking off the job and refusing to complete the building) in reliance on the landowner's agreement to the modification.

Question 2

To encourage her neighbor to continue pursuing her avocation of photography, an art patron promised to buy her first photographic work that wins a prize in a juried art show. To show that she was serious, the art patron gave her neighbor a contract to sign which stated that she agreed to buy and the neighbor agreed to sell the neighbor's first framed photograph that wins a ribbon (first, second, or third prize) in a juried art show, with payment due within 14 days of delivery. Price was not mentioned in the contract, which was enforceable in all other respects. Both parties signed the contract.

Some months later, the neighbor won first prize for one of her photos set in an expensive frame. The parties made arrangements for the art patron to take possession of the piece. The neighbor insisted on a price of $1,200, pointing to the expensive frame and the prestige of the art show that awarded the prize. The art patron instead tendered $700, a good faith approximation of the value of the photo display, and sued when the neighbor refused to deliver it.

If the neighbor defends on the ground that no price was fixed in the contract and the parties have been unable to agree on a price, the court should hold that:

(A) The art patron is entitled to purchase the photograph at whatever price the court determines to be reasonable.

(B) An arbitrator must be appointed to set the price.

(C) The art patron is entitled to purchase the photograph for $700.

(D) The art patron will have to pay $1,200 for the photograph.

Question 3

An interior decorator asked a woodworker she met at a crafts fair to build a curly maple armoire. They entered into a written contract, with a contract price of $6,500 to be paid upon the decorator's receipt of the armoire. When the work was completed, the woodworker shipped the armoire to the decorator. After inspecting it, the decorator felt that it was not of the same high level of workmanship as she was expecting, given the other furniture that the woodworker had showcased at the fair, and a good faith dispute arose between the parties as to the

workmanship. The decorator sent the woodworker a check for $4,000 marked "payment in full."

The woodworker indorses and cashes the check, then sues the decorator to recover the $2,500 balance. Most courts would hold that:

(A) The woodworker's cashing of the check constituted an accord and satisfaction, discharging the decorator's duty to pay the balance.

(B) The woodworker can recover the $2,500 balance from the decorator.

(C) The woodworker is estopped to sue for the balance because he cashed the check knowing that it was being tendered in full settlement.

(D) The woodworker's indorsing a check so marked constituted a written release, thereby discharging the contract.

Question 4

A nonprofit group entered into a written contract with a builder to construct an after-school center in an urban neighborhood plagued by crime, on land that it owned. After the building had been completed except for exterior gutters and downspouts and interior painting, the entire structure was destroyed by a fire set by vandals. The builder's expenses had been so great, and the builder was so frustrated that his work was destroyed by hooligans, that he refused to rebuild the building.

Under traditional contract law principles, the builder can recover from the nonprofit group:

(A) The full contract price, less the value of the work remaining to be done when the building was destroyed.

(B) The actual value of labor and materials expended, plus a proportionate amount of the profits the builder would have earned on completion, his further performance having been excused by impossibility.

(C) Nothing.

(D) The reasonable value of the builder's labor and materials on the building, but without any allowance for profits.

Question 5

A racehorse breeder and a stable owner entered into a contract giving the stable owner first right to purchase all colts foaled out of a particular champion racehorse during the next three years. The agreement provided that price would be determined on the basis of sex, weight, height, and bone structure at time of delivery.

Six months later, the first colt was born to the horse, and it had all the markings of a champion. The stable owner immediately tendered $25,000 to the breeder for the colt, which was a good faith approximation of its value. However, the breeder refused to deliver the colt unless the stable owner paid $100,000. The stable owner sued the breeder.

If the breeder defends on the ground that there is no enforceable contract obligating him to sell, the court would most likely hold:

(A) There is no enforceable contract because the stable owner was not obligated in any way under the signed writing.

(B) There is an enforceable contract because, by signing the document, the stable owner impliedly promised to purchase.

(C) Even if the writing was not an enforceable contract, the stable owner's good faith tender of $25,000 created an enforceable contract.

(D) The agreement is enforceable as a firm offer between merchants under the U.C.C.

Question 6

A yoga instructor entered into a valid written contract with a builder to construct a large yoga studio on some land she owned outside of town.

She agreed to pay the builder $150,000 upon completion of the job. As work progressed, and due to substantial increased building costs, the yoga instructor and the builder orally agreed that the builder may omit installation of the koi pond planned for the atrium (saving the builder $1,000), and that the contract price would be reduced to $149,500. The builder completed the job (minus the koi pond) in reliance thereon.

Most courts would hold that this subsequent oral agreement is:

(A) An enforceable contract.

(B) Unenforceable under the Statute of Frauds.

(C) Unenforceable, because a contract in writing cannot be modified orally.

(D) Unenforceable under the parol evidence rule.

Question 7

The order department of a machine tools manufacturing company received a phone call from a factory owner who placed an order for two of the company's standard "Type-A" machines. The factory owner and the company came to an oral agreement whereby the total price for both machines was agreed to be $10,000. The first machine was to be delivered on May 1, with payment of $5,000 due 30 days after delivery, and the second machine was to be delivered on June 1 on the same terms (payment of $5,000 due 30 days after delivery). Although the company did not carry the machine in stock, no retooling was required because the Type-A machine was a standard model.

The first machine was duly delivered on May 1. The second machine arrived on June 1, but the factory owner refused to accept delivery and also refused to pay for the first machine. Assume that it cost the company $3,000 to manufacture each Type-A machine, and that the company could resell the machine for only $3,000.

The company sues the factory owner on June 2. What damages should be awarded aside from any incidental damages?

(A) $3,000.

(B) $5,000.

(C) $7,000.

(D) $10,000.

Question 8

A property owner decided that she would turn the garage on her property into an exercise area, including a modern sauna and spa. She entered into a written agreement with a contractor who agreed to do the job personally for $12,500, which included all requisite plumbing, electrical, and carpentry work. The contractor was to begin work by May 14. On May 15, he had not yet appeared to start the job. The property owner telephoned the contractor, who told her that he was hired for a big job that was going to pay him "a lot more money than that marginal project of yours, so I'm not going to work on your garage." Over a period of several months, the property owner made many calls to local contractors, but none of them would agree to do the job for the price agreed upon by the original contractor. On June 3 of the following year, the property owner filed suit for specific performance against the original contractor.

Which of the following represents the contractor's best argument in his defense against the property owner's suit?

(A) Specific performance is an equitable remedy, and because the property owner waited for over a year to sue, the equitable defense of laches will apply.

(B) Specific performance is inappropriate, because a contract for personal services is involved.

(C) Specific performance is inappropriate, because nominal legal damages are available to the property owner.

(D) Specific performance is inappropriate, because the property owner's failure to obtain another contractor for the job is an indication that $12,500 was an unfair price.

Question 9

The owner of a factory that uses widgets in making its product and a widget maker entered into negotiations over the telephone and, after a time, reached a general understanding that the factory owner would buy widgets from the widget maker. Following their conversation, the widget maker sent the factory owner a contract, which he had already signed, agreeing to sell 1,000 widgets to the factory owner for a total contract price of $10,000. Upon receipt of the contract in the mail, the factory owner signed the contract and deposited an envelope containing the contract in the mailbox located in front of his workplace.

Before the widget maker received the contract, the factory owner had a change of heart. He telephoned the widget maker and told him that he could not afford to buy the widgets he had ordered, and he was "not interested in that contract we talked about." The widget maker replied, "That's all right, I understand. Maybe we can do business some other time." The next day, the signed contract was delivered to the widget maker's office. The widget maker, also having had a change of mind, decided that he wanted to enforce the contract.

Is the contract enforceable against the factory owner?

(A) Yes, because the acceptance occurred prior to rejection.

(B) Yes, because of the parol evidence rule.

(C) No, because the offer to rescind was accepted and that discharged the original contract.

(D) No, because the rejection by telephone voided the acceptance by mail.

Question 10

On March 1, a health food store owner and a health food distributor entered into a written agreement providing that the distributor would supply the store owner with his natural foods requirements over the next 12 months. In return, the store owner agreed to purchase only from the distributor. The agreement also provided that payment for any purchases made under the agreement during the month of April would be turned over to a nonprofit food research corporation, "to carry on its good works."

On April 1, the store owner ordered and the distributor shipped 20 cases of health food products, at a wholesale price of $4,000, which remains unpaid.

On April 15, the store owner sold his store, inventory, and accounts receivable to a chain operation that also sells health food products. As part of the sale, the store owner assigned to the chain operation the contract with the distributor. The chain operation promptly notified the distributor of the sale and assignment.

The $4,000 for the April 1 transaction remained unpaid and, on May 31, the food research corporation commenced suit to collect the money. Against whom may the action be maintained?

(A) The store owner only.

(B) Both the store owner and the chain operation.

(C) The chain operation only.

(D) Neither the store owner nor the chain operation.

Question 11

A law firm, at its clients' behest, instituted a class action lawsuit against a tobacco company for $100 million. Prior to signing the written contract outlining the parties' rights and responsibilities, including the fee arrangement, the

firm's senior partner told the clients' representative in a moment of goodwill and generosity that if they won or the tobacco company settled, he would turn over half of the attorneys' fees in the case to a particular nonprofit group that funds research on lung cancer and other respiratory illnesses. After the law firm won the case and collected its fee of $33 million, it had second thoughts about turning over half of it to the nonprofit group.

If the nonprofit group sues the law firm in an attempt to collect the $16.5 million, which of the following is the law firm's best defense to such action?

(A) The promise to turn over half of the attorneys' fees was discharged by novation.

(B) A partial assignment (in favor of the nonprofit group) is ineffective.

(C) The promise to turn over half of the attorneys' fees was not in writing.

(D) The law firm was simply attempting to confer a gift upon the nonprofit group.

Question 12

A jeweler sent a fax to a gold dealer offering to sell the dealer 100 ounces of gold at $900 per ounce. The dealer immediately responded via fax, "What are your terms of shipment?" The jeweler faxed back, "F.O.B. my store." The dealer faxed back, "I accept."

Who must pay the freight charge from the shop to the dealer?

(A) The shop owner, because of the F.O.B. term.

(B) The shop owner, because he is a merchant seller.

(C) The gold dealer, because of the F.O.B. term.

(D) The gold dealer, because both parties are merchants.

Question 13

A pet shop entered into a written contract with a distributor of pet products, whereby the distributor agreed to supply the pet shop with whatever quantity of pet food it might order, at a mutually agreed price, for two years, with an option to renew. Also, the contract required that the pet shop buy its pet food from the distributor only. For the first six months of the contract, the pet shop ordered from the distributor 10 cases of pet food per month. In the seventh month, the owner of the pet shop sold the shop, inventory, and accounts receivable to a chain operation. As part of the sale, the pet shop assigned to the chain operation its contract with the distributor. The chain operation promptly notified the distributor of the sale and assignment. That same month, looking to stock the pet food in stores throughout its chain, the chain operation sent the distributor an order for 5,000 cases of pet food "on the terms and conditions of the agreement expressed in the contract which has been assigned to us." The distributor did not have the means to fill such a large order and refused to deliver 5,000 cases.

The chain operation brings suit to compel the distributor to fill the order for 5,000 cases of pet food? Who will prevail?

(A) The chain operation, because it gave the distributor prompt notice of the assignment from the pet shop it purchased.

(B) The chain operation, because it would not be impossible for the distributor to acquire the quantity of pet food that the chain operation requires.

(C) The distributor, because the quantity required by the chain operation is too great compared to the pet shop's needs and, thus, the assignment is not enforceable.

(D) The distributor, because there was no mutuality of obligation in the original agreement between the distributor and the pet shop and hence there was nothing to "assign" to the chain operation.

Question 14

A buyer for a chain of shoe stores ordered 1,000 pairs of shoes from a shoe manufacturer. The shoes cost $50 per pair, so the total contract price was $50,000. It happened that the manufacturer owed $50,000 to a trucking company. The manufacturer assigned, in writing, "all proceeds from the contract with the buyer" to the trucking company. The manufacturer notified the buyer that he had assigned the proceeds of the contract to the trucking company and then shipped the 1,000 pairs of shoes to the buyer. Upon receipt of the shoes, the buyer discovered that 10% of the shoes were defective. He sent a check for 90% of the contract price ($45,000) to the manufacturer, who deposited the check. Shortly thereafter, the manufacturer closed down its business and disappeared without a trace. The trucking company, meanwhile, demanded payment from the buyer, to no avail.

The trucking company sues the buyer for the $45,000 that the buyer paid on the contract. Will the trucking company prevail?

(A) Yes, because the buyer had notice from the manufacturer that the contract had been assigned to the trucking company.

(B) No, because the manufacturer wrongfully took the money that was assigned to the trucking company and is solely liable to the trucking company.

(C) No, because the buyer fulfilled his obligations under the contract by paying the manufacturer.

(D) No, because the trucking company could not have performed the other side of the contract by furnishing the shoes.

Question 15

A wholesale seller of personal digital assistants ("PDAs") entered into a contract with a retailer who was in the business of selling electronics, to sell 50 PDAs at a cost of $200 apiece, or a total cost of $10,000. When the PDAs were delivered, the retailer discovered that 20% of them were defective. The retailer sent the seller a check for 80% of the contract price ($8,000). Did the retailer make a proper rejection?

(A) Yes, because the PDAs were defective.

(B) Yes, because the retailer paid for the PDAs that were not defective.

(C) No, because the retailer accepted the PDAs and failed to seasonably notify the seller of any rejection due to defects.

(D) No, because the retailer kept all of the PDAs and did not return the defective PDAs to the seller.

Question 16

An art collector was interested in buying a painting from his neighbor. The neighbor told the collector that he could have the painting for $30,000. The collector wanted to think the purchase over. Therefore, the two agreed in writing that the neighbor would keep the offer open for 30 days in exchange for $500, which the collector paid. The terms of the written agreement provided that the offer would expire at 11:59 p.m. on September 30 if the collector failed to accept by that time. On September 20, the collector telephoned his neighbor and told him, "The more I think about it, the less I think that I want your painting." The neighbor responded, "That's your decision to make." On September 26, one of the neighbor's friends was visiting him, saw the painting, and offered his friend (the neighbor) $35,000 for it.

On September 27, the neighbor mailed a $50 check to the collector with a letter stating that he was terminating his offer to the collector regarding the painting and refunding 10% of the money that the collector paid him to keep the offer open. He mailed the letter at 11:59 p.m. on September 27. The collector received the letter at 11:30 a.m. on September 29. On September 28, at 9:30 a.m., the collector mailed a letter to his neighbor stating that he had decided to

purchase the painting and a certified check in the amount of $30,000 was enclosed. Two hours later, the neighbor sold the painting to his friend for $35,000. The neighbor received the collector's letter on October 1 and immediately mailed the check back to the collector.

Can the collector maintain a successful legal action against his neighbor?

(A) Yes, because the neighbor sold the painting after the collector's effective acceptance, and before the neighbor's revocation became effective.

(B) Yes, because in his revocation the neighbor did not refund the full $500 to the collector.

(C) No, because the neighbor effectively revoked his offer before the collector accepted.

(D) No, because the collector's power to accept lapsed before he effectively accepted.

Question 17

A landowner advertised in the newspaper that he wished to sell 40 acres of land at $10,000 per acre. A rancher who was looking to expand his holdings was interested, so he came out to inspect the property. After the inspection, the rancher agreed to purchase the land for $400,000. A contract for the sale of the 40 acres was prepared and signed by the landowner and the rancher. The contract failed to state the purchase price. Later, the rancher had a change of heart and refused to complete the purchase.

The landowner now brings a lawsuit for breach of contract. The court should hold for:

(A) The landowner, because the parol evidence rule will not bar testimony that the rancher agreed to pay $400,000.

(B) The landowner, because the Statute of Frauds can be satisfied by combining the original advertisement and the written contract.

(C) The rancher, because the parol evidence rule will bar all evidence that he agreed to pay $400,000 for the land.

(D) The rancher, because the Statute of Frauds would require the contract to contain the price in order to be enforced.

Question 18

On November 3, an investor who had watched his stocks sink to unprecedented low levels sent a fax message to a dealer in precious metals: "Please quote your best price on 800 troy ounces platinum bars for immediate delivery at my bank." At 10 a.m. the next morning (November 4) the dealer replied by fax, "My best price is $475 per ounce." The investor received the dealer's message later on that same day.

The communications between the investor and the dealer are best characterized as:

(A) An offer and an acceptance.

(B) A request for an offer and an offer.

(C) An offer and a price quotation.

(D) A request for an offer and a price quotation.

CONTRACTS ANSWERS - SET 3

Answer to Question 1

(A) The agreement is unenforceable because modification of the contract must be supported by consideration, and the builder has given no consideration. While consideration is generally necessary to modify a contract, even when the modification is in writing, consideration is usually found to exist where the obligations of both parties are varied. However, a modification solely for the benefit of one of the parties is unenforceable. The modification here is solely for the benefit of the builder because he receives the same amount of money from the landowner even though the air conditioning unit will not be installed. The builder is not giving any new or different consideration because he was already obligated to finish the house, and the performance of an existing legal duty is not sufficient consideration. While courts will sometimes find consideration where severe and unforeseen hardships make full performance impracticable, increased construction costs are not within that category. Therefore, the subsequent written agreement is unenforceable. (B) is incorrect because there is no novation here. A novation occurs where a new contract substitutes a new party under the terms of an old contract. Clearly, the agreement here does not involve such a substitution. (C) is incorrect because consideration is required for modification of a construction contract. Modification of a contract for the ***sale of goods*** under the U.C.C. may be effective without consideration [U.C.C. §2-209(1)], but the contract here only incidentally involves the sale of goods (all things movable at the time they are identified to the contract). Primarily, the contract is a construction contract and is not subject to the U.C.C. rule. Therefore, consideration is required for its modification. (D) is incorrect because the builder does not have a legal right to breach the contract. The majority of courts adhere to the view that detriment to the promisee is the exclusive test of consideration. Legal detriment will result if the promisee refrains from doing something that he has a legal right to do. Because the builder does not have a legal right to breach the contract, his refraining from walking off the job is not sufficient consideration to support the modification. While a number of cases have held that unforeseen hardships may justify enforcing an agreement for more than the originally bargained-for consideration, most courts require the hardship to be so severe that the contract could be discharged on impracticability grounds (so that a new promise to perform for more money is supported by refraining from exercising the right to discharge the contract). The test for impracticability requires that the party encounter ***extreme and unreasonable*** difficulty and/or expense and that this difficulty was not anticipated. The substantially increased building costs would probably not be considered an extreme and unreasonable expense. Furthermore, the builder arguably should have anticipated possible increases in costs.

Answer to Question 2

(A) The art patron may purchase the photographic work at whatever price the court determines to be reasonable. In a contract for the sale of goods, the failure to state the price does not prevent formation of a contract if the parties intended to form a contract without the price being settled. In such a case, if the price is left to be agreed to by the parties and they fail to agree, a reasonable price at the time of delivery will be supplied by the court. [U.C.C. §2-305] Here, the parties had a contract for the sale of goods (a piece of artwork), with the price of the artwork not fixed at the time of contracting. Because they have failed to agree on a price, the art patron is entitled under the U.C.C. to purchase the artwork at whatever price the court determines to be reasonable. (B) is incorrect because there is no provision for arbitration in the agreement. As stated above, if the price is left open in a contract for sale of goods, and the parties are unable to agree later on a price, the court will supply a reasonable price. [U.C.C. §2-305] (C) is incorrect because even

though $700 was a good faith tender, it may or may not be the "reasonable" price determined by the court. As discussed above, if the price in a contract for sale of goods is left to be agreed to by the parties at a later point and they fail to agree, the court will supply a reasonable price. [U.C.C. §2-305] (D) is incorrect because, as discussed above, the U.C.C. provides that if the price is left to be agreed to by the parties and they fail to agree, the court will supply a reasonable price. [U.C.C. §2-305] The art patron would have to pay $1,200 only if the court determined that $1,200 was a reasonable price.

Answer to Question 3

(A) Most courts would hold that there is a good faith dispute, and the check thus proposed an accord; the woodworker's act of cashing it is a satisfaction. A contract may be discharged by an accord and satisfaction. An accord is an agreement in which one party to an existing contract agrees to accept, in lieu of the performance that he is supposed to receive from the other party, some other, different performance. Satisfaction is the performance of the accord agreement. An accord and satisfaction generally may be accomplished by tender and acceptance of a check marked "payment in full" where there is a bona fide dispute as to the amount owed. Here, there is a good faith dispute between the parties as to the workmanship on the armoire. Therefore, the decorator's tender of the check marked "payment in full" and the woodworker's cashing of the check constituted an accord and satisfaction, discharging her duty to pay the balance. (B) is incorrect because the debt is unliquidated. Generally, payment of a smaller sum than due will not be sufficient consideration for a promise by the creditor to discharge the debt. However, the majority view is that payment of the smaller amount will suffice for an ***accord and satisfaction*** where there is a bona fide dispute as to the claim. As discussed above, because the parties had a good faith dispute about the workmanship on the armoire, the decorator's tender of the check and the woodworker's cashing of the check constituted an accord and satisfaction, which discharged the decorator's duty to pay the balance. (C) is incorrect because a promissory estoppel situation does not exist in that there was no change of position by the decorator based on any act or statement by the woodworker. Whenever a party to a contract indicates that she is waiving a condition before it is to happen or some performance before it is to be rendered, and the person addressed ***detrimentally relies*** upon the waiver, the courts will hold this to be a binding (estoppel) waiver. Here, there is no indication that the designer detrimentally changed position as a result of the woodworker's cashing of the check. Therefore, his act of cashing the check could not be considered an estoppel waiver. (D) is incorrect because the woodworker's indorsement is not sufficient to meet the writing requirement for a release. A release that will serve to discharge contractual duties is usually required to be in writing and supported by new consideration or promissory estoppel elements. While the good faith dispute between the woodworker and the decorator would meet the consideration requirement for a release, the indorsement does not show the kind of circumspection and deliberateness that the writing requirement was intended to ensure. Therefore, the better answer is that the acceptance of the check by the woodworker was a satisfaction, as discussed above, rather than a release.

Answer to Question 4

(C) The builder will recover nothing because his duty to construct the building for the nonprofit group is not discharged by the fire. Contractual duties will be discharged where it has become impossible to perform them. While contractual duties will generally be discharged if the contract's subject matter is destroyed, a contractor's duty to construct a building is not discharged by destruction of the work in progress unless the other party has assumed that risk. The rationale behind this rule is that the construction is not rendered impossible; the contractor can still rebuild.

The risk of loss during construction, absent contrary provisions, lies with the builder, who is generally in a better position to acquire insurance during the construction process. Therefore, because there is no indication that the builder inserted a provision in the contract relieving him of liability in the case of fire, his duty to build the house is not discharged by the fire. (A) is incorrect because there has not been a breach by the nonprofit during the construction, nor has the nonprofit assumed the risk of the fire. If the owner of property on which the construction is to take place breaches the construction contract during the construction, the builder is entitled to the contract price minus the cost of completion. However, the facts here involve risk of loss from fire, not a breach by the owner (the nonprofit). Also, while the builder might have recovered the contract price less the value of the work remaining to be done if the nonprofit had assumed the risk of a fire, the nonprofit had not done so and the builder's duty to complete the house is not discharged. (B) is incorrect because the builder's duty of performance has not been rendered objectively impossible by the fire, as discussed above. Moreover, even if the construction contract were discharged, the builder would not be entitled to a proportionate amount of the profits he would have earned. At best, he would be reimbursed only for the value of his labor and the materials used on the building (*see* below). (D) is incorrect because, while the builder might be entitled to this recovery if the construction contract were discharged by impossibility, his duty was ***not*** discharged by the fire. When the duties of parties to a contract are excused on account of impossibility, restitution in a quasi-contract action is available to put the parties back into the original status quo to prevent unjust enrichment. However, as discussed above, the builder's duty of performance has not been rendered objectively impossible by the fire. (It is also unlikely that he could show that the nonprofit has been unjustly enriched because the construction was destroyed.) Therefore, the builder can recover nothing from the nonprofit unless and until he builds another house.

Answer to Question 5

(C) An enforceable contract was created because even though the document standing alone does not appear to be supported by any consideration, it still may be construed as an ***offer*** to sell, which was accepted before it was revoked. In general, a contract must be supported by valuable consideration on both sides to be fully enforceable from the moment of formation. The majority of courts adhere to the view that detriment to the promisee in performing an act or making a promise is the exclusive test of consideration. Here, the writing was not supported by consideration on both sides because the stable owner was not clearly obligated to purchase the colts. However, the writing still may be construed as an offer to sell. The fact that the price of the colts was left open to be determined later does not prevent the writing from being considered an offer because a reasonable price at the time of delivery will be supplied by the court. [U.C.C. §2-305] Because the offer had not been revoked, the stable owner's good faith and prompt tender would constitute the acceptance, creating an enforceable contract (although the contract may or may not be enforceable at the price tendered). (A) is incorrect because, as discussed above, the breeder became obligated to sell the colt when the stable owner accepted the offer to purchase the colt by tendering the $25,000. (B) is incorrect because the stable owner did not impliedly promise to purchase a colt by signing the agreement. The terms of the document clearly show that the parties did not intend that the stable owner would be obligated to purchase; he merely was given a right of first refusal. The courts will not infer from the signing of a document a promise that is contrary to the parties' intent. Because the stable owner was not obligated to purchase a colt, the written document was unenforceable as a contract for lack of consideration. (D) is incorrect because the U.C.C. limits the duration of irrevocability of merchants' firm offers to three months. Even without consideration, an offer by a merchant to buy or sell goods in a signed writing that, by its terms, gives assurances that it will be held open is not revocable during the time stated or for a

reasonable time if no period is stated (but in no event may such period exceed three months). [U.C.C. §2-205] The breeder would be considered a merchant under the U.C.C. because he holds himself out as having special knowledge of horses. [U.C.C. §2-104(1)] However, because such an offer can only be considered irrevocable without consideration for three months, the six-month-old written agreement is not enforceable as a firm offer.

Answer to Question 6

(A) The agreement is enforceable because both the builder and the yoga instructor gave new consideration to support the modification. If parties agree to modify their contract, consideration is usually found to exist where the obligations of both parties are varied. It is usually immaterial how slight the change is, because courts are anxious to avoid the preexisting duty rule. Here, the obligations of both the builder and the yoga instructor are varied—he will not install the koi pond and she will pay a construction price reduced by $500. Consideration is therefore found in the promise of both parties to forgo their rights under the original contract—the builder's right to full contract price and the yoga instructor's right to the koi pond. (C) is incorrect because a contract in writing may be modified orally unless the modification brings the contract within the Statute of Frauds or, in U.C.C. cases, the contract provides that modifications must be in writing. The contract here is not within any provision of the Statute of Frauds (*see* below), and does not fall under the U.C.C. Even if the contract had prohibited oral modifications, parties in non-U.C.C. cases may alter their agreement orally in spite of such a provision as long as the modification is otherwise enforceable. (B) is incorrect because this modified construction contract does not have to be in writing, because it is not for the sale of goods valued at $500 or more and can be completed within a year. A promise that by its terms cannot be performed within a year is subject to the Statute of Frauds and must be evidenced by a writing signed by the parties sought to be bound. If the contract can be completed within one year, it need not be in writing. Here, it can be assumed that the builder could complete the studio within a year. Therefore, the modification does not have to be in writing. (D) is incorrect because the parol evidence rule does not apply to ***subsequent*** oral agreements. The parol evidence rule states that where the parties to a contract express their agreement in a writing with the intent that it embody the full and final expression of their bargain, any other expressions—written or oral—made prior to the writing, as well as any oral expressions contemporaneous with the writing, are inadmissible to vary the terms of the writing. Parol evidence can be offered to show ***subsequent*** modifications of a written contract, such as the oral agreement between the builder and the yoga instructor, because the rule applies only to prior or contemporaneous negotiations.

Answer to Question 7

(B) The company should recover $5,000 because the oral contract between it and the factory owner is enforceable to the extent the factory owner received and accepted the goods. A promise for the sale of goods of $500 or more is not enforceable unless evidenced by a writing signed by the party to be charged. [U.C.C. §2-201(1)] However, an oral contract for such goods is enforceable to the extent of goods received and accepted by the buyer. [U.C.C. §2-201(3)(c)] Oral contracts for specially manufactured goods not suitable for sale in the ordinary course of the seller's business also are enforceable when the seller has begun substantially to perform. Here, the parties' agreement was oral. The factory owner accepted one machine, but neither machine was specially manufactured. He is bound to pay the $5,000 contract price for the accepted machine but is not bound to pay for the rejected machine. (A) is incorrect because the company is entitled to the contract price for the machine the factory owner accepted, not just restitution. If a contract is unenforceable because of noncompliance with the Statute of Frauds, a party can generally sue for the restitution of any benefit that has been conferred. However, as discussed above, an oral contract for the sale of goods of $500 or more is enforceable to the extent of goods received and accepted by the buyer. Therefore, because the factory owner accepted one machine, the company is entitled to the $5,000 contract price of that machine, not just $3,000 in restitutionary damages. (C) is incorrect because the company is not entitled to any damages as to the rejected machine. As indicated above, the company is entitled to $5,000 for the first machine. There is no enforceable contract regarding the second machine, and the company is not entitled to damages for that machine. If there were an enforceable contract for the second machine, (C) would state a proper measure of damages—if a buyer breaches by refusing to accept goods, the seller is entitled to recover the difference between the contract price ($5,000) and the market or resale price ($3,000), here, $2,000. Thus, the company would be entitled to $5,000 for the accepted machine and $2,000 for the rejected machine, or $7,000. (D) is incorrect for the same reason that (C) is incorrect—the company is only entitled to the contract price of the machine accepted by the factory owner. If the contract for the second machine were enforceable, (D) would still not be a proper measure of damages. Under the U.C.C., the seller has a right to force goods on a buyer who has not accepted them only if the seller is unable to resell the goods or if the goods have been lost or damaged after the risk of loss passed to the buyer. [U.C.C. §2-709] Because the company can resell the second machine, which has not been lost or damaged, it could not recover the full price of the second machine from the factory owner even if the contract was fully enforceable.

Answer to Question 8

(B) The contractor's best argument is that a personal services contract is not specifically enforceable. Thus, the property owner cannot obtain specific performance of the contractor's agreement to perform personal plumbing, electrical, and carpentry work for her. One of the prerequisites to obtaining specific performance is that a plaintiff must show that the legal remedy is inadequate. Where the plaintiff has contracted for something rare or unique, money damages are inadequate compensation for loss of the bargain. Generally, services to be performed under a personal services contract are not unique and money damages can remedy a breach. Thus, specific performance is not available in such cases. In addition, even in the case of unique services, a court will not order a defendant to work for the plaintiff, in part because of the difficulty of enforcement and because such an order is tantamount to unconstitutional involuntary servitude. Another requirement for specific performance is that enforcement must be feasible. Enforcing a personal services contract generally would create complicated and time-consuming supervision problems that courts are reluctant to undertake. In this case, the contractor agreed to personally perform for the property owner plumbing, electrical, and carpentry work. Thus, this was a personal services contract. However, the services to be performed by the contractor were not unique or capable of being performed solely by him. The property owner could obtain adequate compensation by receiving the amount, above her contract price with the contractor, that it will cost to have someone else perform the required work (plus reasonable compensation for the delay in performance). Thus, specific performance is inappropriate here. (A) is incorrect because circumstances that would permit the defense of laches do not appear to be present. Laches is available as an equitable defense if the plaintiff has unreasonably delayed in bringing the action and the delay is prejudicial to the defendant. There is no automatic invocation of laches by a delay of one year before suit is filed. Here, there is no showing that the property owner's delay in filing suit was unreasonable, given that she spent several months trying to find another contractor, nor that the contractor has been prejudiced by the delay. Therefore, laches will not provide the contractor with a strong defense. (C) is incorrect because nominal damages would not be an adequate legal remedy. Nominal damages are appropriate where there is a breach, but no actual loss. Here,

nominal damages would fail to compensate the property owner for the amount she will have to pay above the price agreed to by the contractor. Thus, the availability of nominal damages would not, by itself, render specific performance an inappropriate remedy. Regarding (D), a court of equity may inquire into the relative values of agreed-upon consideration and deny an equitable remedy if it finds a contract to be unconscionable. Nevertheless, the mere fact that the property owner could not find another contractor to do the job for the price agreed upon by the contractor does not establish that the contract was unconscionable. Thus, the contractor will not be successful in his contention that specific performance should be denied on the basis that the price for which he agreed to do the work was too low.

Answer to Question 9

(A) The contract is enforceable because the mailbox rule applies here. Acceptance by mail creates a contract at the ***moment of posting***, properly addressed and stamped, unless the offer stipulates that acceptance is not effective until received, or an option contract is involved. If the offeree sends an acceptance and then rejects the offer, the mailbox rule applies; *i.e.,* a contract is created upon dispatch of the acceptance. Because no option contract is involved here, and the widget maker's offer did not state that the factory owner's acceptance would be effective only when received, his acceptance was effective the moment he placed the envelope containing the contract in the mailbox. His attempt to reject occurred after acceptance took place. Thus, a valid contract was formed and the widget maker may enforce it. (B) is incorrect because nothing in the parol evidence rule would serve to validate the contract. Ostensibly, this choice implies that there is a contract because the parol evidence rule will prevent the factory owner from introducing the oral rescission. However, as discussed below, the rescission is ineffective because there was no meeting of the minds. The parol evidence rule would not prevent introduction of the rescission if it were otherwise valid. The parol evidence rule of the U.C.C. merely prohibits a party to a goods contract from contradicting an integrated writing with evidence of any prior agreement or contemporaneous oral agreement. Subsequent agreements such as the attempted rescission here can be introduced. Therefore, the parol evidence rule does not serve to validate the contract here. (C) is incorrect because there is no "meeting of the minds" concerning the rescission. A contract may be discharged by an express agreement between the parties to rescind; the agreement to rescind is itself a binding contract. Because the widget maker did not know that the factory owner had accepted the contract, his statement that "that's all right" cannot be construed as acceptance of the factory owner's offer to rescind. Therefore, a contract to rescind was not formed. (D) is incorrect because the telephone rejection did not void the acceptance by mail. As discussed above, if the offeree sends an acceptance first, followed by a rejection, the mailbox rule applies; *i.e.,* a contract is created upon dispatch of the acceptance. Because the factory owner's telephone rejection took place after his acceptance by mail, his acceptance was effective and a contract was created when the letter was mailed. While an ***offeree*** will be estopped from enforcing the contract if the offeror receives the rejection first and changes his position in reliance on it, the widget maker is the one wanting to enforce the contract here.

Answer to Question 10

(B) The store owner remains liable based on his contract with the distributor, and the chain operation is liable based on its assumption of the contract with the distributor. The food research corporation is expressly designated in the contract between the store owner and the distributor as a party to whom payment for any April purchases is to be directly made. Thus, the portion of the contract providing for payment is primarily for its benefit. Consequently, the food research corporation is an intended third-party beneficiary of the store owner's promise to make the April payment. As the third-party beneficiary, it has a right of action against the promisor (the store owner) for enforcement of the promise to pay. When the store owner assigned to the chain operation his contract with the distributor, the distributor was deemed to have assumed the store owner's duties under that contract as well as being assigned the rights thereunder. Thus, the chain operation can be held to the duty to pay for the health food products that were ordered in April. Although the chain operation is deemed to have assumed the duties of the store owner under the contract, the store owner (the delegator) remains liable on the contract. Consequently, the food research corporation has a right of action for the April payment against both the store owner and the chain operation (although it will be limited to only one recovery, *see* below). (A) and (C) are incorrect because they conclude that, as between the store owner and the chain operation, only one of them has the duty to tender the required payment. As explained above, ***both*** the store owner and the chain operation are under this duty. (D) is incorrect because, as discussed above, both the store owner and the chain operation are liable. Of course, there will be only one recovery, so as not to cause a windfall as a result of the breach. Generally, the purpose of contract damages is to put the nonbreaching party it in the position it would have been in had the contract been performed.

Answer to Question 11

(D) The nonprofit group did not give consideration to the law firm in return for the law firm's promise to turn over half of its attorneys' fees to the group in the event it won or settled the class action suit. Thus, the law firm's promise was gratuitous; *i.e.*, it was simply attempting to confer a gift upon the nonprofit group, and the group could not compel the law firm to turn over the money. (A) is incorrect because there was no novation and, hence, no discharge of the promise. A novation substitutes a new party for an original party to a contract, and in the process discharges the old contract and creates a new one. Here, the parties to the contract (the law firm and the clients) did not change when the law firm, through its senior partner, made its gratuitous promise. (B) is incorrect because partial assignments are effective—an assignor may transfer some rights under the contract and retain others. (C) is incorrect because the promise did not fall within the Statute of Frauds, which requires a writing signed by the party to be bound. Although the amount in question was $500 or more, the promise was not for the sale of goods. Moreover, this was not a promise that, by its terms, could not be performed within a year—there was a possibility of completion within one year, for example, if the parties settled. Thus, the promise was not unenforceable due to the lack of a written agreement.

Answer to Question 12

(C) The gold dealer must pay the freight because that is what the offer stated, and he accepted the offer. The term "F.O.B." is a delivery term under the U.C.C., which governs the contract here because it is a contract for the sale of goods. That term means "free on board," and it obligates the seller to get the goods to the location indicated after the term. [U.C.C. §2-319(1)] Here, the term indicates that the goods are "F.O.B. [jeweler's] shop," so the shop owner is not obligated to pay for costs of shipment beyond his shop. Thus, (A) is incorrect. (B) and (D) are incorrect because the parties' status as merchants is irrelevant here. If an acceptance were sent that added the F.O.B. term, whether the parties were merchants would be relevant in determining whether the terms of the contract included only those of the offer or also those of the acceptance. However, we do not have a case where the acceptance added terms. The gold dealer accepted all terms of the offer unequivocally with the fax stating, "I accept."

Answer to Question 13

(C) The chain operation cannot compel the distributor to fill the order for 5,000 cases of pet food, because that amount was not contemplated by the original parties to the contract and is grossly disproportionate to the number of cases ordered by the pet shop during the first six months of its contract with the distributor. An assignment of rights is barred if it will substantially change the obligor's duty. At common law, the right to receive goods under a requirements contract generally was not assignable because the assignment could change the obligation of the parties. Under the U.C.C., such a right is assignable if the quantity requirement is not unreasonably disproportionate to the quantity originally contemplated by the parties or, in the absence of a stated estimate, any normal or otherwise comparable prior requirements. [U.C.C. §2-306] Here, the owner of the pet shop owned only one store and his requirements for the first six months of the contract were only 10 cases per month. The chain operation, on the other hand, owned multiple stores and its requirements are 5,000 cases per month, a disproportionately large increase. Therefore, the assignment here would be unenforceable even under the Code. (A) and (D) are incorrect because prompt notice of the assignment, or the ability to secure the quantity of pet food required by the chain operation, does not obviate the problem of the unreasonably disproportionate requirements. (B) is incorrect because there is mutuality of obligation (consideration on both sides) here. The parties entered into a requirements contract whereby the distributor agreed to sell the pet shop all of its pet food requirements and the pet shop promised to buy its pet food only from the distributor. (Its promise to buy only what it "might order" is not illusory because it agreed to not purchase pet food from any other source.) A requirements contract is not illusory because the U.C.C. imposes a duty to purchase requirements in good faith.

Answer to Question 14

(A) The trucking company will be able to recover the $45,000 from the buyer because the buyer had notice of the assignment. Most contract rights may be assigned, and the right assigned here (to receive money) falls within the general rule. Once the assignment is effective, the assignee (the trucking company) becomes the real party in interest, and he alone is entitled to performance under the contract. (The assignor has been replaced by the assignee.) Once the obligor (the buyer) has knowledge of the assignment, he is bound to render performance to the assignee. Here, the assignment was effective as soon as the assignor (the manufacturer) manifested his intent that the right should be assigned (*i.e.,* in his written assignment to the trucking company). The buyer was given notice of the assignment and, thus, was bound to pay the trucking company. The buyer breached his duty by paying the manufacturer instead of the trucking company. Thus, the trucking company may recover from the buyer for his failure to perform. (B) is wrong because the assignee, as the real party in interest, may enforce its rights against the obligor directly. (C) is wrong because, as stated above, once the buyer had notice of the assignment, he owed the duty to pay to the trucking company (the assignee), and payment to any third party, even the manufacturer (the assignor), does not discharge this duty. (D) is wrong because it is irrelevant whether the assignee could perform under the contract; the relevant question is whether the assignor could and did properly perform.

Answer to Question 15

(C) The retailer did not properly reject, because he accepted the PDAs and failed to give proper notice of rejection. A buyer who receives nonconforming goods generally has the right to accept all, reject all, or accept any commercial units and reject the rest. Here, 20% of the PDAs shipped were defective, so the retailer had a right to reject. To properly reject, the rejecting party must, within a reasonable time after delivery and before acceptance, notify the seller of the rejection. If the notice fails to state a defect, the buyer cannot rely on that defect if the seller could have cured by supplying conforming goods. Here, the retailer failed to notify the seller of the defects. He merely sent a check for less than the contract price. Because the contract did not have a particular delivery date, the seller probably had time to cure and presumably would have. Thus, the retailer cannot rely on the defect in claiming a breach, and his rejection was improper. (A) and (B) are wrong because, although the retailer does not have to accept defective goods or pay for them, he must give the seller notice of the specific defect or he cannot rely on that defect in rejecting. (D) is wrong because, as discussed above, the retailer was required to notify the seller of the defects so that the seller could cure, if possible. Returning, or not returning, the defective goods without explanation would deprive the retailer of his right to rely on the defect in rejecting the goods.

Answer to Question 16

(D) The collector's power to accept lapsed because the power had to be exercised prior to 11:59 p.m. on September 30 and it was not. The mailbox rule does ***not*** apply to the exercise of options. In such cases, acceptance is effective when ***received*** by the offeror, here, on October 1. Thus, (D) is correct. (A) is wrong because, for the reasons discussed above, the collector did not effectively accept before his option expired. (C) is wrong for two reasons: (i) a revocation is not effective until received; and (ii) because the contract is an option, the offeror's power to terminate the offer through revocation is limited. Even if the revocation had arrived earlier, the painter lacked the power to revoke. (B) is irrelevant. Returning the consideration, in and of itself, would not give the offeror the power to revoke in an option situation.

Answer to Question 17

(D) Under the Statute of Frauds, contracts for the sale of land must be in writing. The writing must contain all essential terms, and the price is considered an essential term. (A) is wrong because although the parol evidence rule might not bar the testimony, the Statute of Frauds will prevent recovery. (B) is wrong; the advertisement was not signed by the rancher, the party charged with breaking the contract. Thus, it is not a memorandum. Furthermore, the ad could not be considered part of the contract because there is nothing in the question indicating that it was attached to or referred to in the contract, or that it was assented to by the parties as part of the contract. In fact, an ad is a mere offer to deal; the actual price term may be very different by the time parties to a contract reach an agreement. (C) is wrong; the parol evidence rule would not bar the testimony, and in any event, that is not the reason the rancher will win.

Answer to Question 18

(B) The investor's communication was a request for an offer and the dealer's response was an offer. For a communication to be an offer, it must create a reasonable expectation in the offeree that the offeror is willing to enter into a contract on the basis of the offered terms. The investor's communication does not pass the test because it is clear on its face that he did not want to be bound by whatever price the dealer came up with, but rather wanted to find out what the dealer would offer. The dealer's communication, on the other hand, passes the test. While it said nothing more than the price, it was sent in response to a request containing specific delivery terms and a specific quantity. Under the circumstances, the dealer's response would have created a reasonable expectation in the investor that the dealer was willing to enter into a contract under the terms of the two communications. (A) is wrong because, as indicated above, the investor's communication was not an offer because it did not indicate the requisite intent to be bound. Thus, the dealer's communication could not be an acceptance, because an acceptance must be in response to an offer. (C) and (D) are wrong because, as explained above, the dealer's communication was not merely a price quotation; given that it was sent in response to a very specific inquiry, it was sufficient to be an offer.

Set 4 Answer Sheet

1. Ⓐ Ⓑ Ⓒ Ⓓ
2. Ⓐ Ⓑ Ⓒ Ⓓ
3. Ⓐ Ⓑ Ⓒ Ⓓ
4. Ⓐ Ⓑ Ⓒ Ⓓ
5. Ⓐ Ⓑ Ⓒ Ⓓ
6. Ⓐ Ⓑ Ⓒ Ⓓ
7. Ⓐ Ⓑ Ⓒ Ⓓ
8. Ⓐ Ⓑ Ⓒ Ⓓ
9. Ⓐ Ⓑ Ⓒ Ⓓ
10. Ⓐ Ⓑ Ⓒ Ⓓ
11. Ⓐ Ⓑ Ⓒ Ⓓ
12. Ⓐ Ⓑ Ⓒ Ⓓ
13. Ⓐ Ⓑ Ⓒ Ⓓ
14. Ⓐ Ⓑ Ⓒ Ⓓ
15. Ⓐ Ⓑ Ⓒ Ⓓ
16. Ⓐ Ⓑ Ⓒ Ⓓ
17. Ⓐ Ⓑ Ⓒ Ⓓ
18. Ⓐ Ⓑ Ⓒ Ⓓ

CONTRACTS QUESTIONS - SET 4

Question 1

On November 5, an athletic shoe manufacturer entered into a written contract with a shoe store to carry its running shoes. The contract included a provision that "5% of the proceeds attributable to the sale of the manufacturer's shoes by the shoe store during the month of February (American Heart Month) each year would be donated to the local hospital's new cardiovascular wing." The day after the parties signed their contract, the store owner informed the hospital of the planned donation and indicated that the hospital could expect to receive about $1,500 in early March. In anticipation of the donation, the hospital purchased a new heart monitor on January 5.

On January 15, because the Christmas sales season had been poor, the manufacturer and the shoe store agreed to modify their contract to eliminate the provision for payments to the hospital's cardiovascular wing.

What effect would this subsequent modification have on the hospital's right to institute an action for the lost proceeds (assuming that it otherwise had standing to collect the same)?

(A) It would have no effect, because the hospital's rights vested when it learned of the original agreement.

(B) It would have no effect, because the hospital detrimentally relied on the parties' agreement before finding out that they had changed the agreement.

(C) It would have the effect of cutting off the hospital's right to institute an action under the original agreement.

(D) It would have no effect, because the hospital's rights vested when the contract was made.

Question 2

A farmer who wanted to sell his rye before the growing season was over sent the following fax to a local baker: "Will sell my unprocessed rye, 20 bushels maximum, best price $100 per bushel, firm for 48 hours." Unsure how the baker would respond, and anxious to find a buyer for the rye, the farmer made the same offer to the baker's chief competitor by fax later that same day. The baker was delighted to receive the offer, but needed a day or so to figure out how much rye she needed. When she accepted the farmer's offer the next day, faxing to him an order for 20 bushels, she was aware of the farmer's offer to her competitor, and that her competitor had faxed an order to the farmer for 20 bushels. Unbeknownst to the baker, the farmer does not have enough rye in his fields to sell 20 bushels to each party. The jurisdiction's Uniform Commercial Code includes farmers within the definition of "merchants."

Upon receipt of the baker's order, the farmer has which of the following obligations?

(A) A contract with the baker only, because rye constitutes "goods" under the Uniform Commercial Code.

(B) A contract with the baker's competitor only, because unharvested rye is not within the Uniform Commercial Code's definition of "goods."

(C) A contract with the baker and a contract with her competitor, because the farmer's fax to the baker was a firm offer.

(D) A contract with neither the baker nor her competitor.

Question 3

A steel mill contracted with an appliance manufacturer to sell the manufacturer a 10-ton coil of steel. The written contract specified the quality of the steel to be delivered and also contained a clause that made the agreement contingent upon the appliance manufacturer obtaining a letter of credit from a federally insured bank at an interest rate of no more than 2.5%.

The appliance manufacturer subsequently received a letter of credit from a federally insured bank at 3% interest. Upon hearing of this, the mill refused to ship the steel to the baker.

The appliance manufacturer sues the mill for breach. Who will prevail?

(A) The mill, because the 2.5% is a material term of the contract which the appliance manufacturer breached.

(B) The mill, because the appliance manufacturer breached a duty of good faith.

(C) The appliance manufacturer, because the interest-rate term was included in the contract for his benefit.

(D) The appliance manufacturer, because the .5% differential between the interest rate stated in the contract and the rate actually obtained is not material.

Question 4

The owner of a summer house entered into a written agreement with a plumber. The contract contained a clause requiring all plumbing work to be completed by noon on June 1 and provided that the homeowner would pay the plumber $1,200 for his work. The plumber began working on the job on May 28. When he quit working for the day on the afternoon of May 29, half of the job was completed. Shortly thereafter, it started to rain. The rain continued and became so heavy that a nearby reservoir overflowed and burst the dam restraining the water. A flash flood ensued. The house was in the path of the flood, and the flood struck the house at 2 a.m. on May 30. It was completely washed away.

Which of the following best describes the obligations of the parties to the contract after the flood?

(A) Neither the plumber nor the homeowner is discharged from their obligations under the contract.

(B) The homeowner is obliged to pay the plumber $1,200.

(C) The plumber is discharged from his obligation, but is entitled to recover from the homeowner the fair value of the work he performed prior to the flood.

(D) Both the plumber and the homeowner are discharged from all contract obligations.

Question 5

A recent nursing school graduate mailed a letter to a classmate on July 1 telling her that she was moving to take a nursing position in another city and asking her whether she wanted "the stuff in my house" for $2,500.

The classmate received the letter on July 2, and on July 3 she sent the newly minted nurse a letter accepting the offer. The next day the classmate changed her mind, called the nurse, and told her to forget the deal. Later that same day, the nurse received the letter that her classmate had sent on July 3.

Is there a contract between the nurse and her classmate?

(A) Yes, because the contract is for the sale of goods for more than $500 and the classmate's attempted rejection is oral.

(B) Yes, because the classmate's letter of acceptance was effective when she mailed it.

(C) No, because the classmate's rejection was communicated to the nurse before her letter of acceptance was received.

(D) No, because the description of the subject matter as "the stuff in my house" is not sufficiently definite and certain.

Question 6

The owner of a house put the property up for sale. A surgeon entered into negotiations with the owner to purchase the house, and the parties agreed upon a sale price of $200,000. The owner told the surgeon that she would drop a contract in the mail and have her attorney draw up a deed. The owner signed a land sale contract, which included the property's address but did not contain a metes and bounds legal description. She mailed the contract to the surgeon that afternoon, although it was mailed too late for the last mail pickup of the day. The owner's attorney promptly drew up a deed and dropped it in the mail to his client, who did not sign it. The surgeon received the contract the next day.

After she mailed the contract, the owner received an offer of $250,000 for her property from her next-door neighbor, who wanted to expand beyond his own property line. The owner called her attorney and told him to inform the surgeon that the deal was off. The attorney sent a letter to the surgeon, stating that his client had found another purchaser for the property, and that all matters regarding the surgeon's offer for the property were rescinded. The owner later received the signed contract from the surgeon.

Can the surgeon compel the owner to convey the property to him for $200,000?

(A) Yes, because the owner signed the land sale contract.

(B) No, because the land sale contract does not contain the complete legal description of the property.

(C) No, because the deed was not signed by the party to be charged.

(D) No, because contracts involving land are governed by the Statute of Frauds.

Question 7

On August 1, the owner of a hardware store noticed that he was running low on half-inch carriage bolts and their corresponding nuts. He called a screw manufacturer and ordered 1,000 half-inch carriage bolts and nuts to be delivered by August 15. On August 15, the 1,000 bolts were delivered, but the nuts were missing. The store owner called the manufacturer and was told that they had been temporarily out of nuts when they had filled his order, and had reduced the amount he owed to reflect this, as they had done in the past with him in similar circumstances. The store owner protested and the manufacturer offered to send the nuts by overnight carrier so that he would get them the next day.

May the store owner cancel the contract?

(A) Yes, because he was entitled to a perfect tender.

(B) Yes, because the time for performance has passed.

(C) No, because the one-day delay is not material.

(D) No, because the manufacturer has a reasonable amount of time within which to cure.

Question 8

A sailing enthusiast went to a boat builder and told him that he wanted a yacht built to his specifications. They agreed that the price would be $400,000, and that the sailing enthusiast was to make payment in full within 30 days after he had accepted delivery of the yacht. They further agreed that the boat builder would not subcontract any of the work. The boat builder, however, contacted a master sail maker and subcontracted the sails for the yacht to him. They agreed orally that the boat builder would pay the sail maker $25,000 for the sails within 20 days of receiving them. The boat builder did not tell the sail maker of his agreement with the sailing enthusiast regarding subcontracting. The sail maker made the sails and delivered them to the boat builder, who then completed the yacht and delivered the boat to the sailing enthusiast. Although the yacht was built to his specifications,

the sailing enthusiast refused to accept it after he learned that the boat builder had subcontracted for the sails.

When the 20-day payment period for the sails had expired, the sail maker went to the boat builder and demanded the $25,000. The boat builder told the sail maker that he could not pay the $25,000 unless the sailing enthusiast paid him for the yacht.

The sail maker sues the boat builder for breach of contract. Is there an enforceable contract between the sail maker and the boat builder?

(A) Yes, because they are merchants under the Uniform Commercial Code.

(B) Yes, because the sail maker fully performed.

(C) No, because the boat builder had agreed not to subcontract.

(D) No, because of the Statute of Frauds.

Question 9

A condominium owner hired a cleaning and junk removal service to clean his condo after he moved. The parties agreed in writing that the company was to completely empty out the condo, wash the walls and floors, and clean the appliances in exchange for $1,500. Shortly after beginning performance, the company assigned to a creditor its right to all monies due under the contract (*i.e.*, $1,500), and the creditor promptly notified the young man of the assignment. The condo owner acknowledged the assignment. The company continued working, completely emptying out the condo, washing the walls and floors, and cleaning all of the appliances except for the oven before quitting the job. It would cost $150 to hire a substitute to clean the oven. The condo owner refuses to pay the creditor anything because of the cleaning service's breach.

If the creditor sues the condominium owner, the creditor would be entitled to recover:

(A) $1,500, the amount assigned, and the condominium owner may look to the company to recover for the minor breach.

(B) The reasonable value of the labor and materials expended by the company on the portion of the job it did complete.

(C) $1,350, on a theory of substantial performance.

(D) Nothing, because the condominium owner's duty to pay is subject to a constructive condition precedent, and the assignee takes subject to the defense that the condition has not been satisfied.

Question 10

A builder contracted with a landowner to construct a house on the landowner's property for a contract price of $100,000. The landowner committed a total breach of the contract at a time when the builder had already incurred costs of part performance of $30,000 and would have to spend an additional $60,000 to finish the job.

The builder is entitled to recovery in the amount of:

(A) $10,000.

(B) $30,000.

(C) $40,000.

(D) $60,000.

Question 11

A psychotherapist group hired a construction company to construct a one-story building for $700,000 to use as the group's offices. The contract provided that the group would pay one-third of the contract price (*i.e.*, $233,333) on completion of the foundation, another one-third ($233,333) on completion of the walls and roof, and the balance ($233,334) when the rooms were customized for group and private sessions. After completing work on the foundation, the construction company abandoned the project.

The group hired another contractor to complete the building.

The construction company can recover:

(A) $233,333, the contract price for the work that it completed.

(B) $233,333, offset by whatever damages the consortium suffered in getting the job completed by someone else.

(C) Nothing, because the construction company committed a material breach of the contract.

(D) Nothing on the contract, because this construction contract is not divisible in nature, but it might be entitled to restitution.

Question 12

A jeweler was commissioned by a young man to design and create a set of rings (engagement and wedding) for his fiancée. The jeweler designed and created the rings in 18k gold, leaving room in the engagement ring for a large marquise-shaped diamond. She then entered into an oral agreement with a gemologist under which she would pay him $20,000 for a diamond. The jeweler's agreement with the gemologist was that she would pay him when the young man paid her. The gemologist found and cut a suitable stone and delivered it to the jeweler, who accepted it. The gemologist waited to be paid, and when he was not, he contacted the jeweler, who refused to pay him, arguing that their agreement was unenforceable and, anyway, the young man has not paid her.

The gemologist sues the jeweler for breach of contract. How much can the gemologist recover?

(A) The fair market value of his work, under a quasi-contract theory.

(B) The cost of materials and labor, under a quasi-contract theory.

(C) $20,000, the contract price.

(D) Nothing, because the young man did not pay the jeweler.

Question 13

A dairy farmer hired a local company to assemble milking machines that the farmer had purchased. The written contract between the parties provided that the company would assemble and install the milking machines in the farmer's dairy barn within 30 days, in time for the arrival of the additional cows, and the farmer agreed to pay the company $10,000.

Three weeks into the job, the company realized that it would lose $2,500 on the job, due to a new wage agreement forced on the company by its employees' union after the contract was executed. The company approached the farmer and told him that the job could not be completed for less than $12,500.

After some discussion, the farmer and the company executed an agreement obligating the farmer to pay an additional $2,500 upon completion of the job. The company completes the work on time but the farmer refuses to pay the additional $2,500.

In a suit by the company against the farmer, which of the following would be the farmer's strongest position?

(A) He has no duty to pay the company more than $10,000, because this was a contract for services and the modification was not supported by consideration.

(B) The modification is voidable because the company knew that the farmer needed the machines up and running in 30 days and took advantage of his duress.

(C) The company's mistake regarding the cost of providing its services is not grounds for voiding the original contract.

(D) During initial contract negotiations, the company assured the farmer that the

milking machines would be assembled and installed for no more than $10,000.

Question 14

A building contractor hired an excavator to dig six basements for houses that the contractor was going to construct. The excavator was to receive $36,000 upon completion of the excavations. After digging five of the basements, the excavator realized that because of a recent rise in the cost of fuel, he would lose $2,000 on the contract. He called the contractor to inform him of the situation and the contractor refused to allow the excavator to dig the final basement.

If the contractor sues the excavator for breach of contract, which of the following statements is most correct?

(A) The contractor will lose, because the excavator did not unequivocally repudiate the contract.

(B) The contractor will win because the excavator's actions amount to anticipatory repudiation.

(C) The excavator cannot recover restitution for the value of the materials and labor already provided to the contractor at the time the contractor called a halt to the assembly work.

(D) The excavator will have a valid defense because of the increase in the price of fuel.

Question 15

An elderly woman regularly corresponded with her only niece (her sister's daughter), who lived out of town. One day she sent her niece a letter telling her that she planned to leave everything she owned to her upon her death. When the woman died, her will left her entire estate to her nephew (her niece's brother), valued at $200,000. He wrote his sister a letter telling her that he felt bad about being the only person named in their aunt's will, and added, "I'm going to share her estate with you. We can discuss the details at Auntie's funeral."

The niece spent $800 on a round-trip ticket to attend her aunt's funeral. After the funeral, she spoke to her brother, who told her that he had changed his mind about sharing their aunt's estate with her. He went on to say that he would be willing to share the estate with her if she were willing to share their mother's estate with him, when their mother passed on. The niece responded by telling her brother that their mother had already signed over all her property to her. He replied that, given her attitude, he would keep their aunt's estate for himself.

Later, after the two had returned to their respective homes, no longer on speaking terms, the niece sued her brother for a 50% share of their aunt's estate. What amount should the sister realize from her suit?

(A) Nothing, because the aunt's will left everything to the brother, and the brother's letter is an insufficient basis to compel him to share.

(B) $800, because this represents the sister's actual expenses incurred in reliance on her brother's letter.

(C) $100,000 (half of the aunt's estate), because her brother promised her that in the letter.

(D) $100,000, but only if she shares their mother's estate with her brother.

Question 16

A woman had a developmentally disabled brother who lived in a group home. Nevertheless, the woman ran errands for her brother, took him to the park, and generally made his life pleasant and comfortable. The siblings' grandmother wanted to encourage her granddaughter to continue helping her brother. Therefore, she called her granddaughter and told her that if she continued to take care of her brother for the next five years, she (the grandmother) would give her (the granddaughter) her condominium in Hawaii.

The granddaughter continued to take care of her brother. However, two years after their conversation, the grandmother sold her condominium in Hawaii and told her granddaughter that she would not be able to give her the condominium as a gift, as she had promised. The granddaughter continued to care for her brother and brought suit against her grandmother.

If the court refused to award the granddaughter any damages, which of the following would not be a basis for the court's decision?

(A) The contract was oral and involved the transfer of an interest in real property.

(B) The contract was oral and involved services that could not be performed within a year.

(C) The grandmother's promise did not induce the granddaughter to take action.

(D) The grandmother sold the condominium before the end of the five years.

Question 17

On January 2, a retiree borrowed $1,000 from a friend, agreeing in writing to repay the loan within a year. In September, it became clear to the retiree that he would have difficulty meeting the deadline, and so he approached an acquaintance who owned a print shop with the following proposition: He would perform 200 hours of work for the print shop owner within six months at the special rate of $5 per hour, if the print shop owner would agree to pay $1,000 for the entire 200 hours to the retiree's friend on January 1. The print shop owner agreed. By January 1, the retiree had worked only five hours for the print shop owner, and the print shop owner refused to pay the retiree's friend because the retiree had not worked the agreed-upon number of hours. The retiree told the print shop owner that it was "no problem," and to just hold on to the money until he worked the full 200 hours, and then pay his friend. The print shop owner agreed.

Subsequently, the retiree's friend learned of the arrangements between the retiree and the print shop owner and sued the print shop owner for $1,000. The probable result of this action will be:

(A) Judgment for the friend, because he was a third-party beneficiary to the original contract between the retiree and the print shop owner and there was no consideration for the modification of the contract.

(B) Judgment for the friend, because he was a third-party beneficiary to the original agreement between the retiree and the print shop owner and he did not agree to the modification.

(C) Judgment for the print shop owner, because his contract was with the retiree and therefore he cannot be liable to the friend.

(D) Judgment for the print shop owner, because the original agreement had been modified before the friend knew of the original agreement.

Question 18

A housepainter and a landlord of a two-flat entered into a written agreement whereby the painter would paint both apartments for $2,000, in anticipation of new tenants moving in. The painter told the landlord that after he finished the job, the landlord should pay the $2,000 to the paint store on Main Street, where the painter has an open account and owes the store several thousand dollars. The landlord agreed. The painter informed the store owner of the arrangement. The store owner responded by saying that he did not care who paid him, but the painter's account was seriously overdue, and if he did not get paid by June 1 he would sue. Shortly thereafter, the painter and landlord modified their agreement to push back the work for several months and, as a result, the landlord would not be paying the paint store the $2,000 or any part of it by June 1. The store owner learned about this latest turn of events the next day.

When June 1 rolled around, and neither party paid the store owner the $2,000, the store owner sued the landlord for that amount. Who will prevail?

(A) The store owner, because he was informed of the original agreement and did not participate in the modification.

(B) The store owner, because he assented to the original agreement.

(C) The landlord, because the original agreement was modified before the store owner's rights became vested.

(D) The landlord, because his contract was with the painter and not with the store owner.

CONTRACTS ANSWERS - SET 4

Answer to Question 1

(B) The hospital can still sue because it detrimentally relied on the agreement. An intended third-party beneficiary can enforce a contract only after its rights have vested. Vesting occurs when the beneficiary: (i) manifests assent to the promise in a manner invited or requested by the parties; (ii) brings suit to enforce the promise; or (iii) materially changes position in justifiable reliance on the promise. Here, the hospital purchased the heart monitor in detrimental reliance on the agreement between the manufacturer and the shoe store. The reliance was reasonable because the store owner informed the hospital of the agreement, the approximate amount that they would receive, and the date they would receive it. (A) and (D) are incorrect because, as noted above, the third-party beneficiary's rights do not vest until occurrence of one of the specified conditions. Vesting does not automatically occur on execution of the contract or when the beneficiary learns of the promise. (C) is incorrect because the hospital's right to institute an action under the original agreement could not be cut off once the right vested, and it vested when the hospital purchased the heart monitor ***before*** the parties' executed their new agreement.

Answer to Question 2

(C) Because his fax provided a firm price for 48 hours, the farmer would have a contract with both the baker and her competitor because the offer to the baker was an irrevocable firm merchant's offer during the 48 hours. Under the U.C.C., which governs here because goods are involved, a written offer signed by a merchant giving assurances that it will stay open will be irrevocable for the time stated. The farmer qualifies as a merchant of rye (one who deals in goods of that kind sold) and his offer was written and signed and contained words of firmness ("firm for 48 hours"), so it was irrevocable for 48 hours. The baker accepted the offer within the stated time. Thus, a contract was formed between the baker and the farmer. A contract was also formed between the baker's competitor and the farmer because the competitor accepted the farmer's offer. Therefore, the farmer is obligated to both the baker and her competitor. (A) is incorrect because while rye qualifies as "goods," the result under the U.C.C. is as described above. Also, (A) would probably be incorrect even if rye were not goods, because the baker's acceptance was effective under common law rules. Under the common law, the farmer's offer was revocable despite the words of firmness (because no consideration was given to keep the offer open), but it was not revoked when the baker accepted—her knowledge of the offer to her competitor was not sufficient to revoke the farmer's offer (unless she also knew of the farmer's limited supply, which is not the case here). Thus, even under the common law, the farmer would have a contract with both the baker and her competitor. (B) is incorrect because unharvested grain qualifies as goods, and even if it did not, the farmer would be obligated to both the baker and her competitor, as explained above. (D) is incorrect because, as explained above, the farmer has a contract with both the baker and her competitor.

Answer to Question 3

(C) The appliance manufacturer will prevail because the limitation on the interest rate was placed in the contract for his protection and he was free to waive it. The terms of the contract made the contract contingent upon the appliance manufacturer obtaining a letter of credit from a federally insured bank. Thus, the letter of credit was a condition precedent to the contract. The limit on interest was clearly for the appliance manufacturer—he would not have to enter into the contract unless he could find a satisfactory loan. One having the benefit of a condition may by words or

conduct indicate that he will not insist upon the condition, and the courts will enforce such a waiver. (A) is incorrect because while the 2.5% term was material, it was placed in the contract for the appliance dealer's benefit and he was free to waive it, as discussed above. (D) is incorrect because while the extra .5% may be immaterial, it would be sufficient to prevent the contract; the court would give the condition a literal meaning, and the fact that the variance was immaterial would not alter the fact that the condition precedent was not met. (B) is incorrect because while the U.C.C. (which governs here because we have a contract for the sale of goods) places a duty of good faith on all parties, it is not a breach of the duty for a party to waive a condition that was placed in the contract for that party's benefit.

Answer to Question 4

(C) The destruction of the house discharges the plumber's duties due to impossibility, but the plumber has a right to recover for the reasonable value of the work he performed. Contractual duties are discharged where it has become impossible to perform them. The occurrence of an unanticipated or extraordinary event may make contractual duties impossible to perform. If the nonoccurrence of the event was a basic assumption of the parties in making the contract, and neither party has assumed the risk of the event's occurrence, duties under the contract may be discharged. Impossibility must arise after entering into the contract. If there is impossibility, each party is excused from duties that are yet to be performed. If either party has partially performed prior to the existence of facts resulting in impossibility, that party has a right to recover in quasi-contract at the contract rate or for the reasonable value of his performance if that mode of valuation is more convenient. Here, the house on which the plumber was to perform plumbing repairs was totally destroyed in a flood. The facts indicate that this flood was of such an unexpected nature that its nonoccurrence was a basic assumption of the parties, and neither party was likely to have assumed the risk of its occurrence. Thus, it has become literally impossible for the plumber (or anyone else) to complete the job. This impossibility will discharge both the homeowner and the plumber from performing any contractual duties still to be fulfilled. Therefore, the plumber need not finish the repair work, and the homeowner is not obligated to pay the entire amount of $1,200. (A) and (B) are therefore incorrect for these same reasons. (D) is incorrect because it fails to account for the fact that the homeowner will have to pay the plumber for the value of the work already performed.

Answer to Question 5

(B) The classmate accepted the nurse's offer when she mailed the letter on July 3, and thus, a contract was formed. Under the mailbox rule, acceptance of an offer by mail creates a contract at the moment the acceptance is posted, properly stamped and addressed. If the offeree sends both an acceptance and a rejection, whether the mailbox rule will apply depends on which the offeree sent first, the acceptance or the rejection. If the offeree ***first sends an acceptance*** and later sends her rejection, the mailbox rule does apply. Thus, even if the rejection arrives first, the acceptance is effective upon mailing (and so a contract is formed) unless the offeror changes his position in reliance on the rejection. Here, the classmate first sent an acceptance, then called with her rejection. The mailbox rule applies, and because there is nothing in the facts to show that the nurse relied on the rejection, a contract was formed. (A) is wrong because it implies that a rejection must be in writing. There is no such requirement. Also, the rejection (absent detrimental reliance) has no effect on the contract because the offer had already been accepted and the contract formed. (C) is wrong because, as stated above, under the mailbox rule the fact that the rejection was received before the acceptance is irrelevant (unless there has been detrimental reliance on the rejection, which was not the case here). The contract was formed when the classmate sent her

acceptance. (D) is wrong because the description, although somewhat ambiguous, can be made reasonably certain by evidence of the subjective understanding of the parties and extrinsic evidence of what was in the house, which a court will consider to clarify an ambiguous term.

Answer to Question 6

(A) The surgeon is entitled to specific performance because the homeowner signed the land sale contract. A contract was formed here when the parties orally agreed to the sale of the property. However, the contract was unenforceable at that time because, under the Statute of Frauds, a contract for the sale of land is unenforceable unless a memorandum containing the contract's essential terms is signed by the party to be charged. Here, the party to be charged is the homeowner, and she signed the land sale contract, a writing sufficient to satisfy the Statute of Frauds (a memorandum for the sale of land is sufficient if it contains the price, a description of the property—which need not be a "legal" description—and a designation of the parties). Thus, the contract was enforceable. Specific performance is allowed when the legal remedy (damages) would be inadequate (usually with contracts to purchase land). Therefore, the surgeon is entitled to specific performance (assuming the property has not already been sold to a bona fide purchaser); under the facts the neighbor had made an offer but nothing indicates that the homeowner accepted the offer yet. (B) is incorrect because to satisfy the Statute of Frauds, a description need not be a complete legal description, but need merely be sufficient to reasonably identify the subject of the contract. It is sufficient that the property was identified by its address. (C) is incorrect because it does not matter whether the deed was signed by the homeowner, because the land sale contract was sufficient under the Statute, and the homeowner signed it. (D) is incorrect because while it is true that contracts involving the sale of land are governed by the Statute of Frauds, the Statute was satisfied here by the written sale contract.

Answer to Question 7

(D) The store owner may not cancel the contract, because the manufacturer made a reasonable offer to cure. The general rule in contracts for the sale of goods under the U.C.C. is that the buyer is entitled to a perfect tender. A few exceptions to this rule exist, including where the seller has reason to think that nonconforming goods will be acceptable to the buyer, which reason can arise from the parties' past dealings. In such a case, upon notification of its intention to cure, the seller must be given a reasonable time within which to cure, which may extend beyond the original time for performance. Here, the manufacturer had reason to think the bolt only delivery would be acceptable based on the parties' past dealings. Thus, the manufacturer had a reasonable time to cure and its offer to send the store owner the nuts by overnight carrier is a reasonable offer to cure, negating the store owner's right to cancel the contract. Thus, (A) and (B) are wrong. (C) is wrong because, but for the above exception, the perfect tender rule would apply and the day's delay would be fatal.

Answer to Question 8

(B) There is an enforceable contract between the sail maker and the boat builder because the sail maker fully performed. The contract here was for the sale of goods (sails) for the price of $500 or more; thus, the contract is within the Statute of Frauds. A contract within the Statute of Frauds is generally unenforceable absent a memorandum signed by the party to be charged containing the contract's essential terms. However, there is an exception to the general rule for goods received and accepted. Here, although the contract was oral, the boat builder accepted the sails, and so he is bound despite the Statute. Note that the boat builder might also be bound under another exception

to the Statute—for specially manufactured goods if the sails were made specially for the yacht and were not suitable for sale to others. (A) is incorrect because the U.C.C. does not exempt merchants from the Statute of Frauds. Although it provides a special confirmatory memo rule by which a merchant may be bound even if his signature does not appear on the writing evidencing the contract, here there is no writing at all. (C) is incorrect because it is irrelevant. The fact that the boat builder agreed not to subcontract is relevant to whether he breached his contract with the sailing enthusiast, but it does not affect his contract with the sail maker. (D) is incorrect because, as stated above, the contract here falls within an exception to the Statute of Frauds because the boat builder accepted the sails.

Answer to Question 9

(C) The creditor will be able to recover the contract price less damages for the company's minor breach. Generally, an assignee has whatever rights his assignor would have against the obligor. Similarly, the assignee is subject to any contract-related defenses that the obligor has against the assignor. Thus, the creditor will have whatever rights the company would have against the condominium owner. Here, the company completed all of the tasks that needed to be done except for one (*i.e.*, cleaning the oven). If the work remaining on the contract is minor, the company will be seen as substantially performing its contract, and substantial performance will discharge its duty to perform and obligate payment by the condominium owner. Because the facts state that the cost of finishing the job was relatively small (10% of the cost of the contract), it will probably be seen as a minor breach. Thus, the condominium owner cannot avoid payment of the contract price. However, despite the substantial performance, the other party to the contract may recover damages for the less than complete performance. Thus, the condominium owner will be able to offset his damages from the breach. The creditor then will be able to recover $1,350 (the contract price less the damages). (A) is incorrect because, as stated above, the obligor may offset damages directly against the assignee; he does not have to pay the full contract price and then seek damages from the assignor. (B) is incorrect because this suggests a restitutionary remedy, but as stated above, the creditor, as assignee of the company, would be able to recover the contract price less damages because the company substantially performed. (D) is incorrect because the constructive condition precedent to the condominium owner's duty to pay (the company's performance) has been satisfied here by substantial performance.

Answer to Question 10

(C) The builder is entitled to his profit plus costs. Where an owner breaches a construction contract after construction has been started but before construction is completed, the builder is entitled to recover any profit he would have derived from the contract plus any costs he has incurred to the date of the breach. Here, the builder's profit would have been $10,000 and his costs up to the time of the breach are $30,000. Thus, he can recover $40,000. Another way of saying this is contract price minus the cost of completion. Here, the contract price was $100,000 and the cost of completion was $60,000. Thus, the builder is entitled to $40,000. (A) is incorrect because that amount ($10,000) reflects only the builder's profit and he is also entitled to his costs. (B) is incorrect because that amount ($30,000) reflects only the builder's expenses, and he is also entitled to profits. (D) is incorrect because the builder is not entitled to recover the cost of completion because he has not done the work.

Answer to Question 11

(D) The construction company cannot recover on the contract but it may recover restitution for the work it did. The issue here is whether this contract is divisible. A contract is divisible if: (i) the performance of each party is divided into two or more parts under the contract, (ii) the number of parts due from each party is the same, and (iii) the performance of each part by one party is the agreed-upon equivalent of the corresponding part from the other party. The third requirement is the problem here. There is no indication that the parts the construction company is to perform are the equivalent of the payments the group is to make. Rather, these payments appear to be unrelated to the actual work and merely represent progress payments. Thus, this contract is not divisible in nature. Because the construction company breached the contract by ceasing performance before completion of the entire job, it is not entitled to the contract price. However, it may be entitled to restitution. Modern courts permit a breaching party to recover restitution where the party has conferred a benefit on the other that will result in unjust enrichment of the other if no compensation is paid. Here, the construction company properly completed the foundation, and this conferred a benefit on the group. Therefore, restitution may be available to the construction company. (A) is wrong because, as mentioned, the construction company is not entitled to the contract price, because this is not a divisible contract. Even if it were divisible, (A) would be wrong because the group would be able to offset its damages for the construction company's breach and thus would not be obliged to pay the full contract price. (B) would be the correct answer if the contract were divisible. As explained above, this contract is not divisible merely because it calls for three payments. The payments must be the equivalent of the work performed; otherwise the payments are mere progress payments and the times set for payment are simply convenient times to pay. (C) is wrong because although the breach was material, the construction company could recover something in restitution (*see* above).

Answer to Question 12

(C) The gemologist will be able to recover the full $20,000 contract price. Under the U.C.C., the contract is enforceable, despite the absence of a writing, to the extent of the goods accepted, which here is the entire amount contracted for. The proper remedy is the agreed-upon price of $20,000, which the gemologist will be able to prove by parol evidence. [*See* U.C.C. §2-201, comment 2] (A) is incorrect because the recovery will be under the contract, because the promises are enforceable under the acceptance exception to the Statute of Frauds; thus, the quasi-contract remedy need not be applied. Note that if the contract had been unenforceable, quasi-contract would be a basis for a recovery of restitutionary damages. (B) is incorrect because it also is a possible measure of restitutionary damages in a quasi-contract action, and as stated above, the gemologist will be able to recover under the contract here. (D) is incorrect because the court will construe the jeweler's agreement as a promise rather than an implied condition. If it were a condition, the jeweler would not have a duty to pay because she was not paid. However, where an agreement provides that a duty is to be performed once an event occurs, if the event is not within the control of the promisee, it is less likely that he will have assumed the risk of its nonoccurrence and therefore less likely to be a condition of the promisor's duty to perform. In doubtful situations, courts are more likely to hold that the provision is a promise rather than a condition because this supports the contract and preserves the reasonable expectations of the parties.

Answer to Question 13

(A) The farmer's strongest position is that he came under no duty to pay because this was a contract for services rather than goods. The general rule is that a modification of a contract for services must be supported by consideration. Because a preexisting legal duty is not consideration, for a modification to be enforceable there must be a new promise made by each side. Here, the farmer

agreed to pay an additional $2,500, but the company promised nothing in return. Thus, the modification is unenforceable. Note that the U.C.C. enforces a good faith modification even without consideration, but the U.C.C. applies only in the sale of goods, and the contract here was for services (assembly and installation of the milking machines). (B) is an arguable position, but the majority of jurisdictions would not find duress under the facts here, where one party is merely taking economic advantage of the other party's pressing need to enter into the contract. (C) is wrong because there was no mistake here. Mistakes must exist when the contract is formed, and here the reason for the increased labor costs (the new labor agreement) arose after the contract was formed. (D) is not the best position because what was discussed at the negotiations is irrelevant; the parol evidence rule would prohibit introduction of such statements (when there is an integrated writing, prior and contemporaneous oral statements are inadmissible to vary its terms).

Answer to Question 14

(A) The contractor does not have a valid cause of action because the excavator did not unequivocally repudiate the contract. The contractor refused to allow the excavator to perform under the contract, which itself is a breach of contract that would excuse the excavator from performing its contractual duties. Thus, an action for breach by the contractor will be successful only if the excavator did something to breach the contract before the proprietor breached. The contractor would argue that the excavator breached by anticipatory repudiation when it asked for more money to complete the work. However, the facts do not support this argument because excuse from a contract for anticipatory repudiation is available only where the repudiating party ***unequivocally indicates*** that it will not perform under the contract, and here, nothing in the facts indicates that the excavator unequivocally stated that he would not perform. Thus, (A) is correct and (B) is incorrect. (C) is incorrect because the excavator can pursue a remedy for restitution that may be more favorable than its contract remedy. Restitution may be sought as an alternative to contract damages when the defendant has committed a material breach of contract, in which case the measure of damages is the reasonable value of the benefit conferred on the defendant prior to the breach. Here, the contractor's refusal to allow the excavator to perform under the contract (*i.e.*, to finish digging the basements) would probably be treated as a breach of contract (*see* (A), above) for which the contractor would be liable. However, because the excavator had a losing contract (due to the increased cost of fuel), it likely could recover more in restitution damages than in expectation (benefit of the bargain) damages. (D) is incorrect because, as noted in (A), above, the contractor does not have a valid cause of action against the excavator and, therefore, it would have no need to mount a defense. Had the excavator been required to defend itself, the argument that it would have lost money under the original agreement would fail because it does not fall within any of the traditional categories of defenses (*i.e.*, lack of mutual assent; absence of consideration; illegality; legal incapacity to contract; lack of volitional consent; Statute of Frauds; or unconscionability).

Answer to Question 15

(A) The sister should not recover in her suit because there is no enforceable promise (*i.e.*, no contract) between the brother and sister. Generally, a contract will not be enforced unless consideration has passed between the parties. Consideration is defined as a bargained-for exchange of a benefit to the promisor or a detriment to the promisee. Here, the brother offered his sister half of their aunt's estate, which is certainly a detriment to him, but the sister offered nothing in return. While the brother told the sister that they would discuss the details at the funeral, the sister's purchasing a ticket to attend the funeral is not a bargained-for detriment to her (*i.e.*, it is not the

price of the exchange) because it does not appear that the brother's motive for the promise was to induce his sister to come to the funeral. Rather, the brother's offer was simply to make a gift. Thus, his offer was not an enforceable promise. (B) is incorrect because the sister would be able to recover her reliance damages only under a promissory estoppel theory, and there are no grounds for promissory estoppel here. Under promissory estoppel, a promise is enforceable, at least to the extent necessary to prevent injustice, even though there was no consideration for it, if the promisor should reasonably expect to induce action by his promise and that action is in fact induced. Here, the brother did not promise to give his sister half of their aunt's estate ***if*** she came to the funeral; rather, he only promised to share the estate and said they would talk about it at their aunt's funeral. It is not reasonably foreseeable that, based on the promise, the sister would make a special trip to attend the funeral. Indeed, it is not clear that the sister was induced to go to the funeral by the promise; she may have been planning to attend in any case. (C) is incorrect because, as explained above, the brother's letter was an offer to make a gift; without consideration for that offer, it is unenforceable. (D) is incorrect because it relies on the existence of a contract between the brother and sister (he will share their aunt's estate with his sister in exchange for her sharing their mother's estate with him), and there is no such contract here. The brother certainly made an offer to make such a contract, but the sister probably rejected the offer by saying that their mother's property was already hers. Even if the sister's statement was not sufficient to amount to a rejection, the brother's reply was certainly a revocation. Thus, a contract was not formed by the exchange, and she cannot recover from her brother on that basis.

Answer to Question 16

(D) That the grandmother sold the condominium before the end of five years is not relevant to a decision to deny the granddaughter a remedy. If there were an enforceable contract requiring the grandmother to turn the condominium over to her granddaughter, and the grandmother sold the condominium to a bona fide purchaser for value, that would cut off the granddaughter's right to specific performance, but she would still be entitled to a remedy. Thus, the sale does not support a decision to deny the granddaughter remedy. (A) is a basis for the court's decision. The Statute of Frauds makes certain contracts unenforceable unless they are evidenced by a writing signed by the party to be charged and evidencing the material terms of the contract. Among the contracts that are within the Statute are contracts for an interest in real property. Here the contract was oral and it involved a transfer of real property. Thus, it is unenforceable. (B) would support the court's decision under a similar rationale. Contracts which by their terms cannot be performed within one year are within the Statute of Frauds and are unenforceable without a writing, and, again, the contract here was oral and required five years of performance. (C) would also support the court's decision. Where an oral promise is not enforceable under contract law because of the Statute of Frauds and the promisor should foresee that it will induce the promisee to change position in reliance on the oral promise, promissory estoppel may be used to take the contract out of the Statute of Frauds entirely. If the court finds that the grandmother's promise did not induce the granddaughter to care for her brother (because she was already doing so before the promise was made and after the promise was broken), then the promise is not enforceable under the doctrine of promissory estoppel.

Answer to Question 17

(D) An agreement affecting a third-party beneficiary may be modified without the third party's consent if his rights have not yet vested. If the friend did not know of the original agreement, his rights could not yet have vested. (A) is wrong. It is true that the friend was a third-party beneficiary, but the retiree and the print shop owner are free to modify the agreement without

consideration. (B) is wrong because, as stated, although the friend must agree to the modification if his rights have vested at the time of the modification, his rights had not vested when the agreement was modified. (C) is wrong because it is too broad a statement; under some circumstances, there can be liability to the third party.

Answer to Question 18

(B) A modification of the contract can take place without the consent of the third-party beneficiary prior to the time the third-party beneficiary's rights become vested. The rights become vested when the third party assents in a manner requested by the parties, detrimentally relies on the contract, or brings a lawsuit to enforce it. Here, the painter asked the store owner to assent and, although his answer may have been grumbling, he assented. Because the store owner's rights were then vested, the contract could not subsequently have been modified without his consent. Thus, (C) and (D) are wrong. (A) does not go far enough; mere knowledge of the original arrangement is not enough to vest rights.

Set 5 Answer Sheet

1. Ⓐ Ⓑ Ⓒ Ⓓ
2. Ⓐ Ⓑ Ⓒ Ⓓ
3. Ⓐ Ⓑ Ⓒ Ⓓ
4. Ⓐ Ⓑ Ⓒ Ⓓ
5. Ⓐ Ⓑ Ⓒ Ⓓ
6. Ⓐ Ⓑ Ⓒ Ⓓ
7. Ⓐ Ⓑ Ⓒ Ⓓ
8. Ⓐ Ⓑ Ⓒ Ⓓ
9. Ⓐ Ⓑ Ⓒ Ⓓ
10. Ⓐ Ⓑ Ⓒ Ⓓ
11. Ⓐ Ⓑ Ⓒ Ⓓ
12. Ⓐ Ⓑ Ⓒ Ⓓ
13. Ⓐ Ⓑ Ⓒ Ⓓ
14. Ⓐ Ⓑ Ⓒ Ⓓ
15. Ⓐ Ⓑ Ⓒ Ⓓ
16. Ⓐ Ⓑ Ⓒ Ⓓ
17. Ⓐ Ⓑ Ⓒ Ⓓ
18. Ⓐ Ⓑ Ⓒ Ⓓ
19. Ⓐ Ⓑ Ⓒ Ⓓ
20. Ⓐ Ⓑ Ⓒ Ⓓ
21. Ⓐ Ⓑ Ⓒ Ⓓ
22. Ⓐ Ⓑ Ⓒ Ⓓ
23. Ⓐ Ⓑ Ⓒ Ⓓ
24. Ⓐ Ⓑ Ⓒ Ⓓ
25. Ⓐ Ⓑ Ⓒ Ⓓ
26. Ⓐ Ⓑ Ⓒ Ⓓ
27. Ⓐ Ⓑ Ⓒ Ⓓ
28. Ⓐ Ⓑ Ⓒ Ⓓ
29. Ⓐ Ⓑ Ⓒ Ⓓ
30. Ⓐ Ⓑ Ⓒ Ⓓ
31. Ⓐ Ⓑ Ⓒ Ⓓ
32. Ⓐ Ⓑ Ⓒ Ⓓ
33. Ⓐ Ⓑ Ⓒ Ⓓ
34. Ⓐ Ⓑ Ⓒ Ⓓ
35. Ⓐ Ⓑ Ⓒ Ⓓ
36. Ⓐ Ⓑ Ⓒ Ⓓ

CONTRACTS QUESTIONS - SET 5

Question 1

A young man proposed to his girlfriend but she was reluctant because of his meager income and lack of job potential. The young man told his father about her reluctance. The father told the girlfriend that if she married his son, he would support them for six months and send his son to a six-month computer technology training school. This was sufficient to dispel her reservations and the two were married very soon after. When they returned from their honeymoon, the father refused to go through with his offer. Although the girlfriend is happy in her marriage, she sued the father for damages.

If the father prevails, it will be because:

(A) The father's promise was not supported by valid consideration.

(B) The contract is against public policy.

(C) The contract was oral.

(D) The girlfriend is happy and therefore has incurred no detriment.

Question 2

A manufacturer of desktop and laptop computers decided to purchase a certain model of high-speed printers from a distributor and then offer the printers for sale as part of a complete system with its keyboards and computers. Because printing speed was important, the written agreement between the distributor and the manufacturer provided that the printers must be able to print 30 pages per minute or more. The distributor was to provide, during the term of the agreement, 150 printers for the manufacturer at $300 each. The printers were to be delivered at the rate of 10 per month, commencing March 15, and the manufacturer was to pay for the printers as they were delivered.

When the first shipment arrived, the manufacturer paid for it with a cashier's check for $2,000. However, when the manufacturer put one of the printers on line with its system, it found that the printer was printing at a rate of only 20 pages per minute. The manufacturer then tested the entire shipment and found that none of the printers met the contract specifications. Although the printers did not meet the specifications, the manufacturer was under contract with its own lawyers to deliver two systems by April 1. The manufacturer negotiated with the lawyers, and it was agreed that the manufacturer would install the two systems with the printers, but that the manufacturer would have to deliver by December two high speed printers that met the contract specifications at no extra cost to the lawyers, as replacements for these two printers. Immediately on making this agreement, the manufacturer sent an email to the distributor of the printers telling the distributor that the shipment did not conform to the contract and that no further shipments would be accepted.

Because of the sale of the systems with the nonconforming printers to its lawyers, the manufacturer has accepted:

(A) None of the printers, because it has to replace the two within six months.

(B) The two printers that it sold to its lawyers.

(C) The entire first shipment of 10 printers.

(D) The entire order, because it has shown it is capable of selling the systems with the slower printer.

Question 3

A department store buyer and a manufacturer of food processors entered into a written contract whereby the manufacturer would sell to the buyer 50 of its top-of-the-line models for $100 each. When the delivery arrived on May 15, several days early, the buyer noticed that the food processors were a different model that did not have all of the features as the top-of-the-line model that was ordered. The buyer contacted the manufacturer and told him that he was rejecting the food processors that were delivered to him and expected the manufacturer to send 50 top-of-the-line models immediately. The manufacturer replied that because of a backlog of orders that had not yet been filled, the top-of-the-line models could not be delivered until August 15. Because the department store had contracted with a restaurant to deliver three top-of-the-line models by May 31, the buyer delivered three of the nonconforming food processors along with a promise to replace them with three top-of-the-line models in mid-August. The buyer returned the remaining food processors to the manufacturer.

How much could the department store recover from the manufacturer for the three food processors that it delivered to the restaurant?

(A) Nothing, because they were resold to another.

(B) Nothing, because it accepted them knowing they were defective.

(C) The difference between the contract price and the food processors' actual value.

(D) The difference between the existing food processors' actual value and the cost of the food processors that the department store must provide to the restaurant in mid-August.

Question 4

A large appliance store entered into a written agreement with a television manufacturer for 20 high definition televisions for $300 each. The shipment arrived on time and was paid for with a cashier's check by the appliance store. However, when the appliance store tested the TVs, it found that none of them met the high definition specifications in the contract, even though they functioned fine otherwise. The appliance store notified the manufacturer that it was rejecting the TVs because they were nonconforming, but the manufacturer did not want them returned.

The appliance store may recover:

(A) Nothing.

(B) The money it has already paid for the TVs, and it gets to keep them.

(C) The difference between the value of the TVs and the price it could have obtained for them on the market.

(D) The money it paid for the TVs, but it may sell them for the manufacturer's account.

Question 5

On February 1, the owner of a bowling alley read an ad from a major manufacturer of bowling balls offering 40 balls in various weights and drilled in various sizes for $10 per ball. The owner immediately filled out the order form for the 40 balls and deposited it, properly stamped and addressed, into the mail. On February 2, the bowling alley owner received in the mail a letter from the manufacturer, sent out as part of its advertising campaign, stating in relevant part that it will sell the bowling alley owner 40 bowling balls at $10 per ball. A day later, on February 3, the manufacturer received the bowling alley owner's order. On February 4, the balls were shipped.

On what day did an enforceable contract arise?

(A) February 1, the day the bowling alley owner deposited his order in the mail.

(B) February 2, the day the bowling alley owner received the letter from the manufacturer.

(C) February 3, the day the manufacturer received the bowling alley owner's letter.

(D) February 4, the day the balls were shipped.

Question 6

A steelmaker purchased a tube rolling machine from a manufacturer of heavy machinery.

The machine was sold unassembled for a price of $150,000, with $25,000 payable on delivery and the balance ($125,000) to be paid in 10 monthly installments of $12,500 each. After the machine parts were delivered, the steelmaker contacted an assembly company that specialized in assembly and installation of large and complex manufacturing machinery, and told the company that the machinery had to be up and running within 45 days, or the steelmaker would be in breach of a major contract that it relied on for much of its current revenue. The company agreed, in a written contract with the steelmaker, to assemble and install the tube rolling machine within 45 days at a price of $15,000.

Two weeks later, the manufacturer that sold the tube rolling machine to the steelmaker learned that the assembly company was planning to stop work, due to a strike by its labor union. The manufacturer orally offered the assembly company a $3,500 bonus if it would agree to finish the job for the steelmaker. The company accepted the manufacturer's promise and completed the assembly and installation of the tube rolling machine with supervisory personnel within the 45-day time limit set in the agreement between the company and the steelmaker. However, the manufacturer refused to pay the assembly company the $3,500 bonus, so the company sued the manufacturer.

Which of the following would be the assembly company's strongest argument to prevail?

(A) The assembly company owed the manufacturer no preexisting duty to complete the job for the steelmaker, and such completion was sufficient bargained-for consideration for the manufacturer's promise to pay the additional $3,500.

(B) Because the $3,500 payment was characterized as a "bonus," no further consideration was required and the manufacturer is bound to its promise.

(C) The assembly company would not have completed the job for the steelmaker within the time limit except in reliance on the manufacturer's promise to pay the additional $3,500.

(D) By completing the job for the steelmaker, the assembly company conferred a benefit on the manufacturer worth at least $3,500, because such performance assured the steelmaker's ability to pay the manufacturer the balance on the installment purchase agreement for the tube rolling machine.

Question 7

A married couple entered into a contract with a well-regarded dancing coach to provide dance lessons eight hours a day for two weeks. The coach would be paid only if the couple won a dance contest airing on local television. The couple had already qualified in the opening round, and if they won the local contest, they would join other winners in a dance contest to be televised nationally. The agreement between the couple and the dance coach did not specify an amount of payment. After the dance coach's instruction was completed, the couple performed on the local television show and won the contest. However, they refused to pay the dance coach because they felt it was their talent and long hours of practice, and not his instruction, that had won them the contest.

Can the dance coach recover from the couple?

(A) No, because the coach cannot prove conclusively that his instruction was the reason they won the contest.

(B) No, because the agreement did not specify the amount to be paid.

(C) Yes, the coach will recover a reasonable price for his services under the contract.

(D) Yes, the coach will recover his normal fee for his services.

Question 8

A farmer in a small town suffering a severe drought contacted a scientist in another county

who claimed to have perfected a rainmaking machine. The farmer and the scientist entered into an agreement providing that the scientist would be paid if he made it rain. The agreement did not specify an amount of payment or any deadline by which it must rain. After several days of trying without success, the scientist said that the machine might work better at a higher elevation. A neighbor who lived on higher ground agreed to let the scientist place the rainmaking machine on his land and further told the scientist that if he made it rain before the end of the following day, he would pay him $20,000. The scientist placed the machine on the neighbor's land. By nightfall of the same day, clouds had begun to gather over the town, and the next morning it was pouring rain.

If the neighbor refuses to pay the $20,000 to the scientist, can the latter enforce the promise to pay?

(A) Yes, because the neighbor's promise was supported by the consideration that the scientist make it rain by the next night.

(B) Yes, but only in the amount of the reasonable value of his services.

(C) No, because the scientist had a preexisting duty to make it rain as a result of the agreement with the farmer.

(D) No, because the neighbor's promise constituted no legal detriment to him.

Question 9

The owner of an old car parked it in front of his house with a "for sale" sign in the windshield. In response to an inquiry from his neighbor, the car owner said that he would take $400 for the car. The neighbor responded, "You've got a deal." Because it was a Sunday, and the banks were closed, the neighbor told the car owner that he would come to his house with the $400 the next day at about 6 p.m. The car owner said that was fine. At 9:15 the next morning, the car owner called his neighbor and told him that when they had talked the previous day, he forgot that he had just put two new tires on that car and that he would need an extra $50 to cover their cost. The neighbor agreed to bring $450 in cash to the car owner's house at about six o'clock.

Is the neighbor legally bound to pay the car owner the additional $50?

(A) Yes, because the original contract was not in writing.

(B) Yes, because the contract, as modified, does not need to be in writing.

(C) No, because no additional consideration was given for the oral modification.

(D) No, because neither the neighbor nor the car owner is a merchant.

Question 10

A bulk retailer of accessories for musical instruments placed an advertisement in a trade magazine popular with those in the music business, offering for sale 50-count boxes of a particular type of mouthpiece for use with the French horn, minimum purchase 10 boxes, at $100 per box. In response to the advertisement, the owner of a large store that sold brass and woodwind instruments in its shop and over the Internet sent a written order to the bulk retailer for 12 boxes (50-count) of the mouthpiece. In his letter that accompanied the order, the store owner stated that he would send the bulk retailer his payment of $1,200 upon delivery. The letter also said that the mouthpieces must fit onto three specified models of French horn.

The day after receiving the written order and letter from the store owner, the bulk retailer shipped 12 boxes (50-count) of the mouthpiece to him. Accompanying the invoice on the boxes was a letter from the bulk retailer stating that the mouthpieces are compatible with two of the models of French horn, but that the retailer makes no warranties as to the compatibility of the mouthpieces with any other model of French horn. Shortly after accepting shipment of the boxes, the store owner realized that the mouthpieces did not fit onto the third model of French horn that it had specified and instituted an action against the bulk retailer.

Which of the following statements would offer the strongest support in favor of the store owner's position?

(A) The store owner's letter was an offer, and shipment of the units was an acceptance.

(B) The store owner's letter was an offer, and the bulk retailer's letter accompanying the invoice was an acceptance.

(C) The bulk retailer's letter was an offer, and acceptance of the units by the store owner was an acceptance of the offer.

(D) Shipment of the units was a counteroffer, and acceptance of the units by the store owner was an acceptance of the counteroffer.

Question 11

A contract between a camera store and a distributor of camera lenses called for the sale of 20 standard zoom lenses that would be compatible with a particular manufacturer's film and digital cameras, for a price of $300 per lens. After an employee of the camera store with authority to accept deliveries accepted shipment of the zoom lenses, store personnel learned that the lenses would not work with the manufacturer's film camera, but instead were compatible only with the manufacturer's digital camera. The camera store filed suit. At trial, the store's attorneys established that the nonconforming lenses were worth $200 per lens.

Which of the following should be the measure of damages applied to determine the camera store's loss?

(A) The cost of purchasing lenses compatible with the manufacturer's film camera from another supplier.

(B) The contract price of $6,000, because the camera store has not received the benefit of its bargain.

(C) The difference between the value of the lenses as received and their value if they had been compatible with the manufacturer's film camera—$2,000.

(D) The camera store is not entitled to damages, because its employee accepted the lenses as shipped by the distributor.

Question 12

A manufacturer of electronic game cartridges for use with other manufacturers' electronic game systems received a letter from a buyer for a large toy store chain ordering two 100-unit lots of a particular game cartridge from the manufacturer's catalog. The buyer's letter stated that the cartridges must be compatible with two specified game systems. The manufacturer made no warranties of any type regarding the compatibility of the cartridges with any game systems, but both parties reasonably believed that the cartridges were compatible with both game systems. On receiving the shipment, the buyer discovered that the cartridges did not work with one of the game systems.

Which of the following is the most appropriate remedy for the buyer?

(A) Specific performance of the contract, requiring the manufacturer to ship two 100-unit lots of cartridges compatible with both game systems.

(B) Rescission of the contract.

(C) Restitution by the manufacturer of the purchase price of the two lots.

(D) Restitution by the manufacturer of the value of the cartridges.

Question 13

A downtown department store engaged an electrician to service all electrical appliances

sold by the store for a flat fee of $5,000 per month. Under a written contract signed by both parties, the store was responsible for pick-up and delivery of the appliances to be repaired and the billing for the work. By its terms, the contract would continue until either party gave 180 days' written notice of its intent to terminate. Several months ago the electrician informed the store that he was losing money on the deal and was in financial trouble. He requested in good faith that the fee for the next three months be increased by $1,000 and that this increase be paid to a local bank to help pay off a loan that the bank had made to the electrician. The store orally agreed to so modify the original contract. However, the store did not pay the bank and now the bank is suing the store for $3,000.

Who will prevail?

(A) The store, because there was no consideration to support the promise to pay the bank.

(B) The store, because the bank is only an incidental beneficiary of the modified contract between the store and the electrician.

(C) The bank, because it is an intended creditor beneficiary of the modified contract between the store and the electrician.

(D) The bank, because the electrician exercised good faith in requesting the modification regarding the payment to the bank.

Question 14

On June 1, an uncle whose niece was looking to buy a car wrote a letter to a car dealership, stating that he would guarantee payment of the purchase price for any car that it sold to his niece costing less than $10,000. On June 3, after receiving this letter, the dealership sold a $9,500 car to the niece for $2,000 down, with the balance to be paid by the end of the year. The uncle died unexpectedly on June 17. The dealership was unaware of the uncle's death when it mailed the uncle a letter on June 19 accepting his offer. The letter also stated that the niece was a good customer in the past and that it had, in fact, planned to extend her credit for the purchase before receiving the uncle's letter. In August, the niece was killed and her estate is bankrupt.

Can the dealership succeed in an action against the uncle's estate for the balance of the price of the car when it becomes due?

(A) Yes, because the dealership had accepted the uncle's offer before the uncle died.

(B) Yes, because the dealership reasonably, justifiably, and foreseeably relied on the uncle's promise.

(C) No, because the dealership would have sold the car to the niece even without the uncle's promise.

(D) No, because the uncle died before the dealership mailed the letter notifying him that it had accepted his offer.

Question 15

A general contractor advertised in a trade publication that she planned to bid on the construction of a new building to be located in the town square. The advertisement welcomed bids from subcontractors to perform various functions, including plumbing. The lowest plumbing bid was from a local plumber who bid $10,000. The contractor used the bid in preparing her general bid. One hour after she submitted her general bid, the plumber called her and told her that he made a mistake on the bid he submitted to her, and that he could not do the plumbing work for less than $12,000. The contractor acknowledged that he had done good work for her in the past and said, "I'll just forget you ever made that $10,000 bid." The contractor then hired the second lowest bidder to do the plumbing work for $12,000.

If the contractor sues the plumber for damages, will she prevail?

(A) Yes, because there was no additional consideration to support a release.

(B) Yes, because the dollar amount of the agreement is large enough that the Statute of Frauds applies.

(C) No, because a rescission has taken place.

(D) No, because the contractor and the plumber mutually agreed to a release.

Question 16

A widget manufacturer entered into a written agreement with a retailer to sell the retailer 500 widgets for a total price of $10,000. Prior to the date set for execution of the contract, the price of the raw material essential to manufacture of widgets had soared because of a civil war in the country that produces 80% of the world supply of the material. The manufacturer informed the retailer that it would now cost $11,000 to manufacture the widgets and requested that the contract price be adjusted to $12,000 for the 500 widgets. The retailer agreed orally to pay the $12,000, but no written confirmation was exchanged between the parties.

Shortly thereafter, the civil war ended and the raw material became available again at prewar price levels. The manufacturer shipped 500 widgets to the retailer. On receipt, the retailer sent the manufacturer a certified check in the amount of $10,000, marking it "payment in full." The manufacturer did not cash the check, but telephoned the retailer demanding an additional $2,000. The retailer refuses to pay the additional sum.

May the manufacturer enforce his demand for an additional $2,000 in a court of law?

(A) No, because of the parol evidence rule.

(B) No, because of the Statute of Frauds.

(C) Yes, because the parol evidence rule would allow evidence of a changed price term, as it is material to the contract.

(D) Yes, because a subsequent modification can also be a waiver after the initial agreement.

Question 17

A small processor of specialized steel agreed in writing with a small manufacturer of children's toys that it would supply, and the manufacturer would buy, all of the manufacturer's specialized steel requirements over a period of years at a set price per ton of steel. Their contract did not include a nonassignment clause. Recently, the toy manufacturer decided to abandon its line of steel toys, so it made an assignment of its rights and delegation of its duties under the contract to a toymaker many times larger. The large toymaker notified the steel processor of the assignment and relayed to the processor its good faith belief that its requirements will approximate those of the assignor.

Must the steel processor supply the requirements of the large toymaker?

(A) Yes, because there was no nonassignment clause in the contract.

(B) Yes, because the large toymaker acted in good faith to assure the steel processor that its requirements will approximate those of the small manufacturer into whose shoes it stepped.

(C) No, because requirements contracts are not assignable under the U.C.C.

(D) No, because the steel processor did not give prior approval of the assignment.

Question 18

On April 15, a wholesaler of tulip bulbs from Holland telephoned a local nursery and offered to sell to the nursery 80 gross of tulip bulbs for $8,000, not including delivery charges. The nursery accepted immediately. On April 17, the nursery sent the wholesaler a letter confirming the deal for the sale of 80 gross of tulip bulbs for $8,000, and stating that it anticipated a waiver of the delivery charges because of the size of the order. On May 3, the wholesaler telephoned the nursery and stated that, due to a poor growing season in Holland, it would not be able to supply any tulip bulbs to the nursery.

If the nursery brings suit against the wholesaler and the wholesaler asserts the Statute of Frauds as a defense, will the nursery prevail?

(A) Yes, because its April 17 letter contained the quantity term.

(B) Yes, because its April 17 letter contained the quantity term and the price term.

(C) No, because the nursery's April 17 letter varied the terms of the wholesaler's offer.

(D) No, because the wholesaler is the party to be charged and has signed nothing.

Question 19

On February 1, a tire manufacturer telephoned a car dealership and offered to sell to the dealership 50 sets of its top-of-the-line whitewall tires for $5,000. The dealership accepted immediately. On February 3, the dealership sent the tire manufacturer a letter confirming the deal and stating that it was counting on a 20% discount due to the size of the purchase. The tire manufacturer did not respond to the letter.

What price must the dealership pay for the five sets of tires?

(A) A reasonable price as fixed in good faith by the dealership.

(B) The reasonable value of the goods, because the parties cannot agree on the price.

(C) $5,000, because the discount term is a material alteration of the original deal.

(D) $4,000, because the tire manufacturer did not object to the discount term in the dealership's February 3 letter.

Question 20

A landowner entered into a written agreement with a real estate broker whereby the broker would receive a commission of 10% of the sale price if he procured a "ready, willing, and able buyer" for the landowner's property and if the sale actually proceeded through closing. The broker found a buyer who agreed in writing to buy the property from the landowner for $100,000, the landowner's asking price. The buyer put up $6,000 as a down payment. The agreement between the landowner and the buyer contained a liquidated damages clause providing that, if the buyer defaulted by failing to tender the balance due of $94,000 at the closing date, damages would be 10% of the purchase price. The landowner included that clause because she was counting on using the proceeds of the sale for a business venture that would likely net her at least $10,000.

The buyer became seriously ill and defaulted. When he recovered, he demanded that the landowner return his $6,000, and the landowner refused. The broker also demanded the $6,000 from the landowner and was refused. The broker and the buyer filed separate suits against the landowner, with the buyer pleading impossibility of performance. The two cases are consolidated into a single case.

How should the court rule as to the disposition of the $6,000?

(A) The landowner keeps the entire $6,000 because the liquidated damages clause is reasonable.

(B) The buyer gets the entire $6,000 because his performance was impossible.

(C) The broker gets the entire $6,000, which is 60% of the commission he is entitled to, because he substantially performed his part of the contract by producing a buyer willing to pay the $100,000 asking price.

(D) The broker gets $600 and the landowner gets $5,400, because the damages clause

was reasonable and the broker is entitled to 10% of whatever the landowner realizes from the deal.

Question 21

An aunt agreed to pay for any lace shawl that her niece purchased at a certain local shop if the niece wore the shawl to the town's ethnic festival. The niece despised shawls but she really loved her aunt and did not want to hurt her feelings, so she purchased a $300 lace shawl from the shop. She accompanied her aunt to the ethnic festival wearing the shawl, and the aunt was very pleased. The aunt died shortly after the festival and her estate refused to reimburse the niece for her purchase. The niece filed suit to collect the $300 from the aunt's estate.

Which legal theory will offer the niece her best chance of winning the case?

(A) Quasi-contract.

(B) Bargain and exchange.

(C) Conditional gift.

(D) Account stated.

Question 22

A man shopping for a leather jacket at a clothing store could not decide between two jackets, so the proprietor, who knew the man and his family well, let him take one of the jackets on approval. No mention was made by the proprietor of the method of payment he expected. The man wore the jacket on a visit to his grandfather, who liked it so much that when the man told him what the jacket cost and that he had taken it on approval, the grandfather said he would buy it for him if he promised to give some of his old clothes to a favorite charity for the poor at Christmastime. The man wholeheartedly agreed to donate the clothes to the charity at Christmas. Very pleased, the grandfather called the shop and told the proprietor to send the bill for the jacket to him, which he did. Before the bill was paid and before the Christmas season arrived, the grandfather fell ill and died. The grandfather's executor has refused to pay the bill, and the man has not yet given any old clothing to the charity.

Will the proprietor be able to recover the price of the jacket from the estate?

(A) Yes, because the proprietor was the intended beneficiary of the promise between the man and his grandfather.

(B) Yes, because the man has no duty to give the clothing to the charity.

(C) No, because the grandfather's implied promise to pay the proprietor arising from the phone call is unenforceable.

(D) No, because a condition has not yet occurred.

Question 23

A widow wanting to give her daughter a special wedding gift entered into a written agreement with a contractor to build a house for $300,000 on property she owned. Detailed specifications regarding the layout and materials to be used were included in the written agreement between the widow and the contractor. Just as the contractor was about to begin construction of the house, he discovered that an underground river bisected the widow's property, leaving insufficient subterranean support to construct the house as planned. Given this discovery, the contractor refused to build the house for $300,000.

If the widow files suit demanding specific performance or damages from the contractor, which of the following additional facts, if proven, would most favor her case?

(A) It is physically possible to build the house according to the original specifications, but it would add $1 million to the contractor's costs.

(B) The detailed specifications in the agreement had been drawn up by the contractor,

as were other blueprints and plans for the house.

(C) Neither the widow nor the contractor had reason to know of the underground river before the contract was signed.

(D) The daughter knew of the contract between the widow and the contractor and turned down other opportunities to purchase suitable housing in the area in reliance on the contract.

Question 24

A grandfather told his granddaughter that he was moving to a retirement home and that she could have his house. He promised her that he would have another wing added to the house in the back before turning it over to her, and entered into a written contract with a builder to construct the addition for his granddaughter. Before the grandfather had entered into the contract with the builder, the granddaughter had paid $5,000 for a 60-day option to purchase another house. However, when her grandfather showed her the plans for his house prepared by the builder, she liked it very much and decided to let her option to purchase the other house lapse. Shortly thereafter, but prior to the granddaughter's option lapsing, the builder discovered a latent problem with the soil that would substantially interfere with adding the addition onto the back of the house. The builder offered to put an addition above the existing floor rather than in the back, and the grandfather agreed. After the granddaughter's option had lapsed, she discovered that the addition was now going up rather than in the back. She angrily demanded that the builder either build the house according to the original specifications that she approved or pay her damages. The builder refused and the granddaughter filed suit.

Who is more likely to prevail?

(A) The granddaughter, because she was an intended beneficiary of the contract whose rights had vested.

(B) The granddaughter, because the subsequent agreement between her grandfather and the builder to modify the construction was unsupported by consideration.

(C) The builder, because he may raise all defenses that he had against the grandfather against the granddaughter.

(D) The builder, because the granddaughter is merely an incidental beneficiary of the contract between the grandfather and the builder and, as such, has no power to enforce the contract against the builder.

Question 25

A contractor with a contract to deepen a well in a drought stricken area mistakenly entered onto the wrong property and proceeded to deepen the well there. The owner of the property saw the contractor at work but said nothing. When the contractor completed the job, the property owner refused to pay his bill, and the contractor filed suit. In her answer, the property owner stated that she thought the contractor was employed by the county and that the government was paying for the work because of the drought. She knew, however, that two of her neighbors had recently paid private contractors to deepen their wells.

Which of the following arguments offers the contractor his best chance for winning his lawsuit?

(A) Implied-in-fact contract.

(B) Promissory estoppel.

(C) Mutual mistake.

(D) Unilateral mistake.

Question 26

An insurer offered a plan to cover an insured's catastrophic illnesses for the remainder of the insured's life in exchange for a large one-time payment at the inception of coverage. Because the program was experimental, the insurer would accept only a fixed number of applications during the enrollment period. A recent retiree in good health was one of the applicants accepted, and he enrolled in the program. He paid the one-time premium of $30,000 a few days before coverage began. The day after his coverage started, he was struck by a bus and killed. The executor of the retiree's estate reviewed the policy and immediately notified the bank to stop payment on it. The insurer then filed suit against the retiree's estate.

Will the court compel the estate to pay the premium to the insurer?

(A) Yes, because the insurer necessarily declined to take another applicant during the enrollment period because of the retiree's promise to buy the policy.

(B) Yes, because the risk of the timing of the retiree's death was assumed by both parties and built into the cost of the contract.

(C) No, because the purpose of the contract between the retiree and the insurer had been frustrated.

(D) No, because it is unconscionable for the insurer to have charged the retiree so much for so little value received.

Question 27

The general partner of a two-person partnership committed suicide because of gambling debts. His partner, who was a limited partner and the general partner's uncle, was besieged by creditors of the partnership who wanted their money. The jurisdiction statutorily limited the liability of limited partners for debts of the partnership or acts of the general partner to the extent of their investment in the partnership. However, the limited partner was unaware of this and believed that he was liable to all who had claims against the partnership. The limited partner told an unsecured creditor of the partnership that he would pay the partnership debt if the unsecured creditor would hold off filing an involuntary bankruptcy petition against the partnership. In a bankruptcy action filed by secured creditors, the assets of the partnership, which were very small, were consumed by the costs of the proceedings and no creditor received any payment. The general partner himself left no assets. The unsecured creditor brought an action against the limited partner for the amount of the debt owed to him by the partnership.

Will the unsecured creditor be successful in collecting the debt from the limited partner?

(A) No, because his claim against the partnership was worthless.

(B) No, because the limited partner's only obligation to pay the debts of the partnership was a moral one based on his relationship to the general partner.

(C) Yes, because the unsecured creditor detrimentally relied on the limited partner's promise.

(D) Yes, because the limited partner's promise was supported by a bargained-for exchange.

Question 28

The owner of farm land entered into a written contract with a prospective tenant of the property to erect a barn with a milking station and silo on the property in exchange for the tenant's taking a five-year lease on the property. After the agreement was signed, the tenant moved himself and his family onto the property. The farm owner, who had worked for many years as a skilled building contractor before retiring, began the work of building the barn and the silo. However, an injury prevented him from completing the job when it was about two-thirds done. He told the tenant that he would see to it that the work was completed and that he had already entered into an oral contract with his nephew, a novice contractor, to finish the job. However, the nephew failed to complete the job. The tenant brought an action against the nephew for breach of contract.

Which would be the best defense for the nephew?

(A) His contract was with the farm owner and not with the tenant.

(B) The tenant furnished no consideration.

(C) His agreement with the farm owner was oral.

(D) The building duties which the nephew took on were not delegable.

Question 29

On November 5, an electronics store owner realized that his stock of 15 of the most popular video game of the holiday shopping season would not last until the first of the next month. Seeing an advertisement from the manufacturer of the game in a trade journal listing its price at $3,000 per hundred, with delivery one week from order, the store owner faxed to the manufacturer an order of 100 copies of the game at $3,000 per hundred. There were no further communications between the store owner and the manufacturer. By November 25, the store owner realized that the manufacturer was not going to deliver any of the video games. He thus was forced to obtain additional stock by purchasing from a middleman at a cost of $4,000 per hundred. The store owner brings an action for breach of contract against the manufacturer.

Who will prevail?

(A) The manufacturer, because the communications between the store owner and the manufacturer were not definite or certain enough to form a contract.

(B) The manufacturer, because it never accepted the offer contained in the store owner's fax.

(C) The store owner, because his fax was an acceptance of the offer contained in the trade journal.

(D) The store owner, because he changed his position for the worse in reliance on the manufacturer's offer to deliver the video games within one week.

Question 30

A manufacturer of electric toy trains and a hobby shop owner entered into a written contract providing that the manufacturer will tender to the shop owner four dozen of a popular electric train set at a price of $100 apiece, to be delivered no later than October 31 to take advantage of the holiday shopping season. Shortly after the shop owner placed his order, the manufacturer raised its prices due to a sudden surge in popularity of that train set. Because the manufacturer did not have enough train sets to accommodate everyone due to the surge of orders, it decided to deliver train sets only to those buyers who had ordered them at the increased price. The manufacturer notified the shop owner that it would not deliver the train sets it ordered. The shop owner filed an action to force the manufacturer to deliver the train sets at the agreed-upon price.

Will the court compel the manufacturer to deliver the train sets to the shop owner?

(A) No, because a contract for the sale of goods is not subject to specific performance.

(B) No, because the shop owner can buy them from another dealer.

(C) Yes, because the shop owner will not be able to buy them from another source at the contract price.

(D) Yes, because time is of the essence.

Question 31

A wholesaler persuaded a retailer to order a line of dolls for the Christmas season, even though the retailer was skeptical of the dolls' marketability. The contract provided that the retailer would pay $1,500 for its order of 100 dolls if they sold during the Christmas season.

Some dolls did sell, but on February 12, the retailer had 80 of them in inventory. He sent the wholesaler notice that he would be returning the 80 dolls. The wholesaler replied that it did not want the dolls back, that the retailer should continue to try to sell them. Despite this reply, the retailer sent the wholesaler a check for $300 and shipped the dolls to the wholesaler, who refused to accept them but did accept the check. Thereafter, the retailer held the dolls at his warehouse. The wholesaler brought an action to recover the $1,200 balance.

The wholesaler will:

(A) Recover, because the retailer still has the dolls in his possession.

(B) Recover, because it was not a condition precedent that the dolls be sold during the Christmas season, but merely a convenient time for payment.

(C) Not recover, because sale during the Christmas season was a condition precedent to payment.

(D) Not recover, because accepting the $300 waived any rights that the wholesaler may have had to enforce the contract.

Question 32

The owner of a one-acre parcel of land with a small house on it rented the property to a professor of a nearby college at a monthly rental of $500. Several years later, after the professor got tenure, the parties orally agreed that the professor would purchase the property from the owner for the sum of $60,000, payable at the rate of $500 a month for 10 years. They agreed that the owner would give the professor a deed to the property after five years had passed and $30,000 had been paid toward the purchase price, and that the professor would execute a note secured by a mortgage for the balance. The professor continued in possession of the property and made all monthly payments in a timely fashion. When he had paid $30,000, he tendered a proper note and mortgage to the property owner and demanded that she deliver the deed as agreed. The owner refused because valuable minerals had been discovered on adjacent parcels in recent months, causing the value of this parcel of land to increase to 10 times its former value. The professor brought suit against the property owner for specific performance.

If the property owner wins, it will be because:

(A) The transaction had not proceeded far enough to amount to an estoppel against enforcement of the Statute of Frauds.

(B) The purchase price, given the present value of the land, made the contract unconscionable, providing the property owner with a valid defense to enforcement.

(C) Oral agreements are generally revocable unless expressly made irrevocable.

(D) The professor's payments are as consistent with there being a landlord-tenant relationship between them as with there being an oral contract.

Question 33

The owner of a personal watercraft put an ad for its sale in the paper. Her neighbor saw the ad and told her that he wanted to buy the watercraft but had to arrange for financing. The owner suggested that they write a contract for sale then and there so that they would not have to waste any time while he got his financing. They orally agreed that the contract would not become binding unless the neighbor obtained financing, but the written contract did not mention this and appeared to be a fully integrated document. The neighbor could not obtain financing and the owner brings suit to enforce the written contract.

Who will prevail?

(A) The owner, because the contract was a fully integrated writing.

(B) The owner, because parol evidence is not allowed to contradict a writing.

(C) The neighbor, because the oral agreement that the contract would not be binding if the neighbor did not get financing was made contemporaneous with the writing.

(D) The neighbor, because obtaining financing was a condition precedent.

Question 34

After working in her father's famous restaurant for many years, his daughter had a falling out with him. She decided to open her own establishment using the family name. She wrote to the wine merchant who had supplied the house red wine for her father's restaurant for many years informing him of the opening of the new establishment. She requested that the merchant supply the same wine for the new restaurant's requirements during the next year at $10 per bottle. Although the wine merchant had not directly dealt with the daughter before, he believed, because of the similarity of the names, that the new restaurant would be operated by the father. The wine merchant wrote back that, "in light of our long-standing business relationship," he would ship, as requested, her requirements of the red wine specified in her letter at $10 per bottle, payment due within 30 days of receipt. After receiving the letter, the daughter placed an order for 500 bottles of the wine. Shortly before shipment, the wine merchant discovered that the new restaurant had no connection with her father's restaurant. He faxed a letter to the daughter, telling her that because her restaurant has no relationship with her father's restaurant, the price for the wine in the contract is $15 per bottle.

If the daughter files suit to enforce the original agreement to supply wine at $10 per bottle, which of the following would be the wine merchant's best defense to the action?

(A) The contract is unconscionable.

(B) The daughter intentionally misrepresented the identity of her business.

(C) The daughter should have known that there was a mistake because of the reference to "long-standing business relationship" in the letter.

(D) Unilateral mistake is a basis for rescission by the mistaken party.

Question 35

The owner of a soon-to-be-opened pastry shop wrote to a large supplier of confectioner's sugar about placing a standing order for sugar to meet the pastry shop's frosting and other needs. By return mail, the supplier offered the shop owner a discounted price of $5 per pound—$3 per pound less than its regular price—based on the parties' "many years of pleasant business association." Because the shop owner had not done business with the supplier before, she realized that the supplier had confused her shop with another pastry shop having a similar name. However, the shop owner kept quiet about the mixup and placed an order for 200 pounds of sugar at the discounted price of $5 per pound. Shortly before it shipped the sugar to the shop owner, the supplier discovered that it was mistaken about the identity of the shop owner and that the order was for a new pastry shop that was opening soon. It sent an overnight letter to the shop owner noting its mistake and stating that the price of a pound of confectioner's sugar was $8 per pound. The shop owner, whose grand opening was coming soon, sent the supplier $1,600 and received the 200 pounds of confectioner's sugar in a timely manner. Immediately thereafter, the shop owner filed suit against the supplier for $600 (the difference in price between cost of the sugar at $5 per pound and its cost at $8 per pound) plus any consequential damages. In her pleadings, the shop owner asserted that the supplier violated its contract to sell the sugar at $5 per pound and that it had forced her to pay the higher amount knowing that she needed the sugar for her pastry shop to open.

Will the shop owner win her suit?

(A) Yes, because there was no consideration to change the price term to $8.

(B) Yes, because the supplier, knowing the pastry shop was to open very soon, took unfair advantage of a superior bargaining position to improperly increase the price.

(C) No, because as between merchants, a modification of an original agreement does not need consideration.

(D) No, because $8 per pound was a fair market price for the sugar at the time of the contract.

Question 36

The owner of a stationary bicycle wrote a letter to her friend offering to sell her stationary bicycle to him for $150. The friend received the letter on January 18. On January 19, he mailed a letter back saying that he was not interested in purchasing the bike because he had just purchased a gym membership. However, the friend changed his mind the next day and mailed a letter to the owner accepting her offer to sell the bicycle and enclosing a certified check for $150. The owner received the friend's rejection letter on January 21 but put it aside without reading it. The next day, she received the friend's acceptance letter, which she opened and read immediately.

Do the parties have a contract?

(A) Yes, because under the mailbox rule an acceptance is effective on dispatch, while a rejection is effective on receipt.

(B) Yes, because the friend paid for the bicycle when he accepted the offer to buy it.

(C) No, because the friend rejected the offer first and then accepted it.

(D) No, because the mailbox rule does not apply—whichever is received first controls.

CONTRACTS ANSWERS - SET 5

Answer to Question 1

(C) If the father prevails, it will be because his promise to the young woman was not in writing. The Statute of Frauds requires that a contract in consideration of marriage must be evidenced by a writing to be enforceable. This includes any promise that induces someone to marry by offering something of value. Hence, the father's offer of support and education expenses is unenforceable. (A) is wrong because a promise to marry is a sufficient detriment to constitute valid consideration. (B) is wrong because there is no public policy against ***encouraging*** marriage. (D) is wrong because a person's pleasure or displeasure from performing a contractual duty is irrelevant as to whether performance constitutes consideration. The young woman agreed to do something that she was under no legal obligation to do in exchange for the father's promise of financial support; hence, consideration exists.

Answer to Question 2

(B) The manufacturer accepted the two printers that it sold to its lawyers. Upon receiving nonconforming goods, a buyer may accept all, reject all, or accept any commercial unit and reject the rest. The sale of the two nonconforming printers to its lawyers, even for temporary use only, was acceptance by the manufacturer. Thus, (A) is incorrect. (C) is incorrect because there is no showing that the 10 printers constitute a commercial unit. A commercial unit is not only what unit has been the basis of the contract, but whether the partial acceptance produces so materially an adverse effect on the remainder as to constitute bad faith. (D) is a misstatement of the law. The fact that the manufacturer was able to sell two systems with the slower printer does not create an acceptance of the entire order.

Answer to Question 3

(C) The department store was entitled to recover contract damages from the manufacturer for the three food processors that it accepted. The department store's acceptance of the three food processors ***did not*** waive its right to collect damages for the defect in quality. Thus, (A) and (B) are wrong. Having accepted the nonconforming food processors, the department store's damages would be the difference between the value of the food processors as received and what they would have been worth if they had been as warranted, plus foreseeable incidental and consequential damages. (D) is wrong, because the agreement with the restaurant was to accommodate the department store only and was not foreseeable by the manufacturer.

Answer to Question 4

(D) The appliance store may recover the money it paid for the 13 TVs and resell them for the TV manufacturer's account. A buyer who has rejected goods as nonconforming is entitled to any prepayment, ***or***, if the seller refuses to refund, to resell the goods and apply the proceeds to what is owed him from the seller. The buyer is entitled to offset expenses of selling and get its money back. Hence, (D) is correct and (A) is wrong. The buyer is ***not*** entitled to keep the TVs ***and*** get its money back. Thus, (B) is wrong. (C) is wrong. Had the appliance store accepted the 13 nonconforming TVs, it would be entitled to the difference between the value of the TVs and the value they would have had if they had conformed to the contract. Here, however, the appliance store rejected the TVs.

Answer to Question 5

(D) The offer arose when the balls were shipped. The general rule is that an offer can be accepted by performance or a promise to perform unless the offer clearly limits the method of acceptance. Here, the offer would be the bowling alley owner's order, because a magazine ad is usually held to be merely solicitation to accept offers rather than an offer. Thus, the manufacturer accepted and the contract was formed when it shipped the balls. (A) is wrong because the bowling alley owner's order was an offer to buy, and no contract could be formed until that offer was accepted. (B) is wrong because this is a case of crossing offers; even though both offers contain the same terms, they do not form a contract. (C) is wrong because no contract will be formed until there has been an acceptance, and, as stated, the bowling alley owner's letter was merely an offer.

Answer to Question 6

(A) The assembly company's best argument is that it owed the manufacturer no preexisting duty to complete the job, and such completion was sufficient bargained-for consideration. Generally, a promise is unenforceable unless it is supported by consideration; thus, for the manufacturer's promise to be enforceable, there must be consideration supporting it. Consideration is defined as a bargained-for exchange of something of legal value. Most courts hold that the thing exchanged will have legal value if it causes the promisee to incur a detriment. A minority of courts hold that a benefit to the promisor is also sufficient. Thus, the company's best argument would be one that includes the idea that it incurred a bargained-for detriment, and this is reflected by (A). The problem with (A) is the preexisting legal duty rule. Traditionally, courts have held that performance of an existing legal duty is not sufficient consideration. However, the rule is riddled with exceptions, and one exception recognized in most jurisdictions applies when, as here, the preexisting duty is owed ***to someone other than the promisor***. Thus, (A) is the best argument because it provides for a full contract recovery. (D) is wrong because it merely reflects the fact that the manufacturer received a benefit. As indicated above, it is the presence of consideration—defined as a bargained-for exchange of something of legal value—that permits the contract to be fully enforced. (A) is a better answer than (D) because it more clearly reflects the basis for finding consideration here. (B) is wrong because merely identifying a promise to pay as a "bonus" does not obviate the need for consideration. For a promise to be enforceable, there must be consideration. (C) is wrong because mere reliance on a promise is not enough to make a contract enforceable. For reliance to provide a substitute for consideration, under the doctrine of promissory estoppel, the promisor must reasonably expect that its promise will induce reliance, and such reliance must reasonably be induced. However, the promise will be enforceable ***only to the extent necessary to prevent injustice***. Here, because the company had a duty to complete the work even without the manufacturer's promise, there is no indication that justice would require payment of the $3,500; there is nothing in the facts to show the company incurred more costs, etc. Thus, the recovery to the company under a promissory estoppel theory would undoubtedly be less than the contract recovery possible under (A).

Answer to Question 7

(C) If the couple refuses to pay the dance coach, he will recover a reasonable price for his services as a contract remedy. Generally, an offer must be certain and definite in its terms. However, all terms do not have to be spelled out completely. Most courts today will supply reasonable terms if the terms are consistent with the parties' intent as otherwise expressed. Terms that can be supplied by a reasonableness standard include a price term. Unless the parties have shown at the time of contracting that they do not want a contract until they have agreed on a price, a reasonable price will be supplied by the court. [*See* Restatement (Second) of Contracts §33, comment e] Here, the parties evidenced an intent to enter into a contract: The couple agreed to pay the dance coach to provide dance lessons and to pay him if they won the local contest, and he undertook to perform by providing instruction to them in accordance with their agreement. The dance coach fully performed prior to either party terminating and can therefore enforce the contract. Hence, he can recover a reasonable price for his services. (A) is incorrect because under contract law, a party is entitled to the other party's performance as soon as all conditions precedent have been satisfied; the party need not prove that he caused the conditions to be satisfied, merely that they are in fact satisfied. (B) is incorrect because mere absence of the price term is not sufficient to prevent a contractual remedy; as discussed above, a court could find the offer certain enough and supply a reasonable price term. (D) is incorrect because the contract remedy would be a reasonable price; the court may take into account the dance coach's normal fee when it determines the reasonable price, but it will not be bound by it.

Answer to Question 8

(A) The scientist can enforce the contract with the neighbor because it was supported by consideration. For a contract to be enforceable, there must be an offer, an acceptance, and consideration. Here, there was an offer made by the neighbor (*i.e.,* if the scientist made it rain before the end of the following day, he would pay the scientist $20,000), the scientist accepted the offer by performing, and the performance was valid consideration because the scientist was not under a preexisting duty to make it rain by the next evening (the scientist agreed with the farmer to try to make it rain, but there was no time limitation and no specified consideration). Thus, the neighbor's condition that the scientist had to make it rain by the following day was new consideration and not a preexisting duty. Therefore, the contract is enforceable. (B) is incorrect because a contract is usually governed by the terms agreed on by the parties, and the neighbor and the scientist agreed that if the scientist made it rain by the next day, the neighbor would pay the scientist $20,000. Thus, the scientist should be paid $20,000. (C) is incorrect because, as discussed above, the scientist's making it rain ***by the next day*** was consideration sufficient to support the neighbor's promise to the scientist. Moreover, the scientist probably did not owe any duty to the farmer in the first place, because the offer appears to be for a unilateral contract—an offer looking for performance rather than a promise to perform, which does not become binding until performance is rendered. (D) is incorrect because a promise to pay $20,000 in exchange for performance is a legal detriment.

Answer to Question 9

(B) The neighbor must pay the car owner the additional $50 because the parties have an enforceable contract. A contract for the sale of goods (the car) was formed when the neighbor said, "You've got a deal." The parties then orally agreed to a modification of the contract when the car owner called his neighbor the next morning. Under the Statute of Frauds provision in the U.C.C., which applies to all contracts for the sale of goods, a promise requires a writing signed by the party to be charged to be enforceable if it is for the sale of goods of $500 or more. Here, the contract as modified is under $500, so it is enforceable even though it is not in writing. (A) is incorrect because the fact that the original contract was not in writing is irrelevant to the issue of whether the modified contract is enforceable. If the modification had caused the contract to reach or exceed $500, the car owner could not have collected the additional $50 from his neighbor. (C) is incorrect because under U.C.C. section 2-209, no consideration is needed for a good faith modification of a contract for the sale of goods. (D) is incorrect because the U.C.C. rules on modifications and the Statute of Frauds apply to all contracts for the sale of goods, not just those between merchants.

Answer to Question 10

(A) The store owner's best position is that his letter was an offer, and shipment of the mouthpieces was an acceptance; thus, the shipment of nonconforming goods both created a contract and a breach of that contract, affording the store owner an immediate cause of action. The contract at issue involves the sale of goods, and is thus governed by Article 2 of the U.C.C. Under U.C.C. section 2-206, an offer to buy goods for current or prompt shipment is construed as inviting acceptance either by a promise to ship or by current or prompt shipment of conforming or nonconforming goods. The shipment of goods, even though they are nonconforming, is an acceptance creating a bilateral contract and a breach unless the seller reasonably notifies the buyer that the nonconforming goods are offered only as an accommodation to the buyer. Here, the store owner's letter was an offer that invited the bulk retailer to accept by either a promise to ship or a prompt shipment. The bulk retailer's shipment of the mouthpieces is an acceptance of the store owner's offer, because the bulk retailer's letter accompanying the shipment was probably not sufficient as an accommodation notice (which would have made the shipment a counteroffer rather than an acceptance). The shipment contains nonconforming goods, because the mouthpieces are not compatible with the third type of French horn specified in the store owner's offer. The shipment of nonconforming goods as an acceptance both created a bilateral contract between the parties and constituted a breach of that contract by the bulk retailer, thus allowing the store owner to sue for any appropriate damages for breach of contract. (B) is incorrect because, since the bulk retailer's letter was an acceptance, there is a chance that the store owner will be bound by the terms of the letter. Between merchants, additional proposed terms in an acceptance become part of the contract unless: (i) they materially alter the original contract; (ii) the offer expressly limits acceptance to its terms; or (iii) the offeror has already objected to the particular terms, or objects within a reasonable time after receiving notice of them. [U.C.C. §2-207] The bulk retailer and the store owner are both merchants, in that they deal in goods of the kind involved in the contract. Insofar as the bulk retailer's letter is an acceptance of the store owner's offer, the sentence disclaiming compatibility of the mouthpieces with other models of French horns is an additional proposed term. The store owner's offer did not expressly limit acceptance to its terms, nor did the store owner object to the additional terms. Thus, the additional terms will become part of the contract unless the court finds that they materially alter the original contract. If these terms are held to be part of the contract, the store owner will have no cause of action for the incompatibility of the mouthpieces with one of the French horn models. Because (B) creates a framework in which the store owner might lose (*i.e.,* if it is found that the additional terms do not materially alter the original contract), (B) is not as good an answer as (A). (C) and (D) represent the worst scenarios for the store owner. If the bulk retailer's letter was an offer as stated in (C) and acceptance of the mouthpieces by the store owner was an acceptance of the offer, there is a contract based on the terms in the bulk retailer's letter; *i.e.,* no warranties as to the compatibility of the mouthpieces with any other model of French horn. In that event, the store owner would have no cause of action against the bulk retailer based on the mouthpieces' incompatibility with one of the French horn models. The same result would arise if shipment of the mouthpieces were treated as a counteroffer as stated in (D) (this would be the result if the bulk retailer's letter were held to be a sufficient accommodation notice under U.C.C. section 2-206(1)(b)). Acceptance of the mouthpieces would be acceptance of the counteroffer according to the terms of the letter accompanying the shipment, so that the store owner could not bring an action based on the mouthpieces' incompatibility with one of the French horn models.

Answer to Question 11

(C) The camera store's measure of loss would be the difference between the value of the goods as received and the value they would have had if they had conformed to the contract. When goods

are delivered that do not conform to the parties' contract, the buyer has the option to accept all, reject all, or accept any commercial units and reject the rest. If the buyer chooses to accept the goods, as the camera store did here, the buyer has a right to recover damages for the nonconformity. The standard measure of damages as to accepted goods is the difference between the value of the goods as delivered and the value they would have had if they had been conforming (plus incidental and consequential damages). Here, the goods as delivered were worth $4,000 ($200 per lens for 20 lenses) and they would have been worth $6,000 ($300 per lens for 20 lenses) if they had been as the contract required. Thus, (C) is correct. (A) is incorrect because it describes the remedy of "cover," and cover is available only when the buyer rejects the goods. (If the buyer rejects the goods, he may either cancel the contract or buy substitute goods and charge the breaching seller for the substitutes.) (B) is incorrect because the buyer is entitled to return of the entire contract price only when he cancels the contract. Otherwise, the buyer would get a windfall based on the value of the goods received. (D) is incorrect because, as indicated above, a buyer who accepts nonconforming goods is still entitled to damages.

Answer to Question 12

(B) The buyer is entitled to rescission on the ground of mutual mistake. Rescission is a remedy that discharges the contractual duties of the parties and puts an end to the transaction, leaving the parties as though the contract had never been made. Unilateral rescission results where one of the parties desires to rescind it but the other party refuses to agree to a rescission. For unilateral rescission to be granted, the party desiring rescission must have adequate legal grounds. One ground for unilateral rescission is mutual mistake of a material fact. If the manufacturer reasonably believed that the cartridges were compatible with both game systems when shipped to the buyer, then both parties were operating under a mistake of fact. This mistake concerns a basic assumption on which the contract is made, because the compatibility of the cartridges with both systems was a fact without which the buyer would not have entered into the transaction. The mistake creates a material imbalance in the agreed exchange, and the party seeking avoidance (the buyer) did not assume the risk of the mistake. Because of this mutual mistake of material fact, which existed at the time the contract was entered into, the buyer is entitled to rescission of the contract. (C) and (D) may look attractive because if a plaintiff is entitled to rescission and has paid money to the defendant in an attempt to perform his duties under the contract, he is entitled to restitution. Here, as part of its rescission remedy, the buyer would be entitled to restitution of the purchase price if it has already paid the manufacturer. However, it will also have to return the cartridges to the manufacturer before it will be granted restitution. [*See* Restatement (Second) of Contracts §384] (B) is a better choice than (C) because restitution of the purchase price is dependent on—and just one element of—the remedy of rescission. (D) is additionally incorrect because, if the buyer is entitled to restitution, he will receive the entire amount that he paid to the manufacturer (*i.e.,* the purchase price of the two lots) rather than simply the value of the cartridges. (A) is incorrect because the manufacturer was not obligated to provide adaptors compatible with both systems. Even if it were, this would not be an appropriate remedy because a buyer has a right to specific performance of a sales contract only where the goods are unique or in other proper circumstances. [U.C.C. §2-716] There is no indication that cartridges compatible with both game systems are unique. Thus, a contract for the sale of such goods is not an appropriate subject for specific performance.

Answer to Question 13

(A) The store will prevail, because there was no consideration to support its promise to pay the bank the additional $1,000 per month. This question looks like it concerns third-party beneficiaries,

but it actually presents a consideration issue. Generally, there must be consideration for modification of a contract, and a promise to perform an act that a party is already obliged to do is not sufficient consideration (the "preexisting legal duty" rule). Here, the electrician is promising to do exactly what he was obliged to do under his original contract with the store; thus, there is no consideration to support the promise to increase the fee. (B) is wrong because the bank is an intended beneficiary, not an incidental beneficiary. An intended beneficiary is one who is clearly intended to benefit from the agreement. Hence, the bank was named in the agreement and performance was to be made directly to it, and so it is clearly an intended beneficiary. (C) is wrong even though it is true that the bank is an intended creditor beneficiary. Despite this status, the bank will not recover because there was no consideration to support the modification of the contract. The status of creditor beneficiary does not give the bank any more rights than the electrician would have had to enforce the agreement, and the electrician could not enforce the agreement for the additional money because there was no consideration. (D) is wrong because it is based on the rule of U.C.C. section 2-209, which states that an agreement subject to the U.C.C. does not need consideration to be binding. However, the U.C.C. governs only in cases of the sale of goods, and this question presents a contract for services. Thus, the U.C.C. does not apply and the common law rule requiring consideration controls.

Answer to Question 14

(A) The car dealership will succeed. The uncle made an offer, which was accepted by the car dealership by doing the requested act. The uncle's offer was to guarantee the purchase price, up to $10,000, of a car in exchange for the car dealership's selling a car to the niece. This offer traditionally could be accepted by an act (the sale of the car), but could also be accepted by a promise to sell the car to the niece. Here, the car dealership accepted the offer by selling the car, and it then notified the uncle of the acceptance by mail. A contract was formed when the car dealership sold the car. Therefore, when the niece did not pay for it, the car dealership could collect from the uncle. (B) is wrong because it relies on a promissory estoppel theory, but here the uncle's promise is supported by a bargained-for exchange (his promise in exchange for the car dealership's sale); thus, there is no need to rely on promissory estoppel. (C) is wrong because the car dealership's ***motive*** in selling the car to the niece is not relevant. The car dealership did something it was not under a duty to do (sell the car to the niece) and that is sufficient consideration to support the uncle's promise to guarantee payment. (D) is wrong because the offer was accepted when the car dealership did the act, and the uncle was alive at that time.

Answer to Question 15

(C) The unilateral option contract between the plumber and the contractor to keep the plumber's offer open was effectively rescinded by the contractor's expressed intent to make a gift of the obligation owed her. The typical case of rescission involves a bilateral contract where neither party has yet performed; *i.e.,* the duties of both parties are still executory. However, no contract to do the plumbing work has been created yet, because the contractor has not communicated her acceptance of the bid to the plumber. Despite her use of the plumber's bid to prepare her own bid, the contractor is free to award the plumbing work to someone else if she is awarded the general contract. Hence, the contract to do the plumbing cannot be rescinded because it has not been created. Another contract is present under this fact pattern, however. Under section 87 of the Restatement (Second) of Contracts, the plumber's offer is binding as an option contract because the contractor reasonably relied on it to submit her bid. The option contract here is unilateral: The contractor's acceptance of the option contract by using the bid also constituted

performance of her duties under the option contract. In a unilateral contract case, a rescission promise must be supported by either (i) an offer of new consideration, (ii) elements of promissory estoppel (*i.e.,* detrimental reliance), or (iii) the offeree's manifestation of an intent to make a gift of the obligation owed her. The first two alternatives are absent in these facts, but the gift alternative is indicated by the contractor's statement that she will "forget" that the plumber ever made the bid. The contractor's response was an effective rescission of the option contract. (A) is an incorrect choice even though it is a true statement. A discharge of contractual duties by means of a release requires additional consideration or some substitute, such as a signed writing or reliance by the offeror on the discharge. Here there is no additional consideration to support a release, as choice (A) indicates, but the contractor will not win because a rescission has taken place. (B) is incorrect because a large dollar amount for purposes of the Statute of Frauds is irrelevant unless there is a contract for the sale of goods, which must be in writing if the goods are priced at $500 or more. The agreement between the contractor and the plumber involved a contract for services, which is not within the $500 provision of the Statute. (D) is incorrect because, as discussed above, a release requires additional consideration, a signed writing, or detrimental reliance by the offeror. Because none of these is indicated by the facts, a release has not taken place.

Answer to Question 16

(B) The manufacturer will not be able to enforce his demand because the contract, as modified, is within the Statute of Frauds, and there is no writing evidencing the modification. Because the contract here is for the sale of goods, the Uniform Commercial Code will govern. Under the U.C.C., a modification of a contract is enforceable even though it is not supported by consideration (which is required under the common law), as long as the modification is sought in good faith. Here, the modification was sought in good faith (the civil war raised the price of the raw material needed to manufacture widgets, making the contract unprofitable). Thus, the modification may be enforceable despite the lack of consideration. However, the U.C.C. also provides that contract modifications must comply with the Statute of Frauds if the contract as modified is within the mandate of the Statute. Under the Statute, a contract for the sale of goods for $500 or more must be in writing and signed by the party to be charged to be enforceable. Here, the contract as modified is within the Statute and the modification is not in writing; thus it is unenforceable. (A) is incorrect because the parol evidence rule does not prohibit introduction of the modification here. The rule provides that the terms of a contract set forth in a writing intended as a final expression of the parties' agreement cannot be contradicted by evidence of any prior or contemporaneous oral statement. The agreement to modify the price to $12,000 is neither prior nor contemporaneous, but rather was subsequent to the written contract. Thus, the parol evidence rule will not prevent admission of the modification. (C) is incorrect because even though the modification is admissible under the parol evidence rule, it is unenforceable under the Statute of Frauds. The parol evidence rule does not override the Statute; both hurdles must be overcome before a contract may be varied. (D) is incorrect because there was no reliance on the waiver. It is true that an attempted modification, invalid because it does not comply with the Statute of Frauds, may operate as a waiver of the right to enforce the contract as written. However, waivers may be withdrawn unless the retraction would be unjust because of a material change of position in reliance on the waiver. Here, with prices dropping to prewar levels, the manufacturer will make the same profit that he originally anticipated and there is no other evidence that he materially changed his position in reliance on the waiver. Thus, (D) is incorrect.

Answer to Question 17

(B) Because the large toymaker acts in good faith in setting its requirements to approximately those of the small manufacturer into whose shoes it stepped, the contract may be assigned. The contract

in this question is a "requirements" contract: The steel processor must sell the small manufacturer of children's toys all the specialized steel it requires for its toys. Generally, the right to receive goods under a requirements contract is not assignable because the obligor's duties could change significantly. In fact, here, a significant change would seem possible because the large toymaker is a larger company than the small manufacturer and its needs could be greater. However, the U.C.C. allows the assignment of requirements contracts ***if the assignee acts in good faith*** not to alter the terms of the contract. [U.C.C. §2-306] (The U.C.C. applies here because goods are involved.) Thus, assuming the large toymaker's requirements remain about the same as the small manufacturer's requirements, the steel processor would be required to honor its contract, now assigned to the large toymaker. (A) is wrong because requirements contracts may be nonassignable, even without a nonassignment clause. Thus, the clause would be irrelevant. The only thing that could allow assignment of a requirements contract is a good faith limitation, as addressed in choice (B). (C) is wrong because the U.C.C. does allow requirements contracts to be assigned, as long as the good faith limitation is satisfied. (D) is similarly incorrect. The U.C.C. would allow assignment without approval by the obligor if there is a good faith limitation on the requirements.

Answer to Question 18

(A) Because the quantity was stated in the April 17 letter, the Statute of Frauds is satisfied and the nursery may prevail. This contract is for the purchase and sale of goods; thus, the U.C.C. applies. The Statute of Frauds requires that a contract for the sale of goods for $500 or more be evidenced by a writing signed by the party to be charged. This writing must contain the essential elements of the agreement. The quantity term is the key to the sufficiency of a memorandum, and here the writing includes the quantity term. Thus, the writing complied with the Statute of Frauds. (B) is wrong because all other terms (including price) may be proved by parol evidence. The U.C.C. requires only that the memorandum contain (i) quantity, (ii) the signature of the party to be charged, and (iii) a writing sufficient to indicate that a contract was formed. [U.C.C. §2-201] (C) is wrong because it does not bear on the Statute of Frauds issue, but rather on the issue of the additional terms, which will not prevent a contract from being formed between merchants. (D) is wrong because U.C.C. section 2-201(2) provides that, in a deal between merchants, a writing confirming the deal sent by one party will bind ***both*** parties, unless the other party objects in writing within 10 days. Here, the wholesaler did not object within 10 days and so the nursery's letter confirmed the deal. Thus, the wholesaler can be charged even though the wholesaler has not signed the memorandum.

Answer to Question 19

(C) The dealership must pay the original price because the discount submitted in the confirmation materially alters the original deal. Under the U.C.C., in a deal between merchants, additional terms in the acceptance or in the written confirmation will be included as part of the deal ***unless*** the additional terms materially alter the original deal, the offer expressly limits acceptance to the terms of the offer, or the offeror objects to the terms within a reasonable time. [U.C.C. §2-207(2)] Because variation of the price term by 20% is a material alteration, the discount term is not included in the contract and the dealership must pay the original price. (A) and (B) are wrong because they attempt to use the U.C.C. rules regarding open price terms in a material alteration situation. Under the U.C.C., if the price is not stated in the contract but it appears that the parties intended to form a contract, a reasonable price will be implied. For the price to be implied: (i) there must be nothing about price in the contract; (ii) the price must have been left to be agreed upon later; or (iii) the price was to be fixed by a third party or external factor. None of these situations occurred here; thus, the open price term rules do not apply. (D) is wrong because only an additional term that is ***not a material variation*** becomes a part of the deal in the absence of an objection. Therefore, even without an objection by the tire manufacturer, if the discount materially alters the deal, it is not part of the contract.

Answer to Question 20

(A) The landowner may keep the $6,000 as liquidated damages. A liquidated damages clause is enforceable if: (i) damages are difficult to ascertain at the time of the making of the contract, and (ii) the damages are a reasonable forecast of compensatory damages. Here, the landowner was unsure what her damages would be if she did not receive the sales proceeds from the property, but $10,000 seemed a reasonable amount. Thus, both criteria for valid liquidated damages clauses are met. (B) is incorrect because impossibility must be objective; *i.e.,* performance cannot be accomplished by anyone. Physical incapacity of a person necessary to effectuate the contract may discharge contractual duties ***if*** that person's performance is clearly impossible. (Usually this occurs in personal services contracts, where only that one person can perform the required duty.) Although the buyer was seriously ill, it is not clear that this made it ***impossible*** for him to produce the $94,000. Without more facts, it is reasonable to assume that someone else could have delivered the money or that his mortgage would still have gone through, etc. (C) is incorrect because the conditions for the broker's payment were not met: it is debatable whether he produced a "ready, willing, and able" buyer, and in any event the sale did not actually proceed through closing. (D) is incorrect because the broker was to receive proceeds from the sale of the property; the $6,000 was damages and not sale proceeds.

Answer to Question 21

(B) The legal theory of bargain and exchange would offer the niece her best chance of collecting from her aunt's estate. To be enforceable, a contract must be supported by consideration. Generally, consideration requires a bargained-for exchange of something of legal value from each party. To be bargained-for, the promise must induce the detriment and the detriment must induce the promise. Here, the niece was induced to purchase the shawl and incur a debt in exchange for her aunt's promise to pay, and the aunt was induced to pay in exchange for her niece's promise to purchase the shawl and attend the festival. It does not matter that the aunt did not receive an economic benefit—influencing her niece's mind is sufficient to establish an exchange. Both parties gave something of legal value because the aunt had no legal duty to pay for a shawl for her niece and the niece had no legal duty to purchase the shawl and attend the festival. Therefore, there was a bargained-for exchange of something of legal value and a contract was formed. (A) is wrong because there was a contract that would be enforceable (*see* above). Restitution in quasi-contract is available in cases where a contract is unenforceable and one of the parties has performed, resulting in unjust enrichment to the other party, or in cases where there is no contract but the plaintiff has conferred a benefit on the defendant with the reasonable expectation of being paid, the defendant knew or had reason to know of the plaintiff's expectation, and the defendant would be unjustly enriched if she were allowed to retain the benefit without compensating the plaintiff. This theory would not be appropriate because there is an enforceable contract and an adequate legal remedy is available. (C) is wrong because a promise to make a gift is unenforceable for lack of consideration, and this result is not changed where the promise is conditional and the conditions have been fulfilled. In fact, an argument that there was a conditional gift would negate the bargain and exchange needed to establish an enforceable contract, because it would involve arguing that the aunt did not intend to induce her niece's detriment (*i.e.,* the aunt was not

seeking to trade her promise to pay in exchange for her niece's promise to attend the festival), but rather was merely stating on what conditions the niece could receive her gift. Thus, (C) would not be helpful to the niece's case. (D) is wrong because the theory of account stated is used in cases where the parties to a contract have had a series of transactions and agree to a final balance due from one to the other. Here, the niece is seeking to enforce a single transaction and, thus, the theory would not be appropriate.

Answer to Question 22

(A) The proprietor can recover the cost of the jacket from the grandfather's estate because the proprietor is an intended third-party beneficiary and his right to enforce the contract has vested. The rights of an intended third-party beneficiary vest when the beneficiary (i) manifests assent to the promise in a manner invited or requested by the parties; (ii) brings suit to enforce the promise; or (iii) materially changes his position in justifiable reliance on the promise. Here, the proprietor qualifies as an intended beneficiary of the agreement between the man and his grandfather because the proprietor was expressly designated in the contract, he was to receive performance directly from the grandfather, and he stood in an existing contractual relationship with the man that required the man to either pay for the jacket or return it, making it likely that the young man's purpose in making the arrangement with his grandfather was to satisfy the obligation to the proprietor. The proprietor can enforce the contract because his rights vested when he sent the bill to the grandfather at the grandfather's request. Thus, the proprietor will prevail against the grandfather's estate. (B) is wrong because the man does have a duty to give the clothes to the charity; if he does not do so, he will be in breach of his contract with his grandfather, and this would give his grandfather's estate a defense to payment. However, the man's time for performance (Christmastime) has not yet occurred, and so he is not in breach. Nevertheless, this fact is not the reason the proprietor will recover; he will recover due to his status as an intended beneficiary, not because this possible defense has been negated. (C) is wrong because both the result and the rationale are incorrect. The proprietor is not relying on the grandfather's implied promise to him in the phone call; he is seeking to enforce his rights as a third-party beneficiary of the agreement between the man and his grandfather. Even if the grandfather had not called the proprietor, the proprietor could still have recovered against the grandfather's estate because of his status as a third-party beneficiary. (D) is wrong because the man's giving the clothes to the charity is not a condition that must be fulfilled before the grandfather's estate must pay. The grandfather promised to pay for the jacket if the man promised to donate the clothes; *i.e.*, the consideration for the grandfather's promise was the man's promise, not his actually donating the clothes. As soon as the man made the promise, the grandfather's duty to pay became absolute. (If the man does not donate the clothes, he will be in breach of his contract with his grandfather, but the grandfather's performance was not conditioned on the man's donating the clothes.)

Answer to Question 23

(B) The widow's strongest argument is that the contractor had drawn up both the detailed specifications of the agreement and the plans for the house. When both parties entering into a contract are mistaken about facts relating to the agreement, the contract may be voidable by the adversely affected party if (i) the mistake concerns a basic assumption on which the contract is made; (ii) the mistake has a material effect on the agreed-upon exchange; and (iii) the party seeking avoidance did not assume the risk of the mistake. Here, it is likely that neither party knew that the soil conditions were unsuitable. But if the contractor had drawn up the specifications and plans for the house, it will be more likely that the court will conclude that he has assumed the risk of any mistake as to the sufficiency of the soil to support the house, and will not be able to avoid the contract. (A) might be helpful to the widow, but it might also be harmful to her and so is not as good an answer as (B). The fact that it is physically possible to build the house at an increased cost negates the defense of impossibility (which is also unavailable because the impossibility existed at the time the contract was entered into). However, the argument may aid a defense of impracticability, which is available where the party to perform has encountered extreme and unreasonable difficulty in performing that was not anticipated by either party. While a moderate increase in the cost of building would not be sufficient for impracticability, the fact that performance here will cost over 300% more than the anticipated cost will support the impracticability defense. [*See* Restatement (Second) of Contracts §261, comment d] (C) would not be as helpful to the widow's case as (A) because it only indicates that there was a mutual mistake, and a contract can be avoided for mutual mistake unless the adversely affected party bears the risk of the mistake, which the fact in (B) would establish. (D) is irrelevant because whether the daughter, the third-party beneficiary, knew of the contract affects only her ability to enforce the contract. The widow, as a party to the contract, may enforce regardless of whether her daughter knew of it.

Answer to Question 24

(C) The builder will prevail because he may raise all defenses that he had against the grandfather against the granddaughter. The granddaughter is an intended third-party beneficiary of the contract between the grandfather and the builder. Generally, a third-party beneficiary has rights under the contract as soon as she does something to vest her rights (manifests assent to the promise, brings suit to enforce the promise, or materially changes position by justifiably relying on the promise). Here, the granddaughter materially changed her position by justifiably allowing her option on the other house to lapse. Generally, once the third-party beneficiary's rights have vested, the original contracting parties may not modify the contract without the assent of the third-party beneficiary. However, the third-party beneficiary is subject to any defenses that the promisor could have used against the original promisee, and here the builder could have used the defense of impracticability against the promisee. Therefore, he could use that defense against the granddaughter to avoid having to pay damages for not building the house as he originally agreed. (A) is incorrect because although it is true that the granddaughter's rights had vested, the answer fails to take into account the defenses available to the builder. (B) is incorrect because there was consideration for the modification. Because the original contract was impracticable to perform, the builder would have been discharged. By agreeing to build the addition above, he undertook something that he was not otherwise bound to do. Likewise, because of the impracticability, the grandfather would have been discharged from his original contract to pay. (D) is incorrect because the granddaughter is not an incidental beneficiary; rather she is an intended beneficiary because she was specifically mentioned in the contract as the recipient of the house.

Answer to Question 25

(A) The contractor's best (and only) argument would be that the property owner's silence while the contractor deepened her well was an acceptance by silence of an implied-in-fact contract. An implied-in-fact contract is formed by manifestations of assent other than oral or written language, *i.e.,* by conduct. Where a person knowingly accepts offered benefits, such conduct, viewed objectively, may be said to manifest an agreement to the conferral of such benefits, resulting in a contract implied in fact. While generally an acceptance must be communicated to an offeror to be effective, courts will often find an acceptance where an offeree silently accepts offered benefits. Here, the property owner's purported belief that the work was being done by a county employee at no charge is not plausible. The property owner had no prior notification from or contact with any county employee, and it is not reasonable to believe that anyone, including an employee of the government, would enter upon and disturb private property without prior consent. Moreover, the property owner knew that her neighbors had not had their wells deepened by county workers but had paid private contractors to do the work. Thus, the facts strongly suggest that the property owner's silence as she watched the contractor deepen her well was acceptance by silence of an implied-in-fact contract. (B) is incorrect because promissory estoppel is inappropriate in this case. Under the doctrine of promissory estoppels, as outlined in section 90 of the First Restatement, a promise is enforceable to the extent necessary to prevent injustice if the promisor would reasonably expect to induce action or forbearance of a definite and substantial character and such action or forbearance is in fact induced. Here, the contractor and the property owner whose well he deepened had never met or negotiated for services and had no communications with one another prior to the contractor sending the property owner his bill, and the contractor did not even realize that he was doing the work for ***that*** property owner's benefit. Thus, promissory estoppel is not proper. (C) and (D) are incorrect, because mistake is a defense to ***formation*** of a contract, and it is raised to render a contract voidable by the adversely affected party. Thus, mistake would not be a ground on which relief could be granted. Even if the property owner's purported mistake were treated as credible by the court, there was no "mutual" mistake because the contractor and the property were not mistaken about the ***same*** fact, but rather, each was mistaken about a different fact (the contractor, that he was at the right address, and the property owner, that the contractor was a county employee doing the work without charge). Nor could the facts be characterized as a unilateral mistake, in which only one of the parties is mistaken about facts relating to the agreement, because ***both*** parties were operating under a mistaken belief. Thus, both (C) and (D) are incorrect.

Answer to Question 26

(B) In entering into the contract, the possibility that the retiree would die shortly after paying the premium and therefore receive virtually nothing in return should have been apparent to both parties. Actually, both parties took risks in this regard, as the retiree could have incurred medical expenses for a catastrophic illness during his lifetime that would have required the insurer to make payments far exceeding the one-time $30,000 premium. The retiree and the insurer were equally aware of these various possibilities, yet they freely entered into an agreement with this knowledge and on terms that were apparently acceptable to each of them. Despite the apparent unfairness of the result, a court generally will not interfere with the parties' right to make their own deal. Thus, the insurer is entitled to the premium. (D) is incorrect because the price paid by the retiree was freely arrived at by the parties. There is no indication of any inequality in bargaining power or any other factors indicative of hardship or oppression exerted against the retiree by the insurer. The retiree was free to enter into an agreement that turned out to be a bad one for him. Therefore, there are no factors pointing to the existence of unconscionability. (A) is incorrect because the insurer is entitled to the payment of the premium regardless of whether it declined to take another applicant. As detailed above, the possibility of the retiree's death occurring in the time frame that it did was part of the risk voluntarily undertaken by the parties, and as such, will not afford a basis for preventing the insurer from recovering the premium payment. The payment of $30,000 in return for the insurer's promise of catastrophic insurance coverage was part of a bargained-for exchange. Regarding (C), discharge by frustration of contractual purpose requires that, at the time of entering into the contract, the parties did not reasonably foresee the occurrence of the act or event leading to the frustration. Here, the parties should have foreseen the possibility that the retiree would die shortly after the policy took effect. Consequently, this is not a proper case for the application of frustration of purpose.

Answer to Question 27

(D) The unsecured creditor will prevail because the limited partnership's promise was supported by a bargained-for exchange. Legal detriment will result if the promisee does something he was under no obligation to do or refrains from doing something that he has a legal right to do. The detriment to the promisee need not involve any actual loss to the promisee or benefit to the promisor. Here, there was a bargained-for exchange in the unsecured creditor's forgoing of a claim in which he had a good faith belief, even though the claim might have been worthless. Thus, (D) is correct, and (A) is wrong. (C) is not a good answer because there is no need to rely on promissory estoppel when an enforceable agreement, which can be enforced according to its terms, is present. (B) is wrong because there was more than a moral obligation. Even though the limited partner may have been motivated by a feeling of moral obligation, there was a bargained-for exchange between him and the unsecured creditor.

Answer to Question 28

(D) The nephew's best defense is that the duties were nondelegable. Although, as a general rule, all contractual duties may be delegated to a third person, if the duties involve personal judgment and skill, they may not be delegated. Here, the farm owner, a skilled building contractor for many years, assigned his duties to build the barn, milking station, and silo to his nephew, a novice contractor. The nephew could argue that because the duties to which he was assigned involved personal judgment and skill, the assignment was not proper. (A) is incorrect because it does not matter that the nephew's contract was with the farm owner and not with the tenant. The tenant was an intended third-party beneficiary of their contract. An intended beneficiary can enforce the contract once his rights have vested, such as by manifesting assent to the promise in a manner invited or requested by the parties. Here, the tenant's rights would have vested when he assented to have the nephew do the work. (B) is incorrect because the fact that the tenant furnished no consideration is immaterial, because consideration was furnished by the farm owner. (C) is incorrect because the contract does not raise any Statute of Frauds issues; hence, it is enforceable even though it was oral.

Answer to Question 29

(B) The manufacturer will prevail because it never accepted the offer. For a communication to be an offer, it must contain a promise, undertaking, or commitment to enter into a contract, rather than a mere invitation to begin negotiations. The broader the communicating media, *e.g.*, publications, the more likely it is that the courts will view the communication as merely the solicitation of an offer. An advertisement in a trade journal generally is construed as an invitation to submit offers, not an offer itself. It is an announcement of the price at which the seller is willing to receive offers. Thus, the store owner's fax was an offer that was never accepted by the manufacturer. (A) is wrong because if the communication were otherwise a contract, the less formal requirements for certainty in contracts under the U.C.C. (which governs here because goods are involved) would not be a bar to enforcement. (C) is wrong because, as discussed above, the ad is not an offer. (D) is wrong because the ad in the trade journal was not a promise; hence, the store owner cannot rely on promissory estoppel or detrimental reliance to recover.

Answer to Question 30

(B) Because the shop owner can cover (*i.e.*, buy the train sets from another source), a court will not grant specific performance. If the seller fails to deliver goods under a valid contract, the buyer

has a number of remedies available, including the right to cover and the right to obtain specific performance if appropriate. A buyer may obtain specific performance of a contract for the sale of goods if the goods are unique or in short supply, but that is not the case here. The facts state that other dealers are selling the train sets (albeit at a higher price). Thus, the shop owner can buy the train sets from another dealer and get the difference between the cost of the substitute goods and the contract price. Thus, (B) is correct. (A) is incorrect because, as discussed above, under certain circumstances a seller of goods may be subject to specific performance. (C) is incorrect because, as discussed above, the shop owner can buy the train sets from another dealer and then sue for damages for the difference in cost. Thus, specific performance is not the appropriate remedy. (D) is irrelevant to whether specific performance is granted and is unsupported by the facts.

Answer to Question 31

(C) The wholesaler will not recover the $1,200 because sale during the Christmas season was a condition precedent. A condition precedent is one that must occur before an absolute duty of immediate performance arises in the other party. Based on the facts here, the intent of the parties was that the retailer would have to pay for the dolls only if they sold during the Christmas season. Sale during that time was a condition precedent to payment. Thus, the retailer had no obligation to pay for the 80 dolls that had not sold by February 12 (well after the Christmas season). Thus, (C) is correct, and (B) is wrong. (A) is wrong because the wholesaler refused the retailer's tender of the dolls, and the retailer is just holding them awaiting the wholesaler's instructions. (D) is wrong because accepting the check did not result in a waiver of any rights the wholesaler may have had. If a monetary claim is uncertain or subject to a bona fide dispute, an accord and satisfaction can be accomplished by a good faith tender and acceptance of a check when that check (or an accompanying document) conspicuously states that the check is tendered in full satisfaction of the debt. Here, there is no indication that the retailer stated that the check was payment in full.

Answer to Question 32

(D) If the property owner wins, it will be because the payments by the professor may be based on a valid landlord-tenant relationship. A promise creating an interest in land must be in writing to be enforceable. This includes not only agreements for the sale of real property or an interest therein, but also leases for more than one year. However, under the part performance doctrine, conduct that unequivocally indicates that the parties have contracted for the sale of land will take the contract out of the Statute of Frauds. Here, the parties had originally created a landlord-tenant relationship, and the lease would be enforceable even without a writing as a month-to-month tenancy. The continuation of the monthly payments can as readily be explained by a continuation of the lease relationship as by an oral agreement for an installment land sale contract. Thus, because the conduct does not unequivocally indicate a contract for the sale of land, the Statute of Frauds requirements will not be excepted. (A) is wrong because while part performance may create an estoppel, the professor will have a hard time proving it because the parties' conduct is consistent with a lease relationship as well. (B) is wrong because unconscionability is measured at the time the contract is formed, and there is nothing in the facts to indicate that the price was not fair at that time. Moreover, the property owner was not in a weaker bargaining position vis-à-vis the professor that would have forced her to accept an unfair price for the property; the parties were of roughly equal bargaining position and, as discussed above, the price was not unfair when the deal was struck. (C) is wrong because it states an incorrect position of the law; other than Statute of Frauds requirements, oral agreements are no more revocable than written agreements.

Answer to Question 33

(D) The neighbor will prevail because obtaining financing was a condition precedent. When the parties to a contract express their agreement in a writing with the intent that the writing embody the full and final expression of their bargain, no other expression made prior to or contemporaneous with the writing is admissible to vary the terms of the writing. Nevertheless, a party can still attack the validity of the contract through parol evidence, and this includes an argument that the writing never became enforceable because a condition precedent to enforceability had not been fulfilled. In such a case, all evidence of the understanding may be offered and received. The rationale is that the written agreement is not being altered by means of parol evidence if the written agreement never came into being. While (A) and (B) are true statements, they are wrong because the neighbor will not try to vary the writing, but rather he will show that the writing never became effective. (C) is wrong; if the neighbor were seeking to vary the writing with the oral agreement, the fact that it was made contemporaneous with the writing would not make it admissible. Any oral expressions contemporaneous with the written agreement are inadmissible under the parol evidence rule.

Answer to Question 34

(C) Because the daughter should have known of the wine merchant's unilateral mistake as to the identity of her business, the wine merchant is entitled to rescind the original agreement. Unilateral mistake as to a material fact is generally not a basis for rescission by the mistaken party unless the nonmistaken party knew or should have known of the mistake. To use this defense, the wine merchant does not need to establish that the daughter did in fact know of its mistake. The wine merchant need only show, based on an objective standard, that the daughter should have known of the mistake. Here, the wine merchant accepted the daughter's offer "in light of our long-standing business relationship." In conjunction with the similarity in the names of the two restaurants, this statement should have alerted the daughter to the mistake of identity. It also indicates that the presumed connection between the two restaurants was a material factor in the wine merchant's acceptance of the terms of the daughter's proposal. Thus, the wine merchant's rescission of the original agreement was justified. (A) is incorrect because, notwithstanding the fact that the daughter got a 50% discount in the price of the wine she ordered, the wine merchant apparently offered such discounts to long-standing customers. Thus, it not the price itself, but the wine merchant's unilateral mistake and the daughter's knowledge of it that made the price unfair. The unconscionability concept is often applied to one-sided bargains where one of the parties has substantially superior bargaining power and can dictate the terms of the contract to the other party with inferior bargaining power. That is not how the daughter got a highly favorable price on the wine; rather, it was because of the wine merchant's unilateral mistake. (B) is not as good a defense as (C) even though misrepresentation by one party may allow the other party to rescind the contract. To use the defense of misrepresentation, the wine merchant would need to show, at a minimum, that the daughter had ***actual knowledge*** that he had agreed to the contract only because he believed the two restaurants were connected, creating a duty on her part to disclose the true facts. Because the wine merchant has a right to rescind based on unilateral mistake without having to establish the daughter's state of mind, (C) offers a better defense than (B). (D) is incorrect because it is an incomplete statement of the law. Unilateral mistake is a basis for rescission by the mistaken party only if the other party knew or should have known of the mistake.

Answer to Question 35

(D) The fact that $8 per pound was a fair market price for the sugar at the time of the contract—it was the regular price it charged its customers—suggests that the change in the price term was not

extorted in bad faith. This is a contract for the sale of goods controlled by U.C.C. Article 2. Section 2-209 provides that an existing contract may be modified without additional consideration, but this is subject to the general provision of section 1-203 that every U.C.C. contract imposes an obligation of good faith in its performance or enforcement. Comment 2 to section 2-209 specifically states that extortion of a "modification" without legitimate commercial reason is ineffective as a violation of good faith. Here, the facts in the question indicate that the supplier set the $5 per pound price initially because that was the price it charged its long-standing customers, even though it was lower than the price the supplier would charge new customers. Because the supplier is apparently only seeking to charge the pastry shop what it would have charged her at the outset had it known of all the circumstances, its demand meets the test of good faith. (C) is not as good a choice as (D), even though it is a correct statement of law, because it does not address the good faith requirement, an issue raised by the shop owner in her pleadings. (D) is better because it tends to negate the claim of lack of good faith made by the shop owner. (A) is incorrect even though it is a true statement of fact. As noted above, U.C.C. section 2-209 explicitly authorizes modification of contracts for the sale of goods without additional consideration. (B) is incorrect because the fact that the supplier knew the pastry shop was opening soon does not establish bad faith on its part. The supplier made the demand for the modification as soon as it discovered its mistake. As discussed above, the supplier would have been justified in trying to modify what was a potentially long-term requirements contract if the price per pound of sugar was $3 below what it would have charged the pastry shop had all of the circumstances been known.

Answer to Question 36

(D) The parties do not have a contract, because the mailbox rule does not apply when the offeree sends a rejection, followed by an acceptance. In such a case, whichever is received first controls. Under the mailbox rule, acceptance by mail or similar means creates a contract at the moment of posting, with a couple of exceptions not relevant here. Rejection, on the other hand, is effective when received. So, if the mailbox rule had applied, there would have been a contract, because the friend's acceptance was mailed before his rejection letter was received. But because the mailbox rule does not apply here, and the matter is decided based on which letter was received first, there is no contract, because the friend's rejection letter was received by the bicycle owner a day before his acceptance letter was received by her. (A) is incorrect because, as discussed above, the mailbox rule does not apply when a rejection is sent before an acceptance; rather, whichever is received first controls. The fact that the bicycle owner did not read the rejection does not matter; it still was received by her before the acceptance. [*See* Restatement (Second) Contracts §68] (B) is incorrect because whether the friend paid for the bicycle is irrelevant. He sent the certified check (and his acceptance) after he sent his rejection, and the rejection was received first. (C) is incorrect because when a rejection by mail is followed by an acceptance by mail, the rule is that ***whichever is received first*** controls, ***not*** whichever is dispatched first. Thus, although it is true that there is no contract between the parties, it is because the friend's rejection letter was received by the bicycle owner first, rather than because it was mailed first.

Set 6 Answer Sheet

1.	Ⓐ Ⓑ Ⓒ Ⓓ	19.	Ⓐ Ⓑ Ⓒ Ⓓ
2.	Ⓐ Ⓑ Ⓒ Ⓓ	20.	Ⓐ Ⓑ Ⓒ Ⓓ
3.	Ⓐ Ⓑ Ⓒ Ⓓ	21.	Ⓐ Ⓑ Ⓒ Ⓓ
4.	Ⓐ Ⓑ Ⓒ Ⓓ	22.	Ⓐ Ⓑ Ⓒ Ⓓ
5.	Ⓐ Ⓑ Ⓒ Ⓓ	23.	Ⓐ Ⓑ Ⓒ Ⓓ
6.	Ⓐ Ⓑ Ⓒ Ⓓ	24.	Ⓐ Ⓑ Ⓒ Ⓓ
7.	Ⓐ Ⓑ Ⓒ Ⓓ	25.	Ⓐ Ⓑ Ⓒ Ⓓ
8.	Ⓐ Ⓑ Ⓒ Ⓓ	26.	Ⓐ Ⓑ Ⓒ Ⓓ
9.	Ⓐ Ⓑ Ⓒ Ⓓ	27.	Ⓐ Ⓑ Ⓒ Ⓓ
10.	Ⓐ Ⓑ Ⓒ Ⓓ	28.	Ⓐ Ⓑ Ⓒ Ⓓ
11.	Ⓐ Ⓑ Ⓒ Ⓓ	29.	Ⓐ Ⓑ Ⓒ Ⓓ
12.	Ⓐ Ⓑ Ⓒ Ⓓ	30.	Ⓐ Ⓑ Ⓒ Ⓓ
13.	Ⓐ Ⓑ Ⓒ Ⓓ	31.	Ⓐ Ⓑ Ⓒ Ⓓ
14.	Ⓐ Ⓑ Ⓒ Ⓓ	32.	Ⓐ Ⓑ Ⓒ Ⓓ
15.	Ⓐ Ⓑ Ⓒ Ⓓ	33.	Ⓐ Ⓑ Ⓒ Ⓓ
16.	Ⓐ Ⓑ Ⓒ Ⓓ	34.	Ⓐ Ⓑ Ⓒ Ⓓ
17.	Ⓐ Ⓑ Ⓒ Ⓓ	35.	Ⓐ Ⓑ Ⓒ Ⓓ
18.	Ⓐ Ⓑ Ⓒ Ⓓ	36.	Ⓐ Ⓑ Ⓒ Ⓓ

CONTRACTS QUESTIONS - SET 6

Question 1

A church deacon led his church's young adults group. One afternoon, the deacon saw a young woman who was a member of his church group walking down the street with a white cylinder in her mouth. He assumed that she was smoking a cigarette. In fact, she was eating a piece of candy that looked like a cigarette. Shortly after he saw the young woman on the street, the deacon took his young adults group to a weekend religious retreat. At that time, the deacon told the young woman that he would give her $50 if she did not smoke a single cigarette during the weekend of the retreat. The young woman agreed and did not smoke that weekend. On Sunday evening, the deacon told the church's pastor how he had helped turn the course of a young person in the right direction through his stratagem with the young woman. The pastor correctly informed the deacon that the young woman never smoked cigarettes. The deacon now refuses to pay the young woman $50.

Is the deacon legally obligated to pay the young woman $50?

(A) Yes, because the young woman fulfilled the deacon's terms and her motive for doing so is unimportant.

(B) Yes, because the deacon's anti-tobacco and alcohol activities morally obligate him to pay the young woman.

(C) No, because not smoking during the weekend religious retreat was good for the young woman's health and in no way a detriment to her.

(D) No, because the young woman would not have smoked during the weekend religious retreat in any case and cannot be said to have been induced into abstinence by the deacon's offer.

Question 2

A breeder of quarter horses entered into an agreement with a rancher to sell and deliver two quarter horses, one to the rancher and the other to the rancher's fiancée as a gift. Although the fair market value of each horse was $3,000, the horse breeder agreed to sell both horses together for a total price of $5,000. Under the agreement that the rancher wrote out and both parties signed, the horse breeder agreed to deliver one horse to the rancher on August 1, at which time the rancher agreed to pay the horse breeder $5,000. The horse breeder further agreed to deliver the other horse to the rancher's fiancée on August 12.

On August 1, the horse breeder delivered the first horse to the rancher and, at the same time, the rancher gave the horse breeder a certified check for $5,000. On August 12, the horse breeder brought the second horse to the residence of the rancher's fiancée and told her that the horse was a gift from the rancher. The rancher's fiancée told the horse breeder that she loathed quarter horses and she refused to take the horse. The horse breeder brought this horse back to his farm and sent an e-mail to the rancher, informing him that his fiancée refused delivery and that he (the horse breeder) could not keep the horse. Two weeks later, after not hearing from the rancher, the horse breeder sold the horse to an interested party for $3,000.

If the rancher sues the horse breeder, he should recover:

(A) $3,000, the value of the second horse.

(B) $2,000, the difference between the value of the horse delivered to the rancher and what the horse breeder received from the rancher.

(C) Nothing, because the rancher was not financially harmed.

(D) Nothing, because the horse breeder performed his part of the contract.

Question 3

A man borrowed $5,000 from his colleague to purchase stock and agreed in writing to repay the loan on or before August 1.

On July 15, the man notified his colleague that he would be unable to pay back the $5,000 on August 1. He told her that he could send her a check for $2,500 and that in addition, he could give her an antique diamond ring that had been recently appraised at $2,200. The colleague liked the ring and agreed to accept it plus $2,500 in cash as payment for the loan.

On August 1, a courier delivered the ring and a certified check for $2,500 to the colleague. She took the check, but told the courier to return the ring to the man. The man received the ring back the same afternoon. Meanwhile, the colleague deposited the check in her bank, and the next day filed suit against the man for $2,500. The man consulted an attorney as to whether he has a valid defense against his colleague's suit.

Assuming there are no Statute of Frauds issues, the attorney should advise the man that:

(A) The man has no defense against his colleague's suit, because the amount of the debt was undisputed.

(B) The man has no defense against his colleague's suit, because she properly exercised her right to enforce the original agreement by refusing tender of the ring.

(C) The man has no defense at law, but he may successfully defend in equity under a specific performance theory because the ring is unique.

(D) The man has the option of defending in equity under a specific performance theory or waiting until his colleague obtains a judgment against him and then suing her for breach.

Question 4

One Saturday, the owner of an art gallery and her friend were discussing art after the friend had helped the owner move some furniture in her home. The friend mentioned that he was very fond of a particular artist. The gallery owner asked her friend if he would like to buy a painting by the artist, entitled "Tears of a Clown," recently consigned to the gallery. The friend said that he would love it, but he only had $2,700. The gallery owner told her friend that she would let him have the painting for that price. The friend knew that the painting was priced at $7,000. He immediately wrote out a check for $2,700 and gave it to the gallery owner, who told him to visit the gallery on Monday to pick up the painting. On Sunday, a salesperson at the gallery sold "Tears of a Clown" to a gallery customer. Neither the salesperson nor the customer knew of the agreement between the gallery owner and her friend. The customer took the painting with him on Sunday. When the friend arrived at the gallery on Monday, the painting was gone.

Can the friend obtain specific performance from the gallery owner?

(A) Yes, because there was a bargained-for exchange of promises between the friend and the gallery owner.

(B) Yes, because the friend's assistance to the gallery in moving her furniture should be considered part of the quantum of adequate consideration.

(C) No, because the painting was sold to a bona fide purchaser for value and enforcement against the gallery owner is no longer feasible.

(D) No, because the gallery owner's promise was essentially a gift to her friend that she was free to revoke.

Question 5

A widget manufacturer sent out a circular describing its various models of widgets, specifying that "Model Z16" widgets were $3,500 per 100 widget lot "C.I.F." A recipient of the circular faxed an order for "two 100 widget lots, Model Z16, at $3,500 per lot per your circular, with delivery by August 6." The manufacturer mailed back its standard confirmation form, confirming quantity, price, and delivery date. However, the purchasing agent for the company that placed the order noticed that a rubber stamp impression in red ink had been placed on the bottom of the manufacturer's confirmation, stating that acceptance of the order was conditioned on a crating charge of $150 per 100 widget lot.

Assuming no additional facts, which of the following best represents the relationship between the manufacturer and the company that placed the order, immediately after the company received the manufacturer's confirmation?

(A) There is a valid, enforceable contract between the manufacturer and the company that includes the crating fee.

(B) There is a valid contract between the manufacturer and the company, but it does not include the crating fee.

(C) There is no contract between the manufacturer and the company, because there has been an alteration of a material term.

(D) There is no contract between the manufacturer and the company, because the manufacturer's confirmation letter was a counteroffer, which the company may accept or reject.

Question 6

A large wholesale dealer in produce had never done business with a certain greengrocer who operated a small chain of markets in the Midwest. They entered into a written agreement whereby the wholesale dealer agreed to supply to the greengrocer the "fuzzy" variety of peaches at $35 per 50 pound lot. The agreement contained a provision stating that the greengrocer will buy "as many 50 pound lots of fuzzy peaches as the greengrocer chooses to order."

Assuming that the greengrocer has not yet placed any orders for peaches with the wholesale dealer, is this agreement between the parties enforceable?

(A) Yes, because it is a valid requirements contract and, as such, is enforceable under the Uniform Commercial Code.

(B) Yes, because the Uniform Commercial Code will imply reasonable terms.

(C) No, because the total quantity of the contract is not specified.

(D) No, because there is no consideration on the greengrocer's part.

Question 7

On February 1, a national department store chain entered into a written agreement with a canoe manufacturer providing that the manufacturer would sell the department store any quantity of 16-foot aluminum canoes that the department store desired at a price of $250 per canoe, deliveries to be made 30 days after any order. The agreement was signed by authorized agents of both parties. On March 1, the department store sent the manufacturer an order for 500 canoes to be delivered in 30 days. The manufacturer immediately e-mailed the department store a confirmation of the order. Ten days later, the department store sent the manufacturer an order for an additional 500 canoes, to be delivered in 30 days. Five days after receiving the department store's second order, the manufacturer e-mailed the department store and explained that a large sporting goods chain was willing to purchase all of the manufacturer's output of 16 foot canoes at $275 per canoe and that the manufacturer would be unable to fill any of the department store's orders.

The department store found another canoe manufacturer willing to provide it with 16 foot

aluminum canoes for $280 per canoe and on April 15 filed an action against the manufacturer seeking damages for the manufacturer's failure to deliver the 1,000 canoes ordered.

How should the court rule?

(A) The department store is not entitled to any damages because no contract was formed by the parties' communications.

(B) The department store is entitled to cover damages of $30 per canoe only for 500 canoes but is not entitled to any damages for breach of the duty of good faith.

(C) The department store is entitled to cover damages of $30 per canoe for 1,000 canoes but is not entitled to any damages for breach of the duty of good faith.

(D) The department store is entitled to punitive damages equal to the lesser of 10% of the total sale price or $500 in addition to any cover damages that are due because the manufacturer breached the duty of good faith.

Question 8

A dairy farm operated a small processing plant that supplied premium ice cream to nearby specialty shops and ice cream parlors. It entered into a written agreement with a local ice cream parlor to sell "all output" of its Extra Rich ice cream to the ice cream parlor, and the ice cream parlor agreed to sell exclusively the dairy farm's Extra Rich frozen desserts. The agreement stated that the ice cream parlor would pay $25 for each five-gallon container of Extra Rich ice cream that it ordered from the dairy farm. Several months after the parties entered into this contract, demand for high-fat ice creams dropped sharply among the health-conscious consumers who had formerly patronized the ice cream parlor, and the proprietor had to throw out some of its product because the reduced demand meant that opened containers were not used up before the taste of the ice cream became affected. The ice cream parlor wanted to stop selling the dairy farm's Extra Rich ice cream and instead sell a frozen yogurt product produced by another dairy.

Can the dairy farm enforce its agreement against the ice cream parlor?

(A) Yes, because changing demand is one of the standard risks of business that both parties assumed.

(B) Yes, because the court will imply a promise on the part of the ice cream parlor to use its best efforts to sell the dairy farm's Extra Rich ice cream.

(C) No, because there was no consideration on the part of the ice cream parlor to support an enforceable contract.

(D) No, because the total price and total quantity terms were never established.

Question 9

A building contractor entered into a contract with the local college to remodel a residence hall during the summer. As specified by the contract, the work had to be completed before the fall semester began at the beginning of September. Because the contractor received a great deal of other maintenance business from the college, his price of $400,000 was significantly lower than other contractors and he was not going to demand payment until the work was completed.

By the end of the first week in August, the contractor had completed 75% of the project and had expended $350,000 in labor and materials. At that time, however, a labor dispute between the contractor and his employees prompted most of the workers to walk off the job. Because prospects for a quick settlement of the dispute were doubtful, the contractor informed the college that he would not be able to meet the completion deadline. A week later, the college obtained another contractor who was able to finish the project by the end of August. The college paid him $150,000, which included a substantial amount of overtime for his workers. The increase in value of the residence hall due to the remodeling was $425,000. The original contractor, who had not been paid, files suit against the college, which files a counterclaim against him.

What should the contractor recover from the college?

(A) Nothing, because the contractor breached the contract.

(B) $200,000 in restitutionary damages, which is the difference between its expenditures and the amount the college paid the other contractor to complete the work.

(C) $250,000 in restitutionary damages, which is the contract price minus the amount the college paid the other contractor to complete the work.

(D) $275,000 in restitutionary damages, which is the difference between the value of the completed remodeling and the amount the college paid the other contractor to complete the work.

Question 10

The owner of an art gallery entered into a written contract with an avid art collector whereby the art collector agreed to buy and the gallery owner agreed to sell for $7,500 any painting in the gallery by artist Alpha. The contract was to be executed on July 6 according to its written terms. The art collector went to the gallery on July 6 with a certified check in the amount of $7,500. The art collector pointed out a painting by a different artist hanging on the wall, and told the gallery owner that that was the painting he wanted, and that he would also take the old fashioned $250 gilt frame to go with it. The gallery owner responded that the painting was by the artist Beta, but that the art collector could have it with the frame if he was willing to pay $250 extra for it. This enraged the art collector, and he filed suit against the gallery owner, asserting in his pleading that he remains able and willing to tender $7,500 to the gallery owner. He also asserts that prior to signing the contract, the parties agreed orally that the art collector could have a painting by Beta if he wanted one and that the gallery owner would throw in a frame worth $250. The gallery owner denied that any such conversation took place. There are no other witnesses.

The court should allow the art collector to testify regarding:

(A) The oral agreement for the painting, but not the oral agreement for the frame.

(B) The oral agreement for the frame, but not the oral agreement for the painting.

(C) Both the oral agreement for the painting and the oral agreement for the frame.

(D) Neither the oral agreement for the painting nor the oral agreement for the frame.

Question 11

A photography buff wrote a letter to his brother-in-law offering to sell him his camera for $1,500, because he knew that he had admired it for a long time. The day after the brother-in-law received the letter, he mailed a letter back to the photography buff agreeing to purchase the camera equipment for $1,500. The next day, after describing the camera to a friend who was very knowledgeable about photographic equipment, the brother-in-law learned that the camera was second-rate and not worth more than $1,200. He immediately telephoned the photography buff and told him that he had no interest in buying the camera. The photography buff received his brother-in-law's letter agreeing to purchase the camera equipment a day after receiving the phone call.

If the photography buff brings an action against his brother-in-law for breach of contract, and the brother-in-law defends on the grounds that no contract was formed, how should the court rule?

(A) For the brother-in-law, because the description of the subject matter of the contract was too indefinite to be enforced.

(B) For the brother-in-law, because the photography buff received the telephone call before he received the letter.

(C) For the photography buff, because his brother-in-law's letter accepting the offer was effective when mailed.

(D) For the photography buff, because the contract is for the sale of goods over $500 in value and his brother-in-law's attempted rejection of the offer was oral.

Question 12

An art gallery owner wrote to one of her regular customers to inform him that she had just acquired a painting by the collector's favorite artist and that she would sell it to him for $1,000. She added that the art collector must let her know whether he was interested within 10 days, because another customer had already offered her $1,000 for the painting and she must get back to him by June 1.

Two days after receiving the letter, on May 25, the art collector mailed a letter back to the gallery owner agreeing to purchase the oil painting for $1,000. Shortly thereafter, the art collector had a change of heart and refused to accept the painting when it was delivered to him. The gallery owner brings an action for breach.

Should the trial court invoke the parol evidence rule to bar the art collector from offering evidence that he was unduly rushed into making a decision because the gallery owner really did not need an answer within 10 days?

(A) Yes, because the proffered evidence contradicts a material term of the contract.

(B) Yes, because the art collector is estopped from denying the truth of a contract that he has accepted.

(C) No, because the proffered evidence does not contradict a material term of the contract.

(D) No, because the proffered evidence establishes a fraud.

Question 13

A licensed doctor sees an unconscious pedestrian bleeding and lying on the shoulder of a highway. Two years earlier, she had witnessed a similar scene and failed to stop. The earlier pedestrian wound up dying, and the doctor promised that victim's wife that if she ever came upon a similar victim, she would stop to help. True to her word, the doctor stopped her car, dashed to the pedestrian's side, and frantically (yet competently) rendered emergency medical care. The pedestrian was stabilized because of the doctor's quick actions and survived. He eventually made a full recovery.

The best argument for the doctor recovering the reasonable cost of her medical care from the pedestrian is:

(A) There was an implied-in-fact contract.

(B) There was an implied-in-law contract.

(C) The doctor acted under extreme duress.

(D) The doctor had a preexisting duty to a third party.

Question 14

A general contractor entered into a written agreement with a subcontractor, whereby the subcontractor agreed to furnish heavy equipment and operators for a new state toll road project that the contractor was overseeing. Among the duties that the subcontractor undertook to perform was the installation of the toll collection booths and automatic toll collection machinery.

The contract contains four clauses of special interest. The first is a time-is-of-the-essence

clause, which states that the subcontractor must have all toll booths and toll collection equipment in place and operable by August 20. The second is a clause concerning modifications—any modification of the contract without written approval by the general contractor would be void. The third is an exoneration clause, which holds the general contractor harmless for any property damage occurring while the subcontractor is placing the toll booths and automatic toll collection machinery. The fourth is a liquidated damages clause, providing for liquidated damages of $1,000 per day chargeable against the subcontractor for each day that the subcontractor fails to complete the job beyond the contract date.

Before the subcontractor began work on the general contractor's project, the subcontractor was offered an extremely lucrative opportunity to work on a construction project in a war-ravaged Middle Eastern oil sheikdom. The rebuilding work would continue for several years and promised to bring the subcontractor far more income than the work for the general contractor. The subcontractor wished to assign his part of the contract with the general contractor to his former employee, who was equally experienced and qualified in heavy equipment contracting.

Which clause in the contract between the general contractor and the subcontractor would be most likely to bar the subcontractor from assigning to his former employee?

(A) The time-is-of-the-essence clause.

(B) The modifications clause.

(C) The exoneration clause.

(D) The liquidated damages clause.

Question 15

A homeowner and a local builder entered into a written contract that called for the builder to build a second story onto the top of the homeowner's one-story residence. When scheduling conflicts arose, the builder asked the homeowner if they could substitute his buddy, an out-of-town builder who had comparable experience and skills, to perform the local builder's part of the contract. All of the parties agreed to the substitution. Unfortunately, the out-of-town builder made a major blunder that will be quite expensive to correct.

Is the local builder liable to the homeowner for the cost of correcting the defect?

(A) Yes, because the substitution in and of itself does not relieve the local builder of liability on the underlying contract.

(B) Yes, because the local builder did not give any consideration on which to base a release.

(C) No, because the local builder transferred his duties to the out-of-town builder.

(D) No, because the local builder was discharged through a novation.

Question 16

A homeowner entered into a written agreement with a contractor whereby the contractor agreed to completely remodel the homeowner's bathroom "to her specifications" at a cost of $10,000. The homeowner's specifications were highly detailed and required custom-made fixtures that would not be usable in other bathroom remodeling jobs. The contractor ordered the custom-made fixtures and paid $4,000 for them when they were delivered to his place of business. Figuring up the cost of the fixtures and labor, the contractor estimated that he would make a total profit of $2,000 on the job after payment for materials and workers. Before the contractor began work on the project, but after he had paid for the fixtures, the homeowner told the contractor that she had had a change of heart and would probably be selling the house the following year, and so would not need a custom bathroom. The contractor made no attempt to sell the fixtures to another contractor and filed suit against the homeowner for damages.

The contractor is likely to recover:

(A) Nothing, because he failed to mitigate damages.

(B) His expectation damages of $2,000.

(C) $4,000, the cost of materials as restitution.

(D) $2,000 as expectation damages, plus $4,000 in reliance damages.

Question 17

A retailer entered into a written contract with a wholesaler whereby the wholesaler agreed to sell and the retailer agreed to buy 100 boxes of sunglasses manufactured by a large corporation located in a neighboring city. The agreed-upon price was $75 per box. Two weeks before the specified delivery date, the wholesaler told the retailer that it would not be able to fill its order, because of unexpected high demand for sunglasses this season. Although the retailer learned that the needed quantity of the same brand of sunglasses could be shipped within two days for $83 per box from a supplier in another area, the retailer instead purchased 100 boxes of the sunglasses locally at a cost of $90 per box. These sunglasses were of a slightly higher quality than the sunglasses that were originally contracted for. A few days before the original delivery date, the wholesaler notified the retailer that it would fill the order, and tendered 100 boxes of the sunglasses on the date of delivery. However, the retailer refused to accept them. At that time, the wholesale market price of the sunglasses had declined to $80 per box.

If the retailer sues the wholesaler for damages based on the wholesaler's alleged breach, the retailer is likely to recover:

(A) $1,500, the difference between the cost of cover and the contract price.

(B) $800, the difference between the contract price and the nonlocal supplier's price.

(C) $500, representing the difference between the contract price and the wholesale market price at the time of performance.

(D) Nothing, because the retailer obtained cover without waiting a commercially reasonable time for the wholesaler to retract the repudiation.

Question 18

An antique lover spotted a beautiful Early American bedroom ensemble at her favorite antique store. The ensemble included a bed, a mirror, and two dressers. Over a period of several weeks, the shop owner and the antique lover negotiated over a price, but they were unable to come to an agreement.

On April 3, the shop owner and the antique lover signed a statement whereby the shop owner offered to sell to the antique lover an Early American bedroom ensemble, recorded as items 20465, 20466, 20467, and 20468 in the shop's registry if the parties agree upon a price on or before April 12.

On April 6, the shop owner sent a letter to the antique lover, telling her that she could have the bedroom ensemble for $22,000. Also on April 6, the antique lover sent a letter to the shop owner telling him that she was willing to pay him $22,000 for the bedroom ensemble. Both parties received their letters on April 7.

Without assuming any additional facts, which of the following statements is most correct as of April 8?

(A) The shop owner and the antique lover had a valid contract from the moment the letters of April 6 were mailed.

(B) A contract exists between the shop owner and the antique lover, because the shop owner, a merchant, sent the antique lover an offer in writing.

(C) A contract exists between the shop owner and the antique lover, because the crossing offers were identical and received before April 12.

(D) No contract exists between the shop owner and the antique lover, because of a lack of mutual assent.

Question 19

A bicycle shop proprietor and a customer entered into a valid contract under which the customer was to purchase a racing bicycle to be delivered on May 20. The contract provided that the bicycle was to be delivered to the customer's nephew as a birthday present. The proprietor sent a photocopy of the contract to the nephew, which the nephew received on May 4. In anticipation of receiving the new bicycle, the nephew immediately donated his old bicycle to a charitable organization. On May 15, the customer told the proprietor that he wanted to cancel the contract for the bicycle. The proprietor assented and promptly sold the bicycle to another customer at twice the price. The nephew called the bicycle shop when the bicycle was not delivered on May 20 and was told of the cancellation of the contract.

Can the nephew compel the customer to honor the original contract or pay him damages?

(A) Yes, because the nephew is an intended beneficiary of a valid contract.

(B) Yes, because the nephew reasonably relied on the contract between the proprietor and the customer.

(C) No, because the nephew was merely an incidental beneficiary.

(D) No, because the nephew was a donee beneficiary and the customer properly revoked the gift.

Question 20

A wealthy sportsman purchased a large old wooden sailing ship for $200,000. Although the boat was a classic, the sportsman wanted it to be modernized and made more comfortable. To that end, the sportsman entered into a written contract with a marine architect-engineer to draw up and then execute the modernization plans, for $7,500.

At the time the parties entered into the agreement, the sportsman told the architect-engineer that his modernization plan would be subject to the approval of the sportsman's sister, that they would, in fact, have no deal unless the plans meet with her approval. The architect-engineer agreed to this. He finished his drawings and submitted them to the sportsman, who was enthusiastic about the designs. The sportsman's sister, a famous yachtswoman, was engaged in a trans-Pacific yacht race at the time and was not expected home for a number of weeks. Cheered by the sportsman's enthusiasm, the architect-engineer went ahead and modernized the ship according to his designs. When he finished the work, he submitted a bill to the sportsman, who refused to pay, pointing out that his sister had never approved the designs.

If the architect-engineer sues the sportsman, which of the following issues of contract law is most likely to be decisive in determining the outcome of the case?

(A) Statute of Frauds.

(B) Parol evidence rule.

(C) Rules of construction.

(D) Conditions precedent.

Question 21

A homeowner and a builder entered into a written contract to build a sauna in a spare room in the homeowner's home at a cost of $3,000. The contract contained a clause stating that the builder will not begin construction without prior approval of the plans by the homeowner's certified public accountant. The builder submitted his designs to both the homeowner and the accountant. The homeowner liked the plans, but the accountant did not and withheld his approval. The builder asked the homeowner

whether she wanted him to submit new designs. The homeowner told the builder orally, "No! Your designs are great! My accountant is crazy! You go right ahead and construct the sauna." The builder constructed the sauna. The homeowner now refuses to pay the builder, citing the clause requiring approval by the accountant.

If the builder sues the homeowner, the builder will recover:

(A) The full contract price, because the accountant's approval was not a condition precedent for the contract to take effect.

(B) The full contract price, because once the builder began building the sauna after speaking to the homeowner, the homeowner did nothing to stop the builder.

(C) The reasonable value of the builder's services and materials, because otherwise the homeowner would be unjustly enriched.

(D) Nothing, because the homeowner's oral statement will be excluded by the parol evidence rule.

Question 22

Two years ago, an expert gemologist told the owner of a sapphire ring that the ring was probably worth about $6,000, although the gemologist never gave a formal appraisal. The ring's owner now is in need of cash and offered to sell it to his friend. She liked the ring but had no idea of its value. She therefore suggested that the owner take it to a reputable jeweler for an appraisal, and if the price was not too high, she would buy it from him. The owner did not tell his friend about the gemologist's opinion because he hoped the ring's value had increased.

The owner took the ring to a reputable jeweler, who told the owner in good faith that there was a tiny flaw in the stone that reduced the ring's value to $4,800. The jeweler noted that if the stone were perfect, the ring would be worth $6,200. Although the ring's owner was disappointed, he told his friend that she could have it for its appraised value: $4,800. Unbeknownst to the friend or the ring's owner, the jeweler was suffering from a minor eye infection that caused him to find a "flaw" where none, in fact, existed. After she purchased the ring from its owner for $4,800, the friend sought her own appraisal for insurance purposes. A reputable jeweler issued the friend an appraisal document accurately stating the ring's value at $6,200. The ring's (now-former) owner learned of this and demanded return of the ring in exchange for the money she had paid for it. The friend refused.

If the original owner of the ring sues his friend to replevy the ring, will the court rule in his favor?

(A) No, because parties to a contract generally assume the risk of determining value.

(B) No, because he should have known the ring was worth more than $4,800 based on his conversation with the gemologist.

(C) Yes, because both parties mistakenly relied on an inaccurate appraisal in determining the ring's value.

(D) Yes, because accuracy of the appraisal was an express condition precedent.

Question 23

A man agreed to sell his large screen television to his neighbor for $2,500. The neighbor made a down payment of $700, took possession of the television and agreed to pay the outstanding balance in 18 equal $100 installments, beginning on June 5, with subsequent installments due on the fifth of each month until the balance was paid in full.

The buyer's friend owed her $2,000. On May 20, the buyer and her friend entered into an oral agreement whereby the friend agreed to make the 18 $100 installment payments to the seller in exchange for the buyer's promise to forgive the friend's $2,000 debt. On June 7, the seller called the buyer to ask her where his first $100

installment payment was, and she told him at that time of her agreement with her friend. The friend has made none of the installment payments.

If the seller files suit against the friend demanding payment, who will prevail?

(A) The seller, because he was a third-party beneficiary of the agreement between the buyer and her friend.

(B) The seller, because he is an assignee of the buyer's rights against her friend.

(C) The friend, because there was no consideration for her promise to the buyer.

(D) The friend, because the surety provision of the Statute of Frauds prevents the seller from enforcing the friend's promise.

Question 24

A neighborhood handyman did some work over the summer for an elderly gentleman who lived down the street. When the work was completed, the handyman sent the elderly gentleman a bill for $500, the price they had agreed to. The elderly gentleman told the handyman that he did not have the money but would make the necessary arrangements to pay him. After the elderly gentleman talked to his brother-in-law, who owed him $500, and extracted a promise from the brother-in-law that he would pay the handyman, the elderly gentleman told the handyman to expect a $500 check from his brother-in-law within the week. In a conference call on the telephone, the handyman expressly agreed with the brother-in-law and the elderly gentleman that the brother-in-law would assume the elderly gentleman's duties under the contract. However, when the bill was sent to the brother-in-law, he inexplicably ignored it and used the $500 to buy a new television instead. The handyman has not yet filed suit against the brother-in-law but is weighing his options.

Does the handyman have a right to recover the debt from the elderly gentleman?

(A) Yes, the elderly gentleman remains liable for the debt.

(B) No, because there has been a novation.

(C) No, because the handyman has not yet attempted to recover from the brother-in-law first.

(D) No, because the original agreement between the elderly gentleman and the handyman for the work that the handyman did was not in writing.

Question 25

A businesswoman entered into a written contract with a general contractor to build a studio and broadcast transmitter for $3 million by July 1. Among his tasks, the contractor was to install underground cables and fiberoptic lines necessary to broadcast.

When digging the deep trench necessary to lay the conduit containing the fiberoptic lines, the contractor encountered a stretch of extremely soggy soil. This was an indication that an offshoot of the nearby city's aquifer underlay the property. This was not indicated on any of the geological survey maps available in the office of the county recorder of deeds. The contractor told the businesswoman that it would cost an additional $50,000 to lay the conduit through that stretch of soil. The businesswoman had already launched an advertising campaign indicating that the station would begin broadcasting on July 4, which was rapidly approaching. Therefore, when the contractor threatened to quit the job without the additional $50,000, the businesswoman reluctantly agreed orally to the contractor's demand as long as he promised that all of the work would be completed by the middle of June. The contractor agreed, proceeded to lay the conduit, and completed building the studio and transmitter by June 15. The businesswoman paid the contractor $3 million, but when the contractor demanded $50,000 more, she refused to pay it. The contractor sues the businesswoman for the $50,000.

Who will prevail?

(A) The businesswoman, because the oral modification was not effective to alter the prior written agreement.

(B) The businesswoman, because no valid consideration was provided for the agreement to pay the additional $50,000.

(C) The contractor, because the modification was supported by consideration.

(D) The contractor, because $3,050,000 was a fair price for the completed job.

Question 26

The owner of several radio stations throughout the Midwest purchased land in a small Midwest town for the purpose of building another radio station. He entered into a written contract with a contractor to build a studio and broadcast transmitter on the property. In response to an engineering survey undertaken before the contract was executed, the contract contained a clause providing that the underground cables be laid in a path that avoided an identified area of magnetized rock, because under certain conditions, such as magnetic storms generated by sunspot activity, a higher than normal level of interference with the radio broadcast signals would occur if the cables were laid there.

After the contractor finished the job, the radio station owner discovered that the contractor had laid a portion of the underground cables through a patch of magnetized rock. Despite the defect, the studio and broadcasting transmitter are now worth about $4 million. Without the defect, their value would be $100,000 more. The radio station owner contracted with an electrical contractor to reroute the cables around the magnetized rock for a cost of $50,000.

How much is the original contractor entitled to collect from the radio station owner?

(A) $2,900,000, because the actual value of the property is $100,000 less than the value it would have been if the contractor had not breached.

(B) $3 million, because the value of the property even with the defect is greater than the contract price.

(C) $2,950,000, because the radio station owner will have to pay $50,000 to correct the contractor's defective performance.

(D) Only the expenses he incurred, but not his expected profit, because he breached the contract with the radio station owner.

Question 27

A man of seemingly modest means died, leaving his nephew as his sole heir. Among the items inherited by the nephew were some old oil paintings. The nephew knew nothing about art and had no place to put the paintings in his home. He placed an ad in the paper offering to sell the paintings at a price to be mutually agreed upon. A buyer for an art gallery responded to the ad. The buyer did not identify himself as an art gallery buyer or tell the nephew that he was knowledgeable about art. Rather, he concocted a story about wanting the paintings for his country estate. The nephew, for his part, revealed his lack of knowledge about art when he told the buyer that his uncle had probably painted the pieces himself. From the signature and the style, the buyer recognized that the artist was a renowned 19th century American portrait artist. The nephew and the buyer agreed upon a price and executed a contract. However, before the nephew delivered the paintings to the buyer, or the buyer paid him, he sought to rescind the contract. The buyer insisted that the nephew deliver the paintings to him and threatened to sue for breach of contract if he did not.

Which argument would give the nephew the best basis for rescinding the contract with the buyer?

(A) The nephew told the buyer that his uncle had probably painted the paintings himself.

(B) The nephew did not know that the buyer was a professional buyer for an art gallery and was knowledgeable about art.

(C) The buyer falsely told the nephew that the paintings were going to be used to furnish his (the buyer's) country estate.

(D) The contract was still executory on both sides.

Question 28

A salvage company offered for sale confederate dollars that had been recovered when the company recently raised a shipwreck off the coast of South Carolina. A purchasing agent for a private west coast museum purchased the bills, but he had represented that he was buying them for himself in hopes of obtaining a lower price.

After purchasing the bills, the agent carefully packaged them and had them shipped to his museum. While the bills were in transit, the museum burned to the ground and its owner decided that she would not rebuild because most of her collections had been destroyed.

When the bills arrived after the fire, the owner opened the package only to discover that the bills were too brittle for shipping by this method—three bills had disintegrated in transit. Undaunted, the owner took the remaining nine bills and had them mounted behind a glass frame so she could display them in her study. While the bills were being framed, the owner read on the Internet that a large cache of similar bills had just been discovered, and the market price for such bills had just been cut in half.

Frustrated but still undaunted, the owner hung the framed bills in her study. Unfortunately, the salt water had reacted with the pigments in the bills in such a way that shortly after they had been exposed to indirect sunlight, all of the color in the bills faded almost completely away. No other confederate bills raised from the ocean before had similar reactions; these bills appear to have been printed using substandard dyes.

Which of the following facts would give the museum owner the best basis for rescinding the contract with the salvage company?

(A) The bills were too brittle for transport.

(B) The discovery of a large cache of similar bills a few days after the sale.

(C) The bills' unusual reaction to indirect sunlight.

(D) The destruction of the museum before the bills arrived.

Question 29

A manufacturer of high-speed computers entered into a written agreement with a distributor whereby the distributor would purchase a specified computer from the manufacturer for $50,000. The parties had orally agreed that the delivery date would be November 4. However, when the agreement was reduced to writing, a glitch in the word processor caused the printout to show the delivery date as "12/4" instead of "11/4." Both parties signed the paper without noticing the incorrect delivery date. Before reducing their agreement to writing, the parties had also orally agreed that the agreement would not become binding unless the distributor notified the manufacturer, in writing, by October 7, that it (the distributor) had obtained a buyer for the computer.

On September 25, the distributor found a buyer who needed the computer for her business and who agreed to buy it from the distributor. However, the distributor did not inform the manufacturer that it had found a buyer until October 30.

In the meantime, due to a strike at the manufacturer's leading competitor, the price of high-speed computers rose rapidly during the month of October. By the end of the month, the market value of the computer in question was $70,000. Because of the increase in the value of the computer, the manufacturer does not want to deliver the specified computer to the distributor for $50,000.

Which of the following provides the best argument that the manufacturer should be discharged from its duties under the contract?

(A) The increase in value of the computer makes the contract unconscionable.

(B) There has been a failure of a condition precedent.

(C) A case of mutual mistake exists because of the word processing error regarding the delivery date.

(D) There has been a failure of a condition subsequent.

Question 30

A buyer and seller entered into a written contract on March 31 for the sale of a beach house. Under the terms of the agreement, the buyer would purchase the house for $275,000, with 10% due at closing on May 1 and a 15-year mortgage. At the time the contract was entered into, the parties agreed orally that the written agreement would not become binding unless the buyer notified the homeowner, in writing, by the end of the day on April 15, that she had secured the proper financing. With the summer season approaching, the seller did not wish to risk any delay in selling the house if the buyer was not in a position to buy it. On the morning of April 15, the buyer's financing was approved. On April 16, the buyer telephoned the seller and told him that her financing had been approved. The buyer also told the seller that she was not able to get written confirmation to him by April 15 because of the postal workers' slowdown and because her fax machine just broke down. The seller assured the buyer that this was not a problem. However, before closing, the seller had a change of heart and decided not to sell the beach house after all. The buyer files an action for breach.

The buyer's best argument would be based on:

(A) Statute of Frauds.

(B) Parol evidence rule.

(C) Waiver of condition.

(D) Excuse of condition by hindrance.

Question 31

A manufacturer of down coats and jackets entered into a written agreement with a distributor, whereby the distributor agreed to distribute the manufacturer's products statewide for a one-year period to begin on June 1. Before the manufacturer signed the distribution contract with the distributor, the distributor told the manufacturer that their deal was exclusive, but nothing to that effect was in the written agreement. However, in the outerwear industry it has been a custom for many years for distributors to distribute only one brand of outerwear.

On September 1, the distributor began distributing coats and jackets manufactured by one of the manufacturer's chief competitors. These coats and jackets were sewn with man-made fabrics, were as warm as the manufacturer's jackets, and were less bulky. The competitor's advertising campaign throughout the state emphasizes that "you don't have to look fat to stay warm." Seasonally adjusted sales figures showed that the manufacturer's sales in the state dropped 6% after its competitor's products were introduced.

The manufacturer of the down coats and jackets complained to the distributor, demanding that it stop distributing the man-made coats and jackets made by the manufacturer's competitor. The distributor refused, and the manufacturer of the down coats and jackets brought suit against the distributor.

Which of the following facts would provide a basis for the manufacturer's best case against the distributor?

(A) The competitor's advertising campaign throughout the state alluding to the unattractive bulkiness of the manufacturer's coats and jackets.

(B) The 6% drop in seasonally adjusted sales figures in the state after the competitor's products were introduced.

(C) The distributor's oral statement to the manufacturer about their deal being exclusive.

(D) The long-standing custom in the outerwear industry for distributors to distribute only one brand of outerwear.

Question 32

The owner of an exclusive clothing salon entered into a written agreement with a customer to sell the customer a certain full-length fake fur coat for $12,000, with delivery by December 7. On December 6, the customer went to the salon at 5:30 p.m., and the salon owner told her that her coat was ready and she could take it home with her. The customer inspected the coat and discovered that a button was missing. She told the salon owner that she would not accept the coat without the missing button. He informed her that the tailor had gone home for the day at 5 p.m. and would not be back at the salon until 8:30 a.m. on December 8, because Congress had enacted a law declaring December 7 to be Pearl Harbor Day, a new federal holiday, and the tailor had the day off. The salon owner assured the customer that the coat could be ready with the button sewn on by 9:15 a.m. on December 8.

Which of the following best states the customer's position?

(A) The customer may reject the coat, because the salon owner failed to provide perfect tender.

(B) The customer may reject the coat, but she must give the salon owner an opportunity to cure.

(C) The customer must accept the coat, because its value is not substantially impaired by the missing button.

(D) The customer must accept the coat, because the defect can be easily cured.

Question 33

On March 5, a seller who regularly deals in the sale of drill bits mailed a signed communication to the buyer for a chain of hardware stores, offering to sell to him 500 diamond core drill bits, priced at $300 each. The communication explicitly stated that it was a firm offer. The buyer received the offer on March 7. On March 8, the seller mailed a notice to the buyer revoking his March 5 offer. The buyer received this notice on March 10. On March 11, the buyer e-mailed the seller, stating that he considered the seller to be bound by his offer. The buyer also placed on order "per your offer" for 500 diamond core drill bits.

The seller refused to tender delivery of the drill bits, and the buyer sues the seller for breach of contract. The seller defends on the ground that there was no contract because it had revoked its offer.

Given these facts, the court probably would hold:

(A) No contract exists because the seller's notice of revocation had been received by the buyer before acceptance was attempted.

(B) Having stated that it was extending a "firm offer," the seller's offer was irrevocable for three months as a matter of law.

(C) The buyer has an enforceable contract with the seller.

(D) Having received no consideration for its declaration that it had made a firm offer, the seller retained an unfettered election to revoke its offer at any time.

Question 34

On September 14, a farmer sent a signed communication to a commercial bakery, offering to sell to the bakery 100 bushels of wheat at

$30 each. This offer was received by the bakery on September 17. On September 18, the bakery e-mailed the farmer to order 50 bushels of wheat, with half to be delivered on October 1 and the other half on November 1. The farmer refuses to deliver the wheat as ordered and defends on the ground that his offer was for the sale of 100 bushels of wheat in one lot only.

The court should hold that:

(A) Because the farmer's offer failed to state that it was a single lot only, it was subject to partial acceptance at the buyer's option.

(B) The farmer should prevail because the farmer specifically offered 100 bushels of wheat and it would be commercially unreasonable to hold him to piecemeal sales at the stated price.

(C) The attempted formation of a contract is flawed by ambiguity so that the minds of the parties never met and no enforceable obligation to sell was created by the bakery's acceptance.

(D) Parol evidence is admissible on the question whether the offer contemplated sale of the wheat as a single lot or piecemeal.

Question 35

On September 15, a highlighter manufacturer faxed a large office supply company offering to sell the supply company 50,000 highlighters for $25,000. The supply company faxed back the following communication: "We accept your offer. Please box 125 highlighters per case in post-consumer cardboard shipping boxes."

Assuming the existence of a valid contract, its terms would include:

(A) Only those terms set forth in the manufacturer's fax of September 15, because the manufacturer did not assent to any enlargement of the shipping terms.

(B) All terms set forth in the manufacturer's offer plus consistent additional terms proposed in the office supply company's acceptance.

(C) All terms set forth in the manufacturer's offer plus those in the office supply company's attempted acceptance that did not amount to a material alteration of the manufacturer's offer.

(D) All terms set forth in the manufacturer's offer plus all those in the office supply company's purported acceptance that did not amount to a material alteration of the manufacturer's offer and to which the manufacturer did not object within a reasonable time.

Question 36

A hardware store ordered 200 cans of wood stain in various shades. The written contract between the store and manufacturer provided that 100 cans of stain would be delivered on April 30, and the remaining 100 cans would be delivered on June 30. Payment would be due at the time of each delivery. The first shipment arrived on April 30. Sales of the stain were brisk, but 25 customers almost immediately returned their stain, complaining that it was not the color indicated on the can. The store owner called the manufacturer and informed it of the problem. The manufacturer truthfully told the owner that they had had a small problem with their labeling machine and a few cans in the store owner's lot must have been mislabeled before they caught the problem. The manufacturer offered to replace all 100 cans from the original order. The store owner refused the offer and told the manufacturer not to deliver the second lot, because he could no longer trust the manufacturer. The owner was very sensitive to the hardware store's good reputation, which he felt was harmed by this incident.

If the manufacturer brings a claim of breach regarding the second shipment which was due on June 30, the court will find that:

(A) The buyer had the right to cancel the second shipment, because of legitimate fears that it would contain the same defects as the first shipment.

(B) The buyer had the right to cancel the second shipment, because the first delivery was defective.

(C) The buyer did not have the right to cancel the second shipment, because the defects in the first shipment did not substantially impair the value of the entire contract.

(D) The buyer did not have the right to cancel the second shipment, because he failed to make a demand upon the manufacturer for adequate assurances that the second shipment would be free of defects.

CONTRACTS ANSWERS - SET 6

Answer to Question 1

(A) The young woman gave up her legal right to smoke cigarettes, thus incurring detriment and fulfilling her agreement with the deacon. As a result, the deacon is obligated to pay her the $50. For a valid contract to exist, there must be (i) mutual assent, and (ii) consideration or an appropriate substitute. Consideration requires two elements: (i) there must be a bargained-for exchange between the parties; and (ii) that which is bargained for must be of legal value. Traditionally, "legal value" has meant that either some benefit passed to the promisor or some detriment was incurred by the promisee. Most courts today hold that detriment to the promisee is the exclusive test of consideration. There is a bargained-for exchange when the promise induces the detriment and the detriment induces the promise; *i.e.,* the detriment must be the price of the exchange, and the promisor's motive must be to induce the detriment. There is legal detriment if the promisee does something she is under no legal obligation to do or refrains from doing something that she has a legal right to do. There is no requirement that detriment entail any actual loss by the promisee. Here, the deacon offered to pay the young woman $50 if she did not smoke during the weekend religious retreat. She accepted this offer. Thus, there was mutual assent between the parties. There was bargained-for exchange, in that the deacon's motive in offering to pay the money was to induce the young woman not to smoke, and in turn the promise of receiving the money induced her to promise not to smoke for the weekend. Finally, the young woman incurred legal detriment in promising to refrain, and in fact refraining, from smoking for the weekend. Although she had never smoked and probably had no intention of smoking that weekend, the fact remains that she had a legal right to smoke if she so chose. By giving up that right at the request of the deacon, the young woman is deemed in the eyes of the law to have incurred a detriment. Hence, the deacon and the young woman have entered into a legally enforceable contract. With the young woman having performed her part of the agreement, the deacon is obligated to pay as per his part of the agreement. (D) is incorrect because, as noted above, the fact that the young woman would not have smoked anyway is not determinative of whether there is legal detriment. Detriment existed in the sense that the young woman gave up her ***right*** to smoke, and was induced to do so by the deacon's offer of money. (C) is incorrect because the detriment to the young woman arose by virtue of her refraining from doing something that she was legally entitled to do. The fact that refraining from smoking was probably beneficial to her health does not change the character of her actions as a legal detriment. (B) is incorrect because the deacon could only be obligated to pay the young woman pursuant to the bargained-for exchange between the parties; *i.e.,* payment would be due upon her fulfillment of her promise not to smoke for the weekend. Had she failed to perform as promised, there is no principle of law that would impose on the deacon a "moral" obligation arising from his anti-tobacco and alcohol activities.

Answer to Question 2

(B) The rancher should recover $2,000 because that is the amount by which the horse breeder would be unjustly enriched. In a proper tender of delivery under U.C.C. section 2-503, the seller must put and hold conforming goods at the buyer's disposition for a time sufficient for the buyer to take possession. The seller must give the buyer notice reasonably necessary to enable him to take possession of the goods. Proper tender of delivery entitles the seller to acceptance of the goods and to payment according to the contract. [U.C.C. §2-507] Having made a proper tender of delivery at the place designated by the rancher and having notified the rancher of his fiancée's nonacceptance, the horse breeder has discharged his duty under the contract. When a party's duty of performance is discharged, the other party is entitled to restitution of any benefits that he has

transferred to the discharged party in an attempt to perform on his side. With the horse breeder's contractual duty to deliver the second horse to the rancher's fiancée discharged, the horse breeder would be unjustly enriched, to the detriment of the rancher, if he were permitted to keep the entire $5,000 paid to him by the rancher. The rancher conferred a benefit upon him by paying him $5,000 in exchange for two horses, one of which was to be delivered to the rancher, the other to the rancher's fiancée. Because delivery to the fiancée cannot be accomplished, the rancher finds himself in a position of having paid $5,000 for one horse, the fair market value of which is $3,000. Thus, if the horse breeder is permitted to retain the sum of $5,000, he will be unjustly enriched by $2,000. Therefore, the rancher should recover restitution of $2,000. (A) is incorrect because $3,000 represents more than the amount by which the horse breeder has been unjustly enriched. Although the value of the second horse is $3,000, keep in mind that the horse breeder's duty to deliver the horse to the rancher's fiancée has been discharged (and the horse breeder still has title to the horse under the U.C.C. rule that title passes on delivery). The rancher received a discount of $1,000 off of the total fair market value of the two horses because he was buying both of them. Once the horse breeder's duty under the contract is discharged, the rancher cannot recover the benefit of that bargain under the contract; he can only recover the benefit conferred upon the horse breeder, the retention of which would unjustly enrich the horse breeder. Because the horse breeder has received $5,000 from the rancher for one horse worth $3,000, the amount of unjust enrichment is $2,000. (C) is incorrect because, if the rancher recovers nothing, he will have incurred financial harm by paying $5,000 for one horse worth $3,000. (D) is incorrect because the fact that the horse breeder tendered performance but was unable to complete delivery of the second horse to the rancher's fiancée, solely due to her refusal to accept the horse, does not justify the horse breeder's keeping the entire $5,000 paid by the rancher, because the horse breeder would be unjustly enriched.

Answer to Question 3

(D) The man has either option available because his colleague is in breach of the accord agreement. An accord is an agreement in which one party to an existing contract agrees to accept, in lieu of the performance that she is supposed to receive from the other party, some other, different performance. The accord must be supported by consideration, but the consideration is sufficient if it is of a different type than called for under the original contract, even if the substituted consideration is of less value. Performance of the accord cuts off the parties' rights to enforce the original contract. Here, the accord was supported by sufficient consideration because the man was giving a ring in lieu of some cash. As with any contract, the man's duties under the accord were discharged when he timely tendered delivery of the ring and cash. By refusing the ring and filing suit for the part of the original debt that has not been paid, the colleague has breached the accord agreement. If a creditor breaches an accord agreement, the debtor has the option of either raising the accord agreement as an equitable defense in the creditor's action and asking that it be dismissed, or waiting until he is damaged (*i.e.,* until the creditor is successful in an action on the original contract) and then bringing an action at law for damages for breach of the ***accord*** contract. (A) is incorrect because the amount of the debt does not have to be in dispute to have an enforceable accord, as long as there was some alteration in the debtor's consideration, as discussed above. (B) is incorrect because the colleague would have the right to enforce the original contract only if the man had breached the accord agreement. Here, the man's tender of the ring discharged his duty under the accord agreement, precluding his colleague from suing on the original contract. (C) is incorrect because the man has both a breach of contract remedy and an equitable defense option available to him. Also, whether the ring is unique does not affect his right to specific performance of the accord agreement; he is simply raising the agreement as an equitable defense to prevent the colleague from continuing with her suit on the original contract.

Answer to Question 4

(C) The salesperson sold the painting in good faith to a customer. Because the gallery owner no longer actually has the painting, there is no way to specifically enforce her agreement to convey it to her friend. Specific performance is granted when: (i) there is a valid contract; (ii) the legal remedy is inadequate; (iii) enforcement is feasible; and (iv) mutuality of remedy is present. The gallery owner and her friend had a contract, pursuant to which the gallery owner promised to sell her friend the painting for $2,700. Although this was an oral contract for the sale of goods for a price exceeding $500 and thus subject to the Statute of Frauds, the contract is removed from the Statute by the fact that the friend tendered full payment for the painting. Thus, the oral nature of the agreement is no hindrance to its validity. Moreover, a painting, by its nature, is unique, rendering the legal remedy (damages) inadequate. However, feasibility of specific performance against the gallery owner is lacking here. The salesperson sold the painting to a customer who paid value for it and was unaware that the gallery owner had already agreed to sell it to her friend. The salesperson also was unaware of the gallery owner's agreement with her friend. With the subject matter of the contract having been transferred in good faith to a third party, there is no feasible means to enforce against the gallery owner her agreement to sell the painting to her friend. Thus, the right to specific performance is cut off. Regarding (A), it is true that there was a bargained-for exchange of promises between the gallery owner and her friend. Nevertheless, specific performance is unavailable because enforcement is not feasible. (B) is incorrect because the friend's assistance to the gallery owner in moving her furniture does not form part of the basis of the consideration. The assistance given by the friend occurred before the gallery owner's promise to sell the painting, and thus was not given in exchange for the promise when made. Also, even if the assistance given did form part of the quantum of adequate consideration, specific performance would still be denied because enforcement is not feasible. (D) is incorrect because a gift is a voluntary transfer of property from one person to another without compensation or consideration. The gallery owner clearly stated that she wanted her friend to pay her $2,700 for the painting. Thus, the donative intent necessary for a gift was absent.

Answer to Question 5

(D) The language of the rubber stamp impression indicates that the manufacturer did not give a definite expression of acceptance; rather, acceptance was conditioned upon assent to the new terms regarding a crating charge. Thus, this was a counteroffer, and there is at this time no contract between the parties. The circular sent by the manufacturer was an announcement of prices at which it was willing to receive offers. Thus, the circular was a mere invitation for offers rather than an offer. The company's order that was faxed to the manufacturer was an offer to purchase the designated number and type of widgets at the specified price, with delivery to be made on the specified date. By referring to the circular, the company's offer also includes a C.I.F. term, meaning that the price would include the cost of the goods, plus insurance and freight. Under U.C.C. section 2-207, a written confirmation is effective as an acceptance even though it states additional terms, unless the acceptance is expressly made conditional on assent to the additional terms. The manufacturer's confirmation form, in stating that acceptance of the order was ***conditioned on*** an additional crating charge, not only states an additional term but also indicates that the manufacturer does not accept the offer unless the company agrees to this term (*i.e.,* agrees to pay a charge for crating in addition to the quoted price figure). Thus, the manufacturer has not expressed a definite acceptance, but rather has communicated a counteroffer. The company is free to accept or reject this counteroffer, but until it does accept (if at all), there is no contract. Because there is no contract at this time, (A) and (B) are both incorrect as stating that there is a contract. (B) is also incorrect because if the manufacturer's response did constitute an acceptance, it probably would have included the crating fee. Between merchants, additional proposed terms in a valid acceptance automatically become part of the contract unless: (i) they materially alter the original contract; (ii) the offer expressly limits acceptance to its terms; or (iii) the offeror has already objected to the particular terms, or objects within a reasonable time after receiving notice of them. Had the manufacturer definitely accepted, the additional term would have become part of the contract because the term probably is not a material alteration (as discussed below) and both parties are merchants. Although (C) correctly states that there is no contract, it reaches this result for the wrong reasons. First of all, it is doubtful whether the term regarding a crating charge materially alters the offer. The crating charge will add $300 ($150 times two lots) to an order that otherwise totals $7,000. This change would probably not be deemed material. Second, even if the alteration were material, its inclusion in the confirmation would mean that a contract was still created, but without this additional term (assuming that the manufacturer had conveyed a definite acceptance rather than a counteroffer). The salient point in determining whether there was a contract is the manufacturer's conveyance of a counteroffer, rather than the materiality of the proposed addition.

Answer to Question 6

(D) The agreement is not enforceable because the greengrocer's promise is illusory. For a contract to be enforceable, consideration must exist on both sides, *i.e.,* each party's promise must create a binding obligation. If one party has become bound but the other has not, the agreement lacks mutuality because one of the promises is illusory. Here, the wholesale dealer has promised to supply the greengrocer with fuzzy peaches at a fixed price. The greengrocer, however, has not promised to order any peaches from the wholesale dealer. Even if the greengrocer decides to sell fuzzy peaches, it has not bound itself to order them from this particular wholesale dealer. The illusory nature of the greengrocer's promise makes the agreement unenforceable on consideration grounds. (A) is incorrect because in a valid requirements contract, both parties' promises create binding obligations: The promisor binds itself to buy from the supplier all that it requires, and the supplier binds itself to sell to the promisor that same amount. Consideration exists because the promisor is suffering a legal detriment; it has parted with the legal right to buy the goods it may need from another source. Under the U.C.C., which governs in this case because a contract for the sale of goods is involved, a good faith term is implied: The buyer's requirements means such actual requirements as may occur in good faith. Thus, if the provision had stated instead that the greengrocer will buy "as many 50 pound lots of fuzzy peaches as the greengrocer shall require," it would be a valid requirements contract under the U.C.C. because it requires the greengrocer to buy fuzzy peaches only from the wholesale dealer and to act in good faith in setting its requirements. (B) is incorrect even though the U.C.C. will imply reasonable terms under certain circumstances. Such terms as price and time for performance need not be spelled out in the contract; the terms will be supplied by a "reasonableness" standard if that is otherwise consistent with the parties' intent. However, supplying reasonable terms will not change the express terms of the contract. The provision that the greengrocer will buy as many peaches as it chooses to order is not sufficiently obligatory to be saved by the court supplying reasonable terms. (C) is incorrect because if the agreement were otherwise a valid requirements contract, the absence of a total quantity term would not matter. As a general rule in sale of goods contracts, the quantity being offered must be certain or capable of being made certain. The U.C.C. provides that an agreement to buy all of one's requirements is sufficiently certain because requirements usually can be objectively determined. Furthermore, the quantity ultimately required in good faith must not be unreasonably disproportionate to any stated estimate or any normal requirements (in the absence of a stated estimate). Hence, if the greengrocer had contracted to buy all of

its requirements from the wholesale dealer, the absence of a term specifying total quantity would not have made the agreement unenforceable.

Answer to Question 7

(B) This question is best answered by eliminating the incorrect choices first. (A) is incorrect. A contract was formed here for 500 canoes. The original "agreement" between the parties was nothing more than an invitation seeking offers. It did not create a contract between the department store and the manufacturer because it was illusory—an agreement to buy only what is desired is not consideration. The "agreement" probably does not even qualify as an offer. An offer must express a commitment to conclude a bargain on the offered terms. Absent some quantity limitation, a court would probably find the "agreement" here too vague to constitute an offer; otherwise, the manufacturer could be committing itself to sell more canoes than it can supply. Thus, the department store's first order will be construed as an offer, and the manufacturer's confirmation will be construed as an acceptance of the offer, thus creating a contract. (C) is incorrect because there was no acceptance of the department store's second offer. If the original agreement did not create a contract, the second order must be construed as an offer. The manufacturer did nothing to accept the department store's second offer. The manufacturer's failure to reject the offer until five days after it was made does not constitute an acceptance. Therefore, no contract was formed for the additional 500 canoes. (D) is incorrect because although it is true that the Uniform Commercial Code ("U.C.C.") imposes a duty of good faith on all parties, and failure to deliver under a contract simply because a better price can be obtained might violate this duty, the U.C.C. does not provide for punitive damages for breach of this duty. When a seller fails to deliver goods, one remedy available to the buyer is cover damages—the difference between the contract price and the price of substitute goods. Because the manufacturer had agreed to sell the department store 500 canoes and failed to deliver, the department store reasonably bought replacement goods for $30 more per unit and is entitled to recover the additional $30 per unit.

Answer to Question 8

(A) The ice cream parlor has no grounds for avoiding its obligations under the contract with the dairy farm. In effect, the ice cream parlor is advancing the position that its duty to perform under the contract is discharged by impracticability. In contracts for the sale of goods under the U.C.C., a party's duty to perform may be discharged where performance would be impracticable. Impracticability exists where a party encounters extreme and unreasonable difficulty and/or expense, and such difficulty was not anticipated. Duties will not be discharged where performance is merely more difficult or expensive than anticipated. The facts giving rise to impracticability must be such that their nonoccurrence was a basic assumption on which the contract was made. Where, as here, parties enter into a contract for the sale of goods to be supplied to the public through a retail outlet, both parties must anticipate the possibility that there will be a change in market conditions, resulting in either an increased or decreased demand for the product. Although the decreased demand results in increased expense to the ice cream parlor in performing its contract because of waste, such difficulties arising from changing demand are to be anticipated. Thus, the ice cream parlor does have the right to no longer buy any of the dairy farm's Extra Rich ice cream. Note that under the U.C.C., a shutdown by a requirements buyer for lack of orders may be permissible if the buyer is acting in good faith [U.C.C. §2-306, comment 2], but this right would only arise only if there were no longer a market for frozen desserts entirely, and that is not the case here. Here, the ice cream parlor simply wants to curtail its losses by selling a more popular type of frozen dessert, which is forbidden by the exclusivity provision. Thus, the ice cream parlor continues to be bound by its duties under the agreement with the dairy farm. (B) is incorrect

because, although a court will imply a promise on the part of the ice cream parlor to use its best efforts to sell the dairy farm's products, the facts do not indicate that the ice cream parlor did not use its best efforts. At issue here is whether, despite those efforts, circumstances exist that were unanticipated and now create extreme and unreasonable difficulty or expense for the ice cream parlor in the performance of its contractual duties. (C) is incorrect because the ice cream parlor relinquished its legal right to sell any frozen desserts other than those of the dairy farm. This giving up of a legal right constitutes legal detriment to the ice cream parlor, so there is consideration. (D) is incorrect because an agreement to buy or sell all of one's requirements or output is capable of being made certain by reference to objective, extrinsic facts (*i.e.,* the buyer's actual requirements or the seller's actual output). There is an assumption that the parties will act in good faith; thus, there may not be a tender or demand for a quantity unreasonably disproportionate to a stated estimate or prior output or requirements. Here, the agreement by the dairy farm to sell all of its output of Extra Rich ice cream to the ice cream parlor can be made certain by referring to such factors as the normal output of such product by the dairy farm. In addition, the ice cream parlor agreed to pay $25 for each container of Extra Rich ice cream, so the total price is also ascertainable. Thus, it is not a ground for avoiding enforcement that the total price and quantity were not established.

Answer to Question 9

(C) The contractor should be able to recover $250,000 in restitutionary damages. Where a builder in a construction contract breaches during the construction, the nonbreaching party is entitled to the cost of completion plus compensation for any damages caused by the delay in completing the building. Most courts, however, will allow the builder to offset or recover for work performed to date to avoid the unjust enrichment of the owner. This restitutionary recovery is usually based on the benefit received by the unjustly enriched party. If substitute performance is readily obtainable, damages are measured by the unpaid contract price minus the cost of completion (up to the value of the benefit received by the defendant). Here, the contractor's duty to complete the project was not discharged by impossibility; he could have hired another contractor to take his place or yielded to his employees' demands. Hence, the contractor's failure to complete the remodeling constituted a breach of contract and resulted in the college having to expend $150,000 to have the building completed on time. However, the contractor did not receive any payments for the work that he did before breaching; the college would be unjustly enriched if it does not have to pay for any of this work. The benefit of the completed remodeling is measured by the contract price, $400,000, because a restitutionary recovery here would be based on the failed contract between the parties and substitute performance is readily obtainable. This amount is reduced by the $150,000 cost of completion that the college can recover from the contractor, leaving a net recovery of $250,000 for him. (A) is incorrect. Most modern courts would permit the contractor to recover in restitution to prevent the college's unjust enrichment from the work that he did. (B) is incorrect because recovery measured by the claimant's detriment (*i.e.,* his reliance interest) is an appropriate alternative only where the standard "benefit" measure would achieve an unfair result; it is not applied where the party seeking restitutionary recovery was the breaching party. (D) is incorrect because courts will always limit relief to the contract price where the claimant is the breaching party. Measuring the benefit to the college in terms of the value of the improvements rather than the contract price will deny to the college the benefit of the bargain that it became entitled to when the contractor breached.

Answer to Question 10

(D) Contractual terms that are set forth in a writing intended as a final expression of the parties' agreement cannot be contradicted by evidence of any prior agreement or contemporaneous oral agreement. Although this parol evidence rule prohibits contradicting the writing, the terms of the writing may be explained or supplemented by consistent additional terms, unless the court finds from all the circumstances that the writing was intended as a complete and exclusive statement of the parties' agreement. To determine whether the parties intended the writing to be the complete and exclusive statement of their agreement, it must be determined whether parties situated as were the parties to this contract would naturally and normally include the extrinsic matter in the writing. Here, the writing at issue states clearly that the painting subject to sale is any painting by Alpha. The art collector's assertion of a prior agreement allowing him to buy a painting by Beta clearly contradicts the terms of the writing. Consequently, the parol evidence rule will render inadmissible testimony as to such an alleged agreement. (A) and (C) are therefore incorrect. The assertion that the parties agreed prior to signing the writing that the art collector could have a $250 frame at no additional cost does not contradict any of the terms of the writing. However, it does supplement those terms. As noted above, such supplementation is permitted unless there is a finding that the writing was intended by the parties as a complete and exclusive statement of the terms of their agreement. It is likely that a court would find that parties situated as were the art collector and the gallery owner would normally and naturally include in their written agreement for the sale and purchase of a painting at a specified price the additional provision that the purchaser could also have a $250 frame at no extra cost. Such a finding would lead to the conclusion that the writing, standing as it is without any reference to the frame, constitutes a complete and exclusive statement of the agreement. Given this finding, evidence of the alleged agreement regarding the frame will not be admissible even for the purpose of supplementing the terms of the writing. Thus, (B) is incorrect. (D) is the only choice correctly stating that testimony as to neither agreement is admissible.

Answer to Question 11

(C) A contract was formed because the brother-in-law's acceptance was effective on dispatch. Under the "mailbox rule," acceptance by mail or similar means creates a contract at the moment of posting, properly addressed and stamped, unless: (i) the offer stipulates that acceptance is not effective until received; or (ii) an option contract is involved. Here, the brother-in-law dispatched first an acceptance and then a rejection of the photography buff's offer. The mailbox rule applies because the photography buff's offer did not specify that acceptance was not effective until receipt, nor is an option contract involved. Because the brother-in-law dispatched his acceptance before he called with his rejection, the mailbox rule applies. Thus, the brother-in-law's acceptance was effective, thereby creating a contract at the moment it was mailed, and his attempted rejection was ineffective. (B) is incorrect because once the acceptance was effective, the fact that the photography buff received the "rejection" by telephone before he received the acceptance letter has no effect on the formation of the contract. (A) is incorrect because the letter from the photography buff indicates that the subject matter of the contract was his camera that the brother-in-law had admired for some time. This description on its face appears to be sufficiently definite that a court would be able to determine with reasonable accuracy which camera is subject to the photography buff's offer to sell. (D) is incorrect even though it is true that, pursuant to the Statute of Frauds, a contract for the sale of goods of $500 or more is not enforceable unless evidenced by a writing. There is no requirement that a rejection of an offer to enter into such a contract must be in writing.

Answer to Question 12

(C) The fact that the gallery owner did not really need an answer within 10 days is not a material term of the contract, only a limitation on the offer, and thus would not be barred by the parol

evidence rule. The parol evidence rule bars evidence of expressions of the parties' agreement, made prior to or contemporaneous with a writing that is the complete embodiment of that agreement, where such expressions vary the terms of the writing. Here, the terms of the agreement between the gallery owner and the art collector are embodied in the gallery owner's letter—the sale of the painting to the art collector for $1,000. The gallery owner's statement in the letter that she needed an answer within 10 days is not a material term of the contract. Thus, the proffered evidence does not—and is not being offered to—contradict or vary the terms of the written agreement of the parties, and is therefore not barred by the parol evidence rule. (A) is incorrect because the gallery owner's time limit on her offer is not a material term of the contract, nor is it even part of the agreement; it is simply a recital of collateral facts. Thus, the proffered evidence does not contradict a material term of the contract. (B) is incorrect because the art collector is not denying the truth of a contract that he has accepted, but is rather contradicting a statement of fact contained in the letter that embodies the agreement. (D) is incorrect. Although evidence of fraud can be admitted into evidence despite the parol evidence rule, the proffered evidence here does not establish a fraud. To constitute fraud, there must be an intentional misstatement of a material fact. Here, although the gallery owner's statement that she needed an answer within 10 days might have been untrue, the statement and the owner's reasons for it do not pertain to a material fact of the contract and, thus, could not be the basis for fraud.

Answer to Question 13

(B) The doctor can recover restitution for the value of her services under an implied-in-law contract theory (*i.e.*, in quasi-contract). When there is no contractual relationship between the parties, an implied-in-law contract action will prevent unjust enrichment of one party to the detriment of another. Here, the doctor conferred a benefit on the pedestrian and the law will presume that the pedestrian would have requested the emergency medical care had he been able to do so, and will allow the doctor to recover reasonable compensation for his services. (A) is incorrect because this was not an implied-in-fact contract situation. An implied-in-fact contract is a contract formed by manifestations of assent other than oral or written language, *i.e.*, by conduct. The manifestations of mutual assent are analyzed ***objectively*** under contract law. Even if there is no subjective "meeting of the minds," the parties will be bound if their conduct objectively appears to manifest a contractual intent. Here, the pedestrian has not manifested assent to an implied-in-fact contract with the doctor (in contrast to a patient who goes to the doctor's office and submits to treatment by her). A court will not find an implied-in-fact contract unless the conduct of ***both*** parties objectively indicates assent to a contract, and in this case one of the parties was unconscious and could not have manifested assent or even been aware of his injuries or the doctor's presence on the scene. Thus, there was no implied-in-fact contract. (C) is incorrect because duress is a defense that is used to make a contract voidable, and not a state of mind used to justify the existence of a contract or payment under it. Thus, even if the doctor acted under duress in administering the emergency medical care to the pedestrian, she could not use that fact to recover the reasonable cost of that care. Duress is raised to avoid a contract, not create one. (D) is incorrect because this is not a proper case to raise the concept of preexisting duty owed to a third party. Whether there is such a duty goes to the question of whether there has been valid consideration when there is a new promise between contracting parties. Because this is an implied-in-law contract and not a traditional contract with offer, acceptance, and consideration, and no promises, let alone ***new*** promises, were exchanged, any such duty would be irrelevant.

Answer to Question 14

(C) The exoneration clause will be the clause most likely to bar the subcontractor from assigning to his former employee, because as a result of the exoneration clause an assignment would substantially alter the general contractor's risks. Here we are dealing with both an assignment of rights (the right to receive compensation for installing the toll booths) and a delegation of duties (the duty to install the booths). The general rule is that most duties are delegable and most rights are assignable. However, assignment and delegation are prohibited when they would substantially alter the obligor's (the general contractor's) risks. An example of a situation where the obligor's risk will be changed occurs where the obligor extends any degree of trust or confidence to the particular obligee. The exoneration clause here amounts to such an extension—by agreeing to hold the subcontractor harmless, the general contractor was acting as an insurer of the subcontractor's performance. It would be unfair to force the general contractor to accept the risk of someone else's performance, because the risk of faulty performance will be different from the risk assumed. It does not matter that the former employee is equally qualified. (A) is incorrect because the time-is-of-the-essence clause merely makes performance on the exact day agreed upon critical. Absent such a clause, a court might allow some damages for late performance, but could find late performance to be only a minor breach. The clause makes late performance a material breach. This would not affect an assignment in any way other than by requiring the assignee to perform in a timely manner. (B) is incorrect because the modifications clause only requires written approval of modifications, and an assignment technically is not a modification—if it were, there could never be unilateral assignment because modification requires mutual assent. Thus, while a contract clause providing that any purported assignment by a party is void may effectively prohibit assignment, the clause here requiring that modifications be approved in writing will not have the same effect Moreover, a requirement that modifications be approved in writing generally is unenforceable (except under the U.C.C.) because the new (modified) contract implicitly includes a mutual agreement to abandon the writing requirement set out in the old contract. (D) is incorrect because the liquidated damages clause merely stipulates the damages to be paid in the event of breach. Assigning the subcontractor's part of the contract to his former employee could mean that the former employee, instead of the subcontractor, would be chargeable with $1,000 per day for failure to complete the job on time. Thus, the liquidated damages clause would not bar the assignment.

Answer to Question 15

(D) The agreement among all of the parties to substitute the out-of-town builder for the local builder operates as a novation which immediately discharged the local builder from any duties he had under the original contract. A novation arises when the parties enter into an agreement to substitute a third party for one of the parties in a contract, releasing the party who was substituted. All parties must agree to the substitution. Here, the facts say that all of the parties agreed that the out-of-town builder would substitute for the local builder. Thus, there was a novation and the local builder was released immediately and is not liable for the out-of-town builder's blunder. (A) states incorrectly that the substitution does not relieve the local builder of liability. If the parties had not all agreed to substitute the out-of-town builder for the local builder, or the facts said that there was merely an assignment of rights and delegation of duties, (A) would reflect the correct result. However, where the parties agree to substitute a new party for an old party, there is a novation that does release the old party. (B) is incorrect because there was consideration to support the release—the local builder implicitly agreed to give up his rights under the original contract, the homeowner implicitly agreed to give up his right to look to the local builder for performance, and the out-of-town builder agreed to perform. (C) is not as good an answer as (D). The mere fact that a contractual duty was transferred does not release the transferor from a duty under the contract. It is only the agreement among the parties to substitute the new party for the old that released the local builder here.

Answer to Question 16

(D) The contractor can recover $2,000 as lost profits plus the $4,000 in costs he incurred before the homeowner breached the contract. The purpose of a damages remedy based on an affirmance of the contract is to give compensation for the breach; *i.e.,* to put the nonbreaching party where he would have been had the promise been performed. In most cases, the plaintiff's standard measure of damages will be based solely on an "expectation" measure, *i.e.,* sufficient damages for him to buy a substitute performance. A reliance measure of damages, on the other hand, awards the plaintiff the cost of his performance, *i.e.,* his expenditures in performing his duties under the contract. In certain situations, an award of compensatory damages will contain both an expectation and a reliance component. In a construction contract, if the owner breaches the contract after the builder has already begun his performance, the builder will be entitled to any profit he would have derived from the contract ***plus*** any ***costs*** he has incurred to date. This formula contains an expectation component (the profit the builder would have made) and a reliance component (the cost incurred prior to the breach). This formula is applicable to the facts in this case. The contractor has begun performance by ordering and purchasing the custom-made fixtures at a cost of $4,000. Because they are usable only for the homeowner's purposes, their cost, which is treated just like any other expenditure of labor and material in a partially completed construction contract, can be recovered as reliance damages. The other element of his recovery is the $2,000 profit that he would have derived from the contract—his expectation damages. His total recovery will therefore be $6,000. (A) is incorrect because the homeowner can do nothing further to mitigate his damages. The nonbreaching party is always under a duty to mitigate damages after learning of the other party's breach. In construction contracts, the builder's duty to mitigate generally dictates only that he not continue work after the breach and not incur further expenditures. While the builder would also have a duty to apply any usable materials that he purchased to other jobs or to attempt to resell them to another contractor, the facts specify that the custom-made fixtures here were not usable in other remodeling jobs. Hence, contractor's failure to attempt to sell the fixtures did not amount to a failure to mitigate damages. (B) is incorrect because an award of $2,000 does not put the contractor in the position he would have been in had the contract been performed—the $4,000 that he spent on the fixtures would have been covered by part of the $10,000 that he was to receive as the contract price. Had the homeowner not breached, the contractor would have received the contract price of $10,000, and he would have spent an additional $4,000 in labor and materials to complete the job. The difference, $6,000, consists of the $4,000 that he already spent on materials and the $2,000 profit that he expected to make. (C) is incorrect. Instead of seeking a damages remedy based on an affirmance of the contract, the nonbreaching party may rescind and sue for restitution for any "benefit" that he has transferred to the breacher in an attempt to perform the contract. The restitution recovery is generally based on the fair market value of the benefit transferred. Here, the contractor can provide the homeowner with the fixtures and seek restitution, but there is nothing to indicate that their fair market value is $4,000. Even if that is the case, however, the contractor has a provable compensatory damages remedy on the contract of $6,000; he will elect that remedy rather than the lesser restitution remedy.

Answer to Question 17

(B) The retailer is entitled to recover $800. The wholesaler's notice that it would be unable to fill the retailer's order constituted an anticipatory repudiation, which the retailer was entitled to treat as a total breach. Under the U.C.C., the buyer's basic remedy where the seller breaches by refusing to deliver is the difference between the contract price and either the market price or the cost of buying replacement goods ("cover"). If the buyer intends to fix damages based on the latter measure, the buyer must make a reasonable contract for substitute goods in good faith and without unreasonable delay. Here, the retailer chose to make a contract for a higher quality of sunglasses at a higher price, even though the model that he had originally ordered was available from a supplier outside the area. While the retailer need not find the lowest available price in the country or make a contract for substitute goods with an unreliable supplier, he was aware that he could have obtained the sunglasses in plenty of time from the nonlocal supplier. Absent additional facts that would justify the retailer's decision, he can recover only the difference between the contract cost and a reasonable contract for substitute goods. Hence, (A) is wrong because the retailer's contract for cover probably would not be deemed to be commercially reasonable. (C) is wrong because the retailer's remedy based on market price would be determined at the time the retailer learned of the breach, not necessarily the time of performance. In the case of an anticipatory repudiation such as this, the buyer may either treat the anticipatory repudiation as a total breach and pursue his breach of contract remedies, or suspend his performance and await the seller's performance for a commercially reasonable time. The retailer chose to treat the wholesaler's notice as a total repudiation and breach of contract. Hence, the market price remedy would be measured at that time because that is when the retailer "learned of the breach," rather than at the time of performance. (D) is wrong because the nonrepudiating party need not wait for the repudiating party to retract its repudiation. The retailer exercised its option to treat the repudiation as a total breach and buy substitute goods. Once that occurred, the wholesaler was not entitled to retract its repudiation and force the retailer to accept the sunglasses.

Answer to Question 18

(D) Although the crossing offers as to price were identical, there is no requisite mutual assent absent an acceptance. If offers stating precisely the same terms cross in the mail, they do not give rise to a contract despite the apparent meeting of the minds. An offer cannot be accepted if there is no knowledge of it. Here, the shop owner and the antique lover each sent offers setting the price of the ensemble at $22,000. Despite the fact that these offers were identical, there is no mutual assent without at least one of the parties manifesting acceptance of the terms of the offer, and communicating that acceptance to the other. We are told that this has not yet happened even though the shop owner and the antique lover both have received the letters. Consequently, although there is an apparent meeting of the minds as to price, there has not been a sufficient objective manifestation of this agreement as to denote a mutual assent. (C) fails to account for the principle discussed above, that identical crossing offers do not give rise to a contract. Despite their receipt of identical offers before April 12, there is no agreement between the parties. (A) is incorrect because it misstates the mailbox rule. Acceptance by mail or similar means creates a contract at the moment of posting, properly addressed and stamped, unless the offer stipulates that acceptance is not effective until received, or unless an option contract is involved. This rule does not operate to create a contract from the moment an ***offer*** is mailed (or in this case, two identical offers are mailed). Thus, (A) is incorrect. Regarding (B), the fact that a merchant sends an offer in writing is significant because it will limit the offeror's power to revoke if it gives assurances that it will be held open for a stated time. Here, the written offer by the shop owner is irrevocable at least until April 12, but the issue in the question is whether it has been accepted rather than whether it has been revoked.

Answer to Question 19

(D) Despite his reliance, the nephew has no recourse against the customer. A third-party donee beneficiary has no cause of action against the promisee, because the promisee's act is gratuitous

and he may not be held to it, unless the promisee tells the beneficiary of the contract and should foresee reliance by the beneficiary, and the beneficiary reasonably relies to his detriment. The nephew is a third-party beneficiary of the contract between the proprietor and the customer because he is expressly designated in the contract and performance is to be made directly to him. Because the object was to arrange a gift for the nephew rather than to bring about payment of a debt owed to him by the customer, the nephew is a donee beneficiary. Because the proprietor, and ***not*** the promisee (the customer), told the nephew about the contract, the nephew, as a third-party donee beneficiary, has no cause of action against the customer. (A) is incorrect because, although the nephew is an intended beneficiary of the valid contract, he is a donee beneficiary, and as explained above, has no claim against the promisee. (B) is incorrect because, as explained above, the nephew's reasonable detrimental reliance does him no good because of his status as a donee beneficiary. (C) is incorrect because the nephew was designated in the contract as the party to whom the bicycle was to be tendered. Thus, he was an intended, rather than an incidental, beneficiary.

Answer to Question 20

(D) Approval of the modernization plans by the sportsman's sister is a condition precedent because without such approval the parties have no agreement. Where there is an oral condition precedent, evidence of the condition falls outside the parol evidence rule. The parol evidence rule provides that where the parties to a contract express their agreement in a writing with the intent that it embody the full and final expression of their bargain, any other expressions, written or oral, made prior to the writing, as well as any oral expressions contemporaneous with the writing, are inadmissible to vary the terms of the writing. Certain forms of extrinsic evidence are deemed to fall outside the scope of the parol evidence rule. For instance, a party to a written contract can attack the validity of the agreement. One way of doing so is by asserting that there was an oral agreement that the written contract would not become effective until the occurrence of a condition. Such a condition would be deemed a condition precedent to the effectiveness of the agreement, and evidence of the condition will be freely offered and received. Here, the sportsman and the architect-engineer have entered into a written agreement that apparently embodies the full and final expression of their bargain. However, the sportsman's statement at the time of entering into the agreement indicates quite clearly that the parties had no agreement absent the approval of his sister, and the architect-engineer agreed with this statement. Thus, there is an oral agreement that the written contract would not become effective until the occurrence of a condition precedent. As discussed above, evidence of this oral condition does not come within the purview of the parol evidence rule and is therefore admissible. Consequently, the sportsman can assert the nonoccurrence of a condition precedent as a way to avoid liability on the contract. (B) is incorrect because, as explained above, the nature of the oral agreement takes it outside the scope of the parol evidence rule. Therefore, the rule will not be decisive in determining the outcome of this case. (A) is incorrect because the agreement at issue here is not of a type that is covered by the Statute of Frauds; *i.e.*, it does not involve a promise: (i) by an executor or administrator to pay the estate's debts out of her own funds; (ii) to answer for the debt of another; (iii) made in consideration of marriage; (iv) creating an interest in land; (v) that by its terms cannot be performed within one year; or (vi) for the sale of goods at a price of $500 or more. Therefore, the Statute of Frauds is inapplicable to these facts. (C) is incorrect because the term "rules of construction" refers to rules used by courts when interpreting contracts; *e.g.*, contracts are to be construed as a whole, words are to be construed according to their ordinary meaning, or custom and usage in the particular business and locale should be considered. The facts and issues presented here do not call for the application of any such principles of contract interpretation.

Answer to Question 21

(B) By her statement to the builder, the homeowner waived the benefit of the condition requiring the accountant's approval of the design plans, and the builder detrimentally relied on the statement by building the sauna. Thus, there is a binding waiver of the condition. A condition is an event, other than the passage of time, the occurrence or nonoccurrence of which creates, limits, or extinguishes the absolute duty to perform in the other contracting party. The occurrence of a condition may be excused under a number of different circumstances. One such circumstance is where the party having the benefit of the condition indicates by words or conduct that she will not insist upon it. If a party indicates that she is waiving a condition before it happens, and the person affected detrimentally relies on it, a court will hold this to be a binding estoppel waiver. The promise to waive the condition may be retracted at any time before the other party has detrimentally changed his position. Here, the contract provided that the builder could not begin work without the accountant's prior approval. This approval was a condition that had to be met before the homeowner's duty to pay would arise. When the homeowner told the builder to commence working on the sauna, even though the accountant had withheld his approval, the homeowner was telling the builder that she was waiving the condition of the accountant's approval. The builder then acted in detrimental reliance on this statement by in fact starting and completing the building of the sauna. While the homeowner could have retracted her statement and reinstated the condition prior to the builder's detrimental reliance, she did nothing when the builder began working on the sauna. Under such circumstances, the homeowner made a binding waiver of the condition and will be estopped from asserting it. Thus, the builder is entitled to recover the full contract price. (A) is incorrect because, as discussed above, the accountant's approval was a condition precedent for the parties' contractual duties to arise. The builder's duty to build the sauna and the homeowner's duty to pay for it would not arise without the condition of the accountant's approval either being satisfied or being excused. (C) is incorrect because unjust enrichment is a quasi-contract alternative that the builder could utilize if he did not have a contract remedy. Here, however, the builder can recover the full contract price because the homeowner waived the condition and is estopped from retracting the waiver. (D) is incorrect because the parol evidence rule does not prohibit evidence of a ***subsequent*** modification of a written contract; the rule applies only to prior or contemporaneous expressions. Consequently, it may be shown that the parties altered the integrated writing after its making. The oral agreement between the homeowner and the builder described in the facts was made subsequent to the writing. Therefore, the parol evidence rule is inapplicable to this agreement.

Answer to Question 22

(C) The court should rescind the contract for mutual mistake and order the friend to return the ring to its rightful owner. Mutual mistake of a material fact to a contract is a defense that allows the adversely affected party to rescind as long as that party did not assume the risk of mistake. Mutual mistake arises where both parties are mistaken as to a basic assumption of the contract and the mistake has a material effect on the agreed-upon exchange. Here, both parties were mistakenly operating under the assumption that the ring was worth only $4,800 when in fact it was worth $6,200. While generally courts will not allow mistakes in value to be the basis for rescission, because the courts will presume that both parties assumed the risk of mistake, the facts here are sufficient to take this case out of the general rule—it appears that neither party wanted to assume the risk of determining value, since both agreed to rely solely on the valuation by an independent expert. (A) is incorrect because it does not take into account that the facts here are sufficient to show that neither party assumed the risk of mistake, and so the general rule does not apply. (B) is incorrect because the statement by the gemologist two years ago does not indicate the value of the ring today, both because market conditions could have changed in two years and because the gemologist gave a fairly equivocal and informal valuation. (D) is incorrect because the appraisal was not a condition precedent—an event creating, limiting, or extinguishing the absolute duty to perform—because when the friend requested the appraisal, she did not obligate herself to buy the ring based on the appraisal. Her promise at that time—that if the price was not too high, she would buy it from him—was too illusory to form a contract, because what is "too high" is very subjective. Because there was no contract, the appraisal could not be a condition.

Answer to Question 23

(A) The buyer has delegated her duties under the agreement with the seller to her friend, and the friend has agreed to assume the duties by agreeing to make the 18 installment payments to the seller. Where a delegate's promise to perform the delegated duty is supported by consideration, there results a third-party beneficiary situation, so that the nondelegating party to the contract can compel performance or bring suit for nonperformance. The friend's promise to make the payments to the seller, totaling $1,800, was given in exchange for the buyer's promise to forgive the $2,000 debt owed by the friend to her. The buyer thus relinquished her right to take action against her friend for the full amount owed, thereby incurring legal detriment. Consequently, the promise of the friend was supported by consideration, and a situation arose in which the seller became a third-party beneficiary of the agreement between the buyer and her friend, and able to enforce performance of the friend's promise to pay. (C) is incorrect because, as explained above, the friend's promise to the buyer ***was*** supported by consideration. (B) is incorrect because there was no assignment of the buyer's rights as against the friend; *i.e.,* the buyer did not manifest an intent to transfer to the seller her rights against her friend. Rather, the buyer transferred to her friend the duties that she owed to the seller. (D) is incorrect because the surety provision of the Statute of Frauds requires only that a promise to answer for the debt or default of another be in writing. Such a promise must be collateral to another person's promise to pay rather than a primary promise (a promise to pay directly for the benefits given to another). Here, the friend did not promise the seller that if he sold the entertainment system to the buyer and the buyer did not pay, she (the friend) would pay. Instead, the friend promised the buyer that she would directly perform the buyer's obligation to pay the seller. Thus, this is not the type of promise required by the Statute of Frauds to be in writing.

Answer to Question 24

(A) The elderly gentleman is liable to the handyman for the debt. When a party to a contract delegates his duties to another, the original party (the delegator) remains liable on his contract. This is so even if the delegate expressly assumes the delegator's duties and the obligee agrees to the delegation. A different result would obtain if the parties all agree to substitute a third party for one of the parties in an executory contract. This would constitute a novation. A novation occurs when a new contract substitutes a new party to receive benefits and assume duties that had belonged to one of the original parties under the terms of an existing contract. For a novation to occur, all parties must agree that the contractual duties between the original contracting parties are extinguished. The effect of the novation is to discharge the old contract, and a valid and enforceable new contract takes its place. Here, the contract was not executory—the handyman had completed his work and was not performing any work for the elderly gentleman. Thus, (A) is correct and (B) is incorrect. (C) is incorrect because there is no rule requiring an obligee to seek payment from a delegate before seeking payment from a delgatee. The rule is different when there is a substitute contract (a novation), but as discussed above, there was no delegation here.

(D) is incorrect because their agreement does not fall under the Statute of Frauds. The work was done over a short period (the summer—in less than a year's time), and although the payment was for $500, this was not a contract for the sale of goods but rather for services. Thus, the Statute of Frauds does not apply. Even if the Statute did apply, there was full performance, which would necessitate payment for that performance. Moreover, the greater question is not ***whether*** the elderly gentleman had to pay the handyman but ***who*** (as between the elderly gentleman or the brother-in-law) had to pay him.

Answer to Question 25

(C) The original contract was modified by the parties, and this modification discharged the payment term of the original contract ($3 million) and replaced it with a new payment term ($3,050,000). If a contract is subsequently modified by the parties, this will serve to discharge those terms of the original contract that are the subject of the modification. A modifying agreement must be mutually assented to and supported by consideration. In most cases, consideration is found to be present in that each party has limited her right to enforce the original contract as is. If a modification will benefit only one of the parties, it may be unenforceable without some consideration being given to the other party. Note, however, that if a promisee has given something in addition to what he already owes in return for the promise he now seeks to enforce, or has in some way agreed to vary his preexisting duty, there is consideration. Here, the businesswoman agreed to pay the contractor an additional $50,000 and the contractor agreed to complete the work early—by mid June instead of July 1. Thus, there was sufficient consideration to support the modification. (A) is incorrect because neither the Statute of Frauds nor the parol evidence rule affects the validity of the oral modification. The Statute of Frauds does not require a writing for the modification of a construction contract, and parol evidence can be offered to show subsequent modifications of a written contract. (B) is incorrect because, as explained above, the contractor's agreement to vary his contractual duty by promising to perform all of the work by a date earlier than that originally agreed to constitutes consideration sufficient to support the businesswoman's promise to pay the additional $50,000. (D) is incorrect because it suggests that the court will evaluate the adequacy of consideration. A court of law will not concern itself with the relative values being exchanged. If the businesswoman has agreed to pay $3,050,000 for the job performed by the contractor, the court will not inquire as to whether this is a fair price or otherwise attempt to make a new agreement for the parties.

Answer to Question 26

(C) The contractor who did the original job is entitled to collect $2,950,000 because his breach of contract entitled the radio station owner to offset the amount of money that will be needed to compensate him for the breach. A failure to perform in accordance with contractual terms constitutes a breach of the contract. A breach is minor if the obligee gains the substantial benefit of his bargain despite the defective performance. In the case of a minor breach, the aggrieved party is entitled to a remedy for the breach, such as damages. However, the aggrieved party is not relieved of his duty of performance under the contract. The purpose of contract damages based on affirmance of the contract is to put the nonbreaching party where he would have been had the promise been performed, *i.e.*, sufficient damages to allow him to buy a substitute performance. Because the nonbreaching party in a case involving a minor breach has a duty to tender counterperformance, his claim for damages is usually asserted as a setoff against his liability to the obligor. Here, the contract imposed on the contractor a duty to lay the underground cables so as to avoid magnetized rock. By failing to do so, the contractor breached the contract. Despite this breach, the radio station owner received the substantial benefit of his bargain because the studio

and broadcast transmitter have been built. Therefore, the breach is minor, entitling the radio station owner to a remedy but not relieving him of his duty to pay the contractor under the contract. The radio station owner has suffered damages of $50,000, because he will have to expend that amount to reroute the cables in order to put him in the position he would have been in had the contractor not breached. Thus, the radio station owner can assert the $50,000 claim as a setoff against the $3 million he is under a duty to pay the contractor, leaving $2,950,000. (A) is incorrect because a measure of damages based on the difference between the value of what the radio station owner would have received if the contractor had properly performed the contract and the value of what he actually received is appropriate only if having a third party properly complete the project would be wasteful. Here, correcting the breach will cost only $50,000. (B) is incorrect because the fact that the studio and transmitter are now worth more than the contract price does not put the radio station owner in the position he would have been in had the contractor not breached. The higher value of the property is part of the radio station owner's "benefit of the bargain" and does not reduce the damages that he is entitled to collect from the contractor. (D) is incorrect because it states a reliance measure of damages that is inapplicable here. Had the contractor's breach been material, the radio station owner would not have been under a duty to pay him under the contract, but the contractor could have recovered in quasi-contract for the benefits he conferred in partially performing. Here, however, because his breach was only minor, he can recover the amount he is owed under the contract minus the setoff for the radio station owner's damages.

Answer to Question 27

(A) The nephew may be able to rescind the contract on the grounds of unilateral mistake if the buyer was aware that the nephew was mistaken about the identity of the artist. Where only one of the parties is mistaken about facts relating to the agreement, the mistake usually will not prevent formation of the contract. However, if the nonmistaken party is aware of the mistake made by the other party, he will not be permitted to snap up the offer; *i.e.*, the mistaken party will have the right to rescind the agreement. Under the facts in this choice, the buyer knows that the nephew is mistaken about the identity of the artist, which is a basic assumption of the contract for the paintings. To obtain rescission, the nephew would also have to establish that the mistake creates a material imbalance in the exchange and that he did not assume the risk of that mistake. The facts in choice (A) give him the best grounds for doing so. (B) is incorrect because the fact that one of the parties to the contract has superior knowledge about the subject matter of the contract does not by itself justify rescission, even if the other party is unaware of that fact. The buyer's knowledge or lack of it was not a basic assumption on which the contract was made and was not relied on by the nephew in making the sale. (C) is incorrect because the buyer's misrepresentation to the nephew as to how he will use the paintings does not appear to have been relied on by the nephew. Hence, the misrepresentation is not significant enough to serve as grounds for rescinding the contract. (D) is incorrect because while it is true that a contract must be executory on both sides to be effectively discharged by rescission, this fact alone will not be sufficient to effect a rescission. Rather, when only one of the parties is seeking rescission, as is the case here, that party must prove an adequate legal ground (*e.g.*, mistake, misrepresentation, duress, and failure of consideration). In this case, as discussed above, the ground of unilateral mistake will provide the nephew with the best basis for rescinding the contract.

Answer to Question 28

(C) The circumstances of (C) offer the best grounds for rescinding the contract based on mutual mistake. When both parties entering into a contract are mistaken about facts relating to the agreement, the contract may be voidable by the adversely affected party if (i) the mistake concerns a basic assumption on which the contract is made; (ii) the mistake has a material effect on the agreed-upon exchange; and (iii) the party seeking avoidance did not assume the risk of the mistake. Here, both parties probably believed that the bills would be suitable for display, like other bills that had been raised from the ocean. They had no reason to suspect that the bills would discolor when exposed to indirect sunlight. This occurrence probably rendered the bills nearly worthless, creating a material imbalance in the exchange. Finally, there is nothing to indicate that the museum owner/purchasing agent assumed the risk of what occurred. In contrast to this situation, the circumstances in (A) are not as strong a basis for avoidance. Even assuming that both parties mistakenly believed that the bills were not too fragile to be transported, that risk is more likely to be deemed assumed by the purchaser. (B) indicates only that circumstances changed ***after*** the contract was formed, but assuming the salvage company knew nothing about the impending discovery of the large cache of similar bills (and we should assume this because the facts do not indicate otherwise), the subsequent change in price cannot be considered a mistake that was made at the time the parties entered into their contract. (D) is incorrect because the circumstances do not satisfy the requirements for discharge by frustration. Frustration will exist where the purpose of the contract has become valueless by virtue of some supervening event not the fault of the party seeking discharge. To establish frustration the following must be shown: (i) there is some supervening act or event leading to the frustration; (ii) at the time of entering into the contract, the parties did not reasonably foresee the act or event occurring; (iii) the purpose of the contract has been completely or almost completely destroyed by this act or event; and (iv) the purpose of the contract was realized by both parties at the time of making the contract. Here, the salvage company thought that the purchasing agent was purchasing the bills for himself; thus, it did not realize at the time the contract was made that the purpose of the contract was to procure the bills for the museum that was subsequently destroyed. Therefore, frustration will not be available as a ground for rescission here.

Answer to Question 29

(B) The written agreement between the manufacturer and the distributor was not to take effect unless the distributor notified the manufacturer in writing by October 7 that it (the distributor) had obtained a buyer. This notification was a condition precedent to the manufacturer's absolute duty of performance. Upon failure of this condition, the manufacturer is discharged from its duties under the contract. A condition is an event, other than the passage of time, the occurrence or nonoccurrence of which will create, limit, or extinguish the absolute duty to perform in the other contracting party. A promisor may insert conditions on his promise to prevent his duty of immediate performance from arising until the conditions are met, so that failure of a condition discharges the obligations of the promisor; the obligations on the conditional promise never mature. A condition precedent is one that must occur before an absolute duty of immediate performance arises in the other party. Here, the oral agreement between the manufacturer and the distributor quite clearly states that the written agreement will not take effect unless the distributor supplies the required notification by October 7. The distributor's timely, written notification constitutes a condition precedent, because it is an event that must occur before an absolute duty to deliver the computer arises in the manufacturer. The failure of the distributor to supply the required notification by October 7 thus constitutes a failure of a condition precedent, so that the manufacturer is discharged from any obligations on the contract. (Note that evidence of the oral agreement does not run afoul of the parol evidence rule because where a party asserts the existence of an oral agreement that a written contract would not become effective until the occurrence of a condition, evidence of the oral understanding may be offered and received. This is simply a way of showing that the agreement never came into being, rather than a means of altering the written agreement.) (D) is incorrect because a condition subsequent is an event the occurrence of which cuts off an already existing absolute duty of performance. Here, the manufacturer was not under an absolute

duty unless the distributor fulfilled the terms of the condition. Thus, the condition that failed was precedent rather than subsequent. (A) is incorrect because contractual duties will be discharged by unconscionability only if, at the time the contract was made, it was one-sided and terribly unfair to one of the parties. Unequal bargaining positions are usually required. Here, at the time the contract was made, nothing about it seemed unfair, and the subsequent increase in price does not render the contract unconscionable. (C) is incorrect because the mistake regarding the delivery date is a mere clerical error, rather than a mistake of fact going to a point that is material to the transaction. As such, this is not the type of mistake that would relieve either or both of the parties of their obligations under the contract.

Answer to Question 30

(C) The buyer's best argument is that the seller's assurances that there was no problem with the buyer's failure to provide written notification by April 15 amounts to a waiver of the condition. The buyer's written notification by April 15 that he had obtained the proper financing was a condition precedent to the seller's absolute duty to perform under the contract. It is clear that the buyer did not provide the required notification by April 15; thus, the condition was not fulfilled. However, one having the benefit of a condition may indicate by words or conduct that he will not insist upon it. When a condition is broken, the beneficiary of the condition has an election: (i) he may terminate his liability; or (ii) he may continue under the contract. If a choice is made to continue under the contract, the person is deemed to have waived the condition. The seller was fully aware that the buyer had not satisfied the condition, yet, when speaking with the buyer on April 16, he stated unequivocally that it was not a problem. This is a definite indication that the seller elected to continue under the contract. Having so elected, the seller is deemed to have waived the condition. Therefore, the seller's duty of performance under the contract became absolute. Regarding (A), the only way the Statute of Frauds could bolster the buyer's position would be if the original oral agreement setting forth the condition were required by the Statute to be in writing. If that were the case, the buyer could argue that the condition is unenforceable because it is not in writing. However, the oral agreement is not of a type that falls within the purview of the Statute of Frauds. Therefore, the Statute of Frauds will provide no help to the buyer. Similarly, regarding (B), the parol evidence rule could help the buyer only if it could be used to preclude admissibility of the original oral agreement. Under the parol evidence rule, where the parties to a contract express their agreement in a writing with the intent that it embody the full and final expression of their bargain, any expression made prior to the writing and any oral expression contemporaneous with the writing is inadmissible to vary the terms of the writing. However, where it is asserted that there was an oral agreement that the written contract would not become effective until the occurrence of a condition, evidence of the oral agreement may be offered and received. Because the original oral agreement between the seller and buyer established a condition precedent to the effectiveness of the written agreement, the buyer will be unable to raise the parol evidence rule as a bar to the admissibility of evidence relating to the oral agreement. (D) is unsupported by the facts. If a party with a duty of performance that is subject to a condition prevents the condition from occurring, he no longer has the benefit of the condition. This is referred to as excuse of condition by hindrance. The seller did nothing to prevent the occurrence of the condition regarding written notification by April 15. Consequently, it cannot be said that the condition is excused by hindrance.

Answer to Question 31

(D) Of all the alternatives listed, (D) is the only one that presents any real basis for supporting the manufacturer's case. One of the general rules of contract construction, including contracts for goods under the U.C.C., is that courts will look to see what custom and usage are in the particular business and in the particular locale where the contract is either made or to be performed. [*See* U.C.C. §1-205] The manufacturer could claim that when he and the distributor entered into the distribution contract, both parties implicitly understood that the custom of distributing only one brand of outerwear would be followed in their transaction. Under such circumstances, the manufacturer may be able to successfully assert that the distributor's distribution of the competitor's outerwear constitutes a breach of contract. The fact that the competitor's advertising campaign at least impliedly denigrates the appearance of the manufacturer's outerwear (as in (A)), or that the manufacturer's sales have dropped since the introduction of the competitor's products (as in (B)) establishes no cause of action against the distributor. Absent some provision in the contract, or some reference to custom and usage as mentioned in (D), there is no basis for holding that the distributor was prohibited from distributing other companies' products, or that the distributor can be held liable for a decline in the manufacturer's sales figures due to sales or advertisements made by a company whose products are being distributed by the distributor. (C) is incorrect because the written agreement between the distributor and the manufacturer would probably be deemed to be a full and final expression of the bargain, so that evidence of the distributor's prior expression would be inadmissible to vary or supplement the writing under the parol evidence rule. Under U.C.C. section 2-202, a party cannot offer consistent additional terms if the writing was intended as a complete statement of the terms of the agreement. (In contrast, evidence of custom in the trade can be offered regardless of the completeness of the written agreement.) Also, the distributor's statement about their deal being exclusive is not specific enough on its face to establish whether he meant that the distributor would distribute only the manufacturer's products, or that the manufacturer would have its products distributed in the state only by the distributor, or perhaps some other meaning. The statement, even if admissible, is not definite enough to form a basis for a cause of action against the distributor.

Answer to Question 32

(B) Although the customer is entitled to reject the coat for even a minor defect such as one button being missing, she is required to give the seller an opportunity to cure this defect. Because this is a contract for the sale of goods, the Uniform Commercial Code applies. Pursuant to the U.C.C., if goods or any tender fail in any respect to conform to the contract, the buyer may reject the goods. This rule of perfect tender allows rejection for ***any*** defect, and does not require material breach. However, the perfect tender rule is softened by the rules allowing the seller to cure the defect by giving reasonable notice of an intention to cure and making a new tender of conforming goods within the time originally provided for performance. Also, where the buyer rejects a tender that the seller reasonably believed would be acceptable with or without money allowance, the seller, upon reasonable notification to the buyer, has a further reasonable time beyond the original contract time within which to make a conforming tender. Here, one button missing on a $12,000 coat is a very minor defect. However, pursuant to the perfect tender rule, the customer has the right to reject the coat even for this defect. In turn, the salon owner is entitled to cure the defect by notifying the customer of his intention to do so and by making a conforming tender. The salon owner has told the customer that the tailor will sew on the button, which will result in the coat's conforming to the contract. Although the tailor, due to the holiday, will not be able to sew on the button by the agreed-upon date of delivery, being able to do so early in the morning of the day after falls within a further reasonable time beyond the original contract time within which to make a conforming tender. In any event, at this point the customer must give the salon owner an opportunity to cure. (A) is incorrect because it fails to add that the salon owner must be allowed an opportunity to cure, as discussed above. (C) and (D) are incorrect because with the failure of perfect tender, the customer is not required to accept the coat. This right of rejection is

not affected by the minor nature of the defect, as (C) suggests. Similarly, the buyer's right of rejection is not impaired by the fact that the defect is easily curable, as (D) states.

Answer to Question 33

(C) (C) is correct because the seller extended a merchant's firm offer and the U.C.C. requires that such offers be held open for a reasonable time. Offers not supported by consideration generally can be revoked at will by the offeror, even if he has promised not to revoke for a certain period. However, an offer by a ***merchant*** to buy or sell goods in a signed writing that, by its terms, gives assurances that it will be held open is not revocable for lack of consideration during the time stated, or if no time is stated, for a reasonable time (not to exceed three months). [U.C.C. §2-205] The seller of the drill bits is a merchant as defined by the U.C.C. because he regularly deals in goods such as the drill bits. [U.C.C. §2-104(1)] Therefore, because the written offer by the seller contained assurances that it was a "firm offer," the buyer's acceptance resulted in an enforceable contract with the seller. (A) is incorrect because, as stated above, the seller could not revoke its offer at will, but instead had to hold the offer open for a reasonable time because this was a merchant's firm offer. (A) would be correct if a firm offer were not involved. (B) is incorrect because while the seller's firm offer must be held open for a reasonable time, this period may be less than the U.C.C.'s three-month limit. As discussed above, a merchant's firm offer is not revocable for lack of consideration during the time stated, or if no time is stated, for a reasonable time (but in no event may such period exceed three months). Therefore, while three months is the ***maximum*** period a firm offer can be held open under the U.C.C., a "reasonable" period for the seller's offer might be less than three months. (D) is incorrect because, as discussed above, the U.C.C. abolishes the need for consideration to make a merchant's firm offer irrevocable. While offers not supported by consideration generally can be revoked at will by the offeror, the U.C.C. provides that a merchant's firm offer is not revocable for lack of consideration.

Answer to Question 34

(D) The court should admit parol evidence to construe the ambiguous terms of the contract. The terms of a contract that are set forth in a writing intended as a final expression of the parties' agreement cannot be contradicted by evidence of any prior agreement or contemporaneous oral agreement. However, the terms of a contract may be ***explained*** or ***supplemented*** by parol evidence. [U.C.C. §2-202] The offer does not indicate whether the wheat is to be sold only as a single lot. Therefore, to clear up the ambiguity in the farmer's offer, the court could consider trade practices, past course of dealing, etc., in determining whether the bakery had a reasonable expectation of being able to purchase the goods piecemeal. (A) is incorrect because such a narrow interpretation is not clear from the ambiguous language in the farmer's offer. When a term of a contract is ambiguous in a writing, the term may be explained by course of dealing, usage of trade, or course of performance. Because it is unclear from the language whether the farmer contemplated sale of the wheat as a single lot or piecemeal, the offer is not subject to partial acceptance at the buyer's option, and the court may consider parol evidence to clear up the ambiguity. (B) is incorrect because it is not clear from the language of the farmer's offer whether the wheat was being offered as a single lot only. As discussed above, because the language of the farmer's offer is ambiguous as to whether sale of the wheat as a single lot or piecemeal was contemplated, the farmer is not entitled to judgment solely on the basis of the written offer. Instead, the court will admit parol evidence, such as trade practices and past course of dealing, to clear up the ambiguity. (C) is incorrect because the court may consider other evidence to clear up ambiguities. As discussed above, the U.C.C. provides that a written contract's terms may be explained or supplemented by (i) course of dealing or usage in the trade, or (ii) the course of performance to date, even if the terms appear to be unambiguous. Therefore, the farmer's ambiguous offer to sell the wheat, which comes under the U.C.C., is not fatal to the formation of the contract because parol evidence is admissible on the question of whether the offer contemplated a piecemeal sale of the wheat.

Answer to Question 35

(D) (D) properly states the U.C.C. position regarding the terms of the contract. Under the U.C.C., if both parties to a contract are merchants, additional terms in an acceptance will be included in the contract unless (i) they ***materially alter*** the original contract; (ii) the offer ***expressly limits acceptance*** to the terms of the offer; or (iii) the offeror has already objected to the particular terms, or objects within a reasonable time after notice of them is received. [U.C.C. §2-207(2)] The manufacturer and office supply company are both merchants because they regularly deal in goods. [U.C.C. §2-104(1)] Therefore, under Article 2 the contract will include the terms of the manufacturer's offer plus those in the office supply company's purported acceptance that did not amount to a material alteration of the offer or to which the manufacturer did not object within a reasonable time. Note that the manufacturer's offer did not expressly limit acceptance of its terms. (A) is incorrect because this was a contract between two merchants. Contract formation under the U.C.C. for contracts between merchants is governed by the rule stated above. If one of the parties were not a merchant, (A) would be correct—if one of the parties to a contract for sale of goods is not a merchant and the acceptance includes additional or different terms, such terms are considered to be mere proposals that do not become part of the contract unless the offeror accepts. [U.C.C. §2-207(1)] However, because this is a contract between merchants, the office supply company's terms regarding shipping will be included unless they materially alter the offer, as discussed above. (B) is incorrect because it does not fully state the Code's "battle of the forms" provision. The choice fails to mention the manufacturer's power to object within a reasonable time. (C) is incorrect because, like (B), it does not note the manufacturer's power to object within a reasonable time.

Answer to Question 36

(C) The buyer did not have the right to cancel the second shipment, because the defects in the first shipment did not substantially impair the value of the entire contract. This case involves an installment contract, *i.e.*, the contract authorizes or requires deliveries in separate lots, and the sale of goods, so Article 2 of the U.C.C. applies. Under Article 2, a buyer may declare a total breach of an installment contract only if the defect substantially impairs the value of the entire contract. [U.C.C. §2-612] The problem with the first shipment of the stain was discovered and corrected by the manufacturer. The manufacturer offered to cure the defect in the first shipment. In whole, the defect in the first shipment did not substantially impair the value of the entire contract. (A) is incorrect because legitimate fears, alone, are not enough to justify anticipatorily repudiating a contract, as the buyer did here. Anticipatory repudiation occurs when a promisor, prior to the time set for performance of his promise, indicates that he will not perform when the time comes. If, as here, the promisor is unsure of whether the other party will fulfill his contract obligations, the promisor may seek adequate assurances that performance will be forthcoming. In this case, the manufacturer already provided the buyer with such assurances, which fell on deaf ears. Because the manufacturer assured the buyer and, more importantly, had already corrected the problem at its factory before the second shipment was due, the store owner's fears would not justify canceling the second shipment. (B) is incorrect because, as discussed above, the defects in the first delivery would not warrant cancellation of the entire installment contract unless they substantially impaired the value of the entire contract, which they did not. (D) is incorrect because, as explained, the manufacturer had already given adequate assurances to the buyer.

Criminal Law

Question Sets and Analytical Answers

Set 1 Answer Sheet

1. Ⓐ Ⓑ Ⓒ Ⓓ
2. Ⓐ Ⓑ Ⓒ Ⓓ
3. Ⓐ Ⓑ Ⓒ Ⓓ
4. Ⓐ Ⓑ Ⓒ Ⓓ
5. Ⓐ Ⓑ Ⓒ Ⓓ
6. Ⓐ Ⓑ Ⓒ Ⓓ
7. Ⓐ Ⓑ Ⓒ Ⓓ
8. Ⓐ Ⓑ Ⓒ Ⓓ
9. Ⓐ Ⓑ Ⓒ Ⓓ
10. Ⓐ Ⓑ Ⓒ Ⓓ
11. Ⓐ Ⓑ Ⓒ Ⓓ
12. Ⓐ Ⓑ Ⓒ Ⓓ
13. Ⓐ Ⓑ Ⓒ Ⓓ
14. Ⓐ Ⓑ Ⓒ Ⓓ
15. Ⓐ Ⓑ Ⓒ Ⓓ
16. Ⓐ Ⓑ Ⓒ Ⓓ
17. Ⓐ Ⓑ Ⓒ Ⓓ
18. Ⓐ Ⓑ Ⓒ Ⓓ

CRIMINAL LAW QUESTIONS - SET 1

Question 1

A state statute defines first degree murder as the intentional, premeditated murder of another human being. Murder in the second degree and manslaughter are defined as at common law. The defendant, just having been served with divorce papers, decided to drown his sorrows at the local pub. After drinking heavily and becoming very intoxicated, the defendant became enraged when another patron spilled a drink on him. He took a nearby ashtray and smashed it over the patron's head, killing him instantly.

What is the most likely crime of which the defendant would be convicted?

(A) Murder in the first degree.

(B) Murder in the second degree.

(C) Involuntary manslaughter.

(D) Voluntary manslaughter.

Question 2

A state statute reads in pertinent part: "Any licensed medical doctor who willfully neglects to assist anyone with a life-threatening injury shall be guilty of a crime, subject to punishment of up to two years' imprisonment in the state penitentiary or a fine of $15,000, or both."

A licensed physician, while jogging in a park, heard the sounds of a man moaning in the bushes next to the jogging path. The physician stopped to investigate and found the man bleeding in the bushes. The physician asked the man if he needed help, and the man responded that he would be fine. Not having seen any indications of a serious condition, the physician returned to her morning jog. The man subsequently bled to death an hour later. The coroner's report made clear that the man could have been saved if he had received prompt medical attention, even if only of a "first aid" variety until an ambulance arrived. At trial, the physician testified that she was unaware of the statute, which had been in effect for one week when the incident took place.

Should the physician be convicted of violating the statute?

(A) Yes, because she neglected someone whose life was in danger.

(B) No, because the statute is too vague and raises mere negligence to criminal status.

(C) No, because the physician was unaware of the new statute.

(D) No, because the physician believed that the man's condition was not life-threatening.

Question 3

A state statute defines first degree murder as the intentional, premeditated murder of another human being. A killing committed during the course of a robbery, burglary, arson, or rape is considered to be murder in the first degree. Murder in the second degree and manslaughter are defined as at common law.

The defendant wanted to steal some papers from a business associate's office, and so he arranged to have a meeting with her at her office. When the associate left the room, the defendant put a knockout drug in her coffee. After she passed out from drinking the coffee, the defendant rummaged through her files, finding and stealing the papers that he wanted. Unfortunately, the defendant miscalculated the dosage, and the business associate died.

What is the most serious offense of which the defendant can be convicted?

(A) Voluntary manslaughter.

(B) Involuntary manslaughter.

(C) Murder in the second degree.

(D) Murder in the first degree.

Question 4

A bookie testified before a grand jury regarding allegedly illegal gambling activities. As a result, the bookie was indicted and a warrant was issued for the bookie's arrest, along with a search warrant for the bookie's home. The police went to the bookie's home, informed him of the charges against him, and placed him in handcuffs. The officers then conducted a search of the bookie's home and found a desk calendar, which had possibly incriminating information written on it relating to appointments. They seized the desk calendar and one of the officers asked the bookie what he had to say about their find. The bookie made an incriminating statement in response. Before trial, the prosecutor obtained an exemplar of the bookie's handwriting to compare it with the handwriting on the calendar.

If introduced at trial, which of the following would most clearly violate the bookie's Fifth Amendment self-incrimination rights?

(A) The grand jury testimony.

(B) The bookie's response to the police officer.

(C) The bookie's handwriting exemplar.

(D) The bookie's desk calendar.

Question 5

A divorced father of two with an erratic temper and a drinking problem would sometimes beat his children. Three days after a particularly savage beating of his 17-year-old son, the father came home late from work in a drunken state. The father asked where his dinner was, and the son replied that he had given the food to the dog. The father became angered, telling the son, "I'll teach you to have some respect." Feeling a little unsteady, he added, "after a little nap." The father then collapsed on the couch. The son knew that there would be trouble when his father came to, and so he took his younger brother to a next-door neighbor's house. He then returned home and looked for his father's handgun, but he could not find it. Rather than continue looking for the gun, the son retrieved a large knife from the kitchen drawer, and waited near the couch for his father to awaken. When the father awoke a short time later, he saw his son holding the knife. Worried, he asked the son what he was doing with the knife. The son replied, "You won't hurt us anymore," and jabbed the knife into his father's chest, killing the father instantly. The son is brought to trial as an adult. The jurisdiction generally follows the common law definitions of crimes.

The court is most likely to find that:

(A) The son is guilty of murder, because he intended to kill his father.

(B) The son is guilty of voluntary manslaughter, because his father provoked him.

(C) The son is guilty of voluntary manslaughter, because the beatings by his father constituted a continuing provocation.

(D) The son was justified in killing his father, because he acted in self-defense.

Question 6

While at a party, the defendant ran into an acquaintance. The acquaintance proceeded to ridicule the defendant about his looks. After an hour of verbal abuse by the acquaintance, the defendant suddenly took a champagne bottle that was on a nearby table and struck the acquaintance over the head, killing him instantly. At his arrest, the defendant told the police that voices inside his head told him to shut the acquaintance up, permanently.

The defendant was tried in a jurisdiction that follows the Model Penal Code test for insanity. At trial, the defendant's lawyer introduced psychiatric testimony indicating that the defendant suffered from a mental illness.

The defendant most likely will be relieved of criminal responsibility if the defense can prove that:

(A) The defendant's actions were a product of his mental illness.

(B) The defendant could not appreciate the criminality of killing the acquaintance, or he could not conform his conduct to the requirements of the law.

(C) The defendant did not know that killing the acquaintance was wrong, or he could not understand the nature and quality of his actions.

(D) The defendant was unable to control himself or conform his conduct to the law.

Question 7

A worker was in the habit of carrying a lot of cash with him after payday. His good friend was worried that someday the worker might get robbed. To teach him to be more careful, and intending only to frighten him, the friend purchased a realistic-looking toy gun and a face mask and hid in the bushes one night after payday, waiting for the worker to come home. As the worker passed by, the friend jumped out of the bushes, pointed the toy gun at him, and took all of his money. The worker was badly frightened by the incident. Shortly thereafter, the friend returned the money to the worker and explained why he had staged the holdup.

Which of the following crimes is the most serious crime of which the friend can be convicted?

(A) Robbery.

(B) Armed robbery.

(C) Assault.

(D) Larceny.

Question 8

A woman's boyfriend came to her apartment with a mink coat in his arms and handed it to the woman. After the boyfriend told her that the coat was now hers, the woman asked him where he got the coat. The boyfriend answered, "From the Easter Bunny." After the boyfriend left, she tried on the coat and admired how good it looked on her in the mirror. The next day, the woman read in the newspaper that the home of a well-known socialite had been burglarized the night before. Among the missing items, according to the paper, was a mink coat. The woman took the coat from the closet and rifled through the pockets. She found a handkerchief with the monogram matching the initials of the well-known socialite. The woman decided to keep the fur coat, thinking to herself that the socialite could probably afford to buy another coat.

Which of the following best describes the crime or crimes, if any, the woman has committed?

(A) Accessory after the fact to burglary.

(B) Larceny and accessory after the fact to burglary.

(C) Receipt of stolen property.

(D) The woman has not committed any crime.

Question 9

An underworld informer advised a police investigator that his neighbor was running an illegal bookmaking operation in his apartment, and that the informer had placed bets with the neighbor at this location. The officer obtained a search warrant, based on his affidavit reciting the foregoing facts, and further stating that the underworld informer was a person who had given him accurate information in previous cases, but whose identity could not be revealed because it might jeopardize other criminal investigations being carried on by the police. Armed with the search warrant, police officers went to the neighbor's apartment. They entered when the neighbor opened the door and searched the apartment. They seized various wagering slips and bookmaking apparatus (described in the search warrant) and placed the neighbor under arrest for illegal gambling. At a preliminary hearing, the neighbor challenges the validity of the search warrant.

Was the search warrant valid?

(A) No, because it was based on hearsay information.

(B) No, because the officer failed to disclose the identity of the informer, so that the accuracy of his information could not be verified.

(C) Yes, because the identity of the informer is never required.

(D) Yes, because the affidavit accompanying it is sufficiently detailed to allow a determination of probable cause.

Question 10

A woman called the police to report that she had been raped. She gave the police a detailed description of her attacker, and they picked up a man who matched the description who was found near the site of the alleged attack. The police took the man to the police station and read him his *Miranda* warnings. The man asked for a public defender to be appointed. Before the public defender arrived, the woman came to the police station and was told there would be a lineup as soon as the suspect's lawyer arrived. On the way to the viewing room, the woman passed a holding cell where the man was being held. She pointed at him and said loudly, "That's the man who attacked me!" The man did not respond in any way. The woman later picked the man out of a lineup.

At the trial, if the prosecutor wishes to introduce evidence that the man said nothing when the woman confronted him, would such evidence be admissible?

(A) Yes, because it is the truth.

(B) Yes, because the man had been read his *Miranda* warnings and knew that any behavior could be used against him.

(C) No, because the man's right against self-incrimination would be violated if he were required to speak.

(D) No, because counsel was not present at the time of the incident.

Question 11

A veteran high school teacher shot and killed one of the students in his class on the spur of the moment. Psychiatric examinations indicated that the teacher believed that the student was trying to ridicule him in front of other students in the class and that he had to do something to stop him. The examinations also indicated that the teacher did not comprehend that killing was condemned by society when he shot his student.

If the teacher pleads not guilty by reason of insanity in a jurisdiction that applies the "*M'Naghten* test," his best argument would be that:

(A) He did not know that the act of shooting the student was wrong.

(B) He lacked the substantial capacity to appreciate the criminality of his act.

(C) He did not know the nature and quality of his act.

(D) His act was the result of an irresistible impulse.

Question 12

A stagehand decided to play a practical joke on an actor. The stagehand went to the storage room where stage props were stored and took what he believed to be a stage gun from the locker where such guns were kept. In fact, a week before, an actress had put her real pistol in the stage gun locker and borrowed the stage gun for an amateur theatrical her church group was putting on.

The actress had forgotten to remove the bullets that her husband always kept in the gun. The stagehand went into the actor's dressing room and yelled, "You've stolen the part that I always wanted to play, now die for it!" The actor knew that the stagehand liked to play practical jokes, and, after an initial frightened reaction, the actor broke out laughing. The stagehand laughed too, shouted, "Bang, you're dead!" and pulled the trigger. A bullet hit the actor in the heart, killing him.

Which of the following best describes the stagehand's criminal liability?

(A) He is guilty of second degree murder.

(B) He is guilty of voluntary manslaughter.

(C) He is guilty of involuntary manslaughter.

(D) He has committed no crime.

Question 13

While out walking one evening, a pedestrian was stopped at gunpoint by a robber who demanded all of her money. The pedestrian hesitated in going for her wallet, and so the robber hit her over the head. In doing so, the robber accidentally dropped the gun, panicked, and started to run. The pedestrian was stunned for a second by the blow to the head, but she recovered quickly, grabbed the gun from the ground, and shot at the fleeing robber. The bullet missed the robber, but hit a bystander, killing him instantly. The pedestrian was arrested and charged with murder.

If her attorney asserts at trial that the pedestrian should be charged with voluntary manslaughter rather than murder, this assertion would be:

(A) Correct, because the pedestrian had no intent to kill the bystander.

(B) Correct, because there was adequate provocation for the pedestrian's actions.

(C) Incorrect, because the pedestrian intended to kill the robber.

(D) Incorrect, because the pedestrian was in no danger when she shot at the fleeing robber.

Question 14

The police suspected that a young man who had been convicted of burglary and was out of prison on parole had stolen a rare diamond that was on display at a local museum. They went to the young man's home, where he lived with his mother, the owner of the house. The young man was not at home, but the police asked his mother if they might enter and search the house for the diamond. The mother allowed the police to enter, and she also consented to show them the room where her son slept and kept his personal belongings. There was a locked trunk in the room, and the police asked the mother to open it for them. She told the police that her son had the only key to the trunk, which he always kept locked. She also told them that, as far as she was concerned, they could go ahead and open the trunk if they were able to do so without a key. The police pried the trunk open and found the missing diamond inside.

Did this constitute a valid search?

(A) No, because the police did not inform the mother that she could refuse permission to allow the search.

(B) No, because the mother did not have authority to consent to the search of the trunk.

(C) Yes, under the doctrine of parens patriae.

(D) Yes, because the mother owned the house and thus could consent to the search of the entire premises.

Question 15

After a particularly harrowing week in the stock market, a trader felt she had earned a weekend of complete rest. She drove to her cabin, built a fire, propped up her feet, and began reading a novel. Later that night, a cold front swept into the area, bringing with it blizzard conditions and freezing temperatures. During this time, a traveler's car broke down a couple of miles from the trader's cabin, and he

was not adequately prepared for the cold weather. After spotting the trader's cabin, the traveler made his way to the cabin's door and began pounding on it. The trader got up and looked out the window and saw the traveler at the door. The trader yelled for the traveler to leave, and went back to reading her book. The traveler froze to death that night on the cabin's porch. The trader has been charged with his death.

If properly charged and tried, the trader can be convicted of:

(A) Murder.

(B) Voluntary manslaughter.

(C) Involuntary manslaughter.

(D) No crime.

Question 16

A patient was late for an appointment with her doctor across town. Because of this, she was driving recklessly through traffic at a high speed and ran through a red light. There were a number of people crossing the street at the time, and the patient accidentally hit one of them. The person she hit was seriously injured and was rushed to the hospital. The patient was arrested and charged with attempted murder.

The patient should be:

(A) Acquitted, because she did not intend to hit anyone with her car.

(B) Acquitted, because she had not gone far enough in her actions to constitute attempt.

(C) Convicted, because a person is presumed to intend the natural and probable consequences of her act.

(D) Convicted, because from her recklessness, the intent to inflict serious bodily harm will be presumed.

Question 17

A suspect was arrested for burglarizing an apartment. He was duly given *Miranda* warnings, and invoked his right to remain silent. When the suspect was put into the lockup, the police took from him his wallet, watch, and other personal possessions. Following standard procedure, a police officer immediately began to make an inventory of the suspect's personal effects. During the course of the inventory, the officer noticed that the suspect's watch bore an inscription with the name of a person whose apartment had been burglarized two days earlier. The officer concluded that the suspect had probably burglarized that apartment as well as the one for which he was arrested. She reported the inscription on the watch to the detective who had arrested the suspect, and the suspect was subsequently charged with the earlier burglary as well.

Did the officer violate the suspect's constitutional rights by reading the inscription?

(A) Yes, because items to be inventoried may be listed, but they may not be closely examined.

(B) Yes, because no search warrant was obtained.

(C) No, because the inventory was a routine procedure of the kind the police normally conduct when an incarceration takes place.

(D) No, because it gave her probable cause to believe that the suspect had committed the earlier burglary.

Question 18

A 15-year-old runaway who worked as a prostitute in a city approached a man and offered her services. The man agreed, and the two engaged in sexual intercourse in the back seat of the man's car. These events were noticed by an undercover police officer, who arrested the runaway and the man. The man admitted to having sex with the runaway, and he was charged with statutory rape. The runaway was charged with being an accomplice to statutory rape.

At the runaway's trial, her best defense is that:

(A) Since the man has not yet been convicted, the runaway may not be convicted as an accomplice.

(B) The statutory rape law is designed to protect minors and therefore the runaway cannot be convicted as an accomplice.

(C) As a minor, the runaway does not have the capacity to be an accomplice.

(D) Since the runaway is a prostitute and consented to the sexual acts, the man cannot be convicted of statutory rape; therefore, the runaway cannot be an accomplice.

CRIMINAL LAW ANSWERS - SET 1

Answer to Question 1

(B) The most likely crime that the defendant would be convicted of is murder in the second degree. The jurisdiction defines murder in the first degree as deliberate premeditated murder, whereas all other types of killings are defined as at common law. Deliberation and premeditation requires some time of cool reflection on the idea of killing. In the instant case, there are no facts indicating that the defendant coolly reflected on the idea of killing. The facts indicate an impulse killing rather than any type of deliberate, premeditated killing. Furthermore, the facts indicate that the defendant was very intoxicated, which would serve as a basis for reducing the crime to second degree murder. Thus, (A) is incorrect. The state defines murder in the second degree as common law murder. At common law, murder required malice; *i.e.,* (i) the intent to kill; (ii) the intent to inflict great bodily injury; (iii) reckless indifference to an unjustifiably high risk to human life; or (iv) the intent to commit a felony. Here, the reckless indifference element arguably could be satisfied. By smashing a heavy ashtray over the other patron's head, the defendant unjustifiably disregarded that the blow could be a killing blow. Neither would intoxication be a defense, as there would be no specific intent-to-kill requirement under this type of analysis. (C) is incorrect. Involuntary manslaughter is a killing committed with criminal negligence or during the perpetration of some unlawful act not encompassing a felony for felony murder. Certainly, striking another with a heavy object would constitute criminal negligence sufficient for conviction. However, involuntary manslaughter is a lesser crime than murder in the second degree, and the call of the question asks for the most serious crime of which the defendant could be convicted, making (B) a better choice than (C). (D) is also incorrect. Voluntary manslaughter is an intentional killing committed under the duress of an adequate provocation, and it requires (i) a provocation sufficient to arouse the sudden and intense passion in the mind of an ordinary person such as to cause him to lose self-control; (ii) the defendant to be in fact provoked; (iii) an insufficient time to cool off; and (iv) the defendant did not in fact cool off. In the instant case, the facts do not indicate that the defendant killed intentionally. Thus, there is no intentional killing to reduce to voluntary manslaughter. Furthermore, it is unlikely that having a drink spilled on him would cause an ordinary person to commit murder. As a result, such a provocation is not adequate to reduce the killing to voluntary manslaughter.

Answer to Question 2

(D) Because the physician believed that the man's condition was not life-threatening, she should not be convicted because she lacked the requisite intent for the crime. The statute here makes it a crime for a licensed physician to ***willfully*** neglect someone with a life-threatening injury. A requirement of willful action means that the person must have acted ***knowing*** that her conduct would necessarily cause such a result. Thus, she must be aware of the circumstances and act with the awareness of what the results of her conduct will be. To be convicted under this statute, the physician must have been aware that the man's condition was life-threatening and that leaving him there without any assistance could cost him his life. Because the facts indicate that the physician believed that the man was not in a life-threatening situation, she did not violate the statute by leaving the man unattended. She did not "willfully" neglect him, because she was not aware of the status of his situation. (A) is wrong because it fails to account for the required mental state (*i.e.,* willfulness). Choice (A) would impose a strict liability; a doctor would be liable whether or not she knew of the life-threatening situation. The statute here does not impose strict liability; only willful neglect is punishable. (B) is wrong because the statute is not too vague. The statute gives a person of ordinary intelligence fair notice of what sort of action or

inaction is punishable (*i.e.,* the willful failure of a licensed medical physician to assist someone with a life-threatening injury). (C) is wrong because ignorance of the law is no excuse. It is not a defense to a crime that the defendant did not know that her acts were prohibited by criminal law. This is true regardless of whether her ignorance was reasonable. Thus, despite the fact that the statute was in effect for only one week, the physician may be convicted whether she was aware of it or not.

Answer to Question 3

(C) The most serious offense of which the defendant can be convicted is murder in the second degree. The jurisdiction defines murder in the first degree as deliberate premeditated murder, whereas all other types of killings are defined as at common law. Deliberation and premeditation requires some time of cool reflection on the idea of killing. In the instant case, the defendant did not actually intend to kill; thus, deliberation and premeditation are logically excluded. The facts indicate that murder in the second degree is defined as common law murder. Murder at common law is the unlawful killing of a human being with malice aforethought. Malice aforethought exists if the defendant has any of the following states of mind: (i) intent to kill (express malice); (ii) intent to inflict great bodily injury; (iii) reckless indifference to an unjustifiably high risk to human life ("abandoned and malignant heart"); or (iv) intent to commit a felony (limited in most states to inherently dangerous felonies). Because malice will be implied from the intent to commit the underlying felony, even an accidental killing committed during the course of a felony is murder. Here, the defendant intended to, and did in fact, commit a dangerous felony, robbery, which is the taking of personal property of another from the other's person or presence, by force or intimidation, with the intent to permanently deprive him of it. The knockout drops constituted force sufficient to overcome the business associate's resistance; hence, the defendant has committed a robbery and his intent constitutes implied malice for purposes of felony murder. Furthermore, an argument could be made that a drug that was sufficient to knock someone out cold is a dangerous drug, and the use of such a drug would evidence an indifference to an unjustifiably high risk to human life. This would provide a second basis for a finding of murder in the second degree. Therefore, (C) is correct and (A), (B), and (D) are incorrect.

Answer to Question 4

(B) The bookie's response to the police officer is the only evidence that was clearly taken in violation of the bookie's Fifth Amendment self-incrimination rights. The Fifth Amendment privilege against compelled self-incrimination forms the basis for ruling on the admissibility of a statement obtained while a defendant is in custody. A person in custody must, prior to interrogation (except for standard booking questions), be clearly informed that: he has the right to remain silent, anything he says can be used against him in court, he has the right to an attorney, and if he cannot afford an attorney, one will be appointed for him if he so desires. These *Miranda* warnings are a prerequisite to the admissibility of any statement made by the defendant during a custodial interrogation. Here, the bookie was in custody (handcuffed) and was questioned ("what do you have to say . . .") and the facts do not indicate that *Miranda* warnings were given. Thus, there has been a direct violation of the Fifth Amendment privilege against compelled self-incrimination. (A) is wrong because use of a defendant's grand jury testimony at trial does not violate the Fifth Amendment. Pursuant to the Fifth Amendment, a criminal defendant may invoke the privilege against self-incrimination by refusing to answer grand jury questions on the grounds that it may incriminate him. If he testifies, he has waived his privilege. Here, the bookie testified at the grand jury proceeding and thus waived the privilege. (C) is wrong because the

Fifth Amendment protects only testimonial or communicative evidence, not real or physical evidence. Thus, the state may compel a person to give a handwriting exemplar without violating the Fifth Amendment, even if the evidence may be incriminating. (D) is wrong because the Fifth Amendment protects against being compelled to communicate information, not against disclosure of communications made in the past. Thus, the police may search for and seize documents tending to incriminate a person. Here, the bookie was not compelled to give any testimony. Rather, the police, pursuant to a valid search warrant, seized the calendar with the appointments marked on it.

Answer to Question 5

(A) The court is most likely to find that the son is guilty of murder. Murder is the unlawful killing of a human being with malice aforethought. Malice aforethought (which may be either express or implied) exists if the defendant has any of the following states of mind: (i) intent to kill; (ii) intent to inflict great bodily injury; (iii) awareness of an unjustifiably high risk to human life; or (iv) intent to commit a felony. An intentional killing can be reduced from murder to voluntary manslaughter if the killing occurs while the defendant is acting under a provocation that would arouse sudden and intense passion in the mind of an ordinary person so as to cause him to lose self-control, with insufficient time between the provocation and the killing for the passions of a reasonable person to cool. One type of adequate provocation is exposure to a threat of deadly force. Here, the son's stabbing of his father in the chest with a large knife, while saying "You won't hurt us anymore," indicates the intent to kill his father. The question arises as to whether circumstances exist to reduce this killing to voluntary manslaughter. Because of the previous violence that the father had inflicted on his son, the son most likely found himself exposed to a threat of force at the moment that his father uttered his angry words. Thus, there may have been adequate provocation at that time. However, the son did not kill until some time later. The issues then are whether there was sufficient time for a reasonable person's passions to have cooled and whether the son did cool off. If the time period was sufficient for a reasonable person's passions to cool or if the son did in fact cool off, there can be no reduction of this killing to manslaughter. Here, it is debatable whether the time period was sufficient for a reasonable person to have calmed down; the facts do not specify exactly how much time has passed. However, they state that the son went to a neighbor's house, dropped off his brother there, returned home, looked for a gun, thought about his options when he could not find a gun, and finally got a knife and waited a short time more for his father to awaken. These actions tend to indicate that probably more than a few minutes passed, but it is difficult to tell whether this period would be sufficient time for a reasonable person to cool off. They do indicate that the son was not acting under the heat of passion caused by his father's angry and threatening words; based on his actions, the son seems to have calmly made his plans to kill his father. Thus, the killing does not constitute voluntary manslaughter because the son was no longer acting under sufficient provocation. Therefore, (B) is wrong. (C) is wrong because the consistent beatings by the father do not provide a basis for reducing this crime to manslaughter if, at the time of the killing, the son's passions had cooled. There is no rule of "continuing provocation" that will result in a finding of manslaughter without regard for whether that particular killing was committed under adequate provocation, before a sufficient time for cooling off. (D) is wrong because the son did not have a right to use deadly force here. The use of deadly force in self-defense requires that the defendant reasonably believe that he is faced with ***imminent*** death or great bodily harm. There is no right to use deadly force if harm is merely threatened at a future time. Since the father had collapsed on the couch and the son had already left the house, the son faced no threat of imminent death or great bodily harm, and thus had no right to use deadly force in self-defense.

Answer to Question 6

(B) This choice states the Model Penal Code test. Pursuant to the Model Penal Code, a defendant is entitled to acquittal if he suffered from a mental disease or defect and as a result lacked substantial capacity to either: (i) appreciate the criminality of his conduct; or (ii) conform his conduct to the requirements of law. (A) is wrong because it would be helpful only if the jurisdiction followed the *Durham* insanity test, pursuant to which a defendant is entitled to acquittal if his crime was the product of mental disease or defect. (C) is wrong because it presents a valid defense under the *M'Naghten* rule, which provides for acquittal if a disease of the mind caused a defect of reason, such that the defendant lacked the ability at the time of his actions to either: (i) know the wrongfulness of his actions; or (ii) understand the nature and quality of his actions. (D) is wrong because it presents the irresistible impulse test, which provides for acquittal if, because of mental illness, the defendant was unable to control his actions or to conform his conduct to the law. Note that the Model Penal Code test combines the *M'Naghten* and irresistible impulse tests. Thus, choices (C) and (D) contain elements of the Model Penal Code test, but are not as good as (B) because the question asks for the set of facts that gives the defendant the greatest likelihood of being relieved of criminal liability. Therefore, (B), which sets forth the complete test used in the jurisdiction, is the best choice.

Answer to Question 7

(C) The friend can be convicted of assault. There are two actions covered by the crime of assault: (i) an attempted battery, and (ii) the intentional creation of a reasonable apprehension in the mind of the victim of imminent bodily harm. The friend's conduct fits within the second type of assault. He intended to create an apprehension of imminent bodily harm in the worker's mind, since he used a realistic toy gun and a mask and pretended to rob the worker. Thus, despite the fact that it was only to teach the worker a lesson, the friend committed an assault. (A) is wrong because the friend did not have the requisite intent for robbery. Robbery is a taking of another's personal property from the other's person by force or intimidation with the intent to permanently deprive him of his property. Here, the friend never intended to keep the money; thus, he did not have the intent necessary for robbery. (B) is wrong for the same reason. "Armed robbery" is robbery with a weapon; it also requires the intent to permanently deprive the owner of his property. This also makes (D) wrong, as larceny also requires the intent to permanently deprive the owner of his property.

Answer to Question 8

(D) The woman is not an accessory after the fact to burglary, and has committed neither larceny nor receipt of stolen property by keeping the coat. (A) is incorrect because, assuming that her boyfriend committed burglary to obtain the coat, the woman would be liable as an accessory after the fact only if she assisted him to avoid apprehension knowing that he had committed a felony. Here, even if the woman's acceptance of the fur coat helped the boyfriend by getting the stolen property out of his possession, it is clear that she had no knowledge at that time that he had committed burglary. (B) is incorrect both as to accessory after the fact to burglary (discussed above) and as to larceny. Larceny at common law requires a taking and carrying away of the tangible personal property of another by trespass, with intent to permanently deprive the other of the property. In this case, there was neither a taking and carrying away by the woman nor, at the time she accepted the coat, an intent to deprive the owner of it. Thus, she is not guilty of larceny. (C) is incorrect because, again, the woman's criminal intent was not formulated at the time she accepted the coat. Receipt of stolen property requires that defendant receive possession and

control of stolen personal property knowing it to have been stolen by another person and with the intent to permanently deprive the owner of it. The woman accepted the coat not knowing it to be stolen and not having the intent at that time to deprive the true owner of it. Her later decision to keep the coat does not relate back to her earlier conduct; there must be a concurrence of the mental state and the physical act for the crime to be committed.

Answer to Question 9

(D) The search warrant is valid because the affidavit accompanying it is sufficiently detailed to allow a determination of probable cause. A warrant must be based on a showing of probable cause. Along with a request for a warrant, a police officer must submit to a magistrate an affidavit setting forth sufficient underlying circumstances to enable the magistrate to make a determination of probable cause independent of the officer's conclusions. The affidavit may be based on an informer's statements. The sufficiency of the affidavit is evaluated according to the "totality of the circumstances." There must be sufficient information for the magistrate to be able to make a common sense evaluation of probable cause. Among the factors determinative of probable cause are the informer's reliability, credibility, and basis of knowledge. Here, the officer's affidavit indicates that the informer has previously proved to be reliable by providing accurate information in other cases. This, in turn, enhances the credibility of the informer. Also, the informer's knowledge is based on his having personally placed bets with the neighbor at his apartment. Thus, the officer's affidavit is supported by sufficient underlying circumstances to allow a magistrate's finding that there was a showing of probable cause. (A) is incorrect because probable cause for issuance of a search warrant may be based on hearsay, if the information comes from a reliable informer. (B) is incorrect because the failure to disclose the identity of the informer does not necessarily invalidate the search warrant. The identity of an informer does not have to be revealed to allow the magistrate to make a determination of probable cause. The magistrate may make this determination based on the police officer's information about the informer showing reliability, credibility, and knowledge. The magistrate need not personally question the informer. (C) is incorrect because it is overbroad. An informer's identity need not be revealed only if there is sufficient other evidence to make a probable cause determination.

Answer to Question 10

(C) Introduction of the proffered evidence would in effect penalize the man for exercising his right to be free from compulsory self-incrimination. *Miranda* warnings are given to safeguard the Fifth Amendment right to be free from compelled self-incrimination. Prior to interrogation, a person in custody must be clearly informed that he has the right to remain silent and anything he says can be used against him in court. These warnings implicitly assure that silence will carry no penalty. Thus, a prosecutor may not comment on a defendant's silence after the defendant is arrested and has received the *Miranda* warnings. To allow the prosecutor to introduce evidence of the man's silence in the face of the woman's accusation would run counter to the very purpose of the *Miranda* warnings, which is to allow the defendant to remain silent without fear of being prejudiced by such silence. The man was no more required to respond to the woman's accusation than he would have been to an accusation or question coming from the police. The man's privilege against compelled self-incrimination would be meaningless if he were required to either respond to the woman or have his failure to respond introduced against him. (A) is wrong because the mere fact that evidence is true does not render such evidence admissible. Evidence that runs afoul of some rule of evidentiary exclusion (*e.g.,* a statement that is hearsay not subject to any of the exclusions to the hearsay rule) or that would violate a right of constitutional magnitude is not admissible, regardless of whether it is true. Because evidence of the man's silence would violate

his Fifth Amendment right to be free of compelled self-incrimination, this evidence is not admissible, even though it is true. (B) is wrong because it turns the *Miranda* warnings on their head. The warnings are to apprise the suspect that he has a right to remain silent, and that if he chooses to say something, this statement can be used against him. The warnings do not, as (B) suggests, apprise the suspect that he must respond to questions or accusations, and that a failure to respond can be used against him. As has been explained above, the crux of the *Miranda* warnings is the right to remain silent, and to be free of coercion to speak at all. (D) is wrong for two reasons. (D) implies that the evidence would be admissible if the man's lawyer were present at the time of the incident. Regardless of the presence of counsel, admission of evidence as to the man's silence in the face of the woman's accusation would violate the man's privilege against compelled self-incrimination. Also, events had not yet reached a stage at which the man was entitled to counsel. At the time of this incident, the man was waiting to take part in a lineup. The facts indicate that the man had not yet been charged with a crime. The right to counsel applies to post-charge lineups, but not to pre-charge lineups. Note also that the woman's accusation did not even occur in a lineup setting, but during an inadvertent viewing of the man. Thus, the right to counsel had not yet attached.

Answer to Question 11

(A) If the jurisdiction uses the *M'Naghten* test, the teacher's best argument is that he did not know that his act was wrong. The *M'Naghten* test provides for a defendant's acquittal if he has a disease of the mind causing a defect of reason so that at the time of his actions he lacked the ability to know the wrongfulness of his actions or understand the nature and quality of his actions. (A) states one branch of this test and is consistent with the facts (which state that the teacher did not understand that the killing was wrongful), and so it is the teacher's best argument. (C) is wrong because it is contrary to the facts. Although (C) also states part of the *M'Naghten* test, the teacher's illness has not left him so irrational that he is unable to comprehend that his act would result in the student's death. He seemed to have known that he was killing his student; he just did not know that killing was wrong. (B) is wrong because although the teacher did lack the substantial capacity to appreciate the criminality of his act, this is not a criterion for insanity in a state that follows the *M'Naghten* test; rather, (B) states the Model Penal Code standard. (D) is wrong because it states conduct outside the scope of the *M'Naghten* test. Also, the facts do not show that the teacher's mental illness had deprived him of his volitional controls.

Answer to Question 12

(D) The stagehand cannot be convicted of any of these crimes. Murder is the unlawful killing of a human being with malice aforethought. Malice aforethought exists if the defendant has any of the following states of mind: (i) intent to kill; (ii) intent to inflict great bodily injury; (iii) awareness of an unjustifiably high risk to human life; or (iv) intent to commit a felony. Modern statutes often divide murder into degrees. For instance, a deliberate and premeditated killing (*i.e.,* one in which the defendant made the decision to kill in a cool and dispassionate manner, and actually reflected on the idea of killing) may be designated first degree murder. Second degree murder is generally a killing with malice aforethought that is not specifically made first degree murder. Here, the stagehand did not even realize that he was pointing a real gun at the actor. Thus, the stagehand did not possess any of the states of mind that would constitute malice aforethought (*i.e.,* he did not intend to kill or to inflict great bodily injury, nor was he aware of a high risk to human life). Consequently, the stagehand cannot be convicted of murder, either first or second degree. Thus, (A) is incorrect. Voluntary manslaughter

is an intentional killing distinguishable from murder by the existence of adequate provocation. At the time of the killing, the defendant must have been acting under a provocation that would arouse sudden and intense passion in the mind of an ordinary person so as to cause him to lose self-control, with an insufficient time between the provocation and the killing for the passions of a reasonable person to cool. The stagehand cannot be convicted of voluntary manslaughter because: (i) his killing of the actor was accidental, rather than intentional; and (ii) in shooting the actor, he was not acting under any type of provocation. Therefore, (B) is incorrect. Involuntary manslaughter occurs when a death is caused by criminal negligence. There is negligence when a person fails to be aware that a substantial and unjustifiable risk exists or that a result will follow, and such failure constitutes a substantial deviation from the standard of care that a reasonable person would exercise under the circumstances. Criminal negligence requires a greater deviation from the "reasonable person" standard than is required for civil liability. The stagehand's firing the gun at the actor was probably negligent. However, the stagehand's conduct did not rise to the level of criminal negligence, because he had insufficient knowledge of the true risk posed by his actions. If the stagehand knew he was using a real gun, it would probably have been criminally negligent to have pointed it at the actor and pulled the trigger. However, the stagehand actually believed that he was using a ***stage gun.*** Thus, he cannot be said to have taken the type of very unreasonable risk that would constitute criminal negligence. Therefore, (C) is incorrect.

Answer to Question 13

(B) The pedestrian's actions were motivated by adequate provocation and therefore manslaughter is the more appropriate crime. Voluntary manslaughter is an intentional killing distinguishable from murder by adequate provocation. Provocation is sufficient to reduce the killing from murder to manslaughter if it would arouse sudden and intense passion in an ordinary person, and there has been insufficient time for the passions of a reasonable person to cool. Also, the defendant must actually be provoked and have acted under that provocation (*i.e.,* did not cool off). Here, the pedestrian's use of a deadly weapon under these circumstances shows that she intended to kill the robber or at least inflict great bodily harm. However, the commission of a violent felony (especially one that included a staggering blow) is provocation that would arouse a reasonable person and apparently did arouse the pedestrian. She acted very quickly after her attack, and thus a reasonable person would not have cooled off nor, apparently, had the pedestrian. Thus, she had the intent and provocation for manslaughter. However, she did not intend to kill the bystander. Under the transferred intent doctrine, if a defendant intended injury to a person, and in trying to carry out that intent caused similar injury to another, her intent is transferred from the intended person to the one harmed. In addition, any mitigating circumstances that the defendant could have asserted against the intended victim (such as provocation) will also usually be transferred. Therefore, the pedestrian can be guilty of voluntary manslaughter for the death of the bystander. (*Note:* It is possible that the pedestrian could try to escape conviction altogether in some jurisdictions by claiming that the intent she formed was "justified" as an effort to prevent the escape of a fleeing felon. However, the question asks only whether she has committed murder or manslaughter.) (A) is wrong because it overlooks the transferred intent doctrine. If the pedestrian intended to kill the robber, this intent will be transferred to the bystander and she cannot escape criminal liability simply because she hit the wrong person. (C) is wrong because, as explained above, her intent was mitigated by adequate provocation, and thus manslaughter is the more appropriate crime. (D) is wrong because even though the pedestrian was in no danger when she shot at the robber, she was at least acting under adequate provocation so that she should be convicted of voluntary manslaughter rather than murder.

Answer to Question 14

(B) Although the mother, as the owner of the house, had the authority to consent to a search of the house, she had no right to consent to the search of the trunk. A warrantless search by the police is valid if they have a voluntary and intelligent consent to the search. Any person with equal right to the use or occupation of the property may consent to a search, and any evidence found may be used against the other owners or occupants. The search is valid as long as the police reasonably believed that the consenting party had a right to use or occupy the premises, even if she in fact lacked such right. A parent generally has authority to consent to a search of a child's room (even an adult child) as long as the parent has access to the room. However, depending on the child's age, the parent may not have authority to consent to a search of locked containers in the room. Here, the mother owns the house. As the owner, she clearly had the right to the use and occupation of the house and could thus consent to the warrantless police search. However, the fact that her son kept the trunk locked, with the only key in his possession, indicates that he had the exclusive right of use and access to the trunk. Because the mother told the police that the trunk was always locked and that her son had the only key, they could not have reasonably believed that she had a right of use or access to it. Therefore, consent to search the trunk was not given by a person with a right to give such consent. Absent proper consent, the warrantless search of the trunk was invalid. (D) is incorrect because the mother's ownership of the house does not confer on her a right to use or gain access to the locked trunk. Without such a right, she could not validly consent to a search of the trunk. (A) is incorrect because knowledge of the right to withhold consent is not a prerequisite to establishing a voluntary and intelligent consent (although it is a factor to be considered). Thus, the failure of the police to inform the mother that she could refuse permission for the search does not automatically invalidate her consent (and the subsequent search). (C) is incorrect. *Parens patriae* is a doctrine that allows the government to take the role of a parent or guardian of someone who is under a disability (such as minority). As the mother was actually the suspect's mother, the doctrine has no application here.

Answer to Question 15

(D) The trader is not guilty of any crime because she had no legal duty to help the traveler. For virtually all crimes, including homicides, one element that must be proved is a physical act or an unlawful failure to act by the defendant. Failure to act will constitute a crime only where there is a legal duty to act and it is reasonably possible to perform the act. Here, it would have been very easy for the trader to save the traveler by allowing him into her cabin. However, she had no legal duty to do so. A legal duty can arise by statute, contract, a close relationship between the victim and the defendant, the voluntary assumption of care by the defendant, or the creation of the peril by the defendant. None of these conditions is indicated in the facts here. Thus, the trader can be convicted of no crime. Note that if the trader had allowed the traveler into her cabin but subsequently kicked him out, the result might be different because she would then have voluntarily assumed the care of the traveler. (A), (B), and (C) are all incorrect because each of these homicide crimes requires the element of a physical act or unlawful failure to act.

Answer to Question 16

(A) Although the patient may have been guilty of murder had the pedestrian been killed, it does not necessarily follow that she is guilty of attempted murder when she almost killed the pedestrian. Murder does not require the intent to kill; an awareness of an unjustifiably high risk to human life will suffice. Like all attempt crimes, ***attempted*** murder is a specific intent crime. Thus, the intent to kill is required. Since the patient did not intend to kill the pedestrian, she cannot be convicted of attempted murder. (B) is wrong because, although the patient can avoid guilt for attempted murder, she cannot do so for the reason given here. Attempt requires an act beyond mere preparation for the offense. If the patient had the required intent to kill, her act of running down the pedestrian would be sufficient for attempted murder. (C) is wrong. It is often loosely said that one is presumed to intend the natural and probable consequences of her act. This is not to be taken literally. It means that if a particular result is a natural and probable consequence of what a defendant does, the fact finder ***may*** draw the inference from such circumstance that the defendant intended that result. Here, however, it is likely that the jury would infer that the patient, who wanted to keep a doctor's appointment, never intended to kill a pedestrian. (D) is wrong for the same reason. It is simply another phrasing of (C). But, as explained above, attempted murder requires an actual intent to kill, not a fictitious, imputed, or constructive one.

Answer to Question 17

(C) Because this was an inventory incident to incarceration, the suspect's rights were not violated. After a valid arrest, the police may make a warrantless search of a defendant's personal effects as part of an established procedure incident to incarceration. This type of search is valid under the Fourth Amendment. Here, it appears that the suspect was validly arrested and incarcerated. Therefore, the officer could inventory the suspect's possessions. Her discovery of the inscription on the watch, as she examined it to inventory it, is within the scope of a valid inventory. (A) is wrong because a valid inventory allows an examination of the items so that they can be properly identified in the inventory. As mentioned, the officer's examination of the watch was within the scope of a valid inventory. (B) is wrong because, as mentioned, a warrant is not required for an inventory incident to incarceration. (D) is wrong because the fact that an item gave rise to probable cause to believe that another crime had been committed cannot be used to justify a search of the item. The item must have been searchable in the first instance.

Answer to Question 18

(B) The runaway's best defense is that she cannot be convicted under the statute because it was designed to protect minors. Statutory rape is the crime of carnal knowledge of a female under the age of consent (generally under age 16 or 18). This crime, by definition, limits criminal liability to the male; a female cannot be convicted. However, one who may not be convicted as a principal may be convicted as an accomplice. Therefore, a woman acting as an accomplice to the crime could be convicted. If, however, the legislative intent is to protect members of a class from exploitation or overbearing, members of that class are presumed to be immune from liability, even if they participate in the crime. Here, the runaway can argue that the crime of statutory rape was intended to protect minors from exploitation, and therefore the legislative intent is that she, as a minor, be immune from prosecution. (A) is wrong because an accomplice may be convicted before the principal. Although the common law rule required that the principal's guilt be determined first, or at least at a joint trial, this rule has been abandoned by most jurisdictions. (C) is wrong because it is too broad; a minor may be an accomplice to a crime. To be convicted as an accomplice, a person must have acted with the intent to aid or encourage the principal in the commission of the crime. As long as a child is old enough to be able to form this intent, she could be convicted as an accomplice. A 15-year-old is certainly capable of forming that intent. (Even under the common law presumptions, children over age 14 are treated as adults.) (D) is wrong because the man could be convicted despite the runaway's consent. Consent is not a defense to statutory rape; even if the female willingly participates in the sexual acts, the male may be convicted. Thus, the runaway's consent, or her status as a prostitute, is not the reason she may not be convicted as an accomplice.

Set 2 Answer Sheet

1. Ⓐ Ⓑ Ⓒ Ⓓ
2. Ⓐ Ⓑ Ⓒ Ⓓ
3. Ⓐ Ⓑ Ⓒ Ⓓ
4. Ⓐ Ⓑ Ⓒ Ⓓ
5. Ⓐ Ⓑ Ⓒ Ⓓ
6. Ⓐ Ⓑ Ⓒ Ⓓ
7. Ⓐ Ⓑ Ⓒ Ⓓ
8. Ⓐ Ⓑ Ⓒ Ⓓ
9. Ⓐ Ⓑ Ⓒ Ⓓ
10. Ⓐ Ⓑ Ⓒ Ⓓ
11. Ⓐ Ⓑ Ⓒ Ⓓ
12. Ⓐ Ⓑ Ⓒ Ⓓ
13. Ⓐ Ⓑ Ⓒ Ⓓ
14. Ⓐ Ⓑ Ⓒ Ⓓ
15. Ⓐ Ⓑ Ⓒ Ⓓ
16. Ⓐ Ⓑ Ⓒ Ⓓ
17. Ⓐ Ⓑ Ⓒ Ⓓ
18. Ⓐ Ⓑ Ⓒ Ⓓ

CRIMINAL LAW QUESTIONS - SET 2

Question 1

An officer went to an apartment to execute a properly obtained search warrant during an investigation of an operation making counterfeit watches. When he arrived he shouted, "Police, open up," but he did not wait before entering the apartment through the unlocked front door. The officer found the defendant half-asleep in a back room, with a workbench for assembling counterfeit watches nearby. Along with some completed counterfeit watches, the officer found a toolset used for making watches and receipts for various watch components in a drawer of the workbench, all of which the officer seized as evidence. The defendant was charged with illegal counterfeiting. At a preliminary hearing, his attorney moves to suppress the evidence obtained during the search.

Should the court grant his motion?

(A) No, because regardless of whether the search warrant itself was valid, the evidence was in "plain view" upon entry.

(B) No, because the exclusionary rule does not apply to the officer's Fourth Amendment violation.

(C) Yes, because the officer failed to wait long enough prior to entering the apartment.

(D) Yes, because the door was unlocked.

Question 2

The police of a resort town discovered that a well-known cat burglar was currently living in town under an assumed name. To try to catch her in the act of burglary, an undercover officer approached the burglar with a plan for a burglary. The undercover officer told the burglar that he knew who she was and that he had a plan to steal jewels from someone staying in one of the town's resorts. The burglar initially refused the offer; however, after lengthy cajoling, she finally agreed to the plan.

As the time for the burglary drew near, the burglar had second thoughts. Three hours before the theft was scheduled to take place, the burglar called the police and told them of the plan. She told them that she was not going to show up, but that her cohort (the undercover officer) would be there, and told them how to recognize the undercover officer.

Is the burglar guilty of conspiracy at common law?

(A) Yes, because the burglar made an agreement with the undercover officer to commit the theft.

(B) No, because there was no agreement.

(C) No, because the intended crime was never completed.

(D) No, because the burglar effectively withdrew.

Question 3

A husband and wife were charged with stealing credit cards and charging expensive items on the misappropriated cards. An attorney was appointed by the court to represent the couple jointly. At the preliminary hearing, the judge found that the attorney would have no conflict representing both defendants in the joint trial. Halfway through the trial, however, a conflict arose between the defenses of the husband and wife. At the wife's request, the attorney moved that another attorney be appointed to represent the wife and that a mistrial be declared. The trial judge moved favorably on the attorney's motion.

Another attorney was appointed to represent the wife, and as soon as the wife's trial began, her attorney moved to dismiss the case on the ground that jeopardy had attached during the wife's first trial and that she was being retried in violation of the United States Constitution.

Should the judge grant the wife's attorney's motion?

(A) Yes, because jeopardy attached when the jury began to hear evidence in the first trial.

(B) Yes, because the judge incorrectly ruled that there would be no conflict of interest from the joint representation.

(C) No, because the wife requested the mistrial.

(D) No, because it is premature to move for a dismissal based on double jeopardy until the defendant is convicted.

Question 4

A disgruntled customer of a business entered its factory and announced that the products from the factory were terrible. He set off a device that filled the factory with fumes, and then swiftly ran out the main entrance. He rushed past a visitor who was entering the factory, passing just inches in front of her. She was taken aback, which caused her to trip and strike her head on the pavement. The customer was promptly apprehended and charged with the misdemeanor of breach of the peace for his conduct in the factory and charged with assault against the visitor.

Which of the following represents the customer's best defense to the charge of assault?

(A) The underlying offense was a misdemeanor rather than a felony.

(B) The customer made no physical contact with the visitor.

(C) The visitor's injury was not a foreseeable consequence of the customer's criminal activity.

(D) The customer lacked the requisite mens rea.

Question 5

An employee of the state government always received his state paycheck on the latest workday of the month. The employee was not a good money manager, and just barely managed to make it from paycheck to paycheck each month. On the second to the last workday of the month, the employee had $45 in his checking account, and, needing to buy a birthday gift for his sister, he wrote a check to a gift boutique for $100. He knew that he would be receiving his paycheck the next day, so he could deposit the paycheck before the check would be sent to the bank.

However, unknown to the employee, the state legislature was having a budget impasse. Because the state constitution prohibited any deficit spending, state employees were not paid as usual. Without a paycheck to deposit, the check written to the gift boutique was returned for insufficient funds. The merchant complained to the police, who arrested the employee and charged him under a statute that prohibited "issuing a check knowing that it is drawn against insufficient funds, with intent to defraud the payee of the check."

What should be the outcome of the employee's prosecution?

(A) Not guilty, because the employee intended to deposit his paycheck the next day.

(B) Not guilty, because it was reasonable for the employee to expect that he would receive his paycheck as usual.

(C) Guilty, because the employee knew when he wrote the check that he did not have sufficient funds in his account to honor it.

(D) Guilty, because reliance on a future source of income does not vitiate the employee's violation of the statute when he wrote the check.

Question 6

A political activist, stopped while driving his car by a police officer in a patrol car, believed that the officer had stopped him solely because a large sign painted on the side of his vehicle proclaimed him a member of a controversial political organization. When additional police units arrived at the scene, the activist was convinced it was a setup. Although unarmed and slightly built, the activist swung his fist at the original officer. Another officer, seeing this, drew his revolver and shot the activist in the stomach. The activist then seized the revolver of the officer he had punched and shot at the second officer, missing him and killing an onlooker.

At the activist's murder trial, his expert witness, who was not contradicted at trial, testified that the activist was rendered unconscious by being shot in the stomach. In the absence of a felony murder or misdemeanor manslaughter rule, the most serious crime for which the activist can be convicted if the jury accepts the expert's testimony is:

(A) Murder, because the activist started the fight in which he eventually shot the bystander.

(B) Murder, because although the killing might have been mitigated as to the second officer, no mitigating circumstances would apply to the innocent bystander.

(C) Manslaughter, because the activist did not intend to kill the onlooker.

(D) Neither murder nor manslaughter, because the activist was unconscious when he shot the onlooker.

Question 7

A wife suffered from a particularly virulent form of cancer, and had lapsed into a nearly comatose state. Since the doctors had indicated that any treatment they could prescribe would be of little value, her husband decided to administer various poisons to his wife, thinking that they might stimulate her natural body defenses, or kill the cancer cells, resulting in her recovery. He tried doses of many different types of poison. Despite his ministrations, his wife died three days later. An autopsy performed by the county coroner established the cause of death as cancer.

If the husband is prosecuted for the murder of his wife, the best reason why he would be acquitted is that:

(A) He was trying to save her life.

(B) He did not have the necessary malice for his actions to constitute murder.

(C) Medical science had given her up for dead.

(D) He did not cause her death.

Question 8

At the defendant's prosecution for robbery of a drugstore, the main prosecution witness testified that the defendant had asked her to drive him to the town where the drugstore was located. The witness testified that the defendant did not explain his purpose for going to the town, and that he had stopped at a relative's house along the way to pick up a bundle that could have been the sawed-off shotgun used by the robber. On cross-examination, the defendant's attorney asked a number of pointed questions of the witness, implying that the defendant had asked her to drive to the town so that he could visit relatives there and suggesting that the witness had obtained a sawed-off shotgun for use by a confederate. The defendant did not testify on his own behalf.

In final argument, the prosecutor called the jury's attention to the two versions of events suggested by the witness's testimony on direct examination and the defense attorney's questions on cross-examination, and then said, "Remember, you only heard one of the two people testify who know what really happened that day."

If the defendant is convicted of robbery, his conviction will probably be:

(A) Overturned, because the prosecutor's comment referred to the defendant's failure

to testify, a violation of his Fifth Amendment privilege of silence.

(B) Overturned, because under the circumstances the attack on the witness's credibility was not strong enough to permit the prosecutor to mention the defendant's failure to testify in rebuttal.

(C) Upheld, because the prosecutor is entitled to comment on the state of the evidence.

(D) Upheld, because even if it was error to comment on the defendant's failure to testify, the error was harmless beyond a reasonable doubt.

Question 9

A police officer often visited an art gallery on his lunch break and became friends with one of the gallery's salespersons, whom he found to be honest and forthright. After hearing rumors that the gallery's owner sometimes dealt in stolen artwork, the officer decided to investigate. Acting without a warrant, he snuck into a back room and discovered various crates addressed to and from a country that was a well-known conduit for stolen artwork. The officer questioned his salesperson friend about the crates. She told the officer that she never saw what was inside any of the crates, but that she assumed they contained artwork for the owner's private collection that he maintained at home. The officer obtained a search warrant for the owner's home based on the foregoing information. Upon executing the warrant, the officer found several pieces of stolen artwork at the owner's home. The owner was subsequently tried for receiving stolen property. The salesperson was to be called to testify about what she knew about the gallery owner's activities related to the procurement of artwork.

The salesperson's testimony will most likely be:

(A) Inadmissible, because it is the fruit of the poisonous tree.

(B) Inadmissible, because she is an unindicted co-conspirator.

(C) Admissible, because she is unindicted and therefore has no privilege against compelled self-incrimination.

(D) Admissible.

Question 10

A tenant vacated an apartment because he could no longer afford the rent. To ensure that the delinquent tenant made up for past arrearages, the landlord would not let him remove his personal property from the apartment. The tenant found a temporary place to stay with a friend, who wanted to help the tenant get his property back. The tenant remembered that the apartment would be vacant the upcoming weekend and that the landlord would be out of town, so he suggested that they break into the apartment and take the property then. They drove the tenant's pickup to the apartment, and the friend entered through an unlocked window. The friend then opened the door for the tenant, and the pair collected the personal property. While the tenant was getting ready to drive away, the friend returned to the apartment and carried out some of the fixtures to the apartment. At this point, police officers who had been alerted by neighbors arrived and arrested the pair.

The tenant's best defense to a charge of burglary would be that:

(A) There was no "entry," since as an occupant of the apartment, he consented to the entry.

(B) There was no breaking, since the window was unlocked.

(C) There was no intent to commit a felony.

(D) He only took his own property.

Question 11

A detective obtained a valid search warrant for the home of a man suspected of manufacturing methampetamine and counterfeiting. The man was not at home, but his wife told the detective that he was at their weekend cabin. After announcing his purpose, the detective searched the home and found a large sum of cash, along with a printing plate for $20 bills and several large stacks of fresh $20 bills. Thereafter, the detective went to the man's cabin with an arrest warrant in hand. After knocking on the door, the officer found a note that the man had left for his wife indicating that he had gone out for dinner and would be back late in the evening. No lights were on in the cabin, and no car or other means of transportation were present. The detective entered the cabin and found several boxes of the over-the-counter drugs and other ingredients for making methamphetamine lying out in the open. The man was indicted for various criminal offenses, including the illegal manufacture of methamphetamine and counterfeiting.

As to the search at the man's cabin following the search of his home:

(A) This is a valid warrantless plain view search.

(B) This is a valid warrantless search incident to arrest.

(C) This is an invalid warrantless search because the detective lacked probable cause.

(D) This is an invalid warrantless search because the detective did not have a warrant.

Question 12

A farmer was in the middle of plowing his field when his tractor broke down. While attempting to repair it, he discovered that he needed a special wrench. He knew that his neighbor used the same type of tractor and kept a large cache of tools in his basement. Not wanting to make the long drive into town to buy one wrench that he probably would not use much, the farmer went to his neighbor's house to borrow the wrench. However, no one was home so he decided to look in his neighbor's basement for the wrench, thinking that he would return it before the neighbor came back. To gain entry, the farmer opened an unlocked window and climbed through the opening to the basement. Once inside, the farmer found the tool and took it with him to work on the tractor. His neighbor returned soon after and contacted the police when he discovered that one of his tools was missing. The police determined that the farmer took the tool and he was charged with burglary.

What is the farmer's best defense against that charge in a common law jurisdiction?

(A) Nobody actually lived in the basement.

(B) The farmer knew that the house was unoccupied and would not have entered without permission had the neighbor been home.

(C) The farmer entered the house through an unlocked window.

(D) The farmer intended only to keep the wrench for a couple of hours.

Question 13

The victim owned a cottage in an ocean resort area. He stayed there only during the summer months, and left the cottage unoccupied during the balance of the year. The defendant, a resident of a neighboring cottage, was aware of this practice. For a change in his routine, however, the victim decided to spend a week at the cabin in the off-season. Unaware that the victim was occupying the cottage, the defendant decided to borrow a portable television set that he knew the victim kept in the cottage. To avoid being seen, he entered the cottage late at night, using a key under the front doormat. He found the television set, disconnected it, and headed for the rear of the house to leave. He opened the kitchen door and found the victim seated there in the dark, having a late night snack. Both men were startled and neither man recognized the other in the dark. The defendant assumed that the victim was a burglar, and was afraid that he might be

armed. Trying to flee the kitchen as quickly as possible, the defendant dropped the television set in the middle of the kitchen floor. As the set hit the floor, the picture tube exploded with a loud noise. The noise so frightened the victim that he had an immediate heart attack and died.

If the defendant is charged with felony murder as the result of the victim's death, his best defense would be that:

(A) He did not intend to kill the victim.

(B) His only intent was to borrow the television set for a few days.

(C) Larceny is not an inherently dangerous crime, and it was not being committed in an inherently dangerous manner.

(D) The victim's heart attack was an unforeseeable consequence of the defendant's acts.

Question 14

Two men drinking at a local bar got into a heated argument. The small, slightly built man knew that the large burly man had a short fuse, yet continued to argue with him. The larger man insulted the smaller man's religion and national origin, whereupon the smaller man spat on the other, who responded by pouring a glass of beer over the smaller man's head. The smaller man then punched the larger man in the nose, catching him off guard and knocking him to the floor. The larger man got to his feet, pulled out a knife, and advanced toward the other, who was standing by the door. The smaller man reached inside his boot and drew out a small gun and shot the larger man, killing him instantly. The jurisdiction makes it a crime to carry a concealed weapon. The smaller man is charged with murder.

If the smaller man claims the killing was in self-defense, which of the following is the most helpful to the prosecution?

(A) The smaller man initiated the physical violence by spitting on the larger man, and his punching the larger man in the nose is what caused him to threaten the smaller man with the knife.

(B) The smaller man was standing very close to the door and could have broken off the affray if he had chosen to do so.

(C) The use or possession of the type of gun that the man used is a crime under state law, and carrying any concealed weapon is a separate crime.

(D) Before any violence erupted, the smaller man was aware that the larger man was becoming increasingly quarrelsome and belligerent, and continued to drink and argue with him notwithstanding.

Question 15

The defendant was at a bar with a couple of friends when he spotted a man who had gotten the defendant's friend fired from a job several weeks ago. Since that time, the defendant had been verbally harassing the man and calling him names. This particular night, the defendant went over to the man's table and flirted with his girlfriend. The man was infuriated after having taken the defendant's abuse for so long, so he jumped up and attacked the defendant with a knife. The defendant could have easily run away, but instead grabbed the man and slammed him backwards. The man went crashing through the front window and was severely cut by the broken glass. He died before he could be taken to the hospital.

At common law, the defendant would most likely be guilty of:

(A) Murder.

(B) Voluntary manslaughter.

(C) Involuntary manslaughter.

(D) None of the above.

Question 16

The defendant rented a room for two nights at a motel. The room was equipped with a large color television set. The defendant decided to steal the set, pawn it, and keep the proceeds. To conceal his identity as the thief, he contrived to make his room look as if it had been burglarized. However, he was traced through the pawnbroker and arrested.

On these facts, the defendant is guilty of:

(A) Embezzlement.

(B) False pretenses.

(C) Larceny.

(D) Larceny by trick.

Question 17

The owner of a furnished cottage leased it to another for one year. While this lease was in effect, the cottage owner found herself in immediate need of cash, and decided to burn down the cottage to collect the insurance on it. She waited until one evening when the tenant was away. The cottage owner then used her own key to gain access to it. To make it appear that the fire was caused accidentally by the tenant, she soaked one end of the mattress on the bed in the bedroom with gasoline and then left a lighted cigarette burning at the other end of the mattress. She planned that the cigarette would ignite the mattress and that when the fire smoldered to the area soaked in gasoline, the entire bed would burst into flames, and the resulting fire would destroy the house. However, the tenant returned home earlier than expected and discovered the fire just as the mattress burst into flames. He immediately put it out with a fire extinguisher. A police investigation revealed the cottage owner's activities.

The cottage owner is guilty of:

(A) Burglary as to the house and arson as to the mattress.

(B) Neither burglary nor arson because she owned the structure and its contents.

(C) Burglary and attempted arson.

(D) Attempted arson but not burglary because she entered with her own key.

Question 18

The police suspected that a man was dealing in illegal drugs. They gathered a sufficient amount of evidence and obtained a search warrant. They went to the man's home, arrested him, and conducted a thorough search. They found and confiscated large amounts of cocaine.

At a preliminary hearing, the man brought a motion to suppress the evidence against him. The prosecution informed the court that the warrant had been issued on the basis of information provided by an informant. The man's attorney requested the prosecution to produce the informant for questioning. When the prosecution refused to do so, the attorney made a further motion to suppress all of the evidence against his client obtained from the search on the basis that his client was denied the right of confrontation by the prosecution's refusal to produce the informant.

The attorney's motion to suppress should be:

(A) Granted, because the denial of the right of cross-examination effectively prevents a fair trial.

(B) Granted, because the rights of a defendant override any right of the police to keep an informant anonymous.

(C) Denied, because defendants have no right to know the identity of informants.

(D) Denied, because the prosecution is not required to either name or produce the informant.

CRIMINAL LAW ANSWERS - SET 2

Answer to Question 1

(B) The evidence is admissible because the exclusionary rule does not apply to violation of the "knock and announce" rule. In executing a search warrant, police officers must knock and announce their authority and purpose, and wait a reasonable time for an occupant to respond, except when there is reasonable suspicion, based on facts, that the announcement would be dangerous or futile or would inhibit the investigation (*e.g.*, lead to destruction of evidence). [Richards v. Wisconsin (1997)] Here, the officer knocked and announced his presence, but did not wait for the door to be answered. Nothing in the facts indicates that the officer had any reason to suspect that waiting would endanger him or lead to the destruction of evidence. Thus, the knock-and-announce requirements were violated. However, the Supreme Court has held that the exclusionary rule does not apply to knock-and-announce violations. [Hudson v. Michigan (2006)] Therefore, although the knock-and-announce rule may have been violated, the evidence may nonetheless be admitted into evidence because the search was otherwise valid. (C) is incorrect in that it states the rule prior to *Hudson v. Michigan.* Although the officer may have violated the knock-and-announce rule by failing to wait for a sufficient period before opening the door, the remedy for such a violation is not the suppression of the evidence. (A) is incorrect because the plain view exception to the warrant requirement applies only when the police: (i) are legitimately on the premises; (ii) discover evidence, fruits or instrumentalities of crime, or contraband; (iii) see such evidence in plain view; and (iv) have probable cause to believe that the item is evidence, contraband, or a fruit or instrumentality of crime. Because of the officer's failure to knock and announce, he was not legitimately on the seller's premises. Thus, the seizure cannot be justified under the plain view exception. (D) is incorrect because even though the door was unlocked, it does not mean that the officer was justified in entering without knocking, announcing, and waiting. The "knock and announce" requirement still applies, although the remedy for a violation is not the suppression of evidence.

Answer to Question 2

(B) There was an insufficient agreement for conspiracy liability at common law. Conspiracy consists of: (i) an agreement between two or more persons; (ii) an intent to enter into an agreement; and (iii) an intent to achieve the objective of the agreement. In addition, most states require an act in furtherance of the conspiracy, although an act of mere preparation will usually suffice. The agreement requirement means that the parties must agree to accomplish the same objective by mutual action. There must be a meeting of at least two "guilty minds"; *i.e.,* between two or more persons who are actually committing themselves to the scheme. If one person in a two-party conspiracy is only feigning agreement, the other person cannot be convicted of conspiracy at common law. Here, the officer, in his undercover capacity, was simply trying to set up a situation in which the burglar would be caught in the act. Thus, the undercover officer merely pretended to reach an agreement with the burglar to commit a burglary. At no time did the undercover officer actually commit himself to the burglary. Therefore, there could have been no agreement of two "guilty minds." Absent the requisite agreement, the burglar cannot be guilty of conspiracy. (A) is incorrect because, as explained above, there was no agreement sufficient for a conspiracy conviction, since the undercover officer never intended to commit the burglary. (C) is incorrect because completion of the substantive crime is not necessary for a conviction of conspiracy. Consequently, although the actual burglary was not consummated, this would not preclude a conviction of conspiracy to commit burglary. (D) is incorrect because withdrawal is not a defense to a charge of conspiracy. Note that, by withdrawing, a person may ***limit her liability*** for subsequent

acts of the other members of the conspiracy. However, this question pertains to the burglar's potential guilt for conspiracy. As applied to the conspiracy charge, withdrawal will not afford a defense to the burglar.

Answer to Question 3

(C) Although jeopardy attached in the wife's first trial, her retrial is not barred because she initiated the grant of the mistrial in her first trial. As a general rule, the right to be free of double jeopardy for the same offense bars a retrial for the same offense once jeopardy has attached in the first trial. However, one of the exceptions permitting retrial even if jeopardy has attached is when a mistrial is granted in the first trial at the request of the defendant on any ground not constituting an acquittal on the merits. Here, the wife requested the mistrial because a conflict arose between the defenses of her and her co-defendant in the joint trial, and the judge granted the mistrial solely to allow the wife to obtain another attorney. Thus, no acquittal on the merits occurred and the double jeopardy rule does not apply. (A) is incorrect for several reasons. Merely because jeopardy attaches does not mean that the double jeopardy rule will apply; retrial will be permitted under certain exceptions, one of which is applicable here. Furthermore, (A) is not a correct statement of law. Jeopardy attaches in a jury trial when the jury is impaneled and sworn in, even if it has not yet heard any evidence. (B) is incorrect because the judge's finding at the preliminary hearing stage appears to be an honest error rather than bad faith conduct. In the absence of bad faith conduct by the judge or prosecutor designed to force the defendant to seek a mistrial, the defendant's securing of a mistrial does not preclude a retrial. (D) is incorrect because the right to be free of double jeopardy creates a bar as soon as the defendant is retried for the same offense, rather than on her conviction.

Answer to Question 4

(D) The customer evidently did not have the mens rea for assault. An assault is either: (i) an attempt to commit a battery; or (ii) the intentional creation (other than by mere words) of a reasonable apprehension in the mind of the victim of imminent bodily harm. An attempt to commit a battery would require a specific intent to unlawfully apply force to the person of another, resulting in either bodily injury or an offensive touching. In this question, the customer was simply fleeing from the factory at the time he darted past the visitor, who happened to be in his path. There apparently was no intent on the part of the customer to bring about any sort of bodily injury or offensive touching to the visitor. Thus, the customer did not possess the requisite mens rea (*i.e.,* specific intent) for an attempt to commit a battery. Likewise, the facts indicate that the customer did not intend to create in the mind of the visitor a fear of imminent bodily harm. Thus, the customer also lacked the requisite mens rea for the second of the two types of assault. (A) states a factor that is totally irrelevant to a charge of criminal assault. In determining possible criminal liability for assault, there is no such thing as an "underlying offense," as in felony murder, where a killing occurring during the course of a felony (the underlying offense) is deemed to be murder. Whether the defendant is guilty of assault on these facts does not depend on any other offense that he committed or was in the process of committing. Thus, it is of no significance that the customer's conduct in the factory constituted a misdemeanor rather than a felony. (B) does not state a defense to assault because, where there is an assault, there is no actual touching of the victim (a touching would constitute a battery, not an assault). Consequently, the absence of contact between the customer and the visitor is of no help to the customer. (C) is not helpful to the customer because the foreseeability of the visitor's injury as a consequence of the customer's criminal activity at the factory is irrelevant to a charge of assault. As detailed above, assault requires the ***intent*** to either commit battery or to create fear of imminent bodily harm. "Foreseeability" speaks to negligence rather than intent, and is not applicable to assault. Even if the

visitor's injury ***were*** a foreseeable consequence of the customer's criminal activity at the factory (and it may well have been foreseeable that a passerby would be injured as the customer fled the scene), the customer would not be guilty of assault based on mere foreseeability of injury, absent the presence of the requisite intent on his part.

Answer to Question 5

(A) Given that the employee intended to deposit his paycheck before the checks cleared, he lacked the intent to defraud required by the statute. The statute under which the employee is being prosecuted is a variation of the offense of false pretenses. As with false pretenses, the statute requires a specific intent, *i.e.*, an intent to defraud. If the employee intended to deposit sufficient funds to honor the check before it reached his bank, then the employee did not intend to defraud the gift boutique. Thus, the employee lacked the specific intent that is a necessary element of the crime charged. (B) is incorrect because the employee's expectation that he would receive his paycheck as usual need not have been reasonable. Even if such an expectation were unreasonable, the employee would not be guilty if he did not intend to defraud the payees, as required by the statute. (C) is incorrect because it would result in a verdict of guilty without requiring intent to defraud. Knowledge that the check was drawn against insufficient funds is just one element of the statute. The intent to defraud is also required to convict under the applicable statute. (D) also incorrectly assumes that the employee violated the statute merely by knowingly writing a check on insufficient funds. As explained above, the requisite intent to defraud is absent. Thus, there is no "violation" to be vitiated.

Answer to Question 6

(D) The activist cannot be convicted of either murder or manslaughter in the death of the onlooker because he did not commit a voluntary act. Virtually all crimes, including homicide, require either a voluntary physical act or a failure to act under circumstances imposing a legal duty to act. An act performed while the defendant is unconscious is not voluntary because it does not stem from a conscious exercise of the will. Thus, if the trier of fact accepts the expert testimony, the activist cannot be convicted of the onlooker's homicide. (A) is incorrect because the death of the bystander was not proximately caused by the activist's initial conduct in swinging at the first officer. A crime such as homicide that requires not merely conduct but also a specified result of that conduct imposes liability on the defendant only for results that occur as a "natural and probable" consequence of the conduct. Even if the jurisdiction did apply the felony murder doctrine or misdemeanor manslaughter doctrine to the initial battery of the officer, it would require that the death be a foreseeable result of the felony or misdemeanor, and here it could be argued that it was not foreseeable that other officers would respond to the battery with deadly force and that a gun battle would ensue, causing the death of a bystander; in any event, the battery does not suffice for homicide in the absence of these doctrines. (B) is incorrect because, under the transferred intent doctrine, any mitigating circumstances excusing or justifying the killing of the second officer would generally be transferred to the bystander; if mitigated as to the former, it would be mitigated as to the latter. The same reasoning applies to (C); if the activist had the requisite intent for murder as to the officer, this intent would be transferred to the onlooker, making the activist liable for murder. Nor would the activist's battery suffice for involuntary manslaughter based on criminal negligence, because the proximate cause requirement cannot be established.

Answer to Question 7

(D) The husband cannot be convicted because he did not cause his wife's death. Murder is defined as the unlawful killing of another human being with malice aforethought. To be guilty of murder,

the defendant's action must be both the cause in fact and the proximate cause of the victim's death. The defendant's act will be a cause in fact of death if, but for the defendant's action, the victim would not have died as and when she did. Here, the victim would have died when she did even if the husband had not administered the poison, since she died not from the poison, but only from her cancer. Thus, the husband's actions were not the cause in fact of death, and (D) is correct. (A) and (B) are incorrect because if the other elements of murder are established, administering poison might be sufficient to establish malice aforethought. Malice aforethought for murder can be established by conduct done with the awareness of an unjustifiably high risk to human life, and the husband knew that the poisons were dangerous and could kill. (C) is incorrect because the law forbids shortening a life even for one second, so it is not a defense that medical science had given the victim up for dead. If the defendant's action in any way shortened the victim's life, he can be held liable for murder.

Answer to Question 8

(A) The prosecutor's comment improperly burdened the defendant's assertion of his privilege against self-incrimination. The prosecution is not allowed to comment on the defendant's failure to testify at trial, because the defendant is privileged under the Fifth Amendment to remain silent. (B) is incorrect because no amount of attacks on the credibility of prosecution witnesses will justify such a comment as a rebuttal. (C) is incorrect because the Fifth Amendment privilege outweighs the prosecutor's right to comment on the state of the evidence. (D) is not the best answer even though the harmless error test does apply to improper comments by the prosecution (*i.e.,* the conviction will not be overturned if the prosecution can show beyond a reasonable doubt that the comments did not affect the outcome of the case). Because there is no real indication as to the strength of the case against the defendant, it is impossible to conclude that the error was harmless beyond a reasonable doubt.

Answer to Question 9

(D) The salesperson's testimony will likely be admissible. Although the discovery of the crates as a result of an illegal search may be said to have led to the salesperson's testimony, her testimony will not be excluded as the product of illegal police activity. Under the exclusionary rule, not only must illegally obtained evidence be excluded, but also all evidence obtained or derived from exploitation of that evidence must be excluded. Such derived evidence is called "the fruit of the poisonous tree." Despite this general rule, it is difficult for a defendant to have live witness testimony excluded as the fruit of the poisonous tree, because a more direct link between the taint and the evidence is required than for exclusion of other evidence. Among the factors that a court considers in determining the existence of a sufficiently direct link is the extent to which the witness is freely willing to testify. Here, the officer did not have a search warrant when he looked into the back room. The gallery owner will argue that, because the officer's questioning of the salesperson followed the illegal search of the back room, the testimony of the salesperson is derived from exploitation of the evidence found in the back room. However, there is no indication from the facts of such a direct link between the illegal conduct of the officer and the testimony as would be required to exclude the testimony. Even prior to seeing the crates in the back room, the officer was aware of rumors regarding the gallery owner's illegal activity. Thus, it is entirely possible that at some point the police would have questioned the salesperson as to her knowledge of this matter and obtained from her the same information that now forms the basis of her testimony. Consequently, the link between the proffered testimony and the illegal police conduct is insufficiently direct to render the testimony inadmissible. Because the gallery owner will be unable to have the salesperson's testimony excluded as the fruit of the poisonous tree, (A) is incorrect. (B) is incorrect for two reasons: First, there is no indication that the salesperson was a co-conspirator with the gallery owner. Second, even if the salesperson were a co-conspirator, there is no principle of law that prohibits an unindicted co-conspirator from testifying. (C) is incorrect because a person has a Fifth Amendment right to refuse to testify whenever the testimony may tend to incriminate. A nondefendant witness may not use the privilege to avoid being sworn as a witness or to avoid being asked questions, but may refuse to answer specific questions while on the stand. In any case, the rationale here—that the Fifth Amendment privilege does not apply—is incorrect.

Answer to Question 10

(C) Absence of intent to commit a felony is the best defense. If the tenant intended merely to retrieve his property, he would have had no intent to commit a felony when he entered the apartment and thus could not be convicted of burglary. Common law burglary consists of: (i) a breaking; (ii) and entry; (iii) of the dwelling; (iv) of another; (v) at nighttime; (vi) with the intent of committing a felony therein. The tenant entered the apartment intending to retrieve his own property. Thus, the facts indicate that the only felony the tenant could have intended to commit at the time of entry would be larceny. Larceny consists of: (i) a taking; (ii) and carrying away; (iii) of tangible personal property; (iv) of another; (v) by trespass; (vi) with intent to permanently (or for an unreasonable time) deprive the person of his interest in the property. Larceny element (iv) would be missing here if the tenant intended to retrieve only his own property. Without the intent to commit a felony, no burglary exists. (A) is wrong because the tenant was no longer an occupant of the apartment and so could not consent to the entry. (B) is wrong because opening the closed but unlocked window was a breaking. (D) is not his best defense. The tenant could argue that the landlord did not have superior rights to the tenant's property (despite a possible claim of arrearages) and that therefore he did not take the property of another, and also that he did not take part in his friend's theft. However, he still would be guilty if he entered the apartment with the intent to commit a felony inside; the stronger defense of choice (C) specifically negates that intent.

Answer to Question 11

(D) The search that resulted in the seizure of the methamphetamine supplies at the cabin is invalid because the search was executed without a warrant, and no exception to the warrant requirement is applicable. All warrantless searches are unconstitutional unless they fit into one of the six recognized exceptions to the warrant requirement. To be valid, a warrantless search must meet all the requirements of at least one exception. These exceptions are: (i) search incident to a lawful arrest; (ii) the automobile exception; (iii) plain view; (iv) consent; (v) stop and frisk and other limited intrusions; and (vi) hot pursuit, evanescent evidence, and similar emergencies. When the officer conducted the search of the cabin, he had no warrant for the search. Thus, the validity of the search and seizure depends on whether an exception to the warrant requirement is applicable. Clearly, the automobile exception does not apply, as there was no search involving a vehicle. The police activity cannot be classified as a stop and frisk or other limited intrusion because the facts state that a search took place and because the activity described—searching the cabin—would not be considered a limited intrusion. No person with authority gave consent to the search, so the search and seizure were not justified under the consent exception. The detective was not engaged in arresting someone, which would have permitted him to search the arrestee and areas into which he might reach to obtain weapons or destroy evidence, given that the man was not on the premises. Thus, (B) is incorrect. Pursuant to the plain view exception, the police may make a warrantless seizure when they: (i) are

legitimately on the premises; (ii) discover evidence, fruits, or instrumentalities of crime, or contraband; (iii) see such evidence in plain view; and (iv) have probable cause to believe that the item is evidence, contraband, or a fruit or instrumentality of crime. Here, because the detective lacked a search warrant for the cabin, he was not in the cabin legitimately when he saw the drugs. Therefore, the plain view exception is inapplicable, and (A) is incorrect. The final exception to the warrant requirement, the hot pursuit exception, provides that officers in hot pursuit of a fleeing felon may make a warrantless search and seizure. The scope of such a search may be as broad as is reasonably necessary to prevent the suspect from resisting or escaping. Here, the detective was not hotly pursuing a fleeing felon. In fact, he had not even come into contact with the man at the time he conducted the search and seizure at the cabin. Consequently, the hot pursuit exception does not apply. (C) is incorrect because it is irrelevant. It implies that if the detective had probable cause, he could have executed the warrantless search. Probable cause alone is not grounds to conduct a warrantless search.

Answer to Question 12

(D) Given that the farmer intended merely to borrow the tool, he lacked the intent to commit larceny, and thus would not be guilty of burglary. Common law burglary consists of: (i) a breaking; (ii) and entry; (iii) of the dwelling; (iv) of another; (v) at nighttime; (vi) with the intent of committing a felony therein. The farmer entered his neighbor's house intending to remove the tool. Thus, the facts indicate that the only felony he could have intended to commit at the time of entry would be larceny. Larceny consists of: (i) a taking; (ii) and carrying away; (iii) of tangible personal property; (iv) of another; (v) by trespass; (vi) with intent to permanently (or for an unreasonable time) deprive the person of his interest in the property. At common law, if the defendant intended to return the property within a reasonable time, and at the time of the taking had a substantial ability to do so, such an unauthorized borrowing would not constitute larceny. Consequently, if the farmer intended to keep the tool only for the short time to fix his tractor, then he did not intend to permanently deprive his neighbor of his interest in the wrench. Because the farmer thus lacked the intent to commit a felony in his neighbor's home at the time he entered, the farmer would not be guilty of burglary. (A) is incorrect because, for purposes of the crime of burglary, a structure is deemed to be a dwelling simply if any part of it is used regularly for sleeping purposes. Thus, the fact that nobody lived in the basement is irrelevant. (B) is incorrect because the fact that the house was unoccupied is irrelevant to his culpability for burglary. The crime of burglary would have been complete if the farmer had broken and entered his neighbor's home with the intent of committing a felony therein, regardless of whether the home was currently unoccupied. Consequently, the farmer's knowledge that the house was unoccupied would provide him with no defense to a charge of burglary. (C) is incorrect because the breaking needed for burglary requires only minimal force to gain entry. Opening an unlocked window is a sufficient use of force to constitute a breaking.

Answer to Question 13

(B) By establishing that he only intended to borrow the television set for a few days, the defendant will show that he did not have the intent to commit a felony. Absent such intent, the defendant cannot be guilty of any underlying felony, which guilt is necessary for a conviction of felony murder. A killing (even if accidental) committed during the course of a felony is murder. Malice is implied from the intent to commit the underlying felony. To be guilty of felony murder, a defendant must be guilty of the underlying felony. Here, the possible felonies being committed by the defendant, during which the victim's death occurred, would be larceny and burglary. Burglary requires the intent to commit a felony within the dwelling, and larceny requires the

intent to permanently deprive a person of his interest in property. If the defendant's only intent was to borrow the victim's television set for a few days, then the defendant lacked the intent to permanently deprive the victim of his interest in the set; *i.e.,* the requisite intent for larceny is missing. Likewise, the absence of intent to steal the set would mean that, at the time of breaking and entering the cottage, the defendant did not intend to commit a felony therein. Consequently, the defendant is not guilty of burglary. Because under these circumstances no felony would have been committed, it cannot be said that the death of the victim occurred during the commission of a felony. Therefore, the defendant would not be guilty of felony murder. (D) is tempting, because generally a conviction of felony murder requires that the death must have been a foreseeable result of commission of the felony. However, some courts do not apply a foreseeability requirement and require only that the underlying felony be malum in se. Furthermore, even those courts applying a foreseeability requirement have been willing to find most deaths occurring during the commission of a felony to be foreseeable. Here, the defendant believed that the cottage was unoccupied for the winter. Thus, it was arguably unforeseeable that the defendant's entering the cottage and taking a television set would result in the death of an occupant, but it is by no means certain that a court would agree. Furthermore, in those jurisdictions that do not require foreseeability of death, the defendant could be convicted of felony murder if the death occurred during the commission of a burglary, because burglary is always classified as a malum in se felony. Because the circumstances in choice (B) would assure the defendant of avoiding conviction in all jurisdictions, (B) is a better answer than (D). (A) incorrectly focuses on intent to kill. Intent to kill is one of the states of mind by which a defendant is deemed to have malice aforethought, which is necessary for a killing to constitute murder. However, this question refers to felony murder, wherein malice aforethought exists in the form of intent to commit a felony. Thus, it is irrelevant whether the defendant intended to kill the victim. Regarding (C), it is true that most courts limit the felony murder doctrine to felonies that are inherently dangerous, and that larceny is not considered to be inherently dangerous. However, assuming the existence of the requisite intent, the defendant may have committed burglary, which is deemed to be inherently dangerous. Thus, (C) might provide no defense at all to a charge of felony murder.

Answer to Question 14

(B) The most helpful fact for the prosecution is that the smaller man had an opportunity to retreat safely. The general rule is that one may use deadly force in self-defense even if the use of force could be avoided by retreating safely. This rule, however, does not apply to one who is the initial aggressor. Generally, one who begins a fight has no right to use force in his own defense during the fight. But the aggressor can regain his right to use self-defense either (i) by withdrawing and communicating the withdrawal to the other person or (ii) when the other person suddenly escalates a minor fight into one involving deadly force without giving the aggressor the chance to withdraw. Here, the smaller man was the initial aggressor because he spat on the larger man and struck the first blow when he punched him in the nose. The larger man then escalated the fight into one involving deadly force by pulling a knife. However, the smaller man would not regain his right to self-defense unless "his back was to the wall"; *i.e.,* if he had a chance to withdraw rather than respond to the larger man's deadly force, he had a duty to do so. Thus, the prosecution could overcome the smaller man's claim of self-defense with the fact that he was very close to the door and could have withdrawn from the confrontation. (A) is incorrect because the fact that the smaller man initiated the violence does not necessarily extinguish his right of self-defense here, because the larger man escalated the fight into one involving deadly force. To rebut the smaller man's claim under these circumstances, the prosecution must show that the smaller man had an opportunity to withdraw that he did not use. (C) is incorrect because it is irrelevant to

the smaller man's right to use deadly force in self-defense. The fact that the smaller man is guilty of weapons violations could be used in a separate prosecution against him, but it would have no bearing on his right of self-defense. (D) is also irrelevant to the smaller man's right of self-defense. The smaller man was under no duty to retreat or to refrain from arguing with the larger man despite his belligerence. The only basis for the smaller man's losing his right to defend himself was his initiation of the physical contact.

Answer to Question 15

(D) The defendant would most likely be guilty of none of the listed crimes because the defense of self-defense makes his homicide excusable. A person may use deadly force in self-defense if (i) he is without fault, (ii) he is confronted with unlawful force, and (iii) he is threatened with imminent death or great bodily harm. In a majority of states, a person may use deadly force in self-defense even if this could be avoided by retreating. Here, the defendant's use of force was privileged because it was reasonably necessary to defend him from the man's unlawful attack, and the defendant had no duty to retreat under the majority view. Furthermore, the defendant can claim the privilege of self-defense even though his words triggered the fight—calling someone names would not be considered adequate provocation that would make the defendant the aggressor. Hence, because the defendant's use of force was privileged, he cannot be convicted of any of the listed crimes, making (A), (B), and (C) incorrect.

Answer to Question 16

(C) The defendant is guilty of larceny because, while having mere custody of the television set, he carried it away from the hotel intending to permanently deprive the hotel owner of his interest in the set. Larceny consists of the taking and carrying away of tangible personal property of another by trespass, with intent to permanently (or for an unreasonable time) deprive the person of his interest in the property. Property must be taken from someone who has a possessory interest superior to that of the defendant. If the defendant has custody of the property, rather than possession, his misappropriation of the property is larceny. Possession involves a much greater scope of authority to deal with the property than does custody. Here, the defendant only had the authority to use the television set for viewing purposes while he was staying at the hotel. Thus, the defendant had only enough authority to deal with the set as to indicate that he had custody of it rather than possession. Consequently, the hotel owner had a possessory interest in the set superior to that of the defendant. The defendant took the set by trespass (without the consent of the owner) and carried it away with the intent to permanently deprive the owner of his interest in the set. Thus, the defendant is guilty of larceny. (D) is incorrect because larceny by trick occurs when the victim consents to the defendant's taking possession of the property, but such consent has been induced by a misrepresentation. Here, the hotel owner never consented to give the defendant possession of the television set, through misrepresentation or otherwise. Instead, the defendant simply took the set without the consent of the owner. Therefore, this is not larceny by trick. (B) is incorrect for a similar reason. The offense of false pretenses consists of obtaining title to the property of another by an intentional or knowing false statement of past or existing fact, with intent to defraud the other. The defendant made no misrepresentations to the hotel owner, nor did the owner convey title to the television set to the defendant. Thus, the defendant is not guilty of false pretenses. (A) is incorrect because embezzlement requires the fraudulent conversion of property of another by a person in lawful possession of that property. The defendant never had lawful possession of the television set. The taking of the set without the consent of the hotel owner was trespassory. Thus, the defendant has not committed embezzlement.

Answer to Question 17

(C) The cottage owner is guilty of burglary because the right of occupancy belonged to the tenant. However, the fact that there was no burning of the structure means that the cottage owner is guilty of attempted arson rather than arson. Burglary at common law is a breaking and entering of the dwelling of another at nighttime, with the intent of committing a felony therein. A breaking requires some use of force to gain entry, but minimal force is sufficient. In determining whether the dwelling is that of another, occupancy rather than ownership is material. Thus, an owner can commit burglary of her own structure if it is rented and used as a dwelling by someone else. Here, although the cottage owner owned the cottage, the tenant had the right to occupy it pursuant to a lease. Thus, for purposes of the crime of burglary, the cottage owner is deemed to have entered the dwelling of another. Although the cottage owner used her own key to gain access to the cottage, this was still an unconsented use of force to effectuate entry, thereby constituting a breaking. This breaking and entering of the tenant's dwelling occurred in the evening. At the time of the entry, the cottage owner intended to commit the felony of arson. Consequently, all the elements of burglary are in place, making her guilty of this crime.

Arson consists of the malicious burning of the dwelling of another. There is a requirement of some damage to the fiber of the wood or other combustible material. As with burglary, ownership of the structure is not material for determining whether the dwelling is that of another; rather, the right to occupancy is material. The cottage owner left a lighted cigarette on the mattress, intending to burn down the entire cottage. However, the tenant extinguished the fire before any damage was done to the structure of the cottage, even mere charring. Absent such damage, arson cannot have been committed. The cottage owner did commit attempted arson. A criminal attempt is an act which, although done with the intention of committing a crime, falls short of completing the crime. The defendant must intend to perform an act and obtain a result that, if achieved, would constitute a crime. Also, the defendant must have committed an act beyond mere preparation for the offense. The cottage owner intended to perform an act that would have culminated in the crime of arson. By soaking the mattress with gasoline and leaving a lighted cigarette on it, the cottage owner committed an act that came dangerously close to successfully burning the cottage. This act, in combination with the intent to commit arson, means that the cottage owner is guilty of attempted arson. (A) is incorrect because there can be no arson as to the mattress. Arson requires a burning of a dwelling. Because the cottage was not burned, the cottage owner is not guilty of arson. (B) is incorrect because the key element in determining whether a dwelling is that of another, for both arson and burglary, is the right of occupancy. Under the terms of his lease, the tenant had the right to occupy the cottage for one year. Therefore, the cottage owner's ownership of the cottage will not be a defense to either arson or burglary. (D) is incorrect because, as explained above, the cottage owner's use of a key to gain access to the cottage without the consent of the person who had the right of occupancy is deemed to be a use of force to gain entry, in the same way as if a person who did not own the cottage were to gain entry by means of a key.

Answer to Question 18

(D) The man's motion should be denied. The United States Supreme Court has held that when the only issue is that of probable cause for issuance of a warrant, the name of the informer is a type of privileged information. (Only if the informer were a material witness to the crime might his identity have to be revealed at or before trial.) The validity of a warrant based on information obtained from informers is based on the totality of the circumstances. (A) is incorrect because although the right of cross-examination of one's accusers has been deemed to be a fundamental

right, it does not apply when the issue is only that of probable cause for issuance of a warrant, as compared to guilt or innocence. (B) is incorrect because, as noted above, unless the informer were also a material witness to the crime, his identity need not be revealed. Here, the facts do not indicate that the informer was a material witness to the crime. (C) is incorrect because it is overbroad. As indicated above, there is a right to know the identity of an informant if the informant is also a material witness to the crime.

Set 3 Answer Sheet

1. Ⓐ Ⓑ Ⓒ Ⓓ
2. Ⓐ Ⓑ Ⓒ Ⓓ
3. Ⓐ Ⓑ Ⓒ Ⓓ
4. Ⓐ Ⓑ Ⓒ Ⓓ
5. Ⓐ Ⓑ Ⓒ Ⓓ
6. Ⓐ Ⓑ Ⓒ Ⓓ
7. Ⓐ Ⓑ Ⓒ Ⓓ
8. Ⓐ Ⓑ Ⓒ Ⓓ
9. Ⓐ Ⓑ Ⓒ Ⓓ
10. Ⓐ Ⓑ Ⓒ Ⓓ
11. Ⓐ Ⓑ Ⓒ Ⓓ
12. Ⓐ Ⓑ Ⓒ Ⓓ
13. Ⓐ Ⓑ Ⓒ Ⓓ
14. Ⓐ Ⓑ Ⓒ Ⓓ
15. Ⓐ Ⓑ Ⓒ Ⓓ
16. Ⓐ Ⓑ Ⓒ Ⓓ
17. Ⓐ Ⓑ Ⓒ Ⓓ
18. Ⓐ Ⓑ Ⓒ Ⓓ

CRIMINAL LAW QUESTIONS - SET 3

Question 1

A person about to travel to the United States was approached by a local who asked him to take a package into the United States, and the local would pay the traveler a substantial sum of money. The traveler asked what was in the package; the local said it would be better if the traveler did not know. The traveler asked no further questions. As he entered the United States, the traveler was instructed by the customs agent to open his suitcase. When he did, the customs agent found heroin wrapped in a package covered with transparent paper. The traveler is charged with knowingly importing illegal narcotics.

The traveler is:

(A) Guilty, because strict liability applies to border crossing offenses.

(B) Guilty, because he knew that the package contained some sort of illegal contraband.

(C) Not guilty, because the local could not be apprehended.

(D) Not guilty, because he did not know that the package contained heroin.

Question 2

A liquor store clerk was working the counter when a young girl came up with a bottle of wine to purchase. The clerk thought that she looked too young to buy wine, so he asked her for her driver's license. The young girl reached into her purse as if to get her license. As the clerk reached under the counter to get a bag, the girl grabbed the bottle of wine, threw $10 on the counter, and ran out. In this state, it is a misdemeanor to sell wine or liquor to a person under the age of 21.

If the clerk is prosecuted for violation of this statute, his best defense is that:

(A) He asked for a driver's license.

(B) He did not know that the girl was actually a minor.

(C) He did not sell her the wine.

(D) He was only a salaried employee rather than the owner and benefits in no way from the transaction.

Question 3

Even though the gambling laws of the state prohibit gambling on professional sports games, the defendant placed a bet with a bookie on the outcome of a football game. There was a disputed call near the end of the game that resulted in the defendant losing the bet. However, later films showed that in fact the call should have been for the defendant's team, which would have changed the outcome. The bookie refused to pay the bet to the defendant. Later that night, the defendant broke into the bookie's home and took the amount he would have won.

The defendant's best defense to a charge of common law burglary is that:

(A) He was so enraged that he had an irresistible impulse to take the money.

(B) Since the original gambling agreement was illegal, the two are in pari delicto and the court should not interfere.

(C) He lacked the specific intent necessary for burglary because he believed that the bookie owed him the money.

(D) He had a mistaken belief that the definition of burglary would not apply to a dispute over gambling winnings.

Question 4

A man was tried for the forcible rape of a woman. His defense was that the woman had consented to have intercourse with him. Over his objection, the trial judge charged the jury that while the prosecution must prove the overall case beyond a reasonable doubt, the man had the burden of proving his defense by a preponderance of the evidence.

The judge's instructions were:

(A) Correct, if state law places the burden of proving consent on the defendant.

(B) Correct, as long as the judge emphasized that the state must prove the entire case beyond a reasonable doubt.

(C) Incorrect, because the instruction placed a burden on the defendant that denied the defendant due process of law.

(D) Incorrect, because in a criminal trial the defendant cannot be required to prove any critical issue by a preponderance of the evidence.

Question 5

A husband was very jealous of any contact his wife had with other men, and was particularly suspicious of his wife's relationship with their neighbor, a plumber. Early one morning, the shower in the couple's master bathroom sprang a leak while the wife was getting ready for the day. Fearing permanent damage to their house, and needing to get the repair done quickly, the wife quickly threw on some clothes and called the neighbor. The neighbor immediately went over to the couple's home, and went to the master bathroom. At the same time, the husband unexpectedly came home because he had forgotten something for work. The husband went to the master bedroom and saw the neighbor and his wife with her hair wet and clothes hastily put on. Enraged, he ran to his study, grabbed his gun from the desk drawer, and shot and killed the neighbor.

The jurisdiction defines murder in the first degree to include premeditated and deliberate killings and all killings that take place during the commission of a dangerous felony. Premeditation and deliberation is defined as requiring some meaningful reflection prior to the killing. All other common law murder is classified as murder in the second degree.

If the jury finds that the husband was unreasonable in his erroneous belief that the neighbor and his wife were together for the purpose of adultery, the husband's killing of the neighbor was:

(A) Voluntary manslaughter.

(B) Involuntary manslaughter.

(C) First degree murder.

(D) Second degree murder.

Question 6

A husband was furious after learning that his wife had an affair. He knew that his wife's best friend, who was arriving for a visit, had a history of mental illness and delusions. To enhance the friend's tendency toward delusions, the husband spiked the friend's drink with a hallucinogen before serving it to her. Then, at every opportunity outside of his wife's presence, the husband would suggest to the friend that his wife was out to get her and that the friend should kill the wife first. Eventually, the friend succumbed to the combination of the hallucinogen and the husband's conduct. The friend went into the kitchen, grabbed a knife, and stabbed the wife several times, killing her.

During the friend's murder trial, it was disclosed that her drink had been spiked, and the friend recounted the husband's statements to her on the day of the murder. She was ultimately acquitted at trial by reason of insanity. The husband then is put on trial for first degree murder, which the jurisdiction's statute defines to include premeditated and deliberate killings.

The husband should be found:

(A) Not guilty, because his co-conspirator was acquitted of the crime.

(B) Not guilty, because the murder was done in the heat of the passion.

(C) Guilty, because the friend is not an "innocent actor."

(D) Guilty, because he intended to kill his wife.

Question 7

The police received information linking a man to drug trafficking and went to the man's residence, where he lived with his mother. The police found the mother at home, and she told them that her son was not expected back until later. The police informed the mother that they suspected the man of selling drugs and asked if they could search his room. She replied, "I'm finished with that no-good bum; not only is he into drugs, but he has been stealing my money to pay for them, and all the time I'm making his bed and fixing his food. You can search his room. He likes to keep his private stuff under his pillow. I hope he goes to jail." The police searched the man's room and discovered a quantity of marijuana under the pillow of his bed.

At a preliminary hearing, if the man's attorney moves to suppress the marijuana on grounds that the search was invalid, the court should:

(A) Grant the motion, because the man had a reasonable expectation of privacy in the area searched, and the police did not have a warrant.

(B) Grant the motion, because the man's mother's consent was given at a time when police knew her interests were in conflict with the man's.

(C) Deny the motion, because the man's mother had the authority to consent to the search of his room.

(D) Deny the motion, because with the mother's statement the police had probable cause to search the room.

Question 8

A college student was the sole lifetime beneficiary under a large trust administered by a banker. The student received a large monthly distribution from the trust, and whenever he ran short, he simply called the banker for extra funds, because the trust provided that the student was to receive whatever he needed from income or principal. The student's roommate found out about the trust arrangement and decided to see if he could make it pay off for him. The roommate sent a telegram to the banker, which appeared to be from the student, and which asked for several thousand dollars to cover medical expenses. The telegram further stated that, since he was in the hospital, the student would send his roommate to pick up the cash. The next day, the roommate showed up at the banker's office and obtained the money on the promise that he would take it to the student. The roommate absconded with the funds.

When the roommate obtained the cash from the banker, he committed:

(A) False pretenses.

(B) Embezzlement.

(C) Larceny by trick.

(D) Larceny.

Question 9

An employee worked as a third-shift supervisor at a manufacturing plant. One of his duties was to ensure that all timekeeping records accurately reflected the time his crew actually worked. Workers, including the employee, were then paid for whatever hours the timecards reflected. The employee was also required to assist in submitting budgets for payroll. Needing to leave work early for a second job that he obtained, the employee had one of his trusted co-workers punch his card out at the regular time every day of the week. At the end of the week, he signed the timecard with those hours included, and was paid accordingly. He continued to do this for several weeks before being discovered.

What crime has the employee committed?

(A) Forgery.

(B) Embezzlement.

(C) Larceny by trick.

(D) False pretenses.

Question 10

The defendant fired a bullet at a police officer's heart. Unbeknownst to the defendant, the officer was wearing a bullet-proof vest, and the bullet did not penetrate. The defendant was charged with attempted murder of the police officer. At trial, the defendant's attorney produced an expert who testified that the vest worn by the officer could not have been pierced by the bullet fired by the defendant, or by any other bullet that the defendant could have legally purchased in the jurisdiction. The prosecution did not dispute this testimony.

Assuming the jury finds that the defendant acted with the requisite intent, he should be found:

(A) Not guilty, because it was factually impossible for him to kill the police officer.

(B) Not guilty, because legal impossibility is always a defense.

(C) Guilty, because factual impossibility is not a defense under these facts.

(D) Guilty, because legal impossibility is not a defense under these facts.

Question 11

A student approached a reputed drug dealer at a pool hall to purchase marijuana, although he knew that it was a crime to possess or smoke marijuana. The student bought a "marijuana cigarette," which was in fact only an ordinary tobacco cigarette, from the drug dealer. As the student left the pool hall, he lit the cigarette, whereupon he was immediately apprehended by a detective who was keeping all of the dealer's visitors under surveillance. After the student was advised of his rights and admitted purchasing the "marijuana cigarette" from the dealer, the police determined that there was no marijuana in the cigarette.

If the student is charged with attempt to smoke a marijuana cigarette, the court should rule that:

(A) He is not guilty, because he accomplished all acts he intended to do yet did not commit a criminal offense.

(B) He is not guilty, because there was no corroboration of his statement to the police.

(C) He is guilty, because had the attendant circumstances been as he believed them to be, he would have committed a criminal offense.

(D) He is guilty, because drug offenses are strict liability crimes.

Question 12

An art restorer, after attending art school for a number of years, secured a job restoring the paintings for an art museum. After several years on the job, the artist discovered that he could imitate the artwork of nearly any artist. He decided that he could make some extra money copying the artwork of up-and-coming artists, while staying away from more well-known artists to reduce his chance of getting caught.

An art collector searching for a painting by a new artist saw the restorer at an art fair selling various paintings, one of which appeared to be by the new artist. The restorer was selling the painting for $100. The collector thought that the price was very low and that the painting should probably sell for around $500, but she bought the painting anyway, giving the restorer $100 after the restorer confirmed that the painting was an original from the new artist. After taking it to an art appraiser for insurance purposes, she

discovered that the painting was a forgery. However, she also discovered that the painting's frame was worth about $125.

With which theft offense may the art restorer be charged?

(A) Larceny by trick.

(B) False pretenses.

(C) Embezzlement.

(D) No theft offense.

Question 13

Police officers were executing a search warrant at a home suspected of containing evidence of illegal gambling. No one was at home when the police arrived. After searching the first floor, the officers went upstairs. A friend of the owner then entered the house carrying a briefcase. He set the briefcase on the floor, opened it, and then heard the officers. He became frightened, left the briefcase sitting in the middle of the floor, and hid in a closet. The police officers returned to the first floor and immediately spotted the briefcase, which they knew was not there earlier. Since the briefcase was open, the officers saw its contents—betting slips—and seized them. Because they knew that someone had entered the house since they arrived, they re-searched the first floor. They found the friend and informed him that he was under arrest, clapped handcuffs on him, and read him his *Miranda* warnings. One of the officers patted the friend down to check for weapons. The officer noticed a bulge in the friend's pocket. Although the officer knew that the bulge was unlikely to be a weapon, he reached into the pocket anyway, and discovered a package that appeared to be (and later proved to be) heroin. The friend was charged with possession of narcotics.

At the preliminary hearing, will the court agree with the public defender's contention that the friend's arrest was illegal?

(A) Yes, because the police officer who searched the friend knew that he did not have a weapon in his pocket.

(B) Yes, because the friend's mere presence in the house did not give the police probable cause to believe he had committed a crime, and they had no basis for searching him at all, because he did not act toward them in a threatening manner.

(C) No, because the contents of the briefcase gave the police probable cause to arrest the man.

(D) No, because the police had a right to search the friend for gambling slips, and the discovery of the heroin was merely incidental to a lawful search.

Question 14

A neighbor of a teenager purchased an expensive sports cars and parked it in his attached garage. To get into the garage, the teenager manufactured a radio device that could be programmed to activate any automatic garage door opener, and the teenager used the device to open the neighbor's garage one night. The teenager hotwired the car and drove it away, intending to cruise by a few of his friends' favorite bars and then return it to its owner with no one the wiser. After driving the car to a local bar and having several drinks, the teenager decided to take his friends for a ride to the nearby seacoast. When the party arrived at the bluffs above the beach, the teenager impulsively decided to push the car over the cliff. The jurisdiction's penal statutes have codified the common law without alteration of any kind.

The teenager is guilty of:

(A) No crime.

(B) Burglary.

(C) Larceny.

(D) Both burglary and larceny.

Question 15

A locksmith knew that his friend had been having marital troubles. The friend had told the locksmith that he suspected his wife was having an affair with his rival. One afternoon, the friend, visibly upset, asked to borrow some of the locksmith's tools, telling him that he knew that his rival was going to meet up with his wife later that day. The locksmith gave his friend the tools, advising him not do anything that he would regret later. The friend stated that it would be others who would have regrets. The friend went to his rival's apartment and picked the door lock with the locksmith's tools. He found his wife and rival in bed together. The friend stabbed his rival, seriously wounding him. A few minutes later the locksmith called the apartment to try to warn the rival that his friend might come over. After the friend was arrested, he agreed to plead guilty to aggravated battery and attempted voluntary manslaughter in exchange for testifying against the locksmith, who was charged as an accomplice to attempted murder.

Can the locksmith be convicted of that charge?

(A) Yes, because he recklessly disregarded a substantial risk to human life and was not provoked.

(B) Yes, because his failed attempt to neutralize his assistance did not prevent the crime from occurring and therefore did not constitute an adequate withdrawal.

(C) No, because he did not have the requisite intent to be liable as an accomplice.

(D) No, because an accomplice cannot be found guilty of a more serious offense than that for which the principal has been convicted.

Question 16

While executing a search warrant at the home of a suspected arsonist, the police heard a knock on the door. A plain clothes officer answered the door and found a young woman standing outside with a backpack in her hand. The woman asked for the owner of the home by name and was told that the owner was not available at the moment. The woman replied, "Give him this, and tell him thanks for the $8,000," and she gave the officer the backpack. The officer opened the backpack and found eight hi-tech delay timers. The officer then identified himself as a police officer and placed the woman under arrest. He performed a quick pat down of the woman's outer clothing. In her jacket pocket, the officer found a package that appeared to be (and later proved to be) heroin. In addition to arson-related charges, the woman was charged with possession of heroin. At trial, the woman's attorney moved to have the heroin excluded from evidence.

How should the court rule?

(A) For the woman, because the warrant only entitled the police to search the premises.

(B) For the woman, because the heroin was seized during an unlawful arrest.

(C) For the state, because the heroin was seized during a lawful arrest.

(D) For the state, because searching the backpack was within the scope of the warrant.

Question 17

A robber approached a newsstand, with her knife drawn, in an attempt to rob the attendant. The attendant gave the robber the small sum of money in his possession. As the robber turned away, the attendant grabbed a gun and fired several times. He intended only to wound the robber but instead killed her.

If the attendant cannot be prosecuted for manslaughter, it will be because:

(A) He only intended to wound the robber.

(B) The robbery constituted a provocation.

(C) The attendant was trying to get his money back.

(D) He was apprehending a fleeing wrongdoer.

Question 18

Two robbers planned to rob a local convenience store, with one using a gun to force the clerk to turn over all of the money in the cash register while the other stood lookout near the door. The robbery did not go as planned. Instead of turning over any cash, the store clerk tried to disarm the gunman. During their struggle for the gun, the lookout decided that her best course of action was to grab what she could and flee the scene. The lookout took a newspaper and a bag of potato chips and ran out of the store. On her way out, she heard a gunshot. Later that day, she learned from news accounts that the gun accidentally discharged, killing the gunman. After an investigation, the lookout was arrested.

If the lookout is charged with felony murder, her most promising defense would be:

(A) She did not intend for the gunman to get killed.

(B) The only person killed was the gunman.

(C) The killing occurred after the robbery was over.

(D) The robbery was not a felony because the items that the lookout took had only minimal value.

CRIMINAL LAW ANSWERS - SET 3

Answer to Question 1

(B) A defendant may be deemed to possess the requisite knowledge if he deliberately avoids discovering the facts when he can readily do so. Here, there was ample reason for the defendant to ascertain what was in the package, but he did not do so. Rather, he remained willfully ignorant of the package's true nature. This is not sufficient to avoid the mens rea requirement of "knowingly." (A) is incorrect because the facts state that the mens rea requirement is "knowingly." (C) is incorrect. First, the statement implies that the rule for the ***acquittal*** of co-conspirators applies to the case. It does not, as the traveler here is being charged not with conspiracy, but with knowingly importing illegal narcotics. Second, the rule only applies to acquittals, not when the other alleged co-conspirator has not been apprehended. (D) is incorrect for the reasons discussed above; a defendant may not remain willfully ignorant to avoid acting with a certain mens rea.

Answer to Question 2

(C) In most states, the sale of liquor to someone underage is a strict liability crime. Therefore, the clerk's best defense is that he did not sell the young girl the wine. (A) is not a valid defense, because under a strict liability statute it is illegal to sell to a minor even if she presented a false identification. Thus, if the clerk had actually made a sale to the young girl, he would have violated the statute even if he had asked for her driver's license. Similarly, (B) is a wrong answer because under a strict liability statute it is illegal to sell to a minor even if the defendant did not know that the purchaser was a minor. Even if the statute were not a strict liability crime, (C) would be his best defense. (B) would only be a defense if the statute required knowledge of age. (D) ignores the stated facts that the seller of the liquor is the guilty party, not the seller's employer.

Answer to Question 3

(C) A belief that the money was rightfully his is the defendant's best defense, because the definition of common law burglary requires that the defendant break into the dwelling place with the intent to commit a felony. If the defendant actually believed that the bookie owed him the money, he could not have been committing larceny because there was no intent to deprive another of his property. Absent the intent to commit a felony, the defendant would not have had the specific intent necessary to be found guilty of burglary. (A) is incorrect because the "irresistible impulse" must be a product of some mental disease as opposed to anger. (B) is incorrect because the theory of pari delicto is a tort theory, not a criminal defense. (D) is incorrect because a mistake as to the ***law*** is not an excuse for an act otherwise criminal.

Answer to Question 4

(C) The judge's instructions resulted in a violation of defendant's due process rights. The Due Process Clause requires that in all criminal cases the state prove guilt beyond a reasonable doubt. This requirement means that each element of a crime must be proved beyond a reasonable doubt. The man is charged with rape, which is the unlawful carnal knowledge of a woman by a man not her husband, without her effective consent. Thus, lack of consent is an element of the offense, and the state must prove lack of consent beyond a reasonable doubt. To require the man to prove consent would violate the due process requirement that the state prove all elements of an offense beyond a reasonable doubt. (B) is incorrect because lack of consent is part of the entire case that

the state must prove where the charge is rape. To say that the state must prove "the entire case" is really to say that the state must prove each element of the offense. It is impermissible for a judge to segregate one element of the offense from other elements, and to impose on the defendant the burden of proving that element. (A) is incorrect because if state law were to place the burden of proving consent on the defendant, such a law would violate the Due Process Clause and would therefore be invalid. (D) is incorrect because a state may impose on a criminal defendant the burden of proof regarding certain issues; *e.g.,* an affirmative defense such as insanity or self-defense.

Answer to Question 5

(D) The husband's killing would be second degree murder. The husband intended to kill his neighbor, but he did not act in a deliberate and premeditated manner, nor was he acting under a provocation that would have aroused a sudden and intense passion in the mind of an ordinary person (given the jury finding). Thus, of the crimes listed, the husband can be guilty only of second degree murder. Murder is the unlawful killing of a human being with malice aforethought. Malice aforethought exists if the defendant has: (i) intent to kill; (ii) intent to inflict great bodily injury; (iii) awareness of an unjustifiably high risk to human life; or (iv) intent to commit a felony. Statutes such as the one in this question often divide murder into degrees. Thus, first degree murder here consists of a deliberate and premeditated taking of life, with all other murders relegated to second degree status. An intentional killing is reduced from murder to voluntary manslaughter if: (i) the defendant acts under a provocation that caused him to lose control; (ii) the provocation would arouse sudden and intense passion in the mind of an ordinary person so as to cause him to lose self-control; (iii) there is insufficient time between the provocation and the killing for the passions of a reasonable person to cool; and (iv) the defendant in fact did not cool off between the provocation and the killing. Here, the facts are clear that the husband shot his neighbor with the intent to kill him. This eliminates (B) as a correct answer. Involuntary manslaughter occurs when death is caused by criminal negligence, rather than an intentional act. The husband's shooting of the neighbor goes far beyond mere criminal negligence. (A) is incorrect because of the unreasonableness of the husband's belief that the neighbor and his wife were together for the purpose of committing adultery. For purposes of voluntary manslaughter, the discovery of one's spouse in the act of adultery constitutes adequate provocation. However, as noted above, the provocation must have been such as to arouse the passions of an ordinary person. If, as this question states, the husband's belief regarding the neighbor and his wife was unreasonable, the passions of an ordinary person would not have been aroused on seeing them together. Therefore, the husband's killing will not be reduced to voluntary manslaughter. (C) is incorrect because the quickness and anger with which the husband acted would preclude the notions that he meaningfully reflected on the idea of killing his neighbor, as required by the definition of premeditation and deliberation in the statute. This absence of deliberation and premeditation takes the killing outside the ambit of first degree murder. Consequently, the husband's intentional killing of the neighbor must be considered second degree murder, as choice (D) states.

Answer to Question 6

(D) The husband is guilty of premeditated murder. Premeditated murder means that the defendant committed the killing after reflecting on the idea of killing, even for a short time, in a cool and dispassionate manner. In the instant case, the husband intended to kill his wife, using the friend as the conduit, and his reflection on committing the crime is shown by the fact that he formulated a plan to use the friend as the conduit to commit the crime. Thus, he should be convicted of

premeditated murder. (A) is incorrect. First, the husband is not being tried for a conspiracy to commit murder; rather, he is being tried for murder. As a result, the friend was not a conspirator to the crime, merely the conduit through which the husband committed the crime. Thus, her acquittal is irrelevant to the prosecution of the husband. (B) is incorrect. Although the husband's motive to commit murder stemmed from finding out that his wife was having an affair, the crime should not be reduced to voluntary manslaughter ("heat of passion" murder) because the husband clearly had time to cool off before committing the crime, thus negating that theory. (C) is also incorrect. The husband's guilt is based on the fact that he caused the death of his wife (using the friend as his agent) after premeditation and deliberation. Thus, the husband has committed first degree murder regardless of what crime, if any, the friend is found to have committed in killing the wife.

Answer to Question 7

(C) The man's motion to suppress should be denied because his mother had authority to consent to the search of his room. A search of a residence can be based on the voluntary consent of the occupant. Where a parent has general access to a room occupied by a son or daughter, the parent can give a valid consent to a general search of the room even if the son or daughter is an adult. The facts in the question indicate that the man's mother had general access to his room ("and all the time I'm making his bed"). Therefore, her consent is valid and eliminates the need for probable cause and a warrant. (A) is wrong. The man had a reasonable expectation of privacy in the area searched, but the consent of his mother eliminated the need for a warrant. (B) is wrong. At one time, some courts required an "amicable relationship" between the parties before the police could rely on a third party's consent. The "amicable relationship requirement" is no longer recognized by the courts. (D) is not a good answer. It is true that with the mother's statement the police had probable cause to search the man's room. However, probable cause alone would not validate the search. The police would need probable cause ***plus*** a warrant or a valid consent. In this question the search would have to be based on consent.

Answer to Question 8

(C) The roommate committed larceny by trick because the banker's consent to the roommate's taking the money was induced by the misrepresentation that the roommate would take the money to the student/beneficiary. Larceny consists of a taking and carrying away of tangible personal property of another by trespass, with intent to permanently (or for an unreasonable time) deprive the person of his interest in the property. If the person in possession of property has not consented to the taking of it by the defendant, the taking is trespassory. However, if the victim consents to the defendant's taking possession of the property, but such consent has been induced by a misrepresentation, the consent is not valid. Under such circumstances, the larceny is called larceny by trick. Here, the roommate obtained the money from the banker on the promise that he would take it to the student/beneficiary. This misrepresentation induced the banker to give possession of the money to the roommate. The roommate then proceeded to take the money and carry it away, intending all the while to permanently deprive one who had a possessory interest superior to the roommate's of his interest in the money. Thus, all the elements of larceny are present. Because the original wrongful taking resulted from consent induced by misrepresentation, the specific larceny committed by the roommate is more precisely characterized as larceny by trick. Consequently, although the roommate has in fact committed larceny, (C) is a better answer than (D). Regarding (A), false pretenses consists of obtaining title to the property of another by an intentional (or knowing) false statement of past or existing fact, with intent to defraud the other. If a victim intends to convey only possession of the property to the defendant,

the offense is larceny by trick. However, if the victim intends to convey title, the offense is false pretenses. Here, the banker intended to convey possession of the money to the roommate so that he could give the money to the student/beneficiary. The banker did not intend to convey title to the roommate. Because the roommate did not obtain title by means of his misrepresentation but simply obtained possession, the offense of false pretenses was not committed. (B) is incorrect because embezzlement is the fraudulent conversion of property of another by a person in lawful possession of that property. In embezzlement, the misappropriation of the property occurs while the defendant has lawful possession of it. In larceny, the misappropriation occurs generally at the time the defendant obtains wrongful possession of the property. The roommate did not have lawful possession of the money because his possession of the money resulted from his misrepresentation to the banker. Thus, the roommate's taking of the money was wrongful from the outset. Because the roommate had wrongful, rather than lawful, possession of the money, there was no embezzlement.

Answer to Question 9

(D) The employee has committed theft by false pretenses. At common law, theft by false pretenses occurs when a defendant (i) obtains title; (ii) to the property of another; (iii) by an intentional (or knowing) false statement of past or existing fact; (iv) with the intent to defraud another. In the instant case, the employee's conduct meets all of the elements of the crime. The employee obtained title to the property by falsely misrepresenting the number of hours that he worked, with the intent that the company would pay him for the hours. Thus, he has committed the crime of false pretenses. (A) is incorrect. At common law, forgery consisted of (i) a making or altering; (ii) of a false instrument; (iii) with the intent to defraud. The falsity must be about the instrument itself, not about the contents of the instrument. Here, the timecard is exactly what it purports to be—a timecard containing the hours worked. Thus, the employee has not committed forgery by submitting a false timecard. (B) is also incorrect. At common law, embezzlement was (i) the fraudulent; (ii) conversion; (iii) of the property; (iv) of another; (v) by a person in lawful possession of that property. In the instant case, it is the last element that is lacking. Although the employee was required to maintain the timekeeping cards for his crew and to submit budgets, he was never actually in lawful possession of any funds. Thus, he cannot properly be convicted of embezzlement. Finally, (C) is also incorrect. At common law, larceny by trick occurred when possession of property was conveyed rather than actual title. Here, the company intended to pay the employee for the hours he purportedly worked; thus, it intended to pass title to the money the employee received. As a result, the employee did not commit larceny by trick.

Answer to Question 10

(C) The defendant should be found guilty. In determining whether impossibility is a defense to attempt, a distinction is made between factual and legal impossibility. It is no defense to a charge of attempt that it would have been impossible for the defendant to do all of those things that he intended to do. Such impossibility is characterized as factual impossibility. Legal impossibility, which is a defense, occurs where a defendant sets out to do something he mistakenly believes constitutes a crime. In the defendant's case, it was impossible for him to complete the intended killing of the police officer simply because of the fact that the officer was wearing a bulletproof vest. This is a classic case of factual impossibility, which will not provide the defendant with a defense to the charge of attempted murder. Thus, (A) is incorrect and (C) is correct. (B) is incorrect because, although legal impossibility is a defense, it has no application here. The crime that the defendant intended to commit—murder—is a crime. (D) is incorrect because the impossibility here is factual, not legal.

Answer to Question 11

(C) The student can be convicted of an attempt to smoke a marijuana cigarette. Whether impossibility of success constitutes a defense to a charge of criminal attempt depends on the type of impossibility at issue. It is no defense to a charge of criminal attempt that it would have been impossible for the defendant to do all of those things that he intended to do, had the attendant circumstances been as the defendant believed them to be. This is known as factual impossibility. It is this type of impossibility that is present in the student's case. Had the attendant circumstances been as he believed them to be, *i.e.,* that the cigarette contained marijuana, he would be guilty of the substantive offense. Thus, impossibility is not a defense in this case. (B) is incorrect. Although corroboration of a defendant's confession is required for a conviction, corroboration here could have come from the detective's testimony. (A) is incorrect because it ignores the effect of the attendant circumstances. Under the better view, one must also consider the "facts" as the defendant believed them to be. Here, the student believed that the cigarette contained marijuana. As a result, impossibility here does not provide a defense. (D) is incorrect because attempt crimes are specific intent crimes, not strict liability crimes. Thus, whether the drug offense in question here was a strict liability crime is irrelevant.

Answer to Question 12

(B) The art restorer has committed false pretenses because his misrepresentation concerning the authenticity of the painting induced the collector to convey title to the $100. The offense of false pretenses consists of obtaining title to the property of another by an intentional (or knowing) false statement of past or existing fact, with intent to defraud the other. The art restorer falsely represented to the collector that the painting he sold her was an original from a new artist, intending that the collector would rely on such a misrepresentation by paying money for the painting. The collector, acting in reliance on this misrepresentation, conveyed to the art restorer title to the $100. Thus, all of the elements of false pretenses are present in the restorer's dealings with the collector. Because the restorer has committed false pretenses, which is a theft offense, (D) is incorrect. Monetary loss on the part of the victim is not an element of the crime. Thus, although the lack of damages might prevent the collector from suing in civil court, the fact that the collector suffered no monetary loss from the crime is irrelevant for criminal law purposes. (A) is incorrect because the restorer obtained title to the $100 rather than mere possession. If a victim consents to someone's taking possession of property, but such consent is induced by a misrepresentation, the consent is not valid. The resulting offense is larceny by trick. False pretenses differs from larceny by trick in what is obtained. If the victim intends to convey only possession of the property, the offense is larceny by trick. However, if the victim intends to convey title, the offense is false pretenses. Here, the collector intended to convey title to the $100, acting in reliance on the restorer's false representation that the painting was an original. Because the restorer obtained title, the offense of which he can be convicted is false pretenses rather than larceny by trick. (C) is incorrect because embezzlement consists of the fraudulent conversion of property of another by a person in lawful possession of that property. In embezzlement, misappropriation of the property occurs while the defendant has lawful possession of it. Here, the restorer did not convert the $100 while he was in lawful possession of it; rather, he obtained title to the money by means of a misrepresentation. Because the restorer did not have lawful possession of the money, he has not committed embezzlement.

Answer to Question 13

(C) The contents of the briefcase supplied probable cause to believe that the friend was involved in the gambling operation, and thus, his arrest was constitutional. A police officer may arrest a person without a warrant if she has reasonable grounds to believe that a felony has been committed and that the person before her committed it. The police had searched the house for gambling paraphernalia pursuant to a search warrant. Upon seeing such paraphernalia in the briefcase, which was not previously present, they had reasonable grounds to believe that the person who left the briefcase was involved in the gambling operation. When the officers found the friend, who had not been present during the initial search, they had reasonable grounds to believe that he had left the briefcase and was therefore involved in the commission of gambling offenses. Thus, the friend's arrest was constitutional. (A) focuses on the propriety of the search that uncovered the heroin, rather than on the validity of the arrest itself. Do not be sidetracked. The call of the question concerns the validity of the arrest. As has been explained above, the friend's arrest was constitutional and based on grounds entirely independent of the legality of the subsequent search and seizure. Moreover, because the arrest was valid, it does not matter whether the officer thought the bulge was a weapon. This alludes to whether a valid warrantless frisk was performed. A police officer may frisk a person for weapons without a warrant if the officer has reason to believe the suspect is armed and dangerous. But here, the friend had been placed under arrest. Incident to arrest, a person may be thoroughly searched for weapons or any type of evidence. Thus, (A) is incorrect. Although it is true that, as (B) states, the friend's mere presence in the house did not give probable cause to believe he had committed a crime, his arrest was not based on his mere presence. As has been explained, reasonable grounds to believe that the friend was part of the gambling operation arose from the presence of betting slips in the briefcase and the great likelihood that the friend was the person who brought the briefcase into the house. Thus, (B) incorrectly states the basis for the friend's arrest. Also, (B) incorrectly states that there was no basis to search the friend, because he had not behaved threateningly. In fact, the police may conduct a search incident to a constitutional arrest without actually fearing for their safety. Note also that this second part of (B), similarly to (A), incorrectly focuses on the search of the friend, rather than on the arrest itself. (D) incorrectly asserts a right to search the man independent of any probable cause to arrest him. A search warrant does not authorize the police to search persons found on the premises who are not named in the warrant. However, if the police have probable cause to arrest a person discovered on the premises, they may search him incident to the arrest. Consequently, any right that the police had to search the friend arose from their arrest of him, which was based on probable cause. (D) ignores the necessity of probable cause to arrest. Of course, (D) also attempts the same distraction as (A) and (B); *i.e.,* it focuses on the search of the friend as a means of either justifying or attacking the arrest, rather than on the grounds for the arrest itself.

Answer to Question 14

(C) The teenager is guilty of larceny only. Larceny is the taking and carrying away of the tangible personal property of another by trespass, with the intent to permanently deprive the person of his interest in the property. Under the continuing trespass doctrine, if a defendant takes property with a wrongful state of mind but without the intent to steal, and later, while still in possession of it, forms the intent to steal it, the trespass involved in the initial wrongful taking is regarded as "continuing" and the defendant is guilty of larceny. Here, the teenager's initial wrongful taking continued to the time the teenager intentionally destroyed the car, thereby permanently depriving the owner of possession. Therefore, the teenager committed larceny and (A) is incorrect. Burglary requires the breaking and entering of the dwelling of another at nighttime with the intent to commit a felony therein. The teenager is not guilty of burglary because, when he entered the attached garage, he did not intend to commit a felony therein; he merely intended to borrow the car. Thus, (B) and (D) are incorrect.

Answer to Question 15

(C) The locksmith cannot be convicted as an accomplice because he did not have the requisite intent for attempted murder. To be convicted as an accomplice under the prevailing rule, a person must

have given aid, counsel, or encouragement with the ***intent*** to aid or encourage the principal in the commission of the crime charged. Mere knowledge that a crime would result from the aid provided is generally insufficient for accomplice liability. Here, the locksmith did not provide the tools to the friend with the intent that he kill the rival. His knowledge that the friend might be intending harm to the rival is not sufficient to establish the intent to kill required for attempted murder. (A) is incorrect because even if the locksmith's conduct constituted reckless disregard of high risk to human life, that state of mind is not sufficient for attempted murder. Unlike murder, ***attempted*** murder is a specific intent crime and requires the intent to kill. (B) is incorrect. Although the locksmith's attempt to neutralize his assistance would not have been enough to raise the defense of withdrawal if he had incurred liability as an accomplice, here he did not have the requisite intent for accomplice liability. (D) is an incorrect statement of law; the degree of liability of a principal is irrelevant to the potential liability of an accomplice. If the locksmith had had the intent to aid his friend in killing the rival, the fact that the friend could show adequate provocation to reduce his offense to attempted voluntary manslaughter would have no effect on the locksmith's liability for attempted murder.

Answer to Question 16

(C) The heroin was discovered during a search incident to a lawful arrest and is admissible. A search warrant does not authorize the police to search persons found on the premises who are not named in the warrant. However, if the police have probable cause to arrest a person discovered on the premises, they may search him ***incident to the arrest.*** This search may be of the person and areas into which he might reach to obtain weapons or destroy evidence (his "wingspan"). The arrest of the woman was lawful because the presence of the timers she brought to the house gave the police probable cause to believe that she was involved in the arsons being investigated. Because the arrest of the woman was lawful, the police were entitled to conduct a search incident to that arrest. Such a search was permissible even though the police did not actually fear for their safety. Consequently, the heroin discovered as a result of this search is admissible, and the motion to suppress will be denied. (A) is incorrect because, although the warrant only authorized a search of the premises, this does not preclude the police from also searching persons found on the premises as to whom there exists probable cause to arrest. Once the woman was lawfully arrested, the police were fully entitled to search her incident to the arrest. (B) is incorrect because, as explained above, the arrest of the woman was lawful. Thus, the heroin cannot be suppressed as the product of an unlawful arrest. (D) is not as good a choice as (C) because whether the backpack was covered by the warrant to search the house is irrelevant to the woman's charge. Once the woman relinquished possession of the backpack by giving it to the officer, she did not have a reasonable expectation of privacy in the object, nor did she have an expectation of privacy in the home (as it was not her home and she was not an overnight guest); hence, she did not have standing to object to the backpack being searched, even if it was not covered by the warrant to search the home.

Answer to Question 17

(D) If the attendant cannot be prosecuted for manslaughter, it will be because he was privileged to use deadly force to apprehend a fleeing felon. A private person may use deadly force to apprehend a fleeing felon if the felon threatens death or serious bodily harm and deadly force is necessary to prevent her escape. Also, for a private person to use force to effect an arrest, the person harmed must actually be guilty of the felony for which the arrest was made; *i.e.,* it is not sufficient that it reasonably appeared that the person was guilty. Here, the robber actually committed the felony of robbery. Because she was armed with a knife, the robber threatened death or serious

bodily harm, and deadly force was necessary to prevent her escape. Thus, the newsstand attendant's best argument is that he had the right to use deadly force to apprehend her, and this serves as a defense to a charge of manslaughter. (A) is incorrect because acting with the intent to inflict serious bodily injury is a sufficient mens rea for voluntary manslaughter. Thus, the fact that the attendant intended only to inflict great bodily injury is no defense to manslaughter. (B) is incorrect because the existence of provocation is not a defense to manslaughter. Rather, provocation must be found to reduce a killing from murder to manslaughter. Thus, the fact that the attendant may have been provoked by the robbery would, if anything, provide a basis for a manslaughter prosecution, rather than a defense thereto. (C) is incorrect because deadly force may not lawfully be used merely to regain possession of property. Deadly force could only be justified by another basis of privilege, such as to effectuate an arrest.

Answer to Question 18

(B) The lookout's best defense is that the gunman was the only person killed. Under the felony murder doctrine, a killing committed during the course of a felony is murder, malice being implied from the intent to commit the underlying felony. However, under the majority view, criminal liability for murder cannot be based on the death of a co-felon from resistance by the victim or police pursuit. Thus, given that the gunman's death resulted from an act by the clerk, the victim of the robbery, the lookout cannot be found guilty of the felony murder of the gunman, a co-felon. (A) is incorrect because any desire or lack of desire by the lookout to see her co-felon harmed is irrelevant to liability for felony murder. The only mens rea required is the intent to commit the underlying felony. Here, the lookout had the intent to commit robbery, the underlying felony. From this intent, the malice required for murder is implied. (C) is incorrect because the fact that the felony was technically completed before the gunman's death does not prevent the killing from being felony murder. A death caused while fleeing from the crime is considered to have been caused during the commission of the felony. (D) is incorrect because robbery is a felony regardless of the value of the property that is taken.

Set 4 Answer Sheet

1. Ⓐ Ⓑ Ⓒ Ⓓ
2. Ⓐ Ⓑ Ⓒ Ⓓ
3. Ⓐ Ⓑ Ⓒ Ⓓ
4. Ⓐ Ⓑ Ⓒ Ⓓ
5. Ⓐ Ⓑ Ⓒ Ⓓ
6. Ⓐ Ⓑ Ⓒ Ⓓ
7. Ⓐ Ⓑ Ⓒ Ⓓ
8. Ⓐ Ⓑ Ⓒ Ⓓ
9. Ⓐ Ⓑ Ⓒ Ⓓ
10. Ⓐ Ⓑ Ⓒ Ⓓ
11. Ⓐ Ⓑ Ⓒ Ⓓ
12. Ⓐ Ⓑ Ⓒ Ⓓ
13. Ⓐ Ⓑ Ⓒ Ⓓ
14. Ⓐ Ⓑ Ⓒ Ⓓ
15. Ⓐ Ⓑ Ⓒ Ⓓ
16. Ⓐ Ⓑ Ⓒ Ⓓ
17. Ⓐ Ⓑ Ⓒ Ⓓ
18. Ⓐ Ⓑ Ⓒ Ⓓ

CRIMINAL LAW QUESTIONS - SET 4

Question 1

A defendant was arrested on suspicion of running an illegal "moonshine" operation. After taking the defendant back to the police station, an officer began questioning the suspect, thinking that his partner had already given the defendant a *Miranda* warning. The defendant voluntarily confessed to each and every element of the crime.

At trial, the defendant took the witness stand and testified on his own behalf, declaring that he was innocent and that a distillery that the officers found at his home belonged to someone else. The prosecution, on cross-examination, produced the confession that the defendant gave concerning his illegal activities. The defense counsel objected to the admission of the confession.

How should the court rule on the defendant's objection?

(A) Sustained, because all evidence obtained in violation of *Miranda* rights is inadmissible.

(B) Sustained, because the prosecution did not get permission from the court in advance to use the confession for any purpose.

(C) Overruled, because the prosecution may question the defendant on cross-examination concerning any issue that was brought out in his defense.

(D) Overruled, but the confession should be admitted only for the limited purpose of impeachment.

Question 2

The defendant discovered that his friend had hit and killed a pedestrian while driving that afternoon, and that he had fled from the scene of the crime before the police arrived. To keep his friend out of trouble, the defendant fixed all the dents in the car caused by the collision and had the vehicle painted a different color. The friend, distraught about hitting and killing someone, eventually turned himself in and told the police what he had done and what the defendant had done for him. The defendant was charged as an accomplice to vehicular manslaughter in a state that follows the modern trend regarding accomplice liability.

He should be found:

(A) Not guilty, because he only helped his friend after the crime was already committed.

(B) Not guilty, because he had no affirmative duty to the victim.

(C) Guilty, because he aided his friend in the crime.

(D) Guilty, because as a party to the crime, he is criminally responsible for all crimes committed by his co-felons.

Question 3

The victim was walking out of a store when she saw someone suddenly fall to the street with an apparent heart attack. However, that person was in fact an accomplice of the defendant. With the victim's attention momentarily diverted, the defendant removed the victim's wallet from her purse. Another passerby shouted to the victim, who turned and caught the defendant by his sleeve. The defendant pushed her hand away and started to run, but tripped over a curb and dropped the wallet when he fell, and the victim was able to recover it.

The most serious crime that the defendant could be charged with is:

(A) Attempted larceny.

(B) Larceny by trick.

(C) Attempted robbery.

(D) Robbery.

Question 4

A wife wanted to have her husband murdered in order to collect the proceeds from a life insurance policy. The wife solicited the services of a hitman, agreeing to split the insurance proceeds with him. The plan was for the hitman to shoot the husband at home and make it look like a botched burglary attempt, while the wife would be at her church hall playing bingo that night. However, when the hitman broke into the apartment, the husband was able to subdue him and call the police. The hitman was arrested and implicated the wife, who was arrested in the parish priest's office just after she had confessed the plan to the priest. The wife is charged with attempted murder and conspiracy to commit murder in a state that retains the common law definitions of these crimes. A psychiatric evaluation of the hitman after he was arrested revealed that he was legally insane, and he later committed suicide while awaiting trial.

As to the conspiracy charge against the wife, which of the following would be her most promising defense?

(A) She cannot be tried for both offenses; the prosecutor must choose between them.

(B) The hitman was insane when the conspiracy was formed.

(C) The hitman died in jail before trial.

(D) She had second thoughts about the plan while playing bingo and had revealed it to her priest.

Question 5

As a wife was organizing files on the family computer, she discovered emails and photos showing that her husband was having an affair with his secretary. The wife was incensed, so she went to a drawer where she knew her husband kept his handgun and, assuming it was loaded because he always told her that it was, headed off to her husband's office with the intent to do away with his secretary. When the wife arrived, she burst into the office, pulled the gun out of her purse, and pointed it at the secretary. However, when the wife pulled the trigger, nothing happened, because the handgun contained no ammunition.

The jurisdiction's criminal code defines assault as "(1) an attempt to commit a battery; or (2) the intentional creation of a reasonable apprehension in the mind of the victim of imminent bodily harm." The code uses the common law definitions of homicide crimes.

Of which of the following crimes could the wife be convicted?

(A) Assault and attempted manslaughter, but not attempted murder.

(B) Attempted murder only.

(C) Assault and either attempted murder or attempted manslaughter.

(D) Attempted murder or attempted manslaughter, but not assault.

Question 6

Two partners who operated an electronics retail store hired a thug to intimidate the owner of a discount electronics store that was undercutting their prices and drawing customers away. They told the thug to rob the store owner but not to harm him; they only wanted to scare him out of town. The thug loitered near the discount store, waiting for it to close. When the lights in the store went out, an employee left by the back exit. The thug thought he was the owner and drew his gun, demanding money. The employee resisted, and in the ensuing struggle was fatally shot. The thug ran off, but both he and the partners were eventually arrested.

In addition to conspiracy to commit robbery, the partners are guilty of:

(A) No other crime.

(B) Robbery.

(C) Felony murder.

(D) Robbery and felony murder.

Question 7

The defendant pointed a loaded gun and shot at the victim. The bullet, however, missed the intended victim, but struck a bystander in the stomach. The bystander fully recovered. In a subsequent prosecution for attempted murder of both the victim and the bystander, the defendant testified that he had wanted only to scare the victim.

Assuming that the jury believes this testimony, he may be convicted of attempted murder as to:

(A) The victim.

(B) The bystander.

(C) Both the victim and the bystander.

(D) Neither the victim nor the bystander.

Question 8

A felon intending to rob a market waited outside until there were no customers. When he saw that the market was empty, he went inside and walked up to the counter with his hand in his jacket pocket to simulate a gun. Before the clerk could turn around to see what the felon wanted, another customer entered the market, startling the felon, who turned and ran out the door.

On a charge of attempted robbery, the felon should be found:

(A) Not guilty, because he used no actual force on the clerk nor threatened any.

(B) Not guilty, because he withdrew successfully from the robbery attempt.

(C) Not guilty, because he never entered the zone of perpetration.

(D) Guilty, regardless of whether he totally abandoned his plan when the customer entered the market.

Question 9

A bank robber held up the local bank at gunpoint wearing a nylon stocking over his head to conceal his identity. He ran out of the bank with the money, intending to get to the nearby train station and catch a train out of town. A customer of the bank had left her car running in the parking lot while she had dashed into the bank to make a quick deposit. The robber jumped into the customer's car and sped off to the train station. He left the car in the parking lot and boarded the train, but he was eventually apprehended and charged with bank robbery.

If the robber is also charged with larceny of the customer's car, he should be found:

(A) Not guilty of larceny, because the customer was grossly negligent in leaving the car unlocked and running.

(B) Not guilty of larceny, because he only intended to use it for his escape.

(C) Guilty of larceny, because using the car for his escape subjected it to a substantial risk of loss.

(D) Guilty of larceny, because it was taken to aid in the commission of an inherently dangerous felony.

Question 10

State law required that all businesses in the state to report any deposits of toxic waste discovered on property owned by the reporting firm. Another provision of the law required that the toxic waste reports be made on a specific state form and that duplicate copies of the form be filed with both the state department of labor and the state environmental protection agency. The statute provided that after each report was filed, the relevant state agencies would ensure that any dangerous area was cordoned off and

work out a plan with the reporting firm for the clean-up of the waste deposit. The effective date of the statute was June 15, but the state office did not produce any of the special forms until July 6.

The defendant, a safety inspector employed by a chemical company, was making her first visit to one of the company's plants on June 17 when she noticed a strange substance on the premises. The defendant filed no report to the state agencies regarding the substance because she was not aware of the requirement, nor did she know that the substance was toxic. On June 20, another employee of the chemical company was walking in an area near the substance when he slipped and fell face first into it. The substance turned out to be very toxic. The employee's skin contact with the substance was sufficient to kill him in a matter of minutes. A later investigation revealed that it would have been impossible to clean up the substance to make the area safe before the employee encountered it.

If the defendant is charged with murder, which of the following represents her best defense:

(A) She did not know that the substance was toxic.

(B) She was unaware of the state reporting law.

(C) The state printing office did not produce any copies of the special forms until July 6.

(D) It would have been impossible to clean up the toxic waste deposit before the time that the employee encountered it.

Question 11

A thug approached the defendant on a street, brandishing a gun. He told the defendant that he had to burn down a store across the street or he was going to shoot him. The defendant complied at gunpoint, starting a fire in the store with gas and matches. Soon after, the owner of the store rushed in trying to save her important papers. In doing so, she was overcome by smoke and died in the fire. The defendant is charged with the criminal homicide of the store's owner.

The most likely result is that the defendant will be found to be:

(A) Guilty of murder.

(B) Guilty of manslaughter.

(C) Not guilty of murder, because duress is a defense to arson.

(D) Not guilty of murder, because the defendant never intended to kill anyone.

Question 12

A woman was stopped at a police roadblock to check for drunk drivers. The police were stopping every third vehicle that came through the checkpoint, and the woman's car turned out to be a third vehicle. After failing a field sobriety test, the woman was arrested and charged with driving while intoxicated.

Was the stop of the woman's car legal?

(A) Yes, because the car was stopped at a fixed checkpoint to check for drunk drivers.

(B) Yes, because temporarily stopping a car does not constitute a seizure of the automobile.

(C) No, because not every car was being stopped.

(D) No, because there was no probable cause to stop the vehicle.

Question 13

A man and a woman were traveling in the man's car when they were stopped by the police for running a red light. Before the police came up to the car, the man told the woman, "You owe me a favor. Keep this package for me," and gave the woman a small foil package. The woman put the package in her backpack, saying, "O.K., but don't tell me what's in it." Before the police even began to question the occupants, the man blurted out, "I'm clean, man, but ***she*** has a stash," pointing at the woman. The officers searched the backpack that the woman was holding and found the foil package, which contained heroin. The woman was arrested, but the man was not.

Is the evidence found on the woman admissible?

(A) Yes, under the automobile exception.

(B) Yes, because due process imputes knowledge where there is willful ignorance.

(C) No, because due process forbids granting of immunity to the more culpable defendant.

(D) No, because the woman did not know that the package contained heroin.

Question 14

The defendant broke into his intended victim's home at night intending to burn it down. He poured gasoline on the floor. However, he discovered that he had forgotten matches or a lighter so he left the premises and headed to a nearby convenience store. Just then, a sudden thunderstorm broke, and a bolt of lightning struck the victim's home, burning it to the ground. When the defendant came back to the home, he was arrested by police who had been called to the scene.

The defendant was charged with burglary and arson. At trial, the fire marshal testified that the gasoline in the basement had no effect on the fire, and that the lightning bolt set off a chain of events that would have destroyed the victim's home anyway.

The jury should convict the defendant of:

(A) Burglary only.

(B) Burglary and arson.

(C) Burglary and attempted arson.

(D) Attempted burglary and attempted arson.

Question 15

After learning that she was the sole beneficiary in her wealthy uncle's will, a niece broke into his house while he was away one evening. She brought with her a vial of poison that she believed would be lethal but undetectable. She poured it into a glass of water that her uncle had placed on the bedside table. During the night, the uncle took a drink of water and the poison started to affect his ability to breathe. Thinking he was having a heart attack, the uncle started to go downstairs to call his doctor. On the way, he slipped and fell down the stairs, breaking his neck. He was found dead the next day. An autopsy revealed that the uncle had ingested poison, but not in a sufficient quantity to have caused death. Further investigation led the police to the niece, who was arrested and charged with burglary and murder.

Based on the above facts, the niece should be convicted of:

(A) Burglary only.

(B) Burglary and murder.

(C) Burglary and attempted murder.

(D) Attempted burglary and attempted murder.

Question 16

The state takes a "bifurcated trial" approach to insanity defense cases. The first part of the trial determines the defendant's guilt or innocence, and the second part determines whether the defendant was legally sane at the time the crime was committed. It also has modeled most of its criminal code after the Model Penal Code.

The defendant was on trial for murder. The prosecution produced three witnesses who

testified that they had seen the defendant shoot the victim. The defense put the defendant on the stand, and the defense attorney asked him if he shot the victim. The defendant answered that he did not shoot a man, and that he had shot a tiger instead. The prosecution immediately objected, and moved that the defendant's testimony be stricken.

How should the court rule on that motion?

(A) Granted, because the defendant's purported delusions are only relevant to the second part of the trial.

(B) Granted, if the judge is convinced that the defendant is lying.

(C) Not granted, because the testimony is relevant to the defendant's mens rea.

(D) Not granted, because the testimony is relevant to the defendant's conduct.

Question 17

A defendant who was indigent was charged with a crime for which the maximum punishment is six months in prison and a fine of $500. At a hearing, the defendant told the judge that he wanted to plead not guilty and that he wished to represent himself. The judge told the defendant that the court would appoint an attorney to represent him if he needed counsel. He further explained that the state has a policy of appointing private attorneys to defend indigents, and that if such defendants are acquitted or imprisoned, there is no charge for the court-appointed lawyer. If, however, the defendant is sentenced to probation, the defendant must pay "reasonable attorney's fees," which it is presumed the defendant will be able to pay out of job earnings while on probation. The defendant told the judge that paying for an attorney would be difficult, and that he still wished to defend himself. The judge believed that the defendant was competent to defend himself, but nevertheless appointed an attorney with criminal defense experience to defend him. The defendant fully cooperated with the attorney, who did a highly competent job, but the evidence heavily favored the state. The defendant was convicted, but the attorney's plea for leniency was effective, and the defendant received a suspended sentence and probation.

Two weeks later, the defendant received a bill for $500 for legal services, a figure that represented about half the sum a lawyer not appointed by the court would have charged for similar work. Although the defendant would be able to pay the bill over a long period of time via installments, he was angry that he had been billed at all, and believed that he could have gotten probation if he had been allowed to argue his own case. He consulted another attorney, and asked her to appeal both his conviction and the imposition of the legal fees.

The second attorney should advise the defendant that the appellate court would most likely:

(A) Affirm both his conviction and the imposition of fees, because there is no reversible error, since the trial attorney competently represented the defendant and the state has a right to recoup costs from those able to pay.

(B) Affirm the conviction because there was no reversible error, but reverse the imposition of fees, because the defendant could have gotten probation for himself as easily as the attorney did.

(C) Reverse the conviction, because the defendant was denied the right to defend himself, but affirm the imposition of fees because the attorney was competent and the state has a right to recoup costs from those able to pay.

(D) Reverse both the conviction and the imposition of fees, because the defendant was denied the right to defend himself.

Question 18

After a business lunch at a restaurant, a patron went to the restaurant's cloakroom to get his coat. He removed a coat he believed to be his own from the coat rack. The coat was of similar color and of the same brand as the patron's own coat, but it actually belonged to another customer. The patron walked back to his office and removed the coat. As he was hanging it up, he noticed that another person's name was written on the inside of the collar. He immediately left the office and sprinted back in the direction of the restaurant, intending to return the coat and pick up his own. As he crossed the street, the patron was struck by a car. Although his injuries were minor, the coat was destroyed.

If the patron is acquitted of larceny, what is the best reason for his acquittal?

(A) The coat was destroyed through no fault of his own.

(B) The coat looked so much like the patron's coat that his mistake was reasonable.

(C) The patron thought the coat was his when he took it.

(D) When he realized the coat was not his, the patron tried to return it.

CRIMINAL LAW ANSWERS - SET 4

Answer to Question 1

(D) The defendant's objection should be overruled. A confession obtained in violation of *Miranda*, but otherwise voluntary, can be used for the limited purpose of impeaching a defendant who testifies at trial. In contrast, an involuntary confession cannot be used to impeach. Here, there are no facts to indicate that the defendant's statement was involuntary. Thus, it can be used to impeach the defendant. (A) is too broad a statement. Although a confession obtained in violation of *Miranda* is inadmissible in the state's case-in-chief as evidence of guilt, as discussed above, such evidence is admissible for limited purposes. (B) is wrong. Advance permission from the court is not a requirement if the confession is used to impeach. (C) is a correct statement but it does not speak directly to the issue of whether the confession is admissible and to what extent.

Answer to Question 2

(A) Under modern statutes, parties to a crime are divided into three different categories. Principals are those who, with the requisite mental state, actually engage in the act or omission that causes the criminal result. An accomplice is one who, with the intent that the crime be committed, aids, counsels, or encourages the principal before or during the commission of the offense. Under modern statutes, accomplices are generally treated as principals. A third category is "an accessory after the fact." An accessory after the fact is one who receives, relieves, comforts, or assists another knowing that he has committed a felony, in order to help the felon escape arrest, trial, or conviction. Unlike an accomplice, an accessory after the fact has committed a separate crime with a punishment unrelated to the felony committed. In the instant case, it is clear that the defendant aided his friend in avoiding capture, that he provided no aid to the substantive offense, and that he did not intend the substantive offense to occur. Thus, he is an accessory after the fact and not an accomplice, making (A) the correct answer. (B) is incorrect because, although it is true that one need not prevent a crime from being committed, one cannot help another avoid arrest, as the defendant did in this case. (C) is incorrect. The defendant did not aid his friend in the commission of the crime; his help came afterward. Thus, the aid provided makes him an accessory after the fact, as explained above, and not an accomplice. (D) is incorrect. The criminal liability for other probable or foreseeable crimes arises when one is deemed an accomplice of a principal. As stated above, the defendant is not an accomplice, so, under these facts, he cannot be criminally liable for any other crimes committed by the defendant.

Answer to Question 3

(D) The defendant could be charged with robbery under these facts because of his use of force. Robbery is larceny from the person or presence of the victim by means of violence or intimidation. The use of force constituting a battery is sufficient, and if the perpetrator uses force to overcome the person's resistance to the taking, there is sufficient force to constitute a robbery. All that is required for taking is that the perpetrator have possession of the item, and the slightest movement will suffice for the carrying away. The fact that he subsequently dropped the wallet does not negate his completion of the crime; hence, (C) is incorrect. (B) is incorrect because larceny by trick involves the victim consenting to the defendant obtaining possession of property as a result of a misrepresentation, not the case here.

Answer to Question 4

(B) If the hitman was insane, the wife cannot be said to have conspired with him to commit the murder. A conspiracy consists of: (i) an agreement between two or more persons; (ii) an intent to

enter into an agreement; and (iii) an intent to achieve the objective of the agreement. The parties must agree to accomplish the same objective by mutual action. This agreement requires a meeting of at least two "guilty minds"; *i.e.,* two persons who are actually committing themselves to the scheme. If the hitman was insane, then he lacked the capacity to intentionally enter into an agreement to kill the husband and to intend to achieve the murder. Under this circumstance, the wife was the only one who was actually committed to the crime and who intended to bring it about. Because there was no meeting of the wife's "guilty mind" with at least one other, the wife cannot be convicted of conspiracy under the common law rule. (A) is incorrect because a defendant can be tried and convicted of both conspiracy and the crime she commits pursuant to the conspiracy (here, attempted murder). (C) is incorrect because a conviction of conspiracy does not require that all parties be tried and convicted. While an ***acquittal*** of all persons with whom a person is alleged to have conspired precludes conviction of the remaining defendant, that is not the case here. The hitman was not acquitted. Also, note that a state's decision to discontinue prosecution would not be deemed to be an acquittal, and thus most likely a state's ***inability*** to prosecute because of a co-conspirator's death would not be an acquittal. (D) is incorrect for two reasons: (i) withdrawal from a conspiracy is not a defense to a charge of conspiracy, and (ii) withdrawal is a defense to ***subsequent crimes*** committed by other members of the conspiracy only if the withdrawing party performs an affirmative act notifying all members of the conspiracy in time for them to have the opportunity to abandon their plans. Here, the wife notified the priest, but took no further action to thwart the conspiracy. Thus, she has no defense to the conspiracy, and it is unlikely that merely telling a priest would be a sufficient withdrawal as to subsequent crimes.

Answer to Question 5

(C) The wife could be convicted of assault and either attempted murder or attempted manslaughter. To be liable for either attempted murder or attempted manslaughter, the defendant must have acted with the intent to kill and have committed an act beyond mere preparation for the offense. The fact that it is not possible to complete the intended offense (factual impossibility) is not a defense to liability for attempt. Here, the wife clearly intended to kill the secretary and did everything in her power to carry out the killing. The fact that the gun was not loaded is no defense. (B) and (D) are wrong because the wife could also be convicted of assault. Assault is either: (i) an attempt to commit a battery; or (ii) the intentional creation (other than by mere words) of a reasonable apprehension in the mind of the victim of imminent bodily harm. Here, the wife has committed both types of assault: she attempted to commit a battery against the secretary and intentionally placed her in fear of imminent bodily harm. Although she could not be convicted of the first type of assault if she were also convicted of attempted murder or attempted manslaughter (because that type of assault is a lesser-included offense that merges into the greater offense), she could be convicted of the second type of assault (it does not merge because it contains elements not encompassed by attempted murder or attempted manslaughter). (A) is wrong because the wife could be convicted of attempted murder instead of attempted manslaughter if she cannot establish adequate provocation. An intentional killing can be reduced from murder to voluntary manslaughter if (i) there exists a provocation that would arouse sudden and intense passion in the mind of an ordinary person so as to cause her to lose self-control; (ii) the defendant in fact was provoked; (iii) there was insufficient time for the passions of a reasonable person to cool; and (iv) the defendant in fact did not cool off between the provocation and the killing. Many common law courts recognized the existence of provocation in only two instances: exposure to a threat of deadly force and discovery of one's spouse in bed with another person. Furthermore, some provocations, such as "mere words," were defined as inadequate provocation as a matter of law. Modern courts tend to be more reluctant to take such cases from juries and are more likely to submit to the jury the question of whether "mere words" or similar

matters constitute adequate provocation. These principles apply in this case even though the wife's liability is only for attempted murder or manslaughter rather than the completed offense. Here, the wife's discovery of the emails and photographs might be sufficient to make it a jury question as to whether adequate provocation existed. However, the jury might still conclude that the provocation was not sufficient and find the wife liable for attempted murder rather than attempted manslaughter.

Answer to Question 6

(C) The partners are guilty of felony murder in addition to conspiracy to commit robbery. A killing (even if accidental) committed during the course of a felony is murder. If, in the course of a conspiracy to commit a felony, a death is caused, all members of the conspiracy are liable for murder if the death was caused in furtherance of the conspiracy and was a foreseeable consequence of the conspiracy. Here, although there was to be no physical harm, and the thug mistook the employee for the discount store owner, it was foreseeable that death would result from the commission of a dangerous felony such as robbery. The employee's death occurred in furtherance of the conspiracy to rob the discount store owner. Because this death occurred in furtherance of the conspiracy and was a foreseeable consequence thereof, the other conspirators (the partners) are liable for felony murder. Robbery was not committed here because there was no taking of personal property from the employee. Robbery consists of a taking of the personal property of another from the other's person or presence by force or intimidation with the intent to permanently deprive him of the property. Although the thug demanded the employee's money, the ensuing struggle prevented him from actually taking it. This would be attempted robbery, because the thug committed an act with the intention of committing robbery, but he fell short of completing the crime. However, this is not robbery. Therefore, (A) is incorrect because it fails to account for the fact that the partners are guilty of felony murder as well as conspiracy to commit robbery. (B) and (D) are incorrect because they would find the partners guilty of robbery, despite the fact that there was no taking of personal property. Also, (B) ignores the fact that the partners are guilty of felony murder.

Answer to Question 7

(D) The defendant may not be convicted of attempted murder because he lacked the necessary intent. A criminal attempt consists of: (i) conduct that brings the defendant in close proximity to the completed offense; and (ii) the intent to commit the completed crime. In other words, the defendant must have the intent to perform an act and obtain a result that would constitute the crime charged if achieved. Regardless of the intent required for the completed offense, an attempt always required specific intent. Thus, attempted murder required the specific intent to kill another person, even though the mens rea for murder itself does not require specific intent—had the bystander died, the defendant could have been convicted of murder, given that malice could have been established by the defendant being aware of an unjustifiably high risk to human life (*i.e.,* an "abandoned and malignant" heart) by pointing a loaded gun and shooting at an individual. However, the defendant did not have the intent to kill either victim, so he lacked the intent necessary for attempt. (D) is therefore correct, and (A), (B), and (C) are incorrect. In answering questions such as this one, remember to be objective and answer the question asked. Although the defendant here is surely guilty of some crimes—*e.g.,* assault and battery—he is not guilty of the charged crime.

Answer to Question 8

(D) The felon should be found guilty of attempted robbery. With the specific intent to commit a robbery, the felon went beyond mere preparation for the offense, and having done so, abandonment

is not a defense. A criminal attempt is an act that, although done with the intention of committing a crime, falls short of completing the crime. The defendant must have the intent to perform an act and obtain a result that, if achieved, would constitute a crime. Also, the defendant must have committed an act beyond mere preparation for the offense. If a defendant has, with the required intent, gone beyond preparation, the general rule is that abandonment is not a defense. Even in those jurisdictions in which abandonment is a defense, such abandonment must be: (i) fully voluntary and not made because of the difficulty of completing the crime or because of an increased risk of apprehension; and (ii) a complete abandonment of the plan made under circumstances manifesting a renunciation of criminal purpose, not just a decision to postpone committing it or to find another victim. Here, the felon intended to take money from the clerk at the market by means of the threat of having a gun (*i.e.,* by simulating a gun). Thus, the felon intended to commit a robbery. In walking up to the market counter while simulating a gun with his hand, the felon committed an act that was a substantial step toward commission of the intended crime, and that strongly corroborated his intent and purpose to commit the crime. All that was missing to complete the crime was for the clerk to turn around and, upon seeing the felon apparently armed, be forced to give up the money. Thus, the felon went far beyond mere preparation for the crime of robbery. Having gone beyond mere preparation, with the intent to commit robbery, the felon is guilty of attempted robbery. And, as explained above, even if the felon abandoned his plan when the customer entered the market, such abandonment will not afford him a defense. Even in those jurisdictions in which abandonment is a defense, the felon will not have a defense because his abandonment apparently occurred when the customer's sudden presence increased the risk of apprehension. Thus, the abandonment did not really manifest a renunciation of criminal purpose. (A) is incorrect because, to be guilty of attempted robbery, events need not have progressed to the point where the defendant has used or threatened to use force. Since the felon had the requisite intent for attempt and went beyond mere preparation by standing at the counter and simulating possession of a gun, he should be found guilty of attempted robbery. (B) is incorrect because, as detailed above, abandonment of an attempt does not afford a defense, and in any event, the felon's abandonment here did not really come about by way of renouncing his criminal purpose. (C) is incorrect because a conviction of attempt does not require entry into a "zone of perpetration." Rather, a defendant (with the requisite intent) need only have committed an act beyond mere preparation. The Model Penal Code and most state criminal codes require that the act constitute a substantial step towards commission of the crime and strongly corroborate the actor's criminal purpose.

Answer to Question 9

(B) Because the bank robber only intended to use the customer's car briefly (to get to the train station), he lacked the intent to permanently deprive the customer of the car. Larceny consists of a taking and carrying away of the tangible personal property of another by trespass, with intent to permanently (or for an unreasonable time) deprive the person of her interest in the property. If the defendant intends to deal with the property in a manner that involves a substantial risk of loss, this intent is sufficient for larceny. Although the bank robber wrongfully took and carried away the customer's car, he did not have the requisite intent for larceny. The bank robber intended only to use the car as a means of getting to the train station, and he left it in a public place, where it was likely to be easily and quickly recovered and restored to the customer. Therefore, the bank robber lacked the requisite intent for larceny. (C) is wrong because there is no indication that the circumstances of the escape were such that there existed a substantial risk of loss of the car. The bank robber was not going to drive the car a great distance, nor was he going to abandon it in some dangerous or obscure location. Admittedly, there may have been ***some*** risk of loss involved in the use of the car. However, the risk was not so substantial as to indicate that the bank robber possessed the intent to deprive that is required for larceny. (A) is incorrect because the negligence of the owner of property does not constitute a defense to a charge of larceny. Although it may have been unwise for the customer to leave her car unlocked with the motor running, a taking of the car without her consent would still be wrongful. (D) is incorrect because the taking of property to aid in the commission of an inherently dangerous felony does not in and of itself constitute larceny. (D) implies the existence of a "felony larceny" rule, similar to felony murder. There is no such rule. Therefore, it must be shown that the bank robber possessed the requisite intent before he will be found guilty of larceny.

Answer to Question 10

(A) If the defendant did not know that the substance was toxic, she did not have the state of mind necessary for murder. Ignorance or mistake as to a matter of fact will serve as a defense to a crime if it shows that the defendant did not have the state of mind required for the crime. If the mistake is offered as a defense to a malice crime, the mistake must be reasonable; *i.e.,* it must be the type of mistake that a reasonable person might make under the circumstances. Although the statute itself may create a strict liability offense, for which the defendant's mistake as to the identity of the substance would not be a defense, the defendant here is being charged with murder, which is a malice crime. For the defendant to be convicted of murder, it must be shown that she had: (i) intent to kill; (ii) intent to inflict great bodily injury; (iii) reckless indifference to an unjustifiably high risk to human life; or (iv) intent to commit a felony. If she knew that the substance was toxic, the prosecution would have an argument that she acted with reckless indifference to an unjustifiably high risk to human life by not taking any action. However, if she did not know that the substance was toxic, her failure to act is far less likely to establish reckless indifference. In other words, the defendant was operating under such ignorance as to a matter of fact that she did not have the requisite state of mind for murder. This would provide the defendant with a defense. (B) is incorrect because it is not a defense to crime that a defendant was unaware that her acts were prohibited by the criminal law, or that the law compelled her to do something. Thus, even though the defendant was unaware of the reporting law, such ignorance of the law is no defense. Furthermore, regardless of her awareness of the reporting law, the defendant, as a safety inspector for the chemical company, may have owed a duty to the employee to act to clean up toxic waste. For this reason as well, the defendant's ignorance of the reporting law would not provide her with a strong argument. (C) does not provide a strong defense argument because the requirement of filing the reports on a specified form is a mere administrative detail. The fact that the forms were not yet available would not relieve the defendant of her duty to report any known deposits of toxic waste or to otherwise act to safeguard any employees from such waste. (D) is incorrect because, even if it would have been impossible to clean up the waste deposit by the time the employee encountered it, an immediate report by the defendant on the existence of the deposit would at least have resulted in warning the employees to stay away from the area, perhaps leading also to the cordoning off of the area.

Answer to Question 11

(C) The defendant is not guilty of arson (since he acted under duress) and therefore he is not guilty of the store owner's homicide. A person is not guilty of an offense, other than homicide, if he performs the otherwise criminal act under the threat of imminent infliction of death or great bodily harm and his perception of the threat is reasonable. Here, the defendant set fire to the store because a thug ordered him to do so or he would shoot him. Since the thug had a gun, the defendant's perception of the thug's threat of imminent death or great bodily harm was reasonable. Therefore, the defendant acted under duress and is not guilty of arson. If the defendant is not guilty of

arson, then he cannot be guilty of murder. Murder requires a mental state of malice aforethought (*i.e.,* an intent to kill or inflict great bodily harm, an awareness of an unjustifiably high risk to human life, or the intent to commit a felony). Here, the state's only basis for showing malice aforethought would be to use the felony murder doctrine. Under that doctrine, a killing, even an accidental one, that occurs during the course of a felony is murder. The only felony here is arson (which includes the burning of buildings other than dwellings in most jurisdictions), and since the defendant is excused from criminal liability for that crime due to duress, he cannot be convicted of murder under the felony murder doctrine because he did not commit the underlying felony. Thus, (C) is correct and (A) is incorrect. (B) is incorrect because the defendant did not commit either voluntary or involuntary manslaughter. Voluntary manslaughter is an intentional killing distinguishable from murder by the existence of adequate provocation. As explained above, the defendant did not have the requisite intent for murder (malice aforethought) and thus he cannot be guilty of voluntary manslaughter. Nor is the defendant guilty of involuntary manslaughter. Involuntary manslaughter consists of either criminal negligence or "unlawful act" manslaughter. Since the defendant acted under duress, he was not criminally negligent nor was the burning a "malum in se" (inherently wrongful) act necessary for "unlawful act" manslaughter. Therefore, there is no basis to find the defendant guilty of manslaughter. (D) is incorrect because one can be convicted of murder without intending to kill (*e.g.,* in the case of a felony murder). Thus, if the defendant were guilty of arson, he could be found guilty of murder despite the fact that he did not intend to kill anyone.

Answer to Question 12

(A) Because the stop was at a fixed checkpoint, it was a legal stop. The police may set up roadblocks to stop cars without individualized suspicion that the driver has violated some law, as long as they: (i) stop cars on the basis of some neutral, articulable standard (*e.g.*, every car or every third car); and (ii) are motivated by a particular problem related to automobiles and their mobility (*e.g.*, drunk driving). Here, the police were entitled to stop the woman because the stop was made at a fixed checkpoint to check for drunk drivers and used a neutral standard as the basis for stopping the cars. (B) is incorrect because stopping a car constitutes a seizure for Fourth Amendment purposes. (C) is incorrect because every car need not be stopped at a fixed checkpoint, as long as the roadblock is based on some neutral, articulable standard. Here, the neutral standard was stopping every third car; thus, the roadblock would not be deemed improper for failure to stop every car. (D) is incorrect because, as discussed above, probable cause is not required under these circumstances.

Answer to Question 13

(A) The evidence is admissible because the search was valid. Even though the police have validly stopped an automobile, they cannot search the vehicle without meeting the requirements of one of the exceptions to the warrant requirement, such as the automobile exception (which requires probable cause) or consent. The automobile exception comes into play when the police have probable cause to believe that the vehicle contains evidence of a crime. Under the exception, the police may search anywhere in the vehicle in which the item for which they have cause to search may be hidden, including packages in the vehicle. The statement of the man to the officers gave them probable cause to believe that the car contained evidence of a crime (*i.e.,* that the woman had drugs somewhere in the car). Thus, the requirement for application of the automobile exception was present, providing validity for the warrantless search conducted by the police. Because the search was valid, the evidence found on the woman is admissible. Besides being an incorrect statement of law, (B) is incorrect because it focuses on the woman's knowledge of the contents of the package. Whether the woman knew that heroin (or some other illegal substance) was in the package is irrelevant to the admissibility of the heroin. Even assuming that the woman knew of the contents, the search would not be valid unless there was a ground for the warrantless search. (D) similarly links the woman's knowledge of the package's contents to the admissibility of the evidence. As noted above, the admissibility of the evidence is dependent on the validity of the search that produced the evidence, rather than on the knowledge of the defendant as to the existence of the evidence. (C) is incorrect for three reasons: (i) due process does not prohibit granting of immunity to a more culpable defendant; (ii) there is no indication that immunity was even granted here (immunity from prosecution may be granted to compel a witness to answer questions. The facts merely state that the man was not arrested; this does not necessarily mean that he was granted immunity); and (iii) the call of the question relates to the admissibility of the evidence, and a grant of immunity does not relate to the question of the admissibility of the evidence found ***on the woman***; such admissibility is determined by the validity of the search of the woman by the officers.

Answer to Question 14

(C) The defendant should be convicted of burglary and attempted arson. Burglary is a breaking and entry of the dwelling of another at nighttime with the intent of committing a felony therein. At nighttime, the defendant broke into and entered his victim's home, intending at the time of entry to commit the felony of arson. Whether the arson was ever carried out by the defendant is immaterial to the crime of burglary. What is important is the defendant's intent at the time of entering the house. Thus, all of the elements of burglary are present. Arson is the malicious burning of the dwelling of another. The defendant set out intending to burn the victim's home, but the testimony of the fire marshal indicates that the burning that occurred was not caused by the gasoline that the defendant poured in the basement. When a crime is defined to require not merely conduct but also a specified result of that conduct, the defendant's conduct must be the cause-in-fact of that result; *i.e.*, the result would not have occurred but for the defendant's conduct. Here, the result—the burning—would have occurred regardless of the defendant's conduct. Thus, it cannot be said that the defendant committed arson. Nevertheless, the defendant is guilty of attempted arson. An attempt is an act that, although done with the intention of committing a crime, falls short of completing the crime. Attempt requires a specific intent to commit the completed crime, as well as an act beyond mere preparation for the offense. The defendant certainly had the specific intent to burn the victim's home, and his pouring the gasoline in the basement was an act that went well beyond mere preparation for the crime of arson. It was only due to the fact that he had no means to ignite the gasoline that the defendant did not actually set fire to the house. Consequently, the elements for a conviction of attempted arson are present. (A) is incorrect because the defendant should be convicted of attempted arson as well as burglary. (B) is incorrect because defendant fell short of completing the crime of arson. (D) is incorrect because the crime of burglary was completed at the time of entry. Thus, there was not merely an attempted burglary.

Answer to Question 15

(B) The niece should be convicted of burglary and murder. The niece is guilty of burglary because she broke into and entered the house at night with the intent to commit the felony of murder. Regarding murder, problems of proximate causation arise when the harmful result that is an element of the crime occurs because of the defendant's acts, but in a manner not intended or anticipated by the defendant. The general rule is that a defendant is responsible for all events that occur as a natural and probable consequence of her conduct, even if she did not anticipate the

precise manner in which they would occur. Here, the niece did not actually administer enough poison to kill the uncle. However, the poison did cause the uncle to become ill and led to his falling down the stairs. Thus, the niece's conduct was the cause-in-fact of the uncle's death. In acting as she did, the niece intended to kill the uncle, and his death was within the scope of risk created by the niece's conduct. Although the uncle's death actually occurred in a manner that was unanticipated by the niece, the death was a natural and probable consequence of her pouring poison into the uncle's water, and the harm that resulted is the type that was likely to occur from her actions. Therefore, the uncle's death was proximately caused by the niece. Thus, the niece is guilty of murder, the killing of another human being with malice aforethought. (A) is incorrect because, as detailed above, the niece is guilty of burglary and murder, rather than just burglary. (C) is incorrect because the niece should be convicted of the completed crime of murder, rather than simply attempted murder. (D) is incorrect for the same reason, as well as for the reason that the niece has committed the completed crime of burglary, not just attempted burglary.

Answer to Question 16

(C) The defendant's testimony makes it more likely than not that he did not intend to kill or inflict great bodily injury to a human being, thus negating the malice aforethought required for murder. The events here take place during the first stage of the bifurcated trial process. During this stage, there is a determination of the perpetrator's guilt; *i.e.,* did the perpetrator perform a criminal act with the requisite mental state? Here, the defendant is on trial for murder. Murder is the unlawful killing of a human being with malice aforethought. Malice aforethought exists if the defendant has any of the following states of mind: (i) intent to kill; (ii) intent to inflict great bodily injury; (iii) awareness of an unjustifiably high risk to human life; or (iv) intent to commit a felony. Thus, at this first stage of the bifurcated process, it must be determined whether the defendant shot the victim with malice aforethought, thus causing the death. Although the bifurcated trial process is designed to separate, as much as possible, the issues of his guilt and his sanity, the defendant's testimony is being offered not as evidence of his insanity, but rather as evidence that, because he believed he was shooting at a tiger, he did not have the intent to kill or inflict great bodily injury to a human being. The distinction may be somewhat fine, but is in accord with the modern approach followed by the Model Penal Code. Because the defendant's testimony tends to show that, at the time of the shooting, he did not have the requisite mens rea for murder, such testimony is admissible in the "guilt" phase of the bifurcated trial process, and the prosecution's motion to strike the testimony is denied. (A) is incorrect because, as has been explained, the defendant's purported delusions are relevant to the first phase of the trial, as well as to the second, because they relate to his malice aforethought, or lack thereof. (B) is incorrect because the judge's opinion as to whether a witness is lying does not determine the admissibility of the witness's testimony (but will affect the weight to be given that testimony if the judge is the trier of fact). The defendant's testimony is relevant to his mens rea and is thus admissible even if the judge believes that the defendant is lying. (D) is incorrect because the testimony is not relevant to his conduct, in that it does not make more or less probable anything concerning the conduct itself. It is apparently undisputed that the defendant shot the victim. At issue is the existence of intent on the part of the defendant at the time of the shooting. It is to this matter that the defendant's testimony is relevant.

Answer to Question 17

(D) Although a waiver of the right to counsel will be carefully scrutinized to ensure that the defendant has a rational and factual understanding of the proceeding against him, a defendant has a right to waive counsel and represent himself as long as the waiver is knowing and intelligent, and

the defendant must be found competent to proceed pro se. Where the state provides counsel in cases of indigence, it may then seek reimbursement from a convicted defendant who subsequently becomes able to pay. Here, the judge thought that the defendant was competent to represent himself. Therefore, his waiver of counsel should have been honored. Violation of the defendant's right to represent himself will result in a reversal of his conviction. Although, as stated above, the state may recoup costs of appointed counsel from indigents who become able to pay, the state cannot recover from the defendant because the attorney was appointed against the defendant's will and in violation of his right to represent himself. Had effect been given to the defendant's right to represent himself, there would have been no attorney's fees to be assessed against him. (A) is incorrect because the denial of the defendant's right to represent himself does constitute reversible error, regardless of the competence with which the attorney represented him. Also, as explained above, the state's right to recoup costs from indigents who become able to pay does not extend to those defendants who have had appointed counsel imposed on them against their will. (B) is incorrect because it states that the conviction involved no reversible error, when denial of the defendant's right to represent himself is reversible error. (B) also incorrectly states that the imposition of fees should be reversed because the defendant could have gotten probation for himself as easily as his attorney did. There is no way to know that the defendant could have gotten probation for himself as easily as the attorney did, and it is not really at issue whether the defendant could have done so. What is at issue is that the costs were imposed as part of an unconstitutional forced representation by appointed counsel. Thus, even if the attorney obtained probation for the defendant when the defendant would have been unable to do so, the costs should be reversed, because the defendant should have been free to proceed pro se, even if this meant risking imprisonment. Similarly, (C) is incorrect because it states that the attorney's competence is a reason for affirming the imposition of fees. As stated above, the defendant had the right to proceed pro se if his decision was knowing and intelligent and he was competent to proceed pro se, regardless of the fact that appointed counsel may have been highly competent. The state cannot force a defendant to forgo a constitutionally protected right by accepting appointed counsel, and then further force him to pay for such counsel.

Answer to Question 18

(C) Because the patron believed the coat to be his own, he lacked the intent to commit larceny. Larceny consists of a taking and carrying away of the tangible property of another by trespass, with the intent to permanently deprive the person of his interest in the property. The intent to deprive the owner of his property generally must exist at the time of the taking (except for the continuing trespass situation; *see* below). Here, the patron took and carried away a coat belonging to another. But when he took it, the patron believed that the coat was actually his own coat. Thus, the patron did not take the coat with the intent to permanently deprive the owner of his property. Absent this intent, the patron cannot be guilty of larceny. (A) is incorrect because although the patron did not actually destroy the coat himself, he could still be guilty of larceny. As mentioned, larceny requires the intent to permanently deprive the owner of the property. This intent includes intentionally dealing with property in such a way as to create a substantial risk of loss. Thus, even if the patron did not destroy the property himself, if he dealt with it in a way as to risk its destruction, he could still be guilty of larceny, and so this is not the best reason for his acquittal. (B) is incorrect because the reasonableness of the mistake is not relevant. The test for whether a defendant has the intent for larceny is a subjective one—what this defendant intended. Thus, even if the mistake were unreasonable, the patron would not be guilty of larceny if he believed the coat was his. (D) is incorrect because it attempts to negate the continuing trespass situation, which is not applicable here. Under the continuing trespass theory, if a defendant ***wrongfully*** (*i.e.*, with a "bad" mental state) takes the personal property of another ***without*** the

intent to permanently deprive the owner, but later, while still in possession of the property, decides to keep it, he is guilty of larceny. This theory does not apply here because the patron's taking of the coat was not wrongful. Thus, it is irrelevant that he was trying to return the coat; even if he had decided to keep it, he would not be guilty of larceny, although he would be guilty of some other crime. Therefore, (D) is not the best reason for the patron's acquittal because it raises irrelevant issues.

Set 5 Answer Sheet

1. Ⓐ Ⓑ Ⓒ Ⓓ
2. Ⓐ Ⓑ Ⓒ Ⓓ
3. Ⓐ Ⓑ Ⓒ Ⓓ
4. Ⓐ Ⓑ Ⓒ Ⓓ
5. Ⓐ Ⓑ Ⓒ Ⓓ
6. Ⓐ Ⓑ Ⓒ Ⓓ
7. Ⓐ Ⓑ Ⓒ Ⓓ
8. Ⓐ Ⓑ Ⓒ Ⓓ
9. Ⓐ Ⓑ Ⓒ Ⓓ
10. Ⓐ Ⓑ Ⓒ Ⓓ
11. Ⓐ Ⓑ Ⓒ Ⓓ
12. Ⓐ Ⓑ Ⓒ Ⓓ
13. Ⓐ Ⓑ Ⓒ Ⓓ
14. Ⓐ Ⓑ Ⓒ Ⓓ
15. Ⓐ Ⓑ Ⓒ Ⓓ
16. Ⓐ Ⓑ Ⓒ Ⓓ
17. Ⓐ Ⓑ Ⓒ Ⓓ
18. Ⓐ Ⓑ Ⓒ Ⓓ
19. Ⓐ Ⓑ Ⓒ Ⓓ
20. Ⓐ Ⓑ Ⓒ Ⓓ
21. Ⓐ Ⓑ Ⓒ Ⓓ
22. Ⓐ Ⓑ Ⓒ Ⓓ
23. Ⓐ Ⓑ Ⓒ Ⓓ
24. Ⓐ Ⓑ Ⓒ Ⓓ
25. Ⓐ Ⓑ Ⓒ Ⓓ
26. Ⓐ Ⓑ Ⓒ Ⓓ
27. Ⓐ Ⓑ Ⓒ Ⓓ
28. Ⓐ Ⓑ Ⓒ Ⓓ
29. Ⓐ Ⓑ Ⓒ Ⓓ
30. Ⓐ Ⓑ Ⓒ Ⓓ
31. Ⓐ Ⓑ Ⓒ Ⓓ
32. Ⓐ Ⓑ Ⓒ Ⓓ
33. Ⓐ Ⓑ Ⓒ Ⓓ
34. Ⓐ Ⓑ Ⓒ Ⓓ
35. Ⓐ Ⓑ Ⓒ Ⓓ
36. Ⓐ Ⓑ Ⓒ Ⓓ

CRIMINAL LAW QUESTIONS - SET 5

Question 1

A man was tried in state court for possession of heroin. The prosecution offered in evidence five rolled-up toy balloons containing heroin, which police officers had found on a table in the man's apartment. At a hearing on the defense motion to suppress, testimony was presented that established that the police had put the apartment under surveillance, and had watched a police informant go to the door of the apartment, hand four balloons of heroin to the man, and leave. The police had then knocked on the apartment door, identified themselves as police officers, and demanded entrance. Having heard nothing for 30 seconds, the police had then broken down the door and entered the apartment, discovering the heroin. The police had intended to arrest the man for the purchase of heroin, a felony. When they had gotten inside the apartment, they discovered that the man had left by a back exit. He was later arrested at the nearby newsstand.

The trial court denied the motion to suppress, and the case is on appeal following the man's conviction for possession of heroin. The appellate court should:

(A) Affirm the conviction on the ground that the error, if any, in admitting the heroin was harmless error.

(B) Affirm the conviction on the ground that the police complied with the "knock and announce rule" even though no one was there to admit them.

(C) Reverse the conviction on the ground that the man's Fourth Amendment rights (as applied to the states by the Fourteenth Amendment) have been violated.

(D) Reverse the conviction on the ground that the "knock and announce rule" was not satisfied when the police announced their presence and identity to an empty residence.

Question 2

A plainclothes police officer who frequently ate lunch at a certain deli heard rumors that the deli's owner often placed illegal bets on sporting events. Based on the rumors, the officer peeked into an envelope next to the register and saw betting slips. The officer asked his waitress about the envelope, and she told him that the owner had given it to her and that a man in a brown cap was to pick it up at 2 p.m. The officer stayed at the deli until 2 p.m. and watched the waitress hand the envelope to a man in a brown cap. The officer passed the above information on to a friend in the F.B.I. Several weeks later, based on that information, F.B.I. agents obtained a search warrant for the owner's home—a condominium in a large multi-unit complex. The agents went to the home in the early evening, while the owner was at the deli. After announcing their purpose to the owner's wife, they searched the home and found betting slips and other materials related to illegal gambling.

The owner was indicted for conspiracy to violate a federal statute prohibiting the use of interstate phone lines to conduct gambling, and for the possession of betting slips.

Which of the following would be the best reason for excluding the evidence found at the owner's home?

(A) The owner was not home when the warrant was executed.

(B) The search was conducted in the evening when it easily could have been conducted during daylight hours.

(C) The warrant failed to specify which condominium unit was to be searched.

(D) The waitress had never been used before as an informant.

Question 3

A student and a few of his friends were making their way to spring break. Along the

way, the old van that they were driving broke down. Not wanting to miss any part of spring break festivities, the student asked the mechanic on duty at the repair shop for a rush job. The mechanic provided the student with a repair estimate, and the student, on the basis of the estimate, authorized the repair and promised to pay when he came back to pick up the van. When the mechanic called the student to tell him that the van was repaired, the student, rather than paying for the repair, told one of his friends that the mechanic had agreed to finance the repair charges and that the only thing left to do was pick up the van in the garage's parking lot. The student handed the friend a key to the van and told him to go pick the van up so that they could continue their trip to spring break. The friend did so.

If the mechanic makes a criminal complaint against the student for larceny of the van, the student will most likely be found:

(A) Not guilty, because it was the student's van to begin with.

(B) Not guilty, because the friend took the van.

(C) Guilty, because the friend took the van from the mechanic without the mechanic's knowledge or permission.

(D) Guilty, because the student promised to pay the mechanic for his work when he came to get the van.

Question 4

The defendant, who worked as a gardener for the victim, decided to break into the victim's home to steal some valuables one evening when he knew the victim would not be at home. The defendant, taking a key that the victim hid under a rock for emergencies, unlocked the front door and stepped into the doorway. At that moment, however, a security alarm sounded. On hearing the alarm, the defendant immediately left the premises.

What is the most serious crime for which the defendant may be convicted?

(A) Burglary.

(B) Attempted burglary.

(C) Attempted larceny.

(D) No crime.

Question 5

Two people agreed to steal a valuable painting that they knew was hanging in the victim's home. One would wait in the car with the engine running to ensure a quick getaway, while the other would break into the victim's home and steal the painting. The burglar broke into the home and reached the victim's library, where the painting was hanging. On the desk he noticed a large vial that appeared to contain cocaine. Thinking he could sell the cocaine and split the proceeds with the getaway driver, the burglar grabbed the vial and stuffed it in his pocket. He then took the painting off the wall and hurried back to the waiting car. The police arrived at that moment and apprehended the pair. A search incident to arrest turned up the vial of cocaine in the burglar's possession.

If the getaway driver is charged with being an accomplice to the unlawful possession of cocaine with intent to distribute, she should be found:

(A) Guilty, because she is liable for all crimes resulting from the conspiracy.

(B) Guilty, because the conspiracy was to steal items for resale.

(C) Not guilty, because the conspiracy did not involve the possession or sale of cocaine.

(D) Not guilty, because the burglar was the person who possessed the cocaine.

Question 6

Two teenagers who had recently gotten their driver's licenses agreed to a game of "chicken,"

with the one who turned his car away first having to pay the other $25. The two cars raced toward each other, and when they were about 40 feet apart, the victim suddenly turned his car to the right, but the defendant was going too fast to avoid the victim's car. He crashed into the side of the victim's car, killing the victim instantly.

The homicide statute in this jurisdiction reads in part as follows: "Murder is the unlawful killing of a human being with malice aforethought. Such malice may be express or implied. It is express when there is manifested a deliberate intention to unlawfully take away the life of a fellow creature. It is implied when no considerable provocation appears or when the circumstances attending the killing show an abandoned and malignant heart. All murder that is perpetrated by willful, deliberate, or premeditated killing or committed in the perpetration of or attempt to perpetrate arson, rape, robbery, or burglary is murder of the first degree. All other kinds of murders are of the second degree."

If the defendant is charged with first degree murder, his most effective defense is:

(A) An automobile is not a dangerous weapon, and therefore there can be no deliberate killing.

(B) The defendant, because of his youth, could not have formed the necessary malice aforethought to support a conviction for murder.

(C) The defendant is guilty of murder, but not first degree murder.

(D) The defendant cannot be guilty of any degree of murder because he did not intend to kill the victim.

Question 7

A worker on scaffolding several stories high on a building took a loose brick from the building's façade and threw it off the scaffolding without looking, striking a pedestrian on the sidewalk in the head and killing her instantly.

The homicide statute in this jurisdiction reads as follows: "Murder is the unlawful killing of a human being with malice aforethought. Such malice may be express or implied. It is express when there is manifested a deliberate intention to unlawfully take away the life of a fellow creature. It is implied when no considerable provocation appears or when the circumstances attending the killing show an abandoned and malignant heart."

The manslaughter statute in the jurisdiction reads as follows: "Manslaughter is the unlawful killing of a human being without malice. It is of two kinds: 1. Voluntary—upon a sudden quarrel or heat of passion. 2. Involuntary—in the commission of an unlawful act, not amounting to a felony; or in the commission of a lawful act that might produce death in an unlawful manner or without due caution and circumspection."

If the worker is charged with criminal homicide, the trial judge could properly give a charge to the jury on the following theories:

(A) Involuntary manslaughter only.

(B) Murder and involuntary manslaughter.

(C) Murder and voluntary manslaughter.

(D) First degree murder, second degree murder, and involuntary manslaughter.

Question 8

Under applicable state law, private security guards are allowed to carry a gun on the job and while proceeding between their place of residence and work. While driving home from work one evening, a security guard was involved in a car accident that was clearly his fault. He exited his vehicle, intending to apologize to and exchange insurance information with the other driver. The other driver also left his car, but, because he was upset over the accident, he began swinging his fists wildly at the security guard, twice hitting the security guard in the face. Enraged, the security guard pulled his gun and fired at the other driver, intending only to shoot him in the arm. However, the bullet struck the other driver in the heart, killing him instantly.

In a jurisdiction that follows the common law, the security guard will most likely be found guilty of:

(A) Felony murder, because the shooting of the other driver was a felony.

(B) Voluntary manslaughter, because the security guard was enraged when he shot the other driver.

(C) Involuntary manslaughter, because the security guard did not intend to kill the other driver.

(D) No crime, because the security guard was justified in using deadly force to prevent a physical attack.

Question 9

A father was angry at his son's coach because the coach would never let the son into a game. In order to exact revenge, the father decided to plant an incendiary device on the coach's front porch. The father believed the device would start a fire that would destroy the coach's home and perhaps injure him as well. However, the father made a mistake while assembling the incendiary device, and it was impossible for the device to do any harm. When the device went off, it did nothing more than produce a foul odor.

If the father is charged with attempted murder and attempted arson in a common law jurisdiction, which of the following decisions is most likely to be reached by the court?

(A) The father is guilty of attempted murder and attempted arson.

(B) The father is guilty of attempted murder, but he is not guilty of attempted arson.

(C) The father is not guilty of attempted murder, but he is guilty of attempted arson.

(D) The father is not guilty of attempted murder or attempted arson.

Question 10

The victim and another player regularly played backgammon together. The other player was entered in an upcoming backgammon tournament and asked the victim if she could borrow his attractive custom-made backgammon set. He agreed, provided in return that he could hold her backgammon computer until the backgammon set was returned. After having success at the tournament with the victim's set, the other player decided to travel to the national championship tournament, but she needed her backgammon computer to hone her game. Not wanting to go to the nationals with her own cheap set, she told the defendant, another weekly club player, that her backgammon computer had been borrowed by the victim, and asked him to get it from the victim's car at the next meeting of the club. At the backgammon club meeting, the defendant, who was not aware of the arrangement between the victim and the other player, removed the computer from the victim's car without telling him. The next day, while waiting to meet the player at the airport to give her the computer, the defendant was playing a game on it when a stranger stopped to admire it. The stranger offered the defendant $400 for the computer, and the defendant readily agreed.

If the defendant is prosecuted for larceny of the backgammon computer from the victim's car, he will be found:

(A) Guilty, because the victim was rightfully in possession of the computer when the defendant took it.

(B) Guilty, because the defendant sold the computer to the stranger and pocketed the proceeds.

(C) Not guilty, because the other player was the rightful owner of the computer, and the defendant was acting on the other player's behalf.

(D) Not guilty, because the defendant thought that the other player was entitled to the computer when he took it from the victim.

Question 11

The defendant, in need of money, agreed to give the victim possession of some personal property in exchange for a loan. However, it soon became apparent that the defendant would not be able to repay the loan. Not wanting to lose her property, the defendant asked a friend to go to the victim's home to retrieve the property. The friend, knowing that the property belonged to the defendant, but not knowing of its use as collateral, did so.

If the defendant is prosecuted for larceny of the personal property from the victim, the defendant will be found:

(A) Not guilty, because the defendant did not personally take the property from the victim.

(B) Not guilty, because the defendant is the rightful owner of the property.

(C) Guilty, because the friend took the property from the victim without the victim's permission.

(D) Guilty, because the defendant did not tell her friend that the property was being used as collateral.

Question 12

A man on probation after pleading guilty to possession of cocaine was suspected of selling cocaine out of his home. His probation officer came to his house and rang the bell. As soon as the man opened the door to see who was there, the officer entered the home, despite the man's protests. After searching the home, the probation officer discovered several bags of marijuana in a drawer. The man was arrested and charged with possession of marijuana with intent to sell. A statute in the jurisdiction in which the search took place provides that, as a condition of probation, a probationer is on notice that his probation officer may conduct a search of the probationer's person or home, without probable cause, at any time of the day or night. The man moved to have evidence of the marijuana suppressed by the court, claiming that the state statute that authorized the search was unconstitutional under the Fourth Amendment prohibition of unreasonable searches and seizures.

Will he prevail?

(A) Yes, unless probable cause was established by the officer's tip in conjunction with other circumstances.

(B) Yes, because a search warrant was not obtained and no exception to the warrant requirement applies.

(C) No, because the man had a diminished expectation of privacy and the government has a heightened need to search probationers' homes.

(D) No, because the search was incident to a lawful arrest.

Question 13

Criminal statutes in the state define murder as "the unlawful killing of another human being with malice aforethought, either express or implied," and define voluntary manslaughter as "the unlawful killing of another human being under an extreme emotional disturbance for which there was reasonable explanation or excuse, without express or implied malice aforethought." Another statute provides that "it shall be an affirmative defense to the charge of murder if the defendant proves by clear and convincing evidence that the defendant was unable to control his actions or conform his conduct to the law."

The defendant was charged with murder and tried in state court. At trial, he introduced evidence regarding his state of mind at the time of the homicide, including testimony from a psychiatrist. At the conclusion of the case, the court instructed the jury as follows:

> Any homicide committed without justification or excuse is murder if the prosecution establishes beyond a reasonable doubt that the defendant intentionally and unlawfully killed another human being, and malice aforethought may be presumed from proof of the felonious homicide. However, if the defendant establishes by a preponderance of the evidence that he acted under extreme emotional disturbance for which there was reasonable explanation or excuse, he shall be liable only for voluntary manslaughter, because extreme emotional disturbance is inconsistent with, and negates the existence of, malice aforethought.

The judge further instructed the jury that it could return an acquittal by reason of insanity "if the defendant established by clear and convincing evidence that he was unable to control his actions or conform his conduct to the law." The jury found the defendant guilty of murder. The defendant appealed, claiming that his constitutional rights were violated by the court's instruction as to voluntary manslaughter and by the requirement that he prove insanity by clear and convincing evidence.

The defendant's rights were violated by:

(A) The court's instruction as to voluntary manslaughter, but not the requirement of clear and convincing evidence for insanity.

(B) The requirement of clear and convincing evidence for insanity, but not the instruction as to voluntary manslaughter.

(C) Both the voluntary manslaughter instruction and the clear and convincing evidence requirement.

(D) Neither the voluntary manslaughter instruction nor the clear and convincing evidence requirement.

Question 14

The defendant and an accomplice were on trial together for burglary. Both had given confessions implicating themselves and their accomplice. At trial, the defendant maintained that his confession had been obtained through improper coercion by the police. For the purpose of countering the claim of coercion, the prosecution seeks to place the accomplice's confession into evidence. After objection by the defendant's counsel, the judge agrees to issue a limiting instruction to the jury that the confession is to be considered only with regard to the question of whether the defendant's confession was coerced. The following conditions for admission of the confession are discussed between the judge and counsel.

May the accomplice's confession be admitted under that condition?

(A) No, because admission of the confession violates the defendant's right of confrontation.

(B) No, unless the accomplice takes the stand and subjects himself to cross-examination regarding the confession.

(C) Yes, as long as all portions of the confession referring to the defendant can be eliminated.

(D) Yes, because the judge's instruction limits consideration of the confession only to the issue of coercion.

Question 15

A patient who was mentally incompetent and a ward of the state received extensive rehabilitation for leg and back injuries she suffered in a fall at a state institution. After her rehabilitation was nearly completed, she became entitled to state payments as compensation for her injury,

which her treatment center began applying to her outstanding rehabilitation bill. Thereafter, the legal guardian for the patient sought to remove her from the center despite the fact that the patient had never shown any desire to leave. The director of the center was aware that her departure would prevent the center from directly applying the state payments to her bill. The director was erroneously advised by his attorney that judicial decisions would support his refusal of the guardian's request until the bill was paid. When the guardian arrived at the center, the director refused to allow the guardian to remove the patient. A criminal statute in the jurisdiction defines false imprisonment as knowingly confining a person without valid consent and without authority of law.

If the director is arrested and charged with false imprisonment, can he be found guilty?

(A) Yes, if the director's reliance on the advice of his attorney was not reasonable.

(B) Yes, because the director kept the patient without lawful authority.

(C) No, because the patient was not held against her will and was not harmed by the confinement.

(D) No, because the director's belief in the lawfulness of his conduct precluded him from having the mental state required for the offense.

Question 16

A robber decided to attempt a bank robbery using a realistic-looking toy pistol. He entered a bank, pulled out the toy pistol, and shouted to a bank teller to hand over all the money in the teller's drawer. A security guard immediately pulled out his real pistol and fired in the robber's direction. However, the security guard missed, instead hitting and killing the teller.

In the jurisdiction, homicide crimes are classified as follows:

> Murder in the first degree is the killing of a human being without justification and with premeditation. Murder in the second degree is any murder which is neither a murder in the first degree nor a murder in the third degree. Murder in the third degree is any killing that occurs during and as a result of the commission of a felony.

The jurisdiction also provides that robbery is a felony for purposes of the felony murder rule.

The most serious homicide crime of which the robber can be convicted is:

(A) Murder in the second degree.

(B) Murder in the third degree.

(C) Involuntary manslaughter based on criminal negligence.

(D) No homicide crime.

Question 17

A state statute contains the following provisions:

> Murder in the first degree is the killing of a human being without justification and with premeditation. Murder in the second degree is any murder which is neither a murder in the first degree nor a murder in the third degree. Murder in the third degree is any killing that occurs during and as a result of the commission of a felony.

The jurisdiction also provides that robbery is a felony for purposes of the felony murder rule.

A robber held up a convenience store with a knife. After the store clerk handed over all the money in the register, she retrieved a pistol from a drawer behind the counter. When the robber turned to leave, the store clerk pointed the gun

at the robber and shouted, "Stop or I'll shoot!" The robber ducked behind the end of an aisle, and the store clerk shot three times in the robber's direction. One of the bullets bounced off a pillar and struck the only other customer in the store, who was crouched behind a counter, killing him instantly.

The most serious homicide crime of which the store clerk can be convicted is:

(A) Murder in the second degree.

(B) Murder in the third degree.

(C) Manslaughter.

(D) No homicide crime.

Question 18

A husband's and wife's Social Security retirement benefits came in a single check payable to both each month, two-thirds of which was the husband's retirement payment and one-third of which was the wife's spousal benefit. Each month when the check arrived in the mail, the wife would take it to their bank and cash it, receiving the entire proceeds in cash, which she would use for her and her husband's living expenses. After the husband died, the Social Security check continued to come in the same amount and made payable to both the husband and wife. The wife knew that she was no longer entitled to her husband's benefit, but that her own spousal benefit would increase greatly as a widow's benefit. She also knew that she would receive a one-time "death benefit." She concluded that the continued receipt of the combined check reflected these increases, so for several months after her husband's death she continued to cash the combined check, signing both her and her husband's names when she negotiated it. When the federal government eventually processed the notification of the husband's death provided by the funeral home, it discovered that the wife had negotiated checks containing $2,000 in benefits to which she was not entitled.

Is she guilty of obtaining the payments by false pretenses?

(A) Yes, because her actions constituted a public welfare offense for which she is strictly liable.

(B) Yes, because she should have known that the combined check, payable in part to a deceased person, contained benefits to which she was not entitled.

(C) No, as long as she reasonably believed that she was entitled to the funds in the combined check.

(D) No, because she believed that she was entitled to the total amount of the combined check.

Question 19

The laws of the state provide that "any person who engages in sexual intercourse with a person under the age of 16 shall have committed the crime of statutory rape."

A waitress propositioned the defendant to have a sexual encounter at a nearby hotel. When they got up to the room, she told the defendant that she would be 16 the next week. In fact, the waitress, who had been adopted, was mistaken about her actual birth date; she had actually turned 16 the week before. The waitress and the defendant engage in sexual intercourse, and the defendant is subsequently charged with statutory rape.

The defendant should be found:

(A) Guilty, because he intended to engage in sexual intercourse with a minor.

(B) Guilty, because a mistake of fact is not a defense to a strict liability crime.

(C) Not guilty, because the waitress was older than 16.

(D) Not guilty, because the waitress initiated the sexual encounter.

Question 20

A drug addict armed with a gun broke into a pharmacy during the night and stole a quantity of prescription drugs. The next morning, on discovering the missing drugs, the pharmacist called the authorities, who kept the pharmacy closed while they looked for evidence and had the pharmacist do an inventory. During this time, one of the pharmacy's customers was stricken with a severe asthma attack and needed asthma medication immediately. After being driven to the pharmacy by a family member and finding the pharmacy closed, the customer had the family member drive to another pharmacy a few minutes away. Unfortunately, their car had a flat tire and the customer died from the asthma attack before he was able to get the medicine from the other pharmacy.

Evidence at the burglarized pharmacy led police to the addict, who was charged with burglary under a statute that extends that crime to businesses. He was also charged with felony murder based on the death of the pharmacy's customer. The city's medical examiner will testify that the customer would not have died had he been given asthma medication at the first pharmacy.

As to the felony murder charge, the addict will be found:

(A) Guilty, because the customer's death occurred only because the pharmacy was closed.

(B) Guilty, because it was foreseeable that the pharmacy would have to be closed to investigate the burglary.

(C) Not guilty, because the customer's death did not occur during the commission of a felony.

(D) Not guilty, because the burglary was not inherently dangerous.

Question 21

A former employee and his friend agreed to rob a grocery store. They entered the store just before closing. The former employee held a gun on the store manager and made him empty out the safe, and the friend directed a clerk who was the only other person in the store to a storeroom in the back. Before tying her up, however, the friend raped her at gunpoint. The friend returned to the front of the store, where the former employee had just finished putting the store's money in a large sack. To prevent the store manager from pursuing the pair or from quickly notifying the police, the friend shot the store manager in both knees. Neither the rape nor the shooting were part of the plan between the former employee and the friend.

In a common law jurisdiction, of which of the following crimes is the former employee guilty?

(A) Robbery only.

(B) Robbery and rape only.

(C) Robbery and aggravated battery only.

(D) Robbery, rape, and aggravated battery.

Question 22

A statute in the jurisdiction, which was enacted with the express purpose of preventing public employees from taking advantage of the status of illegal aliens, made it a felony to accept money or other benefits in exchange for issuing a state identification card. During an undercover investigation, an illegal alien was recorded offering $500 to a clerk in exchange for issuance of a card. The clerk agreed to the deal and later that day exchanged the card for the money, after which both parties were arrested.

In a jurisdiction following the common law approach to conspiracy, which of the following statements is correct?

(A) The clerk can be convicted of violating the statute and conspiracy to violate the statute, and the illegal alien can be convicted of no crime.

(B) The clerk can be convicted only of violating the statute, and the illegal alien can be convicted of no crime.

(C) The clerk can be convicted only of violating the statute, and the illegal alien can be convicted as an accomplice to violation of the statute.

(D) The clerk can be convicted of violating the statute and conspiracy to violate the statute, and the illegal alien can be convicted of conspiracy to violate the statute.

Question 23

In an effort to curb underage drinking, the police staked out a liquor store near a college campus that was suspected of selling liquor to minors in violation of state law. They recorded a liquor store clerk being told by a minor that he was an underage student at the local university and that he would pay triple the marked price for a case of beer. The clerk readily agreed to the deal, but both parties were arrested before they could complete the transaction.

In a jurisdiction following the unilateral approach to conspiracy, which of the following statements is correct?

(A) The minor can be convicted of solicitation and the liquor store clerk can be convicted of conspiracy to violate the statute.

(B) Both the minor and the liquor store clerk can be convicted of conspiracy to violate the statute.

(C) The minor cannot be convicted of either solicitation or conspiracy, but the liquor store clerk can be convicted of conspiracy to violate the statute.

(D) The minor cannot be convicted of either solicitation or conspiracy, and the liquor store clerk cannot be convicted of conspiracy.

Question 24

The jurisdiction divides murder into degrees, with all murders being second degree murder unless the prosecution can prove premeditation and deliberation, in which case the killing would be first degree murder. The jurisdiction also uses the *M'Naghten* rule for insanity.

A physician prescribed an experimental drug for the defendant's severe allergies. The physician told the defendant that the medication was experimental, but failed to inform the defendant that the manufacturer had reported a small risk that the medicine caused severe delusions. After taking the medicine the first day, the defendant began to believe that his next door neighbor was spreading false rumors about him to a few of his other neighbors. While still under the influence of the medication, the defendant grabbed a knife from the kitchen, went to his neighbor's house, and rang the doorbell. When the neighbor answered the door, the defendant plunged the knife into his neighbor's chest, killing him instantly.

May the defendant be convicted of first degree murder?

(A) No, because the defendant was temporarily insane under the *M'Nagthen* rule.

(B) No, because the defendant's intoxication was involuntary.

(C) Yes, because the defendant's intoxication was voluntary.

(D) Yes, because the defendant murdered his neighbor without justification and with premeditation.

Question 25

In the final seconds of a playoff football game, the home team's quarterback was knocked to the ground a few seconds after throwing the ball on a critical fourth-down play. A penalty flag was thrown, which the home fans assumed would be a "roughing the passer" call. Instead, the fans saw the referee signal "intentional grounding" against the home team, which resulted in both a loss of yardage and a loss of down, sealing the loss for the home team. To register her displeasure without intending to hit anyone, a fan sitting in the stands threw a bottle onto the field that just missed the head of the referee, who was looking in the other direction and did not see the bottle being thrown. The fan was charged with assault.

The fan should be:

(A) Convicted, because the throwing of the bottle was a substantial step.

(B) Not convicted, because the referee did not see the bottle.

(C) Not convicted, because the fan did not intend to hit anyone.

(D) Not convicted, because the referee did not see the bottle, nor did the fan intend to hit anyone.

Question 26

Acting pursuant to a valid search warrant, the police entered and searched the defendant's garage and discovered a cardboard box containing cocaine in the rafters storage area. The box was securely taped and bore a freight label addressed to the defendant's friend. At his trial for violation of the jurisdiction's statute making it a felony to knowingly possess cocaine, the defendant testified that his friend had brought him the package a week before it was seized by the police, telling him that he needed to store it in the defendant's garage. The defendant also testified that he had not asked the friend what it contained.

What additional facts must the prosecution prove to establish the defendant's liability for the charged felony?

(A) That he knew or believed that the box contained cocaine and had moved or handled the box.

(B) That he knew or believed that the box contained cocaine.

(C) That he should have known that the box contained cocaine and had moved or handled the box.

(D) No additional facts.

Question 27

A robber planned to rob a 24-hour convenience store at a very early hour when there would be only one clerk on duty and very few customers. He called his friend and asked her if she would telephone him to wake him early so he could rob a store. The friend laughed but promised to wake him up. The next morning, the friend called the robber, waking him from a sound sleep. The robber succeeded in robbing the convenience store but was arrested a short time later, and implicated his friend.

The friend is likely to be convicted of:

(A) Robbery only.

(B) Conspiracy to commit robbery only.

(C) Robbery and conspiracy to commit robbery.

(D) Neither robbery nor conspiracy to commit robbery.

Question 28

At a waterfront bar, a college student sought to provoke a fight with a merchant seaman by making insulting remarks. Eventually the seaman had had enough and threw a punch that connected to the student's jaw and sent him sprawling to the floor. The seaman then told the student that he wanted no further trouble. Getting up off the floor, the student pulled a knife out of his pocket and charged at the seaman. Three other students were standing between the seaman and the exit door. The seaman tried to dodge, but was cut on the forearm by the student's knife. The seaman

immediately drew a gun and shot the student, killing him. The seaman was charged with murder.

Which of the following points raised in the seaman's defense will not be helpful for his defense?

(A) The student had no reason to fear serious bodily injury when he drew the knife.

(B) The student's drawing of the knife constituted an escalation of the fight.

(C) Three college students were standing between the seaman and the door, so there was no clear route of retreat.

(D) The student's comments were motivated by a desire to provoke the seaman.

Question 29

The defendant is charged with the burglary of a home. Evidence presented at the defendant's trial indicates that he talked another person into assisting him. The jurisdiction generally follows the common law; the jury is instructed on burglary, solicitation, conspiracy, and attempt.

If the defendant is found by the jury to be guilty of burglary:

(A) He also may be found guilty of conspiracy, but not of solicitation or attempt.

(B) He also may be found guilty of conspiracy and solicitation, but not of attempt.

(C) He also may be found guilty of conspiracy or solicitation but not both, and he may not be found guilty of attempt.

(D) He also may be found guilty of solicitation or attempt but not both, and he may not be found guilty of conspiracy.

Question 30

The defendant's neighbor owned an authentic major league baseball signed by Babe Ruth. The defendant asked if he could show it to some friends who were visiting. The neighbor agreed as long as he kept it in the display case, which the defendant promised to do. In fact, the defendant intended to use the ball in a pickup game. During the game, the ball was hit over the fence and into a yard with a guard dog, which had chewed up several other balls that had previously landed in the yard. The dog did the same to that ball. When the neighbor learned what happened to the ball, he pressed charges against the defendant.

If the defendant is convicted, he will most likely be found guilty of:

(A) Common law larceny.

(B) Embezzlement.

(C) False pretenses.

(D) Larceny by trick.

Question 31

The defendant planned to break into a home, steal any valuables that he could easily pawn, and then burn down the home using gasoline from his lawnmower. When the defendant got to the home that night, he realized that he had forgotten the gas at home. Nonetheless, the defendant broke into the home through a basement window. Unbeknownst to him, the police were alerted by a silent alarm and arrested the defendant just as he was leaving the home with a sack filled with valuables.

At common law, the defendant has committed:

(A) Burglary and attempted larceny.

(B) Burglary, attempted larceny, and attempted arson.

(C) Burglary and larceny.

(D) Burglary, larceny, and attempted arson.

Question 32

An officer on routine patrol noticed a flashlight moving within a darkened house and stopped to investigate. The suspect, who had broken into the home to steal valuables, caught sight of the patrol car, dropped the bag of valuables as he was about to carry them out of the house, and tried to sneak out the back way. The officer saw him sneaking out and seized him. The suspect, who had a lock-picking device in his possession, pulled out two $100 bills from his wallet, stating that he did not take anything and would like to forget the whole thing. The officer took the money, stating that she would give him a break this time around, and let the suspect go.

The officer is:

(A) An accessory after the fact to burglary and larceny.

(B) An accomplice to the crimes of burglary and larceny.

(C) An accessory after the fact to burglary.

(D) Neither an accomplice nor an accessory after the fact.

Question 33

A statute provides "any person who knowingly sells intoxicating liquor to a person under 21 years of age is guilty of a misdemeanor and may be fined $1,000 or sentenced to up to six months in jail, or both." A patron ordered a drink at a bar. The bartender asked for some identification, and the patron produced a driver's license stating that he was 25 years old. In fact, the patron was only 18 years old, but he had some gray hair and was balding. A plain-clothes police officer sitting at the bar witnessed the bartender selling a drink to the patron. The officer knew that the patron was under 21 years old, and demanded to see the patron's driver's license. The officer determined it to be false and arrested the bartender for violation of the statute.

The bartender will be found:

(A) Guilty, because this type of statute is a strict liability statute and the bartender's knowledge of the patron's age is irrelevant.

(B) Guilty, because the bartender knew that the patron was under 21 years old.

(C) Not guilty, because the bartender made a reasonable mistake concerning the age of the patron.

(D) Not guilty, because the patron produced a driver's license that stated that he was 25 years old.

Question 34

The defendant approached a clerk at a local gas station/mini-mart and offered to exchange a pair of sunglasses for some gas. The clerk refused, saying he could only accept cash. The defendant then pulled a knife out of his pocket and told the clerk he wanted a fill up. The clerk, who was quite a bit older than the defendant, gave him some "fatherly advice" that crime does not pay. In response to the advice, the defendant put the knife away. Feeling sorry for the defendant, the clerk then agreed to give him some gas for the sunglasses. The defendant got the gas and then left. The clerk then discovered that the defendant had taken the sunglasses from a display case in the store and clipped the tag off before offering them to the clerk. The defendant was apprehended shortly thereafter.

Which of the following statements is correct regarding the defendant's conduct?

(A) The defendant can be convicted of larceny by trick and attempted robbery.

(B) The defendant can be convicted of false pretenses and attempted robbery.

(C) The defendant can be convicted of larceny by trick but not attempted robbery because he voluntarily abandoned the attempt.

(D) The defendant can be convicted of false pretenses but not attempted robbery because he voluntarily abandoned the attempt.

Question 35

A woman was the subject of a murder investigation. The investigation continued for over two years, with the woman frequently being called in for questioning. Finally, the woman was indicted for the murder. The woman's lawyer filed a motion to dismiss all charges against her, arguing that the excessively long investigatory period violated the woman's constitutional right to a speedy trial.

Despite the pending motion, the woman decided that she wanted to "get it over with," and she told the judge that she wished to plead guilty. The judge then explained the charges to the woman and asked her if she understood them. She replied, "Yes." The judge then asked the woman if she understood that she was not required to plead guilty. She responded in the affirmative. Finally, the judge described the maximum sentence and asked the woman if she understood that she could receive the maximum sentence, which was life imprisonment. She again responded, "Yes," and maintained that she still wished to plead guilty. The judge accepted the woman's plea and sentenced her to 30 years' imprisonment in the state penitentiary. Six months later, the woman filed a motion to set aside the guilty plea.

Which of the following provides the best argument that the woman has a constitutional basis for relief?

(A) The judge did not rule on the pending motion to dismiss before accepting her guilty plea.

(B) The judge did not attempt to determine if the woman had actually committed the murder.

(C) The judge did not determine whether the files in the prosecutor's office contained any undisclosed exculpatory evidence.

(D) The judge did not determine whether the woman understood that she had a right to a trial by jury.

Question 36

After drinking at his favorite bar all day long and becoming very intoxicated, the defendant pulled out a gun to re-enact a scene from a movie he had seen the other day. Pointing his gun at a bystander, he slurred a line from the movie and pulled the trigger. He was shocked to see the bystander fall down dead with a bullet in him. Due to his intoxicated state, the defendant cannot remember pulling out or firing the gun.

In a jurisdiction that has defined degrees of murder in the typical way, what is the most serious crime of which the defendant may be convicted?

(A) First degree murder.

(B) Second degree murder.

(C) Manslaughter.

(D) No crime.

CRIMINAL LAW ANSWERS - SET 5

Answer to Question 1

(C) The appellate court should reverse the conviction on Fourth Amendment grounds. In *Payton v. New York* (1980), the United States Supreme Court held that, absent an emergency, a forcible, warrantless entry into a residence for the purpose of making a felony arrest is an unconstitutional violation of the Fourth Amendment as made applicable to the states by the Fourteenth Amendment. No exigent circumstances justified the warrantless arrest, and searches of a home without a warrant are presumptively unreasonable. Evidence that is the fruit of an unlawful arrest may not be used against the defendant at trial because of the exclusionary rule. (A) is therefore incorrect. (B) and (D) are incorrect because whether or not the "knock and announce rule" was violated will not affect admissibility of the heroin—the exclusionary rule will not apply to evidence resulting from a search violating that rule.

Answer to Question 2

(C) If the warrant was invalid, any evidence obtained thereunder will be excluded. A warrant must be based on a showing of probable cause. When requesting a warrant, officers must submit to a magistrate an affidavit setting forth sufficient underlying circumstances to enable the magistrate to make a determination of probable cause, independent of the officers' conclusions, that evidence of a crime will be found at the premises. Also, a warrant must describe with reasonable precision the place to be searched and any items to be seized. A finding that a warrant was invalid because it was not supported by probable cause will not entitle the defendant to exclude evidence obtained under the warrant if the police have acted in good faith and reasonable reliance on a facially valid warrant. However, a police officer cannot in good faith rely on a defective search warrant if: (i) the affidavit underlying the warrant is so lacking in probable cause that no reasonable police officer would have relied on it; (ii) the warrant is defective on its face (*e.g.,* it fails to state with particularity the place to be searched or the things to be seized); (iii) the affiant lied to or misled the magistrate; or (iv) the magistrate has wholly abandoned his judicial role. Because the deli owner lives in a condominium, the warrant should have specified which unit in the multi-unit dwelling was to be searched. If the warrant did not so specify, then it failed to describe with sufficient particularity the place to be searched. Such an absence of precision renders the warrant defective on its face, so that the F.B.I. agents cannot be said to have relied in good faith on a facially valid warrant. Thus, the evidence obtained pursuant to this facially defective warrant will be excluded. (A) and (B) each incorrectly imply that there was something wrong with the execution of the warrant. A warrant must be executed by the police without unreasonable delay, with the police knocking and announcing their purpose (unless they reasonably believe that such notice will endanger them or lead to the destruction of evidence). The F.B.I. agents conducted themselves in accordance with these standards. The fact that a warrant was executed in the evening or at a time when a particular person was not on the premises will not invalidate a search conducted pursuant to the warrant. Here, the agents announced themselves to the deli owner's wife, and they were not required to wait until the owner returned in order to conduct their search. (D) is incorrect because it states a fact that will not, in and of itself, invalidate a warrant and a search pursuant thereto. The sufficiency of a search warrant affidavit based on an informer's hearsay is evaluated under the totality of the circumstances. The informer's reliability and credibility, as well as her basis of knowledge, are all elements that may illuminate the issue of probable cause, but they are not strictly separate requirements. Had the waitress been used before as an informant, and been previously found to be reliable, this would have been one factor in determining her present reliability. However, the fact that the waitress had not previously

served as an informer does not invalidate the warrant. Given the specificity and accuracy of the waitress's information (a man in a brown cap would pick it up at 2 p.m.), there was enough of a basis for her information to establish sufficient credibility to permit a magistrate to make a determination of probable cause.

Answer to Question 3

(C) The student will most likely be found guilty. Larceny is the taking and carrying away of the personal property of "another" with the intent to permanently deprive the other person of the property. It is possible to commit larceny of your own property if another person, such as a bailee, has a superior right to possession of the property at that time. Since the mechanic had a right to possession of the van until he was paid, the student committed larceny when he had his friend take the van without the mechanic's consent. (B) is wrong because a person can be guilty even though he did not personally engage in the behavior if he acts through an innocent agent. (D) is also incorrect. The student is guilty, but not for the reason stated in (D). He would be guilty even if he had not made the promise to pay for the van; he incurred an obligation to pay by having the repairs done.

Answer to Question 4

(A) The defendant may be convicted of burglary. Common law burglary was the breaking and entering of the dwelling house of another in the nighttime with the intent to commit a larceny or other felony inside. In the instant case, opening the door by use of a key would be sufficient to constitute a breaking, and the facts indicate that the defendant actually entered the house. Furthermore, the defendant intended to steal valuables when he entered the victim's home; thus, the intent to commit a theft inside the home may be established. As a result, the defendant has committed burglary. (B) is incorrect because, although the defendant was unable to complete the theft of the valuables, the crime of burglary is complete on entry. (C) is also incorrect. An attempt is an act that, although done with the intention of committing a crime, falls short of completing the crime. An attempt consists of two elements: (i) the intent to commit the crime, and (ii) an overt act in furtherance of the crime. Here the defendant has committing an attempted larceny, as he had the intent to steal valuables from the victim, and, by breaking into the home, he committed an overt act in furtherance of the crime. However, burglary is a more serious offense, making choice (C) an incorrect answer. (D) is incorrect because the defendant may be convicted of burglary, as explained above.

Answer to Question 5

(C) The getaway driver should be found not guilty. At common law, once a conspiracy has been entered into, each conspirator, by virtue of her participation in the conspiracy, may be charged with "aiding and abetting" the commission of crimes by her co-conspirators and therefore may be liable for those crimes as an accomplice. Even if the conspirator did not have the sufficient mental state for accomplice liability, a separate doctrine provides that each conspirator may be liable for the reasonably foreseeable crimes of all other co-conspirators that were committed in furtherance of the conspiracy. However, in the instant case, the getaway driver did not know of the theft of the cocaine, and, as a result, would not have the requisite mental state as an accomplice. The conspiracy doctrine discussed above also would not apply, as the crime of possession of cocaine with the intent to deliver would neither be in furtherance of the burglary nor a reasonably foreseeable result of the burglary. (A) is incorrect because it is too broad a statement. A conspirator is not criminally liable for ***all*** crimes resulting from the conspiracy. As discussed above, to be charged with a crime that grew out of the conspiracy, the additional crime must be both foreseeable and committed in furtherance of the conspiracy. (B) is also incorrect. Although a bit of a close call, the crime of possessing cocaine with the intent to distribute is a separate act from burglary, and a crime involving drug possession is not a crime ordinarily arising out of this type of burglary. It is this lack of foreseeability that makes (B) an incorrect choice. Finally, (D) is incorrect. The criminal liability of a conspirator for acts of a co-conspirator arises under the theory of accomplice liability. An accomplice need not have performed the criminal act himself to be held criminally liable for the criminal act of the principal. Thus, the fact that the actual burglar meets the definition of a principal is irrelevant.

Answer to Question 6

(C) The most effective argument is that the defendant is not guilty of first degree murder. The only theory of first degree murder applicable here is that the murder was "willful, deliberate, or [and] premeditated." This type of murder requires an actual intent to kill, which the defendant did not have. (A) is wrong because an automobile can be a dangerous weapon when used as one, and the intentional driving of an automobile at another can support and permit, though not require, an inference that defendant intended to kill. (B) is wrong because, at common law, 14 is the cutoff age for youthfulness to be a factor. The facts state that defendant was licensed and thus must be over the age of 14. (D) is clearly wrong. Although the defendant might be able to avoid liability for first degree murder because of his lack of intent to kill, he could be liable for second degree murder.

Answer to Question 7

(B) The judge should instruct the jury on murder and involuntary manslaughter. First, a jury could find the worker guilty of murder under the theory that throwing a brick from scaffolding high above a sidewalk without looking shows an "abandoned and malignant heart." The jury could also find the worker guilty of involuntary manslaughter—either because throwing a brick off scaffolding is an unlawful act not amounting to a felony or because throwing the brick off scaffolding is a lawful act done "without due caution and circumspection." Thus, (A) is wrong; it would be proper to charge the jury on murder as well as manslaughter. (C) is wrong because there is no way that the worker could be guilty of voluntary manslaughter, which would involve an unjustified, unexcused, but mitigated intentional homicide (*i.e.,* an intentional homicide committed under "heat of passion"). The worker did not intend to kill or seriously injure; moreover, if even assuming he did so intend, there is no factor of mitigation present. (D) is wrong because this question is based on a statute following the common law definition that does not divide murder into degrees.

Answer to Question 8

(B) The guard will most likely be found guilty of voluntary manslaughter. Voluntary manslaughter occurs when the actor kills another person but acts in the "heat of passion" after "sufficient provocation." At common law, provocation could be established by showing that the victim had committed a serious battery on the defendant. If as a result of the battery (provocation) the defendant killed the victim while in a rage (heat of passion), the criminal liability was voluntary manslaughter. Therefore, (B) is the correct answer; given that a serious battery was committed on the security guard and that the security guard was enraged when he shot the other driver. (A) is wrong. For criminal liability to attach under the felony murder rule, it must be established that the actor was engaged in a felony "independent" of the homicide when the death occurred. There

was no independent felony here. (C) is wrong because the statement "the security guard did not intend to kill the other driver" is too broad a statement. Even though the security guard did not intend to kill the other driver, he might be guilty of murder under a theory of "intent to cause serious bodily harm" or "depraved heart." Thus, the fact that the security guard did not intend to kill the other driver would not necessarily result in a manslaughter conviction. (D) is also too broad a statement and cannot be correct in light of the facts set out in the question. A person is justified in using deadly force only if he reasonably believes such force is necessary to prevent death or serious physical injury.

Answer to Question 9

(C) The father lacked the specific intent to kill that is required for attempted murder. However, the circumstances surrounding the "incendiary device" constitute factual impossibility and will not afford the father a defense to attempted arson. Criminal attempt is an act that, although done with the intention of committing a crime, falls short of completing that crime. To be guilty of attempt, the defendant must have the intent to perform an act and obtain a result that, if achieved, would constitute a crime. Regardless of the intent that would suffice for the completed offense, attempt always requires a specific intent to commit the target offense. Also, the defendant must have committed an act beyond mere preparation for the offense. Here, to be guilty of attempted murder, the father must have had the specific intent to kill his son's coach, even though the intent to inflict great bodily injury would be sufficient mens rea for murder. However, the facts indicate that the father intended at most only to injure the coach rather than kill him. Thus, the father cannot be guilty of attempted murder. However, the father did intend to burn the coach's home; therefore, he had the specific intent to commit arson by means of placing an incendiary device on the coach's porch, and his placing the device was an act beyond mere preparation for this crime. Although the device could not have actually burned the coach's house, it is no defense to attempt that it would have been impossible for the defendant to complete his plan. This is factual impossibility and is not a defense. Thus, the father is guilty of attempted arson. (A) and (B) are incorrect because the father did not have the specific intent to kill. (D) is incorrect because the father is guilty of attempted arson, as explained above.

Answer to Question 10

(D) Given that the defendant believed that, at the time he took the computer, the victim would have permitted him to take it to return it to the other player, the defendant lacked the intent to permanently deprive the victim of her interest in the computer, which is the necessary intent for larceny. Common law larceny consists of a taking and carrying away of tangible personal property of another by trespass with intent to permanently (or for an unreasonable time) deprive the person of his interest in the property. Larceny is a crime against possession; thus, it is only necessary that the property be taken from someone who has a possessory interest superior to that of the defendant. At the moment of the taking, the defendant must have had the intent to permanently deprive the person from whom the property is taken of his interest in the property. Here, although the other player owned the computer, the victim had the right of possession of the computer until the other player returned the victim's backgammon set. Thus, when the defendant took the computer from the victim's car, he was taking and carrying away tangible personal property in which the victim had a possessory interest. However, the defendant believed that, at the time of the taking, he was merely returning the computer to the other player, and that the victim would want him to do so. Thus, the defendant did not have the intent to deprive the victim of her interest in the computer because he was unaware that the victim had any such interest. Because the intent element of larceny is lacking, the defendant cannot be convicted of larceny.

Alternative (A) is incorrect because, although it correctly states that the victim was rightfully in possession of the computer when the defendant took it, the defendant lacked the intent necessary for larceny (as explained above). (B) is incorrect because the intent to deprive another of her interest in the computer, demonstrated by the defendant's sale of the computer to the stranger, did not exist at the time that the defendant took the computer. The intent and the taking must coincide. The defendant's intent at the airport does not change the earlier innocent taking into larceny (although the defendant might be guilty of embezzlement for intentionally converting the computer while in lawful possession of it). (C) is incorrect because, despite the other player's ownership of the computer, the victim had a superior right to possession at the time that the defendant took the computer (*i.e.*, she had the right to possess the computer, even as against the other player—the owner—until the other player returned the backgammon set). Thus, had the defendant known at the time of the taking that the victim's right to possess the computer was superior to that of the other player, the defendant would have been guilty of larceny because he would have had the requisite intent.

Answer to Question 11

(C) The defendant is guilty because she caused her friend to take and carry away the personal property, to which the victim had a superior right to possession, intending to permanently deprive the victim of her interest in the property. Larceny is a crime against possession rather than ownership, requiring only that the property be taken from someone who has a possessory interest superior to that of the defendant. Even the owner of property can be guilty of larceny, if she takes it from one who, at the time of the taking, has a superior possessory interest in it. Here, the victim had the right to possess the personal property until the defendant repaid the loan. Thus, in taking the property (through her friend), the defendant was taking property to which the victim had a superior possessory interest. Because the rightful owner of property can be guilty of larceny with respect to that property, (B) is incorrect. (A) is incorrect because a taking essential to larceny occurs even if a defendant obtains control of the property through the act of an innocent agent. The defendant's removal of the personal property from the victim's possession through the acts of her friend constitutes a sufficient taking, so that the defendant is guilty despite not having personally taken the property. (D) is incorrect because her friend's knowledge as to the true possessory interest in the personal property, or lack thereof, is irrelevant to the defendant's guilt. With respect to the defendant's guilt, the important point is that she knew that the victim had a superior possessory interest in the personal property, and that, with intent to deprive the victim of that interest, she persuaded her friend to take and carry away the property. Even if the defendant had told her friend about the agreement, the defendant would still be guilty of larceny if her friend took the personal property as her agent.

Answer to Question 12

(C) The man will not prevail in his motion to suppress. To be reasonable under the Fourth Amendment, most searches must be pursuant to a warrant. However, several types of inspections and searches do not require a warrant or even probable cause. The Supreme Court has held that the Fourth Amendment is not violated by a statute authorizing warrantless searches of a probationer's home—even absent probable cause—if a statute provides for such searches. The Court reasoned that in such circumstances, the probationer has a diminished expectation of privacy and the government has a heightened need for searching probationers; thus the search is reasonable in a constitutional sense. (A) is incorrect because while probable cause may be based on this type of tip under the "totality of the circumstances" test, probable cause is not necessary to establish the validity of the search based on the above discussion. (B) is incorrect because a search warrant is

not required for a search of a probationer's home that otherwise complies with procedures. (D) is incorrect because this was not a search incident to a constitutionally valid arrest. There was no basis for an arrest until after the search occurred; if the search were not otherwise independently valid, the fact that the man was arrested after the search revealed the drugs would not make the search valid.

Answer to Question 13

(A) The defendant's rights were violated by the voluntary manslaughter instruction. The Due Process Clause requires in all criminal cases that the state prove guilt beyond a reasonable doubt. The prosecution must bear the burden of proving all of the elements of the crime charged. Thus, the Supreme Court has held that if "malice aforethought" is an element of murder, the state may not require the defendant to prove that he committed the homicide in the heat of passion, because heat of passion negates malice and in effect requires the defendant to disprove the element of malice aforethought. [Mullaney v. Wilbur (1975)] Here, the judge's instructions create the same result with "extreme emotional disturbance." By instructing the jury that extreme emotional disturbance negates the existence of malice aforethought, which otherwise may be presumed from proof of the unlawful killing, and that the defendant bears the burden of proof on that issue, the judge improperly imposed on this particular defendant the burden to disprove an element of murder. Here, this defendant came forward with some evidence on the issue of emotional disturbance, but the prosecution still bore the burden of proving that whatever emotional disturbance he had did not negate malice aforethought. Thus, (B) and (D) are incorrect. Insanity is an affirmative defense for which it is constitutional to impose the burden of proof on the defendant. Although many jurisdictions require a defendant to prove his insanity by a preponderance of the evidence, federal courts require proof by clear and convincing evidence, and one Supreme Court case upheld requiring a defendant to prove insanity beyond a reasonable doubt. [*See* Leland v. Oregon (1952)] Thus, (B) and (C) are incorrect and (A) is correct.

Answer to Question 14

(D) The confession is admissible with the judge's limiting instruction. Where two persons are tried together and one has given a confession implicating the other, the general rule is that the Sixth Amendment right to confront adverse witnesses prohibits the use of such a statement. This problem arises because of the inability of the nonconfessing defendant to compel the confessing co-defendant to take the stand for cross-examination at their joint trial. As exceptions to the general rule, the statement may be admitted if: (i) all portions of the statement referring to the other defendant can be eliminated (so that there is no indication of that defendant's involvement); (ii) the confessing defendant takes the stand and subjects himself to cross-examination with respect to the truth or falsity of what the statement asserts; ***or*** (iii) the confession of the nontestifying co-defendant is being used to rebut the defendant's claim that his confession was obtained coercively, in which case the jury must be instructed as to the purpose of the admission. The accomplice's confession, which the prosecution seeks to introduce into evidence, implicates the defendant in the commission of the crimes charged. Consequently, introduction of this confession raises a problem based on the right of confrontation. However, given that the judge will issue the limiting instruction, the confession is admissible. (D) is therefore correct and (A) is incorrect. (B) and (C) are incorrect because neither of those conditions is necessary for the confession to be admitted as long as the judge issues a limiting instruction, as discussed above.

Answer to Question 15

(D) The director cannot be found guilty under the false imprisonment statute. Despite the general rule that it is no defense to a crime that the defendant mistakenly believed that his conduct was not prohibited by the criminal law, a mistake as to some aspect of law pertaining to the ***elements*** of the crime rather than the ***existence*** of the statute making the act criminal may negate the state of mind required for the crime. When a culpable state of mind is specified by an offense without indicating to which element it applies, the state of mind applies to all material elements of the offense unless a contrary purpose appears in the statute. Thus, the state of mind required here, "knowingly," requires not only that the director know of the patient's confinement, but also that the director know there is no valid consent and that he has no legal authority to confine her. His mistake as to his legal authority to confine her negates the state of mind required for that element of the false imprisonment statute. (A) is wrong because whether the director's reliance on his attorney's advice was reasonable is irrelevant. As long as he believed that he had lawful authority to hold the patient, the director did not have the state of mind required for the offense. (B) is wrong because, as stated above, the director would have had to have knowledge of the absence of lawful authority before he could be found liable under the false imprisonment statute. (C) is wrong because the patient's compliance with her confinement and her absence of harm are not relevant. Valid consent to negate a charge of false imprisonment cannot be obtained from one without capacity to give such consent, and the patient, being mentally incompetent, did not have the capacity to consent to the confinement. Absence of harm may be a defense to a tort action for false imprisonment where the victim is not aware of the confinement, but it is not a defense to the crime of false imprisonment.

Answer to Question 16

(B) The robber can be convicted of third degree murder based on the felony murder statute. The state statute defines murder in the third degree as any killing that occurs during and as a result of the commission of a felony. Hence, even an accidental killing committed during the course of a felony is murder. To be guilty of felony murder under the statute, the defendant must be guilty of the underlying felony and death must have been a foreseeable result of commission of the felony. Under such a statute, a defendant can be held liable for felony murder when resistance by the victim results in the death of a third-party bystander who is not a co-felon; there is no requirement in the statute that the killing be caused by the defendant or an accomplice of the defendant. The robber attempted to commit a robbery of a bank. Even though the robber was armed only with a toy pistol, a jury could find that it was foreseeable that death could result from commission of the robbery, such as by resistance from the victim or police. The killing of the bank teller resulted from the resistance of the security guard. Consequently, the robber can be convicted of third degree murder because the killing occurred during the commission of the robbery. (A) is incorrect because, by implication, murder in the second degree consists of murder as known at common law. Thus, to be guilty of second degree murder, a defendant must have intended to kill or to inflict great bodily injury, or have been recklessly indifferent to an unjustifiably high risk to human life. The facts do not indicate that the robber engaged in any action while intending to kill or seriously injure, or that he acted with the degree of reckless indifference required for murder. Note that the robber did not initiate the shooting and was "armed" only with a toy pistol. Therefore, the robber did not unlawfully kill with malice aforethought (other than intent to commit a felony). Consequently, the robber cannot be convicted of the more serious crime of second degree murder. (C) is incorrect because murder in the third degree, of which the robber can be convicted, is more serious than manslaughter. (D) is incorrect because, as discussed above, the robber can be convicted of third degree murder.

Answer to Question 17

(D) The store clerk can be convicted of no homicide crime because shooting at the robber was authorized by law. A private person has the right to use deadly force to effectuate an arrest when the

felon appears to pose a threat to the person or to others and deadly force is necessary to prevent his escape, as long as the felon was actually guilty of the felony. Similarly, a person has the right to use deadly force in preventing the completion of a crime being committed if the crime is a "dangerous felony" involving risk to human life. Here, the store clerk had the right to use deadly force against the robber, even though she was not directly threatened with imminent death or great bodily harm at the time she fired, because the robber was armed with a deadly weapon and appeared to pose a danger to anyone who might try to stop him. Although this right to shoot at the robber would not justify the killing of the customer if the clerk acted with malice aforethought as to the customer, in this case the customer was not in the line of the clerk's fire. Thus, the clerk's conduct would not constitute reckless indifference to an unjustifiably high risk to human life or any other state of mind constituting malice aforethought. The clerk therefore can be convicted of no homicide crime. (C) is incorrect because the facts do not support a conviction for manslaughter. The clerk is not guilty of voluntary manslaughter because she did not intentionally kill anyone while under legally adequate provocation. She is not guilty of involuntary manslaughter because her shooting at the robber was authorized by law and, given the low probability of anyone else being hit, was not such a great deviation from the conduct of a reasonable person as to constitute criminal negligence. (A) is incorrect because, as discussed above, the clerk did not act with reckless indifference to human life or any other state of mind constituting malice aforethought as to anyone other than the robber. (B) is incorrect because the clerk did not cause a death during the commission of a felony; she was trying to stop the completion of a felony when she shot the gun.

Answer to Question 18

(D) The wife is not guilty because she lacked the intent to defraud the government. The crime of false pretenses consists of obtaining title to the property of another by an intentional false statement of past or existing fact, with intent to defraud the other. This is a crime requiring specific intent, *i.e.,* intent to defraud. The wife believed that she was entitled to the total amount of the combined check, because she thought that the amount of the check equaled what she would have received as a death benefit and an increased spousal benefit. Because the wife believed that she was simply receiving money to which she was entitled, rather than money actually belonging to the government, she lacked the intent to defraud the government. Absent the requisite specific intent, the wife is not guilty of obtaining money by false pretenses. (B) is incorrect because it would hold the wife to a "reasonable person" standard; *i.e.,* imposing liability if she ***should have known*** that she was receiving benefits to which she was not entitled. Even if the wife should have known this, the fact remains that she sincerely believed that she was only receiving money to which she was entitled. This sincere belief, even if unreasonable, will negate the existence of intent to defraud the government. (C) is virtually identical to (B), stating in effect that the wife is guilty if her belief as to her entitlement to the money is unreasonable. As explained above, the reasonableness of the wife's belief is not significant. As long as the wife truly believed that she was entitled to all of the money, she did not intend to defraud the government. (A) is incorrect because the question asks about the offense of false pretenses. As noted above, this offense clearly requires specific intent, and is therefore not an offense to which strict liability would be properly applicable.

Answer to Question 19

(C) The defendant should be found not guilty. The state statute proscribes sexual intercourse with a person under the age of 16. Although the defendant thought he was having sex with someone under the age of consent, the waitress in fact had attained the age of consent. Thus, the defendant has not engaged in the conduct that is prohibited by the statute. (A) is incorrect. Statutory rape, as defined in the jurisdiction, is a strict liability crime. Thus, the defendant's state of mind is largely irrelevant to whether he may be convicted of statutory rape. (B) is also incorrect. The legal proposition in the answer choice—that a mistake of fact is not available against the charge—essentially means that a mistake of fact that negates the defendant's state of mind is irrelevant when the crime has no state of mind requirement. Hence, if the defendant mistakenly believed that the waitress was over age 16 when in fact she was not, the mistake would not be a defense. Here, however, the mistake was the opposite. The fact that she was not a minor precludes the defendant from being found guilty, regardless of his state of mind. (D) is incorrect; whether the victim to a statutory rape initiated the sexual encounter is irrelevant as to whether the crime was committed.

Answer to Question 20

(C) The addict should be found not guilty because the death did not occur during the commission of a felony. Under the felony murder theory, a person is criminally liable for the death of another committed during the course of the felony, even if the death was accidental. However, one limitation is that the death must occur during the commission of the felony. Generally, when a felon reaches a place of temporary safety, the potential for criminal liability for felony murder ceases. Here, the addict committed the burglary at night, and the customer was stricken with asthma the next day, presumably long after the addict returned to his home. Hence, the death is not felony murder and (A) is incorrect. (B) is incorrect because the fact that it was foreseeable that the pharmacy would be closed to customers as a result of the burglary is irrelevant. As explained above, the death did not occur during the commission of the felony. (D) is incorrect because a burglary committed by an armed intruder would be an inherently dangerous felony.

Answer to Question 21

(C) The former employee is guilty of robbery and aggravated battery. Robbery is (i) the taking (ii) of the personal property (iii) of another (iv) from the other person's presence (v) by force or intimidation (vi) with the intent to permanently deprive the person of the property. The former employee clearly committed a robbery by forcing the store manager, at gunpoint, to empty the contents of the safe into a sack. Given that the former employee did not physically commit either the rape or the aggravated battery, criminal liability would hinge on whether he could be held accountable based on a conspiracy theory. Provided that a conspiracy exists, a person will be criminally liable for the acts committed by a co-conspirator that were committed in furtherance of the objectives of the conspiracy and were a natural and probable consequence of the conspiracy (*i.e.*, foreseeable). At common law, a conspiracy exists when there is (i) an agreement between two or more persons; (ii) the intent to enter into the agreement; and (iii) the intent to achieve the objective of the agreement. Here, the former employee and his friend intentionally entered into an agreement to rob the grocery store. Furthermore, the fact that they armed themselves shows that they considered the possibility that they might need to use force during the crime; thus, the fact that the friend actually used force by shooting the store manager was foreseeable. The shooting was also done in furtherance of the conspiracy, as it was intended to aid in the pair's getaway. Thus, the former employee may be found guilty of the aggravated assault on the store manager, and (A) and (B) are incorrect. However, the rape was neither committed in furtherance of the conspiracy (it did nothing to further the robbery or aid in the pair's getaway), nor do the facts indicate that it was foreseeable that the friend would commit such a crime during a robbery. Under these circumstances, criminal liability probably would not attach to the former employee for the acts of his friend in raping the produce clerk, making (B) and (D) incorrect.

Answer to Question 22

(B) The illegal alien cannot be convicted of a crime under the statute because it was enacted for his protection, and the clerk cannot be convicted of conspiracy under the statute because the illegal alien, who would otherwise be liable as an accomplice, is not subject to conviction because of a legislative intent to exempt him. If a statute is intended to protect members of a limited class from exploitation or overbearing, members of that class are presumed to have been intended to be immune from liability, even if they participate in the crime in a manner that would otherwise make them liable. Thus, the illegal alien would not be liable as an accomplice under the statute, making (C) incorrect. The clerk clearly can be convicted for the substantive offense, but he cannot be convicted of conspiracy. One of the implications of the common law requirement that there be at least two guilty parties in a conspiracy arises when the crime involves members of a class protected by the statute. If members of a conspiracy agree to commit an act that violates a statute designed to protect persons within a given class, a person within that class not only cannot be guilty of the crime itself, as discussed above, but also cannot be guilty of a conspiracy to commit the crime. (D) is therefore incorrect. Because the member of the protected class cannot be guilty of conspiracy, if no other guilty party exists, the other member of the agreement cannot be guilty of criminal conspiracy because there were not two guilty parties to the agreement. Thus, since the illegal alien cannot be convicted of conspiracy under the statute, neither can the clerk. (A) is therefore incorrect and (B) is correct.

Answer to Question 23

(C) The liquor store clerk can be convicted of conspiracy in a unilateral jurisdiction even though the minor can be convicted of neither solicitation nor conspiracy. Under the unilateral (Model Penal Code) approach, the crime of conspiracy is shown by proof that the defendant agreed with another to commit a crime (even if that other person does not share the commitment), and does not require proof of an actual agreement between two or more persons. Thus, the fact that no other party to the conspiracy could be found guilty does not prevent the defendant from being convicted of conspiracy. Here, the fact that the minor is a member of the class that the statute was designed to protect prevents him from being found guilty of conspiracy; (B) is therefore incorrect. However, unlike under the common law approach, under the unilateral approach this fact has no bearing on the liquor store clerk's liability for conspiracy. Thus, (C) is correct and (D) is incorrect. (A) is incorrect because the crime of solicitation is treated the same as conspiracy. If the solicitor could not be guilty of the completed crime because of legislative intent to exempt him, he cannot be found guilty of solicitation of the crime. Because the minor is a member of the class intended to be protected by the statute, he cannot be found guilty of soliciting the liquor store clerk to commit it.

Answer to Question 24

(D) The defendant may be convicted of first degree murder because he was not justified in killing the neighbor and it appears that he did have time to premeditate and deliberate on the murder. The facts here point to involuntary intoxication as a possible defense. Intoxication is involuntary if it results from the taking of an intoxicating substance without knowledge of its nature, under direct duress imposed by another, or pursuant to medical advice. Such intoxication is treated as mental illness, in which case the defendant is entitled to acquittal if, because of the intoxication, the defendant meets the applicable test for insanity. Here, the defendant took the medicine without knowing of its hallucinatory properties and pursuant to the advice of his doctor. Thus, the defendant's resulting state of hallucination will be considered to be involuntary intoxication. We are told that the applicable test for insanity is the *M'Naghten* rule. Pursuant to this rule, a defendant is entitled to acquittal if a disease of the mind caused a defect of reason such that the defendant lacked the ability at the time of his actions to either: (i) know the wrongfulness of his actions; or (ii) understand the nature and quality of his actions. If a defendant suffers from delusions (false beliefs), it must be determined whether his actions would have been criminal if the facts had been as he believed them to be. Here, the defendant falsely believed that his neighbor was spreading false rumors about him. Had this delusion been accurate, the defendant obviously would not have been legally entitled to murder the neighbor. As a result, the *M'Naghten* rule would not allow for acquittal based on an insanity defense, which in turn would also negate the viability of an involuntary intoxication defense. Thus, (D) is correct, and (A) and (B) are incorrect. (C) is incorrect because, as explained above, the intoxication was involuntary even though the defendant voluntarily ingested the drugs.

Answer to Question 25

(D) The fan should not be convicted under either definition of assault. Criminal assault is either: (i) an attempt to commit a battery, or (ii) the intentional creation, other than by mere words, of a reasonable apprehension in the mind of the victim of imminent bodily harm. In the instant case, the fan did not intend to hit anyone. Thus, the fan's actions do not constitute an attempt to commit a battery, which would require a specific intent to bring about bodily injury or an offensive touching. In addition, the fact that the referee did not see the bottle being thrown at him means that the defendant did not create in the referee a reasonable apprehension of imminent bodily harm. Consequently, the fan is not likely to be convicted of either type of assault. This also makes (B) and (C) incorrect, in that each answer considers only one type of assault. (A) is incorrect. Although a substantial step, or some overt act showing the defendant's intent to commit the crime, is required to convict for an attempt of a crime, the facts here explicitly state that the fan had no such intent. This makes (A) an incorrect answer choice.

Answer to Question 26

(B) The defendant should be found guilty of the charged felony if he knew or believed that the box contained cocaine. The defendant is being tried for "knowingly" possessing cocaine. A person does not act knowingly unless he is aware that his conduct is of the proscribed nature or that the proscribed circumstances exist. Thus, the defendant could not have acted knowingly unless he knew or believed that the box contained cocaine. (A) is incorrect because criminal statutes that penalize the possession of contraband generally require only that the defendant have ***control*** of the item for a long enough period to have had an opportunity to terminate the possession. Thus, the defendant need not have moved or handled the box. (C) is incorrect for the same reason as (A), and also because the defendant's failure to know when he should have known would constitute negligence—failure to be aware of a substantial risk that prohibited results will follow or that circumstances exist—and negligence is not sufficient to establish knowledge. Note, however, that a defendant may not consciously avoid learning the true nature of the item possessed; knowledge or intent may be inferred from a combination of suspicion and indifference to the truth. (D) is incorrect because, as discussed above, the statute requires that the defendant knew or believed that the box contained cocaine.

Answer to Question 27

(D) The friend did not have the requisite intent to be convicted of either robbery or conspiracy to commit robbery. Because the friend did not actually engage in the act constituting the robbery,

the only way she can be convicted of this crime is as an accomplice. An accomplice is one who aids, counsels, or encourages the principal before or during commission of the crime. To be convicted as an accomplice, a person must have given aid, counsel, or encouragement with the intent to aid or encourage the principal in the commission of the crime charged. Mere knowledge that a crime will result from the aid provided generally is insufficient for accomplice liability. Here, the friend did aid the robber in the commission of the robbery prior to the crime by awakening him at the time he requested. However, the facts do not even establish that the friend believed that the robber intended to carry out his plan. Assuming that she did believe that the robber was going to rob the store, there is no indication that she was interested in the outcome of the plan or had a stake in the robbery (*i.e.,* she did not have the intent to bring about the permanent deprivation of the money from the store). Such mere knowledge that the robber intended to rob the store on being awakened, without a clear indication of an actual intent to aid in the commission of the robbery, will not suffice as the mental state required to be convicted as an accomplice. Therefore, the friend cannot be convicted of robbery. Thus, choices (A) and (C) are wrong. Choice (B) is wrong because the friend is not likely to be convicted of conspiracy to commit robbery. Conspiracy consists of: (i) an agreement between two or more persons; (ii) the intent to enter into an agreement; and (iii) the intent to achieve the objective of the agreement. Here, for much the same reasons as set forth above concerning accomplice liability, the friend probably will be found not to have intended to achieve the objective of robbing the store. Conspiracy is a specific intent crime that requires both the intent to agree and the intent to achieve the objective of the conspiracy. The intent to agree can be inferred from the friend's conduct of providing the robber with the wake-up call. However, it cannot be said that the friend intended to bring about the robbery of the store. Such intent cannot be inferred from mere knowledge that the robber planned to rob the store. As an apparently disinterested bystander, the friend probably will be found not to have the state of mind necessary to be convicted of conspiracy to commit robbery.

Answer to Question 28

(D) Even though the student's words may have been intended to provoke the seaman, this fact alone would not justify the seaman's use of deadly force. A person may use deadly force in self-defense if he is: (i) without fault; (ii) confronted with unlawful force; and (iii) threatened with imminent death or great bodily harm. Generally, one who begins a fight has no right to use force in his own defense during that fight. However, if the victim of the initial aggression suddenly escalates a relatively minor fight into one involving deadly force and does not give the aggressor a chance to withdraw, the aggressor may use force in his own defense. Here, although the student instigated the hostile situation by repeatedly insulting the seaman, the seaman's throwing of a punch probably calls for his being characterized as the aggressor. The student, as the victim of the initial aggression, escalated matters by using a knife, especially since the seaman had said that he wanted no further trouble. This escalation (which is the point stated in choice (B)) entitled the seaman to employ deadly force in his own defense against the imminent threat of death or great bodily harm posed by the student's use of the knife. Thus, (B) presents a point that will be helpful to the seaman. (A) is incorrect because, if the student had no reason to fear serious bodily injury when he drew the knife, his use of the knife constitutes unlawful force, in response to which the seaman was entitled to use deadly force of his own. Consequently, (A) will also be of value in gaining the seaman an acquittal. Regarding (C), many courts hold that a person is not under a duty to retreat before using deadly force. Thus, even if the seaman could have safely retreated, he was still entitled to use deadly force in self-defense, so that he is not required to show why he did not retreat. Other courts, however, do require retreat before the use of deadly force, but only if the retreat can be made in complete safety. The fact that the seaman's route of

retreat was blocked by other students would indicate that a retreat might not be able to be made in safety, and would be significant in a jurisdiction holding that there is a duty to retreat. Therefore, (C) also presents a point that can be helpful to the seaman. (D) is correct because the motive of the student in insulting the seaman is of no help to the defense. Even if the words did provoke him, the seaman would not be entitled to employ deadly force against the student on the basis of the student's desire for trouble. Use of such force would be justified only if the seaman held a reasonable belief that he was faced with imminent death or great bodily harm from one of the students if he did not respond with deadly force.

Answer to Question 29

(A) The defendant may also be found guilty of conspiracy if he is found guilty of burglary. One who solicits another to commit a crime cannot be convicted of both the solicitation and the completed crime. Likewise, one who completes a crime after attempting it may not be convicted of both the attempt and the completed crime. However, if conspirators are successful, they can be convicted of both criminal conspiracy and the crime they committed pursuant to the conspiracy (*i.e.,* conspiracy does not merge with the completed offense). Thus, if the defendant is found guilty of burglary, he cannot also be convicted of either attempt or solicitation. The defendant ***can*** be convicted of conspiracy in addition to burglary (with conspiracy liability being based on the apparent agreement between the defendant and the other person to bring about the burglary of the home. (B) incorrectly states that the defendant may be found guilty of solicitation as well as the principal offense of burglary. (C) and (D) make the same incorrect assertion. In addition, (D) incorrectly states that the defendant may be found guilty of attempt as well as the completed crime, and that he may not be found guilty of conspiracy.

Answer to Question 30

(D) The defendant is guilty of larceny by trick because he obtained possession of the baseball by means of a misrepresentation. Larceny is the taking and carrying away of tangible personal property of another by trespass, with intent to permanently (or for an unreasonable time) deprive the person of her interest in the property. The taking must be without the consent of the person in possession of the property. If such consent is induced by a misrepresentation of a past or existing fact, the consent is not valid. The resulting larceny is called larceny by trick. Here, the defendant obtained possession of the baseball with the owner's consent. However, this consent was obtained by means of the defendant's misrepresentation about friends visiting. This was a false statement of an existing fact, made with the intent that his neighbor rely on the statement, and the misrepresentation induced his neighbor's consent. At the time of this taking, the defendant intended to deal with the baseball in a manner that involved a substantial risk of damage or loss. This suffices as intent to permanently deprive. Therefore, all the elements are in place for larceny by trick. (A) is not as good a choice as (D) because the taking in this case is better characterized as larceny by trick rather than larceny, given that the defendant induced his neighbor to consent to his taking possession of the baseball. (C) is incorrect because the defendant obtained only possession of the baseball, not title. False pretenses differs from larceny by trick in what is obtained. If the defendant obtains only possession of the property, the offense is larceny by trick, whereas obtaining of title means that false pretenses has been committed. What the victim intended to convey to the defendant is determinative. The neighbor intended only to let the defendant borrow the baseball for a short time, not to convey title to him. Consequently, the only thing the defendant obtained was possession of the baseball. Because title to the baseball was not obtained, there can be no conviction of false pretenses. Regarding (B), embezzlement is the

fraudulent conversion of property of another by a person in lawful possession of that property. In embezzlement, misappropriation occurs while the defendant has lawful possession of the property, while in larceny, it occurs generally at the time the defendant obtains wrongful possession of the property. Here, as detailed above, the defendant's taking of possession of the baseball was trespassory due to the manner in which he obtained consent to such possession. The crime of larceny was complete on the defendant's taking possession with the requisite intent to permanently deprive. Thus, at the time the baseball was destroyed, the defendant had already misappropriated it and was not in lawful possession of it. As a result, there can be no conviction for embezzlement.

Answer to Question 31

(C) The defendant has committed burglary and larceny. Burglary consists of a breaking and entry of the dwelling of another at nighttime, with the intent of committing a felony therein. The felony need not be carried out—all that is required is that the person committing the crime have the intent to commit a felony at the time of entry. At night, the defendant broke into and entered the house with the intent to commit the felony of larceny. Regardless of whether the defendant took any property or committed a burning, the burglary was complete on his breaking and entering the dwelling at nighttime with the requisite intent. The defendant has also committed common law larceny. Larceny is the taking and carrying away of the personal property of another, by trespass, with the intent to permanently deprive the owner of his interest in the property. The element of carrying away, or asportation, is satisfied as long as there is some movement of the property as a step in carrying it away. The movement need only be slight as long as it was part of the carrying away process. Here, the defendant placed valuables in a sack and started to leave the home. This movement was sufficient to constitute a carrying away. Having acted with the requisite intent to permanently deprive the true owner of their property, the defendant has committed larceny. (A) is incorrect because, as discussed above, the defendant is liable for the completed crime of larceny rather than attempted larceny. (B) is incorrect for the same reason, and also because the defendant probably has not committed an act sufficiently close to success to be liable for attempted arson. An attempt requires the intent to commit the completed offense and an act beyond mere preparation for the offense. Traditionally, courts used the proximity test, requiring an act that is dangerously close to success. Here, although the defendant was in the house and had at one time intended to burn it, he has done nothing else toward committing the arson. In fact, he left the gas at home. It is also important to note that possession of the gas has another lawful purpose for this defendant; as such, the possession of the gas, by itself, probably would not be sufficient in this case. Hence, the defendant's acts probably are not so dangerously close to success as to make him liable for attempted arson, also making (D) an incorrect answer.

Answer to Question 32

(C) The officer is an accessory after the fact to burglary. An accessory after the fact is one who receives, relieves, comforts, or assists another, knowing that he has committed a felony, in order to help the felon escape arrest, trial, or conviction. The crime committed by the principal must have been completed at the time aid is rendered. Here, the officer had a duty to arrest the suspect and failed to do so, instead letting him go. Her failure to act under these circumstances constituted sufficient assistance to the suspect to make her liable as an accessory after the fact. She almost certainly knew that the suspect had committed the felony of burglary, as she saw him with a flashlight in the darkened house and caught him sneaking out the back way with a lock-picking device in his possession. Under these facts, she can be liable as an accessory after the fact to burglary. (A) is incorrect because the facts do not indicate that the officer knew that the defendant had committed larceny when she let him go. She had stopped him outside of the house, and since he apparently had none of the home's valuables in his possession, she had no reason to doubt his claim that he had not gotten anything from the house. Although she probably surmised that he had broken in with the intent to commit larceny, she had no way of knowing that he had completed the crime of larceny by carrying the bag of valuables almost out of the house. (B) is incorrect because an accomplice is one who, with the intent that the crime be committed, aids, counsels, or encourages the principal before or during the commission of the crime. Because the defendant had already completed his crimes when the officer stopped him, her only liability will be as an accessory after the fact. (D) is incorrect because, as discussed above, the officer can be held liable as an accessory after the fact to burglary.

Answer to Question 33

(C) From the facts, it appears that the bartender made a reasonable mistake as to the age of the patron, and thus he did not have the mental state necessary for the crime charged. In this question, the statute requires a mental state of ***knowingly*** selling to a person under age 21; therefore, a mistake concerning the age of the purchaser would negate criminal liability. (A) is wrong. In many jurisdictions, selling liquor to a minor is a strict liability offense. In such jurisdictions, a person would be guilty if he sold the liquor to a minor even if he made a reasonable mistake about age. The statute in question, however, is not a strict liability offense because it requires a ***knowing*** state of mind. (B) is wrong because it is simply an incorrect statement of the facts. There is nothing in the question indicating that the bartender knew that the patron was younger than 21. (D) is wrong. Although the driver's license would be a consideration in deciding whether the bartender made a reasonable mistake, it would not of itself negate criminal liability: the bartender would be guilty if he knew that the patron was underage even if the patron produced a driver's license stating otherwise.

Answer to Question 34

(B) The defendant can be convicted of false pretenses and attempted robbery. False pretenses consists of obtaining title to the property of another by an intentional or knowing false statement of past or existing fact with intent to defraud another. With regard to the false representation, all that is required is that the defendant create a false impression as to a matter of fact, which is what happened here. In this case, the defendant obtained title to the gasoline by creating a false impression that he owned the sunglasses that he was offering in exchange, and he had the requisite intent to be convicted of false pretenses. He can also be convicted of attempted robbery because he attempted a taking of the property of another in the presence of the victim by force and with the intent to permanently deprive the victim of it. The fact that he was persuaded not to carry out the robbery does not affect his liability for attempt; that crime was completed as soon as he pulled out a knife and demanded the gas. (A) and (C) are incorrect because larceny by trick occurs when ***possession*** of the property is obtained by the defendant's misrepresentations, whereas false pretenses is the appropriate offense when the misrepresentations have prompted the victim to convey ***title*** to the property to the defendant. Here, the clerk intended to convey title to the gas to the defendant in exchange for the sunglasses. (C) and (D) are incorrect because the majority rule is that abandonment is not a defense to attempt. As discussed above, the crime of attempted robbery was completed as soon as the defendant pulled the knife out of his pocket and demanded the gas.

Answer to Question 35

(D) The judge's failure to determine whether the woman understood her right to trial by jury indicates that her guilty plea does not satisfy the constitutional requirement that it be "voluntary and

intelligent." A guilty plea is a waiver of the Sixth Amendment right to a jury trial. To be a valid waiver, the judge must determine on the record that the guilty plea represents a voluntary and intelligent choice among the alternative courses of action open to the defendant. To ensure that this is the case, the judge should make sure that the defendant is informed of the nature of the charge to which the plea is offered, of the maximum possible penalty, that she has a right not to plead guilty, and that by pleading guilty she waives her right to a trial. If the judge did not determine whether the woman understood that she had a right to a trial by jury, her plea will not be a sufficiently intelligent choice to satisfy the constitutional standard, and therefore will not be immune from a post-sentence attack on it. (A) is incorrect because the woman had no legitimate grounds for her motion to dismiss for violation of her right to a speedy trial. The Sixth Amendment right to a speedy trial does not attach until the defendant has been arrested or charged. Pre-arrest delays do not violate this standard, nor do they violate general due process requirements unless they were in bad faith and prejudice the defendant. Otherwise, the only limitation on pre-arrest delay would be the statute of limitations for the particular crime. Thus, the failure of the judge to rule on the motion to dismiss would not be a good argument for setting aside the woman's guilty plea. (B) is incorrect because most jurisdictions do not require that the record contain evidence of the defendant's guilt or other factual basis for the plea. Unless the defendant claims her innocence while offering a guilty plea, the judge need not determine whether there is evidence to indicate that the defendant actually committed the crime. (C) is incorrect. While the prosecutor has a duty to disclose exculpatory evidence to the defendant, the judge may accept a guilty plea without determining whether the prosecutor has satisfied that duty.

Answer to Question 36

(B) The defendant may be convicted of second degree murder. In states that divide murder into degrees, evidence that the defendant was intoxicated may be used to show that the defendant was unable to premeditate and deliberate on the idea of killing, making (A) incorrect. In such jurisdictions, however, the fact that the defendant was intoxicated may not further reduce the killing from second degree murder to manslaughter, given that second degree murder encompasses common law murder and thus includes depraved heart murder. Carrying and firing a gun while intoxicated certainly shows a reckless indifference to an unjustifiably high risk to human life, thus meeting the definition of second degree murder. This makes (B) correct and (C) and (D) incorrect.

Set 6 Answer Sheet

1. Ⓐ Ⓑ Ⓒ Ⓓ
2. Ⓐ Ⓑ Ⓒ Ⓓ
3. Ⓐ Ⓑ Ⓒ Ⓓ
4. Ⓐ Ⓑ Ⓒ Ⓓ
5. Ⓐ Ⓑ Ⓒ Ⓓ
6. Ⓐ Ⓑ Ⓒ Ⓓ
7. Ⓐ Ⓑ Ⓒ Ⓓ
8. Ⓐ Ⓑ Ⓒ Ⓓ
9. Ⓐ Ⓑ Ⓒ Ⓓ
10. Ⓐ Ⓑ Ⓒ Ⓓ
11. Ⓐ Ⓑ Ⓒ Ⓓ
12. Ⓐ Ⓑ Ⓒ Ⓓ
13. Ⓐ Ⓑ Ⓒ Ⓓ
14. Ⓐ Ⓑ Ⓒ Ⓓ
15. Ⓐ Ⓑ Ⓒ Ⓓ
16. Ⓐ Ⓑ Ⓒ Ⓓ
17. Ⓐ Ⓑ Ⓒ Ⓓ
18. Ⓐ Ⓑ Ⓒ Ⓓ
19. Ⓐ Ⓑ Ⓒ Ⓓ
20. Ⓐ Ⓑ Ⓒ Ⓓ
21. Ⓐ Ⓑ Ⓒ Ⓓ
22. Ⓐ Ⓑ Ⓒ Ⓓ
23. Ⓐ Ⓑ Ⓒ Ⓓ
24. Ⓐ Ⓑ Ⓒ Ⓓ
25. Ⓐ Ⓑ Ⓒ Ⓓ
26. Ⓐ Ⓑ Ⓒ Ⓓ
27. Ⓐ Ⓑ Ⓒ Ⓓ
28. Ⓐ Ⓑ Ⓒ Ⓓ
29. Ⓐ Ⓑ Ⓒ Ⓓ
30. Ⓐ Ⓑ Ⓒ Ⓓ
31. Ⓐ Ⓑ Ⓒ Ⓓ
32. Ⓐ Ⓑ Ⓒ Ⓓ
33. Ⓐ Ⓑ Ⓒ Ⓓ
34. Ⓐ Ⓑ Ⓒ Ⓓ
35. Ⓐ Ⓑ Ⓒ Ⓓ
36. Ⓐ Ⓑ Ⓒ Ⓓ

CRIMINAL LAW QUESTIONS - SET 6

Question 1

The defendant and his friend entered a convenience store wearing ski masks and demanded all the money in the register, claiming they had a gun. The clerk promptly complied with that demand. The pair grabbed the money and ran out the door. A police officer saw them running through the parking lot, still wearing their masks, and surmised that a robbery had taken place. Without any warning, the police officer drew out his gun and fired two shots, one of which shattered the defendant's kneecap and sent him tumbling to the ground. The other bullet struck the friend in the head, killing him instantly. The defendant is placed on trial for the friend's death on a felony murder theory.

Which of the following is the best argument for the defendant to make in order to gain an acquittal:

(A) Both the defendant and his friend were unarmed.

(B) The police officer failed to warn the pair before firing.

(C) The felony had already been completed when the friend was killed.

(D) The friend was a co-felon.

Question 2

A police officer was given a tip about a blond male living in a nearby trailer park who was selling narcotics. The officer immediately drove to the trailer park and obtained from the manager the names of six blond males who had trailers or mobile homes in the trailer park. At the first lot, the officer knocked on the defendant's door, announced that he was a police officer, and asked to talk to the defendant. The defendant's girlfriend, who did not live there but had been visiting, told the officer that the defendant would not be back for some time. The officer, believing that the girlfriend lived there, told her that he suspected that the defendant was dealing drugs and asked her if he could look around a little. The girlfriend said, "Sure, why not?" and let the officer in. After seeing nothing in the main living area, he went into the small back bedroom and opened several small storage compartments. In the corner of one of the compartments, he found an opaque bag. On opening it, he observed that it contained what appeared to be marijuana and confiscated the bag. Shortly thereafter, the defendant was arrested and charged with possession of narcotics with intent to distribute, a felony.

On a motion by the defendant's attorney to suppress the introduction of the marijuana into evidence, how is the court likely to rule?

(A) For the defendant, because his girlfriend did not live in the trailer.

(B) For the defendant, because the search exceeded the scope of the consent.

(C) Against the defendant, because mobile homes fall within the automobile exception to the warrant requirement.

(D) Against the defendant, because the officer reasonably believed that the defendant's girlfriend lived in the trailer.

Question 3

Suspecting criminal activity, a police officer acting without a warrant peeked through a small opening in the shutters of an apartment. The officer observed the apartment's tenant and the defendant making methamphetamine. The officer immediately entered the apartment and arrested the tenant and the defendant, and he confiscated the ingredients for the methamphetamine, the tools used for methamphetamine production, and any completed methamphetamine for evidence. The search is later ruled invalid at a preliminary hearing.

May the defendant now claim that her Fourth Amendment rights have been violated by the seizure of the ingredients, tools, and methamphetamine from the apartment?

(A) Yes, because the items will be used in evidence against her.

(B) Yes, if she was an overnight guest of the tenant.

(C) No, because she was not the owner or occupier of the apartment.

(D) No, unless she admits to ownership of the items.

Question 4

A state statute provided for criminal penalties for "knowingly selling alcoholic beverages in violation of the regulations of the State Liquor Commission to any person under the age of 18." One of the State Liquor Commission regulations provided that "before an alcoholic beverage is sold to any person between the ages of 17 and 24, the seller must demand some form of photo identification to determine the buyer's age."

A minor who looked much older than his age of 17 walked into a tavern located in the state and asked the bartender for a beer. The bartender never asked the minor for any form of identification, as he thought that he was at least 25 years old. Had the bartender asked for identification, the minor would have shown him a fake identification card showing that he was 21 years old. The bartender served the beer to the minor, who consumed it on the premises. The bartender was subsequently charged under the state statute for selling the beer to the minor.

The bartender is:

(A) Not guilty, because he reasonably believed that the minor was older than 25 years.

(B) Not guilty, because the minor had fake identification with which he could have obtained the beer.

(C) Guilty, because he sold an alcoholic beverage to a minor, a strict liability crime

(D) Guilty, because he failed to ask for identification, and the regulation does not provide for a mens rea requirement.

Question 5

A police officer saw a car containing three teenagers driving slowly down the street at 1 a.m. She waited for it to go by her and, after it was far enough ahead, started to follow it. Several blocks later, the car rolled through a stop sign. The officer immediately pulled the car over and requested the driver's license. A license check showed that the driver had five outstanding parking tickets. A statute in the jurisdiction permits an arrest to be made if a driver has four or more outstanding parking or traffic violations. The officer decided to take the driver in on the tickets. She informed the driver that he was under arrest and asked him to step out of the car. When the driver got out, the officer patted him down and found a gun in his waistband. Calling for backup, she decided to haul all three teenagers to jail.

Subsequent testing showed that the gun had been used in a recent homicide during a store robbery by three young men. One of the passengers made a motion to prevent the introduction of the gun at his trial for murder and robbery.

The judge should:

(A) Deny the motion, because the officer was legitimately concerned for her own personal safety.

(B) Deny the motion, because the gun was found after the driver had been arrested.

(C) Grant the motion, because the officer had no valid reason to be following the automobile.

(D) Grant the motion, because the officer had not arrested the driver for suspicion of robbing the store or committing the homicide.

Question 6

The defendant entered a bank, planning to rob it. An alert bank employee saw the defendant brandishing her gun and pushed the silent alarm button to summon the police, and most of the employees and customers were successful in fleeing the bank. However, when the police surrounded the bank, the defendant was still inside with a hostage, one of the bank's tellers, whom the defendant had forced to turn over all the money in her drawer. The police obtained only a vague description of the defendant from the fleeing employees and customers as being a white female of average height, but all agreed that she was wearing a bright yellow scarf around her neck. The defendant, hoping to distract the police and escape out a back door, forced the teller to put on the bright yellow scarf and walk in front of a window. A rookie police officer, on seeing the yellow scarf, opened fire, killing the bank teller immediately. The defendant was apprehended shortly thereafter trying to escape out the back door.

If the defendant is prosecuted and found guilty of the teller's murder, it will be because:

(A) The defendant was still in the building and had not yet run out at the time that the teller was killed.

(B) The police officer did not have legal justification to use deadly force under the circumstances.

(C) The defendant caused the death of the victim during the course of a felony.

(D) The defendant's putting the victim in a position of danger shows intent to kill.

Question 7

A coal company developed a new extraction process that enabled it to produce coal at marketable cost from "worn out" mines that it owned, and began operating the mines using the new process. As a cost-cutting measure that increased profits, the corporate officers knowingly permitted the new process to be utilized in such a way that federally and state mandated methane gas detection measures were not complied with, and a consequent methane explosion severely injured several miners. In addition to being prosecuted for felony violations of the methane detection statutes, the corporation and its officers were prosecuted for attempted murder.

What should be the outcome of this prosecution?

(A) Not guilty, because the corporate officers had not proceeded sufficiently beyond the planning stage for their actions to constitute an attempt.

(B) Not guilty, because the corporate officers did not possess the requisite intent to constitute the crime of attempted murder.

(C) Guilty, because the corporate officers' actions created a situation so dangerous to human life or safety that their mental state would be considered an abandoned and malignant heart.

(D) Guilty, because the violation of the federal and state methane detection statutes is a felony.

Question 8

A woman was arrested outside of a house shortly after she had broken in and stolen some jewelry. She was indicted for larceny and later for burglary. She was tried on the larceny indictment and convicted. Thereafter, she was brought to trial on the burglary indictment. Relying on the Double Jeopardy Clause of the Constitution, the woman moves to dismiss the indictment.

Her motion should be:

(A) Granted, because the Double Jeopardy Clause requires that all offenses arising out of the same transaction be adjudicated in the same trial.

(B) Granted, because the Double Jeopardy Clause allows the imposition of separate sentences for separate offenses occurring during the same criminal episode only if the offenses are tried together.

(C) Denied, because larceny and burglary are offenses that may constitutionally be tried and punished separately, even if they arise out of the same transaction, because each requires proof of a fact that the other does not.

(D) Denied, because the only protection double jeopardy affords to a defendant charged with multiple counts is under the doctrine of collateral estoppel.

Question 9

The criminal law of the state uses the common law elements to define the crime of burglary. The state also has a statute making "flashing" (exposing of sexual parts) a felony. One night, the defendant broke into the home of the victim, a young woman who lived in the defendant's neighborhood. He entered the victim's bedroom and opened his trenchcoat to "flash" at her. The victim screamed, and the defendant fled, taking nothing with him from the victim's home. At the time of the "flashing," the defendant was wearing "long john" underwear, which was extremely difficult to remove and which the defendant knew he would not have time to remove. Thus, he did not in fact actually expose his sexual organs to the victim. The defendant knew about the "flashing" statute, but did not know that actual exposure of sexual organs is an element of the crime of "flashing," as defined in the statute.

Can the defendant be convicted of burglary?

(A) Yes, because he broke into the victim's dwelling place in the nighttime with the intent to commit a felony.

(B) Yes, because the defendant's mistake as to the "flashing" law is not a defense.

(C) No, because the defendant did not commit a felony.

(D) No, because the defendant could not have committed the felony while still wearing concealing underwear.

Question 10

A lessee rented from the defendant a building containing a store on the ground floor and an apartment above. The lessee operated a jewelry store on the ground floor and lived in the apartment above. One night as the defendant happened by the store, he saw a light on in the shop and, finding the door unlocked, decided to investigate. While looking around the store, the defendant spotted an expensive piece of jewelry. Recalling that the lessee was much behind in her rent, the defendant decided to take the jewelry and keep it until the lessee paid the rent. Just as the defendant was leaving the store, the lessee entered the store. Afraid of a confrontation, the defendant tossed the lessee the watch and ran out.

The defendant cannot be convicted of common law burglary because:

(A) The door was unlocked.

(B) A different part of the building was used as a dwelling.

(C) The defendant owns the building.

(D) The defendant had no intent to commit any crime until he entered the shop.

Question 11

A mechanic ran a car repair shop that specialized in repairing antique cars, and he also sold antique cars from time to time that he had repaired in the shop. Right before the shop closed, a customer brought her an antique car for repair. Although he knew that he would be unable to repair the car, the mechanic nonetheless wanted to inspect the car and see if there would be any usable parts should customer decide to sell the car. He lied to the customer that he would work on it the first thing in the morning. That night, one of the mechanic's creditors walked by the shop and saw the antique car standing in the shop's parking lot. Remembering that the mechanic had fallen behind on his loan payments, the creditor decided to take the car, believing it to be one that the mechanic was going to sell. Finding the car keys in the visor, the creditor tried to start the car, initially to no avail. However, the car finally started, but it moved only a couple of feet before it stalled again, permanently.

If the creditor is accused of grand larceny, his most promising defense would be:

(A) He did not manage to take away the car.

(B) The mechanic obtained the car by false pretenses, so the defendant cannot be convicted of stealing it, at least from the mechanic.

(C) The defendant honestly thought he was entitled to take the car as security for payment of the loan.

(D) Since the car was standing on a commercial property out in the open, the "by trespass" element cannot be met.

Question 12

A blacksmith ran a small forge in a tourist attraction depicting village life in the 1800s, and produced small metal trinkets for sale as souvenirs. A tourist came into the forge and started ridiculing the blacksmith, telling him that he was foolish for practicing such an out-of-date trade when modern equipment could produce the same trinkets faster and far more cheaply. Although he maintained a calm demeanor, the blacksmith was enraged by the time the customer finished and headed back out the door. He picked up an anvil and hurled it in the general direction of the customer. The anvil fell harmlessly to the ground after traveling maybe a foot.

If the blacksmith is charged with assault, which of the following statements would be most helpful for his defense:

(A) The blacksmith did not succeed in hitting the customer with the anvil, and he knew that it was impossible to do so.

(B) The blacksmith knew that it was impossible to hit the customer with the anvil.

(C) The customer did not see the blacksmith throw the anvil, and the blacksmith knew that it was impossible to hit the customer with the anvil.

(D) The customer did not see the blacksmith throw the anvil.

Question 13

The police received a tip from a reliable informant that a former student at the local university was selling narcotics. A brief investigation revealed that the former student, a college dropout, still hung around the university campus, had no visible means of support, and yet drove a large luxury car and wore flashy clothing and jewelry. The police picked up the former student the next time he showed up on campus, took him to the station, and questioned him all night long without a break and without letting him communicate with anyone else. When the former student tired from the interrogation, he admitted that he sold cocaine to his friend, who is a current student at the university. Based on this information, the police went to the current student's dormitory room. When they arrived, they found the door open but no one was in the room. The police entered, searched the room, and discovered a vial of white powder. Later laboratory tests established the powder to be cocaine. The former student was then charged with the sale of narcotics. At his trial, the prosecution attempted to admit the cocaine discovered in the dormitory room into evidence.

What is the former student's best argument for preventing the cocaine from being admitted into evidence?

(A) The search of the dormitory room was conducted without a warrant and without consent.

(B) The police arrested the former student without a warrant.

(C) The former student's confession was not voluntary under the circumstances.

(D) The police failed to give the former student *Miranda* warnings.

Question 14

A man and a woman were arrested and charged with a series of armed robberies. Each suspect was given *Miranda* warnings, and different interrogation teams questioned each suspect separately. Upon being questioned, the man told the police, "I'm not going to talk until I see a lawyer." An officer responded, "You might want to reconsider, because your partner has already confessed, and she's implicated you in the crimes." The man then told the police that he wanted to talk to the woman privately. The police escorted the man to the woman's cell, locked him in with her, and left. Unbeknownst to either of them, the police had "bugged" the woman's cell and recorded both the man and the woman making self-incriminating statements during their meeting. The man made no further statements to the police on advice of counsel, whom he called immediately after his conversation with the woman. The man was put on trial first, and the prosecution sought to introduce into evidence tapes of the bugged conversation between the man and the woman. The defense made a motion to suppress the evidence.

Should the court grant the motion to suppress?

(A) Yes, because the evidence is the fruit of a wiretap that violated the Fourth Amendment.

(B) Yes, because the police created a situation likely to induce the defendant to make an incriminating statement.

(C) No, because there is no expectation of privacy in a jail cell.

(D) No, because the conversation constituted a waiver of the man's *Miranda* rights.

Question 15

A borrower owed a lender $1,000. The debtor had promised to pay the lender back in one week, but three months passed and no money was forthcoming. The debtor always managed to avoid the lender's calls, so the lender drove to the debtor's house one night, intending to demand repayment in person. The lender rang the debtor's doorbell, knocked on his door, and screamed for the debtor to come out, but no one responded. The lender then tried the doorknob on the closed front door. To her surprise the door was unlocked, and she entered the debtor's house. After yelling several times for the debtor, the lender concluded that the debtor was not at home. Convinced that the debtor had run out the back door to avoid her, the lender went to the debtor's living room, grabbed an overstuffed chair, and carried it to the debtor's front lawn. The lender then doused the chair with lighter fluid and set it afire. Alarmed at the flaming chair, one of the debtor's neighbors called the police. The police found the lender still standing on the lawn next to the smoldering chair.

Assuming that the jurisdiction has not statutorily amended the common law elements of the crimes below, with which of the following may the lender be properly charged?

(A) Arson only.

(B) Larceny only.

(C) Arson and burglary.

(D) Burglary and larceny.

Question 16

A state has a modern theft statute that combines such common law crimes as larceny,

embezzlement, and receiving stolen property into one comprehensive crime. The police arrested a car dealer who had been dealing in stolen cars. When the police suggested strongly that it might be in his best interests to cooperate with a police "sting" operation, the dealer readily agreed. The police told the dealer to continue to purchase stolen autos from thieves, but to inform the police when a buyer was about to purchase a stolen car. The police would then arrest the buyer.

The defendant approached the dealer on his car lot, asking for a late-model used car at a good price. The dealer told the defendant that he had a sedan that he was willing to sell, and he quoted a price that was half "book value" of the car. The dealer told the defendant that the sedan was "hot," to which the defendant responded, "It's none of my business where you got the car; I just asked for a late-model car at a good price." The defendant then gave the dealer the money and the dealer gave the defendant the keys. The dealer went to his office to complete the paperwork and informed the police of the transaction. The defendant was arrested and charged with theft.

As an attorney assigned to the district attorney's felony review group, which decides whether cases should be pursued or dropped, you should advise that the charge should be:

(A) Dropped, because the defendant was entrapped.

(B) Dropped, because the dealer was an agent of the police, and when the stolen car came into his hands it was as if it had been returned to the rightful owner.

(C) Pursued, because the police never recovered possession of the car, and it retained its character as stolen property when the defendant purchased it knowing it had been stolen.

(D) Pursued, because the defendant had the specific intent to purchase a stolen car.

Question 17

The defendant was arrested, given *Miranda* warnings, and charged with burglary. At the police station, he telephoned his mother and asked her to come to the station to post bail. Instead, his mother immediately called the family attorney. In the meantime, the police had begun questioning the defendant. Although he never told the police to stop the questioning, his answers were at first vague or clearly unresponsive. During the course of the questioning, the family attorney phoned the station and told the police that she had been hired to represent the defendant and would be there in half an hour. The police did not inform the defendant of the attorney's call. Ten minutes later, the defendant admitted to committing the burglary, and signed a statement to that effect prepared by the police. The attorney arrived a few minutes later and advised the defendant to remain silent, but he told her that he had already signed a confession.

At the preliminary hearing, how should the court rule on the attorney's motion to exclude the confession as evidence at trial?

(A) Grant the motion, because the police had a duty to inform the defendant that an attorney was coming to represent him.

(B) Grant the motion, because the defendant has been deprived of his Sixth Amendment right to counsel.

(C) Deny the motion, because the defendant's statement admitting the crime was voluntary.

(D) Deny the motion, because the defendant waived his *Miranda* rights.

Question 18

Late one evening, a cook at a diner coming off his shift was grabbed in the parking lot by a large man wearing a ski mask. The man threatened to kill the cook and demanded his wallet. The man then pulled a knife from his pocket and lunged at the cook. The cook, having taken

several self-defense courses, was able to fend off the man's attack. After being struck by the cook several times, the man dropped the knife and fell to the ground. The cook, angry at the assault, took the knife and stabbed the man, killing him instantly.

Should the cook be convicted of murder?

(A) No, because he was acting in self-defense.

(B) No, but he may be convicted of manslaughter.

(C) Yes, because the killing was committed during the course of a felony.

(D) Yes, because the killing was not committed while acting in self-defense.

Question 19

A woman was arrested, given *Miranda* warnings, and questioned about an armed robbery. After she asked to speak with an attorney, the police stopped questioning her about the robbery. Several hours later, the police gave the woman a fresh set of *Miranda* warnings and began to question her about a different robbery. She did not repeat her request for an attorney and instead made several incriminating statements about the robbery. At the woman's trial for the robbery for which she made incriminating statements, the prosecution seeks to have her statements introduced into evidence.

If the woman's attorney objects on appropriate grounds, the court should:

(A) Overrule the objection, because the police did not badger the woman into confessing.

(B) Overrule the objection, because the woman did not renew her request for an attorney after receiving fresh *Miranda* warnings.

(C) Sustain the objection, because the police did not honor the woman's request.

(D) Sustain the objection, because a confession obtained in violation of a defendant's *Miranda* rights but otherwise voluntary may be used against the defendant.

Question 20

While fleeing from an armed robbery he had just committed, a man struck a pedestrian with his car, seriously injuring the pedestrian. The robber was soon apprehended and charged with armed robbery and reckless driving, both felonies. Just prior to trial, the pedestrian died from his injuries. The trial on the robbery and driving charges proceeded, and the robber was convicted of the armed robbery charge and acquitted of the reckless driving charge. The robber was then indicted under the jurisdiction's felony murder statute for causing the death of the pedestrian during the course of committing an armed robbery. The robber moved to dismiss the indictment on the ground that a second trial would violate double jeopardy.

The robber's claim is:

(A) Correct, because he was acquitted of the reckless driving charge.

(B) Correct, because the pedestrian died before the robber's first trial had begun.

(C) Incorrect, because he was convicted of the armed robbery charge.

(D) Incorrect, because felony murder requires proof of an additional element not required by the felony itself.

Question 21

A man and a woman were arrested and charged with conspiring to blow up a federal government building. After being given *Miranda* warnings, they were questioned separately and each of them gave a written confession. The confessions interlocked with each other, implicating both of the defendants as being involved in every stage of the conspiracy. Subsequently, the woman attempted to retract her confession, claiming that it was false. At a preliminary

hearing, the judge rejected her claim. Both defendants were tried together, and the prosecutor introduced both confessions into evidence. At trial, the woman testified that she was not involved in any conspiracy and that her confession was fabricated. Both defendants were found guilty by the jury.

If the woman challenges her conviction on appeal because of the admission of the man's confession, will she likely be successful?

(A) No, because the man's confession was no more incriminatory to her than her own confession.

(B) No, if the jury was instructed to consider the man's confession as evidence only of his guilt and not of the woman's.

(C) Yes, if the man refused to testify at trial and therefore was not subject to cross-examination regarding his confession.

(D) Yes, if the man testified at trial and was subject to cross-examination but denied making the confession attributed to him.

Question 22

Acting on information from reliable informants that drugs were being sold by residents at a certain fraternity house, the police obtained a search warrant that entitled them to search the entire premises for illegal narcotics. The police arrived at the house when a party was in progress and were admitted to the house by the fraternity president after showing the warrant. Officers proceeded to search the house. In an upstairs bedroom, they found a young woman who was a guest of a fraternity member sleeping on the bed. No one else was in the room. The police found a footlocker under the bed and opened it, finding a variety of illegal drugs. The police then seized the woman's purse and found a small quantity of marijuana. The woman was charged with a drug possession offense. At her trial, the prosecution seeks to admit the marijuana seized from her purse over the objection of her attorney.

Should the court admit the marijuana?

(A) Yes, because the footlocker was within the woman's reach.

(B) Yes, because the woman was present in a room where drugs were found.

(C) No, because the woman had no possessory interest in the premises.

(D) No, because the police had no reason to believe that the woman had drugs on her person.

Question 23

An acquaintance asked the defendant to give him a lift downtown because he did not have bus fare. While riding on the defendant's motorcycle, the acquaintance asked to stop at a convenience store to get a bottle of wine, showing the defendant a tire iron in his backpack that he was going to use. The defendant stopped at the store and waited in the parking lot while the acquaintance went in. He demanded money from the clerk, brandishing the tire iron. The clerk tried to grab a gun under the counter while he was filling a bag with money, and a struggle ensued. The gun discharged, killing the clerk. The defendant heard the gunshot and raced off, but was eventually apprehended.

The jurisdiction's criminal code provides that a death caused during the commission of certain felonies, including robbery, is first degree felony murder, for which the death penalty is permitted. The code also permits cumulative penalties for first degree felony murder and for the underlying felony. The defendant was charged and convicted of both robbery and felony murder. After appropriate consideration of all relevant circumstances, the jury imposed the death penalty. On appeal, the defendant challenged both the convictions and the sentence.

Assuming that the above facts were properly admitted into evidence, how should the appellate court rule?

(A) The defendant's conviction for both offenses should be upheld, but imposition of the death penalty was not proper.

(B) The defendant's conviction for both offenses should be upheld, and imposition of the death penalty was proper.

(C) The defendant's conviction should be overturned under double jeopardy principles because robbery is a lesser included offense of felony murder.

(D) The defendant's conviction for felony murder should be overturned because the circumstances do not establish the necessary degree of culpability.

Question 24

Acting with probable cause, the police arrested a man in connection with the armed robbery of a liquor store. After being given *Miranda* warnings, the man confessed to the robbery but denied his involvement with several other recent armed robberies of businesses in the area. He was formally charged with the one robbery and put into a cell with a paid informant working undercover for the police. The informant had been instructed to find out what he could about the other robberies but not to ask any questions. The informant began talking about a convenience store robbery in which a bystander was shot and seriously injured by the robber, and he deliberately misstated how it happened. The man, unaware that his cell mate was an informant, interrupted to correct him, bragging that he knew what really happened because he was there, and proceeded to make incriminating statements about the robbery. The man was subsequently charged with armed robbery and attempted murder in the convenience store robbery.

At a motion-to-suppress hearing on that charge, if the man's attorney moves to exclude the statements made to the informant, should the motion be granted?

(A) Yes, because the informant deliberately elicited incriminating statements in violation of the man's Sixth Amendment right to counsel.

(B) Yes, because the informant's conduct constituted custodial interrogation in violation of the man's Fifth Amendment privilege against self-incrimination.

(C) No, because the man had not yet been charged with the robbery of the convenience store when he made the statements to the informant.

(D) No, because the informant's conduct did not constitute interrogation.

Question 25

The defendant happened to have the same name as a famous attorney in the city. Coincidentally, they also shared the same birthday, and their Social Security numbers nearly matched except for one number. The defendant went to an electronics store to buy a new portable television set, and decided to finance the purchase because he had little money. The defendant truthfully filled out the store's credit application. As had happened previously, the defendant was mistaken for the famous attorney. As a result, he was approved for a credit line well beyond his means. Instead of explaining the situation, the defendant took advantage by purchasing a state-of-the-art high-definition television set with a surround sound system. The defendant knew that he would be unable to make payments on the equipment when due, but he decided to deal with that when the time came. After several months of nonpayments, the defendant received notice that the store was going to repossess the television and sound system. Before it could do so, a fire burned the defendant's home to the ground, destroying all of his property, including the electronics. The electronics store filed a criminal complaint against the defendant, outlining all of the above facts.

The authorities will likely determine that:

(A) The defendant has committed false pretenses, because he improperly gained title to the equipment.

(B) The defendant has committed larceny by trick, because he improperly gained possession of the equipment.

(C) The defendant has committed neither false pretenses nor larceny by trick, because he may have initially intended to pay for the electronics on receipt of the bill.

(D) The defendant has committed neither false pretenses nor larceny by trick, because he was under no duty to disabuse store employees of their mistake as to his true identity.

Question 26

While the defendant was committing a robbery, he shot and killed the victim. The defendant is charged with first degree murder in a state that defines first degree murder as murders committed with premeditation or deliberation or during the commission of burglary, arson, rape, or robbery, and defines second degree murder as all other murders. The state also defines voluntary manslaughter as the unlawful killing of a human being with malice upon a sudden quarrel or heat of passion, and it defines involuntary manslaughter as the unlawful killing of a human being without malice in the commission of an unlawful act, not amounting to an enumerated felony, or in the commission of a lawful act that might produce death in an unlawful manner or without due caution and circumspection.

Assuming evidence to support, what explanation for the shooting would best help the defendant in avoiding conviction for first degree murder?

(A) In an act of resistance, the victim suddenly attacked the defendant and knocked him down, so the defendant pulled the trigger because he was afraid the victim was going to hit him again.

(B) The defendant had the gun for many years, it was old and rusty, and he did not think it would fire.

(C) The defendant had taken "angel dust" before the incident and does not remember getting a gun or holding up the victim.

(D) When the defendant tried to hold up the victim, the victim said, "Get out of here, you dirty bum, or I'll kill you," and the defendant became so upset that he did not know what he was doing.

Question 27

The state has the following homicide statutes:

> Murder is the unlawful killing of a human being with malice aforethought. Such malice may be express or implied. It is express when there is manifested a deliberate intention to unlawfully take away the life of a fellow creature. It is implied when no considerable provocation appears or when the circumstances attending the killing show an abandoned and malignant heart. All murder that is perpetrated by willful, deliberate, or premeditated killing or committed in the perpetration of or attempt to perpetrate arson, rape, robbery, or burglary is murder of the first degree. All other kinds of murders are of the second degree.

The defendant and her associate entered a jewelry store to shoplift a diamond bracelet. Just as the defendant put the bracelet into her pocket, a sales clerk saw her and grabbed her by the wrist. The associate grabbed a knife from one of the silver displays and lunged at the sales clerk, but then a store guard shot and killed her. The defendant is charged with the first degree murder of her associate.

Which of the following is the defendant's strongest argument?

(A) The defendant cannot be convicted of murder because when they went into the

store they were not carrying any weapons; therefore, there was no felony on which the felony murder rule may arise.

(B) The defendant cannot be convicted of murder because the associate's death was not murder but justifiable homicide.

(C) The defendant cannot be convicted of murder because she and her associate had an agreement never to use violence when they stole anything.

(D) The associate did not intend to hurt the sales clerk, but just wanted to scare him so that the defendant could run.

Question 28

A police officer learned from a reliable informant that a major drug deal was about to take place at a local restaurant. The officer obtained a search warrant for the restaurant and arrived with other uniformed officers to search the premises. While conducting the search, the officer searched several of the customers. While searching one of the restaurant's regular customers, the officer felt an object in the customer's pocket and pulled out a container filled with heroin. The customer was arrested and later convicted of possession of heroin. A state statute permits officers executing a search warrant to search persons on the premises if the officers reasonably expect danger to themselves or a risk of disposal or concealment of anything described in the warrant.

If the customer appeals his conviction to the United States Supreme Court, the Court will most likely rule that:

(A) The conviction of the customer must be reversed because the statute is vague and overbroad.

(B) The conviction of the customer must be reversed because his presence in the place to be searched by the police does not negate the requirement of probable cause.

(C) The conviction of the customer must stand because the search was conducted pursuant to a valid search warrant.

(D) The conviction of the customer must stand because the search was authorized by statute.

Question 29

Believing that it is a crime to purchase gunpowder without a state license, a gun shop owner purchased 10 pounds of gunpowder from a man who acquired it in another state. Actually, a state license is required only for the purchase of 20 pounds or more of gunpowder in one year. The owner is charged with attempting to purchase gunpowder without a state license.

May the owner be convicted?

(A) No, because he committed no illegal act.

(B) No, because he has a Second Amendment right to bear arms.

(C) Yes, because ignorance of the law is no excuse.

(D) Yes, because factual impossibility is not a defense to a charge of an attempt of a crime.

Question 30

When the defendant learned that his former wife, to whom he was paying $1,000 per month in alimony, was dating someone else, the defendant encouraged her to get married "for the sake of the children." The former wife said that she would consider it, but she also expressed concern that her boyfriend might already be married. The defendant told his former wife that he would have an acquaintance run a computer check on the boyfriend that would reveal whether he was currently married. However, the defendant did not bother with the computer check; instead he called the boyfriend and offered him $5,000 if he would propose to the defendant's former wife. The defendant then told his former wife that, according to official records, the boyfriend was single. The defendant's former wife and the boyfriend went through a wedding ceremony shortly thereafter. The boyfriend, however, was already married to someone else, a fact that would have been disclosed by a routine check of official records.

If the defendant is charged with being an accessory to bigamy, a strict liability offense in the jurisdiction, he should be found:

(A) Guilty, because the defendant aided, abetted, and encouraged the marriage.

(B) Guilty, because even though the defendant did not know that the boyfriend was married, bigamy is a strict liability offense.

(C) Not guilty, unless the defendant's action in failing to check the records was a breach of duty to his former wife.

(D) Not guilty, because the defendant did not have the mental state necessary for aiding and abetting.

Question 31

A bartender diligently followed the procedure her employer set: She would ask every patron for identification regardless of how old (or young) the patron appeared to be. One day, after asking for identification, the bartender served alcohol to a minor. The identification that the minor gave to the bartender was actually issued by mistake by an appropriate state agency and appeared to show that the minor was of legal age. After another patron, an off-duty police officer, recognized the minor, the bartender was arrested for serving alcohol to a minor. In this jurisdiction, the highest state court has held that, under state law, strict liability is abolished and all crimes require a culpable mental state.

The best reason for finding the bartender not guilty would be:

(A) She did not know that the minor was underage, and she relied on the identification card for proof of age.

(B) She did not know that the minor was underage, and therefore never intended to serve alcohol to a minor.

(C) She made a diligent effort to determine the minor's age.

(D) She checked the minor's state-issued identification card, which showed that the minor was of age.

Question 32

The criminal statutes of the state define manslaughter and murder as they were defined at common law. As to insanity, the state has the following provision:

> Under the defense of insanity a defendant may be entitled to acquittal if, because of mental illness, the defendant was unable to control his or her actions or to conform his or her conduct to the law.

The defendant was put on trial in the state for the murder of his wife and her co-worker. The evidence at trial established that the defendant's wife was having an affair with the co-worker, and that the defendant learned of it and killed the pair. The defendant did not take the stand in his own defense. In his closing statement to the jury, the defendant's attorney made a statement, "Ladies and gentlemen, you must consider that there are some things that would provoke any one of us to kill, and there are things that make one unable to control one's actions." The defendant's attorney requested that the judge give the jury instructions on manslaughter and on insanity, and the judge agreed to do so. The judge also issued the following instructions:

> INSTRUCTION #6: In order to mitigate an intentional killing to voluntary manslaughter, the burden of proof is on the defendant to establish that adequate provocation existed.

> INSTRUCTION #8: Insanity is an affirmative defense and the burden of proof is on the defendant to establish that such insanity existed at the time of the killing.

The jury found the defendant guilty of murder, and he appealed. He asserts that the jury instructions violated his rights under the federal Constitution.

The appeals court should:

(A) Reverse the defendant's conviction, because Instruction #6 was improper.

(B) Reverse the defendant's conviction, because Instruction #8 was improper.

(C) Reverse the defendant's conviction, because both Instructions #6 and #8 were improper.

(D) Uphold the defendant's conviction, because neither Instruction #6 nor Instruction #8 was improper.

Question 33

A teenager stole a car from the homeowner's driveway after she had left the keys in the car overnight. He was stopped for speeding and a license plate check indicated that the car had been reported stolen. The teenager was charged with common law larceny. At trial, his defense was that he intended to return the car to the owner's home the following morning before anyone realized it had been taken. The trial judge instructed the jury that while the state must prove the case beyond a reasonable doubt, the defendant has the responsibility to prove his defense by a preponderance of the evidence. The court further instructed the jury that if it found by a preponderance of the evidence that the teenager intended to return the car, it should find him not guilty. The teenager was convicted; he appealed on the ground that the jury instructions were erroneous.

The teenager's conviction should be:

(A) Reversed, because in a criminal case the state must prove all disputed issues beyond a reasonable doubt.

(B) Reversed, because the instruction placed an improper burden of proof on the defendant.

(C) Affirmed, because intent to return is not a defense to the charge.

(D) Affirmed, because the jury instructions were correct.

Question 34

The defendant, while visiting the victim, asked for permission to borrow the victim's car so he could drive to a convenience store to buy cigarettes. In fact, he intended to keep the car and sell it for cash. The victim agreed, and the defendant took the car and drove off. After thinking about it further, the defendant decided that it would be wrong to sell the victim's car, and headed back to the victim's house. On the way back, the car was destroyed in a collision through no fault of the defendant.

May the defendant be convicted of larceny?

(A) No, because he intended to return the car and therefore lacked the requisite mens rea for the crime.

(B) No, because he abandoned his plan of selling the vehicle.

(C) Yes, because withdrawal is not a defense to the crime.

(D) Yes, because he intended to permanently deprive the victim of the car when he drove off in it.

Question 35

The defendant was fired from his sales job while calling on customers in another city. He failed to return the company car that he was using for his sales visits; instead, he sold the car to a "chop shop" for cash.

The defendant has committed:

(A) Larceny.

(B) Larceny by trick.

(C) Embezzlement.

(D) Theft by false pretenses.

Question 36

A gang member threatened to kill the defendant unless he robbed a convenience store and gave the proceeds to the gang member. The gang member also demanded at gunpoint that the defendant kill the clerk to prevent identification. In abject fear of his life, the defendant did everything that the gang member requested.

If the defendant is arrested and charged with murder and robbery in a common law jurisdiction, what result?

(A) The defendant should be convicted of murder and robbery.

(B) The defendant should be acquitted of the robbery and convicted of murder.

(C) The defendant should be convicted of robbery, and the killing will be reduced to voluntary manslaughter.

(D) The defendant should be acquitted of the robbery, and the killing should be reduced to voluntary manslaughter.

CRIMINAL LAW ANSWERS - SET 6

Answer to Question 1

(D) The defendant's best argument is that, under the majority view, one co-felon is not criminally liable for the death of another co-felon from resistance of the victim or police. A killing committed during the course of a felony is murder, with malice being implied from the intent to commit the underlying felony. Liability under the felony murder doctrine requires that death have been a foreseeable result of commission of the felony. Under the majority view, felony murder liability cannot be based on the death of a co-felon from resistance by the victim or police pursuit. In the instant case, the defendant's friend and co-felon was killed by a pursuing police officer following commission of the robbery. Under the majority rule, the defendant is not guilty of felony murder for such a death. Thus, (D) represents his strongest argument for acquittal. (A) is incorrect because, despite the fact that the defendant and his friend were unarmed, they still committed robbery of the store, in that they took the money from the clerk by means of threats of immediate death or serious physical injury, with the intent to permanently deprive. Certainly, it was reasonable for the clerk to not take a chance that they might not have guns, given that the defendant said they did. Thus, the defendant is guilty of the underlying felony of robbery. Armed resistance by the victim or police that results in death is a foreseeable result of robbery even when the robbers are not armed. Consequently, the fact that the defendant and his friend were unarmed at the time of committing the robbery will have no bearing on his guilt under a felony murder theory. (B) is incorrect because the police officer's failure to warn the fleeing felons before firing is irrelevant to the defendant's liability for felony murder. Even had the police officer given a warning, the defendant would not be guilty of the felony murder of his co-felon killed by the police. The lack of a warning might go to the issue of whether the police officer's shooting was justified, but it does not impact on the defendant's guilt for felony murder. (C) is incorrect because, although death must have been caused during the commission or attempted commission of a felony, the fact that the felony was technically completed before death was caused does not prevent the killing from being felony murder. Deaths caused while fleeing from the crime are felony murder. Although the defendant and his friend had completed the robbery at the time the friend was killed, the killing occurred while the felons were fleeing from the crime. Thus, if all other required factors were present, this would be felony murder.

Answer to Question 2

(D) The court should deny the defendant's motion because the officer reasonably believed that the defendant's girlfriend lived in the trailer, making the search valid. Under the exclusionary rule, evidence obtained from an unconstitutional search must be excluded from trial. To be valid, searches must be reasonable. The Supreme Court has held that most searches are unreasonable unless the police obtain a warrant before searching. However, there are six categories of searches that the Court has held to be reasonable without a warrant. One such category is searches conducted pursuant to consent. To fall within this exception to the warrant requirement, consent must be given by one who appears to have an apparent right to use or occupy the premises and the search cannot go beyond the scope of the consent given. The consent is valid as long as the police reasonably believed that the person who gave the consent had the authority to do so, and the scope of the consent is limited only to areas to which a reasonable person under the circumstances would believe it extends. Here, the girlfriend's consent was valid because the officer believed that she lived there. His belief appears to be reasonable since she answered the door, knew of the defendant's whereabouts, and readily consented to the search. Therefore, the search was valid under the consent exception and the evidence should not be excluded. (A) is incorrect because consent is not invalid merely because the person who gave it did not actually have authority to do so; the police need only reasonably believe that the person had authority to consent, and as explained above, it was reasonable for the officer to believe that the defendant's girlfriend had authority here. (B) is incorrect because the scope of consent extends to any area where a reasonable person under the circumstances would assume it extends, and since the officer told the girlfriend that he suspected the defendant of dealing drugs, it was reasonable to assume that he was looking for drugs and so would probably look in even small containers. (C) is incorrect because it appears that the defendant's trailer would not fall within the automobile exception. Certain searches of automobiles are excluded from the requirement of a warrant because the Supreme Court has held that people have a lesser expectation of privacy in an automobile than in other areas and automobiles are likely to disappear before a warrant can be acquired. The automobile exception extends not only to cars, but also to other vehicles that are readily mobile and as to which there is a lesser expectation of privacy. However, nothing in the facts here indicates that the defendant's mobile home may readily be moved, and since it appears to be the defendant's regular home rather than a vehicle, it is doubtful that the Court would find the requisite lesser expectation of privacy. Therefore, the trailer would not fall within the automobile exception to the warrant requirement.

Answer to Question 3

(B) The defendant can claim a reasonable expectation of privacy for Fourth Amendment purposes if she was an overnight guest of the owner of the place searched. To raise a Fourth Amendment claim of an unreasonable search or seizure, a person must have a reasonable expectation of privacy with respect to the place searched or the item seized. It is not enough merely that someone has an expectation of privacy in the place searched. The Supreme Court has imposed a standing requirement so that a person can complain about an evidentiary search or seizure only if it violates her own reasonable expectations of privacy. The Court has held that a person has a legitimate expectation of privacy any time (i) she owned or had a right to possession of the place searched, (ii) the place searched was in fact her own home, whether or not she owned or had a right to possession of it, or (iii) she was an overnight guest of the owner of the place searched. Thus, the defendant would have standing to challenge the search of the tenant's apartment if she was an overnight guest of the tenant. (A) is incorrect because standing to raise a Fourth Amendment claim does not exist merely because a person will be harmed by introduction of evidence seized during an illegal search of a third person's property. The person must establish that her own legitimate expectation of privacy has been violated. (C) is wrong because the fact that the defendant was not the owner or occupier of the apartment does not preclude her from challenging the search. As discussed above, an overnight guest may also have a reasonable expectation of privacy in the premises for purposes of the Fourth Amendment. (D) is incorrect. Although the defendant may have standing to object to the seizure of items if she claims ownership of them, that is not the only basis for raising a Fourth Amendment claim; she will have standing to object to the search of the apartment under the circumstances in (B) regardless of whether she claims ownership of the marijuana.

Answer to Question 4

(A) The bartender's reasonable belief that the minor is 25 years old is a mistake of fact that negates the state of mind required by the statute. Ignorance or mistake as to a matter of fact will affect criminal guilt only if it shows that the defendant did not have the state of mind required for the crime. In addition, the mistake must be reasonable unless the offense is a specific intent crime. Here, the statute requires that the defendant have acted "knowingly" with respect to each of the material elements of the offense. A person acts knowingly with respect to the nature of his conduct when he is aware that his conduct is of that nature or that certain circumstances exist. At least one of the material elements of the offense here is that the sale be to a person under the age of 18. If the bartender believed that the minor was 25 years old, the bartender has not acted knowingly with respect to the fact that the purchaser was under 18, and he cannot be convicted of violating the statute. (B) is not a good answer. Given that the bartender never asked for any identification, the minor's possession of the driver's license had no effect on the bartender's state of mind. (C) is incorrect. Although some states may make selling liquor to minors a strict liability crime, the state here has added a "knowingly" requirement that must be satisfied beyond a reasonable doubt for a conviction. (D) is not as good an answer as (A). Although the regulation apparently does not have a state of mind requirement, it is not entirely clear that ***criminal*** liability can result from the violation of the ***regulation***. There would have to be a separate statute providing for criminal penalties for failing to check for identification. Furthermore, the criminal statute in question clearly has a state of mind requirement that must be satisfied, as explained above.

Answer to Question 5

(B) The judge should deny the motion. The officer had a valid reason under the statute for arresting the driver after she legally stopped the car for running the stop sign; thus, the search was incident to a constitutional arrest. (A) is wrong because there is no indication that the officer had searched the driver because she was concerned with her personal safety. If she had searched him without having first arrested him under this factual situation, the search would have been unconstitutional. (C) is wrong because whatever the reason she first followed the car, the fact remains that she had a valid reason for stopping it. Note that if an officer has probable cause to believe that a traffic law has been violated, she may stop the car even if her ulterior motive is to investigate whether some other law is being violated. (D) is wrong because the search incident to a constitutional arrest need not have been based on suspicion that the three had committed the crimes for which they have been charged (robbery and homicide); the only requirement is a constitutionally valid arrest. As discussed above, the arrest here was valid because the driver had five outstanding traffic tickets.

Answer to Question 6

(C) If the defendant is found guilty of murder, it will be through application of the felony murder rule as stated in choice (C). Under the felony murder doctrine, a killing—even an unintentional one—committed during the course of a felony is murder. Malice is implied from the intent to commit the underlying felony. For the doctrine to apply, the death must have been a foreseeable result of commission of the felony, but almost any death during an armed bank robbery would be deemed foreseeable by a court. Courts following the "proximate cause" theory of felony murder extend it to situations like the one in this fact pattern, where resistance by the victim or the police results in the death of a third party who is not a co-felon. Although courts following the "agency theory" of felony murder would not apply it here, choice (C) states the only basis for the defendant being guilty of murder because all of the other rationales are wrong. (A) is wrong because it is irrelevant that the defendant had not yet run out of the building at the time the teller was killed; the defendant would be liable even if she had already fled from the building. Only when the felon has reached a place of temporary safety after the felony has ended will the felony murder rule cease to apply. (B) is wrong because the defendant's guilt under the felony murder rule is not dependent on whether the police were justified in using deadly force; it is the defendant's commission of the robbery, rather than the response by the police, that establishes her liability for felony murder. (D) is wrong because the defendant's putting the teller in a position of danger,

although it might be sufficient to imply malice based on reckless indifference to human life, is not sufficient to establish an intent to kill (express malice). Here, malice is established by the felony murder doctrine.

Answer to Question 7

(B) The corporate officers cannot be guilty of attempted murder because criminal attempt requires a specific intent to commit a particular completed crime. A criminal attempt is an act that, although done with the intention of committing a crime, falls short of completing the crime. A defendant must have the intent to perform an act and obtain a result that, if achieved, would constitute a crime. Hence, attempt is a specific intent crime. Guilt of attempted murder requires that a defendant have the specific intent to commit the crime of murder. In contrast to the malice aforethought required for murder, which is satisfied not only by intent to kill but also by awareness of an unjustifiably high risk to human life, intent to inflict great bodily injury, or intent to commit a felony, ***attempted*** murder is satisfied only by intent to kill. Here, the corporate officers, in permitting the mining to proceed without compliance with methane detection measures, subjected the miners to an unjustifiably high risk to their lives. This "abandoned and malignant heart" demonstrated by the officers would suffice to convict the officers of murder if the miners had been killed. However, there were no deaths; the crime charged is attempted murder. Consequently, there must be a showing that the officers specifically intended to cause the deaths of the miners. Because the facts do not indicate such intent, the officers are not guilty of attempted murder. (C) is incorrect because, as explained above, the mental state of an abandoned and malignant heart will not satisfy the intent required for ***attempted*** murder. (D) is incorrect because, even though a felony was committed, the intent to commit a felony (although sufficient to constitute malice aforethought for a murder charge) will not satisfy the intent to kill that is necessary for a conviction of attempted murder. (A) is incorrect because the officers' actions had gone well beyond the planning stage; allowing the mining to proceed without compliance with methane detection measures satisfies the overt act requirement for attempt. Had the other requirements for attempt been satisfied, their actions would be sufficient to support a conviction.

Answer to Question 8

(C) The woman's motion should be denied because the Double Jeopardy Clause does not prohibit the second prosecution. The Double Jeopardy Clause of the Fifth Amendment provides criminal defendants with the right to be free of double jeopardy for the same offense. However, two crimes do not constitute the same offense if each crime requires proof of an additional element that the other crime does not require, even though some of the same facts may be necessary to prove both crimes. [Blockburger v. United States (1932)] Here, larceny requires a taking and carrying away of the property of another, which burglary does not require, and burglary requires a breaking and entry, which larceny does not require. Hence, they are distinct offenses for purposes of the Double Jeopardy Clause. (A) and (B) are incorrect because the Supreme Court does not use a "same transaction" or "same episode" test suggested by these answer choices; instead, the *Blockburger* test is used regardless of whether the two offenses were tried together at a single trial or at separate trials. (D) is incorrect because while double jeopardy also protects against inconsistent factual determinations at a subsequent trial, it protects against multiple prosecutions as well, as long as the crime is the "same offense."

Answer to Question 9

(D) The defendant cannot be convicted of burglary because he lacked the requisite intent. At common law, burglary consists of a breaking and entry of the dwelling of another at nighttime, with the intent of committing a felony therein. Here, the defendant broke and entered the victim's home at night. However, at the time of entry, the defendant intended only to open his trenchcoat and expose his underwear to the victim, knowing that he would not have time to remove his underwear and expose his sexual organs. Although the defendant apparently believed that these actions would constitute the felony of "flashing," commission of this crime requires ***actual exposure*** of sexual organs. Thus, although the defendant was mistaken as to the felonious character of his actions, the fact remains that, at the time he entered the victim's home, he did not have the intent to commit the acts that would constitute the felony. Absent such intent, the defendant cannot be convicted of burglary. (A) incorrectly states that the defendant intended to commit a felony when he broke and entered the victim's home. As explained above, the act that the defendant intended to commit (opening his trenchcoat without exposing his sexual organs) is not a felony, despite the defendant's belief that it was. (This is analogous to legal impossibility.) Therefore, it cannot be said that the defendant acted with the intent to commit a felony. Likewise, (B) is incorrect, because it misapplies the general rule that ignorance of the law is not a defense. While a defendant's conduct generally will not be excused because he was not aware that the conduct was illegal, this case presents the reverse situation; the defendant was not aware that his conduct was legal and did not constitute a felony. (C) is incorrect because a conviction for burglary does not require that a felony actually be carried out. All that is required is that intent to commit a felony exist at the time of entry. Consequently, although the defendant did not actually commit a felony, he could be convicted of burglary if he had entered the home with the intent to commit acts constituting a felony.

Answer to Question 10

(D) The defendant cannot be convicted because he did not have the requisite intent. To be convicted of burglary, the defendant must have intended to commit a felony at the time of entry. The elements of common law burglary are: (i) a breaking; (ii) and entry; (iii) of the dwelling; (iv) of another; (v) at nighttime; (vi) with the intent of committing a felony therein. The intent to commit a felony must exist at the time of entry. If such intent is formed after the entry is completed, common law burglary has not been committed. At the time the defendant entered the lessee's store, the defendant did not intend to commit any crime. Indeed, he probably intended to investigate to determine if a crime was being committed in the shop, because his suspicions had been aroused by seeing a light on in the store at night. Because the defendant did not enter the shop with intent to commit a felony therein, he cannot be convicted of burglary. (A) is incorrect because opening a closed door, although it is unlocked, constitutes a breaking for purposes of common law burglary. A breaking requires some use of force to gain entry, but minimal force is sufficient. Even pushing open a door that is already partially open is considered a breaking under the better view, because some force was used to gain entry. Thus, the fact that the door was unlocked will not provide the defendant with a defense to burglary. (B) is incorrect because the entire building was rented to the lessee, and the building includes a dwelling. As noted above, at common law the breaking and entry had to be of a dwelling. A structure is considered a dwelling if it is used regularly for sleeping. Such a structure remains a dwelling even if it is also used for other purposes, such as conducting a business. The building that the lessee is renting from the defendant includes both an apartment and, directly underneath the apartment, space used as a watch repair shop. This is a dwelling. The fact that the lessee uses another part of the rented premises to conduct a business does not mean that the entirety of the area rented should not be considered a dwelling. Thus, (B) will not afford the defendant a defense to burglary. (C) is incorrect because burglary requires only that the structure be used as a dwelling by someone other than the defendant. Occupancy, rather than ownership, is material. Thus, an owner can commit burglary of his own structure if it is rented and used as a dwelling by others. Here, the lessee has the right of occupancy. Consequently, the defendant's ownership of the building does not mean that he cannot be convicted of burglary with respect to premises rented and used as a dwelling by another.

Answer to Question 11

(C) If the creditor honestly thought he was entitled to take the car as security for payment of the rent, then he lacked the requisite intent for larceny. Larceny consists of: (i) a taking (ii) and carrying away (iii) of tangible personal property (iv) of another (v) by trespass (vi) with the intent to permanently (or for an unreasonable time) deprive the person of her interest in the property. Taking property with the intent to hold it as security for a legitimate debt is not sufficient intent for larceny because the intent is not to permanently deprive the person of the property; rather the intent is to return the property when the debt is paid (or if it is not paid, to sell the property to satisfy the debt, with any excess proceeds going back to the debtor). Thus, if the creditor honestly intended to hold the car as security for the missed loan payments, he lacked the intent to permanently deprive the mechanic of the car. (A) is wrong because the creditor's actions as to the car constituted a sufficient carrying away. Larceny requires a "carrying away" (asportation), but that requirement is met by even a slight movement of the property. Here, the creditor took control of the car and began to leave the parking lot. Although he did not actually leave the lot, he did apparently move somewhat toward the lot's exit. This is sufficient movement for larceny. (B) is wrong because larceny can be committed against a thief. Larceny is a crime against possession—all that is necessary is that the property be taken from someone who has a possessory interest superior to that of the defendant. Thus, even if the mechanic had obtained the car by false pretenses, he had a possessory interest superior to that of the creditor. Therefore, the creditor could be convicted of larceny by taking the car from the mechanic. (D) is wrong because the requirement for larceny of a taking "by trespass" means a wrongful taking (*i.e.*, one without consent). Here, the creditor took the car without the mechanic's consent. The fact that the car was stored on a commercial property to which anyone could enter does not save him.

Answer to Question 12

(C) That the customer did not see the blacksmith throw the anvil, and that the blacksmith knew it was impossible to hit the customer with the anvil, would be most helpful to the blacksmith's defense. For purposes of the MBE, an assault is either (i) an attempt to commit a battery, or (ii) the intentional creation, other than by mere words, of a reasonable apprehension in the mind of the victim of imminent bodily harm. The fact that the blacksmith knew that it was impossible to hit the customer with the anvil negates the specific intent to commit a battery that is required for the first type of assault. (If the blacksmith knew that, when he threw the anvil, it was impossible to hit the customer, the blacksmith's conduct was not motivated by the intent to commit a battery against the customer.) The fact that the customer did not see the blacksmith throw the anvil negates the second type of assault because no apprehension of harm would have been created in the customer if he did not see the blacksmith throw the weight. Since the type of assault is not specified here, (C) is a better choice than (B) or (D) because both types of assaults are negated. Choice (A) is not correct because the fact that the blacksmith failed in his attempt to hit the customer with the anvil establishes only that there was a failure to commit a battery. It does nothing to negate the blacksmith's potential liability for assault/attempted battery.

Answer to Question 13

(C) The former student's best argument for preventing the cocaine from being admitted into evidence is that his confession was not voluntary. This question is difficult because each of the choices appears to present a good argument for the former student. With regard to (A), the search of the current student's dorm room appears to be an unreasonable search under the Fourth Amendment. However, a person's Fourth Amendment rights against unreasonable search and seizure may be enforced by the exclusion of evidence only at the instance of someone whose own protection was infringed by the search and seizure. Here, the former student cannot assert a possessory interest or legitimate expectation of privacy in the current student's dorm room. Thus, the former student cannot successfully exclude the cocaine on the ground that it was seized in violation of the Fourth Amendment. (B) is incorrect because arrest warrants are usually required only for arrests made in the person's home. Police generally do not need to obtain a warrant before arresting a person in a public place, even if they have time to get a warrant, as long as the arrest is based on probable cause. Here the police had probable cause to arrest the former student, and because he was arrested on the grounds of the campus, the failure of the police to obtain an arrest warrant will be of no help to him. Choices (C) and (D) both focus on improper conduct during the former student's interrogation, but (C) is better because the former student will have a better chance of invoking the exclusionary rule if the confession is involuntary. For confessions to be admissible, the Due Process Clause of the Fourteenth Amendment requires that they be voluntary. While voluntariness is a fact question that is assessed by looking at the totality of the circumstances, the duration and manner of the police interrogation here indicate that the confession probably was the result of actual coercion. If the confession is found to be involuntary, the former student can invoke the exclusionary rule to exclude the cocaine as "fruit of the poisonous tree." In contrast to an involuntary confession, a confession obtained without *Miranda* warnings, as long as there was no actual coercion involved, may not be sufficient to justify excluding the nontestimonial "fruits" of the confession. [*See* United States v. Patane (2004)] In *Patane*, although there was no majority opinion on this point, five Justices indicated that suppression was not necessary. Thus, the involuntariness of the confession, rather than the absence of *Miranda* warnings, is the best argument for excluding the cocaine.

Answer to Question 14

(B) The conversation should be suppressed because the police conduct violated the man's Sixth Amendment right to counsel. The Sixth Amendment provides that in all criminal prosecutions a defendant has a right to the assistance of counsel at all critical stages. For Sixth Amendment purposes, a criminal prosecution begins when adversary judicial proceedings have commenced, such as the filing of formal charges in this case. Because interrogation is a critical stage of prosecution, the Sixth Amendment is violated by post-charge interrogation unless the defendant has waived his right to counsel. Interrogation includes not only direct questioning, but also any other conduct by the police intended to elicit a response. The police conduct here (telling the man that the woman had implicated him and then bugging the conversation) constitutes prohibited interrogation. [*See* Maine v. Moulton (1985)] (A) is incorrect because the wiretap was not an illegal search under the Fourth Amendment. Wiretapping and other forms of electronic surveillance are subject to the Fourth Amendment prohibition of unreasonable searches and seizures. However, to have a Fourth Amendment right, a person must have a legitimate expectation of privacy with respect to the place searched or the item seized. In a different context, the Supreme Court has held that prisoners have no legitimate expectation of privacy in their cells or in any personal property that they have in their cells. [Hudson v. Palmer (1984)] Hence, neither defendant can assert a Fourth Amendment claim based on the wiretap, because they had no legitimate expectation of privacy in the jail cell. The fact that there was no expectation of privacy does not make choice (C) correct, however. Even though he probably cannot claim that the bugging was an unreasonable search under the Fourth Amendment, the man can claim that it was an interrogation in violation of his Sixth Amendment right to counsel, as discussed above. (D) is incorrect

because it is irrelevant. The facts probably would not give rise to a *Miranda* violation in light of the Court's ruling in *Illinois v. Perkins* (1990) that *Miranda* does not apply unless interrogation is by someone known to be a police officer (on the rationale that *Miranda* is merely a prophylactic rule designed to offset the coercive nature of a custodial interrogation by a police officer). In any case, *Miranda* rights and Sixth Amendment rights to counsel can only be waived knowingly, and so the man's ignorance of the fact that the cell was bugged precludes a finding of waiver here.

Answer to Question 15

(B) The lender can be charged with larceny, but not the other crimes. Larceny consists of a taking and carrying away of the tangible personal property of another by trespass, with the intent to permanently deprive the person of her interest in the property. Here, the lender took and carried away the debtor's personal property (her chair). The taking was trespassory because it was without the debtor's consent. At the time of the taking, the lender intended to deal with the chair in a manner that involved a substantial risk of loss (*i.e.,* burn it). Such intent is enough for larceny, as the "intent to permanently deprive" includes a substantial risk of loss. Thus, the lender is guilty of larceny. (Note that if the lender had simply taken the chair in the honest belief that she was entitled to it as ***repayment*** of the debt, there would be no larceny. However, setting the chair on fire indicates that the lender intended to permanently deprive the debtor of the chair rather than take it as repayment.) (A) and (C) are wrong because common law arson has not occurred here. At common law, arson is the malicious burning of the ***dwelling*** of another. Here, the burning was of an item of personal property, not of the dwelling itself. (C) and (D) are wrong because the lender did not commit common law burglary. Burglary consists of a breaking and entering of a dwelling of another at nighttime with the intent to commit a felony therein. Here, the lender's unauthorized opening of the unlocked door is sufficient for a breaking, and the breaking and entering of the debtor's dwelling occurred at night. However, at the time the lender entered, she did not intend to commit a felony; she simply wanted to confront the debtor and demand repayment of her money. The lender did not decide to commit the larceny until ***after*** she was already in the house and found that the debtor was not at home. Since she did not have the requisite intent when she entered the house, she cannot be guilty of burglary.

Answer to Question 16

(C) The charge should be pursued. The defendant is liable for theft by receipt of stolen property because the car was still "stolen" when it was received by him. At common law and under modern theft statutes, the crime of receiving stolen property requires (i) receiving possession and control (ii) of "stolen" personal property (iii) known to have been obtained in a manner constituting a criminal offense (iv) by another person, (v) with the intent to permanently deprive the owner of his interest in the property. Here, all of the elements of the prima facie offense have been established: the defendant "received" possession and control when he paid the dealer and received the keys (the fact that he was arrested before he drove away is irrelevant since there is no asportation requirement as there is for larceny); the car qualifies as personal property; the defendant knew that the car was stolen because the dealer informed him that it was "hot"; and the defendant intended to keep the car and not return it to the original owner. In a "sting" operation such as the one in this question, an attendant circumstance of the offense is that the property must still be "stolen" at the time it is received by the defendant. Once stolen property is recovered by the owner or by the police on the owner's behalf, it loses its "stolen" status. Even if the owner consents to the property's use for the purpose of trapping a suspected recipient of stolen goods, the property cannot be the basis of a receipt of stolen property charge because it is no

longer "stolen." This situation is different, however. Here, neither the owner nor the police had recovered the stolen car before the defendant took possession of it. The police have permitted the dealer to continue to obtain stolen autos, but have not obtained the permission of the rightful owner of this car to use it in their operation, since neither they nor the dealer know to whom this particular car belongs. Therefore, the car retained its status as stolen property. [*See, e.g.*, United States v. Muzii, 676 F.2d 919 (2d Cir.), *cert. denied*, 459 U.S. 863 (1982)] Thus, the dealer is liable for receipt of stolen property. (A) is incorrect because, under the majority rule, entrapment requires the defendant to prove that the criminal design originated with and was induced by the police and that he was not in any way predisposed to commit the crime. Here, the police merely offered the opportunity for the defendant to commit the crime. The defendant readily made the deal for the car even though he knew it was stolen. (B) is incorrect. Even though the dealer arguably may have been an agent of the police because he was cooperating with them, the police were not acting on behalf of, and with the permission of, the rightful owner of the car that the defendant purchased. Thus, that car never lost its status as stolen property even during the dealer's possession of it. (D) is wrong because intent is not required for the crime of receiving stolen property. While it is unclear whether the defendant "intended" to purchase a stolen car, it is clear that the defendant ***knew*** he was purchasing a stolen car, and knowledge satisfies the mens rea element of this offense.

Answer to Question 17

(D) The defendant's confession should be admitted because he waived his Fifth Amendment privilege against compelled self-incrimination after receiving *Miranda* warnings. *Miranda v. Arizona* requires that a person in custody be informed of his right to remain silent and his right to the presence of an attorney during questioning. A suspect may subsequently waive his rights by making a confession, as long as the waiver was knowing, voluntary, and intelligent. In this case, the defendant received proper *Miranda* warnings, and there is no indication that he did not understand what his rights were. Although his answers during questioning were initially unresponsive, he never asked for an attorney or indicated that he wished to remain silent, and he voluntarily confessed after a relatively short period of interrogation. Hence, he validly waived his *Miranda* rights. (A) is incorrect because the police have no duty to inform the defendant that an attorney is attempting to see him. The defendant's ignorance of his attorney's efforts has no bearing on whether he made a knowing waiver of his *Miranda* rights. (B) is incorrect because the defendant's right to counsel was not violated. Although the defendant does have a separate Sixth Amendment right to counsel under *Escobedo v. Illinois* because he has already been arrested and charged with the crime, this right would only be violated if the defendant, after being informed of his right to counsel, had requested an attorney or had been prevented from seeing his attorney. Here, he made no request to see an attorney—even when he called his mother—and his attorney was allowed to see him immediately upon her arrival. Thus, his Sixth Amendment right to counsel has not been violated. (C) is incorrect even though it is true that the defendant made a voluntary statement. Due process requires that for confessions to be admissible, they must be "voluntary," based on the totality of the circumstances, and here all of the circumstances indicate that the defendant's confession was voluntary. However, even a voluntary confession will be inadmissible if it was obtained in violation of *Miranda* rights. (D) is therefore a better choice than (C).

Answer to Question 18

(B) The cook may be convicted of manslaughter. At common law, murder was the killing of another human being with malice aforethought. Malice is: (i) the intent to kill; (ii) the intent to inflict

great bodily injury; (iii) a reckless indifference to an unjustifiably high risk to human life; or (iv) the intent to kill to commit a felony. A killing committed in self-defense, however, is not murder. A person may use deadly force in self-defense if: (i) he is without fault; (ii) he is confronted with unlawful force; and (iii) he is threatened with imminent death or great bodily harm. As to a threat of imminent death or great bodily harm, the defendant must reasonably believe that he is faced with imminent death or great bodily harm if he does not respond with deadly force. Additionally, a killing that ordinarily would be murder is reduced to voluntary manslaughter when the killing is committed under the stress of adequate provocation (*e.g.,* being subjected to a serious battery, being confronted with deadly force, or discovering one's spouse in bed with another person). In the instant case, although the cook would have been justified in using deadly force to repel the initial attack, the facts indicate that the cook had successfully repelled the attack, and it appears that the cook no longer was facing a threat of imminent death. Thus, the right to use deadly force had passed. This makes (A) an incorrect answer choice. As a result, at first glance, it would appear that the cook committed murder, in that stabbing another in the heart with a knife indicates, at a minimum, that the defendant had the intent to inflict great bodily harm. However, it appears that the cook was still acting under adequate provocation, as he had just been subjected to a serious battery and had been confronted with deadly force. Thus, the killing that ordinarily would be murder is reduced to voluntary manslaughter, making (B) the correct answer choice. (C) is incorrect. While a killing committed during the course of an independent felony is felony murder, the rule does not apply to the homicide felony itself, such as manslaughter. Since the cook was committing the felony by killing the man, he cannot be guilty of murder based on a felony murder theory. (D) is an incorrect answer because it fails to take into account the reduction to voluntary manslaughter, as explained above.

Answer to Question 19

(C) The court should sustain the objection because the police did not honor the woman's request for an attorney. At any time prior to or during a custodial interrogation, the accused may invoke a *Miranda* (Fifth Amendment) right to counsel. If the accused invokes this right, ***all questioning must cease*** until the accused is provided with an attorney or initiates further questioning himself. Thus, the police questioning of the woman about the robbery was improper, and she can have her statements excluded. (A) is incorrect. After receiving *Miranda* warnings, if an accused invokes the right to remain silent, the police cannot badger the accused. However, courts have ruled that if the police scrupulously honor the request, they can rewarn the accused and later resume questioning, at least about a different crime. Here, however, the accused did not simply invoke the right to remain silent, but rather requested an attorney. After such a request, as indicated above, all questioning must cease. (B) is incorrect because the accused does not need to reassert the right to an attorney; all questioning must stop until the accused is provided an attorney or resumes the questioning herself. (D) is incorrect. It is stating the rule for impeachment—a confession obtained in violation of a defendant's *Miranda* rights but otherwise voluntary may be used against the defendant for purposes of impeachment, but there is no such rule for use of the confession for other purposes.

Answer to Question 20

(B) The robber's claim is correct because the victim died before jeopardy attached for trial on the lesser included offense. The Fifth Amendment right to be free of double jeopardy provides that once jeopardy attaches for an offense, the defendant may not be retried for the same offense. Under the *Blockburger* test, two crimes do not constitute the same offense if ***each*** crime requires proof of an additional element that the other crime does not require. Under this test, a lesser included offense and the greater offense would be considered the "same offense," because the lesser included offense consists entirely of some, but not all, elements of the greater crime. Hence, under double jeopardy rules, attachment of jeopardy for the greater offense bars retrial for lesser included offenses, ***and*** attachment of jeopardy for a lesser included offense generally bars retrial for the greater offense. An exception to this latter rule exists if all of the elements for the greater offense had not occurred at the time of prosecution for the lesser offense, but in this case the final element for the felony murder charge—the death of the victim—occurred before jeopardy had attached in the first trial, so the prosecution could have added a charge of felony murder prior to proceeding with the first trial. Thus, the underlying felony of armed robbery was a lesser included offense of the felony murder and the robber's being placed in jeopardy for it bars the subsequent trial for the felony murder. (A) is incorrect because the reckless driving charge was not the basis for the felony murder charge. Under principles of collateral estoppel embodied in the double jeopardy rule, a subsequent trial would be barred if it would require a factual determination inconsistent with the one in the prior prosecution. If the reckless driving charge were the underlying felony for the felony murder charge, the robber could argue that proving felony murder based on reckless driving would require a determination that he was guilty of the underlying felony, which would appear inconsistent with his acquittal. However, this principle is not applicable here because the armed robbery charge was the underlying felony for the felony murder charge. (C) is incorrect. As discussed above, double jeopardy applies regardless of the outcome of the trial on the robbery charge, because jeopardy attached for the robbery charge as soon as the trial started, barring a second trial for the greater offense of felony murder. (D) is incorrect because, as discussed above, two crimes are not the "same offense" for double jeopardy purposes only if ***each*** crime requires proof of an additional element that the other crime does not require. Because the underlying felony is a lesser included offense of the felony murder charge, *i.e.*, it has no other elements not required by the felony murder charge, it constitutes the "same offense" for purposes of double jeopardy.

Answer to Question 21

(C) The woman will prevail in her challenge to the admission of the man's confession if the man could not be cross-examined regarding his confession. Under the Sixth Amendment, a defendant in a criminal prosecution has the right to confront adverse witnesses at trial. If two persons are tried together and one has given a confession that implicates the other, the right of confrontation generally prohibits the use of that statement because the other defendant cannot compel the confessing co-defendant to take the stand for cross-examination. A co-defendant's confession is inadmissible even when it interlocks with the defendant's own confession, which is admitted. If the man refused to take the stand and subject himself to cross-examination, his confession was not properly admitted because it violated the woman's Confrontation Clause rights. (A) is incorrect because the fact that the man's confession incriminates the woman no further than her own confession is not relevant. The interlocking nature of the man's confession with the woman's confession may make it more damaging by making it harder for the woman to claim that her confession was false. (B) is incorrect because the Supreme Court has held that instructing the jury to consider the confession only as going to the guilt of the confessing defendant is inadequate to avoid Confrontation Clause problems, because the risk that the jury will not follow the limiting instructions is too great in this context. (D) is incorrect. Confessions of a co-defendant may be admitted if (i) all portions referring to the other defendant can be eliminated (so that there is no indication of that defendant's involvement), (ii) the confessing defendant takes the stand and subjects himself to cross-examination regarding the truth or falsity of the statement, or (iii) the confession of the nontestifying co-defendant is being used to rebut the defendant's claim that

his confession was obtained coercively, and the jury is instructed as to that purpose. Even if the co-defendant denies ever having made the confession, as stated in choice (D), the opportunity at trial to cross-examine the co-defendant satisfies the Confrontation Clause.

Answer to Question 22

(D) The court should not admit the marijuana into evidence because it was obtained as a result of an unreasonable search of the woman. Under the exclusionary rule, evidence obtained in violation of a defendant's Fourth Amendment rights is not admissible to establish the guilt of the defendant at trial. The Fourth Amendment protects against unreasonable searches and seizures by government agents. To have a protected Fourth Amendment right, a person must have a reasonable expectation of privacy with respect to the place searched or the item seized. For a search based on a search warrant to be constitutionally valid, the warrant must be based on probable cause and must describe with reasonable precision the place to be searched and the items to be seized. A search warrant does not authorize the police to search persons found on the premises who are not named in the warrant. However, if the police have probable cause to arrest a person discovered on the premises to be searched, they may conduct a warrantless search of her incident to the arrest. If a person is not named in the warrant and circumstances justifying an arrest of that person do not exist, the police may search her for the objects named in the search warrant only if they have probable cause to believe that she has the named objects on her person. Here, the search warrant was issued on the basis of information from reliable informants, and it stated precisely the premises (the fraternity house) to be searched and the items (illegal narcotics) to be seized. Thus, the warrant is valid. However, the search warrant (which did not name the woman) did not authorize the police to search the woman's purse. The search cannot be justified as incident to a valid arrest because: (i) the police searched the purse ***before*** they arrested the woman; and (ii) the police did not have sufficient probable cause to arrest the woman prior to searching the purse. Because the police had no reason to believe that the woman had drugs on her person, they cannot successfully claim that they were searching for the drugs mentioned in the warrant. The woman can challenge the search because she had a possessory interest and a legitimate expectation of privacy in her purse, which was the object of the search. Thus, because the marijuana was seized pursuant to an unreasonable search in violation of the Fourth Amendment, it must be excluded from evidence. (B) is incorrect because mere presence at a place for which the police have a search warrant does not authorize a search of a person not named in the warrant. Only if the police obtain probable cause to arrest a person on the premises may the person be searched (as incident to the arrest). (A) is incorrect. The footlocker was properly searched pursuant to the warrant, not because it was within the woman's reach. However, the marijuana at issue here was seized as a result of a search of the woman's purse. Thus, the proximity of the woman to the footlocker is of no consequence to the admissibility of the marijuana found in her purse. (C) is incorrect because the woman's lack of a possessory interest in the premises does not invalidate a search of her purse. For example, if the police had probable cause to believe that the woman had drugs on her person, they could have searched her for the drugs, regardless of the fact that she had no possessory interest in the fraternity house.

Answer to Question 23

(A) The defendant can be found guilty of robbery and felony murder, but the death penalty cannot be imposed. The defendant can be found guilty of robbery as an accomplice. The Supreme Court has held that, under the Eighth Amendment, the death penalty may not be imposed for felony murder where the defendant, as an accomplice, did not take or attempt or intend to take life, or intend that lethal force be employed. [Enmund v. Florida (1982)] Here, because the defendant's involvement in the crime was only to provide transportation, it cannot be said that he participated in such a major way that he acted with reckless indifference to human life; hence, the death penalty cannot constitutionally be imposed against him. (B) is therefore incorrect. (C) is incorrect because the defendant's conviction of both robbery and felony murder does not raise double jeopardy problems under these facts. Under the rule that lesser included offenses "merge" into greater offenses, a person may not be convicted of both the greater offense and a lesser included offense. While the Supreme Court has held that a subsequent prosecution for robbery is not permitted against a defendant who has been tried for felony murder where the robbery is the underlying felony, this situation is different. Imposition of cumulative punishments for two statutorily defined offenses arising from the same transaction and constituting the same crime does not violate double jeopardy when the punishments are imposed ***at a single trial***, as long as the two offenses were specifically intended by the legislature to carry separate punishments. [Missouri v. Hunter (1983)] Here, the legislature did specifically provide for cumulative penalties for first degree felony murder and for the underlying felony. Thus, the defendant can be convicted of both robbery and felony murder. (D) is incorrect because the jury could properly find the defendant guilty of felony murder. When the felony murder rule is combined with accomplice liability rules, the scope of liability becomes very broad. The felony murder rule provides that a killing—even an accidental one—committed during the course of a felony is murder. All parties to the felony are liable for the murder as long as (i) it was committed during the commission of the felony or in fleeing from the scene, and (ii) it was a foreseeable result of commission of the felony. Courts have been willing to find most deaths committed during a felony to be foreseeable. Here, the jury could reasonably find the shooting death of a store clerk by the acquaintance during a struggle for a gun to be a foreseeable result of the commission of a robbery and impose felony murder liability on the defendant as an accomplice.

Answer to Question 24

(C) The man's motion should be denied because neither his Fifth nor Sixth Amendment rights were violated by the informant's conduct. The Sixth Amendment right to counsel applies to all critical stages of a criminal prosecution, but does not apply in precharge custodial interrogations. Because this right is "offense specific," the fact that the right to counsel has attached for one charge does not bar questioning without counsel for an unrelated charge. Because the man has not been charged with the convenience store robbery, his Sixth Amendment right to counsel has not been violated. The Fifth Amendment privilege against self-incrimination requires *Miranda* warnings and a valid waiver before any statement made by the accused during custodial interrogation can be admitted. However, this requirement does not apply where interrogation is by an informant who the defendant does not know is working for the police, because the coercive atmosphere of police-dominated interrogation is not present. [Illinois v. Perkins (1990)] Because the man was not aware of the informant's status, the informant's conduct did not constitute a police interrogation. (A) is wrong despite the fact that the informant's conduct may have been deliberately designed to elicit incriminating remarks. As discussed above, the man's right to counsel did not attach for purposes of the convenience store robbery. (B) is incorrect because, as discussed above, the *Miranda* warnings need not be given before questioning by a cellmate working covertly for the police. (D) is incorrect because interrogation refers not only to express questioning, but also to any words or actions on the part of the police that the police should know are reasonably likely to elicit an incriminating response from the suspect. Here, the informant, working for the police, made statements about the convenience store robbery that were intended to, and reasonably likely to, prompt a response from his cellmate. Hence, it is not the absence of "interrogation" that avoids the *Miranda* problem, but the fact that the man did not know that his cellmate was working for the police.

Answer to Question 25

(D) The defendant did not make a false representation for purposes of either false pretenses or larceny by trick. Both false pretenses and larceny by trick require a misrepresentation on the part of the defendant. In the case of false pretenses, the victim intends to convey ***title*** to the property, while in the case of larceny by trick, the victim intends to convey only ***possession*** of the property. For both crimes, the misrepresentation required is an intentional (or knowing) false statement of past or existing fact. The defendant must have created a false impression as to a matter of fact. There is no misrepresentation if the defendant merely fails to correct what is known to be a mistaken impression held by the victim, as long as the defendant is not responsible for creating the mistake or has no fiduciary duty to the victim. Here, although this defendant did not obtain unconditional title to the stereo because the seller could repossess it if payments were not made, he probably obtained enough of the title to qualify for the crime of false pretenses. However, he did not create a false impression as to a matter of fact. Although this defendant was aware of the clerk's mistake regarding his identity, this defendant did not create this mistake, nor did he have a fiduciary duty to the clerk. Thus, he had no duty to correct the false impression, and it cannot be said that there was a misrepresentation on the part of this defendant. Absent a misrepresentation, by means of which this defendant obtained either possession of or title to the stereo, he cannot be convicted of either larceny by trick or false pretenses. (C) is incorrect because, in the absence of a misrepresentation on the part of this defendant, his intent to pay for the stereo is not determinative of his guilt of either crime mentioned. Even if this defendant intended to pay at a later point, he would be guilty if he had obtained title to or possession of the stereo by a misrepresentation, with intent to defraud the store. Subjecting the store to a greater risk of loss as a result of the misrepresentation (because the store would otherwise have obtained a down payment) satisfies the intent to defraud element. (A) and (B) are incorrect because, as explained above, this defendant is guilty of neither crime due to the absence of misrepresentation. In addition, (B) is incorrect because most courts would find that title has been transferred under these circumstances, rather than merely possession, making the potential crime false pretenses rather than larceny by trick.

Answer to Question 26

(C) Since the defendant was charged with first degree murder, the theory of the case is most likely felony murder, and (C) is the only choice that sets out a theory to avoid a felony murder conviction. If the defendant was so intoxicated that he could not form the intent to steal, then he is not guilty of robbery, and there would be no "felony" from which the felony murder rule is to arise. (A) and (B) are incorrect because even though the defendant could argue that no premeditation or deliberation was present, he would still be guilty of first degree murder under the felony murder rule because the felony was robbery. (D) is wrong because insulting someone is not adequate provocation that would mitigate a homicide to voluntary manslaughter; neither would this "threat" suffice, in all likelihood. At most, the circumstances might produce the sort of unreasonable anger that would negate premeditation and deliberation. However, since the defendant clearly caused the homicide while committing the felony of robbery, his crime remains first degree murder.

Answer to Question 27

(B) The defendant's strongest argument is that her associate's death was justifiable homicide. Most courts today would not allow the defendant to be convicted on a felony murder theory when a co-felon is killed by a third party during the crime. Some courts base this result on the fact that the person who did the killing was justified in doing so. (A) is wrong. Aside from the fact that the attempt to steal from the jewelry store is probably statutory burglary, the fact that the associate attempted to aid the defendant in stealing the bracelet by attacking the clerk with a knife is probably robbery. When or how the associate came by the dangerous weapon is immaterial. (C) is wrong because the circumstances of one co-felon breaking an agreement not to commit violence would not prevent the application of the felony murder rule if it were otherwise applicable. (D) is wrong because if the felony murder rule is otherwise applicable, the fact that the person who killed the co-felon may have mistaken the co-felon's intentions does not prevent the operation of this rule.

Answer to Question 28

(B) To be reasonable under the Fourth Amendment, most searches must be pursuant to a warrant. The warrant must describe with reasonable precision the place to be searched and the items to be seized. A search warrant does not authorize the police to search persons found on the premises who are not named in the warrant. In *Ybarra v. Illinois* (1979), a case based on similar facts, the Supreme Court held that "each patron of the tavern had an individual right to be free of unreasonable searches, and presence at a location subject to search does not negate the requirement of probable cause to search the person present." (A) is incorrect because the validity of the statute is not the primary issue. Even in the absence of a statute, the search of the customer by the officer violated the customer's Fourth Amendment rights. (C) is incorrect because, as discussed above, the search warrant did not override the customer's Fourth Amendment rights. While the police would be able to search a person discovered on the premises for whom they had probable cause to arrest, because the search would be incident to a lawful arrest, here they searched the customer prior to an arrest and without probable cause. (D) is irrelevant; if a search is unconstitutional, it does not matter that it was authorized by statute. To the extent that the statute authorizes a search in violation of the Fourth Amendment, it is unconstitutional.

Answer to Question 29

(A) Since purchasing 10 pounds of gunpowder without a license is not a crime, the owner cannot be convicted of purchasing gunpowder without a license, ***or*** of attempting to purchase gunpowder without a license, even if the owner believed he was committing a crime. Given that there is no crime on the books to cover the owner's behavior or his intended behavior, he cannot be found guilty of attempt. This is the doctrine of legal impossibility. (B) is incorrect because the Second Amendment right to bear arms is not unlimited, and reasonable restrictions may be placed on the sale and possession of weapons. Limiting the quantity of gunpowder that may be purchased within a year without a license falls within this category. (C) is also incorrect. Generally, it is not a defense that the defendant was unaware that his conduct was prohibited by law. However, the fact scenario in this question presents the opposite situation: the gun shop owner was unaware that his conduct was lawful. (D) is incorrect. Although factual impossibility generally is not a defense to an attempt charge, here the facts raise the issue of legal impossibility, not factual impossibility.

Answer to Question 30

(D) Although the defendant might have been indifferent with respect to the boyfriend's marital status, the facts do not show that the defendant intended to see the offense of bigamy committed. To establish criminal liability under an accomplice theory, it must be established that the defendant helped with the commission of the crime and had the intent to see the crime committed. A

mental state of recklessness would not justify a conviction as an accomplice, regardless of the mental state required by the definition of the principal crime. (A) is incorrect because, although the defendant did aid and encourage the marriage, he cannot be held as an accomplice without the necessary intent, which was lacking. (B) is incorrect. Although bigamy is a strict liability offense when applied to the actual participants in the bigamous marriage, the defendant is not a participant to the marriage. (C) is incorrect because, even if the defendant's actions amounted to a breach of duty, he still did not possess the mental state necessary for accomplice liability.

Answer to Question 31

(A) An honest and reasonable mistake as to a material element of the offense would negate criminal liability for all crimes except strict liability offenses. Thus, if the state had abolished strict liability crimes, the bartender's mistake would be a defense regardless of the mental state required for the crime of serving alcohol to a minor. (B) is not as good an answer as (A). The bartender's lack of intent to commit the crime of serving alcohol to a minor would negate criminal liability if the crime required a specific intent, thus requiring an actual intention to engage in the act of serving alcohol to a minor. The question does not indicate the mental state required for the crime of serving alcohol to a minor. Even though the state had abolished strict liability offenses, the state could punish the crime of serving alcohol to a minor with a "reckless" or "should have known" state of mind. If so, the bartender's lack of intent would not result in a not guilty verdict. (C) is not as good an answer as (A) because the fact that the bartender made a diligent effort to determine the age of the minor would be an important consideration in deciding whether she made an honest and reasonable mistake, but it would not in and of itself automatically negate liability. A similar analysis applies to (D). The fact that the bartender checked the identification card supplied by a state agency would be an important consideration in deciding the nature of her mistake, but it would not by itself negate liability, as the mistake must be both honest and reasonable. For example, if the bartender knew that the minor was not of age despite what the identification card showed, she would commit a crime by serving the minor alcohol.

Answer to Question 32

(A) The court should reverse the defendant's conviction because Instruction #6 requires the defendant to disprove one of the elements of murder. Due process requires in criminal cases that the state prove guilt beyond a reasonable doubt. The prosecution has the burden of proving all of the elements of the crime charged. Thus, if malice aforethought is an element of murder and voluntary manslaughter is distinguished from murder by the existence of adequate provocation, the defendant cannot be required to prove that he committed the homicide in the heat of passion (*i.e.*, with adequate provocation). Such a requirement would impose on the defendant the burden of disproving the element of malice aforethought, since "heat of passion" negates malice. Although the defendant can be given the burden of going forward with some evidence on the provocation issue, once he has done so, the prosecution bears the burden of proving that the killing was not done in the heat of passion. In the case at issue, Instruction #6 requires a defendant to prove that he committed the intentional killing under adequate provocation. At common law, and consequently in the state, malice aforethought is an element of murder. Therefore, this instruction in effect requires the defendant to disprove the element of malice aforethought, thereby relieving the state of its burden of proving all elements of the crime. As discussed above, such an instruction cannot pass constitutional muster. On the other hand, for an affirmative defense such as insanity, it is permissible to impose the burden of proof on the defendant. Thus, Instruction #8 does not affect the state's obligation to prove all elements of the crime, and is permissible under the general principles mentioned above. Thus, (B) and (C) incorrectly state that this instruction is improper. (D) is incorrect because it states that Instruction #6 is proper. As explained above, this is not an accurate statement of the law.

Answer to Question 33

(B) The teenager's conviction should be reversed because the court's charge to the jury required the teenager to prove that he intended to return the car. In a criminal case, the state must prove beyond a reasonable doubt all "elements" of the crime. Elements include the behavior, result, and mental state found in the definition of the crime charged. Because common law larceny requires an "intent to permanently deprive," the state must prove beyond a reasonable doubt that mental state. In this question, the judge incorrectly placed the burden of proof on the defendant to prove an intent to return the car by a preponderance of the evidence. (A) is an incorrect statement of the law. The state is not required to prove ***all*** disputed issues beyond a reasonable doubt, only the basic elements of the crime charged. Many states require a defendant to prove a defense, such as entrapment or self-defense, by a preponderance of the evidence. (C) is wrong because an intent to return the car would show a lack of intent to permanently deprive, which would negate liability for common law larceny. (D) is wrong because the jury instructions were incorrect for the reasons stated above.

Answer to Question 34

(D) The defendant has committed larceny. The defendant's change of heart after taking the car will not provide him with a defense because it is irrelevant. Larceny requires the taking and carrying away of the tangible personal property of another by trespass. In the instant case, the larceny was committed at the time he took the victim's car with the intent to permanently deprive him of possession. (Note that the taking was trespassory because the defendant obtained possession by misrepresentation—larceny by trick.) Given that the crime was complete once the defendant drove off, he is guilty of larceny, which makes (D) the correct answer. (A) is incorrect because the defendant did not intend to return the car at the time of the taking and thus had completed the crime at that time. He had the requisite mens rea at the time of the taking and carrying away, and this is sufficient to convict. (B) and (C) are wrong for similar reasons. Abandonment is a defense to ***an attempt*** of a crime. In the instant case, the defendant had already completed the crime, as described above. Thus, abandonment cannot act as a good defense. Choice (C) speaks of withdrawal, which is sometimes a defense to conspiracy. It has no relevance to the crime of larceny.

Answer to Question 35

(C) The defendant has committed embezzlement because a court will probably find that he had "possession" of the car at the time he appropriated it. Embezzlement is the fraudulent conversion of the property of another by a person in lawful possession of it. In the instant case, the car belonged to the company for which the defendant worked, but the company probably gave the defendant lawful possession of it so that he could make sales calls. When he sold the car rather than return it, he wrongfully converted the car. This is embezzlement. (A) is incorrect. Larceny is the taking and carrying away of the property of another by trespass with the intent to permanently deprive the person of the property. The intent to permanently deprive must be concurrent with the taking and carrying away. In the instant case, the defendant did not have the intent to permanently deprive the company of the car when he was given the car. Thus, the intent element is missing. (B) is also incorrect. Larceny by trick is a specialized form of larceny. For larceny by trick, the defendant must acquire possession of the property by some misrepresentation concerning a present or past fact. The defendant did not come into possession of the car by misrepresentation,

making (B) incorrect. For similar reasons, (D) is also incorrect. The crime of false pretenses is the obtaining title to the property of another by an intentional (or knowing) false statement of past or existing fact with the intent to defraud. As with larceny by trick, the defendant here came into possession of the vehicle without use of a misrepresentation. Furthermore, he also never obtained title to the car. Thus, (D) is an incorrect answer.

Answer to Question 36

(B) The defendant should be convicted of common law murder, but acquitted of the robbery. At common law, murder is the unlawful killing of a human being with malice aforethought. "Malice aforethought" exists if the defendant has any of the following states of mind: (i) the intent to kill (express malice); (ii) the intent to inflict great bodily injury; (iii) a reckless indifference to an unjustifiably high risk to human life ("abandoned and malignant heart"); or (iv) the intent to commit a felony. In the instant case, malice could be found either by the intent to kill (because the clerk was intentionally killed to prevent identification) or by the intent to commit a felony (the killing was committed during the course of a robbery). Robbery is an aggravated form of larceny and consists of the following elements: (i) a taking; (ii) of the personal property of another; (iii) from the other's person or presence; (iv) by force or intimidation; (v) with the intent to permanently deprive him of it. Clearly, the elements for robbery are met here. Thus, at first glance, the defendant has committed both murder and robbery. However, the fact pattern also raises the defense of duress. A person is not guilty of an offense, other than homicide, if he performs an otherwise criminal act under the reasonable belief that another will imminently inflict death or great bodily harm on him or an immediate family member if he does not commit the criminal act. In the instant case, the defendant committed the robbery under duress and thus should be acquitted of that charge, making (A) incorrect. However, duress would not be effective against a murder charge based on an intent-to-kill theory, and here the defendant intentionally killed the store clerk under instructions from the gang member to prevent identification. Thus, because the defendant could be convicted of an intent-to-kill murder, but acquitted of the robbery charge based on duress, (B) is the correct answer. (C) and (D) are incorrect. An argument could be raised that the killing should be reduced to voluntary manslaughter from murder, given that the defendant was acting under the provocation of a threat of deadly force. At common law, provocation would reduce a killing to voluntary manslaughter if (i) the provocation must have been one that would arouse the sudden and intense passion in the mind of an ordinary person such as to cause him to lose self-control; (ii) the defendant must have in fact been provoked; (iii) there must not have been sufficient time to cool off; and (iv) the defendant did not in fact cool off. Provocation includes being subjected to a serious battery or a threat of deadly force. That said, the reduction to voluntary manslaughter occurs only as to the person who provoked the defendant (or the killing of a third person under the transferred intent doctrine). Thus, had the defendant killed the gang member, he might have been able to claim "adequate provocation" to have the killing reduced to voluntary manslaughter (assuming that a straight self-defense issue could not have been raised). However, as discussed above in terms of a duress defense, it would not justify the killing of a third party.

Evidence

Question Sets and Analytical Answers

Set 1 Answer Sheet

1. Ⓐ Ⓑ Ⓒ Ⓓ
2. Ⓐ Ⓑ Ⓒ Ⓓ
3. Ⓐ Ⓑ Ⓒ Ⓓ
4. Ⓐ Ⓑ Ⓒ Ⓓ
5. Ⓐ Ⓑ Ⓒ Ⓓ
6. Ⓐ Ⓑ Ⓒ Ⓓ
7. Ⓐ Ⓑ Ⓒ Ⓓ
8. Ⓐ Ⓑ Ⓒ Ⓓ
9. Ⓐ Ⓑ Ⓒ Ⓓ
10. Ⓐ Ⓑ Ⓒ Ⓓ
11. Ⓐ Ⓑ Ⓒ Ⓓ
12. Ⓐ Ⓑ Ⓒ Ⓓ
13. Ⓐ Ⓑ Ⓒ Ⓓ
14. Ⓐ Ⓑ Ⓒ Ⓓ
15. Ⓐ Ⓑ Ⓒ Ⓓ
16. Ⓐ Ⓑ Ⓒ Ⓓ
17. Ⓐ Ⓑ Ⓒ Ⓓ
18. Ⓐ Ⓑ Ⓒ Ⓓ

EVIDENCE QUESTIONS - SET 1

Question 1

In a personal injury case involving a two-car collision, the plaintiff wishes to introduce a sworn deposition taken from a witness who died two weeks before the case came to trial. In the deposition, the witness stated that she saw the defendant run a red light at the time of the collision with the plaintiff's car. Both the plaintiff's and the defendant's attorneys were present at the deposition. The defendant objects in the appropriate manner to the introduction of the witness's statement.

How should the court rule on the admissibility of the deposition?

(A) Admissible, because the defendant had an opportunity to cross-examine the witness at the time the deposition was taken.

(B) Admissible, as a dying declaration.

(C) Inadmissible, because the statement was not made while the witness was testifying in court.

(D) Inadmissible, because the defendant has no opportunity to cross-examine the witness at trial.

Question 2

The plaintiff hired the defendant as a clerk in his jewelry store. One of the plaintiff's employees reported that he saw the defendant stealing pieces of less expensive jewelry from the store. The plaintiff thereupon discharged the defendant and brought a civil action against her for the value of various pieces of jewelry missing from the store. At the trial, the plaintiff calls his employee as a witness. The witness testifies that he does not remember either having seen the defendant take anything from the store or having told the plaintiff that she had done so. The plaintiff then takes the witness stand and proposes to testify to what the witness had told him about seeing the defendant stealing pieces of less expensive jewelry from the store.

Assuming appropriate objection by the defendant, such testimony by the plaintiff would be:

(A) Admissible as a statement against interest by the witness.

(B) Admissible as proper impeachment of the witness's testimony.

(C) Inadmissible as irrelevant.

(D) Inadmissible hearsay if offered to prove theft by the defendant.

Question 3

A plaintiff brought a civil action against a defendant for embezzlement of funds missing from a trust account, for which the defendant also is being investigated by the district attorney. At trial, the plaintiff calls the defendant as an adverse witness and asks him one question, "Is it not true that you embezzled funds from the trust?" The defendant refuses to answer, claiming a privilege against self-incrimination.

The trial court should:

(A) Order him to disclose to the court in camera what happened to the missing funds so that the court can determine whether he reasonably fears prosecution for a crime.

(B) Order him to answer because the privilege against self-incrimination does not apply in civil proceedings.

(C) Sustain his claim of privilege, because no witness can be compelled to answer questions that may tend to incriminate.

(D) Sustain his claim of privilege because he is a likely subject of criminal prosecution.

Question 4

A plaintiff sues a defendant for serious personal injuries he incurred when the defendant

allegedly drove through a red light and collided with the plaintiff's car. Calling the defendant as an adverse witness, the plaintiff asked her if she had been drinking before the accident. The defendant refused to answer, asserting her privilege against self-incrimination. The plaintiff then offers in evidence a certified copy of a court record indicating that, eight years previously, the defendant had been convicted of reckless driving while intoxicated that caused serious personal injury, a felony.

The trial court should:

(A) Admit the record as relevant character evidence because the plaintiff suffered serious personal injuries.

(B) Admit the record as impeachment evidence.

(C) Exclude the record as irrelevant because as yet the defendant has given no testimony to be impeached.

(D) Exclude the record because the conviction is too remote and does not necessarily reflect on the defendant's credibility as a witness in the present proceedings.

Question 5

A horse breeder offered to sell a colt to his neighbor and subsequently received a note in which the neighbor agreed to pay the agreed-upon purchase price for the colt. The note was addressed to the horse breeder and contained the neighbor's alleged signature. When the horse breeder attempted to set up transfer of the colt, the neighbor denied that she agreed to purchase it. In a breach of contract action against the neighbor, the horse breeder offers into evidence the note. The horse breeder testifies that he is familiar with the neighbor's handwriting and recognizes the signature on the note as being hers.

Assuming appropriate objection by the neighbor, who claims that she did not sign the note, the trial court should:

(A) Exclude the note for lack of foundation because lay opinion testimony regarding handwriting identification is not admissible.

(B) Exclude the note unless its authenticity is established by a preponderance of the evidence.

(C) Admit the note as authentic and instruct the jury accordingly.

(D) Admit the note but instruct the jury that it is up to them to decide whether the note is authentic.

Question 6

In a criminal trial, the prosecutor called a witness to the stand to authenticate the voice in a tape recording as the defendant's. The only other time the witness had heard the defendant's voice was after his arrest.

Assuming a proper foundation has been laid, may the witness properly authenticate the defendant's voice?

(A) Yes, because the witness is now familiar with the defendant's voice.

(B) Yes, because the prosecutor can qualify the witness as an expert on the defendant's voice.

(C) No, because the witness's testimony would be inadmissible hearsay.

(D) No, because the witness did not hear the defendant's voice until after he was arrested.

Question 7

Who, among the following, would *not* be permitted to verify writing as the handwriting of a criminal defendant charged with forgery?

(A) An expert witness who examined it and compared it with a genuine specimen of the defendant's handwriting.

(B) The jury, when offered a comparison with handwriting known to be the defendant's, obtained after her arrest.

(C) A police officer who had a copy of the defendant's true handwriting.

(D) A secretary who had worked for the defendant for five years.

Question 8

At an antiques show, a purchaser who did not speak English asked her brother to communicate her offer to purchase an antique chair to the dealer. The brother and dealer agreed on a purchase price of $15,000, but did not reduce the agreement to writing. The brother told the purchaser of the agreement, and died two days later. The next day, the purchaser brought a certified check for $15,000 to the dealer. She showed the check to the dealer and pointed to the chair but he would not accept the payment. The purchaser sued the dealer on a contract theory. At the trial, the purchaser, through an interpreter, wished to testify to a conversation she had with her brother, where he said, "The dealer has agreed to sell you the chair for $15,000."

If the jurisdiction has a typical "Dead Man Act," what effect will the Act have upon the admissibility of the purchaser's conversation with her brother?

(A) It will render the conversation inadmissible because a civil action is involved.

(B) It will render the conversation inadmissible because the purchaser is an interested party.

(C) None, because the dealer is not a protected party.

(D) None, because a civil action is involved.

Question 9

A husband was driving a motor home late at night while his wife slept in the back. Suddenly, there was a collision and the wife was jolted awake. She rushed to the front of the vehicle and saw that it had struck a small car. The husband said, "I just ran a red light and hit that car." The wife got out of her vehicle and began to inspect the damage to both the motor home and the car. A woman said, "What happened?" Not knowing that the woman was a passenger in and owner of the car that had been struck, the wife said, "My husband ran a red light." At trial of a negligence action against the couple filed by the occupants of the car that was struck, the plaintiff's first witness is the woman, a plaintiff, who will testify as to the wife's statement.

Should the trial court admit this evidence?

(A) Yes, because it will impeach the wife if she denies having said it in her case-in-chief.

(B) Yes, because it is an admission by a party-opponent.

(C) No, because the wife had no foundational knowledge when she made the statement.

(D) No, because the wife did not know she was talking to an occupant of the car when she spoke.

Question 10

An auto mechanic for a local body shop was on a routine test drive for a car that she repaired. During the drive, she exceeded the posted speed limit and collided with the victim's vehicle at an intersection. The victim had failed to stop at the stop sign preceding the intersection. When the mechanic saw that the victim was injured, she ran over and told him, "I'm really sorry. I guess I didn't fix the brakes as well as I thought." Later, she readjusted the brakes of the vehicle she had been driving at the time of the accident. The victim brought an action against the body shop for personal injuries and property damage. At trial, he called a bystander to testify to the mechanic's statement about the brakes after the accident.

The body shop's objection to the bystander's testimony should be:

(A) Sustained, because the mechanic's statement is inadmissible against the body shop.

(B) Sustained, because the victim did not stop at the stop sign.

(C) Overruled, because it is a declaration against interest.

(D) Overruled, because it is an admission of a party-opponent.

Question 11

A plaintiff brought a personal injury action against a defendant, the owner of a small fishing resort, for injuries he suffered when a dockside chair he was sitting on collapsed. At trial, the plaintiff testified that he had reported to the defendant the previous day that one of the chairs had a loose leg, whereupon the defendant tightened the screws holding the leg to the chair body, but that the next day the repaired leg of the chair collapsed while the plaintiff was fishing from it, injuring him. The plaintiff now wishes to offer evidence showing that the defendant had attached a new chair leg after the accident.

The defendant's objection to that evidence should be:

(A) Overruled, because it tends to prove the defendant's negligence.

(B) Overruled, because it is relevant to the defendant's state of mind.

(C) Sustained, because it constitutes assertive conduct.

(D) Sustained, for public policy reasons.

Question 12

A plaintiff brought an action against a defendant for property damages, alleging that the defendant's car nicked the side of the plaintiff's truck while the defendant was changing lanes on an expressway. At trial, the defendant sought to introduce evidence of her good driving record.

The evidence is:

(A) Inadmissible, because it is character evidence.

(B) Inadmissible, because it is self-serving.

(C) Admissible, because it is character evidence.

(D) Admissible, because it is habit evidence.

Question 13

A plaintiff sues a defendant for personal injuries, claiming that while the plaintiff was driving through an intersection at the posted speed limit, the defendant failed to stop at a stop sign and struck her car. At trial, the plaintiff calls the defendant's friend to testify to the fact that the defendant never stops at the stop sign at the accident intersection and invariably "runs" every stop sign.

The defendant's objection to the testimony should be:

(A) Sustained, because it is not the best evidence.

(B) Sustained, because character evidence is inadmissible in a civil case.

(C) Overruled, because it is evidence of habit.

(D) Overruled, because it is self-serving.

Question 14

A victim was struck by a car in a hit-and-run accident. A police officer arrived half an hour after the accident. The victim was in shock and came in and out of consciousness. As the officer applied first aid, the victim muttered, "I know I'm going to die. Oh my, he ran the light!" The victim fell back into unconsciousness, but revived again and muttered, "Why didn't he stop?" The officer heard the comments clearly and made a note of them. Good police work by the officer and others led to the discovery of the driver of the car that struck the victim. The victim survived and filed a tort action against the driver. Before the case came to trial, the victim died of a heart attack. The causes of the heart attack were totally unrelated to the accident. The laws of the jurisdiction allow for survival of personal injury actions. Thus, the victim's estate is substituted for the victim as plaintiff.

If the plaintiff's attorney seeks to have the officer testify to the victim's statements at the time of the accident, how will the court rule?

(A) Inadmissible, because the victim did not die as a result of the accident.

(B) Inadmissible, because this is a civil case and not a criminal matter.

(C) Admissible, because the victim's statements were present sense impressions.

(D) Admissible, because the statements were made at a time when the victim feared impending death.

Question 15

At the trial of a lawsuit that arose out of a collision between the plaintiff's and the defendant's cars, the plaintiff's attorney calls an automobile mechanic as a witness, who testifies that he has 12 years' experience and was the only witness to the accident. The witness also testifies that he arrived at the scene immediately after the accident, which caused both cars to overturn, and saw the wheels on both cars still spinning. He testifies that the wheels of the defendant's car were spinning faster than the wheels of the plaintiff's car. The plaintiff's attorney asks the witness to testify as to what speed the respective cars were traveling at the time of the accident based upon his observations of the spinning wheels. The defendant's attorney objects.

Should the testimony regarding the speed of the cars be admitted?

(A) Yes, as the witness's personal opinion.

(B) Yes, as a matter based upon personal observation.

(C) No, because the witness has not been qualified as an expert in accident reconstruction.

(D) No, because there is not another witness to corroborate the witness's presence at the accident scene.

Question 16

A witness heard a horn sounding while walking down the street. She looked up and saw two cars enter an intersection and collide. In a suit between the drivers of the two cars, the plaintiff's attorney calls the witness to the stand. On direct examination, she is asked to describe the accident scene, position of the cars in the intersection, etc. On cross-examination, the defense attorney goes over the same ground with the witness. He asks her whether there was any broken glass on the pavement, to which she responds, "Yes, lots of it," and before the defense attorney can ask his next question, the witness blurts out, "They had to be going over 50!" The defense attorney moves to strike the statement.

How should the court rule?

(A) Strike it, as unresponsive to any question asked.

(B) Strike it, because the witness had no way of knowing how fast the cars were traveling.

(C) Not to strike, because the defense attorney "opened the door" to anything the witness might say about the accident.

(D) Not to strike, because the statement accuses both drivers of going over 50, and is not prejudicial to only one side.

Question 17

A state court is ***least*** likely to take judicial notice of which of the following?

(A) The blood type that occurs with greatest frequency in the population is O-positive.

(B) Main Street, upon which the courthouse is situated, runs north and south.

(C) The sun rose at 6:52 a.m. on Friday, December 12, of last year.

(D) In Australian law, there is no private action for environmental issues.

Question 18

In its lead editorial in the Sunday edition, a suburban daily newspaper characterized a real estate developer as a "common thief." The developer promptly filed suit against the newspaper for defamation. During the course of the presentation of the plaintiff's case, he sought to put a witness on the stand who is prepared to testify that the plaintiff once saved the life of a fellow soldier in Vietnam.

If the newspaper's lawyer objects, the court should rule that the testimony is:

(A) Admissible, because the plaintiff has a right to introduce evidence of his good character.

(B) Admissible, because the plaintiff's character has been brought into question by the editorial.

(C) Inadmissible, because the witness's testimony is not probative of any material issue.

(D) Inadmissible, because specific instances of conduct are not admissible to prove character.

EVIDENCE ANSWERS - SET 1

Answer to Question 1

(A) The deposition testimony of the now unavailable witness is admissible under the former testimony exception to the hearsay rule. The witness's statement is hearsay because it is a statement, other than one made by the declarant while testifying at the trial or hearing, offered in evidence to prove the truth of the matter asserted. Unless such a statement falls within a recognized exception to the hearsay rule, it must be excluded upon appropriate objection to its admission. [Fed. R. Evid. 802] Pursuant to the former testimony exception to the hearsay rule, the testimony of a now unavailable witness given at another hearing or in a deposition taken in accordance with the law is admissible in a subsequent trial as long as there is a sufficient similarity of parties and issues so that the opportunity to develop testimony or cross-examine at the prior hearing or deposition was meaningful. [Fed. R. Evid. 804(b)(1)] Here, the plaintiff is offering the deposition testimony of the witness to prove the truth of the matter asserted therein; *i.e.*, that the defendant ran a red light at the time of the accident. Thus, the testimony is hearsay. The witness is unavailable because she is dead. Also, because the deposition was taken in connection with the same case that is currently the subject of the trial, there is an exact identity of parties and issues between the deposition and the trial. Thus, the defendant had an opportunity and a motive to develop the testimony of the witness at the time of the deposition by cross-examination. As a result, the elements of the former testimony exception are satisfied, and the deposition testimony of the witness is admissible in the trial. (B) is incorrect because the testimony of the witness does not constitute a dying declaration. In a civil action or a homicide prosecution, a statement made by a now unavailable declarant while believing her death was imminent, that concerns the cause or circumstances of what she believed to be her impending death, is admissible. [Fed. R. Evid. 804(b)(2)] There is no indication that the witness's statements contained in the deposition were made at a time when she believed her death was imminent, or that such statements concerned the cause or circumstances of what she believed to be her impending death. Therefore, the requirements of a dying declaration are not met. (C) is incorrect because a statement need not be made in court to qualify under the former testimony exception to the hearsay rule. Deposition testimony is within the exception if the deposition is taken in compliance with the law and the party against whom it is offered (or his predecessor in interest) had an opportunity and similar motive to develop the testimony. (D) is incorrect because it is not necessary for the defendant to have the opportunity to cross-examine the witness at the trial. It is only necessary that the defendant have had the opportunity to develop the witness's testimony at the prior proceeding; *i.e.*, at the deposition. Having been afforded this opportunity, the defendant cannot now obtain the exclusion of the proffered testimony on the ground that the witness cannot be cross-examined at trial.

Answer to Question 2

(D) If offered to prove that the defendant stole the jewelry, the testimony by the plaintiff would be hearsay and, thus, inadmissible. Hearsay is a statement, other than one made by the declarant while testifying at the trial or hearing, offered in evidence to prove the truth of the matter asserted. [Fed. R. Evid. 801(c)] A hearsay statement, to which no exception to the hearsay rule is applicable, must be excluded upon appropriate objection. [Fed. R. Evid. 802] The proffered testimony of the plaintiff relates to a statement made by the witness other than while testifying at the instant trial. Therefore, if the witness's out-of-court statement is offered to prove that the defendant stole the pieces of jewelry, the statement is hearsay. Since no exceptions to the hearsay rule apply, the statement is inadmissible. (A) is incorrect because the statement is not against the interest of the declarant (the witness). Under the statement against interest exception to the

hearsay rule, statements of a person, now unavailable as a witness, against that person's pecuniary, proprietary, or penal interest when made are admissible. [Fed. R. Evid. 804(b)(3)] Here, the witness may be deemed to be unavailable because he has testified to a lack of memory of the subject matter to which his original statement to the plaintiff relates. However, the statement contained in the proposed testimony of the plaintiff is not against any interest of the witness, who is the declarant, but is rather against the interest, both penal and civil, of the defendant. Therefore, the statement does not qualify for admissibility as a statement against interest. (B) is incorrect because the witness has simply testified that he does not remember either seeing the defendant take the jewelry or telling the plaintiff that she did so. Impeachment refers to the casting of an adverse reflection on the truthfulness of a witness. One form of impeachment is to show that a witness has, on another occasion, made statements that are inconsistent with some material part of his present testimony. If the witness in his testimony had denied seeing the defendant take anything or telling the plaintiff that she had done so, then the testimony of the plaintiff as to the witness's previous statements would be admissible as a prior inconsistent statement, thus serving to disprove the credibility of the witness. However, because the witness has merely testified to a lack of memory concerning these matters, the plaintiff's testimony probably would not be considered a prior ***inconsistent*** statement. Although (B) could be correct in some jurisdictions, most would not consider introduction of a prior inconsistent statement an appropriate response to a claim of lack of memory unless the court believed the witness was being deliberately evasive. Since (D) is a completely accurate statement, it is the better answer. (C) is incorrect because the plaintiff's testimony is relevant. Evidence is logically relevant if it tends to make the existence of any fact of consequence to the determination of an action more probable than it would be without the evidence. [Fed. R. Evid. 401] The plaintiff's testimony that he was told that the defendant stole jewelry from his store would certainly tend to make it more probable that she took the jewelry than would otherwise be the case. This fact is of great consequence to the determination of the plaintiff's action against the defendant for the value of the missing jewelry. Thus, the proffered testimony is relevant. Although relevant, however, the testimony runs afoul of the hearsay rule, and is thus inadmissible.

Answer to Question 3

(C) The Fifth Amendment of the United States Constitution provides that a witness cannot be compelled to testify against himself. Pursuant to this privilege, a witness may refuse to answer any question if its answer might tend to incriminate him. Testimony is incriminating if it ties a witness to the commission of a crime or would furnish a lead to evidence tying the witness to a crime. The privilege against compelled self-incrimination can be claimed at any proceeding, whether civil or criminal, at which the witness's appearance and testimony are compelled. Here, the defendant's answer to a question as to whether he embezzled funds from the trust might tend to incriminate him by tying him to the commission of a crime (*e.g.*, embezzlement). Thus, the defendant is privileged to refuse to answer the question posed by the plaintiff. (B) is incorrect because, as noted above, a witness may claim the privilege against self-incrimination in a civil proceeding. If the testimony might expose the witness to criminal liability, then the privilege applies even in a civil proceeding. (A) is incorrect because, where testimony might be incriminating, the witness may refuse to answer a question, regardless of whether the witness has a reasonable fear of prosecution. There is no basis for the judge predicating her ruling on a determination that the defendant has a reasonable fear of prosecution. Also, the privilege against self-incrimination allows the defendant to refuse to answer any questions at all relating to whether he embezzled trust funds. As a result, he cannot be compelled to disclose such matters, even in an in camera proceeding. Similarly, (D) is incorrect because the applicability of the privilege against self-incrimination does not depend on the likelihood of actual criminal prosecution of the witness.

Testimony that might tend to incriminate the witness triggers the privilege, without regard for whether the witness is a likely target of criminal prosecution.

Answer to Question 4

(C) The record of the conviction should be excluded because the defendant has given no testimony to be impeached. Impeachment involves the casting of an adverse reflection on the truthfulness of a witness. Although the defendant has been called as a witness, she has not given any testimony at this point. Consequently, the plaintiff is unable to introduce evidence that would otherwise constitute proper impeachment evidence. (A) is incorrect because evidence of character to prove the conduct of a person in the litigated event is generally not admissible in a civil case. Circumstantial use of prior behavior patterns for the purpose of inferring that, at the time and place in question, a person probably acted in accord with such patterns raises the danger of unfair prejudice and distraction from the main issues. Consequently, even if the prior conviction resulted from driving while intoxicated, the record of that conviction is not admissible to show that the defendant was intoxicated when she collided with the plaintiff. (B) is incorrect because, as has been noted, evidence cannot be used for impeachment purposes before there is anything to be impeached. (D) is incorrect for two reasons: First, it is unnecessary to address the issue of whether the conviction constitutes proper impeachment evidence, because impeachment is not even called for on these facts. Second, if properly offered to impeach testimony by the defendant, the conviction would not be considered too remote. Under the Federal Rules, a conviction is not too remote if fewer than 10 years have elapsed since the conviction or release from prison.

Answer to Question 5

(D) The court should admit the note and instruct the jury that it is up to the jury to decide whether the note is authentic. Before a writing may be received in evidence, it must be authenticated by proof showing that the writing is what the proponent claims it is. All that is necessary is proof sufficient to support a jury finding of genuineness. The authenticity of a document is a preliminary fact to be decided by the jury. Here, the horse breeder's testimony that he is familiar with the neighbor's handwriting and that he recognizes the signature on the note to be that of the neighbor is sufficient to support a jury finding of genuineness. Thus, the note should be admitted and authenticity should be left to the jury to decide. (A) is wrong because a lay witness who has personal knowledge of the handwriting of the supposed writer may state his opinion as to whether the document is in that person's handwriting. (B) is wrong because authentication of documentary evidence requires only enough evidence to support a jury finding that the matter is what its proponent claims it is. It is not required that the proponent establish its genuineness by a preponderance of the evidence. (C) is wrong because, as noted above, where there is a dispute as to the authenticity of a document, the issue of authenticity is a fact determination for the jury, not the judge, to decide.

Answer to Question 6

(A) The witness may properly authenticate the defendant's voice because she is now familiar with his voice. ***Any*** person familiar with an alleged speaker's voice may authenticate a recording of the voice by giving an opinion as to its identity. Thus, because the witness is now familiar with the defendant's voice, she may give her opinion as to whether it is his voice on the tape. (B) is incorrect because the witness does not need to be qualified as an expert—lay opinion testimony is sufficient to identify a voice (assuming the lay witness is familiar with that voice). Expert testimony is appropriate only when the subject matter is one where scientific, technical, or other

specialized knowledge would assist the trier of fact in understanding the evidence or determining a fact in issue. [Fed. R. Evid. 702] Here, identification of the defendant's voice does not require such specialized knowledge; rather, all that is required is familiarity with his voice. (C) is incorrect because the witness's testimony would not be hearsay at all. Hearsay is a statement, other than one made by the declarant while testifying at the trial or hearing, offered in evidence to prove the truth of the matter asserted. [Fed. R. Evid. 801(c)] The witness is not going to be testifying to an out-of-court statement. Rather, she will testify that, being familiar with the voice of the defendant by virtue of having heard that voice before, she can now identify the voice on the tape as being that of the defendant. Because the witness will not be testifying as to any particular statement made by the defendant, there is no hearsay problem. (D) is incorrect because, as long as the witness is familiar with the voice of the defendant, it makes no difference that she acquired such familiarity only after he was arrested. Thus, the witness may properly authenticate the voice.

Answer to Question 7

(C) Of the persons listed, the police officer is the only one who would not have: (i) personal familiarity with the defendant's handwriting; (ii) a basis for forming an opinion as to the handwriting derived from specialized knowledge; or (iii) a particular fact-finding function, such as that assigned to the jury. (A) and (B) are incorrect because an expert witness or a trier of fact can determine the genuineness of a writing by comparing the questioned writing with another writing proved to be genuine. Since a police officer is neither an expert witness nor a trier of fact, (C) does not come within this rule. (D) is incorrect because lay opinion testimony is admissible to identify handwriting if the witness is familiar with the handwriting. A secretary employed by the defendant for five years would have the requisite familiarity with the defendant's handwriting to permit the secretary to offer an opinion as to the genuineness of the writing at issue. Since the police officer was not previously familiar with the defendant's writing, he cannot testify as a lay witness either.

Answer to Question 8

(C) The Dead Man Act will have no effect on the admissibility of the purchaser's conversation with her brother because the dealer is not a protected party. A typical Dead Man Act provides that a party or person interested in the event, or her predecessor in interest, is incompetent to testify to a personal transaction or communication with a deceased when such testimony is offered against the representative or successor in interest of the deceased. Such statutes are designed to protect those who claim directly under the decedent from perjured claims. Here, the dealer is not a representative or successor in interest of the brother, such as an executor, administrator, heir, legatee, or devisee. Therefore, the dealer is not a protected party for purposes of a Dead Man Act. Because the testimony of the purchaser is not being offered against a representative or successor in interest of the decedent (her brother), the Dead Man Act is inapplicable. Regarding (A), it is true that the bar to competency created by a Dead Man Act applies only to civil cases. However, the mere fact that a civil action is involved will not trigger applicability of a Dead Man Act. As explained above, the absence of someone who is deemed to be a protected party will prevent a Dead Man Act from having any effect. Thus, (A) is incorrect. Regarding (B), it is true that the purchaser is an interested party (*i.e.*, she stands to gain or lose by the direct and immediate operation of a judgment in this case). Nevertheless, (B) is incorrect because a Dead Man Act requires not only an interested person but a protected party. As has been noted, the dealer is not a protected party. (D) is incorrect because it is based on the assumption that a Dead Man Act does not apply to civil cases. In fact, such statutes apply only to civil cases, and not to criminal cases.

Answer to Question 9

(B) The wife's statement was an admission, which is nonhearsay under the Federal Rules. An admission is a statement made or an act done that amounts to a prior acknowledgment by one of the parties to an action of one of the relevant facts. Although the statements would otherwise be hearsay, courts allow admissions by a party-opponent on the theory that if the party said or did something that now turns out to be inconsistent with her contentions at trial, she should be estopped from preventing the earlier statement's admission into evidence. Here, the statement that the plaintiff wants to testify to would ordinarily be barred as hearsay because it was made by an out-of-court declarant (the wife) and is being offered to prove the truth of what was stated; but because the wife is one of the defendants in this action, the statement will be admissible as an admission by a party-opponent. (A) is incorrect because a witness cannot be impeached before she testifies. The woman is the first witness of the plaintiffs, who present their case first, so the wife, a defendant, has not yet testified. If the woman were to testify after the wife, however, she could introduce the statement for impeachment purposes even if it were otherwise hearsay and inadmissible as substantive evidence. (C) is incorrect because lack of personal knowledge does not necessarily exclude a party's admissions. The wife can attempt to discredit her statement in her case-in-chief by explaining that she had no foundational knowledge when she made the statement, but she cannot bar its admission. (D) is incorrect because the admissibility of admissions by a party-opponent is not dependent on whether the party knew she was speaking to a potential trial opponent; it is irrelevant to whom the admission is made.

Answer to Question 10

(D) The mechanic's statement is admissible as an admission of a party-opponent. The Federal Rules treat admissions by a party-opponent as nonhearsay (whereas most states consider admissions to be an exception to the hearsay rule). An admission is a statement made or act done that amounts to a prior acknowledgment by one of the parties to an action of a relevant fact. Such a statement need not have been against interest at the time it was made. Some statements are considered admissions even if not made by the party against whom they are offered. One such vicarious admission is a statement by an agent concerning a matter within the scope of her agency, made during the existence of the agency relationship. [Fed. R. Evid. 801(d)(2)(D)] Here, the bystander's testimony as to the mechanic's statement is offered to prove the truth of the matter asserted therein; *i.e.*, that the mechanic had not properly fixed the brakes. Thus, the mechanic's statement would normally be considered hearsay. However, the statement was made while she was an agent of the body shop, and the statement concerned a matter within the scope of her agency (*i.e.*, whether she had properly performed the job for which she was employed by the body shop). Consequently, her statement may be introduced against the body shop as an admission by a party-opponent of negligence in the repair of the brakes. (A) is wrong because the statement is admissible against the body shop as a vicarious admission. (B) is wrong because it is irrelevant to the issue of whether the bystander's testimony is admissible. The fact that the victim failed to stop at the stop sign, and thus was negligent, will not prevent introduction of testimony that the mechanic admitted that she was negligent. (C) is wrong because the statement against interest exception to the hearsay rule is applicable only where the declarant is unavailable as a witness. Here, the mechanic is available as a witness. In addition, as noted above, a statement is admissible as an admission by a party-opponent even if not against interest when made. Thus, the statement would be admissible against the body shop even if it were not against its interest when made.

Answer to Question 11

(D) Evidence that the defendant had attached a new chair leg after the accident is inadmissible because, for public policy reasons, evidence of repairs or other precautionary measures made

after an injury is inadmissible to prove negligence or culpable conduct. [Fed. R. Evid. 407] The purpose of this rule is to encourage people to make such repairs. Here, the plaintiff is offering the evidence to prove the defendant's negligence in the original repair of the chair, by showing the need to attach a new leg. Thus, this evidence is inadmissible, and the objection should be sustained. (A) is wrong because, as discussed above, the evidence may not be used to show the defendant's negligence. Thus, the tendency of the evidence to prove negligence would constitute a reason for sustaining the objection, rather than overruling it. (B) is wrong because the defendant's state of mind is not at issue. In addition, the proffered evidence does not really tend to prove anything relative to her state of mind. (C) is wrong for two reasons: (i) Even if the act of replacing the chair leg constituted assertive conduct, it would not be hearsay. If the defendant's conduct was a statement, it would be an admission of a party-opponent, and thus it would be nonhearsay. (ii) The act of replacing the leg is not assertive conduct constituting a statement under the hearsay rule. Assertive conduct is conduct intended by the actor to be a substitute for words. The defendant was not trying to communicate anything by replacing the leg.

Answer to Question 12

(A) The driving record is inadmissible because it is being offered as character evidence. In a civil case, evidence of character to prove the conduct of a person in the litigated event is generally not admissible. The slight probative value of character is outweighed by the dangers of prejudice and distracting the jury from the main issues. Therefore, circumstantial use of prior behavior patterns for the purpose of drawing the inference that a person has a particular character trait and that, at the time and place in question, she probably acted in conformity with it is not permitted. Evidence of the defendant's good driving record is being offered to show that she is a careful driver and to raise the inference that, when the accident occurred, she was acting in conformity with that trait. This constitutes impermissible use of character evidence and is inadmissible. (B) is incorrect because evidence is not excludable because it is self-serving. Virtually all evidence is self-serving to the party offering it. (C) is incorrect because it is based on the mistaken assumption that character evidence is admissible. As stated above, character evidence is generally inadmissible in a civil case. It is admissible in a civil case only when a person's character is directly in issue (*e.g.*, in a defamation case). The defendant's character is not in issue, so the driving record is inadmissible. (D) is incorrect because this is not habit evidence. Habit describes one's regular response to a specific set of circumstances. Character describes one's disposition in respect to general traits. The defendant's good driving record describes a general behavior pattern of careful driving, rather than a regular response to a specific set of circumstances. Thus, this is character evidence, rather than habit evidence.

Answer to Question 13

(C) The testimony is admissible as evidence of habit. Habit describes a person's regular response to a repeated specific situation. Evidence of a person's habit is relevant to prove that the conduct of the person on a particular occasion was in conformity with that habit. [Fed. R. Evid. 406] According to the testimony, the defendant regularly fails to obey the stop sign at the intersection at which the collision occurred, and in fact, he regularly disregards any stop sign. This regular response to a specific circumstance constitutes a habit. Consequently, the testimony, which is evidence of this habit, is admissible, and so the defendant's objection should be overruled. (A) is incorrect because the best evidence rule is inapplicable to this question. Under the best evidence rule, where the terms of a writing are material, the original writing must be produced in proving the terms of the writing. Here, there is no writing material to the case; thus, the best evidence rule does not come into play. (B) is incorrect because the offered testimony is not character evidence.

Character describes one's disposition with respect to traits or general patterns of behavior. If the testimony were that the defendant is generally a careless driver, it would be inadmissible character evidence. The testimony, however, describes a repeated response by the defendant to repeated specific circumstances, which is admissible habit evidence. (D) is incorrect because the fact that an objection is self-serving does not form a basis for overruling (or sustaining) the objection. In a sense, all objections are self-serving to the party making them, just as the evidence to which an objection is made is self-serving to the party offering it.

Answer to Question 14

(D) The officer's testimony as to the victim's statements is admissible because the statements were made when the victim feared impending death and so they qualify under the dying declaration exception to the hearsay rule. Hearsay is a statement, other than one made by the declarant while testifying at the trial or hearing, offered in evidence to prove the truth of the matter asserted. [Fed. R. Evid. 801(c)] Upon appropriate objection, a hearsay statement to which no exception is applicable must be excluded. Under the dying declaration exception to the hearsay rule, a statement made by a now-unavailable declarant while believing her death was imminent that concerns the cause or circumstances of what she believed to be her impending death is admissible. [Fed. R. Evid. 804(b)(2)] The declarant need not actually die as a result of the circumstances giving rise to her belief of imminent death. Here, testimony as to the victim's statements would be hearsay, because they are out-of-court declarations offered for the truth of the matter asserted; *i.e.*, that the driver of the car that hit her ran a red light. However, these statements related to the circumstances of what the victim believed to be her impending death and the victim (who is now unavailable due to her death) made these statements under a fear of imminent death, as indicated by her condition and her statement "I know I'm going to die." Consequently, all of the elements of the dying declaration exception are present, and the officer's testimony as to the statements is admissible. (A) is incorrect because the declarant need not actually die as a result of the incident that gives rise to the statements. Indeed, the declarant need not die at all. All that is required is that the declarant be unavailable at the time the statements are offered. (B) is incorrect because it reflects the traditional view, which limited the admissibility of dying declarations to homicide cases, rather than the position of the Federal Rules, which allow such declarations in both civil cases and homicide prosecutions. (C) is incorrect because the statements do not qualify under the present sense impression exception to the hearsay rule. A present sense impression is a comment made by a person while perceiving an event that is not particularly shocking or exciting that concerns the event she is observing. Here, the victim's statements were made at least one half-hour after the accident. This time lapse between the accident and the statements means that such statements were not made either at the time the victim received a sense impression or immediately thereafter; thus, the present sense impression exception is inapplicable to these facts.

Answer to Question 15

(C) The witness's testimony regarding the speed of the cars should not be admitted because he has not been qualified as an expert in accident reconstruction. If the subject matter is such that scientific, technical, or other specialized knowledge is required to render an opinion, expert testimony is admissible and appropriate. In fact, in such an area, opinions by laypersons would not be permitted. To testify as an expert, a person must have special knowledge, skill, experience, training, or education sufficient to qualify him as an expert on the subject to which his testimony relates. The expert must possess reasonable certainty or probability regarding his opinion. Here, the witness is being asked to testify as to the speed of the cars, not based on actually viewing the cars while in motion (in which case lay opinion is often accepted), but on his observation of the spinning wheels after the accident. Determination of the speed of vehicles based upon observation of the spinning wheels of such vehicles after a collision would certainly call for the application of technical or specialized knowledge, thus making the subject matter appropriate for expert testimony. To testify as an expert, the witness must be qualified by virtue of having special knowledge or experience regarding accident reconstruction, which encompasses rendering opinions on the speed of vehicles based on the spinning of their wheels. The witness's experience as an auto mechanic would not suffice to establish him as an expert in accident reconstruction. Since he is not qualified as an expert, his opinion testimony as to the speed of the cars based upon his observation of the spinning wheels will not be admitted. (A) is incorrect because, as has been explained, the witness's personal opinion is not admissible without proper qualification as an expert. (B) is incorrect because, if the witness is not qualified as an expert, the fact that his opinion is supported by a proper factual basis (*i.e.*, personal observation) will not render that opinion admissible. (D) is incorrect because the presence of a witness at the scene of events to which his testimony relates need not be corroborated by another witness.

Answer to Question 16

(A) The court should strike the statement as unresponsive to any question asked. An unresponsive answer by a witness is subject to a motion to strike by examining counsel, but not by opposing counsel. Thus, examining counsel can adopt an unresponsive answer if it is not objectionable on some other ground. Here, the defense attorney asked the witness a question that was very specific and called for a specific answer (*i.e.*, whether there was broken glass on the pavement at the time and place of the accident). Thus, the witness should only have stated whether there was any glass. Her volunteered information regarding the speed of the cars bore no connection to the question posed and was totally unresponsive to that question (or to any other question asked). Therefore, the defense attorney, as examining counsel, is entitled to move to strike the statement, and this motion should be granted. (B) is incorrect for two reasons: (i) The witness's comment should be stricken as unresponsive regardless of whether she could have known how fast the cars were traveling. Even if she was highly experienced in estimating vehicle speeds, her comment was still not in response to any question. (ii) It is not true that the witness could not offer an opinion on the speed of the cars (if she were asked a question on this). A lay witness is permitted to estimate in miles per hour the speed of a moving vehicle if it is shown that she has some experience in observing the rate of speed of moving objects. Thus, if the witness can establish such experience, her statement would be admitted into evidence (providing it was made in response to a question posed by examining counsel). (C) is incorrect because it misstates the concept of "opening the door." One who introduces evidence on a particular subject thereby asserts its relevance and cannot complain, except on grounds other than relevance, if her adversary thereafter offers evidence on the same subject. This is what is meant by "opening the door." The defense attorney is not complaining of evidence being offered by opposing counsel. Rather, the motion to strike is directed at a totally unsolicited comment from a witness. (D) is incorrect because the prejudicial nature (or lack thereof) of an unresponsive answer does not form the basis for a motion to strike. It is true that, in most cases, an attorney would move to strike only if the witness has made a statement harmful to his case. However, as noted above, the option of moving to strike rests entirely with the examining attorney, and he may move to strike based solely on the unresponsive character of the statement, without showing any prejudice.

Answer to Question 17

(D) The state court is least likely to take judicial notice of the Australian law. Most state courts will not take judicial notice of the law of a foreign country. Note that foreign law is a legislative fact and thus would not be covered by Federal Rule 201, which covers only adjudicative facts, even if the case were in federal court. (A) and (B) are incorrect because they are notorious facts (*i.e.*, facts of common knowledge in the community), and (C) is incorrect because it is a manifest fact (*i.e.*, a fact capable of certain verification by resort to easily accessible sources of unquestionable accuracy). Both manifest and notorious facts are appropriate for judicial notice, and under the Federal Rules, notice ***must*** be taken of these facts if so requested by a party.

Answer to Question 18

(C) The witness's testimony is inadmissible because it is not probative of a material issue (*i.e.*, whether the plaintiff is a thief). Relevant evidence tends to prove or disprove a material fact in issue. Here, the testimony tends to prove that the plaintiff is brave and selfless, but it is not relevant as to the fact in issue, which is whether he is honest. (A) is incorrect because character evidence is admissible in a civil suit only when, as here, a person's character is directly in issue, but even when character is in issue, the evidence must be relevant to the particular character trait in issue; here, it is not relevant to the issue of the plaintiff being a thief. (B) is incorrect for the same reason; to be admissible, the evidence must be relevant. (D) is incorrect because proof of specific instances of a person's conduct is admissible when character is directly in issue. [Fed. R. Evid. 405(b)]

Set 2 Answer Sheet

1. Ⓐ Ⓑ Ⓒ Ⓓ
2. Ⓐ Ⓑ Ⓒ Ⓓ
3. Ⓐ Ⓑ Ⓒ Ⓓ
4. Ⓐ Ⓑ Ⓒ Ⓓ
5. Ⓐ Ⓑ Ⓒ Ⓓ
6. Ⓐ Ⓑ Ⓒ Ⓓ
7. Ⓐ Ⓑ Ⓒ Ⓓ
8. Ⓐ Ⓑ Ⓒ Ⓓ
9. Ⓐ Ⓑ Ⓒ Ⓓ
10. Ⓐ Ⓑ Ⓒ Ⓓ
11. Ⓐ Ⓑ Ⓒ Ⓓ
12. Ⓐ Ⓑ Ⓒ Ⓓ
13. Ⓐ Ⓑ Ⓒ Ⓓ
14. Ⓐ Ⓑ Ⓒ Ⓓ
15. Ⓐ Ⓑ Ⓒ Ⓓ
16. Ⓐ Ⓑ Ⓒ Ⓓ
17. Ⓐ Ⓑ Ⓒ Ⓓ
18. Ⓐ Ⓑ Ⓒ Ⓓ

EVIDENCE QUESTIONS - SET 2

Question 1

A plaintiff filed suit against a defendant, asserting that his German shepherd dog had bitten her without provocation. The defendant denied that his dog bit the plaintiff. At the trial, the plaintiff's attorney called the plaintiff to the stand. After asking her name and address, he asked only one further question: "Were you bitten by a German shepherd dog with a white forepaw?" The plaintiff replied in the affirmative and was dismissed from the stand. The plaintiff's attorney then called the defendant to the stand as an adverse witness. After ascertaining his name and address, the attorney asked only one question: "Do you own a German shepherd dog with a white forepaw?" Upon receiving an affirmative answer, the plaintiff's attorney rested. The defense attorney rose to cross-examine the defendant. Her first question was, "Has your German shepherd dog ever displayed anything other than a gentle disposition?" The plaintiff's attorney immediately objected to the question.

What would be the most likely ruling of the court on the objection?

(A) Sustained, because the defense attorney is improperly attempting to introduce character evidence when character has not been called into question.

(B) Sustained, because the defense attorney's question goes beyond the proper scope of cross-examination.

(C) Overruled, because the plaintiff brought up the dog in direct examination.

(D) Overruled, because the testimony sought is relevant and is otherwise admissible.

Question 2

A victim was struck by a car and taken to the emergency room ("ER") immediately after the accident. He was treated by an ER doctor and released 30 minutes later. The victim later went to his own physician for a follow-up. The victim filed suit against the driver of the car that struck him. At trial, the victim testified that he suffered from lower back pains and sought damages from the driver therefor. The defense attorney subpoenaed the ER doctor and put her on the witness stand. After a line of questioning establishing who the ER doctor is and where she is employed, the defense attorney asked the ER doctor to describe the victim's condition when she examined the victim immediately after the accident. The victim's attorney objected on the grounds that his client wished to invoke the jurisdiction's physician-patient privilege.

How should the court rule on the objection?

(A) Sustained, because the patient has the right to invoke the privilege.

(B) Sustained, because the ER doctor's testimony is irrelevant to the victim's present condition.

(C) Overruled, because the victim is suing for personal injuries.

(D) Overruled, because the ER doctor was not the victim's physician prior to the accident.

Question 3

The police arrested the defendant and charged him with murder. After the defendant's arrest, two police officers went to his home, where they found his wife. The victim had been killed on the night of March 13, and the officers asked the wife to give them the jacket that the defendant wore on the evening of March 13. Without saying a word, the wife handed the officers a jacket that was covered with bloodstains. Crime lab tests established that the blood on the jacket matched the victim's blood characteristics. At the defendant's trial for murder, the prosecution seeks to introduce the jacket into evidence.

Assuming the prosecution successfully establishes a foundation, if the defense objects to the jacket's admissibility, the court should rule that the jacket is:

(A) Admissible, as relevant evidence linking the defendant to the crime.

(B) Admissible, because the wife waived the marital privilege by handing over the jacket.

(C) Inadmissible, as hearsay not within any exception.

(D) Inadmissible, because of the privilege against self-incrimination.

Question 4

A plaintiff sues a defendant in a contract dispute. The plaintiff calls a witness to testify as to his personal knowledge of the agreement. The plaintiff now wants a second witness to testify as to her knowledge of the first witness's honesty. The defendant objects and the court sustains the objection.

The plaintiff may not bring the second witness to testify because:

(A) The first witness's credibility has not been questioned.

(B) It would be inadmissible under the hearsay rule.

(C) The second witness may not testify as to an opinion.

(D) Reputation evidence is generally inadmissible in civil cases.

Question 5

A commercial airliner crashed and the entire flight crew and most of the passengers were killed. The executor of the estate of one of the deceased passengers brought suit against the airline and the manufacturer of the aircraft. The Federal Aviation Administration ("FAA") is required by law to investigate the causes of all commercial airline crashes. The FAA prepared a report that indicated that the crash was caused by the pilot's negligence. The executor seeks to introduce the FAA report into evidence.

Should the judge admit the report into evidence?

(A) Yes, because it is a public record.

(B) Yes, but only for impeachment purposes.

(C) No, because it is hearsay, and the pilot is unavailable to testify.

(D) No, because of the best evidence rule.

Question 6

A driver was driving north on a local road when his car went out of control, crossed the center line, and struck the vehicle of another driver who was driving south on the same road. Immediately after the accident, an off-duty officer came by and photographed the accident scene for the police report. In a suit between the drivers, the plaintiff seeks to introduce the photograph taken by the officer. The officer is present in court but has not been called as a witness.

Is the photograph of the scene of the accident admissible?

(A) Yes, because the photograph was taken by a police officer who took the photo for an official report.

(B) Yes, because the officer is available to testify at trial.

(C) No, because a proper foundation has not been laid.

(D) No, because of the best evidence rule.

Question 7

A defendant was charged with the January 12 armed robbery of a grocery store in Texas. His defense is that he was not in Texas on the date of the armed robbery and thus he could not have committed the crime. To show that he was not in the area on January 12, the defendant wishes to introduce into evidence a letter he wrote to his sister stating, "I will see you in Vermont on January 12." The prosecution objects.

The letter is:

(A) Admissible, as evidence of the defendant's intent to go to Vermont on the date in question.

(B) Admissible, as a present sense impression.

(C) Inadmissible, because the statement in the letter is irrelevant.

(D) Inadmissible, because it is hearsay not within any recognized exception to the hearsay rule.

Question 8

A jurisdiction's arson statute has dropped the common law requirement that the intentional burning be of "the dwelling of another." Under this statute, the defendant was charged with first degree felony arson. The indictment alleged that the defendant burned down his own building to collect the insurance. At the trial, the defense called a witness who testified on direct examination that he was with the defendant at the place of business when the fire started and that some cleaning solvent caught fire and spread out of control. The witness testified that the ignition of the fire was purely accidental. The defense also introduced evidence that the witness is of good character. On cross-examination, the prosecutor asks the witness if he is being prosecuted for first degree felony arson in a separate trial for the burning of the same building. The defense lawyer objects.

Should the court allow the prosecutor's question?

(A) Yes, because the defense lawyer has introduced evidence tending to establish that the witness is a person of good character.

(B) Yes, because the question is appropriate to show bias or interest on the part of the witness.

(C) No, because the witness has not been convicted of the crime.

(D) No, because the question violates the witness's Fifth Amendment right to be protected from self-incrimination.

Question 9

In a tort case involving personal injury, a hospital orderly is called to the stand. There is some dispute as to whether the plaintiff ever lost consciousness. The plaintiff's attorney wishes to have the orderly, who was working in the hospital emergency room when the plaintiff was brought in, testify that the plaintiff was unconscious at the time she entered the emergency room.

Would such testimony be admissible over the defendant's objection?

(A) No, because the orderly is not an expert witness.

(B) No, because it impermissibly intrudes upon the province of the jury.

(C) Yes, because it is the best evidence.

(D) Yes, because it is proper opinion testimony by a lay witness.

Question 10

A plaintiff sues a defendant for injuries arising out of a collision between vehicles driven by the parties. The plaintiff alleges that the defendant ran a red light when he struck the plaintiff's vehicle in an intersection. The plaintiff wishes to call a witness to the stand who was near the intersection at the time of the accident. The witness is prepared to testify that the defendant offered to pay the witness $500 to testify falsely in the defendant's favor.

Such testimony should be:

(A) Admitted, as substantive evidence of the weakness of the defendant's case.

(B) Admitted, for the limited purpose of impeachment by specific bad conduct.

(C) Excluded, because it is irrelevant to the case.

(D) Excluded, because although relevant, such evidence is misleading and prejudicial.

Question 11

A plaintiff suffered injuries when her car was struck by the defendant's car. The police arrived on the scene and required the defendant to take a breathalyzer test. The defendant was cited for driving while intoxicated, tried in traffic court, and duly convicted. He received the maximum sentence for driving while intoxicated, which is 90 days' imprisonment in the county correctional facility. The plaintiff brings a civil action against the defendant, seeking compensation for her personal injuries. At the trial of the plaintiff's suit, the plaintiff's attorney offers a properly authenticated photocopy of the court judgment showing that the defendant was convicted of driving while intoxicated.

The evidence is:

(A) Admissible as a public record.

(B) Admissible as a final judgment offered to prove a fact essential to a point in controversy.

(C) Inadmissible, because the crime was punishable by imprisonment of at most 90 days.

(D) Inadmissible, because it is not the best evidence of the defendant's conviction.

Question 12

In a will contest action, the decedent's children, who were not provided for in his will, claim that the decedent was not of sound mind at the time of executing the will. The plaintiffs' attorney calls as a witness the neighbor of the decedent, who was present when the will was executed but did not attest to the will. The attorney asks the neighbor to describe the decedent's mental state at the time of the will's execution. The neighbor states that the decedent appeared to be senile. The defense objects.

How should the court rule?

(A) Sustained, because this is an opinion.

(B) Sustained, because the neighbor has not been qualified as an expert.

(C) Overruled, because this is proper opinion testimony.

(D) Overruled, because this is a present sense impression.

Question 13

At a victory party after a hard-fought election, the campaign director consumed several drinks. A campaign worker who had also been drinking took the director to her hotel room for a nightcap. They later had intercourse. The worker filed a complaint with the police, claiming that the director had intercourse with her against her will, and the director was charged with rape.

Which of the following is ***most likely*** to be admitted in the director's defense?

(A) The worker has a reputation in the community as being sexually promiscuous.

(B) Since the incident occurred, the worker has had sexual intercourse with two other campaign workers.

(C) Two years ago during the candidate's previous campaign, the worker maintained a sexual relationship with the former campaign director.

(D) The director and the worker had had consensual sex on two prior occasions.

Question 14

A defendant is charged with having been one of two men who robbed a bar and its patrons at gunpoint at 5:30 p.m. on December 16. The defendant calls a witness in his defense who testifies that she drove to the defendant's home at 10 a.m. on December 16 and picked up the defendant and his wife, then took them to a birthday party that lasted until 7 p.m. The prosecutor asks on cross-examination, "What is your relationship to the defendant's wife?" Defense counsel objects.

How should the court rule?

(A) Overruled, because the question attacks the witness's truth and veracity.

(B) Overruled, because the question is directed at discovering possible bias in the witness.

(C) Sustained, because the question seeks to elicit irrelevant information.

(D) Sustained, because the answer to the question would create prejudice that would outweigh its probative value.

Question 15

The defendant is on trial for assault with a deadly weapon. The sole prosecution witness is the victim, who testifies as to his version of the events leading up to and including the charged assault. The defense's first witness contradicts the victim's testimony that the defendant engaged in an unprovoked attack. The witness testifies that the victim pulled a knife on the defendant and that the defendant, in defending himself, wrested the knife away and accidentally stabbed the victim. The defense's next and final witness intends to testify that the defendant's reputation in the community for honesty and veracity is very good. Aware of the intended testimony, the prosecutor moves in limine to exclude it.

How should the court rule?

(A) For the state, because the defendant may not introduce evidence of his character to prove that he acted in conformity therewith.

(B) For the state, because the testimony as to the defendant's honesty and veracity is irrelevant.

(C) For the defendant, because a criminal defendant may put his character in issue.

(D) For the defendant, because a criminal defendant's reputation for honesty and veracity is always at issue.

Question 16

At the defendant's trial for rape, he calls a witness who testifies that she was on her patio barbecuing some hamburgers at the time of the charged rape and saw the assailant run from the victim's apartment. She further testifies that the person who ran from the victim's apartment was not the defendant.

On cross-examination by the prosecutor, to which of the following questions would a defense objection most likely be sustained?

(A) "Weren't you convicted of perjury 11 years ago?"

(B) "Weren't you under the influence of heroin at the time you were barbecuing those hamburgers?"

(C) "Haven't you and the defendant known each other since grammar school?"

(D) "Weren't you fired from your job last week because they discovered you were embezzling funds?"

Question 17

A plaintiff was injured when her car was struck broadside by a van driven by the defendant at an intersection controlled in all directions by stop signs. The plaintiff initiated a personal injury action against the defendant. At trial, the plaintiff calls a witness who testifies that he was standing on the sidewalk at the intersection at which the accident occurred and ran to see if the defendant was injured after the collision. He further testifies that as the ambulance was leaving with the plaintiff, the defendant offered him $500 in cash to testify falsely that the defendant had stopped at the stop sign before proceeding into the intersection.

Should this last statement have been admitted into evidence?

(A) No, it is hearsay not within an exception.

(B) No, it is not relevant to the issue of negligence.

(C) Yes, it is relevant and not hearsay.

(D) Yes, it is a declaration against interest by the defendant.

Question 18

A resort hotel provided parking valets to park cars of hotel guests. One valet had been working for the hotel for nine months when a well-known actor handed the valet the keys to his new limited edition sports car. The valet could not resist the urge to take the car for a spin. Unfortunately, he drove the car into a tree when he neglected to slow down for a curve. The valet received only minor injuries but the car was extensively damaged. The actor sued the hotel for damages on theories of respondeat superior and negligent hiring. At trial, the actor's counsel offers evidence that six months before the accident, but three months after the valet was hired, the hotel instituted new hiring procedures for all potential employees, including parking valets. Included in the new rules is a requirement that all persons must pass a thorough background check before being hired. The valet had been required only to have a valid driver's license when he was hired. In fact, he had an extensive record of traffic offenses at the time he was hired.

Is the evidence regarding the new employment requirements admissible?

(A) No, because it is irrelevant.

(B) No, because it is evidence of remedial measures.

(C) Yes, because it is evidence of the hotel's negligence.

(D) Yes, because it is evidence that the valet was incompetent.

EVIDENCE ANSWERS - SET 2

Answer to Question 1

(D) The plaintiff's attorney's objection should be overruled because the testimony sought is relevant and otherwise admissible. Evidence is relevant if it tends to make the existence of a material fact more probable or less probable than it would be without the evidence. The defendant's answer to his attorney's question will tend to make it either more or less probable that his was the dog that bit the plaintiff, and that the defendant had notice of the dog's propensity to bite, both of which are material facts. Thus, this evidence is relevant. Relevant evidence may be admitted unless there is some specific rule against its admission (*e.g.*, hearsay). Here, there is nothing to prohibit the admission of this evidence. (A) is wrong because character evidence relates to human traits. The rules concerning character are completely inapplicable to animals. (B) is wrong because the direct examination concerned the identity of the dog that bit the plaintiff, and this question bears on that issue. Cross-examination is proper on matters brought out on direct examination and the inferences naturally drawn from those matters. Here, the inference from the direct examination is that it was the defendant's dog that bit the plaintiff. On cross-examination, the defense attorney is trying to show that it was not the defendant's dog because his dog has a gentle disposition. (C) is wrong because the mere fact that the dog was brought up on direct examination does not mean that the defendant may be cross-examined on any subject relating to the dog (*e.g.*, how much he paid for his dog, what vet he goes to, etc.); the question must be relevant and concern a matter brought out on direct.

Answer to Question 2

(C) The court should overrule the objection because the victim is suing for personal injuries. A person cannot invoke the physician-patient privilege, which prohibits the doctor from divulging information acquired while attending a patient, where that person has put his physical condition in issue (*e.g.*, by suing for personal injuries). The victim is suing the driver for personal injuries allegedly incurred as a result of being struck by the car driven by the driver. Therefore, the victim himself has put his physical condition in issue and cannot avail himself of the physician-patient privilege. While it is true that the physician-patient privilege belongs to the patient (*i.e.*, the patient decides to claim or waive the privilege), (A) is incorrect because, as discussed above, the privilege does not apply in this situation. (B) is incorrect because the testimony of the ER doctor is relevant to the present condition of the victim. Evidence is relevant if it tends to make the existence of any fact that is of consequence to the determination of an action more probable than it would be without the evidence. [Fed. R. Evid. 401] The testimony of the ER doctor will indicate whether the physical condition of the victim immediately after the accident would suggest that the victim had suffered lower back injuries. For example, if the ER doctor's testimony would indicate the absence of a condition of injury at the time of the observation, then this would make it more probable than not that any current pain experienced by the victim was not caused by the accident. (D) is incorrect because the privilege does not require that the physician be the patient's personal physician prior to an accident or other cause of injury. It is sufficient if the physician attended the patient in a professional capacity, even if she has never seen the patient before. Thus, the fact that the ER doctor was not the victim's personal physician prior to the accident will not constitute a ground for overruling the objection.

Answer to Question 3

(A) The jacket is admissible as relevant evidence linking the defendant to the crime. Generally, all relevant evidence is admissible if offered in an unobjectionable form or manner (*i.e.*, if it is not

subject to an exclusionary rule). Clearly, the bloodstained jacket makes it more probably true that the defendant committed the murder than it would have been without the jacket; therefore, the jacket is relevant evidence. Since it is not subject to an exclusionary rule, the jacket is admissible. (B) is incorrect because neither spousal immunity nor the privilege for confidential marital communications applies in this situation. Spousal immunity prohibits the prosecution from compelling one spouse to testify against the other in a criminal proceeding; that clearly is not at issue here. The privilege for confidential marital communications protects communications (*i.e.*, expressions intended to convey a message) between spouses made in reliance on the intimacy of the marital relationship. Nothing in the facts suggests a confidential communication with respect to the jacket. No privilege applies to observations of a spouse's condition, actions, or conduct. Furthermore, this is a ***testimonial*** privilege and probably would not prevent the wife from handing over real evidence. (C) is incorrect because a jacket is not a "statement," and the hearsay rule excludes out-of-court statements that are offered for their truth. While the wife's conduct in handing over the jacket arguably may be a statement and perhaps hearsay, the jacket itself is not. (D) is incorrect because the jacket does not incriminate the wife, and she is the person who gave it to the police. More importantly, the privilege against self-incrimination applies only to testimony, not real evidence.

Answer to Question 4

(A) The plaintiff may not call the second witness to testify about the first witness's honesty because his credibility has not been questioned. Generally, a party may not bolster or accredit the testimony of her witness until the witness has been impeached. [Fed. R. Evid. 608(a)] Here, the defendant has not tried to cast any adverse reflection on the first witness's truthfulness (*i.e.*, he has not been impeached). Thus, the second witness's testimony as to her knowledge of the first witness's honesty will not be allowed. (B) is incorrect because these facts do not present a hearsay problem. Hearsay is an out-of-court statement offered in evidence to prove the truth of the matter asserted. [Fed. R. Evid. 801(c)] The second witness's testimony will relate only to her knowledge of the first witness's honesty; the second witness will not be testifying as to a statement made by an out-of-court declarant. Consequently, her testimony does not involve hearsay. (C) is incorrect because the credibility of a witness may be supported (if impeached) or attacked by opinion or reputation evidence regarding the witness's truthfulness. [Fed. R. Evid. 608(a)] Thus, if the first witness's honesty had been attacked by the defendant, the second witness could testify as to her opinion of the first witness's character for truthfulness or as to his reputation for honesty. (D) is incorrect because, although evidence of ***character*** to prove the conduct of a person in a litigated event is generally inadmissible in civil cases (except where character itself is in issue in the case), a witness's ***reputation*** for truthfulness is generally admissible for impeachment purposes in both civil and criminal cases.

Answer to Question 5

(A) The judge should admit the FAA report because it clearly qualifies for admissibility under the public records exception to the hearsay rule. Hearsay is an out-of-court statement offered in evidence to prove the truth of the matter asserted. [Fed. R. Evid. 801(c)] If a statement is hearsay, and no exception to the hearsay rule applies, the evidence must be excluded upon appropriate objection to its admission. [Fed. R. Evid. 802] Under the public records exception to the hearsay rule, records, reports, statements, or data compilations in any form of public offices or agencies are admissible if they set forth: (i) the activities of the office or agency; (ii) matters observed pursuant to a duty imposed by law (excluding police observations in criminal cases); or (iii) factual findings resulting from an investigation made pursuant to authority granted by law, in civil actions and against the government in criminal cases. [Fed. R. Evid. 803(8)] The source of information and other circumstances must not be such as to indicate its lack of trustworthiness. In this case, the factual finding of the report (*i.e.*, that the crash was caused by the pilot's negligence) is an out-of-court statement offered to prove the truth of the matter asserted, and thus would be hearsay. However, because these findings result from an investigation made pursuant to authority granted by law, and are contained in a report compiled by a public agency, the elements of the public records exception have been satisfied, and the report is admissible. (B) is incorrect because the FAA report is admissible as substantive, as well as impeachment, evidence. There is nothing in the Federal Rules limiting the use of this type of agency report to impeachment evidence. (C) is incorrect because the report is admissible as a hearsay exception (*i.e.*, a public record). Also, the pilot's unavailability to testify has no bearing on the admissibility of the report. (D) is incorrect because the best evidence rule is inapplicable to these facts. In proving the terms of a writing, where the terms are material, the best evidence rule requires that the original writing be produced. The rule applies where the writing is a legally operative or dispositive instrument such as a contract, deed, or will, or where the knowledge of a witness concerning a fact results from having read it in the document. The rule does not apply where the fact to be proved has an existence independent of any writing. Here, negligence of the pilot (which the executor seeks to prove) does not depend on the FAA report. The report may be very strong evidence of such negligence, but the pilot either was or was not negligent independent of the report. Thus, the report is not the type of legally operative instrument to which the best evidence rule applies. Also, the rule prohibits secondary evidence in the form of copies (unless the original is shown to be unavailable for some reason other than the serious misconduct of the proponent). The executor is not seeking to introduce a copy of the FAA report, but rather the report itself. Thus, even if the best evidence rule were applicable, there is no attempt here to offer prohibited secondary evidence of the contents of the document.

Answer to Question 6

(C) The photograph is not admissible because a proper foundation has not been laid. To be admissible, a photograph must be identified by a witness as a portrayal of certain facts relevant to the issue, and verified by the witness as a correct representation of those facts. It is sufficient if the identifying witness is familiar with the scene or object that is depicted. Here, the photograph taken by the officer must be verified by a witness who is familiar with the accident scene as an accurate representation of that scene. Absent such verification and identification (*i.e.*, a proper foundation), the photograph is not admissible. (A) is incorrect because a photograph's admissibility does not require that the photographer be a police officer or that the photograph be taken for an official report. The identity of the photographer and the purpose for which the photograph was taken are irrelevant to the issue of admissibility of the photograph. (B) is incorrect because the photographer need not be available to testify at trial. To authenticate a photograph, any person familiar with the scene may authenticate the photograph. (D) is incorrect because the best evidence rule (also known as the original documents rule) is inapplicable to these facts. The best evidence rule states that in proving the terms of a writing (including a photograph), where the terms are material, the original writing must be produced. Secondary evidence of the writing, such as oral testimony regarding the writing's contents, is permitted only after it has been shown that the original is unavailable for some reason other than the serious misconduct of the proponent. [Fed. R. Evid. 1002] Here, the admissibility of the original photograph is in issue. A copy of the photograph is not being offered. Thus, no problem arises under the best evidence rule.

Answer to Question 7

(A) The letter is admissible as evidence of the defendant's intent to go to Vermont on January 12. Hearsay is an out-of-court statement offered to prove the truth of the matter asserted. Upon objection, hearsay must be excluded unless it falls within a recognized exception to the rule. The letter is an out-of-court statement, and it is being offered to prove its truth; *i.e.*, that the defendant intended to be in Vermont on January 12. The letter, therefore, is hearsay. However, there is an exception for declarations of state of mind, including declarations of intent offered to show subsequent acts of the declarant; *i.e.*, a statement of intent to do something in the future is admitted as circumstantial evidence that the intent was carried out. This principle was established in the famous *Hillmon* case, which held that state of mind is admissible to show that the declarant acted in conformity with his expressed declaration. The defendant's letter was a statement of intent to go to Vermont on January 12 and is admissible as circumstantial evidence that he did so. (B) is wrong because it states the wrong hearsay exception. A present sense impression is a comment made concurrently with the perception of an event that is not particularly exciting concerning the event perceived. Clearly this exception does not apply to these facts because the defendant was not perceiving an event and describing it in his letter; rather, he was expressing his state of mind at the time he was writing. (C) is wrong because the letter is relevant. Evidence is relevant if it tends to make the existence of a material fact more probable than it would be without the evidence. The defendant's whereabouts on the day of the crime are certainly a fact of consequence to the determination of this action. The letter makes the fact that he was in Vermont on January 12 more probable than it would be without the letter; thus, the letter is relevant. (D) is wrong because the letter falls within the state of mind exception to the hearsay rule (*see* above).

Answer to Question 8

(B) The court should allow the prosecutor's question because it is appropriate to show bias or interest on the part of the witness. Evidence that a witness is biased or has an interest in the outcome of the case tends to show that the witness has a motive to lie. Bias or adverse interest can be proved by cross-examination or extrinsic evidence, and in some cases, both. Here, the fact that the witness is being prosecuted for the same crime tends to show that he has a motive to lie in saying that the fire started accidentally. Thus, it is proper impeachment for the prosecutor to cross-examine the witness about his own prosecution. (A) is wrong because all witnesses are subject to impeachment, and evidence (including character evidence) that bears on truthfulness is always admissible (although the means of proof may be restricted). This choice confuses the basis for the prosecution's introduction of substantive character evidence against a defendant in a criminal trial with valid impeachment of a witness for bias or interest. (C) is wrong because conviction of a crime is not a requisite for introduction of evidence showing bias or interest. A felony conviction or a conviction for a crime involving dishonesty is an entirely separate method of impeachment. (D) is wrong for two reasons: (i) the answer to the question could in no way incriminate the witness; and (ii) even if the answer could tie the witness to the commission of the crime, he could invoke the privilege to refuse to answer—the question itself would not be objectionable.

Answer to Question 9

(D) The orderly's testimony should be admitted because it is proper opinion testimony by a lay witness. Where an event is likely to be perceived as a whole impression, rather than as more specific components, opinions by lay witnesses are generally admitted. Lay opinion testimony is admissible when: (i) it is rationally based on the perception of the witness; (ii) it is helpful to a clear understanding of his testimony or to the determination of a fact in issue; and (iii) it is not based on scientific, technical, or other specialized knowledge. [Fed. R. Evid. 701] One matter about which a lay witness may testify is the general appearance or condition of a person. In contrast, expert opinion testimony is called for when the subject matter is such that technical or other specialized knowledge will assist the jury in understanding the evidence or determining a fact in issue. Here, the orderly is not being asked to describe specific injuries that may have been incurred by the plaintiff; that would more appropriately be left to the specialized knowledge of an expert. Rather, he is being asked to testify as to the plaintiff's general condition (*i.e.*, whether she was conscious or unconscious). Having been on duty in the emergency room when the plaintiff was brought in, the orderly had the opportunity to observe the plaintiff. Thus, he is in a position to offer an opinion as to the plaintiff's unconscious condition based on his own perception. It is easier for the orderly to express his testimony this way than to go into detail about specific manifestations of the plaintiff's condition. Also, this opinion aids in the determination of a disputed factual issue (*i.e.*, whether the plaintiff ever lost consciousness). Therefore, the orderly's testimony is admissible as proper lay opinion testimony. (A) is wrong because, as noted above, this testimony does not relate to a matter the understanding of which requires resort to specialized knowledge. Status as an expert is not necessary to be able to state whether a person was conscious. Therefore, the orderly's status as a nonexpert constitutes no basis for the exclusion of his testimony. (B) is wrong because, if anything, the testimony will assist the jury, rather than intrude upon its province. Generally, the jury is to make fact determinations. The orderly's opinion testimony is helpful to the determination of a disputed fact. The jury relies on such testimony to enable it to reach a conclusion as to whether the plaintiff was unconscious. (C) is wrong because the best evidence rule does not apply to these facts. In proving the terms of a writing, where its terms are material, the best evidence rule requires that the original writing be produced. This question does not involve a writing of any type. The orderly would simply be testifying to what he personally observed. Thus, the best evidence rule does not come into play.

Answer to Question 10

(A) Testimony regarding the defendant's attempt to bribe the witness is admissible as substantive evidence against the defendant. An admission is a statement made or act done that amounts to a prior acknowledgment by one of the parties of one of the relevant facts. Under the Federal Rules, admissions by parties are not hearsay. Various kinds of conduct, including attempts to bribe witnesses, may be held to manifest an awareness of liability or guilt. Since the defendant's liability is the issue (*i.e.*, a relevant fact) in the case, his attempt to bribe the witness is admissible as an admission of a party-opponent. (B) is wrong because, as discussed above, the offer is also admissible as an admission, and thus is not limited to impeachment. Moreover, the witness's testimony would not be admissible as evidence of a specific instance of misconduct to impeach the defendant. A specific act of misconduct can be elicited only on cross-examination; extrinsic evidence is not permitted. The facts do not even indicate that the defendant has testified. (C) is wrong because the offer to bribe the witness is relevant. Evidence is relevant if it tends to make the existence of a fact of consequence to the action more probable than it would be without the evidence. Evidence that the defendant tried to bribe a witness to testify falsely makes it more probable that the accident was his fault; thus, it is relevant. (D) is wrong because the fact that relevant evidence is misleading or prejudicial is not a sufficient reason, by itself, to exclude the evidence. Under Federal Rule 403, the judge has discretion to exclude otherwise admissible, relevant evidence if its probative value is substantially outweighed by the danger of unfair prejudice, confusion of the issues, misleading the jury, or by considerations of undue delay, waste of time, or needless presentation of cumulative evidence. Here, the choice states only that the evidence is misleading and prejudicial; it does not state that the probative value of the evidence is substantially outweighed by these facts. Furthermore, bribing a witness is highly probative of guilt, so it is unlikely to be misleading. Although the evidence is prejudicial, it is not at all clear that the prejudice would be unfair since there are few reasons other than guilt for bribing a witness.

Answer to Question 11

(C) The evidence of the defendant's conviction is inadmissible to prove that the defendant was intoxicated because the crime was punishable by imprisonment of at most 90 days. Despite the fact that copies of judgments are hearsay (because they are out-of-court statements used to prove the truth of the matter asserted), the Federal Rules of Evidence provide that judgments of felony convictions are admissible in both criminal and civil actions to prove any fact essential to the judgment. The Rules define felony convictions as crimes punishable by death or imprisonment in excess of one year. [Fed. R. Evid. 803(22)] Here, the crime for which the defendant was convicted carries a maximum term of imprisonment of 90 days. Thus, the defendant's conviction is not a felony conviction for purposes of the Federal Rule, and the conviction is inadmissible hearsay as proof of the fact asserted (*i.e.*, that the defendant was driving his car while intoxicated when he struck the plaintiff's car). (A) is incorrect because the copy of the judgment of conviction is not a record, report, statement, or data compilation of a public office or agency, setting forth: (i) the activities of the office or agency, (ii) matters observed pursuant to a duty imposed by law, or (iii) factual findings resulting from an investigation made pursuant to authority granted by law. Therefore, the copy of the judgment is not deemed to be a public record for purposes of the hearsay exception for public records and reports. (B) is incorrect because a final judgment offered to prove a fact essential to a point in controversy is admissible under the Federal Rules only if the judgment is a felony conviction. As noted above, the defendant's conviction is not a felony conviction. (D) is incorrect because a properly authenticated copy of a court judgment would be the best evidence of the defendant's conviction. The best evidence rule states that, in proving the terms of a writing, where the terms are material, the original writing must be produced. [Fed. R. Evid. 1002] One class of situations to which the rule applies is that in which the writing is a legally operative or dispositive instrument such as a contract, deed, will, or judgment. Such writings are viewed as essential repositories of the facts recorded therein, and as such are within the rule. Furthermore, duplicates (*e.g.*, photocopies) are admissible the same as originals, unless: (i) the authenticity of the original is challenged; or (ii) circumstances exist that would render it unfair to admit the duplicate in place of the original. [Fed. R. Evid. 1003] Here, a properly authenticated photocopy of the judgment of conviction would be as admissible as the original judgment for purposes of proving that such a judgment has been entered. Therefore, there is no violation of the best evidence rule.

Answer to Question 12

(C) The objection should be overruled because the neighbor's testimony is proper opinion testimony. Although opinions by lay witnesses are generally inadmissible, they may be admitted when an event is likely to be perceived as a whole impression rather than as more specific components. Under the Federal Rules, lay opinion testimony is admissible when: (i) it is rationally based on the perception of the witness; (ii) it is helpful to a clear understanding of her testimony or to the determination of a fact in issue; and (iii) it is not based on scientific, technical, or other specialized knowledge. [Fed. R. Evid. 701] The witness must have had the opportunity to observe the event that forms the basis of her opinion. A witness who has seen a person and is able to describe that person's actions, words, or conduct may express an opinion as to whether that person was lucid or senile. Here, the neighbor had an opportunity to personally observe the decedent and his words and conduct at the time of the will's execution. Her opinion that the decedent appeared senile is helpful to an understanding of her testimony because it is easier and clearer to simply state that the decedent appeared senile than to describe his actions. Also, the neighbor's opinion is helpful to the determination of a fact in issue—*i.e.*, the decedent's mental state at the time of executing his will. Thus, the neighbor's opinion as to the decedent's mental state is proper lay opinion testimony, and the objection by the defense should be overruled. (A) is incorrect because, as has been explained, lay opinion testimony as to whether or not a person who has been observed by the witness was senile is admissible. (B) is incorrect because expert testimony is appropriate and necessary only when the subject matter of testimony is such that scientific, technical, or other specialized knowledge would assist the finder of fact in understanding the evidence or determining a fact in issue. [Fed. R. Evid. 702] A determination as to whether a person was senile can easily be based on observation of that person by a layperson and does not require any technical or specialized knowledge. Therefore, the neighbor's status as an expert or nonexpert has no bearing on the admissibility of her testimony. (D) is incorrect because it states an exception to the hearsay rule, and there is no hearsay problem here. Hearsay is an out-of-court statement offered to prove the truth of the matter asserted. The neighbor is not testifying to an out-of-court statement made by herself or anyone else, but rather is testifying as to what she observed concerning the decedent's mental state.

Answer to Question 13

(D) Evidence of prior consensual sexual relations between the director and the worker is most likely admissible. Although Federal Rule 412 generally excludes evidence of an alleged victim's sexual behavior, evidence of specific instances of sexual conduct between the alleged victim and the accused may be admitted to show consent. Thus, if the director raises consent as a defense to the rape charge, evidence of his previous consensual sexual encounters with the worker is admissible. (A) is incorrect because it presents evidence that Federal Rule 412 specifically intends to exclude; *i.e.*, evidence of the alleged victim's sexual behavior. The Federal Rules also contain an exception for specific instances of the alleged victim's sexual conduct tending to show that someone other than the accused was the source of semen, injury, or other physical evidence. (B) does not fit this exception because the worker had intercourse with two other workers after the incident with the director occurred. Likewise, (C) is not likely to fit this exception as the workers' relationship with the previous campaign director occurred two years ago, and is therefore probably not helpful in explaining the presence of physical evidence.

Answer to Question 14

(B) The prosecutor's question is aimed at discovering bias, which tends to show that the witness has a motive to lie. Impeachment involves the casting of an adverse reflection on the veracity of a witness, and it may take several forms. Evidence that a witness is biased tends to show that she has a motive to lie, and is thus a well-recognized method of impeachment. Inferences of bias may be shown by evidence of family or other relationship. Here, the prosecutor is attempting to show that, due to a family relationship or friendship with the defendant's wife, the witness may be biased and would thus have a motive to lie on behalf of the defendant. Therefore, the prosecutor is engaging in an accepted method of impeachment. (A) correctly states that the prosecutor's question attacks the witness's truth and veracity. However, not all methods of attacking a witness's truth and veracity are admissible. (B) is a better answer than (A) because it identifies the specific method of impeachment that the cross-examiner is using. (C) is incorrect because evidence that tends to prove or disprove the credibility of a witness is relevant. The information sought to be elicited by the prosecutor's question will reflect on a possible motive that the witness may have to lie. Therefore, such information is relevant. (D) incorrectly states that the answer to the prosecutor's question would create prejudice that would outweigh its probative value. Under Federal Rule 403, evidence may be excluded if its probative value is substantially outweighed by the danger of unfair prejudice, confusion of the issues, or misleading the jury. While any material evidence introduced by a party will probably be prejudicial to the adverse party's case, it is only

unfair prejudice (*i.e.*, suggesting a decision on an improper basis) that may be excluded under this rule. Here, the answer to the prosecutor's question would clarify the matter of whether the witness had a motive to lie. This would not be unfairly prejudicial because it would tend to make the witness's testimony as to the defendant's whereabouts at the time of the alleged crime more or less believable, which is the proper basis on which the trier of fact should accept or reject her testimony.

Answer to Question 15

(B) The court should rule for the state. Since the defendant did not testify, and he is charged with a crime of violence, his character for honesty and veracity is not at issue, and the proffered evidence is irrelevant. Thus, (C) is incorrect. A criminal defendant may offer evidence of character relevant to the charges, and so (A) is incorrect. (D) is a misstatement of law.

Answer to Question 16

(A) Federal Rule 609 permits the prosecution to inquire into prior convictions of crimes requiring proof or admission of dishonesty or false statement if they are less than 10 years old. Since the conviction in (A) is more than 10 years old, it would be subject to objection as being too remote. (B) relates to the witness's ability to perceive and would be a legitimate question on cross-examination. (C) shows a possible bias on the part of the witness, which is an acceptable method of impeachment. (D) relates to a prior bad act that shows dishonesty. Such acts may be asked about on cross-examination of the witness.

Answer to Question 17

(C) An admission is a statement made, or an act done, that amounts to a prior acknowledgment by one of the parties of one of the relevant facts. Various kinds of conduct, including attempts to bribe witnesses, may be held to manifest awareness of liability or guilt. The defendant's attempt to bribe the witness would be considered an admission by conduct. Under the Federal Rules, an admission is not considered hearsay. Alternatively, the defendant's conduct could be classified as conduct not intended as an assertion. Such conduct is not considered hearsay under the rules. Thus, (A) is clearly wrong. (B) is wrong. The evidence helps establish that the defendant believed that he acted negligently. (D) is wrong. Since admissions are not hearsay, the evidence would not come in under an exception to the hearsay rule. Also, declarations against interest can only be used when the declarant is unavailable.

Answer to Question 18

(C) The evidence tends to show that the hotel was not acting prudently when it hired the valet, an employee who damaged a guest's car; thus (A) is wrong. (B) is not a good answer because only ***subsequent*** remedial measures (*i.e.*, those taken after the injury to the plaintiff occurred) may not be proven as evidence of negligence. (D) is not accurate—the evidence does not show that the valet was incompetent, but rather that the hotel did not investigate his competence when he was hired, an issue related to the actor's negligent hiring claim.

Set 3 Answer Sheet

1. Ⓐ Ⓑ Ⓒ Ⓓ
2. Ⓐ Ⓑ Ⓒ Ⓓ
3. Ⓐ Ⓑ Ⓒ Ⓓ
4. Ⓐ Ⓑ Ⓒ Ⓓ
5. Ⓐ Ⓑ Ⓒ Ⓓ
6. Ⓐ Ⓑ Ⓒ Ⓓ
7. Ⓐ Ⓑ Ⓒ Ⓓ
8. Ⓐ Ⓑ Ⓒ Ⓓ
9. Ⓐ Ⓑ Ⓒ Ⓓ
10. Ⓐ Ⓑ Ⓒ Ⓓ
11. Ⓐ Ⓑ Ⓒ Ⓓ
12. Ⓐ Ⓑ Ⓒ Ⓓ
13. Ⓐ Ⓑ Ⓒ Ⓓ
14. Ⓐ Ⓑ Ⓒ Ⓓ
15. Ⓐ Ⓑ Ⓒ Ⓓ
16. Ⓐ Ⓑ Ⓒ Ⓓ
17. Ⓐ Ⓑ Ⓒ Ⓓ
18. Ⓐ Ⓑ Ⓒ Ⓓ

EVIDENCE QUESTIONS - SET 3

Question 1

A plaintiff and a defendant were involved in a two-car collision. The defendant was indicted for drunken driving, a crime that carries a maximum sentence of two years' imprisonment. A witness to the collision testified before the grand jury. The defendant pled guilty to the charge of drunken driving and was fined $500. After the criminal charge was disposed of, the plaintiff sued the defendant for negligence and sought personal injury damages. In the negligence action against the defendant, the witness testified for the plaintiff that the defendant was on the wrong side of the highway at the time of the collision. On cross-examination, the defendant seeks to question the witness about his sworn grand jury statement that the defendant was driving normally at the time of the accident.

Upon proper objection, the court should rule the witness's statement before the grand jury:

(A) Admissible for impeachment only.

(B) Admissible as substantive evidence only.

(C) Admissible for impeachment and as substantive evidence.

(D) Inadmissible, because it is hearsay not within any exception.

Question 2

A defendant was arrested for the felony of aggravated battery against a victim. A witness testified before a grand jury that the defendant was with her at a fundraiser at the time the victim claims she was beaten by the defendant. The grand jury refused to indict the defendant. The victim then sued the defendant for personal injuries. The witness could not be located. A second witness, who also attended the fundraiser, was produced and gave alibi testimony similar to that given by the first witness before the grand jury. The defendant's attorney offers as evidence, without prior notice to the victim's attorney, a properly authenticated transcript of the testimony given earlier by the first witness before the grand jury.

The transcript of the grand jury testimony is:

(A) Admissible under the former testimony exception to the rule against hearsay.

(B) Admissible nonhearsay.

(C) Inadmissible to rehabilitate the testimony of the second witness because he has not been impeached by a charge of recent fabrication or improper motive.

(D) Inadmissible hearsay.

Question 3

A defendant was charged with arson (a felony) of an antique shop. Only one corner of the shop was damaged before the fire was extinguished. Under a plea agreement, the defendant pled guilty and received a suspended sentence. Because the owner of the shop had not yet insured a recently acquired 400-year-old refectory table that was destroyed by the fire, he sued the defendant for damages. At trial, the owner offers the properly authenticated record of the defendant's conviction for arson.

The record should be:

(A) Admitted as proof of the defendant's character in order to infer liability.

(B) Admitted as proof that the defendant set the fire.

(C) Excluded, because the conviction was not the result of a trial.

(D) Excluded, because it is hearsay not within any exception.

Question 4

In a criminal trial, the prosecution called an expert witness to the stand. The prosecutor conducted a direct examination of the witness that lasted one-half hour. The defense attorney cross-examined the witness for three days and told the court that he planned to spend at least another day in cross-examination to develop testimony brought up on direct examination. The prosecutor moved that the cross-examination be terminated by the court.

May the court approve the prosecutor's motion?

(A) Yes, unless the testimony is relevant.

(B) Yes, because the defendant had an adequate opportunity for meaningful cross-examination.

(C) No, because the testimony relates to the subject matter of direct.

(D) No, because in a criminal trial the consideration of judicial economy is outweighed by due process.

Question 5

A plaintiff sued a defendant and his employer for personal injuries. The plaintiff claimed that she was struck on the head by a wrench dropped by the defendant from a high scaffold, on which the defendant was working in the course of a construction project. To prove that it was the defendant who dropped the wrench, the plaintiff offers the wrench itself as evidence: The wrench bears the brand name "Craftsman" on the handle, and other evidence shows that the wrenches used by the defendant on the job are "Craftsman" brand wrenches.

Is the wrench admissible?

(A) No, because but for the word "Craftsman" the wrench would be irrelevant, and the word "Craftsman" is inadmissible hearsay.

(B) No, because the wrench is irrelevant as it fails to show that it is more likely than not that the defendant was the person who dropped it.

(C) Yes, because the wrench is relevant direct evidence that it was the defendant who dropped the wrench and is not hearsay.

(D) Yes, because the wrench is relevant circumstantial evidence that it was the defendant who dropped the wrench and is not hearsay.

Question 6

A plaintiff sued a chimney sweeping company for personal injury and property damages resulting from an explosion in her chimney the evening after the company had cleaned it. The explosion, which occurred when the plaintiff lit a fire in the fireplace, caused minor damage to the chimney, roof, and to the plaintiff, who was hit by falling bricks. As evidence that she assumed the risk of injury, the company offers to have its foreman testify that he had told the plaintiff not to use the fireplace for 24 hours to allow certain chemicals to evaporate, and that the plaintiff had replied that she understood.

Is the foreman's proposed testimony hearsay?

(A) No, because the declarant is testifying as a witness at the hearing.

(B) No, because the statement is not offered for its truth.

(C) Yes, but it should be admitted as part of the res gestae.

(D) Yes, but it should be admitted under the present state of mind exception to the hearsay rule.

Question 7

A 54-year-old employee filed an employment age discrimination suit against a corporation, alleging that its personnel director had improperly terminated his employment. In defense, the corporation presents a written report summarizing a meeting between the personnel director and the employee that was prepared directly after the meeting and placed in the employee's personnel file, and that contains several damaging admissions by the employee.

Which of the following is ***not*** among the foundational facts the corporation will have to establish if it wants to have the report admitted under the past recollection recorded exception to the hearsay rule?

(A) That the report was written while the meeting was fresh in the memory of the personnel director.

(B) That the report accurately records what was said by the employee.

(C) That the report was written by the personnel director or adopted by her.

(D) That the personnel director is not available and cannot be called as a witness at trial.

Question 8

A plaintiff sued a defendant for damages suffered when a load of bricks fell off the defendant's truck directly in front of the plaintiff while she was driving on a highway. The plaintiff charged that the defendant was negligent in supplying his truck with a defective load chain clamp, which helped tie the load to the bed of the truck, and in failing to secure the load properly on the truck. The plaintiff calls a witness who testifies that he was formerly employed as a truck driver and is an acquaintance of the defendant. The witness further testifies that immediately prior to the accident he had coffee with the defendant at a cafe, and mentioned to the defendant that the tie chains holding the load of bricks looked kind of loose.

Assuming proper objection by the defendant's attorney, such testimony is:

(A) Admissible under an exception to the hearsay rule.

(B) Admissible nonhearsay.

(C) Inadmissible hearsay.

(D) Inadmissible opinion evidence.

Question 9

A plaintiff sued a city for damages to his motorcycle that occurred when a bolt on the brush of a street sweeper came loose, allowing the brush to become detached and roll onto his driveway. The city has a rule that any employees must file an accident report with the city within 12 hours of any accident. At trial, counsel for the plaintiff demands that the city produce the original handwritten report of the street sweeper operator, which the city does. The plaintiff then calls the operator to the stand as an adverse witness. The operator identifies the report as his and testifies to the existence of the rule requiring such reports and that he routinely fills them out only a few minutes after the accident. However, the operator does not recall all the details in his report. Because the report states that a faulty bumper brush bolt caused the accident, the plaintiff offers it into evidence. The city objects on appropriate grounds.

The report is:

(A) Admissible as nonhearsay.

(B) Admissible, because the operator cannot remember the details in the report.

(C) Inadmissible, because the record was not prepared in the course of the city's primary business.

(D) Inadmissible, because only statements of fact in business records are admissible, and the conclusion that the bolt was "faulty" and that it "caused" the accident are not statements of fact.

Question 10

A victim was raped and beaten by the defendant. The victim called the police and provided an accurate description of the defendant, who was arrested shortly thereafter and charged with the attack. After the attack, the victim was examined by her physician. When the defendant came to trial, the victim refused to cooperate with the prosecution and steadfastly refused to testify against the defendant. To establish that

the victim was raped and beaten, the prosecution put the physician on the stand, planning to have him testify as to the victim's physical condition after the attack and as to how she said she received her injuries. The victim wishes to prevent the physician from so testifying by invoking the jurisdiction's physician-patient privilege, which applies to both civil and criminal proceedings.

Under which of the following circumstances is the court ***least*** likely to allow the victim to use the physician-patient privilege to keep the physician from testifying?

(A) The victim visited the physician for the purpose of diagnosis and treatment, and her statements to him were made for that purpose.

(B) The victim is married to the defendant.

(C) The victim's statements to the physician were made public by the physician in a previous statement to the police.

(D) At the time the victim visited the physician, she knew that his license to practice medicine was revoked two years prior to her visit.

Question 11

A plaintiff sued a defendant to rescind a contract for fraud and damages. The plaintiff alleged in his complaint that, pursuant to a written contract, he had purchased a business from the defendant in reliance on the defendant's fraudulent representations as to the value of the business's inventory and cash on hand. At trial, without objection, the plaintiff introduced the written contract, which included recitals of facts containing the statement: "the company is solvent, with inventory and cash assets valued at $200,000" and a boilerplate integration clause (*i.e.*, "no other representations have been made," etc.). The plaintiff proposes to testify that during negotiations the defendant said the real value of the business in cash and inventory was about $500,000, but that tax laws made it inexpedient to recite the real value. The defendant objects.

The offered evidence is:

(A) Inadmissible, as violative of the parol evidence rule.

(B) Inadmissible, because it is hearsay.

(C) Admissible hearsay, unaffected by the parol evidence rule.

(D) Admissible, because it is neither hearsay nor violative of the parol evidence rule.

Question 12

A defendant is sued by his insurance company for filing a false claim. The insurance company seeks recovery of payment made to the defendant for the alleged theft of his car. At trial, the insurance company seeks to have the defendant's ex-wife testify that he told her that he had really given the car to a friend. The defendant objects on the ground of privilege.

The ex-wife:

(A) Can be called and can testify against the defendant over the objection.

(B) Can be called and must testify because the privilege applies only in criminal cases.

(C) Cannot be directed to testify against the defendant over his objection if the facts were told to her in confidence during the marriage.

(D) Cannot be called as a witness at all over the defendant's objection.

Question 13

The beneficiaries of a trust filed suit to remove the trustee and recover damages, alleging that the trustee improvidently invested trust funds. At trial, the trustee calls a financial expert to testify in his defense. To qualify the witness as an expert, the trustee asks the witness about her education, training, and experience in finance. The witness testifies that she has received a B.A. and Ph.D. in economics and

business finance. On cross-examination concerning qualifications, the beneficiaries' attorney asks, "Isn't it a fact that you flunked out of college at the end of your freshman year?" to which the witness replies, "No." The beneficiaries' attorney then offers the registrar of the college that the witness attended to introduce a transcript of the college's records to show that the witness studied only one year and was awarded no degrees. The trustee objects.

Is the transcript admissible?

(A) Yes, but the judge should instruct the jury that they are to disregard the witness's testimony if they conclude that she is not an expert.

(B) Yes, but the judge should allow the witness to testify further only if he believes the witness to be an expert.

(C) No, because denying the witness's claim that she obtained a B.A. and Ph.D. is impeachment on a collateral matter, which cannot be proved by extrinsic evidence.

(D) No, because whether the witness was awarded a B.A. and Ph.D. is irrelevant to the main issues.

Question 14

The owner of a small business was injured in a traffic accident. A month after the accident, the owner asked an employee to take a photograph of the intersection where the accident occurred. The employee took the photograph and gave it to the owner, who in turn gave it to his lawyer. The lawyer wishes to introduce the photograph into evidence at trial of the owner's lawsuit against the defendant. The lawyer plans to have the employee testify that he took the photograph. The lawyer also plans to call a witness who lives in the neighborhood of the accident scene and arrived at the intersection shortly after the accident occurred. The witness is willing to testify that the scene in the photograph is in fact the intersection where the accident happened.

Whose testimony is necessary to introduce the photograph into evidence?

(A) The employee's testimony is necessary and the witness's is unnecessary.

(B) The witness's testimony is necessary and the employee's is unnecessary.

(C) The testimonies of both the employee and the witness are necessary.

(D) The picture is inadmissible.

Question 15

While working on a construction project, a plaintiff was injured when a heavy object struck his knee. Although the plaintiff was fully compensated for his injuries at the time of the incident, he now seeks disability payments from the construction company because he has developed arthritis in the same knee. The construction company claims that the arthritis has nothing to do with the plaintiff's on-the-job injury and refuses to pay him disability money. The plaintiff sues. A doctor takes the stand to testify for the plaintiff. He is qualified as an expert witness and during direct examination states that in his opinion the blow to the plaintiff's knee caused his arthritis. On cross-examination, the construction company's attorney produces a treatise on arthritis and asks the doctor if the treatise is considered to be authoritative. The doctor responds that the treatise is a standard authority in the field, but that he did not rely on it in forming his professional opinion regarding the plaintiff's condition. The attorney then seeks to introduce into evidence a statement in the treatise that "the idea that arthritis can be caused by a single traumatic event is purely folklore, although it is widely believed by the ignorant who have no scientific basis for their beliefs." The plaintiff's attorney objects.

The court should find the statement from the treatise:

(A) Admissible, but only for the purpose of impeaching the doctor's testimony.

(B) Admissible, but only as substantive evidence.

(C) Admissible, both as substantive evidence and for purposes of impeaching the doctor.

(D) Inadmissible.

Question 16

In the prosecution of the defendant for bank robbery, it is established that as the robber came out of the bank, he was seen entering a car by a group of people, including a witness and his friend. The witness is prepared to testify that as the car drove off, someone yelled, "Get that number," whereupon the friend screamed, "I've got it. The number is 07771!"

The witness's testimony is:

(A) Admissible only if the friend fails or refuses to testify to such facts, because the friend's testimony would be the best evidence thereof.

(B) Admissible hearsay.

(C) Inadmissible hearsay.

(D) Inadmissible, because there is no proper foundation or identification of the hearsay declarant.

Question 17

A defendant is on trial for manslaughter after he hit a victim in a bar, causing the victim to fall and hit his head on the marble bar top. The defendant claims that he hit the victim in self-defense after the victim lunged at him with a knife. During the prosecution's case, a witness testifies that she heard the victim's friend shout at the defendant, "You just killed a helpless man!" A defense witness is called to testify that he was there and does not remember hearing the victim's friend say anything.

The defense witness's testimony is:

(A) Inadmissible as irrelevant to any issue in the case.

(B) Proper impeachment of the prosecution's witness.

(C) Improper impeachment of the prosecution's witness because it relates to a collateral matter.

(D) Improper impeachment because it does not positively controvert the prosecution witness's testimony, as the defense witness merely says he does not remember.

Question 18

A defendant is on trial for murder. The only evidence linking the defendant to the crime is some blood found at the scene. The lead detective testifies that an officer took a vial containing a blood sample that had been retrieved by a crime scene technician and drove off with it. The officer is now dead. Next, the prosecution presents as a witness a crime lab chemist. The chemist will testify that he took a vial of blood that contained a label identifying it as having been retrieved from the subject crime scene, and that he performed tests that established a match between that blood and a blood sample taken from the defendant.

The testimony of the chemist is:

(A) Admissible, because there has been proper authentication.

(B) Admissible, because the chemist qualifies as an expert witness.

(C) Inadmissible, because there is insufficient evidence of chain of custody.

(D) Inadmissible, because he did not take the original blood sample at the scene of the crime.

EVIDENCE ANSWERS - SET 3

Answer to Question 1

(C) The grand jury statement is admissible both as impeachment evidence and as substantive evidence. A prior inconsistent statement made under oath at a prior proceeding or deposition is admissible nonhearsay, and thus may be used as substantive evidence as well as for impeachment. The credibility of a witness may be impeached by showing that the witness has, on another occasion, made statements that are inconsistent with some material part of his present testimony. Because it is made by the declarant other than while testifying at the trial or hearing, a prior inconsistent statement will usually constitute hearsay if offered to prove the truth of the matter asserted therein. Under such circumstances, the statement would be admissible only to impeach the witness. However, where the statement was made under oath at a prior proceeding, including a grand jury proceeding, it is admissible nonhearsay (*i.e.*, it may be considered as substantive proof of the facts stated). [Fed. R. Evid. 801(d)(1)(A)] The witness's sworn statement before the grand jury that the defendant was driving normally at the time of the accident is inconsistent with his later in-court testimony that the defendant was on the wrong side of the highway at the time of the collision. Thus, this statement can be inquired into by the defendant to cast doubt on the witness's credibility. Because the statement was made at a prior proceeding, and was made under oath, it is nonhearsay, and is also admissible as substantive proof that the defendant was in fact driving normally at the time of the accident. (C) is the only answer that reflects the fact that the grand jury statement may be used both for impeachment and for substantive purposes. (A) reflects the view of prior law, which was that prior inconsistent statements were limited to impeachment regardless of the circumstances under which they were made. As noted above, Federal Rule 801(d)(1)(A) deems such statements made under oath at a prior trial or other proceeding to be nonhearsay, and as such, to be admissible as substantive evidence. (B) is incorrect because it precludes use of the witness's grand jury testimony for impeachment purposes. A prior inconsistent statement may always be used to impeach the credibility of a witness. (D) is incorrect for two reasons. First, even if deemed to be hearsay, a prior inconsistent statement would be admissible to impeach the witness. Second, because the prior inconsistent statement of the witness was made under oath at a grand jury proceeding, it is admissible nonhearsay.

Answer to Question 2

(D) The transcript of the first witness's grand jury testimony is inadmissible hearsay. Hearsay is a statement, other than one made by the declarant while testifying at the trial or hearing, offered in evidence to prove the truth of the matter asserted. [Fed. R. Evid. 801(c)] A hearsay statement, to which no exception to the hearsay rule is applicable, must be excluded upon appropriate objection to its admission. [Fed. R. Evid. 802] The transcript of the grand jury testimony is being offered to prove the truth of the matter asserted therein (*i.e.*, that the defendant could not have been the assailant because he was elsewhere at the time of the attack). The grand jury testimony of a person who is not now testifying is deemed neither nonhearsay nor within any recognized exception to the hearsay rule. (A) is incorrect because grand jury testimony does not fall within the former testimony exception. Under that exception, the testimony of a now unavailable witness given at another hearing or in a deposition taken in accordance with law is admissible in a subsequent trial if there is a sufficient similarity of parties and issues so that the opportunity to develop testimony or cross-examine at the prior hearing was meaningful. [Fed. R. Evid. 804(b)(1)] Grand jury proceedings do not afford an opportunity for cross-examination. Consequently, the victim (the party against whom the grand jury transcript is offered) did not have the opportunity to develop the first witness's testimony. Absent a meaningful opportunity to cross-examine the first

witness at the time of her grand jury testimony, the transcript of such testimony will not be admissible under the former testimony exception. (B) is incorrect because the first witness's statement is an out-of-court statement being offered for its truth and does not fall within any special category of nonhearsay under the Federal Rules. Therefore, the grand jury testimony is hearsay. Note that the first witness's testimony cannot be nonhearsay under Rule 801(d) because she is not currently testifying at the defendant's trial; thus, the grand jury transcript cannot be the prior statement of a ***witness***. (C) is incorrect because the rehabilitation of the second witness (if he had been impeached by a charge that he was lying or exaggerating because of some motive) would have to be accomplished through the introduction of a prior consistent statement made by the second witness himself, rather than the first witness. A party may rehabilitate a witness by showing a prior consistent statement if opposing counsel has impeached the credibility of a witness by making a charge that the witness is lying or exaggerating because of some motive. Under Federal Rule 801(d)(1)(B), the prior consistent statement may be used not only to bolster the witness's testimony, but also as substantive evidence of the truth of its contents (*i.e.*, it is nonhearsay). If the second witness had been charged with lying or exaggerating, then defense counsel may rebut such a charge by introducing a prior consistent statement made by the second witness before the time of any such alleged lying or exaggerating. However, a statement by the first witness cannot be used to rehabilitate the second witness.

Answer to Question 3

(B) The record of the defendant's conviction should be admitted to prove that the defendant set the fire. The record of the conviction is hearsay; *i.e.*, it is a statement, other than one made by the declarant while testifying at the trial or hearing, offered to prove the truth of the matter asserted. Under the Federal Rules, however, such judgments fall within the hearsay exception for records of felony convictions. Under the Federal Rules, judgments of felony convictions are admissible in both criminal and civil actions to prove any fact essential to the judgment, whether the judgment arose after trial or upon a plea of guilty. [Fed. R. Evid. 803(22)] For purposes of this Rule, a felony is any crime punishable by death or imprisonment in excess of one year. Arson is a felony. Consequently, a properly authenticated copy of the defendant's conviction of this crime is admissible to prove the fact that the fire that destroyed the table was set by the defendant, a fact essential to the judgment of conviction. Note that the actual plea of guilty is also admissible as an admission of a party-opponent. This type of judicial admission is not conclusive, and the defendant may explain the circumstances of the plea. The plea, being an admission, is nonhearsay under the Federal Rules. (A) is incorrect because, in a civil case, evidence of character to prove the conduct of a person in the litigated event is generally not admissible. Circumstantial use of prior behavior patterns for the purpose of inferring that, at the time and place in question, a person probably acted in accord with such patterns creates a danger of prejudice and distraction from the main issues. Therefore, the record of the conviction cannot be used to infer liability by showing the defendant's character. (C) is incorrect because, as noted above, a judgment of a felony conviction is admissible under Federal Rule 803(22) regardless of whether the conviction resulted from a trial or a guilty plea. (D) is incorrect because, as discussed above, the judgment is within the exception to the hearsay rule for records of felony convictions.

Answer to Question 4

(B) Although a party is entitled as of right to some cross-examination, the extent or scope of cross-examination is a matter of judicial discretion. The judge may exercise reasonable control over the examination of witnesses to aid the effective ascertainment of truth, to avoid wasting time, and to protect witnesses from harassment or undue embarrassment. Specifically, the trial court has the authority to cut off cross-examination when it determines there has been an adequate opportunity for meaningful cross-examination. Here, the defense attorney has the right to cross-examine the adverse witness. However, carrying on such cross-examination for three days, with the prospect of at least one more day, would probably be considered excessive in light of the limited direct examination of the witness. Cross-examination is limited to: (i) matters brought out on direct examination and inferences naturally drawn therefrom; and (ii) matters affecting the credibility of the witness. [Fed. R. Evid. 611(b)] (A) is incorrect because, even if the testimony is relevant, the court may terminate or otherwise control the cross-examination to avoid wasting time or harassing a witness. (C) is incorrect for a similar reason. Although matters relating to the subject matter of direct examination may properly be brought out on cross-examination, the court has the discretion to terminate such questioning to avoid wasting of time or harassment or embarrassment of a witness. Therefore, it is incorrect to state that, if the questioning relates to the subject matter of direct examination, the court lacks the authority to terminate the cross-examination. (D) is incorrect because, although due process considerations are of undisputed significance, the facts here do not appear to present any real conflict between due process and judicial economy. If the defense attorney has had an adequate opportunity for cross-examination of the witness, then there is no deprivation of due process if principles of judicial economy now dictate that the questioning be cut short.

Answer to Question 5

(D) The word "Craftsman" is not hearsay, and the wrench is relevant circumstantial evidence on the issue of whether the defendant dropped the wrench that struck the plaintiff. Evidence is relevant if it tends to make the existence of any fact of consequence to the action more probable than it would be without the evidence. [Fed. R. Evid. 401] If the defendant uses "Craftsman" wrenches on the job, and the wrench that struck the plaintiff bears the brand name "Craftsman," it is more probable than would otherwise be the case that the wrench that struck the plaintiff was dropped by the defendant. Thus, the wrench is relevant to prove that the defendant dropped the wrench. The wrench is circumstantial, rather than direct, evidence because a fact about it is being proved as a basis for an inference that another fact is true; *i.e.*, the fact that the wrench bears the name "Craftsman" is proved to form a basis for inferring that the defendant dropped the wrench. Direct evidence is offered to prove a fact about the object as an end in itself. Here, the wrench bearing the name "Craftsman" is not being offered as a means of proving, *e.g.*, that the wrench is in fact a "Craftsman" brand. Consequently, the wrench constitutes circumstantial evidence. In addition, when offered for the stated purpose, the wrench is not hearsay. Hearsay is a statement, other than one made by the declarant while testifying at the trial or hearing, offered in evidence to prove the truth of the matter asserted. [Fed. R. Evid. 801(c)] The wrench is not being offered to prove the truth of the matter asserted (*i.e.*, that the wrench is actually a "Craftsman"). It is of no significance whether the wrench being offered is a genuine "Craftsman." What is important is that it bears the same name as those wrenches used by the defendant on the job. Thus, introduction of the wrench into evidence will not violate the rule against hearsay. (A) is incorrect because it states that the word "Craftsman" on the wrench creates a hearsay problem. As noted, the wrench is not being offered to prove its genuineness as a "Craftsman," but rather to form the basis for an inference that it was dropped by the defendant. Thus, there is no hearsay problem. (B) reaches the incorrect conclusion that the wrench is not relevant. As has been explained above, the fact that the wrench that struck the plaintiff bears the name "Craftsman" tends to make more probable the material fact that the defendant is the person who dropped the wrench. Therefore, the wrench is relevant. Also, (B) states an incorrect test for relevance. To be relevant, the wrench need not show that it is more likely than not that the defendant dropped it; rather, the wrench must have some tendency to make it more probable than it would be without this evidence that the defendant

dropped it. (C) is incorrect because the wrench is circumstantial, rather than direct, evidence that the defendant dropped the wrench that struck the plaintiff.

Answer to Question 6

(B) The evidence is not hearsay because the statement is not offered for its truth; the statement is offered to show its effect on the plaintiff. Hearsay is a statement, other than one made by the declarant while testifying at the trial or hearing, offered in evidence to prove the truth of the matter asserted. [Fed. R. Evid. 801(c)] If a statement is hearsay, and no exception to the hearsay rule is applicable, the evidence must be excluded upon appropriate objection to its admission. [Fed. R. Evid. 802] A statement that would be inadmissible hearsay to prove the truth of the statement may be admitted to show the statement's effect on the hearer or reader. Thus, in a negligence case, where knowledge of a danger is at issue, a statement of warning is admissible for the limited purpose of showing knowledge or notice on the part of a listener. Here, the defense of assumption of the risk has been raised. Whether the plaintiff knew of the danger involved in lighting a fire within 24 hours of the chimney cleaning is an issue. Consequently, the statement of the foreman is admissible to show that the plaintiff had knowledge of the possible danger. The statement is not hearsay because it is not offered to prove that it was in fact dangerous for the plaintiff to light a fire. (A) incorrectly states that the reason the statement is not hearsay is that the declarant is testifying as a witness. The fact that the declarant is now testifying does not alter the hearsay nature of a statement. Any out-of-court statement offered for its truth is hearsay in most jurisdictions (the Federal Rules have a few specific statements characterized as nonhearsay) regardless of whether the declarant is testifying. The reason hearsay is excluded is that there is no opportunity for cross-examination ***at the time*** the statement was made. The key in this case is not that the declarant is testifying, but that the statement is not being offered for its truth. (C) characterizes the testimony as hearsay, which is incorrect because it is not being offered for its truth. Even if this testimony were hearsay, it is incorrect to state that it is "part of the res gestae." Formerly, a wide class of declarations was loosely categorized under the label of res gestae exceptions to the hearsay rule. This group included the following exceptions: (i) present state of mind, (ii) excited utterances, (iii) present sense impressions, and (iv) declarations of physical condition. The testimony of the foreman would not come within any of these exceptions. (D) incorrectly characterizes the testimony as hearsay. In addition, this statement, even if hearsay, would not come within the present state of mind exception. A statement of a declarant's then-existing state of mind is admissible when the declarant's state of mind is directly in issue and material to the controversy, or as a basis for a circumstantial inference that a particular declaration of intent was carried out. The declarant here is the foreman. There is no indication that his state of mind is at all relevant to this litigation, nor is the statement offered indicative of any particular intent on the part of the foreman. Thus, the present state of mind exception is inapplicable.

Answer to Question 7

(D) The past recollection recorded exception to the hearsay rule is one of a class of hearsay exceptions that do not require unavailability of the declarant. If a witness has insufficient memory of an event to enable her to testify fully and accurately, even after consulting a writing given to her on the stand, the writing itself may be introduced into evidence if a proper foundation is laid for its admissibility. The foundation for receiving such a writing into evidence must include proof that: (i) the witness at one time had personal knowledge of the facts recited in the writing; (ii) the writing was made by or under the direction of the witness or has been adopted by her; (iii) the writing was timely made when the matter was fresh in the mind of the witness; (iv) the writing is accurate; and (v) the witness has insufficient recollection to testify fully and accurately. [Fed. R. Evid. 803(5)] The corporation need not establish the unavailability of the personnel director. (A), (B), and (C) each correspond to one of the foundational requirements. (A) corresponds to requirement (iii), (B) corresponds to requirement (iv), and (C) corresponds to requirement (ii). Because (A), (B), and (C) reflect foundational facts that the corporation will have to establish to have the report admitted under the past recollection recorded exception, they are incorrect.

Answer to Question 8

(B) The witness's testimony is admissible nonhearsay. The statement by the witness is not being offered to prove the truth of the matter asserted therein and thus is not hearsay. Hearsay is a statement made out of court by the declarant, offered in evidence to prove the truth of the matter asserted. [Fed. R. Evid. 801(c)] Although hearsay is inadmissible (unless an exception to the hearsay rule is applicable), a statement that would be inadmissible hearsay to prove the truth thereof may be admitted to show the statement's effect on the hearer or reader. Thus, in a negligence case, where knowledge of a danger is at issue, a person's warning statement is admissible for the limited purpose of showing knowledge or notice on the part of a listener. Here, one of the theories of recovery underlying the plaintiff's lawsuit is that the defendant negligently failed to secure the load. Therefore, the plaintiff must show that the defendant either knew or should have known that the load was not properly secured. Consequently, the witness's statement that the chains looked loose is admissible to show that the defendant had notice of the possible danger. If this same out-of-court statement were offered to show that its contents were true (*i.e.*, that the chains were in fact loose), then it would constitute hearsay, but because the statement is offered to show notice to the defendant of a possible danger, it is nonhearsay and (C) is incorrect. (A) is incorrect because the admissibility of the statement arises from its status as nonhearsay. If a statement is nonhearsay, then there is no need to refer to hearsay exceptions in determining the statement's admissibility. (D) is incorrect for two reasons: First, the statement is not being offered to show the witness's opinion that the chains were loose. Rather, the statement is offered to show that the defendant had notice of a possible danger involving the chains. Because the testimony simply relates this statement made to the defendant, such testimony cannot be characterized as opinion testimony. Second, (D) incorrectly implies that opinion evidence is inadmissible. Even opinions of lay witnesses are admissible when they are: (i) rationally based on the perception of the witness; (ii) helpful to a clear understanding of the witness's testimony or to the determination of a fact in issue; and (iii) not based on scientific, technical, or other specialized knowledge. [Fed. R. Evid. 701] Certainly, the witness would be permitted to testify that the chains looked loose at the time he observed them, because such an opinion would be based on personal observation, would be helpful to the determination of a fact in issue (*i.e.*, whether the load was properly secured), and would not be based on technical knowledge.

Answer to Question 9

(A) The report is admissible nonhearsay. The report is an admission by a party-opponent because it is a statement by an agent concerning a matter within the scope of his agency, made during the existence of the employment relationship. The operator's statement constitutes a prior acknowledgment of a relevant fact, and is admissible against the operator's principal, the city. Such an admission is considered nonhearsay under the Federal Rules. (B) is wrong because, as discussed above, the report is admissible as an admission and no foundation is necessary. If the report were not made by a party, the plaintiff could seek to have it admitted as past recollection recorded, but several foundational requirements would have to be met. A writing may be introduced under this exception to the hearsay rule if: (i) the witness at one time had personal knowledge of the facts

recited in the writing; (ii) the writing was made by the witness or under his direction, or was adopted by the witness; (iii) the writing was timely made when the matter was fresh in the mind of the witness; (iv) the writing is accurate; and (v) the witness is presently unable to remember the facts sufficiently to testify fully. Here, the operator has not testified that the writing is accurate. Without this foundational testimony, the report could not be admitted as a past recollection recorded. (C) is wrong because it implies that the report could be admitted only as a business record, and that one of the elements for that exception is lacking. As discussed above, the writing is admissible as an admission; so there is no need to rely on the business record exception. Furthermore, even if the report was not an admission and the plaintiff was seeking to admit it as a business record, a court might find that it was made in the regular course of business. In *Palmer v. Hoffman*, the United States Supreme Court held that a similar routine accident report was prepared in anticipation of litigation, and litigation was not the railroad's primary business. Most courts, however, have applied this rule only when the report is offered by the preparer's side. If it is offered against the party that prepared it, most courts find it within the regular course of business. The Federal Rules give the trial court discretion to exclude a business record of this nature where its source indicates a lack of trustworthiness. Thus, since the report is being offered against the city, most courts would find it sufficiently trustworthy and admit it. (D) is wrong because, as discussed above, the report is admissible as an admission and thus no foundational requirements for the business record exception need be met. Moreover, even under the business record exception, opinions are allowed as long as they are in the regular course of business.

Answer to Question 10

(D) The court would never permit invocation of the physician-patient privilege if the patient knew that the person she was consulting was not a licensed physician. The physician-patient privilege requires that a licensed physician be present for purposes of treatment, that the information be obtained while attending the patient, and that the information be necessary for treatment (*i.e.*, that it deal with medical matters). While some jurisdictions do not apply the privilege to criminal proceedings, the question indicates that the privilege would be applicable in criminal cases in this jurisdiction. In all jurisdictions, though, the existence of a licensed physician, or the patient's reasonable belief that the consultant is a licensed physician, is a prerequisite for the privilege to apply. (A) is incorrect because it states one of the requirements for the privilege to apply. Thus, under this circumstance the court would be ***most*** (rather than least) likely to allow the victim to use the privilege. (B) is incorrect simply because it is irrelevant. Whether the victim is married to the defendant does not affect the applicability of the physician-patient privilege to the physician's testimony. Thus, that circumstance does not make it either more likely or less likely that the court will allow the privilege. (C) is incorrect because the privilege belongs to the patient and she may decide whether to claim it or to waive it. Hence, the physician's prior disclosure would not make the court less likely to allow the victim to assert the privilege.

Answer to Question 11

(D) The plaintiff's testimony does not violate the hearsay rule or the parol evidence rule. Hearsay is a statement other than one made by the declarant while testifying at the trial or hearing, offered in evidence to prove the truth of the matter asserted. A hearsay statement must be excluded upon objection if no exception to the hearsay rule is applicable. However, an out-of-court statement introduced for any purpose other than to prove the truth of the matter asserted is not hearsay. Thus, a statement that would be inadmissible hearsay if offered to prove its truth may be admitted to show the statement's effect on the person hearing it. Here, the plaintiff is offering to testify to the defendant's out-of-court statement, not to prove the truth of that statement (*i.e.*, that the real value of the business was $500,000), but rather to show the effect of the statement on the plaintiff (*i.e.*, that he relied on the statement in entering into the transaction). Thus, the offered evidence is not hearsay. Under the parol evidence rule, if an agreement is reduced to a writing, all prior or contemporaneous negotiations or agreements are merged into the written agreement. Extrinsic evidence is not admissible to add to, detract from, or alter the agreement as written. However, the parol evidence rule does not bar admission of parol evidence to show that an apparent contractual obligation is not an obligation at all—*e.g.*, to show that a contract was void or voidable. Consequently, parol evidence is admissible to establish or disprove a contract attacked on grounds of fraud, duress, or undue influence inducing consent. The testimony in this case does not violate the parol evidence rule because it is offered to show the existence of fraud that induced the plaintiff to enter into the contract. (A) is wrong because it states that the evidence violates the parol evidence rule, which is not true (*see* above). (B) is wrong because it characterizes the evidence as hearsay and it is not since it is not offered for its truth. (C) is also wrong because it characterizes the evidence as admissible hearsay, and the evidence is not hearsay at all.

Answer to Question 12

(C) If the facts were told to the defendant's ex-wife in confidence during her marriage to the defendant, he has a privilege to prevent her from disclosing such facts. Either spouse has a privilege to refuse to disclose, and to prevent another from disclosing, a confidential communication made between the spouses while they were husband and wife. Both spouses hold this privilege. The communication must be made in reliance upon the intimacy of the marital relationship, and must be made during a valid marriage. Divorce will not terminate the privilege retroactively. If the defendant told his ex-wife of the false claim during their marriage, and he did so in reliance upon the intimacy of their relationship, then he may prevent his ex-wife from disclosing this confidential communication. The divorce of the defendant and his ex-wife subsequent to disclosure of the false claim does not terminate the privilege. (A) is incorrect because it ignores the defendant's privilege to prevent the testimony if the testimony reveals a confidential marital communication. (B) is incorrect because the applicability of the privilege for confidential marital communications extends to civil cases. Thus, the defendant's ex-wife can refuse to disclose the contents of such a communication, or he can prevent her from making such a disclosure. Note that in criminal cases, there is a separate concept of spousal immunity under which a married person may not be compelled to testify against her spouse, and if a spouse is a criminal defendant, the other spouse may not even be called as a witness. In federal court, this privilege belongs to the witness-spouse; *i.e.*, she may not be compelled to testify, but neither may she be foreclosed from testifying (except as to confidential communications). Spousal immunity, unlike that for confidential marital communications, terminates upon divorce or annulment. (Be careful to avoid confusing these two privileges.) (D) is incorrect because it is too broad. The defendant can only prevent his ex-wife's testimony as to matters revealed as a confidential marital communication. He cannot prevent her from being called as a witness.

Answer to Question 13

(B) The qualification of a witness as an expert is a preliminary fact to be determined by the judge. The existence of preliminary facts (*e.g.*, competency of testimony or evidence privilege) other than those of conditional relevance must be determined by the court. These questions are withheld from the jury out of a fear that, once the jury hears the disputed evidence, the damage has been done, rendering ineffective an instruction to disregard the evidence if the preliminary fact is not found. One of these foundational facts that must first be determined by the judge is the

qualification of a witness as an expert. Thus, in this question it is the province of the judge to determine whether the witness is an expert in the field of finance, so as to allow her to testify further. Also, the judge is free to consider any relevant evidence in making the determination; so he should consider the transcript. (A) is incorrect because it assigns to the jury the function of deciding the qualifications of an expert witness, which is a question for the court. The jury decides those preliminary facts where the answer to the preliminary question determines whether the proffered evidence is relevant at all. In such instances, the court may instruct the jury to determine whether the preliminary fact exists, and to disregard the proffered evidence unless the jury finds that the preliminary fact does exist. If the jury were allowed to hear the witness's testimony, it would be virtually useless to instruct the jury to disregard the testimony if it concluded that the witness is not an expert. (C) is incorrect because the witness's claim that she obtained a B.A. and Ph.D. is not a collateral matter. Where a witness makes a statement not directly relevant to the issues in the case, the rule against impeachment on a collateral matter bars the opponent from proving the statement untrue either by extrinsic evidence or by a prior inconsistent statement. However, a witness's competence to testify and credibility are always relevant. A test for deciding whether a matter is collateral is to ask whether the evidence would be admissible absent the contrary assertion by the witness. If it would be, it cannot be excluded as impeachment on a collateral matter. In this case, the beneficiaries could present evidence that the witness is not qualified as an expert regardless of whether she asserted that she had obtained certain degrees. Thus, the transcripts are admissible. (D) is incorrect because the credibility of the witness and her qualifications as an expert witness may be attacked by showing that she did not receive the claimed degrees. Any matter that affects the credibility or competency of the witness is relevant.

Answer to Question 14

(B) Only the witness's testimony is necessary to introduce the photograph. To be admissible, a photograph must be identified by a witness as a portrayal of certain facts relevant to the issue, and verified by the witness as a correct representation of those facts. It is sufficient if the witness who identifies the photograph is familiar with the scene or object depicted. It is not necessary to call the photographer to authenticate the photograph. Here, the actual physical appearance of the intersection is most likely relevant to the manner in which the accident occurred. As a resident of the neighborhood in which the accident took place, and as someone who was at the scene of the accident shortly after its occurrence, the witness is sufficiently familiar with the scene to testify that the photograph is an accurate representation of the accident scene. Such identification by the witness is needed for the photograph to be admissible. (A) incorrectly categorizes the employee's testimony as necessary. Generally, a photographer's testimony is not necessary to authenticate a photo. In this case, it is particularly unhelpful because the employee is not familiar with the scene as it was when the accident occurred. Also, the testimony of the witness is necessary as a verification by one who is familiar with the scene. (C) is incorrect because, as stated above, the testimony of the employee, the photographer, is not necessary. (D) is incorrect because the photograph is admissible if properly identified by the witness.

Answer to Question 15

(C) The statement from the treatise is admissible to impeach and as substantive evidence. Under the Federal Rules, learned treatises can be used either for impeachment or as substantive evidence. One way the credibility of an expert witness may be attacked is by cross-examining him as to his general knowledge of the field in which he is claiming to be an expert. This can be done by cross-examining the expert on statements contained in any scientific publication that is established as reliable authority. Reliability of a publication may be established by: (i) the direct testimony or cross-examination admission of the expert, (ii) the testimony of another expert, or (iii) judicial notice. The Federal Rules recognize an exception to the hearsay rule for learned treatises and admit them as substantive evidence if: (i) the expert is on the stand and it is called to his attention, and (ii) it is established as reliable authority (*see* above). The doctor has admitted on cross-examination that the treatise is authoritative in the field. Thus, the attorney may use the statement in the treatise to attack the doctor's general knowledge of the field of arthritis by showing that the doctor's opinion that the blow to the plaintiff's knee caused his arthritis is considered to be ignorant and unfounded in the text of the treatise. As noted above, such an attack on the doctor's general knowledge of the field is a proper means of impeaching his credibility. In addition, pursuant to the Federal Rules, the statement may be read into the record as substantive evidence (*i.e.*, as a means of proving that the plaintiff's arthritis could not have been caused by a single traumatic event, such as the blow to his knee). The statement may be used as substantive evidence because it has been brought to the attention of the doctor during cross-examination and he established it as a reliable authority, and it will be read into evidence while he is on the stand. (A), which reflects the traditional view, is incorrect because the Federal Rules permit the use of the statement in the treatise as substantive evidence. (B) is incorrect because it precludes use of the statement for impeachment purposes. (D) is incorrect because it would not allow introduction of the statement for either impeachment or substantive evidentiary purposes, and thus it is an incorrect statement of the law.

Answer to Question 16

(B) The friend's statement is admissible under the excited utterance exception to the hearsay rule. Although hearsay is generally inadmissible, certain kinds of hearsay are deemed to be reliable enough to be admitted. Among these exceptions is one for excited utterances. Under this exception, a declaration made during or soon after a startling event is admissible. The declaration must be made under the stress of excitement produced by the startling event (*i.e.*, before the declarant has time to consciously reflect on the occurrence). Also, the declaration must concern the immediate facts of the startling occurrence. [Fed. R. Evid. 803(2)] Here, the friend's statement (to be testified to by the witness) is an out-of-court declaration, offered to prove the truth of the matter asserted (*i.e.*, that the license plate number of the getaway car was 07771). Thus, the friend's statement is hearsay. However, this statement was made during the course of a bank robbery, an event startling enough to produce nervous excitement in the friend. The statement was made under the stress of the excitement produced by the robbery, and concerned the immediate facts of the robbery (*i.e.*, it referred to the car in which the robber was making his escape). Therefore, the statement qualifies as an excited utterance, rendering the witness's testimony admissible. (A) is wrong because it represents an incorrect application of the best evidence rule. The best evidence rule applies only when a party is trying to prove the terms of a writing. Here, there is no writing involved; thus, the best evidence rule is inapplicable. (C) is wrong in characterizing the friend's statement as inadmissible. Although the statement is hearsay, as explained above, it is admissible as an excited utterance. (D) is wrong because no foundation is required for the witness to testify to the excited statement he heard. Also, note that the hearsay declarant (the friend) is, contrary to the language of (D), identified as the person who made the statement.

Answer to Question 17

(B) The defense witness's testimony should be admitted as proper impeachment of the prosecution's witness. Impeachment is the casting of an adverse reflection on the veracity of a witness. A witness may be impeached by either cross-examination or extrinsic evidence, such as by putting

other witnesses on the stand who contradict the witness's testimony. Here, the defense is using the testimony of its witness to impeach the prosecution witness's testimony as to what the victim's friend said. This is proper. (A) is wrong because a witness's credibility is always relevant. Furthermore, the defense witness's testimony relates to a crucial issue in the case; *i.e.*, whether the victim was armed with a knife or was "helpless." Thus, the testimony is relevant. (C) is wrong because this is not a collateral matter. Impeachment on a collateral matter is prohibited, but a collateral matter is one that arises when a witness makes a statement not directly relevant to the issues in the case. The prosecution witness's statement about the victim being "helpless" is directly relevant to the issue of the defendant's self-defense claim and, thus, is a proper subject of impeachment. (D) is wrong because impeachment evidence need not positively controvert the prior testimony; it need only tend to discredit the credibility of the prior witness.

Answer to Question 18

(C) The testimony is inadmissible because it has not been shown what happened to the blood between the time the officer took it and the time the chemist examined it. Real evidence presents an object in issue directly to the trier of fact. One of the general requirements for admissibility of real evidence is that it be authenticated; *i.e.*, that it be identified as being what its proponent claims it is. If the evidence is of a type that is likely to be confused or can be easily tampered with, the proponent of the object must present evidence of chain of custody. The proponent must show that the object has been held in a substantially unbroken chain of possession. It is not necessary to negate all possibilities of substitution or tampering; rather, what is required is to show adherence to some system of identification and custody. Here, the proponent of the blood sample (the prosecution) has not shown what the officer did with it after leaving the crime scene. There is no showing that the vial was placed directly in a properly secured area so as to diminish the possibility of tampering. In short, it has not been demonstrated that there was adherence to some defined system of identification and custody. In the absence of a substantially unbroken chain of custody, the evidence is inadmissible for lack of proper authentication, and (A) is incorrect. (B) is incorrect. Although it may be true that the chemist qualifies as an expert witness (*i.e.*, he has special knowledge, skill, experience, training, or education sufficient to qualify him as an expert on the subject to which his testimony relates), the fact remains that his testimony is inadmissible, as explained above. (D) is incorrect because the chemist would be permitted to testify to the results of the blood comparisons if there were proper authentication of the blood taken from the crime scene. There is no need for the chemist to have taken the original blood sample himself.

Set 4 Answer Sheet

1. Ⓐ Ⓑ Ⓒ Ⓓ
2. Ⓐ Ⓑ Ⓒ Ⓓ
3. Ⓐ Ⓑ Ⓒ Ⓓ
4. Ⓐ Ⓑ Ⓒ Ⓓ
5. Ⓐ Ⓑ Ⓒ Ⓓ
6. Ⓐ Ⓑ Ⓒ Ⓓ
7. Ⓐ Ⓑ Ⓒ Ⓓ
8. Ⓐ Ⓑ Ⓒ Ⓓ
9. Ⓐ Ⓑ Ⓒ Ⓓ
10. Ⓐ Ⓑ Ⓒ Ⓓ
11. Ⓐ Ⓑ Ⓒ Ⓓ
12. Ⓐ Ⓑ Ⓒ Ⓓ
13. Ⓐ Ⓑ Ⓒ Ⓓ
14. Ⓐ Ⓑ Ⓒ Ⓓ
15. Ⓐ Ⓑ Ⓒ Ⓓ
16. Ⓐ Ⓑ Ⓒ Ⓓ
17. Ⓐ Ⓑ Ⓒ Ⓓ
18. Ⓐ Ⓑ Ⓒ Ⓓ

EVIDENCE QUESTIONS - SET 4

Question 1

A 12-year-old child was injured in an automobile accident. The child's father brought the child to see an attorney to bring suit against the defendant. During the paid consultation with the attorney, the seriousness of the child's injuries was discussed with candor. After the discussion, the attorney told the father and child that they would be better off with a lawyer who specialized in personal injury work. Eventually, another attorney was hired to bring the child's lawsuit against the defendant. Defense counsel has reason to believe that the child's injuries are not serious at all. She therefore subpoenas the first attorney for an oral deposition. During the course of the deposition she asks the attorney about his discussion with the child regarding the child's injuries.

May the attorney invoke the attorney-client privilege?

(A) No, because the child never hired the attorney as her counsel.

(B) No, because the privilege is held by the client rather than the attorney.

(C) Yes, because the child paid the attorney for consultation.

(D) Yes, because the presence of a third party did not negate the privilege.

Question 2

Except under extraordinary circumstances, the judge conducting a trial in federal district court:

(A) May not question a sworn witness who is one of the actual parties to the "case or controversy."

(B) May not question a sworn witness regarding ultimate issues of the case.

(C) May not question a sworn lay (nonexpert) witness.

(D) May question a sworn witness in any of the above circumstances.

Question 3

During the course of his trial for assault, the defendant placed a professional sociologist on the stand. The sociologist testified that she had scientifically polled the community in which the defendant lived and that the defendant had a high reputation for being a peaceable man in a rather rough community. On cross-examination, the prosecutor asked the sociologist if she filed a false income tax return last year. The sociologist has in fact been convicted of filing a false tax return; however, the defense immediately objected.

Should the court require the sociologist to answer the question posed to her?

(A) Yes, because the sociologist has been convicted of filing a false tax return.

(B) Yes, because the question is relevant to the truthfulness and credibility of the witness.

(C) No, because specific instances of conduct are inadmissible.

(D) No, because the question does not go to a relevant character trait.

Question 4

A plaintiff was riding up an escalator in a department store, when suddenly the escalator sped up and then came to a very quick stop, throwing people against each other and then down the escalator. The plaintiff was thrown violently to the left, felt a horrible pain in her back, and then tumbled down the escalator to the bottom. When the ambulance arrived, paramedics placed the plaintiff on a stretcher, and just as they picked up the stretcher to take her to the hospital, the plaintiff heard a customer of the store say, "Yesterday I heard my neighbor tell the manager that the escalator was acting funny. You know, speeding up and stopping."

The plaintiff was treated at the hospital and must undergo rehabilitation treatment for her badly injured back. The plaintiff now sues the department store for her injuries, and at trial calls the customer to testify to the neighbor's statement. The neighbor still lives in the area but has not been called as a witness. The lawyer for the department store objects.

How should the court rule?

(A) Admissible, as a statement against interest.

(B) Admissible, as relevant evidence that the department store was aware of the defect and did nothing to correct it.

(C) Inadmissible, because the neighbor is available to testify.

(D) Inadmissible, as hearsay not within any exception.

Question 5

A plaintiff was injured as a result of a defendant's negligence. The plaintiff hired an attorney, who sent the plaintiff to see a physician for the purpose of examining the plaintiff prior to trial and assessing the extent of his injuries. During the course of the examination, the plaintiff made some statements to the physician indicating that he was not completely free from negligence when the accident occurred. The defendant seeks to call the physician to testify to the statements the plaintiff made to the physician. The attorney objects.

The objection should be:

(A) Overruled, because the plaintiff made an admission.

(B) Overruled, because a physician qualifies as an expert witness.

(C) Sustained, because the attorney-client privilege applies.

(D) Sustained, because the jurisdiction's physician-patient privilege applies.

Question 6

A defendant was involved in an accident in which her car struck the rear end of the car driven by the plaintiff. The police issued tickets to the defendant, charging her with reckless driving and speeding. When the defendant's case came before the traffic court, her attorney entered into a plea bargain with the prosecutor. Under the plea bargain, the defendant agreed to plead guilty to speeding and to pay a fine of $100, and the prosecution agreed to drop the reckless driving charge. Accordingly, the defendant pleaded guilty and the court fined her $100.

In the later civil suit, where the plaintiff sues the defendant for personal injuries, is the guilty plea before the traffic court admissible?

(A) Yes, because it is an admission.

(B) Yes, because it is a statement against interest.

(C) No, because there is a public policy in favor of plea bargaining to promote court efficiency.

(D) No, because no felony was involved.

Question 7

A plaintiff sued an elevator company for injuries he suffered when his foot caught in one of its moving walkways. The company's chief engineer prepared a report of the accident at the request of its insurance company, and the report was given to the attorney who was hired to represent the elevator company in this trial. As part of its case-in-chief, the company's attorney seeks to introduce the report into evidence, and states that its expert witness relied on it. The report states that the walkway was in good mechanical condition at the time of the plaintiff's injury. The plaintiff's attorney objects.

The report is:

(A) Admissible, as a business record.

(B) Admissible, because it is relied upon by a testifying expert witness.

(C) Inadmissible, because the insurance company is an interested party.

(D) Inadmissible, because it is hearsay not within any exception.

Question 8

Which of the following statements most accurately states the prevailing view as to the burden of proving consent or lack thereof in a misdemeanor false imprisonment case?

(A) The defendant must establish the victim's consent by a preponderance of the evidence.

(B) The prosecution must establish that the victim did not consent by a preponderance of the evidence, otherwise the defendant's guilt must be proved beyond a reasonable doubt.

(C) The prosecution must prove beyond a reasonable doubt that the victim did not consent even if the defendant remains silent on the issue.

(D) The prosecution must prove beyond a reasonable doubt that the victim did not consent only if the defendant produces some evidence that the victim did consent.

Question 9

In a rape case in which the issue is whether the victim consented, the defense attorney calls a witness and asks him if he knows the victim's reputation in the community for chastity. The witness laughs and then declares, "The victim's reputation for chastity? It's a joke! She's been to bed with everyone—including me!" The prosecution moves to strike the witness's testimony.

The judge should:

(A) Deny the motion as not timely.

(B) Deny the motion, because the witness's testimony is relevant to the issue of consent.

(C) Grant the motion, because the issue is not the victim's reputation, but rather whether she consented.

(D) Grant the motion, because this kind of character evidence is prohibited in rape cases.

Question 10

A defendant is on trial for stealing jewelry from his co-worker. The defendant claims that the co-worker sold the jewelry to him because she needed money to buy medicine for her sick mother. The defense witness is asked to testify as to the co-worker's reputation in the community. The witness testifies that the co-worker is known as a dishonest person who makes her living as a "con artist."

Assuming appropriate objections by defense counsel, which of the following questions would ***not*** be proper on cross-examination of the witness by the prosecutor?

(A) "Isn't it true that you're maligning the defendant's co-worker because she and your wife have been enemies since childhood?"

(B) "Isn't it true that you were charged last year with assault for striking your wife?"

(C) "Have you heard that the defendant's co-worker teaches Sunday School classes on morality and has received an award from her church based on her outstanding moral character?"

(D) "Do you know that the defendant's co-worker teaches Sunday School classes on morality and has received an award from her church based on her outstanding moral character?"

Question 11

A plaintiff applied for a life insurance policy and was required to submit to a physical examination to qualify for the policy. During the course of the examination, the plaintiff told the physician, who was approved by the life insurance company and had never seen the plaintiff before, "I used to have some back trouble, but that's all cleared up now." A few weeks after the examination, the defendant's automobile struck the rear end of a car in which the plaintiff was riding as a passenger. The plaintiff now claims that he suffers persistent lower back pain and sues the defendant for damages. After laying a proper foundation that the plaintiff is attempting to perpetrate a fraud, the defendant calls the physician as a witness and seeks to have her testify as to the plaintiff's statement to her. The plaintiff's attorney objects on the ground of the jurisdiction's physician-patient privilege.

The testimony as to the plaintiff's statement is:

(A) Admissible, because a proper foundation is laid establishing that the plaintiff is attempting to perpetrate a fraud.

(B) Admissible, because the plaintiff was not seeking diagnosis or treatment.

(C) Inadmissible, because the statement was made to a physician who was attending the plaintiff in a professional capacity.

(D) Inadmissible, as irrelevant, because the statement was made prior to the accident.

Question 12

A defendant was on trial for burglary, and he took the stand in his own defense. On direct examination, the defendant vigorously denied having committed the burglary. Also on direct examination, the defense attorney asked the defendant questions about his employment history in an attempt to portray him to the jury as a "solid citizen" who would not commit a burglary. The defendant stated that his last regular employment was as a bookkeeper for a corporation. On cross-examination, the prosecutor asked the defendant if he had embezzled funds from the corporation. The defendant denied that he had embezzled from the corporation or from anyone else. The prosecutor then wanted to call a police officer to the stand to testify that when she arrested the defendant for embezzlement, the defendant admitted to the officer that he had embezzled money from the corporation.

Assuming that the defendant has not yet been tried on the embezzlement charges, may the prosecutor call the officer to the stand?

(A) Yes, but only for purposes of impeachment.

(B) Yes, both for impeachment of the defendant and as substantive evidence.

(C) No, because the defendant has not yet been convicted of embezzlement.

(D) No, because the evidence would be extrinsic.

Question 13

A defendant was visiting with his girlfriend in his apartment when a visitor came to see him. The defendant and the visitor engaged in a conversation relating to the distribution of illegal narcotics in the girlfriend's presence. Two months later, the defendant and his girlfriend married. Subsequent to the marriage, the defendant was arrested and charged under federal law with the sale and distribution of drugs. The prosecutor wants the defendant's wife to testify about the conversation between the defendant and the visitor, but the defendant forbids it.

May she so testify?

(A) Yes, because the conversation occurred prior to their marriage.

(B) Yes, but only if she chooses to do so.

(C) No, because the defendant forbids it.

(D) No, unless both the defendant and his wife agree that she may testify.

Question 14

At trial, questions have been raised as to whether the proposed testimony of the witness is relevant and whether it falls within the present sense impression exception to the hearsay rule.

As to a preliminary determination of the admissibility of the witness's testimony:

(A) A judge should determine whether the proposed testimony falls within the exception before it is heard by the jury, and in making that determination she is limited by the rules of evidence.

(B) A judge should decide whether the testimony falls within the present sense impression exception, but in making that determination she is not limited by the rules of evidence other than privilege.

(C) The jury, after being instructed on the rules of evidence by a judge, should determine whether the testimony falls within the scope of the present sense impression exception.

(D) The jury should determine whether the testimony falls within the scope of the exception and the judge should then instruct the jury on the appropriate uses for that evidence.

Question 15

Two years ago, a woman informed her sister and a friend that she had named the friend beneficiary of a $100,000 insurance policy issued on her life. The sister was very angry. Six months ago, the woman was found strangled in the front seat of her car. The friend was charged with the murder. At trial, the sister testified that she had seen the friend riding in the front seat of the woman's car with the woman driving one hour before she was found dead. The friend was acquitted of the murder. The friend asked the insurance company to pay him the proceeds from the insurance policy on which he was named beneficiary. When the insurance company refused, the friend sued to force payment. The insurance company defended on the grounds that the friend had killed the woman. Because the sister had died by the time of the trial on the insurance policy, the insurance company offers into evidence a duly authenticated transcript of the sister's testimony from the murder trial.

That transcript should be found to be:

(A) Admissible, because it is a record of the sister's former testimony.

(B) Admissible, because it is a past recollection recorded.

(C) Inadmissible, because on the same evidence, the friend was acquitted of murdering the woman.

(D) Inadmissible, because the motive to cross-examine in the former trial was not the same as in this trial.

Question 16

A defendant was arrested and charged with the murder of a member of the local athletic club. The victim was found dead near the locker room inside the club. The defendant allegedly entered the club, killed the victim, and left before anyone discovered the body. At trial, the prosecution called the doorman of the club who testified that, although he could not identify the defendant by sight, he remembered admitting a member the day of the murder who showed a membership card bearing the name of Arnold Kramer. The prosecution then sought to admit the testimony of a police officer that a membership card to the athletic club bearing the name of Arnold Kramer was found on the defendant's person at the time of his arrest.

The defendant's best argument in seeking to exclude the police officer's testimony is that it:

(A) Violates the best evidence rule.

(B) Violates the hearsay rule.

(C) Is about a purely collateral matter.

(D) Violates the defendant's privilege against self-incrimination.

Question 17

A plaintiff sued a defendant for personal injuries sustained when the plaintiff slipped and fell on the floor in the defendant's office. The plaintiff called a witness to testify that he was on duty in the hospital emergency room when the plaintiff was admitted and that he saw a doctor treat the plaintiff's skull. As he was getting ready to testify, the witness refreshed his recollection by studying the plaintiff's copy of the hospital records. These records had not been admitted into evidence.

The witness's testimony concerning the treatment should be:

(A) Admitted, as evidence of the extent of the plaintiff's injury.

(B) Admitted, as past recollection recorded.

(C) Excluded, because it is not the best evidence.

(D) Excluded, because it is based on hearsay not within any exception.

Question 18

A defendant was arrested for driving a car while intoxicated. The police took a videotape of the defendant as he attempted to walk a straight line and touch his nose at the time of the arrest. The prosecution seeks to introduce this tape at the defendant's trial.

The videotape is:

(A) Admissible, because it is more substantive than prejudicial.

(B) Admissible, as an admission.

(C) Inadmissible, because it violates the defendant's privilege against self-incrimination.

(D) Inadmissible, because a specific instance of misconduct cannot be proved by extrinsic evidence.

EVIDENCE ANSWERS - SET 4

Answer to Question 1

(D) The attorney may invoke the attorney-client privilege because the presence of a minor client's parent does not waive the privilege. A client has a privilege to refuse to disclose, and to prevent others from disclosing, confidential communications between herself and her lawyer. The attorney-client privilege requires that, at the time of the communication, the client be seeking the professional services of the attorney. Disclosures made before the lawyer has decided to accept or decline the case are covered if the other requirements of the privilege are met. A communication is confidential if it is not intended to be disclosed to third persons; thus, communications made in the known presence and hearing of a stranger are not privileged. However, statements made in front of third persons whose presence is reasonably necessary to the consultation (*e.g.*, this client's parent) are still considered confidential. Here, the child was consulting with the attorney for the purpose of seeking the attorney's professional services. During this consultation, the child made disclosures concerning her injuries that were not intended to be disclosed to third persons. Thus, the child's communication would be deemed confidential. This confidentiality would not be lost by virtue of the fact that the communication was made in the presence of the father, whose presence was reasonably necessary given the child's age. Because the elements of the attorney-client privilege are thus satisfied, the attorney may invoke the privilege on behalf of the child to refuse to disclose his discussion with the child concerning the child's injuries. (A) is incorrect because the attorney-client privilege does not depend on an actual hiring of the attorney. The requisite relationship exists simply by virtue of the fact that, at the time of the communication, the child was seeking the attorney's professional services. (B) is incorrect because the person who was the attorney at the time of the communication can claim the privilege on behalf of the client. The attorney's authority to do this is presumed in the absence of any evidence to the contrary. (C) is incorrect because application of the privilege does not hinge on payment for services. The confidential communications of a client receiving a professional consultation free of charge are protected to the same extent as those made to a lawyer charging for his time.

Answer to Question 2

(D) The judge may call witnesses upon her own initiative and may interrogate any witnesses who testify. [*See* Fed. R. Evid. 614] The judge has total discretion in this area as long as no partisanship for a particular side is shown. (A), (B), and (C) are incorrect because none of these circumstances would preclude a judge from questioning the witness. As stated above, a judge may question or cross-examine any witness at any time as long as she does not demonstrate partisanship for one side of the controversy.

Answer to Question 3

(B) The court should require the sociologist to answer the question because it is relevant to the truthfulness and credibility of the witness. Any matter that tends to prove or disprove the credibility of a witness is relevant and should be admitted. Specific "bad acts" that show the witness unworthy of belief (*i.e.*, acts of deceit or lying) are probative of truthfulness. Filing a false income tax return reflects on the witness's veracity and, thus, her credibility. Therefore, the sociologist should be required to respond. (A) is incorrect because inquiry into bad acts ***to impeach a witness's credibility*** is permitted even if the witness was never convicted of a crime. (C) is incorrect because Federal Rule 608 permits inquiry about specific acts of misconduct, within the discretion of the court, if they are probative of truthfulness. However, extrinsic evidence is not

admissible to prove the act. (D) is incorrect because the question relates to truthfulness, and a witness's credibility is always relevant.

Answer to Question 4

(B) The court should find the customer's testimony admissible as relevant evidence that the department store was aware of the defect. Hearsay is a statement, other than one made by the declarant while testifying at the trial or hearing, offered in evidence to prove the truth of the matter asserted. [Fed. R. Evid. 801(c)] A hearsay statement to which no exception to the hearsay rule is applicable must be excluded upon appropriate objection to its admission. [Fed. R. Evid. 802] A statement that would be inadmissible hearsay may be admissible to show the effect of the statement on the hearer or reader. For example, in a negligence case where knowledge of a danger is in issue, a third person's statement of warning is admissible to show notice or knowledge on the part of a listener. Here, the neighbor's remark to the manager is an out-of-court statement. However, the statement can be offered to show that the department store had notice of a possible danger posed by the escalator. (Note that the remark would be inadmissible hearsay if offered to prove the escalator was speeding up and stopping.) (A) is incorrect because it states an exception to the hearsay rule, and the testimony offered is not hearsay (*see* above). Even if the testimony were offered to prove the escalator was malfunctioning, this exception would not apply because the declarant (the neighbor) made no statement against ***her*** interest. Also, she is available to testify, which takes her statement out of the exception. (C) is incorrect because the customer's testimony is admissible nonhearsay. In addition, the unavailability of a declarant is only significant with regard to certain hearsay exceptions that require unavailability (*e.g.*, the statement against interest). If the customer's testimony is offered to show notice to the department store of a potential problem with the escalator, there is no hearsay problem. The absence of a hearsay problem precludes resort to a hearsay exception and the availability of the neighbor is of no significance. (D) is incorrect because the neighbor's statement is not hearsay since it is not offered to prove the truth of the matter asserted (*i.e.*, that the escalator was malfunctioning), but to show notice of the defect.

Answer to Question 5

(C) The objection should be sustained because the attorney-client privilege applies. A client has a privilege to refuse to disclose, and to prevent others from disclosing, confidential communications between himself (or his representative) and his lawyer (or her representative). A "representative of a lawyer" is one who is employed to assist in the rendition of legal services. If a physician examines a client at the request of the attorney (*e.g.*, to assess the extent of injury), the attorney-client privilege applies to communications made to the physician because the physician is deemed to be a representative of the attorney. (A) is incorrect because the statements are privileged under the attorney-client privilege. Absent this privilege, the statements would be admissible as admissions of a party-opponent. An admission is a statement made or act done that amounts to a prior acknowledgment by one of the parties of a relevant fact. The plaintiff's negligence is a relevant fact and his statements to the physician constitute an acknowledgment thereof. (B) is incorrect because whether the physician qualifies as an expert is irrelevant. This situation does not call for expert testimony. Expert opinion testimony is appropriate when the subject matter is such that scientific, technical, or other specialized knowledge would assist the finder of fact in understanding the evidence or determining a fact in issue. The physician is not being called to give her opinion on some matter that calls for specialized knowledge, such as matters pertaining to medicine. Rather, she is being called to testify that the plaintiff acknowledged his negligence. Thus, the principles of expert opinion testimony are inapplicable to these facts. (D) is incorrect for two reasons: (i) The physician-patient privilege protects only information that is necessary to enable the physician to act in her professional capacity. Thus, if information given by the patient deals with a nonmedical matter, the information is not privileged. The plaintiff's statements concerning his negligence were not necessary to enable the physician to treat or diagnose his condition. Therefore, this information obtained by the physician is not covered by the privilege. (ii) The privilege is not applicable where the patient has put his physical condition in issue by, *e.g.*, suing for personal injuries. Here, the plaintiff is suing the defendant for personal injuries. Consequently, even if the plaintiff's statements to the physician constituted information that would be deemed privileged, the privilege is not applicable in this case.

Answer to Question 6

(A) The defendant's guilty plea is an admission by a party-opponent and thus is admissible. Under the Federal Rules, an admission by a party-opponent is not hearsay. [Fed. R. Evid. 801(d)(2)] An admission is a statement made or act done that amounts to a prior acknowledgment by one of the parties to an action of a relevant fact. A plea of guilty to a traffic infraction is a formal judicial admission. The admission is conclusive in a prosecution for that infraction, but if the plea is used in another proceeding, it is merely an evidentiary admission (*i.e.*, it is not conclusive and can be explained). Here, the defendant has acknowledged by her guilty plea that she was speeding at the time of the accident. This fact is relevant to the plaintiff's suit for personal injuries because it increases the likelihood that the defendant was at fault in the accident that caused those injuries. Therefore, the defendant's guilty plea is admissible in the current civil action as an evidentiary admission. (B) is wrong because there is no indication that the defendant is unavailable. Statements of a person, now unavailable as a witness, against that person's pecuniary, proprietary, or penal interest when made are admissible under the statement against interest exception to the hearsay rule. [Fed. R. Evid. 804(b)(3)] A declarant is unavailable if: (i) she is exempt from testifying due to a privilege, (ii) she refuses to testify, (iii) she testifies to lack of memory of the subject matter, (iv) she is dead or ill, or (v) she is absent and the statement's proponent has been unable to procure her attendance or testimony by process or other reasonable means. [Fed. R. Evid. 804(a)(1) - (5)] Since the defendant apparently is available as a witness in the suit, the statement against interest exception is inapplicable. Although it may be true that public policy favors plea bargaining, (C) is wrong because there is no attempt here to offer a statement made during the plea bargaining process. Under the Federal Rules, ***withdrawn*** guilty pleas, pleas of nolo contendere, offers to plead guilty, and evidence of statements made in negotiating such pleas are not admissible in any proceeding. [Fed. R. Evid. 410] However, there is no prohibition against admitting the guilty plea itself. This question asks whether the guilty plea is admissible, not whether statements made in negotiation thereof are admissible. Thus, the policy favoring plea bargains is irrelevant. (D) is wrong because the question asks about the admissibility of the plea rather than a copy of the conviction. Convictions may be introduced to prove any fact essential to the case only if they are felony convictions. [Fed. R. Evid. 803(22)] Because the conviction is not being offered, the fact that a felony is not involved is of no consequence. The defendant's ***plea*** is admissible as an admission even though a felony was not involved.

Answer to Question 7

(D) The report is inadmissible hearsay because it is an out-of-court statement being offered for its truth, and it does not fall within any exception to the hearsay rule. It does not qualify as a business record because the report was not made in the course of a regularly conducted business activity. Records prepared in anticipation of litigation, such as at the request of the defendant's liability insurance carrier, generally are not admissible under the rule of *Palmer v. Hoffman*.

Hence, (A) is incorrect. (B) is incorrect because an expert may rely on inadmissible evidence as long as it is a kind reasonably relied on by experts in that field, but relying on it does not make it admissible. (C) is incorrect because interest goes to the weight, not the admissibility, of the evidence. The plaintiff's attorney may elicit on cross-examination information regarding the bias of the party preparing the report.

Answer to Question 8

(C) The prosecution must prove beyond a reasonable doubt that the victim did not consent even if the defendant remains silent on the issue. In a criminal prosecution, the state is required to establish the guilt of the defendant beyond a reasonable doubt. This requirement means that the state must establish every element of the offense beyond a reasonable doubt. The defendant is not required to establish the nonexistence of any element of the crime. This is a false imprisonment case. Under the common law definition, false imprisonment consists of: (i) the unlawful confinement of a person (ii) without his valid consent. Thus, lack of consent by the victim of a false imprisonment is an element of the offense, and as such, must be proven beyond a reasonable doubt by the prosecution. The defendant need not raise the issue to trigger the prosecution's burden of establishing lack of consent. (A) is incorrect because, as explained above, the burden is not on the defendant to establish consent; rather, the burden is on the prosecution to establish lack of consent. (B) is incorrect because the victim's lack of consent is an element of the crime charged, and the prosecution must establish it beyond a reasonable doubt. (D) is incorrect because it would require the defendant to disprove (or at least challenge) the element of lack of consent prior to the prosecution's being required to prove lack of consent.

Answer to Question 9

(A) A motion to strike is effective only where there was no basis or opportunity for an earlier objection. An objection ordinarily must be made after the question is asked, but before the witness answers. If the question is not objectionable, but the answer is, a motion to strike is appropriate. Here, the question was clearly objectionable and the prosecution had time to object. In most states, reputation or opinion evidence of the past sexual behavior of an alleged rape victim or evidence of the rape victim's sexual relations with persons other than the defendant is not admissible. The Federal Rules also exclude such evidence. Thus, the testimony of the witness regarding the victim's reputation for chastity would have been inadmissible. At the time the defense attorney asked this question, it was clear that the witness's answer would necessarily involve inadmissible matter. Therefore, the prosecutor was required to make an objection before the witness answered the question, rather than waiting to see if the answer was damaging to his case. Because the prosecutor failed to make a timely objection despite the opportunity to do so, the testimony of the witness is admissible, and there is no basis for a motion to strike such testimony. (B) reaches the correct result, but for an incorrect reason. While consent is a material issue because the state must prove the absence thereof to establish guilt of rape, whatever probative value the witness's testimony may have is deemed to be outweighed by the dangers of unfair prejudice arising from such evidence of unchastity. Therefore, the relevance of the witness's testimony to the issue of consent would not constitute a basis for denying the motion to strike. As has been explained, the motion is denied because of a lack of timely objection by the prosecutor. (C) is incorrect because, as discussed above, the motion should not be granted because objection to the witness's testimony was not timely. (D), although it states the correct rule of law, is also incorrect because the prosecutor's failure to object to this evidence in a timely manner resulted in its admission, and the motion to strike the witness's testimony is ineffective.

Answer to Question 10

(B) Asking the witness about the assault charge is an improper method of impeachment. A witness may be interrogated upon cross-examination with respect to an act of misconduct only if it is ***probative of truthfulness***. An assault is not probative of truthfulness, so it would not be proper impeachment evidence. Had the witness been convicted of the assault, the conviction would have been admissible, provided it was a felony. (A) is incorrect because it is an example of proper impeachment by showing bias. Evidence that a witness is biased tends to show that he has a motive to lie. The witness's close relationship to his wife gives rise to an inference that he would be hostile toward the co-worker if she and his wife had a longstanding personal enmity. Consequently, the question posed in (A) represents a proper method of impeaching the witness's credibility by probing into a possible bias against the co-worker. (C) and (D) are incorrect because these questions represent proper means of rebutting the evidence of the co-worker's character for dishonesty, as well as trying to impeach the witness's credibility based on lack of knowledge. Evidence of a character trait of the alleged crime victim may be offered by the prosecution to rebut a defendant's evidence of bad character of the victim. [Fed. R. Evid. 404] The prosecution may prove such a trait by reputation evidence as well as by opinion evidence. On cross-examination, the prosecution may inquire into relevant specific instances of conduct. [Fed. R. Evid. 405(a)] Traditionally, asking a witness if he has heard of a particular instance of conduct represents a means of testing the accuracy of the hearing and reporting of a ***reputation*** witness, who relates what he has heard. Asking a witness if he knows of a particular instance of conduct is a means of testing the basis of an ***opinion*** expressed by the witness. Here, the witness's testimony indicates both that he has heard that the co-worker has a bad reputation for honesty and that his own opinion is that she is a dishonest person. Thus, in attempting to rebut this testimony, the prosecution may test the accuracy of what the witness has heard concerning the co-worker's character by asking him if he has heard of specific instances of her teaching Sunday School and receiving a church award. Also, the prosecution may test the basis for the witness's opinion as to the co-worker's dishonesty by asking if he knows of these specific instances that are indicative of her good character.

Answer to Question 11

(B) The physician's testimony regarding the plaintiff's statement is admissible because an examination for insurance purposes is not considered to be for diagnosis and treatment. To be privileged, the information must be acquired by the physician in the course of treatment. Some states have expanded this to include a consultation for diagnosis, but an insurance examination would not qualify as diagnostic either. Thus, the plaintiff's statement to the physician is not privileged. Since it is not privileged and qualifies as an admission by a party-opponent for hearsay purposes, the statement is admissible. (A) is wrong because an attempt by the plaintiff to perpetrate a fraud is not the only way that the physician could testify to the plaintiff's statement. It is true that the physician-patient privilege does not apply if the physician's services were sought or obtained in aid of planning a crime or tort, but that is not the only time it is inapplicable. Moreover, it is nearly impossible to believe that the plaintiff could have been attempting to lay the groundwork for a fraudulent claim, given the facts that the insurance examination occurred before the accident and the statement was against his interest. As noted above, the privilege never attached since the plaintiff was not seeking diagnosis or treatment. Even if it had, the mere fact that the plaintiff has put his physical condition in issue by suing for injuries is sufficient to abrogate the privilege. There would be no need to resort to proof of an attempted fraud. (C) is wrong because the plaintiff's statement, despite having been made while the physician was attending to the plaintiff in a professional capacity, is not privileged for two reasons: (i) the plaintiff was not

seeking diagnosis or treatment, and (ii) he put his physical condition in issue. (D) is wrong because the preexisting back injury is relevant on issues of causation and damages.

Answer to Question 12

(D) The officer may not testify about the embezzlement because it constitutes impeachment by extrinsic evidence of a specific instance of misconduct. A specific act of misconduct offered to attack the witness's character for truthfulness can be elicited only on cross-examination. If the witness denies the act, the cross-examiner cannot refute the answer by calling other witnesses or producing other evidence. Since the alleged embezzlement is admissible, if at all, only as impeachment evidence, when the defendant denied it the prosecutor could not call the officer to testify. (A) is wrong because extrinsic evidence, such as the officer's testimony, of an instance of misconduct is not admissible. (B) is wrong because when a person is charged with one crime, extrinsic evidence of other crimes or misconduct is inadmissible to establish criminal disposition. Since nothing in the facts indicates that such evidence is being offered to prove something other than disposition (*e.g.*, motive, identity, common plan or scheme), the officer's testimony is not admissible as substantive evidence. As discussed above, for impeachment, the prosecutor is limited to inquiry on cross-examination regarding the embezzlement. (C) is wrong because, even if the defendant had been convicted of the embezzlement, the officer's testimony would not be the proper way to introduce it. The fact that a witness has been convicted of a crime is proved by eliciting an admission on cross-examination or by the record of conviction.

Answer to Question 13

(B) The wife may testify if she chooses to do so. In federal court, the privilege of spousal immunity belongs to the witness-spouse. There are two privileges based on the marital relationship. Under spousal immunity, a person whose spouse is the defendant in a criminal case may not be called as a witness by the prosecution, and a married person may not be compelled to testify against her spouse in any criminal proceeding. In federal court, one spouse may choose to testify against the other in a criminal case, with or without the consent of the party-spouse. Spousal immunity lasts only during the marriage and terminates upon divorce. However, as long as a marriage exists, the privilege can be asserted even as to matters that occurred prior to the marriage. Since the defendant is a criminal defendant, his wife cannot be compelled to testify about his conversation with the visitor. She may, however, choose to testify, and the defendant cannot stop her. The other choices reflect elements of the privilege for confidential marital communications. Under that privilege, either spouse (whether or not a party) may refuse to disclose, and may prevent another from disclosing, a confidential communication made between the spouses while they were husband and wife. The communication must be made during a marriage, and must be in reliance upon the intimacy of the marital relationship, which is presumed in the absence of contrary evidence. This privilege is not afforded to a communication that is made in the known presence of a stranger. Both spouses jointly hold this privilege. The conversation between the defendant and the visitor cannot qualify as a confidential marital communication for several reasons. Most importantly, it was not a communication between the defendant and his wife. Moreover, the incident did not occur during the marriage. Thus, the privilege for confidential marital communications does not apply, and the defendant cannot prevent his wife's testimony should she choose to testify. (A) is wrong because it states a reason why the privilege for confidential marital communications does not apply. Spousal immunity still applies; thus (B) is a better choice because it reflects the fact that the wife's testimony cannot be compelled. (C) is wrong because, in federal court, spousal immunity does not permit the defendant-spouse to foreclose testimony by the witness-spouse. As discussed above, the privilege for confidential marital communications, under which both spouses may prevent disclosure, does not apply here. (D) is wrong for the same reason.

Answer to Question 14

(B) The judge determines whether the testimony falls within an exception to the hearsay rule, and is generally not limited by the rules of evidence in making that determination. The Federal Rules of Evidence distinguish between preliminary facts to be decided by the jury, which involve whether the proffered evidence is relevant, and preliminary facts decided by the judge, which involve whether the evidence is competent, *i.e.*, not barred by an exclusionary rule. All preliminary fact questions that determine the applicability of an exception to the hearsay rule must be determined by the judge, because the competency of the evidence will depend on that preliminary fact determination. In making this preliminary fact determination, the trial court may consider any nonprivileged relevant evidence, even though it would not otherwise be admissible under the rules of evidence. [Fed. R. Evid. 104(a)] In this case, then, the judge should decide whether the testimony falls within the present sense impression exception, and she is not limited in making this determination by the rules of evidence other than privilege. (A) is incorrect because the judge's preliminary fact determination does not need to be based on the rules of evidence (other than privilege rules). (C) and (D) are incorrect because, as discussed above, determining whether the testimony falls within the scope of the hearsay exception is a determination of whether the evidence is competent, and this determination is made by the judge rather than the jury.

Answer to Question 15

(A) Prior testimony is admissible as an exception to the hearsay rule if the testimony was given under oath and the party against whom the evidence is now offered either offered the testimony or had the testimony offered against him at the former trial, and had an opportunity and similar motive to develop the testimony either on direct or cross-examination. [Fed. R. Evid. 804(b)(1)] (B) is wrong because a past recollection recorded requires testimony from the witness whose statement was recorded. (C) is wrong because the disposition at the previous trial has no bearing on the admissibility of prior testimony. (D) is wrong because the motive to cross-examine was identical at each trial—to discredit the sister's testimony.

Answer to Question 16

(A) The membership card would be a writing within the meaning of the best evidence rule. As such, secondary evidence as to its existence could only be introduced if the original is shown to have been lost or destroyed, unobtainable, or within the control of the opponent. (B) is incorrect because the police officer's testimony about the name on the card would not violate the hearsay rule. The evidence is not being offered to prove the truth of the matter asserted in the card. It is being offered to show that the defendant possessed the card, and is circumstantial evidence that the defendant committed the crime. (C) is incorrect because the existence of the membership card on the defendant's person is not collateral to the issues involved. (D) is incorrect because the privilege against self-incrimination prevents a witness from being compelled to testify against himself, which is not the case here.

Answer to Question 17

(A) The witness's testimony should be admitted as evidence of the extent of the plaintiff's injury, because it relates to his firsthand observations and is otherwise admissible. (B) is wrong because the witness is not reading from the records as he testifies, and the record is not being introduced.

In addition, a proper foundation has not been laid for the introduction of the records as a past recollection recorded. (C) is wrong because the witness's testimony is about what he saw, not about the contents of the records. (D) is wrong because anything (even hearsay statements) can be used by a witness to refresh his recollection.

Answer to Question 18

(A) The videotape is admissible as relevant and material evidence not excluded by any rule. Furthermore, (A) is the correct pick by process of elimination. (B) is incorrect. The tape is not an admission because it is not a prior acknowledgment by the defendant of a fact in issue. Rather, it is nonassertive conduct offered to show the defendant's mental and physical condition. (C) is incorrect because the privilege against self-incrimination applies only to testimonial evidence. (D) is silly, since almost all crimes (*i.e.*, instances of misconduct) are proven by extrinsic evidence. Note that because this videotape would be considered documentary evidence, a proper foundation will have to be laid before it can be admitted.

Set 5 Answer Sheet

1.	Ⓐ	Ⓑ	Ⓒ	Ⓓ	19.	Ⓐ	Ⓑ	Ⓒ	Ⓓ
2.	Ⓐ	Ⓑ	Ⓒ	Ⓓ	20.	Ⓐ	Ⓑ	Ⓒ	Ⓓ
3.	Ⓐ	Ⓑ	Ⓒ	Ⓓ	21.	Ⓐ	Ⓑ	Ⓒ	Ⓓ
4.	Ⓐ	Ⓑ	Ⓒ	Ⓓ	22.	Ⓐ	Ⓑ	Ⓒ	Ⓓ
5.	Ⓐ	Ⓑ	Ⓒ	Ⓓ	23.	Ⓐ	Ⓑ	Ⓒ	Ⓓ
6.	Ⓐ	Ⓑ	Ⓒ	Ⓓ	24.	Ⓐ	Ⓑ	Ⓒ	Ⓓ
7.	Ⓐ	Ⓑ	Ⓒ	Ⓓ	25.	Ⓐ	Ⓑ	Ⓒ	Ⓓ
8.	Ⓐ	Ⓑ	Ⓒ	Ⓓ	26.	Ⓐ	Ⓑ	Ⓒ	Ⓓ
9.	Ⓐ	Ⓑ	Ⓒ	Ⓓ	27.	Ⓐ	Ⓑ	Ⓒ	Ⓓ
10.	Ⓐ	Ⓑ	Ⓒ	Ⓓ	28.	Ⓐ	Ⓑ	Ⓒ	Ⓓ
11.	Ⓐ	Ⓑ	Ⓒ	Ⓓ	29.	Ⓐ	Ⓑ	Ⓒ	Ⓓ
12.	Ⓐ	Ⓑ	Ⓒ	Ⓓ	30.	Ⓐ	Ⓑ	Ⓒ	Ⓓ
13.	Ⓐ	Ⓑ	Ⓒ	Ⓓ	31.	Ⓐ	Ⓑ	Ⓒ	Ⓓ
14.	Ⓐ	Ⓑ	Ⓒ	Ⓓ	32.	Ⓐ	Ⓑ	Ⓒ	Ⓓ
15.	Ⓐ	Ⓑ	Ⓒ	Ⓓ	33.	Ⓐ	Ⓑ	Ⓒ	Ⓓ
16.	Ⓐ	Ⓑ	Ⓒ	Ⓓ	34.	Ⓐ	Ⓑ	Ⓒ	Ⓓ
17.	Ⓐ	Ⓑ	Ⓒ	Ⓓ	35.	Ⓐ	Ⓑ	Ⓒ	Ⓓ
18.	Ⓐ	Ⓑ	Ⓒ	Ⓓ	36.	Ⓐ	Ⓑ	Ⓒ	Ⓓ

EVIDENCE QUESTIONS - SET 5

Question 1

Undercover police arrested a brother and a sister after a four-month investigation into a series of residential burglaries. During interrogation, the brother admitted that he had committed eight of the burglaries, including one where he stole a valuable painting that he "fenced" to the sister. According to the brother, the sister subsequently sold the painting and gave the brother a share of the sale price. The sister was charged with receipt of stolen property, a misdemeanor offense, and was subsequently convicted. The painting was not recovered and the owners filed suit against the sister for damages. At trial, the brother testified to having "fenced" the painting to the sister.

If the owners' attorney tries to introduce a certified copy of the record of the sister's conviction to corroborate the brother's testimony that the sister possessed and sold the painting, on proper motion this evidence will be:

(A) Excluded, because it is not the best evidence of what happened to the painting.

(B) Excluded, because it is hearsay not within any exception.

(C) Admitted, because a conviction is evidence of the facts necessary to sustain the judgment of the court.

(D) Admitted, because it is an official record.

Question 2

A witness was stopped at an intersection when she saw a car run a red light, strike the victim in the crosswalk, and proceed through the intersection. The witness gave a very detailed description of the driver to the police officer at the scene. Based on this description, the police apprehended the defendant and charged him with several criminal counts for the accident that seriously injured the victim. The witness testified at the trial, but the defendant was acquitted. The victim then filed a civil suit against the defendant to recover for her injuries. Before the trial of the victim's suit, the witness died. In her suit against the defendant, the victim offers into evidence the police report containing the witness's description of the driver. The defendant objects.

The court should find the report:

(A) Admissible, because the report is relevant, and it is not hearsay.

(B) Admissible, because the report falls within the business records exception to the hearsay rule.

(C) Inadmissible, because the report is hearsay not within any exception.

(D) Inadmissible, because the report is not the best evidence.

Question 3

An insured purchased a life insurance policy on his life, naming his brother as beneficiary. Fifteen years ago, the insured traveled overseas on what was supposed to be a six-month trip, but has not been heard from since. The brother contacted the insurance company, which refused to pay the claim on the basis that there was no evidence that the insured was dead. The brother filed suit against the insurance company to collect the proceeds under the policy. The jurisdiction in which the action has commenced has a statute that states that a person is presumed dead if missing from the jurisdiction for seven years, and if no one in the jurisdiction has heard from the person in those seven years.

Assume that no other evidence is admitted at the trial on the issue of the insured's death. Which of the following is the most accurate statement?

(A) The jury will be permitted to find that the insured is alive.

(B) The jury will be permitted to find that the insured is dead.

(C) The judge must rule as a conclusive presumption that the insured is dead.

(D) The jury must find that the insured is dead.

Question 4

A beneficiary has filed a petition in the probate court to contest the validity of a testator's will. The beneficiary contends that when the testator executed the will eight years before, he was an alcoholic and was incapable of forming a valid testamentary intent. In support of this contention, the beneficiary seeks to offer an affidavit prepared by the testator's former attorney, which states that she was asked to prepare a will for the testator just four months before this will was made. The attorney had refused to do so because it was her opinion that the testator suffered from severe mental deficiency as an apparent result of his chronic alcoholism.

The judge should rule this affidavit to be:

(A) Admissible.

(B) Inadmissible, as being violative of the attorney-client privilege.

(C) Inadmissible, because it is hearsay not within any exception.

(D) Inadmissible, because it is improper opinion evidence.

Question 5

A plaintiff was injured in an automobile accident when her car was hit by a pickup truck driven by the defendant. At trial of her personal injury action, the plaintiff alleges that the defendant was driving on the wrong side of the road in excess of the posted speed limit. The defendant denies these allegations and denies liability for the accident. The plaintiff seeks to introduce evidence that the defendant has a reputation in the community for being a daredevil and for being somewhat irresponsible. In fact, the plaintiff's witness would testify that the defendant is known by all his friends as "the Menace."

The proffered testimony is:

(A) Admissible, because reputation evidence is a proper method of proving character.

(B) Admissible, because it is relevant.

(C) Inadmissible, to show that the defendant was negligent on this occasion.

(D) Inadmissible, because the defendant did not introduce evidence of his reputation for carefulness.

Question 6

A brother and a sister were arrested on the federal charge of tax evasion in connection with the family business. Prior to trial, the prosecutor tells the sister that he believes he can get her sentence reduced to probation if she pleads guilty to a lesser charge and agrees to testify against her brother; the sister reluctantly agrees. During the jury trial, the sister is called by the prosecution. On cross-examination, the defense attorney brings out the fact that the sister was arrested on the same charge. The attorney then asks her whether it is true that after her arrest, the prosecutor told her that if she testifies against her brother her sentence can be reduced to probation. The prosecutor objects.

The objection should be:

(A) Sustained, because it is against public policy to reveal information about plea bargains to a jury.

(B) Sustained, because it calls for hearsay.

(C) Overruled, because the question goes to bias or interest.

(D) Overruled, because the sister waived the attorney-client privilege by testifying.

Question 7

A defendant is on trial for violating a statute forbidding possession of a concealed weapon within 100 yards of a government building. The prosecution presents evidence that the defendant was arrested on a street corner with a handgun in his pocket. The building housing the local city hall occupies the entire block on the north and east sides of the two streets where the defendant was apprehended.

Which of the following statements is most accurate regarding judicial notice of the location of the city hall?

(A) The judge may take judicial notice of this fact without resort to a map, and should instruct the jury that it may, but need not, accept this fact as evidence of an element of the offense.

(B) The judge may take judicial notice of this fact only upon reference to an official street map of the city.

(C) The judge may not take judicial notice of this type of fact in a criminal case without a request by the prosecution.

(D) If the judge properly takes judicial notice of this fact, a presumption is created that shifts the burden of persuasion to the defendant to disprove this fact.

Question 8

As the streets of her neighborhood have become more dangerous due to gang warfare, the victim has become very active and vocal in the anti-gang movement. One evening, a brick with the victim's name scrawled on it was thrown through her bedroom window. The brick struck the victim, causing severe injuries. The victim believes that her ex-boyfriend, who is a gang member, threw the brick, but she did not actually see him throw it.

If the ex-boyfriend is arrested and put on trial for battery, which of the following items of the victim's proposed testimony is ***least*** likely to be admitted?

(A) The victim recently moved to a new apartment and only her ex-boyfriend and a few family members knew its location.

(B) The victim had testified against a member of her ex-boyfriend's gang last month in a drug case.

(C) On another occasion, the victim had seen her ex-boyfriend throw a rock through the window of a rival street gang member.

(D) Immediately after the brick went through her window, the victim heard a voice she recognized as her ex-boyfriend's yell, "If you don't start minding your own business, you'll get a lot worse than this next time!"

Question 9

A victim reported to the police that she had been raped by a masked man in her apartment. Although the mask made it impossible for the victim to give the detectives a complete description of her attacker, the police did retrieve a pair of gloves from the tenant's apartment. After a thorough criminal investigation, the police concluded that the defendant had been given a key to the victim's apartment by the manager of the apartment complex, and that the defendant used the key to facilitate the attack on the victim. Warrants were issued against the defendant for rape and conspiracy to commit rape, and against the manager for conspiracy to commit rape. The defendant was successfully apprehended, but the manager disappeared and had not yet been apprehended at the time of the defendant's trial. The defendant's defense is that he never had been in the victim's apartment. The prosecution wishes to call the manager's live-in girlfriend, who is prepared to testify that, two days after the attack, the manager told her, "I never should have given the key to the victim's apartment to the defendant—not only did he not get the stereo like he was supposed to, he also said that he thinks he left his gloves in her apartment."

After appropriate objection by the defense attorney, the court should find the statement:

(A) Admissible, because it is a statement against interest.

(B) Admissible, because it is a statement by a co-conspirator.

(C) Inadmissible, because it is hearsay within hearsay.

(D) Inadmissible, because the statement does not indicate that the manager knew of or agreed to a plan to rape the victim.

Question 10

A defendant is charged with beating a victim to death with a set of brass knuckles during the course of a fight in a tavern. The victim was found to have a pistol on his person at the time of the fight. During the course of the trial, the defendant took the stand in his own defense and testified that the victim threatened him with a gun and the defendant had hit the victim with the brass knuckles in self-defense. To rebut the defendant's claim, the prosecution wishes to place the bartender on the stand, who will testify that two years prior to the attack on the victim, she had seen the defendant approach a customer in her tavern from behind, put on a pair of brass knuckles, and strike the customer a severe blow on the side of the face with a brass-knuckled fist. The prosecutor, in accordance with local court rules, has apprised the defense attorney of the general tenor of the bartender's proposed testimony. As soon as the bartender is sworn in, the defense attorney raises an objection.

The court should rule that the bartender's testimony is:

(A) Admissible, as substantive evidence that the defendant did not act in self-defense in beating the victim.

(B) Admissible, to attack the defendant's credibility.

(C) Inadmissible, because prior bad acts cannot be admitted to prove the defendant's propensity to commit the specific crime with which he is charged.

(D) Inadmissible, because the defendant has not put his character in issue in this case.

Question 11

An expert witness, who has an advanced degree in engineering, is testifying at a jury trial to the possible causes for the failure of an enclosed pedestrian bridge in a shopping mall.

Which of the following data, if relied on by the expert witness in forming his opinion, is admissible on direct examination as substantive evidence?

(A) Statements told to him by witnesses to the collapse, as long as such statements are reasonably relied on by experts in his field.

(B) Statements that he reads from a text on structural engineering that he has testified is authoritative.

(C) Testimony regarding the repair of the bridge one week after the collapse, indicating that it is now equipped with special safety features that were not installed prior to the collapse.

(D) Statements made to him by a former maintenance employee of the shopping mall indicating that the management knew the bridge needed repairs but delayed doing so because the busy holiday season was approaching.

Question 12

Three masked men robbed a convenience store, during the course of which a clerk was killed. An investigation led the police to believe the defendant was one of the robbers and they placed him under arrest. The defendant protested that he was innocent and volunteered to take a lie detector test. The test was conducted by a qualified polygraph expert. According to the expert's analysis of the test, the defendant lied about his participation in the armed robbery. At the defendant's jury trial for the armed robbery, the prosecution calls the expert to the stand to testify as to her analysis of the results of the polygraph test. The defense objects.

If the objection is sustained, it will most likely be because:

(A) The expert's testimony would violate the defendant's right against self-incrimination if he elects not to take the stand in his own defense.

(B) The expert's testimony would violate the defendant's right against self-incrimination, regardless of whether he elects to take the stand in his own defense.

(C) Polygraph evidence is considered to be unreliable and potentially confusing to jurors.

(D) The Federal Rules specifically classify polygraph evidence as irrelevant.

Question 13

A plaintiff sued a defendant for defamation, asserting in her complaint that the defendant had called the plaintiff a thief in front of a number of business associates. The plaintiff calls two witnesses to the stand, both of whom testify that they heard the defendant refer to the plaintiff as a thief in front of the business associates. The plaintiff does not take the stand herself. The defendant pleads truth of the statement as an affirmative defense and calls a witness to the stand. The defense witness is prepared to testify that he was a co-worker of the plaintiff when the plaintiff supplemented her income by tending bar three nights a week. The witness will testify that he saw the plaintiff take a $20 bill from the tavern's cash register and secrete the money in her pocket. The plaintiff's attorney objects.

May the defense witness's testimony be allowed?

(A) Yes, as substantive evidence that the plaintiff is, in fact, a thief.

(B) Yes, because theft is a crime indicating dishonesty.

(C) No, because specific bad acts may not be used to show bad character.

(D) No, because the plaintiff never took the stand.

Question 14

In a trial for bank robbery, a teller has identified the defendant as the robber. Defense counsel offers into evidence a still frame from a video taken by the bank security camera the day after the robbery to show that a column obstructed that teller's view of the defendant.

Such evidence is:

(A) Admissible upon testimony by the camera operator that the still frame was developed from film that was taken from that camera the day after the robbery.

(B) Admissible upon testimony by a bank employee that the photo accurately portrays the scene of the crime.

(C) Not admissible into evidence but usable by a witness for explanatory purposes.

(D) Not admissible if a still frame can be obtained from a video taken at the time of the robbery.

Question 15

A plaintiff sued a defendant over a claimed debt. At the trial, the plaintiff established the existence of the debt and testified that he never received payment. In response, the defendant presents evidence sufficient to establish that she took her check to the post office and sent it to the plaintiff's proper address by certified mail. The defendant offers a certified mail receipt with an illegible signature, which she claims is the plaintiff's signature. The defendant also presents evidence that her basement flooded on March 28, and she claims that she cannot produce a canceled check because her box of canceled checks was destroyed from the water damage. Evidence is also presented that, due to a computer glitch, the defendant's bank cannot reproduce her checking account records for the months of February and March.

After the defendant's testimony:

(A) The burden of persuasion and the burden of going forward with the evidence are on the plaintiff.

(B) The burden of persuasion is on the plaintiff, but he has no burden of going forward with the evidence.

(C) The plaintiff has satisfied his burden of persuasion, but he has a burden of going forward with the evidence.

(D) The plaintiff has satisfied both his burden of persuasion and his burden of going forward with the evidence.

Question 16

A plaintiff was injured in an automobile accident caused by the defendant. The plaintiff sued the defendant for his injuries. In preparation for trial, the plaintiff's attorney hired a doctor to examine the plaintiff. At trial, the defense attorney attempts to call the doctor as a witness to testify about statements the plaintiff made in confidence to the doctor about his injuries, which the doctor then communicated to the plaintiff's attorney. The state recognizes only the common law privileges.

This testimony should be:

(A) Admitted, because the plaintiff's statements are the statements of a party-opponent.

(B) Admitted, because the plaintiff waived the physician-patient privilege by placing his physical condition in issue.

(C) Excluded, because the plaintiff's statements are protected by the attorney-client privilege.

(D) Excluded, because the plaintiff's statements are protected by the physician-patient privilege.

Question 17

While driving home late one night, the defendant struck a child who was playing in the street near the curb. The child was seriously injured. After being questioned by the police and released, the defendant went home and told his wife what had happened. During this conversation, the defendant stated, "Between you and me, just before all this happened, I took a quick peek at the back seat to make sure I brought my briefcase home with me. If I had kept my eyes on the road, I never would've hit the kid." Unknown to either the defendant or his wife, their neighbor overheard this conversation through her open window. The child's parents filed a lawsuit on his behalf against the defendant. Shortly before the trial, the defendant and his wife divorced. Greatly embittered by the circumstances of the divorce, the wife agreed to testify to the statement made to her by the defendant on the night he struck the child.

Assuming a proper objection by the defense attorney, will the wife be permitted to so testify?

(A) Yes, because she and the defendant were divorced during the time between the making of the statement and the trial.

(B) Yes, because the fact that the neighbor heard the statement removes the privileged status of the statement.

(C) No, because the defendant's statement was a confidential marital communication.

(D) No, because the privilege to foreclose such testimony belongs to the party-spouse.

Question 18

A husband and a wife were arrested by federal agents and charged with distributing obscene materials through the United States mails. When called before a grand jury, the wife refused to say anything, invoking her Fifth Amendment right to be protected from compelled self-incrimination. The husband was terrified of the grand jury and readily admitted

under questioning that he sent obscene matter through the mail. He also incriminated his wife in the illegal activity. The thought of a trial and a prison term drove the husband over the edge, and he committed suicide two days before his trial was to begin. A month later, the wife was put on trial in federal district court. The federal prosecutor seeks to introduce a transcript of the husband's grand jury testimony into evidence against the wife. The defense attorney objects.

The court should rule that the grand jury transcript is:

(A) Admissible, as an admission.

(B) Admissible, as former testimony.

(C) Inadmissible, because the wife can invoke the spousal privilege, even though her husband is now deceased.

(D) Inadmissible, because the husband's testimony was not subject to cross-examination.

Question 19

A merchant sued a company for breach of contract, alleging that the products she purchased failed to conform to contract specifications. Shortly before the trial was to begin, the merchant suffered a stroke that left her paralyzed and virtually unable to communicate. Her guardian was properly substituted as the plaintiff in the lawsuit. At trial, following presentation of the plaintiff's case, the company calls as a witness a priest to question him about a conversation he had with the merchant at a church fundraiser. In this conversation, the merchant told the priest in confidence that the products she received were actually quite functional, but that she had become aware of a lower price being offered by another vendor, and thus wanted to get out of her contract with the company. The plaintiff's attorney immediately objects on the basis of clergy-penitent privilege.

The objection should be:

(A) Sustained, because the merchant's statement was made to the priest in confidence.

(B) Sustained, because this is not a criminal case.

(C) Overruled, because the privilege can be invoked only by the person who made the confidential statement.

(D) Overruled, because the circumstances under which the merchant made the statement take it outside the scope of the privilege.

Question 20

A decedent's executor filed a wrongful death suit against a railroad company whose freight train collided with the decedent's automobile, killing him instantly. After the accident it was impossible for experts to tell whether one of the crossing gates was broken because a vehicle drove through it, or if it broke while being lowered suddenly on top of a vehicle entering the grade crossing. A motorist who did not see the accident but who arrived on the scene just seconds later heard a pedestrian standing near the grade crossing exclaim, "That gate didn't come down on time!" The pedestrian collapsed after making his statement. An emergency medical technician tended to the pedestrian. She told the pedestrian that he had probably suffered a mild heart attack. The pedestrian told the medical technician, "Well, I guess I'm a lot luckier than that poor fool who rammed his car right through that crossing barrier into the train." Two months later, the pedestrian suffered another heart attack and died. Four months later, the executor's suit came to trial. The plaintiff called the motorist to the stand, and the court allowed him to testify to what he heard the pedestrian say after the accident. The railroad's attorney wishes to call the medical technician to the stand to testify as to the pedestrian's statement when she was treating him.

The medical technician's testimony should be ruled:

(A) Admissible, but solely for the purpose of impeachment.

(B) Admissible, both for impeachment purposes and as evidence of the positioning of the crossing gate at the time of the accident.

(C) Inadmissible, because the pedestrian is not available to be questioned about the inconsistent statements.

(D) Inadmissible, as hearsay not within any recognized exception to the hearsay rule.

Question 21

A test preparation course sued a rival program for interference with business relations. The rival program had taken the test preparation course's reply cards from various colleges and mailed them in, hoping to swamp the clerks with work and cut the course's profit margin. The rival program also induced a professor under contract with the course to break his contract and lecture with the rival program for a percentage of the profits. The course director caught on to what the rival program was up to after the professor suddenly left the course. The director ordered his clerks to log in, for a two-week period, any and all business reply requests from the rival program's city. Immediately after the tally record was complete, the test preparation course filed its suit. At trial, the course's attorney offers the tally record into evidence. The defense attorney objects.

The court should find the tally record:

(A) Admissible, as past recollection recorded.

(B) Admissible, as a business record.

(C) Inadmissible, because unless it is shown that the clerks are unavailable, their testimony is the best evidence.

(D) Inadmissible, because it is hearsay not within any exception.

Question 22

A decedent was prosecuted for criminal violations of a hazardous waste disposal act and convicted, in part on the testimony of a witness. After the decedent's death, the plaintiff on whose property the decedent dumped the hazardous waste brought suit to recover the cleanup costs against the executor of the decedent's estate. Because the witness is currently incarcerated in another state, the plaintiff seeks to introduce the transcript of the witness's testimony from the decedent's criminal trial in the present action. The executor objects to its admission.

The court should rule that the transcript is:

(A) Admissible, because the witness was subject to cross-examination in the previous action.

(B) Admissible, because the transcript of the criminal trial is a public record.

(C) Inadmissible, because the plaintiff has not shown that the witness is truly "unavailable."

(D) Inadmissible, because the executor was not a party to the previous action.

Question 23

The key witness in the prosecution's case against the defendant is the only eyewitness to have seen the commission of the felony for which the defendant is being charged. The witness, a recent immigrant, has a total hearing impairment and is mute. In addition, the system of "signing" for the deaf is different in the witness's country of origin from the method used in the United States. The only person in the county conversant with the witness's signing method is a clerk in the county prosecutor's office. The clerk had assisted the police in their questioning of the witness prior to the defendant's arrest, and also when the witness identified the defendant in a lineup.

Should the court allow the witness to testify using the clerk as an interpreter?

(A) Yes, because the clerk is qualified.

(B) Yes, if the clerk takes an oath to make a true translation.

(C) No, because as a result of her employment and previous activities, the clerk is inherently biased.

(D) No, unless the clerk discloses to the jury her employment and previous activities in this case.

Question 24

An officer was driving in her squad car when she spotted the defendant, whom the officer knew because she had arrested him for an armed robbery in the past. She followed the defendant for awhile and noted that he kept looking nervously over his shoulder at the squad car and that he was carrying a brown paper bag in his hand. Suddenly, the defendant darted into an alley. A few moments later, he emerged from the alley without the paper bag and began running. The officer put on her siren and pursued the defendant. He was quickly apprehended and searched by the officer. She then drove back to the alley to search it. About six feet from the entrance to the alley, the officer found a paper bag that contained a handgun. She copied the gun's serial number before taking the gun back to the police station. The defendant was charged with illegal possession of a handgun and carrying a concealed weapon. At his trial, while the officer is testifying the prosecution seeks to admit the gun that the officer found into evidence against the defendant. The defense attorney objects on the grounds that the gun lacks proper identification.

The objection should be:

(A) Sustained, because the gun was not in the defendant's possession at the time of his arrest.

(B) Sustained, because there is insufficient proof that the gun belonged to the defendant.

(C) Overruled, because there is sufficient evidence that the gun belonged to the defendant.

(D) Overruled, because the objection should have been based on chain of custody.

Question 25

A defendant and his fiancée were engaged to be married. About two months before the wedding, the fiancée began having an affair with a co-worker. Two weeks before the wedding, the co-worker went to the fiancée's apartment after work. The next morning, the fiancée's body was found in a forest preserve; she had been strangled to death. The fiancée's friend told the police about the affair. The police questioned the co-worker, who readily admitted visiting the fiancée at 6 p.m., but he denied slaying her. The police believed that he was telling the truth. The defendant was subsequently arrested and charged with the murder. At the defendant's trial, the prosecution wants to call the co-worker to the stand to testify that he left the fiancée's apartment at 9 p.m., after she told him that she was going to the defendant's home to tell him that the wedding was off. The defense objects.

The co-worker's testimony is:

(A) Admissible, as a present sense impression.

(B) Admissible, to show the fiancée's state of mind.

(C) Inadmissible, as more prejudicial than probative.

(D) Inadmissible, as hearsay not within any recognized exception.

Question 26

Several members of a small terrorist group are on trial in federal court for conspiring to bomb a military installation. The prosecution would like to introduce the testimony of a military guard at one of the installation's gates. The guard had been present when a bomb that

was being planted by a member of the group had exploded prematurely. The guard will testify that she ran over to administer first aid to the member, who in great pain told her that his group was in the process of planting three other bombs in other areas of the military installation and was going to detonate them all at the same time to get publicity for their cause. The guard will also testify that the member disclosed the locations of the other bombs and the names of two other members of the group. The authorities were able to prevent the other bombings and arrest the other members of the group. The member died from his injuries.

What is the best basis for allowing the guard to testify as to the member's statements?

(A) As a vicarious admission of a co-conspirator.

(B) As a statement against interest.

(C) As a statement of present state of mind.

(D) As a dying declaration.

Question 27

A plaintiff brought a malpractice action against a law firm that had represented him in a personal injury suit. The plaintiff alleges that the firm was derelict in failing to interview a doctor he suggested as a prospective expert witness. The firm's pleadings contend that the doctor was never brought to the attention of anyone at the firm and was never considered as a witness. The plaintiff wants to introduce a "proposed witness list" from his case file at the firm. After the name of the doctor is the notation, "the plaintiff wants us to check this guy out before trial." The notation is in the handwriting of a paralegal with the firm who is responsible for updating various case files as part of his regular duties. The paralegal did no direct work on the plaintiff's case and he cannot remember which attorney in the firm asked him to make the notation. The defense objects to the introduction of the proposed witness list containing the notation.

The proposed witness list and notation are:

(A) Admissible, as past recollection recorded.

(B) Admissible, as a business record.

(C) Inadmissible, as hearsay not within any recognized exception.

(D) Inadmissible, as hearsay within hearsay, and one level is not within an exception.

Question 28

A witness's nephew was visiting her from a foreign country. One evening, the nephew went out with friends. At 11 p.m. that night, he appeared back at the witness's house, pounding loudly on the door. She let him in, and noted that he was panting and out of breath. He immediately told her, "You won't believe what I just saw! I was walking past your neighbor's house just now and the wife ran up to me with a gun in her hand. She looked me straight in the eyes and said, 'I killed the philandering fool' before running off down the street." After the nephew returned to his country, the wife was put on trial for the murder of her husband. The prosecution wants to put the witness on the stand to testify regarding the nephew's statement to her. The defense objects.

Can the witness testify to the nephew's statement?

(A) Yes, because the nephew's statement qualifies as an excited utterance.

(B) Yes, because the nephew is not available to testify.

(C) No, because the wife did not make her admission to the witness.

(D) No, because the witness's testimony would constitute hearsay within hearsay.

Question 29

An elderly woman was the only eyewitness to an automobile accident that occurred one block from her nursing home residence. During the ensuing trial, the plaintiff calls the witness to the stand. After a few questions, it becomes clear that the witness remembers having seen the accident, but her memory of the details has grown fuzzy. The plaintiff's attorney wishes to introduce into evidence the contents of some handwritten notes made by the witness after she returned to her room after witnessing the accident.

Which of the following is a ***false*** statement with respect to the admissibility of the contents of the notes?

(A) The witness must testify that the notes are accurate.

(B) It must be shown that the notes were prepared at a time when the witness was under the stress of excitement of the event and had not had time to reflect on the accident.

(C) The witness must be given the notes to examine to determine if she still has insufficient memory, after consulting the notes, to testify fully and accurately.

(D) The plaintiff's attorney may not introduce the notes into evidence as an exhibit under any circumstances.

Question 30

A plaintiff was severely injured when a car driven by an uninsured driver struck her while she was crossing the street at a busy intersection. The plaintiff subsequently filed an appropriate suit against the city, claiming that it was negligent in not marking the crossing as a pedestrian crossing and in not painting lines on the pavement indicating a crosswalk. The city defends on the ground that the plaintiff was contributorily negligent. The plaintiff's attorney wishes to introduce evidence showing that two weeks after the plaintiff was struck by the vehicle, a city street maintenance crew painted pedestrian crosswalks at the intersection where no such crosswalks existed before and placed pedestrian crossing signs on the two streets at appropriate distances from the intersection. The city's attorney objects.

The court is most likely to rule that evidence regarding the crosswalks is:

(A) Admissible to show that the intersection was within the city's ownership or control.

(B) Admissible to show that the city is attempting to conceal or distort evidence.

(C) Inadmissible, because subsequent repairs are deemed irrelevant under the Federal Rules.

(D) Inadmissible, because public policy favors the encouragement of safety improvements.

Question 31

A defendant is on trial for allegedly burning down her business establishment because it was losing money. Before the defendant takes the stand in her defense, the prosecution seeks to introduce testimony from an insurance agent that the defendant purchased two insurance policies for the building within a month before the fire. Each policy had been purchased from a different insurance carrier and each policy was in the amount of the full value of the business. The defendant's attorney objects to the introduction of this testimony.

The court should rule that the testimony is:

(A) Admissible only for purposes of impeachment when the defendant takes the stand in her own defense.

(B) Admissible as substantive evidence against the defendant.

(C) Inadmissible, because the Federal Rules ban using evidence that a party carried insurance to prove that the party acted wrongfully.

(D) Inadmissible, because the policies themselves are required to be introduced under the original document rule.

Question 32

A plaintiff filed a trademark infringement suit against a defendant company. While the defendant's director of marketing was on the stand, the defendant's attorney produced a "product recognition survey," a document generated by the defendant's marketing division. The plaintiff's attorney objects that the record is hearsay. The defendant's attorney responds that it is a business record admissible under an exception to the hearsay rule. The plaintiff's attorney counters that the document was prepared for this litigation and not made in the ordinary course of business. The plaintiff's attorney demands a hearing to determine whether the document qualifies as a business record.

Which of the following is the most appropriate way for the issue to be decided?

(A) The issue should be decided by the judge after hearing evidence from the defendant's attorney outside the presence of the jury.

(B) The issue should be decided by the judge after hearing evidence from the defendant's attorney and the plaintiff's attorney and may be conducted in the presence of the jury.

(C) The issue should be decided by the jury after hearing evidence from both sides.

(D) The issue should be decided by the judge after hearing evidence from both sides outside the presence of the jury, but if the document is admitted by the judge, the plaintiff may present evidence challenging that finding while presenting his case, and the ultimate decision rests with the jury.

Question 33

A plaintiff brings a federal civil rights action against several members of a police department for near-fatal injuries incurred as a result of an alleged beating administered by the officers. The plaintiff plans to call as a witness his cellmate, who will testify that the plaintiff was in fact beaten by the defendants. The plaintiff also wants to introduce the bloodstained shirt that he wore on the night of the beating. The defendants plan to call an expert to testify that the injuries suffered by the plaintiff were inconsistent with injuries likely to be inflicted by the alleged police beating, and a second expert to testify similarly. The defendants also will call as a witness a fellow officer, who will testify that the defendant was suspected to have AIDS, and as a result the defendants would not have beaten him for fear of being infected by any open wounds.

Which item of relevant evidence is the court ***least*** likely to exclude?

(A) The cellmate's testimony, on the ground that calling this witness constitutes an unfair surprise.

(B) The bloody shirt, on the ground that it will create a danger of unfair prejudice.

(C) The second expert's testimony, on the grounds that it will constitute a waste of time and will unnecessarily present cumulative evidence.

(D) The fellow officer's testimony, on the ground that it may confuse the issues or mislead the jury.

Question 34

During the trial of a personal injury case, the plaintiff calls a witness to testify that he saw the defendant spill a slippery substance in the roadway. Following the testimony of the witness, the defendant calls the witness's neighbor, who testifies that the witness has a poor reputation for truthfulness in the community. The plaintiff's attorney then cross-examines the neighbor asking her, in good faith, if she committed the crime of false pretenses last year. Last year, the neighbor had in fact been charged with and convicted of the crime of false pretenses. The defendant's attorney objects to this question.

The objection should be:

(A) Overruled, because the neighbor was convicted of the crime of false pretenses.

(B) Overruled, because the plaintiff's attorney asked the question in good faith.

(C) Sustained, because an impeaching witness cannot be impeached on collateral matters.

(D) Sustained, because such an inquiry is not proper on cross-examination.

Question 35

A state Yellow plaintiff was travelling to adjoining state Green to visit his relatives. Shortly before crossing the state line, the plaintiff's auto was struck in the rear by a vehicle driven by the defendant, a state Green resident. The plaintiff suffered personal injuries and damage to his vehicle amounting to approximately $90,000. Having managed to obtain proper service on the defendant, the plaintiff filed suit in Yellow federal court. Under the laws of Yellow, the driver of a vehicle that strikes another vehicle in the rear is presumed to have acted negligently, regardless of the surrounding circumstances. Neither the law of Green nor the federal statutes or case law has adopted such a rule.

Regarding the presumption in question, the court should apply:

(A) The Yellow rules of procedure and the federal common law.

(B) The Federal Rules of Civil Procedure and the Yellow substantive law.

(C) The whole law of Yellow, because in a diversity case a federal court must always apply the law of the state in which it sits.

(D) The whole law of Yellow, because the presumption at issue operates upon elements of the prima facie case.

Question 36

A defendant was charged under the Federal Kidnapping Act when he kidnapped his ex-girlfriend and took her across state lines, holding her against her will for five days until she was reported missing and finally found. During the defendant's federal trial, the ex-girlfriend rebuts his assertion that she voluntarily accompanied him by stating that she inflicted severe gashes on his body with her fingernails during her attempts to escape, and that the defendant had to be treated by a physician to prevent infection. The defendant denies seeking treatment for any such injuries. The prosecution calls a physician, who will testify that he treated the defendant's wounds the day after the kidnapping took place. The defendant's attorney objects. The jurisdiction's physician-patient privilege applies to both civil and criminal proceedings.

The court should rule that the physician's testimony is:

(A) Inadmissible, because it violates the privilege against self-incrimination.

(B) Inadmissible, because it violates the physician-patient privilege.

(C) Admissible, as a declaration of past bodily condition.

(D) Admissible, because the physician-patient privilege does not apply.

EVIDENCE ANSWERS - SET 5

Answer to Question 1

(B) The certified copy of the record of the sister's conviction will be excluded because it is inadmissible hearsay. A misdemeanor conviction is hearsay not admissible under any exception. A felony conviction, on the other hand, is admissible under an exception to the hearsay rule. [Fed. R. Evid. 803(22)] Thus, (C) and (D) are incorrect. (A) is incorrect because under the Federal Rules, a certified copy of the record of conviction satisfies the best evidence rule.

Answer to Question 2

(C) The court should not admit the report because it is hearsay not within any exception. The report contains an out-of-court statement being offered for its truth; *i.e.*, that the person who hit the victim fits the description given by the witness. Thus, (A) is incorrect. The report does not fall within any exception to the hearsay rule. It is not a business record because the witness was not under a business duty to convey the information to the police. (B) is therefore incorrect. (D) is incorrect because the report is the original document, and the best evidence rule expresses a preference for originals.

Answer to Question 3

(D) The jury must find that the insured is dead. Since the basic facts that support the presumption were proven at trial, and no other evidence was introduced, the jury must find in accordance with the presumption, because the other party did not meet its burden of going forward with rebuttal evidence. (A) and (B) are therefore wrong. (C) is wrong because the presumption regarding the insured's death is a rebuttable presumption. A rebuttable presumption will have no force or effect when sufficient contrary evidence is introduced. A conclusive presumption is really a rule of substantive law and cannot be rebutted by contrary evidence.

Answer to Question 4

(C) The judge should rule this affidavit to be inadmissible hearsay. This affidavit is clearly hearsay, and there is nothing in the facts that shows that it is admissible under any of the exceptions to this rule. Hence, (A) is wrong. (B) is wrong because, for this purpose, the attorney-client privilege terminates upon the death of the client, and also because the observations of the attorney would not be deemed a "communication received from the client." (D) is incorrect because a lay person could probably testify to her opinion in this situation since it is rationally based on her own perception, it is helpful to a determination of a fact in issue, and it is not based on scientific, technical, or other specialized knowledge.

Answer to Question 5

(C) The testimony of the plaintiff's witness should not be admitted to show that the defendant was negligent. Character evidence as proof of conduct in the litigated event is not admissible in a civil case unless character is directly in issue (*e.g.*, in a defamation action). Character is not directly in issue here, and so (A) and (D) are incorrect. The defendant in a criminal, but not a civil, case can introduce evidence of good character, which can then be rebutted. (B) is incorrect because, although such evidence is clearly relevant, courts exclude this evidence because its slight probative value is outweighed by the danger of unfair prejudice, the possible distraction of the jury from the main question in issue, and the possible waste of time required by examination of collateral issues.

Answer to Question 6

(C) The prosecutor's objection should be overruled because the question goes to the witness's bias or interest. Evidence that a witness is biased or has an interest in the outcome of the suit tends to show that the witness has a motive to lie. A witness may always be impeached by evidence of interest or bias, either on cross-examination or, if a proper foundation is laid, by extrinsic evidence. In a criminal case, it is proper for the defense to ask a prosecution witness whether she has been promised immunity from punishment or a reduction of punishment for testifying. This shows a motive for the witness to curry favor with the state. Here, the defense attorney is trying to impeach the sister by showing that because she was offered an attractive sentence, she has a motive to curry favor with the prosecution. This is perfectly proper. Note that there is no need for a foundation since the attorney is eliciting this evidence on cross-examination, rather than attempting to introduce extrinsic evidence of the deal. (A) is wrong because it misapplies and misstates the rule with regard to plea bargains. Under Federal Rule 410, withdrawn guilty pleas, pleas of nolo contendere, offers to plead guilty, and evidence of statements made in negotiating such pleas are inadmissible against the defendant who made the plea or was a participant in the plea discussions. This rule does not apply in this case because it does not apply to accepted guilty pleas, and the sister is not the defendant. The rule applies only to offers and withdrawn pleas. After the plea is accepted, it is admissible. (B) is wrong for two reasons: (i) the statement by the prosecutor is not hearsay because it is not being offered for the truth of the matter asserted, but rather to show its effect on the hearer; and (ii) even if the statement were hearsay, it would not make the question improper because evidence that is substantively inadmissible may be admitted for impeachment purposes if relevant to show bias or interest. (D) is wrong because no attorney-client privilege arises with respect to communications between the prosecutor and the sister. The attorney-client privilege requires that the attorney-client relationship exist at the time of the communication. To be covered, the client must be seeking the professional services of the attorney at the time of the communication. The sister was not seeking the services of the prosecutor. The prosecutor could not in any way be considered to be her attorney; they are clearly adversaries. Furthermore, even if this were not the case, the client holds the privilege and may waive it. Thus, the question would be proper, and it would be up to the client-witness to decide whether to waive the privilege.

Answer to Question 7

(A) The judge may take judicial notice of this fact because it is a matter of common knowledge in the community, but the jury is not required to accept the fact as conclusive in a criminal case. Judicial notice may be taken of facts that are not subject to reasonable dispute because they are generally known within the territorial jurisdiction of the trial court. [Fed. R. Evid. 201(b)] The facts need not be known everywhere as long as they are known in the community where the court is sitting. The location of the city hall is such a fact. As choice (A) also states, in a criminal case the jury should be instructed that it may, but is not required to, accept as conclusive any fact that is judicially noticed. [Fed. R. Evid. 201(g)] (B) is incorrect. While facts that are not generally known and accepted may be a subject of judicial notice if they are easily verified by resorting to easily accessible, well-established sources (*i.e.*, facts capable of certain verification), facts that are matters of common knowledge in the community, such as the location of the city hall, may be judicially noticed without resort to reference materials. (C) is incorrect because a judge can take judicial notice of matters of common knowledge at any time, whether or not requested by a party, regardless of whether a criminal or civil case is involved. (D) is incorrect because a "presumption" in a criminal case is nothing more than a permissible inference that the jury may make. Because the accused in a criminal case is presumptively innocent until the prosecution proves every element of the offense beyond a reasonable doubt, the burden of persuasion is not shifted to the defendant by a "presumption" or by a fact that has been judicially noticed.

Answer to Question 8

(C) Evidence of the defendant's other crimes or misconduct is admissible only if relevant to some issue other than the defendant's character or propensity to commit the crime charged. Such acts would be admissible to show motive, intent, absence of mistake, identity, or a common plan or scheme. Of these, the only one possibly relevant to these facts is identity. Evidence that the accused committed prior criminal acts that are so distinctive as to operate as a "signature" may be introduced to prove that the accused committed the act in question. Merely throwing an object, such as a brick, through a window could not be considered so distinctive as to operate as a signature. Thus, this evidence would not show identity. The only possible reason for offering the evidence is to show the ex-boyfriend's propensity to commit the crime charged, in which case the testimony will be inadmissible. (A) is wrong because it is circumstantial evidence that the ex-boyfriend threw the brick. It is relevant because it tends to make it more probable that he threw the brick than it would be without the evidence. (B) is wrong because it is relevant and goes to motive. It too makes it more probable that the ex-boyfriend threw the brick than it would be if the victim had not testified against a member of his gang. (D) is wrong because the victim's identification of the ex-boyfriend's voice places him at the scene and is thus relevant. It is more probable that he threw the brick than it would be in the absence of this testimony. The identification of a voice is properly authenticated by the opinion of a person familiar with the alleged speaker's voice. As his ex-girlfriend, the victim would be sufficiently familiar with the ex-boyfriend's voice to make a proper identification.

Answer to Question 9

(A) The manager's statement is admissible under the hearsay exception for statements against interest. Statements of a person, now unavailable as a witness, against that person's pecuniary, proprietary, or penal interest when made, as well as collateral facts contained in the statement, are admissible as an exception to the hearsay rule. [Fed. R. Evid. 804(b)(3)] The declarant must have personal knowledge of the facts, must have been aware that the statement was against his interest, and must have had no motive to misrepresent when he made the statement. In this case, the manager is unavailable because he cannot be located. The statement that he gave the key to the defendant was against his interest when made (exposing him to possible criminal and civil liability), and he should have been aware of that fact. Since the manager was making the statement to his girlfriend, he had no motive to misrepresent the facts when he made the statement. Note that the fact that he is also repeating a statement by the defendant does not cause an admissibility problem. Since the defendant's statement is an admission by a party-opponent, it is not hearsay under the Federal Rules. An admission is a statement made or act done that amounts to a prior acknowledgment by one of the parties of one of the relevant facts. If the party said or did something that now turns out to be inconsistent with his contentions at trial, the law regards him as estopped from preventing its admission into evidence. Here, the defendant's statement that he left his gloves in the victim's apartment is an acknowledgment of the relevant facts that he was in her apartment and that the gloves could be his. Since this is inconsistent with his position at trial, he is estopped from preventing the admission of the statement. (B) is wrong because neither portion of the statement was made in furtherance of the conspiracy. Admissions of one conspirator, made to a third party in furtherance of a conspiracy to commit a crime or tort, at a time when the declarant was participating in the conspiracy, are admissible against co-conspirators as a vicarious admission by a party-opponent. Both the defendant's statement to the manager and the

manager's statement to his girlfriend were made after the conspiracy had ended and in no way were made in furtherance of the conspiracy. (C) is wrong because, as discussed above, the manager's statement to his girlfriend is admissible under the exception to the hearsay rule for statements against interest. Furthermore, under the Federal Rules, admissions by a party are nonhearsay. Thus, technically, this would not be hearsay within hearsay. (D) is wrong because the statement is sufficiently against the manager's interest to qualify under the exception for statements against interest. A full admission to the crime is not required.

Answer to Question 10

(C) The bartender's testimony is inadmissible because the defendant's prior fight in the tavern cannot be admitted to prove his propensity to beat someone to death. The basic rule is that when a person is charged with one crime, extrinsic evidence of his other crimes or misconduct is inadmissible if such evidence is offered solely to establish a criminal disposition. [Fed. R. Evid. 404(b)] The danger is that the jury may convict because of past conduct rather than because of guilt of the offense charged. While evidence of other crimes is admissible if it is independently relevant to some other issue (*e.g.*, motive, intent, or identity), the defendant's prior fight appears to have no relevance other than as evidence of his violent disposition. It is therefore inadmissible. (A) is incorrect because it suggests that the bartender's testimony should be admitted to show the defendant's propensity for violence. As stated above, extrinsic evidence of his prior misconduct is inadmissible if offered solely to establish a criminal disposition. Evidence of specific acts of the person in question as demonstrating that person's character is permitted only in the few instances when character is itself one of the ultimate issues in the case. [Fed. R. Evid. 405(b)] The defendant's propensity for violence is not an ultimate issue in this case. (B) is incorrect because extrinsic evidence of the defendant's previous bad acts cannot be used to impeach him. A specific act of misconduct must be probative of truthfulness (*i.e.*, an act of deceit or lying) and can be elicited only on cross-examination of the witness. Extrinsic evidence is not permitted. Therefore, testimony con-cerning the defendant's prior incident is not admissible for impeachment. (D) is incorrect because it is irrelevant. It is true that the defendant has not put his character in issue in this case simply by pleading self-defense. Even if he had, however, the prosecutor could not rebut by having a witness testify as to prior instances of misconduct; only reputation or opinion evidence would be admissible.

Answer to Question 11

(B) The jury may consider statements from an authoritative text as substantive evidence. Rule 803(18) provides that an expert may base an opinion on facts supplied to him outside the courtroom. One such source is authoritative texts and treatises. Statements from a treatise established as reliable (which may be done by the expert's own testimony) may be introduced on direct examination of the expert and read into the record as substantive evidence under an exception to the hearsay rule. [Fed. R. Evid. 803(18)] Hence, the jury may consider the testimony in (B) as substantive evidence. (A) is incorrect because the evidence may not be considered by the jury as substantive evidence. Rule 703 provides that where an expert bases his opinion on facts made known to him outside the courtroom, the facts need not be of a type admissible in evidence as long as the facts are of a kind reasonably relied on by experts in the particular field. However, the expert will only be permitted to disclose such facts if the court determines that their probative value in assisting the jury to evaluate the expert's opinion substantially outweighs their prejudicial effect. The jury would only be permitted to consider them as the basis for the expert's opinion; the jury could not consider the facts as substantive evidence unless they were independently admissible. Here, the statements made to the expert by witnesses to the collapse are a proper basis of his opinion because they are of a kind reasonably relied on by experts in his field. However, they do not appear to be admissible under any exception to the hearsay rule and therefore could not be considered by the jury as substantive evidence. (C) is incorrect because it is too broad. Generally, evidence of repairs or other precautionary measures made after an incident is inadmissible if used to prove negligence, culpable conduct, product or design defects, or a need for a warning or instruction. Such evidence may, however, be admitted to prove ownership or control, to rebut any claim that precautionary measures were not feasible prior to the incident, or to prove destruction of evidence. Here, admissibility of the expert's testimony regarding the subsequent repair of the bridge will be contingent on the purpose of the testimony, and (C) is incorrect because it does not indicate any purpose. (D) is incorrect. Generally, a statement made by an agent concerning a matter within the scope of his agency is admissible against the principal as a vicarious admission ***if*** it was made during the existence of the employment relationship. In this case, the statement was made by a former employee of the mall, and therefore it was not made during the scope of the employment relationship. Since it does not fall within any of the hearsay exceptions, the statement is inadmissible.

Answer to Question 12

(C) The expert's testimony should not be permitted under Federal Rule 403 because the probative value of polygraph evidence is substantially outweighed by the tendency of its results to mislead and confuse the jury. Federal Rule 702 permits opinion testimony by a qualified expert where the subject matter is one where scientific, technical, or other specialized knowledge would assist the trier of fact in understanding the evidence or determining a fact in issue. However, the methodology underlying the opinion must be reliable (*i.e.*, the proponent must show that the opinion is based on sufficient facts or data, the opinion is the product of reliable principles and methods, and the expert has reliably applied the principles and methods to the facts of the case). Furthermore, Rule 403 gives a trial judge broad discretion to exclude relevant evidence if its probative value is substantially outweighed by the danger of unfair prejudice, confusion of the issues, or misleading the jury. Most jurisdictions have concluded that the probative value of a polygraph test is slight because of its significant rate of error. On the other side of the balancing test, the tendency of jurors to give too much weight to a polygraph test makes the danger of unfair prejudice high. Therefore, the test's unreliability and the risk of confusion from the test's results justify excluding the expert's testimony. (A) is incorrect because the defendant volunteered to take the polygraph test. The Fifth Amendment right against self-incrimination applies only when the defendant is compelled to make the statements. The fact that he did not take the stand in his own defense would not change this result because once a voluntary statement is made, it cannot be kept out of the trial on self-incrimination grounds. (B) is also incorrect because, as discussed above, the defendant volunteered to take the polygraph test. His right against self-incrimination is violated only if he is compelled to testify against himself. Just as a defendant's voluntary confession cannot be kept out of the trial on self-incrimination grounds, so the defendant's voluntary statements during the polygraph test cannot be barred on those grounds. (D) is incorrect because the Federal Rules do not specifically classify polygraph tests as irrelevant; in fact, polygraph evidence ***could*** be relevant under the Federal Rules. Relevant evidence is evidence having any tendency to make the existence of any fact that is of consequence to the determination of an action more probable than it would be without the evidence. [Fed. R. Evid. 401] Polygraph evidence is relevant under this test because it does tend to make the existence of a fact of consequence whether the person is telling the truth more probable. However, as discussed above, this relevant evidence can still be excluded under Federal Rule 403 if the court decides its probative value is substantially outweighed by the danger of unfair prejudice.

Answer to Question 13

(A) The defense witness's testimony is admissible character evidence because the plaintiff's character is directly in issue in the case. As a general rule, evidence of character to prove the conduct of a person in the litigated event is not admissible in a civil case. However, where a person's character itself is one of the issues in the case, character evidence is admissible because it is the best method of proving the issue. Under the Federal Rules, any of the types of evidence—reputation, opinion, or specific acts—may be used. Here, character is an issue in the plaintiff's defamation action because the defendant has pleaded as an affirmative defense that his statement claiming that the plaintiff is a thief is the truth. The defense witness's testimony that he saw the plaintiff take the money from the cash register is relevant because it tends to show that the defendant spoke the truth. Hence, it should be allowed. (B) is incorrect because the fact that theft is a crime of dishonesty would be relevant only if the plaintiff's credibility were being impeached, and only then if proof of an actual conviction were provided. Here, the testimony is admissible because it is being offered as substantive evidence of an aspect of the plaintiff's character that is directly in issue in the case. (C) is incorrect. One of the few cases where testimony as to specific acts of a person may be used to show that person's character is when character itself is one of the ultimate issues in the case, as it is here. (D) is incorrect because the fact that the plaintiff never took the stand only means that she has not placed her ***credibility*** in issue and become subject to impeachment. Here, however, the plaintiff's ***character*** is in issue and the testimony is being offered as substantive evidence of her character rather than to impeach her credibility.

Answer to Question 14

(B) The photo should be admitted into evidence upon testimony that it is an accurate representation of the location depicted. To be admissible, real or demonstrative evidence must not only be relevant but must also be authenticated, *i.e.*, identified as being what the proponent claims it to be. For a photograph that is used as demonstrative evidence, authentication is by testimony that the photo is a faithful reproduction of the object or scene depicted. Here, testimony by a bank employee that the still frame from the video accurately portrays the setting where the robbery took place is sufficient for admissibility. (A) is incorrect because the frame from the video is not being offered as original evidence that played an actual role in the robbery itself, such as a gun used by the robber, which would require the "chain of custody" type of authentication in (A). Here, the still frame is only being used for demonstrative purposes; hence, authentication focuses on whether it is an accurate representation rather than how it was handled. (C) is incorrect. Charts and diagrams that are used solely to help explain a witness's testimony may be permitted at trial but not admitted into evidence where they are not offered as representations of a real object or scene but only as aids to testimony. Here, however, the photo is being offered as a faithful representation of the scene of the crime and should therefore be admissible into evidence. (D) is incorrect because it is a misapplication of the best evidence rule. The best evidence or original document rule, which is made applicable to photographs by the Federal Rules, generally requires that in proving the terms of a writing the original writing must be produced where the terms are material. The terms are material and the rule applies only when (i) the document is a legally operative or dispositive instrument, or (ii) the witness's knowledge results from having seen the fact in the document. Neither situation arises in this case. The location of the columns in the bank and the circumstances of the robbery are facts that exist independently of the document (the videotape on the day of the robbery), and thus may be proved by other evidence.

Answer to Question 15

(A) The burden of persuasion and the burden of going forward with the evidence are on the plaintiff because the defendant's testimony raises a rebuttable presumption that the check had been delivered in the mail. The burden of persuasion is the burden of a party to persuade the jury to decide an issue in its favor. If, after all the proof is in, the issue is equally balanced in the mind of the jury, then the party with the burden of persuasion must lose. The burden of persuasion does not shift from party to party during the course of a trial. Because the plaintiff sued the defendant for the debt, the plaintiff has the burden of persuasion when the time for the jury to make a decision arrives. The burden of going forward with the evidence is the burden of producing sufficient evidence to create a fact question of the issue involved. If a plaintiff makes out a prima facie case, he has met his burden of going forward with the evidence and the burden shifts to the defendant. Here, when the plaintiff made out a prima facie case of the defendant's debt, the burden of going forward with the evidence shifted to the defendant. The defendant met this burden through the use of a presumption. Federal Rule 301 provides that a presumption imposes on the party against whom it was directed the burden of going forward with the evidence to rebut or meet the presumption. The defendant's evidence regarding the proper posting of the check raises a rebuttable presumption that the check was delivered to the plaintiff because a letter shown to have been properly addressed, stamped, and mailed is presumed to have been delivered in the due course of mail. Therefore, the burden of going forward with the evidence has shifted back again to the plaintiff, who must now produce evidence to rebut the presumption (*i.e.*, evidence that he did not receive the check). (B) is incorrect because, as discussed above, the defendant's testimony raised a rebuttable presumption that the check was delivered in the mail, which shifted the burden of going forward with the evidence to the plaintiff. The fact that the plaintiff met his burden of going forward with the evidence of the debt once, when he made out his prima facie case, does not mean the burden cannot shift back to him. (C) is incorrect because the plaintiff has not satisfied his burden of persuasion. As discussed above, the burden of persuasion does not shift from party to party and is only a crucial factor when all the evidence is in. This burden is satisfied when the jury finds a party has been more persuasive in arguing his side of the issue than the other party. Because the defendant's testimony raises a rebuttable presumption that the check was delivered to the plaintiff, the plaintiff's burden of persuasion cannot be met until he offers evidence to prove that the check was not received (a necessary element of his case). (D) is incorrect because, as discussed above, the defendant's testimony raised a rebuttable presumption of delivery of the check in the mail to the plaintiff, which shifted the burden of going forward with evidence of nondelivery back to the plaintiff. The plaintiff's burden of persuasion cannot be satisfied until he comes forward with this evidence because a necessary element of his case is that the defendant never paid him.

Answer to Question 16

(C) The testimony should be excluded because the attorney-client privilege applies to the examination done in preparation for trial. The communication between the doctor and the attorney's client is necessary to help the client convey his condition to the attorney. (A) is incorrect because admissions by party-opponents, while not hearsay under the Federal Rules, are still subject to potential privilege assertions. (B) is a true statement; the physician-patient privilege does not apply to any proceeding in which the condition of the patient has been put in issue by the patient. This is the case in the plaintiff's suit, so (D) is incorrect. However, (B) is incorrect because when a client is examined by a doctor at the attorney's request, the communications involved between the client and doctor (and the doctor and attorney) are not covered by the physician-patient privilege because no treatment is contemplated. Moreover, the physician-patient privilege is a

statutory privilege, and this jurisdiction recognizes only the common law privileges (*e.g.*, the attorney-client privilege).

Answer to Question 17

(C) The defendant's statement to his wife was made in reliance upon the intimacy of what was at that time their marital relationship. Thus, he has a privilege to prevent her from disclosing the statement. Either spouse (whether or not a party) has a privilege to refuse to disclose, and to prevent another from disclosing, a confidential communication made between the spouses while they were husband and wife. Divorce does not terminate this privilege retroactively. At the time that the defendant made the subject statement to his wife, they were married. Given that the statement essentially constituted an admission of liability by the defendant, that he prefaced it with "between you and me," and that he made the statement in the privacy of their home, it seems likely that the statement was made in confidentiality and in reliance upon the intimacy of the marital relationship. Thus, both the defendant and his wife may refuse to disclose, and may prevent the other from disclosing, the statement. Consequently, the defendant can prevent the wife from testifying to the statement. (A) is incorrect because the communication was made during the marriage, and the privilege is not abrogated by a later divorce. (B) is incorrect because the fact that the neighbor heard the statement was unknown to the defendant and his wife. If the communication is made in the ***known*** presence of a stranger, it is not privileged. However, if the statement was not made within the ***known*** hearing of a third party and it is overheard, absent a showing of negligence on the part of the speaker, it remains privileged. Nothing in these facts indicates negligence. Thus, the defendant can prevent his wife from testifying to the statement. (D) is incorrect because the privilege for confidential marital communications belongs to both spouses, rather than to just one. In cases involving spousal immunity (*i.e.*, the privilege not to testify against one's spouse in a criminal case), most state courts hold that the privilege belongs to the party-spouse only. However, the trial here is a civil case, so the spousal immunity is inapplicable; this question involves the privilege for confidential marital communications.

Answer to Question 18

(D) The grand jury transcript is not admissible because the husband's testimony was not subject to cross-examination. The husband's testimony was hearsay because it was an out-of-court statement offered to prove the truth of the matter asserted. [Fed. R. Evid. 801(c)] If a statement is hearsay, and no exception to the rule is applicable, the evidence is inadmissible. [Fed. R. Evid. 802] Under the former testimony exception to the hearsay rule, the testimony of a now unavailable witness given at another hearing is admissible in a subsequent trial as long as there is a sufficient similarity of parties and issues so that the opportunity to develop testimony or cross-examine at the prior hearing was meaningful. [Fed. R. Evid. 804(b)(1)] The party against whom the former testimony is offered must have had the opportunity to develop the testimony at the prior proceeding by direct, cross-, or redirect examination of the declarant. Thus, the grand jury testimony of an unavailable declarant is not admissible as former testimony against the accused at trial. This is because grand jury proceedings do not provide the opportunity for cross-examination. Therefore, because the husband's testimony was in front of the grand jury and was not subject to cross-examination, it is inadmissible as hearsay. (A) is incorrect because the husband's testimony cannot be considered a vicarious admission. An admission by a party-opponent is not hearsay under the Federal Rules. [Fed. R. Evid. 801(d)(2)] An admission is a statement made or act done that amounts to a prior acknowledgment by one of the parties to an action of one of the relevant facts. An admission does not have to be the statement of the party against whom the statement is being offered at trial if it qualifies as a vicarious admission. For example, admissions of one conspirator, made to a third party in furtherance of a conspiracy to commit a crime, may be admissible against co-conspirators. Here, however, the husband's grand jury testimony was not made in furtherance of a conspiracy. Because he was not a party here, and his testimony does not otherwise qualify as a vicarious admission of the wife, it cannot be considered an admission of a party-opponent. (B) is incorrect because the husband's grand jury testimony was not subject to cross-examination. Federal Rule 804(b)(1) allows the former testimony of an unavailable witness to be admitted under circumstances where the opportunity to develop testimony or cross-examine at the prior hearing was meaningful. The husband was an unavailable declarant because he was unable to testify because of death. [Fed. R. Evid. 804(a)(4)] However, as discussed above, his grand jury testimony is not admissible as former testimony because grand jury proceedings do not provide the opportunity for cross-examination. (C) is incorrect because the spousal privilege does not belong to the wife in federal court and because it may only be asserted while the marriage relationship exists. In federal courts, the spousal immunity privilege belongs to the witness-spouse. This means that one spouse may testify against the other in criminal cases, with or without the consent of the party-spouse. Thus, while the husband could not have been compelled to testify against his wife, he could not be foreclosed by her from testifying (except as to confidential communications).

Answer to Question 19

(D) The plaintiff's objection on the basis of the clergy-penitent privilege should be overruled. Pursuant to the clergy-penitent privilege, a person has a privilege to refuse to disclose, and to prevent others from disclosing, a confidential communication by that person to a member of the clergy in the clergy member's capacity as a spiritual adviser. The operation of this privilege is very similar to that of the attorney-client privilege. Here, the merchant made the statement to the priest during a conversation at a social occasion. There is no indication that this was a communication made to the priest in his capacity as a spiritual adviser, as would be the case, for instance, with a statement made in the confessional or during a counseling session. Thus, the matters stated to the priest by the merchant do not come within the clergy-penitent privilege, and the priest cannot be prevented from disclosing the contents of the conversation on the basis of this privilege. (A) is incorrect because, although the merchant undoubtedly made the statement in confidence (*i.e.*, intending and expecting that it would not be disclosed to third persons), as explained above, it was not made to the priest in his capacity as a spiritual adviser. Therefore, the clergy-penitent privilege is inapplicable. (B) is incorrect because it implies that the clergy-penitent privilege does not apply to civil cases. Actually, this privilege applies to both civil and criminal cases. (C) is incorrect because, where the privilege exists, it can be claimed by the person who made the confidential communication, her guardian or conservator, or her personal representative if she is deceased. Thus, if the privilege were applicable, the merchant's guardian (through her attorney) would be able to invoke the protection of the privilege to prevent the priest from disclosing the contents of the conversation with the merchant.

Answer to Question 20

(A) The medical technician's testimony is admissible, but solely for purposes of impeaching the pedestrian, a hearsay declarant. The pedestrian's statement to the motorist, even though hearsay, was admissible as an excited utterance or present sense impression because it was made immediately after the crash. Under Federal Rule 806, the credibility of a hearsay declarant may be attacked by evidence that would be admissible if the declarant had testified as a witness. For the purpose of impeaching the credibility of a witness, a party may show that the witness has, on another occasion, made statements that are inconsistent with some material part of his present testimony. The pedestrian's statement to the motorist may therefore be impeached by proof that he made the inconsistent statement to the medical technician. (B) is incorrect. The pedestrian's statement to the medical technician is hearsay because it is an out-of-court statement offered to prove the truth of the matter asserted, *i.e.*, that the decedent rammed the crossing barrier. [Fed. R. Evid. 801(c)] If a statement is hearsay, and no exception to the rule is applicable, the evidence is inadmissible for substantive purposes. [Fed. R. Evid. 802] The pedestrian's statement does not come within either the excited utterance exception or the present sense impression exception to the hearsay rule because the statement to the medical technician was not made immediately after the accident. Nor does his statement fall under Rule 801(d)(1)(A), which provides that where a prior inconsistent statement was made under oath at a prior trial, hearing, other proceeding, or deposition, it is admissible nonhearsay (*i.e.*, it may be considered as substantive proof of the facts stated). Because the pedestrian's statement to the medical technician was not made under oath, it is hearsay that may only be used to impeach and not as evidence of the position of the crossing gate. (C) is incorrect because a hearsay declarant, such as the pedestrian, does not have to be given an opportunity to explain or deny his alleged prior inconsistent statement. Generally, extrinsic evidence of the prior inconsistent statement of a witness is inadmissible unless the witness was examined so as to give him an opportunity to explain or deny the alleged inconsistent statement, but this foundation requirement may be dispensed with where "the interests of justice otherwise require." [Fed. R. Evid. 613(b)] The courts generally agree that inconsistent statements by ***hearsay declarants*** may be used to impeach despite the lack of foundation. [Fed. R. Evid. 806] Therefore, the medical technician's testimony may be admitted even though the pedestrian is not available to be questioned about the inconsistent statements. (D) is incorrect because the pedestrian's statement to the medical technician, although hearsay, may be used for impeachment purposes. As discussed above, a hearsay declarant may be impeached by evidence of his prior inconsistent statements. The pedestrian's statement to the motorist was properly admitted hearsay, which can be impeached by evidence of his inconsistent statement to the medical technician. However, because the statement to the medical technician is hearsay not within an exception to the hearsay rule, it may be used only for impeachment purposes and not as evidence of the position of the crossing gate.

Answer to Question 21

(D) The tally record should not be admitted because it is hearsay that does not fall within a recognized exception. The Federal Rules define hearsay as "a statement other than one made by the declarant testifying at the trial or hearing, offered in evidence to prove the truth of the matter asserted." [Fed. R. Evid. 801(c)] Any written document, such as the tally record, that is offered into evidence constitutes a "statement" for hearsay purposes. The tally record was prepared out of court by the clerks and is being offered to prove the truth of its assertion, *i.e.*, that the rival program had sent many reply cards. Because the tally record fits the definition of hearsay, and no exception to the rule is applicable, as discussed below, it is inadmissible. [Fed. R. Evid. 802] (A) is incorrect because the tally record is not being used to substitute for the forgotten memory of the clerks. Where a witness states that she has insufficient recollection of an event to enable her to testify fully and accurately, even after she has consulted a writing given to her on the stand, the writing itself may be introduced into evidence if the proper foundation is laid for its admissibility. [Fed. R. Evid. 803(5)] This is the past recollection recorded exception to the hearsay rule. Here, the tally record is not being used to substitute for the insufficient recollection of any witness. It is being offered to stand on its own as evidence, not in connection with a witness on the stand. Therefore, the tally record does not qualify as a past recollection recorded exception to the hearsay rule. (B) is incorrect because the tally record was recorded in preparation for litigation. Any writing or record, whether in the form of an entry in a book or otherwise, made as a memorandum or record of any act or event, is admissible in evidence as proof of that act or event if made in the regular course of a business, as long as it was the regular course of such business to make it at the time. Because the records must have been maintained in conjunction with a business activity to qualify for this exception to the hearsay rule, courts generally exclude reports prepared primarily for litigation. The Federal Rules deal with this problem by giving the trial court discretion to exclude any business record if circumstances indicate the record lacked trustworthiness. [Fed. R. Evid. 803(6)] Because the tally sheet was prepared only in anticipation of litigation instead of in conjunction with a business activity, it does not fall within the business record exception. (C) is an incorrect statement of law. The best evidence rule, also known as the "original document rule," may be stated as follows: In proving the terms of a writing, where the terms are material, the original writing must be produced. [Fed. R. Evid. 1002] The rule does not mean that the "best" evidence must be used to prove a fact. In this case, the test preparation course is not trying to prove the terms of a document. The fact to be proved (*i.e.*, that the rival program was flooding the office with business reply requests) exists independently of any writing. Thus, the best evidence rule does not apply.

Answer to Question 22

(A) The transcript is admissible under the former testimony exception to the hearsay rule. Under this rule, the testimony of a now unavailable witness given under oath at another hearing is admissible in a subsequent trial as long as there is a sufficient similarity of parties and issues so that the opportunity to cross-examine at the prior hearing was meaningful. In a civil proceeding, the parties do not need to be identical, but the party in the original action must be a predecessor in interest to the party against whom the testimony is being offered (*e.g.*, a privity relationship), so that a similar motive existed to develop or cross-examine the declarant's testimony. Here, the decedent was a predecessor in interest of the executor of his estate and had adequate opportunity and motive to cross-examine the witness's testimony against him, which was given under oath at a criminal proceeding. Hence, the testimony is admissible under the former testimony exception. (B) is incorrect because the transcript of the witness's testimony, to the extent that it is being offered to prove the truth of her assertions, does not fall under the public records exception to the hearsay rule. While the Federal Rules also allow a judgment of a felony conviction to be used to prove any fact essential to the judgment, the transcript of a witness is not admissible for that purpose. (C) is incorrect because in civil cases, the unavailability requirement for the former testimony exception is satisfied if the declarant is beyond the reach of the court's subpoena and the statement's proponent is unable to procure her attendance or testimony by process or other reasonable means. (D) is incorrect because, as discussed above, the similarity of issues and parties is sufficient to permit the testimony to be admitted against the executor even though he was not a party to the original action.

Answer to Question 23

(B) The court should allow the witness to testify if the clerk takes an oath to make a true translation. The services of an interpreter may be used where a witness, due to language problems or other reasons, would otherwise have difficulty communicating. Under Federal Rule 604, an interpreter must meet the qualifications required of an expert witness (*i.e.*, by reason of knowledge, skill, experience, training, or education, she is capable of providing a true translation). Also, an interpreter must take an oath or affirmation that she will make a true translation (*i.e.*, that she will communicate exactly what the witness is expressing in his testimony). Here, the witness will have extreme difficulty communicating, due to the fact that he uses a signing method different from that which is used in the United States. Thus, the circumstances allow the use of an interpreter to assist the witness in communicating at the trial. Here, the facts establish that the clerk is the only person qualified to act as an interpreter for the witness. If, as (B) states, the clerk takes an oath to communicate what the witness expresses in his testimony, then the requirements of Rule 604 are met. (A) is incorrect because it omits the requirement of taking an oath or affirming to make a true translation. (C) is incorrect because there is no principle of law that renders the clerk "inherently biased" simply because she works for the prosecutor and has assisted the police in their communications with the witness. If the clerk takes the required oath, she is bound to render a true translation, regardless of her affiliation with the prosecutor's office. (D) is incorrect because there is no requirement that the clerk disclose this information to the jury. Determining whether an interpreter is qualified is a matter within the judge's discretion.

Answer to Question 24

(C) The gun should be admitted into evidence. The gun is a form of real evidence, in that the object in issue is presented for inspection by the trier of fact. To be admissible, the object must be authenticated (*i.e.*, identified as being what the proponent claims it to be). One method of authentication is recognition testimony, in which a witness may authenticate the object by testifying that it is what the proponent claims it is. Here, the officer found the gun in a paper bag in the alley shortly after having seen the defendant run into the alley holding a paper bag and emerge from the alley without the bag. The officer could now be called to identify the gun being offered into evidence as the one she found in the alley. This should be particularly easy in this case since the officer noted the serial number of the gun when she found it. The fact that the gun was found in the alley is circumstantial evidence that the gun was carried by the defendant on the night of the arrest. The evidence here is sufficient to withstand an objection to its admissibility on the ground that the gun has not been properly identified. Thus, (B) is incorrect in concluding that there is insufficient proof that the gun belonged to the defendant. (A) is incorrect. Real evidence may be circumstantial; *i.e.*, facts about the object are proved as a basis for an inference that other facts are true. The circumstances surrounding the discovery of the gun support the inference that it had been in the bag carried by the defendant. It is not necessary for the gun to have been in his possession at the time of his arrest in order to admit the gun into evidence against him. (D) is incorrect because chain of custody problems arise where the evidence is of a type that is likely to be confused or can be easily tampered with (*e.g.*, evidence of a blood alcohol test) after it is in custody. In such a case, the proponent of the evidence must show that the object has been held in a substantially unbroken chain of possession. Here, there is no evidence of a break in the chain of custody after the gun was taken by the police. Furthermore, a gun is generally not a type of evidence that is susceptible to confusion or tampering. Also, if need be, the serial number can be compared with the officer's written copy of the serial number. Thus, there is no viable objection based on chain of custody.

Answer to Question 25

(B) The testimony of the co-worker is admissible to show the fiancée's state of mind, which in turn is circumstantial evidence that she in fact saw the defendant and told him that the wedding was off. Hearsay is a statement, other than one made by the declarant while testifying at the trial or hearing, offered in evidence to prove the truth of the matter asserted. Hearsay to which no exception is applicable is not admissible into evidence. One of the exceptions to the hearsay rule is the present state of mind exception, under which a statement of a declarant's then-existing state of mind, emotion, sensation, or physical condition is admissible. [Fed. R. Evid. 803(3)] Such a statement can be used not only when the declarant's state of mind is directly in issue, but also as a declaration of intent to do something in the future, offered as circumstantial evidence tending to show that the intent was carried out. The prosecution is offering the co-worker's testimony as to the fiancée's statement to prove the truth of the matter asserted therein; *i.e.*, that she was going to see the defendant and tell him that the wedding was off. Thus, the co-worker's testimony is hearsay. However, the statement regarding the fiancée's intent is being offered as a basis for a circumstantial inference that she carried out her intent to see the defendant (the prosecution's theory apparently being that he became enraged and killed her when he was told that the wedding was off). Consequently, the fiancée's statement of her then-existing state of mind is admissible under the present state of mind exception. (A) is incorrect because a present sense impression relates to a person's perception of an event that is not particularly shocking or exciting, but which does move her to comment on what she perceived at the time she perceived it or immediately thereafter. The fiancée's statement to the co-worker simply relates what she is going to tell the defendant, and does not convey a comment on some event then occurring in front of her. Therefore, this is not a present sense impression. (C) is incorrect because, although the testimony will certainly be damaging to the defendant, it cannot be characterized as unfairly prejudicial. Exclusion of evidence on the ground of prejudice is a matter within the trial judge's broad discretion, and Federal Rule 403 requires that the evidence's probative value be ***substantially*** outweighed by the danger of unfair prejudice for it to be excluded. While all evidence is prejudicial to the adverse party, "unfair" prejudice refers to evidence that suggests a decision on an emotional or otherwise improper basis. Certainly, this testimony renders more probably true than would otherwise be the case that the defendant had a motive for killing the fiancée and that he did kill her. Thus, the testimony has probative value that is not substantially outweighed by its prejudicial effect. (D) is incorrect because, as discussed above, the testimony is admissible under the present state of mind exception.

Answer to Question 26

(B) The member's statements are admissible as a statement against interest. Under the Federal Rules, statements of a person, now unavailable as a witness, against that person's pecuniary, proprietary, or penal interest when made are admissible as an exception to the hearsay rule. Here, the member's statements implicating himself in the bombing conspiracy were against his penal interest when he made them; hence, they are probably admissible under that exception. (A) is wrong because for a statement to qualify under the Federal Rules as a vicarious admission of another member of the conspiracy, the admission must have been in furtherance of the conspiracy by a participant in it. Here, the member's statements were not made in furtherance of the conspiracy but instead served to thwart its success. (C) is wrong because the member's statements are not being used to show his then-existing state of mind but rather the scope of the conspiracy and the defendants' participation in it. (D) is wrong because, even assuming that the member made the statements while believing his death was imminent (which the facts do not clearly establish), dying declarations are admissible under the Federal Rules only in a prosecution for homicide or in a civil action, and this case was neither of those.

Answer to Question 27

(B) The witness list should be admitted as a business record. A writing or record made as a memorandum or record of any act, transaction, occurrence, or event is admissible as proof of such act, transaction, occurrence, or event if it was made in the course of a regularly conducted business activity and if it was customary to make the type of entry involved (*i.e.*, the entrant must have had a duty to make the entry). The business record must consist of matters within the personal knowledge of the entrant or within the personal knowledge of someone with a business duty to transmit such matters to the entrant. The entry must have been made at or near the time of the transaction. The list of proposed witnesses and the notation constitute a statement that the law

firm was alerted to the existence of the doctor as a potential expert witness. The plaintiff wants to introduce these documents to prove the truth of this statement (*i.e.*, that he alerted the firm to the existence of the doctor). Thus, the documents present a hearsay problem. Making a list of proposed witnesses would be part of the regular course of business for a law firm, and it would be part of the duties of the paralegal responsible for updating case files to enter the handwritten notation regarding the doctor at the direction of one of the firm's attorneys. The matters contained in the list and notation would be within the personal knowledge of the attorney, who was under a business duty to report the information accurately to the paralegal, who was under a business duty to properly record the information. Thus, all the requirements for a business record are present, and the list and notation, made as records of the firm's having been alerted to the doctor as a potential expert witness, are admissible as proof of that fact. (A) is incorrect because past recollection recorded comes into play when a witness's memory cannot be refreshed by looking at something. At that point, there may be an attempt to introduce a writing made by the witness or under his direction at or near the time of the event. The writing is characterized as past recollection recorded. Here, there is no indication that a witness who has an insufficient memory is testifying, and the list of proposed witnesses and notation are not being offered as a record of anyone's past recollection. Rather, the evidence is offered as a record of the firm's being informed of the doctor as a potential expert witness. Therefore, the evidence will not be admitted as past recollection recorded. (C) is incorrect because, as explained above, the proffered evidence does come within a recognized hearsay exception. (D) is incorrect because the facts do not present any problem of "levels" of hearsay. The list and notation are considered to be an out-of-court statement that the firm was alerted to the doctor as a potential expert witness, and are being offered as proof of that fact. If the notation had simply repeated an assertion made by one outside of the business (*e.g.*, "the doctor says that he will be available to testify on the date of the trial") and been offered to prove the truth of the assertion (that the doctor was available as a witness), a hearsay within hearsay problem would exist. Because the statement within the notation would be hearsay not within any exception, the notation itself, despite the fact that it is a business record, would not be admissible to prove the doctor's availability.

Answer to Question 28

(A) The witness can testify to the nephew's statement because it qualifies as an excited utterance. The statement of the wife that the nephew is relating is admissible as an admission of a party-opponent. The problem presented here is one of hearsay within hearsay. Hearsay is a statement, other than one made by the declarant while testifying at the trial or hearing, offered in evidence to prove the truth of the matter asserted. A hearsay statement to which no exception to the hearsay rule is applicable must be excluded upon appropriate objection. Hearsay included within hearsay is admissible only if each layer of hearsay falls within a hearsay exception. Here, two separate statements are really being offered for the truth of the matter asserted therein: First, the nephew's statement is being offered to prove that he actually said that the wife admitted killing the husband. Second, the wife's statement is being offered to prove that she killed the husband. However, the wife's statement is an admission by a party-opponent, which is traditionally treated as a hearsay exception and is treated as nonhearsay under the Federal Rules. In either case, this statement alone would be admissible. The nephew's statement relating the wife's admission is also admissible; it comes within the excited utterance exception to the hearsay rule. Under this exception, a declaration made during or soon after a startling event is admissible. There must have been an occurrence startling enough to produce a nervous excitement and thus render the declaration an unreflective expression of the declarant's impression of the event. Also, the statement must have been made while the declarant was under the stress of the excitement. Here, the nephew witnessed the wife running with a gun in her hand and declaring that she had killed her husband. The nephew immediately ran back to the witness's house and told her, "You won't believe what I just saw!" The occurrence, including the wife's statement, was certainly a startling event, and the nephew seems to have made his statement to the witness while he was still under the stress of excitement caused by the occurrence. Thus, the witness can testify to the nephew's statement, including the part relating what the wife had told him. (B) is incorrect because the exception to the hearsay rule for excited utterances such as the nephew's statement does not require the declarant to be unavailable to testify. (C) is incorrect because it does not matter in this case that the party-opponent made her admission to someone other than the testifying witness. The witness can repeat what the nephew said—including the wife's admission—because it was an excited utterance. (D) is incorrect because, as discussed above, both parts of the nephew's statement are admissible.

Answer to Question 29

(B) Where a witness has insufficient recollection of an event to enable her to testify fully and accurately, even after she has consulted a writing given to her on the stand, the writing itself may be introduced into evidence if a proper foundation is laid for its admissibility. The foundation for receipt of the writing into evidence must include proof that: (i) the witness had personal knowledge of the facts in the writing; (ii) the writing was made by the witness or under her direction, or adopted by the witness; (iii) the writing was timely made when the matter was fresh in the mind of the witness; (iv) the writing is accurate (the witness must vouch for accuracy); and (v) the witness has insufficient recollection to testify fully and accurately. Under the Federal Rules, if admitted, the writing may be ***read*** into evidence and heard by the jury, but the document itself is not received as an exhibit unless offered by the adverse party. Thus, the witness must vouch for the accuracy of her notes. The notes must be given to the witness on the stand to prove that she still has insufficient memory to testify fully and accurately. Finally, the plaintiff's attorney, who is seeking introduction of this material, is limited to having the contents of the notes read to the jury. While the defendant (the adverse party) may have the notes introduced as an exhibit, the plaintiff's attorney in this case may not do so under any circumstances. Therefore, the statements in (A), (C), and (D) are all true. (B), however, is false because the recorded recollection exception to the hearsay rule does not require that the writing be made while the witness is under the stress of excitement of the event. That is a requirement for the excited utterance exception to the hearsay rule. Under the recorded recollection exception, all that is required is that the writing be made in a timely fashion while the matter is still fresh in the witness's mind.

Answer to Question 30

(D) Evidence of repairs or other precautionary measures made following an injury is inadmissible to prove negligence, culpable conduct, a defect in a product or its design, or a need for a warning or instruction. [Fed. R. Evid. 407] The purpose of this rule is to encourage people to make such repairs. Such evidence is admissible for purposes other than to prove negligence. Among such permissible purposes are: (i) to prove ownership or control where that is at issue, (ii) to rebut a claim that the precaution was not feasible, and (iii) to prove that the opposing party has destroyed or concealed evidence. The painting of the pedestrian crosswalk at the intersection at which the accident occurred and the posting of the signs are subsequent remedial measures of the type contemplated by Rule 407. With none of the circumstances present that would render evidence of subsequent repairs admissible, (D) is the correct answer. (A) is incorrect because the city is not contesting ownership or control of the intersection; its defense is that the plaintiff was contributorily negligent. Hence, this evidence is not admissible for that purpose. (B) is incorrect because the city is not attempting to conceal or distort evidence. It is probably undisputed that there was

no marked crosswalk or signs at the time of the accident. (C) is incorrect because subsequent repairs is a type of evidence that, while relevant, is excluded on the public policy ground that society wishes to encourage immediate repair of dangerous conditions. Therefore, it is incorrect to state that the Federal Rules deem subsequent repairs to be irrelevant.

Answer to Question 31

(B) The testimony is admissible to show that the defendant had a motive to destroy the building. Federal Rule 411, which prohibits the admission of evidence of liability insurance to show a person acted negligently or wrongfully, does not apply to these circumstances. The insurance at issue in this case is not liability insurance; it is casualty insurance. The rationale for the exclusion of evidence of liability insurance (*i.e.*, that a trier of fact might improperly infer that a person acted more carelessly because she knew she was insured) has no application here. Whether a person was negligent is not at issue. The insurance policies are relevant because they make a fact in issue, that the defendant set her building on fire, more likely than it would be without evidence of the policies. Since it is relevant and not subject to any exclusionary rule, the testimony regarding the insurance policies is admissible to show motive for the arson. (A) is wrong because evidence of the insurance policies is admissible as substantive evidence in the prosecution's case in chief; it is not limited to impeachment uses. The rule stated in (A) is the one applicable to character type evidence that may be brought in to impeach a criminal defendant's credibility if she takes the stand. The evidence of the insurance policies, apart from having substantive value in proving the case, is of no help in attacking the defendant's veracity when she takes the stand. Thus, this rule is totally inapplicable to this evidence. (C) is wrong because, as noted above, Rule 411 bans the use of evidence of liability insurance only. Liability insurance is not at issue here. (D) is wrong because the admission of testimony regarding the insurance policies does not violate the original document rule (also known as the best evidence rule). The rule requires the original writing to be produced to prove the terms of the writing, where the terms are material. Here, the testimony is not being sought to prove the terms of the policies, but rather that the defendant obtained them. That fact can be established independent of the policy itself.

Answer to Question 32

(B) The question of the existence or nonexistence of preliminary facts other than those of conditional relevance is to be determined by the court. All preliminary fact questions involving the standards of trustworthiness of alleged exceptions to the hearsay rule are to be determined by the court. Thus, the court, not the jury, must decide whether a purported business record was made in the regular course of business. In the case at bar, the question to be decided is whether the "product recognition survey" was in fact made during the regular course of business. Thus, this issue must be decided by the judge. During the hearing at which the judge makes the preliminary fact determination, both parties must be given an opportunity to present evidence with regard to the fact to be determined. Also, it is within the judge's discretion whether the jury should be excused during the preliminary fact determination. (B) is correct because it calls for the determination as to whether the document is a business record to be made by the judge, it allows for the presentation of evidence by both sides, and holding the hearing in the presence of the jury is within the judge's discretion. (A) is incorrect because it precludes the plaintiff's attorney from presenting evidence on the matter to be decided. (C) incorrectly calls for the jury to decide the issue. There is no question here of conditional relevance. The question is one of competency of the evidence. Therefore, this is not the type of preliminary fact to be decided by the jury. (D) also reaches the incorrect conclusion that the jury has the ultimate decision on this matter. Only the judge may decide whether the document in question qualifies as a business record. Once the decision has been made, this issue cannot be further pursued by the jury.

Answer to Question 33

(A) Under Federal Rule 403, a trial judge has broad discretion to exclude relevant evidence if its probative value is substantially outweighed by the danger of unfair prejudice, confusion of the issues, or misleading the jury, or by considerations of undue delay, waste of time, or needless presentation of cumulative evidence. Although some states list unfair surprise as an additional basis for exclusion, the Federal Rules do not, reasoning that surprise can be prevented by discovery and pretrial conference, or mitigated by granting a continuance. From the foregoing principles, if the cellmate is in fact a surprise witness, this will not suffice as a basis to exclude this otherwise relevant evidence under the Federal Rules, which govern this action. At most, the court should grant a continuance. (B) is incorrect because the bloodstained shirt might be deemed to be inflammatory and capable of producing an unfairly prejudicial effect on the jury. As such, it is within the realm of the judge's discretionary power of exclusion. (C) is incorrect because the second expert's testimony will not add anything to the testimony already given by the first expert. Thus, allowing this testimony will simply waste time and repeat evidence already presented. Pursuant to Rule 403, this constitutes a permissible ground of exclusion. (D) is incorrect because, although the fellow officer's testimony tends to render more probably untrue the allegation of a police beating than it would have been without this testimony, whether the plaintiff has AIDS is not an issue in the case. Thus, the statement referring to the defendants' fears might well cause confusion of the issues or tend to mislead the jury, and is subject to exclusion under the Federal Rules.

Answer to Question 34

(B) The question by the plaintiff's attorney should be allowed because he was acting in good faith. A witness may be impeached by means of being interrogated upon cross-examination, in the discretion of the court, with respect to any act of misconduct that is probative of truthfulness (*i.e.*, an act of deceit or lying). The cross-examiner must act in good faith with some reasonable basis for believing that the witness may have committed the bad act inquired about, but it is not required that the witness have been convicted of a crime. Here, the plaintiff's attorney is attempting to cast an adverse reflection on the truthfulness of the neighbor. The commission of the crime of false pretenses involves the making of a false representation and is therefore an act of misconduct that is probative of the actor's truthfulness. Thus, because the plaintiff's attorney inquired as to this matter in good faith, his question is a permissible method of impeachment, and the objection of the defendant's attorney should be overruled. (A) is incorrect because it implies that the objection could be sustained if the neighbor was not convicted of the crime. As noted above, such an inquiry can be conducted regardless of whether the witness was convicted. Therefore, the objection to the plaintiff's attorney's good faith inquiry would be overruled even if the neighbor was not convicted of false pretenses. (C) is incorrect. Although impeaching witnesses who testify to a witness's reputation for truth and veracity are often impeached by asking the "Have you heard" and "Do you know" questions, that is not the only method of impeachment available. ***Any*** witness who takes the stand puts her character for honesty and veracity in issue and may be impeached by evidence that might show her to be unworthy of belief. Instances of misconduct may properly be inquired into only if they are probative of truthfulness. By taking the stand, the neighbor has put her character for honesty in issue. The crime of false pretenses is probative of truthfulness and is a proper subject for impeachment. (D) is incorrect because a specific act of misconduct offered to attack the witness's character for truthfulness can be elicited ***only*** on cross-examination of the witness. Extrinsic evidence is not permitted. Thus, (D) states the opposite of the correct rule.

Answer to Question 35

(D) The court should apply the law of Yellow with regard to the presumption. In a civil case, the effect of a presumption regarding a fact that is an element of a claim as to which state law supplies the rule of decision is determined in accordance with state law. [Fed. R. Evid. 302] Under the *Erie* doctrine, in a case based on diversity of citizenship, the federal court must apply the substantive law of the state in which the court sits, but usually applies federal law to procedural issues. State procedural law applies only if it would result in an important difference in the outcome of the litigation. With respect to presumptions, the Federal Rule, which follows the *Erie* doctrine, provides that application of state law is appropriate only when the presumption operates on a substantive element of a claim or defense. The presumption at issue here, by presuming negligence on the part of a driver who strikes another vehicle in the rear, impacts on the prima facie case elements of duty and breach of duty. Matters involving elements of a prima facie case are substantive in nature; thus, state law applies to such matters. Because the presumption regards a matter for which state law supplies the rule of decision, the effect of the presumption should be determined according to state law, pursuant to Rule 302. Consequently, both the substantive law of Yellow and the Yellow "procedural" law relative to the presumption of negligence should be applied by the court on this issue. (A) is incorrect because there is no general federal common law. The substantive law to be applied in a diversity case is that of the state. Furthermore, it would not be appropriate to apply all of Yellow's rules of procedure. Except in certain circumstances, such as when the rule applied would be outcome determinative, the Federal Rules of Civil Procedure apply in diversity cases. (B) is incorrect. Although it is true that the Yellow substantive law is to be applied, with respect to the procedural issue in question (the applicability of the state presumption), it is Yellow law, not the Federal Rules of Civil Procedure, that the court should apply. (C) is incorrect because it implies that it is the general rule to apply both the substantive and procedural law of the state in which the federal court sits. As detailed above, state procedural law is applied only in certain instances.

Answer to Question 36

(D) The court should rule that the physician's testimony is admissible because the physician-patient privilege does not apply. Generally, the physician-patient privilege provides that a physician cannot be compelled to disclose information obtained from a patient while treating the patient in a professional capacity if that information is related to the treatment. The privilege does not, however, apply in federal cases where state law does not supply the rule of privilege (*i.e.*, federal question cases). Here, the defendant is before the federal court on charges arising under a federal statute. Thus, the physician-patient privilege does not apply and the physician's testimony is admissible. (B) is incorrect because, although the jurisdiction applies the physician-patient privilege to criminal cases, state privilege law does not apply in this case as explained above. (A) is incorrect because the privilege against self-incrimination prevents a witness from being compelled to testify against himself, which is not the case here. (C) is incorrect because the physician's testimony that he treated the defendant is not hearsay (*i.e.*, he is not testifying to an out-of-court statement). Thus, the exception to the hearsay rule for declarations of past bodily conditions does not apply.

Set 6 Answer Sheet

1.	Ⓐ Ⓑ Ⓒ Ⓓ	**19.**	Ⓐ Ⓑ Ⓒ Ⓓ
2.	Ⓐ Ⓑ Ⓒ Ⓓ	**20.**	Ⓐ Ⓑ Ⓒ Ⓓ
3.	Ⓐ Ⓑ Ⓒ Ⓓ	**21.**	Ⓐ Ⓑ Ⓒ Ⓓ
4.	Ⓐ Ⓑ Ⓒ Ⓓ	**22.**	Ⓐ Ⓑ Ⓒ Ⓓ
5.	Ⓐ Ⓑ Ⓒ Ⓓ	**23.**	Ⓐ Ⓑ Ⓒ Ⓓ
6.	Ⓐ Ⓑ Ⓒ Ⓓ	**24.**	Ⓐ Ⓑ Ⓒ Ⓓ
7.	Ⓐ Ⓑ Ⓒ Ⓓ	**25.**	Ⓐ Ⓑ Ⓒ Ⓓ
8.	Ⓐ Ⓑ Ⓒ Ⓓ	**26.**	Ⓐ Ⓑ Ⓒ Ⓓ
9.	Ⓐ Ⓑ Ⓒ Ⓓ	**27.**	Ⓐ Ⓑ Ⓒ Ⓓ
10.	Ⓐ Ⓑ Ⓒ Ⓓ	**28.**	Ⓐ Ⓑ Ⓒ Ⓓ
11.	Ⓐ Ⓑ Ⓒ Ⓓ	**29.**	Ⓐ Ⓑ Ⓒ Ⓓ
12.	Ⓐ Ⓑ Ⓒ Ⓓ	**30.**	Ⓐ Ⓑ Ⓒ Ⓓ
13.	Ⓐ Ⓑ Ⓒ Ⓓ	**31.**	Ⓐ Ⓑ Ⓒ Ⓓ
14.	Ⓐ Ⓑ Ⓒ Ⓓ	**32.**	Ⓐ Ⓑ Ⓒ Ⓓ
15.	Ⓐ Ⓑ Ⓒ Ⓓ	**33.**	Ⓐ Ⓑ Ⓒ Ⓓ
16.	Ⓐ Ⓑ Ⓒ Ⓓ	**34.**	Ⓐ Ⓑ Ⓒ Ⓓ
17.	Ⓐ Ⓑ Ⓒ Ⓓ	**35.**	Ⓐ Ⓑ Ⓒ Ⓓ
18.	Ⓐ Ⓑ Ⓒ Ⓓ	**36.**	Ⓐ Ⓑ Ⓒ Ⓓ

EVIDENCE QUESTIONS - SET 6

Question 1

A plaintiff sues a hardware store and a manufacturer of leaf blowers for injuries he suffered when his leaf blower gave him an electrical shock the first time he used it. At trial, the plaintiff testified that, although he had purchased the leaf blower several days before using it, he remembered that the purchase date was on his brother's birthday and furthermore, he had a credit card receipt at home that would show that date. The hardware store's attorney objected to the plaintiff's testimony concerning the date on the credit card receipt.

Of the following, how would a judge most likely rule on this objection?

(A) Sustained, because the actual receipt is the best evidence of the date the leaf blower was purchased.

(B) Sustained, because the information in the credit card receipt is hearsay, not subject to any exception.

(C) Overruled, because the date the leaf blower was purchased is not material to any issue at trial, and the plaintiff had independent recollection of the date.

(D) Overruled, because the information in the credit card receipt is admissible under the past recollection recorded exception to the hearsay rule.

Question 2

A plaintiff sued his neighbor over a 10-foot-high stockade fence that the neighbor was building adjacent to the plaintiff's backyard. The local zoning ordinance permitted a fence of this height unless it was a "spite fence," defined as a fence erected solely for the purpose of interfering with neighboring landowners' use and enjoyment of their property. The plaintiff alleged that the neighbor was building the fence to block sunlight to the garden that the plaintiff had planted. The neighbor denied that she was building the fence for that purpose. The plaintiff wishes to introduce evidence that the neighbor had sprayed herbicide towards the garden previously.

Should the judge permit the plaintiff's testimony?

(A) Yes, because the neighbor's character is at issue in the case.

(B) Yes, because it pertains to the neighbor's motivation in building the fence.

(C) No, because the plaintiff's testimony is evidence of specific conduct, which is not admissible in this case because the neighbor's character is not in issue.

(D) No, because character evidence generally is not admissible in a civil case.

Question 3

The guardian ad litem of a minor child filed an appropriate tort suit against a hospital and the resident physician attending the child when he suffered irreversible brain damage due to an excessive fever. The plaintiff alleges that the physician was negligent in not administering a fever-reduction drug, which could only be given when the child's temperature reached 102 degrees Fahrenheit. "Plaintiff's Exhibit F," which has been introduced into evidence, is the chart indicating that the child's temperature reached 103.7 degrees at 3 p.m. on February 26. The chart is signed by the head nurse of the pediatric care division, and the signature has been properly authenticated. Other testimony indicates that it is standard procedure at the hospital for the head nurse of each division to submit medical charts to resident physicians for additional notation before the charts are filed in the hospital's permanent records. Plaintiff's Exhibit F contains no notation, initial, or signature from the physician. When the physician takes the stand she wishes to testify that she was in the room when the child's temperature was taken at 2:30 p.m. on February 26, and at that time his temperature was 101.7 degrees.

Such testimony would be:

(A) Admissible, because the physician has firsthand knowledge of the child's condition at the time in question.

(B) Admissible, because the plaintiff "opened the door" to such testimony by introducing the chart into evidence.

(C) Inadmissible, because the chart is the best evidence of the child's body temperature.

(D) Inadmissible, because the physician had ample opportunity to correct the temperature record and her failure to do so constitutes an adoptive admission.

Question 4

After measuring skid marks and interviewing all eyewitnesses present at the scene of an automobile accident, an officer wrote out in longhand all the pertinent information on the standard police accident report form. The officer turned the report in to the department, where a police typist, according to the prescribed procedure, transcribed the officer's longhand record into a typed record which, after it was checked by the officer, was then placed on file in the police department. Two years later, the plaintiff sued the defendant for her injuries. The plaintiff called the officer to the stand to testify regarding the skid marks. The officer can remember nothing about the specific accident, as he has made at least 200 accident reports since the accident in question. After looking at the report, the officer can remember preparing the report but still cannot remember the accident scene. He wishes to read the information regarding the skid marks in the police report to the jury from the stand. The defense attorney objects.

How should the court rule?

(A) The officer may read from the report, because it is past recollection recorded.

(B) The officer may read from the report, because it is a present sense impression.

(C) The officer may not read from the report, because a police report does not qualify as a business record.

(D) The report should be given to the jury to read, but it should not be read to them by the officer from the stand.

Question 5

A wife was suspected of killing her husband, although she told the police that he was struck by a bullet shot through the window of their home. The wife agreed to undergo a polygraph examination. An experienced polygraph analyst told the police that the wife was telling the truth when she asserted that she had nothing to do with the husband's death. Two weeks later, the police arrested the husband's former business partner. During the partner's trial, the prosecution called the wife to the stand to testify to the happenings on the night the husband was slain and to the "bad blood" that existed between the partner and the husband. The defense attorney, without objection by the prosecutor, asked the wife questions regarding her stormy marital relationship with the husband in an attempt to show that the wife and not his client might have been the slayer. Having seen one of her key witnesses' testimony weakened, the prosecutor on redirect asked the wife, "After your husband was killed, didn't the police have you take a lie detector test?" As soon as the question was asked, the defense attorney objected.

The objection is likely to be:

(A) Sustained, because the scientific reliability of the polygraph evidence is substantially outweighed by its confusing effect on the jury.

(B) Sustained, because the wife is not on trial for murder.

(C) Overruled, because the prosecutor has the right to rehabilitate a witness whose credibility has been impeached.

(D) Overruled, because the defense attorney "opened the door" to the prosecutor's line

of questioning by asking questions that implied that the wife might have killed the husband.

Question 6

A defendant was on trial for the murder of his business partner. The prosecution offered testimony by the telephone operator in the defendant's office that she had listened in without the defendant's knowledge to a telephone call he had received the day before his partner's death, in which an unidentified man said that he heard talk in a bar the previous night that the business partner was going to tell the cops about a phony insurance claim involving the defendant. The defense attorney objects to this testimony.

The trial court should:

(A) Sustain the objection, because the operator was an eavesdropper.

(B) Sustain the objection, because the testimony is hearsay not within any exception.

(C) Overrule the objection, because the statement is relevant to show motive.

(D) Overrule the objection, because the statement constitutes an admission by a co-conspirator.

Question 7

In a criminal battery case brought against the defendant, the prosecutor asked the court to take judicial notice of the fact that a car driven from Chicago to Detroit has to cross state lines. The defense attorney raised no objection, and the judge declared that she was taking judicial notice of the fact as requested by the prosecution.

The effect of such judicial notice is:

(A) To raise an irrebuttable presumption.

(B) To satisfy the prosecutor's burden of persuasion on that issue.

(C) To shift the burden of persuasion on that issue to the defendant.

(D) That the judge should instruct the jury that it may, but is not required to, accept the noticed fact as conclusively proven.

Question 8

While waiting for a flight, a passenger noticed that whenever a bearded man with a large valise passed close to her suitcase, the Geiger counter inside, designed to detect small amounts of radiation, would tick. The passenger informed the airport police, who quickly accosted the bearded man, a medical technician. His suitcase contained some expensive radioactive isotopes used in treating certain forms of cancer. The police were aware that the same type of isotopes had been reported missing from a hospital a few days earlier. The medical technician was charged under a federal statute making it a crime to transport radioactive materials without a license. At the trial, an expert witness testifies as to how the Geiger counter operates. Next, the prosecutor calls the passenger to testify regarding the reaction of the Geiger counter to the medical technician's presence.

The testimony will be allowed only if the prosecution shows:

(A) That there was no other radioactive material in the area that could have set off the Geiger counter.

(B) That the Geiger counter has been held in a substantially unbroken chain of custody.

(C) That the Geiger counter was in sound operating condition at the time of the airport incident.

(D) That the Geiger counter was in the same condition at the time of the airport incident as it is at the trial.

Question 9

A defendant is on trial for the murder of the victim, who was found beaten to death in his home. Evidence already presented has shown that the victim was killed when no one was at home except for the victim and his dog. The prosecution wishes to call a neighbor to the stand who is prepared to testify that she went to the victim's home the day after his murder and that when the defendant came by, the dog ran to a corner, where he cringed and whimpered. The neighbor is also prepared to testify that the dog is normally a very friendly dog, usually greeting visitors to the house, including the defendant, by approaching them with his tail wagging. The defense objects to the neighbor's proposed testimony.

How should the court rule on the neighbor's testimony regarding the dog's behavior?

(A) Admissible, because the dog could be brought into court for a demonstration of his reaction to the defendant.

(B) Admissible, as circumstantial evidence against the defendant.

(C) Inadmissible, because the dog may have been reacting as he did for reasons other than those implied by the neighbor's testimony.

(D) Inadmissible, because even though the testimony has probative value, such value is outweighed by its prejudicial nature.

Question 10

A defendant visited her doctor to seek treatment for a bullet wound. While he was treating the wound, the doctor asked the defendant how she was shot. The defendant replied that she was struck by a police officer's bullet while running away from a jewelry store she had robbed, but she implored the doctor not to tell this to anyone. The doctor promised that he would not. Although the defendant was never charged by the police, the owner of the jewelry store brought suit against her seeking the value of the stolen goods. The defendant denied robbing the store. At the trial, the owner calls the doctor to testify to the statement made to him by the defendant. The defense attorney objects on the ground that such testimony is barred by the jurisdiction's physician-patient privilege.

The objection should be:

(A) Sustained, because the doctor acquired this information while attending the defendant in the course of treatment.

(B) Sustained, because the doctor agreed to the defendant's specific request that this information be kept confidential.

(C) Overruled, because the physician-patient privilege is inapplicable to the defendant's statement.

(D) Overruled, because the doctor is the one who is entitled to either claim this privilege or waive it.

Question 11

A plaintiff has brought suit in federal district court against the Social Security Administration because it denied her retirement benefits on the asserted ground that she had not reached the requisite age to qualify. At trial, the plaintiff introduced into evidence a family Bible given to her by her father in which is inscribed her date of birth, showing her to be 65 years old. The government introduced a certified copy of the plaintiff's birth certificate, which shows her age to be 55. The court admitted both items over objection of the nonpropounding party.

Was this error?

(A) Yes, as to the Bible only, because it contained inadmissible hearsay.

(B) Yes, as to the birth certificate only, because it was not authenticated by the custodian of records.

(C) Yes, as to both, for the reasons stated in the previous answers.

(D) No, both records were admissible.

Question 12

A businessman filed a defamation suit against a newspaper for printing a column that referred to the businessman as "a nasty scoundrel" and "worse than Ebenezer Scrooge," and accused him of "never performing a real act of charity in his life." During the presentation of the businessman's case, he wanted to put an agent of the Internal Revenue Service on the stand. The agent is prepared to testify that the businessman, on his own initiative, reimbursed the IRS for an erroneous overpayment of a tax refund. Counsel representing the newspaper objects.

The court is likely to rule the agent's testimony:

(A) Admissible, because the businessman's character is at issue in the case.

(B) Admissible, because the businessman has a right to defend his good character.

(C) Inadmissible, because the agent's testimony, in and of itself, is not probative of any material issue in the case.

(D) Inadmissible, because specific instances of conduct are not admissible to prove character.

Question 13

A union filed suit against a corporation, known for its antiunion management, asserting that its members were being discharged in retaliation for membership in the union rather than for any failure to perform their jobs properly. Under the pretrial discovery orders, a union employee was allowed to examine all of the records held in the corporation's files concerning discharge of employees for a seven-year period prior to the instigation of suit by the union. The employee sorted through this large volume of material and discovered that persons who were union activists usually had "lack of corporate spirit" listed as their reason for discharge, while other fired workers tended to have more specific grounds for discharge listed, *e.g.*, persistent lateness. The employee developed a chart showing grounds for dismissal of union members versus nonmembers based on the data in the files. At the trial, the union placed the employee on the stand. She testified in some detail regarding how she had conducted her research. The employee brought out the chart and the union's lawyer asked that the chart be admitted into evidence. The corporation's attorney objected.

The court should rule that the chart is:

(A) Admissible, because copies of the original documents upon which the chart was based were available to the corporation prior to trial.

(B) Admissible, because the chart is helpful to the trier of fact.

(C) Inadmissible, because it is hearsay not within any exception.

(D) Inadmissible, in the absence of the underlying records having been first introduced into evidence.

Question 14

A department store and its former manager were being sued for false imprisonment arising from the detention of the plaintiff by a security guard for suspected shoplifting. The plaintiff's attorney wishes to introduce a report from a police officer who was brought back to the store by the plaintiff after she was released. In the report, the manager states that he was not present when the plaintiff was stopped, but that the guard told him that the plaintiff was stopped because of her "shifty eyes," and that she would not have been stopped if she had not looked so suspicious. The attorney for the department store objects to the use of the manager's statement in the police report.

The objection should be:

(A) Overruled, because the manager's statement in the police report was made while he was employed by the department store.

(B) Overruled, because the manager is also a party to the lawsuit.

(C) Sustained, because the manager had neither the authority nor a business duty to relate that statement to the police officer.

(D) Sustained, because the manager's statement was based on hearsay of another person rather than personal knowledge.

Question 15

A defendant was charged with the murder of a victim. During the course of the criminal trial, a witness testified on behalf of the defense that, at the time the murder took place, he saw someone who looked like the defendant dancing at a local nightclub. The defendant is eventually acquitted of the charge. Following the acquittal, the appropriate survivors of the victim bring a wrongful death action against the defendant. As part of her defense, the defendant wishes to introduce the testimony given at the criminal trial by the witness, who the defendant shows is now incarcerated in a prison in another state.

The testimony of the witness is:

(A) Admissible, because the witness testified under oath at another hearing related to the same subject matter.

(B) Admissible, because the defendant is a party to both proceedings.

(C) Inadmissible, because the plaintiffs were not parties to the criminal proceeding.

(D) Inadmissible, because the witness can be subpoenaed to testify.

Question 16

A sportscaster on a local television show interviewed the parent of a child on a high school football team. The interviewee told the sportscaster that the head football coach "openly condones the use of steroids by team members." The coach, who had always conducted a strong antidrug program for his football players, watched and recorded the show daily. He was outraged when he saw the live broadcast, and filed suit for defamation against the interviewee, the sportscaster, and the television station. At the trial of the suit, the coach wishes to testify as to what the interviewee said on the television show. The defense objects.

Should such testimony be admitted?

(A) Yes, because the coach saw the live television broadcast.

(B) Yes, because the matter goes to the ultimate issue of the case and is thus highly relevant.

(C) No, because a videotape of the broadcast is available.

(D) No, because such testimony would be hearsay, not within any recognized exception to the hearsay rule.

Question 17

A beneficiary sued a trustee of a trust for breach of fiduciary duty. During the beneficiary's case in chief, the beneficiary's counsel asks the trustee on direct examination whether the trustee embezzled $50,000 from the bank at which she was a trust officer.

Must the trustee answer this question?

(A) Yes, because by taking the stand she waived her privilege against self-incrimination.

(B) Yes, because the Fifth Amendment has no application to a civil trial.

(C) No, if she has not waived the privilege against self-incrimination.

(D) No, because a witness may always assert the privilege against self-incrimination.

Question 18

During the course of their marriage, a husband told his wife that he stole a famous painting from a federal museum. Six months after the admission, the couple divorced. Shortly after the divorce, the husband was killed in an automobile accident. Later, the wife read in the paper that a man had been charged with the theft of the painting her husband admitting to stealing and was about to be tried in federal district court. She told her friend that the man was probably innocent because the husband told her that he had stolen the painting himself. The friend told several other people what the wife had told her, and eventually the story got back to the defense attorney. The attorney now wants the wife to testify in court to the husband's statement.

Can the wife be compelled to testify?

(A) Yes, but only because the husband is dead and cannot invoke his privilege.

(B) Yes, because there is no privilege when the defendant is not a spouse.

(C) No, because the couple was still married at the time of the disclosure.

(D) No, because her testimony is not essential to prevent a fraud on the court.

Question 19

A defendant was tearing up a stretch of pavement with a jackhammer when a rock flew up and struck a plaintiff in the head, causing him to be hospitalized. Because the jackhammer manufacturer had been out of business for several years, the plaintiff filed a lawsuit for his medical costs, lost work time, and pain and suffering solely against the defendant. At trial, the plaintiff's attorney calls a witness who testifies that, at the time of the incident, the defendant stated, "It was my fault." The defense attorney objects, but the judge overrules the objection on the ground that this is a declaration against interest.

Are the grounds for the judge's decision correct?

(A) Yes, because the statement subjected the defendant to tort liability.

(B) Yes, because the defendant is a party to the litigation.

(C) No, because the statement is not against an important interest.

(D) No, because the defendant is available to testify.

Question 20

A plaintiff read of the success of a box-office hit movie about aardvarks in various entertainment journals. The movie was enormously popular among young children, and cartoon figures from the movie began appearing on T-shirts, soft drink mugs, and other novelties. The plaintiff filed suit against the studio alleging that the production company unlawfully used his ideas for the movie. The studio admitted that it had received a clay model of a cartoon animal from the plaintiff, but denied that the model had any substantial similarity to the now-famous aardvarks. The studio had returned the model to the plaintiff, but he had destroyed it.

For the plaintiff to testify at trial as to the appearance of the model, which of the following is true?

(A) The plaintiff can testify as to the appearance of the model because he has personal knowledge of it.

(B) The plaintiff must show that the destruction of the model was not committed in bad faith.

(C) The plaintiff must introduce a photograph of the model, if one exists.

(D) The plaintiff must give advance notice to the opposing party that he plans to use such oral testimony in his case.

Question 21

A daughter brought suit against an insurer for failure to pay benefits on a policy held by her famous father, who had been missing for years. The insurer had refused to pay because there had been no determination that the father was deceased. At trial, the daughter testifies that she has not heard from her father since prior to New Year's Day seven years ago. On that date, a chartered boat left Florida and has never returned. The ship was last seen near midday on that day sailing into an area known as the "graveyard of ships." No trace of the boat has ever been found. The daughter establishes that the charter operator filed a passenger list with the coast guard, and that one of the names on the list is "Madd Hatter." The daughter wishes to testify that on the day before the disappearance, her father told her that he planned to propose a television pilot for a comedy starring himself as "Madd Hatter."

If the insurer's attorney objects, is the testimony as to the father's alleged statement admissible?

(A) Yes, as circumstantial evidence that the father was on the boat.

(B) Yes, to create a rebuttable presumption that the father was on the boat.

(C) Yes, to create a conclusive presumption that the father was on the boat.

(D) No, the testimony is not admissible.

Question 22

A plaintiff was injured when a portion of a spiral stairway in a shopping mall collapsed. The plaintiff filed suit against both the owners of the mall and the designers of the staircase. At the trial of the case, the plaintiff wishes to call a highly qualified civil engineer to the stand to testify as an expert witness. The expert is prepared to testify that the spiral staircase was improperly designed, and the design defect caused a portion of the staircase to collapse under the plaintiff. The expert's proposed testimony is based in part upon a series of photographs taken by a structural engineer hired by the expert immediately after the expert was engaged by the plaintiff's attorney, and the accompanying report by the structural engineer. It is customary for civil engineers to form professional opinions based on these reports. The photographs are of the collapsed stairway and of an identical stairway located in another part of the mall. Neither the photographs nor the report has been admitted into evidence, but the expert is willing to disclose to the jury the facts on which he relied in forming his opinion.

The expert's testimony should be ruled:

(A) Admissible, because other civil engineers ordinarily reasonably rely on structural engineers' reports in forming professional opinions.

(B) Admissible, because the expert will disclose to the jury the facts on which he based his opinion.

(C) Inadmissible, because the expert based his opinion in part on the structural engineer's opinion.

(D) Inadmissible, because the photographs and report were commissioned solely for the purpose of preparing for litigation and were not admitted into evidence.

Question 23

A victim and his former business partner, the defendant, had a bitter falling out after the victim accused the defendant of embezzling company funds. The defendant threatened to get even. Shortly thereafter, while driving on the expressway, a car swerved suddenly in front of the victim's car. Although the victim applied the brakes immediately, his car failed to stop. To avoid colliding with the car ahead of him, he swerved to the right and smashed into a concrete retaining wall. A passing motorist stopped and came to the aid of the victim. Bleeding profusely from a head wound, and rapidly losing

consciousness, the victim said, "I don't think I'm going to make it. I tried to slow down, but my brakes didn't work. My former partner must have tampered with them to get back at me." With that, the victim lapsed into unconsciousness, and has been in a coma and on life support ever since. A personal injury suit has been filed on his behalf by a court-appointed guardian against the defendant.

At trial, can the motorist testify as to the statement made by the victim?

(A) No, because the victim did not know that the defendant tampered with the brakes.

(B) No, because the victim is still alive.

(C) Yes, because the victim thought he was about to die.

(D) Yes, because this is a civil case.

Question 24

A plaintiff brought a conversion action against a defendant, alleging that the defendant had wrongfully taken a necklace owned by the plaintiff's mother, who had recently died intestate. The defendant's defense is that the mother, who had lived next door to the defendant, had freely given her the necklace because she had often given rides to and run errands for the mother, who did not drive and had trouble getting around. The defendant is cross-examined by the plaintiff's attorney, who challenges the defendant's claim that the mother had given her the necklace. The defendant wishes to testify that, before handing her the necklace, the mother told her, "You've always been so good to me that I want you to have this necklace."

The defendant's proposed testimony is:

(A) Inadmissible, as hearsay not within any exception.

(B) Inadmissible, under the state's Dead Man Act.

(C) Admissible, because it is nonhearsay.

(D) Admissible, because the declarant is unavailable to testify.

Question 25

A defendant is charged with trafficking in firearms, in violation of federal firearms control laws, as well as receiving stolen property. The charges arise from the defendant's having attempted to sell a semi-automatic weapon identified as one of dozens that were stolen from a warehouse a year ago. The defendant denies intending to sell the gun or knowing that it had been stolen.

At trial, which of the following would the court be ***least*** likely to allow the prosecution to introduce as evidence against the defendant?

(A) Evidence that the defendant was once convicted of armed robbery with a semi-automatic weapon.

(B) The testimony of a witness that, the day before the defendant's arrest, he asked the witness how much she would be willing to pay for a semi-automatic weapon.

(C) The testimony of a member of a secret paramilitary group that the defendant had been supplying the group with weapons for several months.

(D) Evidence that the defendant had been previously convicted of receipt of stolen weapons.

Question 26

A local news station broadcast a live interview with a bystander about his views concerning the state of local education. The bystander responded by saying that the principal of his daughter's high school had been embezzling school funds for years. The principal had recorded the telecast and later watched the interview. He sued the owner of the station for defamation. At trial, the principal sought to testify to the defamatory statement made in the interview.

The principal's testimony will most likely be held to be:

(A) Inadmissible, because the testimony would be hearsay not within any exception.

(B) Inadmissible, because a videotape of the interview exists.

(C) Admissible, because the statement is being offered to show its effect on the principal.

(D) Admissible, because the principal personally saw the interview on television.

Question 27

In an action to recover for personal injuries arising out of an automobile accident, the plaintiff calls a bystander to testify. Claiming the privilege against self-incrimination, the bystander refuses to answer a question as to whether she was at the scene of the accident. The plaintiff moves that the bystander be ordered to answer the question.

The judge should allow the bystander to remain silent only if:

(A) The judge is convinced that she will incriminate herself.

(B) There is clear and convincing evidence that she will incriminate herself.

(C) There is a preponderance of evidence that she will incriminate herself.

(D) The judge believes that there is some reasonable possibility that she will incriminate herself.

Question 28

A witness is called in a contract action between a plaintiff and a defendant. The witness takes his oath and testifies. During cross-examination, the defendant's attorney asked the witness this question: "Isn't it true that even though you took an oath to tell the truth so help you God, you are an atheist and don't even believe in God?"

Upon the proper objection, will the judge require that the witness answer this question?

(A) Yes, because the question is relevant to the witness's character for truthfulness.

(B) Yes, because instead of taking the oath, the witness could have requested to testify by affirmation without any reference to God.

(C) No, because evidence of the beliefs or opinions of a witness on matters of religion is not admissible to impair credibility.

(D) No, because an attack on the competency of a witness must be made at the time the witness is sworn.

Question 29

A witness testified against a defendant in a contract action. The defendant then called a friend to the stand, who testified that the witness had a bad reputation for truth and veracity. The defendant then also called the witness's employee to testify that the witness once perpetrated a hoax on an insurance company, for which she was convicted.

The employee's testimony is:

(A) Inadmissible, because it is merely cumulative impeachment.

(B) Inadmissible, because it is extrinsic evidence of a specific instance of misconduct.

(C) Admissible, because the hoax resulted in a conviction of the witness.

(D) Admissible, because a hoax involves untruthfulness.

Question 30

A plaintiff sued a defendant railroad company for injuries sustained when his car was hit at a railroad crossing. The plaintiff testified that just before the accident, a bystander yelled, "Oh no, the crossing signal isn't working!" The defendant wants to place a witness on the stand who

will testify that the bystander, who is now dead, told her that the crossing signal was working.

The witness's testimony is:

(A) Admissible, for the purpose of impeachment only.

(B) Admissible, for the purpose of impeachment and to show that the crossing signal was working.

(C) Inadmissible, because it is hearsay not within any exception.

(D) Inadmissible, because the bystander is not available to explain or deny the contradiction.

Question 31

During the defendant's trial for first degree murder, the prosecution wishes to introduce a tape recording of a telephone call made by the victim to police just before she was killed. The victim was extremely distraught at the time of the call and failed to identify herself. A witness is called to the stand to identify the voice on the recording as that of the victim.

Under which of the following circumstances would the trial court be *least* justified in admitting the tape recording into evidence?

(A) The witness had spoken with the victim numerous times, but had never heard her speak over the telephone.

(B) The witness had spoken with the victim over the telephone many times, but had never met her in person.

(C) The witness had heard the victim's voice in several tape-recorded telephone conversations between the victim and the victim's father, and the father told the witness that the person he was speaking with was his daughter.

(D) The witness had been present with the victim when she made the call to the police, but had heard only the victim's half of the conversation.

Question 32

The defendant is charged with the battery of the plaintiff, a bouncer at a local tavern. At the trial, the plaintiff introduces evidence that while he was attempting to question the defendant about her intoxicated demeanor, the defendant committed a battery on the plaintiff. The defendant attempts to defend against the charge on the basis of self-defense, insisting that the plaintiff used excessive force in stopping her from entering the tavern. The defendant attempts to introduce into evidence an authenticated copy of the tavern records that show that three patrons had written complaints against the plaintiff within the past six months for the use of excessive force. The plaintiff objects on the grounds that the records are inadmissible character evidence.

The court should:

(A) Sustain the objection, because the character of a victim can be established only by reputation or opinion evidence.

(B) Sustain the objection, because there is no evidence that the incidents involving the three patrons were based on the same facts as the defendant's claim.

(C) Overrule the objection, because the records were authenticated.

(D) Overrule the objection, because the character trait of a victim may be established by opinion evidence, reputation evidence, or by specific acts of misconduct.

Question 33

A plaintiff sues her employer for sexual harassment. During the trial, the plaintiff attempts to introduce into evidence company records that include written complaints from other employees alleging that they too were sexually harassed by the employer. The defense objects to the admission of the records on the basis of hearsay.

The objection should be:

(A) Sustained, because the records are hearsay not within any recognized exception.

(B) Overruled, because the records qualify under the business records exception.

(C) Overruled, because the records qualify as a statement against interest.

(D) Overruled, because the records are not hearsay.

Question 34

The defendant is charged with the criminal battery of the victim, a security guard in a drug store. At the trial, the prosecution introduces evidence that while the victim was attempting to question the defendant about a suspected shoplifting incident, the defendant committed a battery on the victim. The defendant claims self-defense, and offers into evidence a judgment for damages against the victim for battery against another person under similar circumstances three months earlier.

Evidence of the judgment would be:

(A) Admissible only in a subsequent civil trial.

(B) Admissible for the purpose of establishing the victim's dangerous propensities.

(C) Inadmissible as hearsay not within any recognized exception.

(D) Inadmissible as irrelevant.

Question 35

A plaintiff sued an airline company for negligence for back injuries she sustained when the airplane in which she was a passenger was involved in an accident. The defendant has answered the complaint with a general denial of negligence as well as of personal injuries. Immediately after the accident, the plaintiff was examined and treated by her physician. The physician made an affidavit stating that he had examined the plaintiff the day after the accident and found her to be suffering from a back injury. The physician is now dead. The plaintiff's counsel seeks to introduce the affidavit.

The judge should rule the affidavit:

(A) Inadmissible, because it is hearsay not within any exception.

(B) Inadmissible, because the affidavit does not state that the injury occurred from the accident.

(C) Admissible, as the prior recorded testimony of the physician.

(D) Admissible, as a statement of present bodily condition made to a physician.

Question 36

A defendant is charged with federal mail fraud based upon misrepresentations in his application for medical insurance coverage and for claims on policies that were subsequently issued. The application and claim forms containing the misrepresentations were mailed to the insurance company through the United States Postal Service. Specifically, the defendant failed to state his previous illnesses on both the application and claim form. The defendant denies the charges of having misrepresented his medical history. The prosecution wishes to offer as proof of his fraud the testimony of the defendant's physician, who will testify as to the defendant's history of previous illnesses. The defendant's attorney objects to the physician's testimony. The jurisdiction's physician-patient privilege applies to both civil and criminal proceedings.

The court should rule that the physician's testimony is:

(A) Admissible, because the physician is qualified to testify as an expert witness.

(B) Admissible, because the physician-patient privilege does not apply.

(C) Inadmissible, because it violates the physician-patient privilege.

(D) Inadmissible, because the defendant's medical records are the best evidence.

EVIDENCE ANSWERS - SET 6

Answer to Question 1

(C) A judge would most likely permit this testimony because (i) the plaintiff had independent recollection of the date, and (ii) the date on which the leaf blower was purchased is really "collateral" to the issues at trial. At most, the two important facts would be that the leaf blower was purchased from the hardware store and that it short-circuited the first time the plaintiff used it. Thus, it seems that the date when he purchased the leaf blower is completely irrelevant, and since the hardware store objected to the testimony only on this point, the trial judge would probably overrule its objection. (A) is incorrect because the best evidence rule is not applicable when the facts "testified" to regard only collateral matters. (B) is weak because the plaintiff is not really testifying as to the facts contained in the credit card receipt, but that he remembered the date independently and could prove it if necessary. Thus, the hearsay rule would probably not apply to what the plaintiff testified to in this instance. (D) is incorrect because even if the credit card receipt were considered hearsay, it would not qualify under the past recollection recorded exception.

Answer to Question 2

(B) The judge should permit the plaintiff's testimony because evidence of specific acts of misconduct is admissible to show motive. Under Federal Rule 404(b), evidence of other acts may be admissible in a criminal or civil case if they are relevant to some issue other than character, such as motive. Here, whether the neighbor was motivated by an improper purpose in building the fence is the key issue in the lawsuit by the plaintiff. The neighbor's prior misconduct in spraying herbicide toward the plaintiff's garden is circumstantial evidence that her hostility toward the garden motivated her to build the fence. (A) is wrong because even though the neighbor's motivation and intent are at issue in the case, her character is not. In the absence of character being directly in issue in the case, evidence of character to prove the conduct of a person in the litigated event is not admissible. (C) and (D) are wrong even though they correctly state general rules: evidence of specific acts of misconduct is generally inadmissible, and character evidence is generally inadmissible in a civil case. However, when the specific acts are being offered for a purpose other than to show bad character or conduct in conformity to character, they are admissible in both criminal and civil cases.

Answer to Question 3

(A) The testimony is admissible because the physician has firsthand knowledge of the child's temperature at the time in question. The best evidence rule requires that in proving the terms of a writing, where the terms are material, the original writing must be produced. [Fed. R. Evid. 1002] This rule applies only where the terms of a writing are at issue or the knowledge of a witness concerning a fact results from having read it in the document. Where the fact to be proved has an existence independent of any writing, the best evidence rule does not apply. Here, the physician's knowledge of the child's temperature at the time in question came from firsthand knowledge, not just from having read it in the chart. The child's temperature on February 26, therefore, is a fact that has an existence independent of the chart and the best evidence rule does not apply. The physician's firsthand knowledge of the child's temperature is obviously relevant to the issue of whether his fever reached 102 degrees and should be admitted. (B) is incorrect because the physician's testimony would have been admissible even if the chart were not in evidence. While the best evidence rule prohibits the material contents of a writing to be proved

by oral testimony rather than by producing the original, the rule does not apply here because the physician's testimony was based on firsthand knowledge instead of the chart, as discussed above. Therefore, whether the chart was in evidence is irrelevant to the admissibility of the physician's testimony. (C) is an incorrect statement of the law. The best evidence rule, as discussed above, requires that original writings be produced to prove their material contents. It does not apply when a fact exists independent of a document. It does not require that the "best" evidence always be used to prove an issue. (D) is incorrect because a prior admission does not make the testimony of the person who made the admission inadmissible. A party may expressly or impliedly adopt someone else's statement as his own, thus giving rise to an "adoptive admission." [Fed. R. Evid. 801(d)(2)(B)] If a defendant makes such an admission, it will not be considered hearsay if offered into evidence. However, such an admission will not bar a defendant from testifying about the matter admitted. Therefore, even if the physician's failure to correct the chart were considered an adoptive admission, his testimony would not be inadmissible as a result.

Answer to Question 4

(A) Because a proper foundation has been laid, the officer may read from the report while on the witness stand. Past recollection recorded is an exception to the hearsay rule. When a witness, after consulting the writing while on the stand, still has insufficient recollection to testify, the writing itself may be introduced into evidence if a proper foundation is laid. The foundation must establish four elements: (i) the witness at one time must have had personal knowledge of the facts in the writing; (ii) the writing must have been made when the matter was fresh in the witness's mind; (iii) the writing must have been made by the witness or under his direction, or adopted by him; and (iv) the witness must be presently unable to remember the facts. [Fed. R. Evid. 803(5)] The officer had personal knowledge of the skid marks. (Note that because of this personal knowledge requirement, any part of the report not relating to the officer's personal observation of the skid marks, such as statements of eyewitnesses, would not be admissible under this exception.) The officer also made the original writing when the facts were fresh in his mind, and he is presently unable to remember the facts. Thus, the record is admissible as a past recollection recorded. (B) is incorrect because a present sense impression is a statement describing or explaining an event made while perceiving the event or immediately thereafter. [Fed. R. Evid. 803(1)] Generally, a present sense impression is an oral statement made to another rather than a written report. Here, the officer's statement was made in a report prepared sometime after he first perceived the skid marks and after he had interviewed all of the witnesses. Thus, the officer's report is not a present sense impression. (C) is incorrect. A police report may qualify as a business record under Federal Rule 803(6) because it was made in the course of a regularly conducted business activity (and "business" is defined very broadly), even though it also qualifies as a public record or report under Federal Rule 803(8) or as past recollection recorded under Federal Rule 803(5). (D) is incorrect because the procedure is exactly the opposite. Under Federal Rule 803(5), a recorded recollection that qualifies under the exception may be read into evidence (because it is a substitute for the witness's testimony) but may not be received as an exhibit for the jury to read unless offered by an adverse party.

Answer to Question 5

(A) The objection is likely to be sustained under Federal Rule 403 because the scientific reliability of polygraph evidence is substantially outweighed by the tendency of its results to mislead and confuse the jury. Testimony concerning the polygraph test would be relevant because it would tend to make the existence of a fact of consequence—whether the wife was telling the truth—more probable. However, Rule 403 gives a trial judge broad discretion to exclude relevant evidence if its probative value is substantially outweighed by the danger of unfair prejudice, confusion of the issues, or misleading the jury. The probative value of a polygraph test depends on its scientific reliability, and its reliability generally is deemed to be slight because of its significant rate of error. On the other side of the balancing test, the tendency of jurors to give too much weight to a polygraph test makes the danger of unfair prejudice high. Therefore, the test's unreliability and the risk of confusion from the test's results justify excluding the prosecutor's question. (B) is incorrect because the credibility of a witness may be attacked by any party and then rehabilitated, regardless of whether the witness is on trial. In terms of relevance, any matter that tends to prove or disprove the credibility of a witness should be admitted. The defense attorney properly asked the wife questions about her marriage because this line of questioning tended to discredit the wife's testimony about what happened the night the husband was slain. A witness, like the wife, who has been impeached may be rehabilitated on redirect by explaining or clarifying facts brought out on cross-examination. While the question about the polygraph test should be excluded under Rule 403, as discussed above, the question may not be barred just because the wife is not on trial. (C) is incorrect because while the prosecutor has the right to rehabilitate the wife's credibility, she may not do so with polygraph evidence. As discussed above, a witness who has been impeached may be rehabilitated on redirect by explaining or clarifying facts brought out on cross-examination. While prior consistent statements generally may not be used for rehabilitation, an exception exists if the opposing counsel has expressly or impliedly charged that the witness is lying or exaggerating because of some motive. The wife can be rehabilitated because her credibility was impeached by the questions concerning her marriage. Because the defense attorney implied that the wife's testimony was biased because she killed the husband, some prior consistent statements may possibly be used for rehabilitation. However, questions about the polygraph test may not be used for this purpose in light of Rule 403, as discussed above. (D) is incorrect because, while the defense attorney's questions opened the door to explanation of the wife's answers concerning her marriage, they do not justify testimony concerning the polygraph test. As discussed above, the defense attorney's questions impeaching the wife by probing into her marriage opened the door to her rehabilitation by the prosecutor. While she may be rehabilitated on redirect by explaining facts brought out on cross-examination, and may even testify as to prior consistent statements if charged with lying or exaggerating because of some motive, she may not be asked questions about the polygraph test. This is because, as discussed above, the slight probative value of the test is substantially outweighed by its tendency to confuse and mislead the jury.

Answer to Question 6

(C) The court should overrule the objection because the testimony is relevant to the issue of motive and is not precluded by any exclusionary rule. Evidence is relevant if it tends to make the existence of any fact that is of consequence to the action more probable than it would be without the evidence. Here, motive is an important fact of consequence to the action; thus, it is relevant. Since no exclusionary rules apply, the statement should come in. (A) is wrong because the operator's status as an eavesdropper has no effect on the admissibility of her testimony. Being an eavesdropper could have some effect if some sort of testimonial privilege (*e.g.*, attorney-client) were at issue, but nothing in the facts indicates such a relationship between the caller and the defendant. (B) is wrong because the statement is being offered for its effect on the hearer, not for the truth of the matter asserted. It does not matter whether the partner was really going to talk to the police. The statement is relevant on the issue of the defendant's motive regardless of whether the statement is true. Therefore, even though the statement would be inadmissible hearsay if offered to prove that the partner intended to talk to the police, it is admissible to show its effect on the defendant, the hearer. (D) is wrong because there is no evidence of a conspiracy, and the

caller's statement could not be construed as a statement made to a third party in furtherance of the conspiracy. The defendant is not a third party.

Answer to Question 7

(D) The effect of the judge's noticing that a car driven from Chicago to Detroit must cross state lines is that the judge will now instruct the jury that it may, but is not required to, accept that fact as conclusively proven. Under the Federal Rules, in a civil case, the court must instruct the jury to accept the judicially noticed fact as conclusive. [Fed. R. Evid. 201(g)] Because this question deals with a prosecution for criminal battery, the applicable rule is that the jury be instructed that the fact that has been judicially noticed may be accepted by it as conclusive, but that the jury is not required to do so. (A) would be correct if this were a civil case. In such an instance, the jury would be instructed to accept as conclusive the judicially noticed fact. This would have the effect of raising an irrebuttable presumption. (B) is incorrect because, in a criminal case, the prosecution has the burden of proving every element of the crime beyond a reasonable doubt. Only the jury can decide, after all of the evidence is in, whether the burden of persuasion is satisfied. (C) is incorrect because the burden of persuasion does not shift from party to party during the course of the trial. The burden of persuasion is never on a criminal defendant.

Answer to Question 8

(C) The prosecution must show that the Geiger counter was in good working condition at the time in question in order for evidence of its reaction to be admissible. Only relevant evidence is admissible. Relevant evidence is evidence having the tendency to make the existence of any fact that is of consequence to the determination of an action more probable than it would be without the evidence. [Fed. R. Evid. 401] Here, the passenger's testimony is being offered to prove that the Geiger counter reacted to the substances in the medical technician's suitcase. The issue of the Geiger counter's reaction to the suitcase is material because the government is claiming that the medical technician had radioactive isotopes in his suitcase, to which the Geiger counter would have reacted. The passenger's testimony of the reaction must be sufficiently probative of the proposition that the Geiger counter reacted to the isotopes in the suitcase. To be sufficiently probative, the evidence must show that the reaction of the Geiger counter was authentic. To authenticate such a reaction, all that is necessary under the Federal Rules is proof sufficient to support a jury finding of genuineness. To establish that the reaction of the Geiger counter was authentic, it would be essential to show that it was in sound operating condition at the time in question. As discussed below, this proof is sufficient to support a jury finding that the machine's reaction was genuine. (A) is incorrect because the passenger's testimony would be relevant without evidence that there was no other radioactive material in the area. To be relevant, evidence must have a tendency to prove or disprove a material issue. While the reaction of the Geiger counter must be shown to be genuine to be sufficiently probative, as discussed above, all that is necessary under the Federal Rules is proof sufficient to support a jury finding of genuineness. It is not required that the prosecution establish the genuineness of the reaction by a preponderance of the evidence as a condition to admissibility. Therefore, while the condition of the Geiger counter must be established, it is not necessary to establish that there was no other radioactive material in the area before the passenger's testimony can be admitted. (B) and (D) are incorrect because they address standards for admitting real evidence. Real evidence must be established as authentic, and is commonly authenticated by establishing a chain of custody. If the condition of the object is significant, it must be shown to be in substantially the same condition at the trial. Here, the Geiger counter itself is not being offered into evidence, but rather the passenger's testimony as to how the Geiger counter reacted at the time in question.

Answer to Question 9

(B) The court should admit the neighbor's testimony because it is relevant circumstantial evidence. The Federal Rules of Evidence define relevant evidence as evidence having any tendency to prove or disprove a fact that is of consequence to the action. [Fed. R. Evid. 401] Generally, all relevant evidence is admissible unless it is barred by a specific exclusionary rule or by the general balancing test of Rule 403, which permits exclusion of relevant evidence if its probative value is substantially outweighed by the danger of unfair prejudice, confusion of the issues, etc. The neighbor's testimony is relevant because the dog's behavior when the defendant came by tends to prove circumstantially (*i.e.*, indirectly) the prosecution's contention that the defendant beat the victim to death (in the dog's presence). The neighbor is competent to testify as to the dog's behavior toward the defendant both before and after the murder, and no other competency rule warrants excluding the testimony; hence, it should be admitted. (A) is incorrect because the availability of other evidence that might demonstrate the dog's reaction more clearly does not preclude the neighbor's testimony on that issue. As long as she is competent to testify regarding the dog's behavior, the dog's availability is irrelevant. (C) is incorrect because it is up to the trier of fact to evaluate the inference for which the circumstantial evidence is being offered. The defense may attack the neighbor's testimony on cross-examination by suggesting other reasons for the dog's reaction, but it cannot exclude the neighbor's testimony on this basis. (D) is incorrect because the balancing test of Rule 403 provides only that a court may exclude relevant evidence if its probative value is ***substantially*** outweighed by the danger of ***unfair*** prejudice. While all evidence is prejudicial to the opposing party, "unfair" prejudice refers to suggesting a decision on an emotional or otherwise improper basis. There is nothing in the neighbor's testimony to justify excluding it on unfair prejudice grounds.

Answer to Question 10

(C) The court should overrule the objection because the physician-patient privilege cannot be invoked for information dealing with a nonmedical matter. Under the physician-patient privilege, a physician is foreclosed from divulging in judicial proceedings information that he acquired while attending a patient in a professional capacity, which information was necessary to enable the physician to act in his professional capacity. Information given by a patient that deals with a nonmedical matter is not protected by the privilege. Hence, the defendant's admission that she was shot while running from a jewelry store that she robbed is not barred by the privilege. (A) is incorrect because, although it is true that the doctor acquired the information while attending the defendant in the course of treatment, the privilege is inapplicable because, as discussed above, the statement deals with a nonmedical matter. (B) is incorrect because a promise to comply with a request by the patient that information be kept confidential will not by itself render the information protectable under the physician-patient privilege. To qualify for such protection, the information must have been necessary for treatment, and there must be no applicable exceptions to the privilege. (D) is incorrect because this privilege belongs to the patient. Thus, the defendant is the one who is entitled to claim or waive the privilege, not the doctor.

Answer to Question 11

(D) It was not error to introduce either item of evidence, even though both contain hearsay. Hearsay is a statement, other than one made by the declarant while testifying at the trial or hearing, offered in evidence to prove the truth of the matter asserted. Here, both items of evidence are being offered to prove the truth of what they are asserting—the date of the plaintiff's birth. However, they both fall within exceptions to the general rule that hearsay is not admissible at

trial. Under Federal Rule 803(13), statements of fact concerning personal or family history contained in family Bibles, engravings on tombstones, etc., are admissible (regardless of whether the declarant is available). The plaintiff's Bible is therefore admissible, and (A) and (C) are incorrect. The certified copy of the birth certificate is also admissible hearsay under Federal Rule 803(9), which admits official records of births, deaths, and marriages. (B) is incorrect because official records are self-authenticating when they are certified [Fed. R. Evid. 902]; the custodian need not authenticate them in court.

Answer to Question 12

(C) The agent's testimony is inadmissible because it is not probative of any material issue in the case. Relevant evidence tends to make the existence of any fact that is of consequence to the determination of an action more probable than it would be without the evidence. [Fed. R. Evid. 401] While evidence tending to prove the businessman's charitable nature, which is a material issue in this case, would be relevant, the evidence here tends to prove only the businessman's honesty, which is not at issue here. Therefore, it is not relevant and should not be admitted. (A) is incorrect because even though the businessman's character has been called into question in this case, only evidence that is probative of the particular character trait in issue may be admitted. When a person's character itself is one of the issues in the case, evidence of specific facts may be used to prove character. [Fed. R. Evid. 405(b)] Because this is a defamation case, the businessman's character as to generosity is directly in issue, and specific acts may be used to prove his generosity. However, as discussed above, the agent's testimony is not probative of the businessman's generosity. (B) is similarly incorrect. The businessman has a right to prove his good character, but only with regard to the particular character trait that has been defamed. (D) is incorrect because specific acts may be used to prove character when character is directly in issue, as discussed above. The businessman's generosity is directly in issue in this case and specific acts of his may be used to prove his generosity. Therefore, the agent's testimony is not inadmissible on these grounds.

Answer to Question 13

(A) The chart is admissible because the original documents are in the corporation's files. The original document or best evidence rule generally requires the original writing to be produced when the terms of the writing are sought to be proved and are material to the case. [Fed. R. Evid. 1002] However, under Federal Rule 1006, the contents of voluminous writings that are otherwise admissible may be presented in the form of a chart as long as the original documents are available to the other party for examination and copying. Here, the underlying documents belonged to the adverse party, and thus the corporation had unlimited access to them. (B) is incorrect because the chart could be helpful to the trier of fact and still be inadmissible, such as if the underlying material were not available to the corporation or the chart were based on inadmissible hearsay. Furthermore, (B) is not as good a choice as (A) because (B) states a generality (it basically states the relevance requirement) whereas (A) applies the law to the specific facts of this case. (C) is incorrect because the chart is admissible provided the underlying documents are admissible. Even if the documents in this case would be hearsay, they would be admissible under the business records exception to the hearsay rule because they are records of events made in the regular course of business. [Fed. R. Evid. 803(6)] (D) is incorrect because Rule 1006 is an exception to the best evidence rule designed to avoid the introduction of voluminous writings into evidence; therefore, it does not require their introduction as a prerequisite to introduction of a chart.

Answer to Question 14

(A) The court should overrule the objection because the manager's statement is a vicarious admission of the department store. Under the Federal Rules, statements made by an agent concerning any matter within the scope of his agency, made during the existence of the employment relationship, are not hearsay and are admissible against the principal. Here, while the police report itself is admissible under the business records exception to the hearsay rule, the manager's statement within the report is not admissible under that exception because he was under no business duty to convey such information to the police officer. However, because he was the manager of the store at the time he made the statement, his statement is admissible against his principal, the department store, as a vicarious admission. Hence, the objection should be overruled. (B) is incorrect because admissions of a party are not receivable against his co-defendants merely because they happen to be joined as parties to the action. Here, the statement is admissible against the department store because of the principal-agent relationship. (C) is incorrect because the Federal Rules have broadened the scope of vicarious admissions by an agent. The statements need not be within the scope of his authority to speak as long as they concerned any matter within the scope of his agency, and the court most likely would find that the reasons for detention of a suspected shoplifter is a matter within the scope of employment of the manager of a department store. (D) is incorrect because the fact that an admission is predicated on hearsay rather than personal knowledge is not a ground for excluding it. Here, the manager was adopting the guard's statement as his own when he related it to the police officer as the justification for stopping the plaintiff; thus, it can be admitted against both him and his employer.

Answer to Question 15

(C) The witness's testimony is inadmissible. Under Federal Rule 804(b)(1), the testimony of a witness who is unavailable, given at another hearing, is admissible in a subsequent trial if there is sufficient similarity of parties and issues so that the opportunity to develop testimony or cross-examination at the prior hearing was meaningful. The former testimony is admissible upon any trial of the same subject matter. The party against whom the testimony is offered or, in civil cases, the party's predecessor in interest must have been a party in the former action. "Predecessor in interest" includes one in a privity relationship with the party, such as grantor-grantee, testator-executor, life tenant-remainderman, and joint tenants. These requirements are intended to ensure that the party against whom the testimony is offered (or a predecessor in interest in a civil case) had an adequate opportunity and motive to cross-examine the witness. In the civil suit here at issue, the survivors of the victim were not parties to the criminal case, nor were they in privity with any such party. (The parties to that case were the defendant and the government.) These survivors, who are the plaintiffs in the instant litigation, are the parties against whom the testimony of the witness is being offered. Because they were not parties to the action in which the witness testified, they had no opportunity to cross-examine him. Even if the government had a similar motive to cross-examine the witness as do the plaintiffs in the current action, that is not sufficient to make the government a predecessor in interest to the plaintiffs. Consequently, the testimony of the witness does not come within the former testimony exception to the hearsay rule, and the testimony is inadmissible hearsay. (A) and (B) incorrectly conclude that the testimony is admissible. Although it is true that the witness testified at an earlier hearing related to the same subject matter, and that the defendant is a party to both proceedings, what is missing is the requisite identity of parties against whom the testimony is being offered. (D) is incorrect because a witness incarcerated in another state is "unavailable" for purposes of civil proceedings. Under the Federal Rules, a witness is unavailable if he is absent from the hearing and the proponent of the statement is unable to procure the declarant's attendance by process or other reasonable

means. The Supreme Court has held that the Confrontation Clause requires a greater showing of "unavailability" in criminal cases than in civil cases. Because all states permit extradition of witnesses against the accused in criminal cases, a mere showing that a witness is incarcerated in a prison outside the state is insufficient to establish "unavailability." In contrast, the reach of process in civil cases is more limited and the Confrontation Clause does not apply. A mere showing that the witness is incarcerated in a prison out of state will suffice to show unavailability in a civil case.

Answer to Question 16

(A) The coach should be allowed to testify as to what the interviewee said because he observed the interviewee making the statements in the television broadcast. To be a competent witness, the witness must have personal knowledge of the matter and be willing and able to testify truthfully. The first requirement is satisfied if the witness observed the matter and has a present recollection of his observation. Thus, the coach would be a competent witness if he observed the publication of the defamation, which occurred through the television broadcast. Even though (B) is a true statement, (A) is a better answer because there are many instances where relevant evidence going to the ultimate issue is excluded (*e.g.*, hearsay). Furthermore, (A) is a better answer because the coach must have personal knowledge to testify, regardless of how relevant the subject matter of his testimony is to an ultimate issue in the case. (C) is incorrect because the availability of the videotape does not preclude independent oral testimony of the statements that the interviewee made. The best evidence rule does not apply here because the fact to be proved (the defamatory statement) exists independent of the recording and the coach's knowledge of the fact was not derived from the recording. (D) is incorrect because the allegedly defamatory statement is not hearsay. The interviewee's out-of-court statement is a verbal act or legally operative fact. It is not being offered to prove the truth of the matter asserted (that the coach condones steroid use by his players), but rather merely to show that the legally actionable statement was made.

Answer to Question 17

(C) The trustee does not have to answer the question unless she has waived the privilege against self-incrimination. A person may assert the privilege against self-incrimination in ***any*** proceeding, civil or criminal, in which testimony that could incriminate the person (*i.e.*, expose her to criminal liability) is sought. Thus, the trustee may raise the privilege unless she has waived it. (A) is incorrect because the privilege here cannot be waived merely by taking the stand. While a criminal defendant may refuse to take the witness stand at all, in a civil action, a witness is required to take the stand if called, but taking the stand is not a waiver of the privilege. The privilege must be raised as to each objectionable question asked and will be waived only if the witness discloses incriminating information. (B) is incorrect because the Fifth Amendment applies to all trials at which the witness's appearance and testimony are compelled. (D) is incorrect because it is too broad; if a witness waives the privilege by testifying as to the subject, and then attempts to raise the privilege later, it is too late. She can no longer assert the privilege.

Answer to Question 18

(A) The wife can be compelled to testify because her husband is dead and cannot invoke the privilege. There are two separate spousal privileges. There is ***spousal immunity***, under which: (i) a married person whose spouse is the defendant in a criminal case may not be called as a witness by the prosecution, and (ii) a married person may not be compelled to testify against her spouse in any criminal proceeding. In federal court, this privilege belongs to the witness-spouse so that she may not be compelled to testify, but neither may she be foreclosed from testifying. This privilege terminates upon divorce. There is also a privilege for ***confidential marital communications***, under which either spouse, whether or not a party, has a privilege to refuse to disclose, and to prevent another from disclosing, a confidential communication made between the spouses while they were husband and wife. Both spouses jointly hold this privilege. Divorce does not terminate this privilege retroactively. Since the communication must be made in reliance upon the intimacy of the marital relationship, if the communication is made in the known presence of a stranger, it is not privileged. Similarly, if one spouse voluntarily reveals the contents of the communication to a stranger, that spouse waives the protection of the privilege as to herself (*i.e.*, she cannot use the privilege to refuse to disclose, or to prevent another from disclosing, the communication), but the other spouse (*i.e.*, the one who did not reveal the communication) retains this privilege. Here, the spousal immunity between the husband and the wife terminated upon their divorce. Thus, the only consideration is the applicability of the privilege for confidential marital communications. The husband's statement to the wife came during their marriage and was made in reliance upon the intimacy of their relationship (marital communications are presumed to be confidential). Thus, the statement was covered by the privilege for confidential marital communications. Their subsequent divorce did not terminate this privilege. However, when the wife revealed to her friend what her husband had told her concerning the theft of the painting, the wife lost her privilege to refuse to disclose the matter. If the husband were alive, he would retain the privilege despite the wife's disclosure and could prevent her from testifying to his statement concerning the theft of the painting. Because the husband is dead, he cannot invoke his privilege. Since the wife has waived her privilege and the husband is unable to foreclose her testimony, she can be compelled to testify. (B) is incorrect because the privilege for confidential marital communications applies to the disclosure of matters communicated during and in reliance on the intimacy of the marital relationship regardless of whether one of the spouses is a defendant in a criminal case. Even spousal immunity is deemed to preclude the compelled testimony of one spouse against the other in any criminal proceeding, regardless of whether the other spouse is a defendant. The difference when a spouse is a criminal defendant is that the other spouse may not even be compelled to take the stand. (C) is incorrect because it does not take into account the fact that the wife waived her privilege when she communicated her husband's admission to her friend, as explained above. (D) incorrectly concludes that the wife cannot be compelled to testify. Due to her knowing and voluntary revelation of the husband's statement to her friend, the wife has waived her privilege and may be compelled to testify. Note that, if the privilege were still applicable (*i.e.*, if the wife had not waived it), she could not be compelled to testify as to the contents of the privileged communication simply on the ground that such testimony would be essential to prevent a fraud on the court.

Answer to Question 19

(D) The ground for the judge's decision is incorrect because the defendant is available to testify. The statement against interest exception to the hearsay rule requires that the declarant be unavailable as a witness. A declarant is unavailable if: (i) she is exempted from testifying on the ground of privilege, (ii) she refuses to testify concerning the statement, (iii) she testifies to lack of memory of the subject matter of the statement, (iv) she cannot testify because she has died or is ill, or (v) she is absent and the statement's proponent is unable to procure her attendance or testimony by process. [Fed. R. Evid. 804(a)(1) - (5)] None of the bases for a finding of unavailability is present here. The defendant, the declarant whose statement is at issue, is available as a witness; thus, the judge was incorrect in basing his decision on this exception. (A) is incorrect because the fact that the statement subjected the defendant to tort liability, and thus was against her interest, is not enough; she must also be unavailable. Also, this choice implies that this exception would be

available only if she were subjected to tort liability, not criminal liability. Although some courts so limit the exception, the Federal Rules include statements against penal interest within the parameters of the statement against interest. (B) is incorrect because the defendant need not be a party to the litigation for her statement to qualify as a statement against interest. Thus, her status as a party would not be a basis for deciding that the statement against interest exception applies here. Of course, this choice is also incorrect because her availability to testify precludes application of this exception. (C) is incorrect because the defendant's statement, which effectively acknowledges liability for the plaintiff's injury, is most certainly against an important pecuniary interest; *i.e.*, it subjects her to the possibility of being held financially liable for the plaintiff's damages. Note that the judge correctly overruled the objection by the defendant's attorney, but for the wrong reason. The defendant's statement constitutes an admission by a party-opponent, which is an act done or statement made that amounts to a prior acknowledgment by a party of one of the relevant facts. Such an admission is nonhearsay under the Federal Rules. [Fed. R. Evid. 801(d)(2)] The defendant is a party, and her statement is a prior acknowledgment of the highly relevant matter of fault. For an admission by a party-opponent, the declarant need not be unavailable. (Don't be confused by the fact that, although the judge was correct in allowing the testimony as to the defendant's statement, the call of the question pertains to the grounds for the ruling, which were incorrect.)

Answer to Question 20

(A) The plaintiff can testify as to the appearance of the model because he has personal knowledge of it. A witness must be competent to testify, which includes the requirement that he have personal knowledge of the matter he is to testify about. Here, the plaintiff has personal knowledge of the model, as he is the person that had submitted it to the studio. Thus, he is competent to testify as to the model's appearance. (B) is wrong because it states the foundation requirement for the admissibility of secondary evidence under the best evidence rule (also called the original document rule), which does not apply under these circumstances. The best evidence rule covers writings and recordings, which are defined as "letters, words, or numbers, or their equivalent, set down by handwriting, typewriting, printing, photostating, photographing, magnetic impulse, mechanical or electronic recording, or other form of data compilation." A clay model clearly does not fit within that definition. Similarly, (C) states an acceptable form of secondary evidence under the best evidence rule, which does not apply here. Note, however, that under the Federal Rules (unlike most states), there are no degrees of secondary evidence. Therefore, this choice would be wrong even if the best evidence rule were applicable, because the plaintiff would not be limited to photographic evidence. (D) is wrong because it incorrectly assumes that notice must be given. This type of notice is not a prerequisite for the plaintiff's testimony even had the best evidence rule been applicable.

Answer to Question 21

(A) The daughter's testimony is admissible as circumstantial evidence that her father was on the boat. The statement is hearsay, but is admissible under the state of mind exception to the hearsay rule. Hearsay is an out-of-court statement offered to prove the truth of the matter asserted. Upon objection, hearsay must be excluded unless it falls within an exception to the rule. Here, the father's out-of-court statement is being offered for its truth—*i.e.*, to prove that he planned to propose a television show starring himself as Madd Hatter. The statement is, therefore, hearsay. Declarations of a declarant's then-existing state of mind, however, are admissible if made under circumstances of apparent sincerity. This exception includes declarations of intent offered to show subsequent acts of the declarant. In this case, the father's statement to his daughter was made under circumstances of apparent sincerity and so may be admitted as circumstantial evidence that he used the name Madd Hatter and was aboard the boat that vanished. (B) is wrong because this evidence would not create a rebuttable presumption that the father was on the boat. A presumption is a rule (established by statute or case law) that requires that a particular inference be drawn from a particular set of facts. There is no indication in the facts, nor is it likely, that such a rule exists in this jurisdiction with respect to the subject matter of the daughter's testimony. Note that the daughter may be offering this testimony as part of her attempt to establish the rebuttable presumption that her father is dead because he has not been heard from in seven years. However, that presumption is distinct from a presumption regarding his presence on the boat. At best, the daughter's testimony allows the jury to find that the father was on the boat; it does not require them to do so. (C) is wrong. A conclusive presumption is a rule of substantive law rather than a true presumption because it cannot be rebutted. There is no conclusive presumption applicable here. (D) is wrong because, as discussed above, the testimony is admissible as circumstantial evidence that the father was on the boat.

Answer to Question 22

(A) The expert's testimony is admissible because other civil engineers ordinarily reasonably rely on structural engineers' reports in forming professional opinions. Expert testimony is admissible if the subject matter is one where scientific, technical, or other specialized knowledge would assist the jury in understanding the evidence or determining a fact in issue. [Fed. R. Evid. 702] The proper design of a spiral staircase would not be a matter of common knowledge, and the testimony of an expert would be of assistance in determining whether the design was faulty. The expert's opinion may be based on facts not in evidence that were supplied to the expert out of court, and which facts are of a type reasonably relied upon by experts in the particular field in forming opinions on the subject. [Fed. R. Evid. 703] The expert may therefore give an opinion based on the photographs and the structural engineer's report if such photographs and reports are of a type reasonably relied upon by civil engineers in forming opinions on structural design. Federal Rule 703 allows the expert's testimony even though the photographs and report are not in evidence. (B) is incorrect because Federal Rule 703 does not require an expert to disclose the facts on which he relied in forming his opinion. In fact, the proponent of the expert opinion must not disclose those facts to the jury (since they may be of a type not admissible in evidence) unless the court determines that their probative value in assisting the jury to evaluate the expert's opinion substantially outweighs their prejudicial effect. (C) is incorrect because the Federal Rules allow the expert to base his opinion on opinions in the structural engineer's report as long as such opinions in reports would be reasonably relied upon by civil engineers in forming opinions. An expert traditionally is not permitted to rely on the opinions of others as a predicate for his own opinion. However, Federal Rule 703 significantly expands the traditional rule and permits an expert to base his opinion on the opinion of others if they are of the type reasonably relied upon by experts in the field, as discussed above. Therefore, if civil engineers ordinarily reasonably rely on such opinions in reports from structural engineers, the Federal Rules allow the expert to base his opinion on opinions in the report. (D) is incorrect because the fact that the report and photographs were commissioned solely for the purpose of litigation and were not admitted into evidence is irrelevant when an expert is basing an opinion on facts reasonably relied upon by experts in that field. When determining whether a report comes under the business records exception to the hearsay rule, the courts sometimes look at whether the report was prepared for litigation in determining if it was a record maintained in conjunction with a business activity. [Palmer v. Hoffman (1943)] Here, whether the report is hearsay is not at issue because an expert may base his opinion on facts reasonably relied upon by experts in that particular field even if those facts are inadmissible hearsay.

Answer to Question 23

(A) Testimony as to the statement made by the victim is inadmissible as a statement under belief of impending death, because the victim did not actually have firsthand knowledge that the defendant was responsible for the collision. The statement is hearsay because it is a statement made by the declarant (the victim), other than while testifying, offered to prove the truth of the matter asserted therein. Here, the plaintiff wants to present this testimony to prove the truth of the statement that the defendant was responsible for the brake failure, and will argue that the statement falls under the hearsay exception for dying declarations. In a civil case or a homicide prosecution, a statement made by a now unavailable declarant while believing his death to be imminent, that concerns the cause or circumstances of what he believed to be his impending death, is admissible. [Fed. R. Evid. 804(b)(2)] For this exception to apply, the declarant need not actually die. Rather, the declarant must be "unavailable" when the statement is offered. A declarant is unavailable if he: (i) is exempted from testifying on the ground of privilege, (ii) refuses to testify despite a court order, (iii) testifies to lack of memory of the subject matter of the statement, (iv) cannot be present or testify because of death or physical or mental illness, or (v) is beyond the reach of the court's subpoena and the statement's proponent has been unable to procure his attendance or testimony by process or other reasonable means. Regarding the statement at issue here, the victim certainly thought he was about to die from his injuries. In addition, he is unavailable, as his physical condition prevents him from testifying. However, the victim's statement represents a mere suspicion that the defendant tampered with the brakes. As well-founded as such a suspicion may be (given the history between the victim and the defendant), a statement based on mere suspicion rather than actual knowledge does not constitute a statement concerning the cause or circumstances of an "impending death" for purposes of the dying declarations exception. Thus, (A) is the correct answer and (C) is incorrect. (B) is incorrect because the declarant's death is no longer required; unavailability is sufficient. Thus, if the victim's statement otherwise qualified under the dying declarations exception, the fact that he is not dead would not render the motorist's testimony inadmissible. (D) is incorrect for the reasons stated above and also because it incorrectly implies that the dying declarations hearsay exception applies only in civil cases. As noted above, the exception also applies to homicide cases. (Note that the traditional view, still followed by some states, would only allow the declaration in a homicide prosecution.)

Answer to Question 24

(C) The mother's statement is admissible as a legally operative fact. Hearsay is a statement, other than one made by the declarant while testifying at trial or a hearing, offered in evidence to prove the truth of the matter asserted therein. Where an out-of-court statement is introduced for any purpose other than to prove the truth of the matter asserted, the statement is not hearsay. One type of out-of-court statement that is not hearsay is evidence of legally operative facts. These are utterances to which legal significance is attached, such as words of contract, bribery, or cancellation. Evidence of such statements is not hearsay because the issue is only whether the statement was made. The defendant is defending the lawsuit on the basis that she received the necklace as a gift, and the statement by the mother contains words that constitute an expression of donative intent, which is essential to a finding of a gift having been made. Thus, (C) is correct and (A) is incorrect. (B) is incorrect because, assuming a Dead Man Act is applicable, its protection has been waived. Dead Man Acts provide that a person interested in an event is incompetent to testify to a personal transaction or communication with a deceased, when such testimony is offered against the representative or successors in interest of the decedent. One who claims under a decedent may waive the protection of the statute by cross-examining the interested person about the transaction. In such a case, the interested person may explain all matters about which she is examined. Here, because the plaintiff's attorney is questioning the defendant about her dealings with the mother, the statute's protection has been waived. (D) is incorrect because unavailability of a declarant controls whether certain kinds of hearsay are admissible as exceptions to the hearsay rule. Because the statement here at issue is not hearsay, the declarant's unavailability is irrelevant.

Answer to Question 25

(A) The defendant's armed robbery conviction is least likely to be admitted. In a criminal case, evidence of the defendant's other crimes or misconduct is inadmissible if offered solely to establish criminal disposition. A broad exception to the general rule permits evidence of other crimes or misconduct to be admitted if such acts are relevant to some issue other than the character of the defendant to commit the crime charged. Such evidence may be used to show motive, opportunity, intent, preparation, plan, knowledge, identity, or absence of mistake. Here, (A) is least likely to be admitted because evidence of the defendant's previous conviction for armed robbery does not come within any permissible use of evidence of other crimes or bad acts. Since the defendant apparently is not contesting the issue of whether he possessed the semi-automatic weapon, it is irrelevant that the robbery conviction shows possession of such a weapon at some earlier time. The only use to which evidence of this conviction can be put is to show the defendant's bad character and disposition to commit the crimes with which he is presently charged. (B) is likely to be admitted because testimony that the defendant apparently tried to interest the witness in buying a semi-automatic weapon tends to show that the defendant had the intent to engage in selling the weapon. For the same reason, (C) is also likely to be admitted. Supplying guns to a paramilitary group is certainly evidence of involvement in a plan of firearms trafficking. (D) is likely to be admitted as evidence of intent or knowledge. Because the defendant has denied knowing that the weapon was stolen, evidence of his prior convictions for receipt of stolen weapons can be introduced to show the likelihood that he knew the weapon was stolen in the present case, negating his claim of good faith.

Answer to Question 26

(D) Since the principal had firsthand knowledge that the statement was made, his testimony will be admissible unless there is a specific rule excluding the evidence. Witnesses are generally presumed competent to testify until the contrary is demonstrated. While a witness may not testify to a matter unless evidence is introduced to support a finding that the witness has personal knowledge of the matter, this evidence may consist of the witness's own testimony. (A) is incorrect. Hearsay is a statement, other than one made by the declarant while testifying at the trial or hearing, offered in evidence to prove the truth of the matter asserted. In a defamation action, evidence of the statement alleged to be defamatory is not hearsay because the evidence is by definition not offered to prove the truth of the matter asserted. It is offered only to show that the actionable statement was made. (B) is incorrect. Since the principal had firsthand knowledge of the event he can testify about the event, even though there might exist a recording that would be better proof of the event. The "best evidence rule" does not apply when the witness is testifying on the basis of firsthand knowledge. (C) is incorrect. Although the statement is not hearsay, it is not being offered to show its effect on the hearer (*e.g.*, knowledge, motive), but rather to show that the statement was made, as explained above.

Answer to Question 27

(D) The judge should allow the bystander to remain silent if there is some reasonable possibility of self-incrimination. Preliminary facts to establish the existence of a privilege must be determined

by the court outside of the presence of the jury. Under the Fifth Amendment, a witness cannot be compelled to testify against herself. The privilege against self-incrimination can be raised by a witness to refuse to answer a question whose answer might incriminate her. Thus, there needs to be only some ***reasonable possibility*** of self-incrimination. (A) is wrong because the judge does not have to be certain that the witness will incriminate herself before granting the privilege. (B) is wrong because it states the standard for the burden of proof (*i.e.*, burden of persuasion) for certain disputed issues in civil cases, such as whether scienter existed in fraud cases or actual malice existed in defamation cases. (C) is wrong because it states the general measure of proof in civil cases, and is defined as requiring the fact finder to be persuaded by the proponent that the fact is more probably true than not true. The standard for determining the application of the privilege against self-incrimination is a lesser standard.

Answer to Question 28

(C) The judge should not require that the witness answer the question because evidence of the religious beliefs of a witness is not admissible to challenge credibility. Lack of religious belief is no longer a basis for excluding a witness. Not only are a person's religious convictions irrelevant in determining the competence of a witness, Federal Rule 610 provides that a witness's religious beliefs or opinions are not admissible to show that the witness's credibility is thereby impaired or enhanced. Thus, (C) is correct and (A) is incorrect. (B) is incorrect. While it is true that the witness could have requested a different type of oath, Rule 610 prohibits this type of question because it would have shown his lack of religious beliefs. (D) is incorrect because, as discussed above, lack of religious belief is no longer a basis for disqualification; thus, this would not constitute an attack on the witness's competency.

Answer to Question 29

(B) The testimony is inadmissible because it is not a permitted way to impeach a witness. A witness may be impeached by ***cross-examining*** her about specific criminal or immoral acts, but extrinsic evidence is not permitted. A specific act of misconduct offered to attack the witness's character for truthfulness can be elicited only on cross-examination of the witness. If the witness denies it, the cross-examiner cannot refute the answer by calling other witnesses or producing other evidence. Thus, the witness could be asked on cross-examination about the hoax, but her employee cannot properly be called to testify about it. (A) is incorrect because there is no specific rule limiting cumulative impeachment. (C) is incorrect. A witness may also be impeached by introducing evidence that the witness was convicted of a crime if the conviction required proof or admission of an act of dishonesty or false statements. However, the prior conviction must be shown by cross-examination of the witness or by introducing the record of the judgment. It is not proper to bring in another witness to testify about the conviction. (D) is incorrect because even though a hoax would impair a witness's credibility, it cannot be shown through testimony of specific acts, as discussed above.

Answer to Question 30

(A) The witness's testimony is admissible for purposes of impeachment only. There are many occasions in which out-of-court statements are admitted into evidence by means of hearsay exceptions. These statements are frequently admitted into evidence even though the person who made the statement does not testify at trial. The party against whom the statement has been admitted may wish to impeach the credibility of the declarant so that the jury will discount the statement.

Under Federal Rule 806, if hearsay statements are admitted, the person who made the out-of-court statements can be impeached the same way any in-court witness could be impeached. (B) is incorrect. Prior inconsistent statements are admissible for impeachment only, unless they were given under oath at a trial or other proceeding. If they were given under oath at a trial or other proceeding, they can be used both to impeach and as evidence to prove the facts contained in the statement. (C) is incorrect. Prior inconsistent statements offered to impeach are not hearsay because they are not being offered for the truth of the matter asserted, only that the declarant made inconsistent statements about the matter. (D) is incorrect. Since the bystander is a hearsay declarant, the statement is admissible to impeach even if he does not have an opportunity to comment on the statement. Even if the bystander were a live witness, the Federal Rules do not always require that he be given an opportunity to comment.

Answer to Question 31

(C) The least likely circumstance for admitting the tape recording into evidence is when the authentication was based in part on hearsay. Before secondary evidence of statements may be received into evidence, it must be authenticated by some evidence showing that it is what its proponent claims it to be. A voice, whether heard first-hand or through a device (such as a tape recording), may be identified by the opinion of anyone who has heard the voice at any time. However, the identification must be based on the first-hand knowledge of the listener. In (C), the father's statement to the witness that the person who was on the telephone was his daughter is hearsay, because it is being offered to prove its truth. Thus, the witness's knowledge of the victim's voice is based on hearsay and not personal experience, and this would not be sufficient to authenticate the tape recording. (A) and (B) are wrong because whether the witness had heard the victim in person or over the phone goes to the weight rather than the admissibility of the evidence. She can still authenticate that the recording contains the voice of the victim. (D) is wrong because if the witness had heard the conversation recorded, even if only the victim's half, she could obviously authenticate it.

Answer to Question 32

(A) The court should sustain the objection because the records are evidence of specific bad acts. The Federal Rules permit a defendant to introduce evidence of a bad character trait of the alleged victim if it is relevant to the charge or the defense, but limit it to reputation and opinion evidence. Evidence of specific acts of the person in question as demonstrating that person's character is permitted only in a few instances, such as when character itself is one of the ultimate issues in the case. Here, such evidence would not be admitted. (A) is therefore correct and (D) is wrong. (B) is wrong because the facts do not have to be identical. If evidence of bad acts were admissible, the conduct would be relevant as long as it involved the same bad character trait as the one at issue. (C) is wrong; documentary evidence, even if fully authenticated and relevant, may be excluded if it violates a rule of competency, such as the rule for character evidence. Here, the objection should be sustained because the document is improper evidence of a specific bad act.

Answer to Question 33

(A) The court should sustain the objection because the records are hearsay not within any recognized exception. Hearsay is a statement, other than one made by the declarant while testifying, offered into evidence to prove the truth of the matter asserted. Here, the records are being offered to prove that the employer sexually harassed other employees, to support the plaintiff's contention that the employer sexually harassed her. Since the statements are offered to prove the truth of the

matter asserted, they are hearsay, and since there is no recognized exception that would allow the records to be admitted, they must be excluded. Therefore, (D) is incorrect. (B) is incorrect. The business records exception applies to records or writings made in the course of a regularly conducted business activity by one who was under a duty to do so. Here, because the employees were not under a business duty to file their claims, the business records exception does not apply to their statements. (C) does not agree with the facts. A statement against interest is a hearsay exception allowed when a declarant is unavailable. Here, there is no showing of unavailability, and also the employees said nothing against their interests.

Answer to Question 34

(C) Evidence of the judgment would be inadmissible hearsay. Hearsay is a statement, other than one made by the declarant while testifying, offered into evidence to prove the truth of the matter asserted. While the Federal Rules create an exception to the hearsay rule for judgments of felony convictions used in any subsequent criminal or civil actions, it is not applicable for judgments in civil actions. The general rule is that a civil judgment is inadmissible in a subsequent criminal trial due to the differing standards of proof. Since the prior judgment in the civil case would be offered to prove the truth of the matters determined in the judgment (that the victim had previously committed battery), it would be inadmissible hearsay. (A) is wrong because, even in a subsequent civil trial, the evidence would still be hearsay that is not within the exceptions of Federal Rule 803(23). The narrow statutory exceptions to the rule of inadmissibility do not apply to these facts. (B) is wrong. Evidence of the victim's dangerous propensities would be inadmissible character evidence. (D) is wrong; the evidence is relevant but it would be inadmissible as hearsay.

Answer to Question 35

(A) The affidavit constitutes hearsay. Hearsay is a statement, other than one made by the declarant while testifying, offered into evidence to prove the truth of the matter asserted. Here, the affidavit is an out-of-court declaration offered to prove the truth of the assertion that the plaintiff suffered a back injury. Because none of the listed exceptions is applicable, the affidavit should be excluded. (B) is incorrect because stating a conclusion as to causation is not a prerequisite for admissibility. If the affidavit were otherwise admissible, the fact that it did not address the cause of the back injury would only go to the weight of the evidence, not its admissibility. (C) is incorrect because an affidavit does not constitute former testimony; the party against whom it is offered did not have an opportunity to develop the testimony by direct or cross-examination. (D) is incorrect because the exception to the hearsay rule for declarations of physical condition applies to the ***declarant's*** own bodily condition. The physician's declaration of someone else's bodily condition does not fall under this exception.

Answer to Question 36

(B) The court should rule that the physician's testimony is admissible because the physician-patient privilege does not apply. Generally, the physician-patient privilege provides that a physician cannot be compelled to disclose information obtained from a patient while treating the patient in a professional capacity if that information is related to the treatment. The privilege does not, however, apply in federal cases where state law does not supply the rule of privilege (*i.e.*, federal question cases). Here, the defendant is before the federal court on charges arising under a federal statute. Thus, the physician-patient privilege does not apply and the physician's testimony is admissible. (A) is incorrect because it implies that the testimony of an expert witness supersedes

the physician-patient privilege. The privilege applies regardless of whether the physician is testifying as an expert witness. (C) is incorrect because, although the jurisdiction applies the physician-patient privilege to criminal cases, state privilege law does not apply in this case as explained above. (D) is incorrect because the best evidence rule does not apply in this situation. The best evidence rule applies when a party is seeking to prove the terms of a writing. In this case, the prosecution is not seeking to prove the terms of any writing (*e.g.*, the medical records), but is rather offering the oral testimony of the physician to establish that the defendant did in fact have a medical history that he fraudulently concealed in his application and claim form.

Real Property

Question Sets and Analytical Answers

Set 1 Answer Sheet

1. Ⓐ Ⓑ Ⓒ Ⓓ
2. Ⓐ Ⓑ Ⓒ Ⓓ
3. Ⓐ Ⓑ Ⓒ Ⓓ
4. Ⓐ Ⓑ Ⓒ Ⓓ
5. Ⓐ Ⓑ Ⓒ Ⓓ
6. Ⓐ Ⓑ Ⓒ Ⓓ
7. Ⓐ Ⓑ Ⓒ Ⓓ
8. Ⓐ Ⓑ Ⓒ Ⓓ
9. Ⓐ Ⓑ Ⓒ Ⓓ
10. Ⓐ Ⓑ Ⓒ Ⓓ
11. Ⓐ Ⓑ Ⓒ Ⓓ
12. Ⓐ Ⓑ Ⓒ Ⓓ
13. Ⓐ Ⓑ Ⓒ Ⓓ
14. Ⓐ Ⓑ Ⓒ Ⓓ
15. Ⓐ Ⓑ Ⓒ Ⓓ
16. Ⓐ Ⓑ Ⓒ Ⓓ
17. Ⓐ Ⓑ Ⓒ Ⓓ
18. Ⓐ Ⓑ Ⓒ Ⓓ

REAL PROPERTY QUESTIONS - SET 1

Question 1

A landowner and her neighbor owned large adjoining properties. The boundary line between the properties was never clearly marked. Twenty-five years ago, the landowner dug a water well on a section of the property that she thought was hers, but in fact was the neighbor's. The landowner has continued to use the water and to maintain the well on a regular basis ever since.

The neighbor was adjudicated mentally incompetent 15 years ago. He died recently, and his executor has filed suit to eject the landowner and quiet title. The jurisdiction's statute of limitations for adverse possession is 20 years.

With respect to the land on which the water well was dug:

(A) The landowner has acquired title by adverse possession.

(B) The landowner cannot claim title as an adverse possessor because she did not enter with hostile intent.

(C) The landowner has not acquired title because the statute of limitations was tolled by the neighbor's incompetency.

(D) The landowner has an implied easement in the land.

Question 2

A farmer owned a large tract of land. She divided the tract into two parcels: Parcel 1 comprised the northern half on which the farmer built her home, and Parcel 2 comprised the southern portion containing a large orchard of fruit trees. First, the farmer conveyed Parcel 1 by grant deed to her friend "for life, and then to his widow for her life, remainder to his children then alive." Later, the farmer conveyed Parcel 2 to the orchard manager. Subsequently, the farmer died intestate, leaving her sister as her sole heir at law.

The house on Parcel 1 is old and in need of repair. The friend proposes to tear down the house and plant fruit trees. The property would be worth substantially more as a fruit orchard than in its present condition. However, the sister feels that the farmer's old house has sentimental value and wants the friend to leave the land as it is. At the time of the deed and at present, the friend is married and has two children. The common law Rule Against Perpetuities is unmodified by statute in the jurisdiction.

Does the sister have standing to sue to enjoin the friend from tearing down the house?

(A) Yes, because she holds a reversion by operation of law that will take effect on the death of the friend's widow.

(B) Yes, because she holds an executory interest that will become possessory if the friend dies without surviving children.

(C) No, because the sister has no interest in Parcel 1.

(D) No, because the friend was married at the time of the farmer's conveyance and had children.

Question 3

A man and a woman purchased a parcel of land, taking title as joint tenants. Two years later, the woman became pregnant. The man and the woman married, and soon after the wedding a son was born. The man and the woman had strong disagreements as to how their son should be raised. These disagreements led to heated arguments, which led to a divorce. After the divorce, the woman and her son continued to occupy the land, although title remained in the names of both the man and the woman. The man moved out of the state and conveyed all of his title and interest in the land by deed to the son. Shortly thereafter, the man was killed in an automobile collision. The man died intestate.

Who has title to the land?

(A) The woman.

(B) The woman owns one-half and the man's heirs own one-half.

(C) The woman and her son as joint tenants.

(D) The woman and her son as tenants in common.

Question 4

A seller entered into a written contract to sell his factory to a manufacturer. Before the closing date, the manufacturer found an alternate site that was better suited to her business. The manufacturer notified the seller that she would not be going through with the closing. The seller sued the manufacturer for specific performance.

If the court rules in favor of the manufacturer, it will be because:

(A) The factory does not comply with the city building code.

(B) The factory violates the setback requirement of the zoning ordinance by one foot.

(C) The zoning ordinance forbids the use of the type of truck that the manufacturer uses in shipping her goods.

(D) Access to the factory is by way of an easement over adjoining property.

Question 5

A buyer entered into a written contract to purchase a seller's house for $250,000. The contract called for the seller to deposit a deed in escrow forthwith, and for payment of the purchase price and delivery of the deed through escrow within 30 days thereafter. The seller immediately deposited the deed with the escrow holder. On the 29th day, the seller was injured in a snowmobile accident and rendered comatose; he remains in this state to date. On the 30th day, the sale closed pursuant to the contract; the seller's deed was delivered to the buyer, and the $250,000 was paid over to the seller's account.

The seller's incapacity:

(A) Has no effect on the buyer's title.

(B) Constitutes a lien on the buyer's title.

(C) Allows his court-appointed guardian to set aside the buyer's deed.

(D) Prevented passage of title to the buyer.

Question 6

A retiree purchased a rustic cabin on a small plot of land near the center of a landowner's large parcel of land. The deed to the land, which the landowner delivered to the retiree for fair consideration, did not specifically grant an easement over the landowner's property to reach the public highway bordering her land. There were two means of access to the cabin from the public roads: a driveway from the county road on the south, and a private road from the highway on the east. The landowner told the retiree that he could use the private road from the highway. Twice during his first two years at the cabin, the retiree took the driveway from the county road instead; all other times he used the private road.

At the end of his second year at the cabin, the retiree began reading tarot cards to supplement his retirement income. He had a steady stream of clients coming to his home at all hours of the day and night. Most of the clients came in on the driveway from the county road, which ran close to the landowner's home. The landowner objected, and told the retiree that neither he nor his clients had any right to use that driveway. She instructed him to advise his clients that they must use the private road from the highway. The retiree refused, and he and his clients continued to use the driveway from the county road for three years. Finally, the landowner began blocking off the driveway from the county road. The retiree brought suit to enjoin this practice. The prescriptive period in this jurisdiction is five years.

Who will most likely prevail?

(A) The landowner, because the tarot business has changed the nature of the use of the easement by necessity.

(B) The landowner, because she may select the location of the easement.

(C) The retiree, because he has a valid easement by necessity in the driveway from the county road.

(D) The retiree, because he has acquired an easement by prescription in the driveway from the county road.

Question 7

An elderly aunt executed a deed to her farm "to my nephew for his life, and on my nephew's death to his children, except that if my nephew becomes bankrupt, to my niece." The nephew is alive and well and not bankrupt.

At the time of the grant, the nephew's interest is best described as:

(A) An estate for indefinite period.

(B) A life estate.

(C) A life estate subject to an executory interest.

(D) A defeasible nonfreehold estate.

Question 8

A father executed a deed to his art gallery "to my daughter for her life, and on my daughter's death to her children; provided, however, that if my daughter stops painting, to my brother." The daughter has two children and is still painting.

At the time of the grant, the interest of the daughter's two children is best described as:

(A) A contingent remainder.

(B) A vested remainder subject to open and to total divestment.

(C) A vested remainder subject to open.

(D) An executory interest.

Question 9

A landlord owned an apartment building. Needing money to make some repairs and improvements, he went to a bank and applied for a loan. The bank loaned the landlord $100,000, secured by a mortgage on the apartment building. Last month, the landlord defaulted on his mortgage payments. The bank instituted foreclosure proceedings and wishes to take possession of the apartment building in order to collect the rents from the property.

Does the bank have the right to take possession of the apartment building before foreclosure?

(A) Yes, if the jurisdiction follows the lien theory.

(B) Yes, if the jurisdiction follows the title theory.

(C) No, because the landlord has a right to redeem the property before foreclosure.

(D) No, unless the landlord consents to the possession.

Question 10

A bank sold one of its mortgages and the accompanying note to a finance company. Shortly thereafter, the finance company sold both the mortgage and the note to a brokerage firm. The brokerage firm duly recorded the assignment in the offices of the county recorder of deeds, as prescribed by state statute. However, the brokerage firm decided to use the finance company as its collection agent for the payments as they came due. Therefore, the brokerage firm left the mortgage and note documents in the hands of the finance company.

The finance company developed cash-flow and liquidity problems. To try to save the finance company from bankruptcy, its president

sold the mortgage and accompanying note to an investor. This transaction was not enough to save the finance company from insolvency. During the winding up of the finance company's affairs, the brokerage firm discovered the finance company's sale of the mortgage and note to the investor. The brokerage firm also learned that the finance company never told the investor about the brokerage firm's interests in the mortgage and note. The brokerage firm files suit against the investor for the return of the mortgage and note.

The court will decide that:

(A) The brokerage firm owns both the mortgage and the note.

(B) The investor owns both the mortgage and the note.

(C) The brokerage firm owns the mortgage, but the investor owns the note.

(D) The investor owns the mortgage, but the brokerage firm owns the note.

Question 11

A developer owned 100 acres of land that he developed into a residential subdivision. Seventy-five acres were divided into one-acre lots on which single-family homes were built, and the remaining 25 acres were left undeveloped as a "recreational area." In the deeds to each of the one-acre lots, the developer granted the homeowners a 10-year easement to use the recreational area. Ten years later, the developer sold the 25-acre tract to a waste disposal company, which plans to use the tract to dispose of low-level radioactive waste. The statute of limitations for adverse possession and prescriptive rights is 10 years.

If the subdivision homeowners seek to enjoin this use, they will:

(A) Prevail, because they have acquired an easement by prescription for recreational use.

(B) Prevail, because they have acquired the tract by adverse possession.

(C) Not prevail, because they have no interest in the property.

(D) Not prevail, because damages, not an injunction, is the appropriate remedy.

Question 12

A businesswoman owned an office building. She sold the building to an investor, who paid her a fair price for the property. The investor failed to record the deed and left for an extended trip. Two days after he departed, the businesswoman died suddenly. Her will devised the office building to her daughter. The daughter knew nothing about the sale of the building to the investor, and she properly recorded her title to the building in the county recorder of deeds office. The daughter, who had no prior experience in business, applied to a lender for a $50,000 loan to start up her own business, offering a mortgage on the office building as collateral. The lender checked the recorder's records showing the daughter to have sole title to the building, and the loan and mortgage were executed.

Unfortunately, the daughter's business failed and she was unable to repay her loan to the lender. The lender instituted foreclosure proceedings. Just as the building was about to be sold, the investor returned from his trip, deed in hand. The state in which the building is located has the following statute: "No conveyance or mortgage of an interest in land is valid against any subsequent purchaser for value without notice thereof, unless it is recorded."

May the lender successfully take the office building?

(A) Yes, because the lender succeeds to the daughter's rights in the building.

(B) Yes, because the lender is a mortgagee for value.

(C) No, because the daughter never owned the building.

(D) No, because the lender was imprudent in lending the money in the first place.

Question 13

A landowner and his neighbor own adjoining properties. The landowner decided to build an addition on his home. Prior to construction of the addition, surface waters flowed across the neighbor's property to the landowner's property and then to a drainage ditch. After the addition was completed, surface waters no longer flowed to the ditch but accumulated on the neighbor's property. The standing water attracted so many mosquitoes that the neighbor was unable to enjoy her backyard.

If the neighbor prevails in a lawsuit against the landowner, it will most likely be because the jurisdiction follows the:

(A) Riparian doctrine.

(B) Prior appropriation doctrine.

(C) Common enemy theory.

(D) Natural flow theory.

Question 14

A husband and wife own a vineyard as tenants by the entirety. Without consulting each other, the husband transfers his interest in the vineyard to his brother by quitclaim deed, and the wife mortgages her interest to her sister in exchange for a loan.

What interest, if any, does the sister have?

(A) A secured interest against the wife's one-half interest as a tenant by the entirety with the brother.

(B) A secured interest against the wife's one-half interest as a tenant in common with the brother.

(C) A secured interest against the wife's one-half interest as a tenant in common with the husband.

(D) No interest.

Question 15

Thirty years ago, a power company constructed a power dam on a river. At the time the dam was constructed, the power company solicited easements from all of the landowners in the river valley, including a farmer. The power company paid fair value for the easements, which would allow the company to release water from the dam at certain times of the year, resulting in flooding of the land in the river valley.

In the 30 years since the dam was constructed, the farmer's property has never been flooded, and the farmer has been using his land in the same way as he did 30 years ago. Now, however, the power company wants to substantially increase power production from the dam. All landowners in the valley were notified by the company that henceforth all 200,000 acres (including the farmer's 200 acres) would be flooded in accordance with the company's rights under the easement. The farmer reviewed the easement for his property and discovered that it lacked the requisite grantor's acknowledgment and thus was improperly recorded. The state's adverse possession statute requires hostile occupation for a period of 20 years.

May the power company properly flood the farmer's land under the terms of the easement?

(A) Yes, because the company has a valid easement, and such flooding is within the terms of the easement.

(B) Yes, because the state's adverse possession statute requires hostile occupation for a period of only 20 years.

(C) No, because the company has failed to exercise its rights under the easement for 30 years, and the easement has lapsed.

(D) No, because the easement was not properly acknowledged and recorded.

Question 16

For many years, a landowner owned a parcel of land bordered on the west by a public road, and his neighbor owned a parcel of land located immediately to the east of that parcel. The neighbor had an easement to cross the west parcel to enter the public road bordering it. Because the neighbor's east parcel is surrounded by swampland on the north, south, and east, the only route of ingress to and egress from that parcel over dry land passed through the west parcel. Subsequently, the neighbor sold the east parcel to the landowner, who proceeded to use both lots as a common tract. Last year, the landowner sold the east parcel to his friend.

Does the friend have an easement over the landowner's west parcel?

(A) Yes, she has an easement in gross.

(B) Yes, because her only access to her parcel from the public road is across the west parcel.

(C) No, because the easement was extinguished when the landowner purchased the east parcel.

(D) No, because she has not used the property long enough to gain an easement by prescription.

Question 17

A driller owned a large tract of land on which she began to drill for oil, but all of her exploratory wells were nonproductive "dry holes." The driller was certain that there was oil in the area, and she asked the neighboring landowner to grant her a lease to drill on his land. The landowner turned down the driller's offer. After the landowner's refusal, the driller drilled an exploratory well on her property. However, the driller drilled the well on a slanted angle, so that she was actually drilling under the landowner's land, even though her rig was located on her property. The driller struck oil, but shortly thereafter the landowner discovered that the oil was coming from underneath his land.

Does the landowner have an action for damages against the driller?

(A) Yes, because the driller has invaded the landowner's subterranean rights.

(B) Yes, but only if the driller's drilling interferes with the landowner's use and enjoyment of his land.

(C) No, because oil is a free-flowing liquid and may be captured wherever it flows.

(D) No, because the driller's action does not interfere with the landowner's right to drill for oil on his land.

Question 18

A buyer purchased a house from a seller. It turned out that the concrete used to pour the foundation had been improperly mixed and the foundation was crumbling. The buyer discovered that the cost of repairing the defective foundation would be over $10,000. She filed suit against the seller for the cost of repairs.

If the court rules in the buyer's favor it will be because:

(A) The crumbling foundation makes the house unsafe or uninhabitable.

(B) The seller was the builder of the house.

(C) The buyer took title to the house by warranty deed.

(D) The buyer had no knowledge of the defect when she purchased the house, and the defect was not reasonably apparent.

REAL PROPERTY ANSWERS - SET 1

Answer to Question 1

(A) The landowner has acquired title to the land by adverse possession. She has been in possession of the land on which the well was dug exclusively, openly, hostilely, and continuously for a period in excess of the statutory limitations period for adverse possession. Such title results from the running of the statute of limitations for trespass to real property. If an owner of real property fails to take legal action within the statutory period to eject a possessor who claims adversely to the owner, title to the property vests in the possessor, and the owner is barred from suing for ejectment. Adverse possession must be actual and exclusive (*i.e.*, the possessor is not sharing with the true owner or the public at large). Also, the possession must be open and notorious (*i.e.*, such as the usual owner would make of the land and sufficiently apparent to put the true owner on notice that a trespass is occurring). The possessor must occupy the property and enter without the owner's permission. The possessor need not believe that she has a right to possession. Finally, the possession must also be continuous throughout the statutory period. Here, the landowner has possessed the subject property openly and notoriously by digging a well. This is something that the usual owner would do on the land, and it is sufficiently apparent to put the neighbor on notice that a trespass is occurring. The landowner's possession has also been exclusive because she has not shared it with the neighbor or the public. This possession has been hostile because the landowner has entered the land without the neighbor's permission and has acted as would an owner. Finally, possession has been continuous for 25 years, which is longer than the limitations period of 20 years. Thus, the landowner has satisfied all of the elements required to obtain title by adverse possession. (B) is incorrect because hostile intent does not require that the possessor realize that the land is not her own. For purposes of adverse possession, the landowner's possession was hostile by virtue of the fact that it was without permission and in derogation of the neighbor's rights. (C) is incorrect because the statute of limitations for adverse possession is tolled by the owner's disability only if he was under the disability at the time his cause of action accrued (when the claimant begins the adverse possession). The neighbor was not adjudicated to be mentally incompetent until 10 years after the landowner began her possession of the well property. Thus, the neighbor's disability will not toll the statute. (D) is incorrect because the landowner has acquired title to the land by adverse possession. The holder of an easement has only the right to use the land, but has no right to possess and enjoy the land. Moreover, implied easements arise when a parcel is divided and (i) there was an existing use prior to the severance, or (ii) the severance deprives one lot of access to a public road or utility line. Here, there is no evidence that the landowner's and neighbor's properties were severed from a unified parcel.

Answer to Question 2

(A) The sister has standing to sue because she holds the reversion by operation of law that will take effect on the death of the friend's widow. The remainder to the friend's children is void under the Rule Against Perpetuities. Thus, the sister inherits the farmer's reversionary interest, giving her standing to enjoin the friend. A person owning an estate in real property can create and transfer a lesser estate. The residue left in the grantor, which arises by operation of law, is a reversion. A reversion is transferable, devisable by will, and descendible by inheritance. The holder of a reversion may sue a possessory owner for waste. Pursuant to the Rule Against Perpetuities, no interest in property is valid unless it must vest, if at all, not later than 21 years after one or more lives in being at the creation of the interest. The validity of an interest under the Rule is determined at the time the interest is created, taking into account the facts then existing. In circumstances involving a deed, the perpetuities period begins to run on the date the deed is delivered with the intent to pass title. If a situation can be imagined in which the interest might not vest within the perpetuities period, the interest is void. One such problem is presented by the situation of the unborn widow. The term "widow" is a technical term referring to the person to whom someone is married at the time of death. A widow cannot be identified until the husband's death. Here, the friend has a life estate. The friend's widow has a contingent remainder in a life estate because, until her identity and existence are ascertained, there is no one to take possession should the friend's life estate come to an end. Also, there is a contingent remainder in fee simple in the friend's children, because their interest is contingent on their surviving the friend and his widow. This remainder violates the Rule Against Perpetuities because the friend (even though he is presently married) might (after divorce or death of his current spouse) marry someone who was not alive at the time the interest was created. The friend might have a child by this person, after which everyone now connected with the vesting of this interest might die. Then, the friend's widow might live for more than 21 years after the death of all lives in being, leaving at her death the afterborn child as the friend's "children then alive." Thus, the interest of the child (or children) would, under these circumstances, vest outside the perpetuities period, rendering the interest void. When the farmer conveyed Parcel 1, she had a reversion by operation of law. This reversion was inherited by the sister, the farmer's only heir. Because the interest of the friend's children is void, the property will revert to the farmer (or her successors) on the death of either the friend or the friend's widow. As the holder of the reversion, the sister will have standing to attempt to enjoin the life tenant from committing waste on the property. (B) is incorrect because the sister holds a reversion rather than an executory interest. An executory interest is a future interest created in a transferee that is ***not*** capable of taking on the natural termination of a preceding life estate. An executory interest divests the preceding interest or follows a gap in possession. Neither situation applies here. Furthermore, the sister is not a transferee of Parcel 1. Rather, the sister derives her interest by virtue of inheriting it from the farmer under the laws of intestacy. (C) incorrectly states that the sister has no interest in Parcel 1, when in fact she holds a reversion. (D) is incorrect because, as detailed above, even though the friend was married at the time of the conveyance and has some children now living, there is a scenario under which the friend might eventually die leaving a widow who was not yet born at the time of creation of this interest. In turn, this widow might die at such a time as to result in the vesting of the children's interest outside the perpetuities period.

Answer to Question 3

(D) The woman and her son have title to the land as tenants in common. The man and the woman took title to the land as joint tenants. An inter vivos conveyance by one joint tenant of his undivided interest severs the joint tenancy, so that the transferee takes the interest as a tenant in common and not as a joint tenant. Here, there was an inter vivos conveyance by the man to the son of all of the man's interest in the property held in joint tenancy with the woman. This conveyance destroyed the joint tenancy, so that the son takes his interest in the property as a tenant in common with the woman, rather than as a joint tenant. (A) is incorrect because the severance of the joint tenancy destroyed the right of survivorship. A joint tenancy carries with it a right of survivorship, whereby the death of one joint tenant frees the property from his concurrent interest, so that the surviving joint tenant retains an undivided right in the property that is no longer subject to the interest of the decedent. Had the man died without having conveyed his interest in the land, the woman would have held an undivided interest in the property, free of the man's interest. However, because the joint tenancy had been terminated prior to the man's death, there is no right of survivorship. Note also that the estate held by the man and the woman was ***not*** a tenancy by the entirety, which is a marital estate similar to a joint tenancy between a husband

and wife. This estate arises presumptively (in some states) in any conveyance made to a husband and wife, and carries a right of survivorship. Here, the man and the woman took title to the land prior to their marriage, and their subsequent marriage does not affect the nature of their title. This is important because in a tenancy by the entirety, one spouse cannot convey any interest. (B) is incorrect because the man conveyed his interest in the land to the son. Thus, there is no interest or right in the land to which the heirs of the man can succeed under the intestacy laws. In addition, even if there had been no conveyance, the man's heirs would not have succeeded to his interest in the land. Rather, the woman would have taken an undivided interest in the property by means of the right of survivorship. (C) is incorrect because one joint tenant cannot convey his right of survivorship. When a joint tenant conveys his interest, it automatically becomes a tenancy in common interest. This is because the unity of time (one of the four unities required for creation of a joint tenancy) is lacking. To be joint tenants, the interests of the co-tenants must vest at the same time. Here, the woman and the man's interest vested at the same time, but the son's vested much later. Thus, the woman and her son cannot be joint tenants.

Answer to Question 4

(B) If the factory violates the setback allowance in the zoning ordinance, the seller cannot successfully sue for specific performance because title is unmarketable. There is an implied warranty in every land sale contract that at closing the seller will provide the buyer with marketable title, *i.e.*, title reasonably free from doubt. Generally, zoning restrictions do not affect the marketability of title, but an existing violation of a zoning ordinance does render title unmarketable. (A) is incorrect because it is generally held that the violation of subdivision, housing, or building codes does not constitute an encumbrance on title. Zoning is treated differently. (C) is incorrect because only an existing violation of the zoning ordinance, not a potential one, will render title unmarketable. Moreover, the truck restriction will not make the manufacturer's intended use impossible (she can use different trucks); thus, that contract argument also fails. (D) is incorrect because although an easement is an encumbrance that renders title unmarketable, this easement does not encumber the factory, but rather the adjoining property.

Answer to Question 5

(A) The seller's incapacity has no effect on the buyer's title. Generally, in an escrow transaction, title does not pass to the grantee until performance of the specified conditions (*e.g.*, the payment of money). When a deed is placed in escrow, there is a valid conditional delivery, and title will transfer automatically on the occurrence of the condition. However, if justice requires, the title of the grantee is deemed to relate back to the time of the deposit of the deed in escrow. One situation in which the relation-back doctrine applies is when the grantor becomes incompetent (to avoid the rule that an incompetent cannot convey title). Here, title would ordinarily not have passed to the buyer until the purchase price was paid, at which time the deed would be delivered through escrow. However, at the time the money was paid and the deed was delivered to the buyer, the seller was comatose and incompetent to actually convey title. This situation would lead to the unjust result that the buyer would be prevented from taking title simply due to the unfortunate circumstances of the seller's sudden incapacitation. Such a result triggers application of the relation-back doctrine, so that title is deemed to have passed to the buyer at the time the seller deposited the deed in escrow. Therefore, the seller's incapacity has no effect on the buyer's title to the house. (D) is incorrect because the prevention of passage of title is precisely the result designed to be avoided by application of the relation-back doctrine. (B) and (C) both incorrectly assume that the seller's incapacity somehow interferes with or prevents the passage of title to the buyer. As explained above, pursuant to "relation back," the buyer has clear title going back to the

time at which the deed was deposited with the escrow holder, prior to the seller's incapacity. Thus, there is no basis for concluding (as does (B)) that the seller's incapacity constitutes a lien encumbering the buyer's title, or that (as (C) states) the seller's guardian is entitled to set aside the deed.

Answer to Question 6

(B) The landowner will prevail in a suit because she, as the holder of the servient estate, has the right to choose the location of an easement by necessity. An easement by necessity arises when the owner of a tract of land sells a part of the tract and by this division deprives one lot of access to a public road or utility line. The owner of the servient parcel has the right to locate the easement, provided the location is reasonably convenient. The landowner has chosen the private road from the highway; thus, the retiree has no right to use the driveway from the county road. Both (A) and (C) are incorrect because the retiree has no easement by necessity in the driveway. As stated above, the owner of the servient parcel (the landowner) has located the easement in the private road; thus, no easement in the driveway exists. (D) is incorrect because the retiree's use has not been continuous for the five-year period. To acquire an easement by prescription, the use must be: (i) open and notorious, (ii) adverse, and (iii) continuous and uninterrupted for the statutory period. Continuous adverse use does not mean constant use. Periodic acts that put the owner on notice of the claimed easement fulfill the requirement. In this case, however, two uses in the first two years would not be sufficient to put the landowner on notice that the retiree intended to claim an easement in the driveway. Therefore, the retiree has not acquired a prescriptive easement in the driveway from the county road.

Answer to Question 7

(C) The nephew has a life estate subject to an executory interest. A life estate is an estate that is not terminable at any fixed period of time, but which is limited to the life or lives of one or more persons. Life estates may be indefeasible, ending only when the life tenant dies, or may be made defeasible, ending before the life tenant's death if the limiting condition occurs. Here, the life estate is clear, and the language "except that if" indicates a condition subsequent. On the happening of that condition, the nephew's estate is divested in favor of the niece, who holds an executory interest (*i.e.*, one that divests the interest of another). Although it is true that the nephew's interest is of indefinite duration, (A) is not the best description of his interest. Several kinds of interests are estates for indefinite periods. Thus, this choice is too broad. (B) is not the best answer because it is incomplete. The life estate is also subject to an executory interest. (D) is incorrect because a life estate is a freehold estate; possession is under title or right to hold.

Answer to Question 8

(B) The daughter's two children have a vested remainder subject to open and subject to complete divestment. A remainder is a future interest created in a transferee that is capable of taking in possession on the natural termination of the preceding estate. A remainder is vested if the beneficiaries are ascertainable and their taking in possession is not subject to a condition precedent. A vested remainder created in a class of persons that is certain to take but is subject to diminution by reason of others becoming entitled to take is a vested remainder subject to open. Vested remainders may be subject to total divestment if possession is subject to being defeated by the happening of a condition subsequent. Here, the daughter's two children have a remainder because, on the expiration of the daughter's life estate, they will be entitled to possession of the property. The remainder is not subject to a condition precedent and the beneficiaries are in

existence and ascertained, so the remainder is vested, not contingent. The remainder is subject to open because the daughter may have more children. Finally, the remainder is subject to total divestment because the daughter's children's right to possession is subject to being defeated by the daughter's ceasing to paint. (A) is wrong because the remainder is vested, not contingent; *i.e.*, it is not subject to a condition precedent, and the beneficiaries are ascertainable. (C) is not the best answer because it is incomplete. The vested remainder here is also subject to total divestment. (D) is wrong because the children's interest does not divest the daughter's estate, which would indicate an executory interest. Rather, their interest is capable of taking in possession on the natural termination of the daughter's estate, and thus is a remainder.

Answer to Question 9

(B) The bank may take possession of the apartment building before foreclosure if the jurisdiction follows the title theory. Under the title theory, title is in the mortgagee (lender) until the mortgage has been satisfied or foreclosed. Thus, the mortgagee is entitled to possession on demand at any time. (A) is incorrect because under the lien theory, title remains in the mortgagor (debtor) and the mortgagee holds only a security interest in the property. Thus, the mortgagee may not have possession before foreclosure in these jurisdictions. (C) is incorrect because, although the mortgagor has the right to redeem the property by paying off the amount due before the foreclosure sale, the equitable right of redemption does not affect the bank's right to possession before foreclosure. (D) is incorrect because, although the mortgagee may take possession if the mortgagor gives his consent, the bank would be entitled to possession before foreclosure in a title theory jurisdiction without the landlord's consent.

Answer to Question 10

(A) The brokerage firm owns both the mortgage and the note. A mortgage is a security interest in property and a note is evidence of the underlying debt. Physical possession of the mortgage and note is not required for ownership. Thus, because the brokerage firm bought the mortgage and note and recorded its interest, the brokerage firm is the owner of both, even though it left possession of the documents with the finance company. The investor has no interest in the mortgage and note because he had record notice of the brokerage firm's interest (because the brokerage firm recorded the mortgage). Having notice of the brokerage firm's interest, the investor cannot claim the protection of the recording act. Also, the investor cannot claim holder in due course status, because that status requires no notice of any other claims to the property. Therefore, the investor has no interest in the mortgage and note. (B) is wrong because, even absent the protection of the recording act or holder in due course status, the first in time rule governs. The brokerage firm was the first to purchase the mortgage and note, and so it prevails. (C) and (D) are wrong because, as stated above, the brokerage firm owns both the mortgage and note, which were never separated.

Answer to Question 11

(C) The homeowners will not prevail because they have no enforceable property interest. This answer is reached by the process of elimination. Although the homeowners may be able to get an injunction against the proposed use, it would not be because they have a property interest in the 25-acre tract, and the other options assume this fact. (A) is wrong because the homeowners have not acquired an easement by prescription. To acquire an easement by prescription, the use must be open and notorious, adverse, and continuous and uninterrupted for the statutory period (here 10 years). The use by the homeowners was ***with*** the developer's permission and, thus, was not

adverse. (B) is wrong for similar reasons. Adverse possession requires the same basic elements as a prescriptive easement plus actual and exclusive possession. As explained above, the homeowners' use was not adverse. Also, they did not have actual possession (only the right to use the property), nor did they have exclusive possession because the developer could also use the property. Therefore, the homeowners did not acquire the property by adverse possession. (D) is wrong because the homeowners have no claim at law, which would make damages, rather than an injunction, the appropriate remedy.

Answer to Question 12

(B) The lender may successfully take the office building. A purchaser for value without notice of the prior conveyance at the time of the transaction is protected by the recording statute, which is a "notice" type of statute. Under a notice statute, a subsequent bona fide purchaser (*i.e.*, one who gives valuable consideration and has no notice of the prior instrument) prevails over a prior grantee who failed to record. Mortgagees are considered "purchasers"; thus, the lender is a bona fide purchaser ("BFP") and is entitled to the protection of the recording act. Because the investor was a prior grantee who failed to record his deed, and because the lender did not have any notice of the investor's interest in the office building, the lender will prevail over the investor under the notice statute. (A) is wrong because the daughter's rights would be insufficient to protect the lender because she was not a BFP and would not be protected by the notice statute. The daughter was not a BFP because she did not pay value for the building; she inherited it under the businesswoman's will. (C) is wrong because, even though the investor could have successfully challenged the daughter's right to ownership of the building because she was not a BFP for value, a subsequent mortgagee for value and without notice is protected by the recording statutes. (D) is wrong because it is irrelevant to a determination of one's interest under any of the recording acts. Even if the lender was imprudent in loaning money to the daughter in the first place, when it lent the money it satisfied the requirements of the notice statute to acquire a priority interest in the office building.

Answer to Question 13

(D) If the neighbor prevails, it will be because the jurisdiction follows the natural flow theory. Under the natural flow theory, a landowner cannot alter the rate or manner of natural flow of surface waters (*e.g.*, rainfall, melting snow) where such actions would injure others above or below him. Here, the landowner's addition caused the surface waters to stop flowing over his land to the ditch and instead to accumulate on the neighbor's land. Therefore, under the natural flow theory, the landowner would be liable. (A) and (B) are incorrect because the riparian and prior appropriation doctrines apply to watercourses (*e.g.*, rivers, lakes), not surface waters. Under the riparian doctrine, owners of land bordering watercourses have riparian rights to use the water; their rights depend on the theory (natural flow or reasonable use) followed by the jurisdiction. Under the prior appropriation doctrine, landowners may acquire the right to divert and use water even though their property might not abut to a watercourse. (C) is incorrect because under the common enemy theory, surface water is a common enemy and any owner can change its course to get rid of it. Thus, the landowner would prevail under this theory.

Answer to Question 14

(D) The sister has no interest in the vineyard. The husband and wife hold their property in a tenancy by the entirety. This type of tenancy is a special joint tenancy held by a married couple. It carries the right of survivorship, and can be terminated only by death of a spouse, divorce of the spouses,

mutual agreement, or execution by a joint creditor of both spouses. Both spouses must join in a mortgage, because one spouse acting alone cannot convey or encumber the property. Thus, the wife lacked the power to grant the sister any interest in the vineyard. (A) is wrong because the wife could not mortgage the property to the sister, and the husband could not convey the property to the brother. Furthermore, a tenancy by the entirety is created by a conveyance to ***spouses***; so the sister could not hold the property as a tenant by the entirety with the brother. (B) would be the correct answer if the husband and wife held the vineyard as joint tenants. An inter vivos conveyance by one joint tenant of his undivided interest destroys the joint tenancy so that the transferee takes the interest as a tenant in common and not as a joint tenant. However, the husband and wife hold title as tenants by the entirety, and an individual spouse cannot convey or encumber his or her interest. Thus, (C) is also wrong.

Answer to Question 15

(A) The power company has a valid easement entitling it to flood the farmer's property. To create an easement by express grant, there must be a writing signed by the grantor. If validly created, an easement is presumed to be of perpetual duration. All of these requirements were complied with in the case of the easement to flood the farmer's property. The farmer signed the writing granting the easement, which is presumed to be of perpetual duration. (B) is incorrect because the requirements for extinguishing an easement by adverse use for the prescriptive period have not been fulfilled. To extinguish an easement by prescription, the owner of the servient tenement must so interfere with the easement as to create a cause of action in favor of the easement holder. The interference must be open, notorious, continuous, and nonpermissive for the prescriptive period. The farmer has done nothing (such as using his land in a different manner) that would indicate an interference with the power company's easement so as to give rise to a cause of action in favor of the company. (C) is incorrect because mere nonuse will not terminate an easement. To terminate an easement, the nonuse must rise to the level of abandonment, which requires physical action by the easement holder that manifests an intention to permanently abandon (*e.g.*, construction of a structure on the easement holder's property that would make it impossible to use the easement). The power company has taken no physical action that could be characterized as an abandonment of the easement. (D) is incorrect because improper recordation does not affect the rights of the original parties to the transaction. Although an unacknowledged instrument does not impart constructive notice to subsequent purchasers, it has absolutely no effect on the validity of the easement as between the original parties.

Answer to Question 16

(B) The friend has an easement by necessity over the landowner's west parcel, because only by crossing over that parcel can she gain access to her parcel. When the owner of a tract of land sells a part of the tract and by this division deprives one lot of access to a public road, a right-of-way by absolute necessity is created by implied grant over the lot with access to the public road. The facts state that the east parcel is surrounded by swampland on the north, south, and east. Thus, when the landowner sold that parcel to the friend, there was an implied grant of an access easement across the landowner's parcel because it was clearly her only access to a public road. (A) is wrong because an easement in gross does not have a dominant tenement. The holder of an easement in gross has a right to use the servient tenement independent of her ownership or possession of another tract of land. Here, the easement over the west parcel arises solely as a consequence of the friend's ownership of the adjacent east parcel. Thus, the easement is appurtenant, not in gross. (C) is wrong because even though the neighbor's easement was extinguished, the friend has acquired a new easement by necessity. When the ownership of the easement and

the servient tenement is in one person, the easement is extinguished. Thus, when the landowner bought the east parcel, the neighbor's easement was extinguished. After the easement was extinguished, however, a new easement was created by operation of law when the land was again subdivided into two lots and as a result of this subdivision one of the lot owners was deprived of access to a public road. (D) is wrong because the friend has an easement by necessity, which can arise any time the appropriate circumstances exist. The friend need not wait out the prescriptive period to gain the legal right to pass over the landowner's parcel.

Answer to Question 17

(A) The driller's action constitutes a trespass. A possessor of real property has the exclusive right to the use and possession of the surface, the air above the surface, and the land below the surface (including minerals). A trespass is a tangible physical intrusion that interferes with the possessor's right to exclusive possession of the land, and the possessor will be entitled to relief upon a showing of intentional, unprivileged physical intrusion. Here, the driller, without the landowner's permission, physically invaded by drilling into property in which the landowner had a right of exclusive possession. Thus, the landowner would be entitled to damages resulting from the driller's trespass. Note that even if the driller had not struck oil, the landowner could maintain a trespass action because trespass does not require actual damages to be established. (B) is incorrect because it states the nuisance grounds as the ***only*** theory of recovery. As noted above, the landowner may also recover damages under a trespass theory. A nuisance is an activity that substantially and unreasonably interferes with a possessor's use or enjoyment of the property. Because the driller's conduct was unreasonable, and the landowner's potential use of his mineral rights is being substantially interfered with (*e.g.*, by reducing the value of a lease he could make with another driller), the landowner probably could recover damages under a private nuisance theory. However, as explained above, the landowner may recover damages under a trespass theory, which would allow a recovery even though his use and enjoyment were not interfered with; the physical invasion alone is sufficient for a recovery. (C) is a true statement of law and would be the correct answer if the well was entirely under the driller's property and oil from under the landowner's land was flowing into it. The driller's slanted well, however, is a trespass onto the landowner's land, and the "rule of capture" does not apply to cases of trespass. (D) is incorrect because it is irrelevant whether the landowner's right to drill for oil is interfered with. The landowner may recover damages for trespass simply because the driller has violated his right to exclusive possession of the land.

Answer to Question 18

(B) If the court rules in the buyer's favor it will be because the seller was the builder of the house. Generally, a conveyance of real property contains no warranties of quality or fitness for the purpose intended, but there is a recognized exception for the sale of a new house by the builder. There is an implied warranty that the new house is designed and constructed in a reasonably "workmanlike" manner and suitable for human habitation. Thus, in this case, the buyer would appear to have no claim against the seller unless he was the builder, in which case she could claim that the house was not constructed in a reasonably "workmanlike" manner. (A) is wrong because the fact that the house was unsafe and uninhabitable would not by itself result in the seller's liability unless he was the builder. (C) is wrong because the covenants contained in a warranty deed are covenants for title (*i.e.*, they protect the purchaser against competing claims for the title to the property); they offer no protection against defects on the property. (D) is wrong because the buyer's knowledge of the defect is not relevant to the seller's liability under these facts. While a seller may be liable if he purposely conceals defects on the property or, in many

states, if he does not disclose serious defects that he is aware of, he is not generally liable for defects in the absence of these circumstances. Because the facts do not indicate that the seller acted to conceal the crumbling foundation, or was even aware of the problem, he will not be liable for the conditions unless he was the builder.

Set 2 Answer Sheet

1. Ⓐ Ⓑ Ⓒ Ⓓ
2. Ⓐ Ⓑ Ⓒ Ⓓ
3. Ⓐ Ⓑ Ⓒ Ⓓ
4. Ⓐ Ⓑ Ⓒ Ⓓ
5. Ⓐ Ⓑ Ⓒ Ⓓ
6. Ⓐ Ⓑ Ⓒ Ⓓ
7. Ⓐ Ⓑ Ⓒ Ⓓ
8. Ⓐ Ⓑ Ⓒ Ⓓ
9. Ⓐ Ⓑ Ⓒ Ⓓ
10. Ⓐ Ⓑ Ⓒ Ⓓ
11. Ⓐ Ⓑ Ⓒ Ⓓ
12. Ⓐ Ⓑ Ⓒ Ⓓ
13. Ⓐ Ⓑ Ⓒ Ⓓ
14. Ⓐ Ⓑ Ⓒ Ⓓ
15. Ⓐ Ⓑ Ⓒ Ⓓ
16. Ⓐ Ⓑ Ⓒ Ⓓ
17. Ⓐ Ⓑ Ⓒ Ⓓ
18. Ⓐ Ⓑ Ⓒ Ⓓ

REAL PROPERTY QUESTIONS - SET 2

Question 1

A landlord owned a three-story brick building. He entered into a five-year written lease with a butcher, which provided as follows:

> The tenant may alter the building for use as a meat processing, refrigeration, and vending business. At the expiration of this lease, the tenant shall have the right to remove any and all items he may have installed.

The butcher promptly installed a refrigeration system. He placed in the basement compressors, machinery, tanks, and piping that extended to the second and third floors; fitted the rear end of those floors with refrigerator doors; and filled in all of the windows in the refrigeration rooms with special insulating bricks. Near the end of the lease term, the landlord died. His will devised the building to his wife. The wife learned that the butcher planned to remove all of the above items that he had installed.

If the wife brings suit to enjoin the butcher from removing the items, what items, if any, should the court allow him to remove?

(A) None of the items.

(B) The refrigerator doors only.

(C) The refrigerator doors and refrigeration system only.

(D) All of the items.

Question 2

A farmer conveyed a 60-acre parcel of land to a rancher. A private gravel road ran through the center of the parcel. The southern half consisted of arable land, which the farmer, and later the rancher, used for farming. The northern half was undeveloped woodland. The rancher never used the northern half for timbering or for anything else. On very rare occasions, the rancher would take a walk in the woods, but outside of those occasions she never set foot on the northern half.

Fifteen years after the farmer conveyed the parcel to the rancher, a landowner appeared, claiming ownership of the northern half of the parcel. Unbeknownst to either the farmer or the rancher, the landowner's name had been forged on the deed purporting to convey the parcel to the farmer, and the landowner was, in fact, the true owner of the property at that time. The state in which the parcel is located has a 10-year statutory adverse possession period. The landowner admits that the rancher now has title to the southern half of the parcel by adverse possession.

In an action to quiet title, the court will determine that the northern half of the parcel belongs to:

(A) The landowner, because the rancher did not actually occupy the northern half.

(B) The landowner, because one may not obtain color of title through a forged deed.

(C) The rancher, because her farming of the southern half was constructive occupation of the entire parcel, including the northern half.

(D) The rancher, because the farmer did not know his deed to the parcel was forged, and he acted in good faith when he conveyed to the rancher.

Question 3

A brother and a sister each hold an undivided one-half interest in a tract of land. By the terms of their agreement, each has the right to possess all portions of the property and neither has the right to exclusive possession of any part. The brother wrongfully ousts the sister from the property.

In an action against the brother, the sister can recover:

(A) The fair rental value of the property for the time excluded.

(B) One-half of the fair rental value of the property for the time excluded.

(C) One-fourth of the fair rental value of the property for the time excluded.

(D) Nothing, because each co-tenant has the right to possess all portions of the property and neither has the right to exclusive possession of any part.

Question 4

A accountant borrowed $30,000 from a bank to help set up a small business. There was an acceleration clause in the loan agreement, which the bank could exercise any time after six months unless the accountant provided security for the loan. A few years later, the bank invoked the acceleration clause. The accountant did not have the cash on hand to repay the loan, so he offered the bank a $30,000 mortgage on property he owned. The bank accepted the mortgage and duly recorded it. There were no other mortgages on the property, which the accountant had inherited from his parents. The following year, a buyer offered the accountant $200,000 for the property, and the accountant promptly accepted. They entered into a written land sale contract, setting the closing date as May 24. The buyer contracted to tender the $200,000 on that date and the accountant contracted to convey "marketable title, free of encumbrances."

On May 15, the buyer's title search in the county recorder's office revealed the mortgage on the property. The buyer immediately contacted the accountant, who said that he planned to use the money he obtained at closing to pay off the mortgage. The buyer found this unacceptable and failed to appear at the appointed time and place of closing, although the accountant was there on time with a deed of conveyance in hand.

If the accountant files an appropriate suit against the buyer demanding specific performance and wins, it will most likely be because:

(A) A mortgage used to secure a debt does not constitute a legal "encumbrance."

(B) The vendor of real property need not have marketable title until the time of the closing.

(C) The mortgage was unenforceable ab initio, because a preexisting debt is not adequate consideration.

(D) A mortgage of the type described does not follow the land, so the buyer would have taken the land free of the mortgage even if the accountant did not pay it off.

Question 5

A husband and wife wanted to buy an expensive home. They asked the wife's mother to help them with the down payment by advancing them one-third of the money that the bank required. In return, they would put the mother's name on the title and keep it there until she was paid back. The mother advanced the money, and title was issued in the name of the husband, the wife, and the mother "as joint tenants with rights of survivorship." Over the next three years, the mother voluntarily paid one-third of all the upkeep expenses of the house, including state and local real estate taxes.

The wife died suddenly of a stroke. Her will devised all of her interests in real property to her son from a previous marriage. The probate court has been asked to rule on the distribution of the house. The husband tells the court that he can prove orally that the mother's name was put on the title only to give her a security interest.

The court should rule that title to the property belongs to:

(A) The husband, as sole tenant.

(B) The husband and the mother, as joint tenants.

(C) The husband and the mother, as tenants in common.

(D) The husband, the mother, and the son, as tenants in common.

Question 6

An investor owned an office building and an apartment building, which were connected to each other. There was no access to the second floor of the apartment building other than a common stairway located entirely within the office building. The investor conveyed the apartment building to a landlord. The landlord, her tenants, and their guests continued to use the common stairway. Subsequently, the investor conveyed the office building to an accounting firm. There was no mention of the stairway in the accounting firm's deed. Both the landlord's deed and the accounting firm's deed were properly recorded.

A few years later, the stairway had become dilapidated. The landlord was concerned about the stairway's condition of disrepair, which she felt reduced the value of the apartment building and posed a risk of injury to her tenants and their guests using the stairs. The landlord approached the accounting firm about repairing the stairs, and even offered to pay for half the cost. The firm refused. After getting an estimate from a reputable construction company, the landlord told the accounting firm she was willing to pay the entire cost of fixing the stairs. The firm again refused.

If the landlord files suit against the accounting firm, can she compel it to allow her to repair the stairs?

(A) Yes, because the landlord has an easement, which implies the power to repair.

(B) Yes, because the landlord may protect herself from the possibility of tort suits from her tenants and their guests.

(C) No, because the landlord's interest in the stairs is only for the reasonable lifetime of the structure.

(D) No, because the landlord has no right to enter the firm's property.

Question 7

A developer owned a large urban property, which she subdivided into 10 lots. The developer conveyed Lot 1 to an architect by a deed that contained a restriction banning commercial use of the property. The developer subsequently conveyed Lots 2 through 7 to six separate purchasers. Each of the deeds to these purchasers also contained the restriction on commercial use. The architect left Lot 1 undeveloped, but the purchasers of Lots 2 through 7 all used their lots for commercial purposes. The developer subsequently conveyed Lot 8 to a florist. The florist's deed contained the restriction banning commercial use of the lot, but he decided that he wished to use Lot 8 commercially. The developer retains ownership of Lots 9 and 10. The florist wants to bring suit to establish his rights to use Lot 8 for commercial purposes.

Which of the following best describes the parties the florist should join in his lawsuit?

(A) The developer only.

(B) The developer and the architect only.

(C) The other commercial users only.

(D) All landowners in the subdivision.

Question 8

A mother was in a nursing home and asked her attorney to draft a deed that would give her farm to her son. The attorney drew the deed, had the mother properly execute it, and thereafter properly recorded the deed. The attorney then told the son what she had done. The son immediately went to the nursing home and told the mother that he did not want the farm so she should take back the deed. A week later, the mother returned home to the farm. Shortly thereafter, the son died without a will, leaving his wife as his only heir. The mother has brought an action against the wife to quiet her title to the farm.

If the mother is successful in this action, it will be because:

(A) The son's statement to the mother was a constructive reconveyance of the farm.

(B) The attorney's recording of the deed had no effect because the son was unaware of what was happening.

(C) The wife is subject to a constructive trust to carry out the son's intent.

(D) The son never effectively accepted delivery of the deed.

Question 9

A vintner owned a vineyard, which adjoined a public road. His neighbor owned the adjoining undeveloped lot, which was from a different original tract. The easiest practical access to the undeveloped lot was from the public road adjoining the vineyard. This required, however, that the neighbor cross the vineyard to reach the road. The vintner granted an easement to the neighbor, allowing her to "pass through" the vineyard on her journeys between the undeveloped lot and the road. The neighbor also wanted to develop her lot but no power lines had been installed to provide it with utility service. The neighbor consulted the vintner, but he refused to alter the wording of the easement. Although a power company had a statutory power of eminent domain, it refused to run power lines to the neighbor's property without the vintner's permission.

Can the neighbor require the vintner to allow the power lines to be installed through the vineyard?

(A) Yes, by exercising the power company's right of eminent domain.

(B) Yes, because the need for utility service is a sufficient basis for an easement by necessity.

(C) No, because the neighbor's easement is for a different purpose.

(D) No, because the property is undeveloped and there is no established necessity for power service.

Question 10

A landlord leased an apartment to a tenant for five years. The lease provided that the landlord will: (i) keep the apartment building at a comfortable temperature 24 hours per day, and (ii) have the carpets cleaned once a year. Two years later, the landlord began turning off the air conditioning at 10 p.m. The tenant's apartment became hot and stuffy, and she demanded that the landlord honor the covenant. The landlord refused. The following month, the pipes burst in the tenant's only bathroom, rendering it unusable. The resultant flooding soiled some of the carpeting, which had not been cleaned in the past 12 months. The tenant reported the problems to the landlord, who did not return the tenant's phone calls.

If the tenant successfully terminates the lease, it will be because the landlord did not:

(A) Keep the apartment building at a comfortable temperature 24 hours per day only.

(B) Fix the bathroom pipes only.

(C) Keep the apartment building at a comfortable temperature 24 hours per day or fix the bathroom pipes.

(D) Keep the apartment building at a comfortable temperature 24 hours per day, have the carpets cleaned, or fix the bathroom pipes.

Question 11

A landowner conveyed a parcel of land to a buyer by warranty deed. The buyer did not record the deed. One year later, the landowner entered into a written contract with a friend, who had performed many favors for the landowner over the years, to convey the land to the friend for "one dollar." On the closing date provided in the contract, the friend handed the landowner a certified check for one dollar. The landowner handed the friend a quitclaim deed conveying the land to him. The friend promptly recorded the deed.

A statute of the state in which the land is located provides: "Any conveyance of an interest in land, other than a lease for less than one year, is not valid against any subsequent purchaser for value without notice thereof whose conveyance is first recorded."

In an action to establish ownership of the land, the friend's greatest obstacle to prevailing will be that:

(A) A quitclaim deed is not a valid transfer of title.

(B) The transaction must be shown to be a transfer for value.

(C) Warranty deeds are superior in right to quitclaim deeds.

(D) A quitclaim deed is not a recordable instrument.

Question 12

An uncle's will devised his lakefront estate "to my butler for life, remainder to my niece." The 40-acre estate includes a mansion, a 20-acre orchard, a beach, and gardens. At the time of the uncle's death, the butler was 40 years old and of modest means. The niece was 18 years old and quite wealthy. The estate was encumbered by a mortgage that was not entitled to exoneration. After the first year, the butler could no longer make the mortgage payments, so the niece paid them.

Ten years after the uncle's death, the town in which the estate was located became a hot resort area. A major resort chain approached the butler with a multimillion-dollar offer for the easternmost 20 acres of the estate, which included the residence and beach. The resort chain planned to raze the mansion to erect a high-rise hotel. The butler approached the niece about the offer. He proposed to give her most of the money from the sale and offered to build any house she desired on the remaining land. The niece refused to go along with the plan. The butler decided to proceed with the sale, and the niece brought a suit to enjoin the butler's proposed actions.

Which of the following is the niece's best argument?

(A) The eventual use of the property by the remainderman will be as a residence.

(B) Destruction of the mansion constitutes waste.

(C) Because the niece paid the mortgage payments, the butler is subrogated to her rights.

(D) The butler has no right to transfer his life estate.

Question 13

A developer owned a 240-acre parcel of land zoned for commercial and residential use. He prepared and recorded, after obtaining approval from all appropriate agencies, a subdivision plan that included a commercial center and a number of lots for single- and multi-family residences. The list of covenants, conditions, and restrictions recorded with the plan included provisions that required every building constructed in the subdivision to be of "simulated adobe style" architecture approved in advance by an association. A year later, the developer sold many of the lots in the commercial center, including several to a real estate firm. Each deed prepared by the developer contained a reference to the design restriction in the recorded plan. The developer also sold almost all of the residential lots, whose deeds contained the same reference to the restriction. The following year, the real estate firm sold one of its lots to a burger franchise. The deed contained no reference to the design restriction. The franchise's prefabricated restaurant, complete with a giant burger logo mounted on the roof, was constructed over the weekend.

A merchant, an original purchaser of one of the commercial lots, owned the lot next to the burger franchise. She did not learn of construction of the restaurant until she came in to work on Monday, and saw the giant burger logo. The merchant brings an action seeking a mandatory

injunction compelling the burger franchise to demolish the restaurant. At trial, the merchant proves that the burger franchise did not seek or obtain approval of the association for its building.

Should the court issue the injunction?

(A) No, because destruction of the restaurant would be a tremendous waste of resources.

(B) No, because the burger franchise's deed contained no restriction on the type of building that could be constructed on the lot.

(C) Yes, because the restrictive covenant runs with the land.

(D) Yes, unless the burger franchise can establish to the court's satisfaction that its restaurant design has at least as much aesthetic merit as any "simulated adobe style" design.

Question 14

An investor owned two adjacent lots in a downtown area, one fronting directly on a public street and the other behind the first. The investor ran a small dry cleaning business on the lot next to the street, and had built a café on the rear lot. Because the rear lot had no access to any public street, the investor used the parking lot of the dry cleaning business, which extended from the street all the way back to the rear lot, for access to the café. The café was only open during the tourist season, from May through September. After several years, the investor sold the rear lot to a chef by a deed that granted an easement over the dry cleaning business's parking lot, to be used as an accessway to the café for the chef and her customers. The chef promptly recorded the deed.

Two years later, in February, the investor sold the dry cleaning lot to a sub sandwich franchise. The deed did not mention the easement previously granted to the chef. The franchise immediately demolished the small dry cleaning building and constructed its own restaurant. An outdoor patio area completely blocked access to the chef's rear lot. Because the chef's café was closed for the winter, nothing came of the franchise's construction until April, when the chef returned to open her café for the summer season. The shortest alternate route over other parcels from the chef's lot to a public street would have to pass through several buildings and lots.

If the chef brings an action to compel the sub sandwich franchise to demolish the outdoor patio, how should the court rule?

(A) For the franchise, because its deed contained no mention of the access easement.

(B) For the franchise, because construction of the outdoor patio extinguished the chef's rights to the access easement.

(C) For the chef, because ownership of the easement gives her the right to use it for access to her lot.

(D) For the chef, because she has no other access to her lot.

Question 15

A developer owns 2,000 acres of land. She wants to develop 1,500 acres as a residential subdivision and hold the remaining 500 acres for a long period, hoping they will appreciate in value. In the meantime, she plans to use the tract as an inducement in the marketing of the lots in the 1,500-acre subdivision by designating the 500 acres as an area in which purchasers in the subdivision can ride horseback, hike, camp, and fish. Business judgment indicates that the developer can make these 500 acres available for these purposes for 20 years if she can be assured that, after such period, she will be free to do with the land as she chooses.

The best device to implement the purpose of the developer with respect to the 500 acres (assuming that any device chosen will receive judicial recognition and enforcement) is:

(A) Covenant.

(B) Easement.

(C) Leasehold.

(D) Personal contractual obligation of the developer.

Question 16

A father owned a parcel of land in fee simple. Shortly after his wife died, the father conveyed the land to his sister for life, remainder to the children of his son in fee simple. The son was married but had no children.

What interest, if any, is created in favor of the son's unborn children at the time of the conveyance?

(A) None.

(B) A contingent remainder.

(C) A vested remainder subject to open.

(D) A vested remainder subject to total divestment.

Question 17

A seller owned a two-acre tract of land, on which he built a single-family residence. The seller entered into a contract to sell the land to a buyer for $200,000. One week before closing, the buyer had a survey of the property made. It revealed that a portion of the seller's house was 5.98 feet from the sideline. The applicable zoning ordinance requires a six-foot sideline setback. The buyer refused to go ahead with the purchase of the land on the ground that the seller's title was not marketable.

If the seller brings suit against the buyer for specific performance, will he prevail?

(A) Yes, because any suit against the seller concerning the setback would be frivolous.

(B) Yes, because the setback violation is *de minimis*.

(C) No, because any variation, however small, amounts to a breach of contract.

(D) No, because the seller's title is unmarketable.

Question 18

A large field, owned by a city, was used as a municipal parking lot for many years. When a new parking facility was constructed, the field was no longer used for that purpose. The city officially vacated the property, except for a small parcel of land at the easterly end of the field. The adjoining owner on both sides of the field went into possession of the parcel, fenced it, and cultivated the parcel for a period of time in excess of the period required for adverse possession. A statute of the jurisdiction in which the field is located provides that real property interests can be lost by a municipality through adverse possession.

In an appropriate action brought by the adjoining owner to establish his title to the parcel, which of the following must he establish if he is to prevail?

(A) The adjoining owner's use of the parcel was proof of his assertion of dominion over the parcel.

(B) Fee interests in real property can be abandoned by a municipality without an official vote.

(C) Lack of use of the parcel by the municipality created an irrevocable license in the adjoining owner.

(D) The adjoining owner believed that he owned the parcel.

REAL PROPERTY ANSWERS - SET 2

Answer to Question 1

(C) The court should allow the butcher to remove only the refrigerator doors and refrigeration system. A fixture is a chattel that has been so affixed to the land that it becomes part of the realty. In divided ownership cases, where the chattel is owned and brought to the realty by someone other than the landlord, the lease controls whether the chattel was intended to become a fixture. To the extent that the landlord and tenant specifically agree that such annexation is not to be deemed a fixture, the agreement controls. However, regardless of any agreement, items that have become incorporated into the structure of the realty always become part of the realty. Here, the lease between the landlord and the butcher clearly states that at the end of the lease the butcher may remove any items he installed. Thus, the butcher may remove the refrigeration system and refrigerator doors. The insulating bricks, on the other hand, were built into the structure of the building and may not be removed. (A) is incorrect because, as explained above, the butcher will be allowed to remove some of the items. (B) is incorrect because the butcher will also be permitted to remove the refrigeration system. Even though removal of the refrigeration system will likely cause damage to the realty, the lease controls whether it is a fixture; here, it is not. However, the butcher will be responsible for repairing the damage. (D) is incorrect because the butcher may not remove the insulating bricks, which were incorporated into the building's structure.

Answer to Question 2

(A) The landowner will prevail in an action to quiet title to the northern half of the parcel because the rancher did not actually occupy the northern half. An adverse possessor will gain title only to the land she actually occupies. Actual possession is the kind of use the true owner would make of the parcel and is designed to give the owner notice of the trespass and the extent of the adverse possessor's claim. The gravel road divides the parcel into two distinct lots, and the rancher's use of the northern half was not sufficient to put the landowner on notice of her trespass. (B) is wrong for two reasons: (i) The rancher has color of title. Color of title merely means possession of a document purporting to convey title. (ii) Color of title is not necessary to gain title by adverse possession. In most jurisdictions, the possessor need not believe she has a right to possession; she can be a trespasser. (C) is wrong because the rancher's possession and use of the southern half was not sufficient to constitute constructive possession of the northern half. Possession of a portion of a unitary tract is sufficient adverse possession of the whole if there is a reasonable proportion between the part actually possessed and the whole, and if the possessor has color of title. The rancher has color of title, but she only occupied one-half of the parcel. Moreover, the parcel consists of two lots separated by a road, so it is unlikely that it constitutes a unitary tract. In any case, the rancher's possession of the southern half was not sufficient to put the landowner on notice of possession of the northern half. (D) is wrong because, regardless of whether the farmer acted in good faith, he did not have any title to convey to the rancher. As noted above, color of title is not necessary for adverse possession, which is the only theory under which the rancher could have title to the northern half.

Answer to Question 3

(B) If one co-tenant wrongfully ousts another co-tenant from possession of the whole or any part of the premises, the ousted co-tenant is entitled to receive her share of the fair rental value of the property for the time she was wrongfully deprived of possession. The sister was wrongfully ousted and therefore, as one of two co-tenants with the right to possess all portions of the property, she would be entitled to one-half of the fair rental value of the property during the period when she was ousted. (A) is incorrect because the sister is entitled only to her share (*i.e.*, one-half) of the fair rental value. (C) is incorrect because it also misstates the share of rental value to which the sister is entitled. She is entitled to one-half, not one-fourth, of the fair rental value of the property. While (D) makes a correct statement, it addresses only the right of possession of the property. It is the share of ownership of the property, however, that determines the share of rents and profits. Because the sister owned an undivided one-half interest in the property, she is entitled to one-half of the fair rental value for the time she was excluded.

Answer to Question 4

(B) If the accountant is granted specific performance, it will be because he was prepared to deliver marketable title to the buyer at closing. The seller of real property need not have marketable title until the closing; *i.e.*, the buyer cannot rescind prior to that date on grounds that the seller's title is not marketable. In fact, the seller has the right to satisfy and eliminate title defects, such as a mortgage, at the closing with the proceeds from the sale. As long as the purchase price is sufficient and the mortgage is paid simultaneously with the transfer of title (*e.g.*, by use of an escrow), the buyer cannot claim that the title is unmarketable. The closing will result in marketable title. In this case, the accountant intended to pay off the $30,000 mortgage at closing with a portion of the $200,000 purchase price. Thus, the buyer cannot claim that the accountant's title is unmarketable; she must proceed to closing. (A) is wrong because ***any*** mortgage or lien constitutes an encumbrance on the property. An encumbrance is any interest in land that diminishes its value. (C) is wrong because the fact that the mortgage was given for a preexisting debt does not mean it is unenforceable. The only possible negative effects of granting the mortgage for an antecedent debt is that the mortgagee is not considered a purchaser for value and, thus, is not protected by the recording statute. In this case, however, the recording statute does not even come into play. Even if it did, the buyer had notice of and could not cut off the bank's interest. The bank's loss of protection would only be a problem as against ***prior*** (of which there are none), rather than subsequent, grantees. Furthermore, it is not clear from the facts that the mortgage was granted merely in exchange for an antecedent debt. The bank agreed to forgo the immediate payment of the debt in exchange for the mortgage on the property. (D) is wrong because all mortgages follow the transfer of land. Had the mortgage not been paid off and the sale proceeded, the buyer would not have been personally liable on the mortgage, but the property would remain subject to foreclosure for default.

Answer to Question 5

(B) The husband and the mother hold the property as joint tenants. A joint tenancy carries the right of survivorship. When one joint tenant dies, the property is freed from her concurrent interest. The survivors retain an undivided right in the property, which is no longer subject to the interest of the deceased co-tenant. Because the husband, the wife, and the mother held the property as joint tenants with rights of survivorship, the wife's death freed the property of her interest and the husband and the mother each hold an undivided one-half interest in the property. Their rights of survivorship continue. (A) is incorrect because, as stated above, the mother also has an interest in the property. (A) might be a correct choice if the husband were successful in proving his contention that the mother's interest was only intended to be a security interest. The facts do not support this argument, however. The fact that the deed specified that the mother had a right of survivorship is evidence that she was intended as a joint tenant, not merely a secured lender. The mother's payment of upkeep and taxes is further evidence that her interest was greater than that of a creditor. (C) is incorrect because the joint tenancy was not severed or partitioned. A conveyance by one joint tenant may sever a joint tenancy, resulting in a tenancy in common. However, a testamentary disposition by one joint tenant has no effect (*see* below) and thus does not work a severance. (D) is incorrect because the son does not have an interest in the property. A will is effective only at death and is inoperative as to joint tenancy property because, at the instant of death, the decedent's rights in the property evaporate. Thus, the wife had no interest in the property to convey to the son at her death.

Answer to Question 6

(A) The landlord has a right to repair the stairs because she has an easement. An easement by implication is created by operation of law rather than by written instrument. It is an exception to the Statute of Frauds. An easement is implied if, prior to the time the property is divided, a use exists on the "servient part" that is reasonably necessary for the enjoyment of the "dominant part," and the parties intended the use to continue after division of the property. The use must be continuous and apparent at the time the property is divided. Reasonable necessity is determined by many factors, including the cost and difficulty of alternatives, and whether the price paid reflects the expected continued use. The use of the stairs was continuous, apparent, and reasonably necessary to the use of the apartment building when the investor conveyed it to the landlord. Although the facts do not give enough information to determine whether the accounting firm's purchase price reflected the continued use of the stairs, it seems clear that the alternatives would be very costly. Because there was no change in the use after the landlord bought the apartment building and the investor was still in possession of the office building, it appears that they intended the use to continue. Thus, the implied easement from existing use arose when the investor conveyed the apartment building to the landlord. The burden of that easement passes with the transfer of the servient tenement, the office building. The holder of an easement has a right, even a duty, to make repairs. Therefore, the landlord has a right to repair the stairs in the office building. (B) is wrong because no such right exists apart from the rights of an easement holder. Absent an easement, the landlord would not have any right to enter the accounting firm's property regardless of whether she would be subject to liability for injuries. (C) is wrong because easements are of perpetual duration, unless limited by the terms of a writing. Here there is no writing, so the landlord's easement is perpetual. (D) is wrong because, as explained above, the landlord has an easement implied from existing use. An easement gives the landlord the right to enter the accounting firm's property.

Answer to Question 7

(D) The florist should join all of the landowners in the subdivision in a suit to terminate the servitude on the grounds of abandonment. If a covenant in a subdivision deed is silent as to who holds its benefit, any neighbor in the subdivision will be entitled to enforce the covenant if a general scheme or plan is found to have existed at the time she purchased her lot. In addition, a prior purchaser can enforce a restriction in a subsequent deed from a common grantor under either a third-party beneficiary theory or an implied reciprocal servitude theory. Under the implied reciprocal servitude theory, an implied reciprocal servitude attaches to the grantor's retained land at the moment she deeds a lot with the restriction. Thus, all of the other landowners in the subdivision could potentially enforce the covenant as an equitable servitude against the florist. All parties would probably fail in an attempt to enforce the servitude, but the florist should join them now to avoid multiple litigation. (Note that had the other landowners tried to enforce the equitable servitude against the florist, they would all have been subject to the equitable defense of acquiescence, which provides that if a benefited party acquiesces in a violation of the servitude

by one burdened party, he may be deemed to have abandoned the servitude as to other burdened parties. In addition, the other commercial users are subject to the defense of unclean hands. It is important to remember that these are defenses and do not terminate the servitude; therefore, it would be best for the florist to join all possible complainants in a suit to have the servitude declared extinguished.) (A) is wrong because, as explained, the other landowners also could try to enforce the covenant. (B) is wrong for the same reason. Although the architect has not violated the covenant and thus is not subject to the defenses possible against the other landowners, he and the developer are not the only possible plaintiffs (remember the question in effect asks who can bring suit, not who can win it). (C) is wrong because the developer and the architect can also bring suit. (Note that the above discussion applies only to sparing the florist from the enforcement of the restriction as an equitable servitude. The developer may try to enforce the restriction as a real covenant. She will, however, be limited to recovering damages, which might be very difficult to prove under the circumstances.)

Answer to Question 8

(D) If the mother prevails, it will be because the son never effectively accepted delivery. A deed is not effective to transfer an interest in realty unless it has been delivered, and there must be acceptance by the grantee to complete the conveyance. (D) is the best answer because even though most states presume acceptance, the presumption is rebutted when the grantee expressly refuses to accept the conveyance. (A) is wrong because there is no such thing as a "constructive reconveyance" of land. (B) may look good at first, but it is a minority rule. In most states, acceptance is presumed if the conveyance is beneficial to the grantee, regardless of whether the grantee has knowledge of the conveyance. (C) is wrong because neither the son nor the wife is guilty of any wrongdoing and there is no ground to impose a constructive trust.

Answer to Question 9

(C) The neighbor cannot require the vintner to permit power lines to be installed on the vineyard. A basic change in the nature of use (scope) of an easement is not allowed. Thus, a power line cannot be added to the neighbor's private easement of way across the vineyard. (A) is incorrect because the neighbor cannot exercise the power company's right of eminent domain. (B) is incorrect because easements by necessity arise only when the owner of a single tract sells a portion of the tract that has no access to a public road or utility line. The facts in this question do not indicate that the vintner ever owned both the vineyard and the undeveloped lot; therefore, no easement by necessity can arise. (D) is incorrect because prior necessity is irrelevant. Necessity is determined at the time the parcel is divided. As noted above, the facts here indicate that the land was not part of a unitary tract; thus, a necessity analysis is impossible.

Answer to Question 10

(B) The tenant will be successful in terminating the lease because the landlord breached the implied warranty of habitability by failing to fix the bathroom pipes. The general rule at common law was that the landlord was not liable to the tenant for damages caused by the landlord's failure to maintain the premises during the period of the leasehold. Today, however, a majority of jurisdictions, usually by statute, provide for an implied warranty of habitability for residential tenancies. In the absence of a local housing code, the standard applied is whether the conditions are reasonably suitable for human residence. If the landlord breaches the implied warranty, the tenant may: (i) terminate the lease, (ii) make repairs and offset their cost against future rent, (iii) abate rent, or (iv) seek damages. Here, a court is likely to consider the lack of a functioning bathroom as

making the premises unsuitable for human residence, allowing the tenant to terminate the lease. (A) is therefore incorrect. (C) would be a stronger answer if the tenant had vacated the premises within a reasonable time. The doctrine of constructive eviction provides that where a landlord does an act or fails to perform some service that he has a legal duty to provide, and thereby makes the property uninhabitable, the tenant may terminate the lease and seek damages. However, a tenant cannot claim a constructive eviction unless: (i) the injurious acts were caused by the landlord, (ii) the premises are uninhabitable, and (iii) the tenant vacates the premises within a reasonable time. Here, the landlord's failing to keep the apartment building at a comfortable temperature 24 hours per day meets conditions (i) and perhaps (ii), but the tenant remains in possession. Therefore, the tenant cannot claim constructive eviction and (C) is incorrect. (D) is incorrect for the same reason and also because covenants in a lease are independent of each other. Thus, if one party breaches, the other can recover damages but must still perform his promises and cannot terminate the landlord-tenant relationship. Here, the tenant can recover damages from the landlord for failure to clean the carpets, but must continue to pay rent and cannot terminate the lease.

Answer to Question 11

(B) To be a bona fide purchaser for value, and thus entitled to the protection of the recording statute, the purchaser must prove that real—not merely nominal—consideration was paid. In other words, the friend must prove that he is a purchaser rather than a donee. The consideration need not be adequate or the market value, but it must be of substantial pecuniary value. Generally, past consideration (*e.g.*, favors) is not sufficient. Thus, the friend will have a difficult time proving that one dollar meets this test. (A) is wrong because title can be conveyed by quitclaim deed. (C) is wrong because a warranty deed is not superior in right to a quitclaim deed. The only difference between the two is that a warranty deed normally contains covenants for title, the breach of which gives rise to a cause of action against the grantor, and a quitclaim deed contains no assurances by the grantor. (D) is wrong because all instruments affecting title to real property are recordable and should be recorded.

Answer to Question 12

(B) The niece's best argument is that destruction of the residence constitutes waste. The other choices do not present arguments giving her a chance of success. A life tenant is entitled to all ordinary uses and profits of the land, but he cannot lawfully do any act that would injure the interests of the remainderman. A grantor intends that the life tenant have the general use of the land in a reasonable manner, but that the land pass to the owner of the remainder, as nearly as practicable, unimpaired in its nature, character, and improvements. Even ameliorative waste, which actually increases the value of the land, is actionable if there is no reasonable justification for the change. A life tenant can substantially alter or even demolish existing buildings if (i) the market value of the future interests is not diminished and ***either*** (ii) the remainderman does not object, or (iii) a substantial and permanent change in the neighborhood conditions has deprived the property in its current form of reasonable productivity or usefulness. Here, the market value of the property would not be diminished. The remainderman (the niece), however, is objecting, making option (ii) unavailable. Furthermore, although the neighboring properties have been sold for hotels and resorts, it does not necessarily follow that the conditions have changed to such a degree that the estate should be similarly converted. The property is large enough to be somewhat isolated from the changes in the surrounding areas; thus, despite the surrounding hotels, an owner could still enjoy the land as a private residence, orchard, and beach. Therefore, the property is still useful and option (iii) is also unavailable. In this case, the life tenant's desire to raze the mansion is not

because the changes in the neighborhood have made the mansion uneconomical or impractical. The life tenant can make more money by tearing the mansion down, but its usefulness and value are apparently unaffected by the changes in the neighborhood. Thus, the niece will be able to enjoin the butler from allowing the resort chain to raze the mansion and build a hotel. (A) is wrong because the fact that the niece intended to use the property as a residence is irrelevant. Even if the niece intended to change the use of the property, she is still entitled to receive the land in the condition in which it passed to the butler. (C) is wrong because the fact that the niece made mortgage payments does not affect the butler's rights. The niece had to make the payments to protect her remainder interest. (D) is wrong because life estates generally are alienable. The transferee merely takes the same interest as the life tenant. In this case, the butler may convey his interest in the property. Of course, anyone taking the butler's interest would have only an estate for the butler's life, *i.e.*, a life estate pur autre vie.

Answer to Question 13

(C) The court should issue the injunction because the covenant runs with the land. A covenant will be enforceable as an equitable servitude—allowing a covenantee, covenantor, or successor to enforce the covenant in equity by way of injunction—when there is (i) a covenant in a writing satisfying the Statute of Frauds, that (ii) touches and concerns the land (*i.e.*, the effect of the covenant makes the land more useful or valuable to the benefited party) and that (iii) indicates an intention that the servitude exists, and (iv) notice is given to future owners of the burdened land. Here, the covenant was in writing in the subdivision plan and presumably it satisfied the Statute of Frauds. It touches and concerns the land—benefiting all of the lots and burdening all of the lots. The intention to create the servitude is established by the writing and can also be implied from the common scheme for development. There was sufficient record notice of the covenant because the plan was recorded and was noted in all of the original deeds prepared by the developer, including the one in the burger franchise's chain of title. Thus, the covenant is enforceable and (C) is the best answer. (A) is incorrect because although an injunction is equitable in nature—so equitable principles govern—it is not a defense in equity merely to claim that granting an injunction will result in a waste of assets. (B) is incorrect because the burger franchise had record notice of the restriction. The deed from the developer to the real estate firm, which contained a reference to the restriction in the recorded plan, was in the burger franchise's direct chain of title and could have been discovered by it. (D) is incorrect because a court will not modify the covenant—it will enforce it or not enforce it, but will not substitute its judgment of what is aesthetically pleasing for the requirements of the covenant.

Answer to Question 14

(C) The court should rule for the chef because her easement gives her the right to use the sub sandwich franchise's property for access to her lot. An easement is an interest in land which gives the holder a right to use the land for certain purposes. Here, the investor granted the chef an easement to use a portion of his property for access to her lot. The presumption when an easement is granted is that it is perpetual unless otherwise stated. Thus, the chef's easement was perpetual and was not destroyed by the transfer of the servient tenement (the investor's property) to the sub sandwich franchise. Moreover, the easement is valid against the franchise because it was recorded. Easements, like other interests in land, are good against subsequent holders of the burdened (servient) tenement as long as the interest is recorded. The facts here state that the chef properly recorded her easement, so it is good against the franchise; thus, (C) is correct. (A) is incorrect because the chef's recorded deed is deemed to be constructive notice of the easement; mention of the easement need not be included in the sub sandwich franchise's deed. A thorough search of the title index would have revealed that the investor, the franchise's predecessor in title, gave the easement to the chef. (B) is incorrect because the obstruction of the chef's easement did not continue for the statutory period required to terminate easements by prescription. To terminate an easement by prescription, the owner of the servient tenement must openly and nonpermissively interfere with the use of the easement for the same statutory period as is necessary to acquire an easement by prescription. Although statutes vary, it would never be less than one year, and most statutes set the period at 10 or 20 years. (D) is incorrect. An easement by absolute necessity may be implied when the purchaser of part of a tract has no outlet to a public road or utility line except over the remaining land of the seller, but here, the chef does not need to rely on an implied easement because she has an express easement from the investor.

Answer to Question 15

(B) A 20-year easement for recreational purposes, granted to the homeowners of the subdivision, will best achieve the developer's goals. The holder of an easement has the right to use the tract of land for a special purpose, but has no right to possess or enjoy the land. If the developer grants the homeowners a 20-year easement, she may limit the permitted uses to whatever she wishes, and at the end of the 20 years, the homeowners' right to use the land ends. The developer may then dispose of the land as she wishes, free of the easement. (A) is incorrect because a real covenant is a promise to do, or refrain from doing, something on one's property that one would otherwise be privileged to do. A covenant does not grant a right to use or possess someone else's property. Therefore, a covenant would not be the appropriate legal device to allow the homeowners the use of the 500-acre tract. (C) is incorrect because a lease is not as effective as an easement in accomplishing the developer's goal. A leasehold is a possessory interest in land; so the developer would be giving up her right to possess the land. Thus, a lease to the homeowners would result in the developer's unnecessarily relinquishing much of her control over the tract, whereas the easement option allows her to do as she pleases with the property while granting the homeowners the right to use the tract. (D) is incorrect because the personal contract obligation of the developer does not adequately protect the homeowners' interests. It will not be much of an inducement if a prospective purchaser realizes that the right to use the land will terminate if the developer dies or sells the land. In the case of a land sale, the homeowners could be entitled to damages, but in contrast to the easement situation, would not be able to enforce the right to use the tract.

Answer to Question 16

(B) The son's unborn children have a contingent remainder. A remainder is a future interest created in a transferee that is capable of taking on the natural termination of the preceding estate. A remainder must be expressly created in the instrument creating the prior possessory estate. The interest in the son's children follows naturally upon the termination of the sister's estate; thus, it is a remainder. It is a contingent remainder because we do not know whether there will be any takers. A remainder created in favor of an unborn person has to be a contingent remainder. (A) is incorrect because the children do have an interest, a remainder. The remainder is valid under the Rule Against Perpetuities because the children's interest will vest, if at all, within 21 years after the death of the son (a life in being at the creation of the interest). (C) and (D) are incorrect because a vested remainder can only be created in an existing person. A vested remainder may be subject to partial or total divestment, but it cannot be vested unless there is at least one remainderman in existence and ascertained.

Answer to Question 17

(D) The seller will not prevail because his title was unmarketable. There is an implied warranty in every land sale contract that at closing the seller will provide the buyer with title that is marketable.

It need not be perfect title, but it must be free from questions that might present an unreasonable risk of litigation. Because the placement of the seller's house violated the zoning ordinance, the buyer could be subject to suit. (A) and (B) are therefore incorrect. (C) is an incorrect statement of law.

Answer to Question 18

(A) The adjoining owner's claim to the parcel would be based on adverse possession. Adverse possession must be (i) open and notorious, (ii) actual and exclusive, (iii) continuous throughout the statutory period, and (iv) hostile (*i.e.*, without the true owner's permission). Although government land generally cannot be obtained through adverse possession, such an action is permitted against a municipality in this jurisdiction. The adjoining owner must also establish that his use shows the assertion of dominion required for adverse possession. Thus, (A) is correct. (B) is incorrect because abandonment by the record owner (the city) is not an element of adverse possession. (C) is incorrect because a license need not be established, and could not be established by mere nonuse. A license, in fact, cuts against acquiring title by adverse possession because it basically constitutes the owner's permission to use the land. (D) is incorrect because the state of mind of the adverse possessor is irrelevant. By the large majority view, it does not matter whether the possessor believes he is on his own land, knows he is trespassing on someone else's land, or has no idea who owns the land.

Set 3 Answer Sheet

1. Ⓐ Ⓑ Ⓒ Ⓓ
2. Ⓐ Ⓑ Ⓒ Ⓓ
3. Ⓐ Ⓑ Ⓒ Ⓓ
4. Ⓐ Ⓑ Ⓒ Ⓓ
5. Ⓐ Ⓑ Ⓒ Ⓓ
6. Ⓐ Ⓑ Ⓒ Ⓓ
7. Ⓐ Ⓑ Ⓒ Ⓓ
8. Ⓐ Ⓑ Ⓒ Ⓓ
9. Ⓐ Ⓑ Ⓒ Ⓓ
10. Ⓐ Ⓑ Ⓒ Ⓓ
11. Ⓐ Ⓑ Ⓒ Ⓓ
12. Ⓐ Ⓑ Ⓒ Ⓓ
13. Ⓐ Ⓑ Ⓒ Ⓓ
14. Ⓐ Ⓑ Ⓒ Ⓓ
15. Ⓐ Ⓑ Ⓒ Ⓓ
16. Ⓐ Ⓑ Ⓒ Ⓓ
17. Ⓐ Ⓑ Ⓒ Ⓓ
18. Ⓐ Ⓑ Ⓒ Ⓓ

REAL PROPERTY QUESTIONS - SET 3

Question 1

A landowner borrowed $30,000 from a bank, secured by a mortgage on his land. The mortgage papers were signed by the landowner and by the chief loan officer as agent for the bank on March 18. The loan officer filled out the appropriate recording form and gave it to a bank clerk on March 19, instructing him to file the papers at the county recorder's office. The bank clerk inadvertently misplaced the papers. He discovered the papers on April 10 and filed them with the county recorder.

At the recorder's office, the bank clerk discovered a conveyance of the landowner's land from the landowner to a buyer dated April 5 and recorded on April 8. Subsequent inquiry revealed that the buyer paid the landowner $150,000 for the land after a diligent title search and that the buyer had no knowledge of the mortgage on the property until the loan officer contacted her on April 11. The jurisdiction in which the land is located follows the lien theory of mortgages, and has a statute providing: "Any conveyance of an interest in land shall not be valid against any subsequent purchaser for value without notice thereof who first records."

If the bank seeks a declaration from the court that the buyer owns the land subject to a $30,000 mortgage with the bank, is the bank likely to prevail?

(A) Yes, because the bank's interest was acquired for value prior to the date when the buyer recorded.

(B) Yes, because the mortgage was merely security for a loan.

(C) No, because the buyer recorded first.

(D) No, because the jurisdiction follows the lien theory.

Question 2

On April 15, a seller entered into a valid written agreement to sell her home to a buyer for $175,000. The provisions of the agreement provided that closing would be at the buyer's attorney's office on May 15, and that the seller would deliver to the buyer marketable title, free and clear of all encumbrances.

On the date of closing, the seller offered to the buyer the deed to the house, but the buyer refused to go ahead with the purchase because his attorney told him that a contractor who had done work on the house had recorded a lis pendens on May 1 against the property regarding a $10,000 contract dispute he had with the seller. The seller indicated that she was unaware of the lien, but that she was willing to go ahead with the sale and set aside funds from the purchase price to cover the contractor's claim until the dispute was resolved. The buyer still refused to proceed, stating that the seller had breached the contract.

If the seller brings an action against the buyer for specific performance, the probable result will be:

(A) The buyer prevails, because the title to the property was not marketable as of the date of closing.

(B) The buyer prevails, because an encumbrance was on the title as of the date of closing that was subject to litigation.

(C) The seller prevails, because under the doctrine of equitable conversion, the buyer was the owner of the property when the lis pendens was recorded, and therefore it was invalid.

(D) The seller prevails, because an implied term of their contract was that she could use the proceeds to clear any encumbrance on the title.

Question 3

A woman and her friend lived together in the woman's home for 20 years. Subsequently, the

woman became disabled because of a heart ailment and the friend had to take care of her. The woman told the friend that she wanted to be sure that the friend got her house after she died, so she gave the friend a quitclaim deed. The friend did not record the deed, but put it in his safe deposit box.

Four months later, the woman's son found out about this and told his mother that if she would sell the house to him, she could live there for the rest of her life. The woman, who wanted the money, agreed and carried out the transaction. She told the friend that she had changed her mind and decided to leave the home to her children. The friend promised to destroy the deed, and the next day, he did. Several days later, however, as the friend and the woman were driving to the store, their car was hit by a train and they both died. The woman's and the friend's heirs claim title to the house.

In an appropriate action to resolve this dispute, the most likely finding by the court will be:

(A) The friend was the owner of the house, because the woman did not tell him the truth about why she was revoking her agreement.

(B) The friend was still the owner, because he did not retransfer title to the woman.

(C) The woman was the owner, because the friend agreed to return the title, and did in fact destroy the deed.

(D) The woman was the owner, because the friend, as a donee, would not be able to prevail against the son, who was a bona fide purchaser.

Question 4

A landlord leased a house to a tenant for five years. Under the terms of the lease, the tenant was to pay a fixed monthly rent plus all taxes and reasonable maintenance charges for the upkeep of the house. Three years into the lease, the tenant assigned her lease to a friend by written agreement. Although the tenant properly set forth the terms concerning the rent and maintenance charges, she failed to properly state that the friend was liable to pay the taxes on the residence during the period of the lease. A year later, the landlord received notice that a tax lien would be placed on the residence unless the taxes were immediately paid. The landlord paid the taxes and brought suit against the tenant's friend for the amount. The suit extremely upset the friend, who abandoned the residence.

Can the landlord successfully bring a suit against the tenant for this breach of the lease?

(A) No, because the tenant is no longer a tenant.

(B) No, because the tenant is no longer in privity of estate with the landlord.

(C) Yes, because the tenant's assignment to the friend did not terminate the tenant's obligations.

(D) Yes, because the tenant had caused the problem by failing to include the tax payment provision in her assignment.

Question 5

A landowner owned a large parcel of land in a rural area. He built his home on the northern half of the property, and developed a large orchard of fruit trees on the southern portion. A county road ran in front of the northern portion. To service his orchard, the landowner built a driveway directly from the county road across the northern portion of the property to the orchard. To provide electricity to his house, the landowner ran an overhead power line across the orchard property to hook up to the only available electric power pole located on the far southern side of the property.

Subsequently, the landowner conveyed the northern parcel to his brother and the southern parcel to his daughter, who said that she did not mind having the power line on the property. Recently, the brother has begun parking his car on the driveway, thus blocking the daughter's access to the southern parcel. Finding no recorded document granting an easement for the power line, the daughter has decided to remove it.

If the brother is successful in preventing the daughter from removing the power line, it will be because:

(A) The daughter knew that the power line ran across the land when she accepted the deed from the landowner.

(B) The brother's alternative access to power is much less convenient and would cost 100 times as much.

(C) The daughter told the landowner that she did not mind having the power line on the property.

(D) The daughter is acting in retaliation against the brother for blocking the driveway, and not in any good faith belief that she has the right to remove the power line.

Question 6

A photographer borrowed $100,000 from a bank, secured by a mortgage on his home, to build a studio and darkroom in the home. The bank properly recorded the mortgage. After completing this project, the photographer decided to remodel his kitchen and borrowed $25,000 from a lending company, also securing the loan with a mortgage on his home. The lending company did not record its mortgage. After the remodeling was complete, the photographer borrowed $15,000 from an investor, secured by a mortgage on his home, to redo his in-ground pool. Learning of this transaction, the lending company raced to the recording office and recorded its mortgage. The next day, the investor recorded its mortgage.

A few months later, the photographer defaulted on all three mortgages, having not made any principal payments. The lending company brought a foreclosure action, joining the investor in the proceeding. The foreclosure sale resulted in $150,000 in proceeds after all expenses and fees were paid. A statute of the jurisdiction in which the photographer's home is located provides: "Any conveyance of an interest in land shall not be valid against any subsequent purchaser for value, without notice thereof, unless the conveyance is recorded."

Which of the following statements is true?

(A) The bank is entitled to $100,000 of the foreclosure proceeds, the lending company is entitled to $25,000 of the proceeds, the investor is entitled to $15,000 of the proceeds, and the buyer at the foreclosure sale is entitled to the remaining $10,000 in proceeds.

(B) The buyer at the foreclosure sale will take the home subject to the bank's mortgage, the lending company is entitled to $25,000 of the proceeds, the investor is entitled to $15,000 of the proceeds, and the photographer is entitled to the remaining $110,000 in proceeds.

(C) The buyer at the foreclosure sale will take the home subject to the bank's and the investor's mortgages, the lending company is entitled to $25,000 of the proceeds, and the photographer is entitled to the remaining $125,000 in proceeds.

(D) The buyer at the foreclosure sale will take the home subject to the bank's and the investor's mortgages, the lending company is entitled to $25,000 of the proceeds, and the buyer at the foreclosure sale is entitled to the remaining $125,000 in proceeds.

Question 7

A developer created an exclusive residential subdivision. In his deed to each lot, the following language appeared:

> Grantee agrees for himself and assigns to use this property solely as a single-family residence, to pay monthly fees as levied by the homeowners' association for upkeep and security guard services, and that the backyard of this property shall remain unfenced so that bicycle paths and walkways may run

through each backyard, as per the subdivision master plan [adequately described], for use by all residents of the subdivision.

The developer sold lots to an actuary, a baker, and a coroner. All deeds were recorded. The actuary in turn sold to an accountant by a deed that omitted any mention of the covenants above, and the accountant had no actual knowledge thereof. Shortly thereafter, the accountant started operating a tax preparation business out of his home. The baker in turn sold to a barber, who knew of, but refused to pay, the monthly fees levied by the homeowners' association. The coroner leased her property for 10 years to a chiropractor, who erected a fence around the backyard, unaware of the covenant against such fencing.

According to common law principles, which of the following statements is correct?

(A) If the developer, still owning unsold lots, sues the accountant to have him cease operating the tax preparation business, the accountant would win because there is no privity between the developer and the accountant.

(B) If the homeowners' association sues the barber to collect the monthly fees for upkeep and security guard services, the homeowners' association would win because the covenant regarding fees is enforceable in equity against the barber.

(C) If the barber sues the chiropractor to obtain removal of her backyard fence, the barber would win because the covenant regarding fencing is enforceable in equity against the chiropractor.

(D) If the chiropractor sues the accountant to have him cease operating the tax preparation business, the chiropractor would win because the covenant regarding single-family use is enforceable at law against the accountant.

Question 8

A landowner executed a will, devising a parcel of land "to my sister for life, then to my brother for life, then to my nieces and nephews." When the landowner died, he was survived by the sister and the brother's son. The sister and the brother's son contracted to sell the land to a buyer for $225,000. At the time set for closing, the sister and the brother's son tendered a quitclaim deed to the buyer, who refused to complete the sale. The sister and the brother's son bring suit against the buyer for specific performance. The jurisdiction in which the land is located does not follow the Doctrine of Worthier Title.

Specific performance will be:

(A) Granted, because a quitclaim deed conveys whatever interest the grantors have in the property.

(B) Granted, because the interests involved are freely alienable.

(C) Not granted, because the jurisdiction does not follow the Doctrine of Worthier Title.

(D) Not granted, because title is unmarketable.

Question 9

A landlord leased office space to a businessman for five years, ending on November 1, reserving a yearly rent of $24,000, payable monthly. On October 1 of the fifth year, the businessman notified the landlord that he was preparing to move, but would greatly appreciate if the landlord could extend the lease for a month or two. On October 10, the landlord wrote to the businessman that she thought they could reach a satisfactory arrangement, but did not hear back from the businessman. The businessman did not vacate the office until November 20. On November 30, the landlord received a check from the businessman in the amount of $1,333 for "November's rent" and a note that he had vacated the premises.

If the landlord brings an action against the businessman for additional rent, the court will rule that:

(A) The businessman is bound to a year-to-year tenancy, because he did not vacate the premises until November 20.

(B) The businessman is bound to a tenancy through December because one month's advance notice was required to terminate.

(C) The businessman is not bound, because the $1,333 check discharged him from his obligations.

(D) The businessman is not bound if the court admits parol evidence of the October 10 letter from the landlord.

Question 10

A merchant had a serious cash flow problem and needed cash to buy the inventory required to fill orders. A friend offered to loan the merchant $50,000 if he would put up adequate collateral to assure her that she would not lose her money. To guarantee the loan, the merchant gave the friend a deed to a property worth $100,000 that he had inherited. The friend recorded the deed. The friend gave the merchant $50,000, and the merchant signed a promissory note agreeing to repay the $50,000 within eight months. The merchant continued to occupy the property, and the friend agreed to reconvey the property to the merchant as soon as he repaid the $50,000. The merchant was unable to pay the friend when the note came due. He asked the friend for an extension, but she refused.

If the friend seeks to take possession of the property, may she do so?

(A) Yes, because she has clear record title.

(B) Yes, but only if she institutes foreclosure proceedings and is the successful purchaser at the foreclosure sale.

(C) No, because $50,000 does not reflect the fair market value of the property.

(D) No, the friend is limited to a contract claim against the merchant because the law does not recognize this type of security agreement.

Question 11

A man and a woman lived together for many years, but never married. The state in which they lived did not recognize common law marriages. One day, the man went with the woman to his bank and showed her a deed to a hotel he owned. The deed was properly executed and named the woman as grantee. The man handed the deed back to the banker, stating, "When I die you are to give the deed to her." The banker accepted the deed, and assured the woman that he would handle everything. A few months later, the man and the woman had a violent quarrel. The man prevailed on the banker to return the deed.

In a suit by the woman against the man to establish her claim to an interest in the hotel:

(A) The woman will win because the deed gave her a present right to possess the hotel.

(B) The woman will win because the facts show that the man intended her to have an interest in the hotel when he gave the deed to the banker.

(C) The man will win because there was no lawful consideration given for the deed and hence it was revocable.

(D) The man will win because the agreement with the banker did not satisfy the Statute of Frauds.

Question 12

A seller owned a large parcel of land. The western half was undeveloped, and the eastern half contained a grove of apple trees. The seller gave a buyer a deed conveying "the western half of the parcel from the western boundary to the grove of apple trees, comprising 220 acres." It was subsequently determined by survey that the land conveyed to the buyer was in fact 229 acres.

In a dispute between the seller and the buyer as to the mistake, which of the following is most accurate?

(A) The deed is invalid because of the mutual mistake of the parties.

(B) The deed is invalid unless the court admits parol evidence as to the amount of acreage conveyed.

(C) The deed is valid, and the buyer is the owner of 220 acres.

(D) The deed is valid, and the buyer is the owner of 229 acres.

Question 13

A landowner needed money. A neighbor agreed to loan him the money he needed if the landowner would give adequate security for the loan. The landowner made out a note payable to the neighbor and secured it with a first trust deed on his house, which the landowner owned free and clear of monetary encumbrances. The neighbor recorded the trust deed. Subsequently, the landowner sold his house to a buyer, who took the house subject to the mortgage. A few months later, the buyer needed money to build a swimming pool and borrowed it from a lender, securing the loan with a second trust deed on the house. This trust deed was recorded.

Several years later, the buyer got into financial trouble and was unable to make payments to either the neighbor or the lender on the notes they held. Both the neighbor and the lender commenced foreclosure proceedings. To protect his credit, the landowner paid the neighbor, and the neighbor assigned him the note and first trust deed. The landowner recorded the assignment of the trust deed.

Which of the following arguments offers the ***least*** support for the landowner's position that his interest has the first priority?

(A) The landowner is subrogated to the rights of the neighbor to the extent of the landowner's payment to the neighbor.

(B) The landowner, as assignee, may enforce the note and trust deed that were owned by the neighbor.

(C) If the landowner were denied a first priority, the buyer or the lender would be unjustly enriched.

(D) Even though the landowner was the maker of the note, the landowner's payment to the neighbor did not discharge the note.

Question 14

A father purchased a tract of land, financing a large part of the purchase price by a loan from a bank that was secured by a mortgage on the land. A provision in the mortgage agreement provided that a defaulting borrower waives his right to redeem once foreclosure proceedings have started. The bank properly recorded its mortgage. Several years later, the father needed money to send his twin daughters to college, so he obtained a loan from a credit union, also secured by a mortgage on the land. The credit union properly recorded its mortgage.

The following year, the father became ill and was unable to make payments to either the bank or the credit union due to his high medical bills. The balance on the loan from the bank was $75,000, and the balance on the credit union loan was $25,000. The bank instituted foreclosure proceedings in a jurisdiction that provides a statutory right of redemption. The day before the judicial sale, the father inherited $100,000 from his aunt. He quickly contacted the bank and offered to pay off both loans in full. The bank refused because it was hoping to buy the now valuable property at the judicial sale.

If the father seeks to force the bank to accept his offer, he will:

(A) Win, because the jurisdiction has a statutory right of redemption.

(B) Win, because equity requires a creditor to accept such an offer.

(C) Lose, because his agreement with the bank waived his right to redeem once foreclosure proceedings started.

(D) Lose, because he lost all of his rights in the property when he defaulted on the loan.

Question 15

An investor rented his property to a pottery maker, who intended to use the back part of the building for living quarters, and the front part as a pottery studio. The pottery maker installed a kiln, some lights, and some storage units in the front part of the building for her use. Sometime later, the investor mortgaged the property to a bank to secure a loan. The mortgage was recorded, but the investor did not personally tell the pottery maker that he had done so. In fact, she only learned of it when the investor defaulted on the loan and the bank foreclosed on the mortgage and told the pottery maker that she would have to quit the premises. The pottery maker began removing the equipment and fixtures that she had installed in the building. The bank objected and sought an injunction to prevent her from doing so.

Under these circumstances, the court should deny the bank the injunction because:

(A) There was no contrary provision in the agreement between the investor and the pottery maker, so the pottery maker is entitled to remove any personal property which belongs to her.

(B) The bank had no perfected security interest in the personal property belonging to the pottery maker.

(C) The equipment was installed for the pottery maker's exclusive benefit and she did not intend for it to stay.

(D) The investor had never given the pottery maker notice of the mortgage.

Question 16

The owner of a hotel in a resort town was approached by a seminar speaker who wanted to lease space in which to conduct a two-week seminar. The owner leased to the speaker the hotel's grand ballroom, the period of the lease being August 1 through August 14. To provide the proper atmosphere for the seminars, the speaker attached curtain rods to the walls of the ballroom, using lightweight screws to attach the rods. The speaker then strung light blue ring curtains through the rods. After the seminar, on August 16, the speaker arrived to remove the curtains and rods. The owner brought an action to enjoin the speaker from removing the curtains and the rods from the grand ballroom.

The court should rule:

(A) In favor of the speaker, because he had a short-term lease and the curtains and rods were easily removable.

(B) In favor of the speaker, because curtains and rods are trade fixtures.

(C) In favor of the owner, because the curtain rods were attached by screws, and as such were fixtures, which became part of the realty.

(D) In favor of the owner, because the speaker did not remove the curtains and rods before the lease expired.

Question 17

A landowner owned a tract of land, and his brother owned the adjoining property. The landowner drew up an instrument that stated:

> Upon my death, I wish the land to pass to my wife; but should she or her heirs ever attempt to sell the land, the right of first refusal is hereby granted to my brother, his heirs and assigns.

The brother drew up a similar instrument granting the landowner the same rights over the adjoining property. Both instruments were executed with all proper formalities.

The landowner died, and the wife enjoyed possession of the land. Subsequently, she offered to sell the land to a buyer for $200,000. The brother learned of this and demanded that he be allowed to exercise his option to purchase the land. The wife refused. The brother filed suit to compel the wife to sell him the land.

Assuming that the state in which the property is located strictly follows the common law Rule

Against Perpetuities and the common law rule against restraints on alienation, will the brother prevail?

(A) Yes, because his arrangement with the landowner was reciprocal.

(B) Yes, because he has the equivalent of a possibility of reverter in the land.

(C) No, because the right of first refusal violates the Rule Against Perpetuities.

(D) No, because a right of first refusal is an improper restraint on alienation.

Question 18

On December 1, a landlord rented an apartment to a tenant for one year, commencing January 1. The tenant paid the first and last month's rent. Both the landlord and the tenant realized that, at the time of the making of the lease, an occupant resided in the apartment with a lease on the premises until December 31. The occupant refused to leave the apartment on December 31, and the landlord served the appropriate legal notices to vacate the premises. The occupant still did not vacate the apartment, and the landlord was therefore forced to institute an unlawful detainer action against the occupant. The landlord was successful in the action and succeeded in getting the marshal to enforce the judgment and take possession of the apartment. The tenant received possession of the apartment on February 1. The lease between the landlord and the tenant contained the following statement: "The tenant, on payment of the monthly rent and compliance with all of the covenants and conditions stated herein, shall have the quiet enjoyment of the premises."

If the tenant now sues the landlord for damages resulting from the delay in the tenant's possession of the premises, which of the following would provide the tenant with the best argument?

(A) The landlord expressly promised the tenant that possession of the premises would be available on January 1.

(B) The landlord breached the covenant of quiet enjoyment stated in the lease by not delivering up possession of the premises to the tenant at the beginning of the term of the lease on January 1.

(C) The jurisdiction follows the majority view, and the landlord was required to deliver actual possession.

(D) The tenant took no part in the hold-over tenancy or the attempts to terminate the hold-over tenancy of the occupant.

REAL PROPERTY ANSWERS - SET 3

Answer to Question 1

(C) The bank's position will not be upheld because the buyer, a bona fide purchaser, recorded first. The applicable recording statute is a race-notice statute, under which a subsequent purchaser for value without notice of any prior conveyance is protected if she records before the prior grantee. Here, the bank, as mortgagee, is a grantee of an interest in the land prior to the buyer. However, the buyer purchased the land for valuable consideration and without notice (either actual, record, or inquiry) of the prior conveyance to the bank. The buyer recorded her conveyance on April 8, prior to the time the bank clerk filed on behalf of the bank. Consequently, the buyer satisfies the statutory requirements, and she is protected against the bank's claim. (A) is incorrect because, to prevail, the bank must have ***actually*** recorded prior to the buyer. It is of no significance that the bank acquired its interest in the property—even for value—prior to the date of the buyer's recordation. The bank is not protected by the recording statute because it recorded its interest after recordation by another bona fide purchaser. (B) is incorrect because, although a mortgage is a security interest for a loan, it is still an instrument creating an interest in land. As such, a mortgage comes within the scope of the recording acts, so that a grantee thereof must record in order to give notice of the conveyance to subsequent purchasers. Having failed to record in time, the bank will lose against a subsequent bona fide purchaser who records first. (D) is incorrect because whether the jurisdiction is a lien theory or a title theory state is irrelevant to this question. Under either theory, the bank's mortgage is an instrument creating an interest in land, and is thus subject to the recording statute.

Answer to Question 2

(D) The seller will likely prevail because she is entitled to clear the encumbrance with the proceeds of the sale. In a contract for the sale of real property, the seller of the land is entitled to use the proceeds of the sale to clear title if she can ensure that the purchaser will be protected. The seller's offer to escrow the funds in this case should act as such guarantee. Thus, (A) is incorrect. (B) is incorrect because, although there will be litigation over the contract dispute, the litigation will not affect the title to the land because the contractor is claiming only money damages and not an interest in the property. (C) is incorrect because the doctrine of equitable conversion is only applicable as against the seller and the buyer, and does not affect the right of some third party with regard to attaching property held in the name of a debtor.

Answer to Question 3

(B) The court will most likely find that the friend was still the owner of the house because he did not retransfer title to the woman. The deed, once delivered, merely evidences title to the property, and its destruction has no effect on the title. Thus, the friend was still the owner, and (C) is incorrect. (A) is incorrect because the woman cannot affect the ownership of the property after she delivered the deed to the friend, regardless of the truth or falsity of her subsequent reasons for the attempted revocation. (D) is incorrect because the son was not a bona fide purchaser: He was aware of the friend's deed. Also, it is only the ***subsequent*** bona fide purchaser, a purchaser for ***value*** and ***without notice***, who gets the protection of the recording act. The friend was the ***first*** grantee and, thus, his status as a donee would be irrelevant to the applicability of the recording act.

Answer to Question 4

(C) The landlord can sue the tenant for breach because the tenant's assignment to the friend did not terminate the tenant's obligations. An assignee is in privity of estate with the landlord and is

liable for all covenants that run with the land, including the covenant to pay rent. The original tenant (assignor) remains in privity of contract with the landlord and is liable for the rent reserved in the lease if the assignee abandons the property. Therefore, the tenant is liable to the landlord for the remaining rent. (A) is incorrect because the tenant's status as a tenant is immaterial. (B) is incorrect because, although the assignor's privity of estate with the landlord ends upon assignment, the assignor remains liable on the original contractual obligations. (D) is incorrect because the tenant's failure to include the tax payment provision in her assignment to the friend does not affect the tenant's liability as assignor under privity of contract.

Answer to Question 5

(B) If the brother is successful in preventing the daughter from removing the power lines, it will be because the brother's alternative access to power is much less convenient and would cost 100 times as much as the current arrangement. This helps to prove that there was an easement implied by operation of law ("quasi-easement"). An easement may be implied if, prior to the time the tract is divided, a use exists on the "servient part" that is reasonably necessary for the enjoyment of the "dominant part," and a court determines that the parties intended the use to continue after division of the property. To give rise to an easement, a use must be apparent and continuous at the time the tract is divided. In this case, the landowner used the servient part of his property (the southern parcel) to run an overhead power line to the dominant part of his property (the northern parcel). Overhead wires are clearly visible and would be readily discoverable on reasonable inspection. The lines are, therefore, apparent. The use must also be reasonably necessary. Whether a use is reasonably necessary depends on many factors, including the cost and difficulty of the alternatives. This use was reasonably necessary to the enjoyment of the dominant parcel because electricity is important to the enjoyment of the property, and the cost (100 times as much) and difficulty of the alternatives are excessive. Thus, the fact that the use of the southern parcel is reasonably necessary would bolster the brother's case. (A) is wrong because the daughter's actual knowledge is irrelevant. The daughter need not be aware of the use; it need only be shown that the use was apparent (*see* above). (C) is similarly wrong. Oral statements made to the grantor after the northern parcel had been conveyed have little effect. They show the daughter's knowledge, but as discussed above, that has little relevance with respect to an implied easement. (D) is wrong because the daughter's motive for removing the power line is also irrelevant. If no easement is established, the daughter may remove the lines for whatever reason she likes. If, however, the requirements for an implied easement are satisfied, the daughter may not remove the lines regardless of how good her reasons are.

Answer to Question 6

(C) The buyer at the foreclosure sale will take the home subject to the bank's and the investor's mortgages, the lending company is entitled to $25,000 of the proceeds, and the photographer is entitled to the remaining $125,000 in proceeds. When an interest is foreclosed, after the expenses and fees are paid, the proceeds of the sale are first used to pay the principal and accrued interest on the loan that was foreclosed, next to pay off any junior liens, and finally any remaining proceeds are distributed to the mortgagor. (A) is wrong because the bank's interest, an interest senior to the lending company's, is not affected by the foreclosure. As a senior interest, the bank was not a necessary party to the foreclosure action and did not need to be named in the foreclosure action. Thus, the bank is not entitled to a share of the proceeds, and its lien continues on the property in the buyer's hands. (B) is wrong because the investor's mortgage is also senior to the lending company's, and as a result, the buyer also takes subject to the investor's mortgage. Under a notice statute, which this jurisdiction has, a subsequent bona fide purchaser prevails over

a prior grantee who fails to record. The important fact under a notice statute is that the subsequent purchaser had no actual or constructive notice ***at the time of the conveyance (or mortgage)***, not at the time of recording. Mortgagees for value are treated as "purchasers." Here, when the mortgage on the property was granted to the investor, it had neither actual nor constructive notice of the mortgage given to the lending company. The fact that the lending company recorded its mortgage first is irrelevant. Thus, the investor was a bona fide purchaser and would be entitled to protection under the statute. (A) and (D) are wrong because the mortgagor (the photographer) rather than the buyer at the foreclosure sale is entitled to the surplus proceeds.

Answer to Question 7

(C) If the barber sues the chiropractor to remove her backyard fence, the barber would win because the covenant regarding fencing is enforceable against the chiropractor as an equitable servitude. An equitable servitude is a covenant that, regardless of whether it runs with the land at law, equity will enforce against the assignees of the burdened land who have notice of the covenant. The benefit of an equitable servitude runs to successors if: (i) the original parties so intended, and (ii) the servitude touches and concerns the land. The burden runs if (i) and (ii) are met ***and*** (iii) the subsequent purchaser has actual or constructive notice of the covenant. Privity of estate is not needed to enforce an equitable servitude because it is enforced not as an in personam right against the owner of the servient tenement, but as an equitable property interest in the land itself. Here, the original parties intended for the fencing covenant to be enforceable by and against assignees, as shown by the specific language of the covenant ("Grantee agrees for himself and assigns") and its purpose to provide bicycle paths and walkways running through each backyard for the use of all subdivision residents. The benefit of the covenant touches and concerns the barber's property because it increases his enjoyment thereof by providing him with such paths and walkways. Therefore, the barber is entitled to enforce the covenant. The burden of the covenant touches and concerns the land occupied by the chiropractor because it restricts the landholder in her use of the parcel (*i.e.*, her rights in connection with the enjoyment of the land are diminished by being unable to fence in the backyard). The chiropractor also has constructive notice of the restriction because all of the original deeds were recorded, and thus the restriction is in the chiropractor's chain of title. In addition, the chiropractor could be deemed to have inquiry notice of the restriction if the subdivision is sufficiently developed, does not have fences, and the bicycle paths and walkways running through each backyard are in place in accordance with a general plan for the subdivision. Moreover, any neighbor in a subdivision can enforce a covenant contained in a subdivision deed if a general plan existed at the time he purchased his lot. As has been noted, the maintenance of access to all backyards for use as bike paths and walkways was part of such a general plan. Finally, the fact that the chiropractor did not succeed to the coroner's entire estate, but rather a leasehold interest, is irrelevant because privity is not required to enforce an equitable servitude. Therefore, all of the requirements are in place for the existence of an equitable servitude, which can be enforced by the barber against the chiropractor. (A) is incorrect because there is privity between the developer and the accountant. There was horizontal privity between the original covenanting parties because, at the time the actuary entered into the covenant with the developer, they shared an interest in the land independent of the covenant (*i.e.*, they were in a grantor-grantee relationship). The accountant holds the entire interest held by the actuary at the time the actuary made the covenant; thus, there is vertical privity. (B) is incorrect because the remedy sought is the payment of money. Breach of a real covenant, which runs with the land at law, is remedied by an award of money damages, whereas breach of an equitable servitude is remedied by equitable relief, such as an injunction or specific performance. Because the homeowners' association seeks to obtain from the barber the payment of money, it is inaccurate to refer to this as a situation involving an equitable servitude. (D) is incorrect because, as

explained above, if equitable relief is sought, the covenant must be enforced as an equitable servitude rather than a real covenant.

Answer to Question 8

(D) The sister and the brother's son will not prevail in a suit against the buyer for specific performance because title is unmarketable. Marketable title is title reasonably free from doubt, *i.e.*, title that a reasonably prudent buyer would be willing to accept. Title may be unmarketable where the owners of the present and future interests attempt to convey a fee simple absolute title if the future interests are held by persons who are unborn or unascertainable. Here, the sister has a life estate, and the brother's son has a vested remainder subject to open because there may be other nieces and nephews born during the sister's life who become entitled to share in the remainder. Life estates and vested remainders are freely transferable, which means that the sister and the brother's son together can transfer the land to a purchaser, but the title is not marketable. It may turn out that the sister has a child, who is entitled to share in the remainder, but who did not join in the conveyance to the buyer. Because the child would not be bound by the conveyance, he would own an interest in the land. Thus, although the interests are considered alienable, the sister and the brother's son cannot convey good title because there are outstanding interests in the unborn nieces and nephews. (A) is incorrect because, although a quitclaim deed does convey whatever interest the grantors have in the property, it does not affect the warranty to provide marketable title. (B) is incorrect because, although the interests involved are transferable (as explained above), the interests of the unborn nieces and nephews are not represented in the conveyance. While most courts will appoint a guardian ad litem to represent unborn persons in litigation, such an appointment will not be made for purposes of conveying land. (C) is incorrect because the Doctrine of Worthier Title is inapplicable here. The doctrine invalidates remainders that are limited to the grantor's "heirs." Here, the remainder is in the grantor's nieces and nephews.

Answer to Question 9

(A) The court will rule that the businessman is bound to a year-to-year tenancy because he is a hold-over tenant. When a tenant fails to vacate the premises after the termination of his right to possession, the landlord may: (i) treat the hold-over tenant as a trespasser and evict him; or (ii) bind the tenant to a new periodic tenancy. The terms and conditions of the expired tenancy apply to the new tenancy. At least in commercial leases, the new tenancy will be year-to-year if the original lease term was for one year or more. Here, the businessman was a tenant for years because his lease was for a five-year fixed period of time. A tenancy for years ends automatically on its termination date. Therefore, as of November 1, the businessman became a hold-over tenant and the landlord had a right to bind him to a new periodic tenancy. Because the original lease was for more than one year, the businessman may be held to a year-to-year tenancy, at the stipulated rent of $24,000 per year. (B) is incorrect because even though the rent is payable monthly, the majority view is that reservation of an annual rent results in a year-to-year periodic tenancy. Hence, his notice of termination on November 30 would not take effect until the end of the new tenancy. (C) is incorrect because the businessman's mere continuance in possession after November 1 gave the landlord the right to bind him to another year's term. This right was not affected by the fact that the businessman paid 20 days' worth of rent. Moreover, although a tenancy for years may terminate on surrender, surrender requires the landlord's acceptance, which is not evident here. (D) is incorrect because even if the court admits the October 10 letter, it merely indicates the landlord's willingness to consider an extension. Because the businessman did not respond and no agreement was reached by the parties, the letter is not enough to allow the businessman to avoid the additional tenancy.

Answer to Question 10

(B) The friend may take possession of the property only if she institutes foreclosure proceedings and is the successful purchaser at the foreclosure sale. The friend must institute foreclosure proceedings because the deed is, in reality, an equitable mortgage. A landowner needing to raise money may "sell" the land to a person who pays cash and may give the lender an absolute deed rather than a mortgage. However, if a court concludes that the deed was really given for security purposes, it will treat it as an equitable mortgage and require that the creditor foreclose it by judicial action, like any other mortgage. The following factors indicate an equitable mortgage: (i) the existence of a debt or promise of payment by the deed's grantor; (ii) the grantee's promise to return the land if the debt is paid; (iii) the fact that the amount advanced to the grantor/debtor was much lower than the value of the property; (iv) the degree of the grantor's financial distress; and (v) the parties' prior negotiations. Here, the merchant has agreed by his promissory note to repay the friend the amount she purportedly paid to purchase the property, and the friend has promised to return the property upon repayment. The sum of money given by the friend to the merchant is only one-half of the value of the property. In addition, the merchant was in fairly serious financial condition at the time of his dealings with the friend. Finally, the discussions between the merchant and the friend prior to the exchange of money and the deed indicate quite clearly that the parties intended that the property serve as security for the friend's loan to the merchant. These facts give rise to the conclusion that the deed, absolute on its face, is really an equitable mortgage, thus requiring the friend to foreclose it by judicial action. At a foreclosure sale, the highest bidder takes the property. Therefore, to take possession of the property, the friend must not only institute foreclosure proceedings but also be the successful bidder at the sale. (A) is incorrect because, pursuant to the foregoing analysis, the deed given to the friend will not be dealt with by the court as an absolute deed conveying title, but rather as an equitable mortgage giving the friend a security interest in the property. Consequently, the friend does not have clear record title. (C) is incorrect because, while the fact that the friend gave the merchant a sum of money lower than the market value of the property will be considered as one of several factors indicating that this is an equitable mortgage situation, it will not, by itself, preclude the friend's taking possession of the property. If this were a situation involving a true absolute conveyance of the property, the conveyance would not be set aside simply because the purchase price is less than the market value. No consideration is necessary for a valid deed. (D) is incorrect because, as discussed above, the court will treat this as an equitable mortgage.

Answer to Question 11

(B) The woman will win because the facts show that the man intended her to have an interest in the hotel when he gave the deed to the banker. To effectively transfer an interest in realty, a deed must be delivered. There is a delivery when there are words or conduct evidencing the grantor's intention that the deed have some present operative effect—*i.e.*, that title pass immediately and irrevocably, even though the right of possession may be postponed until the future. A conditional delivery becomes effective only upon the occurrence of a condition, but the transfer then relates back to the date of the conditional delivery. When the grantor gives the deed to a third party (rather than directly to the grantee), conditional delivery is permissible. If the grantor executes a deed to the grantee and gives it to a third party with instructions to give it to the grantee upon the grantor's death, most courts hold that the grantor cannot get the deed back because his intent was to presently convey a future interest to the grantee (either a remainder with a life estate reserved in the grantor, or an executory limitation). Here, the facts indicate the man intended that the deed have the effect of immediately conveying to the woman a future interest in the hotel (although the woman's taking of possession of the hotel and of the deed itself were to be postponed until

the man's death). Consequently, the delivery is irrevocable and the man is precluded from taking back the deed. (A) is incorrect because the facts actually indicate that the man had no intention of transferring to the woman a present possessory right in the hotel. The entire purpose of the man's words and conduct was to convey some immediate right in the hotel, but to postpone the actual right of possession until the future (*i.e.*, upon the man's death). Thus, the woman will prevail in establishing an interest in the hotel, not because she is entitled to presently possess the hotel, but because she was given a future interest in the property. (C) is incorrect because the revocability of this deed is not affected by the fact that no consideration was given. Consideration is not required to render a deed valid, nor is consideration required to render the delivery of a deed irrevocable. (D) is incorrect because instructions to a person acting as custodian for the donee (in this case, the banker) can be oral. Even though a deed is unconditional, the general rule is that parol evidence is admissible to show the conditions and terms on which a deed was deposited with a third party.

Answer to Question 12

(D) The deed is valid and the buyer owns 229 acres. When there is a mistake or inconsistency in the description of property in the deed, one of the rules of construction is that the physical description takes precedence over the quantity description unless there are grounds for reformation of the deed. Reformation is an equitable action in which the court rewrites the deed to make it conform to the intention of the parties. It is granted when the deed does not express the agreement of the parties due to mutual mistake or a scrivener's error, and may also be granted when there is a unilateral mistake if misrepresentation is involved. Here, the facts indicate that the seller and the buyer were bargaining for a specific physical location ("the western half of the parcel from the western boundary to the grove of apple trees") and not for a specific number of acres. Thus, there appear to be no grounds for reformation. A conflict in description does not invalidate a deed, so (A) and (B) are incorrect. While parol evidence may be admissible to ascertain the parties' intent, the absence of parol evidence will not invalidate the deed as long as rules of construction may be applied to resolve any inconsistency. (C) is incorrect because, as discussed above, physical descriptions prevail over quantity.

Answer to Question 13

(D) The least support for the landowner's position that his interest has the first priority is the argument that his payment to the neighbor did not discharge the note. The note is considered to embody the security obligations, and payment of the note by the maker discharges the note. The best way to get the correct answer is to use a process of elimination. (A) is wrong because it supports the landowner's position: The purchaser of a note and trust deed is subrogated to (*i.e.*, takes over) the interest of the seller, thus giving the landowner the neighbor's priority. (B) is wrong because it is saying essentially the same thing as (A). (C) is wrong because it is the policy reason behind the rules stated in (A) and (B). Thus, (A), (B), and (C) are wrong because they do offer support for the landowner's priority position, while the argument in (D) would not support the landowner's position.

Answer to Question 14

(B) The father will win because he is exercising his equity of redemption rights. The equity of redemption gives the borrower the right to free the land of the mortgage by paying off the amount due, plus any accrued interest, at any time ***prior to*** the foreclosure sale. If the borrower has defaulted on a mortgage, he must pay the full balance in order to redeem. Here, the father's offer to pay both the bank's and the credit union's loans is adequate to redeem the land. (A) is incorrect because a statutory right of redemption, recognized in about half the states, gives the borrower a right to redeem for the foreclosure price ***after*** the foreclosure sale. (C) is incorrect because this right to redeem cannot be waived in the agreement establishing the security interest. This would be "clogging the equity of redemption." However, the right can be waived later for consideration. (D) is similarly incorrect because a defaulting debtor does not lose the equity of redemption.

Answer to Question 15

(C) The court should deny the bank the injunction because the pottery maker did not intend for the equipment to stay. Because the pottery maker installed the equipment without any intention to benefit her landlord (the investor), she is entitled to remove it when the lease terminates, provided that she repairs any damage such removal may cause. (A) is incorrect because personal property attached to real property may become a fixture (and thus a part of the realty, not to be removed) if the one who attached it intended that it become part of the real property. It is presumed that chattels used in a trade or business are not intended to be fixtures and, thus, may be removed. (B) is incorrect in that, but for the fixtures being trade fixtures, they would have been considered part of the real property and subject to the bank's mortgage. (D) is immaterial because notice to the tenant is not necessary. The mortgagee stands in the same position as the landlord-mortgagor, so the issue involved in this case could arise without there being a mortgage at all.

Answer to Question 16

(D) The court should rule in the owner's favor. A tenant must remove annexed chattels before the termination of the tenancy or they become the property of the landlord. Although the seminar speaker was probably entitled to remove the curtains and rods at the end of the lease, he forfeited them by waiting for two days after the lease expired to remove them. (A) is wrong because it goes to whether the curtains and rods were intended to be fixtures. Because of the delay in their removal, whether the curtains or rods were fixtures is irrelevant. This choice would be correct, however, had the speaker attempted to remove the curtains on August 14. The short-term lease and the fact that the rods are easily removable constitute evidence that the speaker lacked the requisite intent to permanently improve the property, and thus he could have removed them if he had acted promptly. (B) is wrong for the same reason. The delay in the removal of the items results in their becoming the property of the landlord regardless of whether they are trade fixtures. Trade fixtures (*i.e.*, fixtures installed for the purpose of carrying on a trade or business) are removable prior to the end of the lease term. Thus, because the speaker installed the curtains to carry on his business, this would have been a correct choice had the speaker attempted to remove the curtains prior to the end of his lease term. (C) is wrong because the mere fact that the curtain rods were attached by screws does not make them fixtures that must remain with the realty. "Fixtures" are chattels affixed to the land that become part of the land. The intent of the person affixing the chattel is relevant. The curtains and rods would probably not be considered fixtures because the speaker did not have the requisite intent to permanently improve the property, as evidenced by the short-term lease and the easily removable nature of the attached chattels. In the absence of an express agreement to the contrary, if removal of the chattel does not cause substantial damage to the premises or destruction of the chattel, the tenant has not manifested an intention to permanently improve the property. Here, removing the screws, rods, and curtains would not result in substantial damage to the premises or destruction of the chattels. Also, even if the curtains and rods were found to be fixtures, they would be trade fixtures, which are removable by the tenant.

Answer to Question 17

(C) The brother will not prevail because the right of first refusal created in the instrument executed by the landowner violates the Rule Against Perpetuities. Under the common law Rule Against Perpetuities, no interest in property is valid unless it must vest, if at all, within 21 years after a life in being at the time the interest is created. Because a right of first refusal is specifically enforceable, it is considered an equitable interest in property. As such, rights of first refusal are subject to the Rule Against Perpetuities. Thus, if the right may be exercised beyond the perpetuities period, it is void. In this case, the right of first refusal extends to the brother's heirs and assigns. These heirs and assigns could exercise the right well after the perpetuities period of a life in being plus 21 years. Therefore, the brother's right is void. (A) is wrong because it suggests that the reciprocity of the arrangement resulted in an enforceable contract. Even if the instrument was a contract, it is not enforceable because it creates an interest in land that violates the Rule Against Perpetuities. (B) is wrong because the brother's interest is nothing like a possibility of reverter aside from the fact that his interest and a possibility of reverter are both future interests. A possibility of reverter is the reversionary interest left in the grantor after he conveys a fee simple determinable. The brother is not a grantor, and his interest is not one retained upon the granting of a lesser estate. The most important difference between a possibility of reverter and a right of first refusal, however, is that a possibility of reverter is vested and not subject to the Rule Against Perpetuities, while a right of first refusal is subject to the Rule. (D) is wrong because rights of first refusal are generally excepted from the application of the common law rule against restraints on alienation, which prohibits any restriction on the transferability of property.

Answer to Question 18

(C) Under the majority view, the landlord has a duty to deliver actual possession of the premises to the tenant. One of the tenant's remedies for a breach of this duty is to continue the lease and recover damages that accrue until the landlord delivers possession. (A) is incorrect because it misstates the facts. (B) is incorrect because the right of quiet enjoyment is interfered with when a tenant is actually evicted by the landlord or someone with paramount title, or is constructively evicted by acts of the landlord or those claiming under her. Here, the tenant's possession is being interfered with by the occupant, who is not the landlord or one claiming under her (because his tenancy has terminated) and who does not have paramount title. Thus, the covenant was not breached by the landlord. (D) is incorrect because under either the majority view or the minority view, in which the landlord does not have the obligation to put the tenant in actual possession, the tenant's inactivity in the unlawful detainer action is irrelevant to the issue of liability.

Set 4 Answer Sheet

1. Ⓐ Ⓑ Ⓒ Ⓓ
2. Ⓐ Ⓑ Ⓒ Ⓓ
3. Ⓐ Ⓑ Ⓒ Ⓓ
4. Ⓐ Ⓑ Ⓒ Ⓓ
5. Ⓐ Ⓑ Ⓒ Ⓓ
6. Ⓐ Ⓑ Ⓒ Ⓓ
7. Ⓐ Ⓑ Ⓒ Ⓓ
8. Ⓐ Ⓑ Ⓒ Ⓓ
9. Ⓐ Ⓑ Ⓒ Ⓓ
10. Ⓐ Ⓑ Ⓒ Ⓓ
11. Ⓐ Ⓑ Ⓒ Ⓓ
12. Ⓐ Ⓑ Ⓒ Ⓓ
13. Ⓐ Ⓑ Ⓒ Ⓓ
14. Ⓐ Ⓑ Ⓒ Ⓓ
15. Ⓐ Ⓑ Ⓒ Ⓓ
16. Ⓐ Ⓑ Ⓒ Ⓓ
17. Ⓐ Ⓑ Ⓒ Ⓓ
18. Ⓐ Ⓑ Ⓒ Ⓓ

REAL PROPERTY QUESTIONS - SET 4

Question 1

A developer owned a large parcel of land, which she subdivided into 25 separate lots. The developer sold lots 1 - 24, retaining lot 25 for herself to live on. The deeds for each of the 24 lots sold by the developer restricted the use of the land to residential purposes only. The purchasers of lots 1 - 24 each built residences on their property. The developer lived on lot 25 in the subdivision until her death, when it was sold without any restrictions to a buyer. Several years ago, the buyer sold lot 25 to a merchant, without any restrictions. Last month, the merchant decided to build a convenience store on lot 25. An adjoining owner in the subdivision informed the merchant of the restriction and told him that he would be unable to build the convenience store.

If the restriction to use the land for residential purposes only is held to apply to lot 25, it will be because the restriction is:

(A) An equitable servitude.

(B) A covenant running with the land.

(C) A reciprocal negative servitude.

(D) Part of a general plan.

Question 2

A landowner deeded her real property to her neighbor "for so long as the property is used for residential purposes, but if the property ceases to be used for residential purposes, it is to go to the American Cancer Society." A year later, the landowner died. Her will left all of her property, including real property, to her friend. The landowner's only heir is her son, whom she purposely excluded from her will. The next year, the neighbor began operating a business on the property.

State probate laws provide that future interests or estates in real property may be passed by will or descent in the same manner as present or possessory interests.

Who owns the property?

(A) The neighbor.

(B) The American Cancer Society.

(C) The friend.

(D) The son.

Question 3

An uncle executed a warranty deed granting a parcel of land to his nephew. The uncle placed the deed in his bedroom closet and told his friend to get the deed and give it to the nephew if the nephew survived the uncle. Several years later, the uncle conveyed the land by quitclaim deed to a purchaser for $20,000. The uncle told the purchaser about the earlier deed to the nephew, and he told the purchaser that he planned to tear it up, but the uncle never did so. The purchaser properly recorded her deed.

The uncle died the following year, leaving the nephew as his sole surviving heir. The friend thereupon delivered the uncle's deed to the nephew, which was the first time the nephew knew of the deed. A statute of the jurisdiction in which the land is located provides: "No conveyance or mortgage of real property shall be good against subsequent purchasers for value and without notice whose conveyance is first recorded according to law."

The deed from the uncle to the purchaser was:

(A) Effective as a conveyance of title when delivered.

(B) Effective on recordation, to cut off the nephew's interest in the property.

(C) Ineffective as against the nephew, because the purchaser knew of the deed from the uncle to the nephew when she became a grantee.

(D) Ineffective as against the nephew, because the purchaser took by quitclaim deed and thus stands in the shoes of the uncle.

Question 4

A landowner and his neighbor owned adjoining properties. The landowner erected an oddly shaped building in the northeast corner of his property and opened a private detective agency. The building cost the landowner $20,000 to build, but due to its unusual design did not really enhance the value of the property at all. Four years and only one client later, the landowner decided to retire from the detective business and tear down the building. As he raised the sledge hammer to the building, the neighbor ran out of her home exclaiming that the building was on her property and it was hers.

Assuming that the building is on the neighbor's property, as between the parties:

(A) The neighbor is entitled to retain the building and can also recover the reasonable rental value for the landowner's use and possession of the property.

(B) The neighbor is entitled to retain the building, but must reimburse the landowner for the $20,000 it cost him to build it.

(C) The landowner is entitled to remove the building.

(D) The landowner is entitled to a lien on the neighbor's property for $20,000, less the fair rental value of the landowner's use and possession of the property.

Question 5

A man and a woman lived together for many years but never got married. Although the state in which they reside does not recognize common law marriage, it has statutes that prohibit discrimination on the basis of marital status. The man and the woman purchased a large property, taking title as joint tenants. Subsequently, the woman accumulated a $20,000 debt. She was too embarrassed to tell the man but was able to convince a bank to hold a mortgage on the property in exchange for the money. The bank was also willing to accept the woman's signature alone, and the man never learned about the mortgage. Two years later, the woman died without having paid off the mortgage. She left no will, and her only heir at law is her sister. The state in which the property is located is a "lien theory" mortgage state.

Who has title to the property?

(A) The man.

(B) The man and the bank.

(C) The man and the sister.

(D) The man, the sister, and the bank.

Question 6

A landowner granted to his adjoining neighbor an easement in a driveway that crosses the southwest corner of the landowner's property. The easement was not recorded. A statute of the jurisdiction in which the landowner's and neighbor's properties are located provides: "No unrecorded interest in real property shall be good against subsequent purchasers for value without notice unless the conveyance is recorded."

In which of the following cases has the neighbor's easement been terminated?

(A) The neighbor constructs her own driveway and ceases to use the one across the landowner's property.

(B) The landowner sells his property to a purchaser for value who is unaware of the easement.

(C) The neighbor begins to hold pottery classes in her home, resulting in increased traffic over the driveway.

(D) The neighbor tells the landowner that she will no longer be using the driveway, and the landowner thereafter builds a garage over the driveway.

Question 7

On February 10, an owner took out a $10,000 mortgage on her land with a bank. On February 15, the owner conveyed the land for $50,000 to a buyer who was not aware of the mortgage. On February 17, the bank recorded its mortgage interest in the land. On February 21, the buyer recorded his deed to the land.

Does the buyer hold the land subject to the bank's mortgage?

(A) Yes, in a race-notice jurisdiction.

(B) Yes, regardless of the type of recording statute.

(C) No, in a race-notice jurisdiction.

(D) No, because the buyer was a bona fide purchaser for value who bought the land before the bank recorded its mortgage.

Question 8

A wealthy philanthropist owned a mansion built to his exact specifications, featuring a pipe organ built into the wall of the music room. The organ was impressive, with beautiful hand-carved wood scrollwork. The accompanying bench was made from the same wood as the organ and was carved to match the patterns on the organ. The bench was fully movable and could be slid into a niche beside the organ when not in use, although the philanthropist usually left the bench in front of the organ for its matching effect, even when the organ was not being played.

The philanthropist died, and his will left all of his personal property to his daughter and all of his real property to a local charity. After the will was admitted to probate, the daughter removed all of the furniture and other movables from the mansion, including the organ bench. The daughter refused the charity's request to return the bench to the mansion.

If the charity brings suit against the daughter to replevy the bench, the court will rule in favor of:

(A) The daughter, because the bench is personalty since it was not bolted to the floor.

(B) The daughter, because removing the bench does not damage the real property.

(C) The charity, because the bench is integrally connected to the organ.

(D) The charity, because removal of the bench reduces the value of the devise to the charity.

Question 9

A seller with a very leaky roof was told that she would need it replaced before she could sell the home. Instead, the seller painted the shingles that could be seen from the street to make them appear new, and covered the watermarks on the interior. A buyer entered into a written contract with the seller that included a clause making the buyer's obligation to tender the purchase price at the closing date "subject to approval by an inspector of the buyer's choosing." Prior to closing, the buyer inspected the property with his friend, a local tradesman with a good reputation. Neither the buyer nor the friend climbed onto the roof, but the friend mentioned that the roof looked fairly new. The friend also looked for signs of water damage to the ceilings and walls on the interior, but found none. At closing, the seller conveyed the property to the buyer by warranty deed. Three months after the buyer moved into the home, a major rainstorm occurred. The roof leaked like a sieve and much of the buyer's personal property was damaged. The buyer replaced the roof at a cost of $8,000. The buyer's homeowner's insurance covered the cost of the water damage to his floors and personal property, but would not reimburse his expenses incurred in installing the new roof, which the insurance carrier deemed "normal maintenance and repair."

If the buyer sues the seller for the $8,000 cost of installing a new roof, the court is likely to rule in favor of:

(A) The buyer, because the seller breached an implied warranty that the house was fit for the purpose intended.

(B) The buyer, because the seller concealed the defects in the roof from the buyer.

(C) The seller, because the buyer had an ample opportunity to inspect the property before tendering the purchase price, and the seller had no duty to disclose defects to him.

(D) The seller, because the property conveyed to the buyer was not a new house constructed by the seller.

Question 10

A developer subdivided his rural parcel of land into 10 lots and rented them out to tenants. To supply the domestic needs of all 10 homes, the developer drilled a well on the land. The well provided an adequate water supply and none of the tenants ever had reason to complain of water shortages. Subsequently, the owner of property adjacent to the developer built a home on her property, drilling a well to supply her water needs. Although all of the owner's water usage was domestic, she drew a large quantity of water from her well. Six months later, the well on the developer's land ceased producing enough water to adequately supply his tenants. Both wells draw percolating water.

If the developer sues the owner, asking that the court enjoin her from interfering with the developer's supply, what is the court likely to order the owner to do?

(A) Cut back her water use sufficiently so that the developer's tenants can be adequately supplied.

(B) Pay money damages to the developer.

(C) Transfer water from the owner's well to the developer's property.

(D) Nothing.

Question 11

A grandfather conveyed a parcel of land "to my granddaughter and her heirs, but should my granddaughter or her successors attempt to convey the property, then to my grandson and his heirs."

During his lifetime, the grandson's interest in the property is best described as:

(A) An executory interest.

(B) A contingent remainder.

(C) A vested remainder.

(D) No interest.

Question 12

The respective deeds of a farm and a ranch established the boundary between them as "a line drawn along the middle of the river." Over time, the river changed its course so that 10 acres of land that was formerly on the farm's side of the river are now on the ranch's side.

Who owns the 10 acres?

(A) The owner of the ranch, because accretion belongs to the riparian owner.

(B) The owner of the ranch, if the requirements for adverse possession of the 10 acres have been satisfied.

(C) The owner of the farm, because accretion does not change property rights.

(D) The owner of the farm, because avulsion does not change property rights.

Question 13

A mother conveyed her real property "to my friend for life, then to the heirs of my son." At the time of the conveyance, the son had not yet married and had no children. Subsequently, the friend died. At the time of her death, the mother was still living, and the son was still unmarried and childless.

At the friend's death, who is entitled to possession of the property?

(A) The son.

(B) The mother.

(C) The friend's heirs.

(D) The son's heirs.

Question 14

A father drew up a deed conveying his land to his son. The father never recorded the deed and left it in the top drawer of his desk in his study. Two years later, the father died. He left a will, which declared that all of his property be divided equally between the son and the father's daughter.

While going through his father's personal effects, the son discovered the deed to the land. He showed the deed to his sister and the two of them agreed not to record the deed. The son put the deed in a desk drawer in his home. A year later, the son died. As the executor perused the son's personal papers, he came across the deed and promptly recorded it. He then entered into a contract to sell the land to a buyer. The daughter discovered this and promptly filed suit, claiming an interest in the land. A statute of the jurisdiction provides: "No conveyance is good against a subsequent purchaser for value, without notice, who first records."

The court will rule:

(A) In favor of the daughter, because there was no proper delivery of the deed to the land.

(B) In favor of the daughter, because the executor violated his fiduciary duty when he recorded.

(C) Against the daughter, because the executor and the buyer are protected by the recording act.

(D) Against the daughter, because she is not a bona fide purchaser.

Question 15

An owner purchased a home in a new subdivision, paying 20% of the purchase price as a down payment and financing the rest of her purchase through a mortgage with a lender. The owner lived in her home for three years and always made her mortgage payments promptly. She then decided to put her house on the market. While the house was being marketed, the owner continued to make all mortgage payments promptly. She sold the house to a buyer, who purchased the property subject to the mortgage. After the buyer took possession, the lender received no further mortgage payments from either the owner or the buyer.

In most states, which of the following best describes the remedy or remedies available to the lender?

(A) The lender may foreclose on the land, but may not sue either the owner or the buyer on the underlying debt.

(B) The lender may foreclose on the land or it may sue the owner on the underlying debt.

(C) The lender may foreclose on the land or it may sue the buyer on the underlying debt.

(D) The lender may foreclose on the land or it may elect to sue either the owner or the buyer on the underlying debt.

Question 16

A landlord leased an office building to a tenant for 10 years. The tenant, a second-year law student, was familiar with the state's recording act, which provided:

> No conveyance is valid against any subsequent purchaser for value without notice unless the conveyance is recorded. No lease for three years or more is valid against a subsequent purchaser for value without notice unless the lease has been recorded.

Believing it would be obvious to any prospective purchaser that the tenant was in possession of the property, she failed to record the lease.

Shortly thereafter, the landlord entered into a contract to sell the leased property to a buyer.

Before purchasing the property, the buyer merely drove by it, and thus did not notice the tenant's occupancy. The standard title search did not reveal the lease because it was unrecorded. The buyer tendered the purchase money to the landlord, and the landlord conveyed to the buyer the property by warranty deed. The buyer subsequently found the tenant in possession of the premises and ordered her to vacate. The tenant refused and asked the buyer where she should send the rent checks.

In an action by the buyer to evict the tenant, the court should rule that:

(A) The tenant wins, because the buyer's drive-by inspection will be deemed to confer actual notice on him.

(B) The tenant wins, because the buyer had a duty to properly inspect the property.

(C) The buyer wins, because the buyer is a subsequent purchaser for value and the tenant failed to record.

(D) The buyer wins, because the tenant knew of the statute and willfully failed to record.

Question 17

A landowner owned a large piece of property containing an inn and a bakery. She entered into a contract to sell the property to a purchaser for $1 million. The contract was recorded. The purchaser gave the landowner $200,000 as earnest money. The closing date was set for September 10, two months after the signing of the contract.

On August 10, an arsonist set fire to the inn, which burned to the ground. On September 10, the landowner appeared at the closing and tendered the deed to the property. The buyer refused to tender the remaining $800,000 of the purchase price and demanded the return of his earnest money. The landowner sued the buyer for specific performance of the contract. The buyer countersued for the return of his earnest money. Both parties stipulate that the value of the property without the inn is $600,000.

At trial, the landowner will most likely:

(A) Not prevail on the issue of specific performance, but will be allowed to keep the earnest money.

(B) Not prevail on the issue of specific performance and will be ordered to return the earnest money.

(C) Prevail on the issue of specific performance, but the price will be abated to $600,000.

(D) Prevail on the issue of specific performance for the full contract price.

Question 18

A farmer owned a 70-acre farm on the outskirts of a rapidly growing town. She conveyed the farm to a developer by a deed that contained no restrictions. The developer divided the property into two tracts, a 40-acre parcel and a 30-acre parcel. He then subdivided the 40-acre parcel into 80 half-acre lots and put them on the market. Under the town's liberal land-use provisions, there was no zoning code limitation on the use of either parcel, nor was the developer required to file a plat map with local officials. However, the deed that each purchaser of a half-acre lot received contained a clause restricting the use of the lot to "no more than one single-family dwelling and one garage." In addition, the developer gave every prospective purchaser a brochure depicting the 80-lot subdivision on its completion, with a drawing of a house on each lot. The lots sold briskly and soon a number of homes were constructed thereon.

Two years later, an original owner of one of the lots sold his home to a buyer. The buyer's deed did not contain the restrictive covenant. Soon after, when the last subdivision lot was sold, the developer sold the adjacent 30-acre parcel to a car dealer by a deed that contained no restrictions as to the use of the parcel. Two weeks after the buyer moved into her home, the car dealer began building an auto mall on his parcel. The buyer was angry that the busy mall was to be right next door to her home. She filed suit against the car dealer to enjoin his construction of the auto mall.

Which of the following is the best argument in the car dealer's defense?

(A) The developer did not expressly promise in writing that he would restrict the remaining lots when he conveyed the lot to the owner.

(B) The buyer and the car dealer are not in each other's chain of title.

(C) The buyer's deed contained no restrictive covenant.

(D) The 30-acre parcel was not part of a common scheme of development.

REAL PROPERTY ANSWERS - SET 4

Answer to Question 1

(C) If the restriction applies to lot 25, it will be because the restriction is a reciprocal negative servitude. When a developer subdivides land into several parcels and some of the deeds contain negative covenants, but some do not, negative covenants or equitable servitudes, binding all of the parcels in the subdivision, may be implied under the doctrine of reciprocal negative servitudes. To enforce a reciprocal negative servitude, the court will need to find: (i) a common scheme for development, and (ii) notice of the covenants. A common scheme may be evidenced by a general pattern of prior restrictions. Notice may be actual (*i.e.*, direct knowledge of covenants in prior deeds), inquiry (*i.e.*, neighborhood appears to conform to common restrictions), or record (*i.e.*, prior deeds containing covenants are in grantee's chain of title). Here, although there were no restrictions on lot 25, all of the other parcels were subject to a negative covenant limiting their use to residential purposes only. Thus, a court would likely determine that all parcels in the subdivision were developed according to a common scheme. It does not appear that the merchant had actual notice of the restriction or that it was in his chain of title; however, the merchant will be deemed to have inquiry notice of the restriction because of the uniform residential character of the other lots in the subdivision. Thus, the restriction may be enforced as a reciprocal negative servitude. (A) is incorrect because it is not as complete an answer as (C). Reciprocal negative servitudes are equitable servitudes implied from a common scheme. (B) is incorrect because the remedy sought here is an injunction (*i.e.*, prohibiting the merchant from building a convenience store), and a breach of a real covenant is remedied by an award of damages, not an injunction. (D) is incorrect because it is incomplete. In order to enjoin the merchant from building the convenience store there must not only be a general plan, but he must have had notice of the restriction.

Answer to Question 2

(C) The friend owns the property. The executory interest in the American Cancer Society is void under the Rule Against Perpetuities because it might vest beyond lives in being plus 21 years; the charity-to-charity exception to the Rule Against Perpetuities does not apply because the neighbor is not a charitable organization. Therefore, (B) is wrong because the void interest is struck, leaving the landowner with a possibility of reverter, which need not be expressly retained in the conveyance. Because all future interests are devisable under the state statute, the landowner's interest passed to the friend on the landowner's death. On the happening of the stated event, *i.e.*, when the neighbor ceased to use the property for residential purposes, the friend's interest became possessory. Thus, (A) is wrong. (D) is wrong because the landowner's interest passed through her will, which did not include her son.

Answer to Question 3

(A) The purchaser's deed was effective to convey title from the uncle to the purchaser immediately on delivery. A quitclaim deed transfers whatever right, title, or interest in the property the grantor has. Thus, when the purchaser took by quitclaim deed, she acquired the uncle's interest in the land. Because the deed from the uncle to the nephew was never validly delivered, the conveyance is ineffective and the uncle was the sole owner of the property. If a grantor executes a deed but fails to deliver it during his lifetime, no conveyance of title has occurred. "Delivery" refers to the grantor's intent; it is satisfied by words or conduct showing that the grantor intended that the deed have a present operative effect—*i.e.*, that title pass immediately and irrevocably, even though the right of possessing the land may be postponed until some future time. To make an

effective delivery, the grantor must relinquish control. Here, the uncle clearly did not intend to relinquish the land because he executed the deed but retained it, and merely told his friend to deliver it at his death to his nephew, provided that the nephew was still alive. Thus, because the uncle did not intend to relinquish control of the land until his death, there was no valid delivery of the deed. Note that the deed did not convey a future interest to the nephew. To convey a future interest (*i.e.*, a present interest in the property, but where possession is postponed until some future time), there must also be a ***present intent*** to convey an interest. Here, the uncle showed no intent to presently convey an interest because he retained the deed. Generally, in cases where the grantor has retained the deed, the condition that title will not pass until the grantor's death must be contained in the language of the deed itself for a future interest to be conveyed. Therefore, the purchaser took full title to the land. (B) is wrong because recordation of the purchaser's deed is irrelevant. The nephew never had an interest that could be cut off (*see* above). Thus, the purchaser prevails because she acquired valid title from the uncle, rather than because of any priority in recording. Had the purchaser not recorded her deed, she would still have prevailed. (C) is wrong because it is irrelevant that the purchaser knew of the earlier deed to the nephew. The earlier deed to the nephew was not a valid conveyance of the property because there was no delivery. Because no interest passed to the nephew, the purchaser's notice of the deed is meaningless. (D) is wrong because the fact that the conveyance was by quitclaim deed is not important; the purchaser is the full owner of the land. This choice implies that the purchaser's quitclaim deed is somehow ineffective against the nephew's warranty deed, but the fact that the purchaser took by quitclaim does not in any way lessen her interest in the land. A quitclaim deed effectively conveys all interest in the property the grantor has. In this case, the uncle had a fee simple absolute, and so that is what passed to the purchaser under the deed. The nephew's warranty deed was never delivered, and thus it was worthless.

Answer to Question 4

(A) The neighbor is entitled to retain the building erected by the landowner and can also recover the reasonable rental value for the landowner's use and possession of the property. Even though the landowner was acting in good faith when he built the building, he was still a trespasser. Whether installed in good faith or not, in the absence of a statute, trespassers' annexations on the property of another are lost to them. This follows from the intention test; *i.e.*, the good faith trespasser, believing the land to be his own, normally intends annexation of an item to be permanent. Therefore, the annexed item becomes part of the property. Here, there is no mention of a statute changing this rule, so the landowner loses his building despite the fact that he believed in good faith that he owned the land. A trespasser can also be held liable for the reasonable rental value of the property. (B) is wrong. Although some courts allow a good faith improver to recover in a case like this, those courts limit such recovery to the ***value added*** to the land by the improvement, rather than the cost to construct the improvement. As noted in the facts, the landowner's building added no value to the land. Thus, he cannot recover his $20,000. (C) is wrong because, as explained above, a trespasser may not recover his annexed item. (D) is wrong. Because the neighbor is entitled to retain the building and the landowner cannot recover any monetary amount because he added no value to the land, the landowner therefore would not be entitled to a lien on the property.

Answer to Question 5

(A) The man takes sole title to the property under his right of survivorship. A joint tenancy carries the right of survivorship. Thus, when one joint tenant dies, the property is freed of her interest and the surviving joint tenant holds the entire property. Therefore, the man owns the property.

(B) is wrong because the bank has no interest. Most states, like the one in this question, regard a mortgage as a lien on title. In these states, a mortgage of the property by one joint tenant does not, by itself, sever a joint tenancy until default and foreclosure proceedings have been completed. The bank's rights were lost when the woman died prior to foreclosure. When the woman died, her interest in the property evaporated, and with it the bank's security interest. On the other hand, in a title theory state, a mortgage is considered to be an actual transfer of title to the property, rather than just a lien on the property. Thus, a mortgage by a joint tenant transfers the legal title of the joint tenant to the mortgagee (the money lender). This action destroys the unity of title and thus severs the joint tenancy. (C) is wrong because the sister has no interest in the property. Surviving joint tenants, rather than heirs at law, succeed to a deceased joint tenant's interest. Even if the woman had left a will naming the sister as devisee of the property, the joint tenancy between the man and the woman would not have been terminated. A will is a testamentary conveyance (effective only at death) and hence is inoperative as to joint tenancy property, because at the instant of death the decedent's rights in the property evaporate. (D) is wrong because, as discussed above, only the man has title to the property.

Answer to Question 6

(D) If the neighbor tells the landowner that she will no longer be using the driveway, and the landowner thereafter builds a garage over the driveway, the easement has been terminated by estoppel. Although an oral release is ineffective because it does not comply with the Statute of Frauds, it may become effective by estoppel. For an easement to be extinguished by estoppel, there must be (i) some conduct or assertion by the owner of the easement, (ii) a reasonable reliance by the owner of the servient tenement, coupled with (iii) a change of position. Here, even though the neighbor's release of the easement was oral, the landowner changed his position in reliance on that release in building the garage over the driveway. Thus, the easement has been terminated. (A) is incorrect because mere nonuse of an easement will not result in its extinguishment. An easement can be extinguished where the holder demonstrates by a physical action that she intends to permanently abandon the easement. However, nonuse of the easement, without more, will not constitute a manifestation of an intent never to make use of the easement again. (B) is incorrect because, just as the benefit of an easement appurtenant passes with a transfer of the benefited land (regardless of whether the easement is mentioned in the conveyance), so also does the burden of an easement appurtenant pass with the servient land when transferred. Note that a subsequent purchaser without actual or constructive notice of an easement may take free of the easement by virtue of the recording act. In this case, however, the notice statute will not aid a purchaser. The mere existence of the driveway across the landowner's property to the neighbor's property puts any purchaser on inquiry notice of an easement. Thus, even if the landowner's property is sold to a purchaser for value who is unaware of the easement, the burden of the driveway easement passes with the transfer of the servient land. (C) is incorrect because, if a court were to find that there is now an unreasonably excessive use of the easement, the proper remedy would be to enter an order conforming use of the easement to a proper scope. Excessive use would not, however, result in the extinguishing of the easement.

Answer to Question 7

(A) The buyer takes subject to the bank's mortgage in a race-notice jurisdiction because it was recorded first. All recording acts apply to mortgages as well as deeds. Thus, a subsequent purchaser of the property will take subject to a prior mortgage unless the recording act changes the result. A race-notice recording act would change this result only where a subsequent purchaser did not have notice of the mortgage at the time of purchase ***and*** recorded his deed before the

mortgage was recorded. Here, the buyer did not have notice of the mortgage but he recorded *after* the bank; thus, he takes subject to the bank's interest. (C) is wrong because the buyer did not win the race to record, which is one of the two requirements for a subsequent purchaser to prevail in a race-notice jurisdiction. (B) is wrong because the buyer would not take the land subject to the bank's mortgage in a pure notice jurisdiction. Under a notice recording act, a subsequent bona fide purchaser with no actual or constructive notice prevails over a prior grantee or mortgagee who has not recorded at the time of the conveyance to the subsequent purchaser. (D) is not the best answer because it would only be true in a notice jurisdiction. The buyer would take subject to the mortgage in a pure race or race-notice jurisdiction because the mortgage was recorded before the buyer's deed (even though the buyer did not have notice of the mortgage when he bought the land).

Answer to Question 8

(C) The charity will win because the organ is a fixture and the bench is integrally connected to the organ. Under the concept of fixtures, a chattel that has been annexed to real property is converted from personalty to realty. As an accessory to the land, it passes with ownership of the land rather than with a transfer of the personal property of an estate. The manifest intent of the annexor determines whether the chattel becomes a fixture. The factors for evaluating the annexor's intent are: (i) the relationship between the annexor and the premises, (ii) the degree of annexation, and (iii) the nature and use of the chattel. Under this analysis, the organ itself is clearly a fixture: (i) the philanthropist was the fee owner of the mansion and had the organ built to his specifications when the mansion was constructed; (ii) the organ was built into the wall of the mansion and could not be easily removed; and (iii) the appearance of the organ and how it complemented the rest of the mansion probably were more important to the philanthropist than its function. Constructive annexation occurs when an article of personal property (an "accession") becomes an integral part of the property, even though it is not physically annexed to the property, in the same sense that a fixture becomes an integral part of the realty. The doctrine is fully applicable in this case even though the accession goes with an item of property that is itself converted from personalty to realty, as the organ was here. The bench is an accession because it was created as an integral part of the organ and significantly contributes to an important aspect of the organ: its overall appearance. Removing the bench and replacing it with a bench made of different wood or carvings would damage the aesthetic value of the organ. Thus, the charity will succeed in obtaining the bench because it is not severable from the organ. (A) is incorrect because the fact that the bench was not bolted to the floor is not determinative. The bolting goes to whether the bench alone is a fixture. This is irrelevant because it is an accession to (and thus a part of) the organ, which is clearly a fixture. (B) is incorrect because the fact that removing the bench does not damage the building itself does not give the daughter the right to remove it. Removing the bench will damage the organ because the bench is an accession to the organ. The organ, as a fixture, is part of the real property; thus, removal of the bench will damage the property. (D) is incorrect because harm to the parties is not an issue in determining whether an item is a fixture. The relevant question is whether removal damages the real property. If the bench were found to be personalty, the fact that its removal would reduce the value of the charity's gift would have no impact on the daughter's right to remove it.

Answer to Question 9

(B) The court is likely to rule in favor of the buyer because the seller concealed the defects in the roof from the buyer. Although the general rule is that a sale of real property carries no implied warranties of quality or fitness, a seller may be liable where she has actually concealed conditions on the property. Here, the seller knew the roof was in need of major repair, yet she made

inexpensive, cosmetic repairs to the roof. These repairs hid from casual inspection the defects that caused the roof to leak. Thus, the seller concealed from the buyer a defective condition on the property. Had the buyer known of this condition, he would have either refused to purchase the property or would have insisted that appropriate repairs be made at the seller's expense. Therefore, the buyer will prevail in his lawsuit. (A) is incorrect because the implied warranty of fitness or quality applies only to the sale of a new house by the builder. (This is an exception to the general rule of no such warranties, above.) The property is not new, nor (as far as we know) is the seller its builder. Thus, the implied warranty does not cover the sale from the seller to the buyer. Although (C) states the general rule, it is incorrect as applied to these facts because of the seller's act of concealment. A seller is generally not required to disclose defects (at least those easily discoverable upon inspection), but she may not make misrepresentations or conceal known defects. Consequently, the rule stated in (C) does not apply here. Although (D) correctly sets forth grounds for the non-applicability to these facts of an implied warranty of fitness, the seller's concealment of the defects will make her liable for damages. Therefore, (D) is incorrect in concluding that the court will rule in favor of the seller.

Answer to Question 10

(D) Under the reasonable use theory, which is followed in most states, the owner can use as much percolating water as she wants as long as it is used for beneficial purposes of the overlying land. She will be liable only if the purpose is malicious or the water is simply wasted. (Note that the result is the same under the absolute ownership theory, still followed in several eastern states, which permits the owner to extract as much water as she wishes for any nonmalicious purpose, including export.) (A) is wrong because the owner may take as much water as she wishes for use on her property. This answer might be correct under the prior appropriation doctrine, a minority approach employed by some western states, because the developer's beneficial use was first in time. (B) is also wrong under the majority view, although it would probably be the best answer under the minority prior appropriation view. Because domestic use is a preferred beneficial use, the owner probably would be allowed to extract the water under that theory, but because water rights are considered property rights, she would have to compensate the developer for diminishing his supply. (C) is wrong under all theories of water law.

Answer to Question 11

(D) The grandson has no interest in the land. The language of the grant creates a fee simple subject to a condition subsequent in the granddaughter and an executory interest in the grandson. The condition subsequent, however, attempts to restrict the transferability of a legal interest in property. This restriction is an invalid restraint on alienation and therefore is void. When the condition is stricken, the granddaughter has a fee simple absolute, and the grandson is left with nothing. Thus, (A) is incorrect because, as explained, the grandson's interest is void. (B) and (C) are incorrect for the same reason, and also because a remainder cannot follow a fee simple interest; it can only follow a fee tail or a life estate. Here, the granddaughter was conveyed a fee simple estate.

Answer to Question 12

(A) The owner of the ranch owns the 10 acres because accretion belongs to the riparian owner. Accretion is the increase of riparian land by the ***slow and imperceptible*** change in course of a river serving as a boundary; any resulting deposit of soil belongs to the owner of the abutting (riparian) land. Here, the facts indicate that the river changed its course "over time," depositing 10 acres on the ranch's side. Thus, the owner of the ranch is entitled to the accretion. (B) is incorrect because adverse possession does not apply here. The land that is gradually added through accretion automatically becomes part of the property at the time it occurs. (C) is a misstatement of the law because accretion does change property rights, as discussed above. (D) is incorrect because although avulsion does not change property rights, avulsion is a ***sudden and perceptible*** loss or addition to land by the change in course of a river, which is not the case here.

Answer to Question 13

(B) The mother is entitled to possession of the property at the friend's death. A reversion is a future interest left in the grantor after she conveys a lesser vested estate than she has. If the reversion was not expressly retained, it will arise by operation of law where no other disposition is made of the property after expiration of the lesser estate. Because the son is still living at the friend's death, meaning his heirs are unascertained and so unable to take possession when the friend dies, the mother acquires possession of the property under a reversionary interest by operation of law. Note that at common law, the heirs' contingent remainder would have been destroyed because no one was ready to take possession when the prior life estate ended. Today, however, most states have abolished the destructibility doctrine. Thus, if the son later dies survived by heirs, the heirs will be entitled to the land. The mother's reversion would give way to a springing executory interest (*i.e.*, one that divests the estate of the transferor) in the son's heirs when he dies. (A) is wrong because the conveyance from the mother did not create an interest in the son; it provided only for his heirs. (C) is wrong because the friend's interest, a life estate, terminated on her death. She had no interest to pass to her heirs. (D) is wrong because during the son's life, his heirs do not exist.

Answer to Question 14

(A) The daughter will prevail because the deed executed by the father to the son was never properly delivered. A deed is not effective unless it is delivered. Unless there is some clear expression of intent that the grantor envisioned the passage of title to the grantee (*i.e.*, that the grantor intended to relinquish control over the property), the continued possession of the deed raises a presumption of nondelivery. The father did not do anything to indicate an intent to pass immediate title to the son. The presumption of nondelivery is not rebutted and the father retained title. Therefore, the land was part of the father's estate and the daughter and the son inherited it as tenants in common. (Multiple grantees are presumed to take as tenants in common.) The daughter has an undivided one-half interest in the land. (B) is wrong because whether the executor violated his fiduciary duty has no bearing on the ownership of the land. That fact would be relevant only if the daughter were seeking damages from the executor. The executor's recording of the void deed did not damage the daughter because it did not affect her rights. (C) is wrong for two reasons: (i) The buyer cannot be protected by the recording act because he has not yet recorded and this is a race-notice jurisdiction. To prevail in a race-notice jurisdiction, a party must be a subsequent purchaser for value, without notice of an adverse claim, and must record first. The buyer has not yet recorded. It is not clear from the facts whether he has even received the deed. If he has not, he cannot qualify as a bona fide purchaser because he now has notice of the daughter's claim. (ii) The executor cannot claim the protection of the recording act because he is acting as the son's agent. The son was a donee with notice and as such was outside the protective provisions of the recording act. (D) is wrong because, as explained above, the daughter need not be a bona fide purchaser (*i.e.*, need not turn to the recording act) to prevail. She inherited an undivided one-half interest in the land, which has not been cut off by the subsequent acquisition and recording by a bona fide purchaser.

Answer to Question 15

(B) The lender may foreclose on the land or it may sue the owner on the underlying debt. When a mortgagor sells the mortgaged property and conveys a deed, the grantee takes subject to the mortgage, which remains on the land. However, the mortgagor remains primarily and personally liable on the loan (unless the grantee has signed an assumption agreement). In most jurisdictions, when a sale is made "subject to" the mortgage, the mortgagee has the option of foreclosing on the land or suing the mortgagor (in this case, the owner) on the debt. (A) is incorrect because it fails to allow for the remedy of suing on the debt. (C) and (D) are incorrect because one who purchases subject to a mortgage (the buyer), but does not sign an assumption agreement promising to pay the mortgage loan, is not personally liable on the underlying debt.

Answer to Question 16

(B) The tenant will prevail because the buyer did not properly inspect the property. A title search is not complete without an examination of possession. If the possession is unexplained by the record, the purchaser is obligated to make inquiry. The purchaser is charged with knowledge of whatever an inspection of the property would have disclosed ***and*** anything that would have been disclosed by the possessor. Thus, the buyer is on constructive notice of the tenant's possession and anything that would have been disclosed by inquiring of the tenant. Because the buyer had this notice, he is not protected by the notice recording statute, and he will take subject to the tenant's lease. (A) is wrong because "actual notice" means that the buyer was aware of the tenant's possession. The facts make clear that the buyer did not know of the tenant's possession. Furthermore, the act of driving by has no legal consequence; thus, it would not be deemed to confer anything on the buyer. (C) is wrong because the buyer had constructive notice of the tenant's possession and, therefore, is not protected by the recording statute. (D) is wrong because the tenant's state of mind is irrelevant for purposes of applying the recording statute.

Answer to Question 17

(D) The landowner will succeed in her suit for specific performance at the full contract price. Where property subject to a contract for sale is destroyed without the fault of either party before the date set for closing, the majority rule in the absence of a statute is that the risk of loss is on the buyer. Thus, the buyer must pay the contract price despite a loss due to fire, unless the contract provides otherwise. Here, the inn was destroyed by fire after the landowner and the buyer entered into their contract for the sale of the property, but before the closing date. The contract apparently was silent regarding the risk of loss and there is apparently no applicable statute. Thus, under the majority rule, the risk of loss is on the buyer. As a result, the landowner is entitled to receive specific performance of the contract, meaning that the buyer must pay the full contract price. (A) and (B) are incorrect because they conclude that the landowner is not entitled to specific performance. As explained above, the landowner ***is*** entitled to specific performance because the risk of loss is on the buyer. (B) is also incorrect because it states that the landowner must refund the earnest money. The landowner is entitled to the full contract price; thus, there is no reason for her to return the earnest money. (C) is incorrect because it allows the buyer to tender less than the full contract price. With the buyer bearing the risk of loss, he must pay the $1 million contract price despite the decrease in the property's value due to the fire.

Answer to Question 18

(D) The car dealer's best argument would be that the buyer cannot enforce the restriction against him because the 30-acre parcel was not part of the common scheme of development. Because neither the car dealer's deed to the 30-acre parcel nor any deed in his chain of title contains the restrictive covenant, to succeed the buyer must show the existence of an implied reciprocal negative servitude that can be enforced on the 30-acre parcel. When a developer subdivides land into several parcels and some of the deeds contain negative covenants but some do not, equitable servitudes (negative covenants enforceable by injunction) binding on all of the parcels may be implied if: (i) there is a ***common scheme*** of development, and (ii) the grantee has ***notice*** of the restrictive covenant. In this case, both requirements are lacking. A common scheme of development is proven by evidence that the developer intended that all parcels in a subdivision be developed within the terms of the negative covenant. The key in this case is that the 30-acre parcel was not part of the subdivision intended to be so restricted. The same evidence that proves the common plan for the subdivision shows that the 30-acre parcel was not intended to be included; *i.e.*, the brochure shows only the 80-lot subdivision with single-family homes and nothing at all about the 30-acre parcel. In addition, the mere fact that the developer bothered to divide the property into two parcels before he subdivided the 80 lots shows that he intended to develop the parcels separately. Last, the 30-acre parcel's disproportionate size—30 acres compared with half-acre lots—further shows that, at the time the owner bought his lot (and the buyer's rights are derived from the owner), the developer did not intend to include the 30-acre parcel in the subdivision. Therefore, the common scheme requirement is not met. Also, it is unlikely that the car dealer had the requisite notice to be bound by the covenant. He did not have record notice (because the restriction was not in his chain of title); nothing in the facts shows that he had actual notice; and because his parcel does not appear to be part of the neighborhood (being 30 acres and on the periphery), he did not have inquiry notice. Thus, the car dealer is not bound by the single-family home restriction in the subdivision deeds. (A) is wrong for the above reasons, but would be wrong even if the 30-acre parcel were within the common scheme. A prior purchaser of a burdened lot generally cannot enforce the promise against a subsequent purchaser unless the developer promised the prior purchaser that he would restrict his remaining lots. This promise need not be in writing, however; it may be implied from many things, including: a map or plat shown to the purchaser, oral representations, or sales literature. In this case, the brochure, as well as the overall appearance of the development, would suffice to infer a promise on the part of the developer to restrict his remaining subdivision lots, but not the 30-acre parcel. (B) is wrong because, had the 30-acre parcel been part of the common scheme, the fact that the buyer and the car dealer are not in each other's chain of title would not matter. That is not a requirement for enforcing an equitable servitude; in fact, it is almost never the case that the party seeking enforcement is in the other party's chain of title. If that were true, only the developer could enforce the restraints. (C) is wrong because the fact that the buyer's deed did not contain the restriction is irrelevant. The important thing is that the buyer's property is bound by the restriction. The restriction is in her record chain of title; thus, the buyer took subject to the restriction and is bound by it.

Set 5 Answer Sheet

1. Ⓐ Ⓑ Ⓒ Ⓓ
2. Ⓐ Ⓑ Ⓒ Ⓓ
3. Ⓐ Ⓑ Ⓒ Ⓓ
4. Ⓐ Ⓑ Ⓒ Ⓓ
5. Ⓐ Ⓑ Ⓒ Ⓓ
6. Ⓐ Ⓑ Ⓒ Ⓓ
7. Ⓐ Ⓑ Ⓒ Ⓓ
8. Ⓐ Ⓑ Ⓒ Ⓓ
9. Ⓐ Ⓑ Ⓒ Ⓓ
10. Ⓐ Ⓑ Ⓒ Ⓓ
11. Ⓐ Ⓑ Ⓒ Ⓓ
12. Ⓐ Ⓑ Ⓒ Ⓓ
13. Ⓐ Ⓑ Ⓒ Ⓓ
14. Ⓐ Ⓑ Ⓒ Ⓓ
15. Ⓐ Ⓑ Ⓒ Ⓓ
16. Ⓐ Ⓑ Ⓒ Ⓓ
17. Ⓐ Ⓑ Ⓒ Ⓓ
18. Ⓐ Ⓑ Ⓒ Ⓓ
19. Ⓐ Ⓑ Ⓒ Ⓓ
20. Ⓐ Ⓑ Ⓒ Ⓓ
21. Ⓐ Ⓑ Ⓒ Ⓓ
22. Ⓐ Ⓑ Ⓒ Ⓓ
23. Ⓐ Ⓑ Ⓒ Ⓓ
24. Ⓐ Ⓑ Ⓒ Ⓓ
25. Ⓐ Ⓑ Ⓒ Ⓓ
26. Ⓐ Ⓑ Ⓒ Ⓓ
27. Ⓐ Ⓑ Ⓒ Ⓓ
28. Ⓐ Ⓑ Ⓒ Ⓓ
29. Ⓐ Ⓑ Ⓒ Ⓓ
30. Ⓐ Ⓑ Ⓒ Ⓓ
31. Ⓐ Ⓑ Ⓒ Ⓓ
32. Ⓐ Ⓑ Ⓒ Ⓓ
33. Ⓐ Ⓑ Ⓒ Ⓓ
34. Ⓐ Ⓑ Ⓒ Ⓓ
35. Ⓐ Ⓑ Ⓒ Ⓓ
36. Ⓐ Ⓑ Ⓒ Ⓓ

REAL PROPERTY QUESTIONS - SET 5

Question 1

A landowner devised her parcel of land to her daughter, her heirs, and assigns, "so long as the property is used for residential purposes, then to my niece, her heirs, and assigns." The remainder of the landowner's property passed through the residuary clause of her will to her grandson. The daughter lived on the land for 25 years, then on her death, ownership passed to her husband. In the meantime, the niece had also died, leaving her entire estate to her son. The husband has leased the land to a developer, who has obtained the necessary permits to build a shopping center on it. The grandson and the niece's son both file quiet title and ejectment actions against the husband, and the cases are consolidated.

How should the court, applying common law, rule as to ownership of the land?

(A) For the husband.

(B) For the niece's son.

(C) For the grandson, because he received a right of reversion from his grandmother.

(D) For the grandson, because he received a possibility of reverter from his grandmother.

Question 2

A seller agreed in writing to sell a tract of land to a buyer. The contract called for the seller to deliver good and marketable title to the buyer within 90 days from the date of the contract, and at that time the buyer was to deliver to the seller $50,000 in cash. One month later, the buyer discovered that the seller was not the owner of record. At the time set for closing, the seller tendered a quitclaim deed, as agreed to in the contract. The buyer refused to pay the purchase price or to take possession because the seller was not the record owner of the land. The seller correctly explained that he had been in adverse possession of the land for 25 years, five years longer than the jurisdictional requirement. The buyer still refused to complete the sale.

If the seller brings suit against the buyer for specific performance, the seller will:

(A) Prevail, because the contract called for a quitclaim deed.

(B) Prevail, because the seller has obtained "good and marketable title" by adverse possession.

(C) Not prevail, because the seller's failure to disclose his lack of record title constitutes fraud.

(D) Not prevail, because the buyer cannot be required to buy a lawsuit, even if the probability is great that the buyer would prevail against the record owner.

Question 3

A landlord leased a building to a baker for 10 years, commencing January 1, at a monthly rental of $1,700. The lease stated in part, "The tenant may not sublet or assign this lease without first receiving written permission from the landlord to do so. Any attempt to sublet or assign the lease without first receiving written permission shall constitute a breach entitling the landlord to terminate this lease."

Five years later, an investor approached the baker and offered to purchase the bakery if the baker would agree to sublet the premises to him. The baker agreed and executed a sublease on July 1 of that year. The investor took possession the same day. On July 3, the baker approached the landlord and asked for written permission to sublet the premises to the investor. The landlord said he had no real objection to the sublease and would execute the document requested by the baker, but only if the investor would sign a five-year extension of the existing lease. The investor refused to extend the lease, but remained in possession of the building. At no time did the landlord accept rent from the investor. After notice was given to all parties and the applicable grace period in the lease had elapsed, the landlord brought an appropriate action against the

baker and the investor to evict them from the premises and to declare the lease terminated because it had been breached.

The result of this action should be:

(A) Against the landlord, because his withholding consent is an invalid restraint on alienation.

(B) Against the landlord, because his conditional consent operated as a waiver of the term of the lease requiring the landlord to give written permission for subletting.

(C) For the landlord, because the baker has breached the lease.

(D) For the landlord, because his oral consent to sublet is not enforceable under the Statute of Frauds.

Question 4

A landowner owned a large parcel of land that he divided into two equal parcels. Thirty years ago, the landowner deeded the eastern parcel to a purchaser by warranty deed, including an easement over the south 25 feet of the western parcel for access to the navigable river that ran along the westerly boundary of the western parcel. The landowner acknowledged the deed and easement, and the purchaser recorded the document. The recording officer maintains an alphabetical grantor-grantee index, but no tract index.

The purchaser made no use of the easement until five years ago, one year after her neighbor had purchased the western parcel from the landowner. The neighbor had paid at least market value for the western parcel and was not aware of the purchaser's easement. The neighbor objected to the purchaser's use of the easement shortly after she began using it, but the purchaser paid no attention. The neighbor sues the purchaser to quiet his title and to restrain the purchaser from using the easement over the western parcel. The purchaser has reasonable access to a public highway on the easterly boundary of the eastern parcel.

If the purchaser is successful, it will be because:

(A) The absence of a tract index requires that the neighbor make inquiry regarding the riparian rights of owners abutting his property.

(B) The neighbor and the purchaser trace their title to a common grantor, the landowner, whose covenants for title run with the land and estop the neighbor from denying the purchaser's title.

(C) An easement is a legal and incorporeal interest that is not just attached to an estate in the land, but runs with the land itself and therefore binds successive owners of the servient estate regardless of notice.

(D) The easement is a legal interest in the neighbor's chain of title even though there is no tract index.

Question 5

An owner conveyed his farm to his friend for life, then to a farmer and a rancher as joint tenants with the right of survivorship. One night, the friend, the farmer, and the rancher were riding together in an automobile when it was struck by a truck. They were rushed to the emergency room of a local hospital. While all three were alive when they arrived at the hospital, the hospital records establish that the rancher died at 10:28 p.m., the farmer died at 10:29 p.m., and the friend died at 10:30 p.m. that same night. The jurisdiction has not adopted the Uniform Simultaneous Death Act or any local modification of that Act.

Who takes the farm?

(A) The friend's heirs.

(B) The farmer's heirs.

(C) The rancher's heirs.

(D) The owner or his heirs.

Question 6

A landowner's will left his ranch to a rancher, his heirs, and assigns, so long as the property was used exclusively for ranch purposes, then to the landowner's grandson. The remainder of the landowner's property passed through the residuary clause of his will to the grandson. Seven years after the landowner's death, the rancher began strip mining operations on the ranch. The grandson brought an action to quiet title to the ranch against the rancher, and the rancher counterclaimed on the same theory.

Who should prevail?

(A) The rancher, because the condition imposed on his interest under the will is void as violating the Rule Against Perpetuities.

(B) The rancher, because the condition imposed is a restraint against alienation.

(C) The grandson, pursuant to the residuary clause.

(D) The grandson, because the condition imposed is valid and he takes according to the subsequent provision.

Question 7

A lawyer rented an office building for his law practice and subleased most of the building to three other tenants. The lawyer paid $2,000 per month to the owner and charged his subtenants $600 per month each. After having been in the building for three years, the lawyer and the owner orally agreed that the lawyer would purchase it for a price of $120,000, to be paid in monthly installments of $2,000 over a five-year period. It was further agreed that title would remain in the owner's name until $48,000 had been paid on the total price, whereupon the owner would deliver a deed to the lawyer.

Shortly thereafter, the lawyer spent $4,000 redecorating his suite. During the course of the next two years, the lawyer hired an associate and placed her in one of the offices formerly occupied by one of the subtenants, and raised the monthly rental he charged the other two subtenants to $700. Two years after the agreement with the owner, the lawyer demanded that the owner convey the building by delivery of a deed. The owner refused, denying that any oral agreement for sale had ever existed. The lawyer brings an action for specific performance against the owner, who pleads the Statute of Frauds as a defense.

If the owner wins, it will be because:

(A) The lawyer did not obtain the owner's approval before making the improvements to his offices.

(B) The original violation of the Statute of Frauds was incurable.

(C) The lawyer's actions in paying $2,000 per month and making improvements were as consistent with being a tenant as with the oral contract.

(D) The owner received no unconscionable benefit entitling the lawyer to equitable relief.

Question 8

A landowner validly conveyed a parcel of land to a veterinarian "for so long as the property is used as an animal shelter, but if the property is used for any other purpose, it is to go to the American Cancer Society." Two years later, the landowner died, validly devising all of his property to his friend. The landowner's only heir is his daughter. Although this jurisdiction is a common law jurisdiction with respect to all real property considerations, the state's probate laws provide that future interests or estates in real property may be passed by will or descent in the same manner as present or possessory interests.

Last month, the veterinarian approached the daughter and asked her to join with him to sell the parcel of land, which he had been using as an animal shelter, in fee simple absolute to a developer. The veterinarian and the daughter entered into a contract of sale with the developer.

However, after consultation with an attorney, the veterinarian decided against the sale. The developer sued the daughter and the veterinarian for specific performance.

The requested relief will be:

(A) Denied, because the American Cancer Society did not join in the contract of sale.

(B) Denied, because the friend did not join in the contract of sale.

(C) Granted, because the veterinarian had the power to sell his interest.

(D) Granted, because together, the daughter's and the veterinarian's interests would merge and they would have a fee simple estate.

Question 9

A landowner validly conveyed a small office building to the Green Party "as long as they use it for operating quarters until the next presidential election." After the next presidential election, which was in three years, the building would go to a private organization that monitors and prepares comprehensive listings of gas prices throughout the country. A year after the conveyance, the landowner died, validly devising all of her property to her son. Although this jurisdiction is a common law jurisdiction with respect to all real property considerations, the state's probate laws provide that future interests or estates in real property may be passed by will or descent in the same manner as present or possessory interests. Last week, the Green Party and the gas monitoring organization joined together to sell the office building in fee simple absolute to a developer. The son filed suit to prevent the sale of the property to the developer.

In this action, judgment will be for:

(A) The Green Party and the gas monitoring organization, because together they own a fee simple absolute in the building.

(B) The Green Party and the gas monitoring organization, because the attempted restrictions on the use of the property violate the Rule Against Perpetuities.

(C) The Green Party and the gas monitoring organization, because the deed restriction was an unlawful restraint on alienation.

(D) The son, because he did not sign the contract of sale.

Question 10

A seller owned two properties located in an arid region. A developer, prior to purchasing the southern parcel, hired a highly qualified engineer to conduct a survey of the property. After receiving the engineer's report that the underground aquifer was adequate to supply the developer's needs for his proposed home, the developer went ahead with his purchase of the property. However, he delayed building his planned home. The following year, a family purchased the northern parcel. They built a large house on the land, installed a swimming pool, and planted a large garden. The house, the pool, and the garden were all supplied with water from a well the family had drilled on the northern parcel. A few years later, the family built two small houses on the land and rented them out to tenants. The tenants' needs for water were supplied from the family's well.

Five years later, the developer finally constructed his home and drilled a well on the southern parcel. He moved into the home during the winter and found the supply of water for his personal needs to be adequate. However, during the ensuing summer, when the neighboring family filled the pool and irrigated the garden, the pressure dropped in the developer's well, and many days only a trickle of water came out of his pipes. The jurisdiction applies the reasonable use doctrine in determining rights to underground water.

If the developer brings suit against the family to determine his rights in the aquifer, he will likely:

(A) Prevail, and will recover monetary damages.

(B) Prevail, and will enjoin the family from overusing the water.

(C) Not prevail, because the proper suit was against the seller for rescission.

(D) Not prevail, because the family is making reasonable use of the water.

Question 11

A landowner and her neighbor owned adjoining tracts of land. No public road abutted the neighbor's land, so the landowner granted the neighbor an express easement over the north 25 feet of the landowner's land. However, the following month the county extended the public road to the neighbor's land, and he ceased using the easement for ingress and egress.

Twenty years later, the neighbor conveyed the easement to his friend, who owned the land adjoining the other side of the landowner. The following year, the neighbor conveyed his land to the landowner. None of the parties has used the easement since the public road was extended. The jurisdiction has a 15-year statute of limitations for acquiring property interests by adverse possession.

At what point was the easement extinguished?

(A) When the neighbor attempted to convey the easement to the friend without conveying the dominant tenement itself.

(B) Fifteen years after the neighbor ceased using the easement.

(C) When the neighbor conveyed his land to the landowner.

(D) The easement was not extinguished.

Question 12

An entrepreneur opened a specialized business on her land. After using up most of her capital to purchase inventory, however, the entrepreneur needed more funds and asked her friend for a $30,000 loan, to be secured by the business's inventory. The friend declined the loan. A desperate entrepreneur then told the friend she would convey the land, which had a fair market value of $100,000, to him if he would give her the loan at the current market rate of interest. The friend agreed, and the entrepreneur conveyed the land to the friend the next day. At that time, the friend gave the entrepreneur $30,000 in cash, and the parties orally agreed that the entrepreneur would pay the friend back at the rate of $1,000 per month, and that after the loan was paid in full, the friend would reconvey the land to the entrepreneur. The friend immediately recorded his deed to the land.

The entrepreneur made three $1,000 payments to the friend and then paid no more. She continued to live on the land but, being very much in debt, could not repay the loan. The friend, meanwhile, had received an offer to buy the land for $100,000.

Which of the following most accurately states the friend's right to sell the property?

(A) The friend may sell the land and keep the entire proceeds.

(B) The friend may sell the land, but he must give $73,000 of the proceeds to the entrepreneur.

(C) The friend may sell the land only after formally foreclosing on the property.

(D) The friend may not sell the land.

Question 13

A grantor executed a valid deed conveying a tract of land to a city "for the purpose of constructing a planetarium thereon." The city held the property for a number of years, but decided on another site for the planetarium. When presented an offer to purchase the property by a privately owned garbage collection company, the city accepted and conveyed the land to the company.

Which of the following statements about the title of the tract of land is true?

(A) The grantor's conveyance to the city created a fee simple determinable in the city and a possibility of reverter in the grantor.

(B) Upon conveyance of the land to the company, the property reverted back to the grantor.

(C) The company owns the land in fee simple absolute.

(D) The company owns the land, but it will revert to the grantor or his successors in interest if the property is used for anything other than a planetarium.

Question 14

A developer and an investor had been in the real estate business for many years. Because of their long-standing relationship, the developer and the investor, neither of whom was an attorney, often dispensed with certain legal formalities when dealing with each other, thus saving the costs of lawyers' fees and other attendant expenses. The investor owned a parcel of land that the developer was interested in, and she offered to buy it from him for $50,000. The developer had reason to believe that a new commercial-entertainment complex might be built near the property, which stood a chance to increase quickly in value. The investor accepted the developer's offer, and the parties agreed on June 15 as the closing date. The developer handed the investor a check for $2,500 with "earnest money" written in the memo, and they shook hands on their deal.

On May 28, the developer learned that the complex would be located on the other side of town. She called the investor and told him she had changed her mind about purchasing the land. The investor appeared at the developer's office on June 15 with the deed to the land in his hand. The developer refused to tender the balance due, and the investor sued the developer for specific performance.

Will the investor prevail?

(A) No, because the agreement does not comply with the Statute of Frauds and is, therefore, unenforceable.

(B) No, but the court will allow the investor to keep the $2,500 earnest money as damages.

(C) No, because the developer's purpose for purchasing the land was frustrated by the relocation of the entertainment complex site.

(D) Yes, because the developer and the investor had established a course of dealing.

Question 15

A seller contracted to convey her property to a buyer for $75,000. A title search revealed the following: (i) There were 25 years left on a lease of the property. The buyer agreed to take title subject to the lease but was not aware that the lease gave the lessee, his heirs, and assigns an option to purchase the land. (ii) The roof of the garage on the property extended approximately one-half inch across the property line into the airspace of an adjoining neighbor. The garage did not interfere with any current or future use of the adjoining lot. (iii) The home on the property was subject to a $5,000 lien arising from a dispute involving some remodeling work. The seller promised to pay off the lien at closing with the proceeds from the sale. (iv) The property was subject to an easement by necessity in favor of the adjoining neighbor. Last month, the city extended the main road to the neighbor's land, but the neighbor planned to continue to use the easement because it was more convenient.

In a jurisdiction that has a standard race-notice recording statute and maintains the common law Rule Against Perpetuities without any modern statutory reformation, which encumbrance renders the seller's title unmarketable?

(A) The lessee's option.

(B) The encroachment of the garage's roof.

(C) The $5,000 lien.

(D) The easement.

Question 16

A developer owned a 30-acre tract of farmland. As required by law, the developer filed a plat with the county planning board, but did not record it. The plat divided the parcel into 87 one-third acre residential lots. A one-acre strip on the eastern edge of the parcel that abutted a busy highway was set aside for commercial development. The plat restricted each lot to a single residence and banned all "nonconforming detracting structures or appurtenances," including "free-standing flagpoles more than six feet in height, television antennas and receiving equipment of excessive size and obtrusiveness, and windmills." The restrictive clause was put into the deeds of all the residential lots in the subdivision, except for the deeds to lots 23, 24, and 25. This oversight was due to an error by the developer's secretary. All the other lots had deeds stating that the restriction applied "to the grantee and his or her heirs and assigns."

A homeowner purchased lot 24 and duly recorded her deed in the office of the county recorder of deeds. The developer's salesperson had orally informed the homeowner of the general restrictions applicable to lots in the subdivision. A year later, a sports bar purchased the one-acre commercial strip and installed a large satellite dish. Two years later, the homeowner sold her property to a buyer. The homeowner never mentioned any of the restrictions to the buyer. The buyer put a satellite dish on top of his house. His dish was not as large as the bar's dish, but it was obviously bigger than any of his neighbors' modest antennas. The owners of 15 lots in the subdivision sue the buyer, demanding that he remove the dish.

If the court finds for the buyer, it will probably be because:

(A) The buyer is not charged with record notice based on other deeds given by a common grantor.

(B) The buyer's predecessor in interest, the homeowner, was not bound by the oral restriction told to her by the developer's salesperson.

(C) The property owners suing the buyer all purchased their lots prior to the homeowner's purchase of lot 24.

(D) The existence of a satellite dish on the eastern end of the original parcel indicates that neighborhood conditions have changed to the point where it would be inequitable to enforce the restrictions.

Question 17

A pedestrian who was struck by a landowner's automobile was awarded a judgment in the amount of $115,000. The landowner's insurance carrier paid the pedestrian $100,000, leaving a $15,000 outstanding judgment that the landowner was unable to pay. The pedestrian properly filed the judgment with the county recorder's office. A statute of the state in which the landowner's land is located provides:

> Any judgment against a person properly filed shall attach to all real property owned by that person or acquired by that person within 10 years following the filing of the judgment.

The landowner owned an undeveloped lot in co-tenancy with her cousin, each holding an undivided one-half interest. The landowner and the cousin put the property up for sale and conveyed it to a purchaser via quitclaim deed for $20,000. The purchaser gave the landowner and the cousin $10,000 each. The landowner promptly applied her $10,000 toward payment of the unsatisfied judgment. The pedestrian then brought an appropriate action against the cousin, demanding $5,000 from her share of the proceeds of the sale of the lot to satisfy the judgment against the landowner.

Will the pedestrian prevail?

(A) Yes, if the landowner and the cousin held the lot as joint tenants, but not if they were tenants in common.

(B) Yes, if the landowner and the cousin held the lot as tenants in common, but not if they held it in joint tenancy.

(C) No, because the pedestrian's remedies are limited to a personal action against the landowner and the $5,000 lien on the purchaser's property.

(D) No, because the pedestrian's sole remedy is against the landowner.

Question 18

A cyclist was injured when a driver ran a red light. The cyclist subsequently sued the driver to recover for her injuries, and obtained a money judgment of $50,000. The state where the cyclist and the driver reside has the following statute: "Any judgment properly filed shall, for 10 years from filing, be a lien on the real property then owned or subsequently acquired by any person against whom the judgment is rendered."

The cyclist filed the judgment in the county where the driver owned a valuable ranch. Sometime later, the driver, who was also injured in the accident, undertook to remodel all the buildings on the ranch to make them wheelchair-accessible. The driver borrowed $30,000 from a bank for the improvements, securing the loan with a mortgage on the ranch. The bank properly recorded its mortgage. Before he paid any principal on the bank's loan, the driver decided to build a new barn. He borrowed $20,000 from a financing company for this purpose, also secured by a mortgage on the ranch. The financing company properly recorded its mortgage.

The driver subsequently defaulted on the bank's mortgage, and the bank brought a foreclosure action, joining the financing company in the proceeding. The foreclosure sale resulted in $90,000 in proceeds after all expenses and fees were paid. The driver still owes the cyclist $50,000, the bank $30,000, and the financing company $20,000.

How should the foreclosure proceeds be distributed?

(A) The cyclist is entitled to $50,000, the bank is entitled to $30,000, and the financing company is entitled to the remaining $10,000.

(B) The cyclist is entitled to $50,000, the bank is entitled to $30,000, and the driver is entitled to the remaining $10,000.

(C) The bank is entitled to $30,000, the financing company is entitled to $20,000, and the driver is entitled to the remaining $40,000.

(D) The bank is entitled to $30,000, and the driver is entitled to the remaining $60,000.

Question 19

An owner of a parcel of land instructed his lawyer to draw up an instrument deeding the land to his friend's "nieces." The owner acknowledged the deed and signed it. As directed by the owner, the lawyer recorded the deed and then returned it to the owner. The owner put the deed in the drawer of his desk, intending to present it to the friend's nieces when they came to visit him next month.

The following week, however, the owner died, leaving his daughter as his sole heir at law. The daughter discovered the deed to the land in the owner's desk. She filed an appropriate action to quiet title in the land, naming the friend's only two nieces as defendants. The only evidence presented at the trial was the deed itself, the evidence of recordation, and the lawyer's testimony regarding the owner's intent.

The court should rule that the land is owned by:

(A) The nieces, because recordation is prima facie evidence of delivery.

(B) The nieces, because a deed is prima facie valid absent evidence to the contrary.

(C) The daughter, because the evidence is insufficient to support a valid delivery.

(D) The daughter, because the grantees in the deed are too indefinite.

Question 20

A landlord who owned a strip mall entered into a written five-year lease of one of the units with a discount retail perfumery. The lease provided for a monthly rent of $1,000, payable on or before the first day of each month. The perfumery dutifully paid its rent on time for two years and three months. At that time, with the oral permission of the landlord, the perfumery transferred its interest in the remainder of the lease to a dry cleaner in writing, and added a clause requiring the dry cleaner to get permission from the perfumery for any subsequent assignments. The dry cleaner promptly paid rent to the landlord for 14 months, and then asked the landlord to approve a transfer of its interest in the lease to a video rental store. The landlord gave her oral assent. To obtain the perfumery's approval of the transfer to the video store, the dry cleaner wrote a letter to the perfumery, promising that if any problems arose and anyone tried to go after the perfumery for money, the dry cleaner would "make it good."

After the perfumery sent a letter back to the dry cleaner agreeing to the transfer, the dry cleaner executed a written transfer of its interest to the video store. The video store promptly paid rent for three months. Having failed to make any profits, the video store ceased paying any rent to the landlord and cannot be located. The landlord has been unable to find anyone interested in the unit.

Given that any judgment against the video store would be worthless, the landlord can collect the unpaid rent owed on the lease from:

(A) Either the perfumery or the dry cleaner.

(B) The perfumery only, but the perfumery may recover in turn from the dry cleaner.

(C) The perfumery only, and the perfumery has no recourse against the dry cleaner.

(D) Neither the perfumery nor the dry cleaner.

Question 21

A landowner included in his will a provision giving "all of my property, both real and personal, wherever situated, to my widow for life, and after her death to any of our children who may survive her."

The gift to the children is:

(A) A contingent remainder.

(B) A vested remainder.

(C) A shifting executory interest.

(D) Void, as violating the Rule Against Perpetuities.

Question 22

A landlord leased residential property to a tenant. The written lease was for a period of one year, with the monthly rent of $1,000 payable on or before the first of each month. The termination date set out in the lease was October 1. On August 10 of the first year of her tenancy, the tenant received a letter from the landlord along with a new lease form. The lease was for a period to terminate on October 1 of the following year, and the rent stated in the new lease was $1,200 per month. Both the rent increase and the notice given were in full compliance with relevant state statutes. An accompanying letter, signed by the landlord, asked the tenant to sign the lease on the line marked "tenant." On September 15, the tenant sent the lease back to the landlord unsigned. On September 20, the tenant sent a letter to the landlord by certified mail. The landlord signed the return receipt, which the post office duly sent to the tenant. Enclosed with the tenant's letter was a check for $1,000

for "next month's rent." The landlord deposited the check into his bank account. With the landlord's acquiescence, the tenant remained in possession after October 1.

Which of the following statements is most accurate?

(A) The tenant has a month-to-month tenancy at $1,000 monthly rent.

(B) The tenant has a month-to-month tenancy at $1,200 monthly rent.

(C) The tenant has an annual tenancy at $1,200 per month rent.

(D) The tenant has a tenancy at will.

Question 23

A fee simple owner of a restaurant provided in his will that the property should go on his death "in fee simple to my friend, but if during my friend's lifetime my son has children and those children are alive when my friend dies, then to said living children." When the owner died, the friend took over the restaurant.

If the son has children and one or more of them are alive when the friend dies, who will take title to the restaurant at that time?

(A) The friend's heirs, because the attempted gift to the son's children is invalid under the Rule Against Perpetuities.

(B) The son's children, because their interest is not contingent, being a possibility of reverter.

(C) The son's children, because their interest is vested, subject to defeasance.

(D) The son's children, because their interest will vest, if at all, within a life in being plus 21 years.

Question 24

A seller entered into a written contract with a vintner on April 4, whereby the seller agreed to convey a vineyard to the vintner for $2 million. The terms of the contract set the closing date as June 1. At the time the seller entered into the agreement with the vintner, the seller had no interest in the vineyard. On April 15, the seller entered into a written agreement with a landowner, whom the seller believed to be the owner of the vineyard. According to the terms of the agreement, the landowner was to convey the vineyard to the seller on or before May 25. Another term of the agreement stated "time is of the essence."

On May 24, the landowner conveyed his interest in the vineyard to the seller. When the seller went to record the deed, she discovered from records in the recorder's office that the landowner held clear title to only seven-eighths of the vineyard. It took some time for the seller to remove the cloud from the title and procure ownership in full of the vineyard. She finally did so on July 1, and on that day she tendered a warranty deed to the vineyard to the vintner. The vintner refused to tender $2 million or any other sum to the seller, asserting that the seller had broken her agreement by failing to close on June 1. The seller then sued the vintner for specific performance.

If the vintner prevails it will be because:

(A) Title was unmarketable, because the seller did not own the vineyard at the time she entered into the contract.

(B) Title was unmarketable, because the seller only owned seven-eighths of the vineyard on the closing date.

(C) Time was not of the essence in the seller-vintner contract.

(D) A one-month delay in closing is determined to be unreasonable.

Question 25

A landowner sold his summer home to a neighbor. The deed to the neighbor reserved for the landowner, his heirs, and assigns the right of first refusal to purchase the summer home when it was offered for sale. The neighbor recorded the deed. Twenty-five years later, in an attempt to avoid the consequences of the covenant, the neighbor deeded the summer home to her friend as a "gift." The friend recorded the deed, which did not contain the right of first refusal covenant. The friend then sold the land to a buyer for $150,000, giving the proceeds of the sale to the neighbor. The buyer knew nothing about the right of first refusal because she inspected only the friend's deed from the neighbor. When the landowner learned of what had happened, he filed suit to compel conveyance of the land to him. The jurisdiction in which the property is located has an unmodified common law Rule Against Perpetuities and the following statute: "Any conveyance of an interest in land, other than a lease for less than one year, is not valid against any subsequent purchaser for value and without notice, whose conveyance is first recorded."

The landowner will most likely:

(A) Prevail, because the deed with the covenant granting the right of first refusal was in the buyer's chain of title.

(B) Prevail, because the neighbor and the friend acted in bad faith.

(C) Not prevail, because the covenant is not enforceable.

(D) Not prevail, because the covenant, although enforceable against the neighbor personally, does not run with the land.

Question 26

A landlord owned a three-story apartment building that had a beautiful view of the ocean over a neighbor's vacant lot. The neighbor assured the landlord that he had no plans to develop the vacant lot. Subsequently, the neighbor was killed in an automobile accident, and his will left the lot to his son. Over the landlord's objections, the son began building a 10-story office structure. Once the construction began, the contractor's workers continually swung large girders suspended from a crane over the landlord's building. The landlord complained incessantly because the tenants complained to her that the girders frightened them, but the son did nothing about it. Even when the office structure was only partially completed it put the landlord's apartment building in shadows for the greater part of the afternoon. Her apartments not only no longer had an ocean view, but were dark and devoid of sunlight. The landlord slashed her rents by 40%, but still had difficulty keeping the building fully occupied.

If the landlord brings a suit seeking all available relief, a court will most likely find that she has:

(A) A cause of action for damages or an injunction against the son because the girders repeatedly pass over the landlord's air space.

(B) A cause of action for damages against the son because of the loss of the ocean view.

(C) A cause of action for damages or an injunction against the son because of the loss of sunlight.

(D) No cause of action.

Question 27

A developer purchased a vacant site next to a boutique shop in a downtown area. Two months after the developer constructed a parking garage on the site, the boutique owner noticed that cracks were beginning to appear in the basement and along some of the walls of her shop. A city engineer inspected the premises and told the boutique owner that the land under her building was subsiding. The boutique owner consulted a contractor who told her it would cost $50,000 to repair the damage and that the damage would not have occurred but for the developer's construction of a large structure on the adjacent site.

If the boutique owner brings suit against the developer for damages, the boutique owner will:

(A) Prevail, because proof of causation alone is sufficient.

(B) Prevail, if the developer's project would have damaged the boutique owner's property even if it was unimproved.

(C) Not prevail, unless the damage was intentional.

(D) Not prevail, because a landowner is liable only if his excavation causes adjacent land to subside in its natural state.

Question 28

A seller put her house and lot on the market for $200,000. After receiving several offers within $5,000 of her asking price, the seller entered into a contract to sell the house and lot to a buyer for $200,000. The contract provided that the buyer put up $4,000 in earnest money, which the seller could treat as liquidated damages unless:

> The seller fails to tender marketable title to the buyer by the agreed-upon closing date, the seller commits a material breach of this contract, or the buyer dies prior to the closing date, in which case the earnest money shall be reimbursed to the buyer's estate.

The contract was signed on July 24, and the closing date was set for September 12.

On August 5, the buyer was seriously injured in an accident. On September 10, the buyer was released from the hospital in a wheelchair. He determined that a ranch-style house would make his life much more bearable, but the seller's home was two stories. The buyer asked the seller to cancel the contract and to refund the $4,000 earnest money. The seller refused. The buyer did not appear on the closing date. On September 16, the seller contracted to sell the home to a purchaser for $198,000. The closing occurred as planned on October 20. The buyer files suit against the seller, praying for a refund of the $4,000 earnest money.

The buyer is likely to recover:

(A) The entire $4,000, because the buyer had a justified medical reason for his failure to perform.

(B) $2,000, because the diminution in value of the property was only $2,000.

(C) $2,000 less any of the seller's out-of-pocket costs involved in remarketing the home.

(D) Nothing, because at the time the contract was entered into, $4,000 represented a reasonable estimate of damages in the event of breach.

Question 29

A vintner divided his vineyard into two parcels, drawing the boundaries so that the single well that had irrigated the entire vineyard fell on the border of the two properties. The vintner then conveyed the eastern parcel to his friend by a deed that contained the following covenant:

> If the well located on the boundary of the eastern and western parcels continues to be used for irrigation purposes and becomes in need of repair or replacement, the grantee, his heirs, and assigns and the grantor, his heirs, and assigns each promise to pay one-half of the cost of such repair or replacement. This covenant shall run with the land.

The deed from the vintner to the friend was not recorded, and the vintner did not record a copy of the deed with the records for the western parcel.

The friend later sold the eastern parcel to a farmer. The farmer's deed did not contain the covenant about the well. After 15 years of use by the owners of both the eastern and western parcels, the well began to fail. The farmer took it upon himself to have the well repaired at a cost of $30,000. About two weeks later, the farmer discovered the deed from the vintner to the friend in some old files. By this time, the western parcel had passed to the vintner's son by inheritance and again to the son's daughter by inheritance from the now-deceased son. The

daughter knew nothing of the covenant concerning the well. The farmer presented the daughter with the bill for the well repair with a copy of the vintner/friend deed and a note that said he expected to be reimbursed for $15,000. The daughter refuses to pay, and the farmer sues.

The jurisdiction has a 10-year statute of limitations for acquiring property by adverse possession, and the following recording statute: "Any conveyance of an interest in land shall not be valid against any subsequent purchaser for value, without notice thereof, unless the conveyance is recorded."

The court is most likely to rule in favor of:

(A) The daughter, because the deed from the vintner to the friend was never recorded.

(B) The daughter, because the farmer has acquired the well by adverse possession.

(C) The farmer, because the covenant runs with the land.

(D) The farmer, because he is a bona fide purchaser.

Question 30

A landlord rented an art studio to an artist. Under the terms of the signed, written, two-year lease, the artist agreed to pay the landlord $1,000 per month and to assume responsibility for all necessary repairs. After the first year of the lease, the artist assigned the balance of his lease to a sculptor. The landlord approved the sculptor as a tenant and accepted two rent payments from her, and then the landlord sold the building to an investor. The sculptor had made two payments to the investor when an electrical fire broke out in the studio, injuring the sculptor. The fire was caused by faulty wiring. The landlord was aware that there was a dangerous wiring problem when he leased the property to the artist. But when the landlord discovered how costly repairs would be, he decided it would be more profitable to sell the property than to repair it. The problem was not easily discoverable by anyone other than an expert electrician, and the landlord did not tell the artist, the sculptor, or the investor about the problem. The sculptor sues to recover damages for her injuries.

The sculptor can recover from:

(A) The investor, because she breached the implied warranty of habitability.

(B) The landlord, because he failed to disclose a latent defect.

(C) The artist, because the artist is considered the sculptor's landlord.

(D) No one, because the covenant to repair runs with the land, and the sculptor is bound by it.

Question 31

A landowner owned a silver mine as her separate property. She executed a will that provided: "The silver mine shall pass to my husband for life, then to my children, with the issue of any predeceased child taking that child's share. All the rest, residue, and remainder of my estate I leave to my husband." At that time the landowner had two children—a son and a daughter. The son had two children—the landowner's grandson and granddaughter. Many years later, the landowner, the son, and the grandson were involved in a plane crash. The son was killed instantly. The landowner died a few days later. The grandson lingered for two weeks before dying. They left the following survivors: the husband, the granddaughter, the grandson's widow and sole heir, and the daughter.

The husband validly disclaims any interest he may have in the landowner's estate. Before the estate is distributed, the daughter is killed in a car accident. The daughter left her entire estate to her boyfriend. The jurisdiction retains the common law Rule Against Perpetuities, unmodified by statute.

Who has an interest in the silver mine?

(A) The granddaughter and the boyfriend only.

(B) The granddaughter, the grandson's widow, and the boyfriend.

(C) The granddaughter only.

(D) The granddaughter and the grandson's widow only.

Question 32

A baker executed a will, leaving his bakery to his cousin "for life or until she ceases to operate the bakery, then to my children." The residue of his estate he left to his cousin. The baker died shortly thereafter, survived by his cousin and four children. The cousin took possession and control of the bakery. After a few years, the cousin began to lose her desire to run the bakery. Instead of closing the bakery, however, she converted the bakery into a used book store and held weekly book clubs there. The baker's children are alarmed by this turn of events and seek a court order to remove the cousin and her used book store from the bakery, and to prevent the cousin from taking any more profits from the bakery. The jurisdiction retains the common law Rule Against Perpetuities, unmodified by statute, and the common law destructibility rule.

The court will most likely rule in favor of:

(A) The cousin, because the gifts following the cousin's life estate violate the Rule Against Perpetuities.

(B) The cousin, because her life estate and reversion have destroyed the children's remainder.

(C) The children, because they are the fee simple owners of the bakery.

(D) The children on the ejectment issue, but the cousin can continue to take profits from the bakery for the rest of her life.

Question 33

A farmer executed a valid deed, conveying his orange grove:

> To my brother for life, then to my niece and nephew. My brother shall have no right to convey any interest in the orange grove. Likewise, should my niece or nephew attempt to convey any interest in the orange grove prior to the date that their interest becomes possessory, that niece's or nephew's interest shall pass to the other.

Subsequently, the brother transfers all of his interest in the orange grove to his friend. Several weeks after the brother's conveyance, the nephew finds himself in need of cash and conveys his interest in the orange grove to a loan shark in exchange for $20,000. The niece is outraged by the conduct of the brother and the nephew and brings a suit to quiet title to the orange grove.

Who will the court find has title to the orange grove?

(A) The niece only.

(B) The niece and the loan shark only.

(C) The niece and the loan shark, subject to the brother's life estate.

(D) The niece, subject to the friend's life estate pur autre vie.

Question 34

A landowner owned a large tract of land, which he divided into two parcels. The northern parcel abutted a public highway. The shortest route from the southern parcel to the highway was over a private road that crossed the northern parcel. The other route was over a single-lane dirt and gravel path that wound for over four miles through the woods. The landowner sold the southern parcel to a developer, including an express easement in the private road across the northern parcel. The landowner knew of the developer's plans to open an inn on the property. The developer built the inn but never opened it to the public.

Fifteen years later, the developer sold the southern parcel to an investor, who planned to open the inn to the public. The developer had never properly recorded her deed to the land, but

the investor promptly recorded her deed, which made no mention of a right to cross the northern parcel via the private road. About a week after the investor took possession of the southern parcel, she learned of the provision in the developer's deed to the land. However, the landowner refuses to grant the investor permission to use the road across his property to reach the highway.

Does the investor have a right to cross the northern parcel?

(A) No, because the easement is not mentioned in the investor's deed, and the developer's deed containing the easement was not recorded.

(B) No, because the investor's opening of the inn would increase the use of the easement.

(C) Yes, but only if the developer exercised her right to use the easement when she owned the southern parcel.

(D) Yes, even if the developer never exercised her right to use the easement when she owned the southern parcel.

Question 35

A tenant agreed in writing to lease a retail site in a shopping mall from the owner of the property. The term of the tenancy was two years, and rent was payable in monthly installments at the beginning of each month. At the end of the second year, there had been no discussions between the tenant and the owner regarding renewal or termination. The tenant did not vacate the premises at the end of the term; instead, she sent a check for the next month's rent to the owner. The owner cashed the check and then informed the tenant that he was holding her to a new tenancy and a rent increase of 10%.

What is the status of the tenancy that the owner created?

(A) A month-to-month tenancy for the original rent amount.

(B) A year-to-year tenancy for the original rent amount.

(C) A month-to-month tenancy for the increased rent amount.

(D) A tenancy at will, terminable at any time, for the increased rent amount.

Question 36

A vendor sold his house and lot to a vendee for $60,000 by a written agreement that called for a $10,000 down payment and $10,000 a month on the first of each month thereafter until the balance was paid. The vendee made the down payment and first month's payment on time. He made the second and third months' payments on the 15th of each month, skipped the fourth month entirely, and resumed payments on the 5th of the fifth month. The following week, the vendor filed an unlawful detainer action to have the vendee ousted and the contract forfeited.

Who is likely to prevail?

(A) The vendee, because the vendor waived the strict performance of the contract.

(B) The vendee, if the contract did not provide that time was of the essence.

(C) The vendor, but he will have to refund the vendee the amount of payments made.

(D) The vendor, and he may retain the amount of payments made.

REAL PROPERTY ANSWERS - SET 5

Answer to Question 1

(D) The court should rule for the grandson because he received a possibility of reverter from his grandmother. The landowner attempted to give the daughter and her successors a fee simple subject to an executory interest, with the niece and her successors holding the executory interest. However, the attempted gift to the niece and her successors fails under the Rule Against Perpetuities because the niece's interest could vest in possession more than 21 years after a life in being. Thus, (B) is incorrect. After the void interest is stricken, the daughter and her successors have a fee simple determinable and the landowner retained a possibility of reverter, which passed to the grandson through the residuary clause in the landowner's will. When the husband, the daughter's successor, ceased using the property for residential purposes, the possibility of reverter matured, leaving ownership in the grandson. (A) is therefore incorrect. (C) is incorrect because a possibility of reverter, not a right of reversion, is the interest left in the grantor when a fee simple determinable is created.

Answer to Question 2

(D) The seller will not prevail because his title is not marketable. There is an implied warranty in every land sale contract that at closing the seller will provide the buyer with a title that is marketable. Historically, title acquired by adverse possession was not considered marketable because the purchaser might be later forced to defend in court the facts that gave rise to the adverse possession against the record owner. While most recent cases are contra, for purposes of the bar exam the rule is that one who obtains title by adverse possession must bring an action to quiet title in order for that title to be marketable. Thus, (B) is incorrect. (A) is incorrect because the fact that a contract calls for a quitclaim deed, which does not contain any covenants for title, does not affect the warranty to provide marketable title on the date of closing. (C) is incorrect because the seller's action does not amount to fraud; marketable title can be based on adverse possession (although a quiet title suit may be necessary). The seller never represented that he had record title.

Answer to Question 3

(C) The landlord should prevail because the baker has breached the lease. Generally, if a tenant transfers (assigns or sublets) in violation of a prohibition in the lease against transfers, the transfer is not void. However, the landlord usually may terminate the lease under either the lease terms or a statute. Here, because the baker has breached the provision of the lease prohibiting assignment or sublease, and the lease contains a forfeiture clause, the landlord was within his rights to terminate the lease. (A) is incorrect because clauses restricting assignment or sublease are not considered to be restraints on alienation. (B) is incorrect because a conditional consent is not a waiver where the condition is not agreed to. (D) is incorrect because an oral consent, if made, is sufficient to waive the provision. Here, the landlord's consent was conditioned on the investor signing an extension of the lease, which he did not do.

Answer to Question 4

(D) If the purchaser prevails, it will be because the easement is a legal interest in the neighbor's chain of title. This is a recording act problem. Even though the neighbor had no actual or inquiry notice, the recorded easement by his grantor, the landowner, would give him constructive notice of the purchaser's interest in the western parcel, regardless of the absence of a tract index. (A) is

a misstatement of the law. The absence of a tract index does not require a purchaser to inquire about the riparian rights of abutting landowners. (B) is incorrect because covenants for title are those contained in a general warranty deed. Although the future covenants for quiet enjoyment, warranty, and further assurances run to successive grantees, the present covenants of seisin, right to convey, and against encumbrances are breached, if at all, at the time of conveyance. (C) is incorrect because a bona fide purchaser of the servient parcel with no notice of the easement takes free of the easement.

Answer to Question 5

(B) The farmer's heirs take the farm. The farmer and the rancher held an indefeasibly vested remainder as joint tenants. There is no condition, stated or implied, that they survive the friend in order to take. Because the rancher predeceased the farmer, the farmer took the property interest pursuant to the right of survivorship. Upon the farmer's death, the remainder passed to her heirs. In turn, the farmer's heirs took the farm on the death of the friend, the life tenant. (A) is wrong because the friend had only a life estate; he had no interest to pass to his heirs at his death. (C) is wrong because the farmer survived the rancher and thus owned all of the remainder at her death; the rancher owned nothing. (D) is wrong because the owner, having granted a life estate and an absolutely vested remainder, retained no interest in the farm.

Answer to Question 6

(C) The grandson prevails because the ranch passed through the residuary clause. Under the Rule Against Perpetuities, the attempt to give the grandson an executory interest is void, so (D) is incorrect. However, the courts would simply read the conveyance without the language of the executory gift, leaving a possibility of reverter in the grantor, the landowner. Thus, (A) is incorrect. Because the grandson succeeded to the landowner's interest as grantor via the residuary clause of the will, he will prevail. (B) is incorrect because there is no restraint on alienation contained in the will.

Answer to Question 7

(C) The doctrine of part performance may be used to enforce an otherwise invalid oral contract of sale, provided the acts of part performance unequivocally prove the existence of the contract. Here, the lawyer's actions are explicable even if he had remained a tenant, because he continued to pay the same amount per month as had been previously paid as rent, and the improvements he made are a kind frequently made by long-term tenants. (A) is incorrect because the owner's approval was not needed to make such improvements. (B) is incorrect because if the lawyer had taken actions that clearly indicated the presence of an oral contract, the doctrine of part performance would have applied. The benefit to the owner is irrelevant for purposes of the Statute of Frauds; the issue is part performance. Thus, (D) is not the best answer.

Answer to Question 8

(B) The requested relief will be denied because the friend did not join in the contract of sale. The conveyance purported to create a fee simple determinable subject to an executory interest in the veterinarian and an executory interest in the American Cancer Society. A fee simple subject to an executory interest is an estate that, on the happening of a stated event, is automatically divested in favor of a third person, who holds the executory interest. However, the executory interest in the American Cancer Society is void under the Rule Against Perpetuities because it might vest beyond lives in being plus 21 years. The charity-to-charity exception to the Rule does not apply

because the veterinarian is not a charitable organization. Because any interest that violates the Rule is void and stricken from the instrument, what is left is a fee simple determinable in the veterinarian and a possibility of reverter in the landowner. On the landowner's death, the possibility of reverter passed to the friend. (A) is incorrect because the American Cancer Society does not have any interest in the land. (C) is incorrect because, although the veterinarian had the power to sell his interest, he did not own a fee simple absolute. (D) is incorrect because the daughter does not have any interest in the land. Even if she did, the merger doctrine—which provides that whenever the same person acquires all of the existing interests in land, present and future, a merger occurs and that person holds a fee simple absolute—would not apply because the friend also has an interest in the land.

Answer to Question 9

(D) The son may enjoin the sale because he has an interest in the property. A fee simple determinable is an estate that automatically terminates on the happening of a stated event. The Green Party's interest in the office building is a fee simple determinable because it lasts as long as the Party is using the building for operating quarters. However, the grant does not provide for the contingency of the Green Party ceasing to use the building as operating quarters before the next presidential election. This gap would be filled by a possibility of reverter retained by the landowner. Because the landowner passed that interest to her son in her will, there can be no contract to sell the property without his signature. *Note:* Although the gas monitoring organization appears to have an indefeasibly vested remainder (*i.e.*, it is created in an ascertained company, is certain to become possessory, and is not subject to being defeated, divested, or diminished in size), its interest is not capable of taking on the natural termination of the preceding estate and so is characterized as a springing executory interest. (A) is wrong because the son also has an interest in the land. (B) is wrong because the interest in the office building will pass to the gas monitoring organization, if at all, within 21 years. (C) is wrong because the Green Party is not prohibited from transferring any interest; it could pass a defeasible fee.

Answer to Question 10

(D) Pursuant to both the absolute ownership doctrine and the reasonable use doctrine, which together comprise the majority view with regard to determining rights in underground water, the family is entitled to use the water from the well on their property in the manner described in the facts. Under the absolute ownership doctrine (followed by about 12 states and the common law rule), the overlying owner may extract as much water as he wishes and use it for whatever purpose he desires, including hauling or piping it to other properties. Thus, under the absolute ownership doctrine, the family is entitled to extract as much water from the northern parcel as they wish for any purposes they desire. Under the reasonable use doctrine (followed by about 25 states), a landowner is limited to reasonable use of the underground water for beneficial purposes on the overlying land. "Reasonable" use is just about any use on the land that is not merely malicious or a waste of water. Thus, the use of water for gardening, filling a pool, and for the needs of tenants will constitute a reasonable use for beneficial purposes on the family's overlying land. Thus, under the reasonable use doctrine, the use of the water by the family from their well is permissible. Consequently, the family will be allowed to continue using the water as they presently are doing. The developer will have no right to control, modify, or otherwise affect their use of the water. Because the family is using the water in a manner permitted by law and is not infringing on any legally protectable right of the developer, the developer is not entitled to monetary damages or injunctive relief. Therefore, (A) and (B) are incorrect. (C) is incorrect because the facts do not indicate the existence of any grounds for rescission (*i.e.*, mistake or misrepresentation) as

between the developer and the seller at the time they entered into the contract for the purchase of the southern parcel.

Answer to Question 11

(C) The easement was extinguished when the neighbor conveyed his land to the landowner. An easement is extinguished when the easement is conveyed to the owner of the servient tenement. For an easement to exist, the ownership of the easement and the servient tenement must be in different persons. (By definition, an easement is the right to use the land of ***another*** for a special purpose.) If ownership of the two property interests comes together in one person, the easement is extinguished. Thus, (D) is wrong. (A) is wrong because, although an attempt to convey an easement appurtenant apart from the dominant tenement is ineffective, it does not extinguish the easement. The easement continues despite the attempted conveyance and will pass with the ownership of the dominant tenement. (B) is wrong because mere nonuse does not extinguish an easement. An easement may be extinguished by abandonment, but to constitute abandonment sufficient to extinguish an easement, the easement holder must demonstrate by physical ***action*** an intent to ***permanently*** abandon the easement. Nonuse of the easement is not enough to show the intent never to make use of the easement again.

Answer to Question 12

(C) The friend may sell the land, but only after formally foreclosing on the property. If a deed is given for security purposes rather than as an outright transfer of the property, it will be treated as an "equitable" mortgage and the creditor will be required to foreclose it by judicial action like any other mortgage. In determining whether an absolute deed is really a mortgage, the court considers the following factors: (i) the existence of a debt or promise of payment by the deed's grantor; (ii) the grantee's promise to return the land if the debt is paid; (iii) the fact that the amount advanced to the grantor/debtor was much lower than the value of the property; (iv) the degree of the grantor's financial distress; and (v) the parties' prior negotiations. Here, the entrepreneur owed the friend a debt; the friend promised to return the property if the debt was paid; the amount advanced ($30,000) was much lower than the value of the property ($100,000); the entrepreneur was in great financial distress; and the parties' negotiations reveal that this transaction was intended as security for the loan. Thus, the friend must bring a judicial foreclosure proceeding before he can sell the land. (A) is wrong because a foreclosure is required. Furthermore, even in a foreclosure sale, the friend is not entitled to all of the proceeds. The proceeds are used to first pay the expenses of the sale, attorneys' fees, and court costs; then to pay the principal and accrued interest on the loan that was foreclosed; then to pay off junior interests. Any remaining proceeds are returned to the mortgagor. The friend is entitled only to his expenses and the amount still owing on the $30,000 loan, including accrued interest. Because the friend has a buyer willing to pay $100,000, the entrepreneur should get some money back. (B) is wrong for two reasons: (i) as explained above, the friend cannot sell the property without a judicial foreclosure; and (ii) the entrepreneur would not be entitled to $73,000. The friend is entitled to his expenses of sale and the principal amount owing, plus accrued interest. (D) is wrong because the friend ***can*** sell the land, provided he undertakes formal foreclosure proceedings.

Answer to Question 13

(C) The garbage collection company owns the tract of land in fee simple absolute because the city had a fee simple absolute, which it conveyed to the company. The language in the deed "for the purpose of constructing a planetarium" merely expresses the grantor's ***motive*** for conveying the

property; the city received the estate that the grantor had, a fee simple absolute. Because the city held a fee simple absolute, that is what it conveyed to the company. (A) is wrong because the grant does not create a fee simple determinable. A fee simple determinable is an estate that automatically terminates on the happening of a stated event. To create a fee simple determinable, durational language (*e.g.*, "for so long as," "until") must be used. Here, the grant does not contain the durational language necessary to create a fee simple determinable. Because the interest is not a fee simple determinable, the grantor cannot have a possibility of reverter. (B) is wrong for two reasons: (i) as explained above, a fee simple determinable was not created by the grant; and (ii) even if a fee simple determinable had been created, the transfer of the property would not by itself cause it to revert back to the grantor. Determinable estates are alienable; the successor merely takes subject to the condition. The conveyance of a fee simple determinable would not automatically result in the property reverting to the grantor (*i.e.*, the company could build a planetarium on the property and avoid the property reverting back to the grantor). (D) is wrong because the grant did not create a fee simple determinable. (Had the grant contained the proper durational language, rather than "for the purpose of," (D) would have been correct. In that case, the company would own the land subject to the estate being terminated if the land is not used for a planetarium.)

Answer to Question 14

(A) The investor will not succeed in a suit for specific performance because the agreement is unenforceable under the Statute of Frauds. Under the Statute of Frauds, a land sale contract is unenforceable unless it is in writing and signed by the party to be charged. The Statute of Frauds requires the writing to contain all essential terms of the contract, which are: (i) a description of the property, (ii) identification of the parties to the contract, (iii) the price and manner of payment, and (iv) the signature of the party to be charged. Here, the agreement between the investor and the developer concerns the sale of land; thus, the agreement must be in writing to comply with the Statute of Frauds. The only writing mentioned in the facts is the check given to the investor by the developer. This check contains neither a description of the property that is the subject of the agreement nor the price and manner of payment. Thus, the check is not a writing sufficient to satisfy the Statute of Frauds. Consequently, the agreement is unenforceable, and the investor will not prevail. (Note that, under the doctrine of part performance adopted by some states, a court may grant specific performance of a contract despite the absence of a writing if there has been payment of the purchase price. Even under this view, the developer's payment of $2,500 out of a total price of $50,000 will not constitute sufficient performance to remove this agreement from the purview of the Statute of Frauds.) (B) is incorrect because, if there is no enforceable agreement, there can be no "breach" of the agreement, for which breach the investor would be entitled to damages. Therefore, the investor may not keep the earnest money as damages. (C) is incorrect for two reasons: (i) there is no need to determine whether duties have been discharged by frustration of contractual purpose where the contract itself is unenforceable under the Statute of Frauds; and (ii) frustration of a contract's purpose exists where some supervening event destroys the purpose, which must have been realized by both parties at the time of making the contract. Here, the investor had no idea that the developer wished to purchase the land because she believed a new commercial-entertainment complex was to be built nearby. Thus, both parties did not realize the purpose. Also, it cannot really be said that a superseding event destroyed the contract's purpose. The developer was simply proceeding on the basis of inaccurate information. Finding out that her sources were incorrect hardly constitutes a supervening event. (D) is incorrect because "course of dealing" (*i.e.*, a sequence of previous conduct between the parties that may be regarded as establishing a common basis of their understanding) may be used to explain or supplement the terms of a written contract under the Uniform Commercial Code

("U.C.C."). This question does not involve the sale of goods, so the U.C.C. is inapplicable. Furthermore, here there is no written agreement, the terms of which can be explained or supplemented by showing a course of dealing between the developer and the investor. Although the developer and the investor often dispensed with legal formalities as a cost-saving measure, this "course of dealing" will not confer validity on their oral agreement for the sale of land.

Answer to Question 15

(A) The lessee's option to purchase renders the seller's title unmarketable. Ordinarily, an option of this duration would violate the Rule Against Perpetuities and be stricken. An interest violates the Rule Against Perpetuities if there is any possibility, however remote, that it will vest more than 21 years after some life in being at the creation of the interest. Here, the relevant measuring life would be the lessee. The lessee could die within the next three years, and the option could be exercised by his successors more than 21 years after his death. There is a special exception to the Rule, however, for options to purchase attached to leaseholds. Because the one who holds the option in this case is the current lessee, the Rule does not apply. Thus, the option is valid, and it renders the seller's title unmarketable. (B) is incorrect because only a ***significant*** encroachment will render title unmarketable. A one-half-inch encroachment on airspace would not be considered significant, particularly because it does not interfere with the use of the adjoining property. Thus, this encroachment will not affect marketability. (C) is incorrect because a lien on property will not render title unmarketable if the seller pays the lien at closing. Unless the contract provides otherwise, the seller need not provide marketable title ***until closing***. A seller has the right to satisfy a lien at the closing with the proceeds of the sale. Therefore, as long as the purchase price is sufficient and the lien is satisfied simultaneously with the transfer of title (*e.g.*, by using escrows), the buyer cannot claim that the title is unmarketable. The closing will result in marketable title. In this situation, the $75,000 purchase price is clearly sufficient to satisfy the $5,000 lien. Thus, the seller may satisfy the lien at the closing and convey marketable title to the buyer. (D) is incorrect because although an easement that reduces the value of the property renders title unmarketable, this easement has been terminated. An easement by necessity terminates as soon as the necessity ends. Because the main road now provides access to the neighbor's land, she no longer needs the easement over the seller's land and it is extinguished.

Answer to Question 16

(A) The most likely reason to find for the buyer is that the court is not charging him with record notice of deeds to other lots given by the developer. When a developer subdivides land into several parcels and some of the deeds contain negative covenants but some do not, negative covenants or equitable servitudes binding all the parcels in the subdivision may be implied under the doctrine of "reciprocal negative servitudes." Two requirements must be met before reciprocal negative servitudes will be implied: (i) a common scheme for development, and (ii) notice of the covenants. The second requirement may be satisfied by actual notice, record notice, or inquiry notice. Here, the buyer has not been given actual notice, and the antenna restriction is not so obvious that the appearance of the neighborhood would provide the buyer with inquiry notice. Finally, the buyer has no record of the restriction in his chain of title to establish record notice. If the buyer had been the first purchaser of the lot, some courts might require him to read all deeds given by a common grantor, but the better view does not require such a search. In any case, the buyer's grantor here is the homeowner, and the restriction was not contained in her deed; the buyer thus does not have record notice of it and is not bound. (B) is incorrect because the restriction could have been enforced against the homeowner as an equitable servitude even in the absence of an express restriction (oral or written). A common scheme for development existed and the developer's salesperson gave the homeowner actual notice of the restriction. (C) is incorrect because courts will allow prior purchasers to enforce the restriction against a subsequent purchaser even if the original grantor made no covenant in the deeds that all subsequent parcels would be subject to the restriction. One theory courts use is that an implied reciprocal servitude attached to the common grantor's retained land at the time the first lots were deeded to the prior purchasers, and the prior purchasers are merely enforcing this implied servitude against the purchaser of a subsequent lot. Hence, if the buyer were deemed to have had notice of the restriction, a court would allow prior purchasers to enforce it. (D) is incorrect. While "changed neighborhood conditions" is an equitable defense to enforcement of a servitude, the strip on the eastern edge of the parcel was always earmarked for commercial uses; the presence of a satellite dish on that property is not sufficient to bar enforcement of the restriction against the residential parcels.

Answer to Question 17

(C) The pedestrian's remedies are limited to a personal action against the landowner and the lien that remains on the property. A judgment lien runs with the land and thus is binding on subsequent owners who have notice of it. Because the lien was properly filed in the recording office, the purchaser had notice of it and took the lot subject to it. Of course, the landowner is still personally liable on the amount of the judgment against her until paid. The cousin is not liable. A joint tenant or a tenant in common may encumber her own interest, but may not encumber the other co-tenant's interest. Thus, the lien attached only to the landowner's one-half interest in the property; it did not attach to the cousin's interest. (A) and (B) are wrong because the form of co-tenancy is irrelevant with respect to whether the pedestrian can reach the cousin's proceeds. The lien would not attach to the cousin's interest regardless of the form of co-tenancy. If it were a tenancy in common, the pedestrian could have executed the lien on the landowner's one-half interest. If the cousin and the landowner owned the property as joint tenants with the right of survivorship, execution of the lien would sever the joint tenancy, but would not affect the cousin's one-half interest. Because the pedestrian did not execute his lien, it remains on the land. (D) is wrong because, as stated above, the pedestrian has the lien on the purchaser's property in addition to his personal action against the landowner.

Answer to Question 18

(C) The bank is entitled to $30,000 of the foreclosure proceeds, the financing company is entitled to $20,000 of the proceeds, and the driver is entitled to the $40,000 balance. When an interest is foreclosed, after the expenses and fees are paid, the proceeds of the sale are first used to pay the principal and accrued interest on the loan that was foreclosed, next to pay off any junior liens, and finally any remaining proceeds are distributed to the mortgagor. Here, there are enough proceeds to satisfy the bank's (the foreclosing party's) $30,000 mortgage and the financing company's (the junior lienor's) $20,000 mortgage. The remaining balance ($40,000) is distributed to the driver (the mortgagor). (A) and (B) are wrong because the cyclist's interest, an interest senior to the bank's, is not affected by the foreclosure. Although foreclosure destroys all interests junior to the mortgage being foreclosed, it does not affect any senior interests. The buyer at the foreclosure sale takes subject to such interests. Without the cyclist foreclosing her lien, she is not entitled to a share of the proceeds, and her lien continues on the property in the buyer's hands. (B) and (D) are wrong because the financing company is entitled to have its mortgage fully discharged.

Answer to Question 19

(A) The nieces own the land because recordation is prima facie evidence of delivery. To be valid, a deed must be "delivered," which means that the grantor must have taken some action (not necessarily a manual handing over of the deed) with the intent that it operate to pass title immediately. Recording the deed is such an action and is presumed to carry with it the requisite intent. Even without the knowledge of the grantee, delivery to the recorder's office will satisfy the delivery requirement. If the grantor intends the recording of the document to be the final act in vesting title in the grantee, then such recording constitutes delivery. (B) is wrong because a deed alone is not prima facie valid absent delivery. There must be evidence of delivery. (C) is wrong because recordation can constitute valid delivery, and there is sufficient evidence that the deed was recorded. Note that a rebuttable presumption of no delivery may arise from the grantor's retention of the deed. However, this presumption is rebutted by the recording of the deed. (D) is wrong because a description of the grantees in a deed is sufficient if it describes the grantees with sufficient particularity that it can be determined who is to take the property. The grantee need not actually be named. Because the friend has a finite number of nieces and they are easy to locate and identify, the deed from the owner satisfies this requirement.

Answer to Question 20

(A) The landlord may collect the unpaid rent from either the perfumery or the dry cleaner. A complete transfer of the tenant's entire remaining term is an assignment of the lease. However, the original tenant can still be held liable on his original contractual obligation in the lease to pay rent; *i.e.*, on privity of contract. (D) is therefore incorrect because the perfumery is liable for the rent. (B) and (C) are also incorrect. Because the covenant to pay rent touches and concerns, and hence runs with the tenant's leasehold estate, an assignee owes the rent directly to the landlord. If the assignee reassigns the leasehold interest, his privity of estate with the landlord ends, and he generally is not liable for the subsequent assignee's failure to pay rent in the absence of a specific promise to the landlord. However, even if the assignee made no promise to the landlord but did promise the original tenant that he would pay all future rent, the landlord may sue the assignee as a third-party beneficiary of the promise to the original tenant. Here, while the dry cleaner made no promise to the landlord, the dry cleaner did make a promise to the perfumery regarding the obligation that the perfumery owed to the landlord. Thus, the landlord can sue either the perfumery or the dry cleaner for the unpaid rent.

Answer to Question 21

(A) The children have a contingent remainder. A remainder is a future interest created in a transferee that is capable of taking in present possession on the natural termination of the preceding estate created in the same disposition. Note that as a rule of thumb, remainders always follow life estates. A remainder will be classified as contingent if its taking is subject to a condition precedent, or it is created in favor of unborn or unascertained persons. Here, the interest in the children follows a life estate and is a remainder because it is capable of taking in possession on the natural termination of the preceding estate. It is subject to the condition precedent of surviving the landowner's widow and, additionally, is in favor of unascertained persons (the children who survive the landowner's widow will not be ascertained until her death). Thus, the interest is a contingent remainder. (B) is incorrect because a vested remainder can be created in and held only by ascertained persons in being, and cannot be subject to a condition precedent. As discussed above, the will provision clearly does not satisfy these requirements because the takers are not ascertained and their interest is subject to a condition of survival. (C) is incorrect because a shifting executory interest is one that divests the interest of another transferee; *i.e.*, it cuts short a prior estate created by the same conveyance. The gift to the children does not divest the interest of the widow; she retains a life estate in the property. The children's interest takes in possession only on the natural termination of the widow's estate (*i.e.*, at her death). (D) is incorrect because the interest does not violate the Rule Against Perpetuities. The children's interest will vest, if at all,

not later than 21 years after the lives in being. The landowner's widow and the children themselves are lives in being. There is no unborn widow problem because the instrument takes effect on the landowner's death and the gift is to his own widow. She must be in being at his death. Likewise, his children would be in being at his death. Thus, the vesting will be within the period of the Rule.

Answer to Question 22

(B) The tenant has a month-to-month tenancy at $1,200 per month. When a tenant continues in possession after termination of her right to possession, the landlord may bind the tenant to a new periodic tenancy. While the terms and conditions of the expired tenancy generally apply to the new tenancy, if the landlord notifies the tenant before termination that occupancy after the termination date will be at an increased rent, the tenant will be held to have acquiesced to the new terms if she does not surrender. This is so even if the tenant objects to the increased rent, as long as the rent increase is reasonable. (A) is therefore incorrect. (C) is also incorrect. In commercial leases, where the original lease term was for a year or more, a year-to-year tenancy results from holding over. In residential leases, however, most courts would rule that the tenant is a month-to-month tenant, irrespective of the term of the original lease. Hence, the tenancy would be month-to-month rather than annual. (D) is incorrect because a tenancy at will generally arises from a specific understanding between the parties that either party may terminate the tenancy at any time. Unless the parties expressly agree to a tenancy at will, the payment of regular rent will cause a court to treat the tenancy as a periodic tenancy.

Answer to Question 23

(D) The interest given to the son's children does not violate the Rule Against Perpetuities because the interest will vest, if at all, within 21 years after the life of the friend. Pursuant to the Rule Against Perpetuities, no interest in property is valid unless it must vest, if at all, not later than 21 years after one or more lives in being at the creation of the interest. In the case of a will, the perpetuities period begins to run on the date of the testator's death, and measuring lives used to show the validity of an interest must be in existence at that time. Here, the interest given to any of the son's children who are born during the friend's lifetime and who survive the friend must vest, if at all, on the death of the friend (who is a life in being at the time of the owner's death). Thus, this interest will vest, if it does vest, within 21 years after the friend's life, and is therefore not in violation of the Rule Against Perpetuities. (A) is therefore incorrect; if one or more of the son's children is alive at the time of the friend's death, the friend's heirs will get nothing because their fee simple will be divested. (B) incorrectly characterizes the interest of the son's children as a possibility of reverter. A possibility of reverter is the future interest left in a grantor who conveys a fee simple determinable estate. Although under different circumstances the son's children could acquire a possibility of reverter as heirs of the grantor (the owner), their interest in this case was conveyed directly to them in the owner's will. (C) is incorrect because the interest of the son's children is not vested. Their interest is a shifting executory interest rather than a remainder because it divests the fee simple determinable estate of the friend and his heirs. The friend has a fee simple determinable because the estate will remain with his heirs if none of the son's children are alive when the friend dies. The friend's death while the son's children are alive divests the interest of the friend's heirs; it is therefore a shifting executory interest rather than a remainder.

Answer to Question 24

(D) If the vintner prevails, it will be because the court determines that the seller's one-month delay in closing was unreasonable. Generally, courts assume that time is not "of the essence" in real estate contracts. This means that the closing date stated in the contract is not absolutely binding

in equity, and that a party, even though late in tendering her own performance, can still enforce the contract if she tenders within a reasonable time after the date. Here, if the court finds that a one-month delay is unreasonable, the seller will not be able to specifically enforce the contract. (A) is incorrect because contracts for the sale of land do not require the seller to hold title at the time she enters into the contract. She is only required to have marketable title at the date of closing so that she can deliver it to the buyer. Hence, the seller did not breach her contract with the vintner by not having an interest in the vineyard at the time of the contract. (B) is incorrect because the seller has a reasonable time after the date set for closing to tender performance unless the contract or circumstances indicate that time is of the essence. Here, nothing in the contract or the surrounding circumstances indicates that time was of the essence in the seller-vintner contract. Moreover, although title was unmarketable on June 1, the seller was able to clear title to the remaining one-eighth of the vineyard and tender performance to the vintner one month after the closing date. A delay of one month after the closing date has been deemed acceptable by courts where the buyer has been delayed in obtaining financing or the seller has been delayed in obtaining marketable title. (However, if the court finds that one month is an unreasonable delay, as in (D), then it will not grant the seller specific performance.) (C) is incorrect because it supports a finding in favor of the seller, as explained above.

Answer to Question 25

(C) The landowner will not prevail because the covenant will be rendered unenforceable by either: (i) the application of the Rule Against Perpetuities, or (ii) imposition of a reasonable time limit of less than 21 years to avoid application of the Rule Against Perpetuities. A majority of jurisdictions would probably hold that the covenant granting the right of first refusal is void because it violates the Rule Against Perpetuities. Under the Rule, no interest in property is valid unless it must vest, if at all, no later than 21 years after a life in being at the creation of the interest. If the right might be exercised later than the perpetuities period, it is void. In this case, there was no limit on the landowner's right of first refusal because it ran to his heirs and assigns. The right clearly could be exercised beyond the perpetuities period and so violates the Rule. Note that there is mixed opinion as to whether a court will avoid a right of first refusal that has an unlimited life, as this one purportedly has. There is a substantial body of opinion to the effect that the court should treat the right as exercisable only for a reasonable time, which is less than 21 years. Hence, under this analysis, the right is valid, but becomes unenforceable by the passage of time. In this case, the right has not been exercised in 25 years; therefore, even under this analysis, the right is no longer enforceable. (A) is incorrect. The recording statute quoted by the question is a race-notice statute. Under a race-notice statute, a subsequent bona fide purchaser, such as the buyer, is protected if she records before the prior grantee. To qualify as a bona fide purchaser, a person must, at the time of conveyance, take without actual, constructive, or record notice of the prior interest. Because the deed to the neighbor was recorded, the buyer had record notice of the right of first refusal because it was in her chain of title. Had the covenant been within the perpetuities period, the buyer would not have been protected by the recording act. However, because the covenant is void, the landowner has no right to the property. Similarly, (B) is incorrect. The bad faith transaction of the neighbor and the friend would not have overcome the covenant had the covenant not violated the Rule. In light of the fact that the covenant is void, however, their bad faith is irrelevant. (D) is incorrect because the covenant runs with the land. The requirements for the burden of the covenant to run are met in this case: The fact that the original covenanting parties intended the right of first refusal covenant to run to their successors is indicated by the use of the language "heirs and assigns." The notice requirement was fulfilled by recording the deed. The horizontal privity requirement is satisfied by the fact that the landowner and the neighbor share an interest in the land independent of the covenant, *i.e.*, as grantor and grantee.

The necessary vertical privity is also present because the friend and the buyer held the entire durational interest held by the landowner when the covenant was made. Last, the covenant runs with the land because it "touches and concerns" the land; *i.e.*, it diminishes the landowner's right with respect to the summer home.

Answer to Question 26

(A) A court will most likely find that the landlord has a cause of action for nuisance because of the girders passing over her property. If land is repeatedly invaded by someone without permission, the possessor has a choice: she may sue for trespass (the intentional invasion of a person's land, which includes the space above the land, by a physical object) or for nuisance (a substantial and unreasonable interference with the use of property). Here, the continual swinging of the girders over the landlord's land constitutes a repeated invasion by a physical object that interfered with the landlord's right of exclusive possession of the space over her building and with her enjoyment and use of her land. The interference is shown by her tenants' complaints. Thus, the landlord has the option of suing for trespass or nuisance to remedy this continuing invasion. (B) and (C) are incorrect because there is no generally recognized cause of action for loss of sunlight or loss of a particular view. Courts do recognize negative easements for light and air. However, the facts of this question do not indicate that any such easement arose. Easements are interests in land and generally must be in writing to be enforceable. The neighbor's oral statement that he would not develop his land would not give rise to an easement or to any other type of legally enforceable right on the part of the landlord to prevent construction of the office structure or otherwise obtain redress for its construction. Note also that even if there were a negative easement, this would merely entitle the landlord to compel the son to refrain from engaging in the construction on his property and would not necessarily entitle the landlord to damages as called for by (B) and (C). (D) is incorrect because, as explained above, the landlord would have a cause of action for trespass or nuisance.

Answer to Question 27

(B) The boutique owner may recover damages for the subsidence if the developer's project would have damaged the boutique owner's property even without the weight of the shop. A landowner has a right to have her land supported in its natural state by adjoining land. If, however, the land has buildings on it, an excavating neighbor is liable for damage to the buildings caused by the excavation if: (i) the excavating landowner was negligent; or (ii) the excavation would have caused the land to subside even in its natural state (*i.e.*, without buildings). Here, the facts indicate that the developer's excavation caused the damage to the boutique owner's shop. Thus, the boutique owner can recover if the subsidence would have occurred even if her land had been unimproved. (A) is wrong because proof of damage to the property with nothing more would not be a basis for recovery in this case. If the land had been unimproved, then the excavating landowner would be strictly liable for injury to neighboring land, but because the boutique owner's property was improved, to recover she must prove more than the fact that the damage was caused by the developer. (C) is wrong because intentional damage is not a requirement for recovery. Even if the damage to the property is unintentional, a landowner may recover if she proves causation and one of the two requirements above. (D) is wrong because an excavating landowner is liable for damage to the buildings on adjacent land even if the land would not have collapsed in its natural state if his excavation is found to have been done ***negligently***.

Answer to Question 28

(D) The buyer will most likely recover nothing because, at the time of the contract, $4,000 represented a reasonable estimate of damages in the event of breach. When a sales contract provides

that a seller may retain the buyer's earnest money as liquidated damages, courts routinely uphold the seller's retention of the money upon breach if the amount appears reasonable in light of the seller's anticipated and actual damages. Many courts uphold retention of earnest money of up to 10% of the sales price without inquiry into its reasonableness. In this case, the earnest money represented 2% of the purchase price. Given the fact that the seller had received other offers within $5,000 of the price offered by the buyer, $4,000 would be a reasonable estimate of damages if the seller were forced to accept another offer. (A) is wrong because the fact that the buyer had a good reason for not performing does not change the fact that he is in breach. The contract is not impossible for the buyer to perform; it is just not as attractive a purchase as it was before the accident. He cannot escape liability on this basis. (B) and (C) are wrong because if there is a valid liquidated damages clause, it will be enforced and actual damages are irrelevant. (If the liquidated damages clause were not enforceable, (C) would be a better choice than (B) because the seller would be entitled to her expenses in remarketing the property.) Thus, because the liquidated damages clause is enforceable, the buyer will not be able to recover any of the $4,000 he paid as earnest money.

Answer to Question 29

(C) The farmer will most likely prevail in his suit for one-half the cost of the well repairs because the covenant runs with the land. When a covenant runs with the land, subsequent owners of the land may enforce or be burdened by the covenant. If all of the requirements for the burden to run are met, the successor in interest to the burdened estate will be bound by the arrangement as effectively as if he had himself expressly agreed to be bound. To be bound: (i) the parties must have intended that the covenant run with the land; (ii) the original parties must have been in horizontal privity; (iii) the succeeding party must be in vertical privity with the original promisor; (iv) the covenant must touch and concern the land; and (v) generally, the burdened party must have actual or constructive notice of the covenant. Here, the intent is shown by the express language of the covenant, which says that it is intended to run with the land. Even without that language, the use of the words "heirs" and "assigns" would show the intent for the covenant to run. The original parties were in horizontal privity because at the time the vintner entered into the covenant, he and the friend shared an interest in the land independent of the covenant—as grantor and grantee. The daughter is in vertical privity with the vintner because she holds the entire interest in the western parcel held by the vintner. The covenant touches and concerns the land because promises to pay money to be used in a way connected with the land are held to touch and concern the property. Because the daughter was unaware of the covenant, the required notice seems to be missing. While it is generally true that the owner of the burdened land must have notice, it should be remembered that the requirement is a function of the recording statute. (At common law, the covenant was enforceable in an action for damages regardless of notice; this was changed by the recording statutes.) However, because the daughter is a donee (an heir) and not a bona fide purchaser, she is not protected by the recording statute and thus is subject to the covenant even without notice. For that reason, (A) is wrong. (B) is wrong because the farmer's possession does not satisfy several of the requirements for adverse possession. Because the farmer had a legal right to use the well, his use was not adverse or hostile to the rights of the vintner's son and the son's daughter, but was rather permissive. The farmer's possession also fails the exclusivity requirement because the facts state that the well was used to irrigate both parcels for most of the statutory period. (D) is wrong because the farmer's status as a bona fide purchaser has no effect on his ability to enforce the covenant. A successor in interest to the original promisee may enforce the covenant (enjoy the ***benefit***) if there was intent and vertical privity, and the covenant touches and concerns the land. Notice is ***not*** required for the benefit to run. Thus, because the above requirements are met here, the farmer may enforce the covenant regardless of his status as a bona fide purchaser. Had the farmer taken the property as a donee, the above analysis would be the same.

Answer to Question 30

(B) The landlord is liable for the sculptor's injuries because he failed to disclose a latent defect. If, at the time the lease is entered into, the landlord knows of a dangerous condition that the tenant could not discover upon reasonable inspection, the landlord has a duty to disclose the dangerous condition. Failure to disclose the information about the condition results in liability for any injury resulting from the condition. Because the landlord knew of the dangerous electrical problem at the time he leased the premises to the artist and did not disclose it to either the artist or the sculptor, he is liable for any injuries resulting from that condition. (A) is wrong for two reasons: (i) the implied warranty of habitability does not apply to commercial leases; and (ii) even if this were a residential lease, it is doubtful that the investor would be liable for a condition of which she had no knowledge or notice. (C) is wrong because it describes the relationship between the artist and the sculptor as though there had been a sublease, when the facts clearly state that the artist assigned the balance of the lease to the sculptor. If a tenant sublets the premises (*i.e.*, the tenant retains part of the remaining term), the tenant is the landlord of the sublessee. The sublessee cannot sue or be sued by the landlord. However, if there has been an assignment (*i.e.*, the tenant makes a complete transfer of the entire term remaining), the assignee is substituted for the original tenant and can sue or be sued by the landlord. The original tenant's relationship to the assignee is at most that of a surety. Here, because the artist transferred the balance of his lease to the sculptor, there was an assignment and thus the artist cannot be considered the sculptor's landlord. (D) is wrong because, as stated above, the sculptor can recover from the landlord. The statement that the covenant to repair runs with the land and binds the sculptor is true, but the landlord's failure to disclose a dangerous preexisting condition renders the landlord liable for the sculptor's injuries despite the covenant; *i.e.*, the sculptor's covenant does not relieve the landlord of his tort liability.

Answer to Question 31

(B) The granddaughter, the grandson's widow, and the boyfriend all have an interest in the silver mine. The landowner's will created a life estate in her husband, with a vested remainder in her children. The will further provided that if a child predeceased her, that child's issue would take the predeceased child's share. When a person renounces a gift in a will, he is treated as having predeceased the testator. Thus, in this case, because the husband renounced his gift, his life estate would be stricken, leaving the gift to the landowner's children, with the issue of any predeceased child taking in the stead of their parent. Because the gift of the silver mine was by will, it was of no effect until the landowner's death. At the landowner's death, the daughter was still alive and so is entitled to an interest in the silver mine. There is no requirement that she survive until the administration of the estate is completed; thus, her share will go to her estate and pass by will to her boyfriend. The son did not survive the landowner but did leave issue. Therefore, his issue will split his share. The grandson and granddaughter were both alive at the landowner's death and so they are entitled to take the son's share. When the grandson died, his share passed through his estate to his widow. Therefore, the interests in the silver mine are: one-half to the boyfriend (taking through the daughter), one-fourth to the granddaughter, and one-fourth to the grandson's widow (taking through the son). (A) is wrong because, as explained above, the grandson's widow is entitled to the grandson's share. (C) is wrong because it omits the boyfriend and the grandson's widow, and as explained above, the boyfriend takes the daughter's share and the grandson's widow takes the grandson's share. The daughter and the grandson had to survive the

landowner to take but they did not have to survive the administration of the estate. Therefore, the daughter and the grandson were entitled to shares in the silver mine and their shares passed through their estates to the boyfriend and the grandson's widow, respectively. (D) is wrong because it omits the boyfriend, who is entitled to the daughter's share.

Answer to Question 32

(C) The children are the owners of the bakery in fee simple absolute. The grant here gave the cousin a defeasible life estate, which would end at her death or when she ceased to operate the bakery. In this case, the cousin's life estate ended upon her conversion of the bakery to a used book store, and at that time the baker's children took the bakery in fee simple. Because the cousin no longer has any right to the bakery, she became a trespasser and could be forcibly removed. Obviously, as a trespasser, she is not entitled to any profits from the bakery. (A) is wrong because none of the gifts violates the Rule Against Perpetuities. The Rule states that an interest is not valid unless it must vest, if at all, within a life in being at its creation plus 21 years. Because the grant to the cousin and the children was made in the baker's will, it did not take effect until the baker's death. At that time, the gifts became vested. The cousin takes a present possessory life estate upon the baker's death (when the will speaks). It is not a future interest, and consequently, the Rule Against Perpetuities has no effect on it at all. The gift to the children will vest within the perpetuities period. The children have both a remainder following the cousin's life estate and an executory interest (which will divest the cousin's life estate if she ceases to operate the bakery). The remainder became vested at the baker's death because at that time his children would be ascertainable (he can have no more children) and there was no condition attached to the grant. The executory interest would also be valid under the Rule because it will vest, if at all, within the cousin's lifetime (*i.e.*, when she ceases to operate the bakery). Therefore, the gifts are valid under the Rule. (B) is wrong because, as explained above, the children have both a vested remainder and an executory interest, neither of which is subject to the destructibility rule (which applies to contingent remainders) or to the related doctrine of merger (which takes effect when one person owns all interests in the land except perhaps for a contingent remainder). (D) is wrong because when the cousin converted the bakery into a used book store, her entire interest in the bakery, not just her right to possession, ended. Thus, because she no longer has any interest in the bakery, she no longer has any right to the profits from the bakery.

Answer to Question 33

(D) The orange grove is owned by the niece, subject to the friend's estate for the life of the brother. The farmer's deed attempted to restrain alienability of the interests in the orange grove. A ***disabling restraint*** is one that renders any attempted transfer ineffective. All disabling restraints on legal interests (*e.g.*, a fee simple or life estate) are void. Here, the brother's life estate, a legal interest, is subject to a disabling restraint. The restraint prohibiting him from transferring his interest is void; therefore, the brother's conveyance to his friend is valid. The friend takes what the brother had: an estate for the brother's life. In contrast to a disabling restraint, a ***forfeiture restraint*** on alienation, under which an attempted transfer forfeits the interest, is valid if placed on a future interest only for the period when the interest is a future interest. In this case, any attempt by the niece or nephew to transfer her or his interest while the interest was still a remainder caused a forfeiture. Because the restraint ended when the interest became possessory (and thus a present interest), it is a valid restraint. Thus, the nephew's attempted transfer to the loan shark was invalid and caused a forfeiture of the nephew's remainder in favor of the niece. Consequently, the niece owns the orange grove, subject to the friend's life estate pur autre vie. (A) is wrong because it does not include the friend's life estate pur autre vie. (B) is wrong because, as

noted above, the forfeiture restraint on the transfer of the nephew's remainder was valid. Thus, the attempted transfer to the loan shark was void. (C) is wrong because, as discussed above, the disabling restraint on the transfer of the brother's interest was void and therefore the brother's life estate was freely transferable. Because the brother conveyed his interest to his friend, the brother no longer has any interest in the orange grove.

Answer to Question 34

(D) The investor has an easement to cross the northern parcel even if the developer never exercised her right to use the easement. The original easement granted to the developer was an easement appurtenant, the benefit of which passes with a transfer of the benefited land. An easement is deemed appurtenant when the right of special use benefits the easement holder in her physical use or enjoyment of another tract of land. The land subject to the easement is the servient tenement, while the land having the benefit of the easement is the dominant tenement. The benefit of an easement appurtenant passes with transfers of the benefited land, regardless of whether the easement is mentioned in the conveyance. All who possess or subsequently succeed to title to the dominant tenement are entitled to the benefit of the easement. The easement granted to the developer was an easement appurtenant because the right to use the private road across the northern parcel (the servient tenement) benefited the developer in her use and enjoyment of the southern parcel (the dominant tenement) by providing her with the most convenient access to the public highway. Thus, when the developer sold the benefited land to the investor, the benefit of the easement also passed to the investor as an incident of possession of the southern parcel. (A) is incorrect because, as explained above, this benefit passed to the investor despite the fact that the deed to the investor made no mention of the easement. The failure to record does not affect the validity of the easement. Recordation is not essential to the validity of a deed, but only serves to protect the interests of a grantee against subsequent purchasers. Here, the dispute is between the original grantor and the successor of the original easement holder. The purpose of most recording statutes is to provide notice to a ***burdened*** party. The person who granted the easement is in no need of notice. The only relevance of recording in this situation is with respect to the servient tenement, the northern parcel. The grant of easement should be recorded on the northern parcel, or bona fide purchasers from the landowner will take free of it. However, no such purchasers are involved in this question. (B) is incorrect because the investor's use of the easement would not be a change in its use. This choice goes to the scope of the easement. The key for determining the scope is the reasonable intent of the original parties, including the reasonable present and future needs of the dominant tenement. Here, because the landowner knew of the developer's plans to open an inn, he knew that she and her guests would use the road across the northern parcel. The investor's use of the easement would be the same—her use and that of her guests. This is not a change in intended use sufficient to allow the landowner to legally prevent the investor's use of the easement. (C) is incorrect because nonuse does not extinguish an easement. Abandonment, which does terminate an easement, requires a physical act by the easement holder that manifests an intent to permanently abandon the easement (*e.g.*, erecting a building that blocks access to an easement of way). Because there is no indication of such an act by the developer, the easement continues to benefit the southern parcel even if the developer never used it.

Answer to Question 35

(B) The owner can hold the tenant to a year-to-year tenancy for the original amount. When a tenant continues in possession after the termination of her right to possession, the landlord has two choices of action: He may treat the hold-over tenant as a trespasser and evict her under an unlawful detainer statute, or he may, in his sole discretion, bind the tenant to a new periodic tenancy, in

which case the terms and conditions of the expired tenancy apply to the new tenancy. Unless a residential lease is involved, a year-to-year tenancy results from holding over if the original lease term was for a year or more. The new tenancy has the same terms as the original tenancy unless the landlord notified the tenant before termination of the original tenancy that occupancy after termination will be at an increased rent. Here, the original lease was a commercial lease for a two-year term, so the owner's decision to hold the tenant to a new tenancy makes it a year-to-year tenancy. However, because the owner did not notify the tenant of the rent increase prior to the end of the term, the new tenancy is at the original amount of rent. (A) is wrong because the lease here is not a residential lease; thus, the periodic tenancy created is a year-to-year tenancy rather than a month-to-month tenancy. (C) is wrong for the same reason that (A) is wrong and also because the new tenancy is at the original amount of rent, as discussed above. (D) is wrong because when a landlord elects to bind a hold-over tenant to a new tenancy, it will be a periodic tenancy rather than a tenancy at will.

Answer to Question 36

(A) The vendee is likely to prevail because the vendor waived the strict performance of the contract. In an installment land contract, the vendee signs a contract with the vendor, agreeing to make regular installment payments until the full contract price has been paid. Only at that time will the vendor give a deed transferring legal title to the purchaser. In case of default, the contract usually contains a forfeiture clause providing that the vendor may cancel the contract, retain all money paid to date, and retake possession of the land. However, where a vendor has established a pattern of accepting late payments from the vendee, he cannot suddenly insist on strict on-time payment and declare a forfeiture if such payment is not forthcoming. Such a pattern is said to constitute a waiver of strict performance. Here, the vendor accepted the vendee's late payments for at least three months. Thus, he is deemed to have waived the strict performance of the contract. (B) is incorrect because even if the contract provided that time was of the essence (*i.e.*, that payments had to be made on the first of the month), the vendor will be deemed to have waived this provision by accepting the vendee's late payments. (C) is incorrect because the vendor will not prevail and because even if he did, he would not have to refund to the vendee the amount of payments made. Thus, (D) would be the correct answer if the vendor had not waived the strict performance of the contract.

Set 6 Answer Sheet

1. Ⓐ Ⓑ Ⓒ Ⓓ
2. Ⓐ Ⓑ Ⓒ Ⓓ
3. Ⓐ Ⓑ Ⓒ Ⓓ
4. Ⓐ Ⓑ Ⓒ Ⓓ
5. Ⓐ Ⓑ Ⓒ Ⓓ
6. Ⓐ Ⓑ Ⓒ Ⓓ
7. Ⓐ Ⓑ Ⓒ Ⓓ
8. Ⓐ Ⓑ Ⓒ Ⓓ
9. Ⓐ Ⓑ Ⓒ Ⓓ
10. Ⓐ Ⓑ Ⓒ Ⓓ
11. Ⓐ Ⓑ Ⓒ Ⓓ
12. Ⓐ Ⓑ Ⓒ Ⓓ
13. Ⓐ Ⓑ Ⓒ Ⓓ
14. Ⓐ Ⓑ Ⓒ Ⓓ
15. Ⓐ Ⓑ Ⓒ Ⓓ
16. Ⓐ Ⓑ Ⓒ Ⓓ
17. Ⓐ Ⓑ Ⓒ Ⓓ
18. Ⓐ Ⓑ Ⓒ Ⓓ
19. Ⓐ Ⓑ Ⓒ Ⓓ
20. Ⓐ Ⓑ Ⓒ Ⓓ
21. Ⓐ Ⓑ Ⓒ Ⓓ
22. Ⓐ Ⓑ Ⓒ Ⓓ
23. Ⓐ Ⓑ Ⓒ Ⓓ
24. Ⓐ Ⓑ Ⓒ Ⓓ
25. Ⓐ Ⓑ Ⓒ Ⓓ
26. Ⓐ Ⓑ Ⓒ Ⓓ
27. Ⓐ Ⓑ Ⓒ Ⓓ
28. Ⓐ Ⓑ Ⓒ Ⓓ
29. Ⓐ Ⓑ Ⓒ Ⓓ
30. Ⓐ Ⓑ Ⓒ Ⓓ
31. Ⓐ Ⓑ Ⓒ Ⓓ
32. Ⓐ Ⓑ Ⓒ Ⓓ
33. Ⓐ Ⓑ Ⓒ Ⓓ
34. Ⓐ Ⓑ Ⓒ Ⓓ
35. Ⓐ Ⓑ Ⓒ Ⓓ
36. Ⓐ Ⓑ Ⓒ Ⓓ

REAL PROPERTY QUESTIONS - SET 6

Question 1

A landowner conveyed his land "to my son for life, then to my son's widow for her life, then to my son's children." At the time of the conveyance, the son was 20 years old and unmarried. The son eventually married and had two children, the landowner's grandson and granddaughter.

Many years later, the landowner and the grandson were involved in a train accident. The landowner was killed instantly. The grandson died a short time later of his injuries. The landowner left his entire estate by will to his friend. The grandson's will devised his entire estate to the city zoo. The son's wife was so grief-stricken that she became ill and died the next year, leaving her entire estate to her husband.

Eventually the son met and married a 21-year-old. Ten years later, the son died, leaving everything to his second wife. When the second wife moved onto the land, the granddaughter filed suit to quiet title to the land, joining all of the appropriate parties.

If the jurisdiction recognizes the common law Rule Against Perpetuities, unmodified by statute, the court will most likely find that title to the land is held:

(A) One-half in the granddaughter and one-half in the city zoo, subject to the second wife's life estate.

(B) One-half in the granddaughter and one-half in the second wife, because the second wife took the son's interest.

(C) Entirely in the friend, subject to the second wife's life estate, because the gift to the son's children violates the Rule Against Perpetuities.

(D) Entirely in the granddaughter, subject to the second wife's life estate, because the grandson did not survive the son.

Question 2

A buyer entered into a written contract with a seller to purchase his commercial property for $100,000. The contract did not specify the quality of title to be conveyed, and made no mention of easements or reservations. The closing was set for November 25, three months from the signing of the contract. Shortly thereafter, the buyer obtained a survey of the property, which revealed that the city had an easement for the public sidewalk that ran in front of the store. Because this actually enhanced the value of the property, the buyer did not mention it to the seller.

Subsequently, the buyer found a better location for her business. On November 1, the buyer notified the seller that she no longer intended to purchase the property. The seller told her that he intended to hold her to her contract. At closing, the buyer refused to tender the purchase price, claiming that the seller's title is unmarketable and citing the sidewalk easement as proof of that fact.

In a suit for specific performance, the seller will most likely:

(A) Prevail, because the contract did not specify the quality of title to be conveyed.

(B) Prevail, because the buyer was aware of the visible easement and it enhanced the value of the property.

(C) Not prevail, because an easement not provided for in the contract renders title unmarketable.

(D) Not prevail, because the buyer gave the seller sufficient notice of her change in plans and yet he made no effort to try to find another purchaser.

Question 3

A buyer agreed to purchase a portion of a seller's parcel for $25,000. The buyer and the seller orally agreed that the property included in the purchase would be the westerly third of the parcel, and the eastern boundary would be a stone fence that ran from the northern border of the parcel to the southern boundary. Due to a clerical error by the seller's secretary, when the agreement was reduced to writing, the eastern boundary was stated to be the picket fence, which is 275 yards east of the stone fence.

If the buyer sues for specific performance of the contract conveying the additional strip of land, the buyer will likely:

(A) Not prevail, because the court will reform the contract.

(B) Not prevail, because natural monuments prevail over artificial monuments.

(C) Prevail, because the language in the contract controls.

(D) Prevail, because evidence of the oral agreement is inadmissible under the Statute of Frauds.

Question 4

A buyer purchased a parcel of land from a seller for $500,000. The buyer financed the purchase by obtaining a loan from the seller for $300,000 in exchange for a mortgage on the land. The seller promptly and properly recorded his mortgage. Shortly thereafter, the buyer gave a mortgage on the land to a creditor to satisfy a preexisting debt of $100,000 owed to the creditor. The creditor also promptly and properly recorded its mortgage. Within a year, the buyer stopped making payments on both mortgages, and the seller brought an action to foreclose on his mortgage. The creditor was not included as a party to the foreclosure action. The seller purchased the property at a public foreclosure sale in satisfaction of the loan. The creditor subsequently discovered the sale and informed the seller that it was not valid.

Who has title to the land?

(A) The seller, because he gave a purchase money mortgage and the creditor's mortgage was for a preexisting debt.

(B) The seller, because the public foreclosure sale extinguished the creditor's interest.

(C) The seller, but he must redeem the creditor's mortgage to avoid foreclosure.

(D) The buyer, because the seller's foreclosure action was invalid without the inclusion of the creditor as a necessary party.

Question 5

A brother and a sister held real property as joint tenants. The sister was involved in an automobile accident and was sued by a motorist who had received serious bodily injuries. The jury ruled against the sister and assessed a large damages award that the sister was unable to pay in full. Therefore, the motorist went back into court and secured a statutory lien on the property. Shortly thereafter, the sister died.

What are the respective interests of the brother and the motorist in the property?

(A) The brother is the sole owner of the property, but the property is subject to the motorist's statutory lien.

(B) The brother is the sole owner of the property, and the property is not subject to the motorist's statutory lien.

(C) The brother and the motorist own the property as tenants in common.

(D) The brother and the motorist own the property in joint tenancy.

Question 6

A rancher entered into a written contract to buy a farm from a farmer for $100,000. The contract stipulated for closing on September 30. In addition, the contract contained the following provision: "The taxes shall be prorated as agreed to by the parties at a later date." Upon the signing of the contract, the rancher gave the farmer a check for $10,000 as a down payment.

On September 28, the rancher notified the farmer that he would not be able to close on the farm until October 2, because the closing on his current home, the proceeds from which were to be applied to his purchase of the farm, was unavoidably delayed due to his buyer's illness. Meanwhile, the farmer had difficulty finding a home she liked as well as the farm. She decided that she would rather not sell the farm and wished to avoid the contract with the rancher. On October 2, the rancher showed up at the closing with the $90,000 to tender to the farmer. The farmer did not show up. The rancher sues for specific performance.

The court will most likely rule in favor of:

(A) The farmer, because the tax provision is an essential term of the contract, and it is not specific enough to satisfy the Statute of Frauds.

(B) The farmer, because the rancher materially breached by not tendering performance on September 30.

(C) The rancher, because of the operation of the doctrine of equitable conversion.

(D) The rancher, because time was not of the essence.

Question 7

To satisfy a debt owing to a creditor, a son executed and delivered to the creditor a warranty deed to a large tract of undeveloped land. The creditor promptly recorded the deed. Shortly thereafter, she built a house on the property and has lived there ever since. The son never actually owned the land. It belonged to his father, but the father had promised to leave the property to the son.

Later, the father died and his will devised the property to the son. Pressed for money, the son then sold the land to an investor by warranty deed, which the investor promptly recorded. Although the investor paid full value for the property, he purchased it strictly for investment and never visited the site. He therefore did not realize that the creditor was living there, and knew nothing of the son's earlier deed to the creditor.

The jurisdiction in which the land is located has the following statute: "A conveyance of an estate in land (other than a lease for less than one year) shall not be valid against any subsequent purchaser for value without notice thereof unless the conveyance is recorded."

Which of the following is the most likely outcome of a quiet title action brought by the creditor against the investor?

(A) The creditor prevails, because the son had no title to convey to the investor.

(B) The creditor prevails, because the investor was not a purchaser for value without notice of the creditor's interest.

(C) The investor prevails, because under the doctrine of estoppel by deed, title inures to the benefit of the original grantee only as against the grantor.

(D) The investor prevails, because under the recording acts, the deed from the son to the creditor was not in the chain of title and hence did not constitute notice to the investor.

Question 8

An owner leased her studio to a photographer under a written lease for a term of five years at $1,250 per month. The lease provided that the photographer was prohibited from assigning or subletting without the owner's consent. Later, the photographer sold all his rights under the lease to an artist. The owner executed a signed writing consenting to the assignment of the photographer's interest to the artist. The deal went through.

Subsequently, the owner sold the studio to an investor. A few months later, the artist transferred her interest under the lease to a pottery maker by a writing providing that the artist could reenter if the pottery maker failed to make rental payments to the investor. The investor, however, refused to consent to the pottery maker's becoming a tenant. As a result, the pottery maker refused to pay any rent.

The transfer from the artist to the pottery maker was:

(A) Effective even though the investor refused to consent.

(B) Effective, because the investor had no reasonable basis to withhold consent.

(C) Effective, because the covenant against assignment is void as a restraint on alienation.

(D) Ineffective.

Question 9

A landowner was declared insane and committed to a state mental hospital 30 years ago. Five years after that, a trespasser entered onto the landowner's 200-acre parcel of land, which was enclosed by a barbed wire fence. A solid wood fence ran through the middle of the land, separating the property into approximately equal east and west parcels. The trespasser began grazing cattle on the west parcel; no one else has been in possession of any part of the 200 acres. The period of time to acquire title by adverse possession is 15 years, but insanity is considered a disability that tolls the running of the time period. Thirteen years ago, the landowner was released from the hospital, but he did nothing until this year, when he brought an action to eject the trespasser. The trespasser counterclaimed to quiet title in him.

In this action, the trespasser will:

(A) Win, because he has acquired title to the 200 acres by adverse possession.

(B) Win, but only as to the west parcel, because that is the portion of the land he actually occupied during his adverse possession.

(C) Lose, because the landowner can assert the defense of laches, as the trespasser did not bring an action to quiet his title within a reasonable time after the statute had run.

(D) Lose, because the landowner was insane for 12 of the 25 years that the trespasser was in possession.

Question 10

A landowner devised her campground in her will "to my niece, her heirs, and assigns, so long as it is used for camping and recreational purposes; if used for any other purpose during her lifetime, then to the Girl Scouts of America." Subsequently, the landowner died. The residuary clause of her will left all property not devised in the remainder of the will to her daughter and sole heir. Soon thereafter, the daughter died intestate, her only heir being her son.

Last month, the niece entered into a contract to sell the campground to a buyer for its reasonable market value. After the buyer received the title report called for in the contract, he refused to proceed with the purchase, claiming that the niece could not convey good title. The niece, the Girl Scouts of America, and the buyer then execute a new contract calling for the former two parties to sell the property at the same price to the latter. The jurisdiction follows the common law Rule Against Perpetuities, and a statute provides that future estates and interests are alienable, and may be devised or inherited, all in the same manner as possessory estates or interests.

Should the buyer proceed with the new purchase transaction?

(A) Yes, because good title can now be conveyed by the sellers.

(B) Yes, if the Girl Scouts of America promises never to use its right of entry should the buyer use the property for other than camping and recreational purposes.

(C) No, because the daughter's son has not been included as a party selling the property.

(D) No, because no one can convey good title to the property during the niece's lifetime.

Question 11

To secure a loan of $100,000 from a bank, the owner in fee simple of a parcel of land conveyed a deed of trust for the land to the bank. The deed of trust contained a "power of sale" clause, permitted by the jurisdiction, which allowed the bank to sell the property in the event of default without the necessity of a judicial foreclosure action. After several years, the owner defaulted on his loan payments to the bank. The bank informed the owner that it was exercising its power of sale. After appropriate notices, the bank conducted a public sale of the land. The bank was the sole bidder and obtained the property for $80,000, which was $10,000 less than the outstanding balance on the loan plus the expenses of the sale. One month later, the owner notified the bank that he wanted to pay off the loan and extinguish the deed of trust, and was prepared to tender $80,000 to do so. The bank insisted that the owner must tender $90,000 to pay off the loan.

If a court in the jurisdiction will require the bank to accept only $80,000 under the circumstances above, it will be because:

(A) The owner had the power to revoke the trust as long as he was alive.

(B) The bank did not have the authority to bid on the property at other than a judicial foreclosure sale.

(C) The owner was exercising a statutory power rather than an equitable power.

(D) The bank does not have the power to clog the equity of redemption.

Question 12

A landowner devised her home "to my daughter for life, then to the eldest survivor of her two children, my grandson and granddaughter, for life, remainder to the eldest surviving offspring of the two grandchildren who is alive at the death of the last life tenant." After the landowner's death, the daughter lived in the family home for 15 years. Upon the daughter's death, both of her children were alive, so the home passed to the grandson, the eldest. He lived in the house for three years, and then conveyed it to the city historical society, which converted it into its headquarters and museum. Eight years later, the grandson died. At the time of his death, he was survived by his widow, his two sons, the granddaughter, and the granddaughter's daughter, who was the eldest of the niece and nephews. Four years after the grandson's death, the granddaughter's daughter brought an action for ejectment and to quiet title against the city historical society. The jurisdiction has a statutory period of adverse possession of 10 years, or five years if entry was made by the adverse possessor under color of title.

How should the court rule in the granddaughter's daughter's action?

(A) For the society, because it has occupied the home for the statutory period required for adverse possession.

(B) For the society, because it purchased the home in fee simple absolute from the grandson.

(C) For the granddaughter's daughter, because the society has not been in adverse possession for the requisite period.

(D) For the granddaughter's daughter, because a purchaser of property from a life tenant cannot acquire a fee simple absolute through adverse possession.

Question 13

A landowner owned a beachfront lot and home in a subdivision occupying several hundred acres near a lake. The recorded subdivision plan grants to each owner in the subdivision an easement to use the private roads therein for personal ingress and egress.

Following seismic activity in the area, the level of the lake dropped substantially, exposing a considerable amount of land between the new shoreline and the old beachfront. It was judicially determined that this "new" land belonged to the county, which put portions of it up for sale. The landowner purchased the land extending from her old property line to the new shoreline, and constructed a boat launching ramp on the new property. She then permitted persons who did not own land in the subdivision to drive through her old property to reach the boat launching ramp on her new property, and thus to utilize the lake, for a small fee. The homeowners' association brought suit against the landowner, seeking to enjoin her from using or permitting nonresidents of the subdivision from traveling its streets to reach the boat launching ramp.

How should the court rule?

(A) For the homeowners, because the scope of the easement granted to the landowner as an owner in the subdivision does not extend to the use that she is making of the new property.

(B) For the landowner, because she has an express easement over the streets of the subdivision.

(C) For the landowner, because she has an easement by necessity as to the new property over the streets of the subdivision.

(D) For the landowner, because she has an implied easement over the streets of the subdivision benefiting the new property since it abuts her old property.

Question 14

A tenant rented an apartment in a large multi-unit building. One day vandals broke into several of the building's apartments, including the tenant's, and smeared excrement into the carpets and on the walls, and broke out all of the windows. The jurisdiction provides by statute that if a tenant notifies her landlord in writing of a repair that is needed to keep the premises in a habitable condition and the landlord does not repair it within 15 days, the tenant may, at her option, either repair it herself and withhold the expenses from rent, or consider herself constructively evicted and terminate her tenancy. The tenant wrote a letter to the landlord informing him that her walls, carpets, and windows had been damaged and needed repair, and after eight days she received a letter in reply stating that such damages to her apartment were her responsibility to repair.

After waiting another week, the tenant paid to have her carpets and walls cleaned and to have her windows replaced. She then withheld the entire next month's rent of $400, because the cleaning and repair bills had totaled $750. After sending her the required statutory notices, the landlord commenced unlawful detainer litigation, seeking to have the tenant evicted for nonpayment of rent.

How should the court rule?

(A) For the landlord, because the damage was the result of the criminal acts of a third party.

(B) For the landlord, because the damage was to a private apartment and not to the common areas of the apartment complex.

(C) For the tenant, if she can show that the landlord was negligent in connection with the vandalism.

(D) For the tenant, because she satisfied the requirements of the statute.

Question 15

A chef purchased a restaurant for $100,000. As part of his financing, he obtained a purchase money mortgage from a bank for $60,000. Due to a clerical error by the bank, the mortgage was not recorded in the county recorder's office.

A statute in the jurisdiction provides: "No conveyance of an interest in land, other than a lease for less than one year, shall be valid against any subsequent purchaser for value, without notice thereof, whose conveyance is first recorded."

After the chef's restaurant had been in operation for five years, business dropped dramatically. To stay in business, the chef obtained a mortgage from a financing company for $30,000. The financing company was not informed by the chef of the mortgage held by the bank. The next day, the chef contacted the bank about renegotiating its mortgage. Checking its records, the bank discovered that the original mortgage was not recorded and immediately recorded it. Later that day, the financing company recorded its mortgage. A few days later, the chef and the bank agreed to a modification of their mortgage agreement to allow the chef to make lower monthly payments in exchange for a higher interest rate and a longer period of repayment.

Despite this agreement, the chef was unable to make payments on the financing company mortgage. The financing company instituted a foreclosure action six months later, but failed to include the bank as a party to the foreclosure action.

If the financing company takes title to the restaurant at the foreclosure sale, which of the following statements most correctly describes the bank's interest?

(A) The bank's mortgage on the restaurant survives under its original terms.

(B) The bank's mortgage on the restaurant survives under its modified terms.

(C) The bank's mortgage is extinguished because when it was modified it became junior to the financing company's mortgage.

(D) The bank's mortgage is extinguished regardless of the modification because it had not recorded before the financing company obtained its mortgage interest.

Question 16

A landlord entered into a written lease of a bakery for a term of 25 years with a baker. The parties agreed to a right of first refusal if the bakery was offered for sale during the term of the lease. The lease also permitted assignments and subleases on notice to the landlord. Three years later, the baker retired and, after notifying the landlord, transferred the lease to a chocolatier. Twenty-one years later, the landlord entered into a contract with a buyer for the sale of the bakery for $100,000. The landlord had informed the buyer of the lease but had forgotten about the right of first refusal. When the chocolatier learned of the sale to the buyer, she informed both the landlord and the buyer that she wanted to exercise her option and was prepared to purchase the bakery for the contract price. The jurisdiction's Rule Against Perpetuities is unmodified by statute.

Can the chocolatier enforce the option?

(A) Yes, because an option held by a tenant on leased property cannot be separated from the leasehold interest.

(B) Yes, because the option touches and concerns the leasehold estate.

(C) No, because the transfer to the chocolatier made the option void under the Rule Against Perpetuities.

(D) No, because the option was not specifically included when the lease was transferred to the chocolatier.

Question 17

An owner of a 240-acre tract of land entered into an agreement to sell 20 acres of the land to his neighbor. The land the neighbor wanted was located in the northwest quarter of the land. The owner wrote out the following statement:

> The owner agrees to sell to the neighbor, for $50,000, 20 acres in the northwest quarter of the owner's land, the owner's land beginning at a point in the northeast quadrant of the county on the 16th county survey line, six minutes west of the 98th Meridian, and then proceeding due east 1,320

> yards and from that point due south to the creek, and then westward along the creek to the point at which it intersects the public road, and then northward along the eastern edge of the public road until the road ends, and then due northward from that point to the original starting point of the survey.

The owner had copied the language describing the land from his own deed. The owner then signed the paper and gave it to the neighbor. On the date set for closing, the neighbor tendered $50,000 to the owner. The owner refused to accept the money and refused to convey 20 acres to the neighbor.

If the neighbor sues the owner for specific performance:

(A) The owner will prevail, because the writing did not adequately describe which 20 acres were to be sold.

(B) The owner will prevail, because the writing was not signed by both parties.

(C) The neighbor will prevail, because metes and bounds are a sufficient way to legally describe property.

(D) The neighbor will prevail, because the writing satisfies the Statute of Frauds.

Question 18

A landowner inherited a parcel of land, free of encumbrances, and promptly recorded his deed. The landowner took out a $100,000 mortgage on the land with a bank to pay for improvements to the property. The instrument was properly recorded. The landowner regularly made the scheduled payments on the mortgage. Subsequently, the landowner decided to further improve the property and took out another mortgage with a financing company for $50,000. The instrument was properly recorded. The landowner then sold the land to a buyer subject to both mortgages.

The buyer procured another loan of $100,000 secured by a mortgage on the land from a lender. The lender knew about the bank's mortgage, but the buyer did not inform her of the financing company's mortgage. The lender lent the money to the buyer on the understanding that the buyer would use the money to pay off the bank's mortgage, placing the lender in first priority. The buyer promptly paid off the bank but made no further payments to the financing company. The financing company initiated steps to foreclose on the land. The lender brings an appropriate action seeking to have her rights declared superior to those of the financing company.

The state in which the land is located has the following statute: "Any conveyance of an estate in land, other than a lease for less than one year, shall not be valid against any subsequent purchaser whose conveyance is first recorded."

If the court rules in the lender's favor, it will be because:

(A) The lender could reactivate the first mortgage and step into the shoes of the bank.

(B) The balancing of equities clearly favors the lender.

(C) The lender lacked actual knowledge of the second mortgage.

(D) The lender received no benefit from the financing company, and therefore cannot be burdened by the financing company's demands.

Question 19

A seller entered into a written contract to sell a tract of land to a buyer. The buyer was to pay $1,500 per month for five years, at which time the seller would deliver a warranty deed. The contract was silent as to the quality of title to be conveyed. After making 12 payments, the buyer discovered that a neighbor had an easement of way over the land, which was not discussed at the time the seller and buyer entered into the contract. The neighbor had not used the easement over the previous year because she had

been out of the country. On the basis of the easement, the buyer wishes to cancel the contract.

Which party is more likely to prevail?

(A) The seller, because the neighbor's easement has been extinguished.

(B) The seller, because the buyer has no basis on which to rescind the contract.

(C) The buyer, because the obligation to convey marketable title is implied.

(D) The buyer, because the seller has breached the covenant against encumbrances.

Question 20

A landowner owned a large tract of land in an area zoned for medium residential use. Permitted uses in this zone are single-family dwellings, condominium and townhouse developments, and moderate density apartment complexes. The landowner subdivided her land into 10 lots and conveyed each lot by a deed restricting the land to single-family use. All deeds were duly recorded and all lots were developed as single-family homes.

The owner of lot 1 died and his property passed by will to his niece. Some time later, the owner of lot 3 sold his property to a buyer by a deed that did not contain the covenant limiting use to single-family dwellings. The buyer subsequently sold lot 3 to her friend, and did not include the covenant in the deed. Both deeds were duly recorded. A storm destroyed the friend's home, and in its place he began to build a three-unit townhouse.

May the niece sue to enforce the covenant against the friend to prevent him from building the townhouse on lot 3?

(A) No, because there is no privity with the friend.

(B) No, because the zoning laws have not been violated.

(C) No, because there was no restriction in the friend's deed.

(D) Yes, because the friend's townhouse would alter the landowner's common scheme.

Question 21

A father conveyed his land to his son by warranty deed. The deed stated that the son paid $125,000 for the land but, in fact, the son had not. However, the son and the father agreed orally that the son would not record the deed until he paid the father the $125,000. The son neither paid the father nor recorded the deed for three years, at which time the property values in the area began to climb rapidly. Wishing to turn a fast profit, the son recorded the deed from the father and one week later conveyed the land to a buyer for $200,000. The buyer promptly recorded the deed. When the father discovered what had transpired, he filed a lawsuit, and the court determined that the son owed the father $125,000. Unfortunately, the son and his $200,000 from the buyer are nowhere to be found. The father asked the court to levy on the land, which the buyer opposed. The jurisdiction in which the land is located has the following statute: "No interest in land shall be good against a subsequent purchaser for value, without notice, unless the interest is recorded."

If the father cannot levy on the land, it will be because the buyer's best defense against the levy is based on:

(A) The Statute of Frauds.

(B) The rights of a bona fide purchaser.

(C) The buyer's recording of the deed, which gave her protection under the recording act.

(D) The parol evidence rule.

Question 22

A landowner and his neighbor purchased adjoining undeveloped lots. After both built homes on their respective lots, the landowner suggested to the neighbor that a common

driveway be built where the two lots joined. The neighbor agreed. The landowner and the neighbor split the cost of constructing the driveway and entered into a written agreement to equally share the costs of its upkeep and maintenance. The agreement was recorded in the county recorder's office.

Two years later, the neighbor built a new driveway located entirely on his lot. The common driveway, which the landowner continued to use but which the neighbor no longer used, began to deteriorate. The landowner asked the neighbor for money to maintain the common driveway, but the neighbor refused to contribute. Three years later, the neighbor conveyed his lot to a friend. The friend entered into possession and used only the driveway built by the neighbor. By this time, the common driveway had deteriorated badly and contained numerous potholes. The landowner asked the friend to pay half of what it would take to repair the common driveway. The friend refused. The landowner repaired the driveway and sued the friend for 50% of the cost of repairs.

Will the landowner prevail?

(A) Yes, because easements run with the land.

(B) Yes, because the agreement between the landowner and the neighbor was recorded.

(C) No, because the neighbor abandoned use of the easement.

(D) No, because the landowner is not in privity of contract with the friend.

Question 23

The owner in fee simple of a tract of land sold it to a farmer for $850,000. To finance the purchase, the farmer obtained a mortgage loan from a financing company for $600,000. The deed from the owner to the farmer was promptly and properly recorded, but due to an oversight the mortgage from the financing company was not immediately recorded. A few months later, the farmer approached the financing company about getting a second mortgage. The financing company turned him down, so he contacted a bank. Not having knowledge of the previous mortgage on the property, the bank agreed to loan the farmer $300,000 secured by a mortgage on the land, which it promptly and properly recorded. One day later, the financing company, having discovered that its original mortgage had not been recorded, properly recorded it.

The jurisdiction's recording statute provides: "Any conveyance or mortgage of an interest in land, other than a lease for less than a year, shall not be valid against any subsequent purchaser for value, without notice thereof, whose conveyance is first recorded."

The farmer struggled to keep up with his mortgage payments, and finally stopped making payments altogether on both mortgages. The bank began foreclosure proceedings, but did not include the financing company as a party. At the foreclosure sale, a buyer purchased the land, having no actual knowledge of the mortgage with the financing company. Soon after, the financing company declared its loan in default and sought to foreclose on the land.

May the financing company foreclose against the buyer?

(A) Yes, because the holder of a senior mortgage interest is unaffected by foreclosure of a junior interest.

(B) Yes, because the holder of a junior mortgage interest is a necessary party that must be included in a foreclosure proceeding by the holder of a senior interest.

(C) No, because its failure to promptly record extinguished its rights against all parties except the farmer, the original mortgagor.

(D) No, because the buyer succeeds to the farmer's right of redemption.

Question 24

A seller conveyed her residential city property to a buyer by a general warranty deed. On taking possession of the property, the buyer discovered that the garage of his neighbor encroached six inches onto his property.

If the buyer wishes to compel the seller to assist him in a suit against the neighbor, which of the following covenants may he rely on to do so?

(A) Seisin and encumbrances.

(B) Warranty and further assurances.

(C) Seisin and warranty.

(D) Encumbrances and further assurances.

Question 25

A mother purchased 80 acres of desert land over 30 years ago. The deed was properly recorded. Although her family had never even visited the land, the mother had described to them the little two-room cabin that sat in the middle of the parcel near the dry streambed. Ten years ago, the mother's son found what he was certain was the little cabin, and over the next few years he built a barn, a greenhouse, and some corrals, all enclosed by a sturdy wire mesh fence. The area bounded by the fence, containing all the structures, occupied about two acres of the 80 owned by the mother.

Three years ago, the mother died, validly devising the 80 acres to the son. The son entered into a contract for sale of the two acres, describing it in detail with reference to the structures and nearby landmarks. The purchaser's surveyor discovered that the son had settled onto a completely different parcel from the one owned by the mother. The purchaser immediately announced that he would not proceed with the sale contract. The state's statutory period for establishing adverse possession is five years.

If the son brings an action for specific performance of the sale contract, for whom should the court rule?

(A) The purchaser, because the son does not own the land he is purporting to sell.

(B) The purchaser, because the son does not have marketable title to the land he is purporting to sell.

(C) The son, if he conveys by quitclaim deed.

(D) The son, because the description in the contract of sale is sufficient to identify the property and need not be as accurate as one contained in a deed conveying land.

Question 26

As a result of a personal injury lawsuit, a victim obtained a judgment against a tortfeasor for $100,000. The tortfeasor, who had few assets, did not pay the judgment. On April 1 of the following year, the tortfeasor inherited a parcel of land from her uncle. On May 1, the tortfeasor entered into a contract with a buyer to sell the land for $120,000. The contract was not recorded. The buyer immediately applied to a bank for a loan of $100,000. The bank approved the buyer's loan, and on May 15, a closing was held. The tortfeasor deeded the land to the buyer, and the buyer executed a mortgage for $100,000 to the bank. Due to an error by the title company, the deed from the tortfeasor to the buyer was not recorded, although the mortgage to the bank was recorded. Neither the buyer nor the bank had any knowledge of the victim's judgment. On May 20, the victim recorded his judgment in the county recorder's office where the land was located. At that time, he had no knowledge of the buyer's or the bank's rights. When he learned about them, he immediately brought a proceeding to foreclose his judgment lien, naming the tortfeasor, the buyer, and the bank as parties.

The jurisdiction has a typical grantor/grantee recording index, and has enacted the following statute:

> Any judgment properly filed in the county recorder's office shall, for 10 years from filing, be a lien on the real property then owned or subsequently acquired by any person against whom the judgment is rendered. No conveyance or mortgage of real property shall be good against subsequent bona fide purchasers for value and without notice unless the same be recorded according to law.

As between the victim and the bank, which party's interest in the land will be given priority?

(A) The bank, because the bank recorded its mortgage before the victim recorded his judgment lien.

(B) The bank, because the victim is not protected by the recording statute.

(C) The victim, because the victim's judgment was filed in the recorder's office before the buyer's deed was recorded.

(D) The victim, because the judgment lien extends to after-acquired property.

Question 27

An owner obtained a loan of $60,000 from a bank in exchange for a promissory note secured by a mortgage on his land, which the bank promptly and properly recorded. A few months later, the owner obtained another loan of $60,000 from a lender, in exchange for a promissory note secured by a mortgage on the land, which the lender promptly and properly recorded. Subsequently, the owner sold the land to a buyer for $150,000 and conveyed a warranty deed. The buyer expressly agreed with the owner to assume both mortgages, with the consent of the bank and the lender. A few years later, the bank loaned the buyer an additional $50,000 in exchange for an increase in the interest rate and principal amount of its mortgage on the land. At that time, the balance on the original loan from the bank was $50,000. Shortly thereafter, the buyer stopped making payments on both mortgages and disappeared. After proper notice to all appropriate parties, the bank instituted a foreclosure action on its mortgage, and purchased the property at the foreclosure sale. At that time the principal balance on the lender's mortgage loan was $50,000. After fees and expenses, the proceeds from the foreclosure sale totaled $80,000.

Assuming that the jurisdiction permits deficiency judgments, which of the following statements is most accurate?

(A) The bank keeps the entire $80,000 and can proceed personally against the owner for its deficiency, while the lender's mortgage remains on the land.

(B) The bank keeps the entire $80,000, the lender's mortgage on the land is extinguished, and both the bank and the lender can proceed personally against the owner for their deficiencies.

(C) The bank keeps $50,000, the lender is entitled to $30,000, and only the lender can proceed personally against the owner for its deficiency.

(D) The bank keeps $50,000, the lender is entitled to $30,000, and neither the bank nor the lender can proceed personally against the owner for their deficiencies.

Question 28

A landlord leased half of the units in her shopping center to various merchants. Subsequently, the landlord borrowed $50,000 from an investor. The landlord gave the investor a promissory note for $50,000, payable in five years, and secured by a mortgage on the shopping center. The note and mortgage contained an assignment of the rents and profits from the shopping center. The investor promptly and properly recorded the note and mortgage. Within one month, the landlord leased the remainder of the units in the shopping center. At the end of five years, the landlord defaulted on the note.

In the absence of an applicable statute, the investor is entitled to collect rents as they accrue from:

(A) All of the tenants.

(B) None of the tenants, unless their leases with the landlord permitted assignment of the rent.

(C) Only those tenants whose leases became effective before the investor's mortgage was recorded.

(D) Only those tenants whose leases became effective after the investor's mortgage was recorded.

Question 29

An investor owned a 100-acre parcel that contained several natural asphalt lakes. A construction company was erecting highways for the state in the vicinity of the investor's land and needed a supply of asphalt. The investor executed a document that, in return for a payment of $1 per barrel, gave the company the right to enter on the land and take asphalt in whatever quantities the company desired. The investor reserved the right to remove asphalt herself and to grant this right to others. Last year, the state commenced an action in eminent domain to take the investor's land for a public park.

Is the construction company entitled to compensation?

(A) No, because the nonexclusive nature of the company's right makes it a license, which is not an interest in property.

(B) No, because a nonexclusive profit, although an interest in property, has no value separate and apart from the land itself.

(C) Yes, because the company has a nonexclusive profit, which is a property right for which it is entitled to compensation.

(D) Yes, because the company has a license coupled with an interest, which is a property right for which it is entitled to compensation.

Question 30

A homeowner's will provided, among other things, that his home would pass upon his death "to my gardener for life, remainder to my housekeeper if my housekeeper survives my gardener; if my housekeeper predeceases my gardener, then to my grandchildren, share and share alike." The homeowner's will contained a residuary clause providing that any of his property not specifically devised would pass to his friend. Upon the homeowner's death, he was survived by two children, the gardener, the housekeeper, and the friend. The homeowner had no grandchildren at the time of his death. The jurisdiction has not modified the common law with any relevant statutory rules.

Upon the gardener's death, predeceased by the housekeeper, if the homeowner's children have still produced no issue, who has the right to possession of the home?

(A) The gardener's heirs.

(B) The friend.

(C) A trustee appointed by the court to hold the home for the benefit of any children born to the homeowner's children.

(D) The homeowner's two children.

Question 31

A landowner owned a large tract of undeveloped land in fee simple. Although no excavation had been done on the land, it was believed to contain gold. The landowner therefore began to mine the land, financing his operation with a $100,000 mortgage to a bank. Subsequently, the landowner sold all of the interest in gold on the land to a miner. Shortly thereafter, the landowner conveyed his ownership in the land to a mining company. Realizing that none of their interests had been recorded, the bank recorded its mortgage first, the miner recorded her deed second, and the mining company recorded its deed third. None of the parties dealing with the landowner had any knowledge of the others at the time of their transactions.

The jurisdiction in which the land is located has the following statute: "No conveyance or mortgage of an interest in land is valid against any subsequent purchaser for value without notice thereof, unless it is recorded."

If the mining company brings an action to quiet title in the land, the most likely result is:

(A) Because the rights of the bank, the miner, and the mining company are different in nature, the court would most likely validate all of the interests, with the mining company having the ownership subject to the payment of the mortgage to the bank.

(B) The mining company would be successful in quieting title to the land.

(C) The bank's mortgage would be declared valid because it is first in time to all of the grants by the landowner concerning the land.

(D) The bank's mortgage would take priority over the miner and the mining company because the bank had no notice at the time it recorded its mortgage.

Question 32

A landowner owned a large tract of land containing numerous coal mines. To finance the renovation of some of the buildings on the land, the landowner obtained a $50,000 mortgage from a bank. Shortly thereafter, the landowner conveyed the surface of the land to his sister and the mineral rights to a utility company. The bank recorded its mortgage the next day; the day after that, the utility company recorded its deed; the following day, the sister recorded her deed. None of the parties dealing with the landowner had any knowledge of the others at the time of their transactions.

The jurisdiction in which the land is located has the following statute: "No conveyance or mortgage of an interest in land is valid against any subsequent purchaser for value without notice thereof whose conveyance is first recorded."

If the sister brings an action to quiet title to the land, the most likely result would be:

(A) The sister would have only a reversionary interest.

(B) The bank's mortgage would be valid and superior because it was first in time.

(C) The sister would be deemed the owner in fee simple absolute and subject only to the payment of the mortgage held by the bank.

(D) The sister would have a fee simple interest subject to the mineral rights of the utility company and the mortgage held by the bank.

Question 33

A corporation was in the business of purchasing real property at below-market prices and reselling the properties to investors. The bylaws of the corporation authorized the chief executive officer ("CEO") and the director of the marketing division to enter into contracts on behalf of the corporation for the purchase or sale of properties. The corporation had recently purchased a large parcel of beachfront property for resale. The CEO secretly opened negotiations with an amusement park to sell the property. However, unknown to the CEO or anyone else in the corporation, the marketing director had already reached an agreement with a hotel for the sale of the property.

On April 23, the marketing director and the hotel signed a written contract providing for sale of the property by the corporation to the hotel for $35 million. On April 25, the board of directors amended its bylaws, effectively depriving the marketing director of authorization to bind the corporation in purchase or sale transactions. This action was immediately publicized and became known to both the marketing director and the hotel. On April 26, the hotel duly recorded its contract. On May 1, the CEO, still unaware of the marketing director-hotel agreement, approved sale of the property to the amusement park for $39 million. The necessary documents of title were prepared and properly recorded by the amusement park on May 5. Two days later, the amusement park learned of the marketing director-hotel agreement. On May 10, the date scheduled for closing of the hotel's sale agreement, the CEO refused to accept the hotel's tender of $35 million and refused its demand for a deed to the property.

In a subsequent action by the hotel against the corporation and the amusement park for specific performance of the contract signed by the marketing director and to quiet title to the property, judgment will likely be for:

(A) The defendants, because the board of directors had deprived the marketing director of authority to bind the corporation in the sale of real property.

(B) The defendants, because the amusement park is the only purchaser who properly recorded a deed to the property.

(C) The hotel, because the amusement park had constructive notice of the hotel's interests in the property when the agreement with the CEO was made.

(D) The hotel, because the attempt to divest the marketing director of authority to approve sales of the corporation's property was invalid.

Question 34

A landlord owned a prestigious downtown office building. A law firm leased the entire building from the landlord for a term of 20 years. The lease included a provision that taxes on the building would be paid by "the lessee, his successors, and assigns." The law firm occupied the building and paid the rent and taxes for eight years. At the end of the eight-year period, the law firm assigned the balance of the lease to an accounting firm and vacated the premises. The assignment was written, but there was no provision concerning the accounting firm's assumption of the duties under the lease.

The accounting firm occupied the building and paid the rent and taxes for five years. At the end of the five-year period, the accounting firm subleased the building for five years to an investment company and vacated the premises. The sublease was written, but there was no provision concerning the investment company's assumption of the duties under the lease. The investment company now occupies the building and has paid the rent but not the taxes. The landlord has sued all three (*i.e.*, the law firm, the accounting firm, and the investment company) for failure to pay the taxes.

The landlord should prevail against whom?

(A) The law firm only.

(B) The law firm and the accounting firm, but not the investment company.

(C) The accounting firm and the investment company, but not the law firm.

(D) The law firm, the accounting firm, and the investment company.

Question 35

A landowner conveyed her parcel of land to "my brother and my sister jointly, with right of survivorship." Shortly thereafter, the brother was in an automobile accident. The driver of the other vehicle sued the brother on a theory of negligence, and obtained a judgment in the amount of $250,000. Because the brother did not have insurance or enough cash to satisfy the judgment, the driver levied on the brother's interest in the land.

The driver will get:

(A) Nothing, because the brother's interest in the land cannot be partitioned.

(B) An undivided one-half interest, regardless of whether the brother and the sister's title to the land is construed as a joint tenancy or a tenancy in common.

(C) An undivided one-half interest, assuming the brother and the sister's interest is construed as a tenancy in common and not a joint tenancy.

(D) A contingent right of survivorship that will vest if the brother survives the sister.

Question 36

A mother executed a will, devising a vacant parcel of land to her daughter. The daughter moved her mobile home onto the land. Two years later, the mother conveyed the land to an investor for $25,000 by a quitclaim deed. The investor, knowing nothing of the mother's will, recorded the deed but has never visited the land. The following year, the mother died, survived by her daughter. The jurisdiction in which the land is located has a five-year limitations period for adverse possession along with the following statute:

> No conveyance of an interest in land, other than a lease for less than one year, shall be valid against any subsequent purchaser for value, without notice thereof, unless the conveyance is recorded.

If the daughter sues to quiet title to the land, for whom should the court rule?

(A) The daughter, because a quitclaim deed conveys whatever interest the seller has.

(B) The daughter, because the investor was not a bona fide purchaser.

(C) The investor, because the daughter's mobile home is not a fixture.

(D) The investor, because the daughter has no interest in the land.

REAL PROPERTY ANSWERS - SET 6

Answer to Question 1

(A) The granddaughter and the city zoo each own one-half of the land, subject to the second wife's life estate. At the time of the conveyance by the landowner, the son had a life estate, the son's widow had a contingent interest (because the son's "widow" cannot be ascertained until the son's death), and the son's children had a contingent remainder (because they have not yet been born). When the grandson and the granddaughter were born, however, their interests became vested subject to open (*i.e.*, if the son had more children). Thus, when the grandson died, he had a vested remainder subject to open that he was free to devise by will; the city zoo took his vested remainder subject to open. At the son's death, the class of his "children" closed (because the son could not have any more children), and the granddaughter's and the zoo's vested remainders subject to open became indefeasibly vested. Also at the son's death, his widow was ascertained and her interest vested in possession. Because the second wife was the son's widow, she is entitled to the valid life estate. Thus, the granddaughter and the city zoo hold one-half interests, subject to the second wife's life estate. (B) is wrong because the son had no interest in the land when he died. He merely had a life estate, which ended at his death. He did not inherit any interest in the property from anyone else. The only person he inherited from in these facts was his first wife, and she had no interest in the land. Furthermore, this choice overlooks the city zoo's interest, which was inherited from the grandson. (C) is wrong because the son's children's interest does not violate the Rule Against Perpetuities. To be valid under the Rule, an interest must vest if at all within a life in being at its creation plus 21 years. The son is a life in being. At the son's death, his children's interest is certain to vest or fail: If the son had any children, at his death, the children's interest would become indefeasibly vested (*i.e.*, the class would close and the children's interest would no longer be subject to open). Note that the children need not come into possession within the perpetuities period; the only requirement is that their interests vest within the period. Likewise, if the son had no children, the gift to them was certain to fail at his death. Thus, the children's interest does not violate the Rule. Because the son had children and their interest was valid, there was no interest to revert to the landowner and to be devised to the friend. Note that the unborn widow aspect of this question is a red herring. The fact would be relevant only if the children's gift were conditioned on their surviving the widow, in which case the takers would remain unascertained and their interest would remain contingent until that time. But because the children's interest vested at the son's death, it is irrelevant that the son's "widow" was not a life in being at the creation of the interest. (D) is wrong because the gift to the son's children was not conditioned on their survival of the son. The law does not imply such a condition. The grandson's interest was vested subject to open and could be disposed of by his will.

Answer to Question 2

(B) The seller will prevail in his suit for specific performance because the easement was visible, the buyer was aware of it at the time she entered into the contract (*i.e.*, she knew a public sidewalk ran in front of the store), and the easement enhanced the value of the property. There is an implied warranty in every land sale contract that, at closing, the seller will provide the buyer with marketable title. Marketable title is title reasonably free from doubt, which generally means free from encumbrances and with good record title. Easements are generally considered encumbrances that render title unmarketable; so if an easement is not provided for in the contract, it usually renders the seller's title unmarketable. There is an exception, however. A majority of courts have held that a ***beneficial*** easement that was ***visible or known*** to the buyer does not constitute an encumbrance. In this case, the sidewalk was visible, known to the buyer, and

beneficial to the property. Thus, the sidewalk easement does not impair the marketability of the seller's title. Therefore, the buyer's excuse for her nonperformance is not valid, and because land is involved, the seller can get specific performance of the contract for purchase of the property. (A) is wrong because, as noted above, the warranty that the seller will convey marketable title is ***implied*** in ***every*** land sale contract. So here, the fact that the contract did not specify the quality of title does not relieve the seller from providing marketable title. Thus, (A) reaches the correct result for the wrong reason. (C) is wrong because, as noted above, there is an exception to the general rule, stated in (C), for beneficial easements that are visible or known to the buyer. (D) is wrong because the buyer cannot escape the contract merely by giving notice of her intent to breach it. It apparently was a valid contract that can be enforced against her. Failure to mitigate damages might prevent the seller from recovering avoidable damages but would not negate the breach.

Answer to Question 3

(A) The buyer will not prevail in a suit for specific performance of the contract conveying the additional strip of land because the court will reform the contract. Reformation is the remedy whereby the writing setting forth the agreement between the parties is changed to make it conform to the original intent of the parties. Reformation may be available where there is a mutual mistake (*i.e.*, the writing does not conform to the original agreement and the parties are not aware of the discrepancy). As long as the parties were in agreement as to the terms before the contract was reduced to writing, reformation can be had regardless of whether both parties signed the contract without noticing the deviation from the oral agreement or one party knew of the deviation and the other did not. Here, both parties intended that the stone fence constitute the eastern boundary of the buyer's parcel. There was no mistake in the oral agreement, merely in putting it in writing. Thus, the court will reform the contract so as to indicate the stone fence as the eastern boundary of the buyer's parcel. (B) is incorrect because there is no mistake or inconsistency in the written description (*e.g.*, two different measurements) that would warrant applying the rules of construction to carry out the parties' probable intent. Here, the parties' intent that the stone fence serve as the eastern border of the buyer's parcel is clear. (C) is incorrect because if the contract does not express what the parties agreed to, the court will reform it to conform to their original intent. (D) is incorrect because the general rule is that parol evidence is admissible to explain or supplement a written description or to clear up an ambiguity.

Answer to Question 4

(C) The seller has title to the land, but he must redeem the creditor's mortgage to avoid foreclosure. As a general rule, the priority of a mortgage is determined by the time it was placed on the property. When a mortgage is foreclosed, the purchaser at the sale will take title as it existed when the mortgage was placed on the property. Thus, foreclosure will terminate interests junior to the mortgage being foreclosed but will not affect senior interests. However, if a lien senior to that of a mortgagee is in default, the junior mortgagee has the right to pay it off (*i.e.*, redeem it) to avoid being wiped out by its foreclosure. Thus, those persons with interests subordinate to those of the foreclosing party are necessary parties to the foreclosure action. Failure to include a necessary party results in the preservation of that party's interest despite foreclosure and sale. Hence, the seller's failure to include the creditor as a party to the foreclosure action preserved the creditor's mortgage on the property. To avoid the creditor's foreclosing (because the buyer was in default of the creditor's mortgage as well), the seller will need to pay off the creditor's mortgage. (A) is wrong because it is irrelevant. While a purchase money mortgage ("PMM"), given when the mortgagor buys the property, is considered to have priority over non-PMM mortgages executed at about the same time, even if the other mortgages are recorded first, that rule is not applicable here because the facts indicate that the seller's PMM was executed and recorded before the creditor's mortgage came into existence. (B) is wrong because the creditor was not included as a party to the foreclosure action. Thus, as discussed above, its interest is not extinguished by the seller's foreclosure action. (D) is wrong because the failure to include the creditor in the foreclosure action does not invalidate the action, it just preserves the creditor's junior mortgage on the property.

Answer to Question 5

(B) The motorist's lien was extinguished at the sister's death, leaving the brother as the sole owner of the property. The distinguishing characteristic of a joint tenancy, which is how the brother and the sister held the property, is the right of survivorship. When one joint tenant dies, the property is freed of her concurrent interest and the survivor continues to retain an undivided right in the property no longer subject to the interest of the deceased co-tenant. The survivor does not succeed to the decedent's interest; he holds free of it. Hence, as long as the joint tenancy is still intact, the decedent's devisees, heirs, and judgment creditors have no claim on the joint tenancy property that the decedent held. For the joint tenancy to remain intact, the unities of time, title, interest, and possession that were necessary to create the tenancy must be undisturbed. Any disturbance of the unities causes a severance of the joint tenancy, and thereafter the parties whose unities are disturbed hold as tenants in common. In most jurisdictions, however, the fact that a creditor has obtained a lien on one joint tenant's interest does not by itself result in severance; there must also be at least a judicial sale of the property. Thus, judgment and other lien creditors easily can lose their security interests by the death of the debtor. That is what happened to the motorist in this case. He obtained a statutory lien on the property through the sister's interest as a joint tenant. This did not cause a severance of the joint tenancy; the brother and the sister remained joint tenants. When the sister died, the property was freed of her concurrent interest and any claims arising through that interest. The motorist, not having caused a judicial sale of the property, loses his security interest. Thus, (A) is incorrect because the brother is the sole owner of the property, and the property is ***not*** subject to the motorist's statutory lien. (C) would be the correct answer if the motorist had foreclosed on his lien. The sheriff's deed issued to the buyer at the judicial sale would have severed the joint tenancy. However, a transferee takes his interest as a tenant in common and not as a joint tenant. Thus, (D) is incorrect.

Answer to Question 6

(D) The rancher will prevail because there is no evidence that time was of the essence. In general, courts presume that time is not of the essence in real estate contracts. Thus, the closing date stated in the contract is not absolutely binding in equity, and a party, even though late in tendering his own performance, can still enforce the contract if he tenders within a reasonable time. (One to two months is usually considered reasonable.) Time will be considered of the essence only if: (i) the contract so states, (ii) the circumstances indicate it was the parties' intention, or (iii) one party gives the other notice that he desires to make time of the essence. The contract in this case made no mention that time was of the essence. The facts do not indicate any circumstances, such as rapidly fluctuating prices or the need for the money to close another critical transaction, that would indicate that the rancher and the farmer intended time to be of the essence. The farmer did not give the rancher reasonable notice before September 30 that she wanted to make time of the essence. Thus, the court will not find that time is of the essence here. Because time is not of the essence, the rancher is not in material breach and is entitled to specific performance. (A) is wrong because the Statute of Frauds is not violated here. Contracts for the

sale of land must be in writing to be enforceable. The essential terms for purposes of the Statute of Frauds are: the description of the property, the identification of the parties, and the price. The tax provision is not an essential term. It is an incidental matter, which need not appear in writing or even be agreed upon. (B) is wrong because, as discussed above, the rancher is not in material breach. Time was not of the essence, so the fact that the rancher did not tender his performance on September 30 did not constitute a breach of the land sale contract. (C) is wrong because the doctrine of equitable conversion will not affect the rights of the parties in this situation. The doctrine of equitable conversion holds that once an enforceable contract of sale is signed, the purchaser's interest is real property, and the seller's interest (the right to proceeds) is personal property. This is important with respect to which party bears the risk of loss if the property is damaged before the date set for closing or if one of the parties dies prior to closing. It has no effect in situations like this one where the question in issue is the enforceability of the contract itself.

Answer to Question 7

(B) The creditor will prevail in a suit to quiet title because the investor had notice of the creditor's interest in the property and, thus, is not a bona fide purchaser for value. When a grantor purports to convey property that he does not own, his subsequent acquisition of title to that property vests in the grantee under the doctrine of estoppel by deed. Most courts, however, hold that this is personal estoppel, which means that title inures to the grantee's benefit only as against the grantor, not a subsequent bona fide purchaser. If the grantor transfers his after-acquired title to an innocent purchaser for value, the bona fide purchaser gets good title. There is a split of authority as to whether the original grantee's recordation of the deed imparts sufficient notice to prevent a subsequent purchaser from being a bona fide purchaser, but the majority view is that it does not because it is not in his chain of title. Thus, it is not the fact that the creditor recorded that prevents the investor from being a bona fide purchaser. The fact that the creditor built a home and was living on the property gave the investor constructive notice of her interest. A title search is not complete without an examination of possession. If the possession is unexplained by the record, the subsequent purchaser is charged with knowledge of whatever an inspection of the property would have disclosed and anything that would have been disclosed by inquiring of the possessor. Therefore, the investor is charged with knowledge of the creditor's possession and with what the creditor would have told him about her possession; *i.e.*, that the property was conveyed to her by the son prior to his conveyance to the investor. Consequently, the investor does not qualify as a bona fide purchaser, and (C) is an incorrect choice. (A) is incorrect because, although the son is estopped to deny that he acquired title for the benefit of the creditor, he could have conveyed valid title to a subsequent purchaser for value who had no notice of the creditor's interest. Therefore, it is not exactly correct to say that the son had no title to convey. (D) is incorrect because the investor will not prevail. It is true that under the recording acts the creditor's deed was not in the chain of title, but the investor still does not qualify as a bona fide purchaser. The investor is on inquiry notice arising from the creditor's possession of the property.

Answer to Question 8

(A) The transfer from the artist to the pottery maker was effective even though the investor refused to consent. If a landlord grants consent to one transfer, she waives her right to avoid future transfers unless she expressly reserves the right to do so. The reservation of this right must take place at the time of granting consent. Here, the owner consented to the transfer from the photographer to the artist, without reserving her right to prohibit future transfers without her consent. Thus, the provision barring assignment and sublease is deemed waived, and cannot be enforced by the investor. Furthermore, even if the provision were effective, it would not make the transfer from the artist to the pottery maker ineffective. The transfer itself is valid, but the landlord may usually terminate the lease under either the lease terms or a statute. Here, there is no mention of such lease terms or a statute that would permit the investor to terminate the lease. He would be left with an action for damages (if he can prove any) for breach, but the transfer would be effective. Because the transfer is effective, (D) is wrong. (B) is wrong because it states the wrong reason that the transfer is effective. Even if the provision were not deemed waived, the reasonableness of the investor's withholding of his consent would not affect the outcome. First, the limitation that a landlord may not unreasonably withhold consent is a minority position. Second, as discussed above, a transfer in violation of a lease provision prohibiting transfer is not void, but would affect only the landlord's remedies; therefore, defenses to compliance with the provision are not necessary to uphold the transfer's effectiveness. (C) is wrong because restrictions on the transferability of leaseholds are valid restraints on alienation. A provision in a lease prohibiting the lessee's assignment or sublease of her leasehold interest without the consent of the landlord is given effect in all jurisdictions.

Answer to Question 9

(D) The trespasser will lose because the landowner's insanity tolled the running of the time period. The insanity disability tolls the running of the statute of limitations for adverse possession if the disability existed on the day the adverse possession began. Because the landowner was insane when the trespasser began the period of adverse possession, the clock did not begin to run until the landowner was free of the disability 12 years later; thus, the clock has run 13 years to the present. That is not enough to satisfy the statute, so the trespasser gets nothing. (A) is incorrect because the disability keeps the trespasser from getting any of the property. In the absence of the disability, however, the trespasser could have obtained title only to that portion of the land that he actually possessed, the west portion. He did not enter under a color of title, which could have given him title to all of the land even though he actually possessed only a part of it. Thus, (B) is also incorrect. (C) is incorrect because there is no specified time in which an adverse possessor has to bring an action to quiet title; the doctrine of laches does not apply.

Answer to Question 10

(C) Good title cannot be obtained without the daughter's son's inclusion in the conveyance. All contracts for the sale of land contain, unless the contract expressly provides otherwise, an implied warranty by the seller that she will deliver to the buyer a marketable title at the date of closing. Private restrictions or encumbrances, including executory interests and possibilities of reverter, will render title unmarketable unless the holders of those interests join in the transaction. Here, the Girl Scouts have a valid executory interest that does not violate the Rule Against Perpetuities because their interest must vest, if at all, during the niece's lifetime. However, the niece's fee simple determinable is not limited in duration like the interest of the Girl Scouts. Thus, the niece's heirs will only have a fee simple determinable rather than a fee simple absolute. Because the Girl Scouts' interest vanishes on the niece's death, and no other provision was made for the property if it should thereafter be used for noncamping or nonrecreational purposes, the transferor (the landowner) retained a possibility of reverter. This interest passed to the daughter and then to the daughter's son, and so the son's interest must be included in the conveyance. (A) is wrong because the buyer has contracted to receive good title to a fee simple absolute without any restrictions on the use of the property. Unless the son joins in the contract to convey his possibility of reverter, good title cannot be conveyed. (B) is wrong because the son's interest is the one blocking good title; the Girl Scouts have already agreed to sell their interest. Furthermore,

their interest is not a right of entry but a shifting executory interest that would automatically divest the buyer's interest if he violated the use restriction, and so their promise would be meaningless. (D) is wrong because the niece, the Girl Scouts, and the daughter's son together can validly convey a fee simple absolute to the buyer.

Answer to Question 11

(C) If the owner can compel the bank to accept his offer, it will be because he has a statutory power to redeem the property after the foreclosure sale has occurred. In all states, the equity of redemption provides the borrower with an equitable right, at any time ***prior to*** the foreclosure sale, to redeem the land or free it of the mortgage or lien by paying off the amount due or, if an acceleration clause applies, the full balance due. Only about half the states, however, give the borrower a statutory right to redeem for some fixed period ***after*** the foreclosure sale has occurred; the amount to be paid is generally the foreclosure sale price, rather than the amount of the original debt. Thus, if the owner can redeem the land for $80,000, it will be based on the jurisdiction's statutory power of redemption. (A) is wrong because the deed of trust is a security interest (similar to a mortgage) to which the revocation rules for trusts do not apply. The deed of trust was created in part to allow the lender to foreclose on the property without going through a judicial foreclosure proceeding. (B) is wrong because, in states that permit a nonjudicial sale with deeds of trust containing a power of sale, the lender may bid at the sale, and in many cases the lender is the sole bidder. (D) is wrong because the prohibition against "clogging the equity of redemption" refers to the rule that a borrower's right to redeem his own mortgage cannot be waived in the instrument itself. Here, there is nothing to indicate that the owner's deed of trust prohibited him from redeeming the property prior to foreclosure. However, it is only through a statutory right of redemption that the owner would be able to redeem the property for $80,000 after the foreclosure sale had occurred.

Answer to Question 12

(C) The granddaughter's daughter prevails because the statutory period for adverse possession did not begin to run against her until the grandson died. The doctrine of adverse possession provides that possession for a specified statutory period in the requisite manner will establish the possessor's title to the land. For possession to ripen into title, it must be: (i) actual; (ii) open and notorious (*i.e.*, such as the usual owner would make of the land and sufficient to put the true owner or the community on notice of the fact of possession); (iii) hostile (*i.e.*, without the true owner's permission); and (iv) continuous. The statute of limitations that determines the time period for adverse possession does not run against the holder of a future interest (*e.g.*, a remainder) until that interest becomes possessory, because the holder of the future interest has no right to possession (and thus no cause of action against a wrongful possessor) until the prior present estate terminates. Here, the society has possessed the home for eight years; however, as against the granddaughter's daughter, the holder of the remainder, the statute did not begin to run until the death of the grandson. Prior to the termination of the grandson's life estate, the granddaughter's daughter had no cause of action against the society because she had no right to possession. Upon the grandson's death, when the granddaughter's daughter's interest became possessory, the statute began to run against her. Thus, as against her, the society has not been in adverse possession for the requisite period. (A) is incorrect because it fails to account for that fact; as against the granddaughter's daughter, the applicable statute did not begin to run until her interest became possessory (on the termination of the grandson's estate). (B) is incorrect because the society could not purchase from the grandson a fee simple absolute; the grandson was only a life tenant in the home. Consequently, when the grandson conveyed the home to the society, the society

received a life estate pur autre vie (for the life of the grandson) rather than a fee simple absolute—the society could not receive from the grandson what he did not own. (D), on the other hand, is incorrect because the society could eventually obtain title in fee simple absolute by means of adverse possession, even though it could not receive a fee simple absolute by means of the conveyance from the grandson. If, *e.g.*, the society had maintained its possession for the statutory period starting at the grandson's death, such possession would have ripened into title against the granddaughter's daughter. Thus, (D) is not an accurate statement.

Answer to Question 13

(A) The express easement for the landowner's old property benefits that property only and cannot be used for the landowner's expanded access to the new property. An easement is a liberty, privilege, or advantage that one may hold in the lands of another. The holder of an easement has the right to use a tract of land (called the servient tenement) for a special purpose; *e.g.*, laying utility lines, or for ingress and egress. An easement can be created, as in this question, by express grant. If the parties to the original creation of the use specifically state the location of the easement, its dimensions, and the special use or limits to such use, the courts will honor this expression of specific intent. Absent specific limitations, it will be assumed that the parties intend that the easement meet both present and future ***reasonable*** needs of the dominant tenement. However, a basic change in the nature of the use is not allowed. The landowner's easement by express grant merely allows her to use the private roads in the subdivision for her personal ingress and egress to and from her beachfront property. The use of the easement for access to a new boat launching ramp for which a fee is charged goes beyond the specific language of the grant (and arguably beyond the reasonable needs of the dominant tenement). Therefore, the homeowners will be able to prevent use of the subdivision streets to reach the boat launching ramp. (B) is incorrect because even if the landowner's express easement over the streets of the subdivision is construed to benefit the property that was recently acquired as well as her old property, the scope of the easement will not be expanded beyond the language of the grant. (C) is incorrect because the elements of an easement by necessity are missing. Where the owner of a tract of land sells a part of the tract and by this division deprives one parcel of access to a public road or utility line, a right-of-way by absolute necessity is created by implied grant over the parcel with access to the public road. The landowner has not purchased her new property from the subdivision owners. Thus, she has no implied right-of-way by necessity over the subdivision streets to reach her new property. (D) is incorrect because the elements of an easement by implied grant are missing. Where an owner sells a portion of his property, and prior to the conveyance a use had been made, the existence of the prior use may give rise to an easement by implication, even though no reference is made to a continuation of that use. Here, when the landowner purchased her original property from the original owner of the subdivision, there was no prior use of the subdivision land to reach her new property (because it did not even exist at that time). Consequently, no such use can now be implied simply by virtue of the fact that the landowner's new property abuts her old property. The new property was purchased from a different owner, and there is no basis for implying a grant to use the land of the subdivision to benefit land purchased from the county.

Answer to Question 14

(D) The tenant will win because she had a right under the statute to withhold the rent. The general rule at common law was that the landlord was not liable to the tenant for damages caused by the landlord's failure to maintain the premises during the period of the leasehold. Today, however, a majority of jurisdictions, usually by statute, provide for an implied warranty of habitability for residential tenancies. The statute in this question allows the tenant to make the repairs and

withhold the cost of the repairs 15 days after notifying the landlord in writing. The statute is applicable because the damage done by the vandals makes the apartment unfit for habitation under whatever standard the court would apply. The tenant has complied with the terms of the statute; she therefore cannot be evicted for nonpayment of rent. (A) is incorrect. The fact that the damage was caused by a third party would be relevant only if the tenant were relying on the judicially developed remedy of constructive eviction, which requires that the damage making the premises uninhabitable have been caused by the landlord. The warranty of habitability is not limited in this way. (B) is incorrect because the statute has extended the common law duty of the landlord, which applied only to the common areas of a multiunit building. (C) is incorrect because the tenant does not need to show that the landlord was negligent.

Answer to Question 15

(B) The bank's mortgage survives under its modified terms because the financing company did not include the bank in the foreclosure action. The general rule is that when a mortgage is foreclosed, the buyer at the sale will take title as it existed when the mortgage was placed on the property. Thus, foreclosure generally will destroy all interests junior to the mortgage being foreclosed, but will not discharge senior interests. However, those with interests subordinate to those of the foreclosing party are necessary parties to the foreclosure action. Failure to include a necessary party results in the preservation of that party's interest despite foreclosure and sale. Here, the bank's original mortgage was senior to the financing company's mortgage. However, where the landowner enters into a modification agreement with the senior mortgagee, raising its interest rate or otherwise making it more burdensome, the junior mortgagee will be given priority over the modification. Thus, the bank's modification would not have priority over the financing company's mortgage. Nevertheless, because the financing company failed to include the bank in its foreclosure action, the bank's mortgage interest survives under its modified terms, even though the modification did not have priority. (B) is therefore correct and (A) is incorrect. (C) is incorrect because the modification of a senior mortgage does not nullify its original senior status; it only means that the junior mortgage will be given priority over the ***modification***. Because the buyer at the foreclosure sale ordinarily will take title as it existed when the mortgage was placed on the property, the senior mortgage ordinarily survives in its original form. (As noted above, here the mortgage survives in its modified form despite its junior status because of the failure to include the bank in the foreclosure action.) (D) is incorrect because the recording statute applicable here is a race-notice statute rather than a notice statute. Under a race-notice statute, a subsequent bona fide purchaser (including a mortgagee) is protected only if it records before the prior grantee or mortgagee. Here, the bank recorded its mortgage before the financing company recorded its mortgage. The fact that the financing company had no notice of the bank's interest at the time it granted the mortgage on the restaurant does not help the financing company because it did not record first.

Answer to Question 16

(B) The chocolatier can enforce the option to purchase because it is a covenant that runs with the land. When a tenant makes a complete transfer of the entire remaining term of his leasehold interest, it constitutes an assignment. The assignee and the landlord are then in privity of estate, and each is liable to the other on all covenants in the lease that run with the land. The covenant runs with the land if the original parties so intend and the covenant "touches and concerns" the leased land, *i.e.*, burdens the landlord and benefits the tenant with respect to their interests in the property. Here, the transfer of the lease to the chocolatier was an assignment, making all covenants

in the lease that run with the land enforceable by the assignee. The right of first refusal burdens the landlord's power of alienation over the bakery, and there is nothing to indicate that the parties intended the option to be personal to the baker. Hence, the chocolatier can enforce the option and purchase the property. (A) is incorrect because most courts do not bar an option from being separated from the leasehold interest if that is the parties' intent. The tenant may transfer the leasehold interest while retaining the option to purchase, or vice versa. Whether the option in this case stayed with the leasehold interest depends on whether it was a covenant that runs with the land. (C) is incorrect because options and rights of first refusal are not subject to the Rule Against Perpetuities when connected to leaseholds. If the option had been separated from the leasehold estate, so that it was no longer exercisable by the tenant, the Rule would have become applicable to the option (and it would have invalidated the option here because it could have been exercised more than 21 years after a life in being). Here, however, the option was not severed from the leasehold; the entire interest was transferred to the chocolatier as the new tenant. Hence, the Rule Against Perpetuities is not applicable. (D) is incorrect because, as discussed above, the option is a covenant that runs with the land regardless of whether it was specified in the assignment to the chocolatier. The chocolatier, as the assignee of the leasehold, can enforce the option on privity of estate grounds.

Answer to Question 17

(A) The owner will prevail because the writing did not adequately describe the 20 acres to be sold. For a court to grant specific performance, there must be a valid and enforceable contract. The Statute of Frauds requires that the writing contain a description of the land to be sold sufficient to identify it. If the description is too indefinite, the contract is not enforceable. In this case, the description given is 20 acres from the northwest quarter of the owner's land. The land consists of 240 acres; therefore, the northwest quarter of the land contains 60 acres. Because there is no guidance as to which 20 acres were intended by the parties, the contract is not enforceable and the owner will prevail. (B) is wrong because the writing need not be signed by both parties. To be enforceable under the Statute of Frauds, the writing need only be signed by the party to be charged. In this case, the owner is the party to be charged, and the writing was signed by him. Thus, the Statute of Frauds was satisfied in this regard. (C) is wrong because the metes and bounds description here described the whole of the land, rather than the property to be conveyed. It is true that metes and bounds is a sufficient way to describe property. In this instance, however, this method was used to describe the wrong property. (D) is wrong because, as discussed above, the description of the property does not satisfy the Statute of Frauds.

Answer to Question 18

(A) The only way that the lender could prevail would be to step into the shoes of a party with an interest senior to that of the financing company. A second mortgagee's rights are subject to the rights of the first mortgagee. Thus, a foreclosure by the second mortgagee will not cut off the first mortgagee's rights. The lender's only way to win would be to acquire the bank's rights. (B) is incorrect because the balance of equities does not clearly favor the lender. She had record notice of the financing company's mortgage (because it was properly recorded). The financing company did nothing wrong. Furthermore, there is no legally recognized right being infringed by the financing company. (C) is incorrect because, in a pure race recording jurisdiction, as here, notice is irrelevant; whoever records first has priority. (Note that even in a notice jurisdiction, record notice is sufficient—actual notice is not required.) (D) is incorrect because benefit to a subsequent purchaser or mortgagee is not a consideration in a foreclosure action.

Answer to Question 19

(B) The seller is more likely to prevail because the buyer has no basis on which to rescind the contract. Absent a provision to the contrary, a contract for the sale of land contains an implied promise by the seller that she will deliver to the buyer a marketable title at the time of closing. This promise imposes on the seller an obligation to deliver a title that is free from reasonable doubt; *i.e.*, free from questions that might present an unreasonable risk of litigation. Title is marketable if a reasonably prudent buyer would accept it in the exercise of ordinary prudence. An easement that reduces the value of the property (*e.g.*, an easement of way for the benefit of a neighbor) generally renders title unmarketable. If the buyer determines, prior to closing, that the seller's title is unmarketable, he must notify the seller and allow a reasonable time to cure the defect. If the seller is unable to acquire title before closing, so that title remains unmarketable, the buyer can rescind, sue for damages caused by the breach, or obtain specific performance with an abatement of the purchase price. However, the buyer cannot rescind prior to closing on grounds that the seller's title is unmarketable. Where an installment land contract is used, the seller's obligation is to furnish marketable title ***when delivery is to occur***, *e.g.*, when the buyer has made his final payment. Thus, a buyer cannot withhold payments or seek other remedies on grounds that the seller's title is unmarketable prior to the date of promised delivery. Here, there is a valid easement on the property (*see* below), but the seller has four years in which to cure this defect. Thus, the buyer cannot yet rescind on grounds that title is unmarketable. (A) is incorrect because the neighbor's easement has not been extinguished. An easement can be extinguished where the owner of the privilege demonstrates by physical action an intention to permanently abandon the easement. Mere nonuse is not sufficient to terminate an easement, unless the nonuse is combined with other evidence of intent to abandon it. Here, the fact that the neighbor did not use the easement for a year because she was out of the country does not establish her intent to abandon the easement. (C) is incorrect because, although the law implies in every land sale contract a covenant that title will be marketable, the seller has until the time of delivery to cure the defect. (D) is incorrect because the deed has not yet been delivered. The covenant against encumbrances is a covenant contained in a general warranty deed which assures that there are neither visible encumbrances (*e.g.*, easements) nor invisible encumbrances (*e.g.*, mortgages) against the title or interest conveyed. This covenant is breached, if at all, at the time of conveyance. Here, the deed has not yet been delivered, and thus this covenant has not yet been breached.

Answer to Question 20

(D) The niece may enforce the covenant as an equitable servitude against the friend because the friend's townhouse would alter the common scheme the landowner created by using restrictive covenants in all of her deeds. For successors of the original promisee and promisor to enforce an equitable servitude, both the benefit and burden of the servitude must run with the land. For the burden to run and thus bind the successor of the promisor (the friend): (i) the covenanting parties must have intended that the servitude be enforceable by and against assignees; (ii) the covenant must touch and concern the land; and (iii) the party to be bound must have had actual, constructive (record), or inquiry notice. The common scheme (all 10 lots were developed as single-family homes) is evidence that the original parties intended that the restriction be enforceable by assignees. The covenant touches and concerns the friend's property because it restricts him in his use of the property. The friend had constructive and inquiry notice because the restriction is in his chain of title. Therefore, the burden of the servitude runs with the land. The next issue is whether the benefit of the servitude runs with the niece's land. For a benefit to run, it must be so intended by the original parties and the covenant must touch and concern the land. As noted above, intent may be inferred from the common scheme. The benefit touches and concerns the niece's land because it benefits her in her use and enjoyment of the lot. Thus, the niece may enforce the covenant. (A) is incorrect for two reasons: (i) privity is not a requirement for the enforcement of equitable servitudes; and (ii) if privity were a requirement, both horizontal and vertical privity would be satisfied. Horizontal privity requires that, at the time the promisor entered into the covenant with the promisee, the two shared some interest in the land independent of the covenant. The landowner and each of the 10 original owners, as grantor and grantees, shared an interest in the land independent of the covenant. Vertical privity exists when the successor in interest to the covenanting party holds the entire interest that was held by the covenantor at the time she made the covenant. Here, the niece and the friend took the entire interest (fee simple absolute) from their predecessors. (B) is incorrect because both zoning laws and restrictive covenants must be complied with. (C) is incorrect because, as discussed above, the restriction runs with the land and is enforceable against successors of the original parties. Actual notice is not required; constructive or inquiry notice is sufficient, and the friend had both.

Answer to Question 21

(B) The buyer's best defense against the father's attempt to levy on the land is her bona fide purchaser status. By purchasing the land for value and without notice of any prior claim or interest, the buyer cut off the father's interest in the property. The father's remedy is exclusively against the son. (A) is incorrect for two reasons: (i) If the father could enforce his claim for the money, the Statute of Frauds would not be a defense. The Statute would not apply to the son's subsequent promise not to record until he paid the money; because the property had already been conveyed, the promise no longer involved a conveyance of an interest in land. Therefore, the promise does not fall within the Statute. (ii) Any writing between the father and the son would have no effect on the rights of the buyer, a bona fide purchaser. (C) is not as good a choice as (B) because the buyer does not need the recording statute for protection. The father's interest in the property was cut off by the buyer's bona fide purchaser status even without resort to the recording act. The recording act, which is a pure notice statute, protects those who purchase property for value and without notice of prior claims against prior unrecorded conveyances. The father's lien against the property was not recorded so as to give the buyer notice at the time she purchased the property. Thus, the father could not win under the recording statute because the father's lien was never recorded at all. (B) is a better choice, however, because the mere fact that the buyer complied with the statute is not the basis of the buyer's rights in the property. Even under the statute, the buyer's recording would be irrelevant because her status as a bona fide purchaser allows her to prevail against the father. Thus, it is the buyer's status as a bona fide purchaser and full owner of the land that prevents the father from levying on the property. (D) is incorrect because the oral agreement between the father and the son is irrelevant for purposes of defending the buyer's rights in the land. Even if the agreement could be proven, the father would not be able to levy on the land, so the parol evidence rule does not matter.

Answer to Question 22

(B) The landowner will prevail because recording the agreement gave the friend constructive notice, thus preventing her from claiming the protection of the recording act as a defense to enforcement of the covenant. A covenant at law will run with the land and be enforceable against subsequent grantees if: (i) the contracting parties intended it to run; (ii) there is privity of estate between the original promisor and promisee (horizontal privity), as well as between the promisor and his successor (vertical privity); (iii) the covenant touches and concerns the property; and (iv) the burdened party has notice of the covenant. If common driveway owners agree to be mutually responsible for maintaining the driveway, the burdens and benefits of these covenants will run to

successive owners of each parcel. The implied cross-easements for support satisfy the horizontal privity requirement because they are mutual interests in the same property. Each promise touches and concerns the adjoining parcel. So here, where the friend is in vertical privity with the neighbor (holding the same interest he held) and has constructive notice, she will be bound by the agreement to maintain the driveway. Although easements appurtenant, such as those involved in these facts, pass with the transfer of the estates involved, (A) is wrong because the easements are not at issue here. The easements involved are implied cross-easements for support and allow each party the right to enter the other's property when using the driveway. The issue here is the accompanying covenant to pay for the maintenance of the driveway. (C) is wrong for the same reason. Whether the easement has been abandoned does not affect the enforceability of the separate covenant. (D) is wrong because privity of estate, not privity of contract, is required for the burden of the covenant to run.

Answer to Question 23

(B) The financing company may foreclose against the buyer because it was not included as a party in the foreclosure proceeding brought by the bank. Generally, the priority of a mortgage is determined by the time it was placed on the property. When a mortgage is foreclosed, the buyer at the sale will take title as it existed when the mortgage was placed on the property. Thus, foreclosure will terminate interests junior to the mortgage being foreclosed but will not affect senior interests. However, the junior mortgagee has the right to pay the senior interest off (*i.e.*, redeem it) in order to avoid being wiped out by its foreclosure. Thus, those with interests subordinate to those of the foreclosing party are necessary parties to the foreclosure action. Failure to include a necessary party results in the preservation of that party's interest despite foreclosure and sale. Here, even though the financing company created its mortgage first, its interest was junior to the bank's interest by virtue of the recording statute. Hence, when the bank brought its foreclosure action, it should have included the financing company as a necessary party. Because the financing company was not included, its mortgage interest on the land is preserved and it may bring a foreclosure action. (A) is incorrect because the financing company did not hold the senior mortgage interest at the time of the foreclosure by the bank. Mortgagees for value such as the bank are treated as "purchasers" under recording statutes. By failing to record its mortgage before the bank executed and recorded its mortgage for value, the financing company became the junior mortgagee under the jurisdiction's race-notice recording statute. Thus, had it been made a party to the foreclosure proceeding by the bank, its interest would have been wiped out. (C) is incorrect because the financing company's delay in recording only affected its rights vis-a-vis the bank. By the time of the foreclosure sale, the financing company's mortgage interest was recorded; hence, the buyer will take subject to it because he had constructive (record) notice of it. (D) is incorrect because the fact that the buyer obtained the right to redeem the property when he purchased it does not preclude the financing company from beginning foreclosure proceedings. To redeem the property, the buyer must pay off the financing company's mortgage prior to the date set for the foreclosure sale.

Answer to Question 24

(B) The buyer would rely on the covenants of warranty and further assurances to compel the seller to assist him in a suit against his encroaching neighbor. Under the covenant of warranty, the grantor agrees to defend, on behalf of the grantee, any lawful or reasonable claims of title by a third party, and to compensate the grantee for any loss sustained by the claim of superior title. The covenant for further assurances is a covenant to perform whatever acts are reasonably necessary to perfect the title conveyed if it turns out to be imperfect. These covenants are "continuous" (run

with the land) and require the grantor to assist the grantee in establishing title. The covenants of seisin and encumbrances do not require such assistance. A covenant of seisin is a covenant that the grantor has the estate or interest that she purports to convey. Both title and possession at the time of the grant are necessary to satisfy this covenant. The covenant against encumbrances is a covenant assuring that there are neither visible encumbrances (easements, profits, etc.) nor invisible encumbrances (mortgages, etc.) against the title or interest conveyed. While the seller may have violated these two covenants because of the garage encroachment, they do not provide the basis to compel her to assist the buyer in a title suit. Instead, the buyer merely has a cause of action against the seller for their breach. Therefore, (A), (C), and (D) are wrong.

Answer to Question 25

(B) The purchaser prevails because the son's acquisition of the land by adverse possession does not satisfy his implied warranty to deliver a marketable title. Unless expressly provided otherwise, all contracts for the sale of land contain an implied warranty by the seller that he will deliver to the buyer at closing a marketable title. Title is marketable if a reasonably prudent buyer, ready and able to purchase, would accept it in the exercise of ordinary prudence. Generally, inability to establish a record chain of title will render title unmarketable. If a seller attempts to rely on adverse possession to establish marketable title, many courts will hold that such title is not marketable until the adverse possessor has perfected it by a judgment quieting title. In other words, the buyer is not required to "buy a lawsuit." Other states require only that the seller provide written evidence or some other proof that the buyer can use in court to defend any lawsuit challenging title. Even under the latter approach, it does not appear that the son can provide enough evidence to make his title marketable. Thus, although the son has acquired title to the land by occupying it in an open, notorious, hostile, and continuous manner, for a period exceeding that prescribed by statute, the fact that he has acquired title only by adverse possession renders his title unmarketable. Because the son has thus breached his warranty of marketable title, implied in the sale contract, his action to specifically enforce that contract will fail. (A) is incorrect because the son ***does*** own the two acres he is trying to sell. The son's fencing of the land and building structures on it qualifies as open and notorious possession because it is such as the usual owner would make of the land and puts the true owner or the community on notice of the fact of possession. His possession was continuous for more than the five-year statutory period, and it was hostile because it was without the permission of the true owner. Under the majority view, the son's good faith belief that he was possessing the land described by the mother's deed is irrelevant. Thus, the son acquired title by adverse possession. However, as explained above, such title, as far as the purchaser is concerned, is not marketable. (C) is incorrect because the type of deed by which title is transferred does not affect the seller's warranty of marketable title, which is implied in the contract. It is true that the implied warranty of marketability is no longer assertable once a deed has been delivered (absent fraud or mistake), so that if the son delivered a quitclaim deed (*i.e.*, without making any assertions relative to the title being transferred), the purchaser could no longer assert the implied contractual warranty of marketable title. However, no deed has yet been delivered; the warranties under the contract are still in effect. (D) is incorrect because the fact that a contract describes land with sufficient specificity does not establish the marketability of title to that land.

Answer to Question 26

(B) The victim will not likely prevail against the bank because a majority of courts hold that the judgment lienor is not protected by the recording statute. If the statute here, which is a notice statute, were applicable to protect the victim, he would have priority over the bank because his

judgment lien was recorded before the buyer's deed was recorded. Under this view, the bank's mortgage would have been considered "wild" and would be deemed unrecorded because the preceding conveyance, the buyer's deed, was actually unrecorded. A searcher in the public records would therefore have been unable to find the mortgage. Hence, if the statute were applicable to protect the victim, he would have priority over the bank. However, most courts reason that either (i) a judgment creditor is not a bona fide purchaser because he did not pay contemporaneous value for the judgment, or (ii) the judgment attaches only to property "owned" by the debtor, and not to property previously conveyed away, even if that conveyance was not recorded. Under the statute in the present question, a judgment does not attach until it is recorded. Here, the victim's judgment did not attach to the land until after the bank obtained a mortgage on it, and the recording statute does not change that result. The failure of the buyer to record, and the resultant treatment of the bank as unrecorded, is irrelevant. Thus, the bank's mortgage is superior to the victim's lien. (A) is wrong because it does not matter whether the bank's mortgage was recorded, as against a subsequent judgment lien creditor. The judgment lien creditor is not protected by the recording statute, so the bank prevails even though its mortgage would be deemed unrecorded, as discussed above. (C) is wrong because, as discussed above, a majority of courts hold that the judgment lienor is not protected by the recording statute. (D) is wrong because the land was not after-acquired property, because the judgment lien was not filed until the tortfeasor had obtained—and conveyed away—an interest in the property. However, if the victim had in fact recorded his lien before the tortfeasor inherited the land, the after-acquired property provision of the statute would have applied, the victim would have had a recorded lien on the land as soon as the tortfeasor acquired it, and the victim would have gained priority over the bank.

Answer to Question 27

(C) The bank's original mortgage has priority in the proceeds, followed by the lender's mortgage, and only the lender can proceed against the owner because the bank modified its mortgage after the owner had transferred to the buyer. Generally, the priority of a mortgage is determined by the time it was placed on the property, and the proceeds of a foreclosure sale will be used to pay off the mortgages in the order of their priority. However, if the landowner enters into a modification agreement with the senior mortgagee, raising its interest rate or otherwise making the agreement more burdensome, the junior mortgage will be given priority over the modification. Thus, if the first mortgage debt is larger because of the modification, the second mortgage gains priority over the increase in the debt. Here, the bank and the buyer modified the original mortgage by increasing the principal amount and the interest rate. This modification is not given priority over the lender's mortgage, and foreclosure proceeds will not be applied against it because the senior lender's mortgage was not fully satisfied from the proceeds. With regard to the deficiency, the owner is liable to the lender because when a grantee signs an assumption agreement, becoming primarily liable to the lender, the original mortgagor remains secondarily liable on the promissory note as a surety. Here, the buyer assumed the lender's mortgage but is no longer available to satisfy the deficiency; hence, the owner will be liable as surety to pay off the rest of the lender's mortgage loan. On the other hand, the owner will not be liable to pay off the balance of the bank's loan, because when a mortgagee and an assuming grantee subsequently modify the original obligation, the original mortgagor is completely discharged of liability. The owner had nothing to do with the modification agreed to by the bank and the buyer that increased the amount of the mortgage debt, and will not be even secondarily liable for that amount. (A) and (B) are incorrect because the bank is not entitled to the entire $80,000 in proceeds from the sale and because the owner is not liable to the bank for more than the original loan amount. (D) is incorrect because, as discussed above, the owner is secondarily liable to the lender for the $20,000 deficiency on its mortgage.

Answer to Question 28

(A) The investor can collect rents from all of the tenants. A landlord may assign the rents to a third party at any time. Unless required by the lease (which is very unlikely), consent of the tenants is not required. Assignment is usually done by an ordinary deed from the landlord to the new owner of the building, but it can also be accomplished as part of a security interest given for a loan, as in these facts. The assignment clause in the note and mortgage did not become effective until the landlord defaulted on the note. At that time, the investor would be entitled to recover rent from all tenants. (B) is incorrect because, as discussed above, consent of the tenants is not required unless specifically stated in the lease. If assignment of leases is not addressed in the lease, it is presumed to be permitted. (C) and (D) are incorrect because the recording of the investor's mortgage does not affect which of the leases are subject to the assignment of rent. The date of recording would be relevant only if the landlord had made another assignment of the rents from the shopping center.

Answer to Question 29

(C) The construction company is entitled to compensation because it has a property right to enter and remove minerals. Like an easement, a profit is a nonpossessory interest in land. The holder of the profit is entitled to enter on the servient tenement and take the soil or the substance of the soil (*e.g.*, minerals, timber, oil, or game). When an owner grants the sole right to take a resource from her land, the grantee takes an exclusive profit and is solely entitled to the resources, even to the exclusion of the owner of the servient estate. By contrast, when a profit is nonexclusive, the owner of the servient estate may grant similar rights to others or take the resources herself. Although here the profit is nonexclusive, it is nevertheless an interest in property for which the company is entitled to compensation in any condemnation proceeding. (A) is incorrect because a license is merely revocable permission to enter on another's land. Unlike a profit, a license is not an interest in land; it is merely a privilege, ordinarily terminable at the will of the licensor. (B) is incorrect because a profit is the right to take something from another person's land; it has a value apart from the land itself and is alienable. (D) is incorrect because a license coupled with an interest has the effect of making the license irrevocable, but it does not convert the license into an interest in land for which compensation is required.

Answer to Question 30

(B) The friend has the right to possession of the home. A remainder is contingent if its taking in possession is subject to a condition precedent or if it is created in favor of unborn or unascertained persons. The gift to the homeowner's grandchildren was a contingent remainder because it followed a life estate and was conditioned on the housekeeper's not surviving the gardener. At common law under the doctrine of destructibility of contingent remainders, a contingent remainder had to vest prior to or on termination of the preceding estate or it was destroyed. In other words, termination of the estate preceding a contingent remainder prior to vesting destroyed the remainder. Here, the contingent remainder did not vest because no grandchildren of the homeowner had been born when the life estate terminated (on the gardener's death). Thus, title to the home reverted to the homeowner's estate and passed through the residuary clause to the friend. (A) is wrong because the gardener had only a life estate—*i.e.*, nothing that could pass to his heirs. (C) is wrong because the court will not wait to see if grandchildren are born under the common law rule; if there is no grandchild at the gardener's death, the gift to the grandchildren fails. (D) is wrong; the homeowner's two children never received any interest under the will, which had a valid residuary clause.

Answer to Question 31

(B) The mining company would likely be successful. Under a notice statute, which the jurisdiction in this question has, a subsequent bona fide purchaser prevails over a prior grantee who fails to record. The important fact under a notice statute is that the subsequent purchaser had no actual or constructive notice ***at the time of the conveyance***, not at the time of recording. When the property was conveyed to the mining company, it had neither actual nor constructive notice of the conveyances to the bank or the miner, whose interests were not recorded at that time. Therefore, the mining company was a bona fide purchaser and would be entitled to protection under the statute. (A) is incorrect because the recording statute applies to all conveyances and mortgages of an interest in land, including a conveyance of the mineral interests. Thus, both the bank's and the miner's interests are not enforceable against the mining company. (C) is incorrect because that would be the result in the absence of a recording statute—priority is given to the grantee who was first in time. The recording statute changes this result. (D) is wrong because, as discussed above, the mining company did not have notice of the bank's interest at the time of its conveyance from the landowner, so it takes free of that interest under the statute.

Answer to Question 32

(D) The sister's fee simple ownership of the land would be subject to the bank's mortgage interest and the utility company's mineral interest. Under a race-notice statute, which the jurisdiction in this question has, a subsequent bona fide purchaser (*i.e.*, one who takes for value and without notice) is protected only if she records before the prior grantee. Notice is measured ***at the time of the conveyance***, not at the time of recording. The rationale of this type of statute is that the best evidence of which interest was created first is to determine who recorded first. As an inducement to record promptly, race-notice statutes impose on the bona fide purchaser the additional requirement that she record first. Because the bank was the first to receive a conveyance, the bank could not be held to have knowledge of any other conveyance, and when the bank recorded its conveyance first, the bank won out over the sister and the utility company under the statute. The utility company owns the mineral interest in coal on the land because it recorded before the sister. (A) is incorrect because the sister has a present ownership interest in the land, but it is subject to the bank's mortgage and the utility company's mineral interest. (B) is incorrect because the jurisdiction has a race-notice statute. Thus, the bank's interest is superior only if it is first in time and without notice of all other interests. (C) is incorrect because, as discussed above, the sister does not have a fee simple absolute; the utility company owns the mineral interest.

Answer to Question 33

(C) Judgment should be for the hotel regardless of whether the jurisdiction has a notice statute or a race-notice statute. Under either type of recording statute, the only persons protected by the statute are bona fide purchasers. To attain this status, the person must take without notice—either actual, constructive, or inquiry—of the prior instrument. Because the marketing director-hotel contract was properly recorded, the amusement park had constructive notice of the hotel's interest in the property. Thus, the park could not become a bona fide purchaser when it entered into its contract. (A) is wrong because the marketing director had not been deprived of authority to bind the corporation at the time she signed the agreement with the hotel, and any subsequent change in her powers did not affect the validity of that agreement, nor the hotel's power to subsequently record the agreement. (B) is wrong because the hotel recorded its contract of sale. Any instrument creating or affecting an interest in land (*e.g.*, deed, mortgage, contract to convey) can be recorded, providing constructive notice to subsequent purchasers. Thus, the hotel's failure

to record a deed does not deprive it of protection of the recording statute. (D) is wrong because regardless of the validity of the board's attempt to divest the marketing director of authority, it is immaterial to the hotel's rights; it came after the valid marketing director-hotel contract was properly signed by the marketing director.

Answer to Question 34

(B) The law firm and the accounting firm are liable. After an assignment, the original tenant is no longer in privity of estate with the landlord. However, a tenant may still be held liable on its original contractual obligations to the landlord on privity of contract grounds. Here, the law firm is liable because it made the original deal with the landlord, which included the obligation to pay taxes on the building. The law firm remains in privity of contract with the landlord throughout the term of the lease unless it is otherwise discharged. In an assignment, the assignee stands in the shoes of the original tenant in a direct relationship with the landlord. Each is liable to the other on all covenants in the lease that run with the land, which would include the obligation of the lessee to pay taxes on the property. Here, the accounting firm is liable because as an assignee it is in privity of estate with the landlord. The accounting firm remains in privity of estate until it assigns to someone else. The sublease to the investment company is not an assignment. A sublessee is not personally liable to the landlord for rent or for the performance of any other covenants made by the original lessee in the main lease (unless the covenants are expressly assumed) because the sublessee does not hold the tenant's full estate in the land (so no privity of estate). Here, the investment company is not liable because, as a nonassuming sublessee, it is not in privity of contract or estate with the landlord. Therefore, (B) is the correct choice, and (A), (C), and (D) are wrong.

Answer to Question 35

(B) The driver will get an undivided one-half interest in the land regardless of the status of the brother and the sister's title. A joint tenancy is a concurrent estate with a right of survivorship, while a tenancy in common does not have a right of survivorship. At common law, the conveyance here would qualify as a joint tenancy because the unities of time, title, interest, and possession are present in the conveyance. Although under modern law a joint tenancy must be created with specific language or else it will be presumed to be a tenancy in common, the conveyance here still would probably qualify as a joint tenancy, even though it did not use the words "joint tenancy," because it contained the "right of survivorship" language. However, regardless of whether the estate is characterized as a joint tenancy or a tenancy in common, one tenant's interest may be transferred without the consent of the other tenant, and a creditor may levy on the interest. In most jurisdictions, a lien against one joint tenant's interest does not sever the joint tenancy until the lien holder proceeds to enforce it by foreclosure. At that point, the purchaser at the foreclosure sale will hold the property as a tenant in common with the other tenant, but will still have an undivided one-half interest in the property unless and until he brings an action to partition the estate. (A) is incorrect because both joint tenancies and tenancies in common may be subject to partition. (In contrast, tenancies by the entirety cannot be terminated by involuntary partition.) (C) is incorrect because, as discussed above, a joint tenant may validly convey or encumber his interest in the property. (D) is incorrect because the driver does not have a contingent interest; she has a present lien on the brother's interest that can be enforced immediately by foreclosure, which would sever the joint tenancy.

Answer to Question 36

(D) The court should rule for the investor because the daughter has no interest in the land. If property is specifically devised or bequeathed in the testator's will, but the testator no longer owns that

property at the time of death, the gift is adeemed; *i.e.*, it fails. Here, the mother specifically devised the land to the daughter in her will. However, the mother conveyed the same land to the investor prior to her death. Thus, the land was no longer in the mother's estate at her death, so the daughter takes no interest in the land under the will. Moreover, the daughter has not obtained title to the land by adverse possession because she has only been in possession for three years, two years less than that required by the statute. (A) is a correct statement of the law—quitclaim deeds do convey whatever interest (if any) the seller has—but here the seller (the mother) owned the land in fee simple, and thus conveyed a fee simple interest to the investor. (B) is incorrect because the daughter has no interest in the land and because the investor was a bona fide purchaser. A bona fide purchaser is a purchaser who takes without actual, constructive, or inquiry notice of a prior conveyance and pays valuable consideration. Because a will takes effect only at the testator's death, there was no prior conveyance here. Thus, the investor will not be held to have inquiry notice of the daughter's interest due to her being in possession of the land. (C) is incorrect because whether the mobile home is a fixture is not at issue here. However, if the mobile home is a fixture (*i.e.*, a chattel that has been so affixed to land that it has ceased being personal property and has become part of the realty), the trespassing daughter risks losing it to the investor. Trespassers normally lose their annexations whether installed in good faith or not. Moreover, the trespasser can be held liable for the reasonable rental value of the property on which she annexed the item.

Torts

Question Sets and Analytical Answers

Set 1 Answer Sheet

1. Ⓐ Ⓑ Ⓒ Ⓓ
2. Ⓐ Ⓑ Ⓒ Ⓓ
3. Ⓐ Ⓑ Ⓒ Ⓓ
4. Ⓐ Ⓑ Ⓒ Ⓓ
5. Ⓐ Ⓑ Ⓒ Ⓓ
6. Ⓐ Ⓑ Ⓒ Ⓓ
7. Ⓐ Ⓑ Ⓒ Ⓓ
8. Ⓐ Ⓑ Ⓒ Ⓓ
9. Ⓐ Ⓑ Ⓒ Ⓓ
10. Ⓐ Ⓑ Ⓒ Ⓓ
11. Ⓐ Ⓑ Ⓒ Ⓓ
12. Ⓐ Ⓑ Ⓒ Ⓓ
13. Ⓐ Ⓑ Ⓒ Ⓓ
14. Ⓐ Ⓑ Ⓒ Ⓓ
15. Ⓐ Ⓑ Ⓒ Ⓓ
16. Ⓐ Ⓑ Ⓒ Ⓓ
17. Ⓐ Ⓑ Ⓒ Ⓓ
18. Ⓐ Ⓑ Ⓒ Ⓓ

TORTS QUESTIONS - SET 1

Question 1

A missile company was engaged in research and development of an interplanetary space shuttle, under contract with the United States government. Over a period of years, it developed the prototype of a huge, solid-fuel rocket engine for use in this program. To evaluate the performance of this engine, it conducted a static test of the engine at a remote desert test site. The rocket engine was mounted on a concrete test stand, with the thrust of the engine directed downward into the ground. When the engine was fired up, huge clouds of flame and smoke filled the air, and particles of debris from the rocket fell onto an adjoining farm.

If the farmer files an action against the company for trespass, which of the following facts, if proved, would be most helpful to the company in avoiding liability?

(A) The farmer bought and operated his farm knowing that the company used the adjoining property for testing its rocket engines.

(B) Neither the company nor anyone in its employ set foot upon the farmer's land.

(C) The company had no reason to anticipate that the tests would cause any of the results that occurred.

(D) The rocket testing program is essential to national security, so that the company's conduct was completely privileged as a public necessity.

Question 2

In response to the latest energy crisis, an oil company began testing a new method of extracting oil from certain types of subsurface rock. The process used concentrated sound waves to pulverize the rock and draw out the oil. The tests, conducted in a sparsely populated area, caused heavy vibrations in the ground and the slumping of subsurface earth structures surrounding the test site. This led to the collapse of a water well on a rancher's property.

If the rancher brings a negligence action against the oil company, which of the following would be most helpful to the oil company in avoiding liability?

(A) The subsurface earth structures that collapsed as a result of the tests were unstable before the tests took place.

(B) The rancher's property is located at such a far distance from the test site that no risk to the rancher was foreseeable.

(C) The oil company exercised due care in selecting the personnel who chose the test site and conducted the tests.

(D) The oil company built its test site and conducted the tests in conformity with safety procedures and standards used by all other companies engaged in similar tests.

Question 3

A car owner lent her automobile to her girlfriend for the specific purpose of picking up a pizza that the owner and the girlfriend had ordered for dinner. The girlfriend drove to the shopping mall where the pizzeria was located and parked the owner's car there. Instead of going directly to the pizzeria, the girlfriend went into a bookstore, browsed, and eventually purchased a book. The girlfriend then went to the pizzeria and picked up the pizza, which had been ready for 15 minutes. Just as the girlfriend left the pizzeria to return to the car, another car struck the owner's parked car, causing extensive damage to the car. The owner did not carry collision insurance, and the car required $800 worth of body work.

If the owner sues the girlfriend on a negligence theory for damage to the car, who will prevail?

(A) The owner, because the girlfriend exceeded her authority when she went to the bookstore.

(B) The owner, because but for the girlfriend's delay in getting the pizza, the owner's car would not have been damaged.

(C) The girlfriend, because she did not create a foreseeable risk of damage to the owner's car.

(D) The girlfriend, because the family car doctrine imputes any of the girlfriend's negligence to the owner.

Question 4

Two high school girls were seated in a booth near the front of a restaurant engaged in conversation when a boy from their high school sat down at the booth immediately adjacent to theirs. The boy had a "crush" on one of the girls, who was seated with her back toward him, and wanted to scare her slightly to draw attention to himself. Therefore, he shot a spitball from his straw toward her. The shot went astray and struck the other girl in the eye, causing her to suffer corneal damage.

If the injured girl sues the boy, she can recover for:

(A) Assault.

(B) Battery.

(C) Intentional infliction of emotional distress.

(D) Nothing, because the boy did not intend to harm her.

Question 5

When a diner began choking on a piece of shrimp, a waitress rushed to the diner's assistance. Before she could reach the diner, the waitress slipped on some pudding that a busboy had failed to remove from the floor. The waitress fell on top of another restaurant patron, injuring him.

If the injured patron sues the waitress for his injuries, can he recover?

(A) Yes, because the waitress had no duty to rescue.

(B) Yes, because the waitress assumed the risk.

(C) No, because the touching was unintentional.

(D) No, but he may recover against the restaurant.

Question 6

A cyclist was riding on a sidewalk when someone in a parked car suddenly opened the door of the car into her path. She swerved to avoid the car door and rode onto a landowner's property, damaging some plastic lawn ornaments of waterfowl placed in his front yard.

In a suit by the landowner against the cyclist for the damage to his lawn ornaments:

(A) The cyclist is liable because she had no privilege to enter onto the landowner's property.

(B) Whether the cyclist is liable depends on whether she was exercising due care.

(C) The cyclist is liable for the damage to the lawn ornaments.

(D) The cyclist is not liable for the damage to the lawn ornaments because her entry was privileged.

Question 7

A pedestrian walking along an unpaved road on his way to work saw a school bus coming in the opposite direction suddenly begin to careen toward him. The bus driver had momentarily lost control of the bus while attempting to light a cigarette.

To avoid being hit by the bus, the pedestrian jumped off the road into a landowner's yard. Unfortunately, he landed in a bed of prize-winning zinnias and damaged them extensively.

In a suit by the landowner against the bus driver for the damages to her zinnias:

(A) The bus driver is liable for trespass because his driving caused the pedestrian to enter the landowner's yard and damage her zinnias.

(B) The bus driver is liable on the theory of negligence.

(C) The bus driver is not liable because the landowner's zinnias were not within the scope of any duty he owed in operating a bus on a public road.

(D) If the bus driver is held liable on any theory, he is entitled to indemnity from the pedestrian, who did the damage.

Question 8

A boy was playing softball in a neighborhood park when a ball was hit over the fence and into a neighbor's yard. The boy knocked on the neighbor's door and obtained permission from her to retrieve the ball from her yard. As he bent to retrieve the ball in some bushes, the boy brushed against an exposed electric wire that was partially hidden by the bushes and received a severe electric shock and burns. The neighbor had failed to maintain the bushes, allowing them to become overgrown, and was not aware of the exposed wire.

In a suit by the boy against the neighbor for these injuries:

(A) The neighbor is liable because the boy entered with her permission.

(B) The neighbor is liable because she failed to repair a dangerous condition on her property.

(C) The neighbor is liable because she failed to reasonably inspect the property, which would have made her aware of the dangerous condition of the wire.

(D) The neighbor is not liable because she did not know of the condition of the wire.

Question 9

A mapping service on the Internet that provided maps and satellite images of urban areas developed a "tourist view" option that offered street level views on its website of many downtown locations in major cities. In one of the street view images posted by the mapping service, a pedestrian could be seen on the steps heading into a business while smoking a cigarette. He was recognized on the website by his supervisor, who was surprised to see him smoking because he had obtained an employee health insurance discount by affirming that he was a nonsmoker.

If the pedestrian sues the mapping service for invasion of privacy, how should the court rule?

(A) For the mapping service, because the disclosure was of someone in a public place.

(B) For the mapping service, unless the pedestrian's employer canceled his health insurance discount.

(C) For the pedestrian, because there was widespread public disclosure by the mapping service of a private fact.

(D) For the pedestrian, because he had stepped from the public sidewalk onto the business's property when the image was taken.

Question 10

A worker at a petrochemical plant was severely burned when a pipe carrying hot oil exploded. The worker brought a negligence action against the company that manufactured and installed the pipe. At trial, the worker established what happened and the injuries he suffered. He also presented evidence that the pipe burst because it had corroded at a higher than normal rate, which according to testimony of the worker's experts indicated a defect in the manufacture of the pipe. At the close of the worker's case, the manufacturer moved for a directed verdict.

The court should:

(A) Deny the motion, because the pipe was defective and injured the worker.

(B) Deny the motion, because the jury could find that the premature corrosion of the pipe would not have occurred absent negligence by the manufacturer.

(C) Grant the motion, because the worker has not established that the manufacturer was negligent.

(D) Grant the motion, because the pipe was in the petrochemical plant's possession when it exploded.

Question 11

A company let an employee borrow one of its company cars for a cross-country vacation trip which the employee had planned for his family. While driving through a remote stretch of farmland, the employee decided to see how much power the car really had, and was driving in excess of 90 m.p.h. when he came to a curve. He applied the brakes and attempted to slow down, but the car went across the double line and struck head-on a minivan coming in the opposite direction. The driver of the minivan was killed in the accident and the minivan was destroyed.

A "permissive use" statute is in effect making the bailor of an automobile liable for personal injury, death, or property damage caused by any person operating the automobile with his consent, up to a maximum of $25,000. The jurisdiction follows traditional contribution rules.

If the driver's estate files suit against the company pursuant to the "permissive use" statute, and recovers the full $25,000, what rights, if any, would the company have against the employee?

(A) None, unless there was a written agreement with the employee that obligated him to assume any such liability imposed on the company.

(B) The company may obtain contribution from the employee to the extent of $12,500, but not indemnity.

(C) The company may obtain indemnity against the employee for the full $25,000.

(D) The company may obtain contribution from the employee to the extent of the employee's relative fault, but not indemnity.

Question 12

The owner of a speedboat let his friend operate it in a busy channel. While operating the boat, the friend collided with a canoe that had the right of way, injuring its occupant. The canoeist filed suit against both the owner and the friend, alleging that the friend was negligent in operating the boat and that the owner was negligent in letting him operate it, having reason to know that the friend was not qualified to operate a boat.

The jurisdiction follows traditional rules for joint and several liability and contribution. There is no other applicable statute.

If the jury finds both defendants liable and assesses the plaintiff's damages at $100,000, how should the judgment be entered?

(A) $50,000 against each defendant.

(B) $25,000 against the owner and $75,000 against the friend.

(C) $100,000 against the owner only.

(D) $100,000 against both defendants.

Question 13

The owner of a collection of old anvils lent it to the local museum and hired professional movers to transport the anvils to the second floor of the museum, where they would be displayed. The movers used a rope and pulley apparatus to lift the anvils on the outside of the building to a second-story window. While one of the largest anvils was being lifted, it slipped and fell, crashing to the ground. However, the anvil was not even dented.

If the owner brings a negligence action against the movers for allowing the antique anvil to fall, he can recover:

(A) Nominal damages.

(B) Punitive damages.

(C) Both nominal damages and punitive damages.

(D) Neither nominal damages nor punitive damages.

Question 14

The owner of a valuable painting hired professional movers to transport it to an auction house when she decided to sell it. As the movers were carrying it to their van, a window air conditioner that a tenant had been trying to install fell out of his second floor window and crashed through the painting and onto the ground. The owner had been watching from her apartment across the street and saw her painting destroyed. She became extremely upset and needed medical treatment for shock

If the owner brings a claim for negligent infliction of emotional distress against the tenant, she would:

(A) Recover, because she suffered physical symptoms from her distress.

(B) Recover, because she was a foreseeable plaintiff.

(C) Not recover, because she was not within the zone of danger.

(D) Not recover, because there was no impact.

Question 15

A student conducting an experiment with gases that caused facial distortions mixed them together near a public sidewalk, causing the fumes to be breathed in by pedestrians on the sidewalk. The gas caused their faces to become grossly distorted, but the effect was temporary and none of the pedestrians suffered any permanent damage.

The pedestrians have a cause of action against the student for:

(A) Assault.

(B) Battery.

(C) Intentional infliction of emotional distress.

(D) Invasion of privacy.

Question 16

A visitor to a cooking demonstration in a neighborhood park was allowed to sample some of the cuisine that was prepared. After sampling one dish, the visitor immediately developed an allergic reaction that caused his face to swell up. A photographer from the local newspaper who was taking photos of the event took a close-up shot of the visitor shortly thereafter. The newspaper ran a story on the cooking event with photos, including the visitor's photo. It just showed his face and made him appear extremely obese.

If the visitor sues the newspaper for invasion of privacy, he will:

(A) Prevail, because the photo made him appear to be extremely obese.

(B) Prevail, because the newspaper disclosed a private fact.

(C) Not prevail, because he was in a public park when the photo was taken.

(D) Not prevail, because he suffered no permanent harm.

Question 17

A 14-year-old was the youngest licensed pilot in the state. On a foggy day when pilots were being advised to fly only if necessary, the pilot took his plane out so that he could fly low over the football field where his friends were practicing.

When he attempted to land on his return to the airport, he ran off the runway due to the fog and damaged an executive's airplane, which was in the parking area.

If the executive sues the pilot for damage to his airplane and prevails, it will be because:

(A) A reasonable pilot would not have flown that day.

(B) A pilot with the same age, education, and experience would not have flown that day.

(C) It was not necessary for the pilot to fly that day.

(D) The flying of a plane by a 14-year-old is an inherently dangerous activity, and the pilot is strictly liable for the damage.

Question 18

A 16-year-old teenager was playing baseball in a sandlot when the ball was hit over his head and onto a landowner's adjacent property. Ignoring "beware of dog" signs, the teenager climbed over the fence into the landowner's yard to retrieve the ball and was attacked by a vicious guard dog belonging to the landowner. The dog bit the teenager, causing him to suffer severe lacerations that required numerous stitches.

If the teenager brings an action against the landowner to recover damages for his injuries, he will:

(A) Prevail, because the landowner may not use a vicious dog to protect only his property.

(B) Prevail, because the landowner is strictly liable for injuries caused by the vicious dog.

(C) Not prevail, because the teenager was trespassing on the landowner's property.

(D) Not prevail, because the landowner had posted signs warning about the dog.

TORTS ANSWERS - SET 1

Answer to Question 1

(C) If the company had no reason to anticipate that the tests would cause the results that occurred, then it cannot be said that the company intended to commit the act constituting trespass. Absent such intent, there is no cause of action for trespass. A prima facie case for trespass to land consists of: (i) an act of physical invasion of the plaintiff's real property by the defendant; (ii) intent on the defendant's part to bring about a physical invasion of the plaintiff's real property; and (iii) causation. The intent required is not intent to trespass; thus, mistake as to the lawfulness of an entry onto another's land is no defense as long as the defendant intended the entry upon that particular piece of land. Here, the company, in firing the rocket engine, caused debris to fall onto the farmer's property. This would be a sufficient physical invasion for purposes of a trespass action. However, maintenance of this action requires a showing that the company intended to send this debris onto the land of the farmer. If (as stated in (C)) the company had no reason to anticipate that its rocket engine tests would cause the debris to fall onto the farmer's property, then the company did not intend to make any entry onto the farmer's property (*i.e.,* the company neither acted with the goal of sending debris onto the farmer's land nor did it know with substantial certainty that such a consequence would result from its tests of the engine). Consequently, under the circumstances set forth in (C), the element of intent would be missing, thereby precluding the farmer from establishing a prima facie case for trespass. (A) is incorrect because the fact that the farmer bought and operated the farm with knowledge that the company used the adjoining land for engine tests will not allow the company to commit an act that would otherwise be characterized as a trespass. The farmer's knowledge of the use to which the company put the adjoining property cannot be taken as implied consent to the scattering of debris on the farmer's land. (B) is incorrect because a physical invasion does not require that the defendant personally come onto the land. There is a trespass if, *e.g.,* the defendant floods the plaintiff's land or, as here, causes debris to settle on the plaintiff's land. (D) is incorrect because the defense of public necessity arises where the public good is threatened with injury, and the defendant's actions are reasonably and apparently necessary to avoid such injury. Also, the threatened injury must be substantially more serious than the defendant's interference with the plaintiff's property that seeks to avoid such injury. This defense presupposes a situation in which immediate action is required by the defendant to ward off an imminent threat to the public good. Testing rocket engines for eventual military use does not rise to the level of conduct necessary to avoid an impending injury to the public good. Thus, the company cannot successfully claim that its conduct is privileged as a public necessity.

Answer to Question 2

(B) The distance from the test site to the rancher's property is most helpful to the oil company. Where an action is based on negligence, the plaintiff is alleging that the defendant has breached its duty of acting as an ordinary, prudent, reasonable person, and that such breach has actually and proximately caused injury to the plaintiff. No duty is imposed upon a person to take precautions against events that cannot reasonably be foreseen. Thus, if at the time of the defendant's conduct, no foreseeable risk of injury to a person in the position of the plaintiff is created by the defendant's act, the general duty of care does not extend from the defendant to the plaintiff. If (as (B) states) the rancher's property is located so far from the test site that no risk to the rancher was foreseeable, then there would be no duty imposed upon the oil company to take precautions against the damage to the rancher's property. Thus, the general duty of reasonable care would not extend from the oil company to the rancher with respect to the oil company's testing operations.

Absent such a duty, there can be no liability for negligence. (A) is incorrect because the prior instability of the subsurface earth structures will almost certainly not help the oil company. Such instability addresses the matter of causation of injury. Even assuming the instability of the structures, the facts indicate that the structures would not have slumped but for the penetration of the sound waves caused by the oil company. Thus, the oil company's conduct was the cause in fact (actual cause) of the damage to the water well on the rancher's property. The testing by the oil company was also the proximate cause of the rancher's injury because the damage was the direct result of the oil company's conduct. Hence, it will be of no help to the oil company to show that the subsurface structures were already unstable. (C) is incorrect because, even if the oil company exercised reasonable care in selecting the personnel involved in the testing, such personnel may still have acted negligently in the manner in which they conducted the tests or chose the test site. Under such circumstances, the oil company would be vicariously liable for the negligence committed by its employees within the scope of the employment relationship. (D) is incorrect because industry standards of conduct do not establish a conclusive test for determining whether specific actions constitute a breach of duty owed to someone. Industry standards are admissible as evidence of an appropriate standard of care, but they are not conclusive on this point (in fact, such standards may actually represent conduct that is negligent).

Answer to Question 3

(C) The girlfriend is not liable for the damage to the car because a reasonable person would not have foreseen damage arising from the delay in getting the pizza. A prima facie case for negligence consists of: (i) a duty on the part of the defendant to conform to a specific standard of conduct for the protection of the plaintiff against an unreasonable risk of injury; (ii) breach of such duty by the defendant; (iii) that such breach is the actual and proximate cause of the plaintiff's injury; and (iv) damage to the plaintiff's person or property. No duty is imposed upon a person to take precautions against events that cannot reasonably be foreseen. Here, it is true that, had the girlfriend gotten the pizza immediately, the owner's car would not have been at the location it was at the time it was struck. However, a mere delay in picking up a pizza while leaving a car properly parked does not create a foreseeable risk of damage to the car. Thus, there is no basis for holding the girlfriend liable in negligence. (B) is incorrect because, as noted above, the fact that the owner's car would not have been damaged if the girlfriend had not delayed in getting the pizza is not enough to establish liability for negligence. The fact that the damage to the owner's car was unforeseeable will preclude a finding that the girlfriend acted negligently by delaying in getting the pizza. Likewise, (A) is incorrect because the mere fact that the girlfriend stopped at the bookstore, when the owner loaned her the car specifically to pick up the pizza, will not mean that the girlfriend acted in a manner that created an unreasonable risk of damage to the car. The concept of "exceeding one's authority" might be relevant in the context of an employer trying to avoid vicarious liability for the tortious conduct of an employee by arguing that the employee acted outside the scope of her employment. However, in the context of this question, the girlfriend's having stopped at the bookstore will not subject her to liability. (D) misstates the family car doctrine, which holds an automobile owner liable for tortious conduct of immediate family or household members who are driving with the owner's permission. This doctrine would not be used to relieve the girlfriend of liability for any negligence on her part by imputing such negligence to the owner. Note also that the girlfriend and the owner are not members of the same family or household.

Answer to Question 4

(B) The boy is liable for battery under the doctrine of transferred intent. Pursuant to this doctrine, where a defendant intends to commit a tort against one person but instead: (i) commits a different tort against that person; (ii) commits the same tort as intended but against a different person; or (iii) commits a different tort against a different person, the intent to commit a tort against one person is transferred to the other tort or to the injured person for purposes of establishing a prima facie case. Transferred intent may be invoked where the tort intended and the tort that results are both among the following: (i) assault; (ii) battery; (iii) false imprisonment; (iv) trespass to land; and (v) trespass to chattels. Assault requires: (i) an act by the defendant creating a reasonable apprehension in the plaintiff of immediate harmful or offensive contact to the plaintiff's person; (ii) intent on the part of the defendant to bring about in the plaintiff such apprehension; and (iii) causation. Battery requires: (i) an act by the defendant that brings about harmful or offensive contact to the plaintiff's person; (ii) intent on the part of the defendant to bring about such contact; and (iii) causation. Here, the boy intended either to commit battery against the girl he targeted (if he intended to hit her with the spitball) or to commit assault (if he merely intended to put her in apprehension of immediate harmful or offensive contact with the spitball). When the boy actually hit the other girl, his intent as to the first girl was transferred to the other girl. Thus, the boy is liable to the girl he injured for battery. (A) is incorrect because, with harmful contact having occurred, the tort for which the boy is liable is battery. Also, there is no indication that the girl he injured was placed in apprehension of any harmful or offensive contact, as she apparently was unaware of what the boy was doing until she was struck by the spitball. (C) is incorrect because the boy's conduct is not so extreme and outrageous (*i.e.,* transcending all bounds of decency) as to qualify for the tort of intentional infliction of emotional distress. Also, the boy did not intend to cause severe emotional distress to anyone. The boy intended only to mildly frighten the girl he targeted, not to cause her (or the girl he injured) to suffer severe emotional distress. The doctrine of transferred intent does not apply where an assault or battery is intended toward one person, and emotional distress occurs in another person. (D) is incorrect because it fails to account for transferred intent. As detailed above, the fact that the boy did not intend to harm the girl he injured will not relieve the boy of liability for battery, because his intent to commit a tort against the girl he targeted is transferred to the tort actually committed against the other girl.

Answer to Question 5

(D) The waitress is not liable because there is no indication of any fault on her part in injuring the patron. However, the restaurant is vicariously liable for the negligence of the busboy in failing to remove the pudding. The waitress fell on top of the patron because she slipped on the pudding. Slipping and falling were not volitional acts by the waitress, so it cannot be said that she acted with the intent to bring about any harm to the patron, or that she knew with substantial certainty that such harm would occur. In addition, the facts do not indicate that the slip and fall occurred because the waitress was not exercising ordinary, reasonable care. In her rush to assist a restaurant patron in distress, the waitress inadvertently stepped on a slippery substance, the presence of which she had no reason to know. Thus, she did not act negligently. Because the waitress's conduct was neither intentional nor negligent, she is without fault in the infliction of injury to the patron. Consequently, she will not be held liable for the injury. However, the busboy who failed to remove the pudding from the floor did act negligently. The busboy owed a duty to restaurant patrons to act as an ordinary, reasonable person for the protection of the patrons against an unreasonable risk of injury. By leaving the pudding on the floor, the busboy created an unreasonable risk that a patron would be injured either by directly falling or by being near someone else who fell. Thus, the busboy breached his duty of due care. This breach, which caused the waitress to fall on the patron, actually and proximately caused physical injury to the patron, who was a foreseeable plaintiff. This negligence on the part of the busboy was committed within the scope of his employment relationship with the restaurant. Under the doctrine of respondeat superior, the restaurant is vicariously liable for this tortious act of its employee. Thus, (D) correctly states

that the waitress is not liable, but the restaurant is liable. (A) is incorrect for two reasons: First, restaurateurs and others who gather the public for profit have a duty to use reasonable care to aid or assist their guests. Therefore, as a restaurant employee, the waitress was under a duty to use reasonable care to assist a diner who was apparently in great distress and in need of assistance. Second, even if the waitress was not under a duty to aid, her attempt to provide help will not render her liable for the patron's injury. As noted above, the waitress was not at fault in inflicting the injury on the patron. Providing help despite not having a duty to do so is not a basis for imposing liability on the waitress for the injury that befell the patron. (B) is incorrect because it misapplies the principle of assumption of risk. A plaintiff may be denied recovery if she assumed the risk of any damage caused by the defendant's acts. Thus, assumption of the risk provides a defense to a plaintiff's claim, rather than a basis on which to hold a person liable. It is therefore meaningless to speak of the waitress, the defendant, as having "assumed the risk." (C) is incorrect because, despite the fact that the waitress's touching of the patron was unintentional, she could still be held liable for his injuries if she had been negligent in causing them. Thus, the unintentional nature of the waitress's conduct will not by itself relieve her of liability.

Answer to Question 6

(C) The cyclist is liable for damage to the lawn ornaments even though she had a privilege to enter the landowner's yard. Pursuant to the privilege of necessity, a person may interfere with property of another where it is reasonably and apparently necessary to avoid threatened injury from a natural or other force and where the threatened injury is substantially more serious than the invasion that seeks to avert it. In cases of private necessity (where the act is solely to benefit a limited number of persons rather than the public as a whole) the defense is qualified, so that the actor must pay for any injury she causes. The cyclist was faced with serious injury from being struck by the car door opening. Apparently the only way to avoid this injury was to swerve into the landowner's yard. The threatened injury to the cyclist was substantially more serious than the cyclist's entry into the landowner's yard. Thus, the cyclist was privileged to enter the yard. However, because this is a private necessity situation, she will be required to pay for the damage she caused to the lawn ornaments. (A) correctly states that the cyclist is liable for the damage, but incorrectly states that she was not privileged to enter upon the landowner's land. On the other hand, (D) is incorrect because it concludes that the cyclist's privilege absolves her of liability for the damage she caused, which is not true in private necessity cases. (B) is incorrect because the cyclist's exercise of due care is irrelevant. The landowner will be proceeding against the cyclist on a theory of intentional tort (either trespass or conversion). Due care is a concept that is applicable to a negligence action, but is not relevant to an action sounding in intentional tort. Therefore, the cyclist's liability is unaffected by whether she was exercising due care.

Answer to Question 7

(B) The bus driver is liable to the landowner in a negligence action. The driver of a vehicle on a public road owes to foreseeable plaintiffs a duty of ordinary, reasonable care to refrain from creating an unreasonable risk of injury in the operation of the vehicle. In trying to light a cigarette while driving the bus, the bus driver created an unreasonable risk that he would lose control of the bus, thus endangering the physical safety and the property of other drivers on the road, pedestrians, and owners of property adjoining the road. There was a foreseeable risk of injury to the landowner or her property arising from the manner in which the bus driver drove the bus; thus, the duty of care extended from the bus driver to the landowner. This duty was breached when the bus driver drove the bus so as to create an unreasonable risk of injury to the landowner or her property. It was reasonably foreseeable that a pedestrian endangered by the manner in which the bus driver drove the bus would be compelled to enter the landowner's property and would damage the zinnias. By forcing the pedestrian to jump off the road to save his life, the bus driver actually and proximately caused the damage to the zinnias; where a defendant's actions cause another to react, liability will attach for any harm inflicted by the reacting person on another. Thus, the bus driver can be held liable in negligence for the damage to the landowner's zinnias. (C) is incorrect because the manner in which the bus driver operated the bus created a foreseeable risk of injury to the person or property of someone who owns property adjoining the road. Therefore, the general duty of due care owed by the bus driver in his operation of the bus extended to the landowner and her zinnias. (A) is incorrect because the bus driver lacked the intent to bring about a physical invasion of the landowner's property. Absent such intent, there can be no liability for trespass. The bus driver was negligent in his operation of the bus, and this caused the pedestrian to enter the landowner's land. However, the bus driver neither acted with the goal of forcing the pedestrian onto the landowner's land nor did he act knowing with substantial certainty that this consequence would result. Therefore, the bus driver did not have the intent needed to support an action for trespass. (D) is incorrect because none of the circumstances in which indemnity is available is present. Indemnity involves shifting the entire loss between or among tortfeasors. One held vicariously liable may obtain indemnification from the person whose conduct actually caused the damage. The bus driver will be held liable for his own negligence in driving the bus, not vicariously for any conduct of the pedestrian's. Thus, this basis for indemnity does not apply. It is also possible for one tortfeasor to recover against a co-joint tortfeasor where there is a considerable difference in degree of fault. Here, the bus driver is primarily at fault. He was negligent in driving the bus, while the pedestrian merely reacted to save himself from death or serious injury, and was apparently not negligent at all. Thus, it is the bus driver who is the "more wrongful" tortfeasor, thereby precluding recovery of indemnity from the pedestrian on this basis as well.

Answer to Question 8

(D) The neighbor is not liable because she did not know of the condition of the wire and the boy was a licensee. A licensee is a person who enters land with the owner's permission, for his own purpose or business rather than for the owner's benefit. The owner or occupier of land has a duty to warn a licensee of a dangerous condition known to the owner or occupier that creates an unreasonable risk of harm to the licensee and that the licensee is unlikely to discover. However, the owner or occupier has no duty to a licensee to inspect for defects nor to repair known defects. The boy was a licensee because he entered the neighbor's land with her permission for his own purpose (retrieving the ball) rather than for any benefit of the neighbor's. The exposed electric wire created an unreasonable risk of death or serious injury to the boy as he reached into the bushes. Because the neighbor did not know of the presence and condition of the wire, she had no knowledge of any risk of harm to the boy. Thus, no duty to warn the boy of the wire was triggered. (A) is incorrect because the mere fact that the neighbor gave the boy permission to enter her land will not subject her to liability for his injuries incurred thereon. The neighbor is not strictly liable for injuries to a licensee, but only for any injuries caused by a breach of her duty to warn of dangerous conditions known to her and that the licensee is unlikely to discover. (A) would impose liability even where the neighbor had no knowledge of the condition of the wire. (B) is incorrect because, as noted above, an owner of land does not owe a duty to a licensee to repair defects or dangerous conditions. Likewise, (C) is incorrect because the owner of land is not under a duty to a licensee to make an inspection to discover defects or dangerous conditions.

Answer to Question 9

(A) The mapping service should prevail because the pedestrian was in a public place when the photo was taken. To establish a prima facie case for invasion of privacy involving public disclosure of

private facts about the plaintiff, the plaintiff must show that the publication was of private information about the plaintiff that a reasonable person would object to having been made public. There is no liability for publication of matters occurring in a public place. Here, the pedestrian was in public when he was photographed smoking. Even though he might not have wished that to be publicized, he was in a public place at the time, so he cannot claim invasion of privacy. (B) is incorrect because the fact that the pedestrian suffered economic damages is irrelevant. He cannot prevail because he cannot establish the prima facie case; if he were able to establish the prima facie case, he could prevail even without proof of economic damages. (C) is incorrect because the scope of the disclosure does not matter if it is not a private fact; a photograph of someone in a public place is not actionable no matter how widely it is disseminated. (D) is incorrect because a "public place" is not limited to property owned by public authorities; it includes all areas open to the public, including the entrance to a business's premises.

Answer to Question 10

(B) The court should deny the motion because the jury may draw an inference of negligence from the plaintiff's evidence. The plaintiff's action against the manufacturer is a products liability action based on a negligence theory. In such a case, the prima facie case consists of: (i) a legal duty owed by the defendant to this plaintiff; (ii) breach of the duty; (iii) actual and proximate cause; and (iv) damages. Breach of duty requires showing (i) negligent conduct by the defendant leading to (ii) the supplying of a defective product by the defendant. The plaintiff may invoke res ipsa loquitur against the manufacturer if the error is usually something that does not occur without the negligence of the manufacturer. Here, the plaintiff has presented evidence that the manufacturer supplied a pipe that was so defective as to be unreasonably dangerous (because of its premature corrosion). The plaintiff can use res ipsa loquitur to show negligence because the manufacturer fabricated and installed the pipe and the premature corrosion would not likely have occurred without negligence on its part. Because the plaintiff has presented evidence of the other elements of the prima facie case, it should withstand the defendant's motion for directed verdict. (A) is incorrect because it implies liability without fault. As a plaintiff in a negligence action, the plaintiff must show that the manufacturer breached a duty owed to him, and that such breach caused his injuries. The mere fact that a pipe manufactured by the manufacturer exploded does not satisfy this burden. It is possible that the pipe could have exploded without any fault on the part of the manufacturer. (C) is incorrect because, as discussed above, the worker may rely on res ipsa loquitur here to establish an inference of negligence. (D) is incorrect because, despite the fact that the pipe was in the petrochemical plant's possession at the time of the explosion, the explosion itself may have been caused by negligence on the part of the manufacturer. Because the manufacturer fabricated and installed the pipe, the plaintiff may rely on res ipsa loquitur even though the manufacturer was not in possession of the pipe when the explosion occurred.

Answer to Question 11

(C) The company may obtain indemnity from the employee. One who is held liable for damages caused by another simply because of his relationship to that person may seek indemnification from the person whose conduct actually caused the damage. The company has been held liable for the damages caused by the employee solely because it loaned a car to the employee. Such vicarious liability (imposed pursuant to the permissive use statute) being imposed on the company will entitle it to be indemnified from the employee, whose conduct actually caused the damage. Thus, the entire loss will be shifted from the company to the employee. (A) is incorrect because a contractual promise to indemnify is not the only means by which a right of indemnification can come into existence. For example, a right of indemnity exists as a matter of law in the circumstances here, as detailed above. Thus, the absence of any obligation of the employee contained in a written agreement will not mean that the company has no rights against the employee. (B) is incorrect because contribution is a device whereby responsibility is apportioned among those who are at fault. Contribution allows any defendant required to pay more than his share of damages to have a claim against any other jointly liable parties for the excess. The company is not really at fault in bringing about the harm here. Rather, the company can only be held liable by virtue of the permissive use statute. There is no responsibility to be apportioned here; instead, the entire loss should be shifted from the company to the person who actually caused the damage. Thus, indemnity is available, and contribution is not appropriate. (D) is incorrect for the same reasons that (B) is incorrect. In addition, (D) incorrectly provides for comparative contribution. Traditional contribution rules require all defendants to pay equal shares regardless of their respective degrees of fault.

Answer to Question 12

(D) The judgment should be entered in the full amount against both defendants. Where two or more tortious acts combine to proximately cause an indivisible injury to the plaintiff, each tortfeasor will be jointly and severally liable for that injury. Joint and several liability of such parties means that each is liable to the plaintiff for the entire damage incurred, so that the plaintiff may recover the entire judgment amount from any defendant (with the plaintiff of course being limited to one total recovery). The owner and the friend have been found jointly and severally liable for the harm caused to the canoeist by their tortious acts. Thus, the entire damage amount of $100,000 is recoverable from either of these defendants. As a result, judgment in the amount of $100,000 should be entered against both the owner and the friend. (A) and (B) incorrectly provide for each defendant to be liable for less than the entire damage incurred. It is only where the actions of each defendant are independent, the plaintiff's injury is divisible, and it is possible to identify the portion of injuries caused by each defendant that each will only be liable for an identifiable portion. Here, there is an indivisible injury, and the defendants have been found to be jointly and severally liable. Thus, there is no basis for entering judgment against either defendant for less than the entire amount of damages. (C) is incorrect because both defendants have been found liable, so there is no basis for entering judgment against the owner only.

Answer to Question 13

(D) The owner cannot recover damages because his property was not harmed and because there are no grounds for punitive damages. The prima facie case for negligence requires damage to the plaintiff's person or property. Damages are not presumed in negligence cases; there must be ***actual*** harm or injury. In cases involving property damage, the measure of damages is the reasonable cost of repair, or, if the property has been almost or completely destroyed, its fair market value at the time of the injury. Punitive damages are recoverable only if the defendant's conduct was reckless, malicious, or willful and wanton. Here there is no indication that the movers intended injury to the anvils; this is merely a case of negligence. Thus, the owner must show damage. The anvil has not been damaged in any way, so there are no actual damages available, and because nominal damages are not allowed for negligence, the owner cannot recover ***any*** compensatory damages from the movers, making (A) and (C) wrong. Also, there is no indication of willful and wanton, reckless, or malicious behavior on the part of the movers, so the owner cannot recover punitive damages, making (B) and (C) wrong.

Answer to Question 14

(C) Because the owner was across the street at the time of impact, she was not within the zone of danger, thus precluding her recovery for negligent infliction of emotional distress. A defendant breaches a duty to avoid negligent infliction of emotional distress when he creates a foreseeable risk of physical injury to the plaintiff through causing a threat of physical impact that leads to emotional distress. Damages are recoverable only if the defendant's conduct causes some physical injury, rather than purely emotional distress (although a severe shock to the nervous system that causes physical symptoms is sufficient). If plaintiff's distress is caused by threat of physical impact to her, she must have been within the zone of danger. Here, the owner witnessed the air conditioner striking her painting from across the street. This vantage point placed her outside the zone of danger from the falling air conditioner. Thus, the owner cannot recover for negligent infliction of emotional distress. It is true that, as implied by (A), there can be no recovery for this tort absent some accompanying physical consequences. However, even though the owner did suffer physical symptoms, she cannot recover because she was not within the zone of danger. Therefore, (A) is incorrect. (B) is incorrect because the owner's distance from the accident makes her an unforeseeable plaintiff, because it is unforeseeable that someone on the other side of the street would suffer physical impact or the threat thereof. (D) is incorrect because physical impact is not required for this tort; the threat of impact is enough. Therefore, even in the absence of impact, the owner could recover if she had been within the zone of danger from the tenant's negligence.

Answer to Question 15

(B) The student has committed a battery because she intentionally caused an offensive contact to the pedestrians. In order to establish a prima facie case for battery, the following elements must be proved: (i) an act by the defendant that brings about harmful or offensive contact to the plaintiff's person; (ii) intent on the part of the defendant to bring about harmful or offensive contact to the plaintiff's person; and (iii) causation. Certainly a reasonable person of ordinary sensibilities would consider contact with the gas to be offensive. The defendant is liable not only for "direct" contact, but also "indirect" contact; *i.e.,* it will be sufficient if she sets in motion a force that brings about harmful or offensive contact to the plaintiff's person. Thus, even though the student did not have direct contact with the pedestrians, she allowed the chemical fumes to pass across the sidewalk and thereby caused the offensive contact to them. The fact that she went to an area with pedestrian traffic to release the gases evidences her intent to bring about the offensive contact. (A) is incorrect. In order to establish a prima facie case for assault, the following elements must be proved: (i) an act by the defendant creating a reasonable apprehension in plaintiff of immediate harmful or offensive contact to plaintiff's person; (ii) intent on the part of the defendant to bring about in the plaintiff apprehension of immediate harmful or offensive contact with the plaintiff's person; and (iii) causation. Here, the student's actions created actual contact but did not create an apprehension of contact on the pedestrians' part; they were evidently not aware of the gas until coming into contact with it. Hence, the applicable tort is battery, not assault. (C) is incorrect. To establish a prima facie case for intentional infliction of emotional distress, the following elements must be proved: (i) an act by defendant amounting to extreme and outrageous conduct; (ii) intent on the part of defendant to cause plaintiff to suffer severe emotional distress, or recklessness as to the effect of defendant's conduct; (iii) causation; and (iv) damages. Actual damages are required. But it is not necessary to prove physical injuries to recover. It is, however, necessary to establish severe emotional distress (*i.e.,* more than a reasonable person could be expected to endure). According to the facts, the effect of the gas was temporary and none of the pedestrians suffered any permanent damage. Furthermore, the facts do not indicate that the pedestrians suffered severe emotional distress. (D) is obviously incorrect, as the student has in no way tortiously interfered with the privacy of the pedestrians, who were on a public sidewalk at the time. The tort of privacy includes the following four kinds of wrongs: (i) appropriation by defendant of plaintiff's picture or name for defendant's commercial advantage;

(ii) intrusion by defendant upon plaintiff's affairs or seclusion; (iii) publication by defendant of facts placing plaintiff in a false light; and (iv) public disclosures of private facts about the plaintiff by the defendant. The facts do not suggest that the student committed any of these four kinds of wrongs.

Answer to Question 16

(A) The visitor will prevail because unauthorized use of his picture that falsely makes him appear extremely obese would be objectionable to a reasonable person and constitute a false light invasion of privacy. To establish a prima facie case for invasion of privacy based on publication by defendant of facts placing plaintiff in a false light, the following elements must be proved: (i) publication of facts about plaintiff by defendant placing plaintiff in a false light in the public eye; and (ii) the "false light" must be something that would be objectionable to a reasonable person under the circumstances. Here, the visitor's facial swelling created the false impression in the picture that he was extremely obese. Publication of the picture conveying this false impression of the visitor's physical appearance would be objectionable to a reasonable person under the circumstances. (B) cannot be correct because it is couched in terms of disclosure of private facts about the plaintiff. To establish a prima facie case for invasion of privacy based on public disclosure of private facts about plaintiff, the following elements must be proved: (i) publication or public disclosure by defendant of private information about the plaintiff; and (ii) the matter made public is such that a reasonable person of ordinary sensibilities would object to having it made public. Here, no private facts were disclosed, and therefore an action based on public disclosure of private facts will not succeed. (C) is incorrect. Because the visitor was placed in a false light, it makes no difference that the picture was taken in a public park. An invasion of privacy based on false light can occur on public property as well as private property. (D) is incorrect. The absence of a permanent harm to the visitor has no bearing on a privacy action. In an action for invasion of right to privacy, the plaintiff need not plead and prove special damages, providing the elements of a prima facie case are present. In other words, emotional distress and mental anguish are sufficient damages.

Answer to Question 17

(A) If the executive prevails, it will be because a reasonable pilot would not have flown that day. When the tortfeasor is a child, the applicable standard of care generally imposed by the courts in negligence actions is that of a child of like age, education, intelligence, and experience. This permits a subjective evaluation of these factors. However, when a child is engaged in an activity that is normally one that only adults engage in, such as flying an airplane, most cases hold that he will be required to conform to the same standard of care as an adult in such an activity. Thus, if the executive prevails, it will be because the pilot did not conform to the standard of care of a reasonable adult pilot. (B) is wrong because it states the general standard of care applied to children; the standard is different when the child is engaged in adult activities. (C) is incorrect because it does not establish that the pilot breached his duty of care. The fact that it was not necessary for the pilot to fly that day does not establish that a reasonable pilot would not have flown that day, which is the standard of care applicable to the pilot's conduct (as stated in choice (A)). (D) is incorrect because regular aviation activity, regardless of the age of the pilot, is not considered inherently or abnormally dangerous; hence, strict liability does not apply. The pilot will not be liable if he acted as a reasonably prudent adult pilot.

Answer to Question 18

(A) The teenager will prevail because the landowner may not intentionally use a vicious dog to protect only his property. One may use only reasonable force to defend property. A landowner

may not use force that will cause death or serious bodily harm. Furthermore, one may not use indirect deadly force such as a trap, spring gun, or vicious dog when such force could not lawfully be directly used, *e.g.,* against a mere trespasser. (B) is incorrect because strict liability in such cases generally is not imposed in favor of undiscovered trespassers against landowners. Trespassers cannot recover for injuries inflicted by the landowner's abnormally dangerous domestic animals in the absence of negligence. (C) is incorrect because a landowner who protects his property from intruders by keeping a vicious watchdog he knows is likely to cause serious bodily harm may be liable even to trespassers for injuries caused by the animal. The liability is based on intentional tort principles: Because the landowner is not entitled to use deadly force in person to protect only property, he also may not use such force indirectly. (D) is incorrect because even though the landowner put up warning signs, he can still be liable under intentional tort principles because he intentionally used the dog to protect his property, knowing that the dog is likely to cause serious bodily harm.

Set 2 Answer Sheet

1. Ⓐ Ⓑ Ⓒ Ⓓ
2. Ⓐ Ⓑ Ⓒ Ⓓ
3. Ⓐ Ⓑ Ⓒ Ⓓ
4. Ⓐ Ⓑ Ⓒ Ⓓ
5. Ⓐ Ⓑ Ⓒ Ⓓ
6. Ⓐ Ⓑ Ⓒ Ⓓ
7. Ⓐ Ⓑ Ⓒ Ⓓ
8. Ⓐ Ⓑ Ⓒ Ⓓ
9. Ⓐ Ⓑ Ⓒ Ⓓ
10. Ⓐ Ⓑ Ⓒ Ⓓ
11. Ⓐ Ⓑ Ⓒ Ⓓ
12. Ⓐ Ⓑ Ⓒ Ⓓ
13. Ⓐ Ⓑ Ⓒ Ⓓ
14. Ⓐ Ⓑ Ⓒ Ⓓ
15. Ⓐ Ⓑ Ⓒ Ⓓ
16. Ⓐ Ⓑ Ⓒ Ⓓ
17. Ⓐ Ⓑ Ⓒ Ⓓ
18. Ⓐ Ⓑ Ⓒ Ⓓ

TORTS QUESTIONS - SET 2

Question 1

A large mansion was purchased as a residence by a vice-president of one of the three major banks in the town. The local newspaper published an article about the purchase, including the $600,000 sale price, after obtaining the information from the county recorder of deeds office. The article included a photograph of the mansion which had been taken from the sidewalk in front.

If the vice-president sues the newspaper for invasion of privacy, will he recover?

(A) Yes, because he did not consent to publication of information about himself and his private residence.

(B) Yes, if a reasonable person of ordinary sensibilities would have been upset by publication of the story.

(C) No, because the newspaper printed public facts.

(D) No, because the story in the newspaper was true.

Question 2

A homeowner hired a computer repair technician to fix his computer. The technician discovered that she needed a different type of memory card than she had, so she drove to the local electronics store to get what she needed. On the way back, she stopped at a liquor store to get a bottle of wine for a dinner party she was attending that night. When she was backing out of the parking lot, she negligently knocked over a pedestrian who was walking on the sidewalk adjacent to the parking lot.

In a negligence action by the pedestrian against the homeowner, the pedestrian will most likely:

(A) Recover, because a principal is vicariously liable for the negligence of his agent.

(B) Recover, because the technician was on a detour and not a frolic.

(C) Not recover, because the technician was on a frolic and not a detour.

(D) Not recover, because the technician is an independent contractor.

Question 3

A professional painter and his apprentice, in business as a partnership, were hired to paint a store. Midway through the job they ran out of paint, so the painter lent his truck to the apprentice to pick up more. On his way to pick up the paint, the apprentice decided to go to the library to get a book. After leaving the library he negligently ran into a parked car, causing extensive damage.

If the car owner brings a negligence action against the painter, will she prevail?

(A) No, because the apprentice is an independent contractor.

(B) No, because a bailor is not vicariously liable for the torts of his bailee.

(C) Yes, if the apprentice's stop at the library was not a frolic.

(D) Yes, because the painter and the apprentice are partners.

Question 4

The owner of a car sold it to a purchaser. The seller had previously bought four new tires for the car from a tire shop and had put 2,000 additional miles on the car before she sold it. The purchaser of the car immediately took it on a long trip, often driving it over the posted limit. As he approached his destination, he was driving 10 m.p.h. over the speed limit when his left front tire suddenly blew out because of a defect. The car went out of control, crashed into another vehicle, and the purchaser was severely injured.

The defect in the tires could have been discovered by the seller by a reasonable inspection at the time she selected them.

If the purchaser sues the seller on a strict liability theory, the purchaser should:

(A) Recover, because the tire was defective when the seller sold the car to the purchaser.

(B) Recover, because the seller could have discovered the defect with a reasonable inspection.

(C) Not recover, because the purchaser misused the tire by exceeding the posted speed limit on his trip.

(D) Not recover, because the seller is not a commercial supplier.

Question 5

A man and a woman were playing tennis. The woman became highly irritated because every time she prepared to serve, the man started talking loudly. The man's loud talk distracted the woman from her game, and she usually faulted on her serves. The woman told the man to "cut it out," but he persisted in the behavior.

Standing several feet away, the woman swung her tennis racket toward the man's head to scare him and get him to stop. However, the woman slipped as she swung the racket, and it flew out of her hand as she lost her balance. The racket flew through the air and struck the man in the head. The woman slipped because the owner of the tennis court had not cleaned the court properly after some maintenance work.

Does the man have grounds for a battery action against the woman?

(A) Yes, because the woman intended to create a reasonable apprehension in the man.

(B) Yes, because the racket struck the man.

(C) No, because the woman did not intend the racket to strike the man.

(D) No, because the owner of the tennis court had not maintained the court properly and this caused the woman to slip.

Question 6

The sales representative of a hot dog company gave the proprietor of a corner hot dog stand a poster of an actress endorsing those hot dogs, which the proprietor put in the window. Sales picked up, but the actress filed suit against the proprietor for invasion of privacy because, in fact, she was a spokesperson for a rival hot dog company.

Will the actress prevail?

(A) No, because the actress is a public figure.

(B) No, because the proprietor was reasonably justified in believing the poster was authorized.

(C) Yes, because the actress had not given her permission to use the poster.

(D) Yes, because the proprietor gained profit from using the poster.

Question 7

The superintendent of a waste management company that operated a landfill noted that some children who lived in a nearby residential development had taken to sledding down the snow-covered mounds of dirt that were piled on the site. A construction company needing dirt fill for a highway project had offered to remove the mounds of dirt at minimal cost but the superintendent had not yet arranged for their removal. In the meantime he posted numerous signs around the landfill site that stated in bold letters, "NO TRESPASSING—NO SLEDDING." Despite the signs, which he saw and read, a 10-year-old neighborhood child sledded down one of the mounds of dirt and was propelled onto a busy highway adjacent to the landfill, where he was struck by a car and seriously injured

In a jurisdiction that retains traditional contributory negligence rules, is the waste management company liable for the child's injuries?

(A) Yes, because the company could have had the piles of dirt removed at minimal cost.

(B) Yes, because the company created a public nuisance.

(C) No, because the child was a trespasser.

(D) No, because the child read and understood the warning signs and appreciated the danger.

Question 8

A driver struck a 10-year-old boy who had darted into the road during a game of tag. After the accident, the boy's mother refused to take him to a physician because of moral scruples against the medical profession. As a result, the boy's injuries were more severe than they would otherwise have been.

The boy's best chance to recover for all of his injuries is to argue that:

(A) The doctrine of avoidable consequences at most bars recovery for the aggravation of but not for the original injury itself.

(B) Any negligence on the mother's part is not to be imputed to her child.

(C) Victims have no duty to take steps for their own safety after the accident.

(D) Defendants must take their victims as they find them, including their mothers' attitudes toward physicians.

Question 9

An eight-year-old girl was playing catch on the sidewalk with her friend when her friend made an errant throw over the girl's head. The ball hit a pedestrian, who was walking on the sidewalk in the other direction. The pedestrian angrily threw the ball into the street. The girl ran out into the street to retrieve it and was hit and seriously injured by a car.

If the girl's guardian brings an action on her behalf against the driver of the car, which of the following best states the pedestrian's liability?

(A) The girl may have a personal injury claim against the pedestrian for negligence.

(B) The girl may have a personal injury claim against the pedestrian for an intentional tort.

(C) The girl has no claim against the pedestrian, but the driver may obtain contribution from the pedestrian.

(D) The girl has no claim against the pedestrian, but the driver may obtain indemnity from the pedestrian.

Question 10

A motorist noticed that one of her tires was almost flat. She decided to return the tire to the tire retailer that sold it her two weeks previous, but first she went to a local service station to inflate the tire. As she began to inflate the tire, she noticed that one spot on the tire was beginning to bulge. She checked the air pressure with a gauge and determined that the tire still needed seven pounds more pressure, so she continued to inflate the tire. The bulge then ruptured, and a piece of rubber flew off the tire and struck her in the face, causing severe eye injuries and lacerations. The motorist filed a lawsuit based on strict liability against the tire retailer in a jurisdiction that follows traditional contributory negligence rules.

If the retailer prevails in this lawsuit, it will be because:

(A) The tire was properly installed by retailer's employees.

(B) The motorist knew that the bulge was dangerous.

(C) A reasonable person would not have driven the car with the tire close to being flat.

(D) The defect in the tire could not have been discovered by a reasonable inspection by the retailer.

Question 11

A motorist driving her brand new SUV was exceeding the posted speed limit by 15 m.p.h. on a curving road when she lost control. The vehicle rolled over, causing her to suffer severe injuries. She brought an action against the manufacturer of the SUV based on strict liability in tort. At trial, the facts of the accident were entered into evidence. The motorist also presented expert testimony that stability control technology, which was available in other similar sized SUVs, could have been incorporated into the model she owned and likely would have prevented the vehicle from tipping over. The manufacturer presented evidence that incorporating the stability control technology would have added almost $2,000 to the cost of manufacturing each vehicle. At the close of all of the evidence, the manufacturer moved for a directed verdict. The jurisdiction has not adopted a comparative fault rule in strict liability cases.

The manufacturer's motion should be:

(A) Granted, because incorporating the stability control technology would have increased the cost of the vehicle.

(B) Granted, because the motorist's speeding constituted contributory negligence per se.

(C) Denied, because the jury could find that the vehicle was defectively designed if a feasible alternative design could have incorporated stability control technology.

(D) Denied, because the jury could find that the manufacturer should have known that the vehicle was not safe without the stability control technology.

Question 12

A homeowner heard a loud bang against the bay window one evening. He looked out the window and saw a 12-year-old boy from the neighborhood packing a large snowball. Fearful that he would break the window with another throw, the homeowner went outside and said, "Come here, I want to talk to you." The boy ran in the other direction and jumped over the fence belonging to a neighbor. Because it was dark, the boy landed on a birdbath and knocked it over, breaking it. The neighbor brought an action against the homeowner for trespass.

If the homeowner prevails, it will most likely be because:

(A) The homeowner confronted the boy in order to defend his property.

(B) The homeowner did not enter onto the neighbor's land.

(C) The boy was the one who made the decision to jump over the fence.

(D) The homeowner did not intend to frighten the boy onto the neighbor's property.

Question 13

A homeowner looked out his front window one day and saw a neighbor standing on a narrow ledge on the second story of the house across the street. He also saw a ladder lying on the ground beneath where the neighbor was stranded. The homeowner ran out and picked up the ladder and placed it against the side of the house. However, he set it atop a patch of ice. As the neighbor started down the ladder, a rotten rung broke and he fell to the ground and was injured.

If the neighbor sues the homeowner for damages for his injuries, will he recover?

(A) Yes, because the homeowner's action caused the injury to the neighbor.

(B) Yes, because the homeowner assumed the duty of aiding the neighbor.

(C) Yes, because it was foreseeable that the neighbor would be injured as a result of the homeowner's negligent conduct.

(D) No, because the homeowner's negligence did not cause the injury to the neighbor.

Question 14

A law enforcement officer was transporting a prisoner on a plane to testify in a criminal case. Unknown to those on the plane, an assassin hired to kill the prisoner had bribed an airport baggage handler to sneak a timed-release crate of poisonous snakes into the cargo hold of the plane. Once the crate was triggered to open, the snakes were able to slither into the passenger compartment through gaps in the conduits between the cargo hold and the passenger compartment. In the ensuing panic caused by the snakes, the officer was struck in the head by a fire extinguisher that another passenger threw at a snake, and suffered a severe concussion.

The officer filed suit against numerous parties, including the person who designed the conduit system on that type of plane. At trial, evidence established that the design for the conduit system that he used had been rejected in the industry because of the danger of pressure loss between the cargo hold and the passenger compartment. An industry-approved design that the designer could have used would have kept the snakes from getting into the passenger compartment of the plane.

As between the officer and the designer, which party is likely to prevail?

(A) The officer, because the designer is strictly liable for designing the conduit system of the plane.

(B) The officer, because of the high degree of care owed to passengers of a common carrier.

(C) The designer, because the assassin's actions were an unforeseeable intervening force.

(D) The designer, because the officer was injured by another passenger rather than a snake.

Question 15

An architect who specialized in the design of large buildings designed a resort hotel for a hotel chain. The architect took into account weather conditions where the hotel was to be built, and came up with two designs that would cost approximately the same amount to construct to specifications. One of them had the four large supporting pylons set so that it could withstand winds 20% higher than the region had experienced in the 85 years that the weather bureaus kept records for the area. The other design set the pylons farther apart, but they would withstand winds 50% higher than the region had experienced. The architect decided to go with the first (20% margin) design, because he felt it was more aesthetically pleasing, and also because a 20% safety margin was usually considered adequate. Officers of the hotel chain reviewed and approved the architect's plans, and the hotel was constructed according to the plans. Two years after the hotel opened, a freak storm struck, bringing with it winds of hurricane force. The hotel suffered significant damage, which would have been avoided had the supporting pylons been placed farther apart.

If the hotel chain sues the architect for the damage to the hotel, who will prevail?

(A) The architect, because the hotel chain reviewed and approved the plans.

(B) The architect, because innkeepers, rather than architect, are subject to strict liability.

(C) The architect, if he acted in the manner of a reputable member of his profession.

(D) The hotel chain, because the placement of the pylons resulted in extensive damage to the hotel.

Question 16

In a state with a comparative negligence statute, a motorcyclist was injured in a collision and suffered $100,000 worth of injuries, including $20,000 in hospital and physician's bills. The motorcyclist's medical insurance company

paid her $20,000 to cover hospital and medical expenses. Later, she filed suit against the driver of the car that struck her motorcycle. When the case came to trial, the jury agreed with the motorcyclist's contention that her injuries were worth $100,000. The jury also determined that the motorcyclist was 30% negligent and that the driver was 70% negligent.

How much should the motorcyclist recover from the driver?

(A) $100,000.

(B) $70,000.

(C) $56,000.

(D) $50,000.

Question 17

A diner was enjoying a steak in a local restaurant when he started to choke. A waiter ran over to a doctor sitting at a nearby table and asked her to help the diner. The doctor stood up and told the waiter that she did not want to become involved, and she left the restaurant. The diner survived but suffered brain damage due to lack of oxygen. The diner brought a suit against the doctor seeking damages for his injuries. At trial, the diner's medical expert testified that had he received prompt medical attention, there would have been no injuries at all. The jurisdiction in which this accident occurred has a statute relieving doctors from malpractice claims when they give emergency first aid

Can the diner recover damages from the doctor?

(A) Yes, because the jurisdiction in which this accident occurred had a statute relieving doctors from malpractice claims when they give emergency first aid.

(B) Yes, if a reasonable doctor in the doctor's position would have rendered first aid.

(C) No, because the doctor was not responsible for the diner's condition.

(D) No, because the diner did not show that the doctor knew that he was substantially certain to suffer injury unless he received assistance from a doctor.

Question 18

A worker who missed his ride home because he was working late walked across the street to a tavern to get a drink. He chatted with a patron of the tavern and discovered that he lived only a short distance from the worker. The patron offered to give the worker a ride home. Although he knew the patron was probably too drunk to drive, he reluctantly agreed. On the way home, the patron, driving in a dangerous manner, was involved in a collision with another car, whose driver was also driving negligently, and the worker was injured. The jurisdiction retains the traditional rules of contributory negligence.

If the worker asserts a claim against the patron, the worker will:

(A) Prevail, because the patron drove in a dangerous manner.

(B) Prevail, because the patron's negligence was a proximate cause of the worker's injury.

(C) Not prevail, because the other driver involved in the collision was negligent.

(D) Not prevail, because the worker knew that the patron was drunk.

TORTS ANSWERS - SET 2

Answer to Question 1

(C) The disclosure of public facts about the plaintiff cannot be the basis of an invasion of privacy lawsuit. There are four categories of invasion of privacy: (i) appropriation of plaintiff's picture or name for defendant's commercial advantage; (ii) intrusion upon plaintiff's affairs or seclusion; (iii) publication of facts that place the plaintiff in a false light; and (iv) public disclosure of private facts about plaintiff by defendant. The first category would not be applicable here because the use of a person's name or photo in a newspaper article is not considered a commercial appropriation, in contrast to the use of his name in an advertisement of a product. The second category is inapplicable because the newspaper gathered its information from public sources and took the picture of the house from a public sidewalk; it did not intrude on the plaintiff's private affairs or seclusion. The third category does not apply because the publication of these facts did not place the plaintiff in a false light. The fourth category is the most likely basis for the vice-president's invasion of privacy action, but it would not succeed because none of the facts published about him could be considered private. The sale price of a piece of property and the identity of the purchaser are matters of public record. A person's occupation would not be considered a private fact, nor would any description of the mansion in the article. Hence, the vice-president will not recover against the newspaper for invasion of privacy. (A) is incorrect. While the fact that the vice-president did not consent to publication of the story would prevent the newspaper from using the defense of consent, he has not established a prima facie case here. The fact that the mansion is now the vice-president's "private residence" does not make information about it "private facts." (B) is incorrect because the fact that a reasonable person would be upset by publication of the story is just one element of the prima facie case for the public disclosure action. The disclosure must also have been of private facts about the plaintiff; this element is not satisfied here. (D) is incorrect because the fact that the story is true is not a defense to invasion of privacy actions. Public disclosure of private facts may subject the defendant to liability even if the facts are true.

Answer to Question 2

(D) The homeowner is not liable for the tortious actions of the technician because the technician is an independent contractor. When there is an employer-employee relationship between a principal and his agent, the employer is vicariously liable for torts committed by the employee within the scope of the employment relationship. This is the doctrine of respondeat superior. On the other hand, the general rule is that a principal is not liable for tortious acts of an agent who is an independent contractor. An agent is likely to be an independent contractor if she: (i) is engaged in a distinct business of her own; (ii) controls the manner and method by which she performs her tasks; (iii) is hired to do a particular job; (iv) supplies her own tools and materials; (v) is paid a given amount for the job; and (vi) is hired to do a short-term, specific job. Despite the general rule, a principal can be held liable for the tortious acts of an independent contractor if: (i) the independent contractor is engaged in inherently dangerous activities; or (ii) the principal has a duty that is nondelegable on public policy grounds (*e.g.,* a land occupier's duty to keep his land safe for business invitees). Also, a principal can be held liable for his own negligence in selecting an incompetent independent contractor. Here, the homeowner hired a computer repair technician to perform one particular job (fixing the homeowner's computer). From the facts, it appears that the technician provided her own materials and controlled the manner and method in which she did her job. Therefore, the technician is, with respect to the homeowner, an independent contractor rather than an employee. The technician was not engaged in an inherently dangerous activity,

nor is there any nondelegable duty of the homeowner involved. In addition, it does not appear that the homeowner was negligent in hiring the technician. Thus, the general rule applies, and the homeowner is not liable for the tortious conduct of the technician. (A) is wrong because a principal is vicariously liable only if the agent is an employee or the exceptions for independent contractors apply. As explained above, neither of these factors is present here. (B) and (C) are wrong because the frolic-detour distinction is inapplicable to these facts. For an employer to be vicariously liable, the tort must have occurred within the scope of the employee's employment. To determine whether the tortious acts occurred within the scope of employment, a distinction is made based on whether the tortious conduct was committed while the employee was on a frolic or on a detour. Small deviations from an employer's directions (a detour) fall within the scope of employment, while major deviations (a frolic) fall outside the scope. Because the technician was not an employee of the homeowner, there is no "scope of employment" issue to be analyzed.

Answer to Question 3

(C) The car owner can recover if the apprentice was acting within the scope of the partnership business when he drove negligently. Vicarious liability for the conduct of another can arise in partnership and joint venture situations. Each member of the partnership is vicariously liable for the tortious conduct of another partner committed in the scope of the partnership's affairs. As with respondeat superior situations, if the tortfeasor has gone off on a frolic of his own, he is no longer acting within the scope of the partnership and the other partners will not be liable. On the other hand, a minor deviation from the partnership activity will not take it outside of the scope of the partnership's affairs. Here, the painter and the apprentice are partners in their painting business. If, as choice (C) indicates, the apprentice's detour to the library did not take his activity outside the scope of the partnership's affairs, the painter is vicariously liable simply because of his status as a partner. (A) is incorrect because the apprentice's status as an independent contractor is irrelevant to this question. While the apprentice is, with respect to the person who hired him, an independent contractor, the apprentice is a partner rather than an independent contractor as to the painter. Because this question concerns the car owner and the painter, the apprentice's status as to the person who hired him is irrelevant and would not save the painter from liability. (B) is a true statement (a bailor is not vicariously liable for the torts of his bailee). However, (B) is incorrect because it does not take into account the status of the apprentice and the painter as partners. It is because of their partnership status rather than their bailor-bailee status that the car owner might be able to recover. (D) is incorrect because the painter's status as the apprentice's partner is not enough to make him liable for the apprentice's torts. As discussed above, the apprentice must have been acting within the scope of the partnership business when he committed the tort for the painter to be liable.

Answer to Question 4

(D) The seller is not strictly liable to the purchaser because the seller is not a commercial supplier of tires. The purchaser's lawsuit is alleging that the seller is strictly liable for selling him a car with a defective tire. To establish a prima facie case for a defective product based on strict liability, the plaintiff must show: (i) a strict duty owed by a commercial supplier; (ii) breach of that duty by the sale of a product in a defective condition unreasonably dangerous to users; (iii) actual and proximate cause; and (iv) damages. While the purchaser might be able to establish the other elements, he cannot establish that the seller is a commercial supplier of either tires or automobiles. A casual seller who is not in the business of manufacturing, distributing, or selling the product does not owe a strict duty to subsequent purchasers; thus, the purchaser will not recover against the seller. (A) is incorrect because the fact that the tire was defective would establish

breach of duty only if the seller were a commercial supplier. Because she is only a casual seller, she has not breached a strict duty to the purchaser. (B) is incorrect because the seller's failure to discover the defect, even if negligent, has no relevance to whether she has a duty in strict liability. (C) is incorrect because misuse that is reasonably foreseeable, such as exceeding the posted speed limits, is not a defense to a strict products liability action. If the seller were in breach of a strict duty owed to the purchaser, the purchaser's conduct would not preclude his recovery.

Answer to Question 5

(A) Because the woman had the requisite intent for assault (creation of reasonable apprehension), that intent is sufficient for battery if contact occurs as the result of the woman's actions. This is one ramification of the doctrine of transferred intent. The transferred intent doctrine applies where the defendant intends to commit a tort against one person but instead commits a different tort against that person. The intent to commit the one tort is transferred to the other tort. Here, the woman's intent to commit an assault would satisfy the intent requirement for battery. (B) is incorrect because mere offensive contact will not suffice for battery if the requisite intent is absent. (C) is incorrect because of the doctrine of transferred intent and the fact that the woman set in motion the process that resulted in the man's being struck. (D) is incorrect because the woman had the requisite intent to commit an intentional tort, making the negligence of a third party irrelevant.

Answer to Question 6

(C) The actress can recover for the unauthorized use of her picture for the proprietor's commercial advantage. There are four branches of the tort of invasion of privacy: (i) appropriation of the plaintiff's picture or name for the defendant's commercial advantage; (ii) intrusion upon plaintiff's affairs or seclusion; (iii) publication of facts that place plaintiff in a false light; and (iv) public disclosure of private facts about plaintiff. Of these four branches, the only one applicable to these facts is the first. To establish a prima facie case for this type of invasion of privacy, a plaintiff need only prove the unauthorized use by the defendant of the plaintiff's picture or name for the defendant's commercial advantage. Generally, liability is limited to the use of the plaintiff's picture or name in connection with the promotion or advertisement of a product or service. The proprietor has used the actress's picture to promote the sale of hot dogs. The actress did not in any way consent to this use by the proprietor of her picture. Therefore, the elements that the actress needs to prove are present, and she will prevail. (A) is wrong because the actress's status as a public figure is irrelevant to this type of privacy tort. Public figure status could affect other types of invasion of privacy (*e.g.*, publication of facts placing the plaintiff in a false light and public disclosure of private facts about the plaintiff) if the published matter was of legitimate public interest. If so, the plaintiff would have to establish that the defendant acted with malice (*i.e.*, with knowledge of falsity or reckless disregard for the truth). If the actress's action were based on one of these other types of privacy tort, her status as a public figure might be relevant. However, public figure status does not alter the elements needed to establish a case for unauthorized use of the actress's picture, nor does it impose upon her the necessity of proving malice. (B) is wrong because mistake (even if reasonable) as to whether consent was given is not a valid defense. Thus, the actress will prevail regardless of whether the proprietor was reasonably justified in believing that the poster was authorized. (D) is wrong because there is no requirement that the defendant have actually gained a profit from using the picture. The proprietor is liable for this tort simply because he used the actress's picture without her permission to promote and advertise the hot dogs.

Answer to Question 7

(A) The waste management company breached its duty of ordinary care to the child because it could have had the piles of dirt removed at minimal cost. Most courts impose upon a landowner the duty to exercise ordinary care to avoid reasonably foreseeable risk of harm to children caused by artificial conditions on his property. Under the general rule, to assess this special duty upon the owner or occupier of land in regard to children on his property, the plaintiff must show the following: (i) there is a dangerous condition present on the land of which the owner is or should be aware; (ii) the owner knows or should know that young persons frequent the vicinity of this dangerous condition; (iii) the condition is likely to cause injury (*i.e.,* is dangerous) because of the child's inability to appreciate the risk; and (iv) the expense of remedying the situation is slight compared with the magnitude of the risk. If all of these elements are present, the child has a cause of action under the "attractive nuisance" doctrine. Under these facts, the mounds of dirt sloping down toward the highway constituted a dangerous condition and the superintendent was aware that children were sledding down the mounds of dirt next to a busy highway. Because the company could have had the dirt removed at minimal cost, the expense of remedying the situation would have been slight compared to the magnitude of the risk, making the company liable under the attractive nuisance doctrine. (B) is incorrect because the mounds of dirt did not constitute a public nuisance, which is unrelated to the attractive nuisance doctrine. A public nuisance is an act that unreasonably interferes with the health, safety, or property rights of the community. The dirt did not unreasonably interfere with the safety rights of the community. The dirt was piled on a site next to a highway and did not create an obstruction for pedestrians or drivers. (C) is incorrect because even though the child was a trespasser, infant trespassers come within an exception to the standard duty of care owed by an owner or occupier of land to a trespasser for artificial conditions. Thus, the child's status as a trespasser does not prevent his recovery. (D) is incorrect because even though the child read the sign, the sign did not alert him to the danger that the piles of dirt created, and there is no other evidence that he was aware of and appreciated the danger of sliding onto the highway. For assumption of the risk to be a defense, the plaintiff must be ***aware of the risk*** and then voluntarily assume that risk.

Answer to Question 8

(B) The boy's best argument is that his mother's refusal to take him to a physician, if deemed to be negligent, is not imputed to him. A plaintiff has a duty to take reasonable steps to mitigate damages. Thus, in personal injury cases, there is a duty to seek appropriate treatment to effect healing and to prevent aggravation. Failure to do so will preclude recovery for any particular item of injury that occurs or is aggravated ***due to the failure to mitigate*** (this is the avoidable consequences rule). Thus, the boy's not consulting a doctor could limit his recovery to the damages for the original injury only. However, the boy is a child and his mother decided not to seek medical help for the boy. If this was negligence on her part, is it imputed to the boy? In actions against a third party, a parent's negligence is not imputed to the child. Thus, the negligence of the boy's mother will not be imputed to the boy, and so the boy should receive a full recovery for ***all*** of his injuries. On the other hand, if the boy uses the argument in (A), then he will probably not recover for the aggravated injuries. (A) presents an accurate statement of law, relative to the effect of the avoidable consequences rule. If the boy avails himself of the avoidable consequences rule, then he will succeed in salvaging merely his right to recover for the original injury. Thus, (A) does not give the boy a chance to recover for ***all*** of his injuries, as does (B). (C) is incorrect because it directly contradicts the rule that a plaintiff must take all reasonable measures to mitigate damages after the original injury is inflicted. (D) is incorrect because it misstates the concept of "taking your victim as you find him." This concept refers to the ***physical***

or mental condition of the victim at the time of the injury (*e.g.*, the "eggshell skull plaintiff"); it does not cover the victim's relationship to others and their attitudes or actions. Thus, the attitude of a victim's mother toward physicians is not included in "taking your victim as you find him."

Answer to Question 9

(A) The girl may have a personal injury claim against the pedestrian for negligence because throwing the ball into the road would expose the children to an unreasonable risk of harm. A prima facie case for negligence consists of: (i) a duty on the part of the defendant to conform to a specific standard of conduct for the protection of the plaintiff against an unreasonable risk of injury; (ii) a breach of that duty by the defendant; (iii) the breach of duty was the actual and proximate cause of the plaintiff's injury; and (iv) damage to the plaintiff's person or property. A person is under a legal duty to act as an ordinary, prudent, reasonable person. It is presumed that an ordinary, prudent, reasonable person will take precautions against creating unreasonable risks of injury to other persons. Thus, if the defendant's conduct creates an unreasonable risk of injury to persons in the position of the plaintiff, then the general duty of care extends from the defendant to the plaintiff. Here, throwing the ball into the road created an unreasonable risk of injury to the girl and her friend. The pedestrian knew, or in the exercise of reasonable care should have known, that one or both of the children would run after the ball, exposing them to the danger of being hit by a car. Thus, the general duty of ordinary, reasonable care extended from the pedestrian to the girl, and he breached this duty by throwing the ball into the road. This breach actually caused the girl's injury because the girl would not have been in the road but for the pedestrian throwing the ball there. The breach also proximately caused the girl's injury, despite the fact that the driver was possibly negligent in not watching the road. The driver's conduct was an independent intervening force; however, it was a foreseeable intervening force that brought about a foreseeable result, because the pedestrian's act of throwing the ball into the road created a foreseeable risk that the girl would be hit by a car when chasing after the ball. Thus, the driver's conduct will not cut off the liability of the pedestrian. The final element of a prima facie case for negligence is made out by the damage to the girl's person. (B) is incorrect because the pedestrian did not intend to bring about the harmful contact suffered by the girl. The intent required for intentional tort liability is present when either: (i) the actor's goal in acting is to bring about the consequences of his conduct; or (ii) the actor knows with substantial certainty that such consequences will result. Here, it does not appear that the pedestrian's goal in throwing the ball into the street was to cause the girl to be hit by a car, nor did the pedestrian know with substantial certainty that such harm would befall the girl. Therefore, the pedestrian did not possess the intent required for intentional tort liability. (C) and (D) are both incorrect for the reason that one from whom contribution is sought or against whom indemnity is sought must be originally liable to the plaintiff. Contribution allows a defendant who is required to pay more than his share of damages to have a claim against other jointly liable parties for the excess. Indemnity involves shifting the entire loss between or among tortfeasors. If, as (C) and (D) state, the girl has no claim against the pedestrian, then the pedestrian cannot be considered a joint tortfeasor with the driver. Consequently, the driver would have no right of contribution against the pedestrian, nor would he be entitled to indemnification from the pedestrian.

Answer to Question 10

(B) If the retailer prevails, it will be because the motorist knew that the bulge was dangerous. The retailer will be able to assert as a defense to strict liability that the motorist voluntarily assumed the risk. Assumption of risk is a valid defense to a products liability action based on strict liability. To have assumed the risk, either expressly or impliedly, the plaintiff must have known of the

risk and voluntarily assumed it. If the motorist knew that the bulge was dangerous, her conduct was unreasonable when she continued to inflate the tire. By voluntarily proceeding with inflating the tire in the face of a known risk, she voluntarily assumed the risk. (A) is incorrect because it implies a necessity to show fault in terms of improper installation. To establish a prima facie case in products liability based on strict liability in tort, the following elements must be proved: (i) strict duty owed by a commercial supplier; (ii) breach of that duty; (iii) actual and proximate cause; and (iv) damages. To establish breach of duty for a strict liability action, the plaintiff need not prove that the defendant was at fault in selling or producing a defective product—only that the product in fact is so defective as to be "unreasonably dangerous." Thus, the element of negligence need not be proved in a strict liability case, and the absence of negligence will not establish that the defendant is not liable. (D) is incorrect for the same reason as (A). (D) implies a necessity to show fault in terms of failure to discover the defect. A retailer, however, may be liable in strict liability even if it has no opportunity to inspect the manufacturer's product before selling it. Again, negligence concepts are irrelevant. (C) is incorrect. Even if it is a true statement, it is not a defense. If the motorist acted contrary to the reasonable person standard, at most she can be deemed contributorily negligent. Ordinary contributory negligence, however, is not a defense to strict liability in a jurisdiction following traditional contributory negligence rules.

Answer to Question 11

(C) The manufacturer's motion should be denied because the jury could conclude that the vehicle was defectively designed if it agrees with the motorist's contention that a reasonable alternative design could have incorporated the stability control technology. To establish a prima facie case in products liability based on strict liability in tort, the following elements must be proved: (i) strict duty owed by a commercial supplier; (ii) breach of that duty; (iii) actual and proximate cause; and (iv) damages. To establish breach of duty for a strict liability action, the plaintiff need prove only that the product in fact is so defective as to be "unreasonably dangerous." For design defects, the plaintiff usually must show a reasonable alternative design, *i.e.*, that a less dangerous modification or alternative was economically feasible. Here, the motorist has made a prima facie case sufficient to withstand a motion for a directed verdict. It is a question for the jury whether a design incorporating the stability control technology was a reasonable alternative and, if so, whether the existing design of the vehicle was defective and unreasonably dangerous. (A) is incorrect because the increased cost of a safety measure does not mean that it is not economically feasible. The trier of fact weighs various factors to make that determination; hence, a directed verdict on that issue is not appropriate under these facts. (B) is incorrect. While the manufacturer may be able to establish that the motorist was contributorily negligent per se based on her violation of the statutory speed limit, ordinary contributory negligence is not a defense to strict liability in a jurisdiction following traditional contributory negligence rules. (D) is incorrect because whether the manufacturer should have known that the vehicle was unsafe is an issue of breach of duty in a negligence action; in a strict liability case, negligence need not be proved and the jury will not be instructed to make that determination.

Answer to Question 12

(D) The homeowner will most likely prevail because he did not intend to frighten the boy onto the neighbor's property. For the neighbor to succeed in his trespass suit, he must show that the homeowner intended to bring about a physical invasion of the neighbor's property. The homeowner did not chase the boy onto the neighbor's yard, nor did the homeowner intend or know with substantial certainty that the boy would enter onto the neighbor's yard as a result of the homeowner's actions. (A) is incorrect because a landowner is not automatically privileged to

chase or otherwise cause third persons to enter onto another's land to prevent the commission of a tort against his property. While the landowner may have a qualified defense if the trespass was reasonable and apparently necessary to protect his property from destruction or serious injury, the interference with the neighbor's property here did not result from necessity. (B) is incorrect because it is not necessary to establish a prima facie case for trespass to land that the defendant personally came onto the land; *e.g.*, trespass exists where the defendant floods the plaintiff's land, throws rocks onto it, or chases third persons upon it. (C) is incorrect because even though the boy made the decision to go over the fence, the homeowner could still be liable for trespass if the homeowner acted with the intention of causing the boy to enter on the neighbor's land.

Answer to Question 13

(D) The neighbor will not recover from the homeowner because even if the homeowner acted negligently in setting the ladder atop a patch of ice, this negligence did not cause the injury to the neighbor. A person generally is under no duty to assist another. Therefore, the homeowner was under no duty to assist the neighbor. However, having gratuitously undertaken to do so, the homeowner came under a duty to act as an ordinary, reasonable person while rendering such assistance. He breached this duty by setting the ladder atop the patch of ice, thus creating an unreasonable risk that the ladder would slip while the neighbor was climbing down, causing him injury. However, the homeowner is not liable for the neighbor's injuries unless the homeowner's breach of duty caused those injuries. Before a defendant's conduct can be considered a proximate cause of the plaintiff's injury, it must first be a cause in fact (actual cause) of the injury. An act is the cause in fact of an injury when the injury would not have occurred but for the act. Here, the neighbor's fall and injuries would not have occurred but for the rotten rung. There is no indication that the homeowner's negligence in placing the ladder on the ice contributed in any manner to the injuries. If the homeowner had carefully placed the ladder on a solid, ice-free surface, the neighbor would have incurred the same injury by stepping on the rotten rung. Therefore, the homeowner's negligence was not a cause in fact of the neighbor's injuries. Because the element of causation is missing, the homeowner will not be liable for the injuries to the neighbor. (A) is wrong because the homeowner's negligent placement of the ladder was not the cause of the neighbor's injury. Rather, the neighbor fell as a result of stepping on the rotten rung. Thus, it cannot be said that the homeowner's negligent conduct caused the injury to the neighbor. (B) is wrong because the homeowner's assumption of the duty to aid the neighbor does not render him absolutely liable for all injuries incurred. As explained, the homeowner did assume the duty to act reasonably in aiding the neighbor, and he did breach his duty by placing the ladder on ice. Nevertheless, this breach of duty did not cause the injuries to the neighbor. Thus, if the homeowner's negligence did not cause the injury to the neighbor, he cannot be held liable, even if he was negligent. Regarding (C), while it is true that it was foreseeable that the neighbor would be injured as a result of the homeowner's negligent conduct (*i.e.,* that the ladder would slip on the ice, causing the neighbor to fall and be injured), it is also true that the neighbor was not injured as a result of the homeowner's negligence. The homeowner cannot be held liable for something that was not in any way caused by his negligent conduct. Therefore, (C) is incorrect.

Answer to Question 14

(C) The designer will prevail because the assassin's actions were an unforeseeable intervening force. To establish a prima facie case for negligence, the following elements must be proved: (i) the existence of a duty on the part of the defendant to conform to a specific standard of conduct for the protection of the plaintiff against an unreasonable risk of injury; (ii) breach of that duty by the defendant; (iii) the breach of the duty by the defendant was the actual and proximate cause of

the plaintiff's injury; and (iv) damage to the plaintiff's person or property. The general rule of proximate cause is that the defendant is liable for all harmful results that are the normal incidents of, and within the increased risk caused by, his acts. An indirect cause case is one where the facts indicate that a force came into motion after the time of defendant's negligent act and combined with the negligent act to cause injury to the plaintiff. Whether an intervening force will cut off the defendant's liability for the plaintiff's injury and be deemed superseding is determined by foreseeability. Here, the designer, as a professional designing a component of a plane, owed a duty of care to passengers such as the officer. He breached that duty of care by using a design for the conduit system that had been rejected in the industry because of the danger of pressure loss. His breach was the actual cause of the officer's harm because, but for his use of that design, the snakes would not have gotten into the passenger compartment of the plane. However, the conduct of the assassin in causing snakes to be placed on the plane is an unforeseeable intervening force. While criminal acts of third persons may be foreseeable if the defendant's negligence increased the likelihood of the crime being committed, there is nothing to suggest that the officer's negligence had any influence on the assassin's conduct. Hence, that conduct cuts off the defendant's liability to the officer for the negligent design of the conduit system. (A) is incorrect. To establish strict tort liability, the plaintiff must prove that the defendant is a commercial supplier of a product. The designer, however, provided a service of designing a conduit system in a plane; because the facts do not suggest that he is a commercial supplier of a product, he cannot be held strictly liable. (B) is incorrect. Even assuming that the designer would be held to the high degree of care that common carriers owe their passengers, the officer must still establish the other elements of the tort. As discussed above, he would not be able to establish proximate cause under these facts. (D) is incorrect because the response by the other passenger is a foreseeable "reaction" force that does not cut off the causal connection between the act and the harm. If the designer were deemed to be a proximate cause of the snakes getting into the passenger compartment, the fact that the officer's injury was caused by the reaction of another passenger rather than a snakebite would not matter.

Answer to Question 15

(C) If the architect acted in the manner of a reputable member of his profession, he will not have breached the duty of care owing to the hotel chain. As the first two elements of its prima facie negligence action, the hotel chain must establish the existence of a duty on the part of the architect to conform to a specific standard of conduct for the protection of the hotel chain against an unreasonable risk of injury, and a breach of that duty. A professional, such as an architect, is required to possess and exercise the knowledge and skill of a member of the profession in good standing in similar localities. If the architect exercised such knowledge and skill, he will have satisfied the applicable standard of care. (A) is incorrect. The hotel chain did not assume responsibility for the damage; it merely reviewed and accepted the plans, relying on the architect's professional opinion. (B) is incorrect because there is no general standard subjecting innkeepers to strict liability and, in any event, this has no bearing on the architect's liability. The hotel chain will prevail if it can establish a prima facie case for negligence. (D) is incorrect. While it may be true that the placement of the pylons resulted in damage to the hotel, there is no indication that the architect breached a duty of care to the hotel chain by choosing this particular design of placement.

Answer to Question 16

(B) The motorcyclist should recover $70,000 from the driver. Under a comparative negligence system, a contributorily negligent plaintiff is allowed to recover a percentage of her damages.

The plaintiff's damages are reduced according to her proportionate share of the fault. Although the various jurisdictions differ as to the levels of a plaintiff's negligence that are allowable before her right to recover is cut off, all comparative negligence states would allow recovery when a plaintiff's negligence is only 30% and the defendant's negligence is 70%. Thus, the motorcyclist can recover 70% of her total of $100,000 in damages, leaving her with a recovery of $70,000. As a general rule, damages are not reduced or mitigated by reason of benefits received by the plaintiff from other sources, such as health insurance. Therefore, the $20,000 paid by the motorcyclist's insurance company will not reduce the $70,000 in damages to which she is entitled. (A) is incorrect because it fails to reflect the reduction in damages required under comparative negligence. Because the motorcyclist was 30% negligent, she cannot recover the entire $100,000. (C) is incorrect because it is derived from an initial reduction of damages by the amount of the insurance payments ($100,000 minus $20,000, leaving $80,000). This $80,000 figure is then reduced by the 30% negligence of the motorcyclist, leaving an amount of $56,000. However, as noted above, the insurance payments are not allowed to reduce damages. Thus, the 30% reduction is made from the figure of $100,000, not from $80,000. Similarly, (D) is incorrect because it is derived from a reduction of the $70,000 proportionate recovery by the $20,000 insurance payment.

Answer to Question 17

(C) Because the doctor did nothing to place the diner in a dangerous position, the doctor had ***no legal responsibility*** to render first aid to the diner. Thus, she cannot be held liable for failing to help him. Therefore, (C) is correct, and (B) is wrong. Similarly, if the doctor had no duty to render aid, it is immaterial that she would suffer no liability if she did render assistance. Likewise, the fact that she was immune from liability does not mean that a ***duty*** to render emergency aid has arisen. Thus, (A) is not the best answer. (D) is a misstatement of the law, because even if the doctor had been shown to have been aware that the diner would suffer brain damage unless he received prompt medical care, she still would have no legal duty to render assistance.

Answer to Question 18

(D) The worker will not prevail because he knew that the patron was drunk. The worker assumed the risk of injury when he allowed the patron to drive him home. Implied assumption of risk requires that the worker knew of the risk and voluntarily chose to encounter it, which is indicated here. Assumption of the risk is a complete defense to a claim based on negligence in a jurisdiction following traditional contributory negligence rules. (A) and (B) are therefore incorrect because the patron can claim assumption of risk as a defense. (C) is incorrect because negligence of other drivers is foreseeable and therefore is not a superseding cause that would cut off the patron's liability for his negligence. The negligence of the other driver cannot be used as an excuse for the patron's negligence; both drivers were actual and proximate causes of the worker's injury.

Set 3 Answer Sheet

1. Ⓐ Ⓑ Ⓒ Ⓓ
2. Ⓐ Ⓑ Ⓒ Ⓓ
3. Ⓐ Ⓑ Ⓒ Ⓓ
4. Ⓐ Ⓑ Ⓒ Ⓓ
5. Ⓐ Ⓑ Ⓒ Ⓓ
6. Ⓐ Ⓑ Ⓒ Ⓓ
7. Ⓐ Ⓑ Ⓒ Ⓓ
8. Ⓐ Ⓑ Ⓒ Ⓓ
9. Ⓐ Ⓑ Ⓒ Ⓓ
10. Ⓐ Ⓑ Ⓒ Ⓓ
11. Ⓐ Ⓑ Ⓒ Ⓓ
12. Ⓐ Ⓑ Ⓒ Ⓓ
13. Ⓐ Ⓑ Ⓒ Ⓓ
14. Ⓐ Ⓑ Ⓒ Ⓓ
15. Ⓐ Ⓑ Ⓒ Ⓓ
16. Ⓐ Ⓑ Ⓒ Ⓓ
17. Ⓐ Ⓑ Ⓒ Ⓓ
18. Ⓐ Ⓑ Ⓒ Ⓓ

TORTS QUESTIONS - SET 3

Question 1

A motorist was driving to a luncheon in a car that he knew did not have operating headlights On the way there he was rear-ended by another driver who had been driving 20 m.p.h. over the speed limit posted on that stretch of road. He suffered personal injuries and his car was extensively damaged. The jurisdiction follows traditional contributory negligence rules and makes it a misdemeanor to drive a vehicle that does not have operating headlights.

If the motorist brings an action against the other driver and establishes the above facts, will he prevail?

(A) Yes, because the misdemeanor statute is intended to protect against cars being driven without headlights.

(B) Yes, because the other driver's violation of the speeding statute constituted negligence per se.

(C) No, because the motorist violated the misdemeanor statute.

(D) No, because the motorist has not established that driving 20 m.p.h. over the speed limit created an unreasonable risk of injury to others.

Question 2

A leading manufacturer of camping products marketed a thermal blanket that incorporated new heat-generating technology. On the blanket's packaging was a label stating that it was recommended by a leading camping association. A camper purchased one of the blankets and took it with her on a fall camping trip. The first night that she used the blanket, it malfunctioned and caused her severe burns.

If the camper maintains an action against the camping association, on which theory is she most likely to recover, if at all?

(A) Express warranty.

(B) Implied warranty of merchantability.

(C) Strict tort liability.

(D) Negligence.

Question 3

After a power outage, the stoplights at a busy intersection were blinking red for traffic going in every direction. By statute, motorists must come to a full stop at a blinking red traffic signal before proceeding through the intersection. Cars driven by the plaintiff and by the defendant arrived at the intersection at the same time. Due to inattention, neither one stopped for the signal and the cars collided in the intersection.

The plaintiff sued the defendant for his injuries in a jurisdiction that has adopted pure comparative negligence. The trier of fact determined that the plaintiff was more at fault than the defendant.

The plaintiff will:

(A) Not recover damages, because the plaintiff did not stop at the blinking red light.

(B) Not recover damages, because the plaintiff's fault was greater than the defendant's.

(C) Recover damages, if the defendant had the last clear chance to avoid the accident.

(D) Recover damages, even though the plaintiff's fault was greater than the defendant's.

Question 4

A bottler markets water in lightweight plastic bottles that are sold by grocery stores, sporting goods stores, and other retail outlets. A hiker purchased several bottles of the water from a retailer and took them with him on a hike. While the hiker left his backpack unattended, a thief took one of the unopened containers without permission and drank some of the water. He immediately became violently ill. Tests were run on the water and showed that it contained impurities.

If the thief maintains a negligence action against the bottler, which of the following arguments would be the most helpful to the bottler in avoiding liability?

(A) The retailer had ample opportunity to test and inspect samples of the bottled water for purity and failed to do so.

(B) The bottler bottled its water in compliance with numerous statutes that regulate the process of bottling water for human consumption.

(C) The thief has failed to introduce any evidence at trial as to how the impurities got into the water he drank, and therefore has not met his burden of proof.

(D) No reasonable person would have foreseen that the water would have been stolen and consumed by a thief.

Question 5

A ballplayer became ill soon after consuming sunflower seeds marketed by a farm products company. The package of seeds was inspected and foreign matter was discovered on the seeds.

If the ballplayer brings an action against the farm products company on the basis of strict tort liability, which of the following would be most helpful for the company to avoid liability?

(A) The foreign matter on the seeds was a rare mold that could not be detected by tests commonly used for establishing that sunflower seeds are safe for human consumption.

(B) The seeds were sold in their natural state, and had not been manufactured or processed by the farm products company in any way.

(C) In answer to an interrogatory, the ballplayer has acknowledged that he has no evidence that his illness was caused by the foreign matter on the seeds.

(D) Although marketed under the label of the farm products company, the seeds had been collected and packaged for distribution by another company and any foreign matter on the seeds was the other company's fault.

Question 6

A company operated a small amusement park on property it owned near a residential neighborhood. On a day when the park was closed, a 10-year-old girl snuck into the park with some friends by climbing over a chain link fence. While climbing on one of the carnival rides, the girl slipped and cut her leg on an exposed gear assembly, sustaining serious injuries.

Through her guardian ad litem, the girl brought suit against the company to recover damages for her injuries. At trial, she presented evidence of the accident and her injuries. In defense, the company established that the girl read and understood the "No Trespassing" signs that were attached to the fence. The company also established that it had not had any previous reports of children sneaking into the park when it was closed. Before submission of the case to the jury, the company moved for summary judgment.

Is the court likely to grant the company's motion?

(A) Yes, because the girl was a trespasser who the company had no reason to anticipate would be on the property.

(B) Yes, because the girl knew she was trespassing and was old enough to recognize the danger.

(C) No, because the jury could find that the company should have foreseen that children would sneak into the park.

(D) No, because the appeal of the carnival rides attracted the girl into the park.

Question 7

A well-known Oscar-winning producer who owned the nation's leading special effects studio employed a creative designer who was recognized throughout the industry as one of the top talents in the special effects field. A competitor of the producer who wanted to hire the designer told him that that the producer was in negotiations to sell his studio to a major Hollywood film company. In fact this statement was not true, and the competitor made the statement without any knowledge of its truth or falsity. The designer, whose employment contract with the producer was terminable at will by either party, agreed to be hired by the competitor. The producer was very upset when he learned of the competitor's action because he knew that the designer would be almost impossible to replace, and brought suit against the competitor.

If the producer establishes the above facts and that he suffered damages, he is likely to:

(A) Recover for intentional interference with business relations, because the competitor used improper means to hire the designer away from the producer.

(B) Recover for defamation, because the producer can show actual damages from the competitor's statement.

(C) Not recover for intentional interference with business relations, because the designer was an at-will employee of the producer.

(D) Not recover for defamation, because the producer did not show that the competitor knew that his statement about the producer's plans was false.

Question 8

A mining company closed down operations at an isolated mine it owned and informed the electric company that electricity in the power poles that led to the mine should be cut off. However, the electric company, following its standard policy, left the power running in the line to deter thieves from stealing valuable transformers and cables. The mining company was unaware that the power was left on.

A hitchhiker who was passing by the entrance to the mine saw that it was closed, so he went onto the property and climbed up a power pole to steal a transformer. He received an electric shock and fell from the pole, suffering serious injuries.

If the hitchhiker sues the mining company, which of the following is the mining company's strongest defense?

(A) The hitchhiker was a trespasser.

(B) The hitchhiker was a thief.

(C) The mining company asked the utility company to turn off the power.

(D) The mining company was unaware that the utility company had not turned off the power.

Question 9

When a hurricane suddenly increased its intensity and changed its path to strike the oceanfront town that a tourist was visiting, she took refuge at the hotel where she was a guest. As the winds increased and the storm surge began to cause the water to rise, the hotel manager advised everyone still in the building to move off of the ground floor. However, the tourist panicked at being trapped by the water and decided to flee the hotel and seek higher ground. She got almost to the main gate of the hotel when she was swept away by the floodwaters and drowned.

In an action by the tourist's estate against the hotel, the likely result is that:

(A) The tourist's estate will prevail because the tourist was a guest at the hotel.

(B) The tourist's estate will prevail because the hotel manager did not prevent the tourist from leaving.

(C) The hotel will prevail because it did not breach any duty it owed to the tourist.

(D) The hotel will prevail because the hurricane was an unforeseeable act of God.

Question 10

A homeowner bought "20-pound test" fishing line for hanging potted plants on his porch. "20-pound test" in the fishing industry means that fishing line will not break under an initial stress of up to 20 pounds when a hooked fish tugs against the line, but not that it will support a constant 20-pound weight. Most sportfishers are aware of this technical meaning, but most laypersons are not, and the manufacturer put no warnings or explanations on the package in which the line was sold. The homeowner hung a 15-pound basket from his front porch, directly above an old-fashioned porch swing. A friend visiting the homeowner was sitting on the swing when the line holding the basket broke, causing the plant to fall and strike the guest on the head.

Will the guest prevail against the homeowner in a suit to recover damages for her injuries?

(A) Yes, because she was a social guest.

(B) Yes, because the homeowner was negligent in hanging the plant.

(C) No, because the homeowner could not be expected to know the technical meaning of "20-pound test."

(D) No, because she was not a foreseeable plaintiff.

Question 11

A collection agent for a wholesale distributor of greeting cards was assigned to collect money owed on a consignment account by the elderly sole proprietor of a card shop. The agent strode into the shop while the proprietor was waiting on some customers and demanded to know why she had not paid her account. She was distressed by his intrusion, and assured him that her account was fully paid and asked him to wait until her customers had left to continue the discussion. The agent became louder and pounded his fist on the counter, threatening to repossess her entire inventory and prosecute her for fraud. By the time he left, the proprietor was in tears.

If the proprietor prevails against the collection agent in a suit to recover damages for her emotional distress, it will be because:

(A) The agent's conduct was extreme and outrageous.

(B) The proprietor felt subjected to a threat of physical injury.

(C) The agent intended for the proprietor to suffer severe distress.

(D) The proprietor did not owe the money that the agent demanded.

Question 12

An only daughter whose father died after a long illness arranged with a mortuary to bury him next to his wife's grave. The daughter selected the most ornate casket available because she wanted it to remain closed during the wake, and she could not bring herself to view the body before the funeral. At the cemetery, however, she decided to view the body just before it was buried. She was horrified to discover that the body in the casket was dressed in a clown costume and a bright orange wig. In fact, it was not her father but a popular circus entertainer who had died the same day as her father and had requested to be buried in his costume. Although the mortuary was able to retrieve her father's body and bury it, the daughter was greatly distressed by the episode and suffered nightmares as a result. However, she did not seek medical or psychiatric care because of it. The mortuary apologized for its error in switching the bodies, but insisted that the daughter pay all of the agreed-to charges for the funeral.

If the daughter brings action against the mortuary to recover for her emotional distress, can she recover damages?

(A) No, because the daughter did not have to obtain medical or psychiatric care.

(B) No, because the daughter suffered no physical injury.

(C) Yes, because of the known sensitivity of people concerning the death of a family member.

(D) Yes, because the mortuary is requiring the daughter to pay the bill for the funeral expenses.

Question 13

Two law students ranked high in their class were competing for one opening at a prestigious law firm. During the interview with the hiring partner, one student was asked what he thought of the other's work as an editor of the law review. The student responded that there was a rumor around the school that the editor got outside help on her law review comment. Based in large part on his statement, that student was chosen over the law review editor, who later accepted a less lucrative position with another firm.

If the law review editor brings a slander action against the other student and establishes the above facts, will she prevail?

(A) Yes, because the student's statement to the hiring partner was defamatory.

(B) Yes, because the law review editor suffered special damages.

(C) No, because the hiring partner asked the student for his opinion.

(D) No, because the law review editor did not establish that the student made the statement with at least negligence.

Question 14

An amateur inventor purchased a laser made for home hobbyist use and set it up on his roof to try to bounce a signal off of a satellite. He attempted to boost its power output with an over-the-counter voltage booster. However, because of a defective voltage regulation device in the laser that was present when it left the factory, the voltage booster caused the laser to overheat and explode. A fragment of molten quartz struck a neighbor, injuring him.

The neighbor brought an action against the laser manufacturer for the physical injuries he suffered as a result of the explosion. At trial, the neighbor presents evidence of the above facts. The manufacturer establishes that its laser was never intended to be used at the power levels necessary to reach a satellite, and that it exercised due care in the manufacture of the laser. The manufacturer moves for a directed verdict after the close of evidence.

The court should:

(A) Grant the motion, because its laser was never intended to be used at the power levels necessary to reach a satellite.

(B) Grant the motion, because it exercised due care in the manufacture of the laser.

(C) Deny the motion, because the jury must determine whether the neighbor is a foreseeable plaintiff.

(D) Deny the motion, because the jury must determine whether the inventor's use of the laser was foreseeable.

Question 15

A patient needing ankle surgery signed standard consent forms and liability waivers covering the surgeon scheduled to perform the surgery. Two hours before the operation was scheduled to be performed, one of the surgeon's patients was brought into the emergency room with numerous orthopedic injuries that required immediate attention. The surgeon requested the head of orthopedic surgery, who was the leading authority on ankle surgery, to perform the ankle surgery for him so he could go to the emergency room. By the time the head surgeon arrived in the

operating room, the patient was already sedated. He performed the operation with his usual skill and the operation was a complete success.

If the patient sues the head surgeon for battery, she will:

(A) Win, but she may be entitled only to nominal damages.

(B) Win, because the head surgeon is vicariously liable for the original surgeon's obtaining a replacement without the patient's consent.

(C) Lose, because the head surgeon performed the operation competently and the patient suffered no harm.

(D) Lose, because a reasonable person similarly situated would have consented to the operation.

Question 16

The owner of a corner lot allowed a hedge on his property to become overgrown, obstructing the view of motorists at that corner. Two motorists were driving inattentively and each ran a stop sign at the intersection bordering the lot. Their cars collided in the intersection and one of the motorists was injured. She sued the owner of the lot in a jurisdiction that has adopted pure comparative negligence. The jury determined that the lot owner was 10% at fault and each of the motorists was 45% at fault.

Will the injured motorist recover damages from the lot owner?

(A) Yes, because she was not more than 50% at fault.

(B) Yes, because it was foreseeable that motorists could be injured if the hedge was not cut back.

(C) No, because the other motorist's negligence was a superseding cause of her injuries.

(D) No, because the lot owner's fault was slight compared with the motorist's fault.

Question 17

A doorman negligently locked a door that an office worker was intending to use to exit an office building, so the worker was forced to use a different exit. As she stepped onto the sidewalk outside the building, a car careened out of control on the street and jumped the curb. The car struck and injured the worker and then drove off. The driver was not found.

The worker brought suit against the doorman, seeking damages for her injuries. At trial, the parties stipulated that the doorman was negligent in locking the door and that the worker suffered injuries when she was struck by the car. The worker also established that if she had exited from the door she was intending to, she would not have been struck by the car. At the end of the worker's case, the doorman moved for a directed verdict in his favor.

The judge should:

(A) Grant the motion, because the driver of the car was the actual cause of the worker's injuries.

(B) Grant the motion, because the car was an unforeseeable intervening force.

(C) Deny the motion, because the jury could find that but for the doorman's negligence, the worker would not have been injured.

(D) Deny the motion, because the jury could find that the doorman's negligence was a foreseeable concurring cause of the worker's injury.

Question 18

Several cars of a freight train transporting nuclear waste derailed as the train neared a street crossing. One of the cars struck a motorist's car as it was waiting at the crossing gate, seriously injuring the motorist. The area around the accident was immediately evacuated, but fortunately none of the freight cars ruptured in the derailment.

In an action alleging strict liability against the railway that operated the freight train, the motorist established the above facts and presented evidence of her injuries. The railway presented evidence that the derailment was caused by a hidden defect in the spikes that anchored the rails to the track. The spikes were manufactured by its regular supplier and had not previously caused any problems. The railroad also presented evidence that the local authorities were supposed to restrict access to roads crossing the freight line while that particular train was in transit, but they had failed to do so.

In this action, the motorist is likely to:

(A) Prevail, because the spikes were in a defective condition that made them unreasonably dangerous.

(B) Prevail, because the railway was engaged in an abnormally dangerous activity.

(C) Not prevail, because the injury did not arise from the dangerous propensity of the activity.

(D) Not prevail, because the negligence of the local authorities in failing to restrict access to roads crossing the freight line was a superseding cause of the motorist's injuries.

TORTS ANSWERS - SET 3

Answer to Question 1

(B) The motorist will recover because the other driver's violation of the statute constituted negligence per se. For a duty created by a criminal statute to replace the more general duty of care, the proponent of the statutory standard must show that (i) he is in a class intended to be protected by the statute, (ii) the statute was designed to prevent the type of harm that was suffered, and (iii) the statutory standards are clearly defined. Here, the motorist can establish that the statutory standard regarding speeding should be applied against the other driver because the motorist, as a fellow driver, is in the class intended to be protected by the statute, it was designed to prevent accidents such as that which occurred, and the speed limit was posted. No excuse for violating the statute is present in the facts; thus, violation of the statute establishes negligence per se (*i.e.*, duty and breach of duty). The motorist has established causation and damages, completing the prima facie case. (A) is incorrect because while an applicable statute may establish plaintiff's contributory negligence, the headlight statute does not apply here. Even though the statute was intended to protect drivers against cars being driven without headlights, it would be very difficult to show that it was designed to prevent rear-end collisions during the day, or that violation of the statute was a cause of the motorist's injury. (C) is similarly incorrect; the motorist's violation of the headlight statute does not establish contributory negligence. (D) is incorrect because the motorist does not need to establish a breach of the general duty of care by the other driver. Here, the speed limit statute's specific duty replaces the more general common law duty of due care, and the other driver's violation of that statute constituted negligence per se.

Answer to Question 2

(D) Liability under (A), (B), or (C) would require that the camping association be either a commercial supplier or a seller of the blanket. Because the association is neither, negligence provides the only possible basis for recovery of the alternatives listed. Here, the association may occupy such a position of prominence in the field of camping equipment and accessories that it was reasonably foreseeable that a person might be influenced by the recommendation on the package into buying the blanket. It might be deemed reasonably foreseeable that such a person would be injured if the association failed to exercise ordinary, reasonable care in checking out the quality of the product being endorsed. If, in fact, the association failed to so investigate, this could create an unreasonable risk of injury to a person in the position of the camper, who would use the product thinking it to be free of defects. Such facts would give rise to a finding that the association had breached a duty of reasonable care owed to the camper, thereby causing her injury. (A) is incorrect because an express warranty arises where a seller or supplier makes any affirmation of fact or promise to the buyer relating to the goods that becomes part of the basis of the bargain. Here, the association is not a seller or supplier of the blanket, but is simply endorsing the product. Thus, an express warranty did not come into existence. (B) is incorrect because a warranty of merchantability is implied in a sale by a merchant who deals in goods of the kind sold. This warranty is that the goods are generally fit for the ordinary purposes for which such goods are used. As noted above, however, the association did not sell the blanket (nor, for that matter, is the association a merchant dealing in goods of this kind). Consequently, the facts do not give rise to an implied warranty of merchantability on the part of the association. Similarly, (C) is incorrect because strict liability requires that the defendant be a commercial supplier of the product in question (*e.g.*, manufacturer, retailer, assembler, or wholesaler). Because the association is merely an endorser of the blanket rather than a commercial supplier, there can be no recovery against it in strict liability.

Answer to Question 3

(D) The plaintiff can prevail in a lawsuit against the defendant even though his fault was greater than hers. The plaintiff will be able to establish a prima facie case of negligence against the defendant, because her inattentive driving breached her duty of care to other drivers and was a direct cause of the plaintiff's damages. The defendant's defense that the plaintiff's contributory negligence also caused the accident does not bar the plaintiff's recovery; comparative negligence jurisdictions allow recovery despite contributory negligence by the plaintiff, and ***pure*** comparative negligence rules allow recovery no matter how great the plaintiff's negligence is. Even if the defendant also was injured (although not indicated by the facts), the plaintiff could still recover damages. While the defendant could counterclaim against the plaintiff for the percentage of her damages that the plaintiff was responsible for, the plaintiff could still have a net recovery—regardless of his greater fault—if his damages are significantly greater than the defendant's (*e.g.,* if the plaintiff is 60% at fault and has suffered $100,000 in damages, while the defendant is 40% at fault and has suffered $10,000 in damages, the plaintiff would recover $34,000 in damages). (A) is wrong because the plaintiff's failure to stop, whether it is considered negligent or reckless, does not bar him from recovering in most pure comparative negligence jurisdictions; it merely reduces his recovery. (B) is wrong because the jurisdiction follows a ***pure*** comparative negligence approach, which allows recovery no matter how great plaintiff's negligence is. If ***partial*** comparative negligence had been adopted instead, the plaintiff's success would depend on a comparison of his fault and the defendant's fault. (C) is wrong because last clear chance is a mitigation of the "all or nothing" effect of traditional contributory negligence; it permits plaintiff to recover despite his own contributory negligence. Because a comparative negligence jurisdiction rejects the "all or nothing" approach, most comparative negligence jurisdictions do not use the last clear chance doctrine.

Answer to Question 4

(B) Evidence that the bottler complied with applicable statutes will be admissible to show that the bottler acted with ordinary, reasonable care, and is the only one of the listed arguments that would be helpful to the bottler. The bottler is being sued on a negligence theory; thus, the thief must prove that the bottler failed to exercise ordinary, reasonable care in bottling and distributing the water. Violation of a statute will establish a conclusive presumption of duty and breach of duty. However, compliance with an applicable statute does not necessarily establish due care, because due care may require more than is called for by the statute. Nevertheless, compliance with a statute is admissible as evidence that a defendant may have acted with due care. Thus, the bottler could use its compliance with the water bottling statutes as a means of establishing that it conformed with its duty to use ordinary, reasonable care. (A) is incorrect because a products liability action based on negligence uses the same causation analysis as a standard negligence case. Thus, a defendant's liability is not cut off by a foreseeable intervening force that comes into motion after the defendant's original negligent act. Consequently, an intermediary's negligent failure to discover a defect is not a superseding cause, and the defendant whose original negligence created the defect will be held liable along with the intermediary. Hence, the retailer's possibly negligent failure to inspect the water for purity will not relieve the bottler of liability for the consequences of its own negligence, if any. (C) will not be helpful to the bottler because this question allows for use of res ipsa loquitur. Under this doctrine, if a plaintiff shows that his injury is of a type that would not normally occur in the absence of negligence, and that such negligence is attributable to the defendant (*e.g.,* by showing that the instrumentality causing the injury was in the exclusive control of the defendant), the trier of fact is permitted to infer the defendant's negligence. Here, impurities would not normally get into the bottled water in the absence of negligence, and the fact that the container from which the thief drank was unopened allows the trier of fact to infer that the impurity entered the water due to negligence on the part of the bottler. Therefore, the thief is not required to introduce evidence as to how the impurity got into the water in order to prevail. (D) is incorrect because the bottler's duty of due care in the context of products liability arises from having placed the water into the stream of commerce. Having done so, the bottler owes a duty to any foreseeable plaintiff, whether such person be an actual purchaser of the water or merely a user thereof. With the placing of the water into the stream of commerce, the thief is a foreseeable plaintiff as a drinker of the water, regardless of the fact that he obtained the water by means of theft.

Answer to Question 5

(C) The ballplayer's lack of evidence of causation is most helpful to the farm products company. One of the elements of a prima facie case for products liability based on strict liability is causation of some harm to the plaintiff by a defective product. The ballplayer must show that the farm products company owed a strict duty as a commercial supplier of the seeds, and that the farm products company breached such duty by marketing a product that was so defective as to be unreasonably dangerous. In addition, the defect must have actually and proximately caused some harm to the plaintiff, and there must be damages. If, as (C) states, the ballplayer can produce no evidence that the illness he suffered was caused by the seeds' foreign matter, then he cannot prove the element of causation. Absent causation, a cause of action for strict liability will not lie. (A) is not as helpful to the farm products company as (C) because it does not preclude the ballplayer from establishing a prima facie case for strict liability. The fact that the foreign matter in the seeds was a rare mold might allow the farm products company to claim that it was not feasible to supply the seeds in a safer condition than they were (*i.e.,* a "state of the art" defense), but the success of this argument is much less certain than the argument of no causation raised by choice (C). (B) is incorrect because the farm products company owes a strict duty as a commercial supplier to refrain from selling a defective product. There is no requirement that the defendant in a strict liability action have manufactured or processed the product, only that the defendant be a commercial supplier of the product. The farm products company is a commercial supplier of the seeds by marketing them in its packaging. Therefore, the farm products company can be strictly liable even if the seeds were sold in their natural state. (D) is incorrect because, even if the seeds were actually collected and packaged by another company, the farm products company also owes a strict duty as the company that markets the seeds and thus is part of the distributive chain.

Answer to Question 6

(C) The court is not likely to grant the company's motion because the jury must determine whether the attractive nuisance doctrine applies. Under this doctrine, a landowner has a duty to exercise ordinary care to avoid reasonably foreseeable risk of harm to children, including trespassing children, caused by artificial conditions on his property. Here, while the company has presented some evidence against application of the attractive nuisance doctrine, it is ultimately the trier of fact's role to determine whether the doctrine applies and whether the company exercised ordinary care. Hence, the court will likely deny the company's motion and allow the jury to make that determination. (A) is incorrect because the jury could find that even though the company was not aware of children trespassing, it should have anticipated that they might try to sneak onto the property because it was an amusement park operation. (B) is incorrect because even though the girl knew she was trespassing, the jury could find that she did not appreciate the risk of playing on the rides. (D) is incorrect because the fact that the girl was attracted onto the land by the artificial condition is just one factor for determining whether the attractive nuisance doctrine applies. Foreseeability of harm to a child is the true basis of liability.

Answer to Question 7

(A) The producer can recover for intentional interference with business relations because the competitor used improper means to hire the designer away. To establish a prima facie case for interference with contract or prospective economic advantage, the plaintiff must prove: (i) the existence of a valid contractual relationship between the plaintiff and a third party or a valid business expectancy of the plaintiff; (ii) the defendant's knowledge of the expectancy; (iii) intentional interference by the defendant that induces a breach or termination of the relationship or expectancy; and (iv) damage to plaintiff. While an interferor's conduct may be privileged where it is a proper attempt to obtain business for the interferor, not only the ends but also the means used to interfere must be proper. Here, the competitor made an intentional misrepresentation with the intent to induce the designer to leave the producer's employment, and the producer has shown that he suffered actual damage from the designer's departure. (B) is incorrect because the producer cannot recover for defamation even though he can show actual damages. Defamatory language is language that tends to adversely affect one's reputation in the community, such as impeaching the individual's honesty, integrity, virtue, sanity, or the like. The statement that the producer is negotiating to sell his business is not, on the facts presented, defamatory. While the competitor could be liable for the tort of injurious falsehood, he is not liable for defamation. Conversely, if the competitor's statement were defamatory, the producer would not need to show actual damages to recover. The producer, who likely is a public figure, can recover presumed damages under common law rules if he establishes that the competitor made the statement with malice, *i.e.*, knowledge that the statement was false or reckless disregard as to its truth or falsity, which is suggested by the facts. (C) is incorrect because even though the competitor did not induce the designer to breach his contract, because it was terminable at will by either party, the competitor did induce a termination of the contractual relationship and interfered with the producer's business expectancy that the designer would stay in his employ. While the competitor would have been privileged to try to hire the designer away using legitimate means, the privilege does not extend to making intentional misrepresentations about the designer's current employer. (D) is incorrect because, as discussed above, the producer need not show that the competitor knew that the statement was false, as long as he shows that it was made with reckless disregard of its truth or falsity. As discussed above, he cannot recover for defamation because he cannot establish the defamatory language element of the prima facie case.

Answer to Question 8

(A) The hitchhiker's status as a trespasser is the mining company's strongest defense because it means that the mining company owed no duty to the hitchhiker, thereby completely relieving the mining company of any liability for his injuries. An owner or occupier of land owes no duty to an undiscovered trespasser. However, with regard to a discovered trespasser, the owner or occupier must warn of or make safe artificial conditions known to the landowner that involve a risk of death or serious bodily harm and that the trespasser is unlikely to discover. The hitchhiker, having come onto the land owned by the mining company without permission or privilege, is a trespasser. Because the mining company had no notice of the hitchhiker's presence on the property, the hitchhiker is deemed to be an undiscovered trespasser. Consequently, the mining company owes no duty to the hitchhiker with regard to the injuries incurred on its property. (C) and (D) each present factors that would be helpful to the mining company, but they are not as strong as (A). The fact that the mining company asked the power company to turn off the power, as well as the mining company's being unaware that it had not turned off the power, would be indicative of the exercise of due care on the part of the mining company (*i.e.*, it took every reasonable step to see that the power was not left running in the abandoned mine, and could not reasonably have known that in fact the power was still on). However, if it is shown that no duty of care extended from the mining company to the hitchhiker, then the first element of a prima facie case for negligence is absent, thus eliminating any need for the mining company to attempt to show that it acted with ordinary, reasonable care. As a result, (A) is a much stronger defense than (C) or (D). (B) is incorrect because the fact that the hitchhiker tried to commit theft of the power company's transformers is not relevant to any duty that may have been owed to him by the mining company. It is relevant that the hitchhiker was a trespasser, because this means that the mining company owed him no duty. However, the hitchhiker's status as a thief is of no significance.

Answer to Question 9

(C) The hotel will prevail because it did not breach any duty owed to the tourist. The tourist's estate may claim that the hotel owed the tourist an innkeeper's high duty of care to its guests or a land occupier's duty to make the premises safe for invitees, and breached that duty when the tourist drowned on the hotel's property. However, even though the tourist was a guest of the hotel and an invitee of the hotel, the facts do not establish any breach of duty by the hotel. The hotel manager advised those still in the hotel to move to a higher floor, which may have been the only reasonable course of action under the circumstances, and the danger of leaving the building should have been obvious to the tourist. Hence, the tourist's estate will not prevail. (A) is incorrect because, as discussed above, the hotel did not breach its innkeeper's high duty of care. (B) is incorrect because the hotel had neither the duty nor the right to prevent the tourist from leaving, even though it was an unwise decision. (D) is incorrect because the hotel's liability does not turn on whether the hurricane was foreseeable. Even if the hurricane were foreseeable, nothing in the facts indicates that the hotel breached its duty to the tourist.

Answer to Question 10

(C) The guest will not prevail in a suit against the homeowner. As a social guest of the homeowner's, the guest is deemed to be a licensee; *i.e.*, one who enters onto land with the owner's permission for her own purpose or business rather than for the owner's benefit. The owner has a duty to warn a licensee of a dangerous condition known to the owner that creates an unreasonable risk of harm to the licensee and that the licensee is unlikely to discover. The owner has no duty to a licensee to inspect for defects nor to repair known defects. The homeowner, as a person who was not involved with fishing, had no reason to suspect that a fishing line that was "20-pound test" could not support the constant weight of a 15-pound basket. Thus, the homeowner did not know of the dangerous condition present in the form of the basket overhanging his porch. Because the homeowner was unaware of the danger, he was under no duty to warn the guest, a licensee, of the dangerous condition. Having violated no duty owed to the guest, the homeowner will not be held liable for her injuries. (A) is accurate in stating that the guest was a social guest. However, as detailed above, the duty owed to a guest is simply to warn of concealed dangerous conditions of which the owner is aware. The homeowner had no duty to warn of a danger of which he neither knew nor had reason to know. (B) is incorrect because there is no indication either that the homeowner hung the basket in a negligent manner or that he was negligent in failing either to warn the guest or to be aware of the danger. The homeowner appears to have acted as would a reasonable person with no knowledge of the meaning of technical terms of fishing. (D) is incorrect because a social guest would indeed be a foreseeable plaintiff. If the homeowner had been negligent in hanging the basket directly above the swing, it would have been reasonably foreseeable that an injury would befall any person who sat on the swing. Thus, (D) reaches the correct result that the guest will not prevail, but for an incorrect reason.

Answer to Question 11

(A) If the proprietor recovers, it will be because the collection agent's conduct is judged to be extreme and outrageous. To establish a prima facie case for intentional infliction of emotional distress, plaintiff must prove (i) an act by defendant amounting to extreme and outrageous conduct, (ii) intent to cause severe emotional distress or recklessness as to the effect of defendant's act, (iii) causation, and (iv) damages, *i.e.*, severe emotional distress. If the agent's conduct is judged to be extreme and outrageous, he is liable because the other elements of the tort are present: Given his conduct and the proprietor's response, he was at least reckless as to whether his conduct would cause severe distress, and the facts indicate that it did cause such distress. Thus, if she prevails it will be because his acts were extreme and outrageous. (B) is incorrect because a threat of physical injury is not required to establish intentional infliction of distress. Nor would threat of physical injury be sufficient to create liability for negligent infliction of emotional distress—that tort requires also that some physical symptoms arise from the distress, which is not the case here. (C) is incorrect because the agent could be liable even if he did not intend for the proprietor to suffer emotional distress, as long as he was reckless as to the effect of his conduct. (D) is incorrect because even if the proprietor did owe the money, she could recover as long as the agent's conduct was extreme and outrageous.

Answer to Question 12

(C) The daughter can recover damages for her emotional distress, even though she suffered no physical injury and did not require medical care, because of the known sensitivity of people concerning the death of a family member. In the usual case, the duty to avoid negligent infliction of emotional distress is breached when defendant creates a foreseeable risk of physical injury to plaintiff, typically by causing a threat of physical impact that leads to emotional distress, and plaintiff can recover for physical injury caused solely by the distress. In special situations, however, courts have permitted plaintiff to recover in the absence of physical symptoms where defendant's negligence creates a great likelihood of severe emotional distress. One of these situations is the mishandling of a relative's corpse, because it is certainly foreseeable that a person will suffer severe emotional distress if the corpse of a family member is negligently mishandled. In this case, the mortuary was negligent in putting the wrong body in the casket, creating a foreseeable risk of severe emotional distress to the daughter under the circumstances. Despite the fact that she suffered no physical injury, she can recover damages from the mortuary. (C) is therefore correct and (B) is incorrect. (A) is incorrect because the fact that the daughter did not obtain medical or psychiatric care does not prevent her from recovering damages. She can establish proof of her emotional distress through her own testimony and the testimony of others. (D) is incorrect because the fact that the mortuary is charging the daughter for the funeral is irrelevant. Regardless of the mortuary's conduct regarding the bill, its negligence in handling the body of her father makes it liable for her emotional distress.

Answer to Question 13

(A) The student's statement constitutes slander per se and therefore the student will be liable. To establish a prima facie case for defamation, the following elements must be proved: (i) defamatory language on the part of the defendant; (ii) the defamatory language must be "of or concerning" the plaintiff (*i.e.,* it must identify the plaintiff to a reasonable reader, listener, or viewer); (iii) publication of the defamatory language by the defendant to a third person; and (iv) damages to the reputation of the plaintiff. Here, the student's suggestion that the law review editor received outside help on an article she authored impeaches her integrity and legal skills. The defamatory language directly related to the editor. The publication requirement is satisfied because the student made the statement to the hiring partner. To recover damages for slander, special damages must be pleaded and proved unless the spoken defamation falls within one of four categories, characterized as slander per se. Hence, a defamatory statement adversely reflecting on the plaintiff's abilities in his business, trade, or profession is actionable without pleading or proof of special damages. The student's statement adversely reflected on the law review editor's honesty and capability in her profession, and as such is slander per se. (B) is incorrect because, as noted above, the student's defamatory statement adversely reflecting on the editor's abilities in her profession is actionable without proof of special damages. (C) is incorrect because the mere fact that the interviewer asked the student his opinion does not justify a defamatory response. The student did not have a common law qualified privilege to make the statements because he was not a former employer of the law review editor and was not yet a member of the hiring partner's firm (negating any common interest privilege). Furthermore, once publication is established, it is no defense that the defendant had no idea that the publication was defamatory. It is the intent to publish, not the intent to defame, that is the requisite intent. Thus, even if the student thought that his comments did not constitute defamation because they were in response to the interviewer's question, he could still be found liable for defamation assuming all other elements of the tort were satisfied. (D) is incorrect because it states a standard for private persons suing on matters of public concern. Private plaintiffs must show that the defendant was at least negligent as to truth or falsity in making the statement, but here no matter of public concern is involved, so fault need not be shown. Also, since a matter of public concern is not involved, the plaintiff does not need to establish that the statement was false; a defamatory statement is presumed false at common law.

Answer to Question 14

(D) The court should deny the motion because the jury must determine whether the inventor's use of the laser was a reasonably foreseeable misuse. The manufacturer of an unreasonably dangerous defective product is strictly liable to foreseeable plaintiffs injured by the product. To establish a prima facie case in products liability based on strict liability in tort, the following elements must be proved: (i) strict duty owed by a commercial supplier; (ii) breach of that duty; (iii) actual and proximate cause; and (iv) damages. All of those elements are satisfied here. The manufacturer was a commercial supplier of the lasers. To hold the commercial supplier strictly liable for a product defect, the product must be expected to, and must in fact, reach the user or consumer without substantial change in the condition in which it is supplied. The facts establish that the defective voltage regulation device was present in the laser when it left the manufacturer's production facilities. Courts extend the protection from defective products to all foreseeable plaintiffs, including members of the buyer's family, guests, friends, and employees of the buyer, and bystanders, such as the neighbor here. While the neighbor has presented evidence of the prima facie case, the manufacturer has established that its laser was not intended to be used in the manner it was. Nevertheless, courts have required suppliers to anticipate reasonably foreseeable uses even if they are "misuses" of the product. Thus, misuse of the product will not preclude a products liability claim by the neighbor if the misuse was reasonably foreseeable, which is a determination to be made by the jury. Thus, (D) is correct and (A) is incorrect. (B) is incorrect because one need not be a consumer or user of the defective product to recover in products liability. As noted above, foreseeable bystanders can sue under strict liability. (B) is incorrect. To establish breach of duty for a strict liability action, the plaintiff need not prove that the defendant was at fault in selling or producing a defective product—only that the product in fact is so defective as to be "unreasonably dangerous." Thus, the manufacturer's exercise of due care is irrelevant. (C) is incorrect because the facts establish that the neighbor was a foreseeable plaintiff,

and the manufacturer presented no evidence to the contrary. Hence, that would not be an issue for the jury to decide.

Answer to Question 15

(A) The patient can establish a prima facie case for battery. The fact that the operation was a success and that she may not be able to prove actual damages will not bar her recovery. The prima facie case for battery requires: (i) an act by defendant that brings about a harmful or offensive contact to plaintiff; (ii) intent on the part of defendant to do the act; and (iii) causation. Here, the head surgeon's performing the operation on the patient's ankle would be harmful or offensive contact because the patient had selected another surgeon to perform the operation and did not consent to the head surgeon's participating in any way. Even if evidence of her distress is not adequate to prove actual damages, she will still be entitled to a judgment in her favor and nominal damages, because damages is not an element of the prima facie case for battery. (B) is wrong because the head surgeon is directly liable to the patient for battery. The patient does not need to establish vicarious liability based on the original surgeon's conduct. (C) is wrong because the fact that the head surgeon performed the operation competently is irrelevant because the patient did not consent to his involvement at all. As discussed above, the prima facie case for battery does not require harm (damages) to be shown. Even if she cannot prove actual harm, she will be entitled to a judgment for nominal damages. (D) is wrong because the fact that a reasonable person would have consented is irrelevant in a nonemergency situation. If the patient had been brought into the emergency room requiring immediate surgery, her consent to the operation would be implied by law if she was incapable of consenting and a reasonable person similarly situated would have consented. Here, however, the operation was not an emergency and the patient's express consent should have been obtained.

Answer to Question 16

(B) The injured motorist may recover damages from the lot owner because the jury found that the lot owner should have foreseen that motorists could be injured if the hedge was not cut back. The lot owner owes the duty of an owner and occupier of land to those off the premises for unreasonably dangerous artificial conditions. In contrast to overgrown weeds, which are a natural condition for which no duty is owed absent a statute, a hedge is considered an artificial condition, analogous to a fence. Hence, by letting the hedge become so large that it created a foreseeable danger to motorists by obstructing their vision, the lot owner has breached his duty to the motorist. The other elements of the motorist's negligence action (besides a duty and a breach of the duty) are actual and proximate cause, and damages. The motorist can establish actual cause by showing that, although she failed to notice the stop sign, she would have noticed another car traveling on a collision course with hers; *i.e.,* but for the overgrown hedge, the motorist would have been able to avoid the accident. Proximate cause in an indirect case such as this can be established by showing that any intervening forces were foreseeable and not superseding. The other motorist's negligent failure to stop may also have been caused in part by the overgrown hedge and is a foreseeable intervening force that does not break the chain of causation. Hence, (C) is incorrect. Because the jurisdiction has adopted pure comparative negligence, the injured motorist can recover 10% of her damages even though her fault was greater than that of the lot owner. (A) is incorrect because a pure comparative negligence jurisdiction allows a plaintiff to recover no matter how great her negligence is. Thus, even though the motorists are both 45% at fault and the lot owner is only 10% at fault, the motorist can recover 10% of her damages from the lot owner. (D) is incorrect because, as discussed above, the lot owner is still liable for some damages in a pure comparative negligence jurisdiction even if his fault was only slight.

Answer to Question 17

(B) The court should grant the motion because the evidence establishes that the car was a superseding force that cut off the doorman's liability for his negligence under proximate cause principles. The general rule of proximate cause is that the defendant is liable for all harmful results that are the normal incidents of, and within the increased risk caused by, his acts. An indirect cause case is one where the facts indicate that a force came into motion after the time of defendant's negligent act and combined with the negligent act to cause injury to the plaintiff. Whether an intervening force will cut off the defendant's liability for the plaintiff's injury and be deemed superseding is determined by foreseeability. Here, nothing in the facts suggests that a car jumping the curb was a foreseeable consequence of the doorman's negligently locking the door. Hence, the judge should grant the motion because the worker has failed to establish the proximate cause element of his prima facie case. (A) is wrong because the doorman was also an actual cause of the worker's injuries—but for the doorman's negligence, the worker would not have been on the sidewalk where the car jumped the curb. (C) is wrong because it establishes only actual cause. A directed verdict is appropriate because no evidence establishes the proximate cause element of the worker's case. (D) is wrong because the facts do not establish foreseeability. While the doorman's negligence was a concurring actual cause of the worker's injury, it was not a proximate cause because the injury that occurred was unforeseeable.

Answer to Question 18

(C) The motorist is not likely to prevail ***in a strict liability action*** because her injury did not arise from the abnormally dangerous propensity of the railway's activity. The railway's transport of nuclear waste likely qualifies as an abnormally dangerous activity because: (i) it involves a risk of serious physical harm; (ii) this risk is present even when reasonable care is exercised by the actor; and (iii) the activity is not a matter of common usage. However, the strict duty is limited to the dangers that would be anticipated from the activity involved; strict liability does not apply to harms that were not caused by the normally dangerous propensity of the activity. Here, the railway's activity is subject to strict liability because of the danger of radioactivity inherent in nuclear waste, but not from a derailment by itself. Because the motorist's injuries were not caused by the release of radioactivity, strict liability does not apply. The railway would be liable for the injuries from the derailment only if the motorist established negligence. (A) is incorrect because it states the standard for strict liability for defective products, which requires that the defendant be a commercial supplier of the defective product, *i.e.* someone in the chain of distribution of the product. Here, the railway is not a commercial supplier of the spikes that failed; rather, it is the purchaser or consumer of the spikes. (B) is incorrect because, as discussed above, strict liability does not apply to the harm that occurred here. (D) is incorrect. It is questionable whether the negligence by the local authorities could be considered an intervening force, which must come into play ***after*** the culpable conduct by the defendant. Even if it were an intervening force, it likely would not be considered so extraordinary as to be an unforeseeable intervening force. Hence, it would not constitute a superseding force that would break the causal connection between the motorist's injury and the railway's actions.

Set 4 Answer Sheet

1. Ⓐ Ⓑ Ⓒ Ⓓ
2. Ⓐ Ⓑ Ⓒ Ⓓ
3. Ⓐ Ⓑ Ⓒ Ⓓ
4. Ⓐ Ⓑ Ⓒ Ⓓ
5. Ⓐ Ⓑ Ⓒ Ⓓ
6. Ⓐ Ⓑ Ⓒ Ⓓ
7. Ⓐ Ⓑ Ⓒ Ⓓ
8. Ⓐ Ⓑ Ⓒ Ⓓ
9. Ⓐ Ⓑ Ⓒ Ⓓ
10. Ⓐ Ⓑ Ⓒ Ⓓ
11. Ⓐ Ⓑ Ⓒ Ⓓ
12. Ⓐ Ⓑ Ⓒ Ⓓ
13. Ⓐ Ⓑ Ⓒ Ⓓ
14. Ⓐ Ⓑ Ⓒ Ⓓ
15. Ⓐ Ⓑ Ⓒ Ⓓ
16. Ⓐ Ⓑ Ⓒ Ⓓ
17. Ⓐ Ⓑ Ⓒ Ⓓ
18. Ⓐ Ⓑ Ⓒ Ⓓ

TORTS QUESTIONS - SET 4

Question 1

A sailor steering his sailboat through a channel was nearly swamped by a large cabin cruiser. The sailor made an obscene gesture and shouted epithets at the captain of the larger boat, who responded by swinging his boat around and heading at high speed directly at the sailboat's bow. The sailor was convinced that the boats would collide, so he steered close to the edge of the channel and abruptly ran aground on a shallow sand bar. The sailor was extremely upset but otherwise uninjured. His boat was not damaged by hitting the sand bar.

If the sailor brings an appropriate action against the captain for damages, the probable outcome will be:

(A) The sailor will win, because he suffered severe emotional distress from the captain's conduct.

(B) The sailor will win, because he believed that the captain's maneuvers threatened imminent danger of harm to him.

(C) The captain will win, because the sailor suffered no physical injury or property damage.

(D) The captain will win, because the sailor was responsible for provoking the captain during the relevant events.

Question 2

A six-year-old girl went with her father to look at Christmas decorations in the neighborhood. One house had a variety of displays in the yard, including a large mechanical Santa Claus figure that waved its arm and moved its head. While the father was talking to the homeowner about his electricity bill, the girl climbed up on the Santa. It toppled over and she hit her head on the ground, suffering a serious injury.

The girl, through her guardian ad litem, brought a products liability action based on strict liability against the manufacturer of the Santa figure in a jurisdiction that follows traditional contributory negligence rules.

Which of the following would provide the best defense for the manufacturer?

(A) The girl is unrelated to the purchaser of the Santa figure.

(B) The girl was contributorily negligent in climbing on the Santa figure.

(C) The girl's misuse of the Santa figure was not reasonably foreseeable.

(D) The girl's father was negligent in his supervision of her.

Question 3

A homeowner purchased a product that makes it easy to remove vinyl tile by chemically breaking down the bonding properties of the adhesive. The label on the product instructed users to allow several hours for the product to be absorbed before attempting removal of the tile and warned not to use the product other than in compliance with the instructions and not to use any other product in conjunction with it. The homeowner believed that she could hasten the absorption process by heating the tile, so she used an industrial strength blow dryer set on high shortly after applying the product. The heat caused toxic fumes to be released by the product, damaging her lungs.

The homeowner brought an action against the manufacturer of the product based on strict liability in tort for failure to warn. The jurisdiction does not apply its comparative negligence rules to strict liability. At trial, the homeowner presented evidence of her use of the product and its manufacture by the manufacturer, the injury she suffered, and that the label bore no warning regarding applying heat to the product. The manufacturer presented evidence that it had received no reports of persons injured by fumes from the product in the 10 years that the product had been on the market.

If the manufacturer moves for a summary judgment at the close of all of the evidence, the court should:

(A) Deny the motion, because a jury could find that the product was in a defective condition unreasonably dangerous to users based on the absence of warnings regarding the use of heat.

(B) Deny the motion, because the homeowner has established that she suffered injury as a result of her use of the product.

(C) Grant the motion, because the homeowner's failure to follow the instructions constituted contributory negligence as a matter of law.

(D) Grant the motion, because the long history of no injuries demonstrates that the warnings on the label were adequate and the product was not defective.

Question 4

A homeowner purchased a ladder from a home supply retailer. While he was using the ladder, an improperly installed bolt fastening one of the rungs gave way, causing him to fall and break his leg. The homeowner sued the manufacturer of the ladder to recover damages for his injury.

If it is established at trial that the home supply retailer could have discovered the defectively installed bolt if it had conducted a reasonable inspection of the ladder, the retailer's failure to inspect:

(A) Has no legal effect on the manufacturer's liability.

(B) Is a superseding cause that relieves the manufacturer of liability to the homeowner.

(C) Is attributable to the manufacturer under the doctrine of respondeat superior.

(D) Will allow the manufacturer to bring an action for indemnity against the home supply retailer if the manufacturer is found liable to the homeowner.

Question 5

A three-year-old girl attending nursery school punched a boy in the face because he was teasing her about wearing glasses. The blow knocked out the boy's newly acquired front teeth.

If the boy's parents sue the girl's parents for the injury, the best defense would be:

(A) The boy was the initial aggressor.

(B) The girl is too young to be responsible for her actions.

(C) A parent cannot be liable for damages due to the child's conduct.

(D) The parents were unaware of any potentially violent behavior by the girl.

Question 6

A physician who was photographically documenting the deterioration of a terminally ill patient came into his room to take more photos as the patient's wife was saying her final goodbye. Ignoring the wife's protests, the physician lifted the patient's head and slid a sheet of blue cardboard underneath for a better background, and then took some photos as the patient expired. The wife is the patient's sole heir.

The wife can recover against the physician for:

(A) Battery and intrusion on seclusion.

(B) Battery only, because a privacy tort does not survive the death of the plaintiff.

(C) Intrusion on seclusion only, because the physician did not cause a harmful or offensive contact with the patient.

(D) Neither battery nor intrusion on seclusion.

Question 7

The wife of the president of a small but prestigious private college was also an instructor at the college. While researching an article about the college president, a reporter discovered and revealed in a published news story that while the wife was dating the president, she had falsified her academic credentials on her application for a position with the college. As a result of the news story, the wife was subject to verbal attacks and innuendo among her colleagues. She asserted a cause of action against the newspaper for defamation and established at trial that the story about her was not accurate.

For the wife to prevail, she also will need to show that:

(A) She suffered special (economic) damages as a result of the story.

(B) The story revealed facts about her private affairs not generally known to the public.

(C) The newspaper published the story with knowledge that it was false or with reckless disregard for its truth or falsity.

(D) The newspaper was negligent in publishing the story.

Question 8

The seller of a three-year-old house showed it to the niece of a potential buyer. The niece told the seller that her aunt was looking for extra space to store some valuable antiques and asked whether the large detached garage would be safe. The seller stated that all of the garage's lumber and wallboard had been treated with a flame retardant that made the garage almost impervious to an accidental fire. At the time he said this, the seller had no knowledge of whether the materials used for the garage had been treated with anything; in fact, they had not. The niece told her aunt that the garage was extremely fire resistant, so the aunt decided to purchase the house and moved all of her antiques into the garage. Three months later, the garage caught fire and burned to the ground.

In an action by the aunt against the seller to recover for the loss of her antiques, will she prevail?

(A) Yes, because the niece was acting as an agent for the aunt.

(B) Yes, because the niece relied on the statements made by the seller.

(C) No, because the seller's statements were not made in a business or professional capacity.

(D) No, because the seller owed no duty to the aunt regarding his statements.

Question 9

A homeowner invited guests over for an evening pool party. One of the guests jumped into the pool without seeing that a swimmer was in the water right below him. He struck the swimmer on the head, knocking her unconscious. Other guests pulled the swimmer out of the water and attempted to revive her. She survived but suffered permanent injury.

The swimmer brought an action against the homeowner for her injuries. At trial, evidence established that when the guest jumped into the pool, he did not see the swimmer in part because a light in the pool near the point of impact was not working at the time, but the homeowner was not aware that it was not working. No other evidence was presented regarding the condition of the pool. Other evidence established that the rescue efforts of the other guests caused greater injury to the swimmer than the initial impact. At the end of the presentation of the evidence, the homeowner moved for a directed verdict.

Should the homeowner's motion be granted?

(A) Yes, because the swimmer's injuries were caused by the conduct of third persons.

(B) Yes, because the homeowner was not aware that the light in the pool was not working.

(C) No, because the jury could determine that the homeowner failed to exercise reasonable care in activities on the property.

(D) No, because the jury could find that any negligence on the part of the rescuers was foreseeable and therefore does not cut off the homeowner's liability.

Question 10

As a motorist was driving on a road, a driver on an intersecting road failed to see a stop sign at the intersection and crossed into the motorist's path. The motorist would have had time to avoid the driver's vehicle except that he was making a call on his cell phone. He slammed on the brakes as soon as he saw the driver, so the impact occurred at a low speed. The driver's car sustained only minor damage, but the motorist's car sustained such heavy damage that it was a total loss.

If the motorist sues the driver in a jurisdiction following traditional contributory negligence and assumption of the risk rules, what is the driver's best defense?

(A) The driver's running the stop sign was unintentional.

(B) The motorist was negligent in purchasing a car that would suffer heavy damage when struck at low speed.

(C) The motorist was contributorily negligent.

(D) The motorist had the last clear chance to avoid the accident.

Question 11

A salesman in a highly visible and competitive field went to the police station to post bond for his son, who had been arrested for possession of a small quantity of narcotics. A photographer for the local newspaper who was at the police station took a picture of the salesman flanked by two bulky police officers. The photo, which looked like the pictures of alleged criminals being taken into custody, ran on a quarter of the front page because it was a slow news day. The photo was accompanied by a very small caption giving the salesman's name and stating that his son had been arrested for possession of narcotics. The salesman's boss was hypersensitive about the reputation of his company and fired the salesman after he saw the picture in the newspaper.

If the salesman sues the newspaper, he will:

(A) Recover for intrusion upon seclusion.

(B) Recover for false light publicity.

(C) Not recover, because the caption was true.

(D) Not recover, because printing the picture was in the public interest.

Question 12

On the way home from a nightclub, a passenger began yelling at the designated driver claiming that he was not taking the best route back to her house. The driver disagreed and contended that his route was the quickest. The passenger impulsively grabbed the steering wheel, causing the car to swerve and strike a pedestrian, injuring him. At trial, the pedestrian established that the driver's license had expired the day before the accident. The driver's traffic record qualified him for an automatic renewal of his driver's license, but he had forgotten to submit it in time. A statute in the jurisdiction makes it an offense to drive a vehicle on any public road in the state without a valid driver's license.

The pedestrian will:

(A) Prevail, because the driver violated a statute by driving without a valid license.

(B) Prevail, because the driver failed to control his passenger.

(C) Not prevail, because the driver did not start the argument.

(D) Not prevail, because the passenger's action was the proximate cause of the injury.

Question 13

In a negligence action against two joint tortfeasors, the jury determined that the plaintiff suffered $100,000 in damages and that she was 10% at fault. The first defendant was judged to be 60% at fault and to have suffered $200,000 in damages. The second defendant was judged to be 30% at fault and to have suffered no damages.

If all parties assert their respective valid claims and the plaintiff ends up with an award of $40,000 from the first defendant, which of the following statements is most likely to be true?

(A) The jurisdiction follows traditional joint and several liability and traditional contribution rules.

(B) The jurisdiction follows traditional joint and several liability rules and comparative contribution rules.

(C) The jurisdiction has abolished joint and several liability.

(D) The jurisdiction has not adopted pure comparative negligence.

Question 14

A motorist was negligently driving close to the shoulder of a highway when his vehicle skidded and hit a support column of a bridge that crossed over the highway. The impact from the car caused structural damage to the support column, which caused the bridge to drop 18 inches. The sag of the bridge was clearly visible from the highway. The motorist died in his heavily damaged car as a result of the accident. A rescuer, who had been five miles away at the time of the accident, came on the scene and pulled his car off the road to see if he could render assistance. Shortly thereafter, a trucker approached the scene of the accident. The trucker saw that an accident had occurred, and had adequate time to slow down or stop, but he proceeded ahead without reducing speed. Under ordinary circumstances, his truck could have passed easily under the bridge, but the 18-inch drop caused the top of the truck to strike the bridge. A chunk of concrete fell from the bridge, striking the rescuer in the head and seriously injuring him.

If the rescuer sues the motorist's estate in a jurisdiction that follows traditional contributory negligence rules, who will prevail?

(A) The motorist's estate, because the trucker's actions caused the rescuer's injuries.

(B) The motorist's estate, because the rescuer was five miles away when the initial accident occurred and therefore not a foreseeable plaintiff.

(C) The rescuer, because he stopped to render assistance.

(D) The rescuer, because the motorist's negligence was the proximate cause of the rescuer's injuries.

Question 15

A farmer employed a 16-year-old high school student for a summer agricultural labor job. One afternoon, a violent storm suddenly erupted as the farmer was driving a tractor up a hill in an open field with the student in the wagon behind. When loud claps of thunder erupted, the farmer stopped his tractor, jumped off without saying anything, and ran swiftly down the hill toward the low ground, which he knew would be safer. The student, who lived in a nearby city and had never seen an electrical storm in open country (except as a passenger inside an automobile), had never been told how to act safely during such a storm. Once the storm began, the student was struck by lightning and seriously injured as he stood at the crest of the hill watching the farmer run.

Is the farmer liable to the student for the injuries caused by lightning?

(A) Yes, because the student was an employee, acting within the scope of his employment.

(B) Yes, because the student was a minor.

(C) No, because the student was injured by an act of God.

(D) No, because lightning is never foreseeable.

Question 16

While at a party, a wife came up behind a younger woman, grabbed her by her arm, and accused her of having an affair with the wife's husband. The wife knew that her accusation was not true.

Of the following facts, which would be most helpful to the younger woman in a suit against the wife for intentional infliction of emotional distress?

(A) The wife knew that the younger woman is very religious, and her religious beliefs strongly condemn adultery.

(B) When the wife grabbed her arm, it caused the younger woman great pain and she has suffered an upset stomach from the trauma of it.

(C) Other people at the party overheard the wife's accusation.

(D) The younger woman's employer heard of the accusation and did not give her a promotion.

Question 17

A recently retired detective who had been instrumental in solving many important crimes in his community and had received many commendations from his police superiors was the subject of a docudrama aired on network television. The credits for the show indicated that it was based on the life of the detective but stated that not every event depicted in the show actually happened. The detective saw the show and was furious because, while most parts of the show dealt fairly accurately with some of the crimes he had helped solve, other parts portrayed his character as being involved in James Bond-type sexual escapades.

If the detective sues the network for invasion of privacy, who will prevail?

(A) The detective, because his name was appropriated by the network for a commercial purpose.

(B) The detective, because the seclusion of his retirement has been upset.

(C) The detective, because he has been portrayed in a false light.

(D) The network, because the show as a whole was complimentary to the detective.

Question 18

A former college baseball player who played in the College World Series 20 years ago was named in a radio broadcast as committing a key error that cost his team the championship. In fact, it was another ballplayer who committed the error.

If the ballplayer brings a defamation action against the broadcaster and the court finds that he was defamed, to what damages would he be entitled?

(A) Nominal damages only, unless the ballplayer can show actual pecuniary loss.

(B) General damages, even without proof of actual injury.

(C) Only damages based on competent evidence of actual injury.

(D) No damages, unless the ballplayer can prove actual malice on the part of the broadcaster.

TORTS ANSWERS - SET 4

Answer to Question 1

(B) The sailor will win because the captain's actions constituted an assault. A prima facie case for assault consists of: (i) an act by the defendant creating a reasonable apprehension in the plaintiff of immediate harmful or offensive contact; (ii) intent on the part of the defendant to bring about that apprehension; and (iii) causation. Here, if the sailor reasonably believed that the captain's boat was about to hit his boat (and thus cause a harmful or offensive contact with him), there is a basis for assault because the other elements (intent on the part of the captain and causation) were present. The only issue is whether the belief was reasonable. In determining whether the apprehension was reasonable, the courts usually apply a reasonable person test. Here, a reasonable person certainly could believe that the captain's actions constituted a threat of an immediate harmful contact (*e.g.*, a crash). Thus, there would be a basis for assault. (A) is wrong because the sailor can prevail on an assault claim regardless of whether he can establish all the elements of a claim for intentional infliction of emotional distress. That tort will require the sailor to prove not only that he suffered emotional distress but also that the captain's conduct was extreme and outrageous. While a trier of fact might find that to be the case, intentional infliction of emotional distress should be considered a fallback tort position, to be chosen only if there is no other tort available from the facts and answer choices. (C) is wrong because damages are recoverable for assault without the plaintiff's suffering actual physical injury. Assault is the causing of ***apprehension*** of contact; it does not require actual contact. (D) is wrong because, unless the sailor's initial actions were such as to justify the captain's acting in self-defense, it is immaterial that the sailor made insults provoking the captain's tortious conduct. Self-defense is permitted when a person reasonably believes he is being or is about to be attacked. Here, it is clear that the sailor's conduct would not justify the captain's actions in self-defense. Also, self-defense would not apply because the captain's conduct was clearly not defensive; he came after the sailor even though the sailor was not a threat at that point.

Answer to Question 2

(C) The manufacturer's best defense is that the girl's climbing on the Santa figure constituted a misuse of the product that was not reasonably foreseeable, thus relieving the manufacturer of any potential strict liability. A prima facie case in products liability based on strict liability in tort consists of: (i) a strict duty owed by a commercial supplier, (ii) breach of that duty, (iii) actual and proximate cause, and (iv) damages. Breach of duty is established by showing that the defendant sold or produced the product in a defective condition unreasonably dangerous to users. Some products are safe if used as intended, but may pose serious dangers if used in other ways. Thus, suppliers must anticipate reasonably foreseeable uses (even if they are misuses) of the product. Here, there is no indication that the Santa figure was defective and unreasonably dangerous for the purpose for which it was designed. The product was not designed for climbing and the manufacturer at least can make the argument that it was not reasonably foreseeable that a child would do so. Hence, the manufacturer's best defense is that the product was not dangerously defective for reasonably foreseeable use. (A) is incorrect because it raises a privity defense. Privity is not required to apply the protection of strict liability. The strict duty is owed not only to purchasers but also to family, guests, friends, and employees of the purchaser, as well as foreseeable bystanders such as the girl here. Thus, the manufacturer cannot raise the lack of privity between itself and the girl as a defense. (B) is incorrect because ordinary contributory negligence is not a defense to a strict products liability action in contributory negligence jurisdictions. Only voluntarily and unreasonably encountering a known risk or misusing the product in an unforeseeable manner (as (C) states) would serve as a defense. (D) is incorrect because, even if the father were negligent in his supervision of his

daughter, such ordinary negligence will not be deemed a superseding intervening force that would break the causal connection between any initial wrongful conduct by the manufacturer and the ultimate injury. Hence, this would not serve as a defense for the manufacturer.

Answer to Question 3

(A) The court should deny the motion because a jury could find that the product was defective. To establish a prima facie case in products liability based on strict liability in tort, the following elements must be proved: (i) strict duty owed by a commercial supplier; (ii) breach of that duty; (iii) actual and proximate cause; and (iv) damages. To establish breach of duty for a strict liability action, the plaintiff need prove only that the product in fact is so defective as to be "unreasonably dangerous." Here, the homeowner has presented evidence that she was injured by a product supplied by the manufacturer, and alleged that the product was in a defective condition unreasonably dangerous to users because of inadequate warnings. In failure to warn cases, the plaintiff is entitled to a presumption that an adequate warning would have been read and heeded, although the jury could very well reject that presumption based on the homeowner's conduct. Nevertheless, whether inadequate warnings made the product so defective as to be unreasonably dangerous is a question of fact for the jury; hence, the motion should be denied. (B) is wrong because the homeowner must also establish as part of her prima facie case that the product was defective. (C) is wrong because the homeowner's failure to follow instructions is at most ordinary contributory negligence, which is not a defense to strict liability actions. (D) is wrong because the absence of previous injuries does not establish the adequacy of the warnings. While it may help the manufacturer's case, it is not sufficient to take that determination away from the jury.

Answer to Question 4

(A) The failure of the home supply retailer to inspect the ladder has no legal effect on the manufacturer's liability, regardless of whether the plaintiff is suing in negligence or strict liability. ***Note that when a question does not supply the plaintiff's theory of liability, you have to consider both negligence and strict liability.*** Under either theory, an intermediary's negligent failure to discover a defect is ***not*** a superseding cause, so the defendant who supplied the defective product will still be liable. Thus, even if the home supply retailer were negligent in not discovering the defect, it would not relieve the manufacturer of liability. (B) is incorrect because an intervening force must be unforeseeable for it to be superseding. Here, the failure of the retailer to discover the defect was ordinary foreseeable negligence that does not break the causal connection between the initial wrongful conduct and the ultimate injury. (C) is incorrect because there is no evidence of an employer-employee relationship for which respondeat superior liability would apply. The only relationship between the two companies appears to be a contractual one; hence, the manufacturer will not be vicariously liable for the negligence of the retailer under respondeat superior principles. (D) is incorrect because it is a reversal of one of the situations in which indemnity is available. When strict liability applies, each supplier of a defective product is liable to an injured person, but each supplier has a right of indemnification against all ***previous*** suppliers of the defective product in the distribution chain, with the manufacturer of the defective product ultimately liable. Here, both the home supply retailer and the manufacturer may be liable as suppliers in a strict liability action if they supplied a defective product. However, the manufacturer, as the previous supplier in the chain, would be liable to the home supply retailer for indemnity, rather than the other way around as (D) states.

Answer to Question 5

(D) The best defense of the girl's parents is that they were unaware of any potentially violent behavior by the girl. At common law, parents are not vicariously liable for the torts of their child.

(Statutes in most states allow for limited liability for intentional torts, but there is no indication of such a statute here.) Parents can be liable, however, for their own negligence, *i.e.,* in not exercising due care under the circumstances. Thus, if the parents know their child may be violent, they could be negligent if they do not take precautions to prevent that behavior or injury from that behavior. However, if the parents have no reason to know their child could be violent, they have no duty to protect against such behavior. Here, if the girl had never done anything like this before, and her parents had no idea that she would be violent, they were not negligent in allowing her to attend nursery school. (A) is wrong because, although the boy's teasing may have provoked the girl, he did not initiate the violence. He did nothing to allow the girl a right of self-defense, and so his actions would not provide the girl's parents with a good defense. (B) is wrong because there is no general tort immunity for children. As long as the child is old enough to intend the act, she can be held liable. Here it seems that the girl intended to cause a battery. She either intended or knew with substantial certainty that swinging her fist would strike the boy in the face, *i.e.,* would cause a harmful or offensive contact. Thus, this choice does not present the best defense for the defendants. (C) is wrong because parents can be liable for damages due to their child's conduct. As explained above, although the parents are not vicariously liable at common law, they can be liable based on their own negligence (*e.g.,* for negligent supervision).

Answer to Question 6

(A) The wife is likely to recover for both torts. Battery requires: (i) an act that brings about harmful or offensive contact; (ii) intent to bring about the harmful or offensive contact; and (iii) causation. Whether a given contact can be considered harmful or offensive is judged by how it would be viewed by a reasonable person of ordinary sensibilities. Most contact that a doctor has with his patient is for purposes of treatment and would not be considered offensive; in fact, the law implies consent to the contact in such cases. However, the physician's lifting of the patient's head during his dying moments for a purpose unrelated to treatment went far beyond the scope of any implied consent. Most persons would judge his act to be an offensive contact. Intent for battery is satisfied by showing that the physician knew with substantial certainty that the offensive contact would occur. He need not have intended injury or committed the act for a bad motive. Causation is easily established, and actual damages are not required. Also, actions for battery do not expire on the victim's (the patient's) death. Thus, the wife can recover in an action for battery to the patient, making (C) and (D) incorrect. The wife's other action would be her own action for intrusion on plaintiff's seclusion. This tort requires an act of intruding on the seclusion of the plaintiff in her private matters, and that the intrusion be objectionable to a reasonable person. While a doctor usually is not intruding on seclusion by entering a patient's room, the physician ignored the wife's protests as her husband was dying just so he could take more photographs. This kind of intrusion would be highly objectionable to a reasonable person. Hence, she can recover for the physician's intrusion on her seclusion, making (B) and (D) incorrect.

Answer to Question 7

(D) For the wife to prevail, she will need to show that the newspaper was negligent. Although at common law defamation liability could be strict, a number of Supreme Court decisions based on the First Amendment now impose a fault requirement in cases involving public figures or matters of public concern. A defendant may not be held liable for defamation on a matter of public concern not involving a public figure unless, in addition to publishing a false story, it was at least negligent in ascertaining the truth or falsity of its facts. Here, a story about an instructor at a prestigious college falsifying her academic credentials is a matter of public concern. (C) is

incorrect because knowledge or reckless disregard is the standard applicable to public figures, and the wife does not qualify as such merely because she is married to someone who may be a public figure. (A) is incorrect because libel does not require proof of special damages; actual damages (which includes noneconomic damages) is enough. (B) is incorrect because it describes a type of invasion of privacy—public disclosure of private facts. Invasion of privacy is not relevant to a defamation action.

Answer to Question 8

(B) The aunt will recover against the seller because she relied on his statements to the niece. The elements of a prima facie case for intentional misrepresentation consist of: (i) a misrepresentation, (ii) scienter, (iii) an intent to induce plaintiff's reliance, (iv) causation (*i.e.,* actual reliance), (v) justifiable reliance, and (vi) damages. Here, the seller made a false statement knowing that he did not know whether it was true; this satisfies the scienter requirement. Regarding intent to induce reliance, statements made to one person can be the basis of an intentional misrepresentation action by another person where the defendant could reasonably foresee that that person would rely on the statement. Based on what the niece had said, the seller had reason to foresee that the niece's aunt might rely on his assertions of fire resistance in storing her antiques. Because the aunt responded to the assertions by purchasing the house and storing her antiques in the garage, she can establish causation (actual reliance). Reliance on the misrepresentation would be justified here because only where the facts are obviously false is reliance not justified. Thus, she can recover for any pecuniary damages she suffered as a result of the fire. (A) is incorrect. As long as reliance by a third party is reasonably foreseeable, the third party need not be in an agency relationship with the recipient of the misrepresentation. (C) is incorrect because the fact that the seller did not make the statements in a business or professional capacity will only preclude recovery for ***negligent*** misrepresentation. The fact that the seller knew that he did not know the truth or falsity of his statement establishes the scienter required for intentional misrepresentation. (D) is incorrect because, as stated above, the seller owed a duty to the aunt because he could reasonably foresee that she would rely on his statements to the niece.

Answer to Question 9

(B) The homeowner's motion should be granted because the homeowner was not aware that the light was not working and there is no other evidence of negligence on his part. The swimmer, a social guest, had the status of a licensee on the homeowner's property. An owner or occupier of land owes licensees a duty to warn of a dangerous condition known to the owner or occupier that creates an unreasonable risk of harm to the licensee and that the licensee is unlikely to discover. The owner has no duty to inspect for defects. Here, the only potentially dangerous condition on the premises was the pool light not working, but the homeowner was not aware of that. The swimmer has presented no other evidence of breach of duty on the homeowner's part; hence, the homeowner's motion should be granted. (A) is incorrect because the fact that the swimmer's injuries were caused by third persons does not establish that the landowner was not liable. If the landowner were aware of a dangerous condition on the property that was a cause of the injury, the fact that third persons were also a cause of the injury would not cut off his liability. (C) is incorrect because there is no evidence that the landowner failed to meet his duty to exercise reasonable care in activities on the property. The only evidence pertaining to the homeowner's duty was the pool light not working, which is a condition on the land rather than an activity. Because the homeowner was not aware of the condition, he has not been shown to have breached a duty to his guest. (D) is incorrect even though negligence of rescuers is often foreseeable. The swimmer has not established that the homeowner breached a duty, so the homeowner has no liability regardless of the conduct of the rescuers.

Answer to Question 10

(C) Because the motorist was not driving attentively, the motorist was contributorily negligent. Under traditional rules, plaintiff's contributory negligence is a complete defense to negligence; *i.e.,* it completely bars plaintiff's right to recover. Here the motorist is contributorily negligent because he was not paying attention to his driving. If he had been paying attention, the facts indicate that he would have had adequate time to either stop his car or swerve to avoid the driver's vehicle. (A) is incorrect because even if the driver alleges that his running the stop sign was unintentional, that defense would apply only for intentional torts and not to torts based on negligent conduct. (B) is incorrect. The motorist was not under any duty to purchase a car that would be able to sustain minimal damage when struck at a low speed; therefore, the first element for establishing a prima facie case of negligence is absent—the existence of a duty to conform to a specific standard of conduct to protect against an unreasonable risk of injury. (D) is also incorrect. The doctrine of last clear chance permits the plaintiff to recover despite his own contributory negligence because the defendant had the last clear chance to avoid the accident. (In effect, last clear chance is plaintiff's rebuttal to the defense of contributory negligence.) Thus, the doctrine of last clear chance would not be available to the driver as a defense.

Answer to Question 11

(B) The salesman will recover in a suit against the newspaper since the newspaper published facts about the salesman that placed him in a false light. To establish a prima facie case for invasion of privacy based on publication by defendant of facts placing plaintiff in a false light, the following elements must be proved: (i) publication of facts about plaintiff by defendant placing plaintiff in a false light in the public eye; and (ii) the "false light" must be something that would be objectionable to a reasonable person under the circumstances. The large picture of the salesman flanked by two bulky police officers implied that the salesman committed a crime because it looked like pictures that newspapers often print of alleged criminals being taken into custody. This "false light" would clearly be objectionable to a reasonable person under the circumstances. (A) is incorrect. This branch of invasion of right to privacy, intrusion upon plaintiff's affairs or seclusion, requires (i) an act of prying or intruding on the affairs or seclusion of plaintiff by defendant; (ii) the intrusion must be something that would be objectionable to a reasonable person; and (iii) the thing to which there is an intrusion or prying must be "private." Here, the photograph of the salesman was taken at the police station, which is a public place. Hence, the intrusion was not into anything of the salesman's private domain and is not actionable under this branch of invasion of privacy. (C) is incorrect. The impression that the salesman committed a crime was not dispelled by inclusion of the small explanatory caption. As a result, the caption will not serve as a valid defense. (D) is incorrect because printing the picture would probably not qualify as being in the public interest. The salesman was not a public official or public figure; his picture was printed because there was a dearth of news. His posting bond for the arrest of his son for possession of a small quantity of narcotics is not the type of information that is of general public interest.

Answer to Question 12

(D) The pedestrian will not prevail because the passenger's grabbing of the wheel is the negligent conduct that caused the pedestrian's injuries. To establish a prima facie case for negligence, the following elements must be proved: (i) the existence of a duty on the part of the defendant to conform to a specific standard of conduct for the protection of the plaintiff against an unreasonable risk of injury; (ii) breach of that duty by the defendant; (iii) the breach of the duty by defendant was the actual and proximate cause of plaintiff's injury; and (iv) damage to plaintiff's

person or property. Here, the driver's actions were an actual cause of the pedestrian's injury because, but for the driver's driving and the passenger's grabbing the steering wheel, the injury to the pedestrian would not have happened. However, the driver's actions were not a proximate cause of the injury because the passenger's grabbing of the steering wheel was a superseding intervening force. A superseding force is one that serves to break the causal connection between the initial wrongful act and the ultimate injury, and itself becomes a direct immediate cause of such injury. Thus, the first actor would be relieved of liability from the consequences of his antecedent conduct. The passenger's conduct in suddenly grabbing the steering wheel was an unforeseeable intervening force creating an unforeseeable harmful result, and thus constituted a superseding force. Consequently, the driver would be relieved of any negligence liability since the passenger's actions were the proximate cause of the accident. (A) is incorrect. A specific duty imposed by a statute may replace the more general common law duty of due care when (i) the plaintiff is within the class to be protected by the statute, (ii) the statute was designed to prevent the type of harm suffered, and (iii) the statutory standard of conduct is clearly defined. The statute probably does not apply here because it is intended to keep unsafe drivers off the streets, and there is no indication that the driver is an unsafe driver, or that any driver could have prevented the injury when the passenger grabbed the steering wheel. Even if the statutory standard were applicable, a violation means only that plaintiff will have established a conclusive presumption of duty and breach of duty. It does not, however, establish causation or damages. Here, the fact that the driver does not have a valid license is not the proximate cause of the pedestrian's injury, as discussed above. (B) is incorrect because the driver had no way of knowing that the passenger would grab the steering wheel. The driver's conduct will be measured against that of the ordinary, prudent, reasonable person who drives a vehicle. An ordinary, prudent, reasonable person would not have foreseen that one of his passengers would impulsively grab the steering wheel, and therefore there are no special safety precautions that the driver should have taken as part of his duty of care toward pedestrians. (C) is incorrect because, even if the driver had started the argument, this would not justify the passenger's grabbing of the steering wheel. In either case, the passenger's actions rather than the driver's would be considered the proximate cause of the pedestrian's injuries.

Answer to Question 13

(C) The jurisdiction has most likely abolished joint and several liability. Under joint and several liability, each tortfeasor is liable to the plaintiff for the entire damage incurred. In the absence of joint and several liability, each tortfeasor is liable for only the amount of damages that is proportional to his fault. Applied to these facts, the first defendant would be liable to the plaintiff for 60% of her damages, or $60,000. This would be offset by the plaintiff's liability for 10% of the first defendant's damages, or $20,000. This leaves the plaintiff with a net award of $40,000 from the first defendant. (A) and (B) are incorrect because if joint and several liability applied, the plaintiff would be entitled to an award of $90,000 against the first defendant (or $10,000 if the first defendant were allowed to offset his entire amount of damages—$80,000—against the plaintiff under joint and several liability). Note that the type of contribution rule is irrelevant to the plaintiff's recovery against the defendant. Contribution comes into play only after distribution of the plaintiff's award under joint and several liability rules; it allows any tortfeasor required to pay more than his share of damages to have a claim against the other jointly liable parties for the excess. (D) is incorrect because if partial comparative negligence applied, the first defendant would be able to recover nothing from the plaintiff because he was more than 50% at fault, and so the plaintiff's damage award against the first defendant would not be offset by any amount. Therefore, only under pure comparative negligence can the first defendant assert a claim against the plaintiff that would reduce the plaintiff's award to $40,000.

Answer to Question 14

(D) The rescuer will prevail against the motorist's estate because he can establish a prima facie case of negligence. One of the elements of negligence is a showing that defendant's breach of duty was the actual (cause in fact) and proximate cause of plaintiff's injury. An act or omission to act is the cause in fact of an injury when the injury would not have occurred but for the act. The motorist's accident was the actual cause of the rescuer's injury because, but for the accident, the rescuer would not have stopped to assist the motorist. The motorist's accident was also a proximate cause of the rescuer's injury. The general rule of proximate cause is that defendant is liable for all harmful results that are the normal incidents of and within the increased risk caused by his acts. This is an indirect cause case because an independent intervening force (the truck) came into motion after defendant's negligent act and combined with it to cause plaintiff's injury. Independent intervening forces are foreseeable (and thus do not cut off defendant's liability) where defendant's negligence increased the risk that these forces would cause harm to the plaintiff. Once the motorist negligently put himself in peril on the highway, he created a foreseeable risk that a rescuer would be injured in some way by the act of another motorist while the rescuer was assisting the motorist. Thus, the trucker's negligence was a foreseeable intervening force that combined with the motorist's negligence to create a foreseeable harmful result to the rescuer. The motorist's estate, therefore, is not relieved of liability by the trucker's conduct. (A) is incorrect because even if the trucker's actions caused the rescuer's injuries, they were a foreseeable risk created by the motorist's conduct and thus do not constitute a superseding intervening force that would cut off the motorist's liability to the rescuer. (B) is incorrect. The motorist owed a duty of care to the rescuer under the general rule that a rescuer is a foreseeable plaintiff as long as the rescue is not wanton. Hence, a defendant will be liable if he negligently puts himself in peril and plaintiff is injured in attempting a rescue. The fact that, at the time the motorist's car struck the bridge support, the rescuer was five miles from the bridge does not make the driver an unforeseeable plaintiff. He could still be considered a foreseeable rescuer. (C) is incorrect because the fact that the rescuer stopped to render assistance merely establishes him as a foreseeable plaintiff. The critical issue is whether the he can establish proximate cause.

Answer to Question 15

(A) As an employer, the farmer breached his duty of care owing to the student and therefore is liable for the student's injuries on a negligence theory. To establish a prima facie case for negligence, the following elements must be proved: (i) the existence of a duty on the part of defendant to conform to a specific standard of conduct for the protection of the plaintiff against an unreasonable risk of injury; (ii) breach of that duty by defendant; (iii) the breach of the duty by defendant was the actual and proximate cause of plaintiff's injury; and (iv) damage to the plaintiff's person or property. The first issue raised by these facts is whether the farmer owed a duty of care to his employee. As a general matter, no legal duty is imposed upon any person to affirmatively act for the benefit of others. However, the existence of a special relationship between the parties may create a duty. Modern cases extend the duty to employers when employees are injured in the course of employment. Thus, the farmer owed the student a duty to protect him against an unreasonable risk of injury while he was acting within the scope of his employment. The farmer breached this duty by not warning and instructing the student in how to act safely during an electrical storm. The breach of that duty was the cause in fact and proximate cause of the student's injuries. An act or omission to act is the cause in fact of an injury when the injury would not have occurred but for the act. The "but for" test applies where several acts combine to cause the injury, but none of the acts standing alone would have been sufficient. But for any of the acts, the injury would not have occurred. Thus, but for the farmer's failure to instruct the student on how to act

during an electrical storm, the student would not have been injured. The farmer's failure to instruct is also the proximate cause of the student's injuries. The general rule of proximate cause is that defendant is liable for all harmful results that are the normal incidents of and within the increased risk caused by his acts. This is an indirect cause case because an independent intervening force (the lightning) came into motion after Farmer's negligent conduct and combined with it to cause the student's injury. Independent intervening forces are foreseeable (and thus do not cut off defendant's liability) where defendant's negligence increased the risk that these forces would cause harm to the plaintiff. The farmer's negligent failure to instruct the student about the need to seek low ground during an electrical storm greatly increased the risk that the student would be struck by lightning when the storm came up. Because the lightning was foreseeable and brought about a foreseeable harmful result to the student, it was not a superseding force that would cut off the farmer's liability for the student's injuries. (B) is incorrect because the student's minority does not create a duty toward him by the farmer. The duty of care arises out of the employer/employee relationship. (C) is incorrect because, as noted above, the act of God (the lightning) would not be a superseding intervening force since it was foreseeable. Here, the farmer was negligent in not seeking to minimize the chances of the student's being struck by lightning, when the farmer knew that such danger existed and owed the student such duty as a result of his relationship (employer/employee) with the student. (D) is similarly incorrect because lightning can be foreseeable and was foreseeable here. The rain and loud claps of thunder were a clear signal that lightning might occur, and the farmer's failure to warn the student created a foreseeable risk that the lightning would strike him.

Answer to Question 16

(A) The wife's knowledge of the younger woman's religious beliefs would be most helpful in her suit. The tort of intentional infliction of emotional distress requires: (i) an act by defendant amounting to extreme and outrageous conduct; (ii) intent on the part of the defendant to cause the plaintiff to suffer severe emotional distress, or a reckless disregard that the conduct would cause emotional distress; (iii) causation; and (iv) damages—severe emotional distress. The statement in (A) is most helpful to establish reckless disregard because it shows that the defendant knew of plaintiff's peculiar susceptibility to such an accusation. (B) is incorrect because, while one of the damages in an action for battery may be for emotional suffering caused by the battery, the younger woman is suing for intentional infliction of emotional distress, which requires severe emotional distress from the outrageous nature of the conduct. (C) is not the best answer, because while evidence that it happened in front of other people may show the "outrageousness" of the conduct, an act is not outrageous just because it occurs in the presence of others. (D) is incorrect because this tort does not require proof of economic damages.

Answer to Question 17

(C) The detective will prevail in a suit for invasion of privacy since the network published facts about the detective that place him in a false light in the public eye by attributing to him actions that he did not take. To establish a prima facie case for invasion of privacy based on a publication by defendant of facts placing plaintiff in a false light, the following elements must be proved: (i) publication of facts about plaintiff by defendant placing plaintiff in a false light in the public eye; (ii) the "false light" must be something that would be objectionable to a reasonable person under the circumstances; and (iii) malice on the part of defendant where the published matter is in the public interest. A fact will be deemed to present plaintiff in a false light if it attributes to him: (i) views that he does not hold, or (ii) actions that he did not take. Several parts of the network's docudrama portray the detective's character as being involved in James Bond-type sexual escapades. Thus, they attribute to the detective actions he did not take. The general disclaimer that not every event in the show actually happened is not sufficient to dispel the false light liability. Furthermore, this false light would be objectionable to a reasonable person under the circumstances. Finally, the detective does not need to show malice because the episodes he is objecting to are not in the public interest. (A) is incorrect. To establish a prima facie case for invasion of privacy based on an appropriation of plaintiff's name, only one element need be proved: unauthorized use by defendant of plaintiff's picture or name for defendant's commercial advantage. Liability is generally limited to the use of plaintiff's name in connection with the promotion or advertisement of a product or service. The mere use of a personality's name in a television show or magazine story, even though motivated by profit, does not suffice for liability. While the detective's name was listed in the credits, there is no evidence that his name was used in connection with the promotion or advertisement of the program and therefore this particular type of invasion of right to privacy is not as applicable as a false light action. (B) is incorrect. To establish a prima facie case for invasion of privacy based on an intrusion upon the plaintiff's affairs or seclusion, the following elements must be proved: (i) act of prying or intruding upon the affairs or seclusion of the plaintiff by the defendant; (ii) the intrusion must be something that would be objectionable to a reasonable person; and (iii) the thing to which there is an intrusion or prying must be "private." This tort does not provide special protection for the seclusion of a retirement. There is nothing in the facts to suggest that the network invaded plaintiff's private affairs in creating the scenes that he is objecting to. The accurate material in the show was drawn from the detective's crimefighting activities, which are not in his private domain. Thus, this branch of the privacy tort is inapplicable. (D) is incorrect because if the detective's privacy has been invaded, it is no defense that the program as a whole was not offensive. The invasion of privacy torts do not involve a balancing of complimentary and offensive statements to determine overall whether plaintiff's privacy was invaded.

Answer to Question 18

(B) The ballplayer can recover presumed general damages because the defamation was libel and did not involve a matter of public concern. At common law, if all other elements of defamation in the form of libel have been established, plaintiff can recover damages for the general injury to his reputation without offering any proof; *i.e.,* general damages are presumed by law for all libel in most jurisdictions. Defamatory material in a radio broadcast is treated as libel by most courts. Thus, the ballplayer can recover general damages even without proof of actual injury for the defamatory broadcast. (A) is incorrect because it states the rule for slander not within one of the slander per se categories: Plaintiff must show actual pecuniary loss (*i.e.,* special damages) or else he can recover only nominal damages. (C) is incorrect. Under *Gertz v. Robert Welch, Inc.* (1974), a private figure suing on a matter of public concern not only must show that the defendant was negligent in ascertaining truth or falsity but also must prove "actual injury," *i.e.,* competent evidence of some personal or reputational damages. (Presumed damages are barred unless actual malice rather than negligence is established.) Here, however, the defamatory statement is not on a matter of public concern. Thus, the damages rules of *Gertz* do not apply and general damages are presumed according to common law. [Dun & Bradstreet, Inc. v. Greenmoss Builders, Inc. (1985)] (D) is incorrect because the ballplayer is not a public figure. The court will determine that a person is a public figure if he (i) achieves such pervasive fame or notoriety that he becomes a public figure for all purposes and contexts, or (ii) voluntarily assumes a central role in a particular public controversy. Neither situation is present in these facts; the fact that the ballplayer is the subject of a media report does not make him a public figure. Hence, he does not have to prove actual malice on the part of the broadcaster to recover damages.

Set 5 Answer Sheet

1.	Ⓐ	Ⓑ	Ⓒ	Ⓓ	19.	Ⓐ	Ⓑ	Ⓒ	Ⓓ
2.	Ⓐ	Ⓑ	Ⓒ	Ⓓ	20.	Ⓐ	Ⓑ	Ⓒ	Ⓓ
3.	Ⓐ	Ⓑ	Ⓒ	Ⓓ	21.	Ⓐ	Ⓑ	Ⓒ	Ⓓ
4.	Ⓐ	Ⓑ	Ⓒ	Ⓓ	22.	Ⓐ	Ⓑ	Ⓒ	Ⓓ
5.	Ⓐ	Ⓑ	Ⓒ	Ⓓ	23.	Ⓐ	Ⓑ	Ⓒ	Ⓓ
6.	Ⓐ	Ⓑ	Ⓒ	Ⓓ	24.	Ⓐ	Ⓑ	Ⓒ	Ⓓ
7.	Ⓐ	Ⓑ	Ⓒ	Ⓓ	25.	Ⓐ	Ⓑ	Ⓒ	Ⓓ
8.	Ⓐ	Ⓑ	Ⓒ	Ⓓ	26.	Ⓐ	Ⓑ	Ⓒ	Ⓓ
9.	Ⓐ	Ⓑ	Ⓒ	Ⓓ	27.	Ⓐ	Ⓑ	Ⓒ	Ⓓ
10.	Ⓐ	Ⓑ	Ⓒ	Ⓓ	28.	Ⓐ	Ⓑ	Ⓒ	Ⓓ
11.	Ⓐ	Ⓑ	Ⓒ	Ⓓ	29.	Ⓐ	Ⓑ	Ⓒ	Ⓓ
12.	Ⓐ	Ⓑ	Ⓒ	Ⓓ	30.	Ⓐ	Ⓑ	Ⓒ	Ⓓ
13.	Ⓐ	Ⓑ	Ⓒ	Ⓓ	31.	Ⓐ	Ⓑ	Ⓒ	Ⓓ
14.	Ⓐ	Ⓑ	Ⓒ	Ⓓ	32.	Ⓐ	Ⓑ	Ⓒ	Ⓓ
15.	Ⓐ	Ⓑ	Ⓒ	Ⓓ	33.	Ⓐ	Ⓑ	Ⓒ	Ⓓ
16.	Ⓐ	Ⓑ	Ⓒ	Ⓓ	34.	Ⓐ	Ⓑ	Ⓒ	Ⓓ
17.	Ⓐ	Ⓑ	Ⓒ	Ⓓ	35.	Ⓐ	Ⓑ	Ⓒ	Ⓓ
18.	Ⓐ	Ⓑ	Ⓒ	Ⓓ	36.	Ⓐ	Ⓑ	Ⓒ	Ⓓ

TORTS QUESTIONS - SET 5

Question 1

A pedestrian was struck and seriously injured by a car driven by an intoxicated driver. The driver had been served several alcoholic drinks by a bartender at a local bar. The pedestrian sued the bartender in a jurisdiction that does not have a dramshop act.

Is the bartender vicariously liable for the pedestrian's injuries?

(A) No, because the driver acted recklessly by driving while intoxicated.

(B) No, because there is no dramshop act in the jurisdiction to impose liability.

(C) Yes, because there is no dramshop act in the jurisdiction to limit liability.

(D) Yes, because the intoxicated driver caused the pedestrian to suffer personal injuries.

Question 2

When a crowded city bus braked suddenly, the standing passengers were thrown together, and a woman wearing very high-heeled shoes began to stumble. A man who was unacquainted with her kept her from falling by reaching his arm around her waist.

If the woman sues the man for battery, will she recover?

(A) Yes, because the man intended to put his arm around her waist.

(B) Yes, because the man touched her without her permission.

(C) No, because the man prevented her from harm.

(D) No, because his conduct was socially acceptable.

Question 3

A manufacturer of insecticides vital to the local agriculture generated very foul-smelling fumes during the operation of its plant. When the plant was built many years ago, the surrounding area was completely agricultural, but now much of the area around the plant is residential, although the plant itself is zoned for manufacturing activities. In response to complaints, the manufacturer's engineers investigated whether it would be possible to install machinery to filter and scrub the plant emissions, but determined that the project would be too costly. Residents of nearby homes brought an action for nuisance against the manufacturer.

If the manufacturer prevails, it will be because:

(A) The plant was there first, and the residents came to the nuisance.

(B) The area is zoned for commercial and manufacturing activities.

(C) The fumes from the plant do not unreasonably interfere with the residents' use and enjoyment of their property.

(D) The insecticides are vital to the local agriculture.

Question 4

The owner of a small computer consulting firm was attending the annual trade meeting of the computer industry and spoke with the owner of a second consulting firm about doing joint projects. The owner of the second firm replied by rejecting the idea immediately, stating that she believed that the first owner was incompetent. A sales representative of a computer supply firm overheard the remark. The owner of the first firm sued the owner of the second firm for defamation.

If the first owner does not prevail in this lawsuit, it will be because:

(A) It was not reasonably foreseeable that the second owner's remark would be overheard.

(B) The second owner did not know that her remark would be overheard.

(C) There was no publication.

(D) The sales representative was not a party to the conversation.

Question 5

A shopper at a grocery store slipped and fell when he stepped in some water that had seeped out from a malfunctioning freezer case. The fall caused the shopper to break an ankle. He filed suit against the store in a jurisdiction that has adopted pure comparative negligence. At trial, the shopper presented evidence of the above facts, and testified that the floor around the water appeared dirty.

To survive a motion for summary judgment by the store, what additional evidence must the shopper present?

(A) No additional evidence.

(B) He was planning to make a purchase at the store.

(C) The store employees knew that the freezer case was leaking.

(D) His attention was diverted by store displays so that he did not notice the water on the floor.

Question 6

A driver in the local racing circuit brought his customized yellow stock car to a body shop to have it repainted before the new racing season began. When the driver returned to pick up the car, he was horrified to discover that it was repainted pink instead of yellow. The owner of the body shop apologized and offered to repaint the car, but the driver refused because the first race was in two days. The driver lost a couple of endorsements because the endorsers' ads did not work with the new color. He was also subjected to ridicule at the track, but he felt better after he drove the car to victory in the first race.

If the driver sues the body shop for their treatment of his car, will he prevail?

(A) No, because he won the race with the car.

(B) No, unless he can prove that the body shop breached a duty of care owed to him.

(C) Yes, because the value of his car was reduced.

(D) Yes, because he suffered severe distress as a result of the conduct of the body shop.

Question 7

A student borrowed her roommate's car to pick up a pizza that they had ordered. On the way and without permission from the roommate, the student drove the car to a bookstore approximately two miles from the pizzeria and spent 10 minutes in the store finding and purchasing a book she needed for a class. She arrived at the pizzeria 10 minutes after the pizza was supposed to be ready but had to wait a few more minutes for it to be done. She brought it back to the car, which she had parked on the street in a marked parallel parking space, and saw to her dismay that the car had been struck by a hit-and-run driver. There were a number of dents in the back of the car, amounting to $900 in damages.

If the roommate sues the student for the damage to her car, she will recover:

(A) Nothing, because the student had to wait for the pizza even after her 10-minute detour.

(B) The value of the car before the accident, because the student used the car for unauthorized purposes.

(C) $900, because the car was under the student's control.

(D) $900, because the student used the car for unauthorized purposes.

Question 8

After their marriage, a wife and husband went for genetic counseling because of a hereditary incurable genetic disease in both of their families. When it was determined that their offspring were certain to inherit the disease, they decided not to have children of their own. The wife went to a doctor to have her fallopian tubes tied to ensure that she would not become pregnant; for religious reasons, abortion was not an option for her. The doctor did not properly perform the surgery. Tests taken after the surgery indicated that it was not successful, but the doctor failed to inform the wife of that fact. Two years later, the wife became pregnant and gave birth to a child who was afflicted with a disabling version of the genetic disease. Furthermore, the pregnancy left the wife partially disabled because of an internal condition that could not have been foreseen by her or her doctor.

The wife sues the doctor, seeking to recover the medical expenses of her pregnancy and her pain and suffering during labor, her lost future earnings because of her disability, the future costs of raising her child, and the extraordinary medical expenses to treat her child's disease.

Under current law, which element of damages is the wife least certain to recover?

(A) Medical expenses and pain and suffering for her labor.

(B) The future costs of raising the child.

(C) The additional medical expenses to treat the child's disease.

(D) Lost future earnings because of her disability.

Question 9

An article in a newspaper reported that the city's professional basketball franchise announced that financial difficulties have forced them to sell the franchise to a group of investors who will probably move the team to another state. The article stated that, according to inside sources, the main reason for the financial difficulties is that the general manager of the team has been siphoning off proceeds from ticket sales to support his gambling habits. The general manager, who is well-known in the community, brought an action against the newspaper for defamation.

If the newspaper stipulates at trial that the statement regarding the general manager is false, what additional facts does he have to prove to recover?

(A) That the newspaper was at least negligent in verifying the story.

(B) That the general manager suffered pecuniary damages from publication of the story.

(C) That the newspaper acted with actual malice in publishing the story.

(D) That the general manager suffered actual injury as a result of the story.

Question 10

A company that was the leading supplier of home water filtration systems had a network of sales promoters who were under contract for two- or three-year terms and were compensated solely by commissions earned from sales and by occasional bonuses. Veteran promoters also earned commissions by recruiting other promoters for the company. One of the company's veteran promoters was contacted by a former top sales representative for an air cleaner manufacturer who was looking for similar sales opportunities in the region. The sales rep knew that the promoter might be able to get her a position with his company, which was looking for additional promoters. At the time he met with the sales rep, the promoter's contract with the company had one more month to run. When the promoter's contract with the company expired, he announced that he was forming his own business to market a different line of water filtration systems manufactured by a competitor of the company, and that the sales rep would be in charge of his promotional network.

The company brought an action against the promoter for interference with business relations. At a preliminary hearing, the parties stipulated to the above facts and that the promoter was an independent contractor rather than an employee of the company. The promoter then filed a motion for a summary judgment in his favor.

Should the court grant the promoter's motion?

(A) Yes, because the sales rep had no business relationship with the company at the time the promoter's alleged interference occurred.

(B) Yes, because the promoter was an independent contractor rather than an employee of the company.

(C) No, because the jury could find that the means the promoter used to obtain the sales rep were not privileged.

(D) No, because the jury could find that the promoter breached his contract with the company by meeting with the sales rep.

Question 11

A motorcycle enthusiast who lived in a state wilderness area with rugged terrain purchased a motorcycle that was promoted as an all-terrain motorcycle in advertisements showing it going over very rugged terrain. However, the shock absorbers that were sold with the motorcycle as standard equipment were not designed for rough terrain and would not provide a safe ride under these conditions. The owner's manual that came with the motorcycle stated that it should not be driven over rough terrain without equipping it with heavy-duty shock absorbers designed for that purpose. The next day, the purchaser took his motorcycle to the wilderness area and rode onto a trail. He crested a hill and landed hard, causing his shock absorbers to fail. The purchaser lost control and crashed, suffering serious and permanent injuries.

The purchaser brought a lawsuit against the motorcycle's manufacturer in a jurisdiction that retains traditional contributory negligence. At trial, he presented evidence of the advertisements and the fact that the shock absorbers installed on the motorcycle were dangerously inadequate under off-road conditions. The manufacturer presented evidence that the purchaser had received the owner's manual with the warning about the shock absorbers and had disobeyed a posted state statute in the wilderness area forbidding motorized vehicles from leaving the roadway. At the close of the evidence, both parties move for a directed verdict.

The court should:

(A) Deny both motions, because the jury could determine that the purchaser's use of the motorcycle over rough terrain was foreseeable.

(B) Grant the manufacturer's motion, because the owner's manual adequately warned of the unsuitability of the shock absorbers for off-road use.

(C) Grant the manufacturer's motion, because the purchaser was in violation of the law when he drove off of the road.

(D) Grant the purchaser's motion, because the shock absorbers were dangerously inadequate for the off-road conditions shown in the motorcycle's advertisements.

Question 12

A woman loaned her car to a friend to use while his car was in the shop for repairs. When the friend's car was repaired, he let his neighbor borrow the woman's car instead of returning it to the woman. The neighbor took the woman's car for several days on a 900-mile trip. While the neighbor was gone on the trip, the woman discovered that the friend had gotten his car repaired and asked him for her car back. She was furious when he told her that he had lent the car to his neighbor. The neighbor eventually returned the car to the friend, who then attempted to return the car to the woman. The woman refused to accept the car even though it was undamaged, and sued the friend for conversion of the car.

Which of the following would be the most likely result of this suit?

(A) The woman will not recover for conversion.

(B) The woman cannot recover for conversion, but can recover for trespass to chattel.

(C) The woman will recover the rental value of the car for the 900-mile trip.

(D) The woman will recover the fair market value of the car from the friend.

Question 13

A store security guard who reasonably but mistakenly thought that a shopper had tried to steal a scarf directed her to accompany him to the manager's office, which had an interior window overlooking the sales floor. Because the blinds were up on the window, the occupants of the office could be seen from the sales floor. After the security guard described what he had seen, the manager began to berate her for trying to steal the scarf and threatened to prosecute her as a shoplifter. However, the manager had neglected to make sure that the public address system that he used to announce specials was turned off, and his statements were broadcast to everyone in the store.

In an action against the store for defamation, the shopper will:

(A) Not recover, because the manager was speaking directly to the shopper.

(B) Not recover, because the manager did not intend for others to hear his statements.

(C) Recover, because the manager should have checked that the public address system was not on.

(D) Recover, because the manager's belief that the shopper had stolen the scarf was reasonable based on the security guard's information.

Question 14

A hockey player who was playing in the final game of the season before a hostile crowd in the opponent's packed stadium had an opportunity to get his team into the playoffs, but he missed a shot into an open net as the horn sounded, ending the game. As the crowd cheered and jeered, the puck bounced back to him and he shot it in anger toward the stands. A fan who had been looking the other way turned back toward the rink just in time to be struck in the face by the puck. He suffered a broken nose and a severe gash under his eye. After the game, the league commissioner fined the player for violating league rules by intentionally directing the puck out of the playing area.

If the fan sues the player for battery, will the fan likely prevail?

(A) No, because by attending a hockey game, the fan assumed the risk of pucks being shot into the stands.

(B) No, because the player did not have the intent to strike the fan with the puck.

(C) Yes, because the player knew that it was substantially certain that a fan would be hit by the puck.

(D) Yes, because the player violated league rules by intentionally shooting the puck out of the playing area.

Question 15

At the end of the season, the owner of a private beach stacked up his rental canoes onto a trailer, and arranged for them to be moved the next day into a storage shed for the winter. That evening, two nine-year-old boys came onto the owner's property even though they knew that the lake was closed to the public for the season. Both of them had used the canoes (with an adult) several times during the past summer. They unhooked one of the canoes from the rack, lifted it down, and pushed it into the water. Although the life vests were sitting in an open bin nearby, neither boy put one on. When they

were out in the middle of the lake with the canoe, they tried to switch seats and caused the canoe to capsize. They both tried to swim to shore. One was able to make it, but unfortunately the other boy could not make it and he drowned. Had he been wearing a life vest, he would have survived. The boy's parents bring a wrongful death action against the beach owner.

If the beach owner prevails, it will be because:

(A) Children of the boy's age, intelligence, and education would not likely take the canoe out without a life vest.

(B) The owner took precautions to make the canoes inaccessible.

(C) The boy appreciated the risk of taking the canoe out onto the lake without a life vest.

(D) The boy was not lured onto the owner's property by the canoes.

Question 16

A homeowner born on the fourth of July celebrated his birthday in his backyard with an assortment of fireworks and skyrockets, despite a severe drought and watering ban that left the grass extremely dry. One of the fireworks landed in a pile of dry grass clippings behind his garage, but the homeowner neglected to check whether it was extinguished. The grass clippings ignited, and the fire eventually spread to the rear wall of the garage. By the time the homeowner discovered the fire and called the fire department, the flames were reaching as high as the vacant apartment on the second floor of the garage. The first firefighter to arrive rushed with a hose to the back of the garage. As he went up the outside stairs leading to the back door of the apartment, one of the steps broke, causing him to fall to the ground and break his leg. Unbeknownst to the homeowner, the wood on the underside of the step had rotted away.

In a suit by the firefighter against the homeowner, the firefighter will:

(A) Prevail, because the homeowner was negligent in allowing the fire to start.

(B) Prevail, because it was foreseeable that the homeowner's shooting off the fireworks would necessitate the assistance of the fire department.

(C) Not prevail, unless the jury determines that the homeowner could have discovered the condition of the step with a reasonable inspection.

(D) Not prevail, because a firefighter cannot recover for negligent conduct of another that causes him to be injured while performing his duties.

Question 17

A mother instructed her son to bring their lawn mower to a local mechanic when it began running poorly. The mechanic replaced some parts and reassembled the mower. When the son started it up the next day in the backyard, a metal bracket that the mechanic had negligently installed flew off, striking the son in his eye and injuring him. The mother was watching her son from the back porch and saw the piece of metal strike him. She became greatly distressed as a result. She sued the mechanic for negligent infliction of emotional distress in a jurisdiction in which the modern "foreseeability" approach for bystander recovery has been adopted. After the mother established the facts above and rested her case, the mechanic moved for a directed verdict.

Should the court grant the motion?

(A) Yes, because the mother was too far away from the accident to be a foreseeable plaintiff.

(B) Yes, because the mother did not introduce evidence that she suffered physical injury.

(C) No, because the jury could find that severe distress to the mother was a foreseeable result of the mechanic's negligence.

(D) No, because the plaintiff was the victim's mother.

Question 18

A dentist filling a child's cavities used a newly developed local anesthetic that was more effective than Novocain. However, it carried a 1% risk of causing a serious seizure when administered to children, which the dentist did not mention to the child's mother. The child's dental work was completed without any problem, but the mother looked up the anesthetic on the Internet and learned about the risk. She complained to the dentist that she would not have consented to use of the anesthetic had she known of the risk, but the dentist argued that using the new anesthetic was justified in the child's case because otherwise he would not have been willing to sit still for the dental work.

Does the mother have a cause of action on behalf of the child against the dentist?

(A) Yes, because a reasonable person would have considered information about the risk important.

(B) Yes, because the mother would not have consented to the use of the anesthetic if she had known of the risk of seizure.

(C) No, because the dentist used his best judgment in deciding that the benefits of using the anesthetic outweighed the risk.

(D) No, because the child suffered no harm from use of the anesthetic.

Question 19

The governor of an arid western state owned a vacation home and permitted his son to have a party there. At the end of the night the son failed to properly extinguish a bonfire that he and his friends had built, and within a few hours, wind-blown cinders had spread the fire to the trees east of the lodge. At the same time several miles away, a worker at a lumber mill was making emergency repairs to a pipe running between two mill buildings. He did not notice some of the sparks from his welding torch land in a pile of dried lumber and catch fire, and he failed to check the area after he was finished. By the time the fire was noticed by another employee, it was out of control. The wind blew both fires toward a landowner's hunting lodge. They merged a mile away and shortly thereafter totally consumed the lodge. Either fire alone would have destroyed the lodge as well.

For political reasons, the landowner did not bring a lawsuit against the governor or his son. He did, however, file a lawsuit against the lumber mill, alleging that its employee's negligence caused the destruction of his lodge. The state in which the landowner is located follows the traditional rules regarding joint tortfeasors.

Can the landowner recover from the lumber mill?

(A) No, because the landowner's lodge would have been destroyed regardless of the conduct of the lumber mill's employee.

(B) No, because the damage is indivisible and cannot be apportioned unless the landowner adds the other tortfeasor to the lawsuit.

(C) Yes, because the negligence of the lumber mill's employee was a cause of the landowner's injury.

(D) Yes, but the landowner can recover only 50% of his damages from the lumber mill.

Question 20

A trainer of homing pigeons brought several of them to a park that he often used for training. He had trained this group of pigeons carefully and was confident that they would readily find their way home. When they were released, one of the pigeons inexplicably turned in the opposite direction from home. Several blocks away at the other end of the park, it collided with a radio-controlled model airplane that its owner had just purchased and was trying out for the first time. The collision sent the airplane out of control; it dipped low across a highway and was struck and run over by a truck.

The airplane owner sued the pigeon trainer for the destruction of his airplane. The parties stipulated to the above facts and the airplane owner presented evidence of his damages. The trainer then moved for a directed verdict.

Should it be granted?

(A) No, because the trainer's pigeon caused the destruction of the airplane.

(B) No, because the jury could find negligence on the trainer's part under the doctrine of res ipsa loquitur.

(C) Yes, because the truck, rather than the pigeon, was the direct cause of the airplane's destruction.

(D) Yes, because the trainer took reasonable care in training his pigeons.

Question 21

At the request of local police, airport security officials made random searches of passenger luggage for contraband as it was being sent to the baggage claim area, although they did not have legal authority to search bags without a warrant. The searches were conducted so that there was no delay in the luggage being released to those claiming their bags. A traveler went to the baggage claim area but his luggage, which contained a number of valuables but no contraband, did not appear. It had been selected for a search but the X-ray machine had malfunctioned and security officers were having difficulty getting it unlocked to search it by hand. When the traveler inquired about the luggage, he was told that it was being inspected and that he would have to remain in the area if he wanted to claim it when it was released, and that its return could not be guaranteed if he was not around when it was released. About 30 minutes later, the luggage was returned to the traveler with an apology for the delay. The delay caused the traveler to miss his train to the city, so he had to pay for cab fare.

Assuming there are no issues of governmental immunity, can the traveler bring an action against the airport security officials for false imprisonment?

(A) Yes, because the traveler suffered harm as a result of the delay in releasing his luggage.

(B) Yes, because the traveler reasonably believed that he would not get his luggage back if he left the airport.

(C) No, because the traveler was not restrained from leaving the airport.

(D) No, because the delay in releasing the luggage was not done for the purpose of restraining the traveler.

Question 22

A patient troubled by an irritating skin rash consulted a dermatologist for treatment. The dermatologist diagnosed the rash as a genetic condition that had no cure and would ultimately spread and lead to disfigurement. The patient was shocked and upset by the diagnosis. On the advice of her family, a week later the patient consulted another doctor. That doctor immediately diagnosed the skin rash as a common bacterial infection and prescribed an ointment that cleared up the condition in a few days. Because the doctor was a friend of the family, the patient was not charged for that visit.

Can the patient recover from the dermatologist for the emotional distress caused by his erroneous diagnosis?

(A) No, because the dermatologist's conduct did not create a foreseeable risk of physical injury to the patient.

(B) Yes, because the misdiagnosis by the dermatologist caused the patient actual harm.

(C) No, because the patient did not have to pay for the second doctor visit.

(D) Yes, if the patient's distress caused her some physical injury.

Question 23

A wife who maintained a joint checking account with her husband was surprised by an alert from her bank that their account was overdrawn. When she called the bank for an explanation, the bank representative told her that the transaction records showed a large amount of funds withdrawn from the account through a debit card for local escort services, which according to media reports were being investigated by the authorities for prostitution offenses. The wife told the bank representative that the bank must have made a mistake, but he insisted that the records were accurate. After the call, the wife confirmed that her debit card was in her purse and that her husband's was in his wallet, and then accused her husband of infidelity. He denied being responsible for the charges and claimed that the bank must have made an error. Because the bank had just closed for a holiday weekend, the husband endured a couple of days of strained relations with his wife before he could go to the bank and have the transaction records reviewed. On further review, the bank discovered that the charges were erroneous and should have been charged to another account.

Can the husband recover damages from the bank for defamation?

(A) No, because the bank representative made no defamatory statement about the husband.

(B) No, because the bank representative made the statements for the wife's benefit.

(C) Yes, if the husband can show pecuniary harm to him from the bank representative's statements.

(D) Yes, because the bank representative's statements constituted slander per se.

Question 24

A plumber working for a company providing plumbing services to commercial and industrial establishments was required to be "on call" for emergency plumbing services 24 hours a day, and was required to drive his company van home each night so he would have all of his tools and equipment at hand for any calls. However, he was not permitted to use the company van for personal errands. On his way home one afternoon, he took a detour toward a supermarket a few blocks away to pick up some items for dinner. While entering the supermarket parking lot, he drove negligently and struck a pedestrian, seriously injuring him. The pedestrian filed suit against the plumber's company in a jurisdiction that maintains traditional common law rules regarding contribution and indemnity, and the jury awarded him $100,000 in damages, which the company paid.

If the company sues the plumber to recoup its loss in the lawsuit, which party will prevail?

(A) The company can recover 100% of the judgment as an indemnity, because the plumber was negligent, not the company.

(B) The company will prevail, because the company had a rule against using company vehicles for personal errands.

(C) The company will not prevail, because the company has already been found liable under principles of vicarious liability in the lawsuit by the pedestrian.

(D) The company will not prevail, because the company required the plumber to be "on call" 24 hours a day.

Question 25

An impatient driver who was fed up with jaywalking pedestrians drove straight at one of them, leaning on the horn and intending to make her jump. She did not hear him or change her pace, however, because her music player was turned to full volume. A bystander on the curb rushed out to pull her to safety. She tripped as she was being pulled to the curb, fracturing her kneecap.

If the pedestrian sues the driver for assault, the likely result will be:

(A) The driver wins, because the pedestrian did not know at the time that she was in danger from the driver.

(B) The driver wins, because he did not intend for the pedestrian to be injured by his conduct.

(C) The pedestrian wins, because the driver intended to create in her an apprehension of immediate harmful contact.

(D) The pedestrian wins, because the driver's conduct was a substantial factor in causing her injury.

Question 26

A 13-year-old boy who lived on a farm with his parents in a rural area had learned to drive the family's tractor when he was 11. A state statute permitted persons without a driver's license to operate farm vehicles on public roads for short distances. One morning the boy took the tractor onto a public road to reach one of the outlying fields a few hundred yards away. As he neared the field he was distracted by a girl riding by on a bicycle, and cut in front of a milk delivery truck that was starting to pass him. The truck swerved off the road, injuring the driver.

If the driver sues the boy to recover damages for his injuries, which of the following statements is most correct regarding the standard of care to be applied?

(A) The state statute replaces the general common law standard of care with a statutory standard.

(B) The trier of fact should take into account the boy's experience at driving a tractor when considering the applicable standard of care.

(C) Persons 13 years of age or older are held to the same standard as adults.

(D) An adult standard of care will not be applied because it is common in that region for children of that age to be operating tractors.

Question 27

The owner of a small fleet of taxicabs had his cabs serviced by a national chain of auto service centers. One of his cabs went through a stop sign when its brakes failed without warning. The ensuing collision seriously injured the passenger. An investigation revealed that brake repairs had been made on the cab a week before, but the service center's mechanic had used the wrong parts and had made numerous errors in reassembling the brakes.

If the passenger sues the cab company owner for her injuries:

(A) The passenger should prevail, unless the jury determines that the owner exercised a high degree of care in selecting the service center for maintenance of his cabs.

(B) The passenger should prevail, because the owner breached his duty to her to provide a safe vehicle in which to ride.

(C) The owner should prevail, because he had no reason to know that the service center's mechanic would be negligent.

(D) The owner should prevail, because he is not vicariously liable for the negligence of an independent contractor.

Question 28

A dog owner lived next door to a day care center. Because he had a large yard and there were no applicable zoning restrictions, he installed a kennel and began training attack dogs to sell to businesses. As soon as he opened the business and posted signs in front advertising the exceptional ferocity of the dogs, some parents who had children enrolled in the day care center became alarmed at the prospect of the dogs right next to the yard where the children played, especially since the children could see the training area where the dogs were taught to attack people. Within a few months of the dogs' arrival next door, the owner of the day care lost 10% of her enrollment.

If the day care owner brings a nuisance action against the dog owner, what will be the most critical factual issue that the trier of fact must resolve to determine who should prevail?

(A) Whether the day care owner suffered other damages in addition to her economic losses.

(B) Whether the day care owner's use of her property makes her business abnormally sensitive to the presence of the dogs.

(C) Whether the dog owner conducted his business with reasonable care.

(D) Whether the dog owner was apprised of the day care owner's concerns and did nothing to alleviate them.

Question 29

An investor who owned several thriving shopping malls was negotiating to purchase a local mall from the company that currently owned it. A staff attorney for the state transportation department who shopped at the mall regularly learned of the negotiations and contacted the investor. The mall had deteriorated noticeably during the time the current company had owned it and the attorney believed that new ownership would revitalize the mall considerably. Although the attorney had no information to support this, she told the investor that the state was currently planning to construct a new interchange for the turnpike only three blocks from the mall. The investor went ahead with the purchase, believing that the new interchange would boost sales. In fact, no interchange was being considered by the state at that time, and nothing that the investor did after he purchased the mall could stem the decline in sales. He ended up selling the property at a substantial loss several years after the purchase.

Does the investor have a cause of action against the attorney for his losses?

(A) Yes, for negligent misrepresentation, because the owner made a business transaction in reliance on the attorney's statements.

(B) Yes, for intentional misrepresentation, because the attorney was aware that she did not know whether the state was planning an interchange.

(C) No, because the attorney's statement pertained to a future event that may not be justifiably relied upon.

(D) No, because the attorney made her statement to the owner gratuitously.

Question 30

A nervous man was persuaded by his girlfriend to go with her to a haunted house. He saw the signs in front of the haunted house warning that this attraction has live "monsters" who will be trying to scare people and is not for the faint of heart, and he also noticed the same warning printed on the tickets. He paid for his ticket and reluctantly went into the darkened house with his girlfriend. In the first room, an actor dressed as a large monster came at them with a shriek, and the man dove through one of the plate glass windows to the outside, severely lacerating his arms and face in the process.

If the man brings an action against the actor in a jurisdiction that has adopted a "pure" comparative negligence statute, will he recover?

(A) No, because the man expressly assumed the risk of injury.

(B) No, unless the jury determines that the actor was negligent in trying to scare the man.

(C) Yes, because the actor intended to cause apprehension on the part of man.

(D) Yes, but the man's recovery will be reduced by a certain percentage if the trier of fact determines that he was also at fault.

Question 31

The owner and manager of a large office building contracted its elevator maintenance to an

elevator repair company that did not have a good reputation for safety. One of its employees incorrectly set a switch while repairing an elevator. As a result, the elevator dropped suddenly when an office worker in the building used it the next day.

The worker sued the elevator company in a jurisdiction that has adopted comparative contribution rules but has retained joint and several liability. The trier of fact determined that the elevator company was 70% at fault and the building owner was 30% at fault in causing the worker's damages. After the worker had obtained a full recovery of his damages from the elevator company, the company sued the building owner to obtain reimbursement for the damages it paid to worker.

The company should recover from the building owner:

(A) All of the damages through indemnity because the building owner owed a nondelegable duty to occupants of its building.

(B) None of the damages because the company was more at fault than the building owner for the worker's injury.

(C) 30% of the total damages because the building owner is jointly liable for the injury to the worker.

(D) 50% of the total damages because joint tortfeasors are liable for contribution in equal shares.

Question 32

A landowner operated a honey farm on her property adjacent to a busy state highway. The landowner had numerous hives for her honeybees that she carefully maintained and operated in compliance with all appropriate regulations. A motorist was driving his sports car on the highway at a high rate of speed after a rain shower when he lost control on the wet pavement. His car crossed in front of a motorcyclist who was going in the opposite direction, causing the motorcyclist to crash into a ditch on the side of the road. The motorist's car continued off the road onto the landowner's property and smashed into one of the beehives, driving an angry swarm of bees out of the hive. The motorcyclist, who suffered only a few bruises when his motorcycle crashed, saw the swarm of bees heading toward him and started to run across the road to get away from them. He stumbled and was struck by a truck, causing him to suffer several broken bones and serious internal injuries.

Can the motorcyclist recover any damages from the landowner?

(A) Yes, because the landowner is strictly liable for injury caused by the honeybees.

(B) Yes, because the motorcyclist was a traveler on a public road.

(C) No, because the honeybees did not directly inflict injury on the motorcyclist.

(D) No, because the landowner exercised due care in her operation of the beehives.

Question 33

A hiker in an isolated area encountered a cross-country skier who had broken her leg. The hiker created a makeshift sled and began pulling the skier to the nearest road. As the hiker was pulling her across the ice of a lake, the ice gave way and they went into the water. The hiker was unable to get out of the water and drowned. The skier was able to pull herself to shore and eventually was rescued. However, she suffered severe hypothermia and lost some of her toes to frostbite as a result of being in the water.

Does the skier have a cause of action for damages against the hiker's estate?

(A) No, because the hiker had no duty to come to the skier's aid.

(B) No, because the hiker did not survive the accident.

(C) No, unless the hiker acted negligently in attempting to cross the ice.

(D) No, unless the hiker acted with gross negligence in his attempt to cross the ice.

Question 34

A boater taking his new powerboat out on a large lake ran out of gas because of a defective seal in the gas tank. The defect was not discoverable by an ordinary inspection. His frantic signaling alerted the captain of a sightseeing boat passing by. The captain pulled up alongside to assist and attempted to restart the boat. A spark ignited a pool of gas that had leaked from the gas tank and collected in the lower part of the boat, causing an explosion and fire. The captain was severely burned and died from his injuries. The captain's estate brought a wrongful death action based on strict liability against the powerboat dealer and the manufacturer. Evidence at trial established that the dealer had sold the manufacturer's boats for years without any problems reported by customers.

Can the captain's estate recover any damages from the dealer?

(A) Yes, unless the jury finds that the boater was negligent in failing to investigate where the gas had gone.

(B) Yes, because harm to someone in the captain's position was a foreseeable result of the gas leak.

(C) No, because the dealer had no reason to anticipate that the manufacturer assembled the gas tank improperly.

(D) No, because the captain did not have a sufficient relationship to the boater to make the dealer liable for the boater's death.

Question 35

A swimmer went to a privately owned lake resort whose owner charged a fee for admission. The beach had a roped-in swimming area and large signs directing swimmers not to swim anywhere but within the ropes. The lifeguards regularly enforced this rule. The resort also rented canoes and rowboats to its patrons, who could take them anywhere on the lake. The swimmer and two of his friends had rented a canoe and started to paddle out toward the other side of the lake when the swimmer saw a volleyball game starting on the beach that he wanted to join. He left his friends in the canoe and started swimming to shore. He was only a few yards outside of the roped-in swimming area when he started, but he angled away from the swimming area toward the area of the beach where the volleyball net was set up. Although the lifeguard on duty saw him, she did not warn him to return to the swimming area. When the depth of the water was about four feet, he put his foot down and was severely cut by the jagged edge of a rusted metal stake protruding a few inches out of the bottom of the lake. The swimmer had not seen the stake even though the water was clear and it was visible if he had looked down.

If the swimmer sues the resort for his injury, he will:

(A) Not recover, because the stake could have been seen by the swimmer.

(B) Not recover, because he was swimming outside of the roped-in area.

(C) Recover, because the lifeguard on duty saw him and did not warn him to return to the swimming area.

(D) Recover, because he is a public invitee of the resort.

Question 36

A golfer and her instructor were playing golf in a foursome when the golfer became very annoyed with critical comments made by the instructor. To show the other golfers in the group how annoyed she was with her instructor, the golfer stood a few yards behind him while the instructor was teeing off and swung a club at him. The instructor, who was focusing on his shot, was not within range of the club but unfortunately the club slipped out of the golfer's hands and struck the instructor in the head, injuring him.

If the instructor brings a battery action against the golfer, will he recover?

(A) Yes, because the golfer acted intentionally and caused harmful contact to her instructor.

(B) Yes, because the golfer intended to cause the instructor reasonable apprehension of imminent harmful contact.

(C) No, because the golfer did not intend to cause harmful or offensive contact.

(D) No, unless the golfer acted unreasonably in swinging the club at her instructor.

TORTS ANSWERS - SET 5

Answer to Question 1

(B) Because the jurisdiction does not have a dramshop statute, the bartender will not be liable for the injuries caused to the pedestrian by the intoxicated driver. At common law, no liability was imposed on vendors of intoxicating beverages for injuries resulting from the vendee's intoxication, whether the injuries were sustained by the vendee or by a third person as a result of the vendee's conduct. Many states, in order to avoid this common law rule, have enacted "dramshop acts." Such acts create a cause of action in favor of any third person injured by the intoxicated vendee. Without a dramshop act, the bartender will not be vicariously liable. (A) is incorrect because it implies that the bartender would be vicariously liable if the driver was not reckless. Without a dramshop act, however, there can be no vicarious liability imposed on the bartender regardless of whether the driver's actions are characterized as reckless or simply negligent. (C) is incorrect because a dramshop act exists to ***impose*** liability on, rather than ***limit*** liability of, a tavernkeeper. (D) is incorrect. While several courts have imposed liability on tavernkeepers even in the absence of a dramshop act, this liability is based on ordinary negligence principles (the foreseeable risk of serving a minor or obviously intoxicated adult) rather than vicarious liability. The question here is attempting to establish liability based on vicarious liability principles rather than negligence principles. Thus, without a dramshop act, the bartender cannot be vicariously liable for any personal injuries caused by the driver.

Answer to Question 2

(D) The woman will not recover in a suit for battery because the man's contact did not constitute a harmful or offensive contact. In order to establish a prima facie case for battery, the following elements must be proved: (i) an act by the defendant that brings about harmful or offensive contact to the plaintiff's person; (ii) intent on the part of the defendant to bring about harmful or offensive contact to the plaintiff's person; and (iii) causation. Judged by this standard, the man's conduct in trying to keep the woman from falling in a crowded bus would not be harmful or offensive. Contact is deemed "offensive" if the plaintiff has not expressly or impliedly consented to it. Consent may be implied from custom, conduct, or words, or by law. Under these facts the consent would be inferred as a matter of usage or custom. A person is presumed to consent to the ordinary contacts of daily life, which would include contact resulting from assistance to a fellow passenger in a crowded bus. (A) and (B) are incorrect. Even though the man intended to put his arm around the woman's waist and touched the woman without her permission, the touching was not harmful or offensive and therefore the man cannot be deemed to have committed a battery. (C) is incorrect. The fact that the man prevented her injury is not the determining factor for him to prevail; rather, it is that he acted with implied consent.

Answer to Question 3

(C) If the manufacturer prevails, it will be because the fumes from the plant do not constitute an unreasonable interference with the residents' use and enjoyment of their property. Private nuisance is a substantial, unreasonable interference with another private individual's use or enjoyment of his property. A substantial interference is one that is offensive, inconvenient, or annoying to an average person in the community. For an interference to be characterized as unreasonable, the severity of the inflicted injury must outweigh the utility of the defendant's conduct. In balancing these respective interests, courts take into account that every person is entitled to use his own land in a reasonable way, considering the neighborhood, the values of the respective properties,

the cost to the defendant to eliminate the condition complained of, and the social benefits from allowing the condition to continue. Here, the interference is substantial because the horrible smells are offensive and annoying to average residents who do not appear to be hypersensitive. However, if the fumes are deemed not to constitute an unreasonable interference with the residents' use and enjoyment of their property, the requirements for establishing a private nuisance have not been satisfied and the manufacturer will prevail. (A) is incorrect. The mere fact that an activity creating a nuisance existed before the plaintiff came within its scope is ordinarily not a defense. The prevailing rule is that, in the absence of a prescriptive right, the defendant may not condemn surrounding premises to endure the nuisance; *i.e.,* the purchaser is entitled to reasonable use or enjoyment of his land to the same extent as any other owner as long as he buys in good faith and not for the sole purpose of a harassing lawsuit. (B) is incorrect. Conduct consistent with what a zoning ordinance or other legislative license permits is highly persuasive, but not necessarily conclusive proof that the use was not a nuisance. Thus, even though the area is zoned for commercial and manufacturing activities, courts will still balance the hardships to determine if injunctive relief should issue. (D) is incorrect because the fact that the insecticides are vital to the local agriculture is just one factor among several that the courts must weigh in determining whether a defendant's conduct is unreasonable. (C) is a better choice because it states the legal standard that will enable the manufacturer to avoid liability.

Answer to Question 4

(A) If the plaintiff does not prevail, it will be because it was not reasonably foreseeable that the defendant's remark would be overheard, and therefore the fault requirement for the publication element would not be satisfied. To establish a prima facie case for defamation, the following elements must be proved: (i) defamatory language on the part of the defendant; (ii) the defamatory language must be "of or concerning" the plaintiff (*i.e.,* it must identify the plaintiff to a reasonable reader, listener, or viewer); (iii) publication of the defamatory language by the defendant to a third person; and (iv) damage to the reputation of the plaintiff. The second owner's statement constitutes defamatory language because it adversely affects the first owner's reputation by attacking his competency. The publication requirement is satisfied when there is a communication to a third person who understands it. However, the communication to the third person must be made either intentionally or negligently; if it was not reasonably foreseeable that the defamatory statement would be overheard by the sales representative, the fault requirement for the publication element is not satisfied. (B) is incorrect. The plaintiff could prevail even if the defendant did not know that her remark would be overheard as long as it was reasonably foreseeable that it could be overheard. (C) is incorrect because there in fact was a publication, *i.e.,* there was a communication, albeit not intentionally made, to the sales representative, who would reasonably have understood it to be defamatory. (D) is incorrect because there is no requirement that the third party be a party to the conversation—the third party need only be a reader, listener, or viewer.

Answer to Question 5

(A) The shopper's lawsuit will survive a motion for summary judgment by the store without any additional evidence. Under the facts here, the shopper was an invitee as to the store because he came onto the premises for a purpose connected with the store's business. The store therefore owed him the duty to warn of nonobvious dangerous conditions ***and*** to make reasonable inspections to discover dangerous conditions and make them safe. The shopper's testimony that the floor around the water appeared dirty suggests that the floor had not been swept or mopped for some time. This is enough evidence to allow the jury to decide whether the store employees failed to reasonably inspect or make safe an area in which its invitees would walk, which would breach its duty to the shopper. (B) is incorrect because the shopper need not show that he planned to make a purchase to have the status of an invitee. Even if he came just to return an item or browse the aisles and compare prices, he qualifies as an invitee. (C) is incorrect because the store could be liable even if its employees did not know that water was leaking onto the floor. Because the shopper was an invitee, the store owed a duty to make reasonable inspections to discover unsafe conditions. (D) is incorrect because the shopper need not establish his due care here. Even if the shopper was not distracted by displays and should have seen the water had he been watching where he was walking, he can still recover some damages because the jurisdiction has adopted "pure" comparative negligence, which allows recovery against a negligent defendant no matter how great plaintiff's negligence is. It will be an issue for the jury to determine whether and to what extend the shopper was at fault.

Answer to Question 6

(C) The driver can recover for trespass to chattels because he can show that the value of his car has been reduced as a result of the conduct of the body shop. Trespass to chattels requires (i) an act of defendant that interferes with plaintiff's right of possession in the chattel, (ii) intent to perform the act bringing about the interference with plaintiff's right of possession, (iii) causation, and (iv) damages. The act of interference may be either dispossession of or damage to the chattel. Here, the body shop employees interfered with the driver's possession of his car by painting it contrary to his instructions, and they intended to do the act (painting) that caused the interference. The driver suffered damage because that conduct reduced the value of his car for advertising purposes. Hence, the driver will be able to satisfy the prima facie case for trespass to chattels. (A) is wrong because the fact that the driver won the race with the car does not establish absence of actual damages. Any loss in value of the chattels will suffice. (B) is wrong because it is not necessary for the driver to show negligence on the part of the body shop to recover. The driver can recover damages for trespass to chattels without proof of breach of duty. (D) is wrong because emotional distress alone is not sufficient to satisfy the actual damages requirement for the tort of trespass to chattels, and the facts do not establish the requisite extreme and outrageous conduct for an intentional infliction of distress action.

Answer to Question 7

(A) Because the student had to wait for the pizza even after her detour, she is not liable because any tortious conduct on her part did not cause the damage to the car, as explained in the discussion for the wrong answer choices. (B) is wrong because the student is not liable for conversion. Conversion requires an act by defendant interfering with plaintiff's right of possession that is serious enough to require defendant to pay the full value of the chattel. In this case, the student's unauthorized use of the car was not significant enough to constitute a serious interference with the roommate's right to possession; it was a short detour that did not prolong the use of the car beyond the time period for which it was originally lent. (C) is wrong because it appears to impose liability on a bailee in the absence of fault. The roommate's loan of her car to the student created a bailment situation. It was a bailment for the mutual benefit of the bailor and bailee, because the pizza was for both of them, and therefore the bailee is only required to exercise ordinary due care, and there is no evidence of negligence here. (D) is wrong. It suggests liability for trespass to chattels, because the appropriate measure of damages for this tort would be the actual amount of the damage, and the interference with the roommate's right to possession does not need to be as serious as for conversion. However, no actual damages flowed from the student's detour, even assuming that it exceeded the use to which the roommate had consented.

The $900 worth of damage occurred while the student was using the car for the purpose for which it had been lent. Hence, a trespass to chattels action would not lie for this damage.

Answer to Question 8

(B) The element of damages that the wife is least certain to recover is the future costs of raising her child. The wife is suing the doctor for "wrongful pregnancy," which is a recognized basis for a negligence action in most states. The doctor owed a duty to the wife to properly perform the contraceptive procedure. He breached that duty by improperly performing it and failing to inform her that it was ineffective. This breach of duty was the actual and proximate cause of the wife's pregnancy because it would not have happened but for the doctor's negligence, and it was foreseeable that she would become pregnant after being led to believe that the surgery was successful. While the wife certainly suffered damages as a result of the doctor's breach of duty, completing the prima facie case, the law is unsettled as to the extent of damages recoverable, particularly over whether parents can recover future child-rearing expenses for the child. Some permit recovery of these expenses but offset them against the benefits of raising a child. Other courts deny recovery, reasoning that the intangible benefits of raising a child cannot be reduced to a monetary figure. Hence, the wife is least certain to recover future child-rearing expenses. In contrast, most courts do permit recovery of the additional expenses of treating the child's disease (choice (C)). These expenses were part of what the wife was trying to avoid when she underwent the surgery, and are not offset by the benefit of having the child. (A) is also incorrect. All courts recognizing a wrongful pregnancy action permit the mother to recover the damages from the pregnancy itself. Similarly, (D) is incorrect because the wife's impaired earning capacity is a direct result of her pregnancy. The fact that these damages were unforeseeable does not prevent their recovery (*i.e.*, the tortfeasor takes his victim as he finds her).

Answer to Question 9

(C) The general manager will have to prove that the newspaper acted with actual malice because he is a public figure. The facts indicate that all of the elements are present to establish a prima facie case of defamation at common law: a defamatory statement of or concerning the general manager was published to others by the newspaper. Because it is libel, damage to reputation, the final common law element, is presumed. However, the general manager is a public figure: he is the general manager of a professional basketball franchise and is well-known in the community. Thus, he has to prove two additional elements: falsity of the defamatory language and fault amounting to "actual malice" on the part of the newspaper. Given that the parties will stipulate that the statement regarding the general manager is false, the only fact not established is that the newspaper acted with actual malice. (A) is incorrect because negligence is the fault standard that private figures have to establish when suing on a matter of public concern. The general manager, as a public figure, has to prove a higher level of fault. (B) is incorrect because pecuniary or special damages do not need to be established in a libel case; the common law presumes damages. (D) is incorrect because proof of actual injury is required by the Constitution only when a fault standard of negligence is applicable. If actual malice is established, the common law rules regarding presumed damages apply.

Answer to Question 10

(C) The court should not grant the promoter's motion because the jury could find that the promoter used improper means, while working for the company, to divert the sales rep for his own purposes. To establish a prima facie case for interference with business relations, the following elements must be proved: (i) existence of a valid contractual relationship between plaintiff and a third party ***or*** a valid business expectancy of plaintiff; (ii) defendant's knowledge of the relationship or expectancy; (iii) intentional interference by defendant that induces a breach or termination of the relationship or expectancy; and (iv) damage to plaintiff. Thus, a plaintiff has a cause of action for interference with probable future business relationships for which the plaintiff has a reasonable expectation of financial benefit. On the other hand, an interferor's conduct may be privileged where it is a proper attempt to obtain business for the interferor, particularly if the interference is only with plaintiff's prospective advantage rather than with an existing contract. What is proper depends on both the interests that the interferor is advancing and the means used to interfere. Here, the promoter's conduct would not be privileged if the jury were to find that he improperly used his position with the company to develop a relationship with the sales rep. (A) is incorrect because even though the company did not have an existing contractual relationship with the sales rep, it could very well show that it had a reasonable expectation of signing a contract with the sales rep that the promoter knew of and intentionally interfered with. (Note that courts do not permit recovery for negligent interference with business relations.) Whether the company could prove its expectancy to a sufficient degree to establish actual damages would be a question for the trier of fact; hence, summary judgment would not be appropriate on this basis. (B) is incorrect because the promoter can be liable for interference with business relations regardless of whether he was an independent contractor or an employee of the company, as long as he used improper means for steering the sales rep away from the company. (D) is incorrect because a defendant's breach of his own contract with the plaintiff is not a basis for the tort of interference with business relations. If the promoter breached his contract with the company, the company's cause of action would be in contract and its remedy would be governed by contract rules. Here, the tort action that the company is suing on does not require establishing a breach of the promoter's contract with the company.

Answer to Question 11

(A) The court should deny both motions because the jury should determine whether the purchaser's misuse of the motorcycle was foreseeable. A strict products liability action requires plaintiff to establish: (i) a strict duty owed by a commercial supplier, (ii) breach of that duty, (iii) actual and proximate cause, and (iv) damages. A supplier has breached its duty when it supplies a product that is so defective as to be "unreasonably dangerous." If the product was dangerous beyond the expectation of the ordinary consumer ***or*** a less dangerous alternative or modification was economically feasible, the supplier has breached its duty. Furthermore, while some products may be safe if used as intended, they may involve serious dangers if used in other ways. Courts require suppliers to anticipate reasonably foreseeable uses even if they are misuses of the product. In this case, the manufacturer has supplied its motorcycle with standard shock absorbers that are probably safe for use on the road. However, the advertisements promoted use of the motorcycle for off-road purposes, and purchasers may not have taken note of the warning in the owner's manual. It is a question for the trier of fact to determine whether the manufacturer should have foreseen that purchasers would use the motorcycle on rough terrain without buying different shock absorbers. (B) is wrong because a simple warning of danger in an owner's manual is not sufficient under the "feasible alternative" approach if it would not be effective to deter users of the motorcycle from using it on rough terrain. The jury will need to determine whether the manufacturer should have provided different shock absorbers or changed the way the motorcycle was advertised. (C) is wrong. The fact that the purchaser was in violation of the law when he drove off of the road may establish that his conduct was contributorily negligent. However, ordinary contributory negligence such as failing to discover a defect or guard against its existence is not a defense to a products liability action based on strict liability in jurisdictions retaining traditional contributory

negligence rules. The type of contributory negligence where one voluntarily and unreasonably encounters a known risk, which is essentially assumption of risk, would be a defense to strict liability, but there is no indication that the purchaser learned of the risk (such as by reading the owner's manual) and decided to take a chance anyway with the shock absorbers that he had. Hence, the purchaser's driving off the road does not warrant granting the manufacturer's motion. (D) is wrong because the fact that the shock absorbers were not safe for off-road use does not establish that they were so defective as to be unreasonably dangerous. The jury will need to determine whether the off-road use was sufficiently foreseeable to make the motorcycle unreasonably dangerous to users.

Answer to Question 12

(D) The woman most likely will recover the fair market value of the car. The tort of conversion does not require that the defendant damage or permanently deprive the owner of the chattel. All that is required is that defendant's volitional conduct result in a serious invasion of the chattel interest of another in some manner. In this case the friend could be considered the bailee of the woman's car. A bailee is liable to the owner for conversion if the bailee uses the chattel in such a manner as to constitute a material breach of the bailment agreement. A substantial interference with the woman's possession, such as is shown by the facts in this question, would constitute a material breach. Hence (A) and (B) are wrong, because the woman could recover for conversion, and (D) is correct rather than (C) because (D) states the correct measure of damages.

Answer to Question 13

(C) The shopper can recover against the store for defamation because the store manager negligently communicated his defamatory statements to third persons. A prima facie case for defamation at common law consists of (i) defamatory language by defendant (ii) of or concerning the plaintiff, (iii) publication of the defamatory language by the defendant to a third person, and (iv) damage to the reputation of the plaintiff. The publication requirement is satisfied when there is a communication of the defamatory statement to a third person who understood it. The communication to the third person may be made either intentionally or negligently. Here, the store manager's statements were defamatory, they were of or concerning the shopper because those hearing the statement could see that the manager was talking to her, and damage to the shopper's reputation is presumed by law because the allegation that she was a thief is slanderous per se. Because the manager neglected to check that the public address system was not on, his broadcasting of the statements to third persons was negligent. Hence, the publication requirement is satisfied. The store, as the employer of the store manager, will be vicariously liable for the manager's defamation because it was committed within the scope of his employment. (A) and (B) are wrong because a publication may occur even when the defendant is not speaking to third persons or does not intend that third persons hear his statements, as long as he was negligent in letting third persons overhear him. (D) is wrong because the manager's reasonable belief in the truth of his statements is irrelevant in a common law defamation action. Because the statements here did not involve a matter of public concern, the shopper does not need to establish that the manager was negligent in his belief as to the truth or falsity of his statements.

Answer to Question 14

(C) The fan will prevail in his battery action because the player had the requisite intent for battery. A prima facie case for battery requires plaintiff to prove (i) an act by defendant that brings about a harmful or offensive contact to the plaintiff's person, (ii) intent on defendant's part to bring about harmful or offensive contact, and (iii) causation. The intent element is satisfied as long as the defendant knew with substantial certainty that the harmful or offensive contact would result. Here, the player's conduct caused a harmful contact to the fan, because the player set into motion the force that caused injury to the fan. His intentionally shooting the puck into the crowded stands is enough to establish that he knew with substantial certainty that the puck would strike a spectator. (Note that even if he only intended to cause apprehension of contact, which is the intent for assault, this intent would suffice for liability for battery under the doctrine of transferred intent.) (A) is wrong because assumption of risk is not a defense to intentional torts. The fan may have assumed a risk of injury from a hockey puck's being accidentally or even negligently shot into the stands, but he did not assume the risk of a player's intentionally shooting the puck at a spectator. (B) is wrong because the player need not have intended to strike that fan to be liable. As long as he knew with substantial certainty that a fan would be struck, he is liable even if he did not single out the fan as the target. (D) is wrong. The fact that the player violated league rules when he shot the puck into the stands tends to establish only that a spectator does not impliedly consent to a puck's intentionally being shot at him, thus negating the defense of consent in a battery action. It does nothing to establish that the player did have the intent to commit a battery.

Answer to Question 15

(C) If the beach owner is not liable to the boy's parents, it will be because the boy appreciated the risk of using a canoe without a life vest. A landowner owes a higher duty of care to a child trespasser than to an adult trespasser. Under the "attractive nuisance" doctrine, a landowner has a duty to exercise ordinary care to avoid reasonably foreseeable risk of harm to children caused by artificial conditions on his property. To assess this special duty on the landowner, the following elements must be shown: (i) there is a dangerous condition on the land of which the owner is or should be aware; (ii) the owner knows or should know that children frequent the vicinity of this dangerous condition; (iii) the condition is dangerous because the child is unable to appreciate the risk; and (iv) the expense of remedying the situation is slight compared with the magnitude of the risk. The third element would be negated by showing that the boy appreciated the risk of taking the canoe out onto the lake without a life vest. In that case, the attractive nuisance doctrine would not apply and the boy would be treated like an adult trespasser, and leaving the canoes out would not constitute a breach of the owner's limited duties to adult trespassers. (A) is incorrect even though showing that children of like age, etc., would likely use a life vest is some evidence that the canoes might not be an attractive nuisance. However, (C) is the stronger answer because it focuses on the boy's own appreciation of the risk. If he had sufficient familiarity with the canoes to appreciate the risk of not using a life vest, the condition would not be an attractive nuisance as to him, as discussed above. (B) is incorrect because the precautions that the owner took might not be sufficient to avoid liability under the attractive nuisance doctrine. The owner would have to show that the expense of taking further precautions to remedy the situation was so great as to outweigh the magnitude of the risk. (D) is incorrect because most jurisdictions do not require a showing that the child was lured onto the property by the dangerous condition. Foreseeability of harm is the true basis of liability; the element of attraction is important only insofar as it indicates that the presence of children should have been anticipated by the landowner. Hence, it is not relevant that the boy was not lured onto the property by the canoes.

Answer to Question 16

(D) The homeowner is not liable because the "firefighter's rule," based on assumption of risk or public policy grounds, generally will preclude a firefighter from recovering for injuries occurring

on duty that are caused by another's negligence. One engaged in the activity of firefighting is deemed to know of the risks inherent in that activity, including the fact that a landowner may have failed to inspect or repair dangerous conditions on the land. (D) is therefore correct. (A) is incorrect because a common cause of fires is negligence by the property owner; that does not affect application of the rule. Thus, even if the homeowner acted negligently in allowing the fire to start, he is not liable. (B) is incorrect because the fact that it was foreseeable that the homeowner's conduct would start a fire establishes only that he was negligent in setting off the fireworks. Despite his negligence, the homeowner has a complete defense because of the "firefighter's rule." (C) is incorrect because the firefighter would not be treated as an invitee under these circumstances. A landowner such as the homeowner owes a duty to invitees not only to warn of nonobvious dangerous conditions known to him but also to make reasonable inspections to discover and rectify dangerous conditions. However, under the "firefighter's rule," firefighters and police officers are generally treated under the same standard as licensees because they are likely to enter the property at unforeseeable times and under emergency circumstances. As such, they cannot hold the landowner liable for failing to make reasonable inspections to discover a dangerous condition.

Answer to Question 17

(B) The court should grant the motion because the mother has offered no evidence of physical injury from her distress. In the majority of jurisdictions that have abandoned the "zone of danger" approach for bystander recovery of emotional distress damages, a plaintiff can recover as long as (i) plaintiff and the person injured by defendant are closely related, (ii) plaintiff was present at the scene of the injury, and (iii) plaintiff personally observed or perceived the event. Regardless of which approach is used to determine the scope of the duty, however, the bystander plaintiff can recover damages only if defendant's conduct resulted in some physical injury from the distress; emotional distress alone is insufficient in the usual case. Thus, despite the fact that the mother has satisfied all of the requirements for the "foreseeability" test, the court should grant the motion in the absence of evidence of physical injury to the mother. (A) is wrong because the mother does not need to be within the zone of danger to recover under the foreseeability approach, and whether the mother was a foreseeable plaintiff in the location she was in is a question of fact for the jury. (C) is wrong because even though it is a jury issue as to whether the mother's distress was foreseeable, the mother also has to show that her distress caused her physical injury. (D) is similarly wrong; while the mother's close relationship with the son is a necessary element of the foreseeability test, it does not substitute for the requirement of physical injury.

Answer to Question 18

(D) The mother has no cause of action because the child suffered no damages from the dentist's breach of duty. One of the duties that doctors, dentists, and other health professionals owe their patients is the duty to provide a patient with enough information about the risks of a proposed course of treatment or surgical procedure to enable the patient to make an "informed consent" to the treatment. If an undisclosed risk was serious enough that a reasonable person in the patient's position would have withheld consent to the treatment, the health care professional has breached this duty. However, breach of duty is only one element of a cause of action for negligence. The plaintiff must also establish actual and proximate cause and some damage to plaintiff's person or property. Damage means actual harm or injury. Unlike for some intentional torts, damage will not be presumed and nominal damages are not available. While a complete absence of consent to a medical or surgical procedure may in some cases constitute battery, which does not require

damage as an element, a nondisclosure of the ***risks*** of the procedure is characterized instead as a breach of the duty of care. Here, the child's dental work was completed without any problem and no other injury is apparent from the facts; the mother's possible distress at not being informed of the risk is not, standing alone, a compensable injury. [Restatement (Second) of Torts §436A] Hence, the mother does not have a cause of action against the dentist. (A) is incorrect even though it is the key factor for establishing that the dentist breached his duty by not disclosing the risk of seizure. As discussed above, breach of duty is just one element of the prima facie case. (B) is incorrect. If the child had suffered harm from the anesthetic, the element of actual cause would be established because the mother could show that she would not have consented to the use of the anesthetic had she known of the risk (*i.e.*, but for the dentist's nondisclosure, the child's injury would not have occurred). However, in the absence of the injury element, the prima facie case is not complete. (C) is incorrect because the fact that the dentist used his best judgment in deciding not to disclose the risk would not be a defense if the child had been harmed by the anesthetic.

Answer to Question 19

(C) The landowner can recover the full amount of his damages from the lumber mill because the negligence of its employee caused the destruction of the lodge. Before a defendant will be liable for a breach of duty to the plaintiff, it must be shown that the breach was the actual and proximate cause of the injury. The general test for determining whether an act or omission is the actual cause of the injury is the "but for" test, *i.e.*, whether the injury would not have occurred ***but for*** the act or omission. Under certain circumstances, however, the "but for" test is inadequate to determine actual cause. Where several causes combine to bring about an injury—and any one alone would have been sufficient to cause the injury—the actual cause requirement is satisfied if defendant's conduct was a substantial factor in causing the injury. Under this analysis, the fire started by the lumber mill employee was an actual cause of the destruction of the landowner's lodge because it was a substantial factor in causing the harm. It was also a proximate cause of the harm because no intervening forces broke the causal connection between the act and the harm. Because its employee was acting within the scope of his employment when he caused the fire to start, the lumber mill is vicariously liable for the injury that resulted. (A) is incorrect because the "but for" test is not applicable to these facts. Under that test, neither fire would be the actual cause of the harm because, looking at either fire alone, the harm would have occurred even without it. However, under the substantial factor test, both fires are actual causes of the injury. (B) is incorrect even though it is true that the damage is indivisible. The landowner can still recover from the lumber mill even if he does not sue the other tortfeasor. (D) is incorrect because traditional joint and several liability rules allow the landowner to recover his full damages from the lumber mill. Where two or more tortious acts combine to proximately cause an indivisible injury to plaintiff, each tortfeasor will be jointly and severally liable for that injury, even though each defendant acted entirely independently. The effect of joint and several liability is that the plaintiff may recover the entire amount of the damages from any tortfeasor, who then may have a right of contribution from the other tortfeasor. Hence, even though the negligence of another tortfeasor was also an actual cause of the destruction of the landowner's lodge, the landowner is entitled to recover all of his damages from the lumber mill.

Answer to Question 20

(D) The court should grant a directed verdict for the trainer because the airplane owner has not shown that the trainer breached any duty that he owed to him. A prima facie case of negligence requires plaintiff to show the following elements: (i) the existence of a duty on the part of the

defendant to conform to a specific standard of conduct for the protection of the plaintiff against unreasonable risk of injury, (ii) breach of that duty by the defendant, (iii) that the breach of duty was the actual and proximate cause of plaintiff's injury, and (iv) damage to plaintiff's person or property. Here, it is doubtful that the trainer's releasing his pigeons created any duty to other users of the park. To the extent that it did, the fact that he had taken great care to train them to return directly to their roosts indicates that he did not breach his duty to the airplane owner. Because the airplane owner has offered no other evidence of negligence, nor any reason to impose strict liability on the trainer (as discussed below), the trainer's motion for a directed verdict should be granted. (A) is incorrect because that choice indicates the imposition of a strict liability standard on the trainer. The owner of a domestic or inherently non-dangerous animal is not strictly liable for the injuries it causes. The conduct of the trainer's homing pigeon would not make the trainer liable in the absence of some negligence on his part. (B) is incorrect because the doctrine of res ipsa loquitur applies only to situations where the fact that a particular injury occurred itself establishes that defendant breached a duty. If the doctrine is applicable, no directed verdict may be given for defendant because plaintiff has established a prima facie case. However, the accident must be the type that would not normally occur unless someone was negligent. The collision between the trainer's homing pigeon and the model airplane is not that type of accident; by itself, it provides no suggestion that anyone was negligent. (C) is incorrect because the truck is not a superseding force that breaks "the causal connection" between the action of the trainer's pigeon and the airplane's destruction. In indirect cause cases, where a force came into motion after defendant's act and combined with it to cause injury to plaintiff, defendant will still be potentially liable for foreseeable intervening forces that are within the increased risk caused by his acts. Even if the intervening force is independent (*i.e.,* not a natural response or reaction to the situation), it will be foreseeable where defendant's negligence increased the risk that the independent force would cause harm. Hence, if the trainer were negligent in releasing his pigeon, the fact that the destruction of the airplane was directly caused by the truck would not relieve the trainer from liability, because the initial collision with the pigeon caused the airplane to go out of control and created a substantial risk that it would be damaged by an intervening force.

Answer to Question 21

(B) The traveler can bring an action for false imprisonment because the delay in releasing his luggage had the effect of confining him to the airport against his will. To establish a prima facie case for false imprisonment, a plaintiff must prove (i) an act or omission to act on defendant's part that confines or restrains plaintiff to a bounded area, (ii) intent on the part of defendant to confine or restrain plaintiff to a bounded area, and (iii) causation. The act or omission can be directed against plaintiff's property if its effect is to restrain plaintiff from leaving. Here, airport officials, who had no legal authority to conduct a search of the traveler's luggage, were under a duty to release it to him when he requested it. Requiring him to remain in the area to claim it when it was released was a sufficient confinement or restraint for purposes of false imprisonment. (A) is wrong because harm is not an element of the prima facie case for false imprisonment. The traveler could recover at least nominal damages even if he had suffered no harm from the delay in releasing his luggage. (C) is wrong because the seizure of the traveler's luggage did have the effect of restraining him because he believed that he would not get it back if he left the airport. (D) is wrong because, for purposes of intentional torts, an actor "intends" the consequences of his conduct if he knows with substantial certainty that these consequences will result. Even if the delay in releasing the luggage was not done for the purpose of restraining the traveler, it was substantially certain that he would remain in the area rather than risk losing his luggage. Hence, the security officials had a sufficient intent for false imprisonment liability.

Answer to Question 22

(B) The patient's distress is a recoverable element of damages caused by the dermatologist's breach of duty to her. A professional generally owes a duty to possess and exercise the degree of knowledge and skill of other doctors in similar localities. However, as a medical specialist, the dermatologist will be held to a "national" standard of care, and he also owes a duty to exercise the superior knowledge and skill that he possessed in his area of specialty. He breached that duty by misdiagnosing a common skin infection that another doctor was able to diagnose immediately. His failure to properly diagnose the condition was the actual and proximate cause of injury to the patient; but for the misdiagnosis, she would not have had to continue suffering from the rash until the other doctor properly treated it. The continuation of the rash and any pain and suffering from it are compensable damages that she can recover from the dermatologist. Also compensable is the emotional distress that she suffered because of the misdiagnosis. While recovery for emotional distress is restricted when there is no other injury caused by the breach, these restrictions do not apply when plaintiff is the victim of another tort that causes physical injury. Plaintiff can "tack on" damages for emotional distress because they attach to the physical injury damages. (A) is incorrect. Given the patient's physical condition, a failure to make a proper diagnosis did create a foreseeable risk that she would continue to suffer from a condition that could otherwise have been alleviated. Thus, the dermatologist's conduct did constitute a breach of the duty he owed the patient. (C) is incorrect because the patient has suffered compensable injury regardless of whether she had to pay for the second doctor visit. The continuation of the skin rash until she saw the other doctor suffices as the damage element of the prima facie case. (D) is incorrect because it states a requirement for recovery in cases where the only harm caused was through the negligent infliction of emotional distress. Here, the dermatologist's negligent diagnosis directly caused the patient physical injury in addition to emotional distress. Hence, the emotional distress is recoverable as a "parasitic" element of damages even if the distress itself did not cause physical injury.

Answer to Question 23

(B) The husband cannot recover damages from the bank for defamation because the bank representative's statements were made under a qualified privilege. To prove defamation, the husband must show (i) defamatory language by the defendant (ii) of or concerning the plaintiff (iii) published to a third person (iv) that causes damage to reputation. Because a public figure or matter of public concern is not involved, falsity and fault are not part of the prima facie case. In this case, the defamatory element of the bank representative's statement is that someone with access to the account used a large amount of funds to purchase escort services. The statement can be shown to be of or concerning the husband through pleading extrinsic facts, *i.e.*, colloquium. The extrinsic fact to be pleaded is that only he and his wife had access to the account. The statement was published by communicating it to the wife, and damage to reputation is likely to be presumed because the implication from the statement is that the husband may have paid for prostitution services, which falls under the slander per se category for crimes involving moral turpitude. While this completes the prima facie case for defamation, the bank representative has a qualified privilege that excuses his utterance of a defamatory statement. A qualified privilege is recognized when the recipient has an interest in the information and it is reasonable for the defendant to make the publication of the statement. Here, it was certainly in the wife's interest to receive an explanation of why her joint account was overdrawn. While the privilege does not encompass the publication of irrelevant defamatory matter that the speaker does not reasonably believe to be connected with the interest entitled to protection, here it was reasonable for the bank representative to identify the entities that charged the account. Therefore, even though the statements may have defamed the husband, they are protected by a qualified privilege under the circumstances. (A) is wrong because, as discussed above, the bank representative's statement would be perceived by a reasonable listener as implying that the husband transacted for these escort services. (C) is wrong because the husband does not need to show pecuniary harm (*i.e.*, special damages). Because the statements are likely slander per se, damage is presumed. (D) is wrong even though the statements may be slander per se. The bank representative is not liable because he has a qualified privilege.

Answer to Question 24

(A) The company can recover 100% of the judgment under common law indemnity rules. The principle of indemnity permits a shifting between the tortfeasors of the entire loss (*i.e.*, the payment made to satisfy plaintiff's judgment). This is in contrast to contribution, which apportions the loss among those who are at fault. Indemnity is available in vicarious liability situations, where one party is held liable for damages caused by another simply because of his relationship to that person. Hence, an employer such as the plumber's company that has been held vicariously liable under the doctrine of respondeat superior can obtain indemnification from the employee (the plumber) whose conduct actually caused the damage. (B) is incorrect because the company need not show that the plumber breached a company rule before it can obtain indemnity. The fact that the plumber's negligence caused the injury and that the company was liable for the judgment solely because of its relationship to the plumber permits indemnification here. (C) is incorrect because vicarious liability is one of the most common areas where indemnity is available. (D) is incorrect because the company's requirement that the plumber be on call 24 hours a day merely establishes that the company will be vicariously liable for the plumber's negligence; it does not bar the company from recovering from the plumber because the plumber's negligence actually caused the damage.

Answer to Question 25

(A) The driver is not liable for assault because he did not cause the pedestrian to reasonably apprehend an immediate harmful contact. The prima facie case for assault requires (i) an act by defendant causing a reasonable apprehension in plaintiff of immediate harmful or offensive contact to plaintiff's person, (ii) intent by defendant to bring about in plaintiff apprehension of that contact, and (iii) causation. For there to be apprehension, plaintiff must be aware of defendant's act at the time that it is occurring. Here, because the pedestrian was oblivious to the driver's attempt to scare her, the driver is not liable for assault. (B) is incorrect because whether the driver had an intent to injure the pedestrian is irrelevant for purposes of assault. (C) is incorrect. While the driver did have the intent to commit an assault, his act does not meet the requirements for the prima facie case because his act did not cause reasonable apprehension. (D) is incorrect even though the driver's conduct was a substantial factor in causing the pedestrian's injury (*i.e.*, the causation element would have been satisfied if damages were required for assault). Because the driver did not cause an apprehension of contact on the pedestrian's part, the driver is not liable for assault.

Answer to Question 26

(B) The most correct statement is that the trier of fact should take into account the boy's experience when considering the applicable standard of care. Regardless of the specific standard of care that is applied, someone with knowledge ***superior*** to that of the average person is required to use that knowledge. Hence, the trier of fact should take into account the fact that the boy had driven a tractor since he was 11 years old. (A) is incorrect. The precise standard of care in a common law negligence case may be established by proving the applicability to that case of a statute providing for criminal penalties, so that the statute's specific duty will replace the more general common law duty of due care, and a violation of the statute will establish duty and breach of duty. Here, nothing in the facts indicates that the boy violated any provisions in the statute, but he still may be liable to the truck driver for breach of a general duty of care. (C) is incorrect. The usual standard of conduct to which a child must conform is that of a child of like age, education, intelligence, and experience. While a child must conform to an adult standard of care when engaging in an activity in which usually only adults engage, there is no blanket rule that children 13 years of age or older are held to the same standard of care as adults. (D) is incorrect because the fact that 13-year-olds commonly drive tractors in that region does not preclude the court from applying an adult standard of care when a tractor is driven on a public road.

Answer to Question 27

(B) The passenger will recover against the owner for her injuries because the owner, a common carrier, owed her a nondelegable duty to provide a safe vehicle in which to ride. The general rule is that a principal will not be liable for tortious acts of his agent if the agent is an independent contractor. However, a major exception to this rule applies when the duty, because of public policy considerations, is nondelegable. In these cases, the principal is vicariously liable for the agent's negligence despite the principal's own exercise of due care. A common example of these types of duties is the duty of a business to keep its premises and instrumentalities safe for its customers. This includes the duty of a common carrier, such as a taxi company, to keep its vehicles in safe working order. Thus, the owner's duty to the passenger, a passenger in his cab, was nondelegable. The negligent conduct of the mechanic is deemed to be that of the owner. The negligent conduct was the actual and proximate cause of the passenger's injuries. Thus, the owner is vicariously liable to the passenger for those injuries. (A) and (C) are wrong because the passenger will prevail regardless of how careful the owner was in selecting the service center to maintain his cabs. As a common carrier, the owner owes his passenger, the passenger, a very high degree of care; *i.e.*, he will be liable for slight negligence. However, because his duty to provide a safe taxicab is not delegable, the fact that he was careful in selecting the mechanic is irrelevant. Even though the owner had no reason to know that a service center mechanic would be negligent, he is vicariously liable for that negligence because it caused injury to the passenger. (D) is wrong because, as stated above, the situation here falls within an exception to the general rule of no liability for the torts of an independent contractor.

Answer to Question 28

(B) The determining factor for the day care owner in prevailing will be whether her use of the property is abnormally sensitive to the presence of the dogs. Nuisance is an invasion of private property rights by conduct that is either intentional, negligent, or subject to strict liability. Strict liability will be the basis for a nuisance action (sometimes called an "absolute" nuisance or a "nuisance per se") when wild animals or abnormally dangerous domestic animals are involved, or when defendant is engaged in an abnormally dangerous activity. Thus, dogs known by their owner to be vicious may create a private nuisance when they interfere with the use and enjoyment of the land next door, and the owner may be subject to strict liability because of his knowledge of the dogs' dangerous propensities. [*See* Restatement (Second) of Torts §822, comment j] For the presence of the dogs to be an actionable nuisance, however, they must result in a ***substantial*** interference with the day care owner's use of her land. The interference will not be characterized as substantial if it is merely the result of plaintiff's specialized use of her own

property. [*See* Foster v. Preston Mill Co., 268 P.2d 645 (1954)—D not strictly liable for blasting operations that caused female mink on P's ranch to kill their young in reaction to the vibrations] Hence, (B) states the most critical factual issue. (A) is incorrect because the day care owner does not need to establish other types of damages to recover once she has established that the dog owner's activity is an actionable interference with the use and enjoyment of her land. (C) is incorrect because the exercise of reasonable care by the dog owner is irrelevant; the day care owner's nuisance action arises from an activity for which the dog owner is strictly liable. (D) is incorrect because the dog owner's knowledge of his interference with the day care owner's use of her property would only establish that his conduct might also be an intentional nuisance, which would require the day care owner to show unreasonableness, *i.e.,* that her injury outweighs the utility of his conduct. She does not need to make that showing for a nuisance action based on strict liability.

Answer to Question 29

(B) The attorney acted with scienter for purposes of an intentional misrepresentation action because she was aware that she did not know whether the state was planning an interchange. To establish a prima facie case of intentional misrepresentation or fraud, plaintiff must prove (i) misrepresentation by defendant, (ii) scienter, (iii) intent to induce plaintiff's reliance on the misrepresentation, (iv) causation (actual reliance on the misrepresentation), (v) justifiable reliance on the misrepresentation, and (vi) damages. The element of scienter, which involves defendant's state of mind, requires plaintiff to show that defendant made the statement knowing it to be false or made it with reckless disregard as to its truth or falsity. Because the attorney made her statement even though she had no information that the state was planning an interchange, she acted with scienter. The other elements of intentional misrepresentation are established by the facts. Thus, the investor has a cause of action against the attorney under the condition stated in (B). (A) is incorrect because an action for negligent misrepresentation is not supported by these facts. Negligent misrepresentation requires (i) a misrepresentation made by defendant in a business or professional capacity, (ii) breach of duty toward that particular plaintiff, (iii) causation, (iv) justifiable reliance, and (v) damages. Here, even though the investor was involved in a business transaction, the attorney was not. She was not acting in a business capacity but rather for her own personal interests. Hence, she is not liable for negligent misrepresentation. (C) is incorrect because the attorney's statement was a false representation of an existing fact—that an interchange was currently being planned. If the attorney had instead assured the owner simply that the interchange was going to be built in the future without any assertion of present facts, the investor could not justifiably rely on the statement because it is a statement of a future event over which the attorney did not have control. The statement here is actionable because an interchange was not even being planned. (D) is incorrect. The fact that the attorney made the statement to the owner gratuitously rather than in a commercial transaction absolves her from liability for negligent misrepresentation, but it has no relevance to her liability for intentional misrepresentation.

Answer to Question 30

(A) The man will not recover damages from the actor because the man's express assumption of risk is a complete defense. A plaintiff in a negligence action may be denied recovery if he assumed the risk of any damage caused by defendant's acts. The risk may be assumed by express agreement. Exculpatory language in a consensual agreement between the parties that is intended to insulate one of the parties from liability resulting from his own negligence is closely scrutinized but generally enforceable as long as it is not an adhesion contract situation (*i.e.*, a situation where one party essentially had no choice but to accept the terms set by the other party). Here, the risks were clearly stated on the signs and on the ticket, and the man was aware of them when he purchased the ticket. Because an entertainment rather than a necessity was involved, it was not an adhesion contract—the man was free to decline to enter the haunted house. Even in comparative negligence jurisdictions, express assumption of risk is a complete defense. Thus, the man will not recover damages from the actor. (B) is incorrect because any negligence on the actor's part in trying to scare the man is one of the risks that the man would be deemed to have assumed by purchasing the ticket and entering the haunted house. The disclaimer warned that the "monsters" would be trying to scare people who entered. A failure to predict what a person's reaction would be when scared, even if it amounted to negligence, was the type of risk that was expressly assumed by participants. (C) is incorrect because the actor's intent to cause apprehension does not make his conduct an assault or any other tort. An assault requires an intent to bring about in plaintiff apprehension of immediate harmful or offensive contact to plaintiff's person. Here, the conduct in which the actor engaged was impliedly consented to by the man when he entered the haunted house. His attempt to scare the man did not clearly go beyond the bounds of the implied consent inherent in that activity. (D) is incorrect because most comparative negligence jurisdictions do not treat express assumption of risk like contributory negligence and apportion damages between the parties. As in contributory negligence jurisdictions, express assumption of risk is a complete defense.

Answer to Question 31

(C) The elevator company can recover 30% of its damages from the building owner under a comparative contribution system. Contribution rules allow any defendant required to pay more than his share of damages under joint and several liability to have a claim against the other jointly liable parties for the excess. In states with a comparative contribution system, the traditional method of equal apportionment of damages is rejected; nonpaying tortfeasors are required to contribute only in proportion to their relative fault. Thus, the company should be able to recover 30% of the total damages from the building owner because the building owner was 30% at fault. (A) is incorrect for several reasons. The fact that the building owner may have had a nondelegable duty to occupants of its building would only establish that the building owner would be vicariously liable to the plaintiff (the worker) for the company's conduct even if the building owner were not at fault; that rule does not allow a defendant to recover indemnity from another defendant. Furthermore, if the building owner were only vicariously liable here, the building owner would have had a right of indemnity against the company if the building owner had had to pay damages to the worker, but the company has no such right against the building owner. (B) is incorrect because the fact that the company was more at fault would not preclude it from recovering contribution from the building owner under a comparative contribution system, which replaces indemnification rules based on identifiable differences in degree of fault. (D) is incorrect because, as discussed above, traditional contribution rules based on equal shares are not applied in a comparative contribution system, which apportions contribution based on relative fault.

Answer to Question 32

(D) The landowner will prevail because there is no evidence that she was negligent in her operation or maintenance of her beehives, and she is not strictly liable for the bees getting loose. Honeybees are domestic animals for which strict liability does not apply. In contrast to keepers of wild animals, the owner of a domestic animal is not strictly liable for the injuries it causes. Strict liability would only apply if the owner has knowledge of that particular animal's dangerous propensities (*i.e.*, propensities more dangerous than normal for that species). Here, while honeybees as a class can inflict harm by stinging, there is no indication that any of these particular

honeybees were more aggressive or dangerous than normal. Hence, (A) is incorrect because the landowner would not be strictly liable for the injury to the motorcyclist. (B) is incorrect because the fact that the motorcyclist is a traveler on a public road establishes only that the landowner, as the adjacent landowner, owes a duty of ordinary care as to dangerous conditions and active operations on her property. Here, the facts do not establish that the landowner acted unreasonably in the placement of her beehives. (C) is incorrect because another vehicle on the highway striking the motorcyclist was a foreseeable intervening force that did not break the causal connection between the release of the bees and the motorcyclist's injury. If strict liability were applicable here, the duty owed would be limited to the "normally dangerous propensity" of the animal involved, but fleeing from the perceived danger is part of the risk that the dangerous propensity creates. Similarly, if the landowner were negligent, the fact that the bees did not reach the motorcyclist would not cut off the landowner's liability to the motorcyclist.

Answer to Question 33

(C) The hiker's estate may be liable to the skier if the hiker acted negligently when he was rescuing the skier. As a general rule, no legal duty is imposed upon any person to affirmatively act for the benefit of others. However, one who gratuitously acts for the benefit of another, although under no duty to do so in the first instance, is then under a duty to act like a reasonable person. Here, the hiker was under no duty to come to the skier's assistance. Having done so, however, he was under a duty to use reasonable care in undertaking the rescue. If he acted negligently in doing so, he was in breach of his duty to the skier and the skier would have a cause of action against his estate. To prevail, the skier would also have to establish that her injuries would not have occurred but for the hiker's negligent attempt to cross the ice, and that the skier herself was not at fault. In any case, the skier has a cause of action stemming from the hiker's negligent conduct. Thus, (C) is correct and (A) is incorrect. (B) is incorrect. At common law, a tort action abated at the death of either the tortfeasor or the victim. However, most states have adopted survival statutes that change this result. Thus, the fact that the potential tortfeasor died would not preclude the skier from bringing an action against the tortfeasor's estate. (D) is incorrect because the skier would have a cause of action even for the hiker's ***ordinary negligence***. Many states have "Good Samaritan" statutes that exempt those who gratuitously render emergency assistance from liability for other than gross negligence, but most of these statutes apply only to health care providers rendering emergency medical assistance. Therefore, the skier could recover even if the hiker's negligence did not amount to gross negligence.

Answer to Question 34

(B) The captain's estate can recover from the dealer on a strict products liability ground because the captain was a foreseeable bystander and the dealer is a commercial supplier. Recovery in a wrongful death action is allowed only to the extent that the deceased could have recovered in a personal injury action had he lived. The captain could have recovered from the dealer in a products liability action based on strict liability because the dealer is a commercial supplier of the boat and owes a duty not to sell a product that is so defective as to be unreasonably dangerous. The defect in the assembly of the gas tank was unreasonably dangerous because it allowed gas to leak out and collect where it could be ignited. The duty was owed to the captain, despite the fact that he was not in privity with the dealer, because he was a foreseeable plaintiff. The disabling effect of the gas leak made it foreseeable that someone passing by would come to the boater's assistance and thereby come within the zone of danger from the leak (*i.e.*, danger invites rescue). The explosion that resulted from the leak was the actual and proximate cause

of the captain's death. Therefore, the captain's estate can recover damages from the dealer. (A) is wrong because, as with proximate cause analysis in ordinary negligence actions, the negligence of a subsequent actor is foreseeable and therefore not a superseding cause that would cut off the liability of the original tortfeasor. In any products liability case, the negligent failure of an intermediary to discover the defect or the danger does not void the commercial supplier's strict liability. Hence, the boater's negligence would be irrelevant. (C) is wrong because in products liability actions based on strict liability, the retailer may be liable even if it had no reason to anticipate that the product was dangerous or had no opportunity to inspect the product for defects. While the dealer could assert that defense if the action were based on negligence, the call of the question indicates that the action is based on a strict liability theory. Under strict liability, the dealer is liable simply because it is a commercial supplier of a product with a dangerous defect. (D) is wrong because the fact that the captain was not in privity with the dealer is irrelevant in a products liability action based on strict liability. The strict duty is owed not only to buyers, but also to the buyer's family, friends, and employees, and to foreseeable bystanders. As a rescuer, the captain was a foreseeable bystander to whom the dealer owed a duty.

Answer to Question 35

(B) The swimmer cannot recover from the resort because he did not have invitee status when he was injured. In most jurisdictions, the nature of a duty of an owner or occupier of land to those on the premises depends on the legal status of the plaintiff in regard to the property, *i.e.*, whether the plaintiff is a trespasser, licensee, or invitee. An invitee is a person who enters onto the premises in response to an express or implied invitation of the landowner. Those who enter as members of the public for a purpose for which the land is held open to the public and those who enter for a purpose connected with the business or other interests of the landowner are considered invitees. However, a person will lose his status as an invitee if he exceeds the scope of the invitation—if he goes onto a portion of the property where his invitation cannot reasonably be said to extend. Here, the swimmer was an invitee of the resort in the areas to which it allowed its patrons to go. However, the resort clearly identified the boundaries of the area held open to swimmers, and the swimmer could not reasonably have believed that he was invited to swim in the area where he was injured. Because the swimmer was at most a licensee when he was injured, the resort did not owe him a duty to make reasonable inspections of that area to discover dangerous conditions and make them safe. At most, the resort had a duty only to warn the swimmer of known dangerous conditions that create an unreasonable risk of harm to him and that he is unlikely to discover, and nothing in the facts indicates that any employees of the resort knew of the stake under the water. The swimmer therefore cannot recover against the resort. (A) is not as good a choice as (B). While a landowner is not liable for a dangerous condition that is obvious to the entrant on the land, the fact that the stake was visible does not establish that it was obvious, given that the swimmer was looking forward rather than down. The better reason why the swimmer cannot recover is because he was no longer an invitee. (C) is incorrect because the lifeguard's failure to direct the swimmer to the swimming area would not constitute an invitation to swim in the restricted area; at most, it would establish only that the swimmer was a licensee rather than a trespasser when he swam in that area. A licensee is one who enters onto land with the possessor's permission, express or implied, for his own purpose or business rather than for the possessor's benefit. The lifeguard's conduct may have constituted implied permission for the swimmer to exit the lake in a nonswimming area for his own benefit, but it does not establish that he reasonably believed that he was invited to swim in that area. (D) is incorrect because the swimmer lost his status as an invitee when he exceeded the scope of his invitation by swimming in an area where swimming was not permitted.

Answer to Question 36

(C) The golfer will not be liable because she did not intend to cause harmful or offensive contact. The prima facie case for battery has the following elements: (i) an act by the defendant that brings about harmful or offensive contact to the plaintiff's person; (ii) intent on the part of the defendant to bring about harmful or offensive contact to the plaintiff's person; and (iii) causation. Here, the golfer did not have the intent to cause harmful or offensive contact. Hence, she will not be guilty of battery. (A) is incorrect because even though the golfer had the intent to swing the club, she did not have the intent required for battery—to cause harmful or offensive contact to another. (B) is incorrect because the facts do not support an intent to cause an assault. Under the transferred intent doctrine, an intent to cause an assault (intent to cause apprehension of imminent harmful or offensive contact) will satisfy the intent requirement for battery when the other elements of battery are present. Here, however, the golfer was standing behind the instructor and was intending only to show the other golfers how annoyed she was. No intent to commit assault is apparent here. (D) is incorrect because it describes a negligence standard. The instructor may be able to recover against the golfer in a negligence cause of action if the golfer acted unreasonably in swinging the club, but this does not establish intent for a battery action.

Set 6 Answer Sheet

1.	Ⓐ	Ⓑ	Ⓒ	Ⓓ	19.	Ⓐ	Ⓑ	Ⓒ	Ⓓ
2.	Ⓐ	Ⓑ	Ⓒ	Ⓓ	20.	Ⓐ	Ⓑ	Ⓒ	Ⓓ
3.	Ⓐ	Ⓑ	Ⓒ	Ⓓ	21.	Ⓐ	Ⓑ	Ⓒ	Ⓓ
4.	Ⓐ	Ⓑ	Ⓒ	Ⓓ	22.	Ⓐ	Ⓑ	Ⓒ	Ⓓ
5.	Ⓐ	Ⓑ	Ⓒ	Ⓓ	23.	Ⓐ	Ⓑ	Ⓒ	Ⓓ
6.	Ⓐ	Ⓑ	Ⓒ	Ⓓ	24.	Ⓐ	Ⓑ	Ⓒ	Ⓓ
7.	Ⓐ	Ⓑ	Ⓒ	Ⓓ	25.	Ⓐ	Ⓑ	Ⓒ	Ⓓ
8.	Ⓐ	Ⓑ	Ⓒ	Ⓓ	26.	Ⓐ	Ⓑ	Ⓒ	Ⓓ
9.	Ⓐ	Ⓑ	Ⓒ	Ⓓ	27.	Ⓐ	Ⓑ	Ⓒ	Ⓓ
10.	Ⓐ	Ⓑ	Ⓒ	Ⓓ	28.	Ⓐ	Ⓑ	Ⓒ	Ⓓ
11.	Ⓐ	Ⓑ	Ⓒ	Ⓓ	29.	Ⓐ	Ⓑ	Ⓒ	Ⓓ
12.	Ⓐ	Ⓑ	Ⓒ	Ⓓ	30.	Ⓐ	Ⓑ	Ⓒ	Ⓓ
13.	Ⓐ	Ⓑ	Ⓒ	Ⓓ	31.	Ⓐ	Ⓑ	Ⓒ	Ⓓ
14.	Ⓐ	Ⓑ	Ⓒ	Ⓓ	32.	Ⓐ	Ⓑ	Ⓒ	Ⓓ
15.	Ⓐ	Ⓑ	Ⓒ	Ⓓ	33.	Ⓐ	Ⓑ	Ⓒ	Ⓓ
16.	Ⓐ	Ⓑ	Ⓒ	Ⓓ	34.	Ⓐ	Ⓑ	Ⓒ	Ⓓ
17.	Ⓐ	Ⓑ	Ⓒ	Ⓓ	35.	Ⓐ	Ⓑ	Ⓒ	Ⓓ
18.	Ⓐ	Ⓑ	Ⓒ	Ⓓ	36.	Ⓐ	Ⓑ	Ⓒ	Ⓓ

TORTS QUESTIONS - SET 6

Question 1

A newspaper printed in a news article that a successful businessman running for the state legislature had attempted suicide and had just been released from the hospital, where he had undergone intensive psychotherapy. Actually, the businessman had been hospitalized because he had contracted hepatitis. The businessman's opponent, the incumbent legislator, read the story into the legislative record the next day.

If the businessman sues the incumbent for defamation, the businessman will:

(A) Recover if he establishes at trial that the incumbent acted with actual malice.

(B) Recover because the statement was slander per se.

(C) Not recover because the incumbent was relying on the veracity of the newspaper article.

(D) Not recover because the incumbent was privileged to make the defamatory statements.

Question 2

A dog whistle manufacturer's factory was located near a residential area. The manufacturer used the most effective methods for testing its whistles, but it was impossible to completely soundproof the testing area. A breeder of champion show dogs bought some property near the factory and raised and trained her dogs there. Although the whistles were too high-pitched to be perceived by human ears, they could be heard by the breeder's dogs. Consequently, the dogs often were in a constant state of agitation.

In a suit by the breeder against the manufacturer, the breeder will:

(A) Prevail on a trespass theory, because the sound waves are entering onto the breeder's property.

(B) Prevail on a nuisance theory, because the sound of the whistles is a substantial interference with the breeder's use of her land.

(C) Not prevail, because the sound of the whistles is not a substantial interference with the breeder's use of her land.

(D) Not prevail, because the manufacturer has acted reasonably in testing its whistles.

Question 3

A statute requires that any pilot who flies passengers for hire must have a commercial pilot's license. An experienced pilot who had only a private pilot's license and not the commercial license required by statute was asked by an attorney to fly her to another city to close a deal. The attorney knew that the pilot did not have a commercial license but the only commercial flight to the city was at an inconvenient time. The pilot flew the attorney through bad weather and landed safely, but because of a minor navigational error he landed at an airport a few miles away from the airport he was heading for. As he was going to start taxiing toward the hangar, another plane struck the aircraft. The student pilot of that plane had ignored the control tower's instructions and gone onto the landing runway instead of the takeoff runway. The attorney was injured in the collision.

If the attorney sues the pilot for her injuries, who will prevail?

(A) The pilot, because the attorney knew he lacked a commercial license and voluntarily assumed the risk of flying with him.

(B) The pilot, because the injuries to the attorney were caused by the negligence of the student pilot of the other plane.

(C) The attorney, because the pilot violated a statute designed to prevent persons without commercial licenses from flying passengers for a fee, and such violation imposes liability per se.

(D) The attorney, because the pilot landed at the wrong airport, and but for this mistake the attorney could not have been injured by the other aircraft.

Question 4

A facility for mentally ill patients had a high security area for patients deemed to be dangerous. The doors in that section had sophisticated double locks, and the staff was regularly trained in security procedures. However, one night a newly hired employee, who had not yet been instructed in all of the security procedures and had not finished reading the training manual, was left in charge of the high security area. A dangerous patient escaped from the hospital out of a rear door which the employee had not locked. Without any provocation, the patient brutally beat a resident of the town in which the hospital was located.

If the resident sues the hospital for his injuries, what is the resident's best argument for a recovery?

(A) The hospital is strictly liable for the actions of its abnormally dangerous patients.

(B) Negligence is presumed from the fact of the patient's escape.

(C) The hospital is vicariously liable for the intentional torts of its patients.

(D) The employee acted negligently when he failed to lock the door.

Question 5 Public

A columnist for a major metropolitan newspaper had a very antagonistic relationship with the city's mayor. When a restaurant owned by the columnist's family was shut down by city health inspectors, the columnist responded with a column publicizing the shutdown and asserting that it was in retaliation for his prior columns in which he had criticized the mayor. In fact, the mayor had nothing to do with the action by the city health inspectors. While the columnist had no evidence of the mayor's involvement, he believed that there was a connection because "that's how the city works."

Can the mayor recover against the columnist for defamation?

(A) No, because the columnist did not act with "actual malice."

(B) No, because the columnist had a qualified privilege to explain why he believed his family's business was shut down.

(C) Yes, because the columnist's hostility toward the mayor establishes malice so as to overcome any qualified privilege the columnist had.

(D) Yes, because the columnist should have investigated the accuracy of his claims before publishing the column.

Question 6

A dog owner brought his dog to an open field to practice the lessons the dog learned in the obedience training class that it had just completed. After a few minutes of training routines, the dog ran off and ended up in a neighbor's flower bed, where he dug up many of the flowers. — trespass.

If the neighbor sues the dog owner for the damage to her flower bed and prevails, it will be because:

(A) The damage to the flower bed was a substantial interference with the neighbor's right of possession in the flowers.

(B) The dog owner was negligent in training or supervising the dog.

(C) The dog was owned by the dog owner.

(D) The invasion of the flower bed constituted a trespass to the neighbor's land.

Question 7

A skier broke his leg when he was knocked down by the chair lift as he tried to avoid other skiers who had fallen off while disembarking. The ski resort employee operating the lift had not been paying attention and had failed to stop the lift. Ski patrol personnel placed the skier on a stretcher, which they then hooked up to a snowmobile to bring him down the mountain. The route down ran along the edge of a ski trail. Midway down, a novice snowboarder tried to see how close he could come to the stretcher without hitting it, but he lost control and landed on top of the skier's leg, damaging it further. The skier filed a lawsuit against the snowboarder and the resort in a jurisdiction that has adopted a comparative contribution system in joint and several liability cases. At trial, the skier's physician testified that the skier's leg was permanently disabled, but that neither injury, by itself, would have caused the permanent disability and it was impossible to quantify how much each injury contributed to the disability. The jury determined that the damages from the permanent disability equaled $2 million, and that the snowboarder and the resort were each 50% at fault.

What amount of damages can the skier recover from the snowboarder for his permanent disability?

(A) $1 million, because the jurisdiction follows comparative contribution rules.

(B) $2 million, because it was not possible to identify the portion of the injury that the snowboarder caused.

(C) Nothing for his permanent disability, because the skier has not met his burden of proof as to the amount of damages that the snowboarder caused.

(D) Nothing for his permanent disability, because the injury inflicted by the snowboarder, by itself, would not have caused the disability.

Question 8

In the course of repainting an apartment, the landlord of a small apartment building used a professional strength, stain-killing primer manufactured by a paint company for professional painters. The building's common ventilation system was running as the landlord applied the primer, and some fumes from the primer went through the ventilation system into the apartment of the upstairs tenant, who suffered injuries to her eyes as a result. The warning label on the can, which the landlord read, stated: "Danger. This material is extremely hazardous and volatile. Do not use near open flame. Use only with adequate ventilation." The product contained a chemical known to be harmful to people's eyes, but in the 15 years that the product has been on the market, there were no reported cases of anyone suffering an eye injury from the product. However, professional painters routinely close off or shut down any common ventilation systems in buildings before using the product.

If the tenant brings an action against the paint company on a theory of strict liability, will she recover?

(A) Yes, because the product was used as intended and she was injured thereby.

(B) Yes, because the label on the product did not warn of the risk of the fumes causing eye injury.

(C) No, because the fact that no one had previously been injured demonstrated that the warning label on the product was sufficient.

(D) No, because the landlord acted negligently by leaving the ventilation system on.

Question 9

An automobile, a truck, and a motorcycle were involved in a threevehicle accident. The automobile driver sued the trucker and the motorcyclist, each of whom countersued the driver and sued each other. At trial, it was determined by the trier of fact that the driver suffered $10,000 in damages, the trucker suffered $1,000 in damages, and the motorcyclist suffered $100,000 in damages. It was also determined that the driver was 45% at fault, the trucker was 35% at fault, and the motorcyclist was 20% at fault.

How would damages be assessed in a jurisdiction that has adopted a modified or "partial" form of comparative negligence?

(A) The motorcyclist has a claim for $80,000, and the driver and the trucker have no claims.

(B) The motorcyclist has a claim for $80,000, which she can collect from either the driver or the trucker, the trucker has a claim for $650, which he can collect only from the driver, and the driver has no claim.

(C) The driver has a claim for $5,500, the trucker has a claim for $650, and the motorcyclist has a claim for $80,000.

(D) The driver has a claim for $10,000, the trucker has a claim for $1,000, and the motorcyclist has a claim for $100,000.

Question 10

A college student owned a very popular video game system that was out of stock in most stores. He agreed to let his friend use the system for a few days, on condition that he return the system by the weekend because the student was hosting a small party. On the morning of the party, the friend still had not returned the game system, so the student went to the friend's apartment and demanded it back. The friend refused, so the student grabbed the system and wrestled it out of the friend's hands.

If the friend sues the student for battery, will he recover on this claim?

(A) No, because the student used reasonable force in attempting to seize the game system.

(B) No, unless the student proves that the friend's delay in the return of the game system was unreasonable.

(C) Yes, because the student had originally agreed to lend the game system to the friend.

(D) Yes, because the student had to give the friend a reasonable period of time after demand in which to return the game system.

Question 11

A new homeowner had two dogs that frequently barked at birds and squirrels in the yard, especially during the day while the homeowner was at work. A neighbor who worked nights was aggravated by the barking, which disturbed his sleep, and decided to let the homeowner know how he felt. One evening, upon learning that the homeowner was entertaining her boss and several clients, the neighbor came to her front door with a boombox and started playing a recording of the dogs barking, putting it at full volume. When the homeowner came to the door, he began yelling at her and berating her in front of her guests for having no consideration for her neighbors, while continuing to play the recording. The homeowner was very upset, especially because her guests decided that they had better leave, and she ended up losing a bonus that her boss was going to give her at the end of the evening.

If the homeowner asserts a claim based on intentional infliction of emotional distress against the neighbor, what will be the probable result?

(A) The homeowner will prevail because the neighbor's conduct was extreme and outrageous.

(B) The homeowner will prevail because she suffered pecuniary harm from the neighbor's conduct.

(C) The neighbor will prevail because the homeowner suffered no physical harm.

(D) The neighbor will prevail if the barking from the homeowner's dogs is judged to constitute a nuisance.

Question 12

An attorney came to work on a Saturday. When he signed in, he was advised by the morning security guard employed by the building management that he must be out of the building by 5 p.m., when it closes. However, he stayed past 5 p.m. to complete a brief that had to be filed on Monday morning. At 5:15 p.m., the afternoon security guard set the locks on all the doors of the building and left. Because she was in a hurry, she did not check the sign-in sheet to make sure that everyone had signed out, contrary to mandatory procedures. When the attorney tried to exit 15 minutes later, he discovered that the doors were all locked and could not be opened from the inside. He used his cell phone to call for help, and a supervisor from the building arrived and let him out shortly thereafter.

If the attorney sues the building management for false imprisonment, he will likely:

(A) Win, because the guard acted recklessly by locking the doors and leaving without checking that everyone was out of the building.

(B) Win, unless the attorney became a trespasser by staying in the building past 5 p.m.

(C) Lose, because the guard did not know that the attorney was locked in the building.

(D) Lose, because the attorney suffered no harm from the confinement.

Question 13

The driver of a tanker truck was transporting radioactive waste from a nuclear power plant to a permanent storage facility in a remote western region of the United States. After driving all night, the driver fell asleep at the wheel and the truck crossed over the center line, off the road, and onto a homeowner's property, coming to rest after crashing into several glass cases containing the homeowner's collection of poisonous snakes, the keeping of which was permitted by local ordinance. When the driver exited the truck, he was bitten on the leg by one of the poisonous snakes and became seriously ill.

The driver brought an action against the homeowner for his injuries in a jurisdiction following traditional contributory negligence rules. The parties stipulated to the above facts, and that the driver violated a state statute by driving off of the road. Both parties moved for judgment as a matter of law on the liability issue.

How should the court rule?

(A) Grant the driver's motion and deny the homeowner's motion, because the homeowner is strictly liable for the injury caused by the snake.

(B) Deny the driver's motion and grant the homeowner's motion, because the driver was a trespasser on the homeowner's property.

(C) Deny the driver's motion and grant the homeowner's motion, because the driver's violation of the state statute establishes contributory negligence as a matter of law.

(D) Deny both parties' motions, because both parties were engaged in an activity for which strict liability is imposed.

Question 14

After picking up a load of hazardous chemical waste, a truck driver for a waste management company set out on the road to his next stop. However, he had failed to secure the latch on the back panel of the truck. Consequently, the panel opened while the truck was on the road, and a metal canister full of chemical waste fell onto the road. A car struck the canister, causing the car to veer off the road and injure the driver. The driver filed suit against the company for his injuries.

The jurisdiction in which the above events took place has adopted a rule of partial comparative negligence. At trial, the driver of the car admitted that he had momentarily taken his eyes off the road to look at his speedometer. When he had looked up again, the canister was there and he could not stop in time. The jury found that the company, through its truck driver, had acted willfully and wantonly and was 90%

at fault, while the driver of the car was 10% at fault. The driver filed a motion for judgment notwithstanding the verdict, seeking recovery for 100% of his damages.

If the judge grants the motion, it will most likely be because:

(A) A plaintiff's comparative negligence is not taken into account in cases of willful and wanton conduct by the defendant.

(B) A state ordinance mandating motorists to stay within the posted speed limit requires as a matter of law an occasional glance at the speedometer.

(C) The company was more than 50% at fault.

(D) The company was engaged in an abnormally dangerous activity.

Question 15

A state statute required that any freight train operating within the city limits be able to stop within 200 yards of applying its brakes. No fixed speed limit was established or particular type of braking mechanism required, but through either lowered speed or braking power, the 200-yard limit was required of all trains. Another statute prohibited vehicles from being within the railroad crossing when the lights on the warning signs are flashing or when the gates are lowered. One day, as a freight train was entering the city limits, the engineer saw a car stalled at a street crossing ahead. He immediately applied full braking power, but was unable to stop the train before it had hit and demolished the car. The driver of the car had gotten clear before the impact, but brought suit against the freight line for property damage to the $25,000 car. At trial, the parties stipulated that the car was stalled within the crossing while the warning lights were flashing. Evidence at trial established that the distance from the point at which the engineer applied the train's brakes to the point of impact was 150 yards, and from the braking point to the point at which the train finally stopped was 225 yards. No other evidence of negligence was presented by the driver. At the end of the driver's case, the freight line moved for a directed verdict.

Should the court grant the motion?

(A) No, because the freight line was negligent per se.

(B) No, because the freight line was strictly liable for its violation of the braking statute.

(C) Yes, because the driver's car was on the freight line's tracks in violation of the crossing statute.

(D) Yes, because the freight line's violation of the braking statute was not the cause in fact of the accident.

Question 16

A husband was on his way to meet his wife for lunch at the restaurant in the lobby of a bank building, where she worked. He had just entered the building when he heard screams and the sound of breaking glass. He rounded the corner and saw the wreckage of a large piece of artwork made of stained glass that had fallen onto the seating area of the restaurant. Looking further, he saw several seriously injured persons, including his wife, lying in the wreckage. He fainted and hit his head on the marble floor, fracturing his skull. The artwork had collapsed because the pedestal that the building had provided for the artwork was not properly constructed. The husband sued the bank, which owns and operates the building, for his injury in a jurisdiction following the traditional "zone of danger" approach in bystander cases.

The husband will:

(A) Prevail, because he suffered physical injury as a result of defendant's negligence.

(B) Prevail, because one of the persons he saw lying in the wreckage was his wife.

(C) Not prevail, because he was not personally put at risk by defendant's negligence.

(D) Not prevail, because he did not actually see the accident occur.

Question 17

After enjoying a wonderful meal in a restaurant, a diner went into the kitchen through a door marked "employees only" to personally compliment the chef. However, before he could get the attention of the chef, he slipped on a puddle of bright yellow grease that had congealed on the floor by the stove. He fell, hitting his head and sustaining a severe head injury.

If the diner sues the restaurant for damages, is he likely to recover?

(A) Yes, because the restaurant is a place of public accommodation and breached its duty of care owed to its patrons.

(B) Yes, because a restaurant employee could have discovered the dangerous condition of the floor by making reasonable inspections.

(C) No, because patrons were not allowed in the kitchen.

(D) No, because the puddle of grease was visible on the floor.

Question 18

A homeowner hired a pool contractor to remove an existing pool while the homeowner was out of town. The contractor applied a powder that, when mixed with an alcohol-based solvent, would assist in dissolving the cement used in the construction of the pool. While applying the powder, the contractor spilled some of it on a portion of a nearby wooden deck. He then proceeded with removal of the existing cement structure, leaving the site at 4 p.m., after nine hours of work. When he left for the day, all of the powder had been removed from the pool area except for the portion on the wooden deck, which had not otherwise been affected by the work done that day. The contractor, knowing that no one would be at the house, planned to clean that up the next day. An hour later, the homeowner's friend, who had permission to use the pool anytime, let himself in with a key that the homeowner had given him. When he went outside to the rear pool area, he saw that the pool was dry and that much of the surrounding area was broken up. Rather than go home, he decided to relax on the wooden deck. Noticing the powder on the deck, he decided to hose it off before he set down a lawn chair, but when he turned on the water, the powder exploded into flames, severely burning him.

The powder was a silicate of magnesium that was extremely volatile when exposed to water. The warnings on the container, which the contractor had read because he was using the substance for the first time, stated as follows: "Danger. Extremely caustic. Do not use near any alcohol-based solvent except under professional supervision. Do not use near source of high heat or open flame." The friend brought an action for personal injuries against the contractor.

The likely result is:

(A) The friend will win, because the contractor left the powder on the wooden deck.

(B) The friend will win, because the contractor is held to the same standard of liability as the manufacturer of the powder.

(C) The contractor will win, because he used the powder for the purpose for which it was designed.

(D) The contractor will win, because it was not reasonably foreseeable that the powder would cause injury to anyone.

Question 19

At an intersection of two busy streets, a motorcyclist failed to stop at a stop sign before entering the intersection. A truck driver who had the right of way saw the motorcycle crossing in front of him but was unable to stop because he had neglected to get his brakes repaired, even though he knew they were in poor condition. The two vehicles collided in the center of the intersection, injuring both parties. Immediately after that, a cabdriver who saw the accident decided to try to go around the vehicles, but she ended up colliding with both of them. All three

parties were injured in the second collision. Each of the parties sues the other two in a jurisdiction that retains traditional contributory negligence rules.

If the trier of fact finds that all three parties were at fault, which of the following is the most likely result?

(A) The motorcyclist and the truck driver will be awarded damages against the cabdriver; no other damages will be awarded.

(B) The motorcyclist will be awarded damages against the truck driver and the cabdriver; no other damages will be awarded.

(C) The motorcyclist will be awarded damages against the truck driver and the cabdriver, and the truck driver will be awarded damages against the cabdriver; no other damages will be awarded.

(D) None of the parties will be awarded damages against any of the other parties.

Question 20

A feed store owner agreed to purchase several tons of grain products at a specified price from a large supplier of cattle feeds. The supplier later failed to deliver the promised grains, and the owner was forced to cover by purchasing from local producers at a higher price. The owner contacted a large law firm in the city and obtained their agreement to represent him in connection with his possible claims against the supplier. Due to error, the applicable statute of limitations period passed without the filing of any action on the owner's behalf. The owner retained another lawyer and sued the large law firm for malpractice. The jurisdiction retains traditional contributory negligence.

In addition to the firm's negligence, the owner will also have to establish, as part of his prima facie case, that:

(A) He had a good faith claim against the supplier that was lost by the law firm's dilatoriness.

(B) He would have recovered from the supplier if an action had been timely filed.

(C) He did not contribute to the failure to timely file an action through his own negligence.

(D) The losses resulting from breach of the sales agreement by the supplier severely harmed his financial situation.

Question 21

A professional bicycle racer built a prototype racing bicycle with a new type of rear axle on which a rider could achieve 20% greater speed than was possible with an unmodified bike. Using the new device on his bicycle, he won the next three races he entered. The racer knew he had a chance at the world championship and so prepared to travel to Europe to race, lining up sponsors and making other preparations. He also received several offers to purchase his new axle, and a few racers offered him as much as $30,000 for his modified bicycle, which, without the new axle, was worth about $1,500. The racer dropped out of the remainder of the United States racing circuit to prepare for his trip. His rival asked if he could borrow the modified bike to use in the United States races, and the racer agreed, on the condition that the rival would return the bicycle no later than March 1. The rival agreed and used the bike to win his next two races. On March 1, the rival did not return the bike, and the racer learned that the rival had arranged a match race with the current European champion, who was visiting the United States before the opening of the racing season in Europe. The racer demanded that his bicycle be returned, but the rival refused, and subsequently won the match race and received $10,000.

The racer sued the rival for not returning the bicycle. At the trial several months later, the racer proved that on the day of the match race between the rival and the European champion, the market value of the bicycle was $30,000. The rival presented evidence that the world bicycle racing authority had outlawed use of the racer's new axle in all sanctioned events shortly before the racer had filed his suit, and that the market value of the bicycle as of that date and continuing to the time of trial was $2,000.

What should be the outcome of the racer's claim against the rival?

(A) He will recover $30,000, because the rival refused to return the bicycle on the racer's demand.

(B) He will recover $10,000, because the rival deprived the racer of an opportunity to win that money.

(C) He will recover $2,000, because the rival refused to return the bicycle on the racer's demand.

(D) He will recover nothing, because he is entitled to damages for loss of use of the bicycle, and he had no opportunity to use it during the relevant period.

Question 22

The owner of a boat took two friends out on a lake near his home. One of his friends was driving the boat when it struck a partially submerged rock that the owner of the boat had forgotten to tell him about. The owner of the boat and the other passenger were injured; the driver of the boat was not hurt.

In a jurisdiction that has adopted pure comparative negligence and applies joint and several liability with comparative contribution, the passenger brought suit against both the boat owner and the driver, and the boat owner also sued the driver. The jury determined that the boat owner was 55% at fault and suffered $10,000 in damages, the driver of the boat was 45% at fault, and the injured passenger suffered $100,000 in damages. After entry of judgment, the boat owner paid the passenger her total damages of $100,000, while the driver of the boat has paid nothing.

How much, if anything, can the boat owner recover from the driver?

(A) $45,000, because the driver was 45% at fault.

(B) $49,500, because the driver was 45% at fault and the boat owner suffered $10,000 in damages.

(C) $50,000, because the boat owner and the driver are jointly liable.

(D) Nothing, because the boat owner was more at fault than the driver.

Question 23

A small print shop on the second floor of an older two-story industrial building kept its front door locked for security reasons, so most visitors gained access to the shop by using the shop's freight elevator in the rear of the building. This elevator did not have a call-button for use by the public, so anyone wanting to use it had to wait for one of the shop's employees to send down the elevator. A city fire inspector inspecting the building informed the shop foreman that he was going to inspect the lower floor, the trash area, and the elevator shaft. The foreman said that he would turn the elevator off until the inspector called up from downstairs that he was finished with his inspection. About 10 minutes later, as the inspector was under the elevator in the shaft, the freight elevator suddenly started descending. The inspector tried to get out of the way, but his leg was severed by the elevator.

The inspector sued the print shop for the loss of his leg. At the time of the accident, there were three employees in the shop, but all deny that they pushed the button that would send the elevator to the first floor. Evidence at trial indicated that the foreman had turned the switch to "off" as he agreed to do. The inspector's expert testified that there was nothing wrong with the elevator that would cause it to malfunction and operate when it was turned off.

The inspector most likely will:

(A) Not prevail, because the evidence indicated that the foreman had turned the switch to "off."

(B) Not prevail, because, as a fire inspector, the inspector was merely a licensee and the foreman took steps to protect him from injury.

(C) Prevail, because the foreman must have forgotten to turn the switch to "off."

(D) Prevail, because the printing shop's elevator could not be controlled from the first floor.

Question 24

A pedestrian walking on the sidewalk was struck by a car backing out of a driveway. The driver did not see the pedestrian because her neighbor's bushes obscured her view of the sidewalk. The pedestrian was seriously injured and brought suit against the driver and the neighbor. The pedestrian also included the city in his lawsuit, alleging that the city failed to enforce its ordinance requiring homeowners to provide a clear view of sidewalks where they intersect with driveways. The trier of fact determined that the driver was 60% at fault, the neighbor was 30% at fault, and the city was 10% at fault. The jurisdiction retains traditional joint and several liability rules and has adopted comparative contribution.

Which of the following is a correct statement regarding liability?

(A) The city is liable to the pedestrian for the full amount of the damage award.

(B) Both the driver and the neighbor are liable to the pedestrian for 90% of the damage award.

(C) Each of the three defendants are liable to the pedestrian for one-third of the damage award.

(D) The driver is liable to the pedestrian for 60% of the damage award, the neighbor is liable for 30% of the damage award, and the city is liable for 10% of the damage award.

Question 25

Late one night, a man was walking up a very narrow city street when he noticed that a large garbage truck parked near the top of the hill had begun to roll, driverless, down the street toward him. Seeing that he could not proceed forward and escape the truck, and if he turned and ran downhill, he would soon be overtaken and crushed, he pushed open a window in the apartment building he was passing and climbed inside. The truck narrowly missed him as it careened down the street. The elderly tenant in the apartment, who had a serious heart condition and lived in fear of intruders, thought that the man was a local gang member trying to burglarize his apartment and suffered a major heart attack.

If he sues the man, he can most likely:

(A) Recover damages because of the man's negligent infliction of his emotional distress.

(B) Recover damages because of the man's trespass on his property.

(C) Not recover, because the man had no alternative to avoid the garbage truck.

(D) Not recover, if a reasonable person would not have been frightened.

Question 26

A repair technician employed by a photocopier company was called to a bank to fix a copy machine. It was Friday afternoon, and the technician planned to be on vacation the next week, so he decided to try to complete the repairs on the spot even if it required working past the normal end of the work day at 5 p.m., when he was supposed to leave. He believed that he would be able to exit the building when he was finished. Thus, he continued to work after the bank closed without alerting anyone as to his presence. At 5:30 p.m., the bank's security guard activated its electronic security system, which automatically locked the locks in every door in the building. The guard then went home for the weekend. When the technician completed his work at 5:45 p.m., he attempted to leave the photocopy room, but discovered that the door was locked. There was no phone in the room and his cell phone was dead, and he realized that no one would be back at the bank until Monday. Noticing a smoke detector on the ceiling, he dumped a file of papers into a waste basket and set them ablaze. Eventually, the detector picked up the burning particles from the fire and set off a fire alarm. The fire department arrived soon after and freed the technician. The papers were copies of documents for which the bank had the originals.

What cause or causes of action may the bank assert against the technician?

(A) Conversion and trespass to land.

(B) Conversion but not trespass to land because the technician believed that he would be able to get out when he was finished.

(C) Trespass to land but not conversion because the bank had original copies of the papers that the technician burned.

(D) Neither conversion nor trespass to land.

Question 27

After a sporting event at a stadium, one of the fans sought out the referees to complain about their handling of the game. The fan took out an electronically amplified bullhorn and knocked on the door of the referees' room. When one of the referees opened it, the fan began yelling and berating the referee through the bullhorn. The referee slammed the door shut, striking the bullhorn and jamming it against the fan's mouth, knocking out two of his teeth.

If the fan asserts a claim based on battery against the referee and the referee prevails, it will be because:

(A) The referee did not foresee that the bullhorn would knock out the fan's teeth.

(B) The referee did not know that the door was substantially certain to strike the bullhorn.

(C) The referee was entitled to use force to protect himself.

(D) The fan's conduct provoked the referee's response.

Question 28

A bicyclist was riding his bicycle in the street when a negligently driven car struck the bike, knocking the bicyclist off the bike and breaking his right ankle. The driver of the car immediately stopped and went to his assistance. She got him to his feet and was slowly moving him toward the curb when a negligently driven taxicab struck him in the left leg. The bicyclist required surgery on both his right ankle and his left leg.

If the bicyclist sues the driver and the cabbie in a jurisdiction following the traditional rules for joint and several liability, the bicyclist can:

(A) Recover from either the driver or the cabbie for all of his injuries because the driver and the cabbie are jointly and severally liable.

(B) Recover from the driver only for the injury to his right ankle and recover from the cabbie only for the injury to his left leg.

(C) Recover from either the driver or the cabbie for the injury to his left leg and recover from the driver only for the injury to his right ankle.

(D) Not recover against the driver for the injury to his left leg unless the jury determines that the driver acted negligently when she came to his aid.

Question 29

A backgammon player was upset after losing a match against the club champion. Rushing out of the club, he inadvertently grabbed the champion's board, which looked very much like his own but which was much more expensive. The player left the backgammon board in the trunk of his car, as was his usual practice.

During the night, the car was stolen and along with it, the champion's expensive backgammon board.

In an action by the champion against the player to recover the value of the backgammon board, the champion will likely:

(A) Recover, because when the player took the backgammon board he committed a trespass to the champion's chattel.

(B) Recover, because when the backgammon board was stolen along with the car, the player became liable for conversion of the champion's chattel.

(C) Not recover, because the player believed in good faith that the board was his when he took it from the backgammon club.

(D) Not recover, because the backgammon board was lost through no fault of the player's.

Question 30

A pilot discovered that her twin engine plane was losing fuel at an alarming rate, caused by a latent defect in the fuel system. Realizing that she could not make it to an airport, she saw a highway off to her left and a lake farther off to her right, and decided to try an emergency landing on the highway. As she maneuvered over the highway, the plane's engine quit for good. The plane's wing clipped a car as it landed, causing the car to veer off the road and crash, injuring the driver.

If the driver of the car brings an action for personal injuries against the pilot, judgment will be for:

(A) The driver, if the jury finds that the pilot's selection of the highway rather than the lake was not a reasonable choice under the circumstances.

(B) The driver, because his injuries were the result of the pilot's flying a plane with a dangerously defective fuel system.

(C) The pilot, if the jury finds that she was not negligent in failing to discover the defect in her fuel system.

(D) The pilot, because she made the decision to land on the highway rather than the lake under emergency conditions.

Question 31

A landowner had a swimming pool and a dressing cabana constructed in her spacious backyard. The pool was entirely within the confines of the landowner's property. However, one corner of the cabana extended a few inches onto a far corner of her neighbor's land. At the time of the construction, neither the neighbor nor the landowner was aware that the cabana extended onto the neighbor's property.

Does the neighbor have a cause of action for trespass?

(A) Yes, because the cabana extends onto the neighbor's land.

(B) Yes, because the presence of the cabana on the neighbor's land has caused damage to his property.

(C) No, because the landowner did not actually enter the neighbor's property.

(D) No, because the landowner did not intend to have the cabana encroach on the neighbor's property.

Question 32

A construction company that was putting in a swimming pool for a homeowner left a couple of large pieces of equipment in the backyard overnight. The equipment was not owned by the construction company but was leased from an equipment company, which was responsible for its repair and maintenance. After the workers had left, a seven-year-old boy came onto the homeowner's property to play. The homeowner was aware that the boy often came onto his property to play with his dog. The boy climbed up on one of the pieces of equipment and began pushing buttons and moving levers. The engine started and the equipment began to move because the equipment company had not replaced a defective safety locking device on the ignition. The boy became frightened and jumped off, falling into the hole that had been dug that day, and was injured.

The boy's parents brought suit against the homeowner and the construction company in a jurisdiction that retains traditional joint and several liability rules.

If the construction company is held liable for the boy's injuries, the construction company could:

(A) Obtain indemnity from the equipment company because the equipment was negligently maintained in an unsafe condition.

(B) Obtain contribution from the equipment company because the equipment was negligently maintained in an unsafe condition.

(C) Obtain indemnity from both the equipment company and the homeowner.

(D) Not recover any damages it paid from any other party.

Question 33

A homeowner who was worried about a series of burglaries in her neighborhood purchased a gun for protection. That evening, a homeless person trying to get out of the cold entered her garage through an unlocked door. The homeowner heard him as he was rummaging around for some blankets and opened the door to the garage with her gun in hand. Pointing it in his direction in an attempt to frighten him away, she shouted, "Get out or I'll shoot!" and fired what she thought was a warning shot into the ceiling. Unfortunately, her aim was bad and a bullet struck the homeless person in the shoulder.

If the homeless person sues the homeowner for battery, her best defense is:

(A) The homeless person was a trespasser.

(B) The homeowner used reasonable force to protect her property.

(C) The homeowner did not intend to hit anyone.

(D) The homeowner reasonably feared for her life.

Question 34

A company that owned a tract of land believed to be rich in mineral deposits contracted with a licensed excavator for the removal of soil from the property and delivery of the soil to the company's laboratories. While one of the excavator's trucks was on the way to the laboratory, the rear gate broke loose, dumping three tons of soil onto the highway. A motorist who was driving a short but safe distance behind the truck was unable to stop in time and collided with the soil, causing her serious injury. The rear gate had been negligently secured by one of the excavator's employees.

If the motorist sues the company for his injuries and does not prevail, it will be because:

(A) The rear gate was secured by the excavator's employee.

(B) The excavator had a license to transport soil on the highway.

(C) The company's duty in respect to the movement of its soil on the highway was delegable.

(D) The transportation of soil on the highways was a common practice in the area where the accident occurred.

Question 35

An investor and a sports club owned adjacent parcels of land in an area that was zoned for commercial use. The sports club constructed four tennis courts on its property and equipped them with bright lights for night use. The tennis

court operated 365 days a year and was kept open until 2 a.m. Five years later, a new shopping center was built one mile from their parcels of land, making them highly desirable for residential purposes. The investor decided to construct several residential units on his property and had his property rezoned for residential use, but his architect informed him that, because of the lights, the residences facing the tennis courts would have to be equipped with lightproof draperies that would have to be kept closed until after the tennis courts close each night.

If the investor asserts a claim based on nuisance against the sports club, who is likely to prevail?

(A) The investor, because the residences will constitute higher use of the property than the tennis courts.

(B) The investor, because the glare from the lights interferes with the use and enjoyment of the investor's property.

(C) The sports club, because the area was zoned for commercial use when the tennis courts were built.

(D) The sports club, because the tennis courts were built before the investor planned his residential development.

Question 36

A college student borrowed his roommate's notebook computer without permission because he needed to write a term paper that was due the next day. While the computer was sitting open on the student's desk overnight, a water pipe in the ceiling began leaking and water dripped down on the computer, rendering it inoperable. A computer repair service estimated that it would cost $500 to repair all the damaged components. At the time it was damaged, the computer was worth $700.

If the roommate sues the student for the damage caused to the computer, what will be the extent of his recovery?

(A) Nothing, because the damage occurred through no fault of the student.

(B) Loss of use damages for the time it was in the student's possession.

(C) $500 in damages.

(D) $700 in damages.

TORTS ANSWERS - SET 6

Answer to Question 1

(D) The businessman will not recover against the incumbent because, as a state legislator, she was absolutely privileged to read the story into the record on the floor of the legislature. Under certain circumstances, a speaker will not be liable for defamatory statements because she is afforded an absolute privilege. Such a privilege is ***not*** affected by a showing of malice, abuse, or excessive provocation. Remarks made by either federal or state legislators in their official capacity during legislative proceedings are absolutely privileged. There is no requirement of a reasonable relationship to any matter at hand. The incumbent is a state legislator. When she read the newspaper article into the legislative record, she was speaking in her official capacity as a legislator, on the floor of the legislature. Thus, her reading of the article is cloaked with absolute privilege, and she will be shielded from liability for defamation. (A) is incorrect because, even if the businessman establishes actual malice by the incumbent, he will not recover. The businessman, as a candidate for public office, is a public figure, and information about his health is probably a matter of public concern. Thus, to recover, the businessman must show actual malice (*i.e.,* knowledge of falsity or reckless disregard for truth or falsity). However, this showing of malice still will not provide the businessman a recovery because the incumbent has an ***absolute*** privilege. If she had only a qualified privilege, a showing of malice would defeat the privilege. (B) is incorrect because slander per se will not provide the businessman a recovery. Slander per se is a characterization applied to certain categories of spoken defamation. If defamation falls within one of these categories, injury to reputation is presumed without proof of special damages. One such category is a defamatory statement that adversely reflects on the plaintiff's abilities in his business, trade, or profession. Although statements to the effect that the businessman suffered from severe psychological problems might adversely reflect on his fitness for public office, this would be significant only in terms of establishing that the businessman need not prove special damages. However, proof of damages is of no importance here, because the incumbent is not liable due to her absolute privilege. If the incumbent is shielded from liability, the possible existence of slander per se is of no use to the businessman. Note also that, in any event, any defamation here would be characterized as libel, rather than slander. Libel is a defamatory statement recorded in writing or some other permanent form. Where the original defamation is libel, any repetition, even if oral, is also libel. Here, the original defamation was in a newspaper article and thus was libel. Consequently, the oral repetition of the article would also be libel, if the incumbent were subject to defamation liability. (C) is incorrect because, if the incumbent were not protected by the absolute privilege, the mere fact that she relied on the article would not afford her a defense. A republisher (one who repeats a defamatory statement) is liable on the same general basis as a primary publisher.

Answer to Question 2

(C) The breeder will not recover because there has been no substantial interference with her use or enjoyment of her land, nor has there been a trespass. A private nuisance is a substantial, unreasonable interference with another person's use or enjoyment of her property. The interference must be offensive, inconvenient, or annoying ***to the average person in the community***. It is not a substantial interference if it merely interferes with a specialized use of the land. Here, the testing of the dog whistles did not bother humans, and so it did not disturb the average person in the community. It is disturbing to the breeder's dogs, but this affects only her specialized use of her land. Thus, the manufacturer's actions do not constitute a private nuisance. (Nor do they constitute a public nuisance—an act that unreasonably interferes with the health, safety, or property rights of the community.) Therefore, (C) is correct, and (B) is incorrect. (A) is incorrect because

the sounds reaching the breeder's property do not constitute a trespass. A trespass is an intentional ***physical invasion*** of another's land. Sound waves do not produce a physical invasion. Thus, the facts here do not support a basis for trespass. (D) is incorrect because the manufacturer could be found liable to the breeder even if it acted reasonably. In determining whether there is a nuisance, a court would consider the manufacturer's care in testing its whistles, but that factor alone would not be determinative. If the activities were offensive to the average person, the court might still find there is a nuisance—even if it is impossible to do a better job of soundproofing. The court would have to consider the "reasonableness" of the interference, *i.e.,* balance the injury against the utility of the manufacturer's conduct.

Answer to Question 3

(B) The pilot will prevail because the conduct of the other plane's student pilot constituted a superseding intervening force that relieves the pilot from liability. To establish a prima facie case for negligence, the attorney must show that the pilot's breach of his duty to her was the actual and proximate cause of her injury. The attorney can establish actual cause because but for the pilot's error, she would not have been injured. However, not all injuries "actually" caused by a defendant will be deemed to have been proximately caused by his acts. The general rule of proximate cause is that the defendant is liable for all harmful results that are the normal incidents of and within the increased risk caused by his acts. This rule applies to cases such as this, where an intervening force comes into motion after the defendant's negligent act and combines with it to cause plaintiff's injury (indirect cause cases). Here, the pilot's navigational error did create a greater risk of collision with other planes in the process of landing, but it did not increase the risk of a plane using the landing runway to take off in disregard of the control tower's instructions once the pilot was safely on the ground. Hence, the student pilot's unforeseeable conduct was not within the increased risk created by the pilot's negligence and constitutes a ***superseding force*** that breaks the causal connection between the pilot's conduct and the attorney's injury, enabling the pilot to avoid liability to the attorney. (A) is incorrect because assumption of the risk requires knowledge of the specific risk and the voluntary assumption of that risk. Although the attorney knew that the pilot lacked a commercial license, she also was under the impression that he was a very good pilot. There is no indication that she knew of or voluntarily assumed any risk. Certainly, she did not assume the risk of the type of harm she suffered. (C) is incorrect because even though the pilot may be negligent per se, he would not be liable per se. A specific duty imposed by a statute may replace the more general common law duty of due care when: (i) the plaintiff is within the class to be protected by the statute; (ii) the statute was designed to prevent the type of harm suffered; and (iii) the statutory standard of conduct is clearly defined. The statutory duty arguably applies here because the attorney, as the pilot's paying passenger, is within the protected class, runway collisions and other pilot errors are what the license requirement is officially designed to prevent, and the statutory standard of conduct is clear. There are no grounds for excusing the pilot's violation of the statute, so the pilot's conduct could be seen as "negligence per se." This means that plaintiff will have established a conclusive presumption of ***duty and breach of duty***. However, for the attorney to prevail, she must also establish actual and proximate causation. As explained above, the attorney will not be able to show that the pilot's negligence was the proximate cause of her injuries. Thus, while she may be able to establish "negligence per se," she has not made a case for "liability per se." (D) is true as far as it goes. An act or omission to act is the cause in fact of an injury when the injury would not have occurred but for the act, and this injury would not have occurred but for the pilot's landing at the wrong airport. However, the attorney must also be able to establish that the pilot's conduct was a proximate cause of her injury. As noted above, the pilot's conduct was not a proximate cause of her injury because the student pilot's actions acted as a superseding intervening force.

Answer to Question 4

(B) The resident's best argument is that negligence is presumed from the fact that the patient escaped. This choice raises the doctrine of res ipsa loquitur, which allows the trier of fact to infer negligence simply from the fact that a particular injury occurred. Res ipsa loquitur requires the plaintiff to establish that: the event causing the injury is of a type that would not normally occur unless someone was negligent; the negligence was attributable to the defendant; and plaintiff was not at fault regarding his injury. Here, the event causing injury is due to the patient's escape, and it seems that the patient would not have escaped unless someone was negligent (*e.g.,* the employee in not locking the door or the hospital in not making sure that the employee knew of his responsibility to lock the door). The fact that the hospital had sole control over the patient can be used to show that the negligence is attributable to the hospital (through its employees). Finally, the resident was not at fault regarding his injury. Thus, res ipsa could be used to find negligence and allow the resident to recover. (A) is wrong because the hospital is not strictly liable. Strict liability occurs only where there is an absolute duty on the defendant's part to make safe (*e.g.,* in abnormally dangerous activity situations). Hospitals do not have an ***absolute*** duty to protect against dangerous acts of their patients. (C) is wrong because there is no basis for holding the hospital vicariously liable. A person or entity can be vicariously liable for the acts of others only if there is a relationship between them that gives rise to such liability (*e.g.,* employer-employee). There is generally no such basis for holding a hospital liable for its patients' actions, nor is there any specific reason to do so here. (D) is wrong because it is not clear that the employee acted negligently even if he did fail to lock the door. The employee was under a duty to act reasonably under the circumstances. If he was unaware of the duty to lock the door, he was not negligent in failing to do so. Arguably the employee was negligent in not reading the entire manual, but if the hospital had not told him that it was important for him to read it immediately, he would not be negligent in not finishing the manual.

Answer to Question 5

(A) The mayor cannot recover against the columnist because he did not act with "actual malice." A public official, such as a mayor, may not recover for defamatory words relating to his official conduct unless there is clear and convincing proof that the statement was made with "actual malice," which is defined as knowledge that the statement was false or reckless disregard as to truth or falsity. Reckless conduct is not measured by whether a reasonable person would have investigated before publishing; rather, there must be a showing that the defendant in fact (subjectively) entertained serious doubts as to the truthfulness of his publication. Here, while the columnist had no evidence of the mayor's involvement with the action of the health inspectors, he believed that there was a connection based on his belief as to how the city operates. Hence, he has not acted with actual malice and is not liable to the mayor for defamation. (B) is incorrect because the columnist's qualified privilege applies only to statements made to defend his own actions, property, or reputation. Even if it were to apply to his explanation of why his family's restaurant was shut down, his statements in the column were beyond the scope of the privilege, which does not extend to making a statement to a mass audience whose reading of the statement would not reasonably further his interest in defending himself. Here, the publication in his newspaper column of his explanation as to why the restaurant was shut down was beyond the scope of any privilege he may have had. (C) is incorrect because malice that will result in the loss of a qualified privilege is defined by most courts as knowledge of falsity or reckless disregard as to truth or falsity, rather than hostility or ill-will. As long as the defendant is using a proper occasion for a qualified privilege in a proper way, he will not lose this privilege simply because he bears ill-will toward the plaintiff. (D) is incorrect because the fact that the columnist

should have investigated the accuracy of his assertions and did not only establishes negligence on his part. As discussed above, the mayor, as a public official, must show at least reckless disregard as to truth or falsity to recover in a defamation action.

Answer to Question 6

(B) If the dog owner is liable for the damages to the neighbor's flower bed, it will be because he was shown to have been negligent. The owner of a trespassing animal is strictly liable for damages done by the animal if it is foreseeable that the animal will trespass and cause that damage. Thus, if the animal involved is of a type likely to roam and do damage to another's property (*e.g.,* livestock such as cows or sheep), the owner is strictly liable. Here, it is not foreseeable that the dog owner's dog would damage the neighbor's flower bed because the dog had just completed an obedience class, and therefore it was not foreseeable that the dog would disregard his training and run off for no apparent reason. Also, it was not foreseeable that the dog would do this type of damage. Generally, runaway dogs do not immediately head for the nearest flower bed and start digging. Thus, because the dog's actions and the type of damages caused by him are unforeseeable, the dog owner is not strictly liable; any recovery for the damages must be based on a showing of fault (intentional tort or negligence) on the part of the dog owner. (A) is wrong because it states a requirement for conversion of property. However, for that tort, the defendant must have intended an act that causes the interference with the plaintiff's property. Here, the dog owner did not act with the goal of having the dog destroy the flower bed, nor did he know with substantial certainty that this would happen. Therefore, he did not have the intent necessary for conversion. (C) is wrong because to impose liability on the dog owner simply because he owned the dog would amount to strict liability, and as explained above, the dog owner cannot be strictly liable here because it was not foreseeable that the dog would escape and do this type of damage. (D) is wrong. The dog owner could not be liable for trespass because he lacked the intent for that tort. Trespass requires an intent to make an entry onto that particular parcel of land. Here, the dog owner did not intend for the dog to go onto the neighbor's land, nor did he know with substantial certainty that that would happen. Thus, the dog owner has not committed a trespass.

Answer to Question 7

(B) The skier can recover $2 million from the snowboarder because the snowboarder is jointly and severally liable for the injury. The doctrine of joint and several liability provides that when two or more tortious acts combine to proximately cause an indivisible injury to plaintiff, each tortfeasor will be jointly and severally liable for that injury. This means that plaintiff can recover the entire amount of his damages from any one defendant. The doctrine applies even though each tortfeasor acted entirely independently and at different times. Here, both the snowboarder and the employee of the ski resort breached their duty to the skier to act with reasonable care. Each tortfeasor's act was the actual cause of the skier's disability because but for either one of the acts, his leg would not have been permanently disabled. The snowboarder's act was the proximate cause of the skier's disability because the disability was the direct result of the snowboarder's act. The fact that the extent of the harm was unforeseeable is irrelevant; *i.e.,* the tortfeasor takes the victim as he finds him. Thus, the skier can recover the entire $2 million from the snowboarder. (A) is incorrect because the contribution rules govern only whether a defendant required to pay more than his share of damages has a claim against the other jointly liable parties for the excess. Contribution does not involve the amount of damages that the plaintiff can collect in the first place. (C) is incorrect because the skier has met his burden of proof by establishing that the snowboarder was an actual and proximate cause of his permanent disability. Since the injury caused by the tortfeasors was not divisible, under joint and several liability rules, the snowboarder is liable for the full amount of the damages, including that attributable to the permanent disability. (D) is incorrect because but for the snowboarder's collision with the skier, the skier would not have been disabled. The "but for" test applies in concurrent cause situations—cases where several acts combine to cause the injury, but none of them standing alone would have been sufficient. The fact that the snowboarder's act standing alone would not have caused the disability is irrelevant to the snowboarder's liability.

Answer to Question 8

(B) The tenant will likely prevail because the lack of a warning about eye injuries made the product unreasonably dangerous. A products liability action based on strict liability requires: (i) a strict duty by a commercial supplier; (ii) a breach of that duty by the sale of a product in a defective condition that makes the product unreasonably dangerous; (iii) causation; and (iv) damages. Here, the paint company is a commercial supplier of a "defective" product. Although the primer was not actually defective in that it apparently performed as it was meant to do, it is legally defective if it was unreasonably dangerous and could be made safer by adequate warnings. Here, the paint company knew of the danger and could easily have placed a specific warning on the label. Even though professional users may have known of the danger, it was not obvious, and it could have been avoided at minimal cost by including a specific warning. That would have alerted the landlord to the danger, making it more likely that he would take precautions that would have prevented the tenant from being injured. To prove actual cause where the plaintiff's claim is that the product is defective because of lack of an adequate warning, the plaintiff is entitled to a presumption that an adequate warning would have been read and heeded. Thus, the tenant can likely establish liability on her cause of action. (A) is wrong because even in a strict liability action, liability will be found only if the product is defective, not just because someone was injured when it was used for its intended purpose. (C) is wrong because the manufacturer must warn of the danger, and its duty is not satisfied merely because there have been no injuries to date by following the instructions on the label. (D) is wrong because, given the inadequacy of the warnings, any negligence on the landlord's part would be ordinary foreseeable negligence that would not cut off the paint company's liability for its defective product.

Answer to Question 9

(C) All of the parties would have a claim for a percentage of their damages, measured by their degree of fault. In a partial comparative negligence jurisdiction, a plaintiff can recover damages as long as her negligence was less serious than, or no more serious than, that of the defendant. When multiple defendants have contributed to plaintiff's injury, most of these jurisdictions use a "combined comparison" approach to determine the threshold level, whereby plaintiff's negligence is compared with the total negligence of all of the defendants combined. Here, each of the parties' negligence is less than the combined negligence of the other two parties. Hence, each of them will have a viable claim for damages, reduced by the percentage of their fault, as reflected in choice (C). (A) and (B) are wrong because they do not reflect the "combined comparison" approach, and (D) is wrong because it does not reflect the reduction in their damage claims due to their percentage of fault. → multiple Def. combined comparison. Partial comp. Neg.

Answer to Question 10

(C) The friend will recover for battery because the student did not have the right to use force. The defense of recapture of chattels is limited by the circumstances of the original dispossession. When another's possession of the owner's chattel began lawfully, the owner may use only

peaceful means to recover the chattel. Force may be used to recapture a chattel only when in "hot pursuit" of one who has obtained possession wrongfully (*e.g.*, by theft). Here, the friend's initial possession of the game system was a bailment, because the student consented to his borrowing it. Thus, the student is not entitled to use force to recover it, and his wrestling it away from the friend constituted the requisite harmful or offensive contact to make the student liable for battery. (A) is incorrect. One who is entitled to use force to recapture chattels is only permitted to use reasonable force, but here the student is not entitled to use any force at all because the friend's initial possession of the game system was lawful. (B) is incorrect because it is not relevant whether the friend's delay in returning the game system was unreasonable; the student is not entitled to use force because he lent the system to the friend originally. (D) is incorrect because the requirement that a timely demand to return the chattel must precede the use of force applies only if the owner of the chattel is entitled to use force. Here, as discussed above, the student did not have the right to use force.

Answer to Question 11

(A) The homeowner will probably prevail on a claim for intentional infliction of emotional distress because the neighbor's conduct was sufficiently extreme and outrageous and the other elements of the tort are present. Intentional infliction of emotional distress requires: (i) an act by defendant amounting to extreme and outrageous conduct; (ii) intent to cause severe emotional distress or recklessness as to the effect of defendant's conduct; (iii) causation; and (iv) damages. "Outrageous conduct" is extreme conduct that transcends all bounds of decency. The neighbor's use of the recording and his insults against the homeowner for the benefit of her guests would probably qualify as extreme and outrageous conduct, particularly because there is no evidence that he had previously tried to resolve the problem with the homeowner in a more civilized manner. The neighbor had the requisite intent (either he intended to cause emotional distress or he was reckless as to its effect), there was causation, and the homeowner suffered damages (*i.e.,* she was severely distressed) as a result of the neighbor's actions. (B) is wrong because pecuniary harm is not required for purposes of this tort—all that is required is severe emotional distress. (C) is wrong because, in contrast to negligent infliction of distress, intentional infliction of distress does not require proof of physical harm to recover. (D) is wrong because the fact that the barking constituted a nuisance would not be a defense to conduct amounting to intentional infliction of distress; abatement of a private nuisance by self-help must be preceded by notice to the other party and must be conducted in a reasonable manner.

Answer to Question 12

(C) The attorney will lose because the guard did not know that he was still in the building. For false imprisonment, the plaintiff must show (i) an act or omission on the part of the defendant that confines or restrains the plaintiff to a bounded area, (ii) intent on the part of the defendant to confine or restrain the plaintiff, and (iii) causation. Here, because the guard apparently did not know that the attorney was still in the building, she had no intent to confine him when she locked the doors. (A) is incorrect because recklessness is not enough; while the attorney likely has a cause of action for negligence against the guard, and through respondeat superior, the building, his claim is for false imprisonment. For liability for false imprisonment, there must be an intent to confine. (B) is incorrect because his status as a trespasser, while it may otherwise make him liable to the building for trespass, does not preclude him from recovering for false imprisonment. (D) is incorrect because the attorney need not show harm from the confinement to recover for false imprisonment, as long as he was aware of the confinement.

Answer to Question 13

(B) The court should grant the homeowner's motion for judgment as a matter of law because the driver has not established a prima facie case against the homeowner. An owner of wild (dangerous) animals is strictly liable for injuries caused by those animals as long as the person injured did nothing, voluntarily or consciously, to bring about the injury. However, strict liability generally is not imposed in favor of undiscovered trespassers against landowners in the absence of negligence, such as when the landowner knows that the trespassers are on the land and fails to warn them of the animal. Here, despite the fact that the driver did not intend to enter the homeowner's land (and thus would not be liable for the intentional tort of trespass), his status on the homeowner's land is that of a trespasser rather than a licensee or invitee. The driver has presented no evidence of negligence on the homeowner's part and therefore has not established a prima facie case against the homeowner. (A) is wrong because, as discussed above, the homeowner is not strictly liable to the driver because the driver was a trespasser. (C) is incorrect because the driver will not prevail regardless of whether he was contributorily negligent, because he cannot establish a prima facie case against the homeowner in either negligence or strict liability. (D) is incorrect for several reasons: While the driver's transport of radioactive waste may have been an abnormally dangerous activity, that danger had nothing to do with the accident that occurred. Furthermore, the fact that the driver may have been engaged in an abnormally dangerous activity would not prevent him from recovering damages from another tortfeasor if he established the requisite prima facie case. Finally, the fact that the parties were engaged in activities potentially creating strict liability has nothing to do with whether issues of fact regarding liability still exist that would require denying both motions and going to trial.

Answer to Question 14

(B) If the driver was effectively required by statute to take an occasional quick look at his speedometer to make sure that he was complying with appropriate speed limits, then his momentary glance at the speedometer in the instant case would, as a matter of law, not constitute negligent conduct. Because this is a matter of law, the judge would be authorized to correct this aspect of the jury's verdict. If the driver is thus found to be not negligent in this matter, his recovery will not be reduced. (A) is incorrect because in most states that have adopted comparative negligence, the plaintiff's negligence will be considered even in cases where the defendant has acted willfully and wantonly. (C) is incorrect because the fact that the defendant is more than 50% at fault does not mean that the plaintiff is entitled to receive 100% of his damages from the defendant in a partial comparative negligence jurisdiction. It only means that the plaintiff's recovery is not totally defeated. (D) is incorrect because, although the transportation of chemical waste would probably be considered an abnormally dangerous activity, liability for conducting an abnormally dangerous activity attaches only if the harm results from the kind of danger to be anticipated from such activity; *i.e.,* the injury must flow from the normally dangerous propensity of the activity. The canister falling from the truck is not the "normally dangerous propensity" of transporting chemical waste.

Answer to Question 15

(D) The court should grant the motion because the driver did not establish the cause-in-fact element of his prima facie case against the freight line. The primary test for cause in fact (actual cause) is the "but for" test: An act is the cause in fact of an injury when the injury would not have occurred ***but for*** the act. Even though the freight line had a duty created by the statute to be able to stop its train within 200 yards of first braking, and breached that duty (establishing the first two

elements of the driver's prima facie case), it must still be shown that the collision would not have occurred in the absence of the breach. Because the car was only 150 yards from the point of braking, even a train in compliance with the statute would have struck it. Since no other evidence of negligence has been presented, the motion should be granted. (A) is incorrect because establishing the freight line's "negligence per se" through violation of the statute only establishes a conclusive presumption of duty and breach of duty; the plaintiff must still prove causation. (B) is incorrect because generally violation of a statute does not create strict liability; even if it did in this case, the plaintiff would still have to prove causation as part of the prima facie case for strict liability. (C) is not correct because the court will not reach the issue of the plaintiff's contributory negligence in this case because the prima facie case for the defendant's negligence has not been established. Furthermore, establishing the plaintiff's contributory negligence by violation of a statute uses the same rules that govern whether a statute can establish the defendant's negligence. Hence, the driver's violation of the crossing statute may be excused if the trier of fact determines that compliance was beyond his control because his car stalled.

Answer to Question 16

(C) The husband will not recover for his injuries because he was not in the zone of danger created by the bank's negligence. The duty to avoid negligent infliction of emotional distress is breached when defendant creates a foreseeable risk of physical injury to plaintiff, either by (i) causing a threat of physical impact that leads to emotional distress, or (ii) directly causing severe emotional distress that by itself is likely to result in physical symptoms, and plaintiff suffers some physical injury from distress rather than from physical contact. If plaintiff's distress is caused by threat of physical impact to himself, courts require that plaintiff be within the "zone of danger" of physical harm from defendant's negligent conduct. Jurisdictions applying the zone of danger approach in bystander cases allow recovery from witnessing another person injured as long as the bystander was also in the zone of danger. Here, however, the husband was not in the zone of danger when the artwork collapsed. Merely witnessing someone else suffer injury from defendant's negligence, even though the husband suffered physical injury from his distress, is not sufficient in these jurisdictions for the husband to prevail. (C) is therefore correct and (A) is incorrect. (B) is also incorrect. The modern majority rule allows recovery based on foreseeability even if plaintiff is outside the zone of danger as long as (i) plaintiff and the person injured by defendant's negligence are closely related, (ii) plaintiff was present at the scene of the injury, and (iii) plaintiff personally observed or perceived the event. (Observation may be by sight, hearing, or other senses.) The court in this case, however, still imposes the zone of danger requirement in bystander cases. (D) is incorrect because the fact that he did not see the accident occur is irrelevant in a "zone of danger" approach. Had he been in the zone of danger, he could have recovered even though he only heard the crash and did not see it (such as if he were looking the other way).

Answer to Question 17

(C) The diner is not likely to recover because the restaurant did not permit patrons in the kitchen. The duty owed by an owner or occupier of land to those entering the land depends in most jurisdictions on whether the entrant is characterized as a trespasser, licensee, or invitee. Here, the diner was an invitee of the restaurant while he was dining at the restaurant. However, a person loses his status as an invitee if he exceeds the scope of the invitation—if he goes into a portion of the premises where his invitation cannot reasonably be said to extend. Here, the diner lost the status of an invitee when he entered the kitchen; he became, at best, a licensee, perhaps even a trespasser, because patrons were not permitted in the kitchen. While a landowner owes no duty to an undiscovered trespasser, he owes a discovered trespasser the duty to warn of artificial conditions

known to the landowner that involve a risk of death or serious bodily harm and that the trespasser is unlikely to discover. For a licensee, the duty extends to ***all*** dangerous conditions that create an unreasonable risk of ***any*** harm to the licensee. Had the diner been an invitee, he could have argued that under the duty owed to invitees to make reasonable inspections, a puddle of grease that had time to congeal should have been discovered and cleaned up, or at least been the subject of a warning. Here, however, there are no facts to suggest that anyone in the kitchen knew of the diner's presence or the puddle of grease, even though it had congealed; hence, the facts do not establish a breach of the duty to warn discovered trespassers or licensees of dangerous conditions. (A) is incorrect. While places of public accommodation have an affirmative duty to use reasonable care to aid or assist their patrons, that duty rule does not alter the duty rules pertaining to the condition of the land, which are based on the status of the person on the premises (as discussed above). (B) is incorrect because the failure to exercise reasonable care to discover a dangerous condition breaches a duty owed only to invitees, as discussed above. However, the diner was no longer an invitee when he entered the kitchen area. He was at most a licensee, for whom the duty to make reasonable inspections does not apply. (D) is incorrect. While a duty to warn does not exist where the dangerous condition is so obvious that the invitee should reasonably have been aware of it, just the fact that the grease was visible on the floor does not establish this. "Obviousness" is determined by all of the surrounding circumstances; *e.g.*, one whose attention may have been directed elsewhere may recover even though the condition was visible. In any case, even if the puddle were not visible, the diner would not be able to recover because he did not have invitee status when he entered the kitchen.

Answer to Question 18

(D) The contractor will win, because the facts indicate that he was unaware that anyone would be at the house or that the powder would react as it did when exposed to water. Because the call of the question does not identify the theory of liability that the friend is using, all possible theories of liability must be considered. The contractor did not commit an intentional tort against the friend. He is not a commercial supplier of a product, who would be liable under a strict products liability theory; nor is he strictly liable for engaging in an abnormally dangerous activity, because the activity can be conducted safely if done carefully by professional users. Most likely, this suit is based on negligence. A prima facie case for negligence consists of: (i) a duty on the part of the defendant to conform to a specific standard of conduct for the protection of the plaintiff against an unreasonable risk of injury; (ii) breach of that duty by the defendant; (iii) the breach was the actual and proximate cause of the plaintiff's injury; and (iv) damage to the plaintiff's person or property. When a person engages in an activity, he is under a legal duty to take precautions against creating unreasonable risks of injury to other persons. However, a duty of care is owed only to foreseeable plaintiffs, and no duty is imposed to take precautions against events that cannot reasonably be foreseen. While courts usually conclude that the injured plaintiff in a negligence action was a foreseeable plaintiff, here, it appears that contractor was unaware that the friend had a key to the homeowner's house and might come over at any time. To the best of the contractor's knowledge, no one was going to be at the house before he returned the next day because the homeowner was out of town. In addition, the contractor, who was using the product for the first time, evidently was unaware that the powder was volatile when exposed to water because the manufacturer did not include a warning to that effect. If the contractor could not reasonably have foreseen that the powder would explode upon being sprayed with water, he would have had no duty to take precautions against such an explosion. Thus, the contractor breached no duty to the friend by leaving the powder on the deck and will not be liable for the friend's injuries. (A) is incorrect because the contractor did not know, nor did he have reason to know, of a foreseeable risk of injury to the friend by leaving the powder on the wooden deck. (B)

is incorrect because the contractor is not a commercial supplier of the powder. The manufacturer, as a commercial supplier of the powder, owes a strict duty to refrain from placing in commerce a product that is so defective as to be unreasonably dangerous. The contractor is simply a user of the powder, not a commercial supplier. Thus, the contractor is not held to the same standard of liability as the manufacturer; to recover, the friend must prove some fault on the part of the contractor in leaving the powder on the deck. (C) is incorrect because using the powder for the purpose for which it was designed would not relieve the contractor of liability if he were otherwise at fault. For example, if the contractor knew that a person such as the friend might be harmed by leaving the powder on the deck, the contractor would be liable for his failure to remove the powder despite the fact that he used the powder for its designed purpose.

Answer to Question 19

(A) The motorcyclist and the truck driver can recover damages against the cabdriver because she had the last clear chance to avoid the accident. In traditional contributory negligence jurisdictions, a plaintiff's contributory negligence completely bars his right to recover. However, under the doctrine of last clear chance, the person with the last clear chance to avoid an accident who fails to do so is liable to the other party for negligence despite that party's contributory negligence. Here, the motorcyclist and the truck driver were both negligent in the initial collision and were in a position of helpless peril. The cabdriver was negligent in deciding to try to go around the vehicles and then striking them. Because she had the last clear chance to avoid the accident and failed to do so, she is liable to both the motorcyclist and the truck driver for damages. (B) and (C) are incorrect because the motorcyclist cannot recover damages against the truck driver. For last clear chance to operate, the defendant must have been able to avoid harming the plaintiff at the time of the accident. Courts will not apply last clear chance when the defendant's only negligence (failing to get his brakes fixed) occurred earlier. (D) is incorrect because last clear chance applies, as discussed above. The cabdriver cannot rely on the general rule that a party's contributory negligence bars his recovery because she had the last clear chance to avoid colliding with the other two vehicles.

Answer to Question 20

(B) The owner will have to show that he would have recovered damages in his lawsuit. The following elements must be proved for a prima facie case of negligence: (i) the existence of a duty on the part of the defendant to conform to a specific standard of conduct for the protection of the plaintiff against unreasonable risk of injury, (ii) breach of that duty by the defendant, (iii) that the breach of duty was the actual and proximate cause of the plaintiff's injury, and (iv) damage to the plaintiff's person or property. Here, the owner can establish that the law firm breached its professional duty of care by failing to file a claim within the statute of limitations. He must also establish that this breach was an actual and proximate cause of his damages, which here would be the loss of the contract damages that he could have recovered from the breach by the supplier. (A) is incorrect because merely having a good faith claim that was lost because of the firm's negligence is not sufficient. The owner has to show by a preponderance of the evidence that he suffered damages because of the firm's negligence. (C) is incorrect because it states a defense rather than part of the prima facie case; any contributory negligence on the owner's part must be pleaded and proved by the law firm to either defeat or reduce his recovery. (D) is incorrect because it is irrelevant whether the breach by the supplier severely harmed the owner's financial situation. The only issue is whether he would have been able to recover any of his losses had he timely filed a breach of contract action. If he establishes that he would have recovered, then the law firm's negligence was an actual and proximate cause of his suffering damages.

Answer to Question 21

(A) The racer will recover $30,000 because the rival committed a conversion. The prima facie case for conversion requires (i) an act by defendant interfering with plaintiff's right of possession in the chattel that is serious enough in nature or consequence to warrant that the defendant pay the full value of the chattel, (ii) intent to perform the act bringing about the interference with plaintiff's right of possession, and (iii) causation. If conversion is established, plaintiff is entitled to the fair market value of the chattel ***as of the time and place of conversion.*** Here, the rival refused to return the bike despite a specific request by the racer; this is deemed to be a conversion because it amounts to a claim of dominion and control by the rival over the racer's property. At the time of the conversion, the market value of the bike was $30,000. Thus, this amount is what the racer should recover. (B) is wrong because, even assuming that the other contestant would have agreed to the substitution of racers, the racer may not be able to prove that he would have won the match and the $10,000. The more appropriate remedy is the conversion remedy of $30,000. (C) is wrong because conversion damages based on fair market value are generally measured at the time and place of the conversion, which was when the rival refused to return the bike, and not at the time of trial. (D) is wrong because it states a measure of damages more appropriate to trespass to chattels, which is a less serious interference with a plaintiff's right of possession in a chattel that requires proof of actual damages. Here, the rival's refusal to return the bike despite the racer's demand that it be returned constitutes conversion rather than trespass to chattels.

Answer to Question 22

(B) The boat owner can recover $45,000 through comparative contribution for the passenger's claim and $4,500 on his own claim against the driver of the boat. Most comparative negligence states have adopted a comparative contribution system based on the relative fault of the various tortfeasors. Nonpaying tortfeasors who are jointly and severally liable are required to contribute only in proportion to their relative fault. Here, because the jurisdiction retained joint and several liability, the boat owner had to pay the passenger all of her damages. Under comparative contribution rules, the boat owner can obtain contribution from the driver for 45% of that amount, because the driver was 45% at fault. In addition, the boat owner has a direct claim against the driver for his own damages of $10,000, reduced by 55%, the amount of his fault. Thus, the total amount that the boat owner can recover from the driver is $49,500, making (B) correct and (A) incorrect. (C) is incorrect because it reflects traditional contribution rules, in which all tortfeasors were required to pay equal shares regardless of their respective degrees of fault. (D) is incorrect because a tortfeasor who was jointly and severally liable is not precluded from recovering contribution merely because he was more at fault than the other tortfeasors.

Answer to Question 23

(D) The inspector will likely prevail. Under the doctrine of res ipsa loquitur, the trier of fact is permitted to infer the defendant's breach of duty when the facts strongly indicate that the plaintiff's injuries resulted from the defendant's negligence. The facts here indicate that, because the elevator was not controllable from the first floor, the elevator would not have descended unless someone from the second floor changed it to "on" and pushed the down button. The fact that someone started the elevator while the inspector was in the shaft is circumstantial evidence that either the foreman was negligent (*e.g.,* by failing to apprise his co-workers of the inspector's presence in the shaft) or one of his co-workers was negligent (*e.g.,* by forgetting the foreman's warning and turning the elevator back on). Thus, under the doctrine of res ipsa loquitur, the inspector would be able to show that, through respondeat superior, the print shop breached a duty owing to him.

Thus, (A) is incorrect. (B) is incorrect because the inspector's status is irrelevant. A possessor of land owes a duty of reasonable care in the exercise of all active operations on the property, regardless of whether the plaintiff was a licensee or invitee. Thus, regardless of the inspector's status, the print shop owed a duty of reasonable care in its employees' operation of the elevator. (C) is incorrect because it may have been another employee who was negligent.

Answer to Question 24

(A) The city is liable to the pedestrian for the full amount of the damage award. Where there is joint and several liability, each defendant found by the trier of fact to be at fault for an indivisible injury is liable to the plaintiff for the entire amount of damages incurred, not just a portion of it. (Of course, multiple recovery is not allowed.) Thus, because the city has been found to be at fault for the accident, the pedestrian could recover the full amount of the damage award from the city. (B) is incorrect because both the driver and the neighbor are liable for the full amount of the damage award rather than 90%. Again, each defendant found to be at fault by the trier of fact for an indivisible injury is liable to the plaintiff for the entire amount of damages incurred. (C) and (D) are incorrect because they are not applying joint and several liability. Under a joint and several liability system, contribution allows a defendant who pays more than his share of damages to recover the excess from the other jointly liable parties; responsibility for the total damages is thus apportioned among those at fault. Traditional contribution rules require all defendants to pay equal shares regardless of their respective degrees of fault (choice (C)), while states with a comparative contribution system impose contribution in proportion to the relative fault of the various defendants (choice (D)). Nevertheless, this simply means that the city (assuming it paid the judgment award to the plaintiff) has contribution rights ***against the other defendants*** (*i.e.*, it can recover from the others for damages paid in excess of the amount proportionate to its relative fault). This does not, however, mean that the defendants' liability ***to the plaintiff*** is based on their relative fault. In fact, if one defendant were judgment-proof, the others would still be responsible for the full amount despite the fact that the judgment-proof defendant was mostly at fault.

Answer to Question 25

(B) The tenant can recover damages because of the man's trespass. Under the defense of necessity, a person may interfere with the real or personal property of another when the interference is reasonably and apparently necessary to avoid threatened injury from another force and the threatened injury is substantially more serious than the invasion that is undertaken. However, when the act is done not for the general public good, but to protect the actor or another person from injury, the defense is qualified; *i.e.*, the actor must pay for any injury he causes. Here, although the man was privileged to enter the tenant's apartment to prevent his injury or death (private necessity), the privilege does not extend to the infliction of damages. Thus, he must pay for any injury he caused, including the tenant's damages from his heart attack. (A) is wrong because negligent infliction of emotional distress requires that the distress be caused by negligent conduct by the defendant. These facts give no indication that the man acted negligently. (C) is wrong because, as stated above, the man's privilege is limited. While he cannot be forced off the premises as a trespasser, he is liable for the injury he caused. (D) is wrong because it is irrelevant what a reasonable person would have felt. If the man's actions caused the tenant's injury, he is liable because the defense of private necessity provides only an incomplete privilege.

Answer to Question 26

(A) The bank may assert a cause of action based on both of these theories. Trespass to land requires (i) an act of physical invasion of plaintiff's real property by defendant, (ii) intent on the part of defendant to bring about a physical invasion of plaintiff's real property, and (iii) causation. A trespass to land may exist when defendant remains on plaintiff's land after an otherwise lawful right of entry has lapsed. Thus, because the technician intended to stay beyond the bank's normal hours and did so without permission, he has arguably committed a trespass. Conversion consists of (i) an act by defendant interfering with plaintiff's right of possession in the chattel that is serious enough in nature or consequence to warrant that the defendant pay the full value of the chattel, (ii) intent to perform the act bringing about the interference with plaintiff's right of possession, and (iii) causation. Because the technician did intend to destroy the bank documents that he burned, he is liable for conversion. Thus, (A) is correct and (D) is incorrect. (B) is incorrect because the technician's belief that he would be able to get out is irrelevant to his liability for trespass—he had the intent to stay in the bank knowing he was not permitted to do so. (C) is incorrect because the fact that the bank had originals of the papers does not change his liability for conversion. Because he intentionally destroyed the papers, he is liable for conversion of those papers even if the bank's damages were minimal.

Answer to Question 27

(B) If the referee prevails, it will be because he did not know the door would strike the bullhorn, so he did not have the intent to commit a battery. Battery requires: (i) an act by defendant that causes a harmful or offensive contact to plaintiff's person; (ii) intent to cause the harmful or offensive contact; and (iii) causation. Here, there was a harmful contact caused by the referee. The only consideration is whether the referee had the requisite intent. If a person knows with substantial certainty the consequences of his action, he has the intent necessary for this type of tort. If the referee did not know that the door was substantially certain to hit the bullhorn the fan was holding, the referee did not have the intent necessary for battery. (For purposes of battery, anything connected to or being held by the plaintiff is usually considered part of the plaintiff's person.) (A) is wrong because if the referee intended to cause a harmful contact (a battery), he is liable for all of the consequences of his actions, whether he intended them or not. A defendant need not foresee the extent of the injuries caused by his intentional act to be held liable for them. (C) is wrong because this is not a case of self-defense. Self-defense is appropriate when a person reasonably believes that he is being or is about to be attacked. Nothing in the facts shows any basis for the referee to believe that the fan was going to harm him. Thus, self-defense is not appropriate here. (D) is wrong because it does not provide the referee with a defense. The fan's conduct angered the referee and may have triggered his actions, but because the fan's conduct was not sufficient to allow the referee to act in self-defense, the referee's use of force here is not excused.

Answer to Question 28

(C) The bicyclist can recover from either party for the left leg injury but only from the driver for the right ankle injury. When two or more tortious acts combine to proximately cause an indivisible injury to a plaintiff, each tortfeasor is jointly and severally liable to the plaintiff for the entire damage incurred. Joint and several liability applies even though each tortfeasor acted entirely independently. However, if the actions are independent, plaintiff's injury is divisible, and it is possible to identify the portion of injuries caused by each defendant, then each will be liable only for the identifiable portion. Here, the cabbie would not be liable for the injury to the right ankle, because the cabbie did not cause the injury. (A) is therefore incorrect. With regard to the left leg, the cabbie was not the only cause of that injury. The original tortfeasor is liable for harm caused by the negligence of third persons when such negligence was a foreseeable risk created by the

original tortfeasor's conduct. Here, as a result of the driver's original negligence, the bicyclist was in a position of danger while he was still in the street. The negligence of the cabbie in striking the bicyclist was a foreseeable risk while the bicyclist was in the street; it is therefore a foreseeable intervening force that will not cut off the driver's liability. Hence, both the driver and the cabbie will be jointly and severally liable for that injury. (B) is therefore incorrect. (D) is incorrect because the driver remains responsible for the foreseeable consequences of her original negligence in striking the bicyclist, regardless of whether she acted with due care when she came to his aid.

Answer to Question 29

(B) The champion will recover from the player for conversion. Conversion consists of (i) an act by defendant interfering with plaintiff's right of possession in the chattel that is serious enough in nature or consequence to warrant that the defendant pay the full value of the chattel, (ii) intent to perform the act bringing about the interference with plaintiff's right of possession, and (iii) causation. Intent to trespass is not required; intent to do the act of interference with the chattel is sufficient for liability. Therefore, the player was guilty of conversion when he intentionally (*i.e.*, volitionally) took the champion's board, which resulted in its loss, even though the player did not intend to lose it or even realize that he had taken the property of another. (A) is not the best answer because complete loss of a chattel, permitting the plaintiff to recover its full value, is too serious an interference to be classified a mere trespass. Trespass to chattels consists of: (i) an act by defendant that interferes with plaintiff's right of possession in the chattel, (ii) intent to perform the act bringing about the interference with the plaintiff's right of possession, (iii) causation, and (iv) damages. Had the champion been able to recover the board, and had he been able to show actual damages during the time of dispossession, he might have been able to recover for trespass to chattels. (C) is wrong because the player's good faith is irrelevant. Even if the conduct is wholly innocent, liability will attach when the interference with the chattel is serious in nature. (D) is wrong because the fact that the player's car was stolen does not relieve him of liability. His initial trespassory interference with the champion's backgammon set was a substantial factor in its complete loss, because it would not have otherwise been in the trunk of his car. Thus, the causation element for conversion is satisfied.

Answer to Question 30

(A) The driver will recover from the pilot if she acted unreasonably under the circumstances. A prima facie case of negligence requires proof of: (i) the existence of a duty on the part of the defendant to conform to a specific standard of conduct for the protection of the plaintiff against unreasonable risk of injury, (ii) breach of that duty by the defendant, (iii) that the breach of duty was the actual and proximate cause of the plaintiff's injury, and (iv) damage to the plaintiff's person or property. If the pilot's selection of the landing site was unreasonable, then she has breached her duty of care to motorists on the highway, including the driver, and was the actual and proximate cause of his injuries. (B) would be correct if this were a products liability action based on strict liability. However, the pilot is not a commercial supplier of a product and would not be liable without some evidence of negligence. (C) is incorrect because even if the pilot was not negligent in failing to discover the defect in the fuel system, she could have been negligent in selecting the landing site, as (A) states. (D) is also incorrect. In selection of the landing site, the pilot is held to the standard of care of a reasonable person in an emergency. If she acted unreasonably in selecting the landing site, she will be liable in negligence.

Answer to Question 31

(A) The neighbor will prevail because the cabana extends onto the neighbor's land. The tort of trespass to land requires: (i) an act of physical invasion of the plaintiff's real property by the defendant, (ii) intent by the defendant to bring about a physical invasion of the property, and (iii) causation. The intent required is the intent to enter on a particular piece of land, rather than intent to trespass. Also, it is not necessary that the defendant personally enter the land. It is sufficient if the defendant's act or something set in motion thereby causes a physical invasion of the property. By having the cabana constructed, the landowner acted so as to bring about the physical invasion of the neighbor's land. (C) is incorrect because it makes no difference that the landowner herself did not enter the property that was being violated. For this reason, (C) is incorrect. (D) is incorrect because the landowner's intent to have the cabana built on its current site suffices for purposes of trespass liability. As noted above, the defendant need not have intended to commit a trespass. (B) is incorrect because actual injury to the violated property is not a prerequisite to sustain this cause of action. Damage is presumed.

Answer to Question 32

(B) Because the equipment company negligently maintained the equipment, the construction company could obtain contribution from the equipment company When two or more tortious acts combine to proximately cause an indivisible injury to a plaintiff, each tortious actor will be jointly and severally liable for that injury. Joint and several liability permits a plaintiff to recover the entire judgment amount from any defendant. Contribution allows a defendant required to pay more than his share of damages to recover from the other jointly liable parties for the excess. In other words, contribution apportions responsibility among those who are at fault. Here, if the construction company is held liable for the boy's injuries, it will be because of its negligence in leaving unattended a piece of equipment without a working safety locking device. However, because the equipment company, which was responsible for repair and maintenance of the equipment, negligently performed such maintenance, resulting in the absence of a working safety locking device, then the equipment company's negligence would have combined with that of the construction company to proximately cause the boy's injuries. This would render the companies jointly and severally liable to the boy for the entire damage incurred. Thus, if the construction company is held liable for the injuries, it has a claim against the equipment company, as a jointly liable party, for the amount it pays in excess of its share of damages. (A) is incorrect because indemnity is not available here. Indemnity involves shifting the entire loss between or among tortfeasors, and is available where: (i) there is a contractual promise to indemnify; (ii) there is a special relationship between the defendants that would allow for vicarious liability; or (iii) the defendant is a supplier in a strict products liability case who is liable to an injured customer, thus giving the supplier a right of indemnification against previous suppliers in the distribution chain. In addition, some states allow a joint tortfeasor to recover indemnification from a co-joint tortfeasor where there is a considerable difference in degree of fault. Here, there is no evidence of a contractual right to indemnity between the construction company and the equipment company, there is no relationship between them that causes the construction company to be held vicariously liable for the equipment company's negligence, and this is not a strict products liability case. Also, there is no indication of a considerable difference in degree of fault between the two companies. Therefore, none of the circumstances in which indemnity is available is present. (C) is incorrect because it would allow for indemnity in this situation and, as explained above, the circumstances allowing for indemnity are simply not present here. (D) is incorrect because, as explained above, the construction company can recover from the equipment company based on contribution rules.

Answer to Question 33

(D) The homeowner's best defense is that she reasonably feared for her life. When a person has reasonable grounds to believe that she is being, or is about to be, attacked, she may use such

force as is reasonably necessary for protection against the potential injury; *i.e.*, reasonable mistake does not negate the defense. She may use force likely to cause death or serious bodily injury if she reasonably believes that she is in danger of serious bodily injury. If the homeowner reasonably believed that her life was in danger or that serious bodily harm was likely, she had a right to use even deadly force to protect herself. Thus, (D) is her best defense. (A) is wrong because the fact that the homeless person was a trespasser does not give the homeowner the right to use deadly force against him. One may not use force likely to cause death or serious bodily harm against a trespasser who is not also threatening bodily harm to the owner. (B) is similarly incorrect; without being threatened with death or serious bodily harm, the homeowner is not privileged to use deadly force to protect her property. (C) is incorrect because the homeowner intended to commit an assault (*i.e.*, create the apprehension of an immediate harmful contact) by threatening to shoot and firing a warning shot, and the doctrine of transferred intent will transfer this intent from the assault to the battery claim. Thus, she could still be liable for battery even though she had no intent to shoot anyone.

Answer to Question 34

(C) The strongest basis for the motorist not prevailing is the absence of a nondelegable duty. The general rule is that a principal will not be liable for tortious acts of its agent if the agent is an independent contractor. However, a broad exception will impose liability on the principal if the duty is nondelegable because of public policy considerations. As long as the company was not subject to a nondelegable duty, it would not be liable for the negligence of the excavator's employee in the transportation of its soil. (A) is not as good an answer as (C) because the fact that the accident was caused by the negligence of the independent contractor's employee does not necessarily excuse the company from liability. (C) supplies the additional factor that enables the company to avoid liability. (B) is incorrect because the possession of a license by the excavator would not excuse the company from liability. (D) is incorrect because the fact that the transportation of soil was common to the area is relevant only for a strict liability action for abnormally dangerous activities, and the transport of soil by truck is not such an activity.

Answer to Question 35

(C) The sports club is likely to prevail because the area was zoned for commercial use when the tennis courts were built. Private nuisance is a substantial, unreasonable interference with another private individual's use or enjoyment of property he actually possesses or to which he has a right of immediate possession. While not conclusive, conduct consistent with what a zoning ordinance permits is highly persuasive evidence that the use is not a nuisance. (A) is incorrect because higher use of property may be a factor considered when the courts balance the respective uses, but it is not in itself a conclusive argument. (B) is incorrect because the interference with another's use and enjoyment must be substantial and unreasonable to be actionable. (D) is incorrect because coming to the nuisance is not a good defense. The prevailing rule is that a defendant may not condemn surrounding premises to endure the nuisance; *i.e.*, the purchaser is entitled to reasonable use or enjoyment of his land to the same extent as any other owner.

Answer to Question 36

(D) The roommate can recover $700 in damages from the student for conversion. To establish a prima facie case of conversion, the following elements must be proved: (i) an act by the defendant interfering with the plaintiff's right of possession in the chattel that is serious enough in nature or consequence to warrant that the defendant pay the full value of the chattel; (ii) intent to perform the act bringing about the interference with the plaintiff's right of possession, and (iii) causation. Even if the conduct is wholly innocent, liability may attach where the interference is serious in nature. Accordingly, accidentally causing damage to another's chattel may constitute a conversion when the damage occurred while the defendant was using the chattel without permission. Here, the student interfered with the roommate's right of possession in the computer by taking it without permission, and it sustained damages of over 70% of its value while in the student's possession. Hence, the student has committed a conversion. The plaintiff in a conversion case is entitled to damages for the fair market value of the chattel at the time and place of the conversion, which in this case was $700. (A) is incorrect because even though the student was not at fault in the water pipe leaking, the damage occurred while the computer was wrongfully in his possession. (B) is incorrect. Had the computer not been damaged, the roommate's recovery would be limited to loss of use damages under a trespass to chattels theory. However, the serious damage that occurred while the computer was in the wrongful possession of the student warrants a recovery for conversion. (C) is incorrect because the damages remedy for conversion is the fair market value; in effect, there is a forced sale of the item. The student may keep the computer but he is liable to the roommate for the entire value of the computer rather than just the cost of repairs.

Mixed Subject

Question Sets and Analytical Answers

Set 1 Answer Sheet

1.	Ⓐ	Ⓑ	Ⓒ	Ⓓ	19.	Ⓐ	Ⓑ	Ⓒ	Ⓓ
2.	Ⓐ	Ⓑ	Ⓒ	Ⓓ	20.	Ⓐ	Ⓑ	Ⓒ	Ⓓ
3.	Ⓐ	Ⓑ	Ⓒ	Ⓓ	21.	Ⓐ	Ⓑ	Ⓒ	Ⓓ
4.	Ⓐ	Ⓑ	Ⓒ	Ⓓ	22.	Ⓐ	Ⓑ	Ⓒ	Ⓓ
5.	Ⓐ	Ⓑ	Ⓒ	Ⓓ	23.	Ⓐ	Ⓑ	Ⓒ	Ⓓ
6.	Ⓐ	Ⓑ	Ⓒ	Ⓓ	24.	Ⓐ	Ⓑ	Ⓒ	Ⓓ
7.	Ⓐ	Ⓑ	Ⓒ	Ⓓ	25.	Ⓐ	Ⓑ	Ⓒ	Ⓓ
8.	Ⓐ	Ⓑ	Ⓒ	Ⓓ	26.	Ⓐ	Ⓑ	Ⓒ	Ⓓ
9.	Ⓐ	Ⓑ	Ⓒ	Ⓓ	27.	Ⓐ	Ⓑ	Ⓒ	Ⓓ
10.	Ⓐ	Ⓑ	Ⓒ	Ⓓ	28.	Ⓐ	Ⓑ	Ⓒ	Ⓓ
11.	Ⓐ	Ⓑ	Ⓒ	Ⓓ	29.	Ⓐ	Ⓑ	Ⓒ	Ⓓ
12.	Ⓐ	Ⓑ	Ⓒ	Ⓓ	30.	Ⓐ	Ⓑ	Ⓒ	Ⓓ
13.	Ⓐ	Ⓑ	Ⓒ	Ⓓ	31.	Ⓐ	Ⓑ	Ⓒ	Ⓓ
14.	Ⓐ	Ⓑ	Ⓒ	Ⓓ	32.	Ⓐ	Ⓑ	Ⓒ	Ⓓ
15.	Ⓐ	Ⓑ	Ⓒ	Ⓓ	33.	Ⓐ	Ⓑ	Ⓒ	Ⓓ
16.	Ⓐ	Ⓑ	Ⓒ	Ⓓ	34.	Ⓐ	Ⓑ	Ⓒ	Ⓓ
17.	Ⓐ	Ⓑ	Ⓒ	Ⓓ	35.	Ⓐ	Ⓑ	Ⓒ	Ⓓ
18.	Ⓐ	Ⓑ	Ⓒ	Ⓓ	36.	Ⓐ	Ⓑ	Ⓒ	Ⓓ

MIXED SUBJECT QUESTIONS - SET 1

Question 1

A man offered to sell a piano to a female acquaintance for $400. The woman had been to the man's house and knew that he owned a Steinberg piano, so she accepted. Unbeknownst to the woman, the man also owned a Hairwin piano, and that was the piano that he intended to sell, although he was aware that the woman had only seen the Steinberg.

If the woman sues the man to obtain the Steinberg, who will prevail?

(A) The woman, because the man knew of the ambiguity.

(B) The woman, because that was her objective intent.

(C) The man, because there was a mutual mistake.

(D) The man, because he subjectively intended to sell the Hairwin instead of the Steinberg.

Question 2

During the trial of her personal injury action against a chemical company, the plaintiff testifies in response to a question by her own counsel that, shortly after she and her family were forced to leave their home because of fumes from its plant, the president of the chemical company telephoned her motel room and said, "If you or any member of your family requires medical treatment, our company will pay all medical expenses in full. We will not have it said that our company's negligence resulted in the illness of a local family." The company's counsel makes a motion to strike all of the plaintiff's testimony, and the court does so.

Was the court's action correct?

(A) Yes, because the testimony relates to inadmissible hearsay.

(B) Yes, because the statement was made in connection with an offer to pay medical expenses.

(C) No, because the statement includes an admission by a party-opponent that it was negligent.

(D) No, because the statement is a factual admission made in connection with an offer to compromise.

Question 3

A bookstore owner entered into an agreement with a building contractor to have a facade attached to the front of his bookstore. The contractor constructed the facade and attached it to the storefront, using plans prepared by himself and his own employees. After completing the work, the contractor was paid the contract price by the bookstore owner. A week later, a woman was walking past the front of the bookstore when the facade and a portion of the original building collapsed, striking and injuring her.

The woman sued both the contractor and the bookstore owner for damages arising from her injuries. The parties stipulated that the attachment of the facade to the storefront caused the building to collapse and that the bookstore owner was not negligent in selecting or supervising the contractor.

If the woman recovers against the bookstore owner, does the latter have any right of action against the contractor?

(A) Yes, because the bookstore owner's conduct was not a cause in fact of the injuries to the woman.

(B) Yes, because the woman recovered from the bookstore owner on the basis of vicarious liability.

(C) No, because the bookstore owner selected the contractor to perform the work.

(D) No, because payment for the work without reservation was acceptance by the bookstore owner.

Question 4

After being arrested on suspicion of murder, a suspect was taken to the police station and informed of his constitutional rights as required by the *Miranda* decision. He immediately requested that a lawyer be provided since he had no money to hire one. The arresting officer said that he would get the suspect's lawyer after he was booked, and the officer proceeded to book him. During the booking search, the suspect said to the arresting officer, "I only killed the bastard because he made a pass at me."

If the suspect attempts to prevent introduction of the statement made by him to the officer during booking, he will most likely:

(A) Fail, because booking is not a critical stage of criminal proceedings requiring the assistance of counsel.

(B) Fail, because the statement was not the result of a custodial interrogation.

(C) Succeed, because the statement was the product of illegal police conduct.

(D) Succeed, because the request for an attorney should have been honored immediately.

Question 5

To help reduce a rising crime rate among teenage boys in a city, a priest decided to organize an overnight jamboree to get teens interested in scouting. The priest met with the city's parks commissioner and requested a permit to camp at a large city park located on the oceanfront. The parks commissioner told the priest that a city ordinance prohibited large organized use of the park during the evening and all overnight camping. The commissioner explained that the city wished to keep the park open for general use during the evening, when most people were off work, and the park was cleaned overnight. The priest brought an action in federal district court, seeking to compel the city to allow overnight camping for this one special occasion.

If the court determines that the ordinance is valid, what will be the basis for its decision?

(A) The ordinance is rationally related to a legitimate government interest and burdens the First Amendment rights involved no more than is reasonable under the circumstances.

(B) The ordinance is narrowly tailored to serve a significant government interest and does not unreasonably limit alternative channels of communication.

(C) The ordinance is substantially related to a legitimate government interest and burdens the First Amendment rights involved no more than is reasonable under the circumstances.

(D) The ordinance is rationally related to a legitimate government interest and does not unreasonably limit alternative channels of communication.

Question 6

A landowner with a 40-acre tract of land had inherited 30 acres and had acquired the other 10 acres by adverse possession from a rancher. The landowner entered into a land sale contract promising to convey the 40 acres to a developer. The contract provided that the landowner would convey marketable title. The developer paid the landowner the purchase price and accepted a deed from him. The developer promptly recorded the deed. The rancher, having learned of the sale, brought a successful action against the developer to quiet title. The developer realized for the first time that there were no covenants for title in his deed. The developer brings an action against the landowner.

What is the most likely outcome of the suit?

(A) The developer will win, because the landowner breached the terms of the contract.

(B) The developer will win, because the landowner misrepresented the size of the tract.

(C) The landowner will win, because the terms of the deed control his liability.

(D) The landowner will win, because the developer was negligent in not checking the covenants of title at the time of closing.

Question 7

A boy and his parents sued a driver for $75,000 for injuries they claim were caused when the driver's car hit the boy one night when the boy was out delivering papers. The boy was knocked unconscious in the accident, and the driver claims that it was not his car that hit the boy. Except for damages, the main issue in the suit is whether it was the driver's car that hit the boy. The driver's own attorney asks him, "Could the boy have mistaken your car for another?"

This question is:

(A) Objectionable, because the answer would be hearsay.

(B) Objectionable, because the answer would be an opinion.

(C) Unobjectionable, because the answer would be relevant to the issue of whose car hit the boy.

(D) Unobjectionable, if a proper foundation has been laid.

Question 8

A landowner and a purchaser orally agreed that the landowner would convey 20 acres of his 160-acre farm to the purchaser. At the time of their agreement, the landowner wrote on the back of an envelope, "I hereby promise to convey the northern 20 acres of my farm to [the purchaser] for $10,000." One month later, the purchaser tendered $10,000 to the landowner, but the landowner refused to convey the 20 acres.

If the purchaser sues the landowner to convey the land and the landowner prevails, it will most likely be because the writing:

(A) Was not signed by the landowner.

(B) Was not signed by the purchaser.

(C) Did not describe the property with specificity.

(D) Was on the back of an envelope.

Question 9

A man believed that a woman who was a former roommate had taken a book of his, so he persuaded a mutual friend to help him get it back surreptitiously. He had the friend take the woman out to dinner, leaving her apartment empty so that the man could pick the lock on the woman's front door and take the book back. On seeing the man trying to pick the lock, a neighbor called the police, who found the man still trying to pick the lock when they arrived. The man and the friend were charged with burglary and conspiracy to commit burglary.

If the man and the friend are acquitted of the conspiracy charge, the most likely reason would be that:

(A) There was no overt act.

(B) There was no agreement.

(C) There was no intent to commit burglary.

(D) The man did not actually commit a burglary.

Question 10

A man drove into the parking lot of a bank and was about to pull into an empty spot when a woman cut in front of him with her automobile and took his parking place. The man and woman got out of their cars, and the man started to yell at the woman. After a heated argument, a fight broke out between them. A customer came out of the bank at that moment and saw that the man was getting the better of the woman in the fight. The customer ran to his car, took a gun from the glove compartment, pointed it at the man and said, "Stop this minute or I'll shoot."

If the man asserts a claim against the customer based on assault, who will prevail?

(A) The man, because the customer threatened him with deadly force.

(B) The man, because the customer was unaware of who was the aggressor.

(C) The customer, if the man was the original aggressor by starting the fight with the woman.

(D) The customer, if it was apparent that the man was about to inflict serious bodily harm to the woman.

Question 11

A homeowner and a carpenter formed a valid oral contract in which the carpenter agreed to construct an extension to the homeowner's home, using materials supplied by the homeowner, in exchange for $2,000. After the work had been completed but before the homeowner had made any payment, the carpenter called the homeowner and instructed him to pay the $2,000 due on the extension work to a creditor of the carpenter.

If the creditor thereafter brings an action against the homeowner for $2,000, will the creditor prevail?

(A) Yes, because the creditor was the intended beneficiary of the original contract between the homeowner and the carpenter.

(B) Yes, because there has been a proper assignment.

(C) No, because personal service contracts are not assignable.

(D) No, because the creditor could not perform the construction work done by the carpenter.

Question 12

During the probate of the estate of a decedent who died intestate, the decedent's private nurse made a claim for his art collection. She testified at trial that when she first became employed by him, she and the decedent had entered into a written agreement that stated that if she accepted a lower monthly salary and worked for him for the rest of his life, he would leave the art collection to her in his will. The decedent's heir objects to this evidence.

The best reason for a judge to rule the evidence inadmissible is that:

(A) It is hearsay.

(B) The contract is not a proper will.

(C) The agreement violates the Statute of Frauds.

(D) The evidence violates the best evidence rule.

Question 13

In a real property dispute over a decedent's vacation home, the plaintiff offers a deed to show that the home had been transferred to her two months before the decedent died. The defendant, the decedent's heir, disputes the plaintiff's claim and alleges that the decedent's signature on the deed was forged. The defendant testifies that he is familiar with the decedent's signature and the signature on the deed is not his.

The judge should rule this testimony:

(A) Inadmissible, because the defendant is not a handwriting expert.

(B) Inadmissible, because the defendant has a stake in the outcome and his opinion is unreliable.

(C) Admissible, because the defendant knows the decedent's signature.

(D) Admissible, because he is disputing the genuineness of the document, not seeking to establish it.

Question 14

A county leased its lakefront property to a privately owned corporation. The lease required the corporation to design, build, operate, and maintain a restaurant, marina, and swimming area, and to pay the county 10% of the net profits as rent. The corporation submitted its bylaws to the county for review. The bylaws provided that its facilities would be open to members only and that its membership committee would set "standards" for membership, including membership fees and dues. The county approved the corporation's bylaws. In addition to setting a dues structure, the corporation's membership committee decided that no applications for membership would be accepted from persons of Asian descent. The plaintiff, a citizen of Korea who now legally resides in the United States, was denied membership. The plaintiff immediately brought suit against the corporation on the ground that the membership standards violated his constitutional rights to equal protection.

Who will likely prevail?

(A) The plaintiff, because the standards are not necessary to promote a compelling state interest.

(B) The plaintiff, unless the corporation can prove some rational basis for the denial of membership to Asian-Americans.

(C) The corporation, because the plaintiff is not a United States citizen and therefore lacks standing to raise an equal protection claim.

(D) The corporation, because its bylaws make no mention of race or national origin.

Question 15

A city has many parks, as well as a country club with a golf course. While the city's parks are accessible to all without a fee, the city charges a $1,000 application fee and $100 per month dues to belong to the country club. A resident of the city wishes to join the country club but cannot afford the application fee or monthly dues.

If the resident brings suit against the city on the ground that the fee and dues discriminate against the poor in violation of the Equal Protection Clause, who likely will prevail?

(A) The resident, because a person cannot be deprived of a public right or benefit on the basis of inability to pay.

(B) The resident, because the poor qualify as a protected class.

(C) The city, because only de jure discrimination against the poor has been held to violate the Equal Protection Clause.

(D) The city, because the membership privilege is not an important enough deprivation.

Question 16

To provide low-cost housing to the unemployed, a city has a policy of leasing empty city-owned buildings to social agencies that promise to convert or rehabilitate the buildings into habitable, low-cost apartments and to pay the city 10% of any net profit made from rentals. A church entered into such an agreement with the city and converted one of the city's abandoned office buildings into 50 small, low-cost apartments. The lease agreement used by the church provides, among other things, that the lessee must affirm a belief in God. The lease agreement was submitted to the city for approval prior to its use by the church, and it was approved. On the first day that the church made the apartments available for rent, the plaintiff, an avowed atheist, applied to lease a unit. The plaintiff's application was quickly denied for the sole reason that the plaintiff refused to affirm a belief in God.

If the plaintiff brings suit against the church on the ground that the required affirmation of a belief in God violates the plaintiff's constitutional rights, who likely will prevail?

(A) The plaintiff, because denial of a lease to atheists has been held to hinder the free exercise of religion.

(B) The plaintiff, because the purpose and effect of the church's policy results in a violation of the Establishment Clause.

(C) The church, because freedom of religion is not protected against acts of private individuals or groups or a private institution.

(D) The church, because as an atheist, the plaintiff has no standing to challenge the lease requirement on religious grounds.

Question 17

A woman decided to have a nude painting done of herself. She contracted in writing with an artist, who agreed to paint the woman nude for $10,000. The fee was payable on completion of the painting, provided that the painting was to the woman's "complete and utter satisfaction." On the same afternoon that the artist entered into the contract with the woman, he assigned the contract to his cousin. The artist then painted the woman's picture. After the job was done, the woman told him, "That's a very good likeness of me, but it shows my defects, so I'm not satisfied." She refused to accept the painting or to pay the artist or his cousin.

Can the cousin recover from the woman?

(A) Yes, because the condition in the agreement between the woman and the artist did not apply to his cousin.

(B) Yes, because otherwise an unjust enrichment will occur.

(C) No, because rights arising under personal services contracts are not assignable.

(D) No, because the woman was not satisfied with the painting.

Question 18

A company that provided electrical and communication services to industries determined that its main trunk line of copper conduit needed to be replaced. The line ran through an industrial park, and the company had access to it by an easement. At the end of the workday on Friday, the copper conduit that had not yet been disconnected was left exposed in the trench. In accordance with the company's policy, intended to discourage theft of the copper, the conduit was still electrically charged.

The next morning, a man was walking by the industrial park and saw the construction site. Ignoring the "no trespassing" signs, he came up to the trench and saw the copper conduit, which he decided to try to steal. He climbed over the barriers and climbed partway into the trench to try to pull out some of the conduit. He received an electric shock as he made contact with the conduit, causing him to fall into the trench and suffer severe electrical burns.

If the man sues the company for his injuries, is he likely to prevail?

(A) Yes, because the company used unreasonable force to protect its property.

(B) Yes, because force applied by mechanical devices may not be used to protect property alone.

(C) No, because the company owed no duty to a trespasser.

(D) No, because the man assumed the risk.

Question 19

A landowner conveyed 30 acres of property "To my brother, his heirs and assigns, so long as the premises are used for agricultural purposes, then to my cousin, his heirs and assigns."

As a consequence of the conveyance, the landowner's interest in the 30 acres is:

(A) A right of entry.

(B) A possibility of reverter.

(C) A fee simple absolute because the conveyance violates the Rule Against Perpetuities.

(D) Nothing.

Question 20

A man and woman agreed to burn down a neighbor's house in retribution for some wrong the neighbor allegedly committed against them. Both the man and woman were arrested shortly after they poured gasoline on the neighbor's front porch. The man revealed to the police that he participated in the plan to ensure that nothing bad would happen to the neighbor, and that he had made an anonymous telephone call to the police alerting them to the crime, which enabled the police to arrest him and the woman "in the act." The woman stated that she would not have participated if not for the man's encouragement.

If charged with a conspiracy at common law to commit arson, the woman should be found:

(A) Not guilty, because she was not predisposed to commit the crime but for the man's encouragement.

(B) Not guilty, because the man did not intend to commit arson.

(C) Guilty, because there was an agreement, and pouring gasoline on the front porch was sufficient for the overt act.

(D) Guilty, because arson is not a specific intent crime.

Question 21

When a man purchased his new home, he kept his old residence because he had not yet received any acceptable purchase offers. He agreed to rent it to a woman but told her that he was intending to sell the house in a few months and that she would have to move if the new owners so desired. The woman agreed and moved in, paying the man the agreed rent of $100 per week by dropping off cash at the man's new house every Friday. After serious business losses, the man had to sell his new home for the amount mortgaged and informed the woman that she would have to vacate the old home. The woman refused and the next Friday brought over the $100 rental payment, but the man refused to accept it.

The following Monday, the man's lawyer commenced an action to evict the woman from the man's old home. The jurisdiction requires that a statutory written notice be served on any tenant whose term is for less than month-to-month, or is not for a fixed term, at least three days before commencement of eviction proceedings. No written notice of any kind was given to the woman.

The man is most likely to gain immediate possession of his home by arguing that the woman is:

(A) A tenant from month-to-month.

(B) A tenant at sufferance.

(C) A licensee.

(D) A trespasser ab initio.

Question 22

A man purchased a large flat screen plasma television and decided to mount it on the ceiling over his bed. The manual that came with the product included detailed instructions and illustrations on how to mount the television on different types of walls, along with all the required hardware, but contained neither instructions nor warnings regarding mounting on the ceiling. The man carefully followed the wall-mounting instructions and was satisfied that it would hold. In fact, however, the mounting was not appropriate for ceilings. The next night, a woman who was the man's overnight guest was seriously injured when the television came loose and fell on the bed.

Will the woman prevail in a suit against the company that manufactured the television?

(A) Yes, because the manufacturer had a duty to include warnings for all potential placements of its product.

(B) Yes, if the manufacturer knew that its television was sometimes mounted on ceilings rather than walls.

(C) No, if the manufacturer's manual had all of the customary warnings for this type of product.

(D) No, because the man was negligent in mounting the television on the ceiling.

Question 23

A railroad company operated freight and passenger service over the line running from one city to another for over 70 years, but the increasing use of autos and planes for passenger travel and trucks for freight forced the railroad to cease all rail service 20 years ago. A portion of the rail line ran over the westernmost portion of 40 acres of land owned by a farmer pursuant to an easement granted by the farmer's predecessors in interest. The farmer purchased the land subject to this easement 25 years ago.

Two years ago, the farmer constructed several large structures for use in housing chickens and began operating a chicken farm, producing eggs and fryers. The farmer has now learned that the railroad company intends to reinstitute passenger rail service between the two cities, and he is afraid that the noise and vibration of the passing trains will adversely affect his egg production. He brings an action in state court to quiet title to the area of the rail easement and to enjoin the railroad company from entering onto his property. The statutory prescriptive period is 10 years.

How should the court rule?

(A) For the farmer, because the railroad company has abandoned the easement.

(B) For the farmer, because the railroad company's use of the easement will interfere unreasonably with his egg production.

(C) For the railroad company, because it has not abandoned the easement.

(D) For the railroad company, because the farmer's failure to use the land under the easement precludes him from asserting that the easement has been abandoned.

Question 24

The police entered a neighborhood suffering from increased illegal drug activity, accompanied by a dog trained to sniff out cocaine. The police entered the backyard of a home and brought the dog to an area immediately outside the back door. The dog acted as if it smelled cocaine. The officers knocked on the back door and a man answered the door and let them in. He was immediately placed under arrest. After a brief search, the police officers found and confiscated a small quantity of cocaine from the bedroom closet. The man is charged with possession of cocaine. At trial, he moves to prevent introduction of the cocaine into evidence.

This motion will most probably be:

(A) Granted, because, under the circumstances, the police activity violated the man's reasonable expectation of privacy.

(B) Granted, because this kind of detection by a trained dog has not been scientifically verified and cannot be the basis for probable cause.

(C) Denied, because the man allowed the police officers to enter his home.

(D) Denied, because the search was incident to a valid arrest.

Question 25

To keep election costs manageable, a state law required a candidate in a general election to collect on a petition supporting her candidacy the signatures of at least 4% of the voters eligible to vote for the office for which the candidate was running. Studies revealed that, prior to adoption of the law, a candidate who did not have at least 4% of the voters supporting her initially had never won an election. An independent candidate for governor who had limited campaign resources was supported in the polls by 30% of the voters, but had been able to obtain only 3.5% of the eligible voters' signatures

by the filing deadline. The board of elections refused to put her name on the ballot.

If the candidate sues to have her name placed on the ballot, claiming that the state's petition requirements are unconstitutional, which of the following statements is most accurate?

(A) She will have to show that the petition requirement is not rationally related to a legitimate state purpose.

(B) She will have to show that the petition requirement is not necessary to achieve a compelling state interest.

(C) The state will have to show that the petition requirement is narrowly tailored to achieve a compelling state interest.

(D) The state will have to show that the petition requirement is rationally related to a legitimate state interest.

Question 26

The defendant was on trial for trying to sell a stolen antique ring to an antique dealer. The defendant claims that she had bought the ring from a street vendor earlier on the day of her arrest. The prosecution calls to the stand a woman who had given a party in her home which the defendant attended, and who had discovered later that evening that her antique ring was missing from her bedroom. She seeks to testify that her friend, who is now backpacking in another country, told her three days after the party that she had seen the defendant the previous evening in a restaurant wearing a ring that looked exactly like the woman's ring. The defense attorney objects.

The objection should be:

(A) Overruled, because the statement is a present sense impression.

(B) Overruled, because the statement is relevant and the friend is unavailable, having gone backpacking in another country.

(C) Sustained, because this is circumstantial evidence within circumstantial evidence.

(D) Sustained, because the statement is hearsay not within any exception.

Question 27

A homeowner was trimming his sidewalk-bordering hedge when a wasp began attacking him. The homeowner attempted to hit the wasp. During one of his swats, the homeowner struck a jogger in the face. The jogger, reacting to the unexpected blow to his head, pulled out a knife and stabbed the homeowner, seriously injuring him.

If the jogger is prosecuted for aggravated battery, he probably will be found:

(A) Not guilty, because he believed the homeowner was attacking him.

(B) Not guilty, because his acts constituted an assault, not a battery.

(C) Guilty, because he used a deadly weapon.

(D) Guilty, because he actually injured the homeowner.

Question 28

A rancher owned a 100-acre tract of land. Eighty acres had been devised to him by his father, and the rancher had acquired title to an adjacent 20 acres from a prospector by adverse possession. The rancher entered into a land sale contract in which he promised to convey the 100 acres to an investor. The contract listed the description of the property and was otherwise definite and certain as to the transaction, but the contract did not state the nature of the title that the rancher was to convey to the investor. At the time of closing, the investor paid the purchase price and accepted the deed conveyed by the rancher. Six months later, the prospector returned to the area and brought a successful action in ejectment against the investor for the 20 acres. The investor now sues the rancher for damages.

Which of the following statements would most accurately describe the investor's rights?

(A) The investor's rights are based on the implied covenant contained in a marketable title.

(B) The investor could bring an action for reformation of the deed with an abatement of the price of the land.

(C) The terms of the investor's deed control the rancher's liability.

(D) The investor could bring an action against the rancher for fraud.

Question 29

A builder went to the local lumberyard late Saturday afternoon to purchase some sheets of plywood. He wandered to the back end of the lot where the plywood was stored. While he was looking over the sheets of plywood, the custodian closed and locked the only gate out of the lumberyard, since it was closing time and he believed that all customers and employees had left. The storage area of the lumberyard was surrounded by a 12-foot-high chain link fence. The builder soon discovered that he had been locked in the lumberyard. Since the storage area was located at the back of the property owned by the lumberyard, there was very little chance that he would be seen on the premises. The builder knew that since the lumberyard was closed on Sunday, no one would be back to let him out until Monday morning. Realizing that he had left his cell phone at home, he panicked at the thought of being trapped on the lumberyard property until Monday morning. He tried to climb over the fence and, in doing so, fell and was injured. He asserted a false imprisonment claim against the lumberyard for damages for his injuries.

Will the builder prevail?

(A) Yes, because he was harmed as a result of his confinement.

(B) Yes, because he was confined against his will.

(C) No, unless the custodian knew that someone was in the lot at the time he locked the gate.

(D) No, unless the custodian was negligent in locking the gate.

Question 30

To help alleviate discrimination in private contracts, Congress passed a bill providing:

> It shall be unlawful to discriminate against minority race members in the making and enforcement of any public or private contract, of every kind whatsoever. Any person whose rights under this statute are violated may bring a cause of action against the party that has so violated the person's rights in the federal district court for the district in which he resides, seeking treble damages or $1,000, whichever is greater.

Several large banks that have been accused of discriminatory loan practices challenge the federal statute.

If the court finds that Congress had the power to enact the statute, the court most likely will find that the power arose from:

(A) The Contract Clause.

(B) The Thirteenth Amendment.

(C) The Fourteenth Amendment.

(D) The Commerce Clause.

Question 31

The owner of a sporting goods store noticed that her tent stock was running low. After consulting various manufacturers' catalogues, she decided to order from a large manufacturer of camping equipment whose catalogue listed the 9 x 12 tent that she wanted, at a cost of $70. On April 1, the store owner phoned the manufacturer and placed her order for 10 tents. The next day, the manufacturer mailed the store owner a letter informing her that the tents were now $72 and that they would be shipped to her on April 16. The store owner received the letter on April 4, but she never responded. On April 15, she received a catalogue from another tent company showing tents similar to the ones that she ordered, but for a cost of $50. She immediately called the manufacturer with whom she had placed her order to cancel it. Nevertheless, the manufacturer shipped the tents to her on April 16.

If the manufacturer sues the store owner to enforce the contract, who will prevail?

(A) The store owner, because there was no meeting of the minds regarding the price term.

(B) The store owner, because her promise was not in writing.

(C) The manufacturer, because its April 2 letter was sufficient to bind the store owner.

(D) The manufacturer, because the store owner's phone call on April 15 to cancel is proof that there was a contract.

Question 32

The manager of the shoe department of a large department store noticed that mukluks were flying off the shelf in anticipation of another exceptionally cold winter, and he realized that he needed to order more. On November 1, the manager phoned a local manufacturer of mukluks and placed an order for 100 pairs, at a cost of $90 a pair, the price listed in the manufacturer's catalogue, which the manager had consulted before placing his order. Two days later, the manufacturer mailed the manager a letter stating that the mukluks were now $105 a pair and that they would be shipped to him on November 17. The manager received the letter on November 5, but he never responded. On November 17, the manufacturer shipped the mukluks to the department store, but it was not a perfect tender, and the manager filed suit for breach of contract.

Assuming that the parties' communications were sufficient to form a contract, on what day was the contract formed?

(A) November 1, the day the manager placed his order.

(B) November 3, the day the manufacturer sent its letter.

(C) November 5, the day the manager received the letter.

(D) November 17, the day the mukluks were shipped.

Question 33

After reading an article in a hunting magazine detailing a state's expanded season for the hunting of grizzly bears, a man called his nephew to see if he wanted to take a trip to the state to hunt grizzly bears. His nephew agreed. Unknown to the man and his nephew, the article in the magazine listed an incorrect ending date for the expanded grizzly bear hunting season; the hunting season had expired the day before. While still in their pickup truck driving to a campsite in the state, the man and his nephew were pulled over by a state trooper. They volunteered that they were on their way to hunt grizzly bears and were promptly arrested. A state statute made hunting bears out of season a strict liability offense.

If the man and his nephew are charged with conspiracy to hunt grizzly bears out of season, they will be:

(A) Acquitted, because there was no agreement.

(B) Acquitted, because they had not intended to commit a crime.

(C) Convicted, because hunting grizzly bears out of season is a strict liability offense.

(D) Convicted, because they took action in furtherance of the conspiracy.

Question 34

While practicing their target shooting at the firing range, a man and woman got into an argument that almost erupted into physical combat, except that they were restrained and separated by bystanders. Later, in the parking lot of the range, the man shot the woman in the shoulder. Bystanders who rushed to the scene immediately after hearing the man's shot found the woman on the pavement with a black metal flashlight in her hand. The woman's pistol was in her locker at the firing range. At the trial of the woman's civil action for battery against the man, the latter testified that the woman approached him, saying, "We'll settle this once and for all, right now," and raised an object toward the man. He testified that he feared that the woman was about to shoot him with a pistol, so he fired in self-defense.

If the woman does not prevail in her civil action, it likely will be because the jury decided that:

(A) The man honestly believed that the woman was about to shoot.

(B) A reasonable person in the same circumstances would have believed that the woman was about to shoot.

(C) The woman was at fault in raising a black object toward the man while threatening him.

(D) The woman was the original aggressor.

Question 35

An employee of a grain company brought suit against his employer for injuries that he suffered in a fire and explosion in a grain elevator. The employer filed a counterclaim against the employee for damages, and alleged that the employee was contributorily negligent in that he cut through some electrical wires while working in the elevator, and the sparks from those wires caused the explosion. The employee denies these allegations. His employer calls the grain elevator operator, who was also working in the elevator, and he testifies that he helped the employee and his assistant out of the elevator soon after the explosion. The elevator operator intends to testify that, at that time, the assistant told him that the employee "should have been able to tell that that wire was hot." The injured employee's attorney objects to the elevator operator's testimony concerning this conversation.

The trial judge should rule that the testimony is:

(A) Inadmissible, because it is hearsay not within any exception.

(B) Inadmissible, because it is improper opinion evidence.

(C) Admissible, as an admission.

(D) Admissible, as being a prior inconsistent statement.

Question 36

A man had rented a woman's home from her for seven years. When the time came to sign a new lease, the woman decided that since the man had always been a quiet tenant, she would continue to charge him only $350 per month rent instead of the $500 to $550 she could probably get otherwise. The new lease was for a period of five years, and by its terms, the man was specifically prohibited from assigning the lease without the woman's specific written consent. About a year later, the man got married and moved into his new wife's home. Instead of giving up his lease, the man sublet the property to a friend for $500 a month. The man did not get the woman's permission to sublease the property.

If the woman brings an action to either eject the friend from the premises or to recover damages from the man for subletting the premises without her consent, the woman most likely would:

(A) Be able to recover damages and to eject the new tenant.

(B) Be able to eject the new tenant only, because she has suffered no money damages.

(C) Not be able to eject the new tenant because, although the man did not have the right to sublet, he had the power, but she will be entitled to recover the full rent paid by the new tenant because it would be unfair to let the man profit from his wrongful act.

(D) Have no cause of action for either ejectment or damages.

MIXED SUBJECT SET 1 SUBJECT GUIDE

1. Contracts
2. Evidence
3. Torts
4. Criminal Law
5. Constitutional Law
6. Real Property
7. Evidence
8. Contracts
9. Criminal Law
10. Torts
11. Contracts
12. Evidence
13. Evidence
14. Constitutional Law
15. Constitutional Law
16. Constitutional Law
17. Contracts
18. Torts
19. Real Property
20. Criminal Law
21. Real Property
22. Torts
23. Real Property
24. Criminal Law
25. Constitutional Law
26. Evidence
27. Criminal Law
28. Real Property
29. Torts
30. Constitutional Law
31. Contracts
32. Contracts
33. Criminal Law
34. Torts
35. Evidence
36. Real Property

MIXED SUBJECT ANSWERS - SET 1

Answer to Question 1

(A) The woman will likely prevail because the man knew of the ambiguity. Where the parties' contract seems clear, but because of subsequently discovered facts it can be interpreted in more than one way, there is a latent ambiguity. If one party is aware of the latent ambiguity but the other party is not, a contract will be enforced in favor of the unaware party. (B) is wrong because the woman did not objectively indicate which piano she wanted. (C) is wrong because even though where there is a latent ambiguity it can be said there is a mutual mistake, in this situation the unaware party's intent controls. (D) is a misstatement of the law.

Answer to Question 2

(C) The court's action was not correct. Federal Rule 409 excludes offers to pay medical expenses, but not statements made in connection with such offers. The president of the company, obviously authorized to speak for that entity, has made an admission of negligence, and that admission is admissible against the company as a vicarious admission. Thus, (B) is wrong. (A) is wrong because the statement is an admission, which is nonhearsay under the Federal Rules. (D) is wrong because there was no offer to compromise—the company merely said that it would pay medical expenses, without bargaining for anything in return. In addition, if it were an offer to compromise, a statement made in connection with the offer would not be admissible.

Answer to Question 3

(B) The bookstore owner has an action against the contractor for indemnification because the woman's recovery against the bookstore owner was based on vicarious liability. Where one is vicariously liable for the torts of another, the former has a right of indemnity against the latter. Here, the bookstore owner was not directly liable to the woman in his capacity as owner of the property because he exercised due care in selecting the contractor, so the judgment against him was on the basis of vicarious liability for any negligence by the contractor. Thus, answers (C) and (D) reach a wrong result, and (A) does not provide any information about the theory on which the woman recovered against the bookstore owner.

Answer to Question 4

(B) If, after being given his *Miranda* warnings, the suspect invokes his right to counsel, all interrogation must stop until counsel is present. "Interrogation" includes any words or actions by the police that the police should know are likely to produce an incriminating response. The suspect may volunteer information to the police at any time. (A) is not the best answer. While it is true that booking is not a critical stage for purposes of the right to counsel, that is not the reason the statement will be allowed. The statement would be excluded if it had been the result of interrogation during the booking. (C) is incorrect; there is no illegal police conduct set forth in the facts. (D) is an incorrect statement of the law.

Answer to Question 5

(B) The court will base its decision on its determination that the ordinance is narrowly tailored to serve a significant government interest and does not unreasonably limit alternative channels of communication. While the First Amendment protects the freedoms of speech and assembly, the government may reasonably regulate speech-related conduct in public forums through content-neutral time,

place, and manner regulation. To be valid, government regulations on speech and assembly in public forums must be content neutral and narrowly tailored to serve a significant government interest, and must leave open alternative channels of communication. Here, the ban on camping overnight in the park, a content-neutral regulation of a public forum, would be evaluated by the court using the standard in choice (B). (A) and (D) are incorrect because the rational relationship test is used for restrictions on free speech rights in nonpublic forums. Here, because the park is a public forum, the more restrictive test stated in (B) is used. (C) is incorrect because it misstates both parts of the standard.

Answer to Question 6

(C) The landowner will win because the terms of the deed, not of the contract, control his liability. Under the doctrine of merger, the contract merges into the deed, and the terms of the contract are meaningless. Even though the contract specified a "good and marketable title," it is the deed that controls, and the deed contained no covenants of title. A deed does not incorporate the title terms of a contract. Thus, (A) is wrong. (B) is wrong; it is not supported by the facts. (D) is wrong because the developer's negligence is irrelevant.

Answer to Question 7

(B) The driver's answer could only reflect his opinion of what the boy did or thought, and is thus impermissible opinion evidence. A lay person's opinion is admissible if it is rationally based on the perception of the witness, helpful to a clear understanding of the witness's testimony on the determination of a fact in issue, and not based on scientific, technical, or other specialized knowledge. The driver's opinion does not meet those requirements. (A) is wrong because the question does not call for an out-of-court declaration. (C) is wrong because, although relevant, the answer would still be improper. (D) is wrong because the form of the question is improper.

Answer to Question 8

(A) If the landowner prevails, it will be because the writing was not signed by the landowner. Under the Statute of Frauds, to be enforceable a contract for the sale of land must be evidenced by a writing signed by the party sought to be charged. Here, the landowner is the party that the purchaser is seeking to charge, so his signature is required on the writing. (B) is wrong because the purchaser's signature is not required to bind the landowner. (C) is wrong because the contract need only reasonably describe the subject matter; great specificity, such as a legal description, is not required. (D) is wrong because it does not matter on what substance the writing is made.

Answer to Question 9

(C) They will be acquitted if there was no intent to commit a burglary. At common law, a conspiracy required: (i) an agreement between two or more persons; (ii) the intent to enter into an agreement; and (iii) the intent to achieve the objective of the agreement. Although an overt act traditionally was not required, the majority rule today is that an overt act committed in furtherance of the conspiracy is required, but "mere preparation" usually suffices as an overt act. Thus, conspiracy to commit burglary requires the intent and agreement to commit a burglary. If the intent was only to retrieve the man's property and not to commit a felony, the man and the friend did not have the necessary intent to achieve a criminal objective. (A) is wrong; there was an overt act. (In fact, but for the lack of intent to commit a felony, sufficient steps were probably taken to constitute an attempt.) (B) is also factually wrong; there was an agreement. (D) is wrong; even though the actual burglary was not committed, they could be found guilty of conspiracy if they had the required intent.

Answer to Question 10

(D) The customer will prevail if it reasonably appeared that the man was about to inflict serious bodily harm on the woman. Deadly force in defense of others is acceptable if the other is being threatened with serious bodily harm; choice (D) presents that situation. (A) is therefore incorrect. (C) is wrong because the fact that the man started the fight does not give the customer the right to use deadly force. (B) is wrong because it is irrelevant whom the customer thought was the aggressor; if it was apparent that the man was about to inflict serious bodily harm on the woman, the customer would have the right to intervene.

Answer to Question 11

(B) The creditor will prevail because the carpenter has made a valid assignment of his right to payment from the homeowner. The general rule is that all contractual rights can be assigned, and all the carpenter assigned here was his right to payment. (A) is wrong because it is contrary to the facts; nothing indicates that payment to the creditor was contemplated in the original contract. (C) is a misstatement of the law; the assignment of a right to receive payment is permitted, even in a personal service contract. (D) is irrelevant.

Answer to Question 12

(D) The best reason for not admitting the evidence is that it most likely violates the best evidence rule. Since the plaintiff testified that there was a written agreement, to prove its terms she would be required to produce the written agreement or explain its absence. (A) is wrong; the out-of-court agreement is being offered for its legal effect; *i.e.*, as a "legally operative fact," which is not considered hearsay. (B) is wrong because she is not claiming that the agreement is a will. (C) is wrong because she is testifying concerning the existence of a written agreement.

Answer to Question 13

(C) The judge should rule this testimony admissible because the defendant knows the seller's signature. Lay opinion testimony is permissible and often essential to identify telephone voices and handwriting. Any lay witness who is familiar with the signature of a person may testify as to his opinion as to its genuineness. In such a case, a foundation must first be laid to show familiarity with the handwriting, as was done here by the defendant's testimony. Therefore, (A) is wrong. (B) is wrong because it goes to the weight of the testimony, not the admissibility. (D) is wrong because the lay witness may testify in support of, or against, the genuineness.

Answer to Question 14

(A) The plaintiff will likely prevail. State action can often be found when the state has affirmatively encouraged or facilitated discriminatory acts by private groups. Since the county leased land to the corporation, approved its members-only policy, and stands to profit by the corporation's operations, state action can be found. Generally, state discrimination against lawful aliens is suspect and will be upheld only if it is necessary to promote a compelling state interest. (B) is incorrect because discrimination based on national origin cannot be justified by a mere "rational" basis. (C) is incorrect because resident aliens are "persons" within the meaning of the Fourteenth Amendment. (D) is incorrect because even though the bylaws are nondiscriminatory on their face, the facts show that they are being applied in a discriminatory manner.

Answer to Question 15

(D) The city will prevail because the membership privilege is not a significant enough deprivation to implicate the Equal Protection Clause. Only the denial of particularly important rights (such as a marriage license) to those unable to pay for them has been held to violate equal protection. Therefore, (A) is wrong. (C) is wrong because a number of de facto discriminations against the poor have been held to violate equal protection. (B) is an incorrect statement of the law. The Supreme Court has never held that wealth alone is a suspect classification. Only when the lack of wealth prevents a person from exercising a fundamental constitutional right will equal protection issues be raised.

Answer to Question 16

(B) The plaintiff will likely prevail. The First Amendment prohibits laws respecting the establishment of religion. Governmental action that does not contain a sect preference will pass muster under the Establishment Clause if it has a secular purpose, its primary effect neither advances nor inhibits religion, and it does not require excessive government entanglement with religion. The church's action will be considered to be state action here because of the significant involvement between the church and the city. (The city is leasing the building to the church, the church shares profits with the city, and the church submitted its lease forms to the city for approval). Requiring a lessee to affirm a belief in God appears to have no secular purpose. Moreover, its primary effect probably is to advance religion. Therefore, the church's action will be found to have violated the Establishment Clause. (A) is wrong because there simply is no such Supreme Court holding. (C) is wrong because, as was pointed out above, state action can be found because of the city's significant involvement in the apartment building at issue. (D) is wrong because a person asserting a violation of the Establishment Clause does not have to allege infringement of a particular religious freedom in order to have standing; it is enough that the person is directly affected by the government action challenged.

Answer to Question 17

(D) The cousin will not recover from the woman because she has a defense inherent in the contract. When one of the original parties to a valid contract assigns his rights under the contract to a third party, the assignee may enforce his rights against the obligor directly but is generally subject to any defenses that the obligor had against the assignor. As long as the defense is inherent in the contract, such as failure of a condition, it is always available against an assignee because it was in existence when the contract was made (even if whether the obligor would be able to utilize it was uncertain). Here, the artist (the assignor) and the woman (the obligor) had a valid contract—her promise to purchase the painting only if she was satisfied with it is not illusory because she has to exercise her right of rejection in good faith. When the artist assigned his rights under the contract to his cousin (the assignee), his cousin became subject to the condition in the contract that the woman be satisfied with the painting. Her dissatisfaction with the painting excuses her duty to pay for it; this is a defense inherent in the contract that precludes the cousin's recovering from the woman. (A) is incorrect because the assignee always takes subject to conditions in the original agreement between the obligor and the obligee. The only defenses that the obligor could not raise against the assignee are setoffs and counterclaims unrelated to the assigned contract that came into existence after the obligor learned that the contract was assigned. (B) is incorrect because the woman has not been enriched by the artist's services. She has justifiably refused to accept the painting and has received no benefit from the transaction that would constitute unjust enrichment. (C) is incorrect because the only right that the artist has assigned is the right to receive payment from the woman if she accepted the painting. The woman's duty is the same regardless of to whom she has to pay the money; therefore, the artist could validly assign his right to his cousin. Note that the analysis would be different if the artist had also attempted to delegate his duty of painting the woman to his cousin: duties involving personal judgment and skill may not be delegated. When an assignor assigns "the contract," the words are interpreted as including a delegation of the duties unless a contrary intention appears. Here, the contrary intention is indicated by the fact that the artist did the painting rather than his cousin; hence, there was no attempt by the artist to delegate a nondelegable duty.

Answer to Question 18

(A) The man will prevail because the company used unreasonable force to protect its property. One may use reasonable force to prevent the commission of a tort against one's property, real or personal. However, force that will cause death or serious bodily harm may not be used. In addition, indirect deadly force may not be used when such force could not lawfully be directly used. Here, the company kept the power running to prevent the theft of its copper. In effect, this amounts to the use of indirect deadly force as a means of preventing a tort to personal property. As explained above, use of such force to protect property is not permitted. Thus, the man will prevail in his suit against the company. (B) is incorrect because it is too broad. Force may be used to protect only property if such force is reasonable, regardless of whether it is directly applied or indirectly applied by mechanical devices. The problem here is that the force used by the company was unreasonable because it was deadly force. Regarding (C), it is true that an owner or occupier of land owes no duty to an undiscovered trespasser. However, the company is not an owner or occupier of the land on which the line runs, but simply the owner of the line itself and the holder of an easement across the land. Thus, the company is held to the general duty of due care regardless of the man's status, rather than the more limited duty owed by a landowner or occupier to a trespasser. (D) is incorrect because the facts do not indicate that the man assumed any risk. To have assumed a risk, a plaintiff must have known of the risk and must have voluntarily gone ahead in the face of the risk. Here, the facts do not indicate that the man knew that electrical current was still running through the line. In fact, because it was under construction and exposed, the man likely assumed that the power was not running. Thus, he did not know of the risk and could not have voluntarily assumed such a risk. Note also that, while the question does not indicate the theory on which the man is basing his cause of action, it may be based on a theory of intentional tort (specifically battery), in which case assumption of risk would not be an appropriate defense.

Answer to Question 19

(B) The landowner's interest in the 30 acres is a possibility of reverter. Under the Rule Against Perpetuities, the attempt to give the cousin an executory interest is void because his interest could vest more than 21 years after a life in being. The courts will strike the gift over to the cousin and will then read the rest of the conveyance as it stands. Thus, (C) is incorrect. The "so long as" language creates a fee simple determinable in the brother, meaning that the grantor retains a possibility of reverter. Thus, (A) and (D) are incorrect.

Answer to Question 20

(B) The woman should be found not guilty of a conspiracy to commit arson. To be convicted of a conspiracy, it must be shown that at least two persons agreed to achieve an unlawful objective. Having two or more persons is a necessary element of conspiracy. (This is called the "Wharton rule.") Here, the facts indicate that the man did not intend to achieve the objective of the conspiracy—

to burn the dwelling house of another. Thus, under the Wharton rule, the woman cannot be guilty of conspiracy to commit arson. (C) is incorrect. The man feigned his agreement, making the answer factually inaccurate. (D) is also incorrect. Although it is true that arson is not a specific intent crime, conspiracy is a specific intent crime, in that the prosecution must show that the defendant intended to agree and intended to achieve the unlawful objective. Thus, the fact that the underlying crime is not a specific intent crime is irrelevant. (A) is incorrect. Even if the woman would not have committed the crime without the man's inducement, that is not a defense for the woman. A person cannot be entrapped by a private citizen.

Answer to Question 21

(C) The man's best argument to gain immediate possession of his home is that the woman is a licensee. A license is a privilege to enter onto another's property. It may be revoked at any time merely by a manifestation of the licensor's intent to end it. A tenant at sufferance would be entitled to the statutory notice, and a month-to-month tenant would benefit from the common law right to a period of notice equal to the tenancy, *i.e.*, one month. Thus, (A) and (B) are wrong. (D) is wrong because the woman is clearly not a trespasser ab initio, since she entered onto the premises with permission.

Answer to Question 22

(B) Knowledge on the part of the manufacturer that its television was being mounted on the ceiling would give rise to a duty to include in the manual warnings against the practice or detailed instructions on how to safely mount it. The television hardware and instructions were appropriate for its intended mounting on the wall. However, courts in a strict liability case require a commercial supplier to anticipate reasonably foreseeable uses even if they are misuses of the product. If the manufacturer knew that members of the public were sometimes mounting the television on the ceiling, marketing the product without including either warnings against the practice or appropriate hardware and instructions on how to safely do so made the product so defective as to be unreasonably dangerous if it were improperly mounted. Under a strict liability theory, the manufacturer breached its duty by supplying a defective product. As a guest of a purchaser of the product, the woman is a foreseeable plaintiff; thus, the duty was owed to her. This breach of duty actually and proximately caused the woman to suffer serious injuries. Therefore, the manufacturer is liable to the woman in a strict products liability action based on negligence. (A) is incorrect because the facts do not establish that the manufacturer was under a duty to include the warnings in its manual. Such a duty would exist if the manufacturer knew (as (B) states) or should have known that the television was being mounted on ceilings. (C) is incorrect because industry custom does not conclusively establish the applicable standard of care in a given case (although such customs are admissible as evidence of the standard to be applied). Here, including only the customary warnings in an instruction manual may be violative of the appropriate standard of care (*i.e.*, manufacturers of these televisions may be under a duty to add additional warnings in the manual). Thus, the statement set forth in (C) will not by itself mean that the manufacturer will prevail. (D) is incorrect because, even if the man should have known that the television should not have been mounted on the ceiling, such negligence would not be a superseding cause of the injury because it would be ordinary foreseeable negligence. Consequently, the manufacturer would not be relieved of liability for the results of its own wrongful conduct, but would be held liable along with the man.

Answer to Question 23

(C) The court will rule for the railroad company because it has not abandoned the easement. Easements are presumed to be of perpetual duration, and mere nonuse is not enough to constitute termination by abandonment. To abandon, the easement holder must demonstrate by physical action (*e.g.*, removing the railroad tracks) an intention to permanently abandon the easement; this has not been done here, and so (A) is incorrect. (B) is incorrect because it reaches the wrong result and relies on a factor having nothing to do with abandonment. (D) is an incorrect statement of law—once abandoned, an easement cannot be revived simply because the owner of the underlying fee did not take some affirmative action.

Answer to Question 24

(A) The man's motion will be granted because he had a reasonable expectation of privacy in his bedroom closet. The search of the closet was not based on a valid warrant or circumstances justifying an exception to the warrant requirement. (B) is wrong. There is no such rule of law. (C) is wrong; allowing the police to enter the house is no "consent" to search the bedroom closet. (D) is wrong; a search of the closet would be outside the area of the immediate control of the defendant and could not be justified as a search incident to an arrest.

Answer to Question 25

(C) Most likely, the state will have to show that its petition requirement is narrowly tailored to achieve a compelling state interest. The Supreme Court uses a balancing test in determining whether a regulation of the electoral process is valid: if the restriction on First Amendment activities is severe, the regulation will be upheld only if it is narrowly tailored to achieve a compelling interest. Requiring a candidate to obtain 4% of voters' signatures probably qualifies as a severe First Amendment restriction. Thus, the state must show that the regulation is narrowly tailored to achieve a compelling interest (*e.g.*, running an honest and efficient election system). Note that the Court has approved a requirement that candidates obtain 1% of the voters' signatures before being placed on the ballot. [*See* Munro v. Socialist Workers Party (1986)] In any case, the Court probably would not apply the rational basis standard under these facts, so (A) and (D) are incorrect. (B) is incorrect because when the Court applies heightened scrutiny, it requires the government to bear the burden of persuasion, not the person challenging the government's action.

Answer to Question 26

(D) The friend's comment is an out-of-court statement offered for its truth, and it does not fall within a recognized exception to the hearsay rule. (A) is incorrect because a present sense impression must be communicated while perceiving the event or object, or immediately thereafter. The friend was telling the woman about something she had seen the previous evening. (B) is incorrect because, even if the statement is relevant, it is still hearsay, and the friend's unavailability does not bring it within an exception to the hearsay rule. (C) does not state a reason for excluding the evidence; circumstantial evidence is admissible.

Answer to Question 27

(C) The jogger's act constituted an unlawful application of force to the person of another and is, thus, a battery. Use of a deadly weapon in the commission of a battery elevates the crime to aggravated battery. (A) is wrong because a person must ***reasonably*** believe that he is faced with imminent death or great bodily harm in order to use deadly force. The accidental blow struck by the homeowner would not rise to that level. (B) is wrong because this is clearly battery, not assault. (D) is wrong because battery requires only an offensive touching, not an injury; in any case, this answer does not address the element of aggravation.

Answer to Question 28

(C) The terms of the deed control the rancher's liability. While the contract did not specify the quality of title, the law implies that a marketable title is to be conveyed, and since a title based on adverse possession is not marketable, although it may be good, the investor could have refused to perform. Once the investor accepted a deed, however, the doctrine of merger comes into play and the contract is merged into the deed. Any contract provisions for quality of title, express or implied, are no longer effective. Thus, (A) is incorrect. The investor must look to the terms of the deed for his rights. (B) is incorrect because the court will not rewrite the deed. The facts do not indicate that the rancher made any misrepresentations, and so (D) is incorrect.

Answer to Question 29

(C) The builder will not prevail unless the custodian knew that someone was in the lot. False imprisonment is an intentional tort requiring that the defendant have the intent to confine the plaintiff to a bounded area. (A) and (B) are therefore wrong, because the intent element is missing. (A) is also wrong because the builder does not have to show that he was harmed as a result of his confinement to recover for false imprisonment. (D) is wrong because negligence is not enough for the tort of false imprisonment. While he may have a negligence claim because he was injured, the cause of action stated is false imprisonment.

Answer to Question 30

(B) The court most likely will find that Congress had the power to enact the legislation under the Thirteenth Amendment. The Thirteenth Amendment simply provides that neither slavery nor involuntary servitude shall exist within the United States and gives Congress the power to adopt appropriate legislation to enforce the proscription. Since the amendment is not limited to proscribing state action, Congress may adopt legislation regulating private parties. Under the amendment, the Supreme Court has allowed Congress to prohibit any private conduct that Congress deems to be a "badge" or "incident" of slavery, and has upheld statutes regulating private contracts. [*See, e.g.,* Runyon v. McCrary (1967)] (A) is not a good basis for the statute because the Contract Clause is a limitation on ***states'*** rights to modify contracts retroactively; it is unrelated to Congress's power to regulate private contracts. (C)—the Fourteenth Amendment—is incorrect. The Fourteenth Amendment prohibits ***states*** from discriminating on the basis of race; it does not extend to private conduct. [*See* United States v. Morrison (2000)] (D)—the Commerce Clause—might also be a basis for the legislation here, but it is not as good an answer as (B) because the commerce power is limited to transactions that either in themselves or in combination with other activities have a substantial economic effect on interstate commerce, and by its terms the legislation here can reach wholly intrastate transactions. The interstate commerce requirement is a limit on congressional legislation and no such limit is present under the Thirteenth Amendment. Therefore, the Thirteenth Amendment is a better basis for the legislation here.

Answer to Question 31

(C) The manufacturer will prevail. This fact situation is governed by U.C.C. section 2-207 because it involves an acceptance or written confirmation that varies the original offer. Under common law, no contract would have been formed because of the difference in the price term ($72 vs. $70 in the original offer). However, under section 2-207, a contract was formed when the seller mailed its letter; thus, (A) is wrong. (B) is wrong because, under U.C.C. section 2-201, a writing in confirmation of the contract (even if it varies from the original offer) that is sufficient to bind the sender will also satisfy the Statute of Frauds against the recipient unless a written objection is made within 10 days, which was not done by the buyer here. (D) is wrong because the store owner would be bound regardless of whether she made the phone call to cancel.

Answer to Question 32

(B) The contract was formed on November 3. An offer to buy goods for shipment is generally construed as inviting acceptance either by a promise to ship or by shipment. Here, the letter constitutes a promise to ship and thus is an acceptance. The rule for acceptances is that they are effective as soon as they are dispatched, which was November 3. Thus, (B) is correct, and (C) is wrong. (A) is wrong because the order was an offer, not an acceptance to the catalogue. (D) is wrong because acceptance occurred before shipment when the manufacturer sent its ***promise to ship***.

Answer to Question 33

(B) The man and his nephew will be acquitted. Conspiracy requires (i) an agreement between two or more persons; (ii) an intent to enter into an agreement; and (iii) an intent to achieve the unlawful objective of the agreement. Conspiracy is a specific intent crime. Here, given that the man and his nephew were charged with conspiracy to hunt grizzly bears out of season, it must be established that they had the specific intent to commit that crime. The man and his nephew intended to legally hunt grizzly bears in season. Thus, there was no intent to commit the crime of hunting grizzly bears out of season. (A) is incorrect because there was an agreement. (C) is incorrect because when a defendant is charged with a conspiracy to commit a strict liability crime, specific intent still must be shown. (D) is also incorrect. Even though overt acts in furtherance of their objective have been committed, specific intent would still have to be shown. As stated above, specific intent is lacking here.

Answer to Question 34

(B) If the man prevails, it will be because the jury determined that he acted reasonably under the circumstances. One may act in self-defense not only where there is real danger but also where there is a reasonable appearance of danger. An honest but mistaken belief that the woman was about to shoot would justify the use of deadly force by the man if a reasonable person would have acted similarly under those circumstances. The test is an objective one—an honest belief alone is not sufficient. Thus, (A) is incorrect. (C) is incorrect because the woman's fault is not the determining factor—the reasonableness of the man's belief governs for self-defense. (D) is incorrect because it does not resolve whether the man had the right to use deadly force.

Answer to Question 35

(A) The testimony should be ruled inadmissible because it is hearsay and does not clearly fall within a hearsay exception under the facts given. (B) is wrong because the opinion was based on the perception of the witness and would be helpful to the determination of a fact in issue—the negligence of the injured employee. (C) is wrong because the assistant is not a party. (D) is wrong because the assistant did not testify and therefore the statement cannot qualify as a prior inconsistent statement. The statement is clearly hearsay. It could be argued that it qualifies as an "excited utterance," but there are not enough facts to establish this; also, "admissible as an excited utterance" is not one of the four picks. Therefore (A) is the winner because (B), (C), and (D) are clearly wrong.

Answer to Question 36

(D) The woman will most likely have no cause of action for either ejectment or damages. Restraints on alienation are traditionally strictly construed. Thus, a covenant prohibiting assignment does not prohibit subleasing and vice versa. Hence, this prohibition against assignment would not be read to include a prohibition against subleasing. Therefore, the woman would have no cause of action against the man, and (A) and (B) are incorrect. (C) is incorrect. If a tenant transfers (assigns or sublets) in violation of a prohibition in the lease against transfers, the transfer is not void, but the landlord usually may terminate the lease under either the lease terms or a statute. Here, however, there is no cause of action because subleasing was not prohibited.

Set 2 Answer Sheet

1. Ⓐ Ⓑ Ⓒ Ⓓ
2. Ⓐ Ⓑ Ⓒ Ⓓ
3. Ⓐ Ⓑ Ⓒ Ⓓ
4. Ⓐ Ⓑ Ⓒ Ⓓ
5. Ⓐ Ⓑ Ⓒ Ⓓ
6. Ⓐ Ⓑ Ⓒ Ⓓ
7. Ⓐ Ⓑ Ⓒ Ⓓ
8. Ⓐ Ⓑ Ⓒ Ⓓ
9. Ⓐ Ⓑ Ⓒ Ⓓ
10. Ⓐ Ⓑ Ⓒ Ⓓ
11. Ⓐ Ⓑ Ⓒ Ⓓ
12. Ⓐ Ⓑ Ⓒ Ⓓ
13. Ⓐ Ⓑ Ⓒ Ⓓ
14. Ⓐ Ⓑ Ⓒ Ⓓ
15. Ⓐ Ⓑ Ⓒ Ⓓ
16. Ⓐ Ⓑ Ⓒ Ⓓ
17. Ⓐ Ⓑ Ⓒ Ⓓ
18. Ⓐ Ⓑ Ⓒ Ⓓ
19. Ⓐ Ⓑ Ⓒ Ⓓ
20. Ⓐ Ⓑ Ⓒ Ⓓ
21. Ⓐ Ⓑ Ⓒ Ⓓ
22. Ⓐ Ⓑ Ⓒ Ⓓ
23. Ⓐ Ⓑ Ⓒ Ⓓ
24. Ⓐ Ⓑ Ⓒ Ⓓ
25. Ⓐ Ⓑ Ⓒ Ⓓ
26. Ⓐ Ⓑ Ⓒ Ⓓ
27. Ⓐ Ⓑ Ⓒ Ⓓ
28. Ⓐ Ⓑ Ⓒ Ⓓ
29. Ⓐ Ⓑ Ⓒ Ⓓ
30. Ⓐ Ⓑ Ⓒ Ⓓ
31. Ⓐ Ⓑ Ⓒ Ⓓ
32. Ⓐ Ⓑ Ⓒ Ⓓ
33. Ⓐ Ⓑ Ⓒ Ⓓ
34. Ⓐ Ⓑ Ⓒ Ⓓ
35. Ⓐ Ⓑ Ⓒ Ⓓ
36. Ⓐ Ⓑ Ⓒ Ⓓ

MIXED SUBJECT QUESTIONS - SET 2

Question 1

A driver was operating her car on a city street when she was stopped by a police officer for speeding. As the police officer reached the driver's car, he saw her put something into her purse. The officer told the driver, "Ma'am, you were speeding; that's why I stopped you. I'd like your driver's license, and, by the way, what did you just put into your purse?" The driver responded, "It's just a marijuana cigarette, but don't worry, I've only had two and my driving judgment hasn't been impaired." The officer took her purse, removed the "joint," and charged the driver with possession of marijuana as well as speeding. At the driver's trial for marijuana possession, the prosecution seeks to introduce the marijuana cigarette into evidence. The driver's attorney moves to suppress the evidence.

The defense motion should be:

(A) Granted, because the cigarette is fruit of the poisonous tree.

(B) Granted, because the police officer did not have a valid search warrant.

(C) Denied, because the police officer's asking about the contents of the driver's purse did not constitute custodial interrogation.

(D) Denied, provided the police officer had a reasonable suspicion of criminal activity.

Question 2

A man and a woman met in a bar. The woman told the man that she greatly admired the diamond stickpin he had in his lapel. "Oh this," the man laughed. "It's no diamond; it's only a piece of glass." The woman acknowledged his statement, but kept commenting on how nice it looked. After further conversation, the man orally agreed to sell the stickpin to her for $510. They agreed that in two days, he would bring the stickpin to the same bar, and the woman would bring the $510 in cash. The man duly appeared with the pin, but the woman failed to appear. The man filed suit against the woman for $510.

The woman's best defense is:

(A) $510 was an unconscionable amount to pay for a piece of glass.

(B) The agreement was not supported by consideration.

(C) The agreement violated the Statute of Frauds.

(D) Neither the woman nor the man was a merchant.

Question 3

A landowner conveyed a large tract of land to a man and a woman by a deed that created a co-tenancy in equal shares with right of survivorship. The man, by deed, then conveyed "My undivided, one-half interest" in the tract of land to a third party. The man has since died. The jurisdiction has no statute directly applicable to this situation.

In an action between the woman and the third party, in which both claim sole title to the tract of land, the woman will prevail only if:

(A) The man and woman owned the tract of land as joint tenants.

(B) The woman was once the sole owner of the tract of land.

(C) The man and woman owned the tract of land as tenants in common.

(D) The co-tenancy created in the man and the woman was a tenancy by the entirety.

Question 4

A plaintiff brings suit against a manufacturing company, seeking to recover for damages he suffered when his car's engine burst into flames following the use of an engine additive made by the company. The plaintiff contends that the manufacturing company was negligent and in breach of warranty.

An automobile engineer sat in court while the plaintiff testified to the events concerning the engine fire. The plaintiff's testimony was not challenged or rebutted. The plaintiff calls the engineer to the stand and asks him whether, based on the plaintiff's prior testimony, it was possible for a car engine to burst into flames as it did.

The engineer's testimony would be:

(A) Inadmissible, because the engineer's opinion was not elicited by means of a hypothetical question.

(B) Inadmissible, because the engineer was in the court while the plaintiff testified concerning the engine fire.

(C) Admissible, because the engineer was in the court while the plaintiff testified concerning the engine fire.

(D) Admissible, as long as the engineer's opinion is based only on admissible evidence.

Question 5

A state statute prohibits speechmaking and loud public gatherings within 250 feet of the state's legislative chamber when the legislature is in session, but permits silent picketing at any time, as long as the picketing does not interfere with pedestrians or traffic. The nearest place to the legislative chamber where speeches could be made during a session is a large public park directly opposite the chamber. During a controversial debate on a proposed bill to ban abortions, a man in the park began voicing his support of the ban. As the man spoke, a crowd of about 250 gathered. When fervor built, the man urged the crowd to cross the street to the steps of the legislative chamber to make their voices heard within the legislature. When the chanting crowd reached the front of the chamber, the state police dispersed the crowd and arrested the man, who was subsequently charged with violating the statute.

If the man challenges the constitutionality of the statute under which he was charged, a court will most likely find the statute:

(A) Constitutional on its face and as applied to the man.

(B) Constitutional on its face but not as applied to the man.

(C) Unconstitutional on its face, because a state's citizens have a right to take their complaints to their state legislature.

(D) Unconstitutional on its face, because it permits silent picketing while prohibiting other picketing.

Question 6

Because of budget shortfalls, a state governor recently signed a bill shortening the period for which state unemployment benefits are available. The defendant gave a speech across the street from the governor's mansion, denouncing the law. In his speech, the defendant urged the crowd to rush across the street, drag the governor from his mansion, and show him how it feels to be homeless. A police officer who heard the defendant's speech arrested the defendant and he was charged with violating a state statute that makes it a crime to "make a threat against any state official in the performance of his duty."

If the defendant defends on constitutional grounds, the court will likely find the statute:

(A) Unconstitutional as a prior restraint.

(B) Unconstitutional because it does not require clear and present danger of imminent lawless action.

(C) Constitutional if limited to true threats.

(D) Constitutional under the fighting words doctrine.

Question 7

A patient went to a highly reputable dentist, who honestly told her that she needed a lot of dental work, some of it involving complex procedures. When she asked the dentist what the cost would be, he told her "about $3,500." The patient agreed to use him as her dentist and he began her treatment. When the patient's treatment was finished, the dentist sent her a bill for $4,100, explaining that the higher bill was because more expensive inlays were used, and that he carefully documented the cost of his materials and had sound medical reasons for his decision. The patient honestly believed that it was unfair for the dentist to charge her $4,100. Therefore, she sent the dentist's invoice back to him, along with a check for $3,500. On the check the patient had clearly written "Payment In Full." The dentist read the notation on the check and deposited it at his bank. The dentist made no notation of his own on the check other than his signature on the back as an indorsement. Two weeks later the dentist called his bank to make sure that the patient's check had cleared. He then immediately filed suit against the patient for $600.

Will the court award the dentist $600?

(A) Yes, because the dentist merely estimated the cost of the dental work to be $3,500.

(B) Yes, because the dentist can document that the precious metal inlays were medically necessary and that he charged a fair price for them.

(C) No, because there has been an accord and satisfaction of the original debt.

(D) No, because there is an account stated.

Question 8

A landowner leased 150 acres of farmland to a produce company for 15 years. The produce company used the land for crops along with several other contiguous acres that it owned or leased. About four years into the lease, the state condemned a portion of the leased property because it intended to build a highway. As a result, too little property remained for the produce company to profitably farm, although there still existed the farmhouse on the property, which was being used by one of its foremen. The produce company gave the landowner 30 days' written notice that it considered the lease to have been terminated because of the condemnation.

In a suit for breach of contract, the landowner would probably:

(A) Lose, because the condemnation made it economically undesirable for the produce company to continue to lease the property.

(B) Lose, because when there is a condemnation, the tenant's obligation to pay rent is extinguished.

(C) Win, because the produce company can still use the farmhouse, and the rental value would be adjusted accordingly.

(D) Win, because the condemnation did not affect the produce company's obligation to pay the full rental price, although it is entitled to share in the condemnation award.

Question 9

A man parked his car on a city street and entered a local tavern. While the man was inside, vandals broke the ignition motor on his car and smashed the taillights. Later that night the man left the tavern and attempted to start his car, but was unable to because of the vandals' actions, which he had not been aware of. Police in a patrolling squad car noticed him entering the car and attempting to start it. When the man got out of the car, the police approached him and asked him to identify himself. When he refused, he was arrested and charged with attempting to drive an automobile at night without functioning taillights.

The man's best defense is:

(A) Entrapment.

(B) Legal impossibility.

(C) Factual impossibility.

(D) Lack of requisite intent.

Question 10

To rein in states passing restrictive usury laws, Congress enacted legislation establishing a uniform usury rate. The legislation, in essence, establishes that the usury rate will be determined by the Federal Reserve Board on the date of the loan. The law is intended to be of great assistance to the private home market as well as the commercial market.

One state has a usury law that permits the charging of interest in excess of that which Congress has provided. The state brings an action in federal court seeking to avoid the law with respect to the state. The state presents evidence that loans made in the state during the last two years for the purpose of housing all were at rates exceeding those permissible under the provision of the federal law. The state alleges that enforcing the federal law would bring the housing industry to a stop.

The federal judge should:

(A) Rule that he has no jurisdiction to hear the case.

(B) Rule that the state law is invalid as a result of the Supremacy Clause.

(C) Rule that granting temporary relief by enjoining the federal act pending a decision on the merits would be proper.

(D) Impanel a three-judge court because of the seriousness of the issue.

Question 11

A landowner owned a large commercial building downtown and the vacant lot next to his building. The landowner agreed to let an inner-city Scout troop use the vacant lot to practice outdoor-type activities. One weekend while the landowner was away on business, the Scout leader asked the landowner's building manager if he would permit the Scouts to practice their archery. The building manager agreed, but insisted that the targets be set up against the building so that an errant shot would merely strike concrete and not injure someone on the streets bordering the lot. The building manager supervised the set-up of the targets and ensured that responsible adults were present to assist the Scouts, then left the area. One of the Scouts jokingly shot an arrow up into the sky, and it came down on the street next to the vacant lot, striking and injuring a motorcyclist who was riding past.

If the motorcyclist does not prevail in an action against the landowner for personal injuries, it will be because:

(A) The landowner had no personal knowledge of the archery practice by the Scouts.

(B) The precautions taken by the landowner's building manager were those a reasonable person would have taken.

(C) The Scout acted recklessly by shooting the arrow in the air.

(D) The failure of the adults present to prevent the Scout's action was a superseding cause of the injury.

Question 12

A plaintiff sued a defendant for negligence when the tractor that he was driving at a construction site collided with the plaintiff's car. The plaintiff alleged that she was driving in a proper lane when the tractor collided with her car. The plaintiff's counsel called the responding police officer to testify that the defendant's employee made a statement to the police officer, in the defendant's presence, that the defendant "accidentally went too far into traffic," and the defendant did not say anything.

The trial judge should rule that this evidence is:

(A) Admissible, because the employee was working for the defendant, and as his agent, could make a statement against the defendant's interest.

(B) Admissible, because silence may be deemed an admission.

(C) Inadmissible, because the employee's statement was hearsay, and the defendant's silence is also hearsay.

(D) Inadmissible, because the employee has not yet testified to his statement.

Question 13

In a claim for damages in a personal injury action, a plaintiff's attorney sought to introduce evidence of the plaintiff's testimony made to her boyfriend several days after her accident that "I must have sprained my neck when it happened because it hurts so much." The plaintiff is also planning to offer medical evidence that her neck was sprained.

The judge should rule the testimony:

(A) Inadmissible, because it is hearsay.

(B) Inadmissible, because the plaintiff is not qualified to give testimony as to her medical condition.

(C) Admissible, because the plaintiff is also going to present medical evidence that her neck was sprained.

(D) Admissible, to show that the plaintiff had suffered physical pain.

Question 14

A defendant, on trial for robbing the victim of some jewelry, relied on the defense that he was only trying to recover property that the alleged victim had previously stolen from him. The trial court instructed the jury that the prosecution must prove guilt beyond a reasonable doubt, and that if the jury should find that the defendant had established by a preponderance of the evidence that he was only trying to recover his property, they should find him not guilty. After he was convicted of robbery, the defendant asserts that the instruction to the jury was error.

His conviction should probably be:

(A) Reversed, because the defendant need only convince the jury of any defense to a reasonable certainty, not by a preponderance of the evidence.

(B) Reversed, because the instruction put a burden on the defendant that denied him due process of law.

(C) Affirmed, because the defendant's burden to show that he was trying to recover his property was not one of ultimate persuasion, but only to produce evidence to rebut the legitimate presumption that the robbery was conducted with the intent to permanently deprive the victim of the jewelry.

(D) Affirmed, because the instruction was an accurate statement of the law.

Question 15

A seller, who was married, entered into a written contract with a buyer to sell the buyer a vacation house, which had been purchased by the seller during his marriage but was held in his name alone. The contract expressly required the seller to provide "good, clear, and marketable title" to the vacation home. The buyer paid the purchase price and was given a deed to the property from the seller. According to the jurisdiction's marital property laws, both husband and wife own an interest in any real property purchased during their marriage. However, another statute provides that when real property is held in the name of one spouse alone, that spouse may convey that real property to another, and any interest in the property owned by the spouse whose name does not appear on the recorded title is terminated, unless that spouse brings an action within one year to set aside the conveyance.

Six months later, the seller's wife successfully set aside the conveyance on the ground that the seller had conveyed her marital interest in the vacation home without her consent.

What would be the result of an action for damages by the buyer against the seller for breach of the land sale contract?

(A) The seller would prevail, unless the deed expressly covenanted title.

(B) The seller would prevail, if the buyer had knowledge that the seller was married.

(C) The buyer would prevail, because the seller's wife was able to set aside the conveyance.

(D) The buyer would prevail, because the terms of the contract are incorporated in the deed when the contract requires marketable title.

Question 16

An artist purchased a warehouse in an industrial district that she converted into a studio many years ago. A few months ago, a record company purchased a warehouse next door to the artist's studio and converted it into a recording studio and rehearsal rooms. The recording studio frequently stays open long past midnight, particularly on the weekends. Although the five recording studios are thoroughly soundproofed, the various rehearsal rooms are not. When bands are using them, the sound can easily be heard by the artist when she is working in her studio. The artist had always done her work at night, but since the recording studio next door opened, she has found it very difficult to concentrate on her work. She is distracted by all the noise and activity from the recording studio.

In a private nuisance suit against the record company, the fact that the artist owns her studio and has used it for 15 years is:

(A) Controlling on the issue of whether the record company's use of its property is reasonable.

(B) Not controlling, but relevant to the issue of whether the record company's use of its property is reasonable.

(C) Not controlling, and irrelevant since the surrounding area was used exclusively for industry and manufacturing when the artist bought her property.

(D) Not controlling, and irrelevant since a landowner cannot establish the reasonableness of the use of property simply by being the first in the neighborhood.

Question 17

A defendant is on trial in federal court for the armed robbery of a casino. The defendant claims that he was out of town at the time of the robbery. The defendant calls an alibi witness to the stand to testify that she was with him on the trip. When asked where she was and who she was with on the date in question, the witness stated that she could not recall. She said she recalls spending a weekend at a bed and breakfast this spring, but she does not recall the date or her traveling companion. The defendant's attorney then showed the witness a letter written by her on stationery from the bed and breakfast, and asks her to look at it and try to answer the question again. The prosecution objects.

The objection should be:

(A) Overruled, because this is a past recollection recorded.

(B) Overruled, but the witness cannot depend on the terms of the letter when answering.

(C) Sustained, because the letter is hearsay.

(D) Sustained, because the letter has not been properly authenticated.

Question 18

The owner of a semi-pro baseball team offered a former player a position as the team's manager. During negotiations, the owner agreed to pay the manager $300 per week, but insisted that if the manager quit during the season, he would have to pay a "penalty" of $200 per week for each week that he did not manage the team, because it would cost the owner several hundred dollars to replace him during the season. The parties agreed in writing to those terms. The manager managed the team for 14 weeks with only mixed success. Nevertheless, with 10 weeks left in the season, he was offered and accepted a job as manager of a professional baseball team. Fortunately for the owner of the semi-pro team, the manager's replacement had great success with the team, causing attendance to skyrocket.

If the owner of the semi-pro team brings suit against the manger to recover $2,000, the amount due under the "penalty" provision, the owner will:

(A) Not prevail, because "penalty" clauses in contracts are not enforceable.

(B) Not prevail, because the owner of the semi-pro team was not harmed by his breach.

(C) Prevail, because the manager can be penalized for his willful breach.

(D) Prevail, because the "penalty" provision is enforceable.

Question 19

The manager of a monthly antique market was looking to hire a professional appraiser who would tell patrons, for a fee of $10 per item, what their antique is worth. Because the manager had had problems at other antique markets he had run because appraisers built up a popular following and then abruptly quit for a better job, he emphasized during the hiring interview the importance of honoring the contract to its completion. When the manager offered the job to an experienced appraiser, and the appraiser accepted, the written contract signed by the appraiser contained, in addition to an agreed-to salary, a liquidated damages clause for early terminations of the contract. It also contained another clause providing that the appraiser would receive 5% of all gate receipts to be paid as a bonus at the end of the contract, which ran for one year.

Eight months into the contract, the manager's worst fears were realized when the appraiser got a more lucrative offer and abruptly quit, leaving the manager scrambling to find a replacement for him. In response to the manager's suit for breach of contract, the appraiser brings a countersuit to recover 5% of gate receipts for the antique markets at which he worked.

Will the appraiser be successful in his countersuit?

(A) Yes, because his breach was not substantial.

(B) Yes, because the manager's only remedy was the liquidated damages clause.

(C) No, because working the entire year was an implied condition of the contract.

(D) No, because working the entire year was an express condition of the contract.

Question 20

A gas company offered a generous sum to a landowner in exchange for permission to run pipes over a 15-foot strip of the landowner's property to supply natural gas to a new housing development. The landowner granted the gas company and its "heirs and assigns" an easement over the 15-foot strip of property "for pipeline purposes." The easement was duly recorded. When the housing development was ready for utility services, the gas company laid the pipe across the 15-foot strip of property. Shortly after the gas company finished laying its pipe, the landowner planted a garden of trees and flowers on the 15-foot strip.

For the next 10 years, the gas company supplied natural gas to the housing development through that pipe. When the gas company no longer needed the lines that ran across the property, it sold its rights in the easement to an oil company that wished to run a crude oil pipeline across the same strip of property. Now, although the oil company confined its activities to the strip, it drove trucks onto the land, uprooted the trees, and tore up the flower garden in order to excavate for the laying of a larger pipe than the gas company had installed. The landowner filed suit to enjoin the oil company from further activities on the 15-foot strip and for damages for the destruction wrought on his property.

Is the landowner likely to succeed in this suit?

(A) Yes, because the gas company's sale of the easement to the oil company was without the landowner's permission.

(B) No, because the gas company had the right to assign its interest.

(C) No, as to the injunction, because the oil company is using the land for pipeline purposes, but the landowner is entitled to damages.

(D) No, as to the injunction and damages, because the use is for pipeline purposes and this obviously implies the right to excavate in order to lay pipe.

Question 21

A construction company was employed by the city to repair a broken pipe under a main street of the city. As part of its work, the construction company dug a deep trench down the center of the street. Warning signs and flashing lights were positioned at both ends of the trench to warn cars of the danger, but, except for two unlit warning signs along the sides, no barriers of any kind were put up on either side. A college student was walking home from the bus depot along the same street after dark. A heavy rain started, and in an effort to avoid getting more drenched, the student jaywalked instead of going to the corner to cross the street, which was empty of traffic at the time. In the dark and the heavy rain, the student did not realize that the road was dug up where he was crossing and fell into the trench. The student was knocked out when he hit the bottom of the trench and drowned when the water from the rain gathered at the bottom.

The student's mother brought a wrongful death action against the construction company for the death of her son. The jurisdiction retains traditional contributory negligence rules and has a statute that makes it a misdemeanor for anyone to cross a main street such as this at any place except in the marked crosswalks.

The construction company is likely to:

(A) Prevail, because the student was negligent per se, and thus at fault for his own death.

(B) Prevail, because it had marked off its trench with warning signs.

(C) Not prevail, because a construction company is strictly liable for inherently dangerous conditions.

(D) Not prevail, because it left an open trench unprotected.

Question 22

A husband who believed that his wife was having an affair with his brother hired a known arsonist out on parole to burn down the brother's house. They planned for the husband to take his brother to a ballgame so that the arsonist would be able to set the house on fire without detection. On the day chosen for the arson, however, the arsonist learned that another arsonist he knew had recently been sentenced to life imprisonment. The arsonist decided to abandon the plan and immediately left town without doing anything further. When the husband returned from the ballgame with the brother, he saw the house still standing and blurted out what was supposed to have happened. The brother and the arsonist were arrested and charged with conspiracy

to commit arson. At the arsonist's trial, his attorney argued that he was innocent of the conspiracy because he decided not to go ahead with the plan, and nothing criminal had in fact occurred.

A jury should find the arsonist:

(A) Not guilty of conspiracy, because going to a ballgame is not a criminal overt act.

(B) Not guilty of conspiracy, because the husband, not the arsonist, committed the overt act.

(C) Guilty, because the husband executed his part of the plan.

(D) Guilty, because the arsonist agreed to set the brother's house on fire.

Question 23

Congress enacted legislation providing that, among other things, "federal courts shall not order any public educational institution to establish athletic activities or to modify existing athletic activities on the grounds that such activities are not provided on an equal basis to both men and women."

Which of the following is the strongest argument for the constitutionality of the federal legislation?

(A) Congress provides financial support for public educational institutions and is therefore empowered to place conditions on the expenditure of federal funds.

(B) Athletics involves tremendous amounts of money and the occasional use of interstate means of transportation, thus falling within the commerce power.

(C) Under Article III, Congress may restrict the jurisdiction of the federal courts.

(D) The Fourteenth Amendment authorizes Congress to define governmental conduct that violates the Equal Protection Clause.

Question 24

Congress adopted legislation prohibiting the federal courts from ordering busing as a remedy for past racial discrimination in a public school district.

Which of the following is the strongest argument that the federal legislation is unconstitutional?

(A) The courts, not Congress, have the primary responsibility for defining the minimum requirements of the Equal Protection Clause of the Fourteenth Amendment.

(B) The Privileges and Immunities Clause of the Fourteenth Amendment prohibits Congress from limiting the forms of relief afforded by federal courts.

(C) Congress cannot limit the authority of federal courts to hear and decide cases properly presented for decision.

(D) The legislation unduly burdens interstate commerce.

Question 25

Hoping to gain a position on a campaign staff, an unemployed law student sent a detailed outline of a campaign strategy to a candidate for Congress. The candidate turned the materials over to his campaign manager, who advised the candidate to adopt some of them in his commercials. The candidate wrote the law student, thanking him for his interest in the campaign and stating that although he had a campaign staff and strategy in place, some of the ideas were good and he adopted them. He added, "To say 'thanks' to a future constituent, I'd like to offer to pay you for your expenses in developing the materials you sent me. Send the bill to my campaign headquarters." Nevertheless, the candidate lost the election. One week after election day, the law student's bill for $1,500 arrived at the candidate's campaign headquarters. Campaign debts were high, and the candidate told his campaign manager not to pay the

bill. The law student filed suit against the candidate to obtain payment of the bill plus an additional $10,000 for his ideas.

What additional fact, if true, would most strengthen the candidate's defense against the law student's suit?

(A) The candidate lost the election by a close margin.

(B) The law student is a relative of the candidate.

(C) The candidate did nothing to solicit the law student's proposal.

(D) The law student sent a similar campaign strategy to the candidate's opponent.

Question 26

A buyer entered into a written contract with a farmer to purchase the farmer's dairy farm. The contract contained a provision that the farmer's "land and inventory are valued at $175,000." The contract also contained a provision that stated, "This contract represents the entire agreement between the parties. No other promises or representations have been made."

In a fraud action against the farmer, the buyer alleges that he purchased the farm only because the farmer had assured him that the land and inventory were worth $350,000, when they were in fact worth only $175,000. The buyer seeks to testify that during negotiations the farmer had said repeatedly that the value of the land and the inventory was $350,000, but at the advice of the farmer's attorney, he was going to list the value at $175,000 in the contract for tax purposes. The farmer's attorney objects.

The evidence is:

(A) Inadmissible hearsay.

(B) Inadmissible under the parol evidence rule.

(C) Neither hearsay nor violative of the parol evidence rule.

(D) Admissible hearsay, unaffected by the parol evidence rule.

Question 27

A landowner developed and built a large apartment house on property he owned. After the apartment house was completed, the landowner conveyed the building and the land to his son for life, remainder to his granddaughter; subject, however, to a bank's mortgage. The bank held a mortgage on the building for $17,000, payable in annual installments of $2,000 plus interest.

The son began to manage the day-to-day maintenance of the building as well as to collect rents. Despite the son's best efforts, the vacancy factor reached an unanticipated high and the rental income was not sufficient to cover the annual mortgage payment.

Who is responsible for the mortgage payments and in what amount?

(A) The son pays all.

(B) The granddaughter pays all.

(C) The son pays the interest and the granddaughter pays the principal.

(D) The granddaughter pays the interest and the son pays the principal.

Question 28

A man and a woman decided to get married and made detailed plans accordingly. Unbeknownst to the woman, however, the man was already married. Nevertheless, he was able to get a minister to agree to perform the ceremony even though the minister knew that the man was already married. As the marriage ceremony was about to begin, the man confessed this fact to the woman and the ceremony was called off. The state in which the couple was to be married, and in which both reside, makes bigamy a strict liability crime.

If the woman were to be tried for conspiracy to commit bigamy, she should be found:

(A) Guilty, because bigamy is a strict liability offense.

(B) Not guilty, because she did not intend to commit the crime of bigamy.

(C) Not guilty, because the wedding was canceled.

(D) Not guilty, because the Wharton rule would prohibit a conviction.

Question 29

A reporter received an anonymous tip that the mayor was taking kickbacks on city contracts with a construction company. The reporter eagerly pursued the tip because she had vowed to get even with the mayor after he caused the breakup of the reporter's romance with someone else. The reporter called the construction company and spoke with the owner's secretary. The secretary told the reporter that her employer had admitted to her that he was paying the mayor, but the secretary did not want her name in the paper. The reporter agreed to keep the secretary's name out of print.

The reporter wrote the story and it was published. The story was in fact false. The secretary happened to be cleaning out her desk when the reporter called because she had just been fired. She thought that confirming the rumor would be a good way to get back at her employer.

The mayor sues the reporter for libel and establishes the above facts at trial. His suit should:

(A) Succeed, because the reporter's vow of revenge indicates that she acted with malice.

(B) Succeed, because the story was false and the mayor was damaged by it.

(C) Fail, because the mayor is a public official.

(D) Fail, because newspaper reporters are protected from libel suits by the First Amendment.

Question 30

A homeowner wanted to have his driveway resurfaced. He called a number of commercial establishments which do such work and received bids ranging from $4,200 to $5,000. A handyman submitted a bid to do the work for $4,000, and the homeowner entered into a contract with him to have the driveway resurfaced.

Shortly before the handyman was scheduled to begin work, he called the homeowner and said, "I just found out my secretary made a mistake in adding figures. I know we signed a contract, but I couldn't possibly do the work for less than $4,400 or it would not be worth it."

If the homeowner sues the handyman for breach of contract, who will prevail?

(A) The homeowner, but only if it is too late for the homeowner to accept the bid of the next lowest bidder.

(B) The homeowner, but only if the homeowner did not have reason to know of the error in the handyman's bid.

(C) The handyman, because he had not yet commenced performance under the contract.

(D) The handyman, because he can successfully assert the defense of mistake.

Questions 31

A homeowner whose television reception was regularly interrupted by her neighbor's transmitting on his ham radio got out a ladder one night and climbed on top of her neighbor's two-story house, intending to cut down the antenna. However, her foot slipped and she had to grab hold of one of the antenna's support cables to keep from falling to the street below. The neighbor was unable to hear her cries for help because he was using earphones with his radio, but the driver of a passing car saw her hanging from the roof. The driver immediately came to her rescue and pulled her back onto the roof, and then had her climb down the ladder first.

However, as he was climbing down the ladder after her, he fell and suffered a broken hip.

If the driver sues the homeowner for the injuries he suffered, the driver should:

(A) Not prevail, because he voluntarily assumed the risk of injury.

(B) Not prevail, because the rescue of the homeowner was already over before he was injured.

(C) Prevail, because the homeowner was at fault in slipping from her neighbor's roof.

(D) Prevail, because the homeowner may have been killed if she had fallen to the street.

Question 32

A small cruise ship struck a whale swimming underwater, causing the ship to suddenly lurch sideways. A passenger on the ship who was walking down a corridor lost his balance and bumped his head on the edge of a doorway. Because of a previously existing medical condition that made him susceptible to bleeding on the brain, he suffered a cerebral hemorrhage and permanent mental impairment, despite prompt medical attention on the ship.

The passenger brought suit against the cruise ship owner for his damages. At trial, the passenger presented evidence of how he was injured as he walked down the hallway, his previous medical condition, and his medical expenses and other damages. The cruise ship owner presented evidence that the cruise ship was following its approved route and that the whale could not have been detected before impact, and that the bump would not have injured someone in ordinary health. At the close of the evidence, the cruise ship owner moved for a directed verdict.

The court should:

(A) Grant the motion, because there is no evidence that the crew operated the ship negligently.

(B) Grant the motion, because the cruise ship owner introduced uncontroverted evidence that a person in normal health would not have been injured by the bump.

(C) Deny the motion, because the jury could find that the cruise ship owner, as a common carrier and innkeeper, breached its high duty of care to the passenger.

(D) Deny the motion, because the fact that the severity of the passenger's injuries was not foreseeable does not cut off the cruise ship owner's liability.

Question 33

A scientist overheard from some friends that a young woman was suffering from a rare blood disease. The scientist told the young woman that he could cure her by giving her a special elixir he had invented. The scientist charged the young woman $500 for the elixir. The elixir had no effect on the blood disease. The scientist is charged with obtaining money by false pretenses.

Each of the following, if true, will absolve the scientist of guilt for obtaining money by false pretenses except:

(A) The scientist was playing a practical joke on the young woman and intended to return the money.

(B) The scientist honestly believed that the elixir would cure the blood disease, but his belief was unreasonable.

(C) The young woman honestly believed that the elixir would cure the blood disease, but her belief was unreasonable.

(D) The young woman was an undercover police officer and did not believe that the elixir would cure the blood disease.

Question 34

A farmers' market association filed for an injunction requiring a farmer to cease labeling her produce as "organic." At the hearing, the farmer called a witness to testify about organic farm practices and procedures. To qualify him as an expert, the farmer's attorney asked the witness about his training, education, and experience in the field. The witness responded that he was "certified by the State Board of Agriculture ten years ago as an expert on Organic Farming Management." On cross-examination concerning the witness's qualifications, counsel for the association asked, "Isn't it true that you failed the certification examination given by the State Board of Agriculture on Organic Farm Management ten years ago?" The witness replied, "No!" The association's attorney then attempts to submit into evidence the official pass-fail list published by the State Board for the Organic Farm Management certification exam from 10 years ago. The farmer's attorney objects.

The court should:

(A) Admit the list in order for the trial judge to evaluate whether the witness is qualified as an expert, and permit the witness to testify only if the judge concludes that he is sufficiently qualified.

(B) Admit the list as relevant to the witness's qualifications, and instruct the jury that the list may also be considered in determining the witness's truthfulness.

(C) Exclude the transcript as irrelevant, since it tends to impeach the witness on a collateral issue.

(D) Exclude the transcript because the association's attorney failed to lay a proper foundation for the evidence.

Question 35

An environmentalist divided her 25-acre property into 100 quarter-acre residential lots. At the time the environmentalist sold her lots, there was a recycling center about one mile from the western boundary of the development. She included in the deed of all 100 grantees the following provision:

> Grantee covenants for herself and her heirs and assigns that all aluminum cans, glass bottles, and grass clippings of Grantee and her heirs and assigns shall be recycled. This covenant runs with the land and shall remain in effect as long as there is a recycling center within five statute miles of the development.

A buyer purchased a lot in the development. Her deed contained the recycling clause. Two years later, the buyer decided to give the property to her niece as a gift. The niece's deed to the property contained the recycling covenant. Shortly after the niece took possession of the house, the recycling center moved its location to a new site about four and a half miles from the development. When the niece put the house up for sale, she said nothing to prospective buyers about recycling.

The house was purchased by a veteran who had lost the use of his legs. The veteran's deed did not contain the recycling clause, and he hired a local disposal service to carry away his garbage and a landscaper to maintain the yard. The landscaper bagged the grass clippings and they were removed by the disposal service, which put all the trash and clippings in a landfill. When the veteran's neighbors informed him of his duty to recycle, he told them that he knew nothing of the covenant and that it would be difficult for a person in his physical condition to haul cans, bottles, and clippings to the recycling center. Unfazed, the neighbors filed suit to require the veteran to comply with the covenant or pay damages.

The veteran's best defense is which of the following?

(A) The veteran's deed did not contain the covenant.

(B) The covenant does not touch and concern the land.

(C) An intelligent inspection of the neighborhood would raise no inference that the covenant existed.

(D) The veteran's physical condition requires a balancing of hardships by the court.

Question 36

A worker entered into a written contract with a homeowner to install aluminum siding on the homeowner's residence. The contract called for all work to be completed by the following Tuesday. On that date, the worker finished installing the siding rather late in the day and decided that he would come back the next day to pick up his ladder and tools. The worker could not tell the homeowner of this plan, however, because the homeowner was out of town overnight. During the night, a thief used the worker's ladder and tools to gain entrance to the house and steal the homeowner's television set and stereo. The homeowner has asserted a claim against the worker for damages for the loss of the television and the stereo.

In his claim against the worker, the homeowner will:

(A) Prevail, because by leaving the ladder and tools out, the worker created the risk that a person might unlawfully enter the house.

(B) Prevail, because the worker failed to get the homeowner's permission to leave his ladder and tools on the homeowner's property overnight.

(C) Not prevail, because the act of the thief was an independent superseding cause.

(D) Not prevail, because the homeowner's only recovery would be by way of an action for breach of contract.

MIXED SUBJECT SET 2 SUBJECT GUIDE

1. Criminal Law
2. Contracts
3. Real Property
4. Evidence
5. Constitutional Law
6. Constitutional Law
7. Contracts
8. Real Property
9. Criminal Law
10. Constitutional Law
11. Torts
12. Evidence
13. Evidence
14. Criminal Law
15. Real Property
16. Torts
17. Evidence
18. Contracts
19. Contracts
20. Real Property
21. Torts
22. Criminal Law
23. Constitutional Law
24. Constitutional Law
25. Contracts
26. Evidence
27. Real Property
28. Criminal Law
29. Constitutional Law
30. Contracts
31. Torts
32. Torts
33. Criminal Law
34. Evidence
35. Real Property
36. Torts

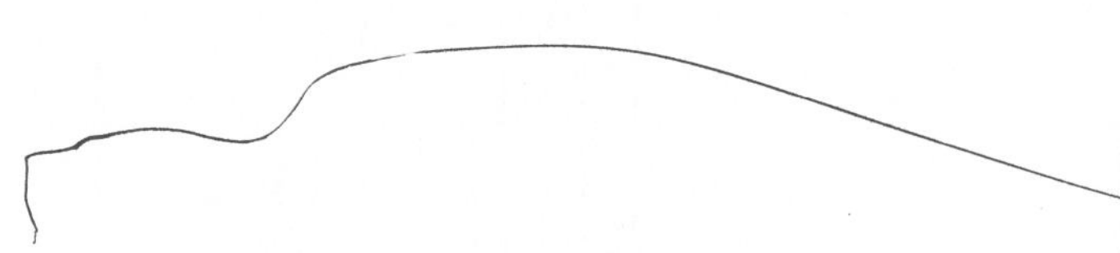

MIXED SUBJECT ANSWERS - SET 2

Answer to Question 1

(C) The defense motion should be denied because the driver was not in custody when she made the statement. Persons temporarily detained for routine traffic stops are not in custody for *Miranda* purposes. Therefore, the driver was not entitled to *Miranda* warnings, and her statement about the marijuana was not tainted. Her statement thus properly provided the probable cause for the search of her purse. (A) is therefore wrong. (B) is wrong because this case falls within the automobile exception to the warrant requirement. (D) states the test for a stop, not a search. An automobile search requires probable cause.

Answer to Question 2

(C) A promise for the sale of goods for $500 or more is not enforceable under the Statute of Frauds unless evidenced by a writing signed by the party to be charged. Uniform Commercial Code section 2-201(1) applies to the agreement between the man and the woman because the stickpin is a tangible, movable item of property, which is the definition of goods under the Code. The Statute of Frauds provision applies regardless of the fact that neither the man nor the woman is a merchant. The woman's promise, therefore, cannot be enforced by the man because it was an oral promise to purchase goods that cost more than $500. (A) is incorrect because the concept of unconscionability allows avoidance of a contract only where the terms are so one-sided as to indicate unfair surprise or a contract of adhesion. Here, neither party had superior bargaining power, and the woman knew exactly what she was buying when she made the agreement. (B) is incorrect because the agreement was a bargained-for exchange in which both parties would suffer detriments by giving something up. Regardless of whether the pin was objectively worth much less than $510, its appearance gave it a higher value in this transaction, and a court will not evaluate the adequacy of the consideration. (D) is incorrect because the parties' status as nonmerchants is irrelevant. While the Code relaxes the Statute of Frauds rule in the case of a written confirmation between merchants [U.C.C. §2-201(2)], that exception does not apply here. Thus, even if the parties were merchants, the agreement would be unenforceable.

Answer to Question 3

(D) The woman will prevail if a tenancy by the entirety was created. The somewhat ambiguous description of the conveyance given in the problem could apply either to a joint tenancy with a right of survivorship or to a tenancy by the entirety. If the conveyance is a tenancy by the entirety, then further conveyance by the man to the third party would not cause a severance and, upon the man's death, the woman would be the sole owner of the land. On the other hand, if it were initially a joint tenancy, the man's conveyance would sever it, converting the estate of the woman and the third party into a tenancy in common. Thus, (A) is incorrect. (B) is irrelevant because the form of concurrent ownership, *i.e.,* tenancy by the entirety or joint tenancy, not the status of prior ownership, is determinative of the rights of the parties. Under (C), the woman and the third party would each have an undivided ***one-half*** interest.

Answer to Question 4

(C) The engineer's testimony is admissible because it is based on knowledge gained by him at trial. Facts or data upon which expert opinions are based may be derived from presentation at trial. One acceptable method of doing this is to have the expert attend the trial and hear testimony

establishing the facts. Thus, (B) is incorrect. (A) is incorrect. Under the Federal Rules, a hypothetical question is not required to elicit an expert's opinion. (D) is incorrect because an expert may also base his opinion on facts supplied to him outside the courtroom, including types of facts not admissible into evidence, as long as they are reasonably relied on by experts in the field.

Answer to Question 5

(A) The statute is likely to be held constitutional on its face and as applied. The First Amendment protects the freedom of speech. Generally, content-based restrictions on speech will be found to violate the First Amendment. However, government may place reasonable restrictions on the time, place, and manner of speech. A speech regulation of a public forum will be found reasonable only if it is content-neutral, it is narrowly tailored to serve a significant government interest, and it leaves open alternative channels of communication. The regulation here passes muster. The area within 250 feet of the legislative chamber probably is a public forum. However, the regulation seems reasonable. It prohibits all loud public gatherings near the chamber when the legislature is in session to vote or debate. Thus, the regulation does not differentiate speech based on content. Moreover, the ban extends only to loud gatherings close to the chamber while the legislature is working. It appears to have the purpose of enabling legislators to hear one another, and it seems to be narrowly tailored to that purpose. Moreover, the regulation leaves other channels of communication open (such as silent picketing). The application of the statute to the man does not make it unconstitutional as applied; there is no reason why he could not have spoken as noisily as he wanted to in the park. Thus, (B) is incorrect. (C) is incorrect because there are many methods to direct complaints to a legislator without yelling through his window. (D) is incorrect because silent picketing can be considered to be reasonable at the same time that loud picketing is prohibited.

Answer to Question 6

(C) The court will likely find the statute constitutional if limited to true threats. The Constitution does not protect true threats, defined as speech meant to communicate an intent to place a person in fear of bodily harm. (A) is incorrect. While prior restraints are disfavored under the First Amendment, because true threats are not protected speech, the statute does not constitute a prior restraint. (B) is incorrect. While a state may forbid speech that poses a clear and present danger of imminent lawless action, that is not the only type of unprotected speech under the First Amendment. (D) is incorrect because the law here does not appear to be a fighting words statute, *i.e.,* personally abusive epithets inherently likely to incite an immediate response.

Answer to Question 7

(C) The dentist will not prevail because the contractual duty was discharged by an accord and satisfaction. An accord is an agreement in which one party to an existing contract agrees to accept, in lieu of the performance that she is supposed to receive from the other party, some other, different performance. Satisfaction is the performance of the accord agreement. The effect of this performance is to discharge both the accord agreement and the original contract. An accord and satisfaction may be accomplished by a good faith tender and acceptance of a check conspicuously marked "payment in full" where there is a bona fide dispute as to the amount owed. The dentist and the patient agreed that the dentist would perform the dental work needed by the patient in return for the patient's promise to pay "about $3,500." The facts indicate that, following the actual dental work, there ensued a good faith dispute as to whether the patient owed only $3,500 or the additional $600 as well. The patient in good faith tendered to the dentist a check marked

"payment in full," which notation the dentist saw before he deposited the check into his account. The dentist's acceptance of the patient's check gives rise to an accord and satisfaction with regard to the disputed original debt. Thus, the dentist is deemed to have accepted the amount tendered by the patient as full payment for the dental services performed, and the patient's duty to pay for the services is discharged. (A) is incorrect because, even if the dentist could have successfully asserted that $4,100 was within the range of the amount "about $3,500," his actions with respect to the check constitute an acceptance of the amount tendered therein. (B) is incorrect because, with the existence of an accord and satisfaction, the patient's duty to pay is deemed to be discharged. Thus, it is irrelevant at this point that the inlays may have been medically necessary or that the dentist charged a fair price for them. (D) is incorrect because an account stated is a contract whereby parties agree to an amount as a final balance due. For an agreement to be an account stated, there must be more than one prior transaction between the parties. The dispute between the patient and dentist involves only one transaction. Thus, there is no account stated.

Answer to Question 8

(D) The landowner probably will win in a breach of contract suit. In partial condemnation cases, the landlord-tenant relationship continues, as does the tenant's obligation to pay the entire rent for the remaining period of the lease. The tenant is, however, entitled to share in the condemnation award to the extent that the condemnation affected the tenant's rights under the lease. Therefore, (B) and (C) are incorrect. (A) is not correct because the law of landlord and tenant traditionally refuses to recognize frustration of purpose as grounds for termination of a lease.

Answer to Question 9

(D) The man's best defense is lack of intent. The crime of attempt is a specific intent crime, requiring the specific intent to carry out the crime in question. Since the man did not know that vandals had smashed his taillights, he never intended to drive an automobile at night without functioning taillights. (A) is incorrect because he did not attempt to drive the automobile at the instigation of the police. (B) is incorrect because legal impossibility is not applicable to these facts. (C) is incorrect because factual impossibility is not a good defense to a charge of attempt.

Answer to Question 10

(B) The court should rule that the Act of Congress is valid under Congress's commerce powers, and that, under the Supremacy Clause of the Constitution, the state law is invalid. While states and the federal government may pass legislation on the same subject matter, the Supremacy Clause provides that federal law is supreme, and any conflicting state law is rendered void. It is possible that the court would enjoin the application of the federal law pending a trial on its merits, but highly unlikely. Thus, (C) is wrong. (A) is wrong; the court has jurisdiction because a federal law is involved. (D) is wrong; no such procedure would apply here.

Answer to Question 11

(B) If the landowner prevails, it will be because his building manager was not negligent. The landowner owed a duty of reasonable care to travelers on highways adjacent to his land, such as the motorcyclist. However, if the landowner's employee was not negligent, the landowner would not be liable. (A) is incorrect because, if the manager was negligent, the landowner's lack of knowledge would not prevent application of respondeat superior. (C) is incorrect because, even though the Scout may have acted recklessly, the landowner could be liable if the employee did not exercise due care. (D) is incorrect because the failure of the adults to stop the Scout, even if it

were considered negligence, would not be so unforeseeable as to cut off any previous negligence by the landowner's employee. The better basis for the result is that the landowner's employee was not negligent.

Answer to Question 12

(B) The judge should rule the evidence admissible as an admission. Although it is arguable that a person who may be liable for negligence would reasonably remain silent when in the presence of a police officer, this is the best answer because silence may be deemed an admission in a situation in which a reasonable person would have responded to an accusation. (D) is wrong because there need be no foundation evidence. (C) is wrong; the silence is deemed the adoption of the statement. Thus, the employee's statement would be an admission. (A) is wrong because, even if the employee is the defendant's agent, the statement against interest exception to the hearsay rule requires the unavailability of the declarant (*i.e.,* the defendant here).

Answer to Question 13

(D) The judge should rule that the plaintiff's testimony is admissible. Although it was hearsay, the plaintiff's testimony was to show she was suffering pain, and is an exception to the hearsay rule as a declaration of present physical sensation. Statements of symptoms being experienced, including the existence of pain, are admissible under the Federal Rules, even if not made to a doctor or other medical personnel. Thus, (A) is wrong. (B) is wrong because the plaintiff's testimony is not to establish that she suffered a "sprained" neck, which would require an expert witness, but just to establish that her neck was in pain. (C) is wrong because the plaintiff's statement would be admissible to show her current physical condition even if she had not planned to introduce medical evidence.

Answer to Question 14

(B) The defendant's conviction should be reversed. Robbery requires an intent to permanently deprive the victim of her property. An intent to recover property that the defendant believes is his would not be a sufficient intent. The prosecution must prove every element of the crime beyond a reasonable doubt, and putting the burden of persuasion to show an innocent intent on the defendant would deprive him of due process of law, since it would relieve the prosecution of its burden to show the required intent for robbery. Thus, the instruction was improper and (D) is wrong. (A) and (C) are wrong. The defendant does not carry any burden of proof with respect to an element of the crime. The burden is on the prosecution to prove each element beyond a reasonable doubt.

Answer to Question 15

(A) The seller would prevail absent express covenants of title in the deed. Under the doctrine of merger, all covenants not collateral to the land sale contract are "merged" in the deed. Thus, acceptance by the buyer of the deed discharges the seller of all liability under the contract. Unless the deed contained the covenants of seisin, right to convey, or right to quiet enjoyment, the seller would prevail. Therefore, (C) and (D) are incorrect. (B) is also incorrect because the buyer's knowledge that the seller was married has no effect on the doctrine of merger or liability on the covenants of title.

Answer to Question 16

(B) The artist's ownership and use of her studio is relevant but not controlling. The fact that one type of land use was entered into before another is relevant but not conclusive evidence of the reasonableness of the use in a private nuisance action. Hence, (A) is incorrect. (C) is not correct because it is relevant what use the neighborhood was put to many years before if the facts show that, subsequently, the neighborhood has changed to another use that would be inconsistent with the record company's use of its property. (D) is incorrect because the fact that the artist was there first is still relevant to the issue of the reasonableness of the record company's use of its property.

Answer to Question 17

(B) The prosecution's objection should be overruled. If a witness's memory is incomplete, the examiner may seek to refresh her memory by allowing her to refer to a writing or anything else—provided she then testifies from present recollection and does not rely on the writing. (A) is incorrect because past recollection recorded is a hearsay exception that applies when a party is seeking to introduce a particular kind of writing. Here, the defendant is not seeking to introduce the writing; he merely wants the witness to look at it. Thus, (A) is incorrect. (C) and (D) are incorrect because the letter is not being offered into evidence.

Answer to Question 18

(D) The owner of the semi-pro team will prevail. Although the $200 per week damages was denominated a "penalty" by the parties, in fact it operates as a reasonable liquidated damages clause. The parties to a contract may stipulate what damages are to be paid in the event of a breach if (i) damages are difficult to ascertain at the time the contract is formed, and (ii) the amount agreed on is a reasonable forecast of compensatory damages in the case of a breach. These conditions have been met here. (A) is wrong because while it is true that penalties will not be enforced, a court would not construe the provision here as a penalty since it meets the requirements above. (B) is irrelevant. (C) is a misstatement of the law.

Answer to Question 19

(C) The appraiser will not recover a percentage of the receipts from the manager. In construing the contract, the court will attempt to give effect to the reasonable expectations of the parties. Even though they did not expressly so provide, the parties probably intended the bonus to be incentive for the appraiser to stay and that it be paid only if he completed the term of the contract. Thus, such a condition will be implied. Therefore, (D) is wrong. (A) is contrary to the facts since there were four months left in the 12-month contract. (B) is wrong because the manager's remedy does not affect the appraiser's right to payment.

Answer to Question 20

(C) The landowner will be unable to obtain an injunction but may recover damages against the oil company. An easement in gross that is commercial may always be transferred, and the permission of the holder of the servient estate is not needed. Thus, (A) is wrong. Since the oil company was within its rights under the terms of the easement, the laying of pipe is permissible and no injunction will lie. It is, however, the obligation of the holder of the easement to reasonably restore the surface following the excavation. Thus, (C) is correct, and (B) and (D) are wrong.

Answer to Question 21

(D) The construction company probably will not prevail in the wrongful death action against it. An excavator near a public road has a duty of due care to protect users of the road from straying and falling in. This duty is satisfied when the excavator has done everything reasonable to protect the open excavation by putting up barriers that are likely to prevent such accidents. The construction company may have reasonably protected cars driving on the street from falling in the trench, but no real step was taken to prevent pedestrians from falling into the trench at nighttime. Hence, (B) is wrong. (A) is wrong because, although the student may have violated the jaywalking statute, the statute is not likely to be applied here because this type of statute was designed to prevent vehicle-pedestrian accidents rather than falling into a trench. In addition, the facts do not establish any other conduct on the part of the student that would constitute contributory negligence. (C) is not the best answer because all that is required with regard to artificial conditions is that the excavator exercise due care to warn persons of the danger.

Answer to Question 22

(D) The arsonist should be found guilty. A conspiracy is a combination or agreement between two or more persons to accomplish some criminal or unlawful purpose, or to accomplish a lawful act by unlawful means. The mens rea required for conspiracy is specific intent, in that both parties must intend to agree to accomplish some criminal or unlawful purpose. Most jurisdictions also require an overt act, but any mere preparation will suffice. Thus, once the arsonist was hired by the husband and they came up with a plan to burn down the brother's house, the crime of conspiracy was completed. (C) is incorrect because it implies that carrying out the plan by at least one party is required; the conspiracy was complete even before the husband fulfilled his duties under the plan. (A) is incorrect. To the extent that an overt act is required, it need not be in and of itself criminal. (B) is also incorrect. To the extent an overt act is required, it need only be performed by one of the co-conspirators, not necessarily the conspirator on trial.

Answer to Question 23

(C) The strongest argument in favor of the constitutionality of the legislation is that Congress is explicitly authorized to restrict the jurisdiction of the federal courts under Article III. (D) is incorrect because Congress cannot define conduct that will violate the Fourteenth Amendment's Equal Protection Clause; it may only enact laws to prevent or remedy violations of rights already recognized by the courts. [City of Boerne v. Flores (1997)] (B) is incorrect because the statute does not regulate interstate commerce, but rather limits the power of the courts to order certain remedies. Neither does the statute affect the expenditure of any federal educational funds, because it is directed at the courts. Therefore, (A) is incorrect.

Answer to Question 24

(A) The strongest argument against the legislation's constitutionality is that Congress cannot usurp the courts' authority to define the scope of the Equal Protection Clause. If the Equal Protection Clause requires a remedy for past racial discrimination, then Congress could not constitutionally interfere with the fashioning of a judicial remedy to achieve constitutionally required conduct. (D) is wrong because Congress may burden interstate commerce, since it has plenary power on that subject. (C) is wrong because Congress may limit the jurisdiction of federal courts. (B) is wrong because the Privileges and Immunities Clause protects individual rights against infringement by state government, it does not limit the powers of Congress vis-a-vis the federal courts.

Answer to Question 25

(C) If true, the fact that the candidate did nothing to solicit the law student's proposal would most strengthen the candidate's defense. Since there is no consideration supporting the candidate's promise to pay the law student, the only way the law student could recover is off contract; *i.e.,* by seeking restitution in a quasi-contract action. Where there is no existing contractual relationship between the parties, restitution may be recovered in a quasi-contract action if: (i) the plaintiff has conferred a benefit on the defendant by rendering services or expending property, (ii) the plaintiff conferred the benefit with the reasonable expectation of being compensated, (iii) the defendant knew or had reason to know of the plaintiff's expectation, and (iv) the defendant would be unjustly enriched if he were allowed to keep the benefits without compensating the plaintiff. Here, the law student conferred his services expecting to be compensated, or at least to obtain employment, and the candidate received the benefit of using the law student's ideas. However, if the candidate did nothing to request that the law student send him ideas, then the third prong of the prima facie case cannot be established. (A) is incorrect because it is irrelevant whether the candidate won or lost the election. The benefit conferred was the use of the law student's ideas, and their value cannot be measured by the candidate's success (*e.g.,* perhaps the results would have been the same absent the suggestions or the candidate would have won without the suggestions; it cannot be known). (B) might be helpful, because if the law student is the candidate's relative there might be a presumption that the idea was a gift. However, the presumption would depend on the closeness of the relationship, and in any case it would be irrelevant if the candidate had requested the law student's services and there was an understanding that the law student was to be paid. (D) is incorrect because even if the law student sent similar suggestions to the candidate's opponent, it does not negate any element of the prima facie case for quasi-contract; *i.e.,* the candidate still received the benefit of the law student's suggestions.

Answer to Question 26

(C) The buyer's offered testimony should be admitted. The statement by the farmer is not hearsay, because it is not offered to prove that the statement was true; rather, it is evidence of words which are a fraudulent representation, and hence themselves actionable. Alternatively, the statement is an admission by the farmer and therefore nonhearsay under the Federal Rules. It is not within the parol evidence rule, because the plaintiff is not trying to prove the meaning of the contract, but rather is alleging fraud. The parol evidence rule does not bar admission of parol evidence to show that what appears to be a contractual obligation is, in fact, no obligation at all. Hence, parol evidence is admissible to attack a contract on the grounds of fraud. (A), (B), and (D) are therefore wrong.

Answer to Question 27

(C) The son is responsible for the interest payments on the mortgage and the granddaughter is responsible for the principal. The doctrine of waste governs the obligations between a life tenant and the holder of the remainder regarding the payment of a mortgage on the property. Under this doctrine, a life tenant is obligated to pay interest on any encumbrances on the land, but he does not have to pay anything on the principal of the debt; reversioners or remaindermen must pay the principal in order to protect their interests. (C) correctly states that rule, and (A), (B), and (D) are necessarily wrong.

Answer to Question 28

(B) The woman should be found not guilty because she did not intend to commit the crime of bigamy. Conspiracy is a specific intent crime. All parties must agree to commit some unlawful

act (or a lawful act by unlawful means). Here, the woman did not know that the man was already married; thus, she was unable to agree to commit bigamy. (A) is incorrect because the state of mind requirement for the target crime is irrelevant. As with attempt crimes, the state of mind required for conspiracy is always specific intent. (C) is incorrect because the answer implies that withdrawal is a valid defense for conspiracy. It is not. (It may be a valid defense for crimes committed in furtherance of the conspiracy, but, in most states, it is not a valid defense to the conspiracy charge itself.) (D) is incorrect. The Wharton rule applies only when the minimum number of actors needed to commit a crime equals the number of conspirators. Here, the minister also appears to be a conspirator, providing the potential third person to the conspiracy, so the Wharton rule does not apply.

Answer to Question 29

(C) The mayor's suit will fail because, as a public official, he has to establish a higher level of fault on the reporter's part than what he has shown. The Supreme Court, in *New York Times v. Sullivan* (1964), held that the First Amendment bars a civil libel judgment for criticism of a public official unless the plaintiff shows actual malice by clear and convincing evidence. "Actual malice" requires a showing that the publication was known to be false or that it was published with reckless disregard as to its truth or falsity. Here, the reporter believed her report was true, and since she confirmed the rumor by talking to an apparently reliable source, she was not reckless as to the truth or falsity of her report. (A) is wrong because traditional malice or ill will is not an element of "actual malice," which has the distinct meaning stated above in defamation cases. (B) is wrong because falsity and damages alone are insufficient; the mayor must also prove actual malice. (D) is wrong because the First Amendment will not protect reporters who act with knowledge of falsity or reckless disregard as to truth or falsity.

Answer to Question 30

(B) If the homeowner knew or had reason to know of the computation error, the mistake will prevent formation of a contract. A mutual mistake going to the heart of the bargain may prevent formation of a contract. However, where only one of the parties is mistaken about facts relating to the agreement, such a unilateral mistake will not prevent formation of a contract. Nevertheless, if the nonmistaken party knows or had reason to know of the mistake made by the other party, he is not permitted to take advantage of the offer. Here, there was such a unilateral mistake, as the handyman (due to his secretary's error) was mistaken as to the price for which he could resurface the homeowner's driveway at a profit. Thus, there is a contract for the price of $4,000. However, if the homeowner had reason to know of the error in the bid, the handyman will be able to successfully defend on the ground that the mistake prevents formation of the contract. (B) is the only answer that reflects this. (D) is incorrect because, as explained above, the handyman ***cannot*** successfully assert mistake as a defense unless the homeowner knew or had reason to know of the error. (A) is incorrect because, even if it is not too late for the homeowner to accept the next lowest bid, the homeowner is still entitled to be put where he would have been had the handyman's promise been performed. Had the promise been performed, the homeowner would have had his driveway resurfaced for $4,000. If the homeowner can still accept the next lowest bid ($4,200), he is entitled to receive as damages the amount above the price of his contract with the handyman that it will cost to resurface the driveway ($200). (C) is incorrect because the handyman is bound to fulfill the terms of his contractual obligation, regardless of whether he has commenced performance under the contract. Had the handyman discovered the error prior to the homeowner's acceptance of the offer, the handyman could have revoked the offer. However, once the contract was formed, the handyman must live up to his contractual duties or be liable for breach.

Answer to Question 31

(C) The driver will prevail because the homeowner was at fault for being on her neighbor's roof and the driver acted reasonably. If a person, because of her wrongful conduct, gets herself into a position from which she must be rescued, that person is liable to the rescuer who suffers injuries while reasonably trying to aid her. (A) is wrong because a rescuer does not "voluntarily" assume the risk where the alternative is to allow the threatened harm to occur. (B) is wrong because although the homeowner had gotten safely back on the ground, the rescue was not "over" until the driver also was safely on the ground again. (D) is not a reason for imposing liability on the homeowner.

Answer to Question 32

(A) The court should grant the cruise ship owner's motion because the passenger has not established a prima facie case of negligence against the cruise ship. To establish a prima facie case for negligence, a plaintiff must show (i) a duty of care, (ii) breach of that duty, (iii) actual and proximate cause, and (iv) damages. As a common carrier and/or an innkeeper, the cruise ship owed its passengers a high duty of care, and therefore would be liable for slight negligence. However, the passenger has offered no evidence to establish that the cruise ship employees breached that duty, and res ipsa loquitur is not applicable here because the collision with the whale swimming underwater is not the type of event that would occur only as a result of negligence. Because the passenger failed to establish breach of duty, the court should grant the cruise ship owner a directed verdict. (B) is incorrect because the cruise ship owner does not need that evidence to prevail. While evidence that a person in normal health would not have been injured by the bump supports the cruise ship's other evidence that it exercised due care, it is not necessary because the passenger has failed to offer evidence that the cruise ship breached its duty. On the other hand, if the cruise ship had breached its duty of care to its passengers, the fact that a person in normal health would not have been injured by the bump on the head would not be a defense to liability. If a defendant's negligence causes an aggravation of a plaintiff's existing physical illness, the defendant is liable for the damages caused by the aggravation. (C) is incorrect because, as discussed above, the passenger has failed to present evidence that the cruise ship breached the high duty of care that it owed to its guests. (D) is incorrect even though it is a true statement of law, as discussed above. The reason the cruise ship owner prevails is because the passenger has failed to establish a prima facie case.

Answer to Question 33

(C) It is of no help to the scientist that the young woman's belief that the elixir would cure her disease was unreasonable. It is not a defense to obtaining money by false pretenses that the victim unreasonably relied on the defendant's misrepresentation. The test for reliance is a subjective one. (A) is incorrect because the obtaining of mere possession that the defendant expects to be temporary does not constitute false pretenses. (B) is incorrect because false pretenses requires that the misrepresentation be knowingly false, and this is not the case when the defendant sincerely, even though unreasonably, believes that the misrepresentation is true. (D) is incorrect because false pretenses requires reliance by the victim to be actionable. (The scientist may be guilty of attempted false pretenses, however.)

Answer to Question 34

(A) The court should admit the list for making a determination whether the witness is qualified as an expert, and refuse to permit the witness to testify if he is not sufficiently qualified. When a

preliminary or foundational fact must be established as a condition to the admissibility of proffered evidence, the judge will determine the existence of the preliminary fact if it involves the competency of evidence that is relevant. The judge must determine whether a witness is sufficiently expert to testify because this is a competency issue. For this purpose, the judge should allow the pass-fail list into evidence. (C) and (D) are therefore wrong. (B) is wrong because the court cannot permit the witness to testify at all until he is qualified.

Answer to Question 35

(B) The veteran's best defense is that the covenant does not clearly "touch and concern" the land. While recycling may benefit the community at large, "touch and concern" involves the relationship between landowners at law. Recycling by the veteran does not directly benefit the other landowners in the use and enjoyment of their land. Thus, (B) is correct. (A) is wrong because even though the veteran's deed does not contain the covenant, he has record notice because the restriction is in his chain of title. (C) is wrong because servitudes implied from a common scheme apply only to negative covenants, and the recycling requirement is an affirmative covenant. Thus, this defense does not go to the point. (D) is wrong because it goes only to issues in equity. The suit includes a claim for damages at law. In any case, balancing of hardships is not generally applied in such cases (although some courts might elect to do so).

Answer to Question 36

(A) The homeowner will prevail in his claim against the worker. The intentional tortious or criminal conduct of a third person is not a superseding cause of the plaintiff's harm if it is foreseeable. The worker's actions have increased the risk that this criminal conduct will occur, making the theft a ***foreseeable*** intervening force; hence, the worker is subject to liability. (C) is therefore wrong. (B) is wrong because it does not go far enough toward establishing liability. The homeowner's claim is based on the fact that leaving the ladder and tools out was negligent, not on the worker's failure to get permission to do so. (D) is wrong because the worker has breached a duty of care he owed to the homeowner, who suffered damages as a result. Hence, the homeowner has a negligence claim against the worker.